THE CHANGING SUPREME COURT

Constitutional Rights and Liberties

THOMAS R. HENSLEY

CHRISTOPHER E. SMITH

JOYCE A. BAUGH

WEST PUBLISHING

A Division of International Thomson Publishing, Inc.

Minneapolis/St. Paul, Albany, NY, Bonn, Boston, Cincinnati, Detroit, Johannesburg, London, Madrid, Melbourne, Mexico City, New York, Paris, San Francisco, Singapore, Tokyo, Toronto, Washington

WEST'S COMMITMENT TO THE ENVIRONMENT
In 1906, West Publishing Company began recycling materials left over from the production of books. This began a tradition of efficient and responsible use of resources. Today, 100% of our legal bound volumes are printed on acid-free, recycled paper consisting of 50% new paper pulp and 50% paper that has undergone a de-inking process. We also use vegetable-based inks to print all of our books. West recycles nearly 27,700,000 pounds of scrap paper annually—the equivalent of 229,300 trees. Since the 1960s, West has devised ways to capture and recycle waste inks, solvents, oils, and vapors created in the printing process. We also recycle plastics of all kinds, wood, glass, corrugated cardboard, and batteries, and have eliminated the use of polystyrene book packaging. We at West are proud of the longevity and the scope of our commitment to the environment.

West pocket parts and advance sheets are printed on recyclable paper and can be collected and recycled with newspapers. Staples do not have to be removed. Bound volumes can be recycled after removing the cover.

Prepress, Printing and Binding by West Publishing Company.

PRODUCTION CREDITS

Production Management: Tobi Giannone, Michael Bass & Associates

Cover and Text Design: Lois Stanfield, LightSource Images

Copyedit: Bonnie Gruen

Artwork: Asterisk Group

Composition: Carlisle Communications

British Library Cataloguing-in-Publication Data. A catalogue record for this book is available from the British Library.

a division of International Thomson Publishing, Inc.
610 Opperman Drive
P.O. Box 64526
St. Paul, MN 55164-0526

Printed in the United States of America
04 03 02 01 00 99 98 97 8 7 6 5 4 3 2 1 0

LIBRARY OF CONGRESS CATALOGING-IN-PUBLICATION DATA
Hensley, Thomas R.
The changing Supreme Court : constitutional rights and liberties / Thomas R. Hensley, Christopher E. Smith, Joyce A. Baugh.
p. cm.
Includes index.
ISBN 0-314-09878-X (alk. paper)
1. Civil rights—United States—Cases. 2. Civil rights—United States—History. 3. United States. Supreme Court—History.
I. Smith, Christopher E. II. Baugh, Joyce A. III. Title.
KF4748.H46 1997
347.73'26—dc20
[347.30735]
96-34468
CIP

CONTENTS

CHAPTER 10

The Fifth Amendment Guarantees Against Compelled Self-Incrimination and Double Jeopardy 464

CHAPTER 11

The Sixth Amendment and Fair Trial Guarantees 511

CHAPTER 12

The Eighth Amendment Guarantee Against Cruel and Unusual Punishments 556

SECTION IV

EQUAL PROTECTION AND PRIVACY: INTRODUCTION, OVERVIEW, AND DOCTRINAL FRAMEWORK 608

CHAPTER 13

Equal Protection and Race 613

Table of Cases

Cases in italic are the principal cases included throughout the chapters. References are to pages.

Table of Tables

Preface

Teaching a course on American civil rights and liberties is fun. The topics covered in this course are important and controversial. Hate speech, flag burning, obscenity, state-sponsored religious activities in public schools, warrantless searches, the exclusionary rule, the *Miranda* warnings, the death penalty, racial equality, gender equality, affirmative action, and abortion are just some of the fascinating topics which are examined.

Our goal in writing this book is to provide students and instructors with a text that captures the excitement of the subject of American civil rights and liberties and at the same time utilizes contemporary approaches and methods of the social sciences. Achieving both of these objectives is not easy. Although our book certainly shares many features in common with most other constitutional law texts, *The Changing Supreme Court: Constitutional Rights and Liberties* contains many unique features that help to capture the excitement of the subject and to draw upon the techniques of contemporary social science.

Capturing the Excitement. American civil rights and liberties is exciting because the issues and cases involve human beings in conflict over important issues of liberty and equality. The individuals who are parties to a case and the attorneys who represent them are central to the human drama, and we begin each chapter with an **in-depth case study** which tells the story of the parties to the case and the attorneys representing them. The justices of the Supreme Court are also important human actors, and we introduce the reader to all of the **justices of the Rehnquist Court** in Chapter 3, where we present a detailed profile of the background, judicial philosophy, and voting record of the fourteen justices who have served on the Court since 1986.

We also seek to convey the excitement and human drama associated with the Court's civil rights and liberties decisions by developing throughout the book an important, **central theme of the effect of membership change on the Court's policies.** In each chapter we examine the extent to which membership change produced a liberal constitutional revolution during the period from 1953 through 1968 when Earl Warren was chief justice, and then we examine the issue of whether membership changes associated with the Burger Court era (1969–1985) and the Rehnquist Court era (1986–present) have produced a conservative counterrevolution in the Court's interpretation of constitutional rights and liberties.

Utilizing Social Science Methods. We have also made a strong effort to utilize **modern social science theories and data** in our book. Although theories and data are sometimes viewed as dull and boring, we think they can be used not only to make an inherently fascinating subject even more interesting but also to add to the intellectual excitement of studying constitutional rights and liberties. We introduce the reader in Chapter 1 to three competing theories of Supreme Court behavior: the legal model, the political model, and the attitudinal model. We take the position that all three theories have both strengths and weaknesses, and we utilize the insights of all three models throughout the text.

We also place great emphasis on providing a systematic, detailed analysis of the issues confronting the Supreme Court today. We provide thorough analysis of the decisions of the Rehnquist Court using unique quantitative and qualitative methods of analysis.

In our quantitative analyses, we utilize the United States Supreme Court Judicial Database throughout our book. These data on the decisions of the Warren, Burger, and Rehnquist Courts have been gathered by Professor Harold Spaeth of Michigan State University and are made available through the Interuniversity Consortium for Political and Social Research. In our analysis of each area of constitutional rights and liberties, we employ these data for three purposes: (1) to compare the liberal/conservative voting records of the Warren, Burger, and Rehnquist Courts to assess ideological shifts as the Court's membership has changed; (2) to describe and compare the individual voting records of the justices of the Rehnquist Court; and (3) to determine bloc voting alignments among the justices of the Rehnquist Court.

Voting data have inherent limitations because they only measure the judgment of the Court and the individual justices, and we have therefore developed a **multidimensional doctrinal framework for measuring policy change** by the Rehnquist Court in each area of civil rights and liberties. This framework involves the simultaneous analysis of four variables for every case decided by the Rehnquist Court: (1) whether the Court's decision was liberal or conservative; (2) whether the Court's opinion involved the application of existing precedent, the modification of existing precedent, or the creation of a new precedent; (3) whether the case was of major or minor importance; and (4) whether the opinion of the Court involved a majority or a plurality of the justices. We argue that the Rehnquist Court can be considered to have engaged in a conservative counterrevolution only if it has issued majority opinions in major cases characterized by the conservative modification of existing precedent or the creation of a new conservative precedent.

Text Organization

The Changing Supreme Court: Constitutional Rights and Liberties is organized into five sections. Section I, "The Supreme Court and American Politics," consists of four chapters. The introductory chapter uses a case study of the nomination of Robert Bork to the Supreme Court to introduce students to the three competing models of Supreme Court behavior: the legal model, the political model, and the attitudinal model. Chapter 2 provides a detailed discussion of the role of the Supreme Court in the American political system. Chapter 3 provides in-depth profiles of the fourteen justices who have served on the Supreme Court since William Rehnquist became chief justice in 1986, and Chapter 4 presents a discussion of the topic of the nationalization of the Bill of Rights. Section II focuses on the First Amendment with separate chapters on the Establishment Clause, the Free Exercise Clause, the freedom of expression guarantees, and obscenity. The constitutional provisions relating to the American criminal justice system are examined in Section III; the section consists of four chapters analyzing the Fourth, Fifth, Sixth, and Eighth Amendments. Section IV examines the subjects of equal protection and privacy with chapters on racial equality, gender equality, affirmative action, other equal protection issues, and privacy/abortion. The fifth section of the book provides a brief summary and conclusion.

Format

A common chapter format is followed throughout Section II, III, and IV of the book.

Introductory Case Study

Each chapter begins with a detailed case study of a leading Supreme Court case. The case is thoroughly analyzed from beginning to end. The parties in the case are introduced, the original conflict giving rise to the case is discussed, the lower court decisions are examined, interest group activity is explained, the attorneys' strategies in presenting their case to the Supreme Court are evaluated, the Court's decision making process and opinion are explained, and the effect of the decision on the parties and on American society is analyzed.

Historic Origins and Contemporary Conflicts

Following the case study, we present an analysis of the historic context within which the constitutional provision was developed. This provides a basis for the reader to assess the "original understanding" of the constitutional provision, which the justices frequently discuss in their opinions. We also present in this section a brief overview of the major contemporary controversies involving the constitutional guarantee.

Supreme Court Decision Making

The focus of this section in each chapter is the tests or doctrines the Court has developed to guide its decision making. We view these judicial tests as important not only in regard to the justices' decision making but also in terms of students' understanding of constitutional law. We stress that although these doctrines are discussed by the justices as embodying neutral, abstract legal principles (the legal model), these doctrines are also the product of the justices' political values (the attitudinal model) and the broader political forces in American society (the political model).

Pre-Warren Court Era

Although we place a heavy emphasis upon social science theory and methods, we also recognize the importance of an historical approach to the study of constitutional law, and thus each chapter has a strong historical framework because we trace the evolution of Supreme Court decision making through four distinctive periods of Supreme Court history: the pre-Warren Court era covering the period from the creation of the Constitution through the first half of the twentieth century, the Warren Court period from 1953–1969, the Burger Court years of 1969–1986, and the contemporary Rehnquist Court period since 1986. In our analysis of the pre-Warren Court era, we typically stress the important changes which occurred in the late 1930s when the Court shifted its agenda from protecting business from government regulation to emphasizing the importance of the Bill of Rights and Fourteenth Amendment.

The Warren Court Era

The Warren Court is widely recognized to have engaged in a liberal constitutional revolution in regard to civil rights and liberties. In each chapter we examine the validity of this proposition. Although we make some use of the Spaeth data, our primary focus is upon the leading precedents and the major doctrines established by the justices of the Warren Court.

The Burger Court Era

President Richard Nixon had the opportunity to remake the Supreme Court when he appointed four justices to the Court in his first term as president from 1969–1973. The central theme we raise in each chapter when we examine the Burger Court era is whether the changes in the Court's membership in this period led to dramatic changes in the Court's civil rights and liberties policies. In this chapter we again utilize both the Spaeth data and traditional doctrinal analysis to assess the extent of the Burger Court's conservative counterrevolution.

The Rehnquist Court Era

Our analyses lead to the conclusion that the Burger Court was substantially more conservative than the Warren Court but that the Burger Court justices did not substantially alter most of the leading precedents and doctrines of the Warren Court era. A central question in each chapter thus becomes whether Presidents Ronald Reagan and George Bush were successful in appointing justices who brought about a conservative counterrevolution in American civil rights and liberties. We make extensive use of the Spaeth data as well as our systematic doctrinal framework to explore this issue in each chapter of the book.

Highlights of the Book

The above discussion illustrates some but not all of the important, and frequently unique, features of *The Changing Supreme Court: Constitutional Rights and Liberties.*

A strong historical basis exists through a discussion of the historic context of the development of each constitutional provision and through an organizational framework tracing the evolution of Court policies through the various eras of Court history.

A central theme is analyzed throughout the book: the effect of changes in the Court's membership on the civil rights and liberties policies of the Court. Special emphasis is given to the question of whether the Rehnquist Court with its conservative appointees has engaged in a conservative constitutional counterrevolution.

Detailed profiles of the Rehnquist Court justices are given in Chapter 3 to provide students with a foundation for understanding how the make-up of the Court affects the decisions made and thus the development of the law.

Statistical analyses utilizing the United States Supreme Court Judicial Database are presented throughout the text. The data help to illustrate trends in the support of civil rights and liberties between the Warren, Burger, and Rehnquist Courts. The statistical analyses also show the voting patterns of individual members of the Rehnquist Court and the voting alignments that exist on the Rehnquist Court.

A unique doctrinal analysis framework is presented for each topic. The framework classifies all decisions of the Rehnquist Court along a six-point continuum to illustrate how specific areas of civil rights and liberties are (or are not) changing. The tables provide a concise overview of the modern Court's decisions in each area and will help students assess the extent to which radical change has taken place.

Cases studies open chapters 4–17. The case studies trace a major decision from beginning to end. This unique method of beginning each chapter serves to pique students' interest and draw them into the chapter discussions.

100 edited cases are integrated throughout each chapter where they are discussed. Each case is preceded by a brief introduction which explains why the case is important and presents questions for students to consider while reading the opinions, which include concurrences and dissents.

Current developments in American civil rights and liberties are covered through an Annual Supplement that covers the Court's 1995–1996 term as well as through a Web Site on the Internet which keeps students and faculty informed of up-to-the-minute developments at the Court.

Teaching Aids/Supplements

Annual Supplement

A supplement written by the authors of the main text will provide a detailed analysis of the Supreme Court's civil rights and liberties decisions in the most recent term. Voting data on the Court as well as on individual justices will be provided and compared with previous terms, all cases will be classified in the doctrinal framework for assessing policy change, the major cases will be discussed, and substantial portions of the opinions in the major cases will be excerpted.

Web Site on the Internet

A Web Site on the Internet will be maintained by the authors of the text. The Web Site will provide continuously updated information regarding the activities of the Court, including decisions to grant certiorari, oral arguments before the Court, and the results of the Court's decisions as they are handed down. The Web Site will be available to adopters of the text using a password via West Educational Publishing Home Page: http://www.westpub.com/Educate. Contact your sales representative for the password.

Instructor's Manual with Test Bank

Prepared by the authors of the text, the Instructor's Manual will contain ideas for teaching constitutional law, lecture material, ideas for class discussion of the questions which precede each case in the text, ideas for videos and other electronic resources, and examination questions for each chapter.

West's Political Science Video Library

Faculty members adopting *The Changing Supreme Court: Constitutional Rights and Liberties* may select videos from West Publishing Company's political science video library. (West sales representatives will provide qualifying information.)

Acknowledgements

We are deeply indebted to many individuals whose scholarship, advice, and assistance have contributed to our knowledge about the Supreme Court and our efforts to present new approaches in this textbook. We owe a special debt to Professor Harold Spaeth of Michigan State University for his efforts in organizing and maintaining the United States Supreme Court Judicial Database. Numerous students at Kent State University have been deeply involved in testing and developing the ideas and approaches in this book. Senior honors theses relating to various aspects of the book have been completed by Marcia Barber, Michele Domen, Rhonda Evans, Kirsten Friedel, Paul Hensley, Deborah Glasgow, Amy Litkovitz, David Oppenheimer, Matt Parrish, Julie Peters, and Chrysanthe Vasilles. Three Kent State graduate students—Scott Johnson, Maureen Oakley, and Jarrod Tudor—assisted the development of this book in a variety of ways. Jennifer Tetreault and Mary Linger of Kent

State University provided valuable typing assistance. Faculty colleagues in the Political Science Department at Kent State, especially chairpersons Byron Lander and Elaine McCoy, provided a supportive environment for the development of this project. At Michigan State University, thanks are due to Merry Morash and other faculty colleagues in the School of Criminal Justice for maintaining an environment conducive to scholarly research, and to Beverly Bockes for her invaluable assistance and support. Several students at Michigan State contributed to gathering material for the book: Roxanne Ochoa, Ed Banks, and Donald Kall Loper. At Central Michigan University, many thanks go to colleagues in the Department of Political Science for their encouragement and support.

The professional staff at the College Division of West Publishing Company has been exceptionally supportive and helpful throughout the preparation of this book. Special thanks go to Elizabeth Hannan, our editor. We deeply appreciate her commitment to this book at its early stages and her unwavering encouragement and assistance at every subsequent stage. We also want to express our appreciation to several other members of the West staff who have provided us with valuable help: Patty Bryant, Holly Henjum, and Ellen Stanton.

A number of professional colleagues provided insightful criticisms and suggestions during the preparation of the book. Whatever the weaknesses of the book, it is substantially stronger because of the contributions of these experts in constitutional law:

Jilda Aliotta
University of Hartford, CT

Robert A. Carp
University of Houston, TX

Donald C. Dahlin
University of South Dakota

Craig Emmert
Texas Tech University

Charles Hersch
Cleveland State University

Robert Jacobs
Central Washington University

Carolyn Johnson
University of Kansas

William P. McLauchlan
Purdue University, IN

Richard Pacelle
University of Missouri

Helen Ridley
Kennesaw State College, GA

Claire A. Smearman
Towson University, MD

Elliot E. Slotnick
Ohio State University

Mary Thornberry
Davidson College, NC

Jim Todd
University of Arizona

Diane Wall
Mississippi State University

This book would never have been completed without the love, support, and especially patience supplied by our families. Our parents—Earl and Ada Hensley, Robert and Carol Smith, and Jeff and Ella Baugh—deserve special credit for the many years of essential education, encouragement, and support that laid the groundwork for our scholarly careers and culminated in the major project that produced this book. Our children—Paul, Brad, and Sarah Hensley, and Alicia and Eric Smith—helped us keep some degree of balance in our lives as we worked on this project. It was, however, our spouses—Jane Hensley, Charlotte Smith, and Roger Hatch—who provided us with the daily support that enabled us to complete this book. We lovingly dedicate this book to them.

The Supreme Court and American Politics

Introduction and Overview

OVERVIEW

Civil rights and liberties can be defined as the constitutional guarantees which help to define the relationship between the governing and the governed in American society in regard to the fundamental values of freedom and equality. The provisions of the Bill of Rights, the first ten amendments to the Constitution, deal with various aspects of freedom, the right of individuals to be free from arbitrary government interference in their lives. The concept of equality is found in the Fourteenth Amendment and provides that the government may not treat people in an arbitrary or unreasonable manner based upon such characteristics as race, ethnicity, or gender.

The ideas of freedom and equality are central to American democracy. One important component of democracy is, of course, majority rule, and a stable democratic society requires that minorities abide by the decisions made through majority rule. Limitations do exist, however, on the principle of majoritarianism. As Justice Jackson stated eloquently in *West Virginia v. Barnette* (1943), "The very purpose of a Bill of Rights was to withdraw certain subjects from the vicissitudes of political controversy, to place them beyond the reach of majorities and officials and to establish them as legal principles to be applied by the courts. One's right to life, liberty, and property, to free speech, a free press, freedom of worship and assembly, and other fundamental rights may not be submitted to vote; they depend on the outcome of no elections" (319 U.S. at 638).

In American society, the United States Supreme Court is ultimately responsible for interpreting the meaning of the constitutional guarantees involving freedom and equality. The temptation exists, therefore, to turn immediately to the Bill of Rights and the Fourteenth Amendment for the purpose of examining the Court's interpretation of these important constitutional provisions. This temptation must be avoided, however, because we must first establish a foundation upon which we can build our subsequent analysis of the Court's interpretation of American civil rights and liberties. This foundation is presented in the four chapters of Section I, which we have entitled "The Supreme Court and American Politics."

Chapter 1 focuses upon three models or approaches regarding Supreme Court decision making in the field of civil rights and liberties. These three models—the legal, the political, and the attitudinal—are each a set of closely related ideas that seek to describe and explain Supreme Court behavior by focusing upon key elements affecting the decision-making behavior of the justices of the Court. The legal model emphasizes the importance of traditional legal criteria, including the language of the Constitution, the historic contexts within which the Bill of Rights and Fourteenth Amendment were adopted, and legal precedent, past decisions of the Court which presumably guide the justices as they hear new cases. The political model stresses the idea that the Supreme Court is part of the broader American political system, and thus the justices are affected significantly by the political forces in American society, including the influence of interest groups, the force of public opinion, and pressures from the other branches of government. Finally, the attitudinal model focuses upon the values and attitudes of the individual justices, which this model maintains is the most important factor in determining Supreme Court decision making. In Chapter 1 these three models will be described, their strengths and weaknesses will be assessed, and their use in our book will be explained.

Each of these three models is discussed further in Chapter 2, which examines the role of the Supreme Court in the American political system. The emphasis in this chapter is on the political model. The discussion focuses on how the Supreme Court operates within not only the larger federal judicial system but also the entire American political system. Special attention is given to the Court's power of judicial review, the authority to declare unconstitutional acts of Congress and actions of the executive branch. We also examine in detail specific factors which influence the justices in their decision making.

The attitudinal model is emphasized in Chapter 3, "The Justices of the Rehnquist Court." A central theme of our book is that important changes in the civil rights and liberties policies of the Court are frequently associated with changes in the Court's membership. Presidents throughout history have attempted to affect the Court's interpretation of the Constitution by appointing justices sharing their political views. In recent years, Republican Presidents Ronald Reagan and George Bush had the opportunity to appoint a majority of the Court's members, and thus a central question is whether the Court's civil rights and liberties policies have been fundamentally altered by these changes in the Court's membership. Thus, Chapter 3 presents an analysis of each justice who has served on the Court since William Rehnquist was appointed chief justice in 1986 by President Reagan. The chapter provides a discussion of each justice's background before coming to the Court, general judicial philosophy, and voting record in civil rights and liberties cases.

The fourth and final chapter of the introductory section analyzes the nationalization or incorporation of the Bill of Rights. Throughout most of American history, the Bill of Rights applied only to the federal government but not to state governments. Beginning in the twentieth century, however, the Supreme Court on a case-by-case basis applied most of the Bill of Rights guarantees to the states, using the Due Process Clause of the Fourteenth Amendment as the basis of this incorporation process. This has been a development of extraordinary significance because the vast majority of the Supreme Court's civil rights and liberties cases involve alleged violations by state and local governments. As we discuss this important topic of nationalization, we will utilize insights from each of the three models—the legal, the political, and the attitudinal.

CHAPTER

1

Approaches to the Study of Civil Rights and Liberties

Introduction

American civil rights and liberties, the constitutional guarantees embodied in the Bill of Rights and the Fourteenth Amendment,[1] are extraordinarily controversial. Should hate speech be outlawed? Should obscene materials be banned from consenting adults? To what extent, if any, can the government provide aid to private, religious schools? Under what circumstances is it constitutional for law enforcement officers to engage in searches and seizures without a warrant or probable cause? Should evidence obtained in violation of constitutional guarantees be excluded from trial? Is the abortion decision a constitutionally protected right even though it is not mentioned in the Constitution? To what extent does the Constitution's guarantee of equal protection of the laws apply to private organizations, businesses, and individuals that are discriminating against individuals based on race, gender, or other characteristics?

In American society, the Supreme Court is the ultimate interpreter of these controversial questions regarding civil rights and liberties. The Court is commonly assumed to approach this difficult task in an objective, impartial manner. It presumably bases its decisions on legal criteria, especially past precedents, thus providing stability and continuity in regard to the meaning of the Constitution. A moment's reflection, however, quickly brings to mind many decisions in which the Court did not adhere to past precedent. In *Brown v. Board of Education* (1954), for example, the Court unanimously overturned the 1896 case of *Plessy v. Ferguson*, ruling that the previous principle of separate but equal facilities for people of different races violated the Constitution's equal protection requirement and invalidating as unconstitutional laws that permitted or required the racial segregation of school children. Another example involves the 1973 decision of *Roe v. Wade* in which the Court created a major, controversial new precedent by ruling that a woman's abortion decision is a fundamental right protected by the Constitution.

Although these cases may be viewed as exceptions to the rule that the Court makes its decisions through the objective interpretation of precedent and other legal criteria, a more accurate view is that the Supreme Court is continually confronted with novel legal issues for which ample precedents may exist on both sides or for

---

[1]Civil liberties are generally considered to be the guarantees in the first eight amendments of the Constitution, and civil rights are the guarantees associated with the Fourteenth Amendment. The terms civil rights and civil liberties are sometimes used interchangeably, however.

which no precedents provide clear guidance. Lacking adequate guidance from legal criteria, the justices may therefore bring their own personal and political views into the decision-making process. This occurs not only because of the types of cases the Court hears but also because of the unique features of the Supreme Court as an institution. The Court issues detailed, written opinions in fewer than 100 cases each year out of approximately 7,000 that they are asked to decide. The justices are therefore careful in selecting these cases, and a dominant characteristic of the cases selected is that substantial disagreement exists regarding the legal issues raised. The justices also have substantial opportunity to introduce their own values and attitudes because they are selected for life tenure on the Court and have no other courts reviewing their decisions.

Because of these realities of the Supreme Court, the composition of the Court is a matter of great significance. If the Court is dominated by liberal justices who place great importance on the protection of individual rights and liberties, then it is likely to issue quite different decisions from a Court dominated by conservative justices who are willing to allow the government substantial authority to regulate such activities. Thus, the Court's policies toward civil rights and civil liberties frequently shift in conjunction with changes in the Court's membership. As a result, the nominations and appointments of Supreme Court justices are extremely important events in American politics and frequently create intense political conflict.

A danger exists, however, in overstating the extent to which the decisions of the Supreme Court depend on the personal values and attitudes of the justices as well as the extent to which new members of the Court may shift constitutional law in new directions. The decision-making process of the Court is a complex activity with numerous factors influencing the justices' behavior. Important legal constraints do exist on the justices. Furthermore, changes in the Court's policies may stem from sources other than the influence of new members. For example, continuing members of the Court have been known to change their views, and the Court may be confronted with new issues that produce different decision patterns from those generated by previous issues.

This book tries to capture this controversy and complexity. The title of the book, *The Changing Supreme Court: Constitutional Rights and Liberties*, identifies a central theme of the book: how has the Supreme Court's interpretation of American civil rights and liberties changed as the membership of the Court has changed? We will thus give substantial emphasis to the importance of the individual justices and to the various coalitions they have formed. But we will also attempt to give full recognition to the complexity of Supreme Court decision making. Thus, we will emphasize the legal constraints that limit the justices' decision making, and we will also attempt to analyze the extent to which changes in the Court's policies are associated with causes other than the addition of new members to the Court.

To achieve these goals, we will employ three models or approaches throughout the book: the legal model, the political model, and the attitudinal model. Given the complexities of Supreme Court civil rights and liberties decision making, no single approach is capable of capturing the variety and richness of the factors that need to be analyzed. The legal model allows us to emphasize the traditional view of the Supreme Court as an institution closely constrained in its decision making by legal factors, such as precedent and the historic intentions of the writers of the Constitution. The political model enhances our ability to recognize that the Court makes it decisions in a broader political context, a context that both affects the Court's decision making and is affected by the Court's decisions. For example, the political model focuses on the influence of interest groups and public opinion on the Court, and the political model also recognizes that Court decisions may be met with resistance and outright defiance. Finally, the attitudinal model allows us to focus on the ideological dimension of Supreme Court decision making, an important key to understanding the behavior of the members of the Court. Thus, the attitudinal model alerts us to the importance of the political values and attitudes of the justices in the decision-making process.

To help illuminate many of the points we have just described, we now turn to a case study of the 1987 nomination of Robert Bork to the United States Supreme Court. This analysis will reveal how intense political conflict and controversy are frequently associated with the Supreme Court and American civil rights and liberties. The case study will also reveal the importance attached to changing membership on the Court because of the effects new members might have on the Court's policies. In addition, the analysis will illustrate the complex factors that operate on the Court to influence the changing directions of the Court's decision making. Finally, the case study will help to illustrate the three approaches to the study of constitutional law, which will be discussed in greater detail following the analysis of the Bork nomination.

The Bork Nomination: A Case Study

When Supreme Court Justice Lewis Powell retired from the Court in 1987, President Ronald Reagan nominated federal Circuit Court Judge Robert Bork to replace Powell. In many ways Bork seemed to be an extraordinarily well-qualified candidate for the position. He had established a distinguished academic record as the Alexander M. Bickel Professor of Public Law at Yale University Law School; he had served in a variety of important government positions, including Solicitor General and Acting Attorney General of the United States; and he became a sitting judge on the U.S. Circuit Court of Appeals for the District of Columbia through a unanimous confirmation vote in the United States Senate. Nonetheless, Bork's nomination to the Supreme Court unleashed a firestorm of controversy; and following a lengthy and bitter confirmation struggle, Bork's nomination was defeated in the Senate by the largest margin of any Supreme Court nominee in American history.

Background

In order to understand the intense controversy that surrounded the Bork nomination, it is necessary to place the event in a broader historical and political context. The replacement of Justice Powell was widely viewed as a potential turning point in American constitutional history, an event that could usher in a conservative counterrevolution regarding American civil rights and liberties. In the 1950s and 1960s the Supreme Court under the leadership of Chief Justice Earl Warren handed down a series of decisions that interpreted the Bill of Rights and the Fourteenth Amendment in ways that significantly expanded the protection of individuals from government control and interference. For example, the Warren Court provided dramatically increased freedom for the press to criticize public officials and public figures, increased the permissible standards regarding the publication of sexually oriented materials, banned government sponsorship of prayers in the public schools, heightened the protection of religious minorities to exercise their religious beliefs, expanded the guarantees of the criminally accused so that they limited not only the federal government but also the states, and sought to end racial segregation in public schools and other public facilities in the South. As two leading experts on the Court have noted, Chief Justice Warren "presided over what can only be described as a constitutional revolution, generated by a group of justices who were perhaps the most liberal in American history" (Walker and Epstein 1993, p. 19).

Although the Warren Court's decisions were supported by political liberals, a strong reaction arose among individuals and groups with more conservative views. In the presidential election of 1968, Republican candidate Richard Nixon made the Supreme Court a focal point of his campaign, and he promised to appoint justices to the Court who would halt and reverse the liberal directions of the Court. Conservatives argued that the liberal decisions of the Court had resulted in a breakdown of law and order in American society, the weakening of America's religious foundations, and a dramatic rise in deviant behavior, including an explosion of pornographic materials.

Nixon won the 1968 election, and because of an unusual series of events he was able in his first term in office to replace four members of the Warren Court with his more conservative appointees. Chief Justice Warren announced his intention to resign in 1968, but Democratic President Lyndon Johnson was unsuccessful in appointing a new chief justice. Upon assuming office in 1969, Nixon named Warren Burger, an outspoken critic of many of the Warren Court's decisions, as the new chief justice. A year later in 1970 Nixon appointed Harry Blackmun, a conservative friend of Burger, to replace one of the Warren Court's most liberal members, Abe Fortas. Finally, in 1971 Nixon had the opportunity to change the Court even further when Hugo Black and John Marshall Harlan resigned for health reasons. Nixon named Lewis Powell, a conservative Southern Democrat from Virginia, to replace Black. Nixon's most controversial nominee was William Rehnquist, who was named to succeed Harlan. Rehnquist had a reputation as a radical conservative, but he was nonetheless confirmed by the Democratically controlled Senate.

Did these more conservative justices engage in a conservative counterrevolution in American civil rights and liberties? The answer is no. Although the Supreme Court during the period of Burger's leadership from 1969 to 1986 was substantially more conservative than the Warren Court, the Court did not engage in dramatic reversals of the major precedents established by the Warren Court (see, e.g., Blasi 1983; O'Brien 1987; and Urofsky 1991).

Indeed, in many areas of constitutional law the Burger Court created major new liberal precedents. In *Roe v. Wade* (1973) the Court recognized the abortion decision as an aspect of the right to privacy protected under the Fourteenth Amendment Due Process Clause, thus providing women the constitutional guarantee of freedom to choose to have an abortion during the first six months of pregnancy. In the area of school desegregation, the Burger Court in *Swann v. Charlotte-Mecklenberg Board of Education* (1971) gave constitutional approval to busing as a means to achieve racially integrated schools; furthermore, the Burger Court expanded the scope of racial integration of public schools from the South to the entire country in *Denver School District No. 1 v. Keyes* (1973). The Burger Court also gave constitutional approval to affirmative action programs in such cases as *Regents of the University of California v. Bakke* (1978) and *Fullilove v. Klutznick* (1980). Finally, the Burger Court in *Craig v. Boren* (1976) created a new sexual equality standard, giving heightened judicial protection to individuals bringing claims of gender discrimination against the government.

The Court's membership changes during the first term of Richard Nixon thus did not result in a dramatic, conservative shift in American civil rights and liberties. Burger and Rehnquist were the only two justices appointed by Nixon who were consistently conservative, and Burger on occasion supported new liberal precedents. Blackmun was initially a member of the conservative camp, but by the early 1980s he had become a liberal member of the Court, frequently joining the Court's two leading liberals from the Warren Court era, William Brennan and Thurgood Marshall. Nixon's fourth appointment, Lewis Powell, was a judicial moderate, who frequently tipped the balance on a Court closely divided between liberals and conservatives, typically but not always in a conservative direction.

Enormously frustrated over the failure of the Nixon appointees to change the direction of the Court,[2] conservatives were hopeful that President Ronald Reagan would be able to make appointments to the Court that would finally bring about a conservative counterrevolution. During his first term in office from 1981 to 1985, Reagan had the opportunity to appoint only one new member to the Court. Potter Stewart, a moderate Republican named to the Court in 1959, resigned in 1981, and Reagan appointed Sandra Day O'Connor to be the first woman ever to sit on the Supreme Court. O'Connor was more conservative than Stewart had been, but her effect on the direction of the Court was relatively modest.

Reagan's next opportunity to change the Court occurred in 1986 when Chief Justice Burger resigned. Reagan nominated the Court's most conservative justice, Rehnquist, to move from his associate justice seat to that of chief justice, and Reagan then nominated a well-known conservative jurist, Antonin Scalia, to Rehnquist's associate justice position. Rehnquist received more opposing votes than any other chief justice in American history, but he was confirmed by the Senate 65–33 on September 17, 1986. Scalia was confirmed overwhelmingly by a 98-0 vote the same day.

An important reason why liberal opposition was not more intense to the 1986 nominations of Rehnquist and Scalia was the perception that these changes would not fundamentally alter the close balance between liberals and conservatives. During the last years of Burger's tenure as chief justice, the Court was widely viewed as containing four liberals—Brennan, Marshall, Blackmun, and John Paul Stevens, a 1976 appointment of President Gerald Ford—and four conservative justices—Burger, Rehnquist, O'Connor, and Byron White, a Kennedy appointee who had become increasingly conservative over the years. Justice Powell, the Southern Democrat, was perceived to be a moderate who frequently held the balance of power on the Court. Thus, Burger's retirement, the elevation of Rehnquist to chief justice, and the appointment of Scalia did not fundamentally alter the liberal-conservative alignment of the Court.

The Court's delicate balance was suddenly threatened, however, by Powell's retirement at the end of the 1986–87 term. Reagan and the conservatives now had the opportunity to complete the conservative counterrevolution that Nixon had started almost two decades before. If a distinctively conservative replacement could be made for Powell, then a conservative majority could not only regularly control the outcome of the Court's decisions but also possibly overturn many of the leading liberal precedents of the Warren and Burger Courts.

The Bork Nomination

Robert Bork was Reagan's choice. Bork was one of the harshest critics of the liberal decisions of the Warren and Burger Courts. In his academic writings, he had strongly attacked the Court's decisions supporting school desegregation, affirmative action, the separation of church and state, expanded protection for the criminally accused, and the right of privacy, including the abortion decision. Perhaps even more significantly, Bork's broader judicial philosophy was in sharp conflict with the views of the leading liberals of the Warren and Burger Courts. Bork advocated a

---

[2]Nixon's immediate successors had little chance to change the Court. Gerald Ford, 1974–1977, appointed one Supreme Court justice, naming John Paul Stevens, a moderate Republican, to replace William Douglas. Jimmy Carter, 1977–1981, did not have the opportunity to appoint any new members to the Court.

philosophy of "original understanding," an approach to constitutional law in which justices would be guided in their decision making by the text of the Constitution, the intent of the drafters of the Constitution, and the general understanding of the constitutional provisions when they were proposed and ratified. Any other approach, Bork argued, would inevitably allow justices to introduce their personal biases into the decision-making process, and Bork maintained that this was precisely what the ultraliberal justices of the Warren and Burger Courts had done.

Bork's nomination was controversial even within the Reagan administration. Moderate conservatives led by White House Chief of Staff Howard Baker argued strongly against Bork. Attorney General Edwin Meese pressed hard for Bork, however. Meese had also been a harsh critic of the liberal decisions of the Warren and Burger Courts as well as an advocate of Bork's approach to constitutional law. Aided by strong support from conservative interest groups, Meese prevailed and Reagan nominated Bork on July 1, 1987, to replace Powell.

Although White House moderates lost the battle over naming Bork, they did succeed in the debate over how to present Bork to the American people and the United States Senate. Under Baker's leadership, the strategy was to recast Bork as a moderate, centrist jurist who would not pose a direct threat to existing Supreme Court precedents. Conservative organizations were discouraged from championing Bork as a radical, Reagan continually emphasized in his speeches that Bork held views similar to those of Justice Powell whom he would replace, and lengthy reports issued by both the White House and the Justice Department portrayed Bork as a judicial moderate.

The White House strategy was not successful, however. Liberal senators and interest groups engaged in a massive, well-coordinated attack on Bork from the day his nomination was announced, and the message of the White House was largely drowned out in the roar of adverse reactions to Bork's nomination.

Liberal interest groups were well-prepared for the fight against Bork. His name had been mentioned prominently for a Supreme Court nomination for more than a decade, but he was passed over in 1975 to replace William Douglas, in 1981 to replace Potter Stewart, and in 1986 when Burger's resignation created an opening on the Court. Thus, liberal groups were well aware of Bork's record, they had long been preparing for the possibility of fighting his nomination, and they were determined to defeat him.

The opposition to Bork by liberal groups was the most massive and intense in the history of Supreme Court nominations. Nearly one hundred interest groups publicly opposed Bork's nomination. Even groups like Common Cause and the American Civil Liberties Union, which historically remained neutral regarding Supreme Court nominations, announced their opposition because of their fear of the impact Bork could have on American civil rights and liberties (Bamberger 1987, p. 880). One estimate places the expenditures of liberal groups at $12 to $15 million in opposing Bork (Baum 1992, p. 35). No stone was left unturned in this campaign. The interest groups mobilized their members to flood the Senate with letters opposing Bork. Radio and TV ads portrayed Bork as a dire threat to American freedom and equality. Senators were threatened with electoral defeat if they supported Bork. Law school professors were mobilized, with almost two thousand faculty members signing letters in opposition to Bork. The interest group campaign against Bork was so extraordinary that a new verb was introduced into the English language; to oppose and strongly attack someone is to "bork" the person.

Conservative interest groups rallied in support of Bork, but their efforts were not effective. They did not have either the numbers or the money possessed by the liberal groups, and the conservative groups were somewhat hamstrung in their efforts to mobilize their supporters because of the White House campaign to portray Bork as a moderate. The conservative groups thus tended to fight a defensive battle, primarily reacting to the charges advanced by Bork's opponents.

Bork's supporters did experience some successes, however. One important development was historically unprecedented support from current and former members of the Supreme Court, including John Paul Stevens, Byron White, and Warren Burger, all of whom announced that they favored his nomination. In addition, in a poll of four hundred state and federal judges by the *National Law Journal*, 50 percent of the judges expressed their support for Bork, 25 percent expressed their opposition, and 25 percent were noncommittal (McGuigan and Weyrich 1993, p. 319). The American Bar Association's Committee on the Federal Judiciary also voted to recommend Bork, but this support was undercut substantially because four of the fifteen members of the ABA Committee voted that he was "not qualified."

The activities of the liberal and conservative interest groups were of great importance, but the ultimate decision on Bork's confirmation would be made by U.S. Senators, initially the members of the Senate Judiciary Committee and ultimately the full Senate. Given this reality, Bork's fate may well have been decided a year earlier on election day in November of 1986. The Republican Party controlled the Senate after the 1984 election by a margin of 53–47. Reagan worked extraordinarily hard in the 1986 election to maintain Republican control of the Senate, and a major campaign theme he stressed was the importance of keeping the Senate Judiciary Committee out of Democratic hands. In a North Carolina speech, Reagan stated a theme he repeated in many states: "Today, Senator Strom Thurmond and Jim Broyhill are in a majority on the Senate Judiciary Committee, overseeing judicial appointments. Without Jim Broyhill and a Republican Senate majority, that job will be turned over to Teddy Kennedy and Joe Biden .... You can strike a blow against drugs, thugs, and hoodlums by casting your vote for Jim and keeping him as a force for law and order in the United States Senate. The future of our country, its safety and security, is in your hands" (quoted in Segal and Spaeth 1993, p. 139). Reagan's efforts were unsuccessful, however, with the Democrats capturing twenty of the thirty-four Senate seats in the 1986 election, giving the Democrats control of the Senate by a 55–45 margin.

Reagan's fears about Democratic control of the Senate quickly became a reality when Biden was selected as chair of the committee and Kennedy gained significant power as a majority party member of the committee. Both men were influential in Bork's defeat. Kennedy denounced Bork immediately from the Senate floor when the nomination was announced and helped to lead the Senate fight against his confirmation. In a widely publicized Senate speech, Kennedy stated: "Robert Bork's America is a land in which women would be forced into back-alley abortions, blacks would sit in segregated lunch counters, rogue police would break down citizens' doors in midnight raids, schoolchildren could not be taught about evolution, writers and artists would be censored at the whim of government, and the doors of the Federal courts would be shut on the fingers of millions of citizens for whom the judiciary is often the only protector of the individual rights that are the heart of our democracy" (quoted in Walker and Epstein 1993, p. 43). Unlike Kennedy, Biden did not immediately oppose Bork. Indeed, following Scalia's confirmation, Biden had gone on public record in support of Bork, stating that he would have voted to confirm Bork if he had been nominated instead of Scalia, regardless of the pressure from liberal interest groups. When this hypothetical situation became a reality, however, Biden changed his view. Under intense pressure from liberal groups and seeking to create the foundation for a presidential bid, Biden announced in early

July that he was opposed to Bork and would make the campaign against Bork his top priority.

Bork's Senate confirmation hearing was one of the longest and most contentious in American history. Senate liberals attempted to raise questions that would result in Bork portraying himself as a dangerous, radical conservative who would be a dire threat to American civil rights and liberties. The strategy of Bork and his White House and Senate supporters was to establish that Bork was an experienced, highly qualified candidate with a well-developed judicial philosophy that would lead to reasonable, moderate judicial decisions.

Bork was successful in articulating his judicial philosophy of original understanding, which he later explained more fully in his best-selling book on his nomination defeat (Bork 1990). Bork argued before the Judiciary Committee that the proper role of federal judges must be carefully controlled because they are given life tenure and thus are not accountable to the people. Because these life appointments given to judges by the Constitution go against the principle of majority rule, federal judges must follow strict legal criteria in their decision making. This is to be achieved, Bork argued, through the approach of original understanding, under which "a judge is to apply the Constitution according to the principles intended by those who ratified the document . . ." (Bork 1990, p. 143). Any other approach, Bork argued, allows judges to substitute their personal values for those of elected representatives. And this is precisely what the United States Supreme Court has been doing in recent decades, Bork argued, thereby enacting an egalitarian political agenda unsupported by the American people and their elected representatives.

Although liberal senators challenged Bork's judicial philosophy, they concentrated their attention on his views on specific constitutional issues. Most Supreme Court nominees refuse to address such specific questions, but Bork could not avoid discussing them because they were so well known through his scholarly publications. However, following the strategy of portraying himself as a moderate, Bork repudiated many of his previous positions. For example, he indicated support for the 1964 Civil Rights Act, he agreed that the Fourteenth Amendment applied to gender as well as racial discrimination, and he stated that the First Amendment should encompass scientific, literary, and artistic speech (Segal and Spaeth 1993, p. 139). These positions were all contrary to views that Bork had stated in his writings as a law professor. Bork did not, however, moderate his view that the right of privacy, including a right of choice for abortion, is not a fundamental constitutional liberty.

Bork and his supporters were caught in a dilemma from which they could not escape. By strongly defending his prior views, Bork would have given ammunition to the liberal critics who labeled him a dangerous radical. By modifying many of his previous views, however, Bork gave the appearance of undergoing a "confirmation conversion," a change in his positions stimulated solely by his desire to become a Supreme Court justice. Bork was thus unsuccessful in satisfying either his conservative supporters or his liberal opponents. Conservatives were disappointed in him for moderating positions on many issues and were uncertain if he would be committed to reversing the liberal trends of the Warren and Burger Courts. Meanwhile, liberals were not convinced that Bork had really altered his views. Thus, when the votes were cast in the Senate Judiciary Committee, Bork lost by a decisive 9–5 margin.

Bork fared no better before the full Senate, which had the final vote on his nomination. Despite frantic efforts by the White House and conservative interest groups, Bork suffered the largest margin of defeat of any candidate in Supreme Court history, losing by a vote of 58–42. The vote followed party lines closely, with fifty-three of fifty-five Democratic senators voting against Bork.

The reasons for Bork's defeat are not difficult to identify. Lawrence Baum's (1992) research on Supreme Court nominees has identified four key variables that can prevent a nominee from being confirmed: (1) the perceived importance of the nomination, (2) the political strength of the president in the Senate, (3) interest group activity, and (4) the qualifications of the nominee. Bork faced severe problems in all four areas. This nomination was widely perceived as one of the most critical in Supreme Court history, a nomination that could profoundly affect the direction of constitutional interpretation of American civil rights and liberties. Reagan had limited influence in the Democratically controlled Senate, and he had directly attacked in his campaign speeches the two leading Democratic members of the Senate Judiciary Committee. Liberal interest groups had mounted a massive, effective campaign that created enormous pressure on moderate senators. Finally, Bork's qualifications, impressive as they were, had been undermined by the negative votes from members of the ABA committee and the outpouring of opposition from the nation's law professors.

Aftermath of the Bork Defeat

Angered by what was perceived to be a highly partisan, ideological attack on an eminently qualified candidate for the Court, Attorney General Meese and other conservatives in the White House pressed once again for a strongly conservative nominee rather than a more moderate candidate. The conservatives prevailed, and Douglas Ginsburg, a federal appeals court judge, was quickly nominated by Reagan. Ginsburg was viewed as a younger Bork in terms of his training, experience, ideology, and judicial philosophy; but unlike Bork, Ginsburg did not have an extensive record of published research that he would have to defend against liberal opponents. Ginsburg's nomination ran into immediate difficulties, however. In addition to the predictable opposition to his conservative views, charges arose of conflicts of interest involving Ginsburg when he was on the White House staff. When Ginsburg admitted to smoking marijuana with his students when he was a professor at Harvard Law School, White House officials decided that their slogan of "Just say no to drugs" forced them to just say no to Ginsburg, and his nomination was withdrawn.

Anthony Kennedy had been passed over twice previously as the Reagan administration sought to replace Powell, but following the Ginsburg fiasco a consensus quickly emerged to send Kennedy's name to the Senate. He possessed strong credentials. Kennedy graduated from Stanford with Phi Beta Kappa honors, and he earned his law degree from Harvard. A successful California attorney, he taught law at McGeorge School of Law and served on the Ninth Circuit Court of Appeals to which he was appointed in 1975. Kennedy's record suggested to the Reagan administration that he would be a consistent conservative, thus creating the desired solid conservative majority on the Court. Kennedy did not, however, have a publication record or a series of judicial opinions associating him with ultraconservative positions. He received strong support from the American Bar Association, and opposition was virtually nonexistent at the Senate Judiciary Committee's hearings. He deflected any potential opposition by rejecting Bork's philosophy of original understanding, indicating that he had no firmly set judicial philosophy that guided him, and refusing to commit himself on more specific, controversial issues. He was unanimously confirmed by the Senate on February 3, 1988.

What effect did Kennedy's appointment have on the civil rights and liberties decisions of the Court? Little effect could be noted in the 1987–88 term[3] because Kennedy was able to participate in only a few decisions due to the lengthy confirmation process; but the 1988–89 term, Kennedy's first full term on the Court, appeared to mark the beginning of a dramatic conservative turn for the Rehnquist Court. Writing in the *Harvard Law Review*, Erwin Chemerinsky (1989, pp. 44–45) provided the following stark assessment of the impact of Kennedy: "Justice Kennedy's first full term on the Court produced a clear and resounding initial answer to his ideology and impact. Joining Chief Justice Rehnquist and Justices White, O'Connor, and Scalia, Justice Kennedy supplied the critical fifth vote in a series of conservative 5–4 decisions in cases concerning abortion, capital punishment, civil rights, and criminal procedure. For conservatives, this is a year of rejoicing. The Reagan legacy of a conservative Court seems secure for many years to come. For liberals, it is a time of despair. The 1988–89 term was devastating for civil rights and civil liberties."

Liberal despair was to increase even further. The Court's two leading liberal voices, William Brennan and Thurgood Marshall, resigned in 1990 and 1991, respectively. Republican President George Bush was thus given the opportunity to ensure even more complete conservative domination of the Court. Bush named David Souter to replace Brennan and then appointed Clarence Thomas to take Marshall's seat. Souter was called the "Stealth" candidate because little was known from public records about his judicial philosophy and positions on civil rights and liberties, and he breezed through the Senate confirmation process, being approved by a vote of 90–9. Thomas, an African American, had a much more difficult time. This was due in part to his widely publicized conservative views that contrasted sharply with those of Marshall's, the Court's first African-American justice. Thomas also encountered serious problems over allegations of sexual harassment by a former aide, Anita Hill. Thomas eventually won confirmation, however, by the narrowest margin in history, 52–48.

Did the addition of Souter and Thomas solidify the conservative majority on the Rehnquist Court and lead to a conservative counterrevolution in civil rights and liberties? This important question is one that will be addressed throughout this book as we examine each area of American civil rights and liberties. For now, we can only observe that the research done thus far on this question does not provide a clear answer, but the evidence does suggest that the appointments of Souter and Thomas did not move the Court in a sharply conservative direction.

Some evidence exists that the addition of Souter and Thomas further solidified the conservative counterrevolution that began with Kennedy's appointment. Studies of both Souter (Johnson and Smith 1992) and Thomas (Smith and Johnson 1993) have shown that both justices were substantially more conservative than their liberal predecessors. O'Brien (1993, p. 5) has observed that "with the retirements of Justices Brennan and Marshall, and the arrival of Justices Souter and Thomas, the conservative majority on the Rehnquist Court further solidified . . . ." Walker and Epstein (1993, p. 21) have noted that with the Reagan and Bush appointees occupying six of the nine seats on the Court, "the counterrevolution that Nixon tried to launch may be in high gear."

---

[3]The Supreme Court's annual term begins on the first Monday of October and typically ends in late June. Thus, the Court's term can be called by either the year in which it began or by the two-year period that it covered. To illustrate, the 1987 term covered the years 1987 and 1988, and this term can be referred to as the 1987 term or the 1987–88 term.

Other research, however, questions whether the Court has become increasingly more conservative in the period since Bork's nomination was defeated and Kennedy, Souter, and Thomas joined the Court. For example, Smith and Hensley (1993) analyzed the Rehnquist Court's civil rights and liberties decisions from the 1986 term through the 1991 term and found a surprising pattern: the Rehnquist Court became increasingly liberal in civil rights and liberties decisions after Souter and Thomas replaced Brennan and Marshall! In a subsequent analysis, Hensley and Smith (1995) suggested that three factors may be primarily responsible for the Court's surprising moderation: (1) the issues before the Court may have changed, in part because lower court judges appointed by Reagan and Bush may have been so ultraconservative that the Rehnquist Court found it necessary to rein them in by overruling them, (2) Souter has not been as conservative as many observers predicted he would be, and (3) O'Connor and Kennedy have become significantly less conservative. Friedelbaum (1994) has also argued that O'Connor, Kennedy, and Souter have emerged as a moderating coalition on the Rehnquist Court.

The appointments of Ruth Bader Ginsburg and Stephen Breyer further complicate efforts to analyze the Rehnquist Court era. Democratic President Bill Clinton appointed Ginsburg in 1993 to replace Byron White. This was the first opportunity in twenty-six years for a Democratic president to appoint a Supreme Court justice, and conservatives expressed deep concern that Ginsburg would bring extremely liberal views to the Court. An initial analysis of Ginsburg's first term on the Court indicated, however, that she was a moderate in civil rights and liberties cases, voting liberally in 53 percent of these decisions, and that she was aligned most closely with another moderate liberal, Justice Souter. (Smith, et al. 1994). Clinton's appointment in 1994 of Breyer to replace Justice Blackmun raised relatively little controversy because Breyer was perceived to be a judicial moderate who was acceptable to groups and individuals across the political spectrum. Many Court observers speculated that Breyer might become another member of a growing, centrist coalition. These predictions were largely confirmed in Breyer's first term when he voted liberally in 57 percent of the Court's civil rights and liberties cases and aligned most closely with Ginsburg and Souter.

Despite Clinton's appointments of Ginsburg and Breyer to the Court, however, many observers have argued that the Court took a dramatic shift in a conservative direction in the 1994 term. In this term, Kennedy and O'Connor frequently joined the Court's three most conservative justices—Rehnquist, Scalia, and Thomas—to create five-person majorities that significantly altered the Court's approaches in the areas of affirmative action, race-based legislative redistricting, and perhaps in church-state relations.

We thus have many more questions than answers. Did Presidents Reagan and Bush succeed in packing the Court with a majority of conservative justices who fundamentally changed the direction of Court policies regarding civil rights and liberties? Has a moderate group of justices emerged in recent years that has maintained continuity with past Supreme Court decisions? We will pursue these central questions throughout this book because one major purpose is to provide insight regarding the effects of the changing membership of the Court on American civil rights and liberties.

Any answers we provide will necessarily be tentative, however, because we are shooting at a moving target. Between the time we write these words and you, the reader, see them, the Court will have handed down numerous additional decisions, and the membership of the Court may have undergone further change.

Three Approaches to the Study of Civil Rights and Liberties

We hope that the analysis of the controversy over Robert Bork's nomination to the Supreme Court has illustrated not only the controversial role of the Court in interpreting American civil rights and liberties but also the potential effect that changing membership patterns can have on the policies of the high court. The case study of the Bork nomination also provides a useful background against which to discuss three major approaches to the study of American civil rights and liberties: the legal model, the political model, and the attitudinal model. We will be discussing all three of these models throughout the book because each approach has strengths and weaknesses. It is therefore important to evaluate these models in some detail, discussing their basic assumptions and ideas as well as analyzing their advantages and limitations in illuminating the study of civil rights and liberties.

The Legal Model

The legal model of Supreme Court decision making is based on the idea that the justices make decisions using a wide variety of legal criteria in an objective manner largely devoid of personal and political considerations. A classical statement of the legal model was advanced by Supreme Court Justice Owen Roberts in the 1936 case of *United States v. Butler*, in which the Court declared unconstitutional the 1933 Agricultural Adjustment Act: "This Court neither approves nor condemns any legislative policy. Its delicate and difficult office is to ascertain and declare whether the legislation is in accordance with, or in contradiction of, the provisions of the Constitution . . . ." And the process by which this is done, according to Roberts, is "to lay the article of the Constitution which is involved beside the statute which is challenged and to decide whether the latter squares with the former" (297 U.S. at 62, 63).

Segal and Spaeth (1993, pp. 33–53) present a more complete description of the legal model. They see the model having four components that are presumably used by the justices in their decision making. One component is the *plain meaning* guideline, which specifies that justices are guided by the explicit language of the Constitution, of laws, and of judicially formulated rules. Thus, the Fifth Amendment Due Process Clause specifies that no person can be denied his or her right to life, liberty, and property without due process; but the plain meaning of this language is that a person's life might be taken if due process is followed, and hence the death penalty is not unconstitutional. A second facet of the legal model involves the *intentions* of the writers of the Constitution. The task of Supreme Court justices is to ascertain this intent and then to apply these intentions to the case in hand in interpreting the Constitution. A third component is *precedent*, the previous decisions of the Court. The justices are to determine which past decisions are most applicable to the case under consideration and then to apply the same principles to reach a decision. The final element of the legal model is *balancing*, a process through which the justices weigh the relative merits of competing claims to assess which side presents the strongest legal arguments in a case.

Probably the most widely discussed and the most influential description of the legal model has been articulated by Robert Bork in both his writings and his appearance before the Senate Judiciary Committee. We briefly discussed his judicial philosophy above, but now it is useful to examine it in greater detail.

Bork (1990) characterizes his approach as a philosophy of original understanding. Bork's judicial philosophy is premised on his analysis of the conflict inherent in the Constitution between the principles of majority rule and minority rights. The popularly elected branches of government, the legislative and executive, reflect majority will, an essential requirement of a democratic society. Civil rights and liberties are also fundamental to a democracy, however, and they are given constitutional protection, thus placing them beyond majority rule. The interpretation of these constitutional guarantees appropriately resides with the courts through their power of judicial review, the authority to declare unconstitutional the acts of the other branches of the government. The federal judiciary is nonelected and serves for life, however, and therefore the power of judicial review must be exercised with extraordinary care in a democratic society. Thus, Bork (1990, p. 2) argues, a judge "must be able to demonstrate that [he] began from recognized legal principles and reasoned in an intellectually coherent and politically neutral way to his result."

Bork specifies a set of guidelines that judges should follow to assure that their decisions are based on neutral principles rather than personal or political values. As a beginning point, where the language of the Constitution is specific, it must be obeyed; and if a purported liberty is not written into the Constitution, judges should not claim that it exists. As a closely related point, where a demonstrable consensus can be ascertained regarding the understanding of a constitutional principle by the writers and ratifiers, then this original understanding must be followed. If ambiguity exists regarding constitutional language and original understanding, then maximum deference must be given by the courts to the majoritarian branches of government, who are sworn to uphold the Constitution. Finally, where no guidance at all can be determined, the courts should refrain from acting and allow the majoritarian branches to determine public policy.

Is the legal model an accurate way to understand Supreme Court decision making? The model does receive substantial support. Most importantly, the justices of the Supreme Court frequently advocate this model as a valid representation of their work. Their written opinions attempt to explain their judgments through careful reasoning based on precedents, legal doctrines, and historical analysis. In their off-the-Court remarks as well, the justices typically argue that their decisions are based on the objective analysis of legal criteria. Support for the legal model also comes explicitly or implicitly from most civil rights and liberties textbooks. Supreme Court decisions are described and analyzed in terms of the controlling legal precedents and doctrines that the Court has established, and students are expected to read lengthy Supreme Court opinions carefully to learn the essence of Supreme Court decision making—carefully crafted legal argumentation.

A great deal of criticism exists of the legal model, however. Bork (1990) represents one form of criticism. He argues that his version of the legal model *can and should be used* in interpreting constitutional law, but he maintains that it unfortunately does not characterize current Supreme Court decision making. Instead, Bork argues, American society has witnessed the "political seduction of the law" through which an intellectual elite and political minority has used the courts to further its own radical, egalitarian political agenda.

A quite different approach to the validity of the legal model—and to the validity of Bork's philosophy of original understanding—rejects the approach as a legal fiction that serves to justify and legitimate judicial power but fails to explain how Supreme Court justices really make their decisions. Segal and Spaeth (1993, pp. 33–64) have developed one of the most recent critiques of the legal model, arguing that none of the major components of the model can effectively guide the justices' decision making. They argue that the plain meaning guideline is inadequate because words rarely have plain meaning but rather multiple possible meanings, the terms used in the Constitution or congressional statutes are rarely defined, and various provisions of the Constitution or a law may conflict with one another. The intent of the writers is also hopelessly vague for many reasons, according to Segal and Spaeth, including the lack of historical documentation and the subjectivity involved in interpreting the relatively limited historical documents that are available. Similarly, precedent provides little clear guidance to the Supreme Court, primarily because ample precedents typically exist for both sides appearing before the Supreme Court. Finally, balancing also is a highly subjective process that provides no clear guidance in judicial decision making.

Despite these criticisms of the legal model as an accurate explanation for the decision-making process of the Supreme Court, the model cannot be rejected completely. Even if "the legal model serves only to cloak—to conceal—the motivations that cause the justices to decide as they do" (Segal and Spaeth 1993, p. 1), attention must still be given to the model. The justices' opinions use the elements of the legal model extensively, and thus a familiarity with the model is necessary in order to read the Court's decisions. In addition, it is not possible to assess the validity of the legal model without becoming closely familiar with its assumptions and methodology.

We do not totally reject the validity of the legal model, however. Valid criticisms can certainly be raised regarding the approach, and Segal and Spaeth (1993) are probably correct that the legal model as described above cannot be subjected to empirically based, quantitative testing. Nonetheless, substantial evidence can be cited that the legal model must be given some consideration. Lawrence Baum (1992, p. 134) has stated this argument effectively: "It would be a mistake . . . to dismiss the law altogether as a factor in Supreme Court decisions, because those decisions are made in a legal context. Justices are trained in a tradition that emphasizes the law as a basis for judicial decisions. They are judged by a legal audience largely in terms of their adherence to what are regarded as good legal principles. Perhaps most important, they work in the language of the law, and this language channels [justices'] thinking and constrains their choices."

Many empirical studies of Supreme Court decision making also give some support to the legal model. Tracy George and Lee Epstein (1992), for example, conducted research on Supreme Court decision making that quantitatively tested the validity of a legal model versus an extralegal model. They found both models to be successful in explaining the justices' voting patterns, but they were most successful when they combined the two models. In a detailed analysis of the Supreme Court's abortion and death penalty cases, Epstein and Joseph Kobylka (1992) found that legal factors were of major significance in explaining changing patterns of Supreme Court decision making. Although they recognized the importance of the justices' attitudes and values as well as the importance of the political environment and the activities of interest groups, Epstein and Kobylka (p. 8) argue that "it is *the law and legal arguments as framed by legal actors* that most clearly influence the content and direction of legal change" (emphasis in original).

We will thus use the legal model as we examine American civil rights and liberties and the changing Supreme Court. But this discussion also alerts us to the limitations and weaknesses of the legal model. We therefore need to use additional models in order to achieve a more complete and accurate understanding of American civil rights and liberties.

The Political Model

Reacting to the almost exclusive focus on the legal model in constitutional law textbooks, several recent studies have broadened the study of civil rights and liberties by emphasizing the broader political context within which Supreme Court decision making occurs (e.g., Fisher 1995; O'Brien 1995; and Epstein and Walker

1995). The political model is based on a very different underlying assumption. The legal model, as we have seen, assumes that the Supreme Court is fundamentally different from the other branches of the federal government because the Court is the nonpolitical branch involved with the neutral interpretation of the Constitution, the laws, and government actions. In contrast, the political model assumes that the Supreme Court is fundamentally similar to the other branches of the federal government because the Court exists in the same political environment, is subject to many of the same political forces, and makes authoritative decisions for the society based not only on legal considerations but also on political considerations.

The case study of the Bork nomination presented earlier in this chapter is an example of the use of the political model to study the Supreme Court. The case study placed the Bork nomination in a broad political context, emphasizing the importance of the nomination in terms of the role of the Court in interpreting American civil rights and liberties. Interest groups in American society were deeply interested and involved in the process, and intense partisan and ideological struggle occurred between the White House and the Senate as well as within the Senate. Bork was ultimately defeated because of fears that his presence on the Court could radically alter the civil rights and liberties policies of the Court, thereby profoundly affecting the lives of millions of Americans.

The political model can be understood more formally by viewing the Court through a systems analysis approach, a theoretical perspective that can be used to study an entire political system (e.g., Easton 1965) or a specific aspect of the political system such as the courts (e.g., Goldman and Jahnige 1976; Bartee 1984). From a systems analysis perspective, politics is the authoritative allocation of values for a society, and the Supreme Court's decisions—like those of Congress and the executive branch—have this authoritative capacity because societal members must follow these decisions or risk government punishment, including the loss of freedom through imprisonment. The Supreme Court, like the other branches of government, exists within a political environment from which demands as well as supports come into the Court. The demands on the Court primarily take the form of legal suits involving a conflict between two parties; these demands are frequently supported by interest groups who often use the courts because they were unsuccessful in pressing their demands on the other branches of the government. Like the other branches of government, the Supreme Court has a variety of methods of gatekeeping, that is, controlling the cases they will agree to hear. Systems theory does not provide specific guidelines regarding the decision-making phase of the political process, but more specific decision-making approaches—e.g., the legal model or the attitudinal model—can be used with the systems analysis approach. The next phase of systems theory involves output, implementation, and impact. This stage focuses on how society reacts to the decisions of the Court and the effects the Court's decisions have on American society. Finally, the systems analysis approach recognizes that the political process is a continuous and dynamic one, and thus the Court receives feedback, which takes the form of new demands and supports. These ideas will be developed in much greater detail in Chapter 2, "The Supreme Court in the American Political System."

Like the legal model, the political model has both strengths and weaknesses in helping us to analyze American civil rights and liberties and the changing Supreme Court. The political model, whether applied through systems analysis or in some other way, is widely accepted by political scientists who study the Supreme Court because it provides a broader, more realistic perspective on the Court than does the legal model. The political model does have limitations, however. Most importantly, the political model is a macrotheory rather than a microtheory; thus, while it does provide an important, broad perspective on the role of the Supreme Court in American society, it does not provide guidance in understanding the decision-making process of the Supreme Court in civil rights and liberties cases. The legal model, which we have already discussed, does provide a perspective on this process, but we have also seen that the legal model has important weaknesses and limitations. We therefore turn our attention now to the attitudinal model of Supreme Court decision making, an approach that helps us address the weaknesses of both the legal and the political models.

The Attitudinal Model

The attitudinal approach is most closely associated with the work of Jeffrey Segal and Harold Spaeth (1993). Their basic idea is that "the decisions of the Court are based on the facts of the case in light of the ideological attitudes and values of the justices" (p. 32). They state the fundamental idea of the attitudinal model even more directly in the following words: "Simply put, Rehnquist votes the way he does because he is extremely conservative; Marshall voted the way he did because he is extremely liberal" (p. 65).

The case study of the Bork nomination provides an excellent example of the acceptance of the attitudinal model by politicians and interest groups in American society. The Reagan administration selected Bork for a seat on the Court because they believed that his basic values and attitudes would lead to extremely conservative decisions on civil rights and liberties, and he was ultimately defeated because liberal politicians and interest groups feared that Bork's strong ideological views could tip a closely divided Court in the direction of a conservative counterrevolution.

Despite the seeming simplicity of the attitudinal model, it is a sophisticated theory based on many decades of research by political scientists and psychologists. The origins of the attitudinal model can be traced to the research of C. Herman Pritchett, who published a pioneering book in 1948 entitled *The Roosevelt Court*, which was based on the assumption that the nonunanimous decisions of the Court were decided by the policy preferences of the justices. Using quantitative techniques to study the voting patterns of the justices, Pritchett found strong support for his ideas. Pritchett's work was developed more fully in subsequent decades by Glendon Schubert (1965 and 1974), who drew on the research of psychologist Clyde Coombs, as well as by David Rhode and Harold Spaeth (1976), who used ideas from psychologist Milton Rokeach. Building on these seminal works, numerous books and scholarly articles have subsequently developed and refined the attitudinal model.

In Segal and Spaeth's (1993) recent book, they argue that the Court's decisions on the merits of the cases can be successfully explained by the attitudinal model. They divide the Court's cases into ten major policy or issue areas, including five civil rights and liberties areas: First Amendment, criminal procedure, civil rights, privacy, and due process. In each of these areas, the outcomes of the cases and the justices' votes can be characterized as "liberal" or "conservative." Segal and Spaeth then offer precise definitions of liberal outcomes and votes, with conservative outcomes and votes being the opposite. In general, a liberal decision is one that supports the individual who is alleging that the government has interfered with a constitutionally protected liberty, whereas a conservative outcome is one that rules in favor of the government, finding no violation of an individual's constitutional right.[4] Using these classification systems, Segal and Spaeth employ a variety of sophisticated quantita-

[4]A more elaborate discussion of the concepts of liberalism and conservatism can be found in Appendix A.

tive techniques to show that Supreme Court justices' ideology is central to their decision making, and thus the attitudinal model is successful in explaining and predicting Supreme Court behavior.

The attitudinal model is widely accepted as the most reliable and valid explanation of Supreme Court decision making (cf. Baum 1992; Barnum 1993; O'Brien 1993; Wasby 1993), but surprisingly the model has not been used extensively in textbooks focusing on American civil rights and liberties. The one exception is the work of Sheldon Goldman (1991); but Goldman's book does not employ the model extensively, and his data do not extend beyond the 1989 term of the Court. There are two possible reasons why the attitudinal model has not been used extensively. First, textbooks on this subject tend to be tradition bound, and this has meant a primary if not exclusive focus on the legal model. Second, a reliable and comprehensive data set on the decisions of the Supreme Court has not been available until recently when the United States Supreme Court Judicial Database became publicly available in late 1990.

Like the legal and political models, the attitudinal model has both strengths and weaknesses. Clearly, the attitudinal model provides important insights into the decision-making behavior of Supreme Court justices, and the model needs to be an integral part of any analysis of the Court's policies regarding civil rights and liberties. The attitudinal model is a somewhat narrow one, however, because it focuses on the psychological dimension of decision making, and thus the political and legal models need to be considered along with the attitudinal model in order to provide a broader understanding of the Supreme Court and American civil rights and liberties.

Utilization of the Three Models

Given the strengths and weaknesses of each model, we will therefore be using all three models to study American civil rights and liberties and the changing Supreme Court. This section briefly discusses the specific techniques we will employ in connection with each of the three models.

In applying the legal model, we will follow the traditional methods of providing excerpts from a large number of leading civil rights and liberties cases, thus providing students with the opportunity to become familiar with the process of legal reasoning used by Supreme Court justices. In addition, we will provide extensive textual commentary about the Court's decisions, tracing the evolutionary development of major Court doctrines and precedents. We will also introduce a unique and innovative approach in regard to the legal model. As we examine the decisions of the Rehnquist Court in each area of civil rights and liberties, we will use Table 1.1 to guide our doctrinal analysis. This table involves three variables: the Court's handling of precedent, the importance of a case, and the presence of a majority or plurality opinion. In regard to the Court's treatment of precedent, we will classify all Rehnquist Court cases into one of six categories along a liberal/conservative continuum:

Creation of a new liberal precedent
Liberal modification of existing precedent
Liberal interpretation of existing precedent
Conservative interpretation of existing precedent
Conservative modification of existing precedent
Creation of a new conservative precedent

The traditional legal model would lead to the prediction that the Court's decisions should be classified roughly equally in the categories of liberal and conservative

TABLE 1.1: Framework for Doctrinal Analysis of the Decisions of the Rehnquist Court

		Treatment of Precedent					
Major or Minor Status	**Majority or Plurality Opinion**	Creation of New Liberal Precedent	Liberal Modification of Existing Precedent	Liberal Interpretation of Existing Precedent	Conservative Interpretation of Existing Precedent	Conservative Modification of Existing Precedent	Creation of New Conservative Precedent
Major	Majority						
	Plurality						
Minor	Majority						
	Plurality						

interpretations of existing precedent. If the Rehnquist Court's decisions are overwhelmingly conservative and frequently involve the modification of existing precedent or the creation of new precedents, then the legal model will be severely undermined. The detailed criteria by which cases will be classified in terms of the three variables in the table can be found in Appendix A.

We will also use the attitudinal model through a variety of techniques. Table 1.1 reveals one important method we will use, for it also has relevance for the attitudinal model. By classifying cases in terms of liberal and conservative outcomes, we are giving explicit recognition to the importance of the attitudinal model. Specifically, the table will enable us to assess the extent to which the Rehnquist Court has engaged in the conservative modification of precedent or the creation of new conservative precedents. A second method of emphasizing the attitudinal model involves our presentation in Chapter 3 of detailed profiles of each member of the Rehnquist Court since 1986. In these profiles, we discuss their social backgrounds prior to joining the Court, their judicial philosophies, and their overall liberal/conservative voting records. A third method associated with the attitudinal model involves the extensive use of the United States Supreme Court Judicial Database, which contains data on the outcomes and the votes of the individual justices for all civil rights and liberties decisions of the Warren, Burger, and Rehnquist Courts. As we analyze each area of civil rights and liberties, we will present a variety of tables containing quantitative data relevant to the attitudinal model. We will compare the overall voting records of the Warren, Burger, and Rehnquist Courts to assess if the high court has significantly changed its civil rights and liberties policies as presidents have attempted to place justices on the Court who share their ideological views. We will also examine the Rehnquist Court justices individually. We will look at the liberal/conservative voting records of each member of the Rehnquist Court, and we will conduct bloc voting analyses to analyze if conservative coalitions of justices have emerged on the Rehnquist Court. The methodological details associated with these analyses of the Supreme Court data are discussed in Appendix B.

Finally, the political model will be integrated into the book in several ways. First, Chapter 2 discusses the place of the Supreme Court in the American political system. Second, we will begin each chapter with a detailed examination of an important Supreme Court case, discussing the origins of the case, the role of any interest groups in supporting the case, the lower courts' treatment of the case, the arguments raised before the Supreme Court, the basis of the Court's decision, the short- and long-term impact of the decision, and the feedback that returned to the Court as a result of the impact of the decision. A third method relevant to the political model involves organizing each chapter around the pre-Warren Court era, the Warren Court period, the Burger Court years, and the Rehnquist Court. This format makes it possible to focus on broad political trends within American society and to give explicit attention to the question of whether membership changes on the Supreme Court have been associated with changes in the Court's civil rights and liberties policies.

REFERENCES

Approaches to the Study of Civil Rights and Liberties

Bamberger, Ruth. "Why Common Cause Opposed the Bork Nomination." *PS:Political Science and Politics* 20(1987): 876-89.

Barnum, David G. *The Supreme Court and American Democracy*. New York: St. Martin's Press, 1993.

Bartee, Alice Fleetwood. *Cases Lost, Causes Won: The Supreme Court and the Judicial Process*. New York: St. Martin's Press, 1984.

Baum, Lawrence. *The Supreme Court*. 4th ed. Washington, D.C.: Congressional Quarterly Press, 1992.

Blasi, Vincent., ed. *The Burger Court: The Counter-Revolution That Wasn't*. New Haven, Conn.: Yale University Press, 1983.

Bork, Robert H. *The Tempting of America: The Political Seduction of the Law*. New York: Free Press, 1990.

Chemerinsky, Erwin. "The Vanishing Constitution." *Harvard Law Review* 103(1989): 43-73.

Easton, David. *A Systems Analysis of Political Life*. New York: John Wiley and Sons, 1965.

Epstein, Lee, and Joseph F. Kobylka. *The Supreme Court and Legal Change*. Chapel Hill, NC.: University of North Carolina Press, 1992.

Epstein, Lee, and Thomas G. Walker. *Constitutional Law for a Changing America: Rights, Liberties, and Justice*. 2d ed. Washington, D.C.: Congressional Quarterly Press, 1995.

Fisher, Louis. *Constitutional Rights: Civil Rights and Civil Liberties*. 2d ed. New York: McGraw-Hill, 1995.

Friedelbaum, Stanley H. *The Rehnquist Court: In Pursuit of Judicial Conservatism*. Westport, Conn.: Greenwood Press, 1994.

George, Tracy E., and Lee Epstein. "On the Nature of Supreme Court Decisionmaking." *American Political Science Review* 86(1992): 323-37.

Goldman, Sheldon. *Constitutional Law: Cases and Essays*. 2d ed. New York: HarperCollins, 1991.

Goldman, Sheldon, and Thomas Jahnige. 2d ed. *The Federal Courts as a Political System*. New York: Harper & Row, 1976.

Hensley, Thomas R., and Christopher E. Smith. "Membership Change and Voting Change: An Analysis of the Rehnquist Court's 1986-1991 Terms. *Political Research Quarterly* 48(1995): 837-56.

Johnson, Scott P., and Christopher E. Smith. "David Souter's First Term on the Supreme Court: The Impact of a New Justice." *Judicature* 75(1992): 238-43.

McGuigan, Patrick B., and Dawn M. Weyrich. "The War Begins." In *American Stories: Case Studies in Politics and Government*, edited by James R. Bowers. Belmont, Calif.: Wadsworth, 1993.

O'Brien, David M. "The Supreme Court: From Warren to Burger to Rehnquist." *PS: Political Science and Politics* 20(1987): 12-20.

__________. *Constitutional Law and Politics: Civil Rights and Civil Liberties*, vol. 2. 2d ed. New York: W. W. Norton, 1995.

__________. *Storm Center: The Supreme Court in American Politics*. New York: W.W. Norton, 1993.

__________. *Supreme Court Watch—1993*. New York: W. W. Norton, 1993.

Pritchett, C. Herman. *The Roosevelt Court*. New York: Macmillan, 1948.

Rhode, David W. and Harold J. Spaeth. *Supreme Court Decision Making*. San Francisco: W. H. Freeman, 1976.

Schubert, Glendon. *The Judicial Mind*. Evanston, Ill.: Northwestern University Press, 1965.

__________. *The Judicial Mind Revisited*. New York: Oxford, 1974.

Segal, Jeffrey, and Harold J. Spaeth. *The Supreme Court and the Attitudinal Model*. New York: Cambridge University Press, 1993.

Smith, Christopher E., and Thomas R. Hensley. "Assessing the Conservatism of the Rehnquist Court." *Judicature* 77(1993): 83-89.

Smith, Christopher E., and Scott Patrick Johnson. "The First-Term Performance of Justice Clarence Thomas." *Judicature* 76(1993): 172-78.

Smith, Christopher E., Joyce Ann Baugh, Thomas R. Hensley, and Scott Patrick Johnson. "The First-Term Performance of Justice Ruth Bader Ginsburg." *Judicature*: 78(1994): 74-80.

Urofsky, Melvin I. *The Continuity of Change: The Supreme Court and Individual Liberties, 1953-1986*. Belmont, Calif.: Wadsworth, 1991.

Walker, Thomas G., and Lee Epstein. *The Supreme Court of the United States: An Introduction*. New York: St. Martin's Press, 1993.

Wasby, Stephen L. *The Supreme Court and the Federal Judicial System*. 4th ed. Chicago: Nelson-Hall, 1993.

CHAPTER 2

The Supreme Court in the American Political System

Introduction

Among the national institutions of government in the United States, the Supreme Court holds a special place in the eyes of the public. Because many Americans believe that the highest court's role is to remain separated from the partisan political influences that affect other branches of government, the judicial branch is often expected to be neutral and detached. According to Robert Bork, whom we met in Chapter 1, the Supreme Court should be "a legal rather than a political institution" (Bork 1990, p. 363). This vision of the Court can be illustrated by comparing the high court to the other branches of government. For example, the legislative and executive branches of government are led by elected officials who are clearly identifiable as "politicians." These officials gain office and become influential decision makers with the help of strategic campaigns by political parties and financial contributions from interest groups. When elected officials make decisions that determine public policies and affect citizens' lives, people usually presume that these leaders are motivated by political self-interest and a desire to gain reelection.

By contrast, the justices on the Supreme Court are lawyers and judges who appear to be specially selected by the president and carefully evaluated by the Senate. Because the Constitution permits them to serve "during good Behaviour," which effectively means a life term in office, justices do not become involved in election campaigns. They appear to make decisions within an institution that has been structurally insulated from the influences of politics. Moreover, their physical surroundings and formal procedures provide the appearance of a special decision-making environment in which decisions are guided by neutral principles of law rather than by political self-interest.

These perceptions of the judicial branch and its differences from other governmental branches should bring to mind the legal model discussed in Chapter 1 and the way it contrasts with the political and attitudinal models for understanding the Supreme Court's decision making. The legal model presumes that the Supreme Court's practices are consistent with its public image. In fact, however, political factors and justices' attitudes and values provide powerful influences over the Supreme Court's decisions.

Despite the general perception that the judicial branch is different than the other branches of government, the Supreme Court, like all of the nation's courts, is a component of the political system. The composition and caseload of the Court are shaped by political elements. The Court interacts with various partisan actors and political institutions, and these interactions shape the decisions produced by the justices.

Many examples can be found of the political elements underlying the Supreme Court's decision making and role in the governing system. Cases are brought to the Supreme Court by interest groups and individuals who often seek to use the justices' authoritative decision-making power in order to achieve their political and public policy goals. Since the 1930s, for example, the National Association for the Advancement of Colored People (NAACP) has sponsored lawsuits against school systems and city governments as a primary strategy for seeking to change discriminatory governmental practices. This strategy developed, in large part, because elected officials in the legislative and executive branches of government failed to use their political power to eliminate racial discrimination against African Americans.

Individual justices are selected to serve on the Supreme Court because they share, or are perceived to share, the president's political philosophy. Justices decide which cases to accept for hearing and eventually author judicial opinions based, in part, on their political values and their perceptions about the Court's proper role in the political system. In addition, the effectiveness of the Court's decisions frequently depends on the support and cooperation of other branches of government.

These political elements do not represent a distortion of Judge Bork's vision of the Court as a "legal institution." In reality, the idealized picture of the justices making decisions based on neutral principles of law is merely an unattainable goal that ignores the pervasiveness and inevitability of politics in shaping the Supreme Court's role and actions. As an authoritative governmental institution empowered to make and change policies affecting the entire nation, the Supreme Court has always been shaped and guided by politics. Although the Supreme Court's performance during the twentieth century has made its political character especially evident, political factors have shaped the Court's decisions since the high court's creation at the end of the eighteenth century.

The political character of the Supreme Court became especially visible and controversial in the aftermath of its accelerated involvement in civil rights and liberties cases during the Warren Court era (1953–1969). During this era, the Court made many decisions concerning controversial issues that divided the nation such as privacy, discrimination, criminal defendants' rights, and religious freedom. In making these decisions, the justices inevitably provoked political backlash and counterattacks by other political actors and institutions. The Supreme Court did not become a political institution by applying its authoritative decision-making power to cases concerning the rights of individuals. It had been equally political in previous eras, especially when making decisions about economic rights and government regulation during the dawn of the twentieth century. The Warren Court merely became more widely recognized—and condemned—as a political institution because many Americans disagreed with its controversial decisions. In deciding controversial cases, the Warren-era justices, just like all of the justices who preceded them as well as those who succeeded them, could not avoid the inevitability of drawing from their own values and attitudes in giving meaning to such vague constitutional phrases as "equal protection," "due process of law," and "cruel and unusual punishments."

The justices' efforts to condemn racial segregation and protect rights for criminal defendants mobilized politicians with opposing views to criticize the Supreme Court and seek strategies for preventing the Court's decisions from being fully implemented. Critics of the Supreme Court's decisions could attempt to seek the "high ground" by claiming that the justices had improperly changed the high court from a legal institution to a political institution by making controversial decisions. Because of the negative connotations associated with the word "politics" in the context of the judiciary, people frequently attempt to show that their preferred judicial outcomes are "correct" by claiming that only the application of politics rather than law could lead to contrary results. In reality, however, all Supreme Court decisions are shaped by politics because of the tactics and motivations of claimants who initiate cases, the political calculations underlying the selection of justices, and the justices' attitudes and values that shape the Court's decisions.

Cases that are brought to the Supreme Court often involve conflicts over values among political interests in American society, especially in cases concerning public policy issues such as abortion, school desegregation, and the death penalty. By presenting these conflicts to the Supreme Court in the form and language of legal cases, claimants are seeking determinations about how entitlements, benefits, rights, and resources will be distributed. In some cases, the Supreme Court simply provides political interests with an alternative forum for pursuing policy objectives that have not been successfully attained through efforts in the legislative and executive branches of government.

CASE STUDY

The Law and Politics of Abortion

The Supreme Court's role as an institution within, rather than set apart from, the political system can be illustrated by examining the Court's actions in defining the nation's policies on abortion.

After the mid-nineteenth century, state legislatures throughout the United States made it a crime to perform abortions. By 1910, every state except Kentucky had made abortion a felony, and Kentucky subsequently added its own prohibition (Craig and O'Brien 1993, p. 9). The political push to enact laws regulating abortions came from people morally opposed to abortion as well as from those concerned about the profiteering of abortionists who lacked any medical training and thereby jeopardized the health of women in undertaking a procedure that was dangerous, even when performed by a doctor, during this early era of modern medicine. In addition, physicians' organizations supported regulatory laws as they sought to establish their control over all medical procedures, including abortion. Women had previously sought the assistance of midwives and pharmacists for abortions (Faux 1988, pp. 56–62).

During the 1960s, several states began to liberalize their laws to permit abortions when a doctor determined that a woman's health would be endangered by a full-term pregnancy. A few states became magnets for women seeking abortions either because the previous restrictive laws had been set aside or because some doctors within those states freely determined that nearly any pregnant woman seeking an abortion qualified under the exception for protecting women's health. Throughout this period, Texas had especially strict criminal laws against doctors performing abortions. In 1969, a poor woman named Norma McCorvey, who claimed that she became pregnant after being raped, found two young lawyers, Linda Coffee and Sarah Weddington, who were eager to challenge the validity of the Texas statute. McCorvey was a twenty-one-year-old divorced mother of a five-year-old girl. She eked out a living as a waitress and as a ticket seller for a traveling carnival. Her daughter lived with McCorvey's mother in Arkansas as Norma struggled to support herself. McCorvey wanted an abortion, but she had no money with which to travel to Colorado, California, or other states that had liberalized their abortion laws. Moreover, these states that had made abortions less difficult to obtain still generally had residency or waiting period requirements that effectively made abortions even more expensive. McCorvey did not wish to consider putting her life in jeopardy, as so many other Texas women did, by going to Mexico for an abortion or by seeking the services of an unlicensed abortionist. McCorvey was four months pregnant by the time she met Coffee and

Weddington. Although the lawyers offered to try to help her find some way to procure an abortion, McCorvey decided to go ahead and have the baby because it was unlikely that they could find a hospital willing to perform the major surgery required at that time for such an advanced stage abortion. Despite being unable to obtain the abortion that she sought for herself, McCorvey agreed to serve as the plaintiff for the lawyers' efforts to challenge the Texas law that had prevented her from obtaining a legal abortion (Faux 1988, pp. 6–10, 23).

Coffee and Weddington sought to persuade the federal courts that the Texas law forbidding abortions violated the constitutional rights of McCorvey and other women. The Texas statute prevented her from obtaining the abortion that she sought, yet she was too poor to be able to afford to travel to other states where abortions were more easily available. Thus the lawyers filed an action seeking to prevent the Dallas district attorney, Henry Wade, from enforcing the Texas antiabortion law. As commonly occurred in cases affecting the personal privacy of litigants, McCorvey's identity was hidden under the pseudonym of "Jane Roe." In June 1970, a special three-judge district court panel declared that the Texas statute violated the constitutional rights of McCorvey and other women. However, the judges declined to issue an injunction to prevent Wade from enforcing the Texas law. Because the judges' opinion did not provide either party with what it wanted, both the State of Texas and McCorvey's attorneys sought to have the U.S. Supreme Court review the case of *Roe v. Wade.*

The Supreme Court did not seek responsibility for defining national policy on abortion. The issue was brought to the Court for its decision. In some cases, a single individual seeking vindication for a perceived violation of a constitutional right can serve as the vehicle for a judicial decision that effectively reshapes policy throughout the nation. In other cases, the judicial decision results from actions by interested attorneys who lack the political power to pressure state legislatures to rewrite abortion laws or other policies. Such attorneys, who frequently work for organized interest groups, initiate cases with the explicit hope that the federal courts, including the Supreme Court, will apply their judicial power to reshape the laws across the entire nation. Thus the judicial branch is often viewed as an alternative policy-making forum in which individuals with little political power can pursue the attainment of broad public policy goals.

Norma McCorvey's case, *Roe v. Wade,* was first argued in 1971 when there were two vacancies on the Supreme Court due to retirements. If "the law" provided a clear answer for the question concerning the constitutionality of statutes prohibiting abortion, the seven remaining justices should have been able to decide the case quite readily. But the Constitution does not mention anything about abortion, so the justices had to apply their individual judicial philosophies in seeking an answer. They faced a difficult interpretive issue. Is there a right to obtain an abortion contained in the stated constitutional right to be free from deprivations of liberty without due process of law? Does the right to privacy include a right to choose whether to have an abortion, notwithstanding the fact that the Constitution does not mention the word "privacy?" The answers to such interpretive questions inevitably depend on the personal values and political attitudes of the individual justices. Moreover, the Supreme Court's ultimate pronouncements concerning such issues depend on the political composition of the high court. In every case, the essential question is: which interpretive approach can garner the support of a majority of justices?

The need to gain majority support in order to prevail on an issue generates strategic thinking and political calculations among the justices on the Supreme Court. In *Roe v. Wade,* the liberal justices who comprised the initial majority within the seven-member Court wanted to decide the case promptly for fear that the addition of two new justices appointed by Republican President Richard Nixon would give their conservative colleagues enough votes to form a new majority in opposition to abortion rights (Epstein and Kobylka 1992, p. 185). The liberal justices recognized, as all justices do, that the outcomes of cases are not dictated by any universally acknowledged principles of law. Instead, they are determined by the political reality of a simple vote count within a frequently divided Court. But the initial four-member majority that formed after the first arguments in the case was not able to decide the case quickly enough to preclude the new appointees' participation and potentially decisive impact on the abortion issue. By the time the Supreme Court considered *Roe,* there were two new justices,

William Rehnquist and Lewis Powell, who were conservative appointees of a president (Nixon) who was opposed to abortion. Nixon had used his opposition to abortion as a means to attract support from working-class and Catholic voters (Tatalovich 1988, p. 197). Because presidents normally attempt to appoint Supreme Court justices whose values and viewpoints conform with their own, Nixon's appointees were expected to be conservative on most issues, including abortion. Upon their arrival, Powell and Rehnquist joined with three sitting justices to form a five-member majority that ordered a reargument in the *Roe* case so that it could be considered by all nine justices, including the two new appointees (O'Brien 1990, p. 31).

As it turned out, the new appointees did not alter the results when *Roe* was reargued in 1972. Powell and Rehnquist each joined opposite sides of the issue, and a seven-member majority, including Powell, issued an opinion in 1973 that invalidated the laws of Texas and every other state that prohibited abortion during the first six months of pregnancy. The Court declared that a woman's right to make choices about abortion during the first two trimesters of pregnancy was protected by the constitutional right of privacy. States were not permitted to restrict abortion choices during the first three months of pregnancy, and they could only enact reasonable regulations to protect a woman's health during the fourth, fifth, and sixth months. Abortions could be prohibited to protect the developing fetus only during the final trimester of pregnancy. The justices' interpretive powers were well illustrated by the *Roe v. Wade* decision (case excerpt on p. 814). Despite the fact that neither privacy nor abortion is mentioned in the Constitution, the justices in the majority used their authority to apply their judicial philosophies in interpreting the Constitution in order to change national policy on abortion. Moreover, they generated great controversy among constitutional scholars through their use of pregnancy trimesters as the basis for defining the scope of a constitutional right.

Although she had served as the catalyst for a landmark Supreme Court decision affecting the rights of women across the nation, the case did not substantially improve Norma McCorvey's life. The pregnancy that generated the case had already produced a child and forced her to make the difficult choice to give the baby up for adoption. McCorvey continued to struggle to make ends meet and ultimately became an apartment house manager. Because her identity was concealed by a pseudonym, even lawyers who assisted Coffee and Weddington with the case did not know "Jane Roe's" real name. Ten years after the Supreme Court's decision, McCorvey publicly revealed that she was "Jane Roe." She sought, with little apparent success, to profit from her historic role in the case by hiring an entertainment lawyer to charge fees for photographs and interviews with her (Faux 1988, pp. 25, 338). Another decade later, McCorvey expressed regret about her role in the abortion issue and she publicly lent her name and support to interest groups seeking to overturn the decision in *Roe v. Wade*. As in many other Supreme Court cases, the individual whose life was most directly involved in the contested legal issue served primarily as the vehicle for legal arguments and judicial policy decisions that grew in scope and importance and thereby superseded her immediate interests.

Although the Supreme Court is considered the final authority on the meaning of the Constitution, its decisions do not resolve constitutional issues once and for all. If Supreme Court decisions were permanent and enduring, then perhaps society could simply accept the Court's pronouncements and the justices could turn their attention to new issues. Because of the Court's connections to the political system, however, decisions on the meaning of the Constitution can change.

In the aftermath of the *Roe* decision, political interest groups mobilized to oppose the new national policy of abortion availability. Right to Life and other groups lobbied Congress, state legislatures, and city councils to urge passage of legislation that would limit, either directly or indirectly, the availability of abortion. Elected officials who disagreed with the Supreme Court's decisions also worked against the policy. Abortion opponents in Congress, for example, attempted without success to initiate a constitutional amendment against abortion that would have effectively altered the Supreme Court's authority over the policy issue. However, they succeeded in enacting legislation to prohibit the use of federal funds to pay for abortions for poor women who rely on public assistance for their medical care. Poor women challenged the legislation in court as an infringement on their right of choice for abortion, but the Supreme Court decided that Congress was not obligated to supply funds for abortions (*Harris v. McRae,* 1980).

State legislatures passed statutes that regulated how abortions must be performed, how doctors must provide counseling and warnings to patients seeking abortions, and other matters that abortion rights advocates viewed as impediments to free choice. The Supreme Court during the Burger Court era consistently struck down such statutes because a majority of justices believed that these laws unjustifiably and improperly interfered with the right of choice. For example, the city council in Akron, Ohio, passed a municipal ordinance purporting to protect the health of the mother. However, because its provisions clashed with the *Roe* opinion by, for example, requiring doctors to tell patients that "the unborn child is a human life from the moment of conception," the Supreme Court struck down the ordinance (*City of Akron v. Akron Center for Reproductive Health,* 1983).

In the first decade after the 1973 decision in *Roe v. Wade,* the Supreme Court revisited the issue of abortion no less than ten times, and additional cases continued to come to the Court thereafter. Abortion became a great national controversy with political candidates making it a primary issue in their campaigns and political parties specifically addressing the issue in their party platforms. The Republican Party adopted positions opposing abortion, and the Democratic Party supported a right of choice. The Supreme Court could not issue a "final word" on the abortion controversy because the governmental reactions created by interest groups and officials in the legislative and executive branches continually generated new kinds of issues that forced the Court to make new decisions concerning abortion. Meanwhile, the composition of the Supreme Court continued to change over the years so that the Court that decided the original *Roe* case had ceased to exist. By 1992, only one justice, Blackmun, remained from the original seven-member majority that created the *Roe* decision.

The composition of the Supreme Court is determined by quirks of fate and depends on who controls the White House at the moment that a justice dies, retires, or resigns. After the *Roe* decision in 1973, the White House was controlled by Republican presidents for all but four of the next twenty years, and no justices left the Court during the one Democratic administration (President Jimmy Carter, 1977–1981). Thus all six appointments to the Supreme Court between 1973 and 1993 were made by Republican presidents and five of them were made by presidents—Ronald Reagan and George Bush—who actively sought to place on the high court people who opposed the Court's decision in *Roe.*

In 1981, Reagan appointed Sandra Day O'Connor to replace retiring Justice Potter Stewart, a member of the original *Roe* majority. In 1986, Chief Justice Warren Burger's retirement and the elevation of *Roe*-dissenter William Rehnquist to chief justice opened a spot for Reagan-appointee and outspoken *Roe* critic, Antonin Scalia. Another member of the *Roe* majority, Justice Lewis Powell, retired in 1987 and was replaced by Reagan-appointee Anthony Kennedy. As we saw in Chapter 1, Kennedy was appointed by Reagan only after the Senate rejected the nomination of Judge Robert Bork. Bork, a critic of the *Roe* decision, was opposed by many liberal interest groups, including pro-choice groups, who spent millions of dollars lobbying in opposition to his confirmation.

Despite Bork's unsuccessful nomination, by 1989 the two dissenters from *Roe* (Rehnquist and Byron White) had been joined by three Reagan appointees. These justices formed a new five-member majority to change abortion policy by approving a Missouri statute that prohibited the performance of abortions at public hospitals, required doctors to conduct specific tests, and proclaimed that human life begins at conception (*Webster v. Reproductive Health Services,* 1989). Because O'Connor did not believe that the Court needed to decide whether or not to overturn *Roe v. Wade,* the new majority still lacked the fifth vote they needed to undo completely the abortion policy established by *Roe.* Even without directly reversing the precedent established by *Roe,* the new five-member majority significantly altered abortion policy by inviting state legislatures to create regulations that previously would have been invalidated as infringements on the constitutional right of choice. Constitutional law and judicial policy making had changed because of developments in the political system. Voters elected abortion opponent Ronald Reagan as president, and Reagan appointed new justices to advance his policy goal of eliminating a constitutional right of choice about abortion.

When two more remaining members of the original *Roe* majority retired in 1990 and 1991 (William Brennan and Thurgood Marshall), they were replaced by two Bush appointees, David Souter and Clarence Thomas. The confirmation hearings for both appointees involved lobbying by abortion interest groups, both for and against choice, and detailed questioning by liberal Democratic senators who feared that one of these candidates would provide the fifth vote to overturn *Roe*. Souter, who had never taken a public stance on the issue during his years as a New Hampshire attorney general and state judge, deflected inquiries about his views on abortion by claiming that he could not discuss issues that he might later have to decide as a justice. Although Democratic senators were unsure about Souter's views on abortion, many voted for his confirmation because he had consistently reassured them that he believed in a constitutional right to privacy and he admired his predecessor, Justice Brennan, as a defender of the Bill of Rights (Smith and Johnson 1992). Unlike Souter, Thomas had made controversial public statements concerning abortion and other issues. When pressed by senators during the confirmation hearings, Thomas claimed that he had never discussed the abortion issue with anyone and indicated that as a judge he would have a completely open mind when considering abortion and other controversial issues. Thomas was ultimately confirmed by the narrowest of margins (52–48) after rancorous hearings concerning allegations that he had sexually harassed a subordinate while serving as an executive branch official in the U.S. Department of Education and later as chairman of the Equal Employment Opportunity Commission in the Reagan administration (Palley and Palley 1992).

When the Supreme Court addressed the abortion issue again in 1992, it was widely believed that the justices eager to overturn *Roe* would find their fifth vote from among either O'Connor, Souter, or Thomas. In fact, Thomas immediately joined Scalia, Rehnquist, and White to advocate reversal of *Roe*, but to the surprise of most observers, Justice Kennedy deserted his previous allies to join O'Connor and Souter in authoring a joint opinion that upheld *Roe* on behalf of a narrow five-member majority (including Harry Blackmun and John Paul Stevens) (*Planned Parenthood v. Casey*, 1992). The opinion by Kennedy, O'Connor, and Souter emphasized that a reversal of *Roe* would threaten the Supreme Court's image and legitimacy by making it appear that national abortion policy had changed merely because the political composition of the Court had changed. Although changes in the composition of the Court had led to abrupt changes in constitutional law concerning many issues, including criminal justice issues in which Kennedy, O'Connor, and Souter participated in dramatic shifts (*e.g.*, *Payne v. Tennessee*, 1991), these justices apparently made a political calculation that the potential backlash from a reversal of *Roe* would place the Court in the middle of an undesirable political firestorm. In doing so, they adopted the classic legal restraintist's position of seeking to protect the image of courts and law by limiting further judicial involvement in controversial issues and the alteration of existing rules.

In 1993, a long-time opponent of *Roe*, Justice White, retired and was replaced by President Clinton's appointee, Ruth Bader Ginsburg. Because Ginsburg was the first Supreme Court nominee to declare forthrightly at her nomination hearings that she recognized the constitutional right of choice for abortion, her appointment solidified the majority supporting choice. Although *Roe*'s author and most ardent defender, Justice Blackmun, retired the following year, President Clinton, a supporter of choice in abortion, appointed Stephen Breyer, who was not expected to alter the strength of the majority supporting a right of choice.

As indicated by the example of abortion, the Supreme Court's decisions are determined by its contacts with the political system and by the political attributes of the Court itself. In seeking to understand the Court's decisions on civil liberties issues, it is impossible to ignore the fact that the cases brought before the Court, the Court's decision-making processes, and the impact of Supreme Court decisions are all shaped by political influences.

The Supreme Court, the Constitution, and Judicial Review

The U.S. Constitution describes the structure and power of the basic institutions of the American national government. In their 1787 efforts to design a workable system of government, the authors of the Constitution sought to accomplish several goals. They wanted a national government that would be sufficiently unified and strong to handle the difficult tasks of taxation, commerce, and national defense. The United States' initial governing system under the Articles of Confederation (1781–89) failed to fulfill these necessary governmental responsibilities because the individual states retained their own authority to handle most matters. The framers feared, however, that if they created a strong national government, a single actor or institution might gain too much power and thereby become capable of depriving citizens of their freedom. Thus they divided the powers of government among three branches and created a system of checks and balances that prevents any branch from becoming too powerful. The Constitution established the Supreme Court as the judicial branch's primary, authoritative institution. Although the framers of the Constitution designed the structure of government and devised ways for the branches to check each other, many aspects of the contemporary high court's important powers and procedures do not come from the words of the Constitution. The Court's authority and role developed over time through its interactions with the other branches of government.

The first three sections of the Constitution describe the structure and powers of the three branches of government, including those of the judicial branch. Article I of the Constitution describes the structure and power of the legislative branch embodied in the Congress; Article II presents the executive power possessed by the president; and Article III discusses judicial power by emphasizing the authority of the Supreme Court. Article III is relatively brief, but several provisions within it laid the groundwork for the development of the Supreme Court's role. For example, only the Supreme Court is established by the Constitution and therefore cannot be abolished without a constitutional amendment. By contrast, however, the rest of the federal court system, which generates many of the cases decided by the high court, is comprised of "such inferior courts as the Congress may from time to time ordain and establish." Thus Congress holds significant power over the design, procedures, and resources of the judicial branch, elements that affect the work and authority of the Supreme Court by shaping the issues brought to the high court and how they are processed and presented.

Article III provides that justices of the Supreme Court and other federal judges "shall hold their offices during good behavior" and shall not have their compensation reduced while they are in office. These protections for judicial officers' tenure and salaries are designed to provide federal judges with sufficient insulation from direct partisan political influences to permit them to make courageous and "correct" decisions. By contrast, judges in many state court systems are elected officials. These states' judicial selection systems emphasize the accountability of public officials by permitting the voters to choose and remove judicial decision makers. Because Article III establishes rules that favor judicial independence over public accountability for federal judges, many observers fear that Supreme Court justices and other federal judges may inappropriately and illegitimately assert their judicial authority over public policy issues that properly belong within the domain of elected officials in the legislative and executive branches of government. In other words, the life tenure granted to federal judicial officers may lead them to behave as "dictators" in violation of the spirit and purpose of the American democratic governing system.

Is it completely "undemocratic" to have judges insulated from direct political pressure and electoral accountability? If democracy is defined as simply citizen control over government and policy making, then the protected tenures of federal judges make them "undemocratic" officials. The U.S. Constitution, however, was written to advance many goals in addition to voter participation and electoral accountability. Thus the American democratic system is not premised on simple majority rule and voters' control of all issues. For example, the Constitution seeks to avoid the risks that the public's attention might be captured by a charismatic demagogue and that the smaller states would feel that their views were not heard in Congress. The Constitution attempts to avoid these respective problems through such "undemocratic" features as an Electoral College instead of the direct election of the president and a Senate in which every state has equal representation without regard to population. As a result, presidents may be elected to office despite having the support of fewer voters than their opponents, and the residents of large states are underrepresented in the Senate. With respect to the responsibilities of judges, the Constitution does not endorse simple majority rule on every issue because of a concern for the rights of individuals who may be out of step with society's majority. By insulating federal judges from direct political accountability, they can enforce constitutional provisions *against* the wishes of the majority of Americans who may, at times, want to limit the rights of individuals.

At the time Article III was drafted to confer life tenure on federal judges, the original Constitution contained few protections for individuals save for the preservation of detained persons' rights to petition the court for release (**habeas corpus**) and protection against **bills of attainder** and **ex post facto laws**. When the Bill of Rights was added to the Constitution in 1791, the life-tenured judges gained broader responsibilities—and, in effect, power—for protecting individuals' rights to speech, religious freedom, due process, and liberty. The scope of judicial responsibility and potential power expanded further with the ratification of the Fourteenth Amendment in 1868, which gave federal judges the opportunity to oversee actions by state and local governments and added the right to equal protection, which has been a vehicle for judicial action on behalf of victimized members of racial minority groups.

Life tenure alone cannot give dictatorial potential to judicial officers if they do not also possess sufficient authority to act on public policy issues. Article III says only that "[t]he judicial power extends to all cases, in law and equity, arising under this Constitution, the laws of the United States, and treaties" as well as to disputes involving the United States, individual states, foreign countries and their officials, and admiralty issues. This general grant of authority had little practical impact on the risk of excessive judicial power until the Supreme Court began to act under the leadership of Chief Justice John Marshall (1801–1835) to define the precise contours of the judicial branch's authority.

Most important among the judiciary's powers is the power of **judicial review.** Judicial review is the power of judges, including justices of the Supreme Court, to review acts by the legislative and executive branches, both federal and state, and declare those acts invalid if they violate the Constitution. In 1803, the Supreme Court decided a case in which a disappointed office seeker sought a judicial order to compel President Thomas Jefferson's secretary of state, James Madison, to deliver a commission for a Washington, D.C. judgeship (*Marbury v. Madison*, 1803). The commission had been signed and sealed but never delivered by President John Adams's administration. The incoming Jefferson administration refused to deliver the commissions because they did not want to place into office more political opponents who were affiliated with Adams. In his opinion for the Supreme Court, Chief Justice Marshall, an Adams appointee who had served as secretary of state in the

Adams administration, deftly avoided the likelihood that Madison and Jefferson would disobey a Supreme Court order to deliver the commission. Marshall asserted that the Court had the authority to issue an order to the president, but he declined to do so because he determined that the case had been brought to the Court under a statutory provision that violated the Constitution and therefore was invalid. In this famous opinion, Marshall asserted that the judicial branch has authority over the other branches of government even though the Constitution's words did not explicitly indicate that the courts had such power. The *Marbury* case established the power of judicial review that subsequently came to be accepted as the legitimate basis for courts' decisions determining whether actions by executive and legislative branch officials are proper under the Constitution. Because most civil rights and civil liberties cases involve disputes between individuals and government officials, this power of judicial review serves as the basis for Supreme Court decisions declaring that government actions violate the constitutional rights of individuals. Thus judicial review has been a central element of controversial case decisions concerning freedom of speech, religious freedom, racial discrimination, abortion, and other civil rights and liberties issues that generated policy-making decisions by the Supreme Court.

If Supreme Court justices (and other federal judges) have life tenure and the power to review actions by other governmental actors and institutions, what keeps the judicial branch from embodying precisely what the framers of the Constitution feared most, namely the excessive accumulation of power in one branch of government? In governing systems that call themselves "democratic," people expect to be able to remove officials who make bad decisions or who attempt to capture too much governmental power. However, in the United States' governing system, unless Supreme Court justices commit crimes that would warrant impeachment proceedings, no method exists for removing these authoritative decision makers from power, even when they overrule the decisions of the citizenry's democratically elected representatives.

On the surface, it appears that the Supreme Court is capable of exerting excessive influence over government and public policy, but the Court's actions are limited and constrained by the structure and operations of the governing political system. Because of the judicial branch's connections to the political system, including those illustrated in the previously discussed example of abortion, the Supreme Court would find it difficult to gain and use an excessive accumulation of power.

Political Limitations on Supreme Court Power

Several aspects of the Supreme Court's structure and procedures limit the risk that the Court will go "too far" in making decisions that shape public policy contrary to the wishes of the public and elected officials. Justices are selected by the president and confirmed by the U.S. Senate. Presidents' choices of new justices are always based on political criteria. Because American society and its political parties could never reach a consensus on any single individual as the "best" or "most qualified" new justice, presidents consider a variety of political questions in sifting through lists of potential nominees. Which potential candidate is most likely to agree with the president on important policy issues? Which candidate is likely to please some important ideological, geographic, religious, racial, or other constituency that the president wishes to cultivate? Which candidate can be confirmed by the Senate without tarnishing the president's political party in an emotional confirmation battle?

As indicated by these expected qualifications, a president is not likely to appoint an extremist to the Supreme Court. Because the voters may hold the president and the president's political party responsible for controversial justices that they place on the Court, presidents and their advisors usually seek to appoint justices who are loyal to the president's party and who possess sufficient experience and respect to win Senate approval. If a nominee seems too extreme, then the Senate has the opportunity to deny confirmation as it has done periodically to candidates throughout American history, most recently in the 1987 vote to reject President Reagan's nomination of Judge Robert Bork. President Clinton, by contrast, consciously sought to appoint noncontroversial candidates with moderate records who would appeal to constituencies on both the liberal and conservative wings of the political spectrum. His appointees, Justice Ruth Bader Ginsburg and Justice Stephen Breyer, were former law professors and federal appellate judges who were respected by both Republicans and Democrats. Thus Supreme Court justices are drawn from the mainstream of the American political establishment. Some may be a bit more liberal than most of society and some may be a bit more conservative than most of society. However, they nearly always come from within the broad mainstream of society rather than from an extremist fringe. Thus, the actual candidate pool from which justices are drawn—lawyers active in mainstream party politics—diminishes the likelihood that any justice would seek to seize excessive power.

The structure of the Supreme Court reduces the potential impact of any single justice. Even if a justice came to the Court with the intention of actively pursuing a radical policy agenda, it would be difficult for the justice to achieve predetermined goals. Because the Court is composed of nine justices, no single justice determines the outcomes of cases. It takes the agreement of five justices to form a majority that will set a new precedent. Moreover, because individual presidents rarely have the opportunity to appoint five like-minded justices, majority opinions must receive the support of justices appointed by different presidents. Extremist opinions are not likely to appeal to five lawyers drawn from the nation's political establishment. Thus, the structure of the Court as a collegial decision-making body of nine members creates incentives to moderate opinions in order to gain majority support.

Supreme Court decisions are also limited by the justices themselves. They each hold conceptions about what their proper role should be as Supreme Court justices. Many justices throughout history have noted that they personally disagreed with government policies challenged in court, but they nonetheless voted to uphold the policies because they believed that their obligation as a judicial officer required them to avoid clashing with elected officials unless absolutely necessary to vindicate a provision of the Constitution. Thus justices restrain themselves. According to a comprehensive survey of research on judicial decision making, judicial officers' decisions are a function of what they prefer to do, tempered by what they ought to do, and constrained by what they believe is feasible to do (Gibson 1983, p. 32). Supreme Court justices' consideration of these issues, namely what they ought to do and what is feasible to do, provides a limitation on the potential scope of the high court's decisions and influence over public policy.

The Supreme Court cannot readily control which public policies it wishes to determine but can only decide the cases that are brought before it. Moreover, it generally considers issues as narrowly framed by the litigants rather than as comprehensive policy questions. For example, in abortion cases, the Supreme Court decides whether specific state statutes or local ordinances violate the constitutional right of privacy. The Court does not purport to provide a complete discussion of the abortion issue that will comprehensively answer all its questions. Thus, the decisions of the Supreme Court are shaped by the Court's agenda which, in turn, is influenced not only by the justices' personal policy interests but also by the kinds of issues brought to the Court by interest groups and other litigants.

Because the Supreme Court is a component of the political system rather than a separate entity, judicial policy making is shaped and limited by the Court's interactions with other branches of government. As indicated by the previous example concerning the issue of abortion, when the Supreme Court issues decisions, other political actors and institutions react. Their reactions may generate new cases for the Court to consider or otherwise influence the outcomes of subsequent decisions. Supreme Court justices are aware of potential reactions by political actors and thus their judicial decisions may be influenced by their anticipation of reactions from external political forces.

When the Warren-era Supreme Court decided in 1954 that racial segregation in public schools was constitutionally impermissible, the justices were concerned about the inevitable political backlash and social upheaval that would result from such a dramatic departure from the previously accepted and pervasive discrimination against African Americans. Chief Justice Warren worked very hard to persuade the other justices to issue a unanimous decision because he knew that segregation supporters would seize upon any division within the Court to claim that the justices really could not agree about the correct interpretation of the Constitution. The price of unanimity may have been a cautious approach to ending school segregation. The Court waited an additional year before announcing that lower courts should proceed to remedy segregation "with all deliberate speed" rather than immediately. The Court's caution was due, in part, to the insistence of Justice Stanley Reed, the final justice to overcome his reluctance to join the controversial decision, who made the delay in remedial implementation a condition of his support (Kluger 1975, p. 698). Thus the justices' anticipatory accommodation of adverse political reactions may have weakened the Court's efforts to end racial segregation and thereby slowed the nation's progress toward reducing discrimination. Alternatively, the Court's cautious approach may have helped the public and policymakers to begin the gradual process of accepting racial equality as a shared ideal. Although it is difficult to know how American history might have been different if the Court had taken a more aggressive approach, it seems clear that the Court's actions are sometimes influenced by the justices' anticipation of public reactions or probable policy consequences.

Legislatures have several options for reacting against and influencing decisions by the Supreme Court. In cases of statutory interpretation, legislators can directly nullify judicial decisions by enacting new legislation that clarifies the meaning of the statute in question. Although the Supreme Court can readily change interpretations of the U.S. Constitution, the justices are supposed to seek to effectuate the intent of Congress when interpreting federal statutes. Thus legislatures, rather than courts, are the ultimate authorities on the meaning and purpose of statutory law. In 1991, for example, Congress enacted a civil rights act concerning employment discrimination in order to reverse several 1989 Supreme Court decisions limiting the scope of antidiscrimination laws (e.g., *Wards Cove Packing Co. v. Antonio*, 1989). President Reagan's final appointee, Justice Kennedy, had given the Court's conservatives the fifth vote they needed to limit the scope of existing employment discrimination laws. A majority in Congress, however, believed that the justices had distorted the intended meaning of the laws, so they passed new legislation that clarified and expanded the coverage of discrimination laws. Legislative supremacy on matters of statutory interpretation limits the potential extent of judicial power over such issues.

Members of Congress may also initiate constitutional amendments when they strongly disagree with Supreme Court decisions. In response to Supreme Court decisions on such civil liberties issues as abortion, school prayer, and school desegregation, the Court's opponents in Congress proposed constitutional amendments that would have nullified the Court's decisions by changing the words of the Constitution. Although recent efforts to amend the Constitution in response to controversial Supreme Court decisions have not succeeded, several previous amendments altered Supreme Court decisions. The Sixteenth Amendment, for example, which approved federal income taxation in 1913, overruled a Supreme Court decision that struck down congressional efforts to implement an income tax by statute (*Pollock v. Farmers' Loan and Trust Co.*, 1895).

By using its power to rewrite the statutes that define the federal court system's structure and authority, Congress can limit the judiciary's jurisdiction over issues. Generally, members of Congress are reluctant to tamper with the judicial branch in this way; but in one notable example after the Civil War, the Supreme Court acquiesced to a congressional withdrawal of appellate jurisdiction in a case that threatened the federal Reconstruction program (*Ex parte McCardle*, 1869). It seems unlikely that the Supreme Court would comply with a statute that sought to withdraw completely its jurisdiction over specific issues. The threat of actions by Congress, however, may make the Supreme Court cautious about whether and how it asserts itself in controversial cases. For example, in 1956 the Supreme Court issued a controversial decision that limited congressional authority to conduct hearings to investigate communism within the United States (*Watkins v. United States*, 1957). Three years later, the Court modified its position in order to grant Congress greater power in such investigations (*Barenblatt v. United States*, 1959). As one scholar observed, "after Congress had threatened to remove the Court's jurisdiction over internal security matters . . ., the Court seemingly backed down" (Wasby 1988, p. 303).

The presidential appointment power represents a significant reactive restraint on the Supreme Court. Presidents Nixon, Reagan, and Bush used their appointments to select justices whom they hoped would slow or reverse the liberal civil rights and liberties decisions of the earlier Warren Court era. The Supreme Court's decisions on criminal justice, abortion, and other issues changed significantly between the early 1970s and the early 1990s because Republican presidents reacted against liberal civil rights and liberties decisions by appointing justices who possessed more conservative policy preferences and judicial philosophies than their Warren-era predecessors. The ability to reshape the Court's composition is not a direct check against objectionable decisions that the justices may produce. Over time, however, the presidential appointment power operates to insure that the Court's composition and decisions generally follow electoral trends. When the voters choose conservative Republican presidents, as they did in every presidential election from 1968 to 1988 with the exception of President Carter's election in 1976, the voters are also insuring, whether they intend to or not, that any Supreme Court vacancies during those presidencies will be filled by appointees who are perceived to share the conservative presidents' values and policy preferences. By placing the appointment and confirmation powers in the hands of elected officials, the Constitution keeps the Supreme Court connected to political and social trends reflected in the electoral process. At specific moments in history, the Supreme Court's decisions may lag behind or move ahead of society, but eventually the appointment process will move the Court back toward the central trends in the United States' continuing political evolution.

Presidents can also adopt the strategy of proposing legislation and constitutional amendments designed to limit the Supreme Court's ability to shape public policy. The most famous example was President Franklin Roosevelt's legislative proposal in 1937 to change the size of the Supreme Court in order to enable him to appoint supporters to the high court whose votes would nullify those of the justices who were blocking his economic and social welfare programs. In the midst of this confrontation between the president and the Court, the high court stopped invalidating Roosevelt's economic legislation and soon thereafter Roosevelt's opponents on the Court began to retire. Roosevelt was then able to appoint supporters of his New Deal program to the Supreme Court.

The Supreme Court's independence and power are also constrained by the judicial branch's limited ability to enforce decisions. The Supreme Court is dependent on other branches of government to enforce judicial decisions. If the other branches of government do not respond to public disobedience of Supreme Court decisions, the justices' opinions are little more than ineffective words on paper. In the 1830s, for example, the Cherokee Nation won Supreme Court cases against the State of Georgia, which had been permitting white settlers to steal Cherokee land. Despite winning legal victories, the Cherokees were brutally expelled from Georgia and forcibly marched to Oklahoma territory because President Andrew Jackson refused to enforce the Court's decisions (Burke 1969). Justices of the Supreme Court can control the written statements in their own opinions, and they can supervise the statements issued by lower court judges. They cannot control effective policy enforcement mechanisms. By contrast, the president controls military and police forces, and Congress controls incentives and punishments through its power to allocate funds and levy taxes.

The Supreme Court's relative weakness was not limited to the nineteenth century. During the social conflicts generated by the Court's desegregation decisions of the 1950s and 1960s, including violent resistance in several cities and states, the high court was dependent on the willingness of Presidents Eisenhower and Kennedy to send military troops to such places as Little Rock, Arkansas, and Oxford, Mississippi, to insure that racial segregation would be dismantled. One study has noted that very little desegregation took place in American public schools in the first decade after the famous 1954 decision in *Brown v. Board of Education*. It was not until Congress and the executive branch actively pressured school systems to end segregation in the 1960s that actual changes took place in the racial composition of schools (Rosenberg 1991). Thus, despite the justices' life tenure, structural independence, and power of judicial review, they are not readily able to effectuate their significant public policy pronouncements.

The Supreme Court's power and effectiveness are also diminished by the implementation process that occurs in response to judicial decisions (Johnson and Canon 1984). Supreme Court decisions are not self-executing. Moreover, justices' opinions are frequently complicated and difficult to understand. Thus the actual implementation of Supreme Court decisions depends on the interpretation and translation of justices' opinions by lower court judges, state attorneys general, city attorneys, and others who must apply general decisions to specific contexts. In addition, implementation depends on the obedience and cooperation of police officers, school principals, corrections officers, and others who must carry out the Supreme Court's instructions. Frequently, these lower level public officials do not implement Supreme Court decisions either out of ignorance about what they are supposed to do or because of outright resistance to the Court's instructions. A study of police officers, for example, found that it took several years for officers in many cities to begin to read criminal suspects their *Miranda* rights because police in small towns did not receive instructions from superiors about what the Supreme Court required them to do in arrest situations (Milner 1970). By contrast, when the Supreme Court barred organized prayer recitations in public schools (*Engel v. Vitale*, 1962), officials in many school districts simply continued to lead their students in prayer anyway (Dolbeare and Hammond 1970). As long as no students within these schools initiated expensive litigation to seek enforcement of the Supreme Court ruling, the school officials could disobey the nation's highest court with impunity.

Because of its connections to other components of the American political system, the Supreme Court is less powerful and effective than most people realize. Despite protected tenure in office and the significant power of judicial review, the Court cannot perform effectively if its decisions are not supported by other government officials and respected by the public. The Supreme Court's composition and the processes that determine its composition operate to keep its decisions within the range of acceptability of mainstream society, and thus the Court is not usually faced with significant public disobedience or overt resistance from executive branch officials. Because of the Court's composition and its dependence on the public and on other branches of government for its effectiveness, it is no surprise that studies of public opinion indicate that the Court's decisions generally comport with prevailing viewpoints in American society (Marshall 1989). Thus, as a practical matter, the Court's connections to the political system limit and shape its decisions in a manner that keeps those decisions roughly on track with the developmental trends in American society.

The Supreme Court's Cases

Unlike the centralized judicial systems of some countries, the United States has a dual court system. Figure 2.1 illustrates the organization of America's judicial system. Each state has its own court system comprised of trial courts and appellate courts. In the federal court system, ninety-four district courts handle the initial processing and

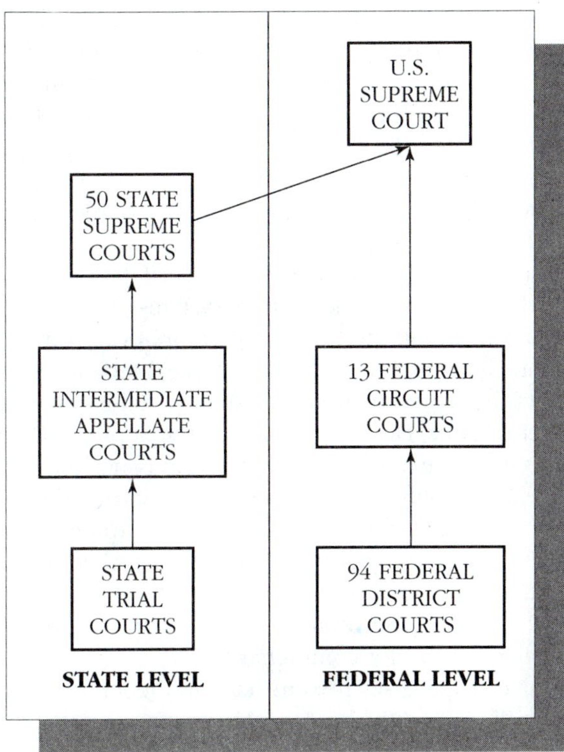

FIGURE 2.1 The Organization of America's Judicial System

trials for federal cases. Some states are within a single district (e.g., U.S. District Court of Massachusetts, U.S. District Court of Connecticut). Larger or more populous states are divided into multiple districts (e.g., U.S. District Court of the Eastern District of Michigan). The ninety-four district courts are supervised by twelve circuit courts of appeals, which are each responsible for reviewing cases from the districts within a specific geographic area. For example, the U.S. Court of Appeals for the Sixth Circuit sits at Cincinnati, Ohio, and reviews cases from the nine districts in Michigan, Ohio, Kentucky, and Tennessee. Each circuit is numbered (one through eleven) with a separate U.S. Court of Appeals for the District of Columbia Circuit, which handles appeals from cases in the nation's capital and from cases concerning federal government agencies. In addition, the Court of Appeals for the Federal Circuit, which was created in 1982, hears specialized appeals in customs, patent, and international trade cases.

The federal court system and its constituent divisions cover precisely the same geographic territory as the individual court systems administered by each state. Thus, for example, the northern half of Ohio has federal trial courts (U.S. District Court for the Northern District of Ohio) in Cleveland, Akron, and Toledo that sit virtually next door to state trial courts. The federal and state courts are distinguishable by their differing **jurisdictions**, namely the kinds of issues over which they have authority. In general, only a few kinds of cases may be filed in federal courts. First, federal courts handle cases concerning federal statutes, which can range from federal crimes such as bank robbery to civil lawsuits concerning federal antidiscrimination laws. Second, federal courts hear cases concerning the U.S. Constitution. Thus, disputes concerning the First Amendment issues of freedom of speech or religion, for example, may be heard by federal judges. Third, federal courts are responsible for cases in which the federal government is one of the disputants. For historical and political reasons, the nation's founders feared that state judges might show favoritism toward state residents or state governments in disputes against the national government. Fourth, the federal courts may also hear "diversity of citizenship" cases, in which a resident of one state, either an individual or a corporation, sues a resident of another state for an amount in excess of $50,000. Virtually all cases that are not within these categories are filed in state courts. Thus state courts handle the lion's share of criminal and civil cases each year. In 1989, for example, there were more than nine million civil cases filed in state courts but only 233,000 civil cases filed in federal courts.

The Supreme Court sits atop the national judicial hierarchy and hears cases generated by both the federal and state court systems. Many cases heard in state courts include issues concerning the U.S. Constitution. Every state criminal case, for example, can potentially raise issues about people's federal constitutional rights concerning speedy trials, representation by counsel, self-incrimination, and unreasonable searches and seizures. However, although the Supreme Court is the nation's highest court, it does not have authority over all legal issues that arise in the United States. The Supreme Court only decides cases that concern the U.S. Constitution, federal law, the U.S. government, state governments, or foreign countries. If a case arises from a dispute between two individuals within the same state who are arguing about the interpretation of a state constitution, then the state's supreme court is the ultimate authority. Thus the U.S. Supreme Court's control over the definition of American law is significant but not comprehensive.

Out of the millions of legal cases filed in state and federal courts each year, only a handful of cases will eventually be accepted for hearing by the U.S. Supreme Court. Most cases end as a result of settlements or dismissals in state and federal trial courts. Only a small fraction receive an actual judicial decision from a judge or jury, and only a fraction of these cases will be appealed to state and federal appellate courts. Many of these cases concern matters of state law and therefore are not eligible for review by the U.S. Supreme Court. Although the U.S. Supreme Court receives about seven thousand petitions annually asking it to review cases, it provides complete reviews and formal opinions in very few cases. Fewer than ninety cases received complete reviews and decisions each year in the Court's most recent terms. In addition, some cases receive a **summary disposition**, which normally involves a brief, decisive order from the justices based on the initial written papers submitted by each side rather than on oral arguments. During the Rehnquist Court era, the Supreme Court decided fewer cases each year than it did in the preceding eras under Chief Justices Warren and Burger. For example, the Court issued 155 full opinions during the 1982 term under Chief Justice Burger but only 75 full opinions during the 1995 term under Chief Justice Rehnquist. This development may reflect the efforts of Justice Scalia and Chief Justice Rehnquist who have sought to reduce the high court's involvement in supervising lower courts (Smith 1990). An overview of the workload of the Court is provided in Figure 2.2.

The high court can hear relatively few cases each year because it is a body of nine people who hear and decide each case as an entire group and who write detailed opinions to explain their decisions. Thus the organization of the Supreme Court

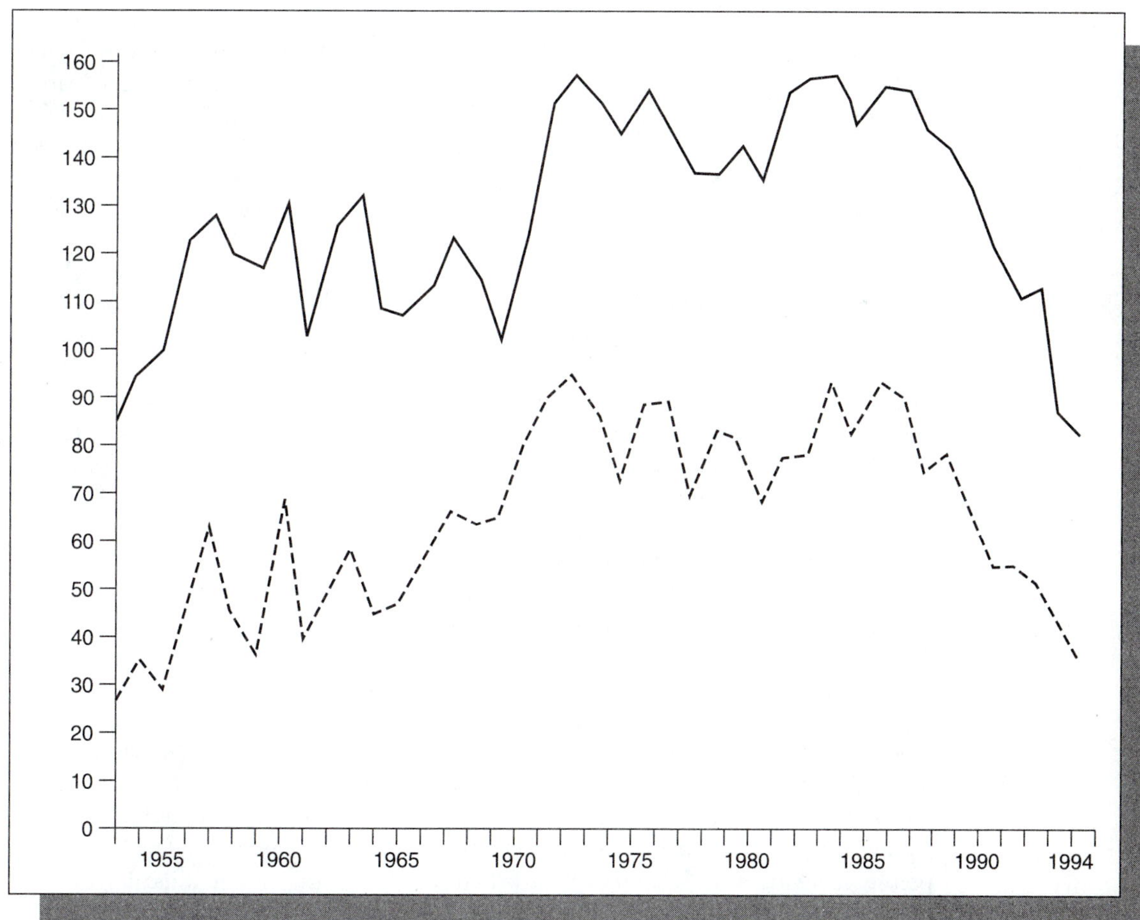

FIGURE 2.2 Plenary Cases Decided by the Supreme Court, 1953–94 Terms
Dark line: All plenary cases
Dotted line: All civil rights and liberties cases
Sources: United States Supreme Court Judicial Database, 1953-1993 Terms and January 1996 *The Third Branch*

limits its ability to handle many cases. The process of producing Supreme Court opinions is extremely time consuming, so only selected cases can receive the Court's attention. In addition, the justices have nearly complete discretion to choose the cases that they wish to hear. Thus they can turn away any cases that they do not wish to decide.

The Constitution gives the Supreme Court **original jurisdiction** over cases involving states, ambassadors, and "other public Ministers and Consuls." In these cases the Supreme Court could act as the trial court for disputes involving such litigants. Because of jurisdiction subsequently granted to lower federal courts by Congress, however, the Supreme Court reserves its original jurisdiction power only for legal cases between two or more states (Abraham 1991, p. 19). The Supreme Court's formal **appellate jurisdiction**, in which the Court is obligated to review cases, is limited to reviews of the small number of cases in which special three-judge federal district courts consider granting injunctions under specific federal statutes. These narrow categories comprise a very small portion of the Court's annual caseload. The overwhelming majority of cases is brought to the Supreme Court through petitions for a **writ of certiorari**. Litigants petition for a writ of certiorari when they want the Supreme Court to call up a case from a lower court. Four or more justices must vote to issue the writ, and they have complete discretion to grant or deny these petitions. The Court declines to "grant cert" to more than 90 percent of the petitions, and the previous decision by the state supreme court or federal appellate court is left undisturbed. The justices reserve their attention and resources for cases that they, or at least four of them, believe to be of greatest significance. Frequently, they focus on accepting cases that will resolve conflicting interpretations of constitutional provisions (or federal statutes) produced by different U.S. circuit courts of appeals. Cases initiated through certiorari petitions are analogous to a kind of discretionary appeal. Although they are not technically appeals, they involve the Court in appellate reviews of lower courts' decisions.

The Supreme Court justices use jurisdictional doctrines to decide which cases are ineligible for acceptance. They can interpret, apply, and alter these doctrines as they wish if they desire to avoid or delay facing controversial issues. Litigants must be the appropriate parties who suffered some harm in order to have **standing** to pursue a case. Standing is not automatically granted to litigants who claim that they are injured. Taxpayers, for example, have only narrow grounds on which they can claim sufficient injury to provide a basis for challenging a government policy or program. The Court has rejected several cases concerning the environment and civil rights issues because it determined that the people initiating the suit did not demonstrate sufficient injury to gain standing to sue.

Several jurisdictional doctrines concern the nature and timing of disputes that can be accepted for decision. A dispute must be **ripe** as a present dispute and not merely anticipate a future conflict. Moreover, disputes that are already over are **moot** and will generally not be considered by the Court. Sometimes the Court will make an exception to the rule if the nature of the legal issue is such that application of the mootness doctrine unfairly or unnecessarily blocks judicial consideration of an important issue. In *Roe v. Wade* (1973), although Norma McCorvey had already given birth to the baby and given it up for adoption, the Court accepted the case for review. It often takes years for cases to work their way through federal or state courts before reaching the Supreme Court. Thus, because of the biological reality of nine-month pregnancies, the mootness doctrine could have blocked the high court from ever considering the abortion issue if the Court had not acted to accept McCorvey's case. Otherwise, no pregnancies would ever have lasted long enough to permit women to challenge abortion regulations before the Supreme Court. In other cases, the Court can avoid deciding controversial issues if the individual litigant's claim has become moot. For example, the Court's first challenge to affirmative action policies in university admissions came from a white male student who asserted that he was denied admission to the University of Washington School of Law because of allegedly discriminatory preferences granted to members of racial minority groups (*DeFunis v. Odegaard*, 1974). By the time the case reached the Supreme Court several years later, the claimant had been accepted for admission into a subsequent class at the law school and was nearing his graduation date. The Court rejected the case despite the fact that the issue of affirmative action remained a significant controversy that would inevitably require the Court's attention.

In addition to concerns about ripeness and mootness, the parties in the case must be actual **adversaries**. The litigants may not undertake a friendly, contrived test of a legal precedent. The Court will not issue **advisory opinions** in friendly test cases or at the request of a public official. The president or members of Congress may be curious about how the Court will react to policies and programs that they contemplate initiating. However, the Court has steadfastly endeavored to limit its decision making to issues that have actually generated disputes within American society rather than spend its time deciding issues in anticipation of possible conflicts.

The Court also will not decide **political questions** that should be left to other branches of government. The Supreme Court decides many cases involving political issues, but it can avoid particularly difficult issues by labeling them "political questions" and leaving them for the other branches of government to decide. Thus, the political question doctrine is actually used as a convenient mechanism to permit the justices to avoid issues that would place them in unwanted confrontations with other governmental branches. For example, the Burger Court cited the political question doctrine in declining to review the constitutionality of the Vietnam War even though Justice William O. Douglas rightly observed that Congress had never exercised its official constitutional authority to "declare war" on North Vietnam (*Schlesinger v. Holtzman*, 1973). If the Court had attempted to determine the legality, or lack thereof, of the Vietnam War, it was very likely that the president and Congress, with the support of a majority of Americans, would have ignored the Court's declarations. The war would have continued to run its course and the Court's impotence in matters of foreign affairs would have been clearly and embarrassingly revealed.

Justices' law clerks handle the job of reviewing the thousands of certiorari petitions filed with the Supreme Court. The law clerks are outstanding recent graduates from the nation's most prestigious law schools who spend a year or two working for a justice, normally after only one prior year of experience working for another federal judge. After reading the petitions, the law clerks write short memoranda to the justices describing the cases, evaluating the importance of the issues presented, and recommending whether or not the Supreme Court should accept the cases for hearing. The law clerks are supposed to look for cases that present issues of sufficient importance to require the attention of the nation's highest court or issues that have been decided in a contradictory manner by two or more federal appellate courts. Over time, the clerks learn to identify the kinds of issues that their supervising justices believe are worthy of the Court's attention. However, the law clerks may have special difficulty in evaluating **pro se** petitions that are submitted by poor people, especially prisoners, without the assistance of attorneys. Such petitions are difficult to understand because they are submitted by people who have little ability to identify and assert appropriate constitutional claims. Because law clerks are inexperienced recent law school graduates, some observers fear that they will overlook important issues contained in the certiorari petitions or that they will assert their own values and policy preferences in making recommendations to the justices. D. Marie Provine's research on case selection in the Supreme Court indicated that although the law clerks' "memos inevitably reflect the backgrounds of the law clerks. . . [t]he extent to which the justices rely on the recommendations of their law clerks seems to vary from issue to issue and justice to justice" (1980, pp. 23–24).

The formation of a "cert pool" in which the law clerks of eight justices divide responsibilities for reviewing petitions has reduced the number of law clerks who read each certiorari petition. Prior to the formation of the pool, one clerk in each justice's chambers read each petition. By 1992, each petition was read and summarized only by one of Justice Stevens' law clerks and one law clerk from the pool in which the other eight justices participated. The cert pool has reduced the law clerks' burden of reviewing thousands of petitions, but it may also have increased the risk that an important issue will be overlooked or mischaracterized. Because justices rarely read certiorari petitions and therefore frequently rely on the clerks' memoranda, the clerks' role in helping to select cases for hearing is especially important.

The chief justice influences case selection by making a preliminary evaluation of each case based on law clerks' memoranda. The chief justice prepares a **discuss list** containing cases that he or she feels are worthy of consideration by the other justices. The chief justice also prepares a separate list of cases that should be summarily rejected. The other justices can ask that cases be added to the discuss list, but the chief justice's initial recommendations may determine which cases are actually considered for hearing by the Supreme Court unless specific excluded cases capture the attention of other justices. In their weekly conferences to discuss which cases they will accept for hearing, the justices follow the so-called **Rule of Four** requiring that at least four justices vote to hear a case in order for it to be accepted for oral argument and decision.

Social scientists who have studied the Court's selection process have hypothesized that the justices and law clerks use cues within the certiorari petitions to help them determine which cases to accept. In particular, the Supreme Court was found to be most likely to accept cases in which the United States government was one of the parties, which contained dissension in the lower court, or which concerned civil liberties or economic issues (Armstrong and Johnson 1982). Researchers have also found that cases in which **amicus briefs** are filed by outside parties are also more likely to be accepted for hearing (Caldeira and Wright 1988). Amicus briefs are written arguments submitted by interested parties—known as amicus curiae, meaning "friend of the court"—who are not directly involved in the case. With the agreement of the justices or the parties to the case, outside parties, including state and local governments, may be permitted to present additional arguments for the Supreme Court to consider. By the late 1980s, amicus briefs were filed in 80 percent of the Supreme Court's cases (Epstein 1991). Such amicus briefs are frequently submitted by interest groups in an effort to persuade the justices to favor the groups' policy preferences. The presence of these written submissions from interested outsiders may indicate to the justices that the underlying case involves a substantial controversy worthy of their attention. Interest groups are also involved in many other cases by providing lawyers for individuals whose claims raise issues that might advance the policy preferences of the interest groups.

Justices apparently do not work together to coordinate their efforts to have the Court accept specific cases for hearing. According to Provine (1980, p. 175), "[t]he [role] concept Supreme Court justices share [about] the scope of behavior suitable to a judge seems to filter [out] judicial attitudes toward [preferred] outcomes." This is not to say that justices never engage in strategic behavior when deciding which cases they ought to hear. Some justices have admitted, for example, that they will not vote to hear a case if they believe that a majority of their colleagues will use the case to set a new precedent with which they do not agree (Provine 1980, p. 127; Perry 1991, pp. 198–207).

When at least four justices vote to hear a case, an oral argument is scheduled for sometime during the Supreme Court's annual term, which runs from October to June. The Court seldom hears oral arguments after April because the justices need the final two months to finish writing opinions for the decisions argued during the term. Cases accepted for hearing in mid-term, which cannot be prepared for argument by April, are scheduled for the Court's next term beginning the following October. Normally, the attorneys for each side are given thirty minutes to present their arguments before the Court. Oral arguments are frequently extended "question and answer" sessions, because the justices pepper the attorneys with questions and arguments. The justices' questions are not merely intended to challenge the attorneys' arguments. They question attorneys to communicate with and attempt to persuade their colleagues about the merits of a particular argument. The justices may also use oral arguments to probe attorneys' minds for additional arguments and justifications that they might use to make their case opinions more complete and persuasive.

After oral arguments, the justices make preliminary decisions on cases during their weekly conferences. They meet in private sessions on Wednesdays and Fridays to vote on certiorari petitions and to decide the cases argued orally on Mondays, Tuesdays, and Wednesdays. No one is permitted in the room except for the justices. Because of their tradition of secrecy concerning case decisions, the justices have the opportunity to argue freely about cases during conferences without fear that outsiders will learn any details of the discussions.

Chief justices play an influential role in these sessions by characterizing each case and then presenting their views first. Scholars have studied how chief justices influence the decision-making process by leading discussions during the conference (Danelski 1989). The chief justice may use the opportunity to characterize the facts and issues in a case in a manner that favors a particular outcome. When the Supreme Court was considering *Brown v. Board of Education* (1954), for example, Chief Justice Warren initiated the discussion by saying that "[s]egregation . . . could be justified only by belief in the inferiority of the Negro; any of the [justices] who wished to perpetuate the practice, he implied, ought in candor to be willing to acknowledge as much" (Kluger 1975, p. 680). His approach may have placed on the defensive any justices who were undecided about the constitutionality of segregation and thereby contributed to the successful attainment of his goal of a unanimous decision favoring desegregation.

The chief justice expresses an initial opinion on the merits of the case, and the other justices then individually express their views in descending order of seniority. After this preliminary vote is tallied by the chief justice, he or she, if a member of the majority, will assign one justice to write the Court's opinion. If it is an important case or one of particular interest to the chief justice, he or she may retain the opinion-writing responsibilities. This presents another opportunity for the chief justice to influence the content and tone of the Court's opinions. Chief Justice Rehnquist, for example, often keeps important opinions for himself as a means of advancing his values and policy preferences. Chief justices can also affect the content of opinions by steering writing assignments to the justices whose views most closely resemble their own. However, Rehnquist has not fully exploited his opportunities to assign opinions to other strongly conservatives justices in order to advance the reasoning that he favors (Davis 1990). He appears to make comparable numbers of majority opinion assignments among colleagues without unduly favoring the most conservative justices.

If the chief justice is not in the majority, the senior justice in the majority makes the opinion assignment. During the first four terms of the Rehnquist era (1986–1990), liberal Justice Brennan frequently assigned opinions for civil liberties cases when Rehnquist and his conservative allies could not muster the necessary five votes to form a majority. The authority to assign opinions can affect both the decision and the reasoning in a case. The chief justice or senior majority justice can choose whether to assign opinions to outspoken justices who will enunciate strongly worded precedents or to moderate justices whose diplomatic tone may persuade undecided or wavering justices to join the majority. Other justices are free to write either **concurring opinions** that support the majority's outcome with alternative reasoning or **dissenting opinions** that express disagreement with the majority's decision. These opinions may attempt to persuade other justices on the current Court, or they may seek to lay the groundwork for future decisions by the Court when new justices have been appointed. Many notable dissenting opinions have later gained support from a majority of justices, often after the opinion's author has passed away. For example, the first Justice John Harlan, the grandfather of a namesake justice who served in the mid-twentieth century, issued a solitary dissenting opinion in *Plessy v. Ferguson* (1896), which included reasoning and conclusions that were later reflected in the Court's opinion in *Brown v. Board of Education.* The composition of the Court had changed and blatant racial prejudice became less acceptable to some segments of American society.

Supreme Court Decision Making

If deciding cases merely required Supreme Court justices to follow clearly established rules, then there would be few disagreements among the justices about the proper outcomes of cases. Constitutional law is not, however, fixed and clear. As Chief Justice Rehnquist has written, "[t]here is simply no demonstrably 'right' answer to the question involved in many of [the Supreme Court's] difficult cases" (1987, p. 291). Justices make choices about how to define the meaning of constitutional provisions and disputed statutory language. The meaning of the law changes and evolves as the human beings wearing the black robes of judicial office make decisions about how to define constitutional and statutory language.

How do the justices of the Supreme Court determine the meaning of constitutional law and the appropriate outcomes for cases? One study of Supreme Court decision making concluded that "[a] stunning and, in some cases, analytically numbing array of forces press contemporaneously on the justices as they work in controversial areas of law" (Epstein and Kobylka 1992, p. 303). Social scientists who study Supreme Court decision making have identified a variety of factors associated with the decision-making tendencies of individual justices. Not surprisingly, for example, Democratic and Republican justices tend to decide civil liberties and economic cases differently. In addition, justices who were previously prosecutors tend to be less supportive of rights for criminal defendants (Tate 1981). Such studies confirm the political underpinnings of Supreme Court decision making. Justices differ in their backgrounds, life experiences, and personal values, and these differences influence the judicial philosophies and policy preferences that they apply in making decisions on the Supreme Court. As we discussed in Chapter 1, most scholars have concluded that human beings' values and attitudes manifest themselves as policy preferences and that "justices' policy preferences are the most important factors that affect Supreme Court decisions" (Baum 1992, p. 145; see also Segal and Spaeth 1993). A primary goal of judicial scholars has been to identify the justices' underlying attitudes, values, social backgrounds, and policy preferences in order to understand, and even predict, decision making by the Supreme Court on civil liberties and other issues. Although social scientists focus on the justices' underlying human characteristics as the driving forces behind the choices they make, other factors also shape their decisions.

The evolution of constitutional law is determined by developments in the political system, such as a president's appointment of conservative rather than liberal justices, but the thinking of judicial decision makers in individual cases is also affected by their beliefs about such things as the nature of law, judges' proper roles in the governing system, and the image of the judicial branch. Thus, the identification of individual justices' underlying attitudes and values does not accurately foretell how they will decide every civil rights and liberties case because "there is substantial evidence that the less ideologically driven justices take [legal] arguments seriously and account for them in explaining the positions they take" (Epstein and Kobylka 1992, p. 310). An understanding of Supreme Court decision making requires recognition of the various factors, both personal and institutional, that shape, constrain, and guide the justices' decisions.

The Constitution and Theories of Interpretation

Supreme Court justices' decisions are shaped and constrained by the words of the Constitution and by the individual justices' beliefs about how the Constitution's words should be interpreted. The justices do not enjoy complete freedom to decide every case before them according to their own preferences. Although they seek to advance their conception of fairness with their decisions, they may not feel free to issue decisions that openly advance their views. If a justice were to decide a case by merely declaring "Side A wins because I think it should be so," the Court's image and legitimacy as a legal institution might be threatened because such a decision is an overt expression of individual preference without any pretense of being based on constitutional law. Justices can determine that "Side A" ought to win, but they must explain their decisions to the legal community and the public through elaborate opinions that purport to show that the outcome is demanded by words or ideas contained in the Constitution.

Although the justices look to the Constitution to guide their decisions and use their interpretations of the Constitution to justify case outcomes, they are not bound by the literal words of the Constitution unless they choose to be. Scholars frequently categorize justices and legal theorists as **interpretivists** and **noninterpretivists** (Ely 1980). Interpretivists seek to base their interpretations of the Constitution on the text and history of specific provisions. In other words, they attempt to confine themselves to the document and its origins when determining the meaning of each provision. Justice Hugo Black, for example, emphasized a literal interpretation of the Constitution's words during his long tenure on the Court from 1937 to 1971. Because the First Amendment of the Constitution says that "Congress shall make no law . . . abridging the freedom of speech," Black tended to take an absolutist position that opposed nearly any government regulation of speech. Black's literalism made him a supporter of broad freedom of speech, but his approach also led him to see civil liberties more narrowly than other Warren Court liberals when asserted rights were not grounded in the literal words of the Constitution. For example, because the word "privacy" does not appear in the Constitution, Black believed that justices should not seek to detect the existence of an implicit right to privacy lurking beneath the text of the Constitution. Black indicated that he personally would like people to enjoy protections for their privacy, but he could not declare that such a right existed if the Constitution's words did not provide it (see *Griswold v. Connecticut*, 1965). Black also could not accept his liberal colleagues' decision that the First Amendment protects symbolic expression, such as the wearing of armbands, because the words of the Constitution explicitly protect "speech" and not other forms of expression (*Tinker v. Des Moines School District*, 1969).

Justice Black was relatively unusual in his adherence to literal interpretation of the Constitution's words. On the Rehnquist Court, Justice Antonin Scalia occasionally resembles the late Justice Black in his willingness to override his ideological policy preferences, which are much more conservative than Black's, when he believes that the text of the Constitution dictates a particular result (Smith, 1992–93). Thus, Scalia has deserted his usual conservative allies on the Court to join the liberal justices in cases concerning freedom of expression (*see Texas v. Johnson*, 1989) and criminal defendants' right to confront their accusers in court (*see Cruz v. New York*, 1987).

By contrast, other justices, both liberal and conservative, tend to use approaches that define the Constitution's meaning without strict adherence to the text. These noninterpretivists believe it is appropriate and necessary to go beyond the Constitution's text in order to define the document's provisions according to the aspirational values that they believe underlie the nation's governing system and legal traditions. These justices may freely disagree with the intentions of the Constitution's authors because they believe the Constitution's meaning needs to change along with American society. Legal issues that were never anticipated by the Constitution's framers, such as abortion, affirmative action, and gender discrimination, are especially likely to generate disputes about the proper approach for determining the Constitution's meaning. For example, in the late 1950s the Supreme Court faced the issue of whether it was cruel and unusual for the United States to punish wartime deserters by declaring that they were no longer citizens of the country. In rejecting this punishment as unconstitutionally excessive, Chief Justice Earl Warren's majority opinion in *Trop v. Dulles* (1958) declared that the Eighth Amendment's prohibition against "cruel and unusual punishments" must "draw its meaning from the evolving standards of decency that mark the progress of a maturing society" (356 U.S. at 101). The words "cruel and unusual" do not, in themselves, clearly define the scope of permissible punishments. Instead of defining those words in accordance with the definitions applied by the Eighth Amendment's authors in 1791, Warren said that the meaning of the words must be judged in accordance with the evolving values and practices of contemporary society.

Obviously, justices who use Warren's approach of looking beyond the text in order to define the Constitution's meaning have a clear opportunity to place their own values within the meanings that they purport to discern from the Constitution's underlying ideals. Justices who use alternative interpretive approaches, however, also have opportunities to impose their personal views into constitutional law. For example, the political conservatives like Judge Bork who advocate interpreting the Constitution in accordance with the original intention of its authors claim that their theory would preclude justices from infusing decisions with personal values and policy preferences. Yet, as we discussed in Chapter 1, even an originalist can select agreeable sources of interpretation to advance preferred policy outcomes because of the lack of definitive evidence about how the Constitution's framers intended to define each provision (Segal and Spaeth 1993, pp. 58–62).

In sum, the Constitution's words and the justices' theories of constitutional interpretation shape decisions but do not necessarily dictate case outcomes. Justices have the opportunity to advance their preferred policy outcomes when the words of the Constitution and underlying ideals of the document provide a plausible justification that can be explained in a written opinion that comports with the style, tone, and reasoning usually found in Supreme Court opinions. If the Constitution does not provide a basis for a reasoned judicial opinion supporting an outcome, the justices may be reluctant to advance their preferences. Moreover, justices make choices about how they believe the Constitution's words should be interpreted. The application of specific interpretive theories limits the freedom of justices to decide cases according to their ideological preferences and may even lead justices to support case outcomes that they personally find distasteful. As Justice Anthony Kennedy, a conservative appointee of President Reagan, wrote when he supported a narrow majority that upheld a protestor's right to burn an American flag as a form of protected political expression: "The hard fact is that sometimes we must make decisions we do not like. We make them because they are right, right in the sense that the law and the Constitution, as we see them, compel the result. And so great is our commitment to the process that, except in the rare case, we do not pause to express our distaste for the result, perhaps for fear of undermining a valued principle that dictates the decision" (*Texas v. Johnson*, 491 U.S. at 420, 1989).

The Facts of the Case

Supreme Court decisions are influenced by the facts underlying each individual case. Civil rights and liberties cases usually involve legal challenges filed by individuals against government laws or actions by government officials. The factual circumstances that gave rise to the conflict between the individual and the government and the particular nature of the government law or action provide the context for the justices' decisions. If justices are seeking to advance their policy preferences concerning particular issues, they cannot decide those issues for hypothetical cases. They must wait for such cases to be brought to them. In hearing the cases, the justices must react to the specific circumstances of the case. They cannot engage in judicial policy making for abstract issues.

For example, in 1991 the Rehnquist Court decided a controversial case concerning the Bush administration's rule that doctors at federally funded family planning clinics could not tell patients about the legal option of obtaining an abortion (*Rust v. Sullivan*, 1991). The Bush administration's so-called "gag rule" for doctors stemmed from the president's opposition to abortion. When the rule was challenged in the Supreme Court, the justices were deeply divided about the issue of abortion, and new appointee Justice David Souter had yet to express any views on the controversial issue. At oral arguments, Souter expressed concern that a "gag rule," which precluded even mentioning abortion as one option, might endanger the health of patients in some cases, such as those in which a woman's health would be jeopardized by pregnancy. Ultimately, Souter provided the decisive fifth vote to uphold the "gag rule," but commentators believed that he did so only because Chief Justice Rehnquist's opinion went to great lengths to emphasize that the Court had not been presented with any specific factual situations concerning the rule's application in cases of medical emergencies (Mincberg 1991). If the Court had faced the issue in a case concerning a specific woman's medical need for information about abortion, Souter might very well have provided the decisive fifth vote to invalidate the rule.

The Court's decisions are also shaped by the nature of the law or governmental official's action that generated the legal action. For example, the first time the Supreme Court faced the controversial issue of whether burning an American flag constitutes protected political expression under the First Amendment, a majority of justices declined to tackle the divisive, emotional issue. Because the New York law that was used to arrest the flag burner stated that someone could be prosecuted not only for burning a flag but also for "cast[ing] contempt upon [the flag] . . . by words," five justices overturned the criminal conviction by claiming that they could not discern whether the individual was arrested for burning the flag or for making statements critical of the United States (*Street v. New York*, 1969). If the arrest had occurred under a statute that limited prosecutions to those people who physically destroyed an American flag, the Court may have had to face the underlying controversy more directly and the case may have been decided differently.

As indicated by the foregoing examples, the Supreme Court focuses on specific government laws and factual situations in issuing decisions about the Constitution's meaning and applicability. The justices do not always have opportunities to decide issues as directly and comprehensively as they may wish, but they can select their own emphasis within the cases argued before them. For example, the Warren Court expanded the scope of the "exclusionary rule" to deter unreasonable searches and seizures in a case (*Mapp v. Ohio*, 1961) in which the attorneys' arguments focused on First Amendment obscenity issues concerning the materials found in the unlawful search (Wasby 1988, p. 151). Despite the interpretive flexibility that the justices can apply to individual cases in deciding which facts or which issues are most important, they are still limited by the necessity of basing their decisions on the concrete disputes presented to them.

Legal Doctrines and Case Precedent

Just as Supreme Court justices must develop their opinions in light of the Constitution's words and ideals, they must also remain cognizant of previously established interpretations of the Constitution that have been "the law of the land" and have served to guide public policy and citizens' behavior. These previous constitutional interpretations are frequently referred to as legal **doctrines** and case **precedent**. Although closely related, these terms refer to somewhat different and distinct bases for Supreme Court decision making. A judicial doctrine is a test or guideline that the justices use to assist them in their legal reasoning. A famous example of a constitutional doctrine in the area of freedom of expression is the clear and present danger test, originally formulated in *Schenck v. U.S.* (1919). This doctrine or test stipulates that freedom of expression is such an important constitutional value that the government may interfere with this liberty only when the danger to society created by the expression is both obvious (clear) and imminent (present). The concept of case precedent refers more narrowly to one or more past Supreme Court cases that hold similarities to a case being considered by the Court and thus can provide assistance to the justices in reaching their decision. Doctrine and precedent can overlap significantly, especially when the Court sets forth a major doctrine in a specific case. For example, in *Lemon v. Kurtzman* (1971), the Court set forth a three-part test by which to analyze claimed violations of the Establishment Clause. This doctrine has come to be known as the *Lemon* test after the case precedent in which it was enunciated.

Legal doctrines and case precedent are used extensively by the members of the Supreme Court in their opinions. In order to protect the Supreme Court's image as a legal institution, the justices must consider how their decision-making processes will appear in the eyes of commentators and the public. If the justices seem simply to make up answers to the cases presented to them, without any linkage between the reasoning in these decisions and the legal reasoning established in prior cases, the public may be less inclined to accept and obey the Court's decisions as representing the true legal definition of the Constitution. Justices regularly mention their concerns about the need to protect the Court's image and legitimacy by insuring that their decisions fit within the framework of established constitutional law and comport with the judicial branch's proper role within the governing system. For example, Justice Felix Frankfurter wrote that "[t]he Court's authority—possessed of neither the purse nor the sword—ultimately rests on sustained public confidence in its moral sanction" (*Baker v. Carr,* 369 U.S. at 267, 1962). Justice Harry Blackmun has expressed similar sentiments: "The legitimacy of the Judicial Branch ultimately depends on its reputation for impartiality and nonpartisanship" (*Mistretta v. United States,* 488 U.S. at 405, 1989). In 1992, three justices, Sandra Day O'Connor, David Souter, and Anthony Kennedy, surprised many commentators by making such concerns the focal point of their coauthored opinion that declined to reverse the controversial 1973 abortion precedent, *Roe v. Wade* (*Planned Parenthood v. Casey,* 1992).

The United States inherited from British legal procedures the common law system of adhering to case precedents. Respect for previously established judicial decisions, also known as ***stare decisis***, has several functional benefits for the judicial system. By relying on previous decisions to guide the resolution of current legal controversies, judges can enhance stability in law, increase the likelihood that similarly situated people will be treated equally, and protect people's behavior undertaken in reliance on established judicial decisions. *Stare decisis* also improves the efficient administration of justice by sparing common law judges from the burden of "starting from scratch" in evaluating and deciding every single dispute. When American judges refer to prior decisions in deciding new cases, they are not obligated to follow the established precedents. They can also distinguish their current case from the prior ruling by asserting that specific facts in the case make it different than prior cases. This creates the opportunity to initiate a new rule. Judges can also alter the rule established in prior cases or, at the appellate level, reverse and rewrite judicially established legal principles. In general, the common law system of relying on case precedents tends to make legal change incremental rather than instantaneous, although the Supreme Court has produced many examples of dramatic changes in legal doctrine produced by a single opinion.

One consequence of justices' concerns about referring to case precedents and maintaining the Supreme Court's image is that even seemingly dramatic changes in the law are shaped, constrained, and slowed by the necessity for justices to address established principles when creating new legal rules. The Supreme Court's monumental 1954 decision in *Brown v. Board of Education* reversed a fifty-eight-year-old precedent (*Plessy v. Ferguson,* 1896) on a single day. Although the decision appeared to be and, in many respects, was a sudden change in constitutional law, the principles of legal segregation abolished by *Brown* had actually experienced legal erosion through prior incremental Supreme Court decisions in the 1940s and early 1950s. In cases concerning higher education, the Court repeatedly found that the purported "separate but equal" educational facilities for African Americans were thoroughly separate but decidedly unequal (*Sipuel v. Board of Regents,* 1948; *Sweatt v. Painter,* 1950). Thus the *Brown* decision might be accurately characterized as the abrupt end of a gradual process in which civil rights groups urged the Supreme Court to advance racial equality and the justices slowly disengaged constitutional law from an undesirable precedent.

In 1990, Justice Antonin Scalia authored a controversial decision that redefined and decisively narrowed the definition of the First Amendment right to exercise freely one's religious beliefs (*Employment Division of Oregon v. Smith,* 1990). Because of the common law process of reliance on case precedent, Scalia could not easily declare that all of the free exercise cases decided by the Supreme Court during the proceeding twenty-five years were wrong. The Supreme Court possesses the authority to make such dramatic declarations, but, because of justices' concerns about stability in law and the image of legal decision making, it would be difficult to gather the necessary support from a majority of justices to do so. Instead, Scalia changed existing principles by declaring that prior Supreme Court decisions actually limited broad Free Exercise Clause protections to a single context, the provision of unemployment compensation for people who lost jobs because they could not work on their religion's Sabbath. Scalia recharacterized the Supreme Court's other decisions concerning free exercise issues as actually "hybrid" cases that involved free exercise issues plus some other right, such as a parent's right to make choices about a child's education. Scalia may have wished to reduce protections for free exercise of religion in all contexts, but the existence of case precedents, especially those involving unemployment compensation, constrained the scope of his opinion.

The norm of expressing support for the importance of case precedent is so great that many justices feel obligated to pay homage to *stare decisis* in decisions that establish entirely new principles. For example, in a 1989 case in which a slim five-member majority on the Supreme Court sharply narrowed the application of an antidiscrimination statute, Justice Anthony Kennedy lauded *stare decisis* even as some aspects of his opinion clashed with the doctrine: "The Court has said often and with great emphasis that 'the doctrine of *stare decisis* is of fundamental importance to the rule of law.'. . . [I]t is indisputable that *stare decisis* is a basic self-governing principle within the Judicial Branch, which is entrusted with the sensitive and difficult task of fashioning and preserving a jurisprudential system that is not based upon 'an arbitrary discretion' " (*Patterson v. McLean Credit Union*, 491 U.S. at 172, 1989).

As indicated by the foregoing examples, established doctrines and precedents do not prevent the Supreme Court from suddenly endorsing new legal principles that clash with those developed in previous decisions. However, the existence of established principles can limit the justices' freedom in deciding cases because their opinions must provide persuasive justifications for their deviations from *stare decisis*. In some instances, case precedents are regarded as so firmly established that even justices who are clearly opposed to existing principles will accept that the relevant constitutional law cannot be changed. For example, even though he expressed his clear disagreement with the Court's decision, Chief Justice Rehnquist concurred rather than dissented in a 1992 case concerning criminal defense lawyers' use of racial considerations in challenging potential jurors (*Georgia v. McCollum*, 1992). In his concurring opinion, Rehnquist acknowledged that the decision was controlled by a strongly supported precedent from which he had previously dissented.

History and Changing Social Conditions

Justices' decisions are influenced by the historical era in which they grew up and by their perceptions of the changing social conditions and problems that will be affected by their decisions. As human beings, they cannot escape being shaped and affected by the events, experiences, and values of their generation.

When the Supreme Court struck down many social welfare and economic regulation laws in the early twentieth century by declaring that such laws violated citizens' freedom to work long hours at low pay, the justices were applying values from an earlier era that ignored the new social conditions affecting the country: "All of the justices who participated in [striking down social welfare laws] were born in the 1830s and 1840s. They grew up in an America ignorant of large-scale industrial organization, urban squalor, and the helplessness of the individual in dealing with organized wealth. The ideas [that these justices] expressed were not unsuited for their early years [when the United States was an agrarian society]. Probably most [judicially created] law must lag slightly behind the march of change" (Cox 1987, p. 136). Decades later, after this generation of justices and its immediate successors retired from the Court, President Franklin Roosevelt was able to appoint younger justices born at the close of the nineteenth century whose values reflected a new generation's recognition of the social problems of a modern industrial society.

Because the justices, as human beings and American citizens, react to the historical events and changing social conditions that surround the cases brought to the Supreme Court, they can become blind to the words of the Constitution or encourage expansive creativity in producing preferred outcomes. A majority of justices appeared blinded during World War II by the government's fears about sabotage, for example, when they approved the wholesale removal and incarceration of Japanese American families living on the West Coast (*Korematsu v. United States*, 1944). Although dissenting justices complained that the Supreme Court was ignoring these citizens' rights to "due process of law" before being deprived of their liberty, most justices apparently permitted their concerns about the country's then-uncertain progress in the war against Japan to dominate their thinking about the case.

By contrast, in the 1960s, when Congress finally acted to pass significant antidiscrimination laws (e.g., the Civil Rights Act of 1964) prohibiting racial discrimination by hotels, motels, restaurants, and other places of public accommodation, the Supreme Court wholeheartedly endorsed these statutes by broadly construing congressional authority to regulate interstate commerce (*Katzenbach v. McClung*, 1964). The Court permitted Congress to prohibit discrimination by businesses that had few demonstrable connections to interstate commerce because "[t]he Civil Rights Act of 1964 represented the moment when the other branches of government finally acted to endorse unambiguously the racial equality goals espoused by the Supreme Court one decade earlier [in *Brown v. Board of Education*]" (Smith 1992, p. 78). The Court responded to a significant national problem, racial discrimination, by interpreting a constitutional concept, "interstate commerce," so broadly as nearly to equate it with *all* commerce.

Attitudes, Values, and Small Group Interactions

Supreme Court justices claim that they persuade each other about case decisions during the process of writing and circulating draft opinions. After the preliminary vote and opinion assignment in conference, the justices return to their chambers and, with the assistance of their law clerks, draft and circulate opinions to explain their preferred outcome and reasoning. Studies of deceased justices' personal papers indicate that justices engage in other kinds of strategic behavior, such as bargaining with each other and cultivating positive personal relationships, in order to persuade their colleagues to join them in decisions (Murphy 1964). Because the Supreme Court is a collegial court in which a group of authoritative decision makers must interact with each other in order to produce decisions, interpersonal relationships and communications shape the outcomes of legal decisions. Justice William Brennan, for example, gained a reputation as a skilled coalition builder within the Supreme Court because he reportedly could be extraordinarily persuasive to his colleagues (Friedelbaum 1991). The interactions among the human beings who serve as Supreme Court justices can significantly affect decision making as majorities form in support of specific case decisions and justices persuade each other through discussions and through the circulation of draft opinions (Baum 1992, pp. 158–60). Personal animosities between justices may also affect decision making by reducing individual justices' inclinations to listen to and agree with each other. Justices Felix Frankfurter and Hugo Black, who served on the Warren Court, irritated each other and several of their colleagues during testy case discussions (O'Brien 1990, pp. 280-83). On the Rehnquist Court, Justice Scalia, the most outspoken, sarcastic, and uncompromising justice, runs the risk of alienating his ideological allies as well as his opponents through the strident, personal attacks contained in his opinions (Smith 1990).

All of the factors that shape Supreme Court decisions are affected by one set of powerful underlying forces: justices' attitudes and values. Each justice comes to the Court with views about the most appropriate public policies for the nation. These policy preferences are determined by the attitudes and values that they gained through such sources as their childhood socialization, personal and professional experiences, and religious beliefs. Attitudes, values, and policy preferences significantly determine which political party individuals choose to join and support and thereby generate detectable differences in the voting patterns of many Republican and Democratic justices (Tate 1981). Similarly, research on judicial decision making has documented that justices' political ideologies, which are comprised of their attitudes, values, and policy preferences, lead conservative and liberal justices to disagree with each other on civil liberties and other issues (Segal and Spaeth 1993). Justices do not simply assert their attitudes and values in deciding case outcomes, because they must decide how to address the Constitution's words, the facts of each case, case precedent, and other influential factors. However, their attitudes and values affect all of these factors because they must choose how to interpret the Constitution, how to characterize the facts in each case, and how much weight to accord to the principle of *stare decisis.*

In the 1986 case of *Bowers v. Hardwick*, for example, a homosexual man challenged Georgia's broad statute that provided criminal penalties for sodomy. Mr. Hardwick asserted that such laws violate the constitutional right to privacy. Under Georgia law, people can receive prison sentences as long as twenty years if convicted. As written, the Georgia statute made no specific references to or exceptions for homosexuals, heterosexuals, men, women, or married couples, and therefore it presumably applied to all people. When the Supreme Court examined the matter in 1986, the justices were deeply divided about characterizing the issue in the case. Justice White, on behalf of a five-member majority, characterized the case as concerning whether homosexuals have a constitutional right to engage in sodomy. Justice Blackmun, for the four dissenters, characterized the issue as whether consenting adults have a constitutional right to privacy for sexual acts within their own homes. The two sets of justices made choices about how to characterize the issue in the case, and their choices ultimately influenced how they determined the case's outcome. By looking at the specific claimant and seeing the case as asking for special protection for presumptively deviant behavior by an unpopular group, Justice White flatly rejected the privacy-based challenge to the Georgia law. The dissenters, however, by recognizing the implications of the statute's broad language for all adults, strongly reaffirmed the Court's twenty-year commitment to protection for adults' decisions about sexual matters within the privacy of one's home, just as previous justices had done for the issues of contraception and private possession of obscene materials (*Griswold v. Connecticut*, 1965; *Stanley v. Georgia*, 1969).

Which fact is more important, the circumstances of the individual claimant's arrest or the words and implications of the challenged statute? Justices make choices about what they think is most important within cases, and these choices affect their reasoning and decisions. Justice White's focus on the individual claimant's sexual preference led his reasoning to rely on historical American traditions proscribing sodomy. Justice Blackmun's emphasis on the statute made his reasoning follow the Court's privacy precedents. The justices' underlying choices about determining factors were shaped by the attitudes and values that colored their views of the issue in the case. Which attitudes and values generated their choices, reasoning, and decisions? It is not always easy to say. In the sodomy case, the justices' choices may have been shaped by their personal attitudes about homosexuality, sex, privacy, or states' authority to write their own criminal laws. In essence, no permanent legal principles dictated to the justices what they must do in the case. Just as in other cases, the individual justices' views in the sodomy case were determined by their views on the Constitution's meaning, American history, societal developments, precedents, and social policy—views which are all shaped by the justices' underlying attitudes and values. Moreover, in the sodomy case, justices' interactions and persuasiveness had a decisive impact on the outcome because during deliberations concerning the case, Justice Lewis Powell originally voted to invalidate the statute but subsequently changed his vote when he found Justice White's opinion more persuasive than Justice Blackmun's (O'Brien 1990, pp. 256–57). Years later, after he had retired from the Supreme Court, Justice Powell admitted that he had made a mistake by switching to provide the decisive vote to support White.

Conclusion

In Chapter 1, we discussed the legal, political, and attitudinal models that scholars use to describe the basis for Supreme Court decision making. As indicated by the discussion in this chapter, although there may be legal factors that influence justices' decisions, political developments and individual justices' values and attitudes are powerful determinants of Supreme Court decisions. The examples and discussions in subsequent chapters will illuminate how the Supreme Court's decisions in civil rights and liberties cases are shaped by political developments and human factors. The Court's composition changes in accordance with electoral trends and strategic political decisions by presidents and senators. The nature and timing of issues confronting the high court are determined by the actions and reactions of various political actors and institutions and by the justices' preferences in choosing cases for decision. The ultimate case outcomes that determine public policy and affect people's lives are the product of both the values of the justices on the Court at any given historical moment and the implementation processes influenced by executive branch officials and the general public. While the Supreme Court is neither as powerful as portrayed by its critics nor as effective as claimed by its supporters, it is an important and highly influential institution in the national government. The Court's image and mystique as a legal institution enhance its effectiveness in making pronouncements on controversial and divisive issues. True understanding of the Supreme Court's decision-making processes and impact on society, however, requires a recognition of the complex political factors that shape the high court's actions and role in the American political system.

REFERENCES

The Supreme Court in the American Political System

Abraham, Henry J. *The Judiciary: The Supreme Court in the Governmental Process*. 8th ed. Dubuque, Iowa: William C. Brown, 1991.

Armstrong, Virginia, and Charles A. Johnson. "*Certiorari* Decision Making by the Warren and Burger Courts: Is Cue Theory Time Bound?" *Polity* 15(1982): 141-50.

Baum, Lawrence. *The Supreme Court*. 4th ed. Washington, D.C.: Congressional Quarterly Press, 1992.

Bork, Robert H. *The Tempting of America: The Political Seduction of Law*. New York: Free Press, 1990.

Burke, Joseph C. "The Cherokee Cases: A Study in Law, Politics, and Morality." *Stanford Law Review* 21(1969): 500-47.

Caldeira, Gregory, and John Wright. "Organized Interests and Agenda Setting in the U.S. Supreme Court." *American Political Science Review* 82(1988): 1109-27.

Cox, Archibald. *The Court and the Constitution*. Boston, Mass.: Houghton Mifflin, 1987.

Craig, Barbara Hinkson and David M. O'Brien. *Abortion and American Politics*. Chatham, N.J.: Chatham House, 1993.

Danelski, David J. "The Influence of the Chief Justice in the Decisional Process of the Supreme Court." In *American Court Systems,* edited by Sheldon Goldman and Austin Sarat. New York: Longman, 1989.

Davis, Sue. "Power on the Court: Chief Justice Rehnquist's Opinion Assignments." *Judicature* 74(1990): 66-72.

Dolbeare, Kenneth, and Phillip E. Hammond. "Inertia in Midway: Supreme Court Decisions and Local Responses." *Journal of Legal Education* 23(1970): 106-22.

Ely, John Hart. *Democracy and Distrust*. Cambridge, Mass.: Harvard University Press, 1980.

Epstein, Lee, and Joseph F. Kobylka. *The Supreme Court and Legal Change*. Chapel Hill, N.C.: University of North Carolina Press, 1992.

Epstein, Lee. "Courts and Interest Groups." In *The American Courts: A Critical Assessment*, edited by John B. Gates and Charles A. Johnson. Washington, D.C.: Congressional Quarterly Press, 1992.

Faux, Marian. *Roe v. Wade*. New York: Macmillan, 1988.

Friedelbaum, Stanley H. "Justice William J. Brennan, Jr.: Policy-Making in the Judicial Thicket." In *The Burger Court*, edited by Charles M. Lamb and Stephen C. Halpern. Urbana: University of Illinois Press, 1991.

Gibson, James L. "From Simplicity to Complexity: The Development of Theory in the Study of Judicial Behavior." *Political Behavior* 5(1983): 7-49.

Johnson, Charles A., and Bradley Canon. *Judicial Policies: Implementation and Impact*. Washington, D.C: Congressional Quarterly Press, 1984.

Kluger, Richard. *Simple Justice: The History* of Brown v. Board of Education *and Black America's Struggle for Equality*. New York: Random House, 1975.

Marshall, Thomas R. *Public Opinion and the Supreme Court*. Boston, Mass: Unwin Hyman, 1989.

Milner, Neal. "Comparative Analysis of Patterns of Compliance with Supreme Court Decisions." *Law and Society Review* 5(1970): 119-34.

Mincberg, Elliot. "The Newest Justice: Stealth Unsheathed." *Legal Times*, July 22(1991), pp. S21, S35.

Murphy, Walter F. *Elements of Judicial Strategy*. Chicago: University of Chicago Press, 1964.

O'Brien, David M. *Storm Center: The Supreme Court in American Politics*. 2d ed. New York: W.W. Norton, 1990.

Palley, Marian Lief, and Howard A. Palley. "The Thomas Appointment: Defeats and Victories for Women." *PS: Political Science and Politics* 25(1992): 473-76.

Perry, H.W., Jr. *Deciding to Decide: Agenda Setting in the United States Supreme Court*. Cambridge, Mass.: Harvard University Press, 1991.

Provine, D. Marie. *Case Selection in the United States Supreme Court*. Chicago: University of Chicago Press, 1980.

Rehnquist, William H. *The Supreme Court: How It Was, How It Is*. New York: William Morrow, 1987.

Rosenberg, Gerald. *The Hollow Hope: Can Courts Bring About Social Change?* Chicago: University of Chicago Press, 1991.

Segal, Jeffrey A., and Harold J. Spaeth. *The Supreme Court and the Attitudinal Model*. New York: Cambridge University Press, 1993.

Smith, Christopher E. "Justice Antonin Scalia and Criminal Justice Cases." *Kentucky Law Journal* 81(1992-93): 187-212.

________. *Politics in Constitutional Law*. Chicago: Nelson-Hall, 1992.

________. "Justice Antonin Scalia and the Institutions of American Government." *Wake Forest Law Review* 25(1990): 783-809.

Smith, Christopher E., and Scott P. Johnson. "Newcomer on the High Court: Justice Souter and the Supreme Court's 1990 Term." *South Dakota Law Review* 37(1992): 21-43.

Tatalovich, Raymond. "Abortion: Prochoice Versus Prolife." In *Social Regulatory Policy: Moral Controversies in American Politics*. Edited by Raymond Tatalovich and Byron W. Daynes. Boulder, Colo.: Westview Press, 1988.

Tate, C. Neal. "Personal Attribute Models of the Voting Behavior of U.S. Supreme Court Justices: Liberalism in Civil Liberties and Economics Decisions, 1946-1978." *American Political Science Review* 75(1981): 355-67.

Wasby, Stephen L. *The Supreme Court in the Federal Judicial System*. 3d ed. Chicago: Nelson-Hall, 1988.

CHAPTER

3

THE JUSTICES OF THE REHNQUIST COURT

INTRODUCTION

Although they occupy positions of extraordinary power and prestige in American society, the members of the Supreme Court are relatively obscure to most Americans. Opinion polls show that only 10 percent of the American public can name the chief justice of the Court, and the other members of the Court are typically even less well known. This anonymity of the Court is not accidental. Appointed for life, the justices have no need to achieve prominence to gain reelection. The justices' daily work schedules require them to work alone or in small groups with the other justices and their law clerks. The popular media give relatively little attention to the activities of the Court compared to Congress and the presidency, and the stories that do appear typically refer to the Court as an institution rather than to the individual justices.

In-depth understanding of the civil rights and liberties policies of the Supreme Court requires knowledge about the individual members of the Court. Presidents, senators, and members of interest groups certainly recognize the significance of each member of the Court, as evidenced by the intense confirmation struggles involving Robert Bork and Clarence Thomas. Numerous studies of Supreme Court decision making provide strong evidence of the effect that individual membership changes can have on the policies of the Court.

Because of both the relative anonymity and the importance of each member of the Court, this chapter provides a detailed profile of each justice who has served on the Rehnquist Court. Presented in order of their seniority, these judicial profiles contain a discussion of the background of each justice prior to being appointed to the Court, the justice's voting record in civil rights and liberties cases, and the justice's judicial philosophy.

A series of tables is presented at the end of this chapter to assist in understanding each justice. Table 3.1 shows the percent liberal/conservative voting of each justice in civil rights and liberties cases during each of the nine terms of the Rehnquist Court from the 1986–87 term through the 1994–95 term, as well as a summary percentage for all the terms. Tables 3.2 through 3.10 contain bloc voting analyses of each Court term from the 1986–87 term through the 1994–1995 term to identify the major alignments among the justices. Finally, Table 3.11 contains data on the percent liberal/conservative voting of each justice in the three major areas of civil rights and liberties: First Amendment, criminal procedure, and civil rights (equality). Although methodological details about these procedures are presented in Appendix B, some brief explanations are appropriate here. In Table 3.1, where we present the liberal/conservative voting records of each justice for every term of the Rehnquist Court, we present a rank ordering of the justices based on their percent liberal voting. We define a liberal vote in a case as one that favors the individual bringing a claim that the government has violated the person's civil rights or liberties, and a conservative vote is one finding in favor of the government. Thus, in Table 3.1 (see p. 84) Justice Rehnquist's score in the 1986 term is 16, which means he voted liberally in 16 percent of the Court's civil rights and liberties cases. In sharp contrast, Justice Marshall's score for the 1986 term is 92 percent liberal. The bloc voting analyses for each term, which are presented in Tables 3.2 through 3.10 (see pp. 84–88), show the extent to which the justices voted together in civil rights and liberties cases each term. The numbers in each matrix are the interagreement scores for each pair of justices, that is, the percentage of cases in which the two justices were in agreement in their voting on the outcome of the case. To illustrate, the information in Table 3.2 shows that Justices Brennan and Marshall voted in agreement in 97 percent of the civil rights and liberties cases in the 1986 term. Two or more justices are considered to form a voting bloc if their average interagreement score is significantly higher than the average interagreement score of all pairs of justices; this is measured by the Sprague Criterion, which is discussed in detail in Appendix B.

WILLIAM J. BRENNAN

During the height of the Warren Court in the late 1950s and 1960s, William Brennan wrote majority opinions in some of the Court's most significant civil rights and liberties cases. As the Court became more conservative under the leadership of Chief Justices Burger and Rehnquist, Brennan's influence began to wane as he frequently found himself authoring dissenting opinions. He continued to be a strong advocate of the liberal civil rights and liberties policies of the Warren Court, and he was successful in helping to preserve many of the precedents of the Warren era. Brennan was replaced in 1990 by David Souter, an appointee of Republican President George Bush.

Background

William Brennan, the second of eight children of Irish immigrants, was born in Newark, New Jersey, on April 25, 1906. In his early years he was educated in parochial schools and then moved on to Newark's public school system. After high school, Brennan was an honor student at the University of Pennsylvania's Wharton School of Finance where he received a B.S. degree in 1928. He earned his LL.B. at Harvard Law School in 1931, graduating in the top 10 percent of his class.

After graduating from law school, Brennan returned to Newark where he joined a prestigious law firm and became a specialist in labor law. His work at the firm was interrupted by World War II. During the war, he served as an officer in charge of military procurement matters.

Following World War II, Brennan returned to his law firm and subsequently became involved in a major state judicial reform movement, which resulted in the creation of a new court system in New Jersey. He later became a member of that court system when he was appointed to a judgeship on the Superior Court in 1949. His work on the Superior Court impressed Arthur Vanderbilt, chief justice of the New Jersey Supreme Court, who influenced Brennan's elevation to higher courts. Brennan was appointed first to the appellate division of the Superior Court in 1950, and then to the state supreme court in 1952 where he served until 1956.

Chief Justice Vanderbilt also influenced Brennan's appointment to the U.S. Supreme Court in 1956–57. When Sherman Minton resigned from the Court in October of 1956, Vanderbilt suggested to President Eisenhower that Brennan would be the perfect choice, given the qualifications that the president had specified: "relative youth, judicial experience, and excellent standing with his state bar as well as the ABA" (Abraham 1992, p. 265).

In addition to Brennan's obvious qualifications, Eisenhower was motivated by important political considerations. Brennan was a Democrat, and because this was an election year, Eisenhower viewed the nomination as an opportunity to maintain the electoral support of the Eisenhower Democrats of 1952. Finally, because Brennan was a Roman Catholic, Eisenhower could use the nomination to fill the "Roman Catholic seat" on the Court, which had been vacant since Justice Frank Murphy's death in 1949.

Eisenhower gave Brennan a recess appointment in October of 1956 and formally nominated him to the Court in January of 1957. Despite Brennan's impressive credentials and the apparent widespread support that he had garnered, the confirmation was delayed. One reason for the delay was related to the recess appointment. Because Brennan had begun serving immediately, some of the questions asked of him at the confirmation hearings touched on issues in cases pending before the Court, and consequently many of Brennan's responses to questions from the Senate Judiciary Committee in February 1957 were vague. Secondly, he was attacked by Senator Joseph McCarthy, whom Brennan had criticized previously for his leadership of the infamous anticommunism crusade. Nonetheless, Brennan was confirmed by the Senate by an overwhelming vote, with McCarthy casting the only negative vote.

Voting Record

Brennan's liberal record had been established early in his career, and it continued in his four terms on the Rehnquist Court until his resignation in 1990. As indicated in Table 3.1, for the four years combined, Brennan voted for a liberal outcome in 86 percent of the cases. His highest level of support for civil rights and liberties claims (92 percent) came in 1986–87, the very first term of the Rehnquist Court.

In addition, Brennan was a member of a liberal voting bloc in each of the four terms, although the composition of the bloc varied, as can be seen in Tables 3.2 through 3.5. In the 1986–87, 1987–88, and 1988–89 terms, the bloc included only Brennan and Marshall, and they were joined by Stevens in the 1989–90 term.

Judicial Philosophy

Brennan was one of the most liberal members of the Supreme Court. His opinions in cases involving the First Amendment, privacy rights, the rights of criminal defendants, and racial and gender equality reflected several major beliefs. First and foremost, Friedelbaum (1991) argues, is Brennan's belief in egalitarianism, a persistent theme in his opinions. Brennan's egalitarianism led him to push for social reform in which the government must play a positive role in "meeting the needs of the deprived and oppressed in American society" (p. 105). As a result, Brennan believed the law could and must be used to remedy various problems in society. He also emphasized that the justices must interpret the Constitution to meet changing societal needs. This theory of an evolving Constitution led to a spirited debate between Brennan and Ronald Reagan's attorney general, Edwin Meese. In a speech to the American Bar Association in July of 1985, Meese maintained that many of the

Court's decisions had been based on the justices' policy preferences rather than on constitutional principles. He stressed further that the Court ought to examine the "original intent" of the Framers in deciding cases. Many observers took Meese's statements to be an attack on the liberal civil rights and liberties record of the Warren and Burger Courts. Three months after this speech, in a paper delivered at a teaching symposium at Georgetown University, Brennan responded to Meese's attack. He argued that the Constitution serves as a framework for government and that it is an ambiguous document that must be interpreted by successive generations. Moreover, he criticized Meese's notion of original intent as "one that 'feigns self-effacing deference' to the framers but, in reality, 'is little more than arrogance cloaked as humility' " (Friedelbaum 1991, p. 121). In Brennan's view, it was not really possible to determine *precisely* what all of the Framers intended when they wrote various provisions of the Constitution. Moreover, the search for original intent distracts justices from their true purpose, namely to effectuate the aspirational ideals of human dignity espoused by the "living Constitution."

BYRON R. WHITE

Byron White's record on the Supreme Court may appear somewhat surprising to Court observers, for although he was appointed by John F. Kennedy, a Democratic president, he became a firm conservative voice on the Court. During his tenure on the Rehnquist Court, he aligned with other conservatives to chip away at liberal precedents of the Warren and Burger Courts. His decision to retire at the end of the 1992–93 term created an early opportunity for President Bill Clinton to affect the composition and direction of the Court. Clinton's choice to replace White was Ruth Bader Ginsburg, the second woman ever to serve on the high court.

Background

Born on June 8, 1917, in Fort Collins, Colorado, White spent his early years and adolescence in the small town of Wellington, Colorado. Academically talented, he was first in his high school class, and in 1934 he won a scholarship to attend the University of Colorado. He proved to be an outstanding scholar-athlete, as he graduated in 1938 at the head of his class, was admitted to Phi Beta Kappa, and won numerous varsity letters in football, basketball, and baseball. Following a brief stint in professional football, White attended Oxford University on a Rhodes Scholarship. During his time in England, he became acquainted with John F. Kennedy, who would later be instrumental in his career opportunities. After returning to the United States, White enrolled in Yale Law School and renewed his career in professional football. When the United States entered World War II, he joined the Navy, serving as a PT boat skipper in the South Pacific where, coincidentally, one of his fellow officers was Kennedy.

After the war, he completed his law degree at Yale, graduating magna cum laude. He then served as a law clerk to Supreme Court Chief Justice Fred Vinson from 1946–47 and, while in Washington, he renewed his acquaintance with Kennedy. In 1947, White returned to Colorado and practiced law for the next fourteen years with a prominent law firm in Denver.

White was heavily involved in Kennedy's 1960 presidential election campaign at both the preconvention stage and after Kennedy won his party's nomination. After Kennedy was elected, White was appointed to serve as deputy attorney general in 1961. In this post, his primary responsibilities entailed conducting investigations of potential judicial nominees and supervising federal marshals and deputies sent to Alabama to protect the Freedom Riders as they attempted to desegregate interstate buses and southern bus terminals.

White's service as deputy attorney general impressed Kennedy and his advisers, and when Charles Whittaker retired from the Supreme Court in 1962, White was nominated to fill the vacancy. He was given a strong endorsement by the American Bar Association, and the nomination was accepted by liberal and conservative newspapers. On April 11, 1962, the Senate confirmed him by a voice vote.

Voting Record

White's voting record in civil rights and liberties cases from the 1986–92 terms makes him the fourth most conservative justice on the Rehnquist Court, behind Rehnquist, Thomas, and Scalia. As shown in Table 3.1, however, White's voting record shows substantial variation. During the first four terms of the Rehnquist Court from 1986–87 to 1989–90, White voted liberally in only 25–30 percent of the civil rights and liberties cases. In his last three terms, however, White increased his liberal voting rather substantially, casting liberal votes in 44 percent of the cases in the 1990 and 1991 terms and voting liberally in 39 percent of the cases in his last term of 1992.

White was aligned with a conservative voting bloc in four of his seven terms, but the composition of the blocs varied substantially. In the 1986–87 term, he joined with Rehnquist, Scalia, and O'Connor to form a four-person bloc, but in the 1987–88 term he was not a member of any bloc. In the 1988–89 term a five-person conservative bloc emerged that included White, Kennedy, Scalia, Rehnquist, and O'Connor, and this bloc continued into the 1989–90 term. This cohesive five-person bloc disintegrated in the 1990 and 1991 terms, however, and White was not aligned with any of the other justices. In the 1992–93 term, however, he did join with Rehnquist in a two-person conservative bloc.

Judicial Philosophy

The major strands of White's judicial philosophy appear to be a view of federalism in which national power is supreme and a belief in some level of judicial restraint. Kramer (1991) asserts that in cases involving conflicts between the national government and states, White most often favored the national power. According to Kramer, some of White's former law clerks refer to him as a "strong nationalist."

In terms of judicial restraint, White's primary concern was judicial deference to the legislative branch. In White's view, legislators are representatives of the people, so courts should take care not to interfere with their work. Moreover, when there are conflicts about social issues, they must be resolved by the accommodation and compromise found in legislative processes. Related to this is the belief that courts are not appropriate agents of social change because "change is too rampant and too demanding, too complex and massive, for either wise or efficient handling in the courts" (Kramer 1991, p. 428).

Finally, Kramer explains that White believed that government is a beneficent institution, that it works for the welfare of the society in general, and that it is a tool to help people. He says that this perspective was shaped by White's experience with the Great Depression and New Deal, his educational experience at a public college established with the aid of federal funds, and his work at the U.S. Justice Department.

THURGOOD MARSHALL

By the time he retired from the Supreme Court in 1991, Thurgood Marshall's role had become primarily that of vocal dissenter. Occasionally, he and Justice Brennan were able to secure a majority to uphold a Warren Court or Burger Court precedent regarding civil liberties or civil rights. Most often, however, Marshall chastised the Rehnquist Court majority for what he perceived as its insensitivity to the needs of the oppressed and disadvantaged in society. Somewhat ironically, Marshall was replaced by Clarence Thomas, an African American who has frequently advocated positions diametrically opposed to those espoused by Marshall.

Background

Marshall, the great-grandson of a slave, was born on July 2, 1908, in Baltimore, Maryland. He was educated in the public schools of Baltimore, including Frederick Douglass High School, the only high school for African Americans in Baltimore. At Lincoln University in Pennsylvania where he graduated with honors in 1930, he gained the reputation as an outstanding debater. Marshall then attended law school at Howard University, graduating first in his class in 1933. It was here that he became acquainted with Charles Hamilton Houston, the dean of the law school and a man with whom he would later collaborate to lead the legal battle against racial segregation in the United States.

After receiving his LL.B. from Howard, Marshall returned to Baltimore where he started a private practice and became associated with the local branch of the National Association for the Advancement of Colored People (NAACP), first as a volunteer, then as counsel. In 1936, Charles Houston named him special assistant legal counsel to the NAACP, and two years later, following an illness, Houston resigned and Marshall became special counsel in charge of litigation. He remained in this position until 1950, when he became director-counsel of the NAACP's Legal Defense and Educational Fund, Inc., the organization which led the attack on racial segregation. In this role, Marshall argued thirty-two cases before the Supreme Court, winning an astonishing twenty-nine of them. The case for which he is best known is the 1954 *Brown v. Board of Education of Topeka* decision, in which the Court ended the "separate but equal" doctrine established nearly sixty years earlier. The *Brown* case paved the way for a number of other legal victories challenging racial segregation in public facilities.

In 1961, President John Kennedy gave Marshall a recess appointment to the Second Circuit Court of Appeals. Despite his impressive credentials and outstanding legal record, he was not confirmed by the Senate for a year because of opposition by southern senators who questioned him repeatedly about his civil rights background. Marshall served on the Second Circuit until 1965, when he was appointed to be solicitor general by President Johnson. This time his confirmation took less than a month. His legal successes continued in both of these positions. In four years on the Court of Appeals, Marshall wrote ninety-eight majority opinions, none of which was reversed by the Supreme Court. In his two years as solicitor general, he argued nineteen cases before the Supreme Court, winning fourteen of them.

President Lyndon Johnson indicated several times during his presidency that he wished to appoint a nonwhite justice to the Supreme Court. Justice Tom Clark's retirement from the Court in 1967 presented Johnson with such an opportunity, and Marshall seemed to be a likely choice. He had a distinguished record, with service both on the court of appeals and as solicitor general. Once again, however, his nomination ran into trouble, with opposition from senators from the Deep South. Nominated on June 13, 1967, Marshall was confirmed on August 30, 1967, by a 69–11 vote.

Voting Record

During his five terms on the Rehnquist Court, Marshall was its most liberal member. As shown in Table 3.1, he voted for a liberal outcome in 88 percent of civil rights and liberties cases. Predictably then, Marshall was a member of a liberal voting bloc in each of those terms, even after William Brennan, his ideological partner, retired following the fourth term of the Rehnquist Court. Marshall was aligned in a two-person bloc with Brennan in the 1986–87, 1987–88, and 1988–89 terms. In his final two terms, he was a member of a changing three-person bloc. The bloc in the 1989–90 term included Marshall, Brennan, and Stevens, while Marshall was joined by Blackmun and Stevens in the 1990–91 term.

Judicial Philosophy

According to Goldman and Gallen (1992), Marshall's judicial philosophy had at its core a belief that the Bill of Rights and the Civil War Amendments must be used expansively, particularly to protect the powerless, the disadvantaged, and the despised in society. Broad phrases such as "due process," "equal protection," "freedom of speech," and "cruel and unusual punishment" should be construed and applied "to protect those outside the political mainstream . . ." (p. 210). Related to this, as Daniels (1991) notes, was a conviction that the Supreme Court is responsible for giving meaning to constitutional rights. Furthermore, as his opinions indicate, Marshall thought the Court's responsibility was to protect people from intrusive and abusive government action, whether such action involved legislators, law enforcement officers, administrative officers in government agencies, or other executive branch officials.

Finally, much like his colleague William Brennan, Marshall believed in the use of the law to correct social injustices. Daniels (1991) argues that although he witnessed the law being used in negative ways to control and oppress people, Marshall nonetheless believed that "legal activism is both a valued and imperative tool in helping the disadvantaged" (p. 235).

HARRY A. BLACKMUN

Following the retirements of Justices Brennan and Marshall in 1990 and 1991, Harry Blackmun became a leading liberal on the Supreme Court, typically aligning closely with John Paul Stevens. His new status reflected a remarkable shift from his early years as the "Minnesota Twin" of Warren Burger, the conservative chief justice. Blackmun's most famous opinion was the controversial abortion decision of *Roe v. Wade* (1973), and he worked vigorously to prevent the more conservative members of the Rehnquist Court from overturning this precedent. Blackmun retired from the Court following the 1993 term, thus allowing Democratic President Bill Clinton to appoint his successor, Stephen Breyer.

Background

Blackmun was born on November 12, 1908, in Nashville, Illinois. He spent his formative years in St. Paul, Minnesota, where he attended kindergarten and elementary school with his friend Warren Burger, whom he would later join on the Supreme Court.

After graduation from high school, Blackmun was a mathematics major at Harvard, where he was elected to Phi Beta Kappa. He graduated cum laude in 1929, and he received his LL.B. in 1932 from Harvard Law School. Upon graduation, he returned to St. Paul and was admitted to the Minnesota Bar.

From 1932–1933, Blackmun served as a law clerk to Judge John Sanborn of the Eighth Circuit Court of Appeals. He then entered private practice in Minneapolis with the firm of Dorsey, Coleman, Barker, Scott, and Barber, working as an associate from 1934–38, becoming a junior partner in 1939 and a general partner in 1943. During these years, he specialized in the fields of estates, taxation, and general civil litigation. Blackmun remained with this firm until 1950, when he became resident counsel for the Mayo Clinic and the Mayo Association in Rochester, Minnesota.

His work with the Mayo Clinic continued until 1959 when he was appointed to the federal bench by President Eisenhower. Ironically, the seat to which he was appointed on the Eighth Circuit Court of Appeals had been held by Judge Sanborn, for whom he had clerked years earlier.

Blackmun's nomination to the Supreme Court followed one of the most bitter and controversial episodes in the history of Supreme Court nominations. Abe Fortas, one of the leading liberals of the Warren Court, had been forced to resign from the Court in 1969 because of a series of allegations regarding improper behavior. President Nixon had already named Warren Burger to replace Earl Warren as chief justice, and now Nixon had another opportunity to alter the Court. Nixon faced formidable opposition, however, from Democratic senators and liberal interest groups who were upset over the treatment of Fortas and concerned about the effect of another conservative addition to the Court. Nixon attempted to name a conservative southerner to the Court as part of a strategy to bring the South into the Republican Party, but the Senate defeated both of his nominees, Clement Haynesworth and G. Harrold Carswell, after bitter confirmation hearings involving various accusations of improprieties against both candidates.

In this highly charged political environment, Nixon then chose Blackmun as a candidate who could gain Senate approval. Although Blackmun's record on the Eighth Circuit was not particularly noteworthy, President Nixon viewed Blackmun as an attractive candidate. Judicial observers had characterized Blackmun as a conservative on civil liberties issues, and most important to Nixon, as a judge who sided with the government in criminal cases and who believed in and practiced judicial restraint. Speculation also exists that Chief Justice Burger, Blackmun's friend from childhood, had a hand in this nomination. Finally, Blackmun was a northerner who did not have any hint of judicial impropriety in his background. Blackmun was nominated on April 15, 1970. The Senate, weary from the previous battles, confirmed Blackmun by a unanimous vote about a month later.

Voting Record

Blackmun, perhaps more than any other justice appointed in recent history, underwent a transformation from his early years on the Court to his later years. According to Wasby (1991), in his first few terms, Blackmun most often voted with the conservative Warren Burger on civil rights and liberties issues; and in nonunanimous cases decided by 5–4 or 5–3 votes, Blackmun and Burger most often took the conservative position. By the mid-1970s, however, Blackmun began to take a more liberal view of civil rights and liberties, and by the early 1980s he was more likely to be found with Brennan and Marshall in close cases. Thus it is not surprising that he was the fourth most liberal justice of the Rehnquist Court. As indicated in Table 3.1, Blackmun's liberalism score for his eight terms of service during the Rehnquist era was 71 percent. His highest support for civil rights and liberties came in the 1990–91 and 1992–93 terms, when he took the liberal position in 78 percent of the cases.

Blackmun has frequently been a member of a liberal voting bloc, but this has varied from term to term as can be seen in Tables 3.2 to 3.9. During the first four terms, Blackmun's agreement scores with the other liberal members of the Court were not high enough for him to be included in the liberal bloc. In the 1990–91 term, however, Blackmun joined Marshall and Stevens to form a bloc, and Blackmun and Stevens constituted a two-person liberal bloc in the 1991–92 and 1992–93 terms. Although the pair's agreement rate was 84 percent in the 1993–94 term, it was not high enough for them to constitute a cohesive voting bloc.

Judicial Philosophy

Blackmun's judicial philosophy, much like his voting record, evolved over time. In his early years on the Court, Blackmun's general trust in governmental institutions led him to believe in judicial deference to the legislative and executive branches of government (Wasby 1991). In Blackmun's view, judges should not overturn the policy judgments of legislators unless absolutely necessary. He also supported only limited judicial review of the actions of federal agencies. As time passed, however, he became more skeptical about the "government's willingness to act appropriately" (Wasby 1991, p. 71). Thus, his position of deference to legislative and executive officials was tempered accordingly.

Blackmun's views on federalism also reflected a moderated approach to construing the extent of national and state powers. He supported a strong role for the federal courts in protecting federal rights, and he rejected attempts by his colleagues to restrict that role. His interpretation of the preemption doctrine led him to uphold federal laws over state laws in most instances. For Blackmun, congressional policies superseded those of states unless there was evidence that this was not the intent of Congress. On the other hand, Blackmun did support states' rights to make policy, particularly in matters involving commerce.

WILLIAM H. REHNQUIST

Since his appointment to the United States Supreme Court in 1971, William Rehnquist has seen dramatic changes in the Court and in his own role on the Court. His conservative legal and political views were well known before he came to the Court, and he has been a strong and consistent advocate of these views throughout his years on the Court. During his first decade on the Court, however, Rehnquist found limited support for his ideas, and he frequently wrote concurring or dissenting opinions that were not joined by any other justices. Rehnquist's role on the Court began to change dramatically during his second decade on the Court and especially when he was appointed chief justice by President Ronald Reagan in 1986. Rehnquist not only assumed formal leadership of the Court but also found the composition of the Court becoming increasingly more conservative with the appointments of Justices Scalia, Kennedy, Souter, and Thomas. Rehnquist has thus moved from a young, relatively isolated conservative to become the undisputed leader of a Supreme Court dominated by more conservative justices. What remains unclear is the extent to which Rehnquist can lead the Court in fulfilling his conservative vision.

Background

Rehnquist established an impressive and somewhat controversial record prior to his appointment to the Court. He was born in a suburb of Milwaukee, Wisconsin, in 1924 and grew up there. He began his undergraduate years at Kenyon College in Ohio, but later joined the Army Air Corps during World War II. Following the war he used the GI Bill, enrolling at Stanford University and graduating with Phi Beta Kappa honors in 1948. He earned M.A. degrees from Stanford in 1949 and Harvard University in 1950, and then he entered law school at Stanford, graduating first in his class in 1952. Rehnquist's first position following law school was a prestigious clerkship with Supreme Court Justice Robert Jackson. During this time, Rehnquist wrote a memorandum regarding the pending case of *Brown v. Board of Education* (1954) in which he argued in favor of maintaining separate but equal schools. This matter resurfaced during Rehnquist's Senate confirmation hearing, where he insisted that these were not his views and that he had been following Jackson's instructions to prepare a memo arguing the separationist position.

Following his clerkship on the Supreme Court, Rehnquist moved to Phoenix, Arizona, where he combined the practice of law with active involvement in the conservative wing of the Republican Party. Rehnquist became involved in politics at the national level during the 1964 presidential campaign when he worked diligently for the Republican candidate, Senator Barry Goldwater. Although Goldwater suffered a crushing defeat, Rehnquist continued his work for the Republican Party. When Richard Nixon won the presidency in 1968, Rehnquist was named an assistant attorney general in charge of the Justice Department's Office of Legal Counsel. In this role, Rehnquist had the responsibility of reviewing constitutional law issues involving the executive branch, and he frequently defended the actions of the Nixon administration before Congress.

Rehnquist's success in his position as assistant attorney general, as well as his strong and frequent criticisms of the liberal decisions of the Warren Court, led Nixon to nominate Rehnquist to replace Justice John Marshall Harlan, who resigned in early 1971. Rehnquist was eventually confirmed by the Senate on December 10, 1971, but it was a confirmation marked by controversy as indicated by the 68–26 vote. Despite the strong opposition by many civil rights and liberties groups, however, his impressive academic credentials, his intellectual abilities, and his performance in the Justice Department gained him sufficient support to win Senate confirmation.

Voting Record

Rehnquist's voting record in civil rights and liberties cases has been consistently conservative throughout his years on the Court. During the Burger Court era from 1969 through 1985, he had the lowest percentage of liberal support in every year except one (Lamb and Halpern 1991, p. 33). Table 3.1 shows that he has maintained this consistent conservatism since becoming chief justice in 1986; his overall record of 23 percent liberal support in civil rights and liberties cases is the most conservative of any justice who has served on the Rehnquist Court.

In addition, Rehnquist has been a member of the conservative bloc in every term but one since he became chief justice, as seen in Tables 3.2 through 3.10. It is important to note, however, that the conservative bloc has shown substantial variation. Rehnquist was a member of a four-person conservative bloc in the

1986–87 term, but the conservative bloc in the next term consisted of only Scalia and O'Connor. In Kennedy's first two full terms, 1988–89 and 1989–90, a five-person conservative bloc existed, providing the conservatives with a working majority of votes. It was widely expected that the replacement of Brennan by Souter in 1990 and of Marshall by Thomas in 1991 would serve to strengthen this conservative majority even further, but the data in Tables 3.6 through 3.10 show this did not occur during the terms 1990 through 1994. Only Rehnquist, Scalia, and Thomas have been consistent members of the conservative voting bloc. These developments illustrate that a great challenge to Rehnquist's leadership as chief justice is forging the consistent, majority conservative bloc necessary to advance his conservative preferences.

Judicial Philosophy

Rehnquist's lack of support for civil rights and liberties claims is directly related to his judicial philosophy. Sue Davis (1986, 1989, 1991) has written extensively about Rehnquist, and she argues that his judicial philosophy is comprised of three main elements: majoritarianism, moral relativism, and original intent. The principle of majoritarianism emphasizes the primacy of majority rule in a democratic system and argues that solutions to societal problems and injustices should be sought primarily through the popularly elected branches of government. Moral relativism is a principle which asserts that no value can be proven to be intrinsically superior to any other value, and therefore judicial officials must look to positive law—that which is written into laws and statutes—rather than relying on abstract theorizing about moral values. The third component of Rehnquist's judicial philosophy involves original intent. This principle emphasizes the importance of interpreting the Constitution based on the language of the document and, when the language itself is not sufficient, the intent of the writers of the Constitution.

Rehnquist's judicial philosophy also involves a hierarchy of values according to Davis (1991), with federalism being the highest value, property rights composing a second level, and individual rights occupying the lowest level of his hierarchy. Rehnquist's view of federalism, the relationship between the national and the various state governments, is of critical importance in his decision making because it relates closely to his views on majority rule and original intent. For Rehnquist, the Constitution embodies a delegation of authority by the citizens to both the national and state governments, but it carefully limits the powers granted to the national government and reserves all other authority to the states or to the people. Furthermore, Rehnquist seems to take the position that laws developed by the smaller units of government, the states, will more faithfully reflect majority will. Thus, Rehnquist advocates a states' rights federalism, which he views as consistent not only with majoritarian principles but also with the language of the Constitution and the intent of its writers.

LEWIS POWELL

As a member of the Burger Court, Lewis Powell earned a reputation for moderation. Although his voting record was generally conservative, he authored important opinions favoring liberal outcomes in civil rights and liberties decisions that sought to balance competing interests and develop compromise positions between the contending views of the Supreme Court's divided liberals and conservatives. Many

Court observers consider Powell to have been the most influential member of the Burger Court because he was frequently the swing vote on a Court closely divided between liberals and conservatives. Powell served as a member of the Rehnquist Court for only one term before he retired in 1987 and was replaced by Justice Anthony Kennedy.

Background

Powell, who was born in 1907, was from a prominent family in Virginia. He was an honor student at Washington and Lee College in Virginia and graduated first in his class from Washington and Lee's law school in 1931 before earning an advanced law degree at Harvard. He spent his pre-Supreme Court career as a partner in a prestigious Richmond, Virginia, law firm. Powell gained prominence through his public service work. During the 1950s, as president of the Richmond Board of Education, he was credited with resisting the efforts of segregationist extremists to close the schools as a means of disobeying the Supreme Court's desegregation orders. Powell served as president of two of the most important national lawyers' associations during the 1960s, the American Bar Association and the American College of Trial Lawyers. He was also an officer in the National Legal Aid and Defender Association and a member of President Lyndon Johnson's National Crime Commission.

In 1971, Powell was appointed by President Richard Nixon to replace Justice Hugo Black, who had died at the age of eighty-five. Nixon was determined to appoint a southerner to the Supreme Court as a component of his strategy to win support from voters in the South. White southerners had traditionally voted for Democratic candidates, but they were becoming increasingly disillusioned with the liberalism of the Democratic Party on civil rights and other issues. Nixon made two attempts to appoint southerners in 1969 and 1970, but both nominees, Clement Haynesworth and G. Harrold Carswell, were rejected by the Senate. Nixon eventually filled the vacant seat with Harry Blackmun, a federal judge from Minnesota, in order to avoid the embarrassment of seeing three consecutive nominees go down to defeat. When Justice Black died in 1971, Nixon had not forgotten about his vow to appoint a southerner. Rather than risk another defeat with this nomination, Nixon appointed Powell, a highly respected, moderate Democrat, despite Nixon's misgivings about Powell's relatively advanced age, sixty-four, and the prospect that the nominee might only serve briefly on the high court. Powell initially declined to accept the appointment, but Nixon repeatedly asked him to reconsider his decision. When Powell reluctantly agreed to be the nominee, he received the American Bar Association's highest endorsement and had a brief, uneventful confirmation hearing before receiving the overwhelming support of the full Senate by a vote of 89 to 1. He took the oath of office on January 7, 1972.

Voting Record

As a justice on the Burger Court, Powell was viewed as a moderate with conservative leanings. Powell's decisions in famous cases gained him a reputation as the Burger Court's "swing voter" who shifted between the liberals and conservatives and thereby cast the decisive vote in many cases. However, Blasecki's (1989) systematic analysis of Powell's voting record demonstrated that he was generally a dependable conservative. During Warren Burger's tenure as Chief Justice, Powell's annual support for liberal civil rights and liberties decisions ranged from 28 percent to 46 percent with an average of 35 percent during his years on the Burger Court (Lamb and Halpern 1991, p. 33). The only justices to support liberal outcomes less frequently than Powell were Chief Justice Burger and Justices Rehnquist and O'Connor.

Powell was the critical swing vote during the first term of the Rehnquist Court. As can be observed in Table 3.1, he supported liberal civil rights and liberties outcomes in 39 percent of the cases. This placed him exactly in the middle of a deeply divided Court, with four justices (Rehnquist, Scalia, White, and O'Connor) supporting conservative outcomes more frequently than Powell and four justices (Marshall, Brennan, Blackmun, and Stevens) voting more liberally than Powell. Powell was not a member of either the liberal or conservative blocs during the 1986–87 term, as can be seen in Table 3.2. He was more likely to vote with the conservative members of the Court than the liberal members, however. His strongest levels of agreement were with White (81 percent) and O'Connor (79 percent).

Judicial Philosophy

Despite Powell's record of conservatism, he failed to fulfill President Nixon's hopes for a southerner who would be a consistent conservative. Powell tended to favor conservative outcomes in most cases, but, unlike his fellow conservatives Rehnquist and Scalia, he did not possess a judicial philosophy that consistently led him to favor such outcomes. Powell sought to balance carefully the competing interests in cases presented to the Court rather than to advance a particular ideology.

One hallmark of Powell's judicial philosophy was his concern for judicial restraint. He sought to permit state and local government officials to retain decision-making authority without undue interference by the judiciary. Powell's emphasis on judicial restraint was drawn from the example of Justice John Harlan, the Warren Court era justice who was perhaps the high court's most famous advocate of restraint. According to Jacob Landynski (1991, p. 278), "Powell seems to have consciously attempted to emulate Harlan; no other justice was cited so frequently in [Powell's] opinions as Harlan, and none more reverently."

Powell also expressed concern about stability in law and the need to respect stare decisis. At the same time, however, he did not bow reflexively to either principle. He was willing to invalidate governmental policies on behalf of individuals' rights and to alter precedents when he believed that a fundamental right was at issue or when his balancing of interests led him to favor individuals.

JOHN PAUL STEVENS

In his first decade as a Supreme Court justice from 1975 to 1985, John Paul Stevens was characterized primarily as an independent, centrist justice, and even as a loner on the Court. He was unlikely to be closely aligned with either the liberal or conservative wings of the Court, and thus he was difficult to categorize. This seems to have changed, however, at least with respect to civil rights and liberties issues. In the first few terms of the Rehnquist Court, Stevens was not aligned with any group, but he was a member of the liberal bloc during the 1989–90 through the 1992–93 terms. With the retirements of Justices Brennan, Marshall, and Blackmun, however, Stevens is the only remaining member of this liberal bloc.

Background

Stevens was born in Chicago, Illinois, on April 20, 1920. Stevens's mother was an English teacher and his father was a wealthy Chicago businessman. He majored in English at the University of Chicago, with plans to become an English teacher. He was an outstanding student, graduating with Phi Beta Kappa honors in 1941.

During World War II, Stevens joined the Navy, serving as a naval officer from 1942–45. Upon returning home, he enrolled in the law school at Northwestern University, where he was coeditor of the law review. After graduating first in his class in 1947, Stevens went to Washington to clerk for Supreme Court Justice Wiley Rutledge from 1947–48. He returned to Chicago in 1948 and practiced law with a firm that specialized in antitrust and commercial law litigation. He remained with this firm until 1951, when he was called back to Washington to serve as an associate counsel to the House Judiciary Committee's Subcommittee on the Study of Monopoly Power.

Stevens returned to private practice in Chicago a year later, forming his own law firm. In addition to his work with the law firm, Stevens taught antitrust law at Northwestern Law School from 1952–54 and at the University of Chicago from 1955–56. He continued this work until 1970 when President Nixon appointed him to the Seventh Circuit Court of Appeals.

When William O. Douglas retired from the Court in 1975, President Ford received his only opportunity to appoint a Supreme Court justice. Edward Levi, Ford's attorney general, had a major role in Stevens's nomination. Ford had given Levi the primary responsibility of evaluating the qualifications of the leading candidates for the seat. Levi's choices came down to Stevens and Judge Arlin Adams, both of whose judicial records impressed him greatly. O'Brien (1991) reports that Levi's professional and personal connections with Stevens in the Chicago Bar Association and at the University of Chicago Law School eventually led him to recommend Stevens for the appointment. Ford accepted Levi's recommendation, nominating Stevens to fill Douglas's seat on November 28, 1975. The Senate Judiciary Committee conducted three days of confirmation hearings, with political opposition to Stevens's appointment coming only from two women's organizations that were concerned about his stance on women's rights. On December 11, the Judiciary Committee unanimously recommended approval of the nomination, and the full Senate confirmed Stevens on December 17 by a vote of 98–0.

Voting Record

Stevens generally provided a moderate level of support for civil rights and liberties during the Burger Court period, but that support increased during the Rehnquist Court era. Canon's (1991) data show that in the period from 1975–85, Stevens voted in favor of civil rights and liberties in 59 percent of the cases that he heard. As Table 3.1 indicates, by the 1990–91 term his support for civil rights and liberties had increased significantly, as he voted for a liberal outcome 81 percent of the time. His overall liberalism score of 72 percent for the first nine terms of the Rehnquist Court made him the third most liberal justice, exceeded only by Brennan and Marshall.

As shown in Tables 3.2 to 3.10, Stevens was not a member of a voting bloc during the 1986, 1987, and 1988 terms of the Rehnquist Court, but he has been aligned in a liberal voting bloc in four of the last six terms. In the 1989–90 term, Stevens joined Brennan and Marshall to form a three-person liberal bloc. After Brennan's retirement, Marshall, Blackmun, and Stevens formed a three-person bloc in the 1990–91 term. By the 1991–92 term, the liberal bloc consisted of only Stevens and Blackmun, who agreed in 89 percent of the civil rights and liberties cases. This Stevens-Blackmun bloc continued in the 1992–93 term; but despite a high agreement rate (84 percent) in the 1993–94 term, the two did not constitute a cohesive voting bloc. Stevens voted 86 percent liberally during the 1994–95 term; this was by far the most liberal extreme on the Court, and thus no other justice joined Stevens in a voting bloc.

Judicial Philosophy

Because Stevens has not been as ideologically predictable as some of his colleagues, many Court observers have found it difficult to discern his judicial philosophy. However, Sickels (1988) disputes this claim by asserting that Stevens's approach to the law has been clear and consistent since his appointment to the federal bench.

After analyzing Stevens's court of appeals and Supreme Court opinions, Sickels writes that Stevens's approach to the law is pragmatic and is characterized by several key elements. First, Stevens believes that it is critical for judges to have clear rules and principles that can be applied to individual disputes. Second, judges must be able to determine the relevant facts in individual cases, and they must carefully consider those facts in reaching decisions. Third, judges must perform the delicate task of balancing the evidence and arguments of the opposing sides to come to a decision. This requires that the rules and facts be considered together; "a decision deficient in principle is ad hoc and arbitrary; a decision deficient in fact is unrealistic and mechanical—a 'mere formula' " (Sickels 1988, p. 31). Fourth, judges must be concerned about the consequences of their decision—on the parties to the case, the courts, other parts of government, and the public. Finally, judges must remember that they do not have the expertise or the time to make sound decisions in all matters. Instead, there are other policymakers whose responsibilities, skills, and information qualify them to make certain kinds of decisions. This latter element, judicial deference to the other branches of government, is referred to as "pluralism" by Sickels.

SANDRA DAY O'CONNOR

When Sandra Day O'Connor became the first woman to serve on the Supreme Court, some women's rights activists were hopeful that she would be very supportive of gender equality. Although O'Connor has refused to overrule *Roe v. Wade* (1973) and has generally voted liberally in gender equality cases, she has not been a strong champion of women's rights during her tenure on the Court. Moreover, in civil rights and liberties issues in general, O'Connor has fulfilled the expectations of the Reagan administration, which appointed her. She has had a conservative voting record in every term of the Rehnquist Court except 1991–92. O'Connor is not easy to classify along liberal/conservative lines, however. After joining the conservative bloc in the first five terms of the Rehnquist Court from 1986 through 1990, O'Connor has been a member of the conservative bloc in only one term since 1990. She therefore occupies an especially key position on the Court, and her vote is frequently critical in 5–4 decisions.

Background

O'Connor, the eldest child of Harry and Ada May Day, was born in El Paso, Texas, on March 26, 1930. She spent summers on her family's ranch in Arizona, but she attended school in El Paso where she lived with her grandparents. After graduation from high school, O'Connor entered Stanford University at the age of sixteen, where she received a bachelor's degree in economics in 1950. Two years later, she received her law degree from Stanford; while there, she was inducted into the Order of the Coif, a national honorary society for outstanding law students.

O'Connor's early career reflected the pervasive sexism that existed in American society. Despite building an impressive record in college and law school, graduating with high honors from both, the only positions offered to her by law firms were those as legal secretary. Her application for employment was rejected by the law firm of Ronald Reagan's first attorney general, William French Smith, who would later be instrumental in her appointment to the Supreme Court.

Unsuccessful in obtaining employment as an attorney in the private sector, O'Connor began her career as a deputy county attorney in San Mateo, California, a post she held for two years. When her husband's position as a lawyer with the Army took them to Germany, she worked for three years as a civilian lawyer for the Quartermaster Corps in Frankfurt.

When they returned to the United States, the O'Connors established residency in Arizona. O'Connor did not immediately resume her legal career on a full-time basis, focusing instead on being a homemaker and mother. She did, however, become active in Republican politics, and she spent several years in a small private practice. In 1965, she became assistant attorney general for the State of Arizona, and she was appointed to the state senate in 1969. In 1970, she was elected to the senate, and she later became the first woman in the country to be chosen as a legislative majority leader. In 1974, she returned to the legal arena, winning a seat on her county superior court, where she served for five years before being appointed to the Arizona Court of Appeals in 1979.

When campaigning for the presidency in 1980, Ronald Reagan pledged that if presented the opportunity, he would appoint a woman to the Supreme Court. Such an opportunity came in 1981, when Potter Stewart retired after serving twenty-three years on the Court. O'Connor was nominated to fill this seat, following a screening process which determined that she had sufficient judicial experience and that her political and judicial philosophies seemed compatible with those of the president. In addition, her nomination was aided by recommendations and endorsements from Barry Goldwater, Warren Burger, and her former law school classmate, William Rehnquist. President Reagan announced the nomination on July 7, 1981, and he formally sent it to the Senate a month later on August 19. The nomination was praised by many moderates and some liberals, but it was criticized by conservatives who believed she was not conservative enough. Anti-abortion groups, in particular, opposed her nomination because they feared she might support *Roe.* After three days of hearings by the Senate Judiciary Committee on September 9, 10, and 11, O'Connor was confirmed on September 21 by a 99-0 vote.

Voting Record

O'Connor's record in civil rights and liberties cases during the Rehnquist era has been generally conservative, although she is not as far to the right as some of her colleagues. In the first nine terms of the Rehnquist Court from 1986 to 1994, she took a liberal position in only 38 percent of the cases as seen in Table 3.1. O'Connor's voting record has been characterized by substantial variation among terms. For example, in the 1989 term O'Connor voted for a liberal outcome in 20 percent of the cases, but in the 1991 term she voted liberally in 58 percent of the decisions.

As can be seen in Tables 3.2 through 3.10, she was aligned with a conservative voting bloc during the 1986 through the 1990 terms, but in three of the four most recent terms she has not been aligned with the Court's most conservative members.

In the 1986–87 term, the conservative bloc included O'Connor, White, Scalia, and Rehnquist; and, in the next term, the conservative bloc consisted of only O'Connor and Scalia. In the 1988–89 and 1989–90 terms, O'Connor was a member of a five-person bloc including Kennedy, Scalia, Rehnquist, and White. The size of this bloc decreased to four members in the 1990–91 term—O'Connor, Souter, Rehnquist, and Kennedy. Since the 1991 term, however, O'Connor has been a member of a conservative bloc only once, joining Thomas, Rehnquist, and Scalia in the 1993 term. Thus, O'Connor has been a frequent but not a consistent member of the conservative voting blocs on the Rehnquist Court.

Judicial Philosophy

Witt (1986) and Cook (1991) assert that two major components of O'Connor's judicial philosophy are federalism and judicial restraint. These two principles, developed before her arrival on the Court, go hand in hand in her analytical framework.

According to Cook, O'Connor's view of federalism emphasizes state sovereignty. She believes that the New Deal and its aftermath have vested too much power in the national government, and that more power and responsibility should be shifted to state and local governments. In this vein, she favors a new reading of the Tenth Amendment that would allow for greater protection of state sovereignty. In addition, she thinks that federal courts must defer to the decisions made by the legislative and executive branches, especially to those officials who have been elected by the people. Furthermore, federal courts should defer to the judgments of state judges because they are as competent as federal judges in making appropriate decisions. Cook notes that O'Connor's commitments to state sovereignty and judicial restraint lead her to frame many civil rights and liberties issues in terms of these principles, typically resulting in conservative decisions.

ANTONIN SCALIA

When Ronald Reagan appointed Antonin Scalia to the Supreme Court in 1986, significant evidence existed that he shared the administration's view that the liberal decisions of the Warren Court had helped to create many societal problems. Scalia was expected to be an important actor in altering the liberalism and judicial activism of the Court. For the most part, he has fulfilled the expectations of the administration that appointed him. He is an important member of the conservative wing of the Rehnquist Court, and has successfully led efforts to alter some of the liberal precedents of the Warren era.

Background

Scalia, the son of a Sicilian immigrant and a first generation Italian American, was born in Trenton, New Jersey, on March 11, 1936. He attended St. Francis Xavier High School, a Jesuit school in lower Manhattan, where he excelled as a student. After graduating first in his class, Scalia attended Georgetown University, where in 1957 he graduated as valedictorian. He then enrolled in Harvard Law School, became note editor of the *Harvard Law Review*, and graduated magna cum laude in the spring of 1960.

After graduating from Harvard, Scalia's first job was at the corporate law firm of Jones, Day, Cockley, and Reavis, in Cleveland, Ohio, where he spent the years from 1961 to 1967 as an associate. He then moved to academia where he combined teaching and government service. First, he accepted a teaching post at the University of Virginia Law School, where from 1967 to 1974 he taught contracts, commercial law, and comparative law. In 1971, he took a leave of absence from the university to become general counsel of the Office of Telecommunications Policy in the Executive Office of the President. After holding this post until 1972, Scalia served from 1972 to 1974 as Chairman of the Administrative Conference of the United States, an advisory group that deals with matters of administrative law and procedure. His service in these capacities resulted in his selection by President Nixon in 1974 as assistant attorney general in charge of the Justice Department's Office of Legal Counsel. In 1977, Scalia returned to academia. Before accepting a position on the faculty at the University of Chicago Law School, he spent one year as a visiting scholar at the American Enterprise Institute (AEI), a Washington-based conservative think tank. In addition to teaching at the University of Chicago, he was a visiting professor of law at Georgetown University and Stanford University, in 1977 and 1980–81, respectively.

By the early 1980s, Scalia's conservative views had made him a favorite of the Reagan administration. Thus, subsequently in 1982 President Reagan appointed him to fill a vacancy on the U.S. Court of Appeals for the District of Columbia Circuit. Scalia's performance on the D.C. court indicated that he shared the Reagan administration's judicial philosophies, and therefore his nomination to fill the vacancy created by Chief Justice Burger's retirement and Rehnquist's subsequent elevation to that seat was not surprising. The nomination was formally announced on June 17, 1986, and the Senate held two days of hearings on August 5 and 6. Opposition came from several civil rights and feminist organizations, for example, the National Organization for Women and the Leadership Conference on Civil Rights. Opposition to Scalia was muted, however, because liberal Senators and interest groups focused most of their attention on the simultaneous appointment of Rehnquist to the position of chief justice. Rehnquist's nomination was confirmed, but it was by the closest margin of any chief justice in American history. Because of the controversy-ridden hearings on the Rehnquist nomination, it was generally accepted that unless major damaging revelations emerged, Scalia's nomination would sail through the Judiciary Committee and the full Senate. This is precisely what happened, as he was recommended for confirmation by an 18–0 vote of the Committee, and he was confirmed by the full Senate on September 17, 1986, by a 98–0 vote.

Voting Record

Scalia's voting record has been decidedly conservative just as most Court observers expected. He is the third most conservative justice on the Rehnquist Court in civil rights and liberties issues, having taken a liberal position in only 31 percent of those cases from the 1986 to the 1994 terms as shown in Table 3.1.

Not surprisingly, then, Scalia was aligned with a conservative voting bloc in all nine of the terms from 1986 through 1994 as can be seen in Tables 3.2 through 3.10. What is somewhat surprising is the fluid nature of the conservative bloc throughout the years of the Rehnquist Court and the failure of a majority bloc of conservative justices to emerge. In the 1986–87 term, Scalia joined White, Rehnquist, and O'Connor to form a four-person bloc, but that bloc diminished to only Scalia and O'Connor in the 1987–88 term. In the 1988 and 1989 terms, a five-person bloc emerged, which included Scalia, Kennedy, Rehnquist, White, and O'Connor. With

Souter replacing Brennan in 1990 and Thomas succeeding Marshall in 1991, a solid conservative bloc seemed assured. This did not occur, however. As can be seen in Tables 3.6 through 3.10, only Scalia, Rehnquist, and Thomas have been consistent members of a conservative voting bloc.

Judicial Philosophy

According to Brisbin (1990), Scalia's judicial philosophy is based on several standards that judges must follow in interpreting the Constitution and statutes. He advocates limited judicial power, stressing that the courts must exercise their powers sparingly to avoid both intruding upon the other branches of government and violating separation of powers. Scalia also believes that decisions about public policy are best left to the discretion of elected officials in the legislative and executive branches because they must make political judgments for which the judiciary is not suited. Thus, the will of the majority must be carried out by leaders who are elected by the people and who can be held accountable for their decisions. Finally, Scalia's view of federalism emphasizes a preference for state powers and prerogatives, and the need for national authorities to respect the decisions of state and local officials.

ANTHONY M. KENNEDY

Anthony M. Kennedy is a pivotal figure on the United States Supreme Court, but it is not yet clear whether he will be a member of a conservative majority that radically alters American constitutional law or a member of a more moderate group of justices that prevents a sharp turn to the right. Kennedy was the third person nominated by President Ronald Reagan to replace Justice Lewis F. Powell, who resigned in 1987. Powell was widely viewed as the swing vote on a Court closely divided between four liberals and four conservatives, and thus Powell's replacement was viewed as critical to the future direction of the Court. Reagan was unsuccessful in his initial bids to appoint two controversial conservatives, Robert Bork and Douglas Ginsburg, but Kennedy was less controversial and gained unanimous Senate approval. In his initial terms on the Court, it appeared that Kennedy was indeed going to provide the critical fifth vote to bring about a conservative counterrevolution in civil rights and liberties, but Kennedy has not been a steady and predictable conservative voice on the Court in the nineties. Kennedy, like O'Connor, has been moderately conservative, and thus he has occupied a critically important pivotal position on the Court.

Background

Kennedy's background prior to his nomination to the United States Supreme Court was one of impressive accomplishments and little controversy. He was born in 1936 in Sacramento, California. He attended Stanford University from 1954–57, studied at the London School of Economics in 1957–58, and returned to Stanford to graduate in 1958 with Phi Beta Kappa honors. He then attended Harvard Law School, earning his LL.B. in 1961. Kennedy returned to California to begin his legal career, joining a San Francisco law firm for two years from 1961–63 and then returning to Sacramento to practice law. In 1975 President Gerald Ford appointed Kennedy to the United States Court of Appeals for the Ninth Circuit in Sacramento, a position he held until his appointment to the Supreme Court in 1988. Kennedy was also a professor of constitutional law at McGeorge School of Law, University of the Pacific, from 1965 to 1988.

Kennedy was nominated to the Supreme Court by President Reagan during one of the most acrimonious confirmation processes in American history. Reagan's first choice to replace Powell was Robert Bork, a judge on the Court of Appeals for the District of Columbia who generated intense opposition from liberal groups throughout the country because of his well-developed conservative judicial philosophy and his outspoken and widely publicized opposition to many liberal Supreme Court precedents, including the abortion decision of *Roe v. Wade* (1973). Following a fierce Senate confirmation hearing, Bork's nomination was defeated 58–42, the largest margin of defeat in history for a Supreme Court candidate. Reagan then nominated another conservative member of the D.C. Circuit Court, Douglas Ginsburg, but this nomination was also unsuccessful. Opposition to Ginsburg arose immediately based not only on his conservative views but also on questions of ethical propriety involving his years serving with the Justice Department and his responses to a questionnaire in 1986 regarding his prior judicial experience. When Ginsburg admitted to using marijuana during the 1960s and 1970s, his fate was sealed, and the president withdrew his nomination.

The intense controversy between the White House and the Senate over the Bork and Ginsberg nominations gave way to a mood of compromise and accommodation with Reagan's nomination of Kennedy to fill Powell's seat. Kennedy's record on the Ninth Circuit suggested to the Reagan Administration that he could become the critical fifth vote needed to create a solid conservative majority, and, equally important, he appeared to be a candidate that the Senate would find acceptable. Kennedy did not have a record of extensive written criticism of the Court like Bork, nor did he have political problems like Ginsburg. Kennedy was given the American Bar Association's highest recommendation, and he was confirmed on February 3, 1988, by a unanimous 97–0 vote after only three days of hearings.

Voting Record

Kennedy's voting record in civil rights and liberties cases is similar in many ways to O'Connor's record. For example, Kennedy has voted liberally in 37 percent of the civil rights and liberties cases, which is nearly identical to O'Connor's 38 percent voting pattern. Kennedy can therefore be classified as a conservative, but, like O'Connor, he is more moderate than the Court's three leading conservatives—Rehnquist, Thomas, and Scalia.

Kennedy has been a frequent but not a consistent member of the Rehnquist Court's conservative bloc. In his first two full terms on the Court, 1988 and 1989, Kennedy joined with Rehnquist, Scalia, White, and O'Connor to provide a majority conservative bloc that sharply shifted the Court in a conservative direction. It appeared that this coalition would grow even larger with Souter replacing Brennan in the 1990 term and Thomas replacing Marshall in the 1991 term, but this did not happen. Part of the explanation for this surprising development is to be found in Kennedy's increased moderation in the nineties. Kennedy remains closer to his conservative colleagues than to his more liberal colleagues, however, and in the 1994 term Kennedy was part of a four-person conservative bloc along with Rehnquist, Thomas, and Scalia. Thus, Kennedy, like O'Connor, plays a pivotal role on the Rehnquist Court, and his votes and opinions frequently determine the direction the Court will take.

Judicial Philosophy

Kennedy does not appear to have a consistent judicial philosophy to guide his decision making. Kennedy emphasized in his Senate confirmation hearings that he did not adhere to any particular theory of constitutional interpretation: "It's somewhat difficult for me to offer myself as someone with a complete cosmology of the Constitution. I do not have an overarching theory, a unitary theory of interpretation. I am searching for the correct balance in constitutional interpretation" (Reagan . . . 1988, p. 115).

Although Kennedy does not appear to have a comprehensive judicial philosophy at this point in his career, two principles of constitutional interpretation seem to be especially important for him: judicial self-restraint and stare decisis. Based on his record on the Ninth Circuit as well as his initial terms on the Supreme Court, Kennedy adheres to a role of judicial self-restraint characterized by a preference to decide issues on statutory rather than constitutional grounds, a literal reading of both statutory and constitutional language, and a strong deference to the majoritarian branches of government (Melone 1990). Kennedy also seems strongly committed to the principle of stare decisis. He emphasized the importance of precedent in his Senate confirmation hearings: "Stare decisis ensures impartiality. And it's a very, very important part of the system. . . . It seems to me that when judges have announced that a particular rule is found in the Constitution, that's entitled to very great weight" (Reagan . . ." 1988, p. 116).

DAVID SOUTER

President George Bush's selection in 1990 of David Souter to replace William Brennan surprised many observers because Souter was virtually unknown in legal circles outside of his native state of New Hampshire. Little was known about Souter's views and judicial philosophy, a factor which probably contributed significantly to his nomination; Bush did not want another confrontation with the Democratic Senate such as occurred when Bork was nominated. During his first term on the Rehnquist Court, Souter had a significant impact on case outcomes because he so frequently cast the decisive vote in 5–4 decisions when the Court was deeply divided. Although he aligned with the conservative bloc in his first term, Souter has become significantly more liberal in subsequent terms, especially in First Amendment cases. Some Court observers see Souter as a key member of an emerging moderate group of justices that may control future decisions of the Court, while other Court watchers see Souter's role as becoming an articulate liberal dissenter on a conservative Court.

Background

Souter was born in Melrose, Massachusetts, in 1939 and his family moved to Weare, New Hampshire, when he was eleven. His father was an assistant bank manager and his mother worked in a giftshop. He was an outstanding student in the Concord, New Hampshire, public schools and later graduated with honors from Harvard College in 1961. After spending two years at Oxford University as a Rhodes Scholar, he returned to Harvard to earn his law degree in 1966. He practiced law briefly with a law firm in Concord before becoming an assistant attorney general for New Hampshire under Warren Rudman, the man who as a U.S. Senator would later urge President Bush to name Souter to the Supreme Court. After Rudman resigned as attorney general in order to run for Congress, Souter was named to replace Rudman as the state's chief legal officer. As attorney general, Souter was involved in controversial cases concerning the separation of church and state. He defended the governor's decision to honor the Christian remembrance of Good Friday by lowering the flags at state office buildings. Souter also undertook prosecution of residents who, for religious reasons, covered the state's motto ("Live Free or Die") on their license plates.

Souter was subsequently appointed to be a state judge in 1978, first on the New Hampshire Superior Court for five years and then on the state's Supreme Court for seven years. President Bush then appointed Souter to serve as a judge on the U.S. Court of Appeals for the First Circuit in Boston during April of 1990. Before Souter could settle into his new position, however, Justice William Brennan announced his retirement from the Supreme Court, and Bush selected Souter to replace the liberal justice.

Unlike Bork, an outspoken conservative who had written many articles outlining his views, Souter had never written any articles, had made few public speeches, and had a reputation as a thoughtful, dependable Republican who was not associated with right-wing groups. Although he was unknown to most people in the country, the quiet, unassuming, and scholarly bachelor was respected by both liberals and conservatives in New Hampshire. Because the Supreme Court appeared to be one vote away from overturning important precedents concerning abortion, affirmative action, and other civil liberties issues, Bush knew that interest groups and liberal senators would be prepared to fight against any nominees who had expressed opposition to these issues. Souter, however, did not have any recorded stance on these issues, and his service as a judge in the courts of a small state had never forced him to address the controversial issues facing the nation's highest court.

Souter's performance during the confirmation hearings before the Senate Judiciary Committee defused any potential organized opposition to his nomination. He impressed the senators with his ability to discuss a wide range of issues and Supreme Court cases without referring to any notes. Souter reassured liberal senators by praising Justice Brennan as the nation's most outstanding defender of the Bill of Rights and by endorsing Warren Court decisions concerning criminal defendants' rights. His own precise views remained a mystery, however, because he spoke in general terms and declined to give specific opinions on abortion and other issues that faced the Supreme Court. With only a handful of liberal senators opposed to his nomination, the full Senate confirmed Souter by a vote of 90 to 9.

Voting Record

As shown in Table 3.1, Souter's overall voting record in civil rights and liberties cases is 54 percent liberal. This suggests that Souter is a judicial moderate. A closer look at his term-by-term voting records leads to a somewhat different conclusion, however, because Souter has become increasingly liberal in recent terms. In his initial term in 1990, Souter voted liberally in only 35 percent of the civil rights/liberties cases, but he has become steadily more liberal each term, reaching a high point of 65 percent liberal voting in the 1994 term. Souter was the second most liberal justice on the Court in the 1994 term, ranking behind only Justice Stevens.

Souter is not closely associated with any distinctive voting bloc. In his initial term in 1990, he was a member of a four-person conservative bloc that included Rehnquist, Kennedy, and O'Connor, but he has not been a member of the conservative bloc since 1990. Souter has had high levels of interagreement with the Court's two most recent appointees, Ginsburg and Breyer, forming a two-person voting bloc with Ginsburg in the 1993 term and with Breyer in the 1994 term.

Souter has thus proven to be a surprise to Court analysts. Appointed by President Bush to replace Justice Brennan, the Court's leading liberal, Souter seemed likely to solidify the Court's conservative majority. Instead, Souter has become increasingly liberal in his voting, and his shift to the left has made it more difficult for the conservative justices of the Rehnquist Court to gain victories and to alter constitutional law.

Judicial Philosophy

Because Souter has had a relatively brief tenure on the Court, it is difficult to discuss with confidence an identifiable judicial philosophy. Discussion is all the more difficult because Souter came to the Supreme Court without any established record on civil rights and liberties issues. In his appearance before the Senate Judiciary Committee, Souter defined himself as a moderate, nondogmatic nominee. Souter appeared to differentiate himself from ideological conservatives because, in response to senators' questions, he could not think of any Supreme Court decisions that went too far in establishing constitutional rights. He explicitly rejected the original intent theory of constitutional interpretation and endorsed the judiciary's responsibility for developing practical decrees to implement constitutional rights. By declaring that he recognized privacy as a fundamental constitutional right, Souter indicated that he supported a flexible interpretation of the Constitution's meaning. His initial performance as a justice provided indications that he did not adhere to a specific judicial philosophy, but that he adopted a pragmatic approach to judicial decision making.

CLARENCE THOMAS

Clarence Thomas joined the Rehnquist Court amid a storm of controversy in 1991. As President George Bush's conservative appointee to replace the Court's most liberal justice, Thurgood Marshall, many observers predicted that the outspoken Thomas would provide the Court's conservative majority with the necessary votes to reverse decisions affecting abortion rights, affirmative action, and other civil liberties issues. As the second African American justice in the history of the Supreme Court, Thomas brought to the Court very different views than those possessed by the first African American, his immediate predecessor Justice Marshall. In his first four terms, Thomas has joined consistently with Chief Justice Rehnquist and Justice Scalia, the Court's most conservative justices. However, his votes did not create an unstoppable conservative majority, because other justices became less inclined to join the Court's most conservative justices during Thomas's initial terms on the Court.

Background

Clarence Thomas grew up in a time and place in American society in which African Americans suffered from blatant racial discrimination and severe segregation.

He was born in Pin Point, Georgia, in 1948. His family was very poor, living in a rundown wooden house that had dirt floors and lacked electricity and plumbing. His father abandoned the family when Thomas was a small child. When his mother struggled to make ends meet while cooking and cleaning for white families in Savannah, Georgia, Thomas went to live with his grandfather, Myers Anderson, the man he later credited with having the greatest influence over his life.

Anderson lived in a more comfortable six-room house with indoor plumbing. He operated his own fuel oil delivery business, but his economic opportunities were limited by the widespread discrimination against African Americans. Anderson was a stern disciplinarian who sent Thomas to strict parochial schools and made him work long hours after school in the delivery business. Later, when his grandfather sent him to a previously all-white, Catholic boarding school for high school, Thomas had to face slights and insults from many classmates who exhibited prejudice against African Americans (Phelps and Winternitz, 1992). Thomas's upbringing instilled him with strong values concerning discipline and hard work. Although other people who experienced harsh racial discrimination during this era advocated government action to remedy inequality, Thomas's values provided a foundation for a conservative philosophy of individual initiative and self-help as the means to success in American society.

After briefly attending a Missouri seminary to train to become a priest, Thomas enrolled for undergraduate studies at Holy Cross College in Massachusetts and subsequently graduated from Yale Law School in 1974. Thomas's first job was in the office of Missouri's Republican attorney general, John Danforth. When Danforth was elected to the U.S. Senate, Thomas worked briefly for Monsanto Chemical Company in St. Louis before joining Danforth's staff in Washington, D.C. During the 1980s, Thomas's Republican connections helped him to become one of the highest ranking African American officials in the Reagan administration, first as assistant secretary for civil rights in the U.S. Department of Education and later as chairman of the U.S. Equal Employment Opportunity Commission (EEOC). At the EEOC, Thomas became a controversial figure. Civil rights groups and liberal members of Congress accused him of reducing enforcement of antidiscrimination laws, and he made many speeches on behalf of the Reagan administration in which he criticized abortion, affirmative action, welfare programs, and other liberal policies.

When President Bush nominated Thomas to be a judge on the U.S. Court of Appeals for the District of Columbia Circuit in 1990, many newspapers speculated that Thomas's credentials were being enhanced in preparation for having a conservative African American judge available to replace the ailing Justice Marshall if the Court's only African American justice should decide to retire. These predictions proved accurate the following year when President Bush nominated the youthful, forty-three-year-old Thomas to replace the retiring Justice Marshall.

During his confirmation hearings before the Senate Judiciary Committee, suspicions were raised about Thomas's truthfulness when he claimed that the strident conservative viewpoints expressed in his speeches did not represent the views he would bring to the Supreme Court as a justice. In attempting to portray himself as an open-minded moderate, Thomas went so far as to claim that he had never discussed the controversial abortion precedent, *Roe v. Wade*, with anyone despite the fact that it had been a burning political issue for eighteen years and Thomas had made a speech praising an article that was critical of the decision.

Despite the questions about his testimony, Thomas appeared headed for confirmation until it was revealed that one of his former assistants felt that he had sexually harassed her when he was at the Department of Education and the EEOC. The entire nation became captivated and polarized by the nationally televised hearings in which his accuser, Professor Anita Hill of the University of Oklahoma College of Law, and other witnesses presented testimony on the sexual harassment allegations. Thomas was eventually confirmed for a seat on the Supreme Court by a narrow 52 to 48 vote in the Senate, but the sexual harassment controversy helped to mobilize angry women voters and thereby contribute to the successful 1992 election campaigns of an unprecedented number of female candidates for Congress and state legislatures (Smith 1993).

Voting Record

During his first four terms, Thomas has established himself as one of the Rehnquist Court's most conservative justices on civil rights and liberties issues. As indicated by Thomas's average level of support for civil liberties (25 percent) in Table 3.1, he was second only to Chief Justice Rehnquist in his conservatism. Thomas joined with Rehnquist and Scalia to form the primary conservative voting bloc during the 1991 and 1992 terms. Their average interagreement rates of 86 and 88 percent shown in Tables 3.7 and 3.8, respectively, indicate that Thomas's views on civil liberties comported with those of the Rehnquist Court's most consistent conservatives.

Thomas's immediate and strong support for the conservative voting bloc coincided with the weakening of the bloc during the 1991 and 1992 terms due to reduced support from previous bloc members Kennedy, O'Connor, and Souter. Observers have speculated that Thomas's strong conservatism and high levels of agreement with Chief Justice Rehnquist and Justice Scalia led the less doctrinaire conservatives to reconsider whether they wanted to overturn long-standing precedents concerning issues such as abortion and school prayer (Smith 1993). In the 1993 term, however, the Rehnquist-Thomas-Scalia bloc regained the support of O'Connor, and in the 1994 term Kennedy joined the Rehnquist-Thomas-Scalia bloc. Thus, Thomas's replacement of Marshall has not yet had a dramatic impact in shifting the Court in a radically more conservative direction.

Judicial Philosophy

Thomas's first-term performance was consistent with his preappointment behavior in delivering strident speeches on behalf of the Reagan and Bush administrations. Thomas brought to the Court values concerning individual initiative and personal responsibility that made him critical of judicial decisions designed to protect politically weak minorities, such as minority ethnic groups and criminal defendants. Thomas consistently supported conservative outcomes in civil liberties cases and used interpretive techniques tailored to enhance his policy preferences. An analysis of Thomas's first-term opinions found that "[h]e seems to be securely anchored in the 'Original Intent' school of constitutional adjudication . . . [because of] his habit of searching the historical record or engaging in close textual analysis in order to find the 'true' meaning of a statute or a provision of the Constitution" (Epperson 1992, p. 28). Like Scalia and Rehnquist, Thomas apparently views a textual approach to interpretation as a means to limit judicial interference in decisions made by other branches of government. Prior to his appointment to the bench, Thomas was an outspoken critic of judicial decisions on affirmative action and other issues that conservatives view as the illegitimate products of liberal judicial activism by the Warren and Burger Courts. Based upon his initial terms on the Court, Thomas seems to have maintained these views.

RUTH BADER GINSBURG

When Byron White announced that he would retire at the end of the 1992–93 term, widespread speculation arose as to whom President Clinton would appoint to fill White's seat. This would be the first appointment made by a Democratic president since Lyndon Johnson's nomination of Thurgood Marshall, the first African American justice, in 1967. After three months of deliberation, Clinton nominated Ruth Bader Ginsburg, a sixty-year-old federal appeals court judge from the District of Columbia circuit. Clinton characterized her as the Thurgood Marshall of women's rights, but he also argued that she would bring a moderate approach to her role as a Supreme Court justice. In her initial two terms on the Court, Ginsburg has fulfilled this moderate expectation, but she has been substantially more liberal than her predecessor, Justice White.

Background

Joan Ruth Bader was born March 15, 1933, in Brooklyn, the second daughter of Nathan and Celia Bader. She was educated in the public schools of Brooklyn, and after graduating sixth in her high school class, she attended Cornell University where she graduated with Phi Beta Kappa honors in 1954. After graduation, she married Martin Ginsburg, a classmate at Cornell who had begun studies at Harvard Law School while Ruth Bader finished her senior year. When Martin Ginsburg received his draft notice, they moved to Oklahoma, where he was stationed for two years. While her score on the civil service exam made her eligible for a GS-5 position in the Social Security Office, when she informed the personnel office of her pregnancy she was denied the GS-5 position and took a GS-2 typist position as her only option.

In 1956 the Ginsburgs returned to Harvard and both enrolled in law school there. Ruth Ginsburg was one of only nine women in her law school class, and, despite being subject to blatant discrimination, she made top grades and earned a place on Law Review.

When her husband graduated and took a job with a New York law firm, she left Harvard and enrolled at Columbia University, where once again she made Law Review. Despite her impressive record, upon graduation in 1959 she received no job offers from the top Manhattan law firms, and she was turned down for a clerkship with Supreme Court Justice Felix Frankfurter in 1960, reportedly because he was not yet ready to hire a woman. After clerking for U.S. District Judge Edmund Palmieri from 1959 until 1961, Ginsburg worked on a special legal project in Sweden until 1963. She then became the second woman on the law faculty at Rutgers University, where she taught constitutional law and the conflict of laws until 1972.

During her years at Rutgers, Ginsburg's awareness of gender discrimination was heightened. On a personal level, mindful of her negative employment experience in Oklahoma, she hid her second pregnancy (by wearing baggy clothes) for fear that it might prevent her from receiving tenure. On a broader level, Ginsburg began working with the state ACLU on lawsuits involving gender discrimination. She then joined the national ACLU in preparing arguments for *Reed v. Reed* (1971), a case that resulted in the Court for the first time declaring a state law unconstitutional because of gender discrimination. After *Reed*, the ACLU established the Women's Rights Project to take on more gender discrimination litigation, with Ginsburg as its first director. By this time, she had become a member of the law faculty at Columbia University.

During her work with the Women's Rights Project, Ginsburg participated in five gender discrimination cases before the United States Supreme Court, winning four of them. She was not successful in convincing the Court to examine gender-based classifications under "strict scrutiny," but she did persuade a majority to adopt an intermediate level of scrutiny, the "important government objective test," for these cases. Her work led legal scholars and commentators to refer to her as the "Thurgood Marshall of gender-discrimination law" (Kaplan and Cohn 1993, p. 29).

In 1980, President Jimmy Carter appointed her to the United States Court of Appeals for the District of Columbia. She earned a reputation as a moderate on this court, which is surprising, given her previous record of liberal activism. Her colleagues and friends insist, however, that her record is consistent. Vivian Berger, dean of Columbia Law School, explains, "She is a judge's judge and a lawyer's lawyer, meaning she has great regard for the role of judges, which is a conservatizing influence, and a great commitment to issues to which she is committed, such as civil rights and liberties" (Coyle 1993, p. 32).

Whatever the appropriate label, Ginsburg became President Clinton's first nominee to the Supreme Court. Clinton announced her nomination on June 14, 1993, and she was confirmed on August 3, 1993, by a 96–3 vote.

Voting Record

Ginsburg's voting record in civil rights and liberties cases in her initial two terms supports the characterization of her as a judicial moderate, although she tends to take the liberal position most frequently. As shown in Table 3.1, she voted liberally in 53 percent of the decisions in the 1993 term and 60 percent in the 1994 term. Ginsburg has been especially liberal in First Amendment cases, for she has taken the liberal side in 90 percent of these cases as shown in Table 3.11. Ginsburg has been aligned most closely with two other recently appointed, moderately liberal justices, Souter and Breyer. Ginsburg and Souter formed a two-person voting bloc in the 1993 term with an 87 percent interagreement rate, and Ginsburg and Breyer formed a voting bloc in the 1994 term with an 86 percent score. Ginsburg's replacement of White seems therefore to have had the effect of reducing somewhat the conservative orientation of the Rehnquist Court. The conservative justices have lost a frequent ally in White, and Ginsburg has been more closely identified with liberal values than conservative ones.

Judicial Philosophy

Ginsburg describes her approach to judicial decision making as "neither liberal nor conservative." It is not surprising, therefore, that it is difficult to discern a distinct judicial philosophy that she espouses. In her confirmation hearings, she emphasized her commitment to judicial restraint, declaring that the judiciary was "third in line" in the Constitution. At the same time, she noted that some decisions by judges are unavoidable because the other branches did not take appropriate action, or simply because legal controversies demand judicial resolution.

STEPHEN G. BREYER

After appointing Ruth Bader Ginsburg to replace Byron White in 1993, President Bill Clinton had his second opportunity to affect the composition of the Court when Harry Blackmun announced his retirement in April of 1994. Clinton decided on

Stephen Breyer, who had been given strong consideration the previous year to replace White. Breyer's record indicated that he would be a moderate, pragmatic justice, and he easily passed Senate confirmation. Based upon his first-term performance in 1994–95, Breyer appears to be another addition to the Court's growing group of moderately liberal justices. Breyer voted liberally in 57 percent of the Court's civil rights and liberties cases, and he was aligned in two-person voting blocs with both Justices Souter and Ginsburg. Breyer wrote few opinions in civil rights and liberties cases, however, and thus it is far too early to offer confident generalizations about his long-term impact on the Court's policies and directions.

Background

Breyer established a superior academic record as a student and then built an impressive legal career combining government work, academic teaching and research, and judicial service. Born in 1938, Breyer grew up in comfortable surroundings in Massachusetts. He enrolled as an undergraduate at Stanford University and then attended Oxford University as a Marshall Scholar, earning a B.A. with first-class honors in 1961. Breyer attended Harvard Law School, serving as articles editor of the Law Review and graduating magna cum laude in 1964. Upon graduation, Breyer clerked for one year at the United States Supreme Court for Justice Arthur Goldberg. Breyer's next job was at the Justice Department where he served for two years as special assistant to the assistant attorney general in the Antitrust Division.

Breyer returned to Harvard Law School in 1967, teaching on a full-time basis until 1980. His areas of expertise included administrative law, antitrust law, and economic regulation. In 1979–80 Breyer took a leave of absence from Harvard to serve as chief counsel for the Senate Judiciary Committee, where he helped write the legislation that deregulated the airline industry.

Breyer's judicial career began in 1980 when President Jimmy Carter appointed him to the Court of Appeals for the First Circuit, where he eventually became chief judge. Breyer remained in a part-time position at Harvard, and he continued to be a productive scholar, authoring books on administrative law and government regulation.

When Blackmun announced his intention to retire in April of 1994, Clinton decided rather quickly on Breyer, nominating him to the high court in May. Clinton had expressed some preference for a candidate who was an experienced politician with a "big heart," but the leading candidate with these credentials, Secretary of the Interior Bruce Babbitt, was viewed as someone who would generate intense opposition from conservatives. With the memories of the Bork and Thomas nominations still fresh in the minds of members of the executive branch as well as the Senate, Clinton chose Breyer instead. Breyer was viewed as an extremely well-qualified candidate, and his moderate reputation promised to negate opposition from conservative Republicans in the Senate.

Breyer sailed through Senate confirmation hearings with relatively little difficulty. He did not advance any overarching theories of the law but rather portrayed himself as taking a moderate, pragmatic approach to the law. Attempting to defuse possible concerns about him as an Ivy League technocrat who was unconcerned about the problems of ordinary people, Breyer emphasized that the law requires judges to use both their heads and their hearts. He indicated his general support for liberal Supreme Court precedents in the area of civil rights and liberties, including *Roe v. Wade* (1973), but he was intentionally vague regarding more specific issues. Opposition to Breyer was limited, but much of it came from liberals who were concerned that Breyer might be too critical of government regulatory power as well as too oriented toward big business over the interests of small businesses and consumers. Most Senate testimony was strongly supportive of Breyer, however, and he was confirmed in July by a vote of 87–9.

Voting Record

Caution must be exercised in discussing Breyer's voting record when the available data cover only his first term on the Court. However, Breyer's first-term performance was consistent with his record and reputation as a moderate appellate judge and with his presentation of himself as a moderate, pragmatic jurist during his confirmation hearings. As shown in Table 3.1, Breyer voted liberally in 57 percent of the Court's civil rights and liberties cases. His liberal voting percentage was close to Ginsburg's (60 percent) and Souter's (65 percent), and as seen in Table 3.10 Breyer formed two-person voting blocs with both of these justices, having an interagreement score of 86 percent with both justices. As further indication of his essentially moderate voting record in his first term, Breyer had much higher levels of interagreement with the Court's moderate conservatives (Kennedy and O'Connor) than with either the Court's three most conservative justices (Rehnquist, Thomas, and Scalia) or the Court's most liberal member (Stevens).

Some evidence does exist, however, that Breyer may be more deeply committed to liberal views than these data suggest. Smith, Baugh, and Hensley (1995, p. 76) examined the sixteen cases in the 1994 term in which the Court divided 5-4, and they found that Breyer consistently joined Ginsburg, Souter, and Stevens in those cases, with the four justices forming a cohesive voting bloc with an average agreement rate of 83 percent. Thus, Breyer's replacement of Blackmun, one of the leading liberals of the Rehnquist Court, may not affect significantly the direction of the Court in civil rights and liberties cases.

Judicial Philosophy

As with the analysis of Breyer's voting record, caution must also be exercised in any attempt to characterize Breyer's judicial philosophy, especially in regard to the area of civil rights and liberties. Breyer's writings have focused on the somewhat technical areas of administrative law and economic regulation, and he wrote opinions in relatively few civil rights and liberties cases as a circuit court judge. In testimony before the Senate, he tended to speak in noncontroversial generalities regarding guiding principles for deciding civil rights and liberties cases. In addition, he wrote opinions in only two civil rights and liberties cases in his first term on the Court, and he provided little insight into broad judicial philosophies in these opinions (Smith et al. 1995, p. 79).

Breyer's testimony in Senate confirmation hearings does suggest, however, that initially he will be more committed to a philosophy of judicial restraint than judicial activism. He assured senators that judges should adhere to established precedent. He also emphasized that popularly elected officials, not nonelected federal judges, should set public policy. Nonetheless, Breyer recognized Justices Brennan and Marshall for their greatness, and he stressed that the Supreme Court must seek to adapt the Constitution to a rapidly changing world, all the while being faithful to its core values.

Court commentators use the term "pragmatist" to summarize Breyer's general approach to the law. Idelson (1995, p. 80), for example, argues that Breyer favors ". . . pragmatic balancing tests between competing rights rather than fixed legal formulas or bold new interpretations of the law." Greenhouse (1994, p. A10) has echoed a similar theme, characterizing Breyer as ". . . a self-described pragmatist more interested in solutions than theories."

TABLE 3.1: A Composite Table of the Individual Voting Records of the Justices of the Supreme Court in Civil Rights and Liberties Cases, 1986-94 Terms (Justices ranked from lowest to highest in terms of total percent liberal voting)

	Terms									
Justices	1986	1987	1988	1989	1990	1991	1992	1993	1994	Average
Rehnquist	16%	30%	22%	12%	22%	33%	27%	25%	19%	23%
Thomas	—	—	—	—	—	26%	31%	20%	24%	25%
Scalia	38%	36%	33%	23%	31%	25%	35%	27%	27%	31%
White	27%	29%	30%	26%	44%	44%	39%	—	—	34%
Kennedy	—	42%	36%	22%	37%	49%	39%	42%	32%	37%
O'Connor	31%	36%	32%	20%	43%	58%	43%	36%	43%	38%
Powell	39%	—	—	—	—	—	—	—	—	39%
Souter	—	—	—	—	35%	54%	57%	58%	65%	54%
Ginsburg	—	—	—	—	—	—	—	53%	60%	56%
Breyer	—	—	—	—	—	—	—	—	57%	57%
Blackmun	75%	65%	67%	58%	78%	73%	78%	71%	—	71%
Stevens	67%	64%	60%	71%	81%	80%	76%	64%	86%	72%
Brennan	92%	83%	85%	85%	—	—	—	—	—	86%
Marshall	92%	84%	86%	89%	87%	—	—	—	—	88%
COURT	46%	49%	36%	33%	43%	51%	39%	42%	40%	42%

TABLE 3.2: Bloc Voting Analysis of Civil Rights and Liberties Decisions, 1986-87 Term of the Supreme Court (Percent agreement rates)

	Bren	**Mar**	**Blkm**	**Stev**	**Pow**	**Whit**	**Rehn**	**Scal**	**OCon**
Brennan	—	97	79	72	46	36	24	38	37
Marshall	97	—	81	71	47	36	23	38	37
Blackmun	79	81	—	75	60	54	42	52	50
Stevens	72	71	75	—	59	57	47	61	57
Powell	46	47	60	59	—	81	78	71	79
White	36	36	54	57	81	—	88	84	79
Rehnquist	24	23	42	47	78	88	—	82	82
Scalia	38	38	52	61	71	84	82	—	81
O'Connor	37	37	50	57	79	79	82	81	—

Court mean=60.67
Sprague Criterion=80.33
Liberal bloc: Brennan, Marshall=97
Conservative bloc: White, Rehnquist, Scalia, O'Connor=83

TABLE 3.3: Bloc Voting Analysis of Civil Rights and Liberties Decisions, 1987-88 Term of the Supreme Court (Percent agreement rates)

	Bren	Mar	Blkm	Stev	Whit	OCon	Scal	Rehn
Brennan	—	99	83	75	57	49	54	45
Marshall	99	—	81	74	55	49	51	44
Blackmun	83	81	—	72	69	55	60	60
Stevens	75	74	72	—	70	64	65	63
White	57	55	69	70	—	81	79	79
O'Connor	49	49	55	64	81	—	85	81
Scalia	54	51	60	65	79	85	—	82
Rehnquist	45	44	60	63	79	81	82	—

Kennedy was not included because he participated in too few decisions.

Court Mean = 67.18
Sprague Criterion = 83.59
Liberal Bloc: Brennan, Marshall = 99
Conservative Bloc: O'Connor, Scalia = 85

TABLE 3.4: Bloc Voting Analysis of Civil Rights and Liberties Decisions, 1988-89 Term of the Supreme Court (Percent agreement rates)

	Bren	Mar	Blkm	Stev	Ken	Scal	Rehn	Whit	OCon
Brennan	—	96	80	73	43	48	39	46	46
Marshall	96	—	78	74	39	44	35	42	44
Blackmun	80	78	—	71	55	56	51	58	58
Stevens	73	74	71	—	61	59	61	62	62
Kennedy	43	39	55	61	—	94	92	85	84
Scalia	48	44	56	59	94	—	88	84	85
Rehnquist	39	35	51	61	92	88	—	91	87
White	46	42	58	62	85	84	91	—	92
O'Connor	46	44	58	62	84	85	87	92	—

Court mean = 65.64
Sprague Criterion = 82.82
Liberal bloc: Brennan, Marshall = 96
Conservative bloc: Kennedy, Scalia, Rehnquist, White, O'Connor = 88

TABLE 3.5: Bloc Voting Analysis of Civil Rights and Liberties Decisions, 1989-90 Term of the Supreme Court (Percent agreement rates)

	Bren	Mar	Stev	Blkm	Whit	Rehn	OCon	Ken	Scal
Brennan	—	96	81	74	41	27	31	35	31
Marshall	96	—	80	70	36	22	26	29	29
Stevens	81	80	—	73	44	40	44	44	44
Blackmun	74	70	73	—	64	53	51	54	49
White	41	36	44	64	—	86	79	78	79
Rehnquist	27	22	40	53	86	—	90	87	87
O'Connor	31	26	44	51	79	90	—	91	91
Kennedy	35	29	44	54	78	87	91	—	88
Scalia	31	29	44	49	79	87	91	88	—

Court mean = 59.00
Sprague Criterion = 79.50
Liberal bloc: Brennan, Marshall, Stevens = 86
Conservative bloc: White, Rehnquist, O'Connor, Kennedy, Scalia = 86

TABLE 3.6: Bloc Voting Analysis of Civil Rights and Liberties Decisions, 1990-91 Term of the Supreme Court (Percent agreement rates)

	Sout	OCon	Rehn	Ken	Scal	Whit	Stev	Mar	Blkm
Souter	—	92	86	82	78	80	49	45	55
O'Connor	92	—	80	83	74	72	54	48	57
Rehnquist	86	80	—	85	87	74	41	31	41
Kennedy	82	83	85	—	80	70	52	43	52
Scalia	78	74	87	80	—	76	43	37	46
White	80	72	74	70	76	—	59	54	59
Stevens	49	54	41	52	43	59	—	91	81
Marshall	45	48	31	43	37	54	91	—	91
Blackmun	55	57	41	52	46	59	81	91	—

Court mean = 64.47
Sprague Criterion = 82.34
Conservation blocs: Souter, O'Connor, Rehnquist, Kennedy = 85
Rehnquist, Kennedy, Scalia = 84
Liberal bloc: Stevens, Marshall, Blackmun = 88

TABLE 3.7: Bloc Voting Analysis of Civil Rights and Liberties Decisions, 1991-92 Term of the Supreme Court (Percent agreement rates)

	Blkm	Stev	OCon	Ken	Sout	Whit	Rehn	Thom	Scal
Blackmun	—	89	78	76	74	67	60	47	49
Stevens	89	—	75	69	74	64	53	44	45
O'Connor	78	75	—	80	76	67	71	58	64
Kennedy	76	69	80	—	81	80	80	60	69
Souter	74	74	76	81	—	76	76	69	69
White	67	64	67	80	76	—	85	72	75
Rehnquist	60	53	71	80	76	85	—	86	85
Thomas	47	44	58	60	69	72	86	—	86
Scalia	49	45	64	69	69	75	85	86	—

Court mean = 70.25
Sprague Criterion = 85.13
Liberal bloc: Blackmun, Stevens = 89
Conservation bloc: Rehnquist, Thomas, Scalia = 86

TABLE 3.8: Bloc Voting Analysis of Civil Rights and Liberties Decisions, 1992-93 Term of the Supreme Court (Percent agreement rates)

	Rehn	Thom	Scal	Ken	Whit	OCon	Sout	Stev	Blkm
Rehnquist	—	92	84	88	88	80	71	51	50
Thomas	92	—	88	84	80	80	67	55	54
Scalia	84	88	—	84	76	76	75	59	50
Kennedy	88	84	84	—	84	73	78	63	58
White	88	80	76	84	—	73	78	59	58
O'Connor	80	80	76	73	73	—	75	63	66
Souter	71	67	75	78	78	75	—	73	72
Stevens	51	55	59	63	59	63	73	—	90
Blackmun	50	54	50	58	58	66	72	90	—

Court mean = 72.08
Sprague Criterion = 86.04
Conservative bloc: Rehnquist, Thomas, Scalia = 88
Liberal bloc: Stevens, Blackmun = 90
Additional blocs: Rehnquist, Kennedy = 88
Rehnquist, White = 88

TABLE 3.9: Bloc Voting Analysis of Civil Rights and Liberties Decisions, 1993-94 Term of the Supreme Court (Percent agreement rates)

	Thom	Scal	Rehn	OCon	Ken	Gins	Sout	Stev	Blkm
Thomas	—	93	91	84	73	67	58	47	40
Scalia	93	—	84	87	80	73	64	53	42
Rehnquist	91	84	—	89	77	70	66	55	48
O'Connor	84	87	89	—	84	82	73	62	56
Kennedy	73	80	77	84	—	84	84	73	62
Ginsburg	67	73	70	82	84	—	87	80	69
Souter	58	64	66	73	84	87	—	80	78
Stevens	47	53	55	62	73	80	80	—	84
Blackmun	40	42	48	56	62	69	78	84	—

Court mean = 71.64
Sprague Criterion = 85.82
Conservative bloc: Thomas, Scalia, Rehnquist, O'Connor = 88
Moderate bloc: Ginsburg, Souter = 87

TABLE 3.10: Bloc Voting Analysis of Civil Rights and Liberties Decisions, 1994-95 Term of the Supreme Court (Percent agreement rates)

	Thom	Scal	Rehn	Ken	OCon	Brey	Gins	Sout	Stev
Thomas	—	92	89	86	70	62	59	49	32
Scalia	92	—	86	89	68	59	62	51	35
Rehnquist	89	86	—	81	76	62	59	54	32
Kennedy	86	89	81	—	78	70	73	62	46
O'Connor	70	68	76	78	—	81	68	78	51
Breyer	62	59	62	70	81	—	86	86	65
Ginsburg	59	62	59	73	68	86	—	78	73
Souter	49	51	54	62	78	86	78	—	73
Stevens	32	35	32	46	51	65	73	73	—

Court mean = 67.25
Sprague Criterion = 83.62
Conservative bloc: Thomas, Scalia, Rehnquist, Kennedy = 87
Moderate blocs: Breyer, Ginsburg = 86
Breyer, Souter = 86

TABLE 3.11: Percentages of Liberal Votes by the Justices of the Rehnquist Court in First Amendment, Criminal Procedure, and Civil Rights Cases, 1986 through 1994 Terms (Justices ranked from lowest to highest in terms of total percent liberal voting)

First Amendment		**Criminal Procedure**		**Civil Rights**	
Justices	% Liberal	Justices	% Liberal	Justices	%Liberal
Rehnquist	22%	Rehnquist	17%	Rehnquist	28%
White	31%	Thomas	19%	Thomas	30%
Scalia	35%	Scalia	26%	Scalia	32%
Thomas	38%	Powell	27%	Kennedy	40%
O'Connor	46%	White	28%	O'Connor	42%
Kennedy	48%	Kennedy	29%	White	45%
Powell	50%	O'Connor	29%	Powell	46%
Stevens	70%	Breyer	35%	Ginsburg	50%
Blackmun	73%	Souter	44%	Souter	58%
Souter	74%	Ginsburg	47%	Stevens	69%
Breyer	83%	Blackmun	62%	Breyer	80%
Brennan	85%	Stevens	72%	Blackmun	83%
Marshall	86%	Brennan	87%	Brennan	91%
Ginsburg	90%	Marshall	88%	Marshall	94%

REFERENCES

Harry A. Blackmun

Blackmun, Harry A. "Movement and Countermovement." *Drake Law Review* 38 (1988/89): 747-58.

Jenkins, John A. "A Candid Talk with Justice Blackmun." *The New York Times Magazine*, 20 February 1983, 20 ff.

Kobylka, Joseph F. "The Judicial Odyssey of Harry Blackmun: The Dynamics of Individual-Level Change on the U.S. Supreme Court." Paper presented at the annual meeting of the Midwest Political Science Association, 1992.

Pollett, Michael. "Harry A. Blackmun." In *The Justices of the United States Supreme Court, 1789-1978: Their Lives and Major Decisions,* edited by Leon Friedman. New York: Chelsea House, 1980.

Wasby, Stephen L. "Justice Harry A. Blackmun: Transformation from 'Minnesota Twin' to Independent Voice." In *The Burger Court,* edited by Charles M. Lamb and Stephen C. Halpern. Urbana: University of Illinois Press, 1991.

William J. Brennan

Abraham, Henry J. *Justices and Presidents: A Political History of Appointments to the Supreme Court.* 3d ed. New York: Oxford University Press, 1992.

Brennan, William J. "Reason, Passion and the Progress of the Law." *Cardozo Law Review* 10 (1988): 3-23.

Friedelbaum, Stanley H. "Justice William J. Brennan, Jr.: Policy-Making in the Judicial Thicket." In *The Burger Court* edited by Charles M. Lamb and Stephen C. Halpern. Urbana: University of Illinois Press, 1991.

Heck, Edward V. "Justice Brennan and the Freedom of Expression Doctrine in the Burger Court." *San Diego Law Review* 24 (1987): 1153-83.

Hopkins, W. W. *Mr. Justice Brennan and Freedom of Expression*. New York: Praeger, 1991.

Stephen G. Breyer

Greenhouse, Linda. "Portrait of a Pragmatist." *New York Times,* 14 July 1994: A1, A10.

Idelson, Holly. "Breyer's Bipartisan Appeal Extinguishes Fireworks." In *Guide to Current American Government*, 60-62. Washington, D.C.: Congressional Quarterly Press, 1994.

Idelson, Holly. "Breyer Affirms Pragmatist Image As He Coasts Toward Court." In *Guide to Current American Government,* 80-83. Washington, D.C.: Congressional Quarterly Press, 1995.

Smith, Christopher E., Joyce A. Baugh, and Thomas R. Hensley. "The First-Term Performance of Justice Stephen Breyer." *Judicature* 79 (1995): 74-79.

Waring, Nancy. "Stephen Breyer: A Look Back at Law School." *Harvard Law Bulletin* 46 (1995): 4-7.

Ruth Bader Ginsburg

Biskupic, Joan. "Nominee's Philosophy Seen Strengthening the Center." *The Washington Post*, June 15 1993: A1+.

Coyle, Marcia. "Nominee's Mettle Will Be Tested Soon." *The National Law Journal*, June 28 1993: 1+.

Kaplan, David A., and Bob Kohn. 1993. "A Frankfurter, Not a Hot Dog." *Newsweek*, 28 June 1993, 29.

Smith, Christopher E., Joyce Ann Baugh, Thomas R. Hensley, and Scott Patrick Johnson. "The First-Term Performance of Justice Ruth Bader Ginsburg." *Judicature* 78 (1994): 74-80.

Von Drehle, David. 1993. "The Quiet Revolutionary." *The Washington Post National Weekly Edition*, 26 July-1 August 1993: 6-7.

Anthony M. Kennedy

Kennedy, Anthony M. "The Constitution and the Spirit of Freedom." *The Gauer Distinguished Lecture in Law and Public Policy*. Vol. 1. Washington D.C.: National Center for the Public Interest, 1991.

Melone, Albert P. "Revisiting the Freshman Effect Hypothesis: The First Two Terms of Justice Anthony Kennedy." *Judicature* 74 (1990): 6-13.

"Reagan Fills Court Vacancy on Third Attempt." *Guide to Current American Government: Fall 1988*, 114-17 Washington, D.C.: Congressional Quarterly Press, 1988.

Smith, Christopher E. "Supreme Court Surprise: Justice Anthony Kennedy's Surprise Move Toward Moderation." *Oklahoma Law Review* 45 (1992): 459-76.

Thurgood Marshall

Bland, Randall W. *Private Pressures on Public Law: The Legal Career of Justice Thurgood Marshall*. Lanham, Massachusetts: University Press of America, 1993.

Daniels, William J. "Justice Thurgood Marshall: The Race for Equal Justice." In *The Burger Court* edited by Charles C. Lamb and Stephen C. Halpern. Urbana: University of Illinois Press, 1991.

Fenderson, Lewis H. *Thurgood Marshall: Fighter for Justice*. New York: McGraw-Hill, 1969.

Goldman, Roger and Davis Gallen. *Thurgood Marshall: Justice for All*. New York: Carroll and Graf Publishers, 1992.

Rowan, Carl T. *Dream Makers, Dream Breakers: The World of Thurgood Marshall*. Boston: Little, Brown, 1993.

Sandra Day O'Connor

Cook, Beverly B. "Justice Sandra Day O'Connor: Transition to a Republican Court Agenda." In *The Burger Court* edited by Charles Lamb and Stephen C. Halpern. Urbana: University of Illinois Press, 1991.

Fox, Mary Virginia. *Justice Sandra Day O'Connor*. Hillside, N.J.: Enslow Publishers, 1993.

O'Connor, Sandra Day. "Our Judicial Federalism." *Case Western Reserve University Law Review* 35 (1984-85): 1-12.

Scheb, John M., and Lee W. Ailshie. "Justice Sandra Day O'Connor and the 'Freshman Effect.'" *Judicature* 69 (1985): 9-12.

Witt, Elder. *A Different Justice: Reagan and the Supreme Court*. Washington, D.C.: Congressional Quarterly Press, 1986.

Lewis F. Powell

Blasecki, Janet. "Justice Lewis F. Powell: Swing Voter or Staunch Conservative?" *Journal of Politics* 52 (1990): 530-547.

Freeman, G. C., Jr. "Justice Powell's Constitutional Opinions." *Washington and Lee Law Review* 45 (1988): 411-65.

Landynski, Jacob. "Justice Lewis F. Powell, Jr.: Balance Wheel of the Court." In *The Burger Court* edited by Charles C. Lamb and Stephen C. Halpern. Urbana: University of Illinois Press, 1991.

Maltz, E. M. "Portrait of a Man in the Middle—Mr. Justice Powell, Equal Protection and the Pure Classification Problem." *Ohio State Law Journal* 40 (1979): 941-64.

Powell, Lewis F., Jr. "Capital Punishment." *Harvard Law Review* 102 (1989): 1035-46.

Urofsky, Melvin I. "Mr. Justice Powell and Education: Balancing of Competing Values." *Journal of Law and Education* 13 (1984): 581-627.

William H. Rehnquist

Davis, Derek. *Original Intent: Chief Justice Rehnquist and the Course of American Church/State Relations*. Buffalo, New York: Prometheus Books, 1991.

Davis, Sue. "Federalism and Property Rights: An Examination of Justice Rehnquist's Legal Positivism." *Western Political Quarterly* 39 (1986): 250-64.

Davis, Sue. *Justice Rehnquist and the Constitution*. Princeton, New Jersey: Princeton University Press, 1989.

Davis, Sue. "Power on the Court: Chief Justice Rehnquist's Opinion Assignments." *Judicature* 74 (1990): 66-72.

Davis, Sue. "Justice William H. Rehnquist: Right-Wing Ideologue or Majoritarian Democrat?" In *The Burger Court* edited by Charles C. Lamb and Stephen C. Halpern. Urbana: University of Illinois Press, 1991.

Jenkins, John J. "The Partisan: A Talk with Justice Rehnquist." *New York Times Magazine*, 3 March 1985: 28-35.

Rehnquist, William H. *The Supreme Court: How It Was, How It Is*. New York: William Morrow, 1987.

Antonin Scalia

Brisbin, Richard A., Jr. "The Conservatism of Antonin Scalia." *Political Science Quarterly* 115 (1990): 1-29.

Kannar, G. "The Constitutional Catechism of Antonin Scalia." *Yale Law Review* 99 (1990): 1297-1357.

Scalia, Antonin. "The Rule of Law as a Law of Rules." *University of Chicago Law Review* 56 (1989): 1175-88.

Scalia, Antonin. "Assorted Canards of Contemporary Legal Analysis." *Case Western Reserve University Law Review* 40 (1989-90): 581-97.

Smith, Christopher E. "Justice Antonin Scalia and the Institutions of American Government." *Wake Forest Law Review* 25 (1990): 783-809.

Smith, Christopher E. "Justice Antonin Scalia and Criminal Justice Cases." *Kentucky Law Review* 81 (1992-93): 187-212.

David H. Souter

Hensley, Thomas R. "Justice Souter and the Rehnquist Court's Conservative Counterrevolution." Paper presented at the annual meeting of the Midwest Political-Science Association, 1992.

Johnson, Scott P., and Christopher E. Smith. "David Souter's First Term on the Supreme Court: The Impact of a New Justice." *Judicature* 75 (1992): 238-43.

Jordan, William S. "Justice David Souter and Statutory Interpretation." *University of Toledo Law Review* 23 (1992): 491-530.

Smith, Christopher E., and Scott P. Johnson. "Newcomer on the High Court: Justice Souter and the Supreme Court's 1990 Term." *South Dakota Law Review* 37 (1992): 21-43.

John Paul Stevens

Arledge, Paula C. "John Paul Stevens: A Moderate Justice's Approach to Individual Rights." *Whittier Law Review* 10 (1989): 563-88.

Canon, Bradley C. "Justice John Paul Stevens: The Lone Ranger in a Black Robe." In *The Burger Court* edited by Charles C. Lamb and Stephen C. Halpern. Urbana: University of Illinois Press, 1991.

O'Brien, David M. "The Politics of Professionalism: President Gerald Ford's Appointment of Justice John Paul Stevens." *Presidential Studies Quarterly* 21 (1991): 103-26.

Sickels, Robert J. *John Paul Stevens and the Constitution: The Search for Balance*. University Park: Pennsylvania State University Press, 1988.

Stevens, John Paul. "Some Thoughts on Judicial Restraint." *Judicature* 66 (1982): 177-83.

Clarence Thomas

Epperson, John W. "Justice Thomas and the Conservative Shift of the Supreme Court." Paper presented at the annual meeting of the American Political Science Association, 1992.

Higginbotham, A. Leon, Jr. "An Open Letter to Justice Clarence Thomas from a Federal Judicial Colleague." *University of Pennsylvania Law Review* 140 (1992): 1005-28.

O'Connor, Karen. "The Effects of the Thomas Nomination on the Supreme Court." *PS: Political Science and Politics* 25 (1992): 492-95.

Phelps, Timothy M. and Helen Winternitz. *Capital Games: Clarence Thomas, Anita Hill, and the Story of a Supreme Court Nomination*. New York: Hyperion, 1992.

Smith, Christopher E., and Scott P. Johnson. "The First-Term Performance of Justice Clarence Thomas." *Judicature* 76 (1993): 172-78.

Smith, Christopher E. *Critical Judicial Nominations and Political Change: The Impact of Clarence Thomas*. Westport, Connecticut: Praeger, 1993.

Byron R. White

Israel, Fred L. "Byron R. White." In *The Justices of the United States Supreme Court, 1789-1969*, edited by Leon Friedman and Fred Israel, Vol. 4. 2951-53. New York: Chelsea House, 1969.

Kramer, Daniel C. "Justice Byron R. White: Good Friend to Polity and Solon." In *The Burger Court* edited by Charles M. Lamb and Stephen C. Halpern. Urbana: University of Illinois Press, 1991.

McLean, Deckel. "Justice White and the First Amendment." *Journalism Quarterly* 56 (1979): 305-10.

Stewart, David O. "White to Right." *ABA Journal* 76 (1990): 40-42.

White, Byron R. "Some Current Debates." *Judicature* 73 (1989): 155-58.

CHAPTER

4 Incorporation of the Bill of Rights

CASE STUDY

Duncan v. Louisiana (1968)

During the 1960s, as the civil rights movement steadily achieved judicial and legislative victories that diminished racial discrimination and segregation, Plaquemines Parish in Louisiana remained under the firm control of segregationist politicians. Led by Judge Leander H. Perez, Sr., the white men who controlled the parish's governing institutions, including the courts, fought against the registration of African American voters and the desegregation of the public schools (Conaway 1973). When a federal judge ordered the parish's schools to end racial segregation, Perez and the other parish leaders attempted unsuccessfully to transfer the public schools to private ownership in order to place them beyond the reach of judicial desegregation orders. Perez succeeded, however, in encouraging the establishment of a private school system for whites that could serve as the vehicle for maintaining racial separation in education (Cortner 1975, p. 9).

Seemingly small events can have a significant impact on the shape of constitutional law. Minor disputes between individual human beings, if passed through the various levels of the American judicial system, can ultimately present the United States Supreme Court with important issues concerning the meaning of the Constitution and the definition of civil rights and liberties. Thus, Gary Duncan, a nineteen-year-old African American man, could never have anticipated that his seemingly minor dispute with several white boys in the racially oppressive environment of Plaquemines Parish would eventually generate an important Supreme Court precedent.

On October 18, 1966, as Duncan, a towboat worker, drove down highway 23, he saw two of his cousins, Bert Grant and Bernard St. Ann, being confronted by four white boys. Grant and St. Ann were new students at the parish's previously all-white public high school, and they had complained that they were being harassed by white students. Duncan stopped his car and asked his cousins about their dispute with the white boys. After hearing that his cousins believed the white boys wanted to start a fight, Duncan told his cousins to get into the car. Duncan then exchanged words with the whites. He claimed that he told one of the boys, Herman M. Landry, Jr., to go home and that he touched Landry on the elbow. Landry, however, claimed that Duncan had slapped him forcefully on the arm (Cortner 1975, p. 10).

The incident was observed by P.E. Lathum, the principal of an all-white private school established to maintain racial separation. Lathum reported the incident to a deputy sheriff who intercepted Duncan's car and returned Duncan to the scene of the incident. The deputy released Duncan shortly thereafter on concluding from questioning the white boys that Duncan had not assaulted Landry.

Three days later, however, Duncan was arrested by parish authorities and charged with cruelty to juveniles (Cortner 1975, p. 10).

Because Duncan's parents believed that their son's arrest was part of a historical pattern of racial discrimination by parish authorities, they contacted lawyers in New Orleans who worked for the Lawyers Constitutional Defense Committee (LCDC). The LCDC, which was organized by liberal civil rights groups, such as the American Civil Liberties Union and the Congress of Racial Equality, placed volunteer lawyers in southern cities to work on civil rights issues. Because Plaquemines Parish officials had previously used intimidation and threats of violence to deter civil rights organizations and their lawyers from entering the parish, the LCDC lawyer in New Orleans, Richard Sobol, was initially not eager to enter what seemed like a minor case. Sobol, a lawyer who had given up a high-paying position with a prestigious Washington, D.C., law firm in order to work on civil rights cases for the LCDC, eventually agreed to represent Duncan in order to combat the anti–civil rights atmosphere in the parish (Cortner 1975, p. 12).

When Sobol argued before the state court that Duncan's case did not fit the intention of the "cruelty to juveniles" statute, parish officials promptly rearrested Duncan and charged him with simple assault, a misdemeanor punishable by a maximum of two years' imprisonment. When Duncan's assault case came to trial in January of 1967, Sobol demanded a jury trial because Duncan faced the possibility of imprisonment if he were convicted of assault. According to Sobol, the Sixth Amendment's grant of a right to "a speedy and public trial by an impartial jury" was applicable to the Louisiana courts as a component of the Fourteenth Amendment's requirement that states respect all persons' rights to "due process of law." However, the state judge rejected Sobol's argument by emphasizing that Louisiana's statutes required juries only in felony cases. Judge Eugene Leon declared: "Misdemeanors are not tried by jury with or without [the possible punishment of] hard labor" (Cortner 1975, p. 12).

The judge's decision reflected the fact that for most of American history the specific rights contained in the Bill of Rights, the Constitution's first ten amendments, protected individuals only against actions by the federal government. State constitutions and statutes provided protections for people against actions by state government, but many states' constitutions protected relatively few civil rights and liberties (Bodenhamer 1992).

During the trial, Duncan and his cousins denied that Duncan hit Landry, but Landry, his friends, and the school principal testified that Duncan hit Landry's arm with sufficient force to knock it upward to the level of Landry's shoulder. Judge Leon found Duncan guilty of simple battery and sentenced him to pay a $150 fine and serve sixty days in the parish prison. Sobol unsuccessfully used his argument about the right to a trial by jury in an appeal to Judge Leon and subsequently to the Louisiana Supreme Court.

After the Louisiana Supreme Court rejected Duncan's appeal, parish authorities asserted their power over the participants in the case as a display of their strident opposition to civil rights advocates. They arrested Sobol and jailed him for several hours on charges that he was not authorized to practice law in Louisiana. In a simultaneous action, Judge Leon revoked Duncan's bail and he "was arrested late at night . . . by Plaquemines Parish officers who generally abused him on the trip to the prison" (Cortner 1975, p. 14). He was later released on bail.

Sobol took Duncan's case to the U.S. Supreme Court. The case was heard by the high court on January 17, 1968. Sobol acknowledged that the Supreme Court had long ago decided that the Sixth Amendment's right to trial by jury did not apply to state courts (*Maxwell v. Dow*, 1900). However, he argued that recent decisions concerning other rights for criminal defendants indicated that fundamental components of due process, such as a jury trial, should protect defendants in state court cases just as these rights protected defendants in the federal courts (Cortner 1975, p. 15).

The Supreme Court issued its opinion on May 20, 1968. By a vote of seven to two, the Court overturned Duncan's conviction (*Duncan v. Louisiana*, 1968) (case excerpt on p. 120). In an opinion written by Justice Byron White, the Court declared that because the right to trial by jury contained in the Sixth Amendment "is fundamental to the American scheme of justice," it must be regarded as a protected right applicable to the states through the Due Process Clause of the Fourteenth Amendment (*Duncan v. Louisiana*, 391 U.S. at 147). White concluded that "in the American States, as in the federal judicial system, a general grant of jury trial for serious offenses is a fundamental right, essential for preventing miscarriages of justice and for assuring that fair trials are provided for all defendants" (391 U.S. at 157). Justices Hugo Black and Abe Fortas each issued concurring opinions that endorsed the right to trial by jury in cases such as Duncan's. In a concurring opinion joined by Justice William O. Douglas, Black reemphasized his long-standing position that all of the rights contained in the Bill of Rights should be applied to the states through the Due Process Clause. Fortas argued that while states should be required to make jury trials available, the states need not be held to the same rules as those applied in the federal courts concerning how jury trials were to be conducted. In dissent, Justice John Harlan, joined by Justice Potter Stewart, asserted that the right to trial by jury was not so fundamental to a free society that it must be considered as a component of the right to due process of law. From Harlan's perspective, it is possible to have a fair trial without a jury, and indeed, many kinds of cases are decided by judges rather than juries. Furthermore, Harlan asserted that the states should be free to develop their own rules and procedures for conducting fair trials in criminal cases. Harlan felt that the Supreme Court should intervene only when states apply procedures that prove to be fundamentally unfair to defendants.

As we will see in Chapter 11's discussion of the Sixth Amendment, the Supreme Court subsequently clarified its *Duncan* opinion by deciding that the right to trial by jury applied only in "serious" cases in which defendants faced six months or more of incarceration (*Baldwin v. New York,* 1970). The right did not apply in "petty" cases with lesser punishments. The Court also decided that juries did not have to contain twelve members (*Williams v. Florida,* 1970), and that jury verdicts did not have to be unanimous (*Apodaca v. Oregon,* 1972).

After the Supreme Court's decision in favor of Duncan, Sobol initiated legal action in federal court to prevent Plaquemines Parish from prosecuting him for unauthorized practice of law in Louisiana and to prevent the parish from making Duncan stand trial yet again on the assault charge. Federal judges issued injunctions to prevent the parish from prosecuting either Sobol or Duncan. With respect to Duncan, the federal court "noted the cancellation of Duncan's bond pending appeal to the Supreme Court, his subsequent arrest late at night, his harassment by the arresting officers, and the rejection of sufficient property pledged as bail for his release" and thereby concluded that the parish was prosecuting Duncan in bad faith for harassment purposes (Cortner 1975, p. 30). The parish appealed the decision through the federal court system, but in 1971 the Supreme Court refused to examine the case.

It took five years of legal action for Gary Duncan's minor incident to pass completely through the stages of the American judicial system. Throughout that time period, an adverse decision by an appellate court would have landed him in jail as a result of the persistent efforts of Plaquemines Parish officials to prosecute anyone who did not defer to the white-dominated status quo. Duncan was very fortunate that he obtained the services of a committed and skilled interest group lawyer who was willing to continue fighting for Duncan through each stage of the judicial process. Most other people are not fortunate enough to have a legal interest group adopt their cause. It is extraordinarily difficult for most people to afford the tens or hundreds of thousands of dollars necessary for pursuing litigation through the multiple layers of the judicial system.

Duncan's good fortune in attracting the support of a civil rights lawyer not only spared him a term in jail; it also helped to reshape constitutional law. Duncan's case provided a vehicle for the Supreme Court's justices to expand the meaning of civil rights and liberties by taking a piece of the Bill of Rights, namely the Sixth Amendment's right to trial by jury, and making it applicable to the states by incorporating that right into the Fourteenth Amendment's Due Process Clause. During the twentieth century, the Supreme Court applied many rights against the states by incorporating them into the Due Process Clause. Duncan's case represented the final stages of this incorporation process at a time when justices eager to expand the scope of civil rights and liberties dominated the Supreme Court's composition. The Warren Court justices who decided in favor of Duncan did not initiate the incorporation process. However, they were responsible for adopting the incorporation concept and using it regularly to insure that people's civil rights and liberties under the Constitution provided protections against actions by state and local governments as well as against those by the federal government.

Origins of the Bill of Rights and Incorporation

The original United States Constitution did not contain a listing of the people's civil rights and liberties when it was ratified in 1789. It contained a few references to protections for individuals, such as the provision in Article I, Section 9 prohibiting bills of attainder and ex post facto laws and restricting the suspension of the writ of habeas corpus. These specific provisions reflected concerns about the potential misuse of governmental power that might lead governmental officials to prosecute and detain people improperly. The framers of the Constitution obviously feared that the government might impose capital punishment on people for treason without proving their guilt through the legal process (bills of attainder), criminalize activities *after* people have done them and try to use that as a basis for prosecution (ex post facto laws), or abolish mechanisms for people in custody to challenge the basis for their incarceration (writs of habeas corpus). Although these provisions addressed the framers' concerns about misuse of governmental power, they did not represent the full range of civil rights and liberties that various leaders and citizens of that era believed to be deserving of protection. When the constitutional conventions in various states ratified the Constitution, many people expressed concerns about the absence in the founding document of other specific protections for civil rights and liberties (Rutland 1955). People in some states would not support ratification of the new Constitution without reassurance that protections would be added to the document.

At its initial session in New York City in 1789, the First Congress submitted twelve constitutional amendments to the states for ratification. The amendments were intended to reassure the citizenry that they retained civil rights and liberties that could not be infringed upon or abolished by the national government. Limitations on national government powers were also intended to reassure the states that their powers would not become subsumed by those of the federal government. Ten of the twelve proposed amendments were ratified by the states. Two proposed amendments concerning the apportionment of representation in Congress and the compensation for members of Congress were not ratified at that time, although the latter amendment was ratified more than two hundred years later. New Jersey became the first state to ratify the ten new amendments to the Constitution on November 20, 1789. By December of 1791, eleven states had ratified the amendments and thereby fulfilled the requirement that three-fourths of the states ratify an amendment before it can take effect.

These first ten amendments to the Constitution are collectively known as the Bill of Rights. The first eight of these amendments list specific rights possessed by people in the United States. Many of the rights listed in the Bill of Rights are quite familiar to twentieth-century Americans. People know that they are supposed to possess freedom of speech, freedom of religion, freedom of the press, and other rights contained in the first eight constitutional amendments. However, the words in the Bill of Rights describing protections for civil rights and liberties have never been self-executing or free from ambiguity. The Fourth Amendment, for example, says that there shall be a "right of the people to be secure in their persons, houses, papers, and effects against unreasonable searches and seizures." It is not clear from the words, however, which searches are "unreasonable." Moreover, the words themselves do not indicate how a statement of rights, which is essentially merely words on paper, will prevent police officers or other government officials from doing whatever it is that they wish to do. Twentieth-century Americans have come to rely on the United States Supreme Court and other courts to define and enforce constitutional rights, but for much of American history the judiciary did not take an active role in such tasks.

After the American colonists' Declaration of Independence from Great Britain in 1776 and subsequent Revolutionary War, the newly independent American states attempted to govern themselves through a document called the Articles of Confederation. The Articles of Confederation established a weak national government that depended on the cooperation of the various states for economic and military matters. Because each state retained the primary power to govern itself, there were frequent disagreements among the states. Their failure to cooperate fully with each other made the new nation economically and militarily vulnerable. Thus the Constitution was intended to remedy the defects in the Articles of Confederation by providing an effective basis for a strong, cohesive national government. It was initially an experimental document.

In the first few decades after the ratification of the Constitution, the nation and its institutions were preoccupied with a variety of problems. Because the young country faced so many questions about the nature and survival of its governing system, as well as continuing threats to its survival from Great Britain, as evidenced by the War of 1812, relatively little attention was directed at the Bill of Rights. In the relatively few cases that it decided each term during the country's first decades, the Supreme Court's most important decisions concerned the definition of both the national government's power and the roles that governing institutions and states were to play under the constitutional system. The early Supreme Court played an important role in translating the Constitution's words into meaningful definitions of institutional relationships and governmental power that would create a strong and stable national government. Under the leadership of the fourth Chief Justice, John Marshall, the Supreme Court's important early decisions established the power of judicial review (*Marbury v. Madison*, 1803), endorsed broad legislative powers for Congress (*McCulloch v. Maryland*, 1819; *Gibbons v. Ogden*, 1824), and confirmed the primacy of the U.S. Supreme Court over state judicial institutions (*Cohens v. Virginia*, 1821). John Marshall and his colleagues on the high court did not turn their attention to the underlying purposes of the Bill of Rights until 1833. In deciding the case concerning John Barron's wharf, Marshall and the other justices established an initial definition of the scope of the Bill of Rights that would last for nearly a century.

John Barron's wharf, which provided his livelihood as an excellent place for ships to load and unload goods, was rendered useless as a result of road construction by the City of Baltimore. During the course of constructing roads, the city diverted several streams, which ultimately deposited sand and gravel in the harbor at Barron's wharf. The sand and gravel accumulated in the water until the water at the wharf was no longer deep enough to permit ships to dock. Barron filed an action against Baltimore claiming that the city's destruction of his wharf's usability violated the Fifth Amendment's prohibition against the taking of private property for public use without just compensation. Barron took his claim to the U.S. Supreme Court after Maryland's appellate court overturned his initial victory in the state trial court.

On behalf of a unanimous Supreme Court, Chief Justice Marshall rejected Barron's claim (*Barron v. Baltimore*, 1833). Marshall and the other justices concluded that the Bill of Rights was intended to protect citizens against actions by the federal government only. According to Marshall, "Each state established a constitution for itself, and, in that constitution, provided such limitations and restrictions on the power of its particular government as its judgment dictated" (7 Peters at 247). The rights contained in each state's constitution protected citizens against actions by that state, and the rights contained in the federal constitution protected citizens against actions by the federal government. Marshall argued that Congress would have explicitly indicated that the Bill of Rights applied to the states if that had been the purpose of the amendments: "Had [C]ongress engaged in the extraordinary occupation of improving the constitutions of the several states by affording the people additional protection from the exercise of power by their own governments in matters which concerned themselves alone, they would have declared this purpose in plain and intelligible language" (7 Peters at 250). Thus Barron could not use a federal constitutional right contained in the Bill of Rights as the basis for an action against a city or state government.

Barron v. Baltimore

32 U.S. (7 Peters) 243, 8 L. Ed. 672 (1833)

■ Barron initiated an action against the city in which he claimed that the loss of his business due to the city's street construction constituted a violation of his Fifth Amendment right to receive just compensation for property taken for public use. A Baltimore county court found in Barron's favor and awarded him $4,500. The Maryland Court of Appeals, however, reversed the judgment of the county court. Subsequently, Barron brought his case to the U.S. Supreme Court.

This case is important because it was the first case in which the Supreme Court determined whether the Bill of Rights applied against state actions. As you read the case, consider the following questions: (1) What did Chief Justice John Marshall look for in the Constitution in order to reach a decision? (2) Did Marshall have an accurate grasp of the intended purposes of the Bill of Rights? (3) After the *Barron* decision, how were people's rights protected against infringement by actions of state and local governments?

Vote:

6 justices found the city's action constitutional (Duval, Johnson, Marshall, McLean, Story, Thompson).

0 justices found the city's action unconstitutional.

[Baldwin did not participate]

Chief Justice Marshall delivered the opinion of the Court.

* * *

The plaintiff in error contends that it comes within that clause of the fifth amendment to the constitution, which inhibits the taking of private property for public use, without just compensation. He insists that this amendment, being in favour of the liberty of the citizen, ought to be so construed as to restrain the legislative power of a state, as well as that of the United States. If this proposition be untrue, the court can take no jurisdiction for the cause.

The question thus presented is, we think, of great importance, but not of much difficulty.

The constitution was ordained and established by the people of the United States for themselves, for their own government, and not for the government of the individual states. Each state established a constitution for itself, and, in that constitution, provided such limitations and restrictions on the powers of its particular government as its judgment dictated. The people of the United States framed such a government for the United States as they supposed best adapted to their situation, and best calculated to promote their interests. The powers they conferred on this government were to be exercised by itself; and the limitations on power, if expressed in general terms, are naturally, and, we think, necessarily applicable to the government created by the instrument. They are limitations of power granted in the instrument itself; not of distinct governments, framed by different persons and for different purposes.

If these propositions be correct, the fifth amendment must be understood as restraining the power of the general government, not as applicable to the states. In their several constitutions they have imposed such restrictions on their respective governments as their own wisdom suggested; such as they deemed most proper for themselves. It is a subject on which they judge exclusively, and with which others interfere no farther than they are supposed to have a common interest.

The counsel for the plaintiff in error insists that the constitution was intended to secure the people of the several states against the undue exercise of power by their respective state governments; as well as against that which might be attempted by their general government. In support of this argument he relies on the inhibitions contained in the tenth section of the first article.

We think that section affords a strong if not a conclusive argument in support of the opinion already indicated by the court.

The preceding section contains restrictions which are obviously intended for the exclusive purpose of restraining the exercise of power by the departments of the general government. Some of them use language applicable only to congress; others are expressed in general terms. The third clause, for example, declares that "no bill of attainder or ex post facto law shall be passed." No language can be more general; yet the demonstration is complete that it applies solely to the government of the United States. . . .

* * *

Had the people of the several states, or any of them, required changes in their constitutions; had they required additional safeguards to liberty from the apprehended encroachments of their particular governments: the remedy was in their own hands, and would have been applied by themselves. A convention would have been assembled in the discontented state, and the required improvements would have been made by itself. The unwieldy and cumbrous machinery of procuring a recommendation from two-thirds of congress, and the assent of three-fourths of their sister states, could never have occurred to any human being as a mode of doing that which might be effected by the state itself. Had the framers of these amendments intended them to be limitations on the powers of the state governments, they would have imitated the framers of the original constitution, and have expressed that intention. Had congress engaged in the extraordinary occupation of improving the constitutions of the several states by affording the people additional protection from the exercise of power by their own governments in matters which concerned themselves alone, they would have declared this purpose in plain and intelligible language.

* * *

* * * In almost every convention by which the constitution was adopted, amendments to guard against the abuse of power were recommended. These amendments demanded security against the apprehended encroachments of the general government—not against those of the local governments.

In compliance with a sentiment thus generally expressed, to quiet fears thus extensively entertained, amendments were proposed by the required majority in congress, and adopted by the states. These amendments contain no expression indicating an intention to apply them to the state governments. This court cannot so apply them.

We are of the opinion, that the provision in the fifth amendment to the constitution, declaring that private property shall not be taken for public use without just compensation, is intended solely as a limitation on the exercise of power by the government of the United States, and is not applicable to the legislation of the states. We are therefore of the opinion that there is no repugnancy between the several acts of the general assembly of Maryland, given in evidence by the defendants at the trial of this cause, in the court of that state, and the constitution of the United States. This court, therefore, has no jurisdiction of the cause; and it is dismissed. . . .

Marshall's opinion was consistent with both the words of the Bill of Rights and the intentions of the drafters of the first ten amendments. The first words of the First Amendment are "Congress shall make no law. . . ," thereby indicating that the Amendment's protections for freedom of speech, freedom of religion, and freedom of the press are directed against the federal government alone. None of the other amendments in the Bill of Rights refer specifically to either the federal government or state governments, but they were written and ratified in conjunction with the First Amendment and share the implications of that amendment's first words. Indeed, scholars agree that the primary advocates of the Bill of Rights, including James Madison and Thomas Jefferson, clearly intended these amendments to limit the power of the federal government (Abraham 1988, p. 39).

The Supreme Court's decision effectively limited the scope of the Bill of Rights. The federal government could not violate people's rights to free speech, religion, press, and other protections, but state and local governments could impinge upon such rights unless their actions were limited by the provisions of their own state constitutions. Chief Justice Marshall's opinion did not leave Americans unprotected against violations of civil rights and liberties because many states' constitutions provided the same kinds of protections within their borders that the Bill of Rights provided against the federal government (Bodenhamer 1992). However, the scope and definition of rights varied from state to state. Thus people in some states could look longingly at specific provisions of the Bill of Rights that were absent from their state constitutions and therefore subject to abuse by local officials.

The decision in *Barron* essentially blocked the Supreme Court from its potential role as supervisor of civil rights and liberties in the states. The relative absence of Supreme Court attention to these issues reflected the high court's preoccupation with other matters during the first decades of its existence. In describing Supreme Court history, many scholars regard the period from 1790 through the end of the Civil War as an era in which the Court assumed responsibility for defining the powers of national governing institutions and the relationship between the state and federal government (Baum 1992, p. 19). The Court's attention to these issues reflected the fragility and uncertainty that accompanied the effort to institute a new system of government. The fragility of the country was well illustrated by the fact that it took a bloody civil war to settle regional differences and finally place the entire country under the control of a unified governing system. Thus constitutional history would have to wait until the next era of the Court's history when amendments to the Constitution began to change the interpretive context in which the Court examined civil rights and liberties claims.

Developments Prior to the New Deal Era

The passage of the Fourteenth Amendment provided a new basis for interpreting the meaning and applicability of the Bill of Rights. Like the other post–Civil War Amendments, the Thirteen and the Fifteenth, the Fourteenth Amendment was written at the historical moment when members of the Reconstruction Congress were concerned about protecting African Americans who were newly freed from the bonds of slavery. The Thirteenth Amendment, which abolished slavery, and the Fifteenth Amendment, which guaranteed voting rights without regard to race, color, or previous condition of servitude, were clearly intended to protect African Americans. The Fourteenth Amendment, by contrast, which was written and ratified during the same era, contains broader language and provisions that also affected people other than African Americans. The most important and controversial sentence in the Fourteenth Amendment says:

> *No State shall make or enforce any law which shall abridge the privileges or immunities of citizens of the United States; nor shall any State deprive any person of life, liberty, or property, without due process of law; nor deny to any person within its jurisdiction the equal protection of the laws.*

The amendment also granted Congress the power to enforce the provisions of the amendment, thus creating the possibility that the federal government would take responsibility for enforcing civil rights and liberties on behalf of people against the state and local governments.

The Fourteenth Amendment clearly intended to protect people against actions by states. The nature of the rights protected, however, was much less clear than the list of rights and liberties in the Bill of Rights that protected people against actions by the federal government. What were the "privileges and immunities of citizens?" What did it mean to have rights to "due process" and "equal protection?" Did these broad rights that provided protection against states effectively include any of the specific rights contained in the Bill of Rights?

Substantial scholarly disagreement exists about whether the authors of the Fourteenth Amendment intended for the amendment to apply the Bill of Rights against the states. Professor Charles Fairman, a prominent law professor in the 1940s, argued strongly that the authors of the Fourteenth Amendment did not intend for it to provide the same protections against actions by states that the Bill of Rights provided against actions by the federal government (Fairman 1949). While some commentators have endorsed Fairman's argument (e.g., Berger 1981), others, including Justice Hugo Black, have argued that the Fourteenth Amendment's drafters intended for their amendment to nationalize the specific rights and liberties specified in the Bill of Rights by applying them against all levels of government (Curtis 1986). Whatever the intentions of the Fourteenth Amendment's authors, the ultimate definition and application of constitutional provisions rests in the hands of judicial officers, especially the justices on the U.S. Supreme Court. Thus the passage of the Fourteenth Amendment did not determine which rights people possessed against the states. It merely provided the ideas and language that could generate court cases that would require the Supreme Court to wrestle with the questions involved in defining the nature and scope of civil rights and liberties.

The Fourteenth Amendment was ratified in 1868, and the first significant case to test its meaning and applicability in protecting people from actions by state governments came in *The Slaughter-House Cases* in 1873. The state of Louisiana had granted a monopoly to one company that gave it the exclusive ability to slaughter livestock in the city of New Orleans. Obviously, this legislative action had immediate adverse impacts on the businesses of the hundreds of butchers in New Orleans whose livelihood depended on their ability to slaughter animals and sell the meat. The butchers of New Orleans filed a legal action to challenge the monopoly. They argued that by granting the monopoly the state violated their basic right to operate their businesses and thereby violated the Fourteenth Amendment's prohibition against states abridging "the privileges and immunities of citizens." If the butchers prevailed, it would open the door for the possibility of interpreting the Privileges and Immunities Clause as providing specific rights against state actions, including perhaps the rights specified in the Bill of Rights. Unfortunately for the butchers, however, a five-member majority on the Supreme Court rejected their argument.

In an opinion by Justice Samuel Miller, the Supreme Court effectively nullified the Privileges and Immunities Clause as a potential vehicle for providing specific rights and liberties. Miller's opinion drew a distinction between national citizenship and state citizenship. It used this distinction to declare that the clause had no effect on states' relationships with their own citizens:

> *It is quite clear, then, that there is a citizenship of the United States, and a citizenship of a State, which are distinct from each other, and which depend upon different characteristics or circumstances in the individual. . . . The argument, however, in favor of the [butchers] rests wholly on the assumption that the citizenship is the same, and the privileges and immunities guaranteed by the clause are the same. . . . [T]he privileges and immunities relied on in the argument are those which belong to the citizens of the States as such, and . . . they are left to the State governments for security and protection, and not by this [amendment] placed under the special care of the Federal government. . . .*
> (The Slaughter–House Cases, *83 U.S. at 74, 78)*

The majority opinion effectively created an implausible interpretation of the Privileges and Immunities Clause by saying that it concerned only the rights of federal citizenship which by their very nature as federal rights could only be violated by the federal government. If the drafters of the Fourteenth Amendment actually intended for the clause to be nothing but a statement unrelated to the amendment's clear purpose of limiting *state* authority, why did they bother placing it into the amendment? Commentators agree that the Court's five-member majority was simply unwilling to use a broad, ambiguous phrase in the Constitution as the basis for reordering the relationship between the federal government and the states because the country was still experiencing chaos and conflict in the aftermath of the Civil War (Abraham 1988, p. 57). If the Court had recognized the clause as granting the butchers specific constitutional rights against the states, it would have made the federal Constitution and the federal government the primary definers and enforcers of the relationships between states and their own citizens. The majority's reluctance to make such a significant change in the governing system at that moment in history is clearly reflected in the majority opinion:

> *[The butchers' argument] would constitute this court a perpetual censor upon all legislation of the States, on the civil rights of their own citizens, with authority to nullify such as it did not approve as consistent with those rights, as they existed at the time of the adoption of this amendment. . . . But when, as in the case before us, these consequences are so serious, so far-reaching and pervading, so great a departure from the structure and spirit of our institutions; when the effects to fetter and degrade the State governments by subjecting them to the control of Congress, in the exercise of powers heretofore universally conceded to them of the most ordinary and fundamental character; when the fact it radically changes the whole theory of the relations of the State and Federal governments to each other and of both these governments to the people; the argument [against the butchers' position] has a force that is irresistible, in the absence of language [in the amendment] which expresses such a purpose too clearly to admit of doubt.* (The Slaughter–House Cases, *83 U.S. at 78)*

By embodying the majority's fears about the potential implications of the butchers' argument, Miller's opinion effectively rendered the Privileges and Immunities Clause useless as a source of substantive civil rights and liberties and protections against the states. The Supreme Court has never corrected the implausible interpretation of the clause that emerged from *The Slaughter–House Cases*, so it remains unusable as a source of rights unless future justices revisit and reinterpret this provision of the Constitution.

Among the dissenters, Justice Stephen Field's opinion was focused narrowly at recognizing "the right to pursue lawful employment in a lawful manner" rather than premised on a broadening of civil rights and liberties generally (Abraham 1988, p. 60). By contrast, Justice Joseph Bradley's dissenting opinion argued that "it was the intention of the people of this country in adopting [the Fourteenth] [A]mendment to provide National security against violation by the States of the fundamental rights of the citizen" (*The Slaughter–House Cases*, 83 U.S. at 122). Bradley's opinion broached the subject that would later become the focus of debates among justices and scholars about whether the Fourteenth Amendment applied the provisions of the Bill of Rights against the states.

Despite the legal defeat experienced by the New Orleans butchers, the division of opinion among the Supreme Court's justices clearly indicated that many people believed that the Fourteenth Amendment should provide specific protections against actions by state and local governments. In 1884, the Supreme Court considered another case that raised the issue of the Fourteenth Amendment's meaning for civil rights and liberties (*Hurtado v. California*, 1884). A man convicted of murder in California objected to that state's use of an information instead of an indictment to initiate a criminal prosecution. The prosecutor in the case had simply filed an information, a statement asserting facts and charges against the defendant, in order to initiate the murder case. After being convicted of the murder charge, the defendant claimed that California should be obligated to follow the Fifth Amendment's requirement of indictment by a grand jury before initiating a serious criminal charge. He argued that the Fifth Amendment's declaration that "No person shall be held to answer for a capital, or otherwise infamous crime, unless on a presentment of a grand jury" should be made applicable to the state of California through the Due Process and Privileges and Immunities Clauses of the Fourteenth Amendment.

By a seven-to-one vote, the Supreme Court rejected the argument. Justice Stanley Matthew's majority opinion noted that the Fifth Amendment contains a Due Process Clause *and* a specific grand jury requirement, and therefore reasoned that the Fourteenth Amendment's Due Process Clause could not encompass the grand jury requirement that is stated separately in the Fifth Amendment. The majority opinion did not preclude the possibility that the Due Process Clause of the Fourteenth Amendment might be used to prevent state infringement of rights contained in the Bill of Rights. According to the majority, the Fourteenth Amendment's Due Process Clause prevented violations by states of "those fundamental principles of liberty and justice which lie at the base of all our civil and political institutions" (*Hurtado v. California*, 110 U.S. at 535). The justices in the majority did not, however, explain which rights were considered "fundamental principles" and therefore protected under the Due Process Clause of the Fourteenth Amendment.

The lone dissenter, Justice John Harlan, whose grandson and namesake would later serve on the Supreme Court when it decided *Duncan v. Louisiana* (1968), forcefully articulated the argument that the Due Process Clause of the Fourteenth Amendment incorporated all of the specific rights from the Bill of Rights and applied them against the states. According to Harlan: "The Fourteenth Amendment . . . evinces a purpose to impose upon the States the same restrictions, in respect of proceedings involving life, liberty and property, which had been imposed upon the general government. 'Due process of law,' within the meaning of the national Constitution, does not import one thing with reference to the powers of the States, and another with reference to the powers of the general government" (*Hurtado v. California*, 110 U.S. at 541).

Hurtado v. California

110 U.S. 516 (1884)

■ The District Attorney in Sacramento County, California, filed an information against Joseph Hurtado charging Hurtado with the murder of Jose Antonio Stuardo. Based on this information and without any presentation of evidence to a grand jury, Hurtado was arraigned on the murder charge. After a jury trial, Hurtado was convicted of first-degree murder and sentenced to death. The California Supreme Court affirmed the conviction. At a hearing to set the date for the execution, Hurtado's attorney argued that the prosecution's procedures had violated the defendant's right to indictment by a grand jury under the Fifth Amendment and as applied to the states by the Fourteenth Amendment. The Superior Court of Sacramento County rejected this argument and a subsequent appeal to the California Supreme Court resulted in the conviction being affirmed once again. Hurtado then brought his case to the U.S. Supreme Court.

This case is important because it illustrates the nineteenth-century Supreme Court's view of the scope of rights provided against state and local government action by the Fourteenth Amendment. As you read the case, consider the following questions: (1) What interpretive approach does the Court employ to define the concept of "due process of law?" (2) What is the Court's definition of "due process of law?" (3) Under the Court's view, what rights might be protected against state infringement by the Fourteenth Amendment's Due Process Clause?

Vote:

7 justices found California's procedures constitutional (Blatchford, Bradley, Gray, Matthews, Miller, Waite, Woods).

1 justice found California's procedures unconstitutional (Harlan).

[Field did not participate]

Justice Matthews delivered the opinion of the Court.

It is claimed on behalf of the prisoner that the conviction and sentence are void, on the ground that they are repugnant to that clause of the Fourteenth Article of Amendment of the Constitution of the United States which is in these words:

"Nor shall any state deprive any person of life, liberty, or property without due process of law."

The proposition of law we are asked to affirm is that an indictment or presentment by a grand jury, as known to the common law of England, is essential to that "due process of law," when applied to prosecutions for felonies, which is secured and guaranteed by this provision of the Constitution of the United States, and which accordingly it is forbidden to the States respectively to dispense with in the administration of criminal law.

The question is one of grave and serious import, affecting both private and public rights and interests of great magnitude, and involves consideration of what additional restrictions upon the legislative policy of the States has been imposed by the Fourteenth Amendment to the Constitution of the United States.

* * *

. . . [I]t is maintained on behalf of the plaintiff in error that the phrase "due process of law" is equivalent to "law of the land," as found in the 29th chapter of Magna Charta; that by immemorial usage it has acquired a fixed, definite, and technical meaning; that it refers to and includes, not only the general principles of public liberty and private right, which lie at the foundation of all free government, but the very institutions which, venerable by time and custom, have been tried by experience and found fit and necessary for the preservation of these principles, and which, having been the birthright and inheritance of every English subject, crossed the Atlantic with the colonists and were transplanted and established in the fundamental laws of the State; that, having been originally introduced into the Constitution of the United States as a limitation upon the powers of the government, brought into being by that instrument, it has now been added as an additional security to the individual against oppression by the States themselves; that one of these institutions is that of the grand jury, an indictment or presentment by which against the accused in cases of alleged felonies is an essential part of due process of law, in order that he may not be harassed or destroyed by prosecutions founded only upon private malice or popular fury.

* * *

It is urged upon us, however, in argument, that the claim made in behalf of the plaintiff in error is supported by the decision of this court in *Murray's Lessee v. Hoboken Land & Improvement Company*, 18 How. 272. There Mr. Justice Curtis, delivering the opinion of the court, after showing, p. 276, that due process of law must mean something more than the actual existing law of the land, for otherwise it would be no restraint upon legislative power, proceeds as follows:

> To what principle, then, are we to resort to ascertain whether this process, enacted by Congress, is due process? To this the answer must be twofold. We must examine the Constitution itself to see whether this process be in conflict with any of its provisions. If not found to be so, we must look to those settled usages and modes of proceeding existing in the common and statute law of England before the emigration of our ancestors, and which are shown not to have been unsuited to their civil and political condition by having been acted on by them after the settlement of this country.

This, it is argued, furnishes an indispensable test of what constitutes "due process of law;" that any proceeding otherwise authorized by law, which is not thus sanctioned by usage, or which supersedes and displaces one that is, cannot be regarded as due process of law.

But this inference is unwarranted. The real syllabus of the passage quoted is, that a process of law, which is not otherwise forbidden, must be taken to be due process of law, if it can show the sanction of settled usage both in England and in this country; but it by no means follows that nothing else can be due process of law. The point in the case cited arose in reference to a summary proceeding, questioned on that account, as not due process of law. The answer was: however exceptional it may be, as tested by definitions and principles of ordinary procedure nevertheless, this, in substance, has been immemorially the actual law of the land, and, therefore is due process of law. But to hold that such a characteristic is essential to due process of law, would be to deny every quality of law but its age, and to render it incapable of progress or improvement. It would be to stamp upon our jurisprudence the unchangeableness attributed to the laws of the Medes and Persians.

* * *

* * * There is nothing in the Magna Charta, rightly construed as a broad charter of public right and law, which ought to exclude the best ideas of all systems and of every age; and as it was the characteristic principle of the common law to draw its inspiration from every fountain of justice, we are not

to assume that the sources of its supply have been exhausted. On the contrary, we should expect that the new and various experiences of our own situation and system will mould and shape it into new and not less useful forms.

* * *

... [The Fifth Amendment] makes specific and express provision for perpetuating the grand jury, so far as it relates to prosecutions for the more aggravated crimes under the laws of the United States. It declares:

> No person shall be held to answer for a capital or otherwise infamous crime, unless on a presentment or indictment of a grand jury, except in cases arising in the land or naval forces, or in the militia when in actual service in time of war or public danger; nor shall any person be subject for the same offence to be twice put in jeopardy of life or limb; nor shall he be compelled in any criminal case to be a witness against himself." (It then immediately adds): "Nor be deprived of life, liberty, or property, without due process of law."

According to a recognized canon of interpretation, especially applicable to formal and solemn instruments of constitutional law, we are forbidden to assume, without clear reason to the contrary, that any part of this most important amendment is superfluous. The natural and obvious inference is, that in the sense of the Constitution, "due process of law" was not meant or intended to include, *ex vi termini* [from or by the force of the term], the institution and procedure of a grand jury in any case. The conclusion is equally irresistible, that when the same phrase was employed in the Fourteenth Amendment to restrain the action of the States, it was used in the same sense and with no greater extent; and that if in the adoption of that amendment it had been part of its purpose to perpetuate the institution of the grand jury in all the States, it would have embodied, as did the Fifth Amendment, express declarations to that effect. Due process of law in the latter refers to that law of the land which derives its authority from the legislative powers conferred upon Congress by the Constitution of the United States, exercised within the limits therein prescribed, and interpreted according to the principles of common law. In the Fourteenth Amendment, by parity of reason, it refers to that law of the land in each State, which derives its authority from the inherent and reserved powers of the State, exerted within the limits of those fundamental principles of liberty and justice which lie at the base of all our civil and political institutions, and the greatest security for which resides in the right of the people to make their own laws, and alter them at their pleasure.

* * *

Tried by these principles, we are unable to say that the substitution for a presentment or indictment of a grand jury of the proceeding by information, after examination and commitment by a magistrate, certifying to the probable guilt of the defendant, with the right on his part to the aid of counsel, and to the cross-examination of the witnesses produced for the prosecution, is not due process of law. It is, as we have seen, an ancient proceeding at common law, which might include every case of an offence of less grade than a felony, except misprision of treason; and in every circumstance of its administration, as authorized by the statute of California, it carefully considers and guards the substantial interest of the prisoner. It is merely a preliminary proceeding, and can result in no final judgment, except as the consequence of a regular judicial trial, conducted precisely as in cases of indictments.

* * *

For these reasons, finding no error therein, the judgment of the Supreme Court of California is *affirmed.*

Justice Harlan, dissenting.

* * *

[The American people] desired a fuller and broader enunciation of the fundamental principles of freedom, and therefore demanded that the guaranties of the rights of life, liberty, and property, which experience had proved to be essential to the safety and security of the people, should be placed beyond all danger of impairment or destruction by the general government through legislation by Congress. They perceived no reason why, in respect of those rights, the same limitations should not be imposed upon the general government that had been imposed upon the States by their own Constitutions. Hence the prompt adoption of the original amendments, by the Fifth of which it is, among other things, provided that "no person shall be deprived of life, liberty, or property, without due process of law." This language is similar to that of the clause of the Fourteenth Amendment now under examination. That similarity was not accidental, but evinces a purpose to impose upon the States the same restrictions, in respect of proceedings involving life, liberty, and property, which had been imposed upon the general government.

"Due process of law," within the meaning of the national Constitution, does not import one thing with reference to the powers of the States, and another with reference to the powers of the general government. If particular proceedings conducted under the authority of the general government, and involving life, are prohibited, because not constituting that due process of law required by the Fifth Amendment of the Constitution of the United States, similar proceedings, conducted under the authority of a State, must be deemed illegal as not being due process of law within the meaning of the Fourteenth Amendment. . . .

* * *

It seems to me that too much stress is put upon the fact that the framers of the Constitution made express provision for the security of those rights which at common law were protected by the requirement of due process of law, and, in addition, declared, generally, that no person shall "be deprived of life, liberty or property without due process of law." The rights, for the security of which these express provisions were made, were of a character so essential to the safety of the people that it was deemed wise to avoid the possibility that Congress, in regulating the processes of law, would impair or destroy them. Hence, their specific enumeration in the earlier amendments of the Constitution, in connection with the general requirement of due process of law, the latter itself being broad enough to cover every right of life, liberty or property secured by the settled usages and modes of proceeding existing under the common and statute law of England at the time our government was founded.

* * *

It is said by the court that the Constitution of the United States was made for an undefined and expanding future, and that its requirement of due process of law in proceedings involving life, liberty, and property, must be so interpreted as not to deny to the law the capacity of progress and improvement; that the greatest security for the fundamental principles of justice resides in the right of the people to make their own laws and alter them at pleasure. It is difficult, however, to perceive anything in the system of prosecuting human beings for their lives, by information, which suggests that the State which adopts it has entered upon an era of progress and improvement in the law of criminal procedure. . . . Thus, in California, nothing stands between the citizen and prosecution for his life, except the judgment of a justice of the peace. . . . In the secrecy of the investigations by grand juries, the weak and helpless—proscribed, perhaps, because of their race, or pursued by an unreasoning public clamor—have found, and will continue to find, security against official oppression, the cruelty of mobs, the machinations of falsehold, and malevolence of private persons who would use the machinery of law to bring ruin upon their personal enemies. . . .

* * *

Now, it is a fact of momentous interest in this discussion, that, when the Fourteenth Amendment was submitted and adopted, the Bill of Rights and the constitutions of twenty-seven States expressly forbade criminal prosecutions, by information, for capital cases; while, in the remaining ten States, they were impliedly forbidden by a general clause declaring that no person should be deprived of life otherwise than by "the judgment of his peers or the law of the land," or "without due process of law." It may be safely affirmed that, when that Amendment was adopted, a criminal prosecution, by information, for a crime involving life, was not permitted in any one of the States composing the Union. So that the court, while conceding that the requirement of due process of law protects the fundamental principles of liberty and justice, adjudges, in effect, that an immunity or right, recognized at the common law to be essential to personal security, jealously guarded by our national Constitution against violation by any tribunal or body exercising authority under the general government, and expressly or impliedly recognized, *when the Fourteenth Amendment was adopted*, in the Bill of Rights or Constitution of every State in the Union, is, yet, not a fundamental principle in governments established, as those of the States of the Union are, to secure to the citizen liberty and justice, and, therefore, is not involved in that due process of law required in proceedings conducted under the sanction of a State. My sense of duty constrains me to dissent from this interpretation of the supreme law of the land.

In 1897, the Supreme Court moved in a different direction in a case concerning economic rights and property. As the city of Chicago used its power of eminent domain to acquire property, the Chicago, Burlington & Quincy Railroad believed that it was not receiving just compensation for its property that the city had acquired. The railroad company, in effect, made the same claim that Mr. Barron had made against Baltimore six decades earlier, except that the railroad company could rely on the Due Process Clause of the Fourteenth Amendment that was enacted in the intervening years and was directed specifically against actions by state and local governments. A potential problem for the railroad company's argument was the fact that the Due Process Clause of the Fifth Amendment directed against the federal government and the Due Process Clause of the Fourteenth Amendment directed against state governments are not identical. The Fifth Amendment says, in part, "No person shall . . . be deprived of life, liberty, or property, without due process of law; nor shall private property be taken for public use without just compensation." Thus the Fifth Amendment explicitly grants a right of just compensation against action by the federal government. By contrast, the relevant portion of the Fourteenth Amendment says only "nor shall any State deprive any person of life, liberty, or property, without due process of law." The absence of any statement in the Fourteenth Amendment concerning just compensation for property provided the opportunity for the Supreme Court to deny the railroad's claim and thereby continue its line of decisions declining to give substantive meaning to the provisions of the Fourteenth Amendment. Instead, the Court decided in favor of the railroad (*Chicago, Burlington & Quincy Railroad v. Chicago*, 1897).

Despite the absence of "just compensation" language in the Fourteenth Amendment, the Court decided to treat the Due Process Clause of the Fourteenth Amendment as incorporating the just compensation right contained in the Fifth Amendment. In a unanimous decision, Justice Harlan had the opportunity to advance his argument about the applicability of the Bill of Rights through the Due Process Clause of the Fourteenth Amendment. Why did the other justices agree to protect the railroad's property rights through the Due Process Clause of the Fourteenth Amendment when they had declined to use that Clause to recognize civil rights and liberties for individuals? Most of the justices on the Supreme Court during that era were especially sympathetic to the claims of businesses concerning economic and property rights. As Archibald Cox has noted, "Nineteenth- and early-twentieth-century lawyers lived almost entirely in the world of business, finance, and property. It is unlikely that many of them could as judges wholly slough off the premises of their earlier years of private practice" (Cox 1987, p. 135). The decision was also consistent with the Supreme Court's focus during the late nineteenth century and early twentieth century. Scholars regard the Court as having been preoccupied with issues concerning economic rights and social welfare legislation during the period of 1865 to 1937 (Baum 1992, p. 21). The Court's attention to these issues reflected the new kinds of problems the country faced during the period of rapid social change due to such forces as industrialization, urbanization, and immigration.

The Supreme Court's recognition of the Fourteenth Amendment's Due Process Clause as a source for economic and property rights did not immediately evolve into a broader use of the clause for recognizing civil rights and liberties. In a 1908 decision, a defendant in a criminal case claimed that the Fifth Amendment right against self-incrimination should apply to the states through the Fourteenth Amendment's Due Process Clause (*Twining v. New Jersey*, 1908). Although Harlan's position remained perfectly consistent as the lone dissenter advocating the incorporation of the entire Bill of Rights into the Fourteenth Amendment's Due Process Clause, the other justices rejected the defendant's argument. Justice William Moody's majority opinion decided that the requirements of due process are met when "a court of justice which has jurisdiction acts, not arbitrarily but in conformity with a general law, upon evidence, and after inquiry made with notice to the parties affected and opportunity to be heard" (*Twining v. New Jersey*, 211 U.S. at 111). Thus specific aspects of criminal proceedings, such as self-incrimination, the use of informations rather than indictments, and trial by jury, were not considered necessary elements of due process because they were not judged to be "immutable principle[s] of justice which [are] the inalienable possession of every citizen of a free government" (211 U.S. at 113). Although the Court rejected the defendant's claim, it opened the door to the possibility of incorporating various rights from the Bill of Rights into the Fourteenth Amendment's Due Process Clause by stating that "it is possible that some of the personal rights safeguarded by the first eight Amendments against National action may also be safeguarded against state action, because a denial of them would be a denial of due process of law" (211 U.S. at 99).

The breakthrough case for the incorporation of civil rights and liberties into the Due Process Clause of the Fourteenth Amendment came in 1925 (*Gitlow v. New York*, 1925). Benjamin Gitlow, a Communist who was active in the Socialist Party, was convicted of violating New York's Criminal Anarchy Act of 1902 when he published pamphlets entitled the "Left Wing Manifesto" and "The Revolutionary Age." Gitlow's "Manifesto" included a call for revolution: "The proletariat revolution and the Communist reconstruction of society—*the struggle for these*—is now indispensable. . . . The Communist International calls the proletariat of the world to the final struggle!" (*Gitlow v. New York*, 268 U.S. at 660 n. 3). Gitlow received a prison sentence for his writings that advocated the overthrow of the American governmental and economic systems. He argued that his conviction violated the First Amendment right of free speech that should be applied against the states through the Fourteenth Amendment's Due Process Clause.

In a six-to-two decision, the Supreme Court upheld Gitlow's conviction because they regarded his writings as "language of direct incitement" that was not protected by freedom of speech. However, in a single conclusory sentence unsupported by analysis or discussion, the majority opinion written by Justice Edward Sanford declared that specific provisions of the First Amendment had been incorporated into the Due Process Clause of the Fourteenth Amendment and therefore applied against actions by state and local governments: "For present purposes we may add and do assume that freedom of speech and of the press—which are protected by the First Amendment from abridgement by Congress—are among the fundamental personal rights and 'liberties' protected by the due process clause of the Fourteenth Amendment from impairment by the states" (268 U.S. at 666).

Gitlow v. New York

268 U.S. 652 (1925)

Benjamin Gitlow was prosecuted under New York's Criminal Anarchy Act that made it illegal for anyone to advocate, advise, or teach the duty, necessity, or propriety of overthrowing the government. During his trial in state court, his attorney argued that New York's statute violated the Due Process Clause of the Fourteenth Amendment. The trial court rejected the argument and denied Gitlow's requests to dismiss the charges against him. Gitlow was convicted of the charges against him and sentenced to imprisonment. On appeal, both the Appellate Division of the New York Supreme Court and the New York Court of Appeals, the state's court of last resort, held the statute to be constitutional. After losing his appeals in the state courts, Gitlow brought his case to the U.S. Supreme Court.

The case is important because it represents the first time that the U.S. Supreme Court applied a personal right, the First Amendment right to freedom of speech, against a state through the Due Process Clause of the Fourteenth Amendment. As you read the case, consider the following questions: (1) Does Justice Sutherland's opinion explain the reasoning for applying freedom of speech against the states through the Due Process Clause? (2) How many rights does Justice Sutherland say are applied to the states through the Due Process Clause? (3) What happens to Gitlow and why does it happen?

Vote:

7 justices found the statute constitutional (Butler, McReynolds, Sanford, Stone, Sutherland, Taft, Van Devanter).

2 justices found the statute unconstitutional (Brandeis, Holmes).

Justice Sutherland delivered the opinion of the Court.

* * *

The indictment . . . charged that the defendant has advocated, advised and taught the duty, necessity and propriety of overthrowing and overturning organized government by force, violence and unlawful means, by certain writings therein set forth entitled "The Left Wing Manifesto"; [and] that he had printed, published, and knowingly circulated and distributed a certain paper called "The Revolutionary Age," containing the writings set forth in the first count. . . .

* * * Sixteen thousand copies were printed, which were delivered at the premises in New York City used as the office of the Revolutionary Age and the headquarters of the Left Wing, and occupied by the defendant and other officials. These copies were paid for by the defendant, as business manager of the paper. Employees at this office wrapped and mailed copies of the paper under the defendant's direction. . . .

There was no evidence of any effect resulting from the publication and circulation of the Manifesto.

* * *

* * * The sole contention here is, essentially, that as there was no evidence of any concrete result flowing from the publication of the Manifesto or of circumstances showing the likelihood of such result, the statute as construed and applied by the trial court penalizes the mere utterance, as such, of "doctrine", having no quality of incitement, without regard either to the circumstances of the utterance or to the likelihood of unlawful sequences; and that as the exercise of the right of free expression with relation to government is only punishable "in circumstances involving the likelihood of substantive evil," the statute contravenes the due process clause of the Fourteenth Amendment. . . .

The precise question presented, and the only question which we can consider under this writ of error, then is, whether the statute, as construed and applied in this case by the state courts, deprived the defendant of his liberty of expression in violation of the due process clause of the Fourteenth Amendment.

* * *

The Manifesto, plainly, is neither the statement of abstract doctrine nor, as suggested by counsel, mere prediction that industrial disturbances and revolutionary mass strikes will result spontaneously in an inevitable process of evolution in the economic system. It advocates and urges in fervent language mass action which . . . through political mass strikes and revolutionary mass action overthrow and destroy organized parliamentary government. It concludes with a call to action in these words: "The proletariat revolution and the Communist reconstruction of society—*the struggle for these*—is now indispensable. . . . The Communist International calls the proletariat of the world to the final struggle!" This is not the expression of philosophical abstraction, the mere prediction of future events; it is the language of direct incitement.

* * *

For present purposes we may and do assume that freedom of speech and of the press—which are protected by the First Amendment from abridgment by Congress—are among the fundamental personal rights and "liberties" protected by the due process clause of the Fourteenth Amendment from impairment by the States. We do not regard the incidental statement in *Prudential Insurance Company v. Cheek*, 259 U.S. 530, 543, that the Fourteenth Amendment imposes no restrictions on the States concerning freedom of speech, as determinative of this question.

It is a fundamental principle, long established, that the freedom of speech and of the press which is secured by the Constitution, does not confer an absolute right to speak or publish, without responsibility, whatever one may choose, or an unrestricted and unbridled license that gives immunity for every possible use of language and prevents the punishment of those who abuse this freedom. . . .

* * *

* * * Freedom of speech and press . . . does not protect publications prompting the overthrow of government by force; the punishment of those who publish articles which tend to destroy organized society being essential to the security of freedom and stability of the State. . . . And a State may penalize utterances which openly advocate the overthrow of the representative and constitutional form of government of the United States and the several States, by violence or other unlawful means. . . .

By enacting the present statute the State has determined, through its legislative body, that utterances advocating the overthrow of organized government by force, violence and unlawful means, are so inimical to the general welfare and involve such danger of substantive evil that they may be penalized in the exercise of its police power. That determination must be given great weight. Every presumption is to be indulged in favor of the validity of the statute. . . . That utterances inciting to overthrow the organized government by unlawful means, present a sufficient danger of substantive evil to bring their punishment within the range of legislative discretion, is clear. Such utterances, by their very nature, involve danger to the public peace and to the security of the State. They threaten breaches of the peace and ultimate revolution. And the immediate danger is none the less real and substantial, because the effect of a given utterance cannot be accurately foreseen. The State cannot reasonably be required to measure the danger from every such utterance in the nice balance of a jeweler's scale. A single revolutionary spark may kindle a fire that, smouldering for a time, may burst into a sweeping and destructive conflagration. It cannot reasonably be required to defer the adoption of measures for its own peace and safety until the revolutionary utterances lead to actual disturbances of the public peace or imminent and immediate danger of its own destruction; but it may, in the exercise of its judgment, suppress the threatened danger in it incipiency. . . .

We cannot hold that the present statute is an arbitrary or unreasonable exercise of the police power of the State unwarrantably infringing the freedom of speech or press; and we must and do sustain its constitutionality.

* * *

And finding, for the reasons stated, that the statute is not in itself unconstitutional, and that it has not been applied in the present case in derogation of any constitutional right, the judgment of the Court of Appeals is *Affirmed.*

Justice Holmes, dissenting.

Mr. Justice Brandeis and I are of opinion that this judgment should be reversed. The general principle of free speech, it seems to me, must be taken to be included in the Fourteenth Amendment, in view of the scope that has been given to the word "liberty" as there used, although perhaps it may be accepted with a somewhat larger latitude of interpretation than is allowed to Congress by the sweeping language that governs or ought to govern the laws of the United States. If I am right, then I think that the criterion sanctioned by the full Court in *Schenck v. United States*, 249 U.S. 47, 52, applies. "The question in every case is whether the words are used in such circumstances and are of such a nature as to create a clear and present danger that they will bring about the substantive evil that [the State] has a right to prevent." It is true that in my opinion this criterion was departed from in *Abrams v. United States*, 250 U.S. 616, but the convictions that I expressed in that case are too deep for it to be possible for me as yet to believe that it and *Schaefer v. United States*, 251 U.S. 466, have settled the law. If what I think the correct test is applied, it is manifest that there was no present danger of an attempt to overthrow the government by force on the part of the admittedly small minority who shared the defendant's views. It is said that this manifesto was more than a theory, that it was an incitement. Every idea is an incitement. It offers itself for belief and if believed it is acted on unless some other belief outweighs it or some failure of energy stifles the movement at its birth. The only difference between the expression of an opinion and an incitement in the narrower sense is the speaker's enthusiasm for the result. Eloquence may set fire to reason. But whatever may be thought of the redundant discourse before us it had no chance of starting a present conflagration. If in the long run the beliefs expressed in proletarian dictatorship are destined to be accepted by the dominant forces of the community, the only meaning of free speech is that they should be given their chance and have their way.

If the publication of this document had been laid as an attempt to induce an uprising against government at once and not at some indefinite time in the future it would have presented a different question. The object would have been one with which the law might deal, subject to the doubt whether there was any danger that the publication would produce any result, or in other words, whether it was not futile and too remote from possible consequences. But the indictment alleges the publication and nothing more. ■

In judicial decisions, only the "holding" or rule of the case establishes precedent for other courts to follow. In the *Gitlow* case, the holding concerned the Supreme Court's determination that his writings contained the "language of direct incitement" and therefore were not protected by freedom of speech against prosecution under New York's law. The majority opinion's statement about the incorporation of the First Amendment for application against the states was merely "dictum" or discussion that was not binding as precedent in subsequent the cases. Thus, after the *Gitlow* decision, the question remained whether the Court would proceed with the incorporation of rights and liberties into the Due Process Clause of the Fourteenth Amendment or, as they did following the *Chicago, Burlington & Quincy Railroad* case (1897) concerning economic and property rights, swing back to a stance of declining to apply additional rights to the states.

Unlike the earlier anomalous case concerning economic rights, the *Gitlow* case actually set into motion a trend of decisions recognizing specific rights incorporated into the Due Process Clause of the Fourteenth Amendment. In *Fiske v. Kansas* (1927), the Supreme Court upheld a freedom of speech claim against a state, and in *Near v. Minnesota* (1931), the justices similarly supported a freedom of the press claim over a state statute permitting injunctions against the publication of newspapers. Thus, in the years immediately following the *Gitlow* decision, the Court's decisions endorsed and gave legal effect to Justice Sanford's dictum and thereby applied the rights to freedom of speech and press against the states.

In subsequent cases, the Court moved beyond the *Gitlow* dictum about speech and press by incorporating additional elements of the Bill of Rights into the Fourteenth Amendment's Due Process Clause. In 1932, the justices acted on behalf of seven indigent, African American youths who were falsely accused of raping two white women on a train in Alabama (*Powell v. Alabama*, 1932). The youths were convicted and sentenced to death in a quick trial without being represented by defense attorneys. According to the Court's opinion, which was supported by seven justices, the quick trial was conducted in a community environment so hostile and threatening to the defendants that "[t]he sheriff thought it necessary to call for the militia to assist safeguarding the prisoners" (287 U.S. at 51). The Court directly addressed the issue of whether the defendants' rights were violated under the Due Process Clause of the Fourteenth Amendment and concluded that the Due Process Clause includes the right to a fair trial and the right to counsel in capital cases. Although the right to counsel provision of the Sixth Amendment, which was previously limited to federal criminal cases, had meant only that defendants must have the opportunity to obtain an attorney if they could afford one, Justice George Sutherland's majority opinion carried the right even farther when applying it to the states: "[U]nder the circumstances [of a death penalty charge against illiterate youths]. . . , the necessity of counsel was so vital and imperative that the failure of the trial court to make an effective appointment of counsel was likewise a denial of due process within the meaning of the Fourteenth Amendment" (287 U.S. at 71). Although the Court's previous incorporation cases had been limited to freedom of speech and press and to economic rights, the justices had now expanded the applicability of the Bill of Rights to the states by incorporating Sixth Amendment rights for criminal defendants. Thus they opened the possibility that additional guarantees, and perhaps even all of the rights in the Bill of Rights, would apply to the states.

The Court's decision on the right to counsel in capital cases made clear that the justices continued to undertake a **selective incorporation** approach to defining the rights embodied in the Due Process Clause of the Fourteenth Amendment. As new cases raised arguments about specific sections of the Bill of Rights that ought to be recognized as incorporated into the Due Process Clause, the Court selectively considered individual rights one at a time to determine whether they should apply to the states.

The New Deal until the Warren Court

As the Court began the gradual process of designating rights for incorporation, the justices had not yet made clear why certain rights were chosen for incorporation while other rights continued to apply only against the federal government. The Court applied two additional rights against the states, freedom of religion (*Hamilton v. Regents of the University of California*, 1934) and freedom of assembly (*DeJonge v. Oregon*, 1937), before clearly articulating a test for determining which rights ought to be incorporated.

In *Palko v. Connecticut* (1937), the Court faced the issue of whether the Fifth Amendment right against double jeopardy should be incorporated into the Fourteenth Amendment's Due Process Clause and applied against the states. Palko faced the death penalty during his trial for the murders of two police officers. The jury found him guilty of second-degree murder and sentenced him to life in prison. A state appellate court granted the prosecution's request for a new trial based on errors in the trial judge's ruling on the admissibility of evidence and on instructions to the jury. After the second trial, Palko was convicted of first-degree murder and sentenced to death. Palko unsuccessfully pursued an appeal through the state courts before bringing to the U.S. Supreme Court his argument that double jeopardy ought to apply against the states through the process of incorporating components of the Bill of Rights into the Fourteenth Amendment. In fact, Palko's attorney argued that all of the rights in the Bill of Rights were applicable to the states through the Fourteenth Amendment (O'Brien 1991, p. 295).

On behalf of an eight-to-one majority, Justice Benjamin Cardozo's opinion rejected Palko's argument. Cardozo endorsed the selective incorporation process in which rights "have been taken over from the earlier articles of the Federal Bill of Rights and brought within the Fourteenth Amendment by the process of absorption" (*Palko v. Connecticut*, 302 U.S. at 326). However, the test he espoused for determining which rights should be incorporated did not, by his application, apply to the Fifth Amendment right against double jeopardy. Cardozo's formulation recognized a hierarchy of rights in which only those that are "of the very essence of a scheme of ordered liberty" would be incorporated into the Fourteenth Amendment's Due Process Clause. To illustrate the application of his approach, Cardozo applied his test to Palko's claim and concluded that Palko's Fourteenth Amendment right to due process was not violated: "Is that kind of double jeopardy to which the [state] statute has subjected him a hardship so acute and shocking that our polity will not endure it? Does it violate those 'fundamental principles of liberty and justice which lie at the base of all our civil and political institutions?' The answer surely must be 'no' " (302 U.S. at 153).

PALKO V. CONNECTICUT

302 U.S. 319 (1937)

■ Frank Palko faced the death penalty during his trial for the murders of two police officers. The jury found him guilty of second-degree murder and sentenced him to life in prison. The state's Supreme Court of Errors granted the prosecution's request for a new trial based on errors in the trial judge's ruling on the admissibility of evidence and on instructions to the jury. After the second trial, Palko was convicted of first-degree murder and sentenced to death. Palko unsuccessfully pursued an appeal through the state's Supreme Court of Errors before bringing to the U.S. Supreme Court his argument that double jeopardy ought to apply against the states through the process of incorporating components of the Bill of Rights into the Fourteenth Amendment.

This case was important because the Court's opinion articulated a test for determining which rights from the Bill of Rights should be incorporated into the Due Process Clause of the Fourteenth Amendment. As you read the case, consider the following questions: (1) What is Justice Cardozo's test for determining whether specific rights from the Bill of Rights should be incorporated? (2) Does Cardozo give any examples of rights that should or should not be incorporated? (3) What happened to Palko?

VOTE:

8 justices found the statute constitutional (Black, Brandeis, Cardozo, Hughes, McReynolds, Roberts, Stone, Sutherland).

1 justice found the statute unconstitutional (Butler).

Justice Cardozo delivered the opinion of the Court.

* * *

The argument for appellant is that whatever is forbidden by the Fifth Amendment is forbidden by the Fourteenth also. The Fifth Amendment, which is not directed to the States, but solely to the federal government, creates immunity from double jeopardy. No person shall be "subject for the same offense to be twice put in jeopardy of life or limb." The Fourteenth Amendment ordains, "nor shall any State deprive any person of life, liberty, or property, without due process of law." To retry a defendant, though under one indictment and only one, subjects him, it is said, to double jeopardy in violation of the Fifth Amendment, if the prosecution is one on behalf of the United States. From this the consequences is said to follow that there is a denial of life or liberty without due process of law, if the prosecution is one on behalf of the people of a state. . . .

* * *

We have said that in appellant's view the Fourteenth Amendment is to be taken as embodying the prohibitions of the Fifth. His thesis is even broader. Whatever would be a violation of the original bill of rights (Amendments 1 to 8) if done by the federal government is now equally unlawful by force of the Fourteenth Amendment if done by a state. There is no such general rule.

The Fifth Amendment provides, among other things, that no person shall be held to answer for a capital or otherwise infamous crime unless on presentment or indictment of a grand jury. This court has held that, in prosecutions by a state, presentment or indictment by a grand jury may give way to informations at the instance of a public officer *Hurtado v. California* [1884]. . . . The Fifth Amendment provides also that no person shall be compelled in any criminal case to be a witness against himself. This court has said that, in prosecutions by a state, the exemption will fail if the state elects to end it *Twining v. New Jersey* [1908]. . . .

On the other hand, the due process clause of the Fourteenth Amendment may make it unlawful for a state to abridge by its statutes the freedom of speech which the First Amendment safeguards against encroachment by the Congress (*DeJonge v. Oregon* [1937]). . . , or the like freedom of the press . . . (*Near v. Minnesota* [1932]), or free exercise of religion (*Hamilton v. Regents of University* [1934]). . . , or the right of peaceable assembly, without which speech would be unduly trampled (*DeJonge v. Oregon* [1937). . . , or the right of one accused of crime to the benefit of counsel (*Powell v. Alabama* [1932]). . . . In these and other situations immunities that are valid as against the federal government by force of the specific pledges in particular amendments have been found to be implicit in the concept of ordered liberty, and thus, through the Fourteenth Amendment, become valid as against the states.

The line of division may seem to be wavering or broken if there is a hasty catalogue of the cases on the one side and the other. Reflection and analysis will induce a different view. There emerges a perception of a rationalizing principle which gives to discrete instances a proper order and coherence. The right to trial by jury and immunity from prosecution except as the result of an indictment have value and importance. Even so, they are not of the very essence of a scheme of ordered liberty. To abolish them is to violate a "principle of justice so rooted in the traditions and conscience of our people as to be ranked as fundamental.". . . Few would be so narrow or provincial as to maintain that a fair and enlightened system of justice would be impossible without them. What is true of jury trials and indictments is true also, as the cases show, of the immunity from compulsory self-incrimination. . . . This too might be lost, and justice still be done. . . . No doubt there would remain the need to give protection against torture, physical and mental. . . . Justice, however, would not perish if the accused were subject to a duty to respond to orderly inquiry. The exclusion of these immunities and privileges from the privileges and immunities protected against the action of the States has not been arbitrary or casual. It has been dictated by a study and appreciation of the meaning, the essential implications, of liberty itself.

We reach a different plane of social and moral values when we pass to the privileges and immunities that have been taken over from the earlier articles of the Federal Bill of Rights and brought within the Fourteenth Amendment by the process of absorption. These in their origin were effective against the federal government alone. If the Fourteenth Amendment has absorbed them, the process of absorption has had its source in the belief that neither liberty nor justice would exist if they were sacrificed. . . . This is true, for illustration, of freedom of thought and speech. Of that freedom one may say that it is the matrix, the indispensable condition, of nearly every other form of freedom. With rare aberrations a pervasive recognition of that truth can be traced in our history, political and legal. So it has come about that the domain of liberty, withdrawn by the Fourteenth Amendment from encroachment by the states, has been enlarged by latter-day judgments to include liberty of the mind as well as liberty of action. . . . Fundamental too in the concept of due process, and so in that of liberty, is the thought that condemnation shall be rendered only after trial. . . . The hearing, moreover, must be a real one, not a sham or pretense. . . . For that reason, ignorant defendants in a capital case were held to have been condemned unlawfully when in truth, though not in form, they were refused the aid of counsel. . . . The decision did not turn upon the fact that the benefit of counsel would have been guaranteed to the defendants by the provisions of the Sixth Amendment if they had been prosecuted in a federal court. The decision turned upon the fact that in the particular situation laid before us in the evidence the benefit of counsel was essential to the substance of a hearing.

Our survey of the cases services, we think, to justify the statement that the dividing line between them, if not unfaltering throughout its course, has been true for the most part to a unifying principle. On which side of the line the case made out by the appellant has appropriate location must be the next inquiry and the final one. Is that kind of double jeopardy to which the statute has subjected him to a hardship so acute and shocking that our polity will not endure it? Does it violate those "fundamental principles of liberty and justice which lie at the base of all our civil and political institutions?". . . . The answer surely must be "no.". . . The state is not attempting to wear the accused out by a multitude of cases with accumulated trials. It asks no more than this, that the case against him shall go on until there shall be a trial free from the corrosion of substantial legal error. . . . This is not cruelty at all, nor even vexation in any immoderate degree. If the trial had been infected with error adverse to the accused, there might have been review at his instance, and as often as necessary to purge the vicious taint. A reciprocal privilege, subject at all times to the discretion of the presiding judge . . . has now been granted to the state. There is here no seismic innovation. The edifice of justice stands, its symmetry, to many, greater than before.

The conviction of the appellant is not in derogation of any privileges and immunities that belong to him as a citizen of the United States. There is an argument in his behalf that the privileges and immunities clause of the Fourteenth Amendment as well as the due process clause has been flouted by the judgment. *Maxwell v. Dow* [1900] . . . gives all the answer that is necessary.

The judgment is affirmed.

Cardozo's approach focused on whether specific rights were so fundamental that a free society could not exist without them and whether they were essential to a fair judicial process. He considered freedom of speech and of the press, which the Supreme Court had already applied to the states, as essential to a free society. By contrast, he pinpointed other rights that he did not see as "fundamental." In his mind these rights were not essential to freedom and justice: "The right to trial by jury and the immunity from prosecution except as the result of an indictment may have value and importance. Even so, they are not of the very essence of a scheme of ordered liberty. To abolish them is not to violate a 'principle of justice so rooted in the traditions and conscience of our people as to be ranked as fundamental.' What is true of jury trials and indictments is true also, as the cases show, of the immunity from compulsory self-incrimination. . . . This too might be lost, and justice still be done" (*Palko v. Connecticut*, 302 U.S. at 325). By using these examples, Cardozo, in effect, justified the Court's earlier decisions declining to incorporate the right to grand jury indictment (*Hurtado v. California*, 1884) and the right against self-incrimination (*Twining v. New Jersey*, 1908).

The *Palko* decision coincided with the Supreme Court's entry into a new historical era. Scholars cite 1937 as the time at which the Court began to shift its primary focus to civil rights and liberties cases (Baum 1992, p. 22). The Supreme Court had been locked in a battle with President Franklin Roosevelt and Congress during the 1930s. Roosevelt attempted to institute his New Deal programs through economic regulation and social welfare legislation, but the Court consistently invalidated Roosevelt's programs by declaring that they impinged upon people's economic liberties. Roosevelt responded by proposing a "court packing plan," which, if implemented, would have permitted him to appoint additional justices to the Court for each sitting justice aged seventy or older. The net effect of the plan would have been to change the balance of power on the Court in favor of Roosevelt's programs. Roosevelt's controversial court-packing proposal was never enacted, but pressure from the proposal apparently influenced Chief Justice Charles Evans Hughes and Justice Owen Roberts to change their votes and begin to support Roosevelt's programs. Shortly thereafter, Roosevelt's elderly opponents began to retire from the Court, and he had the opportunity to appoint new justices from among his political allies. The orientation and composition of the Court changed and thereby ended the conflict between the Court and the other branches of government concerning economic issues. Thereafter the Court turned its attention with increasing frequency to cases concerning civil rights and liberties.

The selective incorporation process moved slowly in the years following the *Palko* decision. The Court reiterated its view that freedom of religion applied to the states by deciding cases specifically incorporating the elements of religious freedom, namely the free exercise of religion (*Cantwell v. Connecticut*, 1940) and the separation of church and state (*Everson v. Board of Education*, 1947). The continuing influence of Cardozo's reasoning in *Palko* was demonstrated when claimants sought to have additional rights incorporated into the Due Process Clause. The incorporation process made it clear that the justices viewed the rights contained in the First Amendment (i.e., speech, press, and religion) as essential, fundamental protections in the American constitutional democracy, but they did not believe that the rights for criminal defendants were as important.

In *Adamson v. California* (1947), a claimant brought to the Supreme Court the claim that the Fifth Amendment right against self-incrimination should be incorporated into the Due Process Clause of the Fourteenth Amendment. This was the same argument that the Court had rejected in the *Twining* (1908) case nearly four decades earlier, but the Court's application of selective incorporation in *Gitlow* and other cases during the intervening years raised the possibility that the Court's view had changed. In the *Adamson* case, the prosecutor had commented on Adamson's failure to testify in his own behalf and implicitly urged the jury to consider the defendant's silence as evidence of guilt. Unfortunately for Mr. Adamson, who was convicted of murder and sentenced to death in California, a five-member majority on the Court rejected his argument by applying the "fundamental rights" test formulated by Cardozo in *Palko* . Justice Stanley Reed's majority opinion relied explicitly on the *Palko* precedent as the basis for rejecting Adamson's claim: "The due process clause of the Fourteenth Amendment, however, does not draw all the rights of the federal Bill of Rights under its protection. That contention was made and rejected in *Palko v. Connecticut*. . . . Specifically the due process clause does not protect, by virtue of its mere existence the accused's freedom from giving testimony by compulsion in state trials that is secured against federal interference by the Fifth Amendment. . . . For a state to require testimony from an accused is not necessarily a breach of a state's obligation to give a fair trial" (*Adamson v. California*, 332 U.S. at 53).

Justice Hugo Black, in a dissenting opinion joined by Justice William O. Douglas, resurrected the arguments first advanced in Justice Harlan's dissenting opinion in *Hurtado* (1884) by asserting that the entire Bill of Rights was intended to be incorporated upon ratification of the Fourteenth Amendment. Black sought to support his argument for the **total incorporation** of the Bill of Rights by attaching to his opinion a thirty-page appendix containing quotations from congressional speeches and committee reports substantiating his claims about the intentions of the Amendment's drafters. In a concurring opinion, Justice Felix Frankfurter attacked Black's total incorporation argument by noting that forty-two of the forty-three justices who ruled on incorporation cases in the first seventy years after ratification of the Fourteenth Amendment had rejected Black's argument. Frankfurter declared that the first Justice Harlan, the lone early advocate of total incorporation, "may respectfully be called an eccentric exception" (332 U.S. at 62).

In a second dissenting opinion, Justice Frank Murphy, joined by Justice Wiley Rutledge, agreed with Black's argument that the entire Bill of Rights should be incorporated into the Fourteenth Amendment. Murphy and Rutledge, however, wanted to go even farther than Black and Douglas by asserting that the Fourteenth Amendment might contain even more rights than those listed in the Bill of Rights: "I am not prepared to say that the [Fourteenth Amendment] is entirely and necessarily limited by the Bill of Rights" (332 U.S. at 124). This argument for **total incorporation plus additional rights** presented the broadest possible view of the Fourteenth Amendment's meaning for protecting individuals' civil rights and liberties from infringement by state and local governments.

ADAMSON V. CALIFORNIA

332 U.S. 46, 67 S. Ct. 1672, 91 L. Ed. 1903 (1947)

Adamson was charged with murder and faced the death penalty if convicted. Because he had prior criminal convictions on his record, he declined to testify at his own trial because, under California law, the prosecutor could have used cross-examination to make him talk about his previous crimes in front of the jury. When he declined to testify, the prosecutor and the judge were authorized under state law to comment to the jury about the defendant's silence as a possible indication of guilt. Adamson was convicted and sentenced to death. His conviction was affirmed by the California Supreme Court. He brought his case before the U.S. Supreme Court to argue that California's procedures violated his Fifth Amendment right against compelled self-incrimination which should be applied to the states through the Fourteenth Amendment's Due Process Clause.

The case was important because it demonstrated the justices' competing approaches to incorporation that were emerging as the Court's composition changed during the mid-twentieth century. As you read the case, consider the following questions: (1) What approach does Justice Reed's opinion take in deciding the incorporation issue presented in the case? (2) Does Justice Black's argument remind you of any prior justices' arguments about incorporation? (3) How does Justice Murphy's approach to incorporation differ from other approaches?

VOTE:

5 justices found the state procedures constitutional (Burton, Frankfurter, Jackson, Reed, and Vinson).

4 justices found the state procedures unconstitutional (Black, Douglas, Murphy, and Rutledge).

Justice Reed delivered the opinion of the Court.

The appellant, Adamson, a citizen of the United States, was convicted, without recommendation for mercy, by a jury in a Superior Court of the State of California. . . . The provisions of California law which were challenged in state proceedings as invalid under the Fourteenth Amendment to the Federal Constitution are those of the state constitution and penal code . . . [which] permit the failure of a defendant to explain or to deny evidence against him to be commented upon by court and by counsel and to be considered by court and jury. The defendant did not testify. . . .

. . . [I]f the defendant, after answering affirmatively charges alleging prior convictions, takes the witness stand to deny or explain away other evidence that has been introduced "the commission of these crimes could have been revealed to the jury on cross-examination to impeach his testimony.". . . This forces an accused who is a repeat offender to choose between the risk of having his prior offenses disclosed to the jury or of having it draw harmful inferences from uncontradicted evidence that can only be denied or explained by the defendant.

* * *

We shall assume, but without any intention thereby of ruling upon the issue, that state permission by law to the court, counsel and jury to comment upon and consider the failure of defendant "to explain or to deny by his testimony any evidence or facts in the case against him" would infringe defendant's privilege against self-incrimination under the Fifth Amendment if this were a trial in a [federal] court. . . . Such an assumption does not determine appellant's rights under the Fourteenth Amendment. It is settled law that the clause of the Fifth Amendment protecting a person against being compelled to be a witness against himself, is not made effective by the Fourteenth Amendment as a protection against state action on the ground that freedom from testimonial compulsion is a right of national citizenship, or because it is a personal privilege or immunity secured by the Federal Constitution as one of the rights of man that are listed in the Bill of Rights.

* * *

* * * A right to a fair trial is a right admittedly protected by the due process clause of the Fourteenth Amendment. Therefore, appellant argues, the due process clause of the Fourteenth Amendment protects his privilege against self-incrimination. The due process clause of the Fourteenth Amendment, however, does not draw all the rights of the federal Bill of Rights under its protection. That contention was made and rejected in *Palko v. Connecticut* [1937]. . . . Nothing has been called to our attention that either the framers of the Fourteenth Amendment or the states that adopted intended its due process clause to draw within its scope the earlier amendments to the Constitution. *Palko* held that such provisions of the Bill of Rights as were "implicit in the concept of ordered liberty" . . . became secure from state interference by the clause. But it held nothing more.

Specifically the due process clause does not protect by virtue of its mere existence, the accused's freedom from giving testimony by compulsion in state trials that is secured to him against federal interference by the Fifth Amendment. . . . For a state to require testimony from an accused is not necessarily a breach of a state's obligation to give a fair trial. Therefore, we must examine the effect of the California law applied in this trial to see whether the comment on failure to testify violates the protection against state action that the due process clause does grant to an accused. The due process clause forbids compulsion to testify by fear of hurt, torture or exhaustion. It forbids any other type of coercion that falls within the scope of our due process clause. . . .

Generally, comment on the failure of an accused to testify is forbidden in American jurisdictions. This arises from state constitutional or statutory provisions similar in character to the federal provisions. . . . California, however, is one of a few states that permit limited comment upon a defendant's failure to testify. That permission is narrow. The California law . . . authorizes comment by court and counsel upon the "failure of the defendant to explain or to deny by his testimony any evidence or facts in the case against him." This does not involve any presumption, rebuttable or irrebuttable, either of guilt or of the truth of any fact, that is offered in evidence. . . . It allows inferences to be drawn from proven facts. Because of this clause, the court can direct the jury's attention to whatever evidence there may be that a defendant could deny and the prosecution can argue as to inferences that may be drawn from the accused's failure to testify. . . .

* * *

It is true that if comment were forbidden an accused in this situation could remain silent and avoid evidence of former crimes and comment upon his failure to testify. We are of the view, however, that a state may control such a situation in accordance with its own ideas of the most efficient administration of criminal justice. The purpose of due process is not to protect an accused against a proper conviction but against an unfair conviction. When evidence is before a jury that threatens conviction, it does not seem unfair to require him to choose between leaving the adverse evidence unexplained and subjecting himself to impeachment through disclosure of former crimes. . . .

* * *

We find no other error that gives ground for our intervention in California's administration of justice. Affirmed.

Justice Frankfurter, concurring.

* * *

Decisions of this Court do not have equal intrinsic authority. The *Twining* case [1908] shows the judicial process at its best—comprehensive briefs and powerful arguments on both sides, followed by long deliberation, resulting in an opinion by Mr. Justice Moody which at once gained and has ever since retained recognition as one of the outstanding opinions in the history of the Court. After enjoying unquestioned prestige for 40 years, the *Twining* case should not now be diluted, even unwittingly, either in its judicial philosophy or in its particulars. As the surest way of keeping the *Twining* case intact, I would affirm this case on its authority.

* * *

* * * I am prepared to agree that, as part of that immunity [against self-incrimination in the Fifth Amendment], comment on the failure of an accused to take the witness stand is forbidden in federal prosecutions. . . . But to suggest that such a limitation can be drawn out of "due process" in its protection of ultimate decency in a civilized society is to suggest that the Due Process Clause fastened fetters of unreason upon the States. . . .

Between the incorporation of the Fourteenth Amendment into the Constitution and the beginning of the present membership of the Court—a period of 70 years—the scope of that Amendment was passed upon by 43 judges. Of all these judges, only one, who may respectfully be called an eccentric exception, ever indicated the belief the Fourteenth Amendment was a shorthand summary of the first eight Amendments theretofore limiting only the Federal Government, and that due process incorporated those eight Amendments as restrictions upon the powers of the States.

* * *

It may not be amiss to restate the pervasive function of the Fourteenth Amendment in exacting from the States the observance of basic liberties. . . . The Amendment neither comprehends the specific provisions by which the founders deemed it appropriate to restrict the federal government nor is it confined to them. The Due Process Clause of the Fourteenth Amendment has an independent potency, precisely as does the Due Process Clause of the Fifth Amendment in relation to the Federal Government. It ought not to require argument to reject the notion that due process of law meant one thing in the Fifth Amendment and another in the Fourteenth. . . .

* * *

Justice Murphy, dissenting (joined by Justice Rutledge).

While in substantial agreement with the views of Mr. Justice Black, I have one reservation and one addition to make.

I agree that the specific guarantees of the Bill of Rights should be carried over intact into the first section of the Fourteenth Amendment. But I am not prepared to say that the latter is entirely and necessarily limited by the Bill of Rights. Occasions may arise where a proceeding falls so far short of conforming to fundamental standards of procedure as to warrant constitutional condemnation in terms of a lack of due process despite the absence of a specific provision in the Bill of Rights.

* * *

Justice Black, dissenting (joined by Justice Douglas).

* * *

This decision reasserts a constitutional theory spelled out in *Twining v. New Jersey* [1908] . . . that this Court is endowed by the Constitution with boundless power under "natural law" periodically to expand and contract constitutional standards to conform to the Court's conception of what at a particular time constitutes "civilized decency" and "fundamental liberty and justice." Invoking this *Twining* rule, the Court concludes that although comment upon testimony in a federal court would violate the Fifth Amendment, identical comment in a state court does not violate today's fashion in civilized decency and fundamentals and is therefore not prohibited by the Federal Constitution as amended.

. . . I think the decision and the "natural law" theory of the Constitution upon which it relies degrade the constitutional safeguards of the Bill of Rights and simultaneously appropriate for this Court a broad power which we are not authorized by the Constitution to exercise. . . .

* * *

My study of the historical events that culminated in the Fourteenth Amendment, and the expressions of those who sponsored and favored, as well as those who opposed its submission and passage, persuades me that one of the chief objects that the provisions of the Amendment's first section, separately, and as a whole, were intended to accomplish was to make the Bill of Rights applicable to the states. With full knowledge of the import of the *Barron* decision, the framers and backers of the Fourteenth Amendment proclaimed its purpose to be to overturn the constitutional rule that case had announced. This historical purpose has never received full consideration or exposition in any opinion of this Court interpreting the Amendment. . . .

* * *

. . . [The Bill of Rights' provisions] may be thought outdated abstractions by some. And it is true that they were designed to meet ancient evils. But they are the same kind of human evils that have emerged from century to century wherever excessive power is sought by the few at the expense of the many. In my judgment the people of no nation can lose their liberty so long as a Bill of Rights like ours survives and its basic purposes are conscientiously interpreted, enforced, and respected so as to afford continuous protections against old, as well as new, devices and practices which might thwart those purposes. I fear to see the consequences of the Court's practice of substituting its own concepts of decency and fundamental justice for the language of the Bill of Rights as its point of departure in interpreting and enforcing that Bill of Rights. If the choice is between the selective process of the *Palko* decision applying some of the Bill of Rights to the States, or the *Twining* rule applying none of them, I would choose the *Palko* process. But rather than accept either of these choices, I would follow what I believe was the original purpose of the Fourteenth Amendment—to extend to all the people of the nation the complete protections of the Bill of Rights. . . .

* * *

The *Adamson* decision illustrated three very important points. First, the Court was continuing the process of selective incorporation by choosing some rights to apply to the states through incorporation while leaving other rights applicable only against the federal government. Second, Cardozo's formulation of "fundamental rights" in the *Palko* case remained highly influential in shaping the Court's decisions about which rights to incorporate. Finally, however, the emergence of four justices who advocated total incorporation, and in the case of Murphy and Rutledge, even more rights than those contained in the Bill of Rights, indicated that changes in the Court's composition had strengthened the position of justices who advocated broader civil rights and liberties protections for people in the United States. The decisions of the Supreme Court are shaped significantly by the viewpoints of the justices who are on the high court at any given moment in history. Thus the appointment of additional libertarian justices after *Adamson* seemed likely to produce even more decisions incorporating rights and applying them to the states.

Soon after *Adamson*, the Court incorporated two additional rights, the Sixth Amendment right to a public trial (*In re Oliver*, 1948) and the Fourth Amendment right to be free from unreasonable searches and seizures (*Wolf v. Colorado*, 1949). Justice Frankfurter, the author of the majority opinion in *Wolf*, followed Cardozo's formulation of "fundamental rights" when determining that the Due Process Clause of the Fourteenth Amendment embodied the right to be free from unreasonable searches and seizures: "The security of one's privacy against arbitrary intrusion by the police—which is at the core of the Fourth Amendment—is basic to a free society. It is therefore implicit in 'the concept of ordered liberty' and as such enforceable through the Due Process Clause" (*Wolf v. Colorado*, 338 U.S. at 27–28). However, Frankfurter's opinion did not apply the right to the states in the same manner that it was applied by the Court to the federal government. In *Weeks v. United States* (1914), the Court had applied the "exclusionary rule" to federal law enforcement agencies by declaring inadmissible any evidence obtained through improper searches. By contrast, the *Wolf* decision did not apply the exclusionary rule to the states, but instead permitted states to develop their own remedies for improper police actions that violated people's rights to be free from unreasonable searches and seizures.

At the dawn of the Warren Court era, the Supreme Court had followed the *Palko* approach by applying selective incorporation to nationalize the application of the First Amendment rights that the justices viewed as "fundamental." However, the Court had done little to apply the Fourteenth Amendment to expand the application of the rights of the criminally accused to the states.

The Warren Court Era

The appointment of Earl Warren as Chief Justice in 1953 quickly placed the Supreme Court in the middle of political controversy when the justices unanimously declared that racial segregation in public schools violated the Fourteenth Amendment's Equal Protection Clause (*Brown v. Board of Education*, 1954). Although the Court earned a reputation for liberalism and activism through its school desegregation decisions, it did not immediately incorporate new rights into the Due Process Clause. It did, however, help to nationalize civil rights through a kind of "reverse incorporation" in which it applied against the federal government a right that the Constitution explicitly guaranteed only against the states. The Fourteenth Amendment contains an Equal Protection Clause that expressly prohibits states from denying people equal protection of the laws. No comparable clause exists to forbid the federal government from engaging in discrimination. When the Court faced the issue of school segregation in Washington, D.C., a jurisdiction controlled by the federal government, the Court had no explicit language in the Bill of Rights to use against the federal government's discriminatory policies. To resolve this dilemma and thereby hold the federal government to the same standard of nondiscrimination applied to the states, the Court simply reversed the usual incorporation process and said that the Fourteenth Amendment's concept of equal protection was embodied in the Due Process Clause of the Fifth Amendment and, thus, was applicable to the federal government (*Bolling v. Sharpe*, 1954).

The Warren Court resumed the incorporation process in 1958 by deciding that freedom of association is a component of the Fourteenth Amendment's Due Process Clause (*NAACP v. Alabama*, 1958). Beginning in the 1960s, the Court accelerated the incorporation process by applying against the states a variety of additional protections from the Bill of Rights. Many commentators have labeled the 1960s as the period in which the Court initiated a "due process revolution" by expanding protections for criminal suspects. In 1961, the Court refined its previous decision in *Wolf v. Colorado* (1949) by applying the same exclusionary rule against state and local governments that already applied against the federal government in cases of improper searches and seizures (*Mapp v. Ohio*, 1961). A six-member majority on the Court concluded that people's rights were inadequately protected when states were permitted to develop their own remedies for illegal searches by police officers. In 1962, the Court incorporated the Eighth Amendment's prohibition against cruel and unusual punishments by striking down a California statute that made it a crime to "be addicted to the use of narcotics" (*Robinson v. California*, 1962). The Court decided that the statute violated Eighth Amendment rights as incorporated into the Due Process Clause of the Fourteenth Amendment by criminalizing a status (i.e., being a drug addict) rather than punishing people for criminal actions.

The Court continued its flurry of incorporation decisions in 1963 by deciding that the Sixth Amendment right to counsel applied to all indigent defendants in state court who faced incarceration for felonies (*Gideon v. Wainwright*, 1963). This right was later extended by the Burger Court to cover all defendants facing the possibility of incarceration (*Argersinger v. Hamlin*, 1972). In the year following the *Gideon* decision, the justices accepted the argument that their predecessors had rejected decades earlier in *Twining* (1908) and *Adamson* (1947) by incorporating the Fifth Amendment right against self-incrimination (*Malloy v. Hogan*, 1964). In 1965, the Court incorporated the Sixth Amendment right to confront witnesses in criminal cases (*Pointer v. Texas*, 1965) as well as the right to privacy (*Griswold v. Connecticut*, 1965). Because the right to privacy is not explicitly mentioned in the Bill of Rights or elsewhere in the Constitution, it appeared to be one of the "other rights" that Justice Murphy alluded to in his *Adamson* (1947) opinion in which he advocated that incorporation include, but not be limited to, the entire Bill of Rights.

In 1966, the Court incorporated the Sixth Amendment's right to an impartial jury (*Parker v. Gladden*, 1966), and in 1967 the Court incorporated the Sixth Amendment rights to a speedy trial (*Klopfer v. North Carolina*, 1967) and to compulsory process for obtaining witnesses (*Washington v. Texas*, 1967). After the *Duncan* decision in 1968, which established the right to trial by jury for serious offenses, the Court reversed the famous *Palko* decision in 1969 by incorporating the Fifth Amendment right against double jeopardy (*Benton v. Maryland*, 1969).

Duncan v. Louisiana

391 U.S. 145 (1968)
[The facts of this case were presented in the case study at the beginning of the chapter.]

■ This case was important because it demonstrated how the Warren Court justices had incorporated most of the Bill of Rights into the Fourteenth Amendment's Due Process Clause by the end of the 1960s. As you read the case, consider the following questions: (1) Is the approach to incorporation applied by Justice White in the majority opinion the same approach applied by justices in any earlier opinions? (2) Has Justice Black's view of incorporation remained consistent? (3) How does the approach of Justice Harlan (II) differ from that of his grandfather?

Vote:

7 justices found the Louisiana practice unconstitutional (Black, Brennan, Douglas, Fortas, Marshall, Warren, White).

2 justices found the Louisiana practice constitutional (Harlan, Stewart).

Justice White delivered the opinion of the Court.

Appellant, Gary Duncan was convicted of simple battery[,] . . . a misdemeanor, punishable by a maximum of two years' imprisonment and a $300 fine. Appellant sought trial by jury, but because the Louisiana Constitution grants jury trials only in cases in which capital punishment or imprisonment at hard labor may be imposed, the trial judge denied the request. Appellant was convicted and sentenced to serve 60 days in the parish prison and pay a fine of $150. . . . [A]ppellant sought review in this Court, alleging that the Sixth and Fourteenth Amendments to the United States Constitution secure the right to jury trial in state criminal prosecutions. . . .

* * *

The Fourteenth Amendment denies the States the power to "deprive any person of life, liberty, or property, without due process of law." In resolving conflicting claims concerning the meaning of this spacious language, the Court has looked increasingly to the Bill of Rights for guidance; many of the rights guaranteed by the first eight Amendments to the Constitution have been held to be protected against state action by the Due Process Clause of the Fourteenth Amendment. That clause now protects the right to compensation for property taken by the State; the rights to speech, press, and religion covered by the First Amendment; the Fourth Amendment rights to be free from unreasonable searches and seizures and to have excluded from criminal trials any evidence illegally seized; the right guaranteed by the Fifth Amendment to be free of compelled self-incrimination; and the Sixth Amendment rights to counsel, to a speedy and public trial, to confrontation of opposing witnesses, and to compulsory process for obtaining witnesses.

* * * Because we believe that trial by jury in criminal cases is fundamental to the American scheme of justice, we hold that the Fourteenth Amendment guarantees a right of jury trial in all criminal cases which—were they to be tried in federal court—would come within the Sixth Amendment's guarantee.[14] * * *

* * *

We are aware of prior cases in this Court in which the prevailing opinion contains statements to the contrary to our holding today that the right to jury trial in serious criminal cases is a fundamental right and hence must be recognized by the States as part of their obligation to extend due process of law to all persons within their jurisdiction. . . . [However,] [i]n neither *Palko* nor *Snyder* [*v. Massachusetts* (1934)] was jury trial actually at issue, although both cases contain important dicta asserting that the right to jury trial is not essential to ordered liberty. . . . These observations, though weighty and respectable, are nevertheless dicta, unsupported by holdings in this Court that a State may refuse a defendant's demand for a jury trial when he is charged with a serious crime. . . . Respectfully, we reject the prior dicta regarding jury trial in criminal cases. . . .

* * *

---

[14]In one sense recent cases applying provisions of the first eight Amendments to the States represent a new approach to the "incorporation" debate. Earlier the Court can be seen as having asked, when inquiring whether some particular procedural safeguard was required of a State, if a civilized system could be imagined that would not accord the particular protection. For example, *Palko v. State of Connecticut* [1937] . . . stated: "The right to trial by jury . . . may have value and importance. Even so, they are not of the very essence of a scheme of ordered liberty. . . . Few would be so narrow or provincial as to maintain that a fair and enlightened system of justice would be impossible without them." The recent cases, on the other hand, have proceeded upon the valid assumption that state criminal processes are not imaginary and theoretical schemes but actual systems bearing virtually every characteristic of the common-law system that has been developing contemporaneously in England and in this country. The question thus is whether given this kind of system a particular procedure is fundamental—whether, that is, a procedure is necessary to an Anglo-American regime of ordered liberty. . . . [T]he question is not necessarily fundamental to fairness in every criminal system that might be imagined but is fundamental in the context of the criminal processes maintained by the American States.

. . . A criminal process which was fair and equitable but used no juries is easy to imagine. It would make use of alternative guarantees and protections. . . . Yet no American system has undertaken to construct such a system. . . .

The State of Louisiana urges that holding the Fourteenth Amendment assures a right to jury trial will cast doubt on the integrity of every trial conducted without a jury. Plainly, this is not the import of our holding. Our conclusion is that in the American States, as in the federal judicial system, a general grant of jury trial for serious offenses is a fundamental right, essential for preventing miscarriages of justice and for assuring that fair trials are provided for all defendants. We would not assert, however, that every criminal trial—or any particular trial—held before a judge alone is unfair or that a defendant may never be as fairly treated by a judge as he would be by a jury. Thus we hold no constitutional doubts about the practices, common in both federal and state courts, of accepting waivers of jury trial and prosecuting petty crimes without extending a right to jury trial. However, the fact is that in most places more trials for serious crimes are to juries than to a court alone; a great many defendants prefer the judgment of a jury to that of a court. Even where defendants are satisfied with bench trials, the right to a jury trial very likely serves its intended purpose of making judicial or prosecutorial unfairness less likely.

. . . Crimes carrying possible penalties up to six months do not require a jury trial if they otherwise qualify as petty offenses. . . . But the penalty authorized for a particular crime is of major relevance in determining whether it is serious or not and may in itself, if severe enough, subject the trial to mandates of the Sixth Amendment. . . . In the case before us the Legislature of Louisiana has made simple battery a criminal offense punishable by imprisonment for up to two years and a fine. The question, then, is whether a crime carrying such a penalty is an offense which Louisiana may insist on trying without a jury.

We think not. . . .

* * * In 49 of the 50 States crimes subject to trial without a jury, which occasionally include simple battery, are punishable by no more than one year in jail. Moreover, in the late 18th century in America crimes triable without a jury were for the most part punishable by no more than a six-month prison term, although there appear to have been exceptions to this rule. We need not, however, settle in this case the exact location of the line between petty offenses and serious crimes. It is sufficient to hold that a crime punishable by two years in prison is, based on past and contemporary standards in this country, a serious crime and not a petty offense. Consequently, appellate was entitled to a jury trial and it was error to deny it.

The judgment below is reversed and the case is remanded for proceedings not inconsistent with this opinion.

Reversed and remanded.

Justice Black, concurring (joined by Justice Douglas).

* * * With [today's] holding I agree for reasons given by the Court. I also agree because of reasons given in my dissent in *Adamson v. California*. . . . In that dissent, . . . I took the position . . . that the Fourteenth Amendment made all of the provisions of the Bill of Rights applicable to the States. . . . And I am very happy to support this selective process through which our Court has since the *Adamson* case held most of the specific Bill of Rights' protections applicable to the States to the same extent they are applicable to the Federal Government. . . .

Justice Harlan, dissenting (joined by Justice Stewart).

* * *

* * * The Due Process Clause of the Fourteenth Amendment requires that those procedures be fundamentally fair in all respects. It does not, in my view, impose or encourage nationwide uniformity for its own sake; it does not command adherence to forms that happen to be old; and it does not impose on the States the rules that may be in force in the federal courts except where such rules are also found to be essential to basic fairness.

The Court's approach to this case is an uneasy and illogical compromise among the views of the various Justices on how the Due Process Clause should be interpreted. . . .

I have raised my voice many times before against the Court's continuing undiscriminating insistence upon fastening on the States federal notions of criminal justice, and I must do so again in this instance. With all respect, the Court's approach and its reading of history are altogether topsy-turvy.

I believe I am correct in saying that every member of the Court for at least the last 135 years has agreed that our Founders did not consider the requirements of the Bill of Rights so fundamental that they should operate directly against the states. . . .

A few members of the Court have taken the position that the intention of those who drafted the first section of the Fourteenth Amendment was simply, and exclusively, to make the provisions of the first eight Amendments applicable to state action. This view has never been accepted by this Court. . . .

* * *

Today's Court still remains unwilling to accept the total incorporationists' view of the history of the Fourteenth Amendment. This, if accepted, would afford a cogent reason for applying the Sixth Amendment to the States. The Court is also, apparently, unwilling to face the task of determining whether denial of trial by jury in the situation before us, or in other situations, is fundamentally unfair. Consequently, the Court has compromised on the ease of the incorporationist position, without its internal logic. It has simply assumed that the question before us is whether the Jury Trial Clause of the Sixth Amendment should be incorporated into the Fourteenth, jot-for-jot, and case-for-case, or ignored. Then the Court merely declares that the Clause is "in" rather than "out."

* * *

The argument that jury trial is not a requisite of due process is quite simple. The central proposition of *Palko*, a proposition to which I would adhere, is that "due process of law" requires only that criminal trials be fundamentally fair. As stated above, apart from the theory that it was historically intended as a mere shorthand for the Bill of Rights, I do not see what else "due process of law" can intelligibly be thought to mean. If due process of law requires only fundamental fairness, then the inquiry in each case must be whether a state trial process is a fair one. The Court has held, properly I think, that in an adversary process it is a requisite of fairness, for which there is no adequate substitute, that a criminal defendant be afforded a right to counsel and to cross-examine opposing witnesses. But it simply has not been demonstrated, that trial by jury is the only fair means of resolving issues of fact.

* * *

That trial by jury is not the only fair way of adjudicating criminal guilt is well attested by the fact that it is not the prevailing way, either in England or in this country. . . . Over all [in England], "the ratio of defendants actually tried by jury becomes in some years little more than 1 per cent."

In the United States, where it has not been as generally assumed that jury waiver is permissible, the statistics are only slightly less revealing. Two experts have estimated that, of all prosecutions for crimes triable to a jury, 75% are settled by guilty plea and 40% of the remainder are tried in court. . . . I therefore see no reason why this Court should reverse the conviction of appellant, absent any suggestion that his particular trial was in fact unfair, or compel the State of Louisiana to afford jury trial in an as yet unbounded category of cases that can, without unfairness, be tried to a court.

* * *

* * * There is no obvious reason why a jury trial is a requisite of fundamental fairness when the charge is robbery, and not a requisite of fairness when the same defendant, for the same actions, is charged with assault and petty theft. The reason for the historic exception for relatively minor crimes is the obvious one: the burden of jury trial was thought to outweigh its marginal advantages. Exactly why the States should not be allowed to make continuing judgments, based on the state of their criminal dockets and the difficulty of summoning jurors, simply escapes me.

. . . [T]he Court has chosen to impose upon every State one means of trying criminal cases; it is a good means, but it is not the only fair means, and it is not demonstrably better than the alternatives States might devise. . . .

As subsequent chapters will discuss with respect to specific constitutional issues, the Warren Court's flurry of activity in incorporating elements of the Bill of Rights to apply against the states through the Fourteenth Amendment coincided with the Court's general decisional patterns during this era. During Chief Justice Warren's tenure, the Court demonstrated a uniquely high level of support for individual civil rights and liberties claimants that was unprecedented in Supreme Court history up to that point and unsurpassed during any subsequent terms (Smith and Hensley 1993). In addition to accelerating the pace of incorporation, the Warren Court justices also decided many other cases that expanded the scope of protections for individuals' rights and liberties in cases concerning religious freedom, criminal defendants' rights, freedom of expression, and other issues that will be examined in detail throughout the book. The Warren Court has been regarded as producing "what can only be described as a constitutional revolution by a group of justices who were perhaps the most liberal in American history" (Walker and Epstein 1993, p. 19).

Incorporation Doctrines

By incorporating provisions of the Bill of Rights into the Due Process Clause of the Fourteenth Amendment, the Supreme Court effectively nationalized the Bill of Rights by making most civil rights and liberties protections applicable against state and local governments as well as against the federal government. During the course of examining the incorporation issue, various justices advocated competing approaches for defining the meaning of the Fourteenth Amendment's Due Process Clause and its relationship to the Bill of Rights.

The first Justice Harlan advocated total incorporation of the Bill of Rights in his *Hurtado* dissent (1884), and his argument was subsequently adopted and advanced by Justice Black in his *Adamson* dissent (1947) and other opinions. Justices Murphy and Rutledge went farther than Harlan and Black, in effect, by arguing that incorporation should include the entire Bill of Rights but not be limited to civil rights and liberties listed in the Constitution's first eight amendments. Thus Murphy's dissent in *Adamson* (1947) urged the adoption of total incorporation *plus* the inclusion of other, unspecified rights.

By contrast, other justices followed less encompassing approaches when defining the meaning of the Due Process Clause. In his famous and influential *Palko* opinion (1938), Justice Cardozo argued for bringing only selected rights "within the Fourteenth Amendment by a process of absorption" (*Palko v. Connecticut*, 302 U.S. at 326). He advocated incorporation of those rights that are "of the very essence of a scheme of ordered liberty" (*Palko v. Connecticut*, 302 U.S. at 325). Thus, Cardozo advocated selective incorporation ("absorption") of fundamental rights from the Bill of Rights into the Due Process Clause of the Fourteenth Amendment.

The second Justice Harlan and Justice Frankfurter claimed to follow Cardozo's test for determining which rights to apply to the states, but they formally rejected the idea that rights from the Bill of Rights were to be incorporated into the Fourteenth Amendment. As Harlan noted in his *Duncan* dissent, "In my view, often expressed elsewhere [in my other opinions], the first section of the Fourteenth Amendment was meant neither to incorporate, nor to be limited to, the specific guarantees of the first eight Amendments" (*Duncan v. Louisiana*, 302 U.S. at 174). Instead, these nonincorporationist justices sought only to determine which protections—whether or not expressed in the Bill of Rights—were so fundamental to liberty and fair procedures that they must be regarded as part of a right to due process. For example, Frankfurter said state and local government officials were barred by the Due Process Clause from taking actions that "shocked the conscience," such as ordering that a suspect be forced to vomit in the course of an improper search for drugs (*Rochin v. California*, 1952). As indicated by Frankfurter's opinion in *Wolf* (1949) concerning the exclusionary rule and Harlan's opinion in *Duncan*, neither justice believed that the states were obligated to adhere to precisely the same restrictions as the federal government in respecting people's civil rights and liberties.

Which of these approaches ultimately prevailed? In practice, the Court followed a selective incorporation process. As indicated by the foregoing discussion, the twentieth-century Supreme Court gradually, but with increasing frequency in the Warren Court era, applied individual rights from the Bill of Rights, one by one, against the states through the Fourteenth Amendment's Due Process Clause. Justice Black, one of the Court's most persistent advocates of total incorporation, acknowledged as much in his concurring opinion in *Duncan*. Although he reaffirmed his support for total incorporation, he wrote: "I am very happy to support this selective process through which our Court since the *Adamson* case held most of the specific Bill of Rights' protections applicable to the States to the same extent they are applicable to the Federal Government" (*Duncan v. Louisiana*, 391 U.S. at 164).

The selective nature of the Court's incorporation process is reflected not only in the incremental approach to incorporation that occurred over several decades, but also in the fact that not all of the provisions of the Bill of Rights were incorporated.

Five specific provisions of the first eight amendments have never been incorporated by the Supreme Court: the Fifth Amendment's right to indictment by grand jury that was initially rejected in the *Hurtado* case (1884); the Seventh Amendment right to a jury trial in civil controversies contesting more than twenty dollars; the Eighth Amendment prohibition against excessive bail and fines; the Second Amendment's controversial provision about keeping and bearing arms; and the Third Amendment's restriction on quartering troops in people's homes (Abraham 1988, pp. 113–16).

While the Supreme Court followed a selective incorporation process, it did not limit itself to selective incorporation according to Cardozo's description in *Palko* of rights "that have been taken over from the earlier articles of the Federal Bill of Rights and brought within the Fourteenth Amendment by the process of absorption" (*Palko v. Connecticut*, 302 U.S. at 326). Instead, the Court effectively undertook an approach that can be appropriately labeled as selective incorporation **plus** the application of additional rights. In several cases, the Supreme Court has applied additional rights against the states that are not expressly listed in the Bill of Rights. For example, the right to privacy (*Griswold v. Connecticut*, 1965) and the right to travel (*Shapiro v. Thompson*, 1969) are not explicitly stated in the Constitution, but the Supreme Court used its interpretive powers to recognize these rights and apply them to the states through the Fourteenth Amendment.

The application of various specific civil rights and liberties to the states through the Due Process Clause of the Fourteenth Amendment is a securely established component of constitutional law. Edwin Meese, the U.S. attorney general during the Reagan administration, publicly questioned the wisdom and desirability of incorporation during the 1980s (Curtis 1986). However, Meese's solitary public criticism of incorporation reflected more about his role as the symbolic point man for conservative jurisprudence than about any effective jurisprudential attack on the nationalization of the Bill of Rights (Caplan 1987). In fact, incorporation is accepted by political conservatives who generally do not favor expansive interpretations of the Bill of Rights. The thorough acceptance of incorporation was well illustrated by the questioning of Justice Ruth Bader Ginsburg by the Senate Judiciary Committee when President Bill Clinton nominated her to replace retiring Justice Byron White in 1993. Senator Orrin Hatch, a Republican from Utah who was among the strongest supporters of conservative presidents Ronald Reagan and George Bush and their appointees to the Rehnquist Court, used Ginsburg's nomination hearings as a platform to advocate that the Second Amendment, which Hatch interprets to provide a right to own firearms, be incorporated to apply against the states just like other rights in the Bill of Rights.

Despite the Supreme Court's slow and controversial efforts to apply the provisions of the Bill of Rights to the states over the course of many decades, the resulting incorporation of rights into the Due Process Clause of the Fourteenth Amendment has become a well-accepted component of constitutional law. In the aftermath of this process, the statutes and policies of state and local governments throughout the country became susceptible to legal challenge by claimants who believed that their constitutional rights had been violated. Most of the cases discussed in subsequent chapters of this book involve assertions of rights that never would have been recognized prior to the Supreme Court's decisions that applied these rights against state and local governments. As a result of the incorporation process, the provisions of the Bill of Rights truly became national in scope as they protected people equally throughout the country against improper governmental actions. It must be noted, however, that U.S. Supreme Court decisions on civil rights and liberties define only the *minimum* rights that state and local governments are required to respect. Many state constitutions provide more expansive protections for rights than those defined through the Supreme Court's interpretation of the Bill of Rights and Fourteenth Amendment. Therefore state supreme court decisions interpreting the provisions of their own states' constitutions have the greatest impact on limiting state and local governments' actions with respect to some rights in individual states.

REFERENCES

Abraham, Henry J. *Freedom and the Court*, 5th ed. New York: Oxford University Press, 1988.

Baum, Lawrence. *The Supreme Court*. Washington, D.C.: Congressional Quarterly Press, 1992.

Berger, Raoul. "The Incorporation of the Bill of Rights in the Fourteenth Amendment: A Nine-Lived Cat." *Ohio State Law Journal* 42(1981):435-66.

Bodenhamer, David J. *Fair Trial: Rights of the Accused in American History*. New York: Oxford University Press, 1992.

Caplan, Lincoln. *The Tenth Justice*. New York: Random House, 1987.

Conaway, James. *Judge: The Life and Times of Leander Perez*. New York: Alfred Knopf, 1973.

Cortner, Richard C. *The Supreme Court and Civil Liberties Policy*. Palo Alto, Calif.: Mayfield, 1975.

Cox, Archibald. *The Court and the Constitution*. Boston: Houghton Mifflin, 1987.

Curtis, Michael Kent. *No State Shall Abridge: The Fourteenth Amendment and the Bill of Rights.* Chapel Hill, N.C.: University of North Carolina Press, 1986.

Fairman, Charles. "Does the Fourteenth Amendment Incorporate the Bill of Rights? The Original Understanding." *Stanford Law Review* 2(1949): 5-139.

O'Brien, David M. *Constitutional Law and Politics: Civil Rights and Liberties*. New York: W.W. Norton, 1991.

Rutland, Robert Allen. *The Birth of the Bill of Rights: 1776-1791*. Chapel Hill, N.C.: University of North Carolina Press, 1955.

Smith, Christopher E., and Thomas R. Hensley. "Assessing the Conservatism of the Rehnquist Court." *Judicature* 77(1993): 83-89.

Walker, Thomas G., and Lee Epstein. *The Supreme Court of the United States: An Introduction*. New York: St. Martin's, 1993.

The First Amendment

Introduction and Overview

OVERVIEW

The First Amendment of the Constitution reads as follows: "*Congress shall make no law respecting an establishment of religion, or prohibiting the free exercise thereof; or abridging the freedom of speech, or of the press; or the right of the people peaceably to assemble, and to petition the Government for a redress of grievances.*" These brief words are well known to most Americans, and they express profound ideas in a simple but eloquent fashion. The apparent brevity and simplicity of the First Amendment is deceptive, however. In this section of the book as we examine the various provisions of the First Amendment in detail, you will become aware of the important and complex nature of the guarantees of the First Amendment.

SPECIFIC GUARANTEES OF THE FIRST AMENDMENT

Six explicit rights are mentioned in the First Amendment: freedom of speech, freedom of the press, freedom of assembly, the right to petition the government, freedom of religion, and the prohibition against the establishment of religion. This list of *explicit* rights does not exhaust the rights that the Supreme Court has found to be within the first Amendment, however, because the Court over time has recognized that certain *implicit* rights are also protected by the First Amendment. One important example is the right of association, which the Court has ruled to be an important corollary guarantee stemming from the explicit guarantees of freedom of speech and assembly. Furthermore, a wide array of particular activities have been determined to fall within the meaning of the guarantees of the First Amendment. These guarantees obviously apply to such traditional activities as the street corner orator, the editor of a daily newspaper, and a group peacefully demonstrating in a public park. The Court has also ruled, however, that a wide variety of other activities also come within the protection of the First Amendment, including such things as camping out on public property and nude dancing.

FREEDOM OF EXPRESSION AND RELIGIOUS RIGHTS

The explicit and implicit guarantees of the First Amendment can be divided into two categories, those dealing with freedom of expression and those concerned with religious activities. In terms of the explicit liberties in the First Amendment, the guarantees of speech, press, assembly, and petition are the ones dealing with freedom of expression, the liberty of a person to communicate ideas without arbitrary government interference. The two religious guarantees of the First Amendment are the Free Exercise and Establishment Clauses. These are fundamentally different from the freedom of expression guarantees because they deal with a specific subject matter—religion. Another important difference between the religious guarantees and the freedom of expression liberties is that they arose from different historical circumstances.

Importance of the First Amendment Guarantees

A widespread consensus exists that the First Amendment freedoms are of truly fundamental importance. They have been called the first freedoms, the indispensable freedoms, the preferred freedoms, and the brightest stars in the constitutional constellation. The First Amendment guarantees are viewed as being so important for two reasons. First, they are considered to be essential for our democratic system of government. A democracy is premised on the idea that ultimate sovereignty resides with the people, and government officials are supposed to represent and carry out the will of the people. This form of government requires an informed citizenry, which can only occur if freedom of expression exists. Second, the freedom of expression guarantees are viewed as being essential to the fullest development of each person's individual character and abilities.

As important as the rights of the First Amendment are, however, they are not absolute. Justice Oliver Wendell Holmes probably made the most memorable statement regarding the limitations of freedom of speech when he observed that freedom of speech does not extend to yelling "fire" in a crowed theater when no fire exists. Similarly, although Americans are deeply committed to freedom of the press, most would agree that libelous and obscene materials can be subjected to government control.

This brings us to a critical question: how can we achieve a proper balance between the important values of the First Amendment and the need to protect individuals and society from extremist abuses of these freedoms? In American society, the Supreme Court has ultimate responsibility to determine the proper balance between competing values of freedom and order, to determine where to draw the line between the exercise of constitutionally protected rights and the overstepping of that line, which creates a severe threat to societal peace, order, and morality.

The Court has developed a series of tests or doctrines over the years to provide guidance in this challenging and important task. These doctrines are guidelines that are based on historical, philosophical, political, and other social ideas and theories that assist the Court in reaching decisions in the difficult issues it confronts. These judicial doctrines can thus provide a principled and consistent basis for Supreme Court decision making. They by no means resolve all issues before the Court, however. The justices are frequently in disagreement over the appropriateness of particular doctrines; they frequently disagree as to which doctrine is applicable in a particular case; and even if agreement exists among the justices on which doctrine to apply in a case, they frequently disagree on how to apply it. Thus, much of our analysis of the various guarantees of the First Amendment will focus on the development and interpretation of various freedom of expression and religious guarantees doctrines.

Organization 

We have chosen to divide our section on the First Amendment into four chapters, dealing respectively with the Establishment Clause (Chapter 5), the Free Exercise of Religion Clause (Chapter 6), Freedom of Expression (Chapter 7), and Obscenity (Chapter 8). A brief explanation for this choice is in order. The religion clauses are treated in separate chapters because they are both of great significance, fundamentally different types of issues are typically raised in cases dealing with the respective clauses, and the Court has developed quite distinct lines of precedents and controlling doctrines for them. We are combining all freedom of expression topics except obscenity into one lengthy chapter. We do this for two reasons. First, clear lines of distinction cannot easily be drawn among the various freedom of expression guarantees. Second, quantitative analysis using the *United States Supreme Court Judicial Database* is an important part of our textbook, and these data can be used most compatibly with the chapter organization we have selected. Thus, Chapter 7 deals with all the Court's freedom of expression areas except obscenity, and Chapter 8 focuses specifically on obscenity, which has occupied an extraordinary amount of the Court's attention.

CHAPTER

5 The Establishment Clause

CASE STUDY

Engel v. Vitale (1962)

"Almighty God, we acknowledge our dependence upon Thee, and we beg Thy blessings upon us, our parents, our teachers, and our country." On November 30, 1951, the New York State Board of Regents, the governing body of the state public school system, voted to recommend that all New York public schools begin the day with this voluntary, nondenominational prayer along with the pledge of allegiance. The Board of Regents also recommended that the schools develop programs stressing the spiritual heritage of the nation. It took the Board, which included Protestants, Roman Catholics, and Jews, several months to reach agreement on these recommendations. The Board's rationale for recommending the prayer and the spiritual training program was that they would contribute to the preservation of American democracy at a time when Americans were deeply concerned about the threat of communism.

Several years later, in July of 1958, a Nassau County school board passed a resolution officially adopting the Regents' Prayer to be said in its schools following the daily flag salute. Less than one year after the adoption of the Regents' Prayer, in January of 1959, the New York Civil Liberties Union (NYCLU) initiated a suit on behalf of five parents of children in the school district. The NYCLU and the parents asserted that the prayer violated the principle of the separation of church and state embodied in the Establishment Clause of the First Amendment, and they petitioned the courts to force the school board to discontinue using it. The petitioners alleged that the saying of the prayer, along with the manner and setting within which it occurred, were religious practices and instruction contrary to the beliefs of both believers and nonbelievers and thus violated the Establishment Clause.

The five parents who initiated the suit on behalf of their school-aged children had various religious affiliations. Steven Engel and Daniel Lichenstein were Jewish, Monroe Lerner was a member of the Society for Ethical Culture, Lenore Lyons was a Unitarian, and Lawrence Roth identified himself as a nonbeliever. The five-member school board named in the suit included William Vitale, Philip Fried, Mary Harte, Anne Birch, and Richard Saunders. The families being represented by the NYCLU immediately became the target of harassment activities. They received critical and sometimes threatening letters, postcards, and telephone calls. For example, the Roth family suffered anti-Semitic epithets as well as threats such as: "Watch out for your family." "We're going to blow up your car." "Keep your eye on your children." (*New York Times,* 28 June 1962, p. 17.)

The NYCLU and the families encountered a series of defeats in the New York courts. The initial petition urging discontinuance of the prayer was filed in the trial court in January of 1959, and a decision was reached on August 24 of that year. In a forty-six-page opinion, Justice Bernard Meyer ruled that the voluntary, nondenominational Regents' Prayer was constitutional, but he remanded the case to the school board for it to develop procedures to make certain that the prayer was truly voluntary and that parents were informed about the adoption of the prayer. Following Justice Meyer's ruling, the petitioners appealed the case to the Appellate Division of the State Supreme Court. In a per curiam decision, five justices unanimously affirmed the lower court decision, expressing their agreement with the views of Justice Meyer. The NYCLU and the parents were not prepared to give up their fight to have the Regents' Prayer declared unconstitutional, so the case was appealed again, this time to the Court of Appeals, New York's highest state court. Once again, they lost. In a 5-2 decision in which the majority wrote three different opinions, the court ruled that it was constitutionally permissible for public schools to open each day with the Regents' Prayer.

Still unwilling to concede defeat and encouraged perhaps by the two dissenters who agreed that the prayer violated the First Amendment, the case was then appealed to the United States Supreme Court, which granted certiorari on December 3, 1961. By this time, the case had attracted national attention, and the Court received and granted numerous requests to file amici curiae briefs.

The Court heard oral arguments on April 3, 1962. William Butler, representing the parent-petitioners, emphasized that despite its voluntary provisions the prayer was a clear violation of the requirements of the Establishment Clause. Although parents could get their children excused from saying the prayer, Butler argued, it was in actuality compulsory because of the manner and setting in which the prayer was conducted along with the children's desire not to be perceived as different from their peers. Butler asked the justices, "Would a parent ask his child to leave the classroom and label himself as a nonconformist?" (*New York Times,* 4 April 1992, p. 45). Representing the school board, Bertram Daiker argued that the prayer was not compulsory and, moreover, that it was simply part of the nation's tradition of expressing faith in a Supreme Being. As evidence of this, he pointed to forty-nine state constitutions that refer to God, as well as to the Declaration of Independence, which speaks of "The Creator." Finally, Porter Chandler, representing the parents who intervened on behalf of the school board, said that his clients wanted the prayer to be continued in the public schools. Noting that the parents were of various religious backgrounds—Jewish, Protestant, Catholic, and unaffiliated—Chandler stressed that those persons who did not like the prayer had the right to be excused but they did not have the right to impose their views on everyone else.

Nearly three months after oral argument, the petitioners' persistence finally proved fruitful. Only seven justices participated because of change that was occurring in the Court's membership. In a 6-1 decision, the Supreme Court ruled that the Regents' Prayer was indeed a violation of the Establishment Clause of the First Amendment. Justice Hugo Black, writing for a five-person majority that included Chief Justice Warren and Justices Clark, Harlan, and Brennan, took an approach of strict separation, arguing that the Establishment Clause requires a high wall of separation between church and state. Black wrote, "The constitutional prohibition against laws respecting an establishment of religion must at least mean that in this country it is no part of the business of government to compose official prayers for any group of the American people to recite as part of a religious program carried on by government" (*Engel v. Vitale,* 370 U.S. at 425, 1962). Responding to the contention of the school board that the nondenominational, voluntary aspects of the prayer made it inoffensive and therefore constitutional, Black replied, "When the power, prestige, and financial support of government is placed behind a particular religious belief, the indirect coercive pressure upon religious minorities to conform to the prevailing officially approved religion is plain" (370 U.S. at 430). Justice Potter Stewart, the lone dissenter in the case, rejected the strict separation approach of the majority and adopted instead an approach willing to accommodate various forms of church-state involvement. Rejecting the wall of separation metaphor, Stewart argued that Americans are a religious people, their institutions assume a Supreme Being, and the Court's decision denied the schoolchildren the chance to share in the nation's spiritual heritage.

The Court's decision resolved the immediate issue for the specific families who brought the suit, and the Court's strong language and overwhelming vote sought to settle the question of government-sponsored religious activities in the public elementary and secondary schools throughout the nation. The families, who had sought anonymity throughout the lawsuit because of the threats they had received, were both relieved and happy to have the suit finished. Despite the community pressure and the harassment they received, the parents did not seem to regret their decision to challenge the prayer and were extremely pleased with the Supreme Court's decision (*New York Times,* 28 June 1962, p. 17).

The Court's decision did not please everyone, however. Indeed, this case provoked the most intense response from the general public and elected officials around the nation since the 1954 *Brown* decision. The Court was deluged with letters critical of the justices for their decision. Some members of Congress took to the House and Senate floors to denounce the Court and its decision. Representative George Andrews from Alabama, for example, proclaimed: "They put the Negroes in the schools and now they've driven God out" (*New York Times,* 26 June 1962, p. 1). Other public officials, from local school board members to state governors, vowed to ignore the Court's ruling and to continue existing practices of having prayers in public schools. In addition to statements of defiance, numerous attempts were made to pass a constitutional amendment to allow religious activities in the public schools. And, not surprisingly given this adverse reaction, the Supreme Court has continuously been challenged since the *Engel* decision with additional cases raising the issue of the constitutionality of government-sponsored religious activities in the country's public schools.

Historical Origins and Contemporary Conflicts

The conflict involving state-sponsored religious activities in the public schools is only one of many difficult issues facing the Court in interpreting the Constitution's provision in the First Amendment that "*Congress shall make no law respecting an establishment of religion. . . .*" In this section some of the modern conflicts involving the Establishment Clause will be introduced, but first it is necessary to look to the historic origins of the clause in order to gain insight into its meaning and the ways in which it can be interpreted.

The historical origins of the Establishment Clause can be traced to seventeenth-century Europe where many countries had an officially established church that enjoyed a sole legal union with the government of the state. In England, for example, the officially established church was the Church of England; in Scotland, Presbyterianism was the established church; and in Italy and Spain, it was the Roman Catholic Church. Individuals who were not members of the established church were subject to discrimination and persecution. The bitter memories of religious intolerance suffered by American colonists before coming to America can be seen in a statement in 1774 by the First Continental Congress declaring that the Church of England (Anglicanism) was ". . . a religion that has deluged [England] in blood, and dispersed bigotry, persecution, murder, and rebellion through every part of the world" (O'Brien 1991, p. 636).

The religious discrimination and persecution associated with the established churches of Europe was a strong factor in the decision of many people to leave Europe and come to the American colonies where they hoped to find religious freedom. Most American colonies, however, established official churches, and religious discrimination and persecution occurred against those who were not members.

Despite some similarities, the American colonial experience with established religion differed in important ways from the European pattern, which involved the formal legal alliance of the government with one church. A pattern similar to the

European model was followed in the five southern colonies (Virginia, Maryland, Georgia, South Carolina, and North Carolina), where the Anglican (Episcopal) Church was the officially recognized church. In the New England colonies of Massachusetts, Connecticut, and New Hampshire, no specific church was recognized. The laws of each of these three states did provide, however, for a general establishment of religion, including provisions to elect and maintain town ministers who would be supported by public tax money, and the Congregational Church predominated for much of the 1700s. New York also had a more general establishment of religion during the 1700s, while four colonies did not have an establishment of any kind: Rhode Island, Pennsylvania, Delaware, and New Jersey.

Despite the variation that existed in the American colonies, religious discrimination and persecution were widespread. Under Virginia law before the Revolutionary War, for example, it was a crime to preach without having Episcopalian ordination. Failure to attend the established church could be punished by jailing. Only clergymen licensed by the church could perform marriage ceremonies. Taxes were used to support the church in various ways, including building and repairing churches. In addition to the official government sanctions of arrests, fines, and jail, religious minorities in Virginia were also harassed and beaten by mobs (Levy 1986, chap. 1).

Substantial resentment and opposition existed to the laws and practices associated with the religious establishments in the American colonies, and the period of the American Revolutionary War gave rise to dramatic changes, including heightened sensitivity to religious freedom and the growing separation of church and state. This was only logical, for the Revolutionary War was fought in part upon such principles as freedom of conscience and no taxation without representation, and the official establishment of religion contradicted both of these principles. Thus, by the time of the writing of the Constitution in 1789, only six states of the original thirteen colonies had establishments authorized by law. Furthermore, all six states had multiple establishments, which included all denominations and sects with sufficient followers to form a church.

Against this brief historical background, it is now possible to look more closely at the specific period when the Establishment Clause of the Bill of Rights was written for the purpose of gaining insight into "original understanding," the meaning of the Clause for those who wrote and supported it. This is important because the various approaches to interpreting the Establishment Clause are based in part upon interpretations of original understanding, and the justices of the Supreme Court frequently use their analysis of this historical period to support their decisions.

While substantial disagreement exists regarding the original understanding of the writers and supporters of the Establishment Clause, some areas of agreement do exist. One important point of consensus is that no clear answer exists regarding this issue. Levy's position is a common one among scholars who have studied this issue: "No scholar or judge of intellectual rectitude should answer establishment clause questions as if historical evidence permits complete certainty. It does not. Anyone employing evidence responsibly should refrain from asserting with conviction that he knows for certain the original meaning and purpose of the establishment clause" (Levy 1986, p. xiii). In addition to agreeing that history provides no clear-cut, definitive answer to the meaning and purpose of the clause, scholars also share a broad consensus regarding two aspects of the meaning of the Establishment Clause. First, the language of the First Amendment and the history of the colonies make it clear that no official church or religion should be established by the national government. Second, the Clause also means that the government should not be involved in any activity in which one church or religion receives preferential treatment over [illegible] e points, however, and we can us [illegible] ups regarding the issue of origir [illegible] preferentialists or accommodatio [illegible]

Separationis [illegible] 36; Alley 1988; and Gunn 1992) t [illegible] dison and Thomas Jefferson in ar [illegible] create a "high and impregnable [illegible] tually all forms of government [illegible] y key figure in the debate becau [illegible] drafting the original Constitution, [illegible] ights in his capacity as a member [illegible] dments in the First Congress, an [illegible] generally and the Establishmen [illegible] ement regarding the relationship of church and state is his 1785 [illegible] emonstrance Against Religious Assessments," written in response to The General Assessment Bill, an act introduced into the Virginia General Assembly that sought to raise public funds to support Christian teachers. Madison strongly opposed this type of government involvement with religion, and his forceful views prevailed. His vigorous arguments in favor of a firm separation between church and state played a key role in his drafting of the language of the First Amendment, and he even sought to have the guarantees of the First Amendment applied to the states as well as to the national government. Alley (1988, p. 13) argues that Madison until his death in 1836 "consistently interpreted the work of the First Congress, and the resulting ratification by the states, as in full accord with his commitment to total and complete separation of church and state." Jefferson was also a strong advocate of strict separation, and he is frequently cited for the "wall of separation" metaphor he wrote in his famous letter of 1802 to the Baptist Association of Danbury.

Important as the views of Madison and Jefferson are to the separationist approach, however, scholars advocating this position also argue that the legislative history of the writing of the clause shows that "Congress rejected a narrow or nonpreferentialist intent" and instead agreed on a central point: "The United States has no power to legislate on the subject of religion" (Levy 1986, p. 89). Furthermore, this strong separation viewpoint was held not only by the Framers but also by the citizens of the United States: ". . . the people of almost every state that ratified the First Amendment believed that religion should be maintained and supported voluntarily. They saw government attempts to organize and regulate such support as a usurpation of power, as a violation of liberty of conscience and free exercise of religion, and as falling within the scope of what they termed an establishment of religion" (Curry 1986, p. 222).

Despite the impressive evidence marshalled by the separationist scholars, a substantial number of scholars reject this position and argue instead that the historical record reveals that the original intent of the drafters and supporters of the Establishment Clause was nonpreferentialism or accommodation. These scholars (e.g., Stokes 1950; Antieau, Downey, and Roberts 1964; Berns 1976; Malbin 1978; and Cord 1982) take the position that the Establishment Clause was intended to allow substantial church-state involvement as long as it was on a nonpreferential basis. The government could not establish a national church or religion, and the government could not provide preferential aid to one church or religion; but beyond these limitations, the government did have substantial leeway and could provide support to religion generally on a nonpreferential basis.

The nonpreferentialists or accommodationists provide a wide variety of support for their position. They deal with the writings of Madison in two ways. One approach argues that Madison's writings can be interpreted to mean that he saw the Establishment Clause as prohibiting only a national church or preferential actions by the government, while the other approach acknowledges that Madison was a strict separationist but argues that Madison's views were atypical of the other drafters and supporters of the Establishment Clause. In regard to the writings of Jefferson, the nonpreferentialists take the position that his views are essentially irrelevant because he was an ambassador to France during this period.

Scholars holding the nonpreferentialist view place great emphasis on the actions of the first Congress, which established Congressional chaplaincies, approved Thanksgiving as a national holiday in which to recognize God's blessings, and approved placing the words "In God We Trust" on our coins. These activities, it is argued, show clearly that the members of the First Congress who drafted and approved the Establishment Clause were not separationists but rather accommodationists who favored government activities supporting religion as long as this was done on a nonpreferential basis. Furthermore, these scholars argue that substantial evidence exists showing that the people throughout the states equated establishment with preferentialism; and while they opposed preferentialism, they favored nonpreferential government support of religion (e.g., Antieau, Downey, and Roberts, 1964, pp. 132–33).

Having reviewed the controversies surrounding the creation of the Establishment Clause, it is now useful to provide a brief overview of some of the most important contemporary issues which surround the Establishment Clause. Unlike the conflicts over the Free Exercise Clause, which typically involve small religious groups and receive little publicity, contemporary Establishment Clause issues are frequently ones which involve major segments of the American population and generate intense public debate. One of these issues was discussed in the introductory case study of *Engel v. Vitale* (1962) involving the constitutionality of state-sponsored religious activities in the public schools. The Court ruled the Regents' Prayer unconstitutional as a violation of the Establishment Clause, but various other forms of state-sponsored religious activities in the public schools have also been brought to the Court, including the posting of the Ten Commandments in classrooms, a moment of silence for prayer or meditation, religious clubs meeting before or after school, and prayers at graduation ceremonies. Do all of these activities violate the Establishment Clause? What guidelines does the Court use to make these determinations?

Another issue area that has frequently confronted the Court is parochial aid, government aid of various kinds to private, religiously affiliated schools. Are all forms of parochial aid unconstitutional, or are certain forms of aid constitutional if they do not support religion directly? For example, does it make a difference if the government aid is to provide transportation to school, to supply textbooks in nonreligious subjects like math, or to provide salaries for parochial teachers? Again, has the Court been able to develop guidelines by which to make these difficult determinations?

Numerous conflicts have also arisen over the issue of government taxation of religious institutions. Does the exemption of religious organizations from taxation constitute a form of government support of religion and therefore a violation of the Establishment Clause? Alternatively, does government taxation of religious institutions create a government hostility toward religion or an excessive involvement of government with religion that is prohibited by the Establishment Clause? On what basis can the Court resolve these questions?

A final major area of Establishment Clause cases involves the use of religious symbols and practices in public places. For example, in the pledge of allegiance to the flag Congress has authorized the words "one nation, under God;" our currency contains the words "In God We Trust;" Congress has chaplains who begin each session with prayer; and each session of the Supreme Court itself begins with an invocation proclaiming "God save this honorable Court." In each of these examples, we see government support for and involvement with religion. Do these activities violate the Establishment Clause?

Supreme Court Decision Making in Establishment Clause Cases

It should be clear by now that the meaning of the Establishment Clause is surrounded by conflicts, both historical and contemporary in nature. In attempting to deal with these issues, the Court has developed a variety of general approaches that help structure and explain the Supreme Court's decision making in specific cases. It should not be surprising to learn, however, that the justices have been in sharp disagreement over which approach is the proper one. Three major approaches have been developed during the past fifty years since the Court has nationalized the Establishment Clause; they are strict separation, accommodation, and neutrality.

The **strict separation approach** was mentioned earlier in the analysis of the history of the Establishment Clause and the subject of original understanding. Justices who advocate this approach support Jefferson's metaphor of a high and impregnable wall of separation between church and state. Under this approach, virtually any form of government assistance, whether preferential or nonpreferential, is viewed as a violation of the Establishment Clause.

Justices advocating strict separation offer a wide variety of reasons to support their position. They argue that separationist scholars have developed the most accurate interpretation of the original intent of the writers of the Establishment Clause. Justices who support strict separation also view this reading of the clause as vital to the preservation of the free exercise of religion. They view government involvement with religion as the greatest single threat to religious freedom, for the inevitable pattern throughout history has been for those in control of government to use its power to promote the favored religion(s) and to discriminate against and persecute those who do not belong. Justices advocating the strict separationist approach frequently make the additional point that government support of religion tends to degrade religion by making it formal and ritualistic. Another important argument frequently advanced by separationist justices is the danger of civil strife that can arise from government aid to religion. Religion and politics are each volatile subjects taken independently; but when they are mixed together, the potential for conflict and violence is dramatically heightened. Given these dangers, it is therefore vital to maintain a strict separation between government and religion. Finally, in response to the argument that limited forms of government support of religion are harmless, justices advocating strict separation tend to argue that even the slightest breach of the wall is dangerous. In the words of Justice Black, quoting Madison, "[I]t is proper to take alarm at the first experiment on our liberties . . ." (*Engel v. Vitale,* 370 U.S. at 436, 1962). The justices most associated with the strict separationist approach have been Black and Douglas, although a variety of other justices have on occasion joined strict separationist opinions. None of the current members of the Rehnquist Court are associated with the strict separationist approach, however.

In sharp contrast to the separationists are the justices who take the **accommodationist** or **nonpreferentialist approach** to Establishment Clause interpretation. As was noted in the earlier historical analysis, accommodationists view the Establishment Clause as prohibiting the creation of a national church or religion as well as prohibiting government favoritism toward any particular religious group, but accommodationists maintain that the clause does not prohibit nonpreferential government aid to religion. Justices taking this approach draw heavily from the writings of the various nonpreferentialist scholars, but they also offer a variety of additional arguments beyond their interpretation of original understanding. Accommodationist justices emphasize that Americans have always been deeply religious people whose government presupposes a Supreme Being, and therefore it is necessary and appropriate for the government to reflect this religious commitment by providing various forms of recognition and support for religion on a nondiscriminatory basis. Accommodationist justices reject the argument of the separationists that government support of religion is dangerous either because it threatens the free exercise of religion through discrimination and persecution or because it creates civil strife and possibly violence. For the accommodationists, government aid to religion serves to enhance rather than undermine the free exercise of religion because government assistance enhances religious activities by promoting religion in the public schools, strengthening parochial schools, and promoting public awareness and acknowledgment of America's religious heritage. In addition, the supporters of accommodation argue that the separationists are alarmists in claiming that government support of religion will lead to civil strife. Accommodationists acknowledge that this could occur and that the Court must be alert to this possibility; but they emphasize that America has a deep tradition of religious tolerance and that few if any programs of government assistance to religion have ever created serious problems of civil strife.

A number of former and current Supreme Court justices are advocates of the accommodationist approach to the Establishment Clause. Chief Justice Burger was one of the early and most influential supporters of accommodation, and during his tenure as chief justice he was joined in this approach by Rehnquist and White. More recently, Scalia, Kennedy, and Thomas have identified strongly with this approach.

Neutrality is a third approach to the Establishment Clause. It does not have the same historical origins and impressive body of scholarship associated with the separationist and accommodationist approaches. Instead, it has evolved during the past fifty years as a middle ground between the other two approaches. Justices advocating the neutralist approach tend to view both strict separation and accommodation as too extreme. For the neutralist, the strict separation approach rejects many deeply rooted American religious traditions and practices, overemphasizes the dangers of many forms of government assistance to religion, and creates a potential hostility of government toward religion. Similarly, advocates of the neutrality approach criticize the accommodationists for going too far in the other direction by their willingness to support programs that are insensitive to the beliefs of religious minorities and nonbelievers, that create a real potential for civil strife, and that may open the door to more serious problems in the future.

Neutralist justices have tended to use a three-part test developed by the Court in the 1960s and set forth explicitly in the 1971 case of *Lemon v. Kurtzman,* in which the Court found various forms of parochial aid to be unconstitutional. The three requirements of the ***Lemon* test** are: "(1) the statute must have a secular legislative purpose; (2) its principal or primary effect must be one that neither advances nor inhibits religion; and (3) the statute must not foster an excessive government entanglement with religion" (403 U.S. at 612, 613). If a challenged government program fails any of the three prongs of the test, then it is declared unconstitutional. It is not difficult to understand why the *Lemon* test is highly compatible with the neutrality approach to the Establishment Clause, because its second prong can reasonably be interpreted to require that any law's primary effect must be neutral toward religion, neither advancing nor inhibiting it. The *Lemon* test is not as compatible with the separationist approach because the test does allow government activities that indirectly advance religion, and the test also allows government entanglement with religion as long as it is not excessive. The *Lemon* test is also not easily compatible with the accommodationist approach, although it was Burger, an accommodationist, who authored the opinion initially setting forth the test. Over the years, however, accommodationist justices like Burger have become disenchanted with the test because it has been used so frequently to reject government laws and actions that accommodationist justices have viewed as constitutional. As a consequence, the accommodationists have sought either to modify the *Lemon* test or to abolish it. The future of the *Lemon* test is thus a critical issue in Establishment Clause jurisprudence.

The neutrality approach has been supported directly or indirectly by many members of the Court even though it was not a well-developed approach until the 1970s. Most members of the Burger Court supported neutrality in the 1970s, but its support eroded in the 1980s and continues to erode under the Rehnquist Court as support for accommodation has grown. Stevens and Ginsburg are the current members of the Court who have given the strongest support to the neutrality approach.

Pre-Warren Court Period

Having examined the historical origins and the major competing approaches to the Establishment Clause, it is now possible to turn to a more detailed analysis of the major case development in this area of constitutional law. Before undertaking this analysis, however, it is important to recognize that the Supreme Court's Establishment Clause decisions have not been characterized by the consistent, logical application of clear constitutional guidelines. Indeed, it has frequently been quite the opposite. Levy (1986, pp. 162–63), for example, has accused the Court of being "inexcusably inconsistent in the interpretation of the Establishment Clause," characterizing the Court's decisions as "erratic and unprincipled. . . ." Similarly, Carter (1991, p. 72) writes, "A thorough review of establishment cases since World War II is one of the most frustrating jurisprudential exercises imaginable."

The Court gave little attention to the Establishment Clause before it nationalized the guarantee in *Everson v. Board of Education* (1947), a process discussed earlier in Chapter 4. The most important reason for the paucity of Establishment Clause cases prior to 1947 was of course that this guarantee limited only the federal government, and it was very unusual for the Congress or executive branch to be involved in legislation or actions that would raise Establishment Clause issues. The matter of standing also presented a barrier to the initiation of Establishment Clause cases. If the federal government did engage in activities aiding religion, those who received the benefits were not likely to raise issues, and those who might initiate a suit frequently lacked standing because they were not directly affected by the government program. Two pre-1947 cases do deserve mention, however. In *Pierce v. Society of Sisters* (1925), the Court ruled unconstitutional a 1922 Oregon Compulsory Education Act requiring that all children must attend public schools through high school. This case was decided under the Due Process Clause of the Fourteenth Amendment rather than the Establishment Clause, but it did have the important effect of providing constitutional support for parochial schools. *Cochran v. Board of Education* (1930) was also a parochial aid case in which the Court upheld a Louisiana law under which state tax monies were used to purchase and supply textbooks dealing with nonreligious subjects to all school children in the state, both public and private. This case was also decided under the Fourteenth Amendment, but the Court in *Cochran* set the stage for the "child benefit theory," which was an important principle in *Everson.*

The Vinson Court heard three major Establishment Clause cases between 1947 and 1952, leaving the Warren Court with a confusing and somewhat contradictory jurisprudential legacy. In *Everson* the Court majority used strict separationist language in arriving at an accommodationist result. In two closely related "released time" cases, the Vinson Court took a strict separationist approach in *McCollum v. Board of Education* (1948) to rule unconstitutional one type of released time program, but then the Court in *Zorach v. Clauson* (1952) used strong accommodationist language to approve a different type of released time activity.

Everson, which involved a New Jersey law that allowed parents to be reimbursed for the cost of sending their children to parochial schools on public buses, is an important case for two reasons. First, the Establishment Clause was nationalized in this case, making the clause applicable to the states through the Due Process Clause of the Fourteenth Amendment. Second, the majority opinion set forth some important principles that have guided the Court since that time.

Although nationalization of the Establishment Clause was important, it was not controversial among the justices. Many Court analysts felt that the Clause had been implicitly nationalized in *Cantwell v. Connecticut* (1940), when the Free Exercise Clause was explicitly nationalized. All nine members of the Vinson Court supported the incorporation of the Establishment Clause in *Everson.* In his majority opinion for the Court, Justice Black simply asserted the applicability of the Clause to the states rather than providing an elaborate rationale for the principle of incorporation. The relative ease with which the Establishment Clause was nationalized does not hide its importance, however, for this case opened the door to a steady flow of cases that continues today and that has thrust the Court into the middle of some of the country's most controversial public policy issues.

Black used predominantly strict separationist language for a five-person majority in this first major analysis of the Establishment Clause. Citing Madison and Jefferson extensively, Black offered the following often-cited interpretation of the Establishment Clause:

> *The "establishment of religion" clause of the First Amendment means at least this: Neither a state nor the Federal Government can set up a church. Neither can pass laws which aid one religion, aid all religions, or prefer one religion over another. Neither can force or influence a person to go to or to remain away from church against his will or force him to profess a belief or disbelief in any religion. No person can be punished for entertaining or professing religious beliefs or disbeliefs, for church attendance or nonattendance. No tax in any amount, large or small, can be levied to support any religious activities or institutions, whatever they may be called, or whatever form they may adopt to teach or practice religion. Neither a state nor the Federal Government can, openly or secretly, participate in the affairs of any religious organizations or groups and vice versa (330 U.S. at 15, 16).*

Black's endorsement of the strict separation approach was emphatic in the conclusion of his opinion: "The First Amendment has erected a wall between church and state. That wall must be kept high and impregnable. We could not approve the slightest breach" (330 U.S. at 18).

Despite the strict separationist language, Black's majority opinion reached an accommodationist result by finding that the challenged law did not violate the Establishment Clause. The basis for this conclusion was the **child benefit theory,** for Black argued that the law "does no more than provide a general program to help parents get their children, regardless of their religion, safely and expeditiously to and from accredited schools" (330 U.S. at 18). Finally, in addition to the strict separationist language and the accommodationist result, Black also employed neutralist language at one point in his opinion. Thus, Black's majority opinion in *Everson* provided support for all three approaches, and justices with sharply different views of the Establishment Clause have subsequently cited *Everson* for support.

The four dissenters agreed with Black's strict separationist interpretation of the Establishment Clause, but they disagreed with his conclusion about the constitutionality of the program. For the dissenters, the New Jersey law clearly breached the wall of separation between church and state.

Everson v. Board of Education of the Township of Ewing

330 U.S. 1, 67 S.Ct. 504, 91 L.Ed 711 (1947)

■ New Jersey had passed a law allowing local school districts to set their own policies regarding the transportation of children to and from schools. Acting under this law, Ewing Township's Board of Education authorized the reimbursement to parents of money spent in sending their children to school on regular buses operated by the public transportation system. This included reimbursement to parents who sent their children to Catholic schools. Arch Everson, a taxpayer in the school district, filed suit challenging the state law and the board policy on the basis that reimbursing parents of parochial school students violated both the state constitution and the Establishment Clause of the First Amendment. The state trial court that initially heard the case ruled that the law violated the state constitution, but the state appellate court reversed, holding that neither the state law nor the board's resolution violated either state or federal constitutional provisions.

This case is important because it was the case in which the Court formally nationalized the Establishment Clause and also because it was the first case in which the Court attempted to interpret the meaning of the Establishment Clause. As you read the case, consider the following questions: (1) Did Justice Black's majority opinion present a convincing argument for a strict separation approach to the Establishment Clause? (2) Were the dissenting justices correct that the strict separation approach should have led to the conclusion that the law violated the Establishment Clause? (3) Does a basis exist in the opinions for the support of all three approaches to the Establishment Clause: strict separation, neutrality, and accommodation?

Vote:

5 justices found the law constitutional (Black, Douglas, Murphy, Reed, Vinson).

4 justices found the law unconstitutional (Burton, Frankfurter, Jackson, Rutledge).

Justice Black delivered the opinion of the Court.

The New Jersey statute is challenged as a "law respecting the establishment of religion." The First Amendment, as made applicable to the states by the Fourteenth, commands that a state "shall make no law respecting an establishment of religion, or prohibiting the free exercise thereof." . . .[T]hese words of the First Amendment reflected in the minds of early Americans a vivid mental picture of conditions and practices which they fervently wished to stamp out in order to preserve liberty for themselves and for their posterity. Doubtless their goal has not been entirely reached; but so far has the Nation moved toward it that the expression "law respecting an establishment of religion," probably does not so vividly remind present-day Americans of the evils, fears, and potential problems that caused that expression to be written into our Bill of Rights. Whether this New Jersey law is one respecting an "establishment of religion" requires an understanding of the meaning of that language, particularly with respect to the imposition of taxes. Once again, therefore, it is not inappropriate briefly to review the background and environment of the period in which that constitutional language was fashioned and adopted.

A large portion of the early settlers of this country came here from Europe to escape the bondage of laws which compelled them to support and attend government favored churches. The centuries immediately before and contemporaneous with the colonization of America had been filled with turmoil, civil strife, and persecutions, generated in large part by established sects determined to maintain their absolute political and religious supremacy. With the power of government supporting them, at various times and places, Catholics had persecuted Protestants, Protestants had persecuted Catholics, Protestant sects had persecuted other Protestant sects, Catholics of one shade of belief had persecuted Catholics of another shade of belief, and all of these had from time to time persecuted Jews. In efforts to force loyalty to whatever religious group happened to be on top and in league with the government of a particular time and place, men and women had been fined, cast in jail, cruelly tortured, and killed.* * *

These practices of the old world were transplanted to and began to thrive in the soil of the new America. The very charters granted by the English Crown to the individuals and companies designated to make the laws which would control the destinies of the colonials authorized these individuals and companies to erect religious establishments which all, whether believers or nonbelievers, would be required to support and attend. An exercise of this authority was accompanied by a repetition of many of the old-world practices and persecutions.* * *

These practices became so commonplace as to shock the freedom-loving colonials into a feeling of abhorrence. The imposition of taxes to pay ministers' salaries and to build and maintain churches and church property aroused their indignation. It was these feelings which found expression in the First Amendment. No one locality and no one group throughout the Colonies can rightly be given credit for having aroused the sentiment that culminated in adoption of the Bill of Rights' provisions embracing religious liberty. But Virginia, where the established church had achieved a dominant influence in political affairs and where many excesses attracted wide public attention, provided a great stimulus and able leadership for the movement. The people there, as elsewhere, reached the conviction that individual religious liberty could be achieved best under a government which was stripped of all power to tax, to support, or otherwise to assist any or all religions, or to interfere with the beliefs of any religious individual or group.

The movement toward this end reached its dramatic climax in Virginia in 1785–86 when the Virginia legislative body was about to renew Virginia's tax levy for the support of the established church. Thomas Jefferson and James Madison led the fight against this tax. Madison wrote his great *Memorial and Remonstrance* against the law. In it, he eloquently argued that a true religion did not need the support of law; that no person, either believer or non-believer, should be taxed to support a religious institution of any kind; that the best interest of a society required that the minds of men always be wholly free; and that cruel persecutions were the inevitable result of government-established religions.* * *

* * *

The meaning and scope of the First Amendment, preventing establishment of religion or prohibiting the free exercise thereof, in the light of its history and the evils it was designed forever to suppress, have been several times elaborated by the decisions of this Court prior to the application of the First Amendment to the states by the Fourteenth. The broad meaning given the Amendment by these earlier cases has been accepted by this Court in its decisions concerning an individual's religious freedom rendered since the Fourteenth Amendment was interpreted to make the prohibitions of the First applicable to state action abridging religious freedom. There is every reason to give the same application and broad interpretation to the "establishment of religion" clause.* * *

The "establishment of religion" clause of the First Amendment means at least this: Neither a state nor the Federal Government can set up a church. Neither can pass laws which aid one religion, aid all religions, or prefer one religion over another. Neither can force nor influence a person to go to or to remain away from church against his will or force him to profess a belief or disbelief in any religion. No person can be punished for entertaining or professing religious beliefs or disbeliefs, for church attendance or non-attendance. No tax in any amount, large or small, can be levied to support any religious activities or institutions, whatever they may be called, or whatever form they may adopt to teach or practice religion. Neither a state nor the Federal Government can, openly or secretly, participate in the affairs of any religious organization or groups and vice versa. In the words of Jefferson, the clause against establishment of religion by law was intended to erect "a wall of separation between Church and State."

We must consider the New Jersey statute in accordance with the foregoing limitations imposed by the First Amendment. But we must not strike that state statute down if it is within the State's constitutional power even though it approaches the verge of that power. New Jersey cannot consistently with the "establishment of religion" clause of the First Amendment contribute tax-raised funds to the support of an institution that teaches the tenets and faith of any church. On the other hand, other language commands that New Jersey cannot hamper its citizens in the free exercise of their own religion. Consequently, it cannot exclude individual Catholics, Lutherans, Mohammedans, Baptists, Jews, Methodists, Non-believers, Presbyterians, or the members of any other faith, *because of their faith, or lack of it,* from receiving the benefits of public welfare legislation. While we do not mean to intimate that a state could not provide transportation only to children attending public schools, we must be careful, in protecting the citizens of New Jersey against state-established churches, to be sure that we do not inadvertently prohibit New Jersey from extending its general state law benefits to all citizens without regard to their religious belief.

Measured by these standards, we cannot say that the First Amendment prohibits New Jersey from spending tax-raised funds to pay the bus fares of parochial school pupils as part of a general program under which it pays the fares of pupils attending public and other schools. It is undoubtedly true that children are helped to get to church schools. There is even a possibility that some of the children might not be sent to the church schools if the parents were compelled to pay their children's bus fares out of their own pockets when transportation to a public school would have been paid for by the State. The same possibility exists where the state requires a local transit company to provide reduced fares to school children including those attending parochial schools, or where a municipally owned transportation system undertakes to carry all school children free of charge. Moreover, state-paid policemen, detailed to protect children going to and from church schools from the very real hazards of traffic, would serve much the same purpose and accomplish much the same result as state provisions intended to guarantee free transportation of a kind which the state deems to be best for the school children's welfare. And parents might refuse to risk their children to the serious danger of traffic accidents going to and from parochial schools, the approaches to which were not protected by policemen. Similarly, parents might be reluctant to permit their children to attend schools which the state had cut off from such general government services as ordinary police and fire protection, connections for sewage disposal, public highways and sidewalks. Of course, cutting off church schools from these services, so separate and so indisputably marked off from the religious function, would make it far more difficult for the schools to operate. But such is obviously not the purpose of the First Amendment. That Amendment requires the state to be a neutral in its relations with groups of religious believers and non-believers; it does not require the state to be their adversary. State power is no more to be used so as to handicap religions than it is to favor them.

This Court has said that parents may, in the discharge of their duty under state compulsory education laws, send their children to a religious rather than a public school if the school meets the secular educational requirements which the state has the power to impose. It appears that these parochial schools meet New Jersey's requirements. The State contributes no money to the schools. It does not support them. Its legislation, as applied, does no more than provide a general program to help parents get their children, regardless of their religion, safely and expeditiously to and from accredited schools.

The First Amendment has erected a wall between church and state. That wall must be kept high and impregnable. We could not approve the slightest breach. New Jersey has not breached it here.

Affirmed.

Mr. Justice Jackson, dissenting.

I find myself, contrary to first impressions, unable to join in this decision. I have a sympathy, though it is not ideological, with Catholic citizens who are compelled by law to pay taxes for public schools, and also feel constrained by conscience and discipline to support other schools for their own children. Such relief to them as this case involves is not in itself a serious burden to taxpayers and I had assumed it to be as little serious in principle. Study of the case convinces me otherwise. The Court's opinion marshals every argument in favor of state aid and puts the case in its most favorable light, but much of its reasoning confirms my conclusions that there are no good grounds upon which to support the present legislation. In fact, the undertones of the opinion, advocating complete and uncompromising separation of Church from State, seem utterly discordant with its conclusion yielding support to their commingling in educational matters. The case which irresistibly comes to mind as the most fitting precedent is that of Julia who, according to Byron's reports, "whispering 'I will ne'er consent,'—consented."

* * *

The New Jersey Act in question makes the character of the school, not the needs of the children, determine the eligibility of parents to reimbursement. . . . [U]nder the Act and resolution brought to us by this case, children are classified according to the schools they attend and are to be aided if they attend the public schools or private Catholic schools, and they are not allowed to be aided if they attend private secular schools or private religious schools of other faiths.

* * *

Justice Rutledge, with whom Justice Frankfurter, Justice Jackson, and Justice Burton agree, dissenting.

* * *

Not simply an established church, but any law respecting an establishment of religion is forbidden.* * *

The Amendment's purpose was not to strike merely at the official establishment of a single sect, creed or religion, outlawing only a formal relation such as had prevailed in England and some of the colonies. Necessarily it was to uproot all such relationships. But the object was broader than separating church and state in this narrow sense. It was to create a complete and permanent separation of the spheres of religious activity and civil authority by comprehensively forbidding every form of public aid or support for religion. In proof the Amendment's wording and history unite with this Court's consistent utterances whenever attention has been fixed directly upon the question.

* * *

Does New Jersey's action furnish support for religion by the use of the taxing power? Certainly it does, if the test remains undiluted as Jefferson and Madison made it, that money taken by taxation from one is not to be used or given to support another's religious training or belief, or indeed one's own. Today as then the furnishing of "contributions of money for the propagation of opinions which he disbelieves" is the forbidden exaction; and the prohibition is absolute for whatever measure brings that consequence and whatever amount may be sought or given to that end.

The funds used here were raised by taxation. The Court does not dispute, nor could it, that their use does in fact give aid and encouragement to religious instruction. It only concludes that this aid is not "support" in law. But Madison and Jefferson were concerned with aid and support in fact, not as a legal conclusion "entangled in precedents." Here parents pay money to send their children to parochial schools and funds raised by taxation are used to reimburse them. This not only helps the children to get to school and the parents to send them. It aids them in a substantial way to get the very thing which they are sent to the particular school to secure, namely, religious training and teaching.

* * *

The judgment should be reversed.

The Vinson Court provided strong support for the strict separationist approach the next year in *McCollum v. Board of Education* (1948). This case involved a released-time program in Illinois, which allowed religious groups, including Protestant, Catholic, and Jewish representatives, to come into the public schools during regular school hours to provide religious instruction. Students were not compelled to attend but instead were allowed to leave their classrooms to pursue their regular work elsewhere in the building. Black again authored the opinion for the Court, but this time he wrote for an eight-person majority. In his opinion, Black explicitly rejected the nonpreferentialist argument that the Establishment Clause prohibited only government preference of one religion over another, not nonpreferential assistance to all religions. Citing *Everson* extensively, Black argued that "the First Amendment has erected a wall between Church and State which must be kept high and impregnable" (333 U.S. at 212). For Black and his seven colleagues, the wall was clearly breached by this released-time program.

A consistency can be seen in the Court's strict separationist language in *Everson* and *McCollum,* but this consistency is difficult to find in the Court's second released time case of *Zorach v. Clauson* (1952), in which the majority of the Court employed strong accommodationist language to approve a New York City released time program. The New York program did differ from the Illinois program because the religious instruction occurred off the public school grounds. Students who wished to receive this religious instruction were allowed to leave the school buildings to go to religious centers where they received religious training or had devotional activities. Justice Douglas authored the six-person majority opinion, which had a primary thrust of accommodation but which also made references to strict separation as well as neutrality. The basis of Douglas's opinion, which led to the approval of the New York program, was contained in the following words: "We are a religious people whose institutions presuppose a Supreme Being. When the state encourages religious instruction or cooperates with religious authorities by adjusting the schedule of public events to sectarian needs, it follows the best of our traditions. For it then respects the religious nature of our people and accommodates the public service to their spiritual needs. To hold that it may not would be to find in the Constitution a requirement that the government show a callous indifference to religious groups" (343 U.S. at 313, 314). Thus, using an accommodationist approach and distinguishing the facts of this case from *McCollum*, the Court ruled that the released time program of New York City did not violate the Establishment Clause.

The Vinson Court thus bequeathed to the Warren Court an Establishment Clause inheritance of confusion and contradiction. It is necessary to guard against being overly harsh in assessing the work of the Vinson Court, however. It can be viewed as a constitutional pioneer exploring new and uncharted areas. No line of precedents existed to guide the Court during this period of time. In addition, the historical record provided mixed guidance. Furthermore, public opinion may also have played an important role, for the *McCollum* decision was met with an outpouring of public criticism. This was heightened between 1948 and 1952 as the cold war and the threat of communism—an atheistic ideology—made the justices especially sensitive to the relationship between religion and the government. It is not possible to measure with any precision the extent to which the majority opinion in *Zorach* was concerned with appeasing public opinion, but the dissenting justices certainly suggested this was a factor. Whatever the reasons for the lack of consistency in its decisions, the Vinson Court did create a foundation upon which future Courts could build by setting forth some of the most important arguments in favor of both the strict separationist and accommodationist approaches as well as hinting at a neutralist approach to the Establishment Clause.

The Warren Court Era

The Warren Court Establishment Clause cases did not show a pattern of complete consistency and clarity, but it is possible to see emerging trends as the justices sought to develop doctrinal guidelines for interpreting the Establishment Clause. An examination of the major cases of the Warren Court shows that the justices rejected an accommodationist approach, but they did not adhere consistently to either a separationist or a neutrality approach. Nonetheless, the Warren Court was most strongly committed to neutrality principles. The justices of the Warren Court also attempted to develop more specific guidelines in Establishment Clause cases, and they were somewhat successful in this effort, developing the first two prongs of what was to become the *Lemon* test.

Some scholars argue that the Warren Court's basic approach to Establishment Clause jurisprudence was the separationist theory, and the case of *Engel v. Vitale* (1962), the case study that began this chapter, is typically cited as the case that best shows the Warren Court's commitment to the high wall approach. It is certainly true that the Court did take a strict separationist approach in this case, which was one of the most publicized and controversial decisions in Supreme Court history. Black, the justice most associated with the separationist approach, authored the opinion, and his forceful language again set forth the basic principles associated with the high wall/no aid theory. He drew extensively upon history, citing again the roles of Jefferson and Madison in contributing to the development of the Establishment Clause. In addressing the specific issue of state-sponsored prayer in the public schools, Black's language was absolutist: ". . . the constitutional prohibition against laws respecting an establishment of religion must at least mean that in this country it is no part of the business of government to compose official prayers for any group of the American people to recite as part of a religious program carried on by government" (370 U.S. at 425). Stewart penned a lone dissent, making a brief accommodationist argument and identifying *Zorach* as the appropriate precedent for this case.

Despite the significance of *Engel* and the strong separationist language in the majority opinion, the other major Establishment Clause cases of the Warren Court in the sixties show an emerging commitment to the neutrality approach and the development of the purpose and effect prongs of the *Lemon* test. This process had its origins in the Sunday closing law case of *McGowan v. State of Maryland* (1961). The Court actually heard four separate cases involving challenges to Sunday closing laws, finding all of the laws constitutional. These cases raised challenges to both the Free Exercise Clause and the Establishment Clause. We will focus here on *McGowan* because the Court gave its fullest exposition of the Establishment Clause in this case. The issue before the Court was whether a Maryland law that prohibited the sale of certain items on Sunday violated the Establishment Clause. The case was initiated by employees of a department store who had been convicted under the law for selling a three-ring loose-leaf binder, a can of floor wax, a stapler and staples, and a toy submarine. The employees' attorneys argued that the law under which they were arrested was passed to promote religious activities and thus was violative of the Establishment Clause. Chief Justice Warren wrote the opinion in this 8-1 case. He rejected the accommodationist view that the Clause was limited only to forbidding the establishment of a national or state church, but he did not present an endorsement of the strict separationist approach. Rather, he argued that the Establishment Clause must be given a broad interpretation to deal with the evils it was designed to suppress, but he also argued that this did not invalidate federal or state laws that coincided with the beliefs of some or all religions. The key distinction, Warren reasoned, involved the purpose and effect of the law, which must not be religious in nature. Warren's lengthy historical analysis of Sunday closing laws led him to conclude that, despite their original religious purpose, current laws as written and administered were secular rather than religious because the state was concerned with setting aside a day of "rest, repose, recreation, and tranquility . . ." (366 U.S. at 450).

The 1963 case of *School District of Abington Township v. Schempp* was closely tied to both the *Engel* and *McGowan* decisions. *Schempp* was directly related to the *Engel* case because both involved the controversial subject of state-sponsored religious activities in the public schools, while *Schempp* and *McGowan* were closely linked because of the Court's emerging doctrinal guidelines involving the Establishment Clause.

As was discussed at the beginning of this chapter, the *Engel* case gave rise to a tremendous outpouring of public criticism of the Court. Substantial evidence suggests that the Court agreed to hear two companion cases the next term—*Schempp* and *Murray v. Curlett* (1963)—in order to blunt some of the criticism. These cases involved more obvious violations of the Establishment Clause because they dealt with state laws requiring Bible reading in the public schools. Thus, while *Engel* involved voluntary, nondenominational religious activities, the 1963 cases concerned compulsory, Christian activities in the public schools.

Warren assigned the majority opinion in this 8-1 decision not to the Court's absolutist, Black, but rather to Tom Clark, a judicial moderate and a Roman Catholic. Clark's opinion went to great lengths to acknowledge the religious nature of the American people, but Clark explicitly rejected the accommodationist approach to the Establishment Clause: ". . .[T]his Court has rejected unequivocally the contention that the Establishment Clause forbids only government preference of one religion over another" (374 U.S. at 216). But Clark certainly did not argue for a high wall/strict separation approach either. Instead, he continually referred to the principle of neutrality as being the proper approach to the Establishment Clause: "In the relationship between man and religion, the State is firmly committed to a position of neutrality" (374 U.S. at 226). Then, drawing from the language of *McGowan,* Clark set forth a two-part test for Establishment Clause cases: "The test may be stated as follows: what are the purpose and the primary effect of the enactment? If either is the advancement or inhibition of religion then the enactment exceeds the scope of legislative power as circumscribed by the Constitution. That is to say that to withstand the strictures of the Establishment Clause there must be a secular legislative purpose and a primary effect that neither advances nor inhibits religion" (374 U.S. at 222). Applying this two-part test to the state-required Bible reading, Clark had little trouble concluding that the Establishment Clause was violated.

School District of Abington Township, Pennsylvania v. Schempp

374 U.S. 203, 83 S.Ct. 1560, 10 L.Ed. 2d 844 (1963)

■ In 1959 Pennsylvania passed a law requiring that at least ten verses should be read from the Holy Bible at the beginning of each class day in the state's public schools. At Abington Senior High School in a suburb of Philadelphia, this law was implemented through standard practices followed each morning between 8:15 and 8:30 A.M. During this homeroom time, a student would read ten verses from the Bible, which were broadcast into each room in the school building through an intercommunication system. Following this, the student would recite the Lord's Prayer, and students in the classrooms were asked to stand and join in unison. Under the provisions of the law, students could choose to leave the classroom or to stay but not participate. This law was challenged in federal district court by Edward Schempp, his wife Sidney, and their two children, Roger and Donna, who were members of the Unitarian Church. Mr. Schempp testified in court that the doctrines associated with a literal reading of the Bible were contrary to the family's religious beliefs, and he also testified that the family decided against excusing the children from the exercises because of concern that this would adversely affect their relationships with their classmates and teachers. A three-judge federal district court panel ruled that the law violated the Establishment Clause of the First Amendment as made applicable to the states through the Due Process Clause of the Fourteenth Amendment. (This case was decided with a companion case from Maryland, *Murray v. Curlett.*)

This is a significant case because the Warren Court embraced a neutralist approach to the Establishment Clause and also because the Court set forth two specific guidelines for the analysis of Establishment Clause cases. In reading the case, consider the following questions: (1) Why did the Court use neutralist language that was so dramatically different from the separationist language in *Everson*? (2) Could the Court have reached the same result using a separationist approach or an accommodationist approach? (3) Do public elementary and secondary schools present an especially sensitive setting for Establishment Clause cases?

VOTE:

8 justices found the law unconstitutional (Black, Brennan, Clark, Douglas, Goldberg, Harlan, Warren, White).

1 justice found the law constitutional (Stewart).

Justice Clark delivered the opinion of the Court.

It is true that religion has been closely identified with our history and government. As we said in *Engel v. Vitale* (1962), "The history of man is inseparable from the history of religion. And . . . since the beginning of that history many people have devoutly believed that 'More things are wrought by prayer than this world dreams of.' " In *Zorach v. Clauson* (1952), we gave specific recognition to the proposition that "[w]e are a religious people whose institutions presuppose a Supreme Being." The fact that the Founding Fathers believed devotedly that there was a God and that the inalienable rights of man were rooted in Him is clearly evidenced in their writings, from the Mayflower Compact to the Constitution itself. * * * It can be truly said, therefore, that today , as in the beginning, our national life reflects a religious people. . . .

This is not to say, however, that religion has been so identified with our history and government that religious freedom is not likewise as strongly embedded in our public and private life. Nothing but the most telling of personal experiences in religious persecution suffered by our forbearers, see *Everson v. Board of Education* (1947), could have planted our belief in liberty of religious opinion any more deeply in our heritage. * * *

Almost a hundred years ago in *Minor v. Board of Education of Cincinnati,* Judge Alphonzo Taft, father of the revered Chief Justice, in an unpublished opinion stated the ideal of our people as to religious freedom as one of "absolute equality before the law of all religious opinions and sects. . . ."

* * *

"The government is neutral, and, while protecting none, it prefers none,and it disparages none."

Before examining this "neutral" position in which the Establishment and Free Exercise Clauses of the First Amendment place our government it is well that we discuss the reach of the Amendment under the cases of this Court.

First, this Court has decisively settled that the First Amendment's mandate that "Congress shall make no law respecting an establishment of religion, or prohibiting the free exercise thereof" has been made wholly applicable to the states by the Fourteenth Amendment. * * *

Second, this Court has rejected unequivocally the contention that the establishment clause forbids only governmental preference of one religion over another. Almost 20 years ago in *Everson,* the Court said that "[n]either a state nor the Federal government can set up a church. Neither can pass laws which aid one religion, aid all religions, or prefer one religion over another." * * *

* * *

The wholesome "neutrality" of which this Court's cases speak thus stems from a recognition of the teachings of history that powerful sects or groups might bring about a fusion of governmental or religious functions or a concert or dependency of one upon the other to the end that official support of the State or Federal Government would be placed behind the tenets of one or of all orthodoxies. This the Establishment Clause prohibits. And a further reason for neutrality is found in the Free Exercise Clause, which recognizes the value of religious training, teaching, and observance and, more particularly, the right of every person to freely choose his own course with reference thereto, free of any compulsion from the state. This the Free Exercise Clause guarantees. Thus, as we have seen, the two clauses may overlap. As we have indicated, the Establishment Clause has been directly considered by this Court eight times in the past score of years and, with only one Justice dissenting on the point, it has consistently held that the clause withdrew all legislative power respecting religious belief or the expression thereof. The test may be stated as follows: what are the purpose and the primary effect of the enactment? If either is the advancement or inhibition of religion then the enactment exceeds the scope of legislative power as circumscribed by the Constitution. That is to say that to withstand the strictures of the Establishment Clause there must be a secular legislative purpose and a primary effect that neither advances nor inhibits religion. *Everson v. Board of Education; McGowan v. Maryland* (1961). The Free Exercise Clause, likewise considered many times here, withdraws from legislative power, state and federal, the exertion of any restraint on the free exercise of religion. Its purpose is to secure religious liberty in the individual by prohibiting any invasions thereof by civil authority. Hence it is necessary in a free exercise case for one to show the coercive effect of the enactment as it operates against him in the practice of his religion. The distinction between the two clauses is apparent—a violation of the Free Exercise Clause is predicated on coercion while the Establishment Clause violation need not be so attended.

Applying the Establishment Clause principles to the cases at bar we find that the States are requiring the selection and reading at the opening of the school day of verses from the Holy Bible and the recitation of the Lord's Prayer by the students in unison. These exercises are prescribed as part of the curricular activities of students who are required by law to attend school. They are held in the school buildings under the supervision and with the participation of teachers employed in those schools. None of these factors, other than compulsory school attendance, was present in the program upheld in *Zorach v. Clauson.* The trial court . . . has found that such an opening exercise is a religious ceremony and was intended by the State to be so. We agree with the trial court's finding as to the religious character of the exercises. Given that finding the exercises and the law requiring them are in violation of the Establishment Clause.

* * *

The conclusion follows that . . . the [law] requires religious exercises and such exercises are being conducted in direct violation of the rights of the appellees. . . . Nor are these required exercises mitigated by the fact that individual students may absent themselves upon parental request, for that fact furnishes no defense to a claim of unconstitutionality under the Establishment Clause. See *Engel v. Vitale.* Further, it is no defense to urge that the religious practices here may be relatively minor encroachments on the First Amendment. The breach of neutrality that is today a trickling stream may all too soon become a raging torrent and, in the words of Madison, "it is proper to take alarm at the first experiment on our liberties."

It is insisted that unless these religious exercises are permitted a "religion of secularism" is established in the schools. We agree of course that the state may not establish a "religion of secularism" in the sense of affirmatively opposing or showing hostility to religion, thus "preferring those who believe in no religion over those who do believe." *Zorach v. Clauson.* We do not agree, however, that this decision in any sense has that effect. In addition, it might well be said that one's education is not complete without a study of comparative religion or the history of religion and its relationship to the advancement of civilization. It certainly may be said that the Bible is worthy of study for its literary and historic qualities. Nothing we have said here indicates that such study of the Bible or of religion, when presented objectively as part of a secular program of education, may not be effected consistent with the First Amendment. But the exercises here do not fall into those categories. They are religious exercises, required by the States in violation of the command of the First Amendment that the Government maintain strict neutrality, neither aiding nor opposing religion.

Finally, we cannot accept that the concept of neutrality, which does not permit a State to require a religious exercise even with the consent of the majority of those affected, collides with the majority's right to free exercise of religion. While the Free Exercise Clause clearly prohibits the use of state action to deny the rights of free exercise to *anyone,* it has never meant that a majority could use the machinery of the State to practice its beliefs. * * *

The place of religion in our society is an exalted one, achieved through a long tradition of reliance on the home, the church and the inviolable citadel of the individual heart and mind. We have come to recognize through bitter experience that it is not within the power of government to invade that citadel, whether its purpose or effect be to aid or oppose, to advance or retard. In the relationship between man and religion, the State is firmly committed to a position of neutrality. Though the application of that rule requires interpretation of a delicate sort, the rule itself is clearly and concisely stated in the words of the First Amendment. Applying that rule to the facts of [this case], we affirm the judgment. . . .* * *

Justice Douglas, concurring. [omitted]

Justice Brennan, concurring. [omitted]

Justice Goldberg, with whom Justice Harlan joins, concurring. [omitted]

Justice Stewart, dissenting. [omitted]

If the Warren Court's purpose in *Schempp* was to blunt public criticism of the Court regarding its stance on state-sponsored religious activities in the public schools, the justices did not succeed. But the Court did experience some success in clarifying the principles by which it would interpret the Establishment Clause, principles that the Court applied in two 1968 cases, *Board of Education v. Allen* and *Epperson v. Arkansas.*

The *Allen* case was another parochial aid controversy, this time involving a New York State program through which state-approved textbooks were lent free of charge to all seventh through twelfth grade students, including parochial students. The Court ruled 6-3 that this program did not violate the Establishment Clause, with White writing the majority opinion. White argued that *Everson* was the most relevant precedent; the Court had approved in *Everson* the public funding of transportation of all students, public and parochial alike, and in this case the Court could approve the loaning of secular textbooks to all students. Unlike *Everson,* however, the majority took a neutrality approach rather than a strict separation approach and applied the purpose and effect prongs of *Schempp,* finding that the New York program had a secular legislative purpose and a primary effect that neither advanced nor inhibited religion. Black, Douglas, and Fortas, the Court's strongest separationists, dissented in the case, with Black chastising the majority for its failure "to keep the wall of separation between church and state high and impregnable. . ." (392 U.S. at 254).

The last major Establishment Clause case of the Warren Court was *Epperson v. Arkansas* (1968) in which the Court ruled unanimously that an Arkansas law prohibiting the teaching of evolution in the public schools and universities violated the Establishment Clause. Fortas wrote the opinion for the Court and followed closely the Establishment Clause guidelines set forth in *McGowan, Schempp,* and *Allen.* He began the opinion with a forceful assertion of the neutrality approach:

"Government in our democracy, state and national, must be neutral in matters of religious theory, doctrine, and practice. It may not be hostile to any religion or to the advocacy of no-religion; and it may not aid, foster, or promote one religion or religious theory against another or even against the militant opposite. The First Amendment mandates governmental neutrality between religion and religion, and between religion and nonreligion" (393 U.S. at 103,104). Fortas then turned to the purpose and primary effect inquiries of *Schempp,* and he had little trouble concluding that the Arkansas law was unquestionably unconstitutional.

Thus, by the end of the Warren Court era, some distinctive directions had emerged in Establishment Clause jurisprudence. The Court had consistently rejected the accommodationist approach. Some support could be found for the separationist view, but the neutrality approach was the dominant one by the late sixties. Consistent with the neutrality approach, the Warren Court had also developed a two-pronged test to assess violations of the Establishment Clause. In order for a government law or action to be constitutional, it had to have a valid secular purpose and its primary effect could neither advance nor inhibit religion.

The Burger Court Era

The Burger Court years were tumultuous ones in Establishment Clause jurisprudence. Under Burger's leadership, the era began with the Court building upon the legacy from the previous Warren Court, embracing a neutrality approach and expanding the two-pronged test of *Schempp* into the three-pronged test of *Lemon.* Burger and other justices became increasingly displeased with the neutrality approach and the *Lemon* test during the seventies, however, because the Court found few government programs to be constitutional. In the early eighties, with Burger and Rehnquist leading the way, the Court shifted from a neutralist to an accommodationist approach and undermined the *Lemon* test. In a remarkable series of cases in 1985, however, the neutralists regained control and reaffirmed the Court's commitment to the *Lemon* test. Our task now is to examine this fascinating period in the history of the Establishment Clause by analyzing the major cases decided by the Burger Court.

It is important at the outset to recognize the important role played by Burger in the Establishment Clause cases. As was seen in Chapter 2, the chief justice has a variety of techniques available by which to lead the Court, and, according to an excellent study by Joseph Kobylka (1989), Burger sought to employ these in Establishment Clause cases during his tenure as chief justice. As evidence of this, Kobylka shows that Burger wrote some type of opinion—majority, plurality, or dissenting—in twenty of the twenty-seven Establishment Clause cases decided during his tenure, a 71 percent rate compared to his overall writing rate of 20 percent. Furthermore, when Burger was in the majority, he assigned himself the opinion 67 percent of the time compared to his 25 percent opinion assignment rate in all important cases (p. 550). Burger championed an accommodationist approach to the Establishment Clause in both his voting patterns and his written opinions, but he nevertheless was not a radical accommodationist. As seen in Table 5.1, showing the voting records of all the justices in the Establishment Clause cases during the Burger Court era (p. 551), Burger supported the accommodationist position 74 percent of the time, a level of support similar to O'Connor's and less than White's (86 percent) and Rehnquist's (91 percent).

Burger exerted his leadership early, writing the majority opinions in three important cases in 1970 and 1971 that set forth the Court's major doctrinal guidelines in Establishment Clause cases. The first case, *Walz v. Tax Commission* (1970),

TABLE 5.1: Levels of Support for Governmental Accommodation of Religion Among Burger Court Justices, 1969-85 Terms

1. Rehnquist	91% (21/23)
2. White	86% (24/28)
3. Burger	74% (20/27)
4. O'Connor	73% (8/11)
5. Powell	46% (10.5/23)
6. Harlan	40% (2/5)
7. Stewart	38% (6.5/17)
8. Blackmun	37% (9.5/26)
9. Black	20% (1/5)
10. Marshall	15% (4/26)
11. Brennan	14% (4/28)
12. Stevens	12% (2/17)
13. Douglas	0% (0/11)

Source: Kobylka, Joseph (1989), p. 551.

involved a challenge to the New York City Tax Commission, which gave property tax exemptions to religious organizations. Writing for an 8-1 majority, Burger argued that the exemption was not a violation of the Establishment Clause. He cast his majority opinion in neutrality language, but Burger wrote of a "benevolent neutrality" that indicated his sympathy for a nonpreferentialist or accommodationist theory of the Establishment Clause. Burger attacked the Court's separationist approach in *Everson* and instead cited with favor Douglas' accommodationist argument in *Zorach*, which must have irritated Douglas who was the lone dissenter in *Walz*. Burger's language regarding the proper approach to the Establishment Clause is worth quoting because it shows the orientation he brought to Establishment Clause cases throughout his tenure as chief justice: "The course of constitutional neutrality in this area cannot be an absolutely straight line; rigidity could well defeat the basic purpose of these provisions, which is to insure that no religion be sponsored or favored, none commanded, and none inhibited. The general principle deductible from the First Amendment and all that has been said by the Court is this: that we will not tolerate either governmentally established religion or governmental interference with religion. Short of these expressly proscribed governmental acts there is room for play in the joints productive of a benevolent neutrality which will permit religious exercise to exist without sponsorship and without interference" (397 U.S. at 669).

Having set forth his benevolent neutrality approach, Burger then turned to the purpose and effect questions of the *Schempp* test, finding the tax exemption to meet both requirements. The exemption did not have a religious purpose or effect, reasoned Burger, because the exemption extended to many nonreligious entities such as hospitals and libraries, all of which contributed in many positive ways to the public interest. Burger also introduced a new question to Establishment Clause analysis, whether a challenged activity creates an excessive government entanglement with religion, for he argued that the Establishment Clause was intended to prevent excessive involvement between government and religion. Burger argued that tax exemptions served to prevent this involvement, whereas government taxation of religious property would have the opposite effect of creating excessive government entanglement with religion.

Lemon v. Kurtzman (1971), decided with a companion case from Rhode Island (*Earley v. DiCenso*), presented the Burger Court with the first of many difficult and controversial parochial aid cases. Numerous state governments during this time period were adopting programs providing substantial forms of support to parochial schools. Ironically, the Court was responsible in part for the dramatic growth in parochial aid programs because of its previous decisions involving school prayer and parochial aid. The decisions in *Engel* and *Schempp* meant that state-sponsored religious activities were prohibited in public schools, and many parents opted for parochial schools so that their children could be educated in a religious environment. Furthermore, the *Everson* and *Allen* decisions suggested that the Court was willing to allow various forms of parochial aid, at least those which primarily benefited the children. The growth in parochial aid programs was also related to two strong arguments in favor of such aid: (1) these schools were reducing the financial pressure on public schools and (2) parochial school parents were paying taxes for the public schools but were not receiving any tax benefits. Pennsylvania's program in this case involved direct reimbursement to nonpublic schools for expenditures for teachers' salaries, textbooks, and instructional materials, and a variety of requirements were written into the law to assure a separation of church and state to meet Establishment Clause challenges.

Burger's majority opinion for the 8-0 Court in *Lemon* formally united the purpose and effect questions from *Schempp* and the excessive government entanglement question of *Walz* into the explicit three-prong inquiry that has come to be known as the *Lemon* test: "First, the statute must have a secular legislative purpose; second, its principal or primary effect must be one that neither advances nor inhibits religion; finally, the statute must not foster 'an excessive government entanglement with religion' " (403 U.S. at 613, 614). In applying this test to the Pennsylvania statute, Burger argued that the law failed the third prong of excessive entanglement in regard to the direct expenditures for teachers' salaries, for the provisions that sought to ensure that the teachers played a nonreligious role involved substantial government monitoring of the activities in the religious schools.

Burger's majority opinion in *Lemon* did not emphasize a particular approach, but it implicitly gave strong support to neutrality. Burger once again attacked the separationist approach, arguing that "our prior decisions do not call for total separation between church and state. . ." (403 U.S. at 614). Instead, Burger argued, "the line of separation, far from being a 'wall,' is a blurred, indistinct, and variable barrier depending on all the circumstances of a particular relationship" (403 U.S. at 614). Nonetheless, Burger concluded: "Under our system the choice has been made that government is to be excluded entirely from the area of religious instruction and churches excluded from the affairs of government. The Constitution decrees that religion must be a private matter for the individual, the family, and the institutions of private choice, and that while some involvement and entanglement are inevitable, lines must be drawn" (403 U.S. at 625).

Lemon v. Kurtzman

403 U.S. 602, 91 S.Ct. 2105, 29 L.Ed.2d 745 (1971)

■ Pennsylvania and Rhode Island both passed laws in the late sixties that provided state financial assistance to church-related elementary and secondary schools. Pennsylvania provided reimbursement to nonpublic schools for various costs associated with teachers' salaries, textbooks, and instructional materials in designated secular subjects. Under this law, the State provided over $5 million in annual assistance to over 1,000 schools, 96 percent of which were church-related. Under the Rhode Island statute, the State provided direct payment of supplemental salaries to teachers of secular subjects in nonpublic elementary schools. Various restrictions were placed on these salaries, including a limit on the amount, which could not exceed 15 percent of a person's salary. Two hundred fifty teachers had applied for benefits under the statute, and all of them were employees of Roman Catholic schools. Both laws were challenged as violating the Establishment Clause of the First Amendment. A three-judge federal district court found the Rhode Island law to be unconstitutional. In the Pennsylvania case, a federal district court ruled 2-1 that the law did not violate the Establishment Clause. The Supreme Court agreed to hear both cases and consolidated them.

This case is important because the Court set forth the three-part *Lemon* test to guide analysis of Establishment Clause cases and because the Court drew lines invalidating some forms of parochial aid. In reading this case, consider the following questions: (1) Did the *Lemon* test represent an innovation in the Court's Establishment Clause cases? (2) Was Burger's analysis convincing that the Pennsylvania and Rhode Island laws were unconstitutional under the *Lemon* test? (3) Does Burger's opinion seem most consistent with the strict separationist, neutrality, or accommodationist approach to the Establishment Clause?

VOTE:

8 justices found the Pennsylvania law unconstitutional (Black, Blackmun, Brennan, Burger, Douglas, Harlan, Stewart, White).

Marshall did not participate.

8 justices found the Rhode Island law unconstitutional (Black, Blackmun, Brennan, Burger, Douglas, Harlan, Marshall, Stewart).

1 justice found the Rhode Island law to be constitutional (White).

Chief Justice Burger delivered the opinion of the Court.

* * *

The language of the Religion Clauses of the First Amendment is at best opaque, particularly when compared with other portions of the Amendment. Its authors did not simply prohibit the establishment of a state church or a state religion, an area history shows they regarded as very important and fraught with great dangers. Instead they commanded that there should be "no law *respecting* an establishment of religion." A law may be one "respecting" the forbidden objective while falling short of its total realization. A law "respecting" the proscribed result, that is, the establishment of religion, is not always easily identifiable as one violative of the Clause. A given law might not *establish* a state religion but nevertheless be one "respecting" that end in the sense of being a step that could lead to such establishment and hence offend the First Amendment.

In the absence of precisely stated constitutional prohibitions, we must draw lines with reference to the three main evils against which the Establishment Clause was intended to afford protection: "sponsorship, financial support, and active involvement of the sovereign in religious activity." *Walz v. Tax Commission,* 1970.

Every analysis in this area must begin with consideration of the cumulative criteria developed by the Court over many years. Three such tests may be gleaned from our cases. First, the statute must have a secular legislative purpose; second, its principal or primary effect must be one that neither advances nor inhibits religion, *Board of Education v. Allen* (1968); finally, the statute must not foster "an excessive government entanglement with religion." *Walz.*

Inquiry into the legislative purposes of the Pennsylvania and Rhode Island statutes affords no basis for a conclusion that the legislative intent was to advance religion. On the contrary, the statutes themselves clearly state that they are intended to enhance the quality of the secular education in all schools covered by the compulsory attendance laws. There is no reason to believe that the legislatures meant anything else. * * *

* * *

The two legislatures, however, have also recognized that church-related elementary and secondary schools have a significant religious mission and that a substantial portion of their activities is religiously oriented. They have therefore sought to create statutory restrictions designed to guarantee the separation between secular and religious educational functions and to ensure that State financial aid supports only the former. All these provisions are precautions taken in candid recognition that these programs approached, even if they did not intrude upon, the forbidden areas under the Religion Clauses. We need not decide whether these legislative precautions restrict the principal or primary effect of the programs to the point where they do not offend the Religion Clauses, for we conclude that the cumulative impact of the entire relationship arising under the statutes in each State involves excessive government entanglement between government and religion.

* * *

In order to determine whether the government entanglement with religion is excessive, we must examine the character and purposes of the institutions that are benefitted, the nature of the aid that the State provides, and the resulting relationship between the government and the religious authority. * * * Here we find that both statutes foster an impermissible degree of entanglement.

(a) Rhode Island program

The District Court made extensive findings on the grave potential for excessive entanglement that inheres in the religious character and purpose of the Roman Catholic elementary schools of Rhode Island, to date the sole beneficiaries of the Rhode Island Salary Supplement Act.

* * *

. . .[T]he District court concluded that the parochial schools constituted "an integral part of the religious mission of the Catholic Church." The various characteristics of the schools make them "a powerful vehicle for transmitting the Catholic faith to the next generation." This process of inculcating religious doctrine is, of course, enhanced by the impressionable age of the pupils, in primary schools particularly. In short, parochial schools involve substantial religious activity and purpose.

* * *

* * * The State must be certain, given the Religion Clauses, that subsidized teachers do not inculcate religion—indeed the State here has undertaken to do so. To ensure that no trespass occurs, the State has therefore carefully conditioned its aid with pervasive restrictions. An eligible recipient must teach only those courses that are offered in the public schools and use only those texts and materials that are found in the public schools. In addition the teacher must not engage in teaching any course in religion.

A comprehensive, discriminating, and continuing state surveillance will inevitably be required to ensure that these restrictions are obeyed and the First Amendment otherwise respected. Unlike a book, a teacher cannot be inspected once so as to determine the extent and intent of his or her personal beliefs and subjective acceptance of the limitations imposed by the First Amendment. These prophylactic contacts will involve excessive and enduring entanglement between state and church.

There is another area of entanglement in the Rhode Island program that gives concern. The statute excludes teachers employed by non-public schools whose average per-pupil expenditures on secular education equal or exceed the comparable figures for public schools. In the event that the total expenditures of an otherwise eligible program exceed this norm, the program requires the government to examine the school's records to determine how much of the total expenditures is attributable to secular education and how much to religious activity. This kind of state inspection and evaluation of the religious content of a religious organization is fraught with the sort of entanglement that the Constitution forbids. * * *

(b) Pennsylvania program

The Pennsylvania statute also provides state aid to church-related schools for teachers' salaries. The complaint describes an educational system that is very similar to the one existing in Rhode Island. * * *

As we noted earlier, the very restrictions and surveillance necessary to ensure that teachers play a strictly nonideological role give rise to entanglements between church and state. The Pennsylvania statute, like that of Rhode Island, fosters this kind of relationship. * * *

The Pennsylvania statute, moreover, has the further defect of providing state financial aid directly to the church-related school. This factor distinguishes both *Everson* and *Allen,* for in both those cases the Court was careful to point out that state aid was provided to the student and his parents—not to the church-related school. * * *

A broader base of entanglement of yet a different character is presented by the divisive political potential of these state programs. In a community where such a large number of pupils are served by church-related schools, it can be assumed that state assistance will entail considerable political activity. Partisans of parochial schools, understandably concerned with rising costs and sincerely dedicated to both the religious and secular educational missions of their schools, will inevitably champion this cause and promote political action to achieve their goals. Those who oppose state aid, whether for constitutional, religious, or fiscal reasons, will inevitably respond and employ all of the usual political campaign techniques to prevail. Candidates will be forced to declare and voters to choose. * * *

Ordinarily political debate and division, however vigorous or even partisan, are normal and healthy manifestations of our democratic system of government, but political division along religious lines was one of the principal evils against which the First Amendment was intended to protect. * * *

* * *

The merit and benefits of these schools . . . are not the issue before us in these cases. The sole question is whether state aid to these schools can be squared with the dictates of the Religion Clauses. Under our system the choice has been made that government is to be entirely excluded from the area of religious instruction and churches excluded from the affairs of government. The Constitution decrees that religion must be a private matter for the individual, the family, and the institutions of private choice, and that while some involvement and entanglement are inevitable, lines must be drawn.

The judgment of the Rhode Island District Court . . . is affirmed. The judgment of the Pennsylvania District Court . . . is reversed, and the case is remanded for further proceedings consistent with this opinion.

Justice Douglas, whom Justice Black joins, concurring. [omitted]

Justice Brennan, concurring. [omitted]

Justice White, concurring and dissenting. [omitted]

In another 1971 case the Court drew a sharp distinction between government programs assisting religious-affiliated elementary/secondary schools and those assisting colleges and universities. In *Tilton v. Richardson* the Court approved a federal act that provided construction grants for religious affiliated colleges and universities to use for facilities employed exclusively for secular purposes. Burger, writing for a five-person majority, argued that a variety of significant differences existed between colleges and elementary/secondary schools, differences which meant that government programs assisting colleges did not create the same threats to the purposes of the Establishment Clause. Douglas, joined by Black and Marshall, wrote a sharp dissent, arguing in favor of a high wall, separationist approach.

Burger thus experienced a great deal of success in his initial Establishment Clause cases. He wrote the majority opinion in each of the first three major cases before the Burger Court, and he not only gave support to the neutrality approach but also formalized a three-part test to guide the Court's analysis in Establishment Clause decisions. Burger's idea of neutrality was not a midpoint between the separationist and accommodationist theories, however. He firmly opposed the separationist approach and explicitly rejected the wall of separation metaphor as a useful guideline in Establishment Clause cases. Burger tended to emphasize the idea of "benevolent neutrality," a somewhat vague concept but one that was clearly sympathetic to some forms of government accommodation of religion. Within this approach, he gave substantial emphasis to historical practices, arguing that if certain forms of government involvement with religion had been practiced through much or all of American history, then such forms of church-state involvement bore a heavy presumption of constitutionality, as in the case of property tax exemptions for religious institutions.

The evidence suggests that Burger initially believed that the *Lemon* test was fully compatible with a benevolent neutrality approach, preventing serious abuses of the Establishment Clause while still allowing reasonable forms of government interaction with religion. In a series of parochial aid cases in the seventies, however, a majority of the Burger Court justices interpreted neutrality and the *Lemon* test in a much different manner than Burger desired, frequently striking down parochial aid programs and providing interpretations of the *Lemon* test that threatened to make it difficult for any forms of government involvement with religion to be found constitutional. Two of the most significant of these cases were *Committee for Public Education and Religious Liberty v. Nyquist* (1973) and *Meek v. Pittenger* (1975).

Nyquist involved a New York State law that provided a variety of forms of financial assistance to private elementary and secondary schools, including reimbursing parents for tuition, giving tax credits for tuition expenses to parents who did not qualify for reimbursements, and providing money grants for the maintenance and repair of school facilities and equipment. The Court ruled 6-3 that these forms of financial assistance were unconstitutional, with Burger, Rehnquist, and White in dissent. Writing for the majority, Powell applied "the now well-defined three-part test" (413 U.S. at 772), and he found that the programs failed the second "effect" prong of the test because they advanced and subsidized the religious mission of the parochial schools. In dissent, Burger argued that *Everson* and *Allen* were the appropriate precedents that required the Court to approve the New York programs because the controlling principle of all of these cases was that indirect aid to religion did not violate the Establishment Clause. Burger accused the majority of misinterpreting the effect prong of the *Lemon* test by measuring the number of people who used the money for religious education. *Nyquist* was a highly significant case that tended to characterize Establishment Clause decisions in the seventies; as Kobylka (1989, p. 555) observes, "With *Nyquist,* Burger lost control over the content and application of the test he created. . . ."

Burger's disenchantment with the directions of the Court and especially its use of the *Lemon* test can be seen clearly in the 1975 *Meek* case, which involved Pennsylvania parochial aid programs that sought to loan textbooks to nonpublic students, to lend various instructional materials directly to private schools, and to provide auxiliary services and speech therapy to private school students. Following the logic of *Nyquist* closely, a six-person majority found the Pennsylvania programs unconstitutional on both the effects and entanglement prongs. Burger wrote a bitter dissent in *Meek,* arguing that the majority decision "does not simply tilt the Constitution against religion; it literally turns the Religion Clauses on their heads" (421 U.S. at 387).

The Burger Court decided a substantial number of additional Establishment Clause cases during the late seventies and early eighties, but most of them were relatively minor cases without major doctrinal innovations. The Court tended to find violations of the Establishment Clause when applying the *Lemon* test, although this pattern was certainly not consistent. Throughout these cases, Burger did not conceal his unhappiness with the general direction of the Court's Establishment Clause jurisprudence and his desire to move the Court in a more accommodationist direction. If this meant modifying or even abandoning *Lemon,* then Burger was willing to consider this.

In a series of decisions in 1983 and 1984, Burger finally succeeded in putting together majority coalitions that firmly embraced an accommodationist approach to the Establishment Clause and dramatically undercut *Lemon.* These cases were *Mueller v. Allen* (1983), *Marsh v. Chambers* (1983), and *Lynch v. Donnelly* (1984).

Mueller was a case from Minnesota involving a law that allowed all taxpayers to deduct from their state income taxes certain expenses incurred for tuition, textbooks, and transportation costs in sending their children to elementary and secondary schools. Rehnquist wrote the majority opinion, which found the law not to violate the Establishment Clause, and he was joined by Burger, White, Powell, and O'Connor. Recognizing that the Court's record on parochial aid cases was quite mixed, Rehnquist's basic argument was that this case presented a situation that was closer to the cases where the Court had approved various forms of assistance—for example, *Everson* and *Allen*—than to those cases where the Court had ruled assistance unconstitutional—such as *Nyquist* and *Meek.* A key point in Rehnquist's argument was that the Court had ruled in *Nyquist* against tax benefits that applied only to private school parents whereas the Minnesota law applied to all parents. Rehnquist used the *Lemon* test, but he undermined it by arguing that "our cases have . . . emphasized that it provides 'no more than [a] helpful signpost' in dealing with Establishment Clause challenges" (463 U.S. at 394). Although it was not an easy task to reach an accommodationist decision through the *Lemon* test, Rehnquist argued that the law did not violate the purpose, effect, or entanglement prongs of the test. An especially important point emphasized by Rehnquist involved an analysis of the concern about civil strife underlying the Establishment Clause. He emphasized that a critical purpose of the Clause was to prevent the type of government involvement in religion that could create strain and strife leading a political system to the breaking point, but he argued that these dangers were remote in American society today and that this particular program posed no such danger.

Marshall wrote a strong dissent in *Mueller,* joined by Brennan, Blackmun, and Stevens. Marshall argued that the effect of the Minnesota law was to advance religion. In attacking Rehnquist's key point that the law in this case was different than New York's law in *Nyquist* because the former applied to all parents while the latter applied only to parents of private school children, Marshall ridiculed this as a difference without a distinction. Marshall emphasized that the factual record showed that 95 percent of the children attending private schools in Minnesota were enrolled in parochial schools, and thus the program would clearly have the effect of supporting religious instruction. In concluding, Marshall wrote: "In my view, the lines drawn in *Nyquist* were drawn on a reasoned basis with appropriate regard for the principles of neutrality embodied in the Establishment Clause. I do not believe that the same can be said of the lines drawn by the majority today" (463 U.S. at 416).

The neutrality approach and the *Lemon* test were thus weakened in *Mueller,* but a week later the Court went dramatically further in altering Establishment Clause jurisprudence in *Marsh v. Chambers* (1983). This case involved a challenge to the constitutionality of a practice by the Nebraska legislature of beginning each session with a prayer by a paid chaplain. Burger wrote the six-person majority opinion, with Blackmun now joining the *Mueller* majority of Burger, Rehnquist, White, Powell, and O'Connor. Burger's opinion was based almost entirely on historical analysis. He stated that the practice of legislative prayer had existed continuously from colonial times to the present in both Congress and state legislative bodies; thus, legislative prayer was not violative of the Establishment Clause because the First Congress approved both the First Amendment and the practice of beginning each session of Congress with a prayer. Burger's opinion was couched in accommodationist language, quoting with favor Douglas' comment in *Zorach* that " '[w]e are a religious people whose institutions presuppose a Supreme Being' " (463 U.S. at 792). Finally, Burger made no reference whatsoever to the *Lemon* test, even though the lower federal appeals court had found the practice to violate all three prongs of the *Lemon* test.

Brennan wrote a lengthy dissent joined by Marshall, a dissent that was substantially longer than the majority opinion. He began by arguing that the Court erred by failing to use the prevailing *Lemon* test, under which "if any group of law students were asked to apply [its] principles. . . , they would nearly unanimously find the practice to be unconstitutional" (463 U.S. at 800–1). Brennan then turned to a more general analysis of the Establishment Clause, arguing that Jefferson's wall of separation metaphor supported the argument that the Court must maintain a position of neutrality in analyzing the Establishment Clause. Quoting *Everson,* Brennan wrote: " 'The First Amendment mandates government neutrality between religion and nonreligion' " (463 U.S. at 802). In this case, Brennan argued, the Court was not pursuing neutrality but was approving government support of religion. Brennan also presented a lengthy analysis about the limitations of using historical analysis to guide the Court's decision making.

MARSH V. CHAMBERS

463 U.S. 783, 103 S.Ct. 3330, 77 L.Ed. 2d 1019 (1983)

■ Nebraska's unicameral legislature had created various rules under which each of its sessions began with a prayer offered by a chaplain, who was chosen biennially by the Executive Board of the Legislative Council and was paid by public funds. This position had been held since 1965 by Robert E. Palmer, a Presbyterian minister, who received a salary of $319.75 each month in which the legislature was in session. This practice was challenged in Nebraska Federal District Court by Ernest Chambers, a member of the Nebraska legislature and a Nebraska taxpayer. In his suit, Chambers named as defendants State Treasurer Frank Marsh, Chaplain Palmer, and the members of the Executive Board of the Legislative Council. The District Court held that the prayers did not violate the Establishment Clause but that it was violated by paying the chaplain from public funds. Both sides appealed to the Court of Appeals for the Eighth Circuit. The Court of Appeals considered the prayers and the payments together rather than separately. Applying the three-part *Lemon* test to the challenged practices, the Court of Appeals ruled that the legislative prayer activity violated all three elements of the test: purpose, effect, and entanglement.

This is an important case for several reasons. It was the first Establishment Clause case since *Lemon* in which the Court's controlling opinion did not use the three-part test, and *Marsh* has been cited frequently by accommodationist justices who desire to modify or overturn the *Lemon* test. The case also presents an excellent example of the manner in which a Court majority can use historical analysis to support a decision, and Brennan's dissent represents a strong statement about the limitations and dangers of using history to guide the Court's decision making. In reading this case, consider the following questions: (1) Was it proper for Burger to disregard completely the *Lemon* test? (2) Do you agree with Brennan that the practice of legislative prayer is clearly unconstitutional under the *Lemon* test? (3) Whose historical analysis is most convincing, Burger's or Brennan's?

VOTE:

6 justices found the practice constitutional (Burger, Rehnquist, O'Connor, Powell, Blackmun, White).

3 justices found the practice unconstitutional (Brennan, Marshall, Stevens).

Chief Justice Burger delivered the opinion of the Court.

The opening of sessions of legislative and other deliberative public bodies with prayer is deeply embedded in the history and tradition of this country. From colonial times through the founding of the Republic and ever since, the practice of legislative prayer has coexisted with the principles of disestablishment and religious freedom. In the very courtrooms in which the United States District Judge and later three Circuit Judges heard and decided this case, the proceedings opened with an announcement that concluded, "God save the United States and this Honorable Court." The same tradition occurs at all sessions of this Court.

The tradition in many of the colonies was, of course, linked to an established church, but the Continental Congress, beginning in 1774, adopted the traditional procedure of opening its sessions with a prayer offered by a paid chaplain. * * * Although prayers were not offered during the Constitutional Convention, the First Congress, as one of its early items of business, adopted the policy of selecting a chaplain to open each session with prayer. * * *

On Sept. 25, 1789, three days after Congress authorized the appointment of paid chaplains, final agreement was reached on the language of the Bill of Rights. Clearly the men who wrote the First Amendment Religion Clause did not view paid legislative chaplains and opening prayers as a violation of that Amendment, for the practice of opening sessions with prayer has continued without interruption ever since that early session of Congress. It has also been followed consistently in most of the states, including Nebraska, where the institution of opening legislative sessions with prayer was adopted even before the State attained statehood.

Standing alone, historical patterns cannot justify contemporary violations of constitutional guarantees, but there is far more here than simply historical patterns. In this context, historical evidence sheds light not only on what the draftsmen intended the Establishment Clause to mean, but also on how they thought that Clause applied to the practice authorized by the First Congress—their actions reveal their intent. An act "passed by the First Congress assembled under the Constitution, many of whose members had taken part in framing that instrument, . . . is contemporaneous and weighty evidence of its true meaning." *Wisconsin v. Pelican Ins. Co.* (1888). In *Walz v. Tax Comm'n* (1970), we considered the weight to be accorded to history: "It is obviously correct that no one acquires a vested or protected right in violation of the Constitution by long use, even when that span of time covers our entire national existence and indeed predates it. Yet an unbroken practice . . . is not something to be lightly cast aside." No more is Nebraska's practice of over a century, consistent with two centuries of national practice, to be cast aside. It can hardly be thought that in the same week Members of the First Congress voted to appoint and to pay a Chaplain for each House and also voted to approve the draft of the First Amendment for submission to the States, they intended the Establishment Clause of the Amendment to forbid what they had just declared acceptable. * * *

This unique history leads us to accept the interpretation of the First Amendment draftsmen who saw no real threat to the Establishment Clause arising from the practice of prayer similar to that now challenged. We conclude that legislative prayer presents no more potential for establishment than provision of school transportation, *Everson v. Board of Education* (1947), beneficial grants for higher education, *Tilton v. Richardson* (1971), or tax exemptions for religious organizations, *Walz*.

Respondent cites Justice Brennan's concurring opinion in *Abington School Dist. v. Schempp* (1963), and argues that we should not rely too heavily on "the advice of the Founding Fathers" because the messages of history often tend to be ambiguous and not relevant to a society far more heterogeneous than that of the Framers. Respondent also points out that John Jay and John Rutledge opposed the motion to begin the first session of the Continental Congress with prayer.

We do not agree that evidence of opposition to a measure weakens the force of the historical argument; indeed it infuses it with power by demonstrating that the subject was considered carefully and the action not taken thoughtlessly, by force of long tradition and without regard to the problems posed by a pluralistic society. * * *

This interchange emphasizes that the delegates did not consider opening prayers as a proselytizing activity or as symbolically placing the government's "official seal of approval on one religious view." Rather, the Founding Fathers looked at invocations as "conduct whose . . . effect . . . harmonize[d] with the tenets of some or all religions." *McGowan v. Maryland* (1961). The Establishment Clause does not always bar a state from regulating conduct simply because it "harmonizes with religious canons." Here, the individual claiming injury by the practice is an adult, presumably not susceptible to "religious indoctrination."

In light of the unambiguous and unbroken history of more than 200 years, there can be no doubt that the practice of opening legislative sessions with prayer has become part of the fabric of our society. To invoke Divine guidance on a public body entrusted with making the laws is not, in those circumstances, an "establishment" of religion or a step toward establishment; it is simply a tolerable acknowledgment of beliefs widely held among the people of this country. As Justice Douglas observed, "[w]e are a religious people whose institutions presuppose a Supreme Being." *Zorach v. Clauson* (1952).

* * *

The judgment of the Court of Appeals is, *Reversed.*

Justice Brennan, with whom Justice Marshall joins, dissenting.

The Court today has written a narrow and, on the whole, careful opinion. In effect, the Court holds that officially sponsored legislative prayer, primarily on account of its "unique history," is generally exempted from the First Amendment's prohibition against "the establishment of religion."

The Court makes no pretense of subjecting Nebraska's practice of legislative prayer to any of the formal "tests" that have traditionally structured our inquiry under the Establishment Clause. That it fails to do so is, in a sense, a good thing, for it simply confirms that the Court is carving out an exception to the Establishment Clause doctrine to accommodate legislative prayer. For my purposes, however, I must begin by demonstrating what should be obvious: that, if the Court were to judge legislative prayer through the unsentimental eye of our settled doctrine, it would have to strike it down as a clear violation of the Establishment Clause.

The most commonly cited formulation of prevailing Establishment Clause doctrine is found in *Lemon v. Kurtzman* (1971):

"Every analysis in this area must begin with consideration of the cumulative criteria developed by the Court over many years. Three such tests may be gleaned from our cases. First, the statute [at issue] must have a secular legislative purpose; second, its principal or primary effect must be one that neither advances nor inhibits religion; finally, the statute must not foster 'an excessive government entanglement with religion.' "

That the "purpose" of legislative prayer is preeminently religious rather than secular seems to me to be self-evident. * * * The "primary effect" of legislative prayer is also clearly religious. * * *

Finally, there can be no doubt that the practice of legislative prayer leads to excessive "entanglement" between the State and religion. * * *

* * *

In sum, I have no doubt that, if any group of law students were asked to apply the principles of *Lemon* to the question of legislative prayer, they would nearly unanimously find the practice to be unconstitutional.

The path of formal doctrine, however, can only imperfectly capture the nature and importance of the issues at stake in this case. A more adequate analysis must therefore take into account the underlying function of the Establishment Clause, and the forces that have shaped its doctrine.

* * *

The Establishment Clause embodies a judgment, born of a long and turbulent history, that, in our society, religion "must be a private matter for the individual, the family, and the institutions of private choice. . . ." *Lemon v. Kurtzman.*

"Government in our democracy, state and national, must be neutral in matters of religious theory, doctrine, and practice. It may not be hostile to any religion, or to the advocacy of no-religion; and it may not aid, foster, or promote one religion or religious theory against another or even against the militant opposite. The First Amendment mandates governmental neutrality between religion and nonreligion." *Epperson v. Arkansas* (1968).

"In the words of Jefferson, the clause against establishment of religion by law was intended to erect a 'wall of separation between church and state.'" *Everson v. Board of Education* (1947).

The principles of "separation" and "neutrality" implicit in the Establishment Clause serve many purposes. Four of these are particularly relevant here.

The first, which is most closely related to the more general conceptions of liberty found in the remainder of the First Amendment, is to guarantee the individual right to conscience. * * *

The second purpose of separation and neutrality is to keep the state from interfering in the essential autonomy of religious life, either by taking upon itself the decision of religious issues, or by unduly involving itself in the supervision of religious institutions or officials.

The third purpose of separation and neutrality is to prevent the trivialization and degradation of religion by too close an attachment to the organs of government. * * *

Finally, the principles of separation and neutrality help assure that essentially religious issues, precisely because of their importance and sensitivity, not become the occasion for battle in the political arena. * * *

* * *

Legislative prayer clearly violates the principles of neutrality and separation that are embedded within the Establishment Clause. It is contrary to the fundamental message of *Engel* and *Schempp.* It intrudes on the right to conscience by forcing some legislators either to participate in a "prayer opportunity," with which they are in basic disagreement, or to make their disagreement a matter of public comment by declining to participate. It forces all residents of the State to support a religious exercise that may be contrary to their own beliefs. It requires the State to commit itself on fundamental theological issues. It has the potential for degrading religion by allowing a religious call to worship to be intermeshed with a secular call to order. And it injects religion into the political sphere by creating the potential that each and every selection of a chaplain, or consideration of a particular prayer, or even reconsideration of the practice itself, will provoke a political battle along religious lines and ultimately alienate some religiously identified group of citizens.

* * *

The Court's main argument for carving out an exception sustaining legislative prayer is historical. * * * I agree that historical practice is "of considerable import in the interpretation of abstract constitutional language" *Walz.* This is a case, however, in which—absent the Court's invocation of history—there would be no question that the practice at issue was unconstitutional. And despite the surface appeal of the Court's argument, there are at least three reasons why specific historical practice should not in this case override that clear constitutional imperative.

First, it is significant that the Court's historical argument does not rely on the legislative history of the Establishment Clause itself. Indeed, that formal history is profoundly unilluminating on this and most other subjects. * * *

Second, the Court's analysis treats the First Amendment simply as an Act of Congress, as to whose meaning the intent of Congress is the single touchstone. Both the Constitution and its amendments, however, became supreme law only by virtue of their ratification by the States, and the understanding of the States should be as relevant to our analysis as the understanding of Congress. This observation is especially compelling in considering the meaning of the Bill of Rights. * * *

Finally, and most importantly, the argument tendered by the Court is misguided because the Constitution is not a static document whose meaning on every detail is fixed for all time by the life experiences of the Framers. We have recognized in a wide variety of constitutional contexts that the practices that were in place at the time any particular guarantee was enacted into the Constitution do not necessarily fix forever the meaning of that guarantee. To be truly faithful to the Framers, "our use of the history of their time must limit itself to broad purposes, not specific practices." *Abington School Dist. v. Schempp.* Our primary task must be to translate "the majestic generalities of the Bill of Rights, conceived as part of the pattern of liberal government in the eighteenth century, into concrete restraints on officials dealing with the problems of the twentieth century. . . ." *West Virginia State Bd. of Education v. Barnette* (1943).

The inherent adaptability of the Constitution and its amendments is particularly important with respect to the Establishment Clause. "[Our] religious composition makes us a vastly more diverse people than were our forefathers. . . . In the face of such profound changes, practices which may have been objectionable to no one in the time of Jefferson and Madison may today be highly offensive to many persons, the deeply devout and the nonbelievers alike." *Schempp.* * * * To my mind, the Court's focus here on a narrow piece of history is, in a fundamental sense, a betrayal of the lessons of history.

* * *

I respectfully dissent.

Justice Stevens, dissenting. [omitted]

Burger's accommodationist position was dominant again the next year in *Lynch v. Donnelly* (1984), a Rhode Island case involving a challenge to the city of Pawtucket's annual Christmas display, that included a nativity scene along with a Santa Claus house and sleigh, a Christmas tree, and other seasonal decorations. Burger, joined again by Rehnquist, White, Powell, and O'Connor in the 5-4 decision, boldly asserted his accommodationist approach in this case. Rejecting the wall of separation metaphor yet again, Burger stated that the Establishment Clause "affirmatively mandates accommodation, not merely tolerance, of all religions, and forbids hostility toward any. Anything less would require the 'callous indifference' we have said was never intended by the Establishment Clause" (465 U.S. at 673). Burger then advanced arguments that the Framers wrote the Establishment Clause with an accommodationist intent and that throughout American history the three branches of government had accommodated religion in a variety of ways. Burger did use the *Lemon* test, but he downplayed its importance, arguing that the Court had "often found it useful" but that the Court's justices had "repeatedly emphasized our unwillingness to be confined to any single test or criterion in this sensitive area" (465 U.S. at 679). In applying the three prongs to the Pawtucket case, Burger argued that the practice passed each element.

Brennan authored another lengthy dissent, joined by Marshall, Blackmun, and Stevens. Although pleased that the Court majority had returned to the *Lemon* test after abandoning it in *Marsh,* Brennan expressed his deep concern that "the Court's less than vigorous application of the *Lemon* test suggests that its commitment to those standards may be superficial" (465 U.S. at 696). Even more disturbing to Brennan was the majority's embrace of accommodation and departure from the Constitution's requirement that "government is to remain scrupulously neutral in matters of religious conscience. . . ." (465 U.S. at 714). Brennan especially attacked Burger's position on the intent of the Framers regarding the Establishment Clause, which Brennan called "a fundamental misapprehension of the proper uses of history in constitutional interpretation" (465 U.S. at 718).

By the end of the 1983–84 term, then, Burger appeared to have succeeded in leading the Court away from neutrality and toward an accommodationist approach to the Establishment Clause. How can we account for this dramatic shift in the Court's decision making? It is easy to explain the support for the accommodationist approach by Burger, Rehnquist, and White, for they had consistently supported this interpretation. These three justices gained a fourth vote when O'Connor replaced Stewart in 1981. As can be seen in Table 5.1, Stewart supported the accommodationist position only 38 percent of the time, while O'Connor's support level was 73 percent, which was nearly identical to Burger's. Powell was the key fifth vote, which created the new accommodationist majority in the 1983 and 1984 cases, and it is more difficult to explain his position. Kobylka (1989, p. 558) suggests that Powell may have been affected by a variety of public pressures, including the strong position by the Reagan administration in advocating a wide variety of forms of government assistance to religion.

Whatever the reasons for Powell's support of accommodation, as the 1984–85 term approached, strong evidence existed that the accommodationist majority was going to solidify and indeed dramatically expand their victories from the previous two terms. Although the doctrinal gains had been significant in *Mueller, Marsh,* and *Lynch,* their practical effects were limited. The legislative prayer case did not affect many people, the nativity scene case was mostly symbolic and left open many questions, and the tax deduction case was not going to open the floodgates of tax change among states hard pressed to balance their budgets. But the Court agreed to hear three cases in the 1984–85 term that could have not only enormous doctrinal significance but also major social significance, for *Wallace v. Jaffree* (1985) involved the volatile subject of prayer in the public schools while *Grand Rapids v. Ball* (1985) and *Aguilar v. Felton* (1985) both involved parochial aid programs. Most Court observers seemed to be betting that the new Court majority would use an accommodationist approach to approve these programs and that the *Lemon* test would be further undercut or abolished.

When the dust settled following these three major decisions, Brennan had replaced Burger as the Court leader in the Establishment Clause cases, neutrality had been reestablished as the guiding approach of the Court, and the *Lemon* test had been reaffirmed. Powell was the key vote that enabled the neutralists to triumph in each of the cases, although O'Connor also joined the neutralists in the Alabama school prayer case.

The initial case the Court handed down was *Jaffree,* where the Court ruled 6-3 against an Alabama statute that authorized a one-minute period of silence in the Alabama public schools for meditation or voluntary prayer. Stevens wrote the majority opinion, joined by Brennan, Marshall, Blackmun, and Powell. In a remarkably brief opinion, Stevens made no reference to the accommodationist approach endorsed by the Court in the three major cases of *Mueller, Marsh,* and *Lynch;* instead, he simply asserted "the established principle that the Government must pursue a course of complete neutrality toward religion" (472 U.S. at 60). Stevens utilized the *Lemon* test, citing Burger's statement in *Walz:* " 'Every analysis in this area must begin with consideration of the cumulative criteria developed by the Court over many years' " (472 U.S. at 55). In applying the purpose prong to the Alabama law, Stevens concluded that the law had no secular purpose whatsoever.

Jaffree is also important because of O'Connor's concurring opinion and Rehnquist's dissenting opinion, both of which were to become prominent parts of the Establishment Clause debate in the coming years. O'Connor agreed with the Court's judgment, but she did not join Steven's opinion. She argued that the *Lemon* test should be modified by an **endorsement test** under which the courts would "examine whether government's purpose is to endorse religion and whether the statute actually conveys a message of endorsement" (472 U.S. at 69). O'Connor concluded that Alabama did intend to endorse religion in its law.

Rehnquist's dissent was his fullest discussion of the meaning of the Establishment Clause. After presenting a lengthy historical analysis, Rehnquist concluded by embracing the accommodationist approach to the Establishment Clause:

> *The Framers intended the Establishment Clause to prohibit the designation of any church as a "national" one. The Clause was also designed to stop the Federal Government from asserting a preference for one religious denomination or sect over others. As its history abundantly shows, however, nothing in the Establishment Clause requires government to be strictly neutral between religion and irreligion, nor does the Clause prohibit Congress or the States from pursuing legitimate secular ends through nondiscriminatory sectarian means (472 U.S. at 113).*

No other justice joined Rehnquist's dissent, and some scholars have sharply attacked Rehnquist's analysis, including Levy (1986, p. 155) who argues that "Rehnquist wrote fiction and passed it off as history." Rehnquist does have support in the scholarly community, however, and his views have gained increasing support in recent years as the Court's personnel has changed.

WALLACE V. JAFFREE

472 U.S. 38, 105 S.Ct. 2479, 86 L.Ed. 2d 29 (1985)

In 1981 the Alabama Legislature enacted a law (Alabama Code Section 16-1-20.1) that authorized a brief period of silence for meditation or voluntary prayer at the beginning of each school day in all grades of the state's public schools. The statute read: "At the commencement of the first class of each day in all grades in all public schools the teacher in charge of the room in which each class is held may announce that a period of silence not to exceed one minute in duration shall be observed for meditation or voluntary prayer, and during any such period no other activities shall be engaged in." The law was challenged as a violation of the Establishment Clause by Ishmael Jaffree, a resident of Mobile County, Alabama, on behalf of three of his grade school children. The federal district judge who heard the case handed down a surprising decision that upheld the law as constitutional on the basis that newly discovered historical evidence proved that the Establishment Clause did not prohibit a state from establishing a religion. The court of appeals rejected this interpretation of the applicability of the Establishment Clause to the states and then ruled that the Alabama statute was unconstitutional.

This is an important case because the Court reversed its recent support of the accommodation approach in the cases of *Mueller v. Allen* (1983), *Marsh v. Chambers* (1984), and *Lynch v. Donnelly* (1984). Instead, a five-person majority used the *Lemon* test and a neutrality approach to invalidate the Alabama moment of silence law. As you read this case, consider the following issues: (1) Does Stevens's majority opinion provide a convincing explanation for the use of the *Lemon* test and the neutrality approach in Establishment Clause cases? (2) What is O'Connor's endorsement test for analyzing the Establishment Clause, and how does it relate to the other tests and approaches in this area of civil liberties? (3) Does Rehnquist present a convincing critique of the majority's view of the Establishment Clause, and does he present a valid alternative interpretation? (4) How would the Court have decided this case if the challenged law called just for a moment of silence with no reference to voluntary prayer?

VOTE:

6 justices found the law to be unconstitutional (Blackmun, Brennan, Marshall, O'Connor, Powell, Stevens).

3 justices found the law to be constitutional (Burger, Rehnquist, White).

Justice Stevens delivered the opinion of the Court.

. . .[T]he narrow question for decision is whether 16-1-20.1, which authorizes a period of silence for "meditation or voluntary prayer," is a law respecting the establishment of religion within the meaning of the First Amendment.

* * *

When the Court has been called upon to construe the breadth of the Establishment Clause, it has examined the criteria developed over a period of many years. Thus, in *Lemon v. Kurtzman* . . . we wrote: "Every analysis is this area must begin with consideration of the cumulative criteria developed by the Court over many years. Three such tests may be gleaned from our cases. First, the statute must have a secular legislative purpose; second, its principal or primary effect must be one that neither advances nor inhibits religion . . .; finally, the statute must not foster 'an excessive government entanglement with religion' . . . ."

It is the first of these three criteria that is most plainly implicated by this case. As the District Court correctly recognized, no consideration of the second or third criteria is necessary if a statute does not have a clearly secular purpose. For even though a statute that is motivated in part by a religious purpose may satisfy the first criterion . . . the First Amendment requires that a statute must be invalidated if it is entirely motivated by a purpose to advance religion.

In applying the purpose test, it is appropriate to ask "whether government's actual purpose is to endorse or disapprove of religion." In this case, the answer to that question is dispositive. For the record not only provides us with an unambiguous affirmative answer, but it also reveals that the enactment of 16-1-20.1 was not motivated by any clearly secular purpose—indeed, the statute has *no* secular purpose.

The sponsor of the bill that became 16-1-20.1, Senator Donald Holmes, inserted into the legislative record—apparently without dissent—a statement indicating that the legislation was an "effort to return voluntary prayer" to the public schools. Later Senator Holmes confirmed this purpose before the District Court. In response to the question whether he had any purpose for the legislation other than returning voluntary prayer to public schools, he stated: "No, I did not have no other purpose in mind." The State did not present evidence of *any* secular purpose.

* * *

The legislative intent to return prayer to the public schools is, of course, quite different from merely protecting every student's right to engage in voluntary prayer during an appropriate moment of silence during the schoolday. . . . * * *

We must, therefore, conclude that the Alabama Legislature intended to change existing law and that it was motivated by the same purpose that the Governor's answer to the second amended complaint expressly admitted; that the statement inserted in the legislative history revealed; and that Senator Holmes' testimony frankly described. The legislature enacted [Section] 16-1-20 . . . for the sole purpose of expressing the State's endorsement of prayer activities for one minute at the beginning of each schoolday. The addition of "or voluntary prayer" indicates that the State intended to characterize prayer as a favored practice. Such an endorsement is not consistent with the established principle that the government must pursue a course of complete neutrality toward religion.

* * *

The judgment of the Court of Appeals is affirmed.

Justice Powell, concurring.

I concur in the Court's opinion and judgment that Alabama Code [Section] 16-1-20.1 . . . violates the Establishment Clause of the First Amendment. My concurrence is prompted by Alabama's persistence in attempting to institute state-sponsored prayer in the public schools by enacting three successive statutes. I agree fully with Justice O'Connor's assertion that some moment-of-silence statutes may be constitutional, a suggestion set forth in the Court's opinion as well.

I write separately to express additional views and to respond to criticism of the three-pronged *Lemon* test. *Lemon v. Kurtzman* identifies standards that have proved useful in analyzing case after case both in our decisions and in those of other courts. It is the only coherent test a majority of the Court has ever adopted. Only once since our decision in *Lemon* have we addressed an Establishment Clause issue without resort to its three-pronged test. See *Marsh v. Chambers. Lemon* has not been overruled or its test modified. Yet, continued criticism of it could encourage other courts to feel free to decide Establishment Clause cases on an ad hoc basis.

* * *

Justice O'Connor, concurring in the judgment.

* * * I write separately to identify the peculiar features of the Alabama law that render it invalid, and to explain why moment of silence laws in other States do not necessarily manifest the same infirmity. I also write to explain why neither history nor the Free Exercise Clause of the First Amendment validates the Alabama law struck down by the Court today.

* * *

". . .[I]t is far easier to agree on the purpose that underlies the First Amendment's Establishment and Free Exercise Clauses than to obtain agreement on the standards that should govern their application." *Walz.* It once appeared that the Court had developed a workable standard by which to identify impermissible government establishments of religion. See *Lemon v. Kurtzman.* Under the now familiar *Lemon* test, statutes must have both a secular legislative purpose and a principal or primary effect that neither advances nor inhibits religion, and in addition they must not foster excessive government entanglement with religion. Despite its initial promise, the *Lemon* test has proven problematic. The required inquiry into "entanglement" has been modified and questioned, see *Mueller v. Allen,* and in one case we have upheld state action against an Establishment Clause challenge without applying the *Lemon* test at all. *Marsh v. Chambers.* The author of *Lemon* himself apparently questions the test's general applicability. See *Lynch v. Donnelly.* Justice Rehnquist today suggests that we abandon *Lemon* entirely and in the process limit the reach of the Establishment Clause to state discrimination between sects and government designation of a particular church as a "state" or "national" one.

Perhaps because I am new to the struggle, I am not ready to abandon all aspects of the *Lemon* test. I do believe, however, that the standards announced in *Lemon* should be reexamined and refined in order to make them more useful in achieving the underlying purpose of the First Amendment. We must strive to do more than erect a constitutional "signpost" to be followed or ignored in a particular case as our predilections may dictate. Instead, our goal should be "to frame a principle for constitutional adjudication that is not only grounded in the history and language of the first amendment, but one that is also capable of consistent application to the relevant problems." Last Term, I proposed a refinement of the *Lemon* test with this goal in mind. *Lynch v. Donnelly.*

The *Lynch* concurrence suggested that the religious liberty protected by the Establishment Clause is infringed when the government makes adherence to religion relevant to a person's standing in the political community. Direct government action endorsing religion or a particular religious practice is invalid under this approach because it "sends a message to nonadherents that they are outsiders, not full members of the political community, and an accompanying message to adherents that they are insiders, favored members of the political community." * * * Under this view, *Lemon*'s inquiry as to the purpose and effect of a statute requires courts to examine whether government's purpose is to endorse religion and whether the statute actually conveys a message of endorsement.

* * *

The endorsement test does not preclude government from acknowledging religion or from taking religion into account in making law and policy. It does preclude government from conveying or attempting to convey a message that religion or a particular religious belief is favored or preferred. * * * At issue today is whether state moment of silence statutes in general, and Alabama's moment of silence statute in particular, embody an impermissible endorsement of prayer in public schools.

* * *

The relevant issue is whether an objective observer, acquainted with the text, legislative history, and implementation of the statute, would perceive it as a state endorsement of prayer in public schools. * * * A moment of silence law that is clearly drafted and implemented so as to permit prayer, meditation, and reflection within the prescribed period, without endorsing one alternative over the others, should pass this test.

The analysis above suggests that moment of silence laws in many States should pass Establishment Clause scrutiny because they do not favor the child who chooses to pray during a moment of silence over the child who chooses to meditate or reflect. Alabama Code 16-1-20.1 does not stand on the same footing. However deferentially one examines its text and legislative history, however objectively one views the message attempted to be conveyed to the public, the conclusion is unavoidable that the purpose of the statute is to endorse prayer in public schools. I accordingly agree . . . that the Alabama statute has a purpose which is in violation of the Establishment Clause, and cannot be upheld.

* * *

Chief Justice Burger, dissenting. [omitted]

Justice White, dissenting. [omitted]

Justice Rehnquist, dissenting.

Thirty-eight years ago this Court, in *Everson v. Board of Education* summarized its exegesis of Establishment Clause doctrine thus: "In the words of Jefferson, the clause against establishment of religion by law was intended to erect 'a wall of separation between church and State.' " *Reynolds v. United States,* 1879.

This language from *Reynolds,* a case involving the Free Exercise Clause of the First Amendment rather than the Establishment Clause, quoted from Thomas Jefferson's letter to the Danbury Baptist Association the phrase "I contemplate with sovereign reverence that act of the whole American people which declared that their legislature should 'make no law respecting an establishment of religion, or prohibiting the free exercise thereof,' thus building a wall of separation between church and state." * * *

It is impossible to build sound constitutional doctrine upon a mistaken understanding of constitutional history, but unfortunately the Establishment Clause has been expressly freighted with Jefferson's misleading metaphor for nearly 40 years. Thomas Jefferson was of course in France at the time the constitutional Amendments known as the Bill of Rights were passed by Congress and ratified by the States. His letter to the Danbury Baptist Association was a short note of courtesy, written 14 years after the Amendments were passed by Congress. He would seem to any detached observer as a less than ideal source of contemporary history as to the meaning of the Religion Clauses of the First Amendment.

Jefferson's fellow Virginian, James Madison, with whom he was joined in the battle for the enactment of the Virginia Statute of Religious Liberty of 1786, did play as large a part as anyone in the drafting of the Bill of Rights. He had two advantages over Jefferson in this regard: he was present in the United States, and he was a leading member of the First Congress. But when we turn to the record of the proceedings in the First Congress leading up to the adoption of the Establishment Clause of the Constitution, including Madison's significant contributions thereto, we see a far different picture of its purpose than the highly simplified "wall of separation between church and State."

* * *

It seems indisputable from these glimpses of Madison's thinking, as reflected by actions on the floor of the House in 1789, that he saw the Amendment as designed to prohibit the establishment of a national religion, and perhaps to prevent discrimination among sects. He did not see it as requiring neutrality on the part of government between religion and irreligion. Thus the Court's opinion in *Everson*—while correct in bracketing Madison and Jefferson together in their home State leading to the enactment of the Virginia Statute of Religious Liberty—is totally incorrect in suggesting that Madison carried these views onto the floor of the United States House of Representatives when he proposed the language which would ultimately become the Bill of Rights.

The repetition of this error in *McCollum v. Board of Education* (1948) and, inter alia, *Engel v. Vitale* (1962) does not make it any sounder historically. Finally, in *Abington School District v. Schempp* (1963), the Court made the truly remarkable statement that "the views of Madison and Jefferson, preceded by Roger Williams, came to be incorporated not only in the Federal Constitution but likewise in those of most of our States." On the basis of what evidence we have, this statement is demonstrably incorrect as a matter of history. And its repetition in varying forms in succeeding opinions of the Court can give it no more authority than it possesses as a matter of fact; stare decisis may bind courts as to matters of law, but it cannot bind them as to matters of history.

* * *

Notwithstanding the absence of a historical basis for this theory of rigid separation, the wall idea might well have served as a useful albeit misguided analytical concept, had it led this Court to unified and principled results in Establishment Clause cases. The opposite, unfortunately, has been true; in the 38 years since *Everson* our Establishment Clause cases have been neither principled nor unified. * * *

* * *

* * * The "wall of separation between church and State" is a metaphor based on bad history, a metaphor which has proved useless as a guide to judging. It should be frankly and explicitly abandoned.

The Court has more recently attempted to add some mortar to *Everson*'s wall through the three-part test of *Lemon v. Kurtzman,* which served at first to offer a more useful test for purposes of the Establishment Clause than did the "wall" metaphor. * * *

* * *

The secular purpose prong has proven mercurial in application because it has never been fully defined, and we have never fully stated how the test is to operate. * * *

* * *

The entanglement prong of the *Lemon* test came from *Walz v. Tax Comm'n* (1970). * * *

We have not always followed *Walz'* reflective inquiry into entanglement, however. * * *

* * *

These difficulties arise because the *Lemon* test has no more grounding in the history of the First Amendment than does the wall theory upon which it rests. The three-part test represents a determined effort to craft a workable rule from a historically faulty doctrine; but the rule can only be as sound as the doctrine it attempts to service. The three-part test has simply not provided adequate standards for deciding Establishment Clause cases, as this Court has slowly come to realize. Even worse, the *Lemon* test has caused this Court to fracture into unworkable plurality opinions depending upon how each of the three factors applies to a certain state action. The results from our school services cases shows the difficulty we have encountered in making the *Lemon* test yield principled results.

* * *

If a constitutional theory has no basis in the history of the amendment it seeks to interpret, is difficult to apply and yields unprincipled results, I see little use in it. * * *

The true meaning of the Establishment Clause can only be seen in its history. As drafters of our Bill of Rights, the Framers inscribed the principles that control today. Any deviation from their intentions frustrates the performance of that Charter and will only lead to the type of unprincipled decisionmaking that has plagued our Establishment Clause cases since *Everson.*

The Framers intended the Establishment Clause to prohibit the designation of any church as a "national" one. The Clause was also designed to stop the Federal Government from asserting a preference for one religious denomination or sect over others. * * * As its history abundantly shows, however, nothing in the Establishment Clause requires government to be strictly neutral between religion and irreligion, nor does that Clause prohibit Congress or the States from pursuing legitimate secular ends through nondiscriminatory sectarian means.

The Court strikes down the Alabama statute because the State wished to "characterize prayer as a favored practice." It would come as much of a shock to those who drafted the Bill of Rights as it will to a large number of thoughtful Americans today to learn that the Constitution, as construed by the majority, prohibits the Alabama Legislature from "endorsing" prayer. George Washington himself, at the request of the very Congress which passed the Bill of Rights, proclaimed a day of "public thanksgiving and prayer, to be observed by acknowledging with grateful hearts the many and signal favors of Almighty God." History must judge whether it was the Father of his Country in 1789, or a majority of the Court today, which has strayed from the meaning of the Establishment Clause.

The State surely has a secular interest in regulating the manner in which public schools are conducted. Nothing in the Establishment Clause, properly understood, prohibits any such generalized "endorsement" of prayer. I would therefore reverse the judgment of the Court of Appeals.

Following *Jaffree,* the new majority on the Burger Court used the neutrality approach and the *Lemon* test in *Grand Rapids* and *Aguilar,* closely related parochial aid cases. The *Grand Rapids* case concerned publicly supported classes of a secular nature provided to private school children in private school classrooms, with forty of the forty-one schools being sectarian in nature. The *Aguilar* case involved a New York City program that used federal funds to pay the salaries of public employees who taught remedial programs to educationally deprived children from low-income families in parochial schools. Brennan wrote the five-person majority opinions in both cases, joined by Marshall, Blackmun, Stevens, and Powell. Brennan argued that the Establishment Clause requires "the government to maintain a course of neutrality among religions, and between religion and nonreligion" (473 U.S. at 382), and he utilized the three-part *Lemon* test, emphasizing that "we have particularly relied on *Lemon* in every case involving the sensitive relationship between government and religion in the education of our children" (473 U.S. at 383).

Applying the *Lemon* test, Brennan concluded that both the Grand Rapids and the New York City programs violated the Establishment Clause, but they did so for different reasons. Under the Michigan program, no attempts were made to monitor the classes for religious content, and thus, Brennan argued, they violated the effects prong of the *Lemon* test because religion could be impermissibly advanced in several ways. Under the New York City program, the classes were monitored for religious content, but Brennan concluded that the third prong of *Lemon* was violated here because the monitoring would create excessive government entanglement with religion. The four dissenting justices accused the majority of creating a "Catch 22" situation where programs are unconstitutional with or without monitoring, seeing dangers where none existed, and "rather than showing neutrality the Court boasts of, [exhibiting] nothing less than hostility toward religion and the children who attend church-sponsored schools" (473 U.S. at 420).

As the Burger Court era came to a close, it was difficult to make confident assertions about either the past or the future of the Court's Establishment Clause jurisprudence. The Court's movement toward accommodation in 1983 and 1984 had been halted by the three major neutralist decisions of 1985, and the *Lemon* test had been confidently reasserted in these decisions. Support for the neutrality approach and *Lemon* was shaky, however, because only four justices—Brennan, Marshall, Blackmun, and Stevens—were firmly committed. Burger, Rehnquist, and White were accommodationists, seemingly willing to modify or eliminate the *Lemon* test. Powell had been an unpredictable swing vote in Establishment Clause cases throughout the Burger Court years, and it was not clear why he had switched from an accommodationist to a neutralist position in the 1985 cases. Whatever the reasons for his switch in 1985, Powell was certainly not a firm member of any camp. O'Connor was also not firmly committed to either the neutralist or accommodationist camps, advancing an approach that introduced an endorsement test modification of the *Lemon* test. It is also important to recognize that post-Burger Court justices would have a wide variety of precedents from which to choose, for despite the Court's movement over the years from separation to neutrality to accommodation and back to neutrality, no precedents had ever been explicitly overruled by the Court. If the votes could be found, precedent existed for a majority to go in whatever direction it desired.

The Rehnquist Court Era

A central inquiry of this book is whether the Rehnquist Court has engaged in a conservative counterrevolution in interpreting American civil rights and liberties. In the previous section of this chapter, it was argued that the Burger Court was on the verge of a conservative counterrevolution in the area of the Establishment Clause with its accommodationist decisions in 1983 and 1984, but that the justices favoring a neutralist approach and the *Lemon* test regained control in 1985. Have the personnel changes that have occurred since Rehnquist became chief justice in 1986 brought about fundamental changes in the Court's interpretation of the Establishment Clause?

Throughout the remaining chapters of this book, we will examine the Rehnquist Court's decision making in civil rights and liberties by undertaking both quantitative and qualitative analyses. The quantitative analysis will compare the voting patterns of the Warren, Burger, and Rehnquist Courts to determine if the Rehnquist Court has become dramatically more conservative in its decisions. We will also study the voting behavior of the individual justices of the Rehnquist Court to gain more detailed insights into past, present, and future trends. Our qualitative analysis will use the doctrinal framework introduced in Chapter 1 to examine whether the Rehnquist Court justices have remained committed to major Court precedents or whether they have departed significantly from the Court's existing precedents. Detailed explanations of the methodologies associated with both the quantitative and qualitative analyses can be found in Appendix A and Appendix B, respectively.

The initial inquiry using voting data involves comparing the liberal/conservative outcomes of the Warren, Burger, and Rehnquist Courts. In analyzing Establishment Clause cases, a liberal decision is defined as one that favors the separation of church and state, typically opposing various laws and actions in which the government supports religious organizations and activities. A conservative decision, on the other hand, is one that favors various forms of government involvement with religion. Interpreted from the various approaches to the Establishment Clause, a liberal orientation is one that is consistent with a separationist or neutralist approach, while a conservative position is associated with the accommodationist approach.

Has the Rehnquist Court been distinctively more conservative than the Warren and Burger Courts in Establishment Clause cases? Table 5.2 presents some interesting results, suggesting that the Rehnquist Court has not engaged in a conservative counterrevolution through the 1994–95 term. The data show that the Rehnquist Court has been somewhat more conservative than either the Warren or Burger Courts; the Rehnquist Court has ruled liberally in 33 percent of its cases, compared to a 56 percent liberal record for the Burger Court and a 50 percent liberal pattern for the Warren Court. These differences are not large enough, however, to support the conclusion that the Rehnquist Court has engaged in a conservative counterrevolution in the Establishment Clause area.

It is necessary, however, to take a closer look at the individual voting patterns within the Rehnquist Court before reaching any conclusions. Given the previous results, we do not expect to find a majority of the justices forming a conservative

TABLE 5.2: Liberal/Conservative Outcomes of Establishment Clause Cases for the Warren, Burger, and Rehnquist Courts, 1953-94 Terms

	Outcomes		
Court Era	Liberal	Conservative	Totals
Warren Court, 1953-68 Terms	50% (4)	50% (4)	8
Burger Court, 1969-85 Terms	56% (15)	44% (12)	27
Rehnquist Court, 1986-94 Terms	33% (5)	67% (10)	15
Totals	48% (24)	52% (26)	50

voting bloc, but this is an empirical question that needs to be examined by looking at the data. Furthermore, even if a majority conservative bloc is not found, the data may suggest the potential for the future formation of such a bloc. We begin by looking at the voting records of the individual justices, and then we will move to bloc voting analysis.

The Establishment Clause voting records of the Rehnquist Court justices are found in Table 5.3, and they reveal some interesting results. Five of the members of the Rehnquist Court—Rehnquist, Thomas, Scalia, Kennedy, and White—have strongly conservative records, although Thomas has participated in only six cases. All five of these justices have voted conservatively in at least 80 percent of the Establishment Clause cases. These five justices served together only briefly, however, during the 1991 and 1992 terms. White's resignation from the Court in 1993 was a significant development in regard to Establishment Clause decision making, for Ginsburg replaced White and has thus far voted liberally in every Establishment Clause case.

The information in Table 5.3 suggests the possibility of a distinctive conservative bloc in Establishment Clause cases. Has this occurred? We can examine this question in Table 5.4, which contains a bloc voting analysis showing the extent to which the justices have voted together in the same cases. (Powell, Souter, Thomas, Ginsburg, and Breyer are excluded because they participated in so few cases.) The results in Table 5.4 reveal that the Rehnquist Court has been a deeply divided one, with a four-person liberal bloc (Brennan, Marshall, Blackmun, Stevens) balanced by a four-person conservative group of justices (Rehnquist, Scalia, White, Kennedy). O'Connor is shown by the data in Table 5.4 to be the critical swing vote in Establishment Clause cases because she has not aligned with either bloc. Recent retirements have of course changed the picture presented by the bloc voting results. White has retired, but his place in the conservative bloc seems to have been filled by Thomas, leaving the accommodationists with four solid votes. The liberal bloc has been hit harder by retirements, with Brennan, Marshall, and Blackmun no longer sitting on the Court. Ginsburg appears to be a strong advocate of the neutralist approach to the Establishment Clause, and thus seems to be an ally of Stevens. Souter and Breyer are more difficult to label. They appear to be committed to a neutralist rather than an accommodationist orientation, but they have shown a strong tendency to join O'Connor in the limited number of Establishment Clause cases in which they have participated thus far.

These results suggest that the Court is unlikely in the near future to be dominated by either a liberal or a conservative bloc of justices. Rehnquist, Scalia, Thomas, and Kennedy appear to be a highly cohesive group of accommodationists, but Kennedy has on occasion shown an independence from this bloc. The highly cohesive group of liberal, neutralist justices that tended to control the early Rehnquist Court no longer exists, but Stevens and Ginsburg remain strong advocates of this orientation. The middle ground on the Court seems to be occupied by O'Connor, Souter, and perhaps Breyer. Thus, the voting data suggest a deeply divided Court in the important and controversial area of Establishment Clause jurisprudence.

Having completed our quantitative analysis, the complementary doctrinal analysis of the Rehnquist Court's Establishment Clause cases can now be undertaken. This is necessary because of the significant limitations of quantitative methods of analysis. Most importantly, they do not take into account the relative importance of cases or the legal reasoning supporting the Court's judgments. Thus, we will examine the written opinions of the justices to assess the extent to which the Court has engaged in the modification of existing precedents or the creation of new conservative precedents. As we discussed in Chapter 1, we will classify each Rehnquist Court Establishment Clause case along a six-point continuum from the creation of new

TABLE 5.3: Liberal/Conservative Voting Records of the Justices of the Rehnquist Court in Establishment Clause Cases, 1986-94 Terms

Justices	Liberal Votes	Conservative Votes
Ginsburg	100% (3)	0% (0)
Stevens	73% (11)	27% (4)
Souter	67% (4)	33% (2)
Brennan	62% (5)	38% (3)
Marshall	56% (5)	44% (4)
Blackmun	54% (7)	46% (6)
Breyer	50% (1)	50% (1)
Powell	50% (1)	50% (1)
O'Connor	47% (7)	53% (8)
Kennedy	17% (2)	83% (10)
White	17% (2)	83% (10)
Scalia	7% (1)	93% (14)
Thomas	0% (0)	100% (6)
Rehnquist	0% (0)	100% (15)

TABLE 5.4: Bloc Voting Analysis of the Rehnquist Court Establishment Clause Cases, 1986-94 Terms (numbers are percentages of agreement)

	BR	MA	ST	BL	OC	KE	RE	SC	WH
Brennan	—	100	88	88	75	33	38	38	62
Marshall	100	—	89	89	67	33	44	33	67
Stevens	88	89	—	85	60	33	27	20	50
Blackmun	88	89	85	—	85	60	46	38	67
O'Connor	75	67	60	85	—	75	53	60	67
Kennedy	33	33	33	60	75	—	83	83	78
Rehnquist	38	44	27	46	53	83	—	93	83
Scalia	38	33	20	38	60	83	93	—	75
White	62	67	50	67	67	78	83	75	—

Court mean = 63
Sprague Criterion = 81
Liberal bloc: Brennan, Marshall, Stevens, Blackmun = 90
Conservative bloc: Kennedy, Rehnquist, Scalia, White = 82

liberal precedents to the creation of new conservative precedents; in addition, each case will also be classified as being of major or minor importance, and cases will also be classified based on whether they involved a majority or plurality opinion.

The results, summarized in Table 5.5, support the quantitative analysis because they do not reveal the occurrence of a constitutional counterrevolution. During its first nine terms, the Rehnquist Court handed down five decisions that are classified as liberal interpretations of existing precedents, with three of those decisions being major ones with majority opinions. The Court has rendered ten decisions that can be classified as conservative interpretations of existing precedents; seven of the ten are major decisions, but a conservative majority existed in only four of them. Although

TABLE 5.5: A Framework for the Doctrinal Analysis of the Rehnquist Court's Establishment Clause Cases, 1986-94 Terms

		Treatment of Precedent					
Major or Minor Importance	**Majority or Plurality Opinion**	Creation of New Liberal Precedent	Liberal Modification of Existing Precedent	Liberal Interpretation of Existing Precedent	Conservative Interpretation of Existing Precedent	Conservative Modification of Existing Precedent	Creation of New Conservative Precedent
Major	Majority			Edwards v. Aguillard (1987) Allegheny v. ACLU (1989) Lee v. Weisman (1992)	Bowen v. Kendrick (1988) Lamb's Chapel v. Center Moriches (1993) Zobrest v. Catalina (1993) Rosenberger v. Virginia (1995)		
	Plurality			Kiryas Joel v. Grumet (1994)	Pittsburgh v. ACLU (1989) Board v. Mergens (1990) Capital Square v. Pinette (1995)		
Minor	Majority				Corporation v. Amos (1987) Hernandez v. Commission, (1989) Swaggert v. Board (1990)		
	Plurality			Texas Monthly v. Bullock (1989)			

these results do show a pattern of conservative jurisprudence by the Rehnquist Court, this pattern is certainly not strong enough to support the conclusion that a conservative counterrevolution has occurred.

It is necessary to undertake a more detailed analysis of the cases in Table 5.5 because extremely interesting and important doctrinal developments have occurred in the Rehnquist Court's Establishment Clause cases even though a conservative counterrevolution has not occurred. The focus will be on the major cases.

The first major Establishment Clause case of the Rehnquist Court, *Edwards v. Aguillard* (1987), suggested that the neutrality approach and the *Lemon* test were firmly entrenched. The newest member of the Court, Scalia, did take a strong accommodationist approach in *Edwards,* but he did not change the lineup of the Court because the accommodationists had lost their leader, Burger. It now fell to the new chief justice, Rehnquist, to assume the leadership role in seeking to move the Court to an accommodationist position, a role he seemed willing to accept.

Edwards involved a challenge to the constitutionality of Louisiana's Creationism Act. This law forbade the teaching of evolutionary theory in the public schools unless it was accompanied by instruction in creation science, which follows a rather literal Biblical interpretation of the origins of the earth and the human race. Brennan wrote the Court's majority opinion and was joined by Marshall, Blackmun, Stevens, and Powell. Placing great emphasis on the *Lemon* test, Brennan argued that the Court had used this test in all Establishment Clause cases but one—*Marsh*—since its creation in 1971, and he also emphasized that the Court had been especially vigilant in enforcing the Establishment Clause in regard to elementary and secondary schools. In applying the *Lemon* test, Brennan argued that Louisiana failed the first prong—the purpose prong—because "the preeminent purpose of the Louisiana legislature was clearly to advance the religious viewpoint that a supernatural being created humankind" (482 U.S. at 591). O'Connor and White concurred in the judgment that the law was unconstitutional, but they were not willing to accept Brennan's ringing endorsement of the *Lemon* test.

In his first Establishment Clause case, Scalia wrote a lengthy dissent, joined by Rehnquist, in which he argued vigorously for an accommodationist approach to the Establishment Clause and the rejection of the *Lemon* test. Scalia cited Rehnquist's characterization in *Wallace* of the *Lemon* test as "a constitutional theory [that] has no basis in the history of the amendment it seeks to interpret, is difficult to apply and yields unprincipled results" (482 U.S. at 636). Furthermore, even if the *Lemon* test were to be applied in this case, Scalia argued, the Louisiana law could pass the purpose prong because it requires that a legislature's sole motive must be to promote religion, and the Louisiana legislature did have a secular purpose of promoting academic freedom.

A new Reagan appointee joined the Court in the 1987–88 term when Kennedy replaced Powell. We have seen that Powell had been a moderate, swing vote in the Establishment Clause cases, and thus Kennedy could provide the accommodationists with an additional key voice. The Court heard a major Establishment Clause case during this term, *Bowen v. Kendrick* (1988), and Kennedy's replacement of Powell may have had a major impact on the outcome of this case because Kennedy joined Rehnquist's five-person majority opinion. *Bowen* involved a controversial federal program, the Adolescent Family Life Act, which provided grants to organizations and agencies dealing with adolescent premarital sexual relations and pregnancy. The Act required that grants must provide for the involvement of religious organizations and agencies and also prohibited the use of grant funds for family planning services and the promotion of abortion. The Court ruled 5-4 that the act on its face did not violate the Establishment Clause, and Rehnquist authored the conservative opinion for himself, Scalia, White, Kennedy, and O'Connor. His approach was rather blunt. He gave no attention to the debate over neutrality versus accommodation, and he referred to the *Lemon* test as the standard "which guides 'the general nature of our inquiry in this area. . .' " (487 U.S. at 602). In applying the three-pronged test, Rehnquist argued that the controlling precedents in this case were those involving government funding for religious affiliated institutions of higher education because they were not pervasively sectarian and neither were the institutions receiving grants under the challenged act. Utilizing these precedents as the foundation of his argument, Rehnquist argued that the Act had a primary secular purpose of addressing the problem of teenage pregnancy, the Act's primary effect was not to advance religion, and finally the Act did not involve excessive government entanglement with religion.

Thus, the addition of Kennedy to the Court did give evidence of yet another justice committed to an accommodationist interpretation of the Establishment Clause, even though this case did not involve an analysis of the approaches to the Clause. Although Kennedy did not write in an Establishment Clause case in his first term, in the next term he had the opportunity to make his views known, and it was clear that Rehnquist, Scalia, and White did indeed have a new ally. The major cases of the 1988–89 term were *County of Allegheny v. ACLU* (1989) and *City of Pittsburgh v. ACLU* (1989), both involving religious displays on public property. In these companion cases, which the Court treated together, the neutralists were severely split regarding the proper application of the *Lemon* test, with Blackmun, Brennan, Stevens, and O'Connor each writing an opinion. The accommodationists were of one view, however. Kennedy—joined by Rehnquist, Scalia, and White—launched a broadside attack on the neutralist approach, accusing the neutralists of a latent hostility or callous indifference toward religion and advocating strongly an accommodationist approach to the Establishment Clause.

Kennedy's arguments were so forceful that Blackmun felt compelled in his controlling opinion to address them directly. In response to Kennedy's charge that the Court's neutrality approach bordered on hostility or callousness toward religion, Blackmun responded that Kennedy's "accusations could be said to be as offensive as they are absurd" (492 U.S. at 610). Blackmun further charged that Kennedy's accommodationist approach was "so far-reaching" that it "would gut the core of the Establishment Clause, as this Court understands it" (492 U.S. at 604). Given these strong accusations, we need to examine these cases in much greater detail.

In extraordinarily involved and confusing language—even by Establishment Clause standards—the Court ruled 5-4 in the *Allegheny* case that the religious display by Allegheny County was unconstitutional but voted 6-3 that the display by Pittsburgh did not violate the Establishment Clause. The county had a nativity scene, along with a sign proclaiming "Glory to God in the Highest," in the County Courthouse. Blackmun, Brennan, Marshall, Stevens, and O'Connor found this to violate the basic meaning and purposes of the Establishment Clause. The city of Pittsburgh's display was located just outside the City-County Building and consisted of an eighteen-foot Chanukah menorah, a large Christmas tree, and a sign bearing the words "Salute to Liberty." Because this display had both religious and secular components, a majority found it not to violate the Establishment Clause, with only Brennan, Marshall, and Stevens in disagreement.

In his lead opinion for the fractured Court, Blackmun—joined by Brennan, Marshall, Stevens, and O'Connor—set forth an interesting innovation in the *Lemon* test by embracing the endorsement test that O'Connor had emphasized in some of her earlier opinions. "In recent years," Blackmun wrote, "we have paid particularly close attention to whether the challenged governmental practice has either had the purpose or effect of 'endorsing' religion, a concern that has long held a place in our Establishment Clause jurisprudence" (492 U.S. at 592). Blackmun recognized that the term endorsement was not self-defining, and he sought to clarify it by linking it to government activities favoring, preferring, or promoting either one religion or religion in general. While agreeing on these principles, however, the neutralists disagreed about how to apply them in the two cases.

Kennedy's dissent is extremely important because this was the first time he had written on the Establishment Clause. Kennedy argued that the history and purpose of the Establishment Clause "permits government some latitude in recognizing and accommodating the central role religion plays in our society" (492 U.S. at 657). The neutrality approach of the majority, he argued, bordered on a latent hostility toward religion, a hostility inconsistent with the country's history and the Court's precedents. In examining the Court's accommodationist decisions, Kennedy found two guiding principles in Establishment Clause analysis: "government may not coerce anyone to support or participate in any religion or its exercise; and it may not, in the guise of avoiding hostility or callous indifference, give direct benefits to religion to such a degree that it in fact 'establishes a [state] religion or religious faith, or tends to do so' " (492 U.S. at 659). Thus, Kennedy argued, it is fully permissible within the meaning of the Establishment Clause for the government to accommodate or passively acknowledge religious symbols in a noncoercive way consistent with practices that are an accepted part of our national heritage. Applying these principles, Kennedy argued that the two displays clearly did not violate the Establishment Clause.

Kennedy's opinion also undercut the *Lemon* test and strongly suggested his willingness to overturn it. He argued that the application of the *Lemon* test to this case did lead to the conclusion that the displays were constitutional, but he emphasized that he did not "wish to be seen as advocating, let alone adopting, that test as our primary guide in this difficult area" (492 U.S. at 655). Citing "pervasive criticism" of *Lemon* by Rehnquist, White, and Scalia, he gave this ominous warning regarding the *Lemon* test: "Substantial revision of our Establishment Clause doctrine may be in order; but it is unnecessary for us to undertake that task today. . ." (492 U.S. at 656). Kennedy also launched a strong attack on the endorsement test that Blackmun had emphasized.

Kennedy maintained his strong support of the accommodation theory in the next term as well, where the major Establishment Clause case was *Board of Education of Westside Community Schools v. Mergens* (1990). This case involved the Equal Access Act passed by Congress in 1984. In this law Congress prohibited public schools receiving federal funds and maintaining a limited open forum from denying equal access to all students wishing to meet within this forum. The legislation was particularly directed to religious groups, and a group of students at Westside High School in Omaha, Nebraska, sought permission under the act to form a Christian club at the school. School officials, however, denied the request because they felt the recognition of the club would violate the Establishment Clause. The case came before the Court on two issues: (1) Is Westside a limited, open forum within the meaning of the Equal Access Act such that a denial of the students' request to form a Christian club violates the act? and, if so (2) Does the Equal Access Act violate the Establishment Clause?

A high level of agreement existed on the statutory issue, with all the justices but Stevens agreeing that the school was a limited, open forum within the meaning of the Equal Access Act and that the school's denial of the request to form a Christian club violated the act. This triggered the Establishment Clause issue, and again every justice but Stevens agreed that the act did not violate the Establishment Clause.

The justices were not in agreement, however, regarding the proper interpretation of the Establishment Clause. In an unusual alignment, O'Connor was joined by Rehnquist, White, and Blackmun in the plurality opinion. She relied on the precedent of *Widmar v. Vincent* (1981), in which the Court used the three-part *Lemon* test to rule that a state university's equal access regulation did not violate the Establishment Clause. O'Connor argued that "the logic of *Widmar* applies with equal force to the Equal Access Act," (496 U.S. at 248) and she reasoned that the act passed all three prongs of the *Lemon* test. Kennedy, joined by Scalia, agreed that the act did not violate the Establishment Clause, but he rejected the *Lemon* approach in O'Connor's plurality opinion and reiterated his argument in *Allegheny* that the Court's Establishment Clause decisions should be guided by an analysis of whether a government activity violates either of two principles, the direct benefits principle and the coercion principle. Kennedy saw no violation of either principle in this case. Marshall also wrote a concurring opinion that Brennan joined. Marshall agreed that the Establishment Clause was not violated in this case, but he argued that the plurality opinion by O'Connor did not pay adequate attention to the differences between high school and college settings. To assure a message of neutrality rather than endorsement is given, Marshall contended, the school "must fully disassociate itself from the Club's religious speech and avoid appearing to sponsor or endorse the Club's goals" (496 U.S. at 270).

The Court did not hear any Establishment Clause cases in the 1990–91 term, but a major case was on the docket for the 1991–92 term, *Lee v. Weisman* (1992). This was another case involving the emotional topic of state-sponsored religious activities in the public schools, specifically the offering of prayers referring to God at public junior high graduation ceremonies.

Interest in this case was intense because of changes in the Court's personnel since the last Establishment Clause case was heard. The Court's two most staunch liberals, Brennan and Marshall, had resigned in 1990 and 1991, respectively. Brennan was replaced by Souter, whose views on the Establishment Clause were unknown, and Marshall was replaced by Thomas, who seemed most unlikely to hold liberal views on the Establishment Clause. It appeared that Rehnquist, Scalia, White, and Kennedy would only need to gain the support of either Souter or Thomas, and it was possible that both of these new members of the Court would join the accommodationists in rewriting Establishment Clause jurisprudence. The Bush administration seemed to sense that the moment had arrived, for the Justice Department filed an amicus brief urging the Court to adopt an accommodationist approach and to abandon the *Lemon* test. As the Court heard oral argument in the case on November 6, 1991, Marcia Coyle of the *National Law Journal* probably echoed the views of most Court observers: "The U. S. Supreme Court may be on the brink of a major reconstruction of the wall between church and state in America as it takes up a constitutional challenge pushed by the Bush administration and conservative religious organizations" (*National Law Journal,* November 11, 1991, p. 1).

When the decision was finally announced almost eight months later on June 24, 1992, the accommodationists had gained another supporter in Thomas, but in a startling development Kennedy broke with the accommodationists for the first time and authored a majority opinion joined by Blackmun, Stevens, O'Connor, and Souter, finding the activity to violate the Establishment Clause. Scalia wrote a blistering dissent joined by Rehnquist, White, and Thomas, that emphasized the importance of interpreting the Establishment Clause based on a government accommodation of practices that have historically been a part of the nation's cultural and political heritage.

In his majority opinion, Kennedy certainly did not undergo a sudden conversion from accommodation to neutrality nor did he embrace the *Lemon* test. He began his opinion by sidestepping the invitation to reconsider *Lemon,* arguing that this was not necessary because this case could be decided directly by applying the controlling precedents of *Engle v. Vitale* (1962) and *Abington School District v. Schempp* (1963). He also recognized throughout his opinion that certain accommodations between government and religion are acceptable under the Establishment Clause. But, Kennedy argued, accommodation has its limits, and government may not coerce anyone to support or participate in religious activities. Applying these precedents and principles, Kennedy concluded that the prayers at graduation ceremonies violated the Establishment Clause.

The other members of the majority coalition were undoubtedly happy to have Kennedy's vote, but their concurring opinions indicated that they were far less comfortable with his cautious, narrowly based opinion. Blackmun wrote a concurring opinion joined by Stevens and O'Connor in which he traced the emergence of the *Lemon* test, stressed the Court's use of it in every case since 1971 except *Marsh,* and then concluded that the policy in question clearly violated the principles of the *Lemon* test. Blackmun went on to make the distinction that while government coercion is sufficient to prove an Establishment Clause violation, it is not necessary. Souter also authored a lengthy concurring opinion joined by Stevens and O'Connor, and he appears to have used this opportunity to explicate his Establishment Clause philosophy embracing a neutralist orientation.

Scalia was at his acerbic best in writing the dissent. He began with a less than subtle jab at Kennedy, citing the latter's opinion in *Allegheny County* about the need to base Establishment Clause jurisprudence on long-standing historical practices. Scalia argued that instead of properly relying on history for guidance, the Court majority invented a "boundless, and boundlessly manipulable, test of psychological coercion" as "the bulldozer of its social engineering" (505 U.S. at 632). In using this test, Scalia continued, "the Court has gone beyond the realm where judges know what they are doing" (505 U.S. at 636). Scalia's only faint praise for the majority opinion was its nonutilization of the *Lemon* test; by ignoring it, Scalia argued, the Court had shown the irrelevance of the test.

Lee v. Weisman

505 U.S. 577, 112 S.Ct. 2649 120 L.Ed. 2d 467 (1992)

■ The public school system of Providence, Rhode Island, had a policy under which middle school and high school principals could invite members of the local clergy to give invocations and benedictions at graduation ceremonies. Attendance at the ceremonies was voluntary; but students who did attend entered as a group in a processional under the direction of teachers and school officials, and they sat together apart from their families. Robert E. Lee, school principal at Nathan Bishop Middle School in Providence, invited Rabbi Leslie Gutterman of Temple Beth El in Providence to deliver prayers at the school's June 1989 graduation ceremonies. Daniel Weisman, chair of the social work department at Rhode Island College, acting for himself and his fourteen-year-old daughter, Deborah, who was graduating from Nathan Bishop, objected to the prayers, but school officials rejected his plea. Weisman filed suit in the Federal District Court for Rhode Island seeking a permanent injunction to bar Providence school officials from inviting clergy to deliver invocations and benedictions at further graduation ceremonies. The District Court found the policy to violate the Establishment Clause on the basis that the activity violated the effect prong of the *Lemon* test, making it unnecessary to consider the other prongs of the test. The decision was appealed to the United States Court of Appeals for the First Circuit, which affirmed the decision of the District Court. The majority opinion adopted the District Court's reasoning that the practice violated the effect prong of *Lemon;* a concurring opinion argued that all three prongs of *Lemon* were violated; and a dissenting opinion argued that the policy was constitutional based upon the logic of *Marsh v. Chambers* (1983).

This was one of the most closely watched Establishment Clause cases in Supreme Court history because many experts thought a majority of the justices might reject the neutrality approach and overturn the *Lemon* test, as the Bush Administration urged the Court to do. The Court did not do this, but the majority opinion did not give support to the neutrality approach or the *Lemon* test. This case is also of importance because it was the first Establishment Clause case for the Court's newest members, Souter and Thomas, who took dramatically different positions in the case. As you read the decision, consider the following questions: (1) Should the Court have based its decision in this case on the legislative prayer precedent of *Marsh* or the school prayer precedents of *Engel* and *Schempp*? (2) Did the Court's decision mean that all forms of religious activities at public school graduation ceremonies were prohibited by the Establishment Clause? (3) What was the line-up of justices favoring the continued reliance on the *Lemon* test? (4) Did a majority of the justices agree on a coercion test?

VOTE:

5 justices found the policy unconstitutional (Blackmun, Kennedy, O'Connor, Souter, Stevens).

4 justices found the policy constitutional (Rehnquist, Scalia, Thomas, White).

Justice Kennedy delivered the opinion of the Court.

This case does not require us to revisit the difficult questions dividing us in recent cases, questions of the definition and full scope of the principles governing the extent of permitted accommodation by the State for the religious beliefs and practices of many of its citizens. For without reference to those principles in other contexts, the controlling precedents as they relate to prayer and religious exercise in primary and secondary public schools compel the holding here that the policy of the city of Providence is an unconstitutional one. We can decide the case without reconsidering the general constitutional framework by which public schools' efforts to accommodate religion are measured. Thus we do not accept the invitation of petitioners and *amicus* the United States to reconsider our decision in *Lemon v. Kurtzman* (1971). The government involvement with religious activity in this case is pervasive, to the point of creating a state-sponsored and state-directed religious exercise in a public school. Conducting this formal religious observance conflicts with settled rules pertaining to prayer exercises for students, and that suffices to determine the question before us.

The principle that government may accommodate the free exercise of religion does not supersede the fundamental limitations imposed by the Establishment Clause. It is beyond dispute that, at a minimum, the Constitution guarantees that government may not coerce anyone to support or participate in religion or its exercise, or otherwise act in a way which "establishes a [state] religion or religious faith, or tends to do so." *Lynch*. The State's involvement in the school prayers challenged today violates these central principles.

That involvement is as troubling as it is undeniable. A school official, the principal, decided that an invocation and a benediction should be given; this is a choice attributable to the State, and from a constitutional perspective it is as if a state statute decreed that the prayers must occur. The principal chose the religious participant, here a rabbi, and that choice is also attributable to the State. * * *

The State's role did not end with the decision to include a prayer and with the choice of clergyman. Principal Lee provided Rabbi Gutterman with a copy of the "Guidelines for Civic Occasions," and advised him that his prayers should be nonsectarian. Through these means the principal directed and controlled the content of the prayer. Even if the only sanction for ignoring the instructions were that the rabbi would not be invited back, we think no religious representative who valued his or her continued reputation and effectiveness in the community would incur the State's displeasure in this regard. It is a cornerstone principle of our Establishment Clause jurisprudence that "it is no part of the business of government to compose official prayers for any group of the American people to recite as part of a religious program carried on by government," *Engel v. Vitale* (1962), and that is what the school officials attempted to do.

* * *

The lessons of the First Amendment are as urgent in the modern world as in the 18th Century when it was written. One timeless lesson is that if citizens are subjected to state-sponsored religious exercises, the State disavows its own duty to guard and respect that sphere of inviolable conscience and belief which is the mark of a free people. To compromise that principle today would be to deny our own tradition and forfeit our standing to urge others to secure the protections of that tradition for themselves.

As we have observed before, there are heightened concerns with protecting freedom of conscience from subtle coercive pressure in the elementary and secondary public schools. See *Abington School District v. Schempp* (1963); *Edwards v. Aguillard*

(1987); *Westside Community Bd. of Ed. v. Mergens* (1990). Our decisions in *Engel v. Vitale* and *Abington School District* recognize, among other things, that prayer exercises in public schools carry a particular risk of indirect coercion. The concern may not be limited to the context of schools, but it is most pronounced there. See *Allegheny County v. Greater Pittsburgh ACLU.* What to most believers may seem nothing more than a reasonable request that the nonbeliever respect their religious practices, in a school context may appear to the nonbeliever or dissenter to be an attempt to employ the machinery of the State to enforce a religious orthodoxy.

We need not look beyond the circumstances of this case to see the phenomenon at work. The undeniable fact is that the school district's supervision and control of a high school graduation ceremony places public pressure, as well as peer pressure, on attending students to stand as a group or, at least, maintain respectful silence during the Invocation and Benediction. This pressure, though subtle and indirect, can be as real as any overt compulsion. Of course, in our culture standing or remaining silent can signify adherence to a view or simple respect for the views of others. And no doubt some persons who have no desire to join a prayer have little objection to standing as a sign of respect for those who do. But for the dissenter of high school age, who has a reasonable perception that she is being forced by the State to pray in a manner her conscience will not allow, the injury is no less real. There can be no doubt that for many, if not most, of the students at the graduation, the act of standing or remaining silent was an expression of participation in the Rabbi's prayer. That was the very point of the religious exercise. It is of little comfort to a dissenter, then, to be told that for her the act of standing or remaining in silence signifies mere respect, rather than participation. What matters is that, given our social conventions, a reasonable dissenter in this milieu could believe that the group exercise signified her own participation or approval of it.

Finding no violation under these circumstances would place objectors in the dilemma of participating, with all that implies, or protesting. We do not address whether that choice is acceptable if the affected citizens are mature adults, but we think the State may not, consistent with the Establishment Clause, place primary and secondary school children in this position. Research in psychology supports the common assumption that adolescents are often susceptible to pressure from their peers towards conformity, and that the influence is strongest in matters of social convention. * * *

The injury caused by the government's action, and the reason why Daniel and Deborah Weisman object to it, is that the State, in a school setting, in effect required participation in a religious exercise. It is, we concede, a brief exercise during which the individual can concentrate on joining its message, meditate on her own religion, or let her mind wander. But the embarrassment and the intrusion of the religious exercise cannot be refuted by arguing that these prayers, and similar ones to be said in the future, are of a *de minimus* character. To do so would be an affront to the Rabbi who offered them and to all those for whom the prayers were an essential and profound recognition of divine authority. And for the same reason, we think that the intrusion is greater than the two minutes or so of time consumed for prayers like these. * * *

* * *

The Government's argument gives insufficient recognition to the real conflict of conscience faced by the young student. The essence of the Government's position is that with regard to a civil, social occasion of this importance it is the objector, not the majority, who must take unilateral and private action to avoid compromising religious scruples, here by electing to miss the graduation exercise. This turns conventional First Amendment analysis on its head. It is a tenet of the First Amendment that the State cannot require one of its citizens to forfeit his or her rights and benefits as the price of resisting conformance to state-sponsored religious practice. To say that a student must remain apart from the ceremony at the opening invocation and closing benediction is to risk compelling conformity in an environment analogous to the classroom setting, where we have said the risk of compulsion is especially high. Just as in *Engel v. Vitale* and *Abington School District v. Schempp,* we found that provisions within the challenged legislation permitting a student to be voluntarily excused from attendance or participation in the daily prayers did not shield those practices from invalidation, the fact that attendance at the graduation ceremonies is voluntary in a legal sense does not save the religious exercise.

Inherent differences between the public school system and a session of the State Legislature distinguish this case from *Marsh v. Chambers* (1983). The considerations we have raised in objection to the invocation and benediction are in many respects similar to the arguments we considered in *Marsh.* But there are also obvious differences. The atmosphere at the opening of a session of a state legislature where adults are free to enter and leave with little comment and for any number of reasons cannot compare with the constraining potential of the one school event most important for the student to attend. The influence and force of a formal exercise in a school graduation are far greater than the prayer exercise we condoned in *Marsh*. The *Marsh* majority in fact gave specific recognition to this distinction and placed particular reliance on it in upholding the prayers at issue there. Today's case is different. At a high school graduation, teachers and principals must and do retain a high degree of control over the precise contents of the program, the speeches, the timing, the movements, the dress, and the decorum of the students. In this atmosphere the state-imposed character of an invocation and benediction by clergy selected by the school combine to make the prayer a state-sanctioned religious exercise in which the student was left with no alternative but to submit. This is different from *Marsh* and suffices to make the religious exercise a First Amendment violation. Our Establishment Clause jurisprudence remains a delicate and fact-sensitive one, and we cannot accept the parallel relied upon by petitioners and the United States between the facts of *Marsh* and the case now before us. Our decisions in *Engel v. Vitale* and *Abington School District v. Schempp* require us to distinguish the public school context.

* * *

For the reasons we have stated, the judgment of the Court of Appeals is Affirmed.

Justice Blackmun, with whom Justice Stevens and Justice O'Connor join, concurring.

Nearly half a century of review and refinement of Establishment Clause jurisprudence has distilled one clear understanding. Government may neither promote nor affiliate itself with any religious doctrine or organization, nor may it intrude itself in the internal affairs of any religious institution. The application of these principles to the present case mandates the decision reached today by the Court.

* * *

In 1971 Chief Justice Burger reviewed the Court's past decisions and found: "Three . . . tests may be gleaned from our cases." *Lemon v. Kurtzman*. In order for a statute to survive an Establishment Clause challenge, "[f]irst, the statute must have a secular legislative purpose; second, its principal or primary effect must be one that neither advances nor inhibits religion; finally the statute must not foster an excessive government entanglement with religion." After *Lemon*, the Court continued to rely on these basic principles in resolving Establishment Clause disputes.

Application of these principles to the facts of this case is straight forward. There can be "no doubt" that the "invocation of God's blessings" as delivered at Nathan Bishop Middle School "is a religious activity." *Engel*. In the words of *Engel*, the Rabbi's prayer "is a solemn avowal of divine faith and supplication for the blessings of the Almighty. The nature of such a prayer has always been religious." The question then is whether the government has "plac[ed] its official stamp of approval" on the prayer. As the Court ably demonstrates, when the government "compose[s] official prayers," selects the member of the clergy to deliver the prayer, has the prayer delivered at a public event that is planned, supervised and given by school officials, and pressures students to attend and participate in the prayer, there can be no doubt that the government is advancing and promoting religion. As our prior decisions teach us, it is this that the Constitution prohibits.

I join the Court's opinion today because I find nothing in it inconsistent with the essential precepts of the Establishment Clause developed in our precedents. The Court holds that the graduation prayer is unconstitutional because the State "in effect required participation in a religious exercise." Although our precedents make clear that proof of government coercion is not necessary to prove an Establishment Clause violation, it is sufficient. Government pressure to participate in a religious activity is an obvious indication that the government is endorsing or promoting religion.

But it is not enough that the government restrain from compelling religious practices; it must not engage in them either. See *Schempp*. The Court repeatedly has recognized that a violation of the Establishment Clause is not predicated on coercion. * * *

Justice Souter, with whom Justice Stevens and Justice O'Connor join, concurring.

I join the whole of the Court's opinion, and fully agree that prayers at public school graduation ceremonies indirectly coerce religious observance. I write separately nonetheless on two issues of Establishment Clause analysis that underlie my independent resolution of this case: whether the Clause applies to government practices that do not favor one religion or denomination over others, and whether state coercion of religious conformity, over and above state endorsement of religious exercise or belief, is a necessary element of an Establishment Clause violation.

Forty-five years ago, this Court announced a basic principle of constitutional law from which it has not strayed: the Establishment Clause forbids not only state practices that "aid one religion . . . or prefer one religion over another," but also those that "aid all religions." *Everson v. Board of Education of Ewing* (1947). Today we reaffirm that principle, holding that the Establishment Clause forbids state-sponsored prayers in public settings no matter how nondenominational the prayers may be. In barring the State from sponsoring generically Theistic prayers where it could not sponsor sectarian ones, we hold true to a line of precedent from which there is no adequate historical case to depart.

Petitioners rest most of their argument on a theory that, whether or not the Establishment Clause permits extensive nonsectarian support for religion, it does not forbid the state to sponsor affirmations of religious belief that coerce neither support for religion nor participation in religious observance. I appreciate the force of some of the arguments supporting a "coercion" analysis of the Clause. See generally *Allegheny County.* But we could not adopt that reading without abandoning our settled law, a course that, in my view, the text of the Clause would not readily permit. * * *

* * *

Our precedents may not always have drawn perfectly straight lines. They simply cannot, however, support the position that a showing of coercion is necessary to a successful Establishment Clause claim.

* * *

While the Establishment Clause's concept of neutrality is not self-revealing, our recent cases have invested it with specific content: the state may not favor or endorse either religion generally over nonreligion or one religion over others. See., e.g., *Allegheny County; Texas Monthly; Edwards v. Aguillard; School Dist. of Grand Rapids; Wallace v. Jaffree.* This principle against favoritism and endorsement has become the foundation of Establishment Clause jurisprudence, ensuring that religious belief is irrelevant to every citizen's standing in the political community, see *Allegheny County,* and protecting religion from the demeaning effects of any governmental embrace. Now, as in the early Republic, "religion & Govt. will both exist in greater purity, the less they are mixed together." Our aspiration to religious liberty, embodied in the First Amendment, permits no other standard.

Justice Scalia, with whom The Chief Justice, Justice White, and Justice Thomas join, dissenting.

Three terms ago, I joined an opinion recognizing that the Establishment Clause must be construed in light of the "[g]overnment policies of accommodation, acknowledgment, and support for religion [that] are an accepted part of our political and cultural heritage." That opinion affirmed that "the meaning of the Clause is to be determined by reference to historical practices and understandings." It said that "[a] test for implementing the protections of the Establishment Clause that, if applied with consistency, would invalidate longstanding traditions cannot be a proper reading of the Clause." *Allegheny County v. Greater Pittsburgh ACLU* (1989).

These views of course prevent me from joining today's opinion, which is conspicuously bereft of any reference to history. In holding that the Establishment Clause prohibits invocations and benedictions at public-school graduation ceremonies, the Court—with nary a mention that it is doing so—lays waste a tradition that is as old as public-school graduation ceremonies themselves, and that is a component of an even more longstanding American tradition of nonsectarian prayer to God at public celebrations generally. As its instrument of destruction, the bulldozer of its social engineering, the Court invents a boundless, and boundlessly manipulable, test of psychological coercion. . . . Today's opinion shows more forcefully than volumes of argumentation why our Nation's protection, that fortress which is our Constitution, cannot possibly rest upon the changeable philosophical predilections of the Justices of this Court, but must have deep foundations in the historical practices of our people.

Justice Holmes' aphorism that "a page of history is worth a volume of logic" applies with particular force to our Establishment Clause jurisprudence. * * *

The history and tradition of our Nation are replete with public ceremonies featuring prayers of thanksgiving and petition. * * *

From our Nation's origin, prayer has been a prominent part of governmental ceremonies and proclamations. The Declaration of Independence, the document marking our birth as a separate people, "appeal[ed] to the Supreme Judge of the world for the rectitude of our intentions" and avowed "a firm reliance on the protection of divine Providence." In his first inaugural address, after swearing his oath of office on a Bible, George Washington deliberately made a prayer a part of his first official act as President. . . . Such supplications have been a characteristic feature of inaugural addresses ever since. * * * [The] tradition of Thanksgiving Proclamations—with their religious theme of prayerful gratitude to God—has been adhered to by almost every President.

The other two branches of the Federal Government also have a long-established practice of prayer at public events. * * *

In addition to this general tradition of prayer at public ceremonies, there exists a more specific tradition of invocations and benedictions at public-school graduation exercises. * * *

The Court presumably would separate graduate invocations and benedictions from other instances of public "preservation and transmission of religious beliefs" on the ground that they involve "psychological coercion." I find it a sufficient embarrassment that our Establishment Clause jurisprudence regarding holiday displays . . . has come to "requir[e] scrutiny more commonly associated with interior decorators than with the judiciary. . . ." But interior decorating is a rock-hard science compared to psychology practiced by amateurs. A few citations of "[r]esearch in psychology" that have no particular bearing upon the precise issue here cannot disguise the fact that the Court has gone beyond the realm where judges know what they are doing. The Court's argument that state officials have "coerced" students to take part in the invocation and benediction at graduation ceremonies is, not to put too fine a point on it, incoherent. * * *

* * *

The deeper flaw in the Court's opinion does not lie in its wrong answer to the question whether there was state-induced "peer-pressure" coercion; it lies, rather, in the Court's making violation of the Establishment Clause hinge on such a precious question. The coercion that was a hallmark of historical establishments of religion was coercion of religious orthodoxy and of financial support *by force of law and threat of penalty.* Typically, attendance at the state church was required; only clergy of the official church could lawfully perform sacraments; and dissenters, if tolerated, faced an array of civil disabilities. * * *

* * *

Thus, while I have no quarrel with the Court's general proposition that the Establishment Clause "guarantees that government may not coerce anyone to support or participate in religion or its exercise," I see no warrant for expanding the concept of coercion beyond acts backed by penalty—a brand of coercion that happily is readily discernible to those of us who have made a career of reading the disciples of Blackstone rather than of Freud. The Framers were indeed opposed to coercion of religious worship by the National Government; but, as their own sponsorship of nonsectarian prayer in public events demonstrates, they understood that "[s]peech is not coercive; the listener may do as he likes."

* * *

The Court relies on our "school prayer" cases, *Engel v. Vitale* (1962) and *Abington School District v. Schempp.* But whatever the merit of those cases, they do not support, much less compel, the Court's psycho-journey. * * *

Our religion-clause jurisprudence has become bedeviled (so to speak) by reliance on formalistic abstractions that are not derived from, but positively conflict with, our long-accepted constitutional traditions. Foremost among these has been the so-called *Lemon* test, which has received well-earned criticism from many members of this Court. The Court today demonstrates the irrelevance of *Lemon* by essentially ignoring it, and the internment of that case may be the one happy byproduct of the Court's otherwise lamentable decision. Unfortunately, however, the Court has replaced *Lemon* with its psycho-coercion test, which suffers the double disability of having no roots whatever in our people's historic practice, and being as infinitely as expandable as the reasons for psychotherapy itself.

* * *

The narrow context of the present case involves a community's celebration of one of the milestones in its young citizens' lives, and it is a bold step for this Court to seek to banish from that occasion, and from thousands of similar celebrations throughout this land, the expression of gratitude to God that a majority of the community wishes to make. The issue before us today is not the abstract philosophical question whether the alternative of frustrating this desire of a religious majority is to be preferred over the alternative of imposing "psychological coercion," or a feeling of exclusion, upon nonbelievers. Rather, the question is *whether a mandatory choice in favor of the former has been imposed by the United States Constitution.* As the age-old practices of our people show, the answer to that question is not at all in doubt.

* * *

For the foregoing reasons, I dissent.

History had repeated itself. In 1985, the accommodationist justices appeared to have a majority coalition that would reject both the neutrality approach and the *Lemon* test, but in *Wallace v. Jaffree* (1985) the neutralists prevailed and the *Lemon* test was used to invalidate government programs supporting religion. In 1992, an accommodationist majority once again seemed poised to rewrite Establishment

Clause jurisprudence, and once again this did not occur, much to the dismay of the accommodationists.

Despite the strong similarities between the *Wallace* case of 1985 and the *Lee* decision of 1992, important differences can be observed in their outcomes and aftermath. In *Wallace,* Stevens's majority opinion supported the neutrality approach and the *Lemon* test, but Kennedy's majority opinion in *Lee* embraced neither neutrality nor *Lemon*. Furthermore, while the Court in the aftermath of *Wallace* had at least a short period of majority consensus, the Court since *Lee* has lacked any clear consensus in its interpretation of the Establishment Clause.

We now turn to the five Establishment Clause cases of major importance that the Court has decided since *Lee: Lamb's Chapel v. Center Moriches Union Free School District* (1993), *Zobrest v. Catalina Foothills School District* (1993), *Board of Education of Kiryas Joel Village School District v. Grumet* (1994), *Capital Square Review and Advisory Board v. Pinette* (1995), and *Rosenberger v. Rector and Visitors of the University of Virginia* (1995). These cases are characterized by the severe fragmentation of the Court in regard to a consensus on the principles by which to interpret the Establishment Clause. The *Lemon* test has slowly disappeared without being formally rejected, but no alternative test has emerged in its place. The accommodation and neutrality approaches are given lip service in the justices' opinions, but these approaches seem increasingly irrelevant in the arguments of the justices. Lacking any consensus upon which to interpret the Establishment Clause, the justices have frequently followed the pattern established in *Lee* of basing decisions on the most relevant precedent cases. This approach has also been unsatisfactory, however, because the justices have frequently lacked consensus on which precedents are most relevant and on how to apply these precedents to the cases under consideration.

Lamb's Chapel and *Zobrest* were argued on the same day—February 24, 1993—and provided the Court with the opportunity to bring greater coherence to the analysis of the Establishment Clause. This opportunity was lost, however.

The *Lamb's Chapel* case involved the use of public school facilities to show a six-part film series containing lectures by Dr. James Dobson, a best-selling author on traditional, Christian family values. Pastor John Steigerwald, leader of the Lamb's Chapel evangelical church in Center Moriches, New York, applied to the school district to show these films at a public school, but he was refused permission because the films were religiously oriented. The church brought federal suit, claiming violations of both freedom of speech and the Establishment Clause, but both the district and circuit courts ruled against the church. The Supreme Court unanimously reversed the lower courts, ruling that the school district's decision violated the First Amendment Freedom of Speech Clause and that the Establishment Clause did not require this type of separation.

The majority's analysis of the Establishment Clause issue was surprising because the *Lemon* test, disregarded in *Lee,* was used to guide the decision. The use of the *Lemon* test was especially unexpected because the majority opinion was authored by White, an accommodationist, and joined by the unlikely coalition of Rehnquist, O'Connor, Blackmun, Stevens, and Souter. In applying the *Lemon* test to this case, the Court majority argued that the government action of allowing the movies to be shown would have a valid secular purpose, would not have the primary effect of either advancing or inhibiting religion, and would not constitute an excessive government entanglement with religion.

The majority's use of the *Lemon* test triggered an explosive reaction from Scalia, who concurred in the Court's judgment but not its reasoning. Scalia argued that allowing the church to use the public school facilities was fully consistent with the Court's accommodationist approach to the Establishment Clause, and many precedents existed to support this position. He could not support the use of the *Lemon* test, however: "As to the Court's invocation of the *Lemon* test: Like some ghoul in a late-night horror movie that repeatedly sits up in its grave and shuffles abroad, after being repeatedly killed and buried, *Lemon* stalks our Establishment Clause jurisprudence once again, frightening the little children and school attorneys of Center Moriches Union Free School District" (508 U.S. at 398).

The *Lemon* test had thus rather suddenly appeared in the *Lamb's Chapel* case, and it disappeared again one week later when the Court handed down its second Establishment Clause case of the 1992–93 term, *Zobrest v. Catalina Foothills*. The accommodationist justices won a 5-4 victory in the *Zobrest* case, which involved the question of whether the Establishment Clause would be violated if a public school district paid for a sign-language interpreter to assist a deaf student in a parochial high school. In an opinion written by Chief Justice Rehnquist and joined by Scalia, Thomas, White, and Kennedy, the Court ruled that this type of assistance did not violate the Establishment Clause.

Rehnquist's opinion was remarkably brief and narrow. Although the lower federal courts had relied extensively on the *Lemon* test as did the attorneys for both parties in their briefs to the Court, Rehnquist did not mention the *Lemon* test. Nor did Rehnquist give any attention to the competing approaches of neutrality and accommodation. Instead, the chief justice relied on the precedent cases of *Mueller v. Allen* (1983) and *Witters v. Washington Dep't. of Services for the Blind* (1986), which he argued had established the principle that ". . . government programs that neutrally provide benefits to a broad class of citizens defined without reference to religion are not readily subject to an Establishment Clause challenge just because sectarian institutions may also receive an attenuated financial benefit" (509 U.S. at 8).

Blackmun, Souter, Stevens, and O'Connor dissented. All four justices agreed that the Court should have avoided the constitutional issue in the case, instead returning the case to the lower court for consideration of various, unresolved nonconstitutional issues. Blackmun, joined by Souter, also addressed the Establishment Clause issue. Blackmun's dissent, like Rehnquist's majority opinion, was narrowly argued, with no reference either to the Court's general approaches or to the *Lemon* test. Rather, Blackmun argued that this type of program authorized ". . . a public employee to participate directly in religious indoctrination" (509 U.S. at 18) thereby ". . . stray[ing] . . . from the course set by nearly five decades of Establishment Clause jurisprudence" (509 U.S. at 24).

The *Zobrest* decision did little to resolve the ambiguities plaguing Establishment Clause jurisprudence. The Court was narrowly divided on the outcome of the case, and no majority had emerged to support a distinctive approach to Establishment Clause analysis. An especially noticeable feature of the case was the absence of any reference to the *Lemon* test, even by Blackmun in his dissent, despite the reliance on the test by the Court majority a week earlier in *Lamb's Chapel*.

The Court's next major Establishment Clause case was *Kiryas Joel v. Grumet* (1994). The justices were certainly not successful in this case in working their way out of the maze of Establishment Clause jurisprudence. Indeed, the confusion and ambiguity seemed to grow.

The *Kiryas Joel* case stemmed from an unusual law passed by the New York legislature. Kiryas Joel is a village composed entirely of Satmar Hasidim, practitioners of a strict form of Judaism. The legislature created a separate school district for the village of Kiryas Joel for the purpose of allowing the Satmars to establish a special education program for their handicapped children. This law was challenged as a violation of the Establishment Clause, and the New York state courts found the law unconstitutional under the *Lemon* test.

The Supreme Court ruled 6-3 that the law was unconstitutional, but little consensus existed in regard to the reasoning behind the vote. Six justices wrote opinions to explain their varying views of the Establishment Clause's application to this case. Souter's controlling opinion gained the support of four other justices—Blackmun, Stevens, O'Connor, and Ginsburg—in regard to a narrow argument that *Larkin v. Grendel's Den, Inc.* (1982) could be used as controlling precedent, but Souter's opinion did not command majority support regarding either the neutrality approach or the *Lemon* test.

The Court's reliance in *Kiryas Joel* upon the Burger Court precedent of *Larkin* is a good example of the trend of the Rehnquist Court to base its recent Establishment Clause decisions more on specific precedent cases than on general principles. *Larkin* involved a Massachusetts statute that gave religious groups the power to veto applications for liquor licenses within five hundred feet of any religious premise. The Burger Court used the *Lemon* test to invalidate this law, arguing that the Massachusetts statute had a primary effect of advancing religion and also created an excessive entanglement of government and religion. Without specifically invoking the *Lemon* test, Souter argued that the *Kiryas Joel* case and the *Larkin* case presented "comparable constitutional problems" (62 L.W. at 4667). More specifically, Souter argued that the New York law impermissibly united religious and civic authority and also lacked any effective means of guaranteeing government neutrality.

The Rehnquist Court could not achieve majority consensus regarding either the proper Establishment Clause approach or the use of the *Lemon* test. Indeed, the justices seem to have created even greater confusion than had existed in earlier Establishment Clause cases. Souter's controlling opinion seemed to embrace both the approaches of neutrality and accommodation. The accommodationist justices also lacked consensus. Scalia wrote a lengthy dissent joined by Rehnquist and Thomas, making another appeal for the Court to adopt the accommodation approach. Kennedy did not join Scalia's dissent, however. Instead, he wrote a concurring opinion, agreeing with the judgment of the Court, advocating a moderate form of accommodation, and arguing that the New York law did exceed permissible boundaries of government accommodation of religion.

The Court was equally divided regarding the *Lemon* test, with at least four different positions existing among the justices. Souter—joined by Blackmun, Stevens, and Ginsburg—did not mention the *Lemon* test explicitly, but he did use the effect prong and the entanglement prong in his analysis. In a concurring opinion, Blackmun stated his belief that the *Lemon* test should continue to guide the Court's decision making in Establishment Clause cases. O'Connor wrote a lengthy concurring opinion in which she argued that the Court was clearly moving away from the *Lemon* test and that "a return to *Lemon,* even if possible, would likely be futile" (62 LW at 4675). She suggested that the Court may need to develop a variety of Establishment Clause tests to deal with various types of Establishment Clause issues. Kennedy made no reference to the *Lemon* test in his concurring opinion. Finally, Scalia, joined by Rehnquist and Thomas, cited his earlier criticisms of the *Lemon* test and again urged its abandonment.

Board of Education of Kiryas Joel Village School District v. Grumet

U.S., 114 S.Ct. 2481, 129 L.Ed. 2d 546 (1994)

■ Kiryas Joel is a village in New York State that was incorporated as a religious enclave for Satmar Hasidim, who were practitioners of a strict form of Judaism. The Satmars ran their own private religious schools, but their handicapped children were provided public education services at an annex to one of their private schools. The Supreme Court in *Aguilar v. Felton* (1985) and *Grand Rapids v. Ball* (1985) invalidated this type of arrangement, and this forced the Satmar children from Kiryas Joel to receive their special education at public schools outside their village. This did not prove satisfactory, however, because of severe emotional problems suffered by the Satmar children in these settings. To resolve this problem, the New York State Legislature passed a law creating the Village of Kiryas Joel as a separate school district and enabling them to establish and operate their own special education program for handicapped children. This law was challenged on Establishment Clause grounds, and the New York State courts used the *Lemon* test to find the law unconstitutional.

This is a significant case because it is a recent Establishment Clause case that contains six separate opinions showing the deep divisions among the Rehnquist Court justices over the proper interpretation of the clause. As you read this case, think about the following questions: (1) What is the status of the *Lemon* test based on the justices' opinions in this case? (2) Does Souter's plurality opinion reflect a firm commitment to the neutrality approach? (3) What approaches do O'Connor and Scalia advocate for interpreting the Establishment Clause?

Vote:

6 justices found the law to be unconstitutional (Blackmun, Ginsburg, Kennedy, O'Connor, Souter, Stevens).

3 justices found the law to be constitutional (Rehnquist, Scalia, Thomas).

Justice Souter delivered the opinion of the Court.

* * * The question is whether the Act creating the separate school district violates the Establishment Clause of the First Amendment, binding on the States through the Fourteenth Amendment. Because this unusual act is tantamount to an allocation of political power on a religious criterion and neither presupposes nor requires governmental impartiality toward religion, we hold that it violates the prohibition against establishment.

* * *

A proper respect for both the Free Exercise and the Establishment Clauses compels the State to pursue a course of 'neutrality' toward religion, *Committee for Public Ed. and Religious Liberty v. Nyquist,* (1973), favoring neither one religion over others nor religious adherents collectively over nonadherents. Chapter 748, the statute creating the Kiryas Joel Village School District, departs from this constitutional command by delegating the State's discretionary authority over public schools to a group defined by its character as a religious community, in a legal and historical context that gives no assurance that governmental power has been or will be exercised neutrally.

Larkin v. Grendel's Den, Inc. (1982) provides an instructive comparison with the litigation before us. There, the Court was requested to strike down a Massachusetts statute granting religious bodies veto power over applications for liquor licenses. Under the statute, the governing body of any church, synagogue, or school located within 500 feet of an applicant's premises could, simply by submitting written objection, prevent the Alcohol Beverage Control Commission from issuing a license. In spite of the State's valid interest in protecting churches, schools, and like institutions from " 'the hurly-burly' associated with liquor outlets," the Court found that in two respects the statute violated "the wholesome 'neutrality' of which this Court's cases speak," *School Dist. of Abington v. Schempp* (1963). The Act brought about a " 'fusion of governmental and religious functions' " by delegating "important, discretionary governmental powers" to religious bodies, thus impermissibly entangling government and religion. *Abington School Dist. v. Schempp;* see also *Lemon v. Kurtzman.* And it lacked "any 'effective means of guaranteeing' that the delegated power '[would] be used exclusively for secular, neutral, and nonideological purposes' " (quoting *Committee for Public Ed. and Religious Liberty v. Nyquist*); this, along with the "significant symbolic benefit to religion" associated with "the mere appearance of a joint exercise of legislative authority by Church and State," led the Court to conclude that the statute had a " 'primary' and 'principal' effect of advancing religion." Comparable constitutional problems inhere in the statute before us.

Larkin presented an example of united civic and religious authority, an establishment rarely found in such straightforward form in modern America, and a violation of "the core rationale underlying the Establishment Clause." * * *

The Establishment Clause problem presented by Chapter 748 is more subtle, but it resembles the issue raised in *Larkin* to the extent that the earlier case teaches that a State may not delegate its civic authority to a group chosen according to a religious criterion. Authority over public schools belongs to the State and cannot be delegated to a local school district defined by the State in order to grant political control to a religious group. What makes this litigation different from *Larkin* is the delegation here of civic power to the "qualified voters of the village of Kiryas Joel," as distinct from a religious leader such as the village rov, or an institution of religious government like the formally constituted parish council in *Larkin*. In light of the circumstances of this case, however, this distinction turns out to lack constitutional significance.

* * *

Because the district's creation ran uniquely counter to state practice, following the lines of a religious community where the customary and neutral principles would not have dictated the same result, we have good reasons to treat this district as the reflection of a religious criterion for identifying the recipients of civil authority. Not even the special needs of the children in this community can explain the legislature's unusual Act, for the State could have responded to the concerns of the Satmar parents without implicating the Establishment Clause, as we explain in some detail further on. We therefore find the legislature's Act to be substantially equivalent to defining a political subdivision and hence the qualification for its franchise by a religious test, resulting in a purposeful and forbidden "fusion of governmental and religious functions." *Larkin v. Grendel's Den.*

The fact that this school district was created by a special and unusual Act of the legislature also gives reason for concern whether the benefit received by the Satmar community is one that the legislature will provide equally to other religious (and nonreligious) groups. This is the second malady the *Larkin* Court identified in the law before it, the absence of an "effective means of guaranteeing" that governmental power will be and has been neutrally employed. But whereas in *Larkin* it was religious groups the Court thought might exercise civic power to advance the interests of religion (or religious adherents), here the threat to neutrality occurs at an antecedent stage.

The fundamental source of constitutional concern here is that the legislature itself may fail to exercise governmental authority in a religiously neutral way. The anomalously case-specific nature of the legislature's exercise of state authority in creating this district for a religious community leaves the Court without any direct way to review such state action for the purpose of safeguarding a principle at the heart of the Establishment Clause, that government should not prefer one religion to another, or religion to irreligion. * * *

In finding that Chapter 748 violates the requirement of governmental neutrality by extending the benefit of a special franchise, we do not deny that the Constitution allows the state to accommodate religious needs by alleviating special burdens. Our cases leave no doubt that in commanding neutrality the Religion Clauses do not require the government to be oblivious to impositions that legitimate exercises of state power may place on religious belief and practice. Rather, there is "ample room under the Establishment Clause for 'benevolent neutrality which will permit religious exercise to exist without sponsoring and without interference.' " * * *

But accommodation is not a principle without limits, and what petitioners seek is an adjustment to the Satmars' religiously grounded preferences that our cases do not countenance. Prior decisions have allowed religious communities and institutions to pursue their own interests free from governmental interferences, . . . but we have never hinted that an otherwise unconstitutional delegation of political power to a religious group could be saved as a religious accommodation. Petitioners' proposed accommodation singles out a particular religious sect for special treatment, and whatever the limits of permissible legislative accommodations may be, it is clear that neutrality as among religions must be honored.

This conclusion does not, however, bring the Satmar parents, the Monroe-Woodbury school district, or the State of New York to the end of the road in seeking ways to respond to the parents' concerns. Just as the Court in *Larkin* observed that the State's interest in protecting religious meeting places could be "readily accomplished by other means," there are several alternatives here for providing bilingual and bicultural special education to Satmar children. Such services can perfectly well be offered to village children through the Monroe-Woodbury Central School District. * * * Or if the educationally appropriate offering by Monroe-Woodbury should turn out to be a separate program of bilingual and bicultural education at a neutral site near one of the village's parochial schools, this Court has already made it clear that no Establishment Clause difficulty would inhere in such a scheme, administered in accordance with neutral principles that would not necessarily confine special treatment to Satmars.

* * *

Justice Cardozo once cast the dissenter as "the gladiator making a last stand against the lions." Justice Scalia's dissent is certainly the work of a gladiator, but he thrusts at lions of his own imagining. * * * The license he takes in suggesting that the Court holds the Satmar sect to be New York's established church is only one symptom of his inability to accept the fact that this Court has long held that the First Amendment reaches more than classic, 18th century establishments.

Our job, of course would be easier if the dissent's position had prevailed with the Framers and with this Court over the years. An Establishment Clause diminished to the dimensions acceptable to Justice Scalia could be enforced by a few simple rules, and our docket would never see cases requiring the application of a principle like neutrality toward religion as well as among religious sects. But that would be as blind to history as to precedent, and the difference between Justice Scalia and the Court accordingly turns on the Court's recognition that the Establishment Clause does comprehend such a principle and obligates courts to exercise the judgment necessary to apply it.

In this case we are clearly constrained to conclude that the statute before us fails the test of neutrality. It delegates a power this Court has said "ranks at the very apex of the function of a State," to an electorate defined by common religious belief and practice, in a manner that fails to foreclose religious favoritism. It therefore crosses the line from permissible accommodation to impermissible establishment. The judgment of the Court of Appeals of the State of New York is accordingly *Affirmed.*

Justice Blackmun, concurring.

* * * I write separately only to note my disagreement with any suggestion that today's decision signals a departure from the principles described in *Lemon v. Kurtzman.* The opinion of the Court relies upon several decisions, including *Larkin v. Grendel's Den, Inc.* that explicitly rested on the criteria set forth in *Lemon.* Indeed, the two principles on which the opinion bases its conclusion that the legislative act is constitutionally invalid essentially are the second and third *Lemon* criteria. * * *

I have no quarrel with the observation of Justice O'Connor that the application of constitutional principles, including those articulated in *Lemon,* must be sensitive to particular contexts. But I remain convinced of the general validity of the basic principles stated in *Lemon,* which have guided this Court's Establishment Clause decisions in over 30 cases.

Justice Stevens, with whom Justice Blackmun and Justice Ginsburg join, concurring.

* * *

Affirmative state action in aid of segregation of this character is unlike the evenhanded distribution of a public benefit or service, a "release time" program for public school students involving no public premises or funds, or a decision to grant an exemption from a burdensome general rule. It is, I believe, fairly characterized as establishing, rather than merely accommodating, religion. For this reason, as well as the reasons set out in Justice Souter's opinion, I am persuaded that the New York law at issue in these cases violates the Establishment Clause of the First Amendment.

Justice O'Connor, concurring in part and concurring in the judgment.

* * *

One aspect of the Court's opinion in this case is worth noting: Like the opinions in two recent cases, *Lee v. Weisman,* (1992) and *Zobrest v. Catalina Foothills School Dist.* (1993), and the case I think is most relevant to this one, *Larson v. Valente* (1982) the Court's opinion does not focus on the Establishment Clause test we set forth in *Lemon v. Kurtzman* (1971).

It is always appealing to look for a single test, a Grand Unified Theory that would resolve all the cases that may arise under a particular clause. There is, after all, only one Establishment Clause. * * *

But the same constitutional principle may operate very differently in different contexts. We have, for instance, no one Free Speech Clause test. * * *

And setting forth a unitary test for a broad set of cases may sometimes do more harm than good. Any test that must deal with widely disparate situations risks being so vague as to be useless. * * *

Moreover, shoehorning new problems into a test that does not reflect the special concerns raised by those problems tends to deform the language of the test. Relatively simple phrases like "primary effect . . . that neither advances nor inhibits religion" and "entanglement" acquire more and more complicated definitions which stray ever further from their literal meaning. * * *

Finally, another danger to keep in mind is that the bad test may drive out the good. Rather than taking the opportunity to derive narrower, more precise tests from the case law, courts tend to continually try to patch up the broad test, making it more and more amorphous and distorted. This, I am afraid, has happened with *Lemon.*

Experience proves that the Establishment Clause, like the Free Speech Clause, cannot easily be reduced to a single test. There are different categories of Establishment Clause cases, which may call for different approaches. * * *

As the Court's opinion today shows, the slide away from *Lemon's* unitary approach is well under way. A return to *Lemon,* even if possible, would likely be futile, regardless of where one stands on the substantive Establishment Clause questions. I think a less unitary approach provides a better structure for analysis. If each test covers a narrower and more homogeneous area, the tests may be more precise and therefore easier to apply. There may be more opportunity to pay attention to the specific nuances of each area. There might also be, I hope, more consensus on each of the narrow tests than there has been on a broad test. And abandoning the *Lemon* framework need not mean abandoning some of the insights that the test reflected, nor the insights of the cases that applied it.

* * *

Justice Kennedy, concurring in the judgment.

The Court's ruling that the Kiryas Joel Village School District violates the Establishment Clause is in my view correct, but my reservations about what the Court's reasoning implies for religious accommodations in general are sufficient to require a separate writing. As the Court recognizes, a legislative accommodation that discriminates among religions may become an establishment of religion. But the Court's opinion can be interpreted to say that an accommodation for a particular religious group is invalid because of the risk that the legislature will not grant the same accommodation to another religious group suffering some similar burden. This rationale seems to me without grounding in our precedents and a needless restriction upon the legislature's ability to respond to the unique problems of a particular religious group. The real vice of the school district, in my estimation, is that New York created it by drawing political boundaries on the basis of religion. I would decide the issue we confront upon this narrower theory, though in accord with many of the Court's general observations about the State's actions in this case.

* * *

Justice Scalia, with whom the Chief Justice and Justice Thomas join, dissenting.

The Court today finds that the Powers That Be, up in Albany, have conspired to effect an establishment of the Satmar Hasidim. I do not know who would be more surprised at this discovery: the Founders of our Nation or Grand Rebbe Joel Teitelbaum, founder of the Satmar. The Grand Rebbe would be astounded to learn that after escaping brutal persecution and coming to America with the modest hope of religious toleration for their ascetic form of Judaism, the Satmar had become so powerful, so closely allied with Mammon, as to have become an "establishment" of the Empire State. And the Founding Fathers would be astonished to find that the Establishment Clause—which they designed "to insure that no one powerful sect or combination of sects could use political or governmental power to punish dissenters" *Zorach v. Clauson*—has been employed to prohibit characteristically and admirable American accommodation of the religious practices (or more precisely, cultural peculiarities) of a tiny minority sect. I, however, am *not* surprised. Once this Court has abandoned text and history as guides, nothing prevents it from calling religious toleration the establishment of religion.

* * *

For his thesis that New York has unconstitutionally conferred governmental authority upon the Satmar sect, Justice Souter relies extensively, and virtually exclusively, upon *Larkin v. Grendel's Den, Inc.* Justice Souter believes that the present case "resembles" *Grendel's Den* because that case "teaches that a state may not delegate its civic authority *to a group chosen according to a religious criterion.*" That misdescribes both what that case taught (which is that a state may not delegate its civil authority *to a church*), and what this case involves (which is a group chosen according to cultural characteristics). * * *

* * *

I turn, next, to Justice Souter's second justification for finding an establishment of religion: his facile conclusion that the New York Legislature's creation of the Kiryas Joel School District was religiously motivated. But in the Land of the Free, democratically adopted laws are not so easily impeached by unelected judges. To establish the unconstitutionality of a facially neutral law on the mere basis of its asserted religiously preferential (or discriminatory) effects—or at least to establish it in conformity with our precedents—Justice Souter "must be able to show the absence of a neutral, secular basis" for the law.

There is of course no possible doubt of a secular basis here. * * *

Since the obvious presence of a neutral, secular basis renders the asserted preferential effect of this law inadequate to invalidate it, Justice Souter is required to come forward with direct evidence that religious preference was the objective. His case could scarcely be weaker. * * *

* * *

But even if Chapter 748 were intended to create a special arrangement for the Satmars *because of* their religion . . . it would be a permissible accommodation.

"This Court has long recognized that the government may (and sometimes must) accommodate religious practices and that it may do so without violating the Establishment Clause." *Hobbie v. Unemployment Appeals Comm'n of Fla.,* (1987). Moreover, "there is ample room for accommodation of religion under the Establishment Clause" and for "play in the joints productive of a benevolent neutrality which will permit religious exercise to exist without sponsorship and without interference." *Walz v. Tax Comm'n of N.Y. City,* (1970). Accommodation is permissible, moreover, even when the statute deals specifically with religion and even when accommodation is not commanded by the Free Exercise Clause.

When a legislature acts to accommodate religion, particularly a minority sect, "it follows the best of our traditions." *Zorach.* The Constitution itself contains an accommodation of sorts. Article VI, cl. 3, prescribes that executive, legislative and judicial officers of the Federal and State Governments shall bind themselves to support the Constitution "by Oath or Affirmation." Although members of the most populous religions found no difficulty in swearing an oath to God, Quakers, Moravians, and Mennonites refused to take oaths based on Matthew 5:34's injunction "swear not at all." The option of affirmation was added to accommodate these minority religions and enable their members to serve in government. * * *

In today's opinion, however, the Court seems uncomfortable with this aspect of our constitutional tradition. Although it acknowledges the concept of accommodation, it quickly points out that it is "not a principle without limits," and then gives reasons why the present case exceeds those limits, reasons which simply do not hold water. * * *

* * *

Contrary to the Court's suggestion I do not think that the Establishment Clause prohibits formally established "state" churches and nothing more. I have always believed, and all my opinions are consistent with the view, that the Establishment Clause prohibits the favoring of one religion over others. In this respect, it is the Court that attacks lions of straw. * * *

* * *

The Court's decision today is astounding. Chapter 748 involves no public aid to private schools and does not mention religion. In order to invalidate it, the Court casts aside, on the flimsiest of evidence, the strong presumption of validity that attaches to facially neutral laws, and invalidates the present accommodation because it does not trust New York to be as accommodating toward other religions (presumably those less powerful than the Satmar Hasidim) in the future. This is unprecedented—except that it continues, and takes to new extremes, a recent tendency in the opinions of this Court to turn the Establishment Clause into a repealer of our Nation's tradition of religious toleration. I dissent.

The Court decided two additional Establishment Clause cases in the 1994–95 term, *Capital Square Review and Advisory Board v. Pinette* (1995) and *Rosenberger v. Rector and Visitors of the University of Virginia* (1995). Although the justices labored mightily in their lengthy opinions to bring clarity and consistency to interpreting the Establishment Clause, they did not succeed. As Justice Thomas candidly observed in a concurring opinion in *Rosenberger,* ". . . our Establishment Clause jurisprudence is in hopeless disarray . . ." (63 L.W. at 4714).

In *Capital Square Review and Advisory Board v. Pinette,* the Court ruled 7-2 that Ohio officials had not properly interpreted the Establishment Clause when they refused to allow the Ku Klux Klan to place a cross on the grounds surrounding the Ohio Statehouse. Despite the 7-2 vote in the case, the justices were sharply divided in their reasoning. The central concern in the justices' opinions involved the endorsement test, which they had used in the 1989 case of *Allegheny County v. American Civil Liberties Union,* and they were deeply divided over the interpretation of this test. Thus, the Court produced a plurality opinion, and six justices expressed their divergent views.

The case began in the 1993 Christmas season when the Ohio Ku Klux Klan sought to place a cross on Capital Square, a ten-acre plaza area that surrounds the Statehouse in Columbus, Ohio. This area has been used historically by a wide range of groups and individuals, and the Capital Square Review and Advisory Board has responsibility for regulating public access to the grounds. The Board rejected the

Klan's request on the basis that permitting the cross to be placed on Capital Square would violate the Establishment Clause. Vincent Pinette, leader of the Ohio Klan, filed suit in Federal District Court for Southern Ohio, and the Court ruled in favor of the Klan, allowing it to erect the cross. The decision was affirmed by the Sixth Circuit Court of Appeals.

Scalia authored the plurality opinion and was joined by the Court's other three accommodationists—Rehnquist, Scalia, and Kennedy. Scalia argued that the Statehouse grounds were available to all groups and that allowing the Klan to erect a cross would simply be a neutral act providing equal access for the expression of ideas.

Scalia rejected outright the argument by the attorneys for Ohio that the endorsement test used by the Court in *Allegheny County* was applicable to this case. In *Allegheny County,* a creche scene had been placed in the grand staircase of the county courthouse, and the Court ruled this violated the Establishment Clause because the display conveyed the idea that the county was endorsing Christianity. Similarly, Ohio's attorneys contended, placement of the cross on the Statehouse grounds would indicate the state's endorsement of religion and thus violate the Establishment Clause. As we discussed earlier in this chapter, the accommodationist justices had strongly opposed the endorsement test in *Allegheny County,* and Scalia was not willing to embrace it in this case. Even if the Court had employed the endorsement test in *Allegheny County,* Scalia reasoned, the Ohio case was different. In the Allegheny case, the staircase display area in the county courthouse was not open to all groups and therefore involved government speech, whereas the Ohio Statehouse grounds were open to all and therefore involved private speech. In Scalia's words, "The test petitioners propose, which would attribute to a neutrally behaving government *private* religious expression, has no antecedent in our jurisprudence and would better be called a 'transferred endorsement' test" (63 L.W. at 4687). For Scalia, the transferred endorsement test not only lacked any basis in precedent but also threatened other settled principles of Establishment Clause analysis.

In separate concurring opinions, both O'Connor and Souter agreed with the judgment of the plurality that the placement of the cross on the Statehouse grounds did not violate the Establishment Clause, but they disagreed emphatically with the plurality's view of the endorsement test. For O'Connor and Souter, the endorsement test adopted by the Court in *Allegheny County* was directly applicable to this case, and both justices felt that a reasonable observer—a key concept—would not view the cross on the Statehouse grounds as signaling the government's endorsement of religion. Attacking the plurality's interpretation of the "transferred endorsement" test, O'Connor and Souter argued that the plurality's approach created ". . . an exception to the endorsement test, not previously recognized and out of square with our precedents" (63 L.W. at 4692). In his first Establishment Clause case, Breyer joined the concurring opinions of both O'Connor and Souter.

Justices Stevens and Ginsburg dissented, with Stevens providing yet another interpretation of the endorsement test. Stevens agreed with O'Connor, Souter, and Breyer that the endorsement test from *Allegheny County* did apply in this case, but Stevens disagreed about how to apply it. For Stevens, the test just required that ". . . *some* reasonable observer would attribute a message to the State" (63 L.W. at 4699). Stevens thought it obvious that some observers would see the State endorsing religion by having the cross on Statehouse grounds, and therefore the Establishment Clause was being violated. Perhaps realizing that the endorsement test did not look promising for resolving Establishment Clause issues, Stevens in the conclusion of his dissent quoted extensively from Black's strict separationist language in *Everson* and argued that "this case illustrates the importance of rebuilding the 'wall of separation between church and state' that Jefferson envisioned" (63 L.W. at 4696). Finally, Ginsburg wrote a brief, narrow dissent in which she argued that the Establishment Clause was violated because an adequate disclaimer sign regarding the lack of government endorsement was not provided in this case.

In the second Establishment Clause case of 1995, *Rosenberger v. University of Virginia,* the Court did issue a majority opinion in ruling that the University would not violate the Establishment Clause by providing funding for a religious publication produced by a student group. This case certainly cannot be characterized, however, as one in which the Court arrived at a clear consensus regarding principles by which to interpret the Establishment Clause.

The case began when the University of Virginia withheld payments for the printing of a religious publication—*Wide Awake: A Christian Perspective*—by a student group because of Establishment Clause concerns. Ronald Rosenberger and others associated with the publication filed suit in federal court, and both the district and circuit courts ruled in favor of the University. The Supreme Court reversed the lower courts, however, ruling in favor of the student newspaper.

Kennedy's majority opinion was joined by the Court's other accommodationists—Rehnquist, Scalia, and Thomas—as well as by O'Connor, but it did not contain the language normally associated with the accommodationist justices. Instead, Kennedy seemed to embrace an approach more closely associated with neutrality. Kennedy began the key part of his opinion by stating that it was necessary to set forth general principles to guide the analysis of Establishment Clause cases. He then stated, "A central lesson of our decisions is that a significant factor in upholding government programs in the face of Establishment Clause attack is their neutrality toward religion" (63 L.W. at 4708). In this case, Kennedy argued, the University had violated the principle of neutrality by denying funding to the religious publication. Citing *Board of Education v. Mergens* (1990) and *Lamb's Chapel* (1993) as especially important precedents, Kennedy argued: "More than once have we rejected the position that the Establishment Clause even justifies, much less requires, a refusal to extend free speech rights to religious speakers who participate in broad-reaching government programs neutral in design" (63 L.W. at 4708). The question naturally arises as to why Kennedy used neutralist language in his majority opinion, and one speculative answer is that he could not have obtained O'Connor's support if he had used an accommodationist approach.

Souter wrote a lengthy dissent joined by Stevens, Breyer, and Ginsburg. Souter argued that the Court majority had severely misinterpreted the Establishment Clause by approving for the first time direct funding of religious activities by the government. For Souter, the clear lesson of the historical development of the Clause and the Court's prior cases was that "using public funds for the direct subsidization of preaching the word is categorically forbidden under the Establishment Clause, and if the Clause was meant to accomplish nothing else, it was meant to ban this use of public money" (63 L.W. at 4716).

Conclusion

The Rehnquist Court is deeply divided over how to interpret the Establishment Clause. The neutrality approach supported by the *Lemon* test was controlling doctrine as the Rehnquist Court era began, but personnel changes have dramatically altered the Court's Establishment Clause jurisprudence. The retirements of Powell, Brennan, and Marshall removed from the Court three supporters of neutrality and the *Lemon* test. It appeared that a new majority existed in 1992 in *Lee v. Weisman* to rewrite Establishment Clause jurisprudence, with the Court replacing neutrality with accommodation and overturning the *Lemon* test. This did not happen, but since *Lee* the Court has lacked any consensus regarding guiding principles for interpreting the Establishment Clause. The Court's current difficulties reflect its half-century search for clarity regarding the meaning and purposes of the Establishment Clause.

Areas of agreement have been limited. All of the members of the Court have acknowledged that the Establishment Clause prohibits any government from recognizing an official church or religion and also that the Clause prevents government from favoring one religion or church over another. Beyond this, however, little consensus has existed. The Court has vacillated among the separationist, neutralist, and accommodationist approaches, with neutrality being the predominant but never the unchallenged theory. The three-pronged *Lemon* test has buttressed the neutrality approach; but it has been used on occasion to reach accommodationist decisions, it has been widely criticized, and its status seems doubtful. Further, no alternative to the *Lemon* test has emerged although many have been suggested, including the coercion test and the endorsement test. Perhaps the only safe prediction is that predicting the Court's Establishment Clause decisions will continue to be an unpredictable activity.

REFERENCES

Alley, Robert S. ed. *The Supreme Court on Church and State.* New York: Oxford University Press, 1988.

Antieau, Chester James, Arthur T. Downey, and Edward C. Roberts. *Freedom from Federal Establishment: Formation and Early History of the First Amendment's Religion Clauses.* Milwaukee: Bruce Publishing Company, 1964.

Berns, Walter. *The First Amendment and the Future of American Democracy.* New York: Basic Books, 1976.

Carter, Lief. *An Introduction to Constitutional Interpretation: Cases in Law and Religion.* New York: Longman, 1991.

Cord, Robert L. *Separation of Church and State: Historical Fact and Current Fiction.* New York: Lambeth Press, 1982.

Curry, Thomas J. *The First Freedoms: Church and State in America to the Passage of the First Amendment.* New York: Oxford University Press, 1986.

Gunn, T. Jeremy. *A Standard for Repair: The Establishment Clause, Equality, and Natural Rights.* New York: Garland, 1992.

Kobylka, Joseph. "Leadership in the Supreme Court: Chief Justice Burger and Establishment Clause Litigation." *Western Political Quarterly* 42 (1989):545-68.

Levy, Leonard W. *The Establishment Clause: Religion and the First Amendment.* New York: Macmillan, 1986.

Malbin, Michael J. *Religion and Politics: The Intentions of the Authors of the First Amendment.* Washington, D.C.: American Enterprise Institute, 1978.

O'Brien, David M. *Constitutional Law and Politics: Civil Rights and Civil Liberties.* New York: Norton, 1991.

Pfeffer, Leo. *Church, State, and Freedom.* Boston: Beacon Press, 1967.

Stokes, Anson P. *Church and State in the United States.* 3 vols. New York: Harper and Brothers, 1950.

Urofsky, Melvin I. *The Continuity of Change: The Supreme Court and Individual Liberties, 1953-1986.* Belmont, California: Wadsworth, 1991.

CHAPTER 6

THE [illegible] OF REL[illegible]

CASE STUDY

EMPLOYMENT DIVISION, DEPARTMENT OF HUMAN RESOURCES OF OREGON V. SMITH (1990)

Alfred Smith had lived a troubled life, but he was a survivor. A Native American, Smith was removed from his tribal homeland in Oregon by the government when he was a youth and was relocated into a Christian boarding school. Smith displayed many talents at this school, excelling in such activities as math, art, and science. Upon graduation, Smith moved to Portland, but he encountered many setbacks and became an alcoholic. Eventually, however, he overcame his alcoholism, and he credited his Native American Church with playing a key role in his rehabilitation. Smith then became employed as a counselor with a private drug and alcohol rehabilitation organization in Oregon, the Douglas County Council on Drug and Alcohol Abuse Prevention and Treatment (ADAPT), while continuing his close association with the Native American Church (Kairys 1993, p. 105)

Ironically, two of the most positive components of Smith's life, his religion and his job, came into conflict. Smith's job required him to refrain from the use of alcohol or nonprescription drugs. Smith's religion, however, required him to use peyote, an illegal drug under Oregon law. Peyote is a cactus that grows in the southwestern United States and contains a hallucinogen, mescaline. Peyote has been used as an important sacrament in Native American religious ceremonies for hundreds of years, and the Native American Church uses peyote in its services under the close supervision of trained, elder leaders.

When officials of the Douglas Chapter of ADAPT learned that Smith had used peyote, they fired him from his counseling position. Smith then filed for unemployment compensation from the Employment Division of Oregon's Department of Human Resources, but his claim was denied on the basis that unemployment benefits were available only to persons who lost their job through no fault of their own. Smith, the State Department ruled, had been fired for work-related misconduct.

Smith decided to challenge the state's action on the grounds that his free exercise of religion guarantee of the First Amendment was being violated. In a long and complicated litigative process, the case worked its way through the Oregon courts, reached the United States Supreme Court for the first time in 1988, was remanded to the Oregon Supreme Court for further proceedings, and finally reached the U.S. Supreme Court for a second time in 1989 after the Oregon high court had ruled in favor of Smith.

The central issue confronting the Court was whether the Free Exercise Clause of the First Amendment permitted Oregon to make criminal the religious use of peyote and thus to deny unemployment benefits to a person fired because of the use of peyote in religious activities. Attorneys for Oregon and Smith filed written briefs with the Court in July of 1989, and oral arguments were presented to the Court on November 6, 1989. Virginia Linder, solicitor general for the state of Oregon, was the counsel of record for the state. Craig Dorsey, director of the Native American Program of Oregon Legal Services, represented Smith as well as Galen Black, who was also a member of the Native American Church and had been fired from his counseling position and denied unemployment benefits for using peyote in religious services.

Dorsey argued that the Oregon Supreme Court had correctly interpreted this case by ruling that Oregon's denial of unemployment benefits had violated Smith's constitutional guarantee of free exercise of religion. Dorsey maintained that the Constitution prohibited the government from any interference with religious belief, but he conceded that religious conduct was not totally free from government regulations. Given the importance of the First Amendment's Free Exercise Clause, however, Dorsey argued that government regulation of religious conduct was permissible only when the government was protecting interests of the highest order: "The State may justify an inroad on religious liberty by showing that it is the least restrictive means of achieving some compelling state interest" (Brief for Respondents, *Employment Division v. Smith*, p. 16, citing *Thomas v. Review Board*, 450 U.S. at 718, 1981). Dorsey maintained that this strict scrutiny test had been used consistently by the Court since it was first set forth in *Sherbert v. Verner* (1963). In applying the *Sherbert* test in this case, Dorsey maintained that Oregon did not have a compelling interest in prohibiting the religious use of peyote nor did the State employ the least restrictive means available.

Oregon's attorneys agreed with Dorsey on many key points regarding the proper approach to analyzing the Free Exercise Clause. They agreed that the Constitution protects religious actions as well as beliefs and that the government can only interfere with religious actions if it is promoting a compelling interest through narrowly tailored means. Thus, Oregon accepted the strict scrutiny approach of *Sherbert* as the appropriate means to analyze this case.

Oregon's attorneys applied the strict scrutiny test quite differently than Dorsey did, however. Oregon maintained that regulating the use and availability of dangerous drugs was a state interest of the highest order, and these interests would be seriously compromised by exempting the religiously motivated use of such drugs. Thus, Oregon argued that the Court should overturn the judgment of the Oregon Supreme Court.

The high court's decision in this case thus seemed to depend upon whether a majority of the justices would find that Oregon could meet the requirements of the strict scrutiny test. The Court, however, took an entirely different approach (case excerpt on p. 229). In a five-person opinion authored by Justice Scalia, the Court rejected the strict scrutiny test and instead used a much less exacting test to rule against Smith. Scalia's opinion was probably the most controversial free exercise of religion case in the Court's history because of charges that the opinion reinterpreted the history of the Court's free exercise jurisprudence, overturned controlling precedent, and relegated a fundamental constitutional guarantee to the barest minimum of Court protection.

Scalia began his opinion by addressing the question of whether the Free Exercise Clause protects both religious beliefs and actions. Although acknowledging that the guarantee prohibits all government regulations of religious belief, he took a narrow view of the Constitution's protection of religious acts. Specifically, Scalia argued, the Constitution does not protect a person "from compliance with an otherwise valid law prohibiting conduct that the State is free to regulate" (494 U.S. at 879). Thus, if the government passes a valid law that is neutral and generally applicable, then a person must comply with the law even if it interferes with his or her exercise of religious beliefs. In this case, Oregon had the authority to prohibit totally the use of peyote, and members of the Native American Church could not claim any immunity from this law under the Free Exercise Clause.

Scalia maintained that the Court's precedents for over a century had consistently supported this position. He recognized that the Court had on occasion ruled that neutral, generally applicable laws were unconstitutional under the First Amendment because they interfered with religious practices, but Scalia argued that all of these cases were "hybrid" situations that involved not only free exercise of religion claims but also other constitutional protections such as freedom of speech.

Scalia then turned to the question of the applicability of the strict scrutiny test of *Sherbert*, which had been accepted as the appropriate approach by both the attorneys for Smith and for Oregon. Scalia rejected the application of the strict scrutiny test to this case, and he strongly undermined the use of the test in any free exercise of religion case. Although acknowledging that the Court had used the test in four prior cases to invalidate the denial of unemployment benefits, Scalia reasoned that it could not apply in this case because to do so would "require exemptions from a generally applicable criminal law" (494 U.S. at 884). Scalia was not content, however, simply to distinguish this case from the previous unemployment compensation cases; rather, he attacked the use and validity of the test in free exercise cases more generally. He argued that "although we have sometimes purported to apply the *Sherbert* test in contexts other than [unemployment], we have always found the test satisfied. . ." (494 U.S. at 883). Further, Scalia maintained that the Court had abstained in recent years from using the test at all except in unemployment cases. Finally, Scalia argued, the implications of applying this test in all cases involving the Free Exercise Clause would be ominous: "Any society adopting such a system would be courting anarchy. . ." (494 U.S. at 888).

O'Connor agreed with the Court's judgment that Oregon had not violated the Free Exercise Clause, but she disagreed strongly with the reasoning of the Court majority. O'Connor contended that the Court's opinion ". . . dramatically departs from well-settled First Amendment jurisprudence and . . . is incompatible with our Nation's fundamental commitment to individual religious liberty" (484 U.S. at 890). She acknowledged that the Court had never viewed the Free Exercise Clause as absolute, but she argued that the Court had consistently required the government to justify a substantial burden on religious activity by meeting the standards of the strict scrutiny test. In applying the test to this case, O'Connor reasoned that, although the question was close, Oregon did have a compelling interest in the blanket prohibition of the use of peyote because of the severe problems of drug abuse in American society, and no less restrictive alternative was available to Oregon.

Blackmun, joined by Brennan and Marshall, wrote a dissenting opinion in which he supported O'Connor's rejection of the majority's interpretation of the Free Exercise Clause, but he disagreed with her view that Oregon met the requirements of the strict scrutiny test. Blackmun echoed O'Connor's view that the Court had consistently applied the strict scrutiny test in its free exercise cases and that Scalia's majority opinion ". . . effectuates a wholesale overturning of settled law concerning the Religion Clauses of our Constitution" (484 U.S. at 908). In applying the strict scrutiny test to this case, Blackmun found the arguments of Oregon to be unconvincing, especially when Oregon had never enforced this law against any member of the Native American Church for the sacramental use of peyote.

The Court's opinion generated an immediate and intense outpouring of criticism from the nation's press, constitutional scholars, and religious groups. Nat Hentoff (1990, p. 16), for example, characterized the decision as "the most revolutionary Supreme Court decision in many years [because] it eviscerated a fundamental liberty contained in the First Amendment. . . ." Criticism of the Court's decision mounted as government officials throughout the country interpreted the *Smith* decision to allow them to carry out neutral, generally applicable laws despite religious objections from persons who saw the government actions as violating deeply held religious beliefs and practices. For example, a general law requiring autopsies in traffic deaths was enforced despite objections by Jewish relatives that the practice deeply offended their religious beliefs. In another case, a zoning ordinance was approved that had the effect of blocking homeowners from placing crosses on their private property.

Congress responded immediately to the *Smith* decision. In the fall of 1990, Representative Stephen Solarz, a Democrat from New York, introduced a bill in the House entitled the Religious Freedom Restoration Act, and a similar bill was placed before the Senate. The proposed law sought to express support for the principles of the *Sherbert* test by instructing governments that neutral, uniformly applicable laws should not burden the free exercise of religion unless the law serves a compelling government interest that is being achieved with the least restrictive means available. An extraordinarily diverse coalition of religious and civil rights groups supported the bill, although numerous discussions and negotiations became necessary before passage was assured. The United States Catholic Conference had originally opposed the bill because of concerns that the law could be used to limit state restrictions on abortions or to challenge tax exemptions for religious groups. Eventually, however, the Catholic Conference endorsed the legislation. The bill passed the House overwhelmingly by voice vote in May of 1993, and the Senate approved the legislation 97-3 in October of 1993. President Clinton signed the bill into law the next month. In an editorial on the new legislation, the *New York Times* (October 25, 1993, p. A14) observed: "It's a welcome antidote to the official insensitivity to religion the Court spawned in 1990." The legislation does not, however, invalidate or overturn the *Smith* decision. The most that it does is to provide a statutory basis for a claim that a law interferes with a person's religious beliefs and practices.

Historical Origins and Contemporary Conflicts

Our case study of the *Smith* case illustrates that significant conflict surrounds the seemingly clear language of the First Amendment that "*Congress shall make no laws . . . prohibiting the free exercise [of religion]. . . .*" In this section we will examine the historic origins of the Free Exercise Clause to seek understanding about the meaning of this important constitutional guarantee, and then we will examine some of the contemporary conflicts involving the Free Exercise Clause that the Court has had to confront in modern times.

Compared to the Establishment Clause, the Free Exercise Clause has been subjected to relatively little historical analysis either by justices on the Supreme Court or by scholars. No Supreme Court justice in the twentieth century has presented a detailed historical analysis of the intent of the writers of the Free Exercise Clause, although several members of the Court—for example, Rehnquist, Scalia, Brennan, and Souter—have written detailed analyses of the historic background of the Establishment Clause. Similarly, although a substantial body of scholarly literature exists regarding the historic development of the Establishment Clause, scholars have only begun to give sustained attention to the Free Exercise Clause as well as to the relationship between the clauses.

Despite the limited number of studies, however, the literature is already characterized by contention and disagreement. Substantial consensus does exist that those who wrote and approved the Bill of Rights viewed the threat of government infringement on religion as a serious concern and that the Free Exercise Clause was intended to protect individuals from laws directly interfering with religious liberty. Consensus breaks down quickly, however, regarding whether the clause was intended to provide exemptions from laws of general applicability. The majority of scholars (e.g., McConnell 1990a and 1990b; Neuhaus 1990; and Durham 1992) have taken the position that the Free Exercise Clause was intended to provide broad protection to religious liberty, including exemptions for religious objections to laws that were neutral and general. McConnell (1990a and 1990b) is probably the preeminent scholar of the exemptionist approach. In his detailed studies of the origins and historic understanding of the Free Exercise Clause, he recognizes that the historical record does not provide an unambiguous answer; but he argues that the evidence does support a broad interpretation of the Free Exercise Clause that allows for religious exemptions to general laws.

McConnell identifies three major sources of evidence to support his conclusions. One important element is the state constitutional provisions dealing with religious freedom. By the late eighteenth century, eight states had constitutions that contained explicit language and one state had implicit constitutional language that "appears to be an early equivalent of the 'compelling interest' test" (McConnell 1990a, p. 1117). Another important source of evidence involves the frequent exemptions from generally applicable laws that were made in the colonies for members of religious minorities. These exemptions occurred in regard to such areas as oath requirements, conscription into the military, and ministerial support. McConnell (1990a, p. 1119) observes: "It is noteworthy that from the beginning it was thought that the solution to the problem of religious minorities was to grant exceptions from generally applicable laws." A final source identified by McConnell is the writings of James Madison, the primary author and legislative sponsor of the First Amendment. McConnell argues that Madison's writings revealed the priority of religious duty over civic duty and that Madison advocated various religious exemptions to general laws.

McConnell recognizes, however, that the historical evidence is not fully conclusive in favor of the exemption approach, and some scholars (e.g., Lindsay 1991; Bradley 1991; and Hamburger 1992) have argued that historical evidence supports a narrow interpretation of the Free Exercise Clause that would not allow religious exemptions from neutral, generally applicable laws. Lindsay, for example, argues that Madison's writings relevant to the Free Exercise Clause have been misinterpreted because Madison was hostile to religion, and thus Madison's writings support a narrow interpretation of the Free Exercise Clause that would not allow religious exemptions to valid, general laws. Similarly, although historical examples of exemptions for religious minorities can be cited, such exemptions were far from common in American colonial history (Hamburger).

We can thus conclude that no clear consensus exists regarding the historic intent of those who wrote and ratified the Free Exercise Clause of the First Amendment. Scholars are in disagreement, and no twentieth-century member of the Supreme Court has attempted a detailed historical analysis of the meaning of the clause. This is an important omission in the Court's free exercise jurisprudence, but it seems unlikely that historical arguments by the justices will resolve the disagreements over the proper interpretation of the Free Exercise Clause. Liberal justices would be inclined to find that the historic record supports a broad interpretation of free exercise that requires the Court to consider religious exemptions to neutral, generally applicable laws, and conservative justices would be more likely to read history to show that the Free Exercise Clause should be narrowly interpreted to preclude such exemptions.

Having completed this brief analysis of the historic evidence associated with the creation of the Free Exercise Clause, we now turn to an overview of some of the contemporary controversies involving this provision. It is useful at the outset to contrast Free Exercise Clause issues with Establishment Clause issues. As we saw in the previous chapter, Establishment Clause cases frequently involve major issues of public policy that affect large segments of the American public and generate intense emotional debate. These issues include state-sponsored prayer in the public schools, government aid to parochial schools, religious displays on public property, and the tax status of religious organizations. In addition, laws triggering Establishment Clause cases frequently are adopted by legislators who knowingly and willingly seek to involve government closely in support of religion, thus directly challenging the Establishment Clause. In sharp contrast, free exercise cases typically involve government programs passed without any awareness of their religious effects but that nonetheless interfere with the practices of a religious minority. Free exercise cases, therefore, generate less public controversy because typically only a few members of a small religious group are affected by their outcomes.

Governments will, of course, occasionally pass laws that directly interfere with the free exercise of religion, but the high court has only dealt with two of these in its history, ruling both laws unconstitutional by unanimous votes. In *McDaniel v. Paty* (1978), the Court ruled against a law stating that religious leaders could not serve as delegates to state constitutional conventions, and in *Church of Lukumi Babalu Aye v. Hialeah* (1993), the Court ruled unconstitutional a set of ordinances that were directed against the Santerians, a religious sect that uses animal sacrifices in some of its rituals.

The far more prevalent situation in free exercise cases involves secular laws that are intended to apply neutrally and generally to everyone but that are enforced in a manner that interferes with the religious beliefs and practices of members of minority faiths. Among the religious groups that have appeared with some frequency in cases before the Supreme Court are Jehovah's Witnesses, the Amish, members of Native American religions, and members of the Jewish faith. The typical question in these cases is whether an exemption should be recognized by the Court to prevent members of a religious minority from being forced into a practice contrary to their religious creed. Should a Native American be forced to obtain a social security number for his daughter if this would violate his religion? Should members of the Amish faith be required to send their children to school until the age of sixteen when this contradicts their religious beliefs? Should the Amish be required to pay social security taxes for their employees when this would contradict their belief in self-sufficiency? Can children of Jehovah's Witnesses be compelled to salute the flag against their religious beliefs? These and many other difficult questions have confronted the justices of the Supreme Court in interpreting the Free Exercise Clause of the First Amendment.

One more issue needs to be mentioned: the conflict between the Free Exercise Clause and the Establishment Clause. This conflict arises frequently in free exercise cases; if the Court rules that a member of a religious minority can be exempted from a valid, general law, then the Court is potentially creating a violation of the Establishment Clause because it is favoring one religious group over other religious groups that have to follow the requirements of the law.

An example of this problem can be seen in the case of *Wisconsin v. Yoder* (1972). In his majority opinion, Chief Justice Burger ruled that the Amish could be exempted from Wisconsin's compulsory school attendance law, which required all children to attend school to the age of sixteen. Although this was a secular, neutral, and generally applicable law, the Court ruled that Wisconsin's interests were not sufficiently compelling to require the Amish to send their children to school beyond the eighth grade when to do so would require them to act contrary to their religious beliefs. Burger also acknowledged, however, the potential conflict between this decision and the requirements of the Establishment Clause: "the Court must not ignore the danger that an exception from a general obligation of citizenship on religious grounds may run afoul of the Establishment Clause . . . " (406 U.S. at 220–21).

Although the Court has frequently acknowledged the potential for conflict between the two clauses, the justices have not developed a consensus on the resolution of the conflict. Typically, the Court has simply asserted that the granting of an exception to a religious minority from a general law does not create a violation of the Establishment Clause. Support for this position has been offered by both McConnell (1990b) and Kairys (1993), although they offer different justifications. McConnell argues that the historic record associated with the period when the First Amendment was written and ratified shows that exemptions could be granted in support of the free exercise of religion without violating the Establishment Clause. Kairys makes a more contemporary argument by focusing on equal treatment of all religious groups. He argues that the majoritarian branches of government frequently make exemptions for members of mainstream religious groups, for example, allowing consumption of wine for religious purposes during Prohibition; therefore, principles of equity allow the courts to make exceptions for religious minorities without violating the Establishment Clause.

The Court may have made this issue of the conflict between the two clauses largely irrelevant, however, in its *Smith* decision. Under the guidelines of *Smith*, members of religious minorities must comply with general, neutral laws, even if such compliance interferes with their religious beliefs. This precedent will thus allow few if any exemptions under the Free Exercise Clause, and thus few conflicts will arise with the Establishment Clause.

Supreme Court Decision Making in Free Exercise of Religion Cases

Just as we have seen with the Establishment Clause of the First Amendment, the Free Exercise Clause is surrounded by conflict and controversy regarding not only the intention of those who wrote and ratified the First Amendment but also the manner in which the clause should be interpreted in contemporary American society. And as with the Establishment Clause, the Supreme Court has sought to develop approaches or tests to guide its decision-making process. It should come as no great surprise that the justices have been in frequent disagreement over the proper approaches for interpreting the Free Exercise Clause, and these disagreements continue today.

The Belief versus Action Controversy

One important issue has involved the controversy over whether the Free Exercise Clause applies to religious actions as well as religious beliefs. In one of the Court's first free exercise cases, *Reynolds v. United States* (1879), the Court seemed to suggest that the Free Exercise Clause prohibited government interference with religious belief but not with religious action. In a unanimous opinion, the Court ruled that a federal law prohibiting polygamy did not violate the religious freedom of a Mormon leader, despite the fact that the practice of polygamy was then an integral part of the Mormon religion. In making a distinction between belief and action, Chief Justice Waite wrote: "Laws are made for the government of actions, and while they cannot interfere with mere religious belief and opinions, they may with practices" (98 U.S. at 166). Substantial disagreement exists regarding the meaning of the Court's opinion in *Reynolds*; but whatever the Court intended in the *Reynolds* case, twentieth-century justices have come to accept the principle that the Free Exercise Clause does apply to both beliefs and to practices. Justice Kennedy stated this clearly in the Court's recent 1993 case of *Church of Lukumi Babalu Aye v. Hialeah*: "the principle that government may not enact laws that suppress *religious belief or practice* is so well understood that few violations are recorded in our opinions" (emphasis added) (508 U.S. at 523).

The *Sherbert* Test

Although consensus exists among Supreme Court justices that the Free Exercise Clause protects both beliefs and actions, this consensus breaks down quickly regarding the extent to which the clause protects individuals from engaging in religious conduct that comes in conflict with government laws. The *Smith* case at the beginning of this chapter identified the two basic approaches that have emerged: the ***Sherbert* test** and the ***Smith* test**.

The *Sherbert* test, which is also referred to as the **strict scrutiny test** or the **compelling government interest test**, was originally set forth in *Sherbert v. Verner* (1963), although its origins can be traced directly to a series of earlier free exercise cases. The test has been stated in a variety of ways, but the most common formulation is: *if a government law or action creates a substantial burden on an individual's religious freedom, then the government must show that its policy seeks to achieve a compelling government interest through narrowly tailored means.* This test represents the highest level of protection that the Court gives to a constitutional principle. As we will see in subsequent chapters, this test is also applied to certain forms of freedom of expression that the Court views as most fundamental and to the area of equal protection in regard to discrimination against racial and alien groups. Whenever this test is applied, an extraordinary burden of proof exists on the government to prove that the challenged policy is concerned with a matter of overwhelming significance; and even if government officials meet this challenge, they must also show that they are using methods that have been carefully crafted to achieve only this compelling interest. Thus, governments typically lose cases when strict scrutiny is applied, although the Free Exercise Clause is an exceptional area of constitutional law because governments have had rather frequent successes in meeting the requirements of the *Sherbert* test.

Advocates of the strict scrutiny approach to the Free Exercise Clause offer a variety of arguments in favor of this test. Most importantly, supporters maintain that religious freedom is a fundamental value of the highest order. Few things are more important to people than their religious beliefs, and the freedom to follow one's religious beliefs is viewed as vital to a meaningful and fulfilling life. Religious freedom is also viewed as a critical component of a stable democratic society, because attempts by government to control religious activity breed distrust, contempt, and rebellion. Justice Jackson presented an eloquent statement of the importance of religious freedom in *West Virginia v. Barnette* (1943), when the Court ruled unconstitutional a West Virginia law requiring children to salute the flag because the law violated the religious beliefs of the Jehovah's Witnesses: "If there is any fixed star in our constitutional constellation, it is that no official, high or petty, can prescribe what shall be orthodox in politics, nationalism, religion, or other matters of opinion or force citizens to confess by word or act their faith therein" (319 U.S. at 642).

Defenders of the *Sherbert* test also argue that historical evidence and textual analysis support the strict scrutiny approach. As we saw earlier in this chapter, the preponderance of historical analysis seems to suggest that the writers and ratifiers of the Free Exercise Clause intended it to provide a high level of protection for religious freedom, allowing exemptions from laws for religious minorities unless the government could show a strong interest in enforcing conformity with the law. In addition, both justices and scholars advocating strict scrutiny argue that the language of the text supports their view. The Free Exercise Clause reads: "Congress shall make no law . . . prohibiting the free exercise [of religion] . . . ," and this language can be interpreted to support strict scrutiny in two ways. First, "the natural meaning" of the word *prohibiting* is that it prevents the government from making a religious practice illegal (McConnell 1990b, p. 1115). Second, the language of the First Amendment is absolutist in nature, unlike the language in other sections of the Bill of Rights, for example, the Fourth Amendment, which allows searches if they are reasonable, and the Fifth Amendment, which allows life, liberty, and property to be taken if due process is followed. Based upon these two premises regarding the test, advocates of the strict scrutiny approach maintain that government interference with religious beliefs and practices can only be permitted when narrowly tailored means are used to achieve a compelling government interest.

Finally, advocates of the *Sherbert* test argue that these tough standards do not present a problem to society's legitimate concerns about safety and order. The argument here is that no significant harm is created for the broader society if Native American Indians are allowed limited usage of peyote in religious ceremonies, or if the Amish educate their children at home after eighth grade, or if Jehovah's Witnesses children do not salute the flag to start the school day. Furthermore, the argument continues, the test does allow for society's legitimate concerns with safety and order to be protected, because religious objections cannot prevail if the government interests are truly compelling and no adequate alternative exists.

To what extent has the Court supported the strict scrutiny test of *Sherbert*? Although we will examine this question in detail throughout this chapter, we can offer some generalizations here. A majority of the justices of the Warren Court supported the *Sherbert* test. The Burger Court in its initial years showed strong adherence to the test; this support appeared to decline in the eighties, although a narrow majority continued to advocate it. With the Rehnquist Court, however, a majority of the justices no longer supports the *Sherbert* test, except perhaps in the narrow area of unemployment compensation when criminal laws have not been violated. Currently, only O'Connor and Souter endorse the strict scrutiny approach to the Free Exercise Clause, although Ginsburg and Breyer have not yet participated in a free exercise case.

The *Smith* Test

The alternative approach to the *Sherbert* test is the *Smith* test, which was set forth by Scalia in the 1990 case of *Oregon v. Smith*. It is difficult to state this test with precision because it is so recent and still seems to be evolving, but the basic ideas can be summarized from Scalia's opinion in *Smith* and Kennedy's 1993 majority opinion in *Hialeah*. Scalia argued that although religious beliefs are protected absolutely by the Free Exercise Clause, religious practices are not protected if they conflict with a neutral, general law that has an incidental effect on the free exercise of religion, although Scalia did allow that the *Sherbert* test might still apply in the limited area of unemployment compensation. Kennedy presented a further elaboration on the *Smith* test in the 1993 *Hialeah* case. Writing for a six-person majority, he argued that if a law is general and neutral, then strict scrutiny does not apply. If, however, a law is not general and neutral, than the strict scrutiny test should be applied. Under the *Smith* test, then, an individual claiming government interference with religious activity is going to have a difficult time prevailing. Few laws are directly targeted at a religious group; and if a law is general and neutral, then the government can enforce the law against a free exercise claim regardless of its effect on an individual's religious beliefs and practices.

Advocates of the *Smith* test advance a variety of arguments in defense of this approach to the Free Exercise Clause, rejecting most of the arguments of the proponents of the *Sherbert* test. In regard to the issue of the textual meaning of the Free Exercise Clause, Scalia argued in *Smith* that several interpretations of the language of the clause are possible; one logical and permissible reading is that the First Amendment is not violated when a valid and generally applicable law has the indirect effect of interfering with religious practices. Thus, the language of the Free Exercise Clause does not require government to provide religious exemptions to its laws. With regard to the historical evidence, advocates of the *Smith* test maintain that the historic record supports the position that the Free Exercise Clause was intended to be a narrow provision that did not provide for religious exemptions to neutral and general laws. As was noted earlier, no member of the Court has yet to present a detailed historical justification for the *Smith* test, but some scholars (e.g., Bradley 1991 and Hamburger 1992) have done so.

Yet another point made by Scalia involved the potential threats to societal order and stability that could arise with the strict scrutiny standards of the *Sherbert* test. Quoting the nineteenth-century case of *Reynolds v. United States* (1879), Scalia reasoned that the compelling interest test permits a person "'. . . to become a law unto himself . . .'" (494 U.S. at 886), and later in his opinion Scalia stated the potential danger of the compelling interest test even more strongly: "any society adopting such a system would be courting anarchy . . ." (494 U.S. at 888).

For Scalia and the Court majority in *Smith*, then, the preferable approach to the Free Exercise Clause is the narrower interpretation, which requires conformity to neutral and generally applicable laws, even if they have the effect of interfering with religious freedom. This would leave the recognition of religious exemptions to the majoritarian branches of government, and Scalia expressed optimism that legislators would be sensitive to the rights of religious minorities. Even if religious minorities were not provided exemptions from general laws by the legislative branch, however, ". . . that unavoidable consequence of democratic government must be preferred to a system in which each conscience is a law unto itself or in which judges weigh the social importance of all laws against the centrality of all religious beliefs" (494 U.S. at 890)

The *Smith* test appears to have solid majority support on the Rehnquist Court. Rehnquist, Kennedy, White, and Stevens joined Scalia's majority opinion in *Smith*, and Thomas joined these five justices in the *Hialeah* case to provide six justices in support of the *Smith* test. Thus, even if Ginsburg's replacement of White reduces the number of justices supporting the *Smith* test, a five-person majority will still apparently exist. We must be cautious in this conclusion, however. Further changes in the Court's membership or changes in the views of the continuing members of the Court could lead to further change in controlling doctrine regarding the free exercise of religion.

Pre-Warren Court Period

Having discussed the historic origins, the contemporary conflicts, and the two major competing approaches to the Free Exercise Clause, we can now turn to a detailed analysis of the case development in this important field of constitutional law. The Court ruled on few free exercise of religion cases during most of the pre-Warren Court period, especially during the formative era from 1789–1865 and the era of laissez-faire capitalism from 1865–1932. The primary reason for this paucity of cases was because the Court had not nationalized the Free Exercise Clause, and thus it did not apply to state and local governments. Furthermore, the Court took a very restrictive view of the Free Exercise Clause during this period of American history. With the advent of the New Deal era and the changing role of the Supreme Court as the champion of civil rights and liberties, however, the Court became much more active in hearing free exercise cases. The Court not only nationalized the Free Exercise Clause in *Cantwell v. Connecticut* (1940) but also increased dramatically the level of protection for individuals charging the government with violating their religious freedom.

Pre-New Deal

In the relatively few cases involving the free exercise of religion that the Court heard prior to the New Deal era, the justices provided a very narrow interpretation of the Free Exercise Clause by maintaining that religious beliefs but not religious activities were protected by the clause. The leading case in this period was *Reynolds v. United States* (1879). Reynolds was a leader of the Church of Jesus Christ of Latter-Day Saints, more commonly known as the Mormon Church. Mormon doctrines encouraged men to have more than one wife, but this practice of being married to more than one person at the same time, known as polygamy, was prohibited by federal law. The law criminalizing polygamy carried a fine of $500 and a prison term of up to five years. Reynolds argued that he was protected from prosecution because this law violated his free exercise of religion as guaranteed by the First Amendment, but a unanimous Court rejected his argument.

In his majority opinion for the Court, Chief Justice Waite set forth the Court's first extended analysis of the Free Exercise Clause. Waite began by acknowledging that the United States government was expressly forbidden by the Constitution from passing any laws directly affecting the free exercise of religion. The more difficult question, Waite argued, was whether the Free Exercise Clause also applied to laws that were not directed toward religion but that nonetheless interfered with religious practices. In regard to this question, Waite argued that the original understanding of the Free Exercise Clause was that religious practices were not exempt from valid secular laws.

In applying these principles to Reynold's case, Waite had little trouble in arguing that Congress was clearly within its powers in passing a law prohibiting polygamy. He stated that polygamy had been viewed as an offense against society from the earliest history of English law, it had been considered an odious practice throughout the western and northern countries of Europe, and it had always been void under common law. Thus, Waite concluded , "the statute immediately under consideration is within the legislative powers of Congress" (98 U.S. at 166).

Waite then turned to the critical question of whether Reynolds could be granted an exemption from this law because polygamy was an integral part of his religion. Waite's answer was an emphatic "no." Waite's language would be echoed by Scalia more than a century later in the *Smith* case: "Can a man excuse his practices to the contrary [of the law] because of his religious belief? To permit this would be to make the professed doctrines of religion superior to the law of the land, and in effect to permit every citizen to become a law unto himself. Government could exist only in name under such circumstances" (98 U.S. at 166–67).

Reynolds v. United States

98 U.S. (8 Otto) 145, 25 L.Ed. 244 (1879)

■ A nineteenth-century law applying to both the states and territories prohibited polygamy, or being married to more than one person. This law directly contradicted a fundamental tenet of the Church of Jesus Christ of the Latter-Day Saints, more commonly known as the Mormon Church, which viewed this practice as one commanded of male church members by Biblical scripture. Indeed, church doctrine held that the failure of male members to practice polygamy would result in damnation in the life to come. George Reynolds, a leader in the Mormon Church, was arrested under this statute for marrying two women. He was tried in the District Court of Utah, found guilty, sentenced to imprisonment at hard labor for two years, and fined $500. The Supreme Court of the Territory affirmed the decision, and Reynolds appealed to the United States Supreme Court.

This is an important case because it was the Court's first major decision dealing with the Free Exercise Clause of the First Amendment. As you read the opinion, consider the following questions: (1) Does the opinion state that only beliefs but not actions are protected by the Free Exercise Clause, or does the opinion also allow that religious actions can be protected by the clause? (2) Why did Justice Scalia cite *Reynolds* as support for his majority opinion in the landmark *Smith* case of 1990?

Vote:

The Court unanimously found the law constitutional.

Chief Justice Waite delivered the opinion of the Court.

The assignments of error, when grouped, presents the following questions:

* * *

5. Should the accused have been acquitted if he married the second time, because he believed it to be his religious duty?

* * *

Upon this charge and refusal to charge the question is raised, whether religious belief can be accepted as a justification of an overt act made criminal by the law of the land. The inquiry is not as to the power of Congress to prescribe criminal laws for the Territories, but as to the guilt of one who knowingly violates a law which has been properly enacted, if he entertains a religious belief that the law is wrong.

Congress cannot pass a law for the government of the Territories which shall prohibit the free exercise of religion. * * * The question to be determined is, whether the law now under consideration comes within this prohibition.

The word "religion" is not defined in the Constitution. We must go elsewhere, therefore, to ascertain its meaning, and nowhere more appropriately, we think, than to the history of the times in the midst of which the provision was adopted. The precise point of the inquiry is, what is the religious freedom which has been guaranteed.

* * *

* * * Congress was deprived of all legislative power over mere opinion, but was left free to reach actions which were in violation of social duties or subversive of good order.

Polygamy has always been odious among the northern and western nations of Europe, and, until the establishment of the Mormon Church, was almost exclusively a feature of the life of Asiatic and of African people. At common law, the second marriage was always void, and from the earliest history of England polygamy has been treated as an offence against society. * * *

* * * In the face of all this evidence, it is impossible to believe that the constitutional guaranty of religious freedom was intended to prohibit legislation in respect to this most important feature of social life. Marriage, while from its very nature a sacred obligation, is nevertheless, in most civilized nations, a civil contract, and usually regulated by law. Upon it society may be said to be built, and out of its fruits spring social relations and social obligations and duties, with which government is necessarily required to deal. In fact, according as monogamous or polygamous marriages are allowed, do we find the principles on which the government of the people, to a greater or lesser extent, rests. * * *

In our opinion, the statute immediately under consideration is within the legislative power of Congress. * * * This being so, the only question which remains is, whether those who make polygamy a part of their religion are excepted from the operation of the statute. If they are, then those who do not make polygamy a part of their religious belief may be found guilty and punished, while those who do, must be acquitted and go free. This would be introducing a new element into criminal law. Laws are made for the government of actions, and while they cannot interfere with mere religious belief and opinions, they may with practices. * * *

So here, as a law of the organization of society under the exclusive dominion of the United States, it is provided that plural marriages shall not be allowed. Can a man excuse his practices to the contrary because of his religious belief? To permit this would be to make the professed doctrines of religious belief superior to the law of the land, and in effect to permit every citizen to become a law unto himself. Government could exist only in name under such circumstances.

* * *

Judgment affirmed.

The *Reynolds* decision was reinforced in *Davis v. Beason* (1890), which also involved the Mormon faith. *Davis* involved a free exercise challenge to a law that denied the right to vote and the right to hold public office to any person belonging to an organization that practiced polygamy. The Court, following the *Reynolds* precedent, again ruled that the Free Exercise Clause was not violated by this law.

The *Reynolds* and *Davis* cases left a legacy of ambiguity in regard to the meaning of the Free Exercise Clause as can be seen in the wide variety of interpretations that subsequent Court opinions have given to these decisions. In *Wisconsin v. Yoder* (1972), Justice Douglas in dissent stated the extreme position that these cases established that the Free Exercise Clause protects only religious belief and not religious action under any circumstances. A slightly less stringent meaning was given to *Reynolds* by Scalia in *Oregon v. Smith*, in which he argued that the principle set forth in *Reynolds* is that the Free Exercise Clause does not protect individuals against the enforcement of generally applicable laws. An even more liberal interpretation of *Reynolds* can be found in *Church of Lukumi Babalu Aye v. Hialeah* (1993), where Kennedy's majority opinion interpreted *Reynolds* to mean that the Free Exercise Clause sometimes provides protection for religious minorities against generally applicable laws. Finally, one noted First Amendment scholar (Alley 1988, p. 349) asserts that the Court in *Reynolds* ruled against the Mormons because the government had established a compelling government interest. Alley's interpretation seems the least defensible because Waite's opinion in *Reynolds* is best understood as providing little protection for claims of religious freedom against valid secular policies of the government. *Reynolds* has never been overturned by the Court; and although the case appeared to be a neglected precedent during most of the twentieth century, the Court did breathe new life into it in the *Smith* case of 1990.

New Deal Era

The Court's free exercise jurisprudence underwent dramatic changes as the Court and the country were transformed by the shift from laissez-faire capitalism to the New Deal era. In a variety of cases in the 1940s, the Court nationalized the Free Exercise Clause and interpreted it as a fundamental freedom requiring a high level of protection by the Court. The Court did vacillate somewhat as it searched for an appropriate standard, and *Reynolds* was never overruled; but the Court's opinions set the foundation for the development of the strict scrutiny standard by the Warren Court in the 1963 case of *Sherbert v. Verner.*

The Court nationalized the Free Exercise Clause in 1940 in the case of *Cantwell v. Connecticut.* Jesse Cantwell was a member of Jehovah's Witnesses, a religious group that frequently generated controversy because of its practice of advocating its beliefs in the streets and sidewalks as well as door-to-door. Cantwell stopped two men on the street, asked them if he could play a phonograph record to them, and received permission to do so. The record contained attacks on the Catholic religion and church, to which the two men belonged, and both men testified in court that they were incensed by the record and were tempted to hit Cantwell unless he went away. Cantwell responded by leaving the area, but he was later arrested and convicted under Connecticut laws regarding breach of the peace.

Justice Roberts, writing for a unanimous Court, provided a strong interpretation of the Free Exercise Clause in overturning the conviction of Cantwell. Roberts began his opinion by stating that the Free Exercise Clause applied against the states as well as the federal government. He then recognized that the free exercise guarantee of the First Amendment involved two concepts, the freedom to believe and the freedom to act; and while the freedom to believe is absolute, the freedom to act is subject to appropriate government regulations. Roberts then argued that government laws interfering with religious activity could be sustained only if the government was pursuing a substantial interest through narrowly tailored means: "although the contents of the record not unnaturally aroused animosity, we think that, in the absence of a statute narrowly drawn to define and punish specific conduct as constituting a clear and present danger to a substantial interest of the State, the petitioner's communication, considered in the light of the constitutional guarantees, raised no such clear and present menace to public peace and order as to render him liable to conviction of the common law offense in question" (310 U.S. at 311).

With the *Cantwell* decision, the Court now had two major precedents that seemed to encompass sharply divergent interpretations of the Free Exercise Clause, with *Reynolds* providing a narrow interpretation of the protection of religious liberty from government intervention and *Cantwell* giving much stronger support for religious freedom from government laws and actions. These divergent perspectives appeared in the "flag salute" cases of 1940 and 1943, the Court's most famous and controversial cases of the pre-Warren Court era. In the first decision of *Minersville School District v. Gobitis* (1940), the Court took a narrow view of the Free Exercise Clause, ruling 8-1 that the Constitution was not violated by a law requiring children to salute the flag even though this practice violated their basic religious convictions. Three years later, however, in a remarkably similar case, the Court by a 6-3 vote in *West Virginia State Board of Education v. Barnette* (1943) explicitly overruled *Gobitis*, strongly affirming the importance of religious freedom and the limited circumstances under which government may legitimately interfere with religious practices.

Both *Gobitis* and *Barnette* involved the same basic factual situations. In *Gobitis*, a local Pennsylvania school board required both teachers and children to participate in a flag salute ceremony each day in which participants stood, placed their right hand over their heart, said the pledge of allegiance, and saluted the flag. Lillian Gobitis and her brother William, ages twelve and ten, were members of Jehovah's Witnesses, and they had been taught in their religion that a salute to the flag was forbidden by biblical scripture. They therefore refused to participate in the flag salute ceremony, and they were expelled from school.

Justice Frankfurter wrote the 8-1 opinion for the Court in the *Gobitis* case, with Stone writing a lone dissent. Frankfurter cited the cases of *Reynolds* and *Davis* as providing the guiding principles: "The religious liberty which the Constitution protects has never excluded legislation of a general scope not directed against doctrinal loyalties of particular sects" (310 U.S. at 594). Furthermore, Frankfurter argued, this case involved government interests of the highest order: "National unity is the basis of national security" (310 U.S. at 595). In regard to the possibility of providing a religious exemption to the compulsory flag salute law, Frankfurter relied heavily on the principle of judicial self-restraint in arguing that the legislative branch could reasonably determine that exemptions could create problems of school discipline and create doubts about the flag salute exercise in the minds of the other children.

Three years later Justice Jackson authored the *Barnette* (1943) opinion for the Court, and his words are frequently cited as among the most eloquent ever written in support of First Amendment values: "If there is any fixed star in our constitutional constellation, it is that no official, high or petty, can prescribe what shall be orthodox in politics, nationalism, religion, or other matters of opinion or force citizens to confess by word or act their faith therein. If there are any circumstances which permit an exception, they do not now occur to us" (319 U.S. at 642). Jackson recognized that this case involved an emotional and patriotic issue, but he argued that the Bill of Rights was intended to apply in precisely these types of cases. "[The] freedom to differ is not limited to things that do not matter much. That would be a mere shadow of freedom. The test of its substance is the right to differ as to things that touch the heart of the existing order" (319 U.S. at 642). Jackson firmly rejected Frankfurter's self-restraint argument that the courts should defer to the popularly elected branches of government on this and similar issues: "The very purpose of a Bill of Rights was to withdraw certain subjects from the vicissitudes of political controversy, to place them beyond the reach of majorities and officials and to establish them as legal principles to be applied by the courts. One's right to life, liberty, and property, to free speech, a free press, freedom of worship and assembly, and other fundamental rights may not be submitted to vote; they depend on the outcome of no elections" (319 U.S. at 638). Thus, Jackson concluded, the actions of the West Virginia State Board of Education violated the First Amendment rights of Jehovah's Witnesses' children and "the decision of this Court in *Minersville School District v. Gobitis* . . . [is] . . . overruled" (319 U.S. at 642).

West Virginia State Board of Education v. Barnette

319 U.S. 624, 63 S.Ct. 1178, 87 L.Ed. 1628 (1943)

■ In the aftermath of the 1940 case of *Minersville School District v. Gobitis,* the West Virginia State Board of Education passed a resolution ordering all teachers and pupils to participate in a flag salute activity. As in the *Gobitis* case, children of Jehovah's Witnesses refused to comply with this requirement based on their religious beliefs, and they were expelled from school. A three-judge federal district panel restrained enforcement against the Jehovah's Witnesses, and the State Board appealed to the United States Supreme Court.

The *Barnette* case is significant for several reasons. The Court explicitly overturned one of its precedents, *Gobitis,* which is relatively unusual, especially in such a short period of time. In addition, this case has frequently been cited in subsequent Court decisions as a basis for the strict scrutiny approach not only to the Free Exercise Clause but also to the entire First Amendment. Finally, several memorable quotations can be found in the case, both in Justice Jackson's statements of the importance of the First Amendment liberties and in Justice Frankfurter's views on judicial self-restraint. As you read this opinion, consider the following questions: (1) Are Jackson's criticisms of the *Gobitis* decision convincing? (2) Is this opinion primarily concerned with the Free Exercise Clause, or does the opinion address the First Amendment more generally? (3) Based on your reading of this case, how valid is Scalia's citation of *Gobitis* as an important controlling precedent in the 1990 *Smith* case?

Vote:

6 justices found the law unconstitutional (Jackson, Douglas, Black, Murphy, Byrnes, Rutledge).

3 justices found the law constitutional (Frankfurter, Roberts, Reed).

Justice Jackson delivered the opinion of the Court.

* * *

This case calls upon us to reconsider a precedent decision, as the Court throughout its history often has been required to do. Before turning to the *Gobitis* Case, however, it is desirable to notice certain characteristics by which this controversy is distinguished.

The freedom asserted by these appellees does not bring them into collision with rights asserted by any other individual. It is such conflicts which most frequently require intervention of the State to determine where the rights of one end and those of another begin. But the refusal of these persons to participate in the ceremony does not interfere with or deny rights of others to do so. Nor is there any question in this case that their behavior is peaceable and orderly. The sole conflict is between authority and right of the individual. The state asserts power to condition access to public education on making a prescribed sign and profession and at the same time to coerce attendance by punishing both parent and child. The latter stand on a right of self-determination in matters that touch individual opinion and personal attitude.

* * *

There is no doubt that, in connection with the pledges, the flag salute is a form of utterance. Symbolism is a primitive but effective way of communicating ideas. The use of an emblem or flag to symbolize some system, idea, institution, or personality, is a short cut from mind to mind. Causes and nations, political parties, lodges and ecclesiastical groups seek to knit the loyalty of their followings to a flag or banner, a color or design. * * *

* * *

It is also to be noted that the compulsory flag salute and pledge requires affirmation of a belief and an attitude of mind. It is not clear whether the regulation contemplates that pupils forego any contrary convictions of their own and become unwilling converts to the prescribed ceremony or whether it will be acceptable if they simulate assent by words without belief and by a gesture barren of meaning. It is now a commonplace that censorship or suppression of expression of opinion is tolerated by our Constitution only when the expression presents a clear and present danger of action of a kind the State is empowered to prevent and punish. It would seem that involuntary affirmation could be commanded only on even more immediate and urgent grounds than silence. But here the power of compulsion is invoked without any allegation that remaining passive during a flag salute ritual creates a clear and present danger that would justify an effort even to muffle expression. To sustain the compulsory flag salute we are required to say that a Bill of Rights which guards the individual's right to speak his own mind, left it open to public authorities to compel him to utter what is not in his mind.

* * *

The *Gobitis* decision, however, *assumed*, as did the argument in that case and in this, that power exists in the State to impose the flag salute discipline upon school children in general. The Court only examined and rejected a claim based on religious beliefs of immunity from an unquestioned general rule. The question which underlies the flag salute controversy is whether such a ceremony so touching matters of opinion and political attitude may be imposed upon the individual by official authority under powers committed to any political organization under our Constitution. We examine rather than assume existence of this power and, against this broader definition of issues in this case, re-examine specific grounds assigned for the *Gobitis* decision.

1. It was said that the flag-salute controversy confronted the Court with "the problem which Lincoln cast in memorable dilemma: 'Must a government of necessity be too *strong* for the liberties of its people, or too *weak* to maintain its own existence?'" and that the answer must be in favor of strength. *Minersville School District v. Gobitis*.

We think these issues may be examined free of pressure or restraint growing out of such considerations.

It may be doubted whether Mr. Lincoln would have thought that the strength of government to maintain itself would be impressively vindicated by our confirming power of the state to expel a handful of children from school. Such oversimplification, so handy in political debate, often lacks the precision necessary to postulates of judicial reasoning. If validly applied to this problem, the utterance cited would resolve every issue of power in favor of those in authority and would require us to override every liberty thought to weaken or delay execution of their policies.

Government of limited power need not be anemic government. Assurance that rights are secure tends to diminish fear and jealousy of strong government, and by making us feel safe to live under it makes for its better support. Without promise of a limiting Bill of Rights it is doubtful if our Constitution could have mustered enough strength to enable its ratification. To enforce those rights today is not to choose weak government over strong government. It is only to adhere as a means of strength to individual freedom of mind in preference to officially disciplined uniformity for which history indicates a disappointing and disastrous end.

* * *

2. It was also considered in the *Gobitis* Case that functions of educational officers in states, counties and school districts were such that to interfere with their authority "would in effect make us the school board for the country." [*Gobitis*]

The Fourteenth Amendment, as now applied to the States, protects the citizen against the State itself and all of its creatures—Boards of Education not excepted. These have, of course, important, delicate, and highly discretionary functions, but none that they may not perform within the limits of the Bill of Rights. That they are educating the young for citizenship is reason for scrupulous protection of Constitutional freedoms of the individual, if we are not to strangle the free mind at its source and teach youth to discount important principles of our government as mere platitudes.

* * *

3. The *Gobitis* opinion reasoned that this is a field "where courts possess no marked and certainly no controlling competence," that it is committed to the legislatures as well as the courts to guard cherished liberties and that it is constitutionally appropriate to "fight out the wise use of legislative authority in the forum of public opinion and before legislative assemblies rather than to transfer such a contest to the judicial arena," since all the "effective means of inducing political changes are left free." [*Gobitis*]

The very purpose of a Bill of Rights was to withdraw certain subjects from the vicissitudes of political controversy, to place them beyond the reach of majorities and officials and to establish them as legal principles to be applied by the courts. One's right to life, liberty, and property, to free speech, a free press, freedom of worship and assembly, and other fundamental rights may not be submitted to vote; they depend on the outcome of no elections.

* * *

4. Lastly, and this is the very heart of the *Gobitis* opinion, it reasons that "national unity is the basis of national security," that the authorities have "the right to select appropriate means for its attainment," and hence reaches the conclusion that such compulsory measures toward "national unity" are constitutional. [*Gobitis*] Upon the verity of this assumption depends our answer in this case.

National unity as an end which officials may foster by persuasion and example is not in question. The problem is whether under our Constitution compulsion as here employed is a permissible means for its achievement.

Struggles to coerce uniformity of sentiment in support of some end thought essential to their time and country have been waged by many good as well as by evil men. Nationalism is a relatively recent phenomenon but at other times and places the ends have been racial or territorial security, support of a dynasty or regime, and particular plans for saving souls. As first and moderate methods to attain unity have failed, those bent on its accomplishment must resort to an ever increasing severity. As government pressure toward unity becomes greater, so strife becomes more bitter as to whose unity it shall be. Probably no deeper division of our people could proceed from any provocation than from finding it necessary to choose what doctrine and whose program public education officials shall compel youth to unite in embracing. Ultimate futility of such attempts to compel coherence is the lesson of every such effort from the Roman drive to stamp out Christianity as a disturber of its pagan unity, the Inquisition, as a means to religious and dynastic unity, the Siberian exiles as a means to Russian unity, down to the fast failing efforts of our present totalitarian enemies. Those who begin coercive elimination of dissent soon find themselves exterminating dissenters. Compulsory unification of opinion achieves only the unanimity of the graveyard.

It seems trite but necessary to say that the First Amendment to our Constitution was designed to avoid these ends by avoiding these beginnings. There is not mysticism in the American concept of the State or of the nature or origin of its authority. We set up government by consent of the governed, and the Bill of Rights denies those in power any legal opportunity to coerce that consent. Authority here is to be controlled by public opinion, not public opinion by authority.

The case is made difficult not because the principles of its decision are obscure but because the flag involved is our own. Nevertheless, we apply the limitations of the Constitution with no fear that freedom to be intellectually and spiritually diverse or even contrary will disintegrate the social organization. To believe that patriotism will not flourish if patriotic ceremonies are voluntary and spontaneous instead of a compulsory routine is to make an unflattering estimate of the appeal of our institution to free minds. We can have intellectual individualism and the rich cultural diversities that we owe to exceptional minds only at the price of occasional eccentricity and abnormal attitudes. When they are so harmless to others or to the State as those we deal with here, the price is not too great. But freedom to differ is not limited to things that do not matter much. That would be a mere shadow of freedom. The test of its substance is the right to differ as to things that touch the heart of the existing order.

If there is any fixed star in our constitutional constellation, it is that no official, high or petty, can prescribe what shall be orthodox in politics, nationalism, religion, or other matters of opinion or force citizens to confess by word or act their faith therein. If there are any circumstances which permit an exception, they do not now occur to us.

We think the action of the local authorities in compelling the flag salute and pledge transcends constitutional limitations on their power and invades the sphere of intellect and spirit which it is the purpose of the First Amendment to our Constitution to reserve from all official control.

The decision of this Court in *Minersville School Dist. v. Gobitis* and the holdings of those few per curiam decisions which preceded and foreshadowed it are overruled, and the judgment enjoining enforcement of the West Virginia Regulation is affirmed.

Justice Roberts and Justice Reed adhere to the views expressed by the Court in Minersville School Dist. v. Gobitis, and are of the opinion that the judgment below should be reversed.

Justice Black and Justice Douglas, concurring. [omitted]

Justice Murphy, concurring. [omitted]

Justice Frankfurter, dissenting:

One who belongs to the most vilified and persecuted minority in history is not likely to be [insensitive] to the freedoms guaranteed by our Constitution. Were my purely personal attitude relevant I should wholeheartedly associate myself with the general libertarian views in the Court's opinion, representing as they do the thought and action of a lifetime. But as judges we are neither Jew nor Gentile, neither Catholic nor agnostic. * * * As a member of this Court I am not justified in writing my private notions of policy into the Constitution, no matter how deeply I may cherish them or how mischievous I may deem their disregard. * * * The only opinion of our own even looking in that direction that is material is our opinion whether legislators could in reason have enacted such a law. In the light of all the circumstances, including the history of this question in this Court, it would require more daring than I possess to deny that reasonable legislators could have taken the action which is before us for review. Most unwillingly, therefore, I must differ from my brethren with regard to legislation like this. I cannot bring my mind to believe that the "liberty" secured by the Due Process Clause gives this Court authority to deny to the State of West Virginia the attainment of that which we all recognize as a legitimate legislative end, namely, the promotion of good citizenship, by employment of the means here chosen.

The question naturally arises as to why the Court reversed itself so dramatically in such a short period of time. The *Barnette* decision seems especially puzzling when consideration is given to the historic context surrounding this case, because the United States was in the midst of World War II with nationalism and patriotism at their peaks. Not surprisingly, this topic has been given extensive scholarly attention (see, for example, Bartee 1984; Irons 1990; Barnum 1993; and Kairys 1993), and three explanations have been offered: public criticism of the *Gobitis* decision, the indecisiveness of new justices in the *Gobitis* case, and changes in the Court's membership between *Gobitis* and *Barnette*.

Frankfurter's majority opinion in *Gobitis* was widely criticized throughout the country. Almost two hundred newspaper editorials attacked the Court's decision and logic, and overwhelming criticism also occurred in the nation's law journals. The flames of public and professional criticism were fanned by increased prosecutions and persecutions that were directed against Jehovah's Witnesses in some areas of the country because of the *Gobitis* decision.

A second explanation of the reversal involves the uncertainty of three new members of the Court—Black, Douglas, and Murphy—during the oral conference in the *Gobitis* case. Bartee (1984, pp. 42–69) argues that Chief Justice Hughes dominated the Court's discussion of *Gobitis,* arguing that the case basically involved the issue of the police power of the states under the Tenth Amendment rather than the Free Exercise Clause of the First Amendment. The only other justice to speak was Frankfurter, who lent his strong support to the views of Hughes. Stone, who wrote the lone dissent in *Gobitis,* had intended to speak and to cast his vote in favor of the Jehovah's Witnesses' position; but when Hughes heard no additional comments from any other justices, the chief justice assumed the Court was unanimous in favor of the Minersville School Board, and no vote was taken. Douglas, Black, and Murphy each had strong reservations about the constitutionality of the flag salute activity, and they might have voted with Stone against the policy had they been aware of his position. By the time Stone circulated his dissent, it was too late for Black, Murphy, and Douglas to change their position. They did announce, however, their opposition to *Gobitis* in the 1942 case of *Jones v. Opelika,* another case involving Jehovah's Witnesses.

The final explanation for the *Gobitis/Barnette* reversal involves the changing membership of the Court. During the period between the two cases, President Roosevelt appointed three new members to the Court: Byrnes, Rutledge, and Jackson. Both Jackson and Rutledge voted in favor of the Jehovah's Witnesses in *Barnette,* joining Stone, Black, Douglas, and Murphy to create the six-person majority to overturn *Gobitis*.

Cantwell and *Barnette* were thus the defining free exercise of religion cases for the high court in the decade before Earl Warren became chief justice. The Court did rule occasionally against free exercise of religion claims, as in *Prince v. Massachusetts* (1944) when an 8-1 majority upheld a state law that prohibited minors from selling newspapers on the streets despite objections from Jehovah's Witnesses that this was required by their religion. In the vast majority of cases, however, mostly involving Jehovah's Witnesses, the Court upheld the claims of religious minorities against various types of neutral, generally applicable laws (e.g., *Murdock v. Commonwealth of Pennsylvania,* 1943 and *Martin v. Struthers,* 1943).

Thus, the Warren Court encountered a free exercise jurisprudence characterized by a strong commitment to the free exercise of religion as a fundamental freedom that the government could limit only under exceptional circumstances. Nonetheless, the far more limited view of the Free Exercise Clause espoused in *Reynolds* had not been overturned, and the Court had found some circumstances in which valid, neutral laws prevailed over claims that they encroached upon religious freedom.

The Warren Court Era

Unlike its decisions in many other areas of civil rights and liberties, the Warren Court did not create a liberal revolution in its cases involving the Free Exercise Clause. The Court heard only a handful of free exercise cases during the fifties and sixties, and the outcomes of these cases divided roughly equally between liberal and conservative results. The Warren Court did set forth the strict scrutiny test in *Sherbert v. Verner* (1963), but even this important development was surrounded by inconsistencies and disagreements. Two years before *Sherbert,* Chief Justice Warren in the Sunday closing cases embraced the spirit of *Reynolds* rather the *Cantwell/Barnette* line of precedents in holding that these laws did not violate the free exercise rights of Jewish store owners. In addition, the majority opinion in *Sherbert* was supported by only five justices. Thus, although the Warren Court did establish the strict scrutiny test that provided a high degree of protection for religious liberty, the legacy of the Warren Court was not one of a clear, consistent, and strong level of support for individuals claiming government violations of the Free Exercise Clause.

The first major free exercise cases decided by the Warren Court were the Sunday closing cases of 1961. These separate but closely interrelated cases all involved state laws that provided for the closing of certain businesses on Sundays. At this time in American history, the majority of the states still had Sunday closing laws, but these laws varied enormously in terms of their scope as well as their enforcement. Numerous challenges arose to these laws for both economic and religious reasons, and the Court agreed to hear four of these cases, which involved various legal challenges and lower court decisions. Two cases—*McGowan v. Maryland* (1961) and *Two Guys from Harrison-Allentown, Inc. v. McGinley* (1961)—involved the owners of discount department stores that wanted to open seven days a week. The other two cases—*Gallagher v. Crown Kosher Super Market Association of Massachusetts* (1961) and *Braunfeld v. Brown* (1961)—concerned Orthodox Jewish shop owners who closed their businesses on Saturdays for religious reasons and wanted them open on Sundays. We can focus our attention on *Braunfeld* because this was the only case of the four in which the Court gave detailed consideration to the free exercise of religion question. In *McGowan* and *Two Guys,* the Court ruled that the petitioners lacked standing to bring a free exercise claim; instead, the Court decided the case on Establishment Clause grounds, ruling that the Establishment Clause was not violated because the laws had both a secular purpose and a secular effect, providing a uniform day of rest, relaxation, and family togetherness. The Court also decided *Gallagher* primarily on Establishment grounds, ruling that the free exercise ruling in *Braunfeld* was controlling for the *Gallagher* decision.

The Court was sharply divided in the *Braunfeld* case. The vote was 6-3 that the Sunday closing law did not violate Abraham Braunfeld's constitutional guarantee of the free exercise of religion, but the Court could not agree on an opinion. Chief Justice Warren wrote the four-person plurality opinion; Frankfurter wrote a concurring opinion joined by Harlan; and Douglas, Brennan, and Stewart each authored separate dissenting opinions.

In his plurality opinion, Warren emphasized the *Reynolds* free exercise precedent over *Barnette.* He distinguished the *Barnette* case from *Braunfeld* by arguing that the flag salute case forced individuals to partake in practices contrary to their religious beliefs whereas no such concern was present in regard to Sunday closing laws. Having thus set aside *Barnette,* Warren turned to *Reynolds* as the appropriate controlling precedent: "As pointed out in *Reynolds v. United States,* legislative power over mere opinion is forbidden but it may reach people's actions when they are found to be in violation of important social duties or subversive of good order, even when the actions are demanded by one's religion" (366 U.S. at 603–4). Elaborating on *Reynolds,* Warren argued that governments do not violate the Free Exercise Clause if they enact valid secular laws of general applicability even if the laws have an indirect burden on religious activity; and in the companion Sunday closing cases, the Court had determined that these laws were indeed valid, secular, and general. The only remaining question for Warren was whether the government could accomplish its legislative goal through means that did not impose a burden on religion, and his answer was negative.

Brennan's dissent took sharp exception with Warren's free exercise reasoning, and Brennan's position was to gain majority support two years later in *Sherbert.* He began his dissent by citing Jackson's opinion in *Barnette* regarding the standards to be used in cases where a law is alleged to conflict with a First Amendment liberty, whether it be speech, press, or religion: "'They are susceptible of restriction to prevent grave and immediate dangers to interests which the State may lawfully protect'" (366 U.S. at 612). Brennan argued that the Court had consistently applied this standard in all cases involving the First Amendment until this case, in which ". . . the Court seems to say, without so much as a deferential nod towards that high place that we have accorded religious freedom in the past, that any substantial state interest will justify encroachments on religious practice, at least if those are cloaked in the guise of some nonreligious public purpose" (366 U.S. at 613). In applying this test, Brennan asked what was the "compelling state interest" behind the Sunday closing law, and he argued that the state had none.

Scholarly analysts have been far more supportive of Brennan's reasoning than Warren's in the Sunday closing cases. Urofsky (1991, p. 41), for example, writes that "there is a striking insensitivity, almost callousness, in Warren's opinion . . ." which "showed a complete misunderstanding of the spirit of the Free Exercise Clause." Slightly less critical, Abraham (1988, p. 322) writes that Warren's opinions in the Sunday closing cases ". . . raised professional and lay eyebrows. . . ."

Two years after the Sunday closing cases, Brennan's views triumphed in *Sherbert v. Verner* (1963). The case involved a woman who was fired because she refused to work on her Sabbath, Saturday, and then was denied unemployment compensation by South Carolina.

The Supreme Court ruled 7-2 in Sherbert's favor, and Brennan marshaled enough support, including Chief Justice Warren, to create a five-person majority coalition, which, for the first time, explicitly gave majority support to the strict scrutiny approach to the Free Exercise Clause. Surprisingly, Brennan did not draw upon *Barnette* for support, as he had done in his dissent in *Braunfeld*. Instead, he began his opinion by acknowledging that the Court had in some cases—for example, *Reynolds, Prince,* and *Braunfeld*—rejected free exercise challenges to laws restricting a person's religious activities. In these cases, however, Brennan argued, the religious conduct presented ". . . some substantial threat to public safety, peace, or order" (374 U.S. at 403). The proper test in free exercise cases, according to Brennan, involved a three-fold inquiry. First, the Court must inquire if the government law or action imposes a burden on an individual's free exercise of religion. If a burden does exist, then the second inquiry is whether this burden is ". . . justified by a 'compelling state interest in the regulation of a subject within the State's constitutional power to regulate . . .'" (374 U.S. at 403). The case cited by Brennan regarding the compelling state interest standard was not a Free Exercise Clause case but rather a freedom of expression case (*NAACP v. Button,* 1963). Finally, even if the government could establish a compelling interest in a particular policy, a third inquiry would be whether any alternative means could achieve these compelling interests without violating the free exercise of religion.

In applying these questions, Brennan argued that South Carolina's action was in clear violation of Sherbert's constitutional guarantee of the free exercise of religion. He began by asserting that the state's action in denying Sherbert unemployment benefits was clearly a burden on her free exercise of religion because the ruling forced her to choose between following her religion and forfeiting benefits or abandoning a religious belief in order to accept work. This, Brennan stated, was the same kind of burden as imposing a fine upon her because of her Saturday worship. In addressing the compelling government interest inquiry, Brennan reasoned that the state's only argument, a concern with fraudulent claims, fell far short of being a compelling interest justifying a burden on religious freedom.

The final concern of the majority opinion focused on the question of whether this decision would violate the Establishment Clause by providing support for the Seventh Day Adventist religion in South Carolina. Brennan argued that no conflict arose with the Establishment Clause because the decision simply applied the principle of government neutrality in regard to religious differences, the decision did not create the type of church-state involvement with which the Establishment Clause was concerned, and the result assured the Establishment Clause principle that government should not deny any person the benefits of public welfare legislation because of their religion.

Sherbert v. Verner

374 U.S. 398, 83 S. Ct. 1790, 10 L.Ed. 2d 965 (1963)

■ Adell Sherbert had worked for many years in a Spartanburg, South Carolina, textile mill. Her schedule had required her to work from Monday through Friday, but then her employer changed her schedule to include Saturday. This created a conflict for her because Saturday was the Sabbath Day of her faith, the Seventh Day Adventist Church. She thus refused to work on Saturday, and she was fired. Unable to obtain other employment because she would not work on Saturdays, she filed for unemployment compensation with the state of South Carolina. The Employment Security Commission denied her request, ruling that she had failed without good cause to accept suitable employment available to her. Sherbert filed a suit arguing that this decision violated her First Amendment right to the free exercise of religion, but the South Carolina courts ruled against her. The case was then appealed to the United States Supreme Court.

This case is important because the Court established the strict scrutiny test for the Free Exercise Clause, requiring the government to justify any burden on religious freedom by showing that a compelling interest was being pursued by narrowly tailored means. In reading this case, consider the following questions: (1) Why did Brennan's majority opinion rely upon the precedent case of *Braunfeld v. Brown* (1962) rather than *West Virginia v. Barnette* (1943)? (2) Were Stewart and Harlan correct that the *Braunfeld* and *Sherbert* decisions were fundamentally incompatible? (3) Does the decision in *Sherbert* supporting the strict scrutiny approach to the Free Exercise Clause create potential conflicts with the requirements of the Establishment Clause?

Vote:

7 justices found the government action unconstitutional (Brennan, Warren, Douglas, Stewart, Goldberg, Black, Clark).

2 justices found the government action constitutional (Harlan, White).

Justice Brennan delivered the opinion of the Court.

* * *

The door of the Free Exercise Clause stands tightly closed against any governmental regulation of religious *beliefs* as such. Government may neither compel affirmation of a repugnant belief, nor penalize or discriminate against individuals or groups because they hold religious views abhorrent to the authorities, nor employ the taxing power to inhibit the dissemination of particular religious views. On the other hand, the Court has rejected challenges under the Free Exercise Clause to governmental regulation of certain overt acts prompted by religious beliefs or principles, for "even when the action is in accord with one's religious convictions, [it] is not totally free from legislative restrictions." [*Braunfeld v. Brown*, 1962.] The conduct or actions so regulated have invariably posed some substantial threat to public safety, peace or order.

Plainly enough, appellant's conscientious objection to Saturday work constitutes no conduct prompted by religious principles of a kind within the reach of state legislation. If, therefore, the decision of the South Carolina Supreme Court is to withstand appellant's constitutional challenge, it must be either because her disqualification as a beneficiary represents no infringement by the State of her constitutional rights of free exercise, or because any incidental burden on the free exercise of appellant's religion may be justified by a "compelling state interest in the regulation of a subject within the State's constitutional power to regulate . . . " *NAACP v. Button* [1963].

We turn first to the question whether the disqualification for benefits imposes any burden on the free exercise of appellant's religion. We think it is clear that it does. In a sense the consequences of such a disqualification to religious principles and practices may be only an indirect result of welfare legislation within the State's general competence to enact; it is true that no criminal sanctions directly compel appellant to work a six-day week. But this is only the beginning, not the end, of our inquiry. For "[i]f the purpose or effect of a law is to impede the observance of one or all religions or is to discriminate invidiously between religions, that law is constitutionally invalid even though the burden may be characterized as being only indirect" [*Braunfeld*]. Here not only is it apparent that appellant's declared ineligibility for benefits derives solely from the practice of her religion, but the pressure upon her to forego that practice is unmistakable. The ruling forces her to choose between following the precepts of her religion and forfeiting benefits, on the one hand, and abandoning one of the precepts of her religion in order to accept work, on the other hand. Governmental imposition of such a choice puts the same kind of burden upon the free exercise of religion as would a fine imposed against appellant for her Saturday worship.

Nor may the South Carolina court's construction of the statute be saved from constitutional infirmity on the ground that unemployment compensation benefits are not appellant's "right" but merely a "privilege." It is too late in the day to doubt that the liberties of religion and expression may be infringed by the denial of or placing of conditions upon a benefit or privilege. * * * To condition the availability of benefits upon this appellant's willingness to violate a cardinal principle of her religious faith effectively penalizes the free exercise of her constitutional liberties.

* * *

We must next consider whether some compelling state interest enforced in the eligibility provisions of the South Carolina statute justifies the substantial infringement of appellant's First Amendment right. It is basic that no showing merely of a rational relationship to some colorable state interest would suffice; in this highly sensitive constitutional area, "[o]nly the gravest abuses, endangering paramount interest, give occasion for permissible limitation." *Thomas v. Collins* [1945]. No such abuse or danger has been advanced in the present case. The appellees suggest no more than a possibility that the filing of fraudulent claims by unscrupulous claimants feigning religious objections to Saturday work might not only dilute the unemployment compensation fund but also hinder the scheduling of employers of necessary Saturday work. But that possibility is not apposite here because no such objection appears to have been made before the South Carolina Supreme Court, and we are unwilling to assess the importance of an asserted state interest without the views of the state court. Nor, if the contention had been made below, would the record appear to sustain it; there is no proof whatever to warrant such fears of malingering or deceit as those which the respondents now advance. Even if consideration of such evidence is not foreclosed by the prohibition against judicial inquiry into the truth or falsity of religious beliefs—a question as to which we intimate no view since it is not before us—it is highly doubtful whether such evidence would be sufficient to warrant a substantial infringement of religious liberties. For even if the possibility of spurious claims did threaten to dilute the fund and disrupt the scheduling of work, it would plainly be incumbent upon the appellees to demonstrate that no alternative forms of regulation would combat such abuses without infringing First Amendment rights.

In these respects, then, the state interest asserted in the present case is wholly dissimilar to the interests which were found to justify the less direct burden upon religious practices in *Braunfeld v. Brown*. The Court recognized that the Sunday closing law which that decision sustained undoubtedly served "to make the practice of [the Orthodox Jewish merchants'] . . . religious beliefs more expensive" [*Braunfeld*]. But the statute was nevertheless saved by a countervailing factor which finds no equivalent in the instant case—a strong state interest in providing one uniform day of rest for all workers. That secular objective could be achieved, the Court found, only by declaring Sunday to be that day of rest. Requiring exemptions for Sabbatarians, while theoretically possible, appeared to present an administrative problem of such magnitude, or to afford the exempted class so great a competitive advantage, that such a requirement would have rendered the entire statutory scheme unworkable. In the present case no such justifications underlie the determination of the state court that appellant's religion makes her ineligible to receive benefits.

In holding as we do, plainly we are not fostering the "establishment" of the Seventh-day Adventist religion in South Carolina, for the extension of unemployment benefits to Sabbatarians in common with Sunday worshipers reflects nothing more than the governmental obligation of neutrality in the face of religious differences, and does not represent that involvement of religious with secular institutions which it is the object of the Establishment Clause to forestall. Nor does the recognition of the appellant's right to unemployment benefits under the state statute serve to abridge any other person's religious liberties. Nor do we, by our decision today, declare the existence of a constitutional right to unemployment benefits on the part of all persons whose religious convictions are the cause of their unemployment. This is not a case in which an employee's religious convictions serve to make him a nonproductive member of society. Finally, nothing we say today constrains the States to adopt any particular form or scheme of unemployment compensation. Our holding today is only that South Carolina may not constitutionally apply the eligibility provisions so as to constrain a worker to abandon his religious convictions respecting the day of rest. This holding but reaffirms a principle that we announced a decade and a half ago, namely that no State may "exclude individual Catholics, Lutherans, Mohammedans, Baptists,

Jews, Methodists, Non-believers, Presbyterians, or the members of any other faith, *because of their faith, or lack of it*, from receiving the benefits of public welfare legislation" (emphasis in original) *Everson v. Board of Education* [1947].

* * *

The judgment of the South Carolina Supreme Court is reversed and the case is remanded for further proceedings not inconsistent with this opinion.

It is so ordered.

Justice Douglas, concurring. [omitted]

Justice Stewart, concurring in the result.

Although fully agreeing with the result which the Court reaches in this case, I cannot join the Court's opinion. This case presents a double-barreled dilemma, which in all candor I think the Court's opinion has not succeeded in papering over. The dilemma ought to be resolved.

* * *

I am convinced that no liberty is more essential to the continued vitality of the free society which our Constitution guarantees than is the religious liberty protected by the Free Exercise Clause explicit in the First Amendment and imbedded in the Fourteenth. And I regret that on occasion, and specifically in *Braunfeld v. Brown*, the Court has shown what has seemed to me a distressing insensitivity to the appropriate demands of this constitutional guarantee. By contrast I think that the Court's approach to the Establishment Clause has on occasion, and specifically in *Engel*, *Schempp* and *Murray*, been not only insensitive, but positively wooden, and that the Court has accorded to the Establishment Clause a meaning which neither the words, the history, nor the intention of the authors of that specific constitutional provision even remotely suggests.

But my views as to the correctness of the Court's decisions in these cases are beside the point here. The point is that the decisions are on the books. And the result is that there are many situations where legitimate claims under the Free Exercise Clause will run into head-on collision with the Court's insensitive and sterile construction of the Establishment Clause. The controversy now before us is clearly such a case.

Because the appellant refuses to accept available jobs which would require her to work on Saturdays, South Carolina has declined to pay unemployment compensation benefits to her. Her refusal to work Saturdays is based on the tenets of her religious faith. The Court says that South Carolina cannot under these circumstances declare her to be not "available for work" within the meaning of its statute because to do so would violate her constitutional right to the free exercise of her religion.

Yet what this Court has said about the Establishment Clause must inevitably lead to a diametrically opposite result. * * * The Establishment Clause as construed by this Court not only *permits* but affirmatively *requires* South Carolina equally to deny appellant's claim for unemployment compensation when her refusal to work on Saturdays is based upon her religious creed. * * *

To require South Carolina to so administer its laws as to pay public money to the appellant under the circumstances of this case is thus clearly to require the State to violate the Establishment Clause as construed by this Court. This poses no problem for me, because I think the Court's mechanistic concept of the Establishment Clause is historically unsound and constitutionally wrong. * * * And I think that the guarantee of religious liberty embodied in the Free Exercise Clause affirmatively requires government to create an atmosphere of hospitality and accommodation to individual belief or disbelief. In short, I think our Constitution commands the positive protection by government of religious freedom—not only for a minority, however small—not only for the majority, however large—but for each of us.

* * *

* * * With all respect, I think it is the Court's duty to face up to the dilemma posed by the conflict between the Free Exercise Clause of the Constitution and the Establishment Clause as interpreted by the Court. It is a duty, I submit, which we owe to the people, the States, and the Nation, and a duty which we owe to ourselves. For so long as the resounding but fallacious fundamentalist rhetoric of some of our Establishment Clause opinions remains on our books, to be disregarded at will as in the present case, or to be undiscriminatingly invoked as in the *Schempp* Case, so long will the possibility of consistent and perceptive decision in this most difficult and delicate area of constitutional law be impeded and impaired. And so long, I fear, will the guarantee of true religious freedom in our pluralistic society be uncertain and insecure.

My second difference with the Court's opinion is that I cannot agree that today's decision can stand consistently with *Braunfeld v. Brown*. The Court says that there was a "less direct burden upon religious practices" in that case than in this. With all respect, I think the Court is mistaken, simply as a matter of fact. The *Braunfeld* Case involved a State *criminal* statute. The undisputed effect of that statute, as pointed out by Mr. Justice Brennan in his dissenting opinion in that case, was that "'Plaintiff, Abraham Braunfeld, will be unable to continue in his business if he may not stay open on Sunday and he will therefore lose his capital investment'" [*Braunfeld*]. * * *

The impact upon the appellant's religious freedom in the present case is considerably less onerous. We deal here not with a criminal statute, but with the particularized administration of South Carolina's Unemployment Compensation Act. Even upon the unlikely assumption that the appellant could not find suitable non-Saturday employment, the appellant at the worst would be denied a maximum of 22 weeks of compensation payments. I agree with the Court that the possibility of that denial is enough to infringe upon the appellant's constitutional right to the free exercise of her religion. But it is clear to me that in order to reach this conclusion the Court must explicitly reject the reasoning of *Braunfeld v. Brown*. I think the *Braunfeld* Case was wrongly decided and should be overruled, and accordingly I concur in the result reached by the Court in the case before us.

Justice Harlan, whom Justice White joins, dissenting.

Today's decision is disturbing both in its rejection of existing precedent and in its implications for the future. * * *

* * *

First, despite the Court's protestations to the contrary, the decision necessarily overrules *Braunfeld v. Brown*, which held that it did not offend the Free Exercise Clause of the Constitution for a State to forbid a Sabbatarian to do business on Sunday. The secular purpose of the statute before us today is even clearer than that involved in *Braunfeld*. And just as in *Braunfeld*—where exception to the Sunday closing laws for Sabbatarians would have been inconsistent with the purpose to achieve a uniform day of rest and would have required case-by-case inquiry into religious beliefs—so here, an exception to the rules of eligibility based on religious convictions would necessitate judicial examination of those beliefs and would be at odds with the limited purpose of the statute to smooth out the economy during periods of industrial instability. Finally, the indirect financial burden of the present law is far less than that involved in *Braunfeld*. * * *

Second, the implications of the present decision are far more troublesome than its apparently narrow dimensions would indicate at first glance. The meaning of today's holding, as already noted, is that the State must furnish unemployment benefits to one who is unavailable for work if the unavailability stems from the exercise of religious convictions. * * *

It has been suggested that such singling out of religious conduct for special treatment may violate the constitutional limitations on state action. My own view, however, is that at least under the circumstances of this case it would be a permissible accommodation of religion for the State, if it *chose* to do so, to create an exception to its eligibility requirements for persons like the appellant. The constitutional obligation of "neutrality" is not so narrow a channel that the slightest deviation from an absolutely straight course leads to condemnation. * * * The State violates its obligation of neutrality when, for example, it mandates a daily religious exercise in its public schools, with all the attendant pressures on the school children that such an exercise entails. But there is, I believe, enough flexibility in the Constitution to permit a legislative judgment accommodating an unemployment compensation law to the exercise of religious beliefs such as appellant's.

For very much the same reasons, however, I cannot subscribe to the conclusion that the State is constitutionally *compelled* to carve out an exception to its general rule of eligibility in the present case. Those situations in which the Constitution may require special treatment on account of religion are, in my view, few and far between, and this view is amply supported by the course of constitutional litigation in this area. * * *

For these reasons I respectfully dissent from the opinion and judgment of the Court.

Although the *Sherbert* case did result in a majority of the Warren Court supporting the compelling government interest test, this case certainly did not eliminate controversy over the proper interpretation of the Free Exercise Clause. The concurring and dissenting justices in *Sherbert* raised important and valid concerns about the majority opinion that were to surface in the decisions of both the Burger and Rehnquist Courts.

The Warren Court thus passed a somewhat mixed legacy onto the Burger Court in the area of the Free Exercise Clause. The *Sherbert* case was a major precedent establishing the strict scrutiny test, but this precedent was planted in rather infirm constitutional soil. Only five justices had subscribed to the reasoning in *Sherbert*.

Furthermore, the *Braunfeld* case, which relied upon the *Reynolds* precedent, had not been overturned in *Sherbert* despite their glaring inconsistencies, and Brennan's attempt to reconcile the two had been effectively critiqued by other justices. Furthermore, the continuous and perhaps irreconcilable conflict between the Free Exercise Clause and the Establishment Clause continued to plague the Court in cases like *Sherbert* where providing an exemption to a religious minority to protect religious freedom raised real conflicts with the Court's neutrality approach to the Establishment Clause.

The Burger Court Era

The Burger Court's free exercise decisions have been given relatively little attention by scholars, some of whom simply fail to discuss these cases at all (e.g., Schwartz 1987) while others give only brief attention to the cases (e.g., Abraham 1988 and Urofsky 1991). The reasons for this inattention seem to be that the Burger Court heard relatively few free exercise cases; furthermore, these cases were typically not viewed as major cases in terms of either doctrinal development or social significance. Instead, scholarly and popular attention focused on the Establishment Clause, an area in which the high court handed down a large number of controversial and important decisions, as we saw in the previous chapter.

The neglect of the Burger Court's free exercise cases is unfortunate, however, because some important, albeit subtle, developments occurred in this era, which served to undermine the Court's commitment to the strict scrutiny approach in analyzing the Free Exercise Clause. In the seventies, the Burger Court was strongly supportive of the *Sherbert* compelling government interest test. In the first half of the eighties, however, the Burger Court issued a series of conservative free exercise decisions that raised major challenges to the *Sherbert* test. In two important cases in 1982 and 1983, the Court used the strict scrutiny test but found the government's interests sufficiently strong to override the claimed violations of the Free Exercise Clause. Then in two cases in 1986, the Court's controlling opinions did not even use the *Sherbert* test and strongly questioned its validity.

The leading case of the seventies was *Wisconsin v. Yoder* (1972), in which the Court embraced the strict scrutiny test of *Sherbert* to rule that Wisconsin's compulsory attendance law violated the religious freedom of Amish children who were being forced to attend school beyond the eighth grade. Chief Justice Burger wrote the majority opinion in favor of the Amish. Burger's opinion was joined by five other justices; Powell and Rehnquist had just joined the Court and did not participate in the decision, and only Douglas was in dissent.

In his majority opinion, Burger used the *Sherbert* test in analyzing the case. First, he concluded that a significant interference with the Free Exercise Clause did exist: ". . . enforcement of the State's requirement of compulsory formal education after the eighth grade would gravely endanger if not destroy the free exercise of respondents' religious beliefs" (406 U.S. at 219). Turning to the second question, Burger began by rejecting Wisconsin's argument that religious actions are outside the protection of the First Amendment, ". . . even under regulations of general applicability" (406 U.S. 220). The chief justice then turned to Wisconsin's position regarding its compelling interest in compulsory education, but he argued that these interests were not sufficiently strong in regard to the Amish to justify the interference with their religious freedom. Thus, Burger concluded, the Amish can be granted an exemption from this valid, general law, although he noted that few other religious groups could probably make such a showing.

WISCONSIN V. YODER

406 U.S. 205, 92 S.Ct. 1526, 32 L.Ed. 2d 15 (1972)

■ Jonas Yoder, Wallace Miller, and Adin Yutzy were members of the Amish faith living in Green County, Wisconsin. Under Wisconsin law, all children under the age of sixteen were required to attend school, but Yoder, Miller, and Yutzy refused to send their children, ages fourteen and fifteen, to school beyond the eighth grade. Their decision was based upon tenets of their faith. They believed that their children would be exposed to values sharply contrary to the Amish faith and that going to school would remove the children from the Amish community at a time when they would learn the values and behaviors associated with the Amish religion and way of life. The Amish contended that this law violated their First Amendment guarantee of the free exercise of religion, but a state trial court rejected their claim and found them guilty of violating the Wisconsin compulsory-attendance law. A state appeals court affirmed the convictions, but the Wisconsin Supreme Court ruled in favor of the Amish.

This is an important free exercise of religion case because the Burger Court used the strict scrutiny approach to give strong protection to claims of government infringement upon religious freedom. This showed a continuity with the Warren Court's approach to free exercise cases set forth in *Sherbert v. Verner* (1963). In reading this case, consider the following questions: (1) Does this decision providing an exemption for the Amish create a conflict with the requirements of the Establishment Clause? (2) How valid were Justice Douglas' concerns about the free exercise rights of the Amish children? (3) Is this decision compatible with Justice Scalia's majority opinion in *Smith* (1990)?

VOTE:

6 justices found the law unconstitutional as applied to the Amish (Burger, Brennan, Marshall, White, Stewart, Blackmun).

1 justice dissented in part (Douglas).

2 justices did not participate (Rehnquist, Powell).

Chief Justice Burger delivered the opinion of the Court.

* * *

There is no doubt as to the power of a State, having a high responsibility for education of its citizens, to impose reasonable regulations for the control and duration of basic education. Providing public schools ranks at the very apex of the function of a State. * * * Yet, a State's interest in universal education, however highly we rank it, is not totally free from a balancing process when it impinges on fundamental rights and interests, such as those specifically protected by the Free Exercise Clause of the First Amendment, and the traditional interest of parents with respect to the religious upbringing of their children. . . .

It follows that in order for Wisconsin to compel school attendance beyond the eighth grade against a claim that such attendance interferes with the practice of a legitimate religious belief, it must appear either that the State does not deny the free exercise of religious belief by its requirement, or that there is a state interest of sufficient magnitude to override the interest claiming protection under the Free Exercise Clause. * * *

The essence of all that has been said and written on the subject is that only those interests of the highest order and those not otherwise served can overbalance legitimate claims to the free exercise of religion. We can accept it as settled, therefore, that, however strong the State's interest in universal compulsory education, it is by no means absolute to the exclusion or subordination of all other interests.

We come then to the quality of the claims of the respondents concerning the alleged encroachment of Wisconsin's compulsory school-attendance statute on their rights and the rights of their children to the free exercise of the religious beliefs they and their forebears have adhered to for almost three centuries. * * *

. . . [W]e see that the record in this case abundantly supports the claim that the traditional way of life of the Amish is not merely a matter of personal preference, but one of deep religious conviction, shared by an organized group, and intimately related to daily living. * * *

* * *

The conclusion is inescapable that secondary schooling, by exposing Amish children to worldly influences in terms of attitudes, goals, and values contrary to beliefs, and by substantially interfering with the religious development of the Amish child and his integration into the way of life of the Amish faith community at the crucial adolescent stage of development, contravenes the basic religious tenets and practice of the Amish faith, both as to the parent and the child.

* * *

In sum, the unchallenged testimony of acknowledged experts in education and religious history, almost 300 years of consistent practice, and strong evidence of sustained faith pervading and regulating respondents' entire mode of life support the claim that enforcement of the State's requirement of compulsory formal education after the eighth grade would gravely endanger if not destroy the free exercise of respondents' religious beliefs.

* * *

Wisconsin concedes that under the Religion Clauses religious beliefs are absolutely free from the State's control, but it argues that "actions," even though religiously grounded, are outside the protection of the First Amendment. But our decisions have rejected the idea that religiously grounded conduct is always outside the protection of the Free Exercise Clause. It is true that activities of individuals, even when religiously based, are often subject to regulation by the States in the exercise of their undoubted power to promote the health, safety, and general welfare, or the Federal Government in the exercise of its delegated powers. But to agree that religiously grounded conduct must often be subjected to the broad police power of the State is not to deny that there are areas of conduct protected by the Free Exercise Clause of the First Amendment and thus beyond the power of the State to control, even under regulations of general applicability. This case, therefore, does not become easier because respondents were convicted for their "actions" in refusing to send their children to the public high school; in this context belief and action cannot be neatly confined in logic-tight compartments.

* * * The Court must not ignore the danger that an exception from a general obligation of citizenship on religious grounds may run afoul of the Establishment Clause, but that danger cannot be allowed to prevent any exception no matter how vital it may be to the protection of values promoted by the right of free exercise. By preserving doctrinal flexibility and recognizing the need for a sensible and realistic application of the Religion Clauses "we have been able to chart a course that preserved the autonomy and freedom of religious bodies while avoiding any semblance of established religion. This is a 'tight rope' and one we have successfully traversed." *Walz v. Tax Commission* [1970].

We turn, then, to the State's broader contention that its interest in its system of compulsory education is so compelling that even the established religious practices of the Amish must give way. Where fundamental claims of religious freedom are at stake, however, we cannot accept such a sweeping claim; despite its admitted validity in the generality of cases, we must searchingly examine the interests that the State seeks to promote by its requirement for compulsory education to age 16, and the impediment to those objectives that would flow from recognizing the claimed Amish exemption.

The State advances two primary arguments in support of its system of compulsory education. It notes, as Thomas Jefferson pointed out early in our history, that some degree of education is necessary to prepare citizens to participate effectively and intelligently in our open political system if we are to preserve freedom and independence. Further, education prepares individuals to be self-reliant and self-sufficient participants in society. We accept these propositions.

However, the evidence adduced by the Amish in this case is persuasively to the effect that an additional one or two years of formal high school for Amish children in place of their long-established program of informal vocational education would do little to serve those interests. * * *

* * *

Finally, the State, on authority of *Prince v. Massachusetts* [1944], argues that a decision exempting Amish children from the State's requirement fails to recognize the substantive right of the Amish child to a secondary education, and fails to give due regard to the power of the State as parens patriae to extend the benefit of secondary education to children regardless of the wishes of their parents. * * *

* * *

Contrary to the suggestion of the dissenting opinion of Mr. Justice Douglas, our holding today in no degree depends on the assertion of the religious interest of the child as contrasted with that of the parents. It is the parents who are subject to prosecution here for failing to cause their children to attend school, and it is their right of free exercise, not that of their children, that must determine Wisconsin's power to impose criminal penalties on the parent. The dissent argues that a child who expresses a desire to attend public high school in conflict with the wishes of his parents should not be prevented from doing so. There is no reason for the Court to consider that point since it is not an issue in the case. The children are not parties to this litigation. The State has at no point tried this case on the theory that respondents were preventing their children from attending school against their expressed desires, and indeed the record is to the contrary. The State's position from the outset has been that it is empowered to apply its compulsory-attendance law to Amish parents in the same manner as to other parents—that is, without regard to the wishes of the child. That is the claim we reject today.

* * *

For the reasons stated we hold, with the Supreme Court of Wisconsin, that the First and Fourteenth Amendments prevent the State from compelling respondents to cause their children to attend formal high school to age 16. * * *

* * *

Aided by a history of three centuries as an identifiable religious sect and a long history as a successful and self-sufficient segment of American society, the Amish in this case have convincingly demonstrated the sincerity of their religious beliefs, the interrelationship of belief with their mode of life, the vital role that belief and daily conduct play in the continued survival of Old Order Amish communities and their religious organization, and the hazards presented by the State's enforcement of a statute generally valid as to others. Beyond this, they have carried the even more difficult burden of demonstrating the adequacy of their alternative mode of continuing informal vocational education in terms of precisely those overall interests that the State advances in support of its program of compulsory high school education. In light of this convincing showing, one that probably few other religious groups or sects could make, and weighing the minimal difference between what the State would require and what the Amish already accept, it was incumbent on the State to show with more particularity how its admittedly strong interest in compulsory education would be adversely affected by granting an exemption to the Amish.

* * *

Affirmed.

Justice Stewart, with whom Justice Brennan joins, concurring. [omitted]

Justice White, with whom Justice Brennan and Justice Stewart join, concurring.

* * *

Decision in cases such as this and the administration of an exemption for Old Order Amish from the State's compulsory school-attendance laws will inevitably involve the kind of close and perhaps repeated scrutiny of religious practices, as is exemplified in today's opinion, which the Court has heretofore been anxious to avoid. But such entanglement does not create a forbidden establishment of religion where it is essential to implement free exercise values threatened by an otherwise neutral program instituted to foster some permissible, non-religious state objective. I join the Court because the sincerity of the Amish religious policy here is uncontested, because the potentially adverse impact of the state requirement is great, and because the State's valid interest in education has already been largely satisfied by the eight years the children have already spent in school.

Justice Douglas, dissenting in part.

I agree with the Court that the religious scruples of the Amish are opposed to the education of their children beyond the grade schools, yet I disagree with the Court's conclusion that the matter is within the dispensation of parents alone. The Court's analysis assumes that the only interests at stake in the case are those of the Amish parents on the one hand, and those of the State on the other. The difficulty with this approach is that, despite the Court's claim, the parents are seeking to vindicate not only their own free exercise claims, but also those of their high-school-age children.

* * *

* * * If the parents in this case are allowed a religious exemption, the inevitable effect is to impose the parents' notions of religious duty upon their children. Where the child is mature enough to express potentially conflicting desires, it would be an invasion of the child's rights to permit such an imposition without canvassing his views. * * *

Religion is an individual experience. It is not necessary, nor even appropriate, for every Amish child to express his views on the subject in a prosecution of a single adult. Crucial, however, are the views of the child whose parent is the subject of the suit. Frieda Yoder has in fact testified that her own religious views are opposed to high-school education. I therefore join the judgment of the Court as to respondent Jonas Yoder. But Frieda Yoder's views may not be those of Vernon Yutzy or Barbara Miller. I must dissent, therefore, as to respondents Adin Yutzy and Wallace Miller as their motion to dismiss also raised the question of their children's religious liberty.

The *Yoder* case thus seemed to indicate a firm commitment by the Burger Court to the strict scrutiny test of *Sherbert*. A six-person majority rejected the belief-action dichotomy; accepted the proposition that even neutral laws of general applicability could violate the Free Exercise Clause; used the compelling government interest standard, ruling against the government despite acknowledging the strong interest of the state in promoting education; and explicitly granted a religious exemption to the Amish. The justices were somewhat uneasy about the potential conflict with the

Establishment Clause that was created by this decision, but as in *Sherbert* they dismissed the conflict by simply stating that no Establishment Clause violation existed.

The Burger Court handed down two other important free exercise decisions in the late seventies and early eighties that reaffirmed the Court's support of the *Sherbert* approach of strict scrutiny. In *McDaniel v. Paty* (1978) the Court ruled unconstitutional by an 8-0 vote a Tennessee law that disqualified an ordained minister from being a candidate to a state constitutional convention. Then in *Thomas v. Review Board* (1981) the Court relied directly on *Sherbert* to rule 8-1 against the denial of unemployment benefits to a person who quit his job for religious reasons.

The *Yoder/ McDaniel/ Thomas* cases represented the pinnacle of the Court's support for individuals claiming governmental violations of their free exercise of religion. In the Court's next two major free exercise cases, *United States v. Lee* (1982) and *Bob Jones University v. United States* (1983), the Burger Court utilized the *Sherbert* test but found the federal government's interests sufficiently compelling to deny the free exercise claims.

Edwin Lee, a member of the Old Order Amish religion, was a self-employed farmer and carpenter who employed several other Amish members on his farm and in his carpentry shop. The Amish believe in self-sufficiency and providing for fellow members of their faith, and therefore Lee did not pay social security taxes for his Amish employees. In 1978 the Internal Revenue Service notified Lee that he owed over $27,000 in unpaid social security taxes, and Lee filed suit in federal district court that this requirement violated his and his employees' free exercise of religion rights. The district court agreed with Lee, but the Supreme Court unanimously ruled in favor of the government.

Chief Justice Burger wrote the majority opinion joined by every justice except Stevens. The chief justice acknowledged that the tax requirement did present a significant burden on Lee's free exercise rights; but, citing *Sherbert*, *Yoder*, and *Thomas*, Burger stated that not all burdens were unconstitutional because "the state may justify a limitation on religious liberty by showing that it is essential to accomplish an overriding governmental interest" (455 U.S. at 257). In this case, Burger reasoned, the federal government's interest in the mandatory social security system was very high, and an accommodation of the Amish religion would interfere with the achievement of this interest. This case was different from the Amish case of *Yoder*, according to Burger, because ". . . it would be difficult to accommodate the comprehensive social security system with myriad exceptions flowing from a wide variety of religious beliefs" (455 U.S. at 259–60).

Stevens wrote the lone separate opinion in the case, agreeing with the Court's judgment but not its logic. Stevens argued that the Court's strict scrutiny test inappropriately placed a heavy burden on the government to justify applying neutral and general laws to religious objectors, and in this case Stevens thought that the government could not meet this standard. Stevens argued that a different approach should be taken in free exercise cases: "In my opinion, it is the objector who must shoulder the burden of demonstrating that there is a unique reason for allowing him a special exemption from a valid law of general applicability" (455 U.S. at 262). For Stevens, Lee had failed to meet this burden. Stevens' concurrence was given little notice when he authored it, but this was an important, early indicator that the Rehnquist Court conservatives had a liberal ally in the area of the Free Exercise Clause.

One year later in *Bob Jones University v. United States* (1983), the Court again applied the strict scrutiny test and found that the government met the requirements of the test. This case, and a companion case involving Goldsboro, North Carolina Christian Schools, involved challenges to the Internal Revenue Service, which had denied or revoked tax-exempt status to the two schools because they had racially discriminatory policies in violation of federal law. The cases centered primarily around tax issues, and the Court ruled in favor of the federal government's decisions against providing tax-exempt status for the schools. The free exercise dimension of the case involved the contention that even if the Internal Revenue Service could generally deny tax-exempt status to schools having racially discriminatory policies, the government could not deny the status in these cases because the policies were based upon sincerely held religious beliefs. Burger quickly rejected this claim, arguing that the federal government had a compelling interest in eradicating racial discrimination in education and that no less restrictive means were available to the government.

As the final term of the Burger Court approached in the fall of 1985, all evidence seemed to indicate that the Court's free exercise jurisprudence was settled law. Individuals bringing claims of governmental violation of their free exercise guarantee might not always prevail, but this would be because the government had met the demanding burdens of the strict scrutiny test set forth in *Sherbert.* Two free exercise cases in the 1985 term, however, raised serious questions about the Court's commitment to *Sherbert.*

S. Simeha Goldman, a commissioned officer in the United States Air Force, was prevented from wearing a yarmulke, the traditional Jewish head covering, because Air Force regulations mandated a uniform dress code for all Air Force personnel. Goldman challenged the regulation because it infringed upon his religious beliefs and practices, which required the wearing of the yarmulke. A federal district court ruled in favor of Goldman; but the Court of Appeals for the District of Columbia Circuit reversed, and the Supreme Court in a narrow 5-4 vote upheld the circuit court decision against Goldman.

Rehnquist authored the five-person majority opinion in *Goldman v. Weinberger* (1986), which maintained that the traditional strict scrutiny standard of *Sherbert* could not be applied in this case involving the military. Although he acknowledged that the guarantees of the First Amendment do not disappear entirely in a military context, nonetheless ". . . courts must give great deference to the professional judgment of military authorities concerning the relative importance of a particular military interest" (475 U.S. at 507). Applying this highly deferential standard, Rehnquist argued that the military's concern with uniformity and the subordination of individual needs to the larger group justified the requirement even though it interfered with Goldman's religious freedom.

Brennan, Blackmun, and O'Connor each authored dissenting opinions. They could not agree about the proper standard to be applied in a military case like this one, but they were in agreement that Goldman's religious rights had been violated and that the Court majority had failed to articulate a meaningful standard for judging claims of free exercise violations in a military context. In Brennan's words, "The Court's response to Goldman's request is to abdicate its role as a principal expositor of the Constitution and protector of individual liberties in favor of credulous deference to unsupported assertions of military necessity" (475 U.S. at 513–14).

Goldman has had little impact as a precedent because it involved the unique context of the military environment, but one interesting effect of the case was to stimulate Congress to address a freedom of religion issue. In 1987 Congress passed legislation requiring the Air Force to change its dress regulations to give greater protection to the free exercise of religion.

The final free exercise of religion decision of the Burger Court was its most controversial. Stephen Roy was a Native American, a member of the Abenaki tribe. Roy's family was receiving welfare benefits in the form of food stamps and aid to dependent children, and he was required to provide the government with the social security numbers of all members of his family. In discussions with his tribal chief and religious leader, Roy became convinced that providing this information to the government would rob the spirit of the person whose number was disclosed. Roy had not yet provided the government with the social security number of his two-year old daughter, and he refused to do so on religious grounds. The government then reduced his welfare benefits accordingly, and Roy filed suit that this reduction in benefits was a violation of his First Amendment free exercise of religion. In *Bowen v. Roy* (1986), the Court rejected Roy's claim. The controversy surrounding this case stemmed not so much from the result as from the reasoning of the Court plurality, which explicitly rejected the strict scrutiny test of *Sherbert* and its progeny.

In the critical portion of the controlling opinion, Chief Justice Burger, joined by Rehnquist and Powell, explicitly rejected the application of the strict scrutiny test in cases like this and instead argued that only the minimal scrutiny of the rational basis test needed to be applied. Burger's specific language was as follows:

> *The test applied in cases like* Wisconsin v. Yoder *is not appropriate in this setting. In the enforcement of a facially and uniformly applicable requirement for the administration of welfare programs reaching many millions of people, the Government is entitled to wide latitude. The Government should not be put to the strict test applied by the District Court. . . . [A]bsent proof of an intent to discriminate against particular religious beliefs or against religion in general, the Government meets its burden when it demonstrates that a challenged requirement for governmental benefits, neutral and uniform in application, is a reasonable means of promoting a legitimate public interest (476 U.S. at 707–8).*

Applying this test to the facts of the case, Burger concluded that the federal government was acting neutrally, that the social security number requirement served a legitimate government purpose of preventing fraud, and that the means used were a reasonable approach to this goal.

O'Connor, joined by Brennan and Marshall, wrote a vigorous dissent, attacking the plurality's rejection of the strict scrutiny standard in this case. "[The plurality's] test has no basis in precedent and relegates a serious First Amendment value to the barest level of minimal scrutiny . . . . I would apply our long line of precedents to hold that the Government must accommodate a legitimate free exercise claim unless pursuing an especially important interest by narrowly tailored means" (476 U.S. at 727). O'Connor agreed that the government did have a compelling interest in preventing welfare fraud, but she argued that the government was not using narrowly tailored means. Only four cases had ever been reported in which the social security number requirement had been challenged on religious grounds, and thus the government could grant a religious exemption without harming its compelling interest.

Bowen v. Roy ended the Burger Court's free exercise cases like a bombshell exploding unexpectedly on a peaceful landscape. The strict scrutiny test of *Sherbert* was seemingly a settled part of the Court's free exercise jurisprudence before *Roy*. Although the plurality opinion did not overturn the strict scrutiny approach, the opinion did reject it at least in regard to welfare programs. Furthermore, Burger harshly criticized the strict scrutiny test in footnotes to his opinion. In response to O'Connor's charge that his test had no basis in precedent, Burger argued, "To the contrary, it is the history advanced by the dissenting opinions that is revisionist" (476 U.S. at 706). In addition, Burger said that the strict scrutiny test advocated by the dissenters would make every action by the government potentially susceptible to a free exercise challenge, placing a tough burden of proof on the government. "While libertarians and anarchists will no doubt applaud this result, it is hard to imagine that this is what the Framers intended" (476 U.S. at 707).

Despite the plurality's views in *Roy,* however, the strict scrutiny test of *Sherbert* still seemed secure as the Burger Court era ended and the Rehnquist Court began. Burger was resigning at the end of the 1985 term, and Powell would resign one year later, leaving Rehnquist as the sole remaining supporter of the *Roy* plurality opinion. Furthermore, despite some disagreements over specifics in *Roy,* a majority of the justices in *Roy* did express support for the strict scrutiny test of *Sherbert.* Thus, despite the *Roy* case, it appeared that the strict scrutiny approach to the Free Exercise Clause was secure. Appearances were to prove deceptive, however.

The Rehnquist Court Era

In analyzing the free exercise jurisprudence of the Rehnquist Court, we will again employ both quantitative and qualitative methods of analysis. Both approaches are necessary because they provide differing yet complementary insights into the decision-making patterns of the Rehnquist Court. The necessity of both methods is especially critical in analyzing the Free Exercise Clause, because the quantitative results hide some important results and relationships that can only be understood through careful qualitative analysis.

The initial question in the quantitative analysis is whether the Rehnquist Court has been dramatically more conservative in its free exercise cases than the Warren and Burger Courts. Table 6.1 provides a comparison of the liberal/conservative outcomes for the three Court eras. In this and subsequent tables in this chapter, a liberal decision is one that favors the individual bringing a complaint that the government has interfered unconstitutionally with the person's First Amendment guarantee of free exercise of religion, and a conservative outcome is a Court judgment against the individual and in favor of the government. The data in Table 6.1 show an increase in conservative decisions from the Warren to the Burger to the Rehnquist Courts. The Warren Court ruled liberally in 60 percent of its cases, the Burger Court reached liberal outcomes 50 percent of the time, and the Rehnquist Court gave liberal interpretations in only 33 percent of its free exercise cases. Although these changes are not dramatic, nonetheless the Rehnquist Court does show a more distinctly conservative voting pattern in free exercise cases than the Warren and Burger Courts.

The next inquiry asks how the individual justices of the Rehnquist Court voted in free exercise cases. The data in Table 6.2 do not support the idea that a cohesive group of conservative justices has dominated the Court in this area of constitutional law. Rehnquist is the only justice with a strongly conservative voting record at 78 percent conservative. Three justices—Marshall, Blackmun, and Brennan—established distinctively liberal records, but each of these justices has retired. The

TABLE 6.1: Liberal/Conservative Outcomes of Free Exercise of Religion Cases for the Warren, Burger, and Rehnquist Courts, 1953-94 Terms

	Outcomes		
Court Era	Liberal	Conservative	Totals
Warren Court, 1953-68 Terms	60% (3)	40% (2)	5
Burger Court, 1969-85 Terms	50% (5)	50% (5)	10
Rehnquist Court, 1986-94 Terms	33% (3)	67% (6)	9
Totals	46% (11)	54% (13)	24

TABLE 6.2: Liberal/Conservative Voting Records of the Justices of the Rehnquist Court in Free Exercise of Religion Cases, 1986-94 Terms

Justices	Liberal Votes	Conservative Votes
Souter	100% (1)	0% (0)
Thomas	100% (1)	0% (0)
Brennan	86% (6)	14% (1)
Blackmun	78% (7)	22% (2)
Marshall	75% (6)	25% (2)
Powell	50% (1)	50% (1)
Kennedy	50% (2)	50% (2)
Stevens	44% (4)	56% (5)
O'Connor	38% (3)	62% (5)
Scalia	38% (3)	62% (5)
White	33% (3)	67% (6)
Rehnquist	22% (2)	78% (7)

remaining justices—White, Scalia, O'Connor, Stevens, and Kennedy—tend to show moderately conservative voting records. Three justices—Thomas, Souter, and Powell—participated in too few decisions to make any meaningful comparisons.

Although the results of Table 6.2 do not suggest that distinctive voting blocs have existed on the Rehnquist Court in religious freedom cases, Table 6.3 does show that the Rehnquist Court has been divided sharply into two voting blocs, a six-person conservative bloc and a three-person liberal bloc. Justices Kennedy, O'Connor, Scalia, White, Rehnquist, and Stevens have an average interagreement score of 94 percent; the liberal bloc of Blackmun, Marshall, and Brennan was even more cohesive, showing a 100 percent level of agreement. Several important points need to be made about these results. One critical point is that the liberal bloc no longer exists because of the retirements of Brennan, Marshall, and Blackmun. Another interesting aspect of the bloc voting patterns is the presence of Stevens in the conservative bloc. Stevens typically takes a liberal position in civil rights and liberties cases, but he has expressed his doubts about the liberal strict scrutiny approach in free exercise cases as we saw in his concurring opinion in *Thomas.* A third matter that requires discussion in Table 6.3 is O'Connor's position in the conservative bloc. Although her voting record places her squarely with the conservative coalition, we will see that she has generally embraced the strict scrutiny test in her opinions in key free exercise cases, especially *Smith.* O'Connor has been somewhat of an enigma in the Rehnquist Court's free exercise cases, but she does not seem to fit comfortably into the conservative camp despite her voting record. Finally, White has resigned from the Court, but his replacement—Ginsburg—has yet to participate in a free exercise case.

What, then, can we conclude about the existence of a dominant conservative bloc on the Rehnquist Court in free exercise of religion cases? The answer appears to be that a cohesive, controlling bloc has emerged and may continue for the foreseeable future. Scalia, Rehnquist, Kennedy, and Stevens are the core of the conservative coalition. Although this coalition has lost White because of his retirement, Thomas' acceptance of the *Smith* test in the *Hialeah* case indicates that he will join the conservative bloc. Thus, even if Ginsburg and Breyer accept the strict scrutiny approach to the Free Exercise Clause, a solid, five-person conservative majority could control the Court's free exercise cases for some time.

TABLE 6.3: Bloc Voting Analysis of the Rehnquist Court Free Exercise of Religion Cases, 1986-94 Terms (numbers are percentages)

	KE	OC	SC	WH	RE	ST	BL	MA	BR
Kennedy	—	100	100	100	100	100	75	67	67
O'Connor	100	—	100	100	88	88	50	43	43
Scalia	100	100	—	100	88	83	50	43	43
White	100	100	100	—	89	89	56	50	43
Rehnquist	100	88	88	89	—	78	44	38	29
Stevens	100	88	83	89	78	—	67	62	57
Blackmun	75	50	50	56	44	67	—	100	100
Marshall	67	43	43	50	38	62	100	—	100
Brennan	67	43	43	43	29	57	100	100	—

Court mean = 73
Sprague Criterion = 87
Conservative bloc: Kennedy, O'Connor, Scalia, White, Rehnquist, Stevens = 94
Liberal Bloc: Blackmun, Marshall, Brennan = 100

With this quantitative analysis completed, we can now turn our attention to an in-depth case analysis of the Rehnquist Court's free exercise cases using the doctrinal framework presented in Table 6.4. As the table shows, the Court handed down two decisions—*Lyng* in 1988 and *Smith* in 1990—which were cases of major importance in which a majority of the Court created conservative modifications of existing precedent, specifically *Sherbert v. Verner.* We will focus attention on these two cases because of their significance, but we will briefly discuss the other cases as well in order to comprehend more fully the radical nature of the *Lyng* and *Smith* decisions.

The Rehnquist Court heard two free exercise cases during its first term, and neither case suggested that dramatic departures from the strict scrutiny approach of *Sherbert* were going to occur. *Hobbie v. Florida* (1987) was another unemployment compensation case. Paula Hobbie was fired from her job for refusing to work on her Sabbath based on her religious views, which she developed after she began her job, and she was denied unemployment compensation. Although this case differed factually from the earlier unemployment compensation cases because she adopted her religious beliefs after taking employment, an 8-1 Court majority ruled that the *Sherbert* and *Thomas* precedents controlled and that Hobbie's free exercise rights had been violated. Rehnquist was the lone dissenter. This case is especially noteworthy because Brennan's majority opinion explicitly rejected Florida's appeal for the Court to use the minimal scrutiny test from *Bowen v. Roy* in the previous term: "Five justices expressly rejected this argument in *Roy.* We reject the argument again today. As Justice O'Connor pointed out in *Roy,* '[s]uch a test has no basis in precedent and relegates a serious First Amendment value to the barest level of minimal scrutiny that the Equal Protection Clause already provides'" (480 U.S. at 142).

The second case of the 1986–87 term, *O'Lone v. Shabazz* (1987), involved a conflict between prison regulations and religious freedom for Muslim inmates who could not attend weekly services because of prison security concerns. Although a five-person majority ruled against the Muslims, using a minimal standard of rational basis, Rehnquist's majority opinion indicated that the lower standard was being used rather than the *Sherbert* test because of the unique circumstances associated with a prison environment.

The Rehnquist Court's initial encounter with the Free Exercise Clause thus indicated that the strict scrutiny approach was still solid precedent. Although it was

TABLE 6.4: A Framework for the Doctrinal Analysis of the Rehnquist Court's Free Exercise of Religion Cases, 1986-94 Terms

		Treatment of Precedent					
Major or Minor Importance	**Majority or Plurality Opinion**	Creation of New Liberal Precedent	Liberal Modification of Existing Precedent	Liberal Interpretation of Existing Precedent	Conservative Interpretation of Existing Precedent	Conservative Modification of Existing Precedent	Creation of New Conservative Precedent
Major	Majority			Lukumi v. Hialeah (1993)		Lyng v. Northwest Indian (1988) Employment Division v. Smith (1990)	
	Plurality						
Minor	Majority			Hobbie v. Florida (1987) Frazee v. Illinois (1989)	Employment Division v. Smith (1988) O'Lone v. Shabazz (1987) Hernandez v. Commissioner (1989) Swaggart v. Board (1990)		
	Plurality						

not used in *O'Lone*, this seemed to be an exceptional case just as *Goldman* was a unique case because it involved the military. In *Hobbie* the Court reaffirmed the *Sherbert* test and explicitly rejected the minimal scrutiny test of *Roy*.

The Court heard two more free exercise cases in the 1987–88 term, and by the end of this term the *Sherbert* compelling government interest test was on much shakier grounds. The less controversial of the two cases was *Employment Division v. Smith* (1988), which we already mentioned in the case study to begin this chapter. In this first *Smith* decision, the Court remanded the case to the Oregon Supreme Court for a ruling on whether the religious use of peyote was a violation of state criminal law.

The far more controversial case of the 1987–88 term was *Lyng v. Northwest Indian Cemetery Protective Association* (1988). In this case, the United States Forest Service wanted to link two California towns, Gasquet and Orleans, with a fully paved road, but this required building a six-mile paved segment through the Chimney Rock area, a piece of land of great religious importance to three Native American tribes in northwestern California. The Forest Service commissioned a study to evaluate the environmental impact of the proposed road, and the report recommended against building the road. According to the report the entire area was " . . . significant as an integral and indispensable part of Indian religious conceptualization and practice," and construction of the road " . . . would cause serious and irreparable damage to the sacred areas which are an integral and necessary part of the belief systems and lifeway of Northwest California Indian peoples" (485 U.S. at 442).

Despite this report, the Forest Service decided to build the road, and the Native Americans brought suit in federal district court. The court decided in favor of the Native Americans, ruling that the road construction would violate the Free Exercise Clause and issuing a permanent injunction against the Forest Service. A Ninth Circuit Court of Appeals affirmed the district court decision on the basis that the United States Government had failed to show a compelling interest in completing the road.

In a 5-3 decision in which Kennedy did not participate, O'Connor wrote a remarkable majority opinion ruling in favor of the Forest Service, explicitly rejecting the compelling government interest test, resurrecting the *Bowen v. Roy* precedent, and introducing a new dimension to free exercise jurisprudence, the **coercion test.** O'Connor acknowledged that the construction of the road ". . . will have severe adverse effects on the practice of their religion" (485 U.S. at 447), and indeed she conceded the possibility advanced by the Ninth Circuit that the road would " . . . virtually destroy . . . the Indians' ability to practice their religion . . . " (485 U.S. at 451). Nonetheless, O'Connor argued for the Court majority, the Native Americans' free exercise of religion guarantee was not being violated. Rejecting the compelling interest test, O'Connor cited *Bowen v. Roy* as the controlling precedent. The key element, she argued, was that the government was not *coercing* individuals into violating their religious beliefs; ". . . incidental effects of government programs, which may make it more difficult to practice certain religions but which have no tendency to coerce individuals into acting contrary to their beliefs, [do not] require government to bring forward a compelling justification for its otherwise lawful actions" (485 U.S. at 450).

Brennan wrote a bitter dissent joined by Marshall and Blackmun. He strongly rejected O'Connor's coercion test as inconsistent with both the text of the Constitution and the Court's long line of free exercise precedents, which, he argued, were not limited to protecting individuals from government coercion. Brennan maintained that the Court majority was motivated by a concern that accepting the Native Americans' claim in this case threatened the federal government's control over vast areas of federal property. His answer was that individuals challenging federal land use decisions ". . . should be required to show that the decision poses a substantial and realistic threat of frustrating their religious practices" (485 U.S. at 475). If this is shown, then the government must show a compelling interest to carry out its decision. Brennan concluded:

> *Today, the Court holds that a federal land-use decision that promises to destroy an entire religion does not burden the practice of that faith in a manner recognized by the Free Exercise Clause. Having thus stripped respondents and all other Native Americans of any constitutional protection against perhaps the most serious threat to their age-old religious practices, and indeed to their entire way of life, the Court assures us that nothing in its decision "should be read to encourage governmental insensitivity to the religious needs of any citizen." I find it difficult, however, to imagine conduct more insensitive to religious needs than the Government's determination to build a marginally useful road in the face of uncontradicted evidence that the road will render the practice of respondents' religion impossible (485 U.S. at 476–77).*

Lyng had the promise of being a landmark Supreme Court decision, but subsequent developments suggest that its long-term effects will be limited. In regard to the immediate crisis facing the Native American tribes, Congress passed legislation on October 28, 1990, making the Chimney Rock area part of a protected federal wilderness area, thus assuring that the road would not be completed and the sacred area preserved (Alderman and Kennedy 1991, p. 68). In terms of subsequent constitutional development, *Lyng* has not been used by the Court as a major, guiding precedent. Indeed, *Lyng* was not cited at all in the Court's next three Free Exercise Clause opinions preceding the 1990 *Smith* decision. If *Lyng* did not mark the death of the strict scrutiny approach to the Free Exercise Clause, however, it did turn out to be a warning signal of impending change.

The Rehnquist Court heard three more cases before the landmark *Smith* decision, and the strict scrutiny test was used in each of them. In *Frazee v. Illinois Department of Employment Security* (1989), the Court was faced with yet another unemployment compensation case. In this case, William Frazee refused a job offered by Kelly Services because it required him to work on Sunday. Although he was not affiliated with any specific religious group, he was a Christian and believed that he should not accept Sunday employment. Illinois refused to provide unemployment compensation, and Frazee sued. The Supreme Court ruled 9-0 in his favor, with White writing the unanimous opinion based on the precedents of *Sherbert*, *Thomas*, and *Hobbie.*

The strict scrutiny test was also used by Marshall for a five-person majority in *Hernandez v. Commissioner* (1989). The case involved an Internal Revenue Service decision that individuals could not deduct as charitable contributions the payments they made to branches of the Church of Scientology for services known as "auditing" and "training," which the Internal Revenue Service ruled were not gifts to the church within the meaning of the law. Justice Marshall for the majority cited the strict scrutiny standards of such cases as *Hobbie*, *Thomas*, and *Yoder* as the proper test. He expressed serious doubts that the government action created a substantial burden on the individuals' religious practices; but he said, citing *United States v. Lee* (1982), this was not necessary to decide because the government's interest in a sound tax system free of numerous exemptions was sufficiently compelling.

Strict scrutiny was used yet another time by the Court in *Jimmy Swaggart Ministries v. Board of Equalization of California* (1990). In this case, Jimmy Swaggart Ministries challenged on both establishment and free exercise grounds California's sales and use taxes on the organization's retail sale of religious materials. The Court rejected both arguments by the religious group. In regard to the Free Exercise Clause, O'Connor wrote a unanimous opinion for the Court, which she began with the following statement: "Our cases have established that '[t]he free exercise inquiry asks whether government has placed a substantial burden on the observation of a central religious belief or practice and, if so, whether a compelling governmental interest justifies the burden'" (493 U.S. at 384–85). Applying the strict scrutiny test, she found no violation of the Free Exercise Clause.

The stage was thus set for the landmark *Smith* decision of 1990. Attorneys for both parties as well as Court observers assumed beyond question that this unemployment compensation case would be decided by the Court under the strict scrutiny standard. This was the test the Court had typically used since 1963, and it was the test that had been used in all cases involving the denial of unemployment benefits. Thus, the critical issue seemed to be whether the Court would distinguish this case from *Sherbert, Thomas, Hobbie,* and *Frazee* by finding that Oregon had a compelling interest in enforcing its criminal law regarding illegal drugs and thus could deny unemployment benefits to anyone discharged for the use of illegal drugs.

As we saw in the opening case study to this chapter, however, the Court took a different and totally unexpected direction. Writing for a five-person majority—which included Rehnquist, Kennedy, White, and Stevens—Scalia argued that Oregon had not violated Smith's free exercise rights. Advocating a position of minimal scrutiny, Scalia stated that the Free Exercise Clause is not violated if a valid, religiously neutral, and generally applicable law has an incidental effect of burdening the free exercise of religion, and Oregon met this test. Scalia sharply attacked the *Sherbert* test without explicitly overturning it.

O'Connor, Brennan, Marshall, and Blackmun were outraged by the majority decision, although O'Connor did agree with the result. All four justices argued that Scalia's opinion departed dramatically from the Court's long-standing commitment to the strict scrutiny approach of the *Sherbert* test. Only O'Connor believed that Oregon met the requirements of the *Sherbert* test.

Employment Division, Department of Human Resources of Oregon v. Alfred L. Smith

494 U.S. 872, 110 S.Ct. 1595, 108 L.Ed. 2d 876 (1990)
[The facts of the case are omitted because they were presented in the case study at the beginning of this chapter.]

■ This is an important case because the Court appeared to reject the use of the strict scrutiny test set forth in *Sherbert v. Verner* (1963) and to substitute a new test providing only minimal protection for claims involving alleged violations of the Free Exercise Clause. As you read this case, consider the following questions: (1) Did the Supreme Court's precedents support Justice Scalia's interpretation opposing the strict scrutiny approach to the Free Exercise Clause, or were the precedents supportive of the dissenters' interpretation? (2) Is Justice Scalia correct that the strict scrutiny approach would threaten society with anarchy? (3) Is Justice O'Connor correct that the majority's opinion is incompatible with the Court's and the nation's commitment to religious liberty as a fundamental principle of American society?

Vote:

6 justices found the government action constitutional (Scalia, Rehnquist, White, Kennedy, Stevens, O'Connor).

3 justices found the government action unconstitutional (Brennan, Marshall, Blackmun).

Justice Scalia delivered the opinion of the Court.

This case requires us to decide whether the Free Exercise Clause of the First Amendment permits the State of Oregon to include religiously inspired peyote use within the reach of its general criminal prohibition on use of that drug, and thus permits the State to deny unemployment benefits to persons dismissed from their jobs because of such religiously inspired use.

* * *

* * * The free exercise of religion means, first and foremost, the right to believe and profess whatever religious doctrine one desires. Thus, the First Amendment obviously excludes all "governmental regulation of religious *beliefs* as such." *Sherbert v. Verner* [1963]. The government may not compel affirmation of religious belief, punish the expression of religious doctrines it believes to be false, impose special disabilities on the basis of religious views or

religious status, or lend its power to one or the other side in controversies over religious authority or dogma.

But the "exercise of religion" often involves not only belief and profession but the performance of (or abstention from) physical acts: assembling with others for a worship service, participating in a sacramental use of bread and wine, proselytizing, abstaining from certain foods or certain modes of transportation. It would be true, we think (though no case of ours has involved the point), that a state would be "prohibiting the free exercise [of religion]" if it sought to ban such acts or abstentions only when they are engaged in for religious reasons, or only because of the religious belief that they display. It would doubtless be unconstitutional, for example, to ban the casting of "statues that are to be used for worship purposes," or to prohibit bowing down before a golden calf.

Respondents in the present case, however, seek to carry the meaning of "prohibiting the free exercise [of religion]" one large step further. They contend that their religious motivation for using peyote places them beyond the reach of a criminal law that is not specifically directed at their religious practice, and that is concededly constitutional as applied to those who use the drug for other reasons. They assert, in other words, that "prohibiting the free exercise [of religion]" includes requiring any individual to observe a generally applicable law that requires (or forbids) the performance of an act that his religious belief forbids (or requires). As a textual matter, we do not think the words must be given that meaning. It is no more necessary to regard the collection of a general tax, for example, as "prohibiting the free exercise [of religion]" by those citizens who believe support of organized government to be sinful, than it is to regard the same tax as "abridging the freedom . . . of the press" of those publishing companies that must pay the tax as a condition of staying in business. It is a permissible reading of the text, in the one case as in the other, to say that if prohibiting the exercise of religion (or burdening the activity of printing) is not the object of the tax but merely the incidental effect of a generally applicable and otherwise valid provision, the First Amendment has not been offended. * * *

Our decisions reveal that the latter reading is the correct one. We have never held that an individual's religious beliefs excuse him from compliance with an otherwise valid law prohibiting conduct that the State is free to regulate. On the contrary, the record of more than a century of our free exercise jurisprudence contradicts that proposition. As described succinctly by Justice Frankfurter in *Minersville School Dist. Bd. of Educ. v. Gobitis* [1940]: "Conscientious scruples have not, in the course of the long struggle for religious toleration, relieved the individual from obedience to a general law not aimed at the promotion or restriction of religious beliefs. The mere possession of religious convictions which contradict the relevant concerns of a political society does not relieve the citizen from the discharge of political responsibilities." We first had occasion to assert that principle in *Reynolds v. United States* [1879], where we rejected the claim that criminal laws against polygamy could not be constitutionally applied to those whose religion commanded the practice. * * *

Subsequent decisions have consistently held that the right of free exercise does not relieve an individual of the obligation to comply with a "valid and neutral law of general applicability on the ground that the law proscribes (or prescribes) conduct that his religion prescribes (or proscribes)." [*United States v. Lee* (1982), *Minersville School Dist. Bd. of Educ. v. Gobitis* (1940), *Prince v. Massachusetts* (1944), *Braunfeld v. Brown* (1962), *Gillette v. United States* (1971)]. * * *

The only decisions in which we have held that the First Amendment bars application of a neutral, generally applicable law to religiously motivated action have involved not the Free Exercise Clause alone, but the Free Exercise Clause in conjunction with other constitutional protections, such as freedom of speech and of the press, see *Cantwell v. Connecticut* (1940), *Murdock v. Pennsylvania* (1943), *Follett v. McCormick* (1944), *Wisconsin v. Yoder* (1972). Some of our cases prohibiting compelled expression, decided exclusively upon free speech grounds, have also involved freedom of religion, cf. *Wooley v. Maynard* (1943), *West Virginia Board of Education v. Barnette* (1943). * * *

The present case does not present such a hybrid situation, but a free exercise claim unconnected with any communicative activity or parental right. Respondents urge us to hold, quite simply, that when otherwise prohibitable conduct is accompanied by religious convictions, not only the conviction but the conduct itself must be free from governmental regulation. We have never held that, and decline to do so now. There being no contention that Oregon's drug law represents an attempt to regulate religious beliefs, the communication of religious beliefs, or the raising of one's children in those beliefs, the rule to which we have adhered ever since *Reynolds* plainly controls. * * *

Respondents argue that even though exemption from generally applicable criminal laws need not automatically be extended to religiously motivated actors, at least the claim for a religious exemption must be evaluated under the balancing test set forth in *Sherbert v. Verner* (1963). Under the *Sherbert* test, governmental actions that substantially burden a religious practice must be justified by a compelling governmental interest. Applying that test we have, on three occasions, invalidated state unemployment compensation rules that conditioned the availability of benefits upon an applicant's willingness to work under conditions forbidden by his religion. See *Sherbert v. Verner* (1963), *Thomas v. Review Board* (1981), *Hobbie v. Unemployment Appeals Comm'n. of Florida* (1987). We have never invalidated any governmental action on the basis of the *Sherbert* test except the denial of unemployment compensation. Although we have sometimes purported to apply the *Sherbert* test in contexts other than that, we have always found the test satisfied, see *United States v. Lee* (1982). In recent years we have abstained from applying the *Sherbert* test (outside the unemployment compensation field) at all. [*Bowen v. Roy* (1986), *Lyng v. Northwest Indian Cemetery Protective Assn.* (1988), *Goldman v. Weinberger* (1986), *O'Lone v. Estate of Shabazz* (1987)]. * * *

Even if we were inclined to breathe into *Sherbert* some life beyond the unemployment compensation field, we would not apply it to require exemptions from a generally applicable criminal law. * * *

* * * We conclude today that the sounder approach, and the approach in accord with the vast majority of our precedents, is to hold the test inapplicable to such challenges. The government's ability to enforce generally applicable prohibitions of socially harmful conduct, like its ability to carry out other aspects of public policy, "cannot depend on measuring the effects of a governmental action on a religious objector's spiritual development." *Lyng*. To make an individual's obligation to obey such a law contingent upon the law's coincidence with his religious beliefs, except where the State's interest is "compelling"—permitting him, by virtue of his beliefs, "to become a law unto himself," *Reynolds*—contradicts both constitutional tradition and common sense.

The "compelling government interest" requirement seems benign, because it is familiar from other fields. But using it as the standard that must be met before the government may accord different treatment on the basis of race or before the government may regulate the content of speech is not remotely comparable to using it for the purpose asserted here. What it produces in those other fields—equality of treatment, and an unrestricted flow of contending speech—are constitutional norms; what it would produce here—a private right to ignore generally applicable laws—is a constitutional anomaly.

Nor is it possible to limit the impact of respondents' proposal by requiring a "compelling state interest" only when the conduct prohibited is "central" to the individual's religion. It is no more appropriate for judges to determine the "centrality" of religious beliefs before applying a "compelling interest" test in the free exercise field, than it would be for them to determine the "importance" of ideas before applying the "compelling interest" test in the free speech field. What principle of law or logic can be brought to bear to contradict a believer's assertion that a particular act is "central" to his personal faith? * * *

If the "compelling interest" test is to be applied at all then, it must be applied across the board, to all actions thought to be religiously commanded. Moreover, if "compelling interest" really means what it says (and watering it down here would subvert its rigor in the other fields where it is applied), many laws will not meet the test. Any society adopting such a system would be courting anarchy, but that danger increases in direct proportion to the society's diversity of religious beliefs, and its determination to coerce or suppress none of them. * * * The rule respondents favor would open the prospect of constitutionally required religious exemptions from civic obligations of almost every conceivable kind—ranging from compulsory military service to the payment of taxes, to health and safety regulations such as manslaughter and child neglect laws, compulsory vaccination laws, drug laws, and traffic laws, to social welfare legislation such as minimum wage laws, child labor laws, animal cruelty laws, environmental protection laws, and laws providing for equal opportunity for the races. The First Amendment's protection of religious liberty does not require this.

Values that are protected against government interference through enshrinement in the Bill of Rights are not thereby banished from the political process. Just as a society that believes in the negative protection accorded to the press by the First Amendment is likely to enact laws that affirmatively foster the dissemination of the printed word, so also a society that believes in the negative protection accorded to religious belief can be expected to be solicitous of that value in its legislation as well. It is therefore not surprising that a number of States have made an exception to their drug laws for sacramental peyote use. But to say that a nondiscriminatory religious-practice exemption is permitted, or even that it is desirable, is not to say that it is constitutionally required, and that the appropriate occasions for its creation can be discerned by the courts. It may fairly be said that leaving accommodation to the political process will place at a relative disadvantage those religious practices that are not widely engaged in; but that unavoidable consequence of democratic government must be preferred to a system in which each conscience is a law unto itself or in which judges weigh the social importance of all laws against the centrality of all religious beliefs.

Because respondents' ingestion of peyote was prohibited under Oregon law, and because that prohibition is constitutional, Oregon may, consistent with the Free Exercise Clause, deny respondents unemployment compensation when their dismissal results from the use of the drug. The decision of the Oregon Supreme Court is accordingly reversed.

It is so ordered.

Justice O'Connor, with whom Justice Brennan, Justice Marshall, and Justice Blackmun join [in part], concurring in the judgment.

Although I agree with the result the Court reaches in this case, I cannot join its opinion. In my view, today's holding dramatically departs from well-settled First Amendment jurisprudence, appears unnecessary to resolve the question presented, and is incompatible with our Nation's fundamental commitment to individual religious liberty.

* * *

The Court today extracts from our long history of free exercise precedents the single categorical rule that "if prohibiting the exercise of religion . . . is . . . merely the incidental effect of a generally applicable and otherwise valid provision, the First Amendment has not been offended." Indeed, the Court holds that where the law is a generally applicable criminal prohibition, our usual free exercise jurisprudence does not even apply. To reach this sweeping result, however, the Court must not only give a strained reading of the First Amendment but must also disregard our consistent application of free exercise doctrine to cases involving generally applicable regulations that burden religious conduct.

* * * Because the First Amendment does not distinguish between religious belief and religious conduct, conduct motivated by sincere religious belief, like the belief itself, must therefore be at least presumptively protected by the Free Exercise Clause.

The Court today, however, interprets the Clause to permit the government to prohibit, without justification, conduct mandated by an individual's religious beliefs, so long as that prohibition is generally applicable. But a law that prohibits certain conduct—conduct that happens to be an act of worship for someone—manifestly does prohibit that person's free exercise of his religion. A person who is barred from engaging in religiously motivated conduct is barred from freely exercising his religion. Moreover, that person is barred from freely exercising his religion regardless of whether the law prohibits the conduct only when engaged in for religious reasons, only by members of that religion, or by all persons. It is difficult to deny that a law that prohibits religiously motivated conduct, even if the law is generally applicable, does not at least implicate First Amendment concerns.

The Court responds that generally applicable laws are "one large step" removed from laws aimed at specific religious practices. The First Amendment, however, does not distinguish between laws that are generally applicable and laws that target particular religious practices. Indeed, few States would be so naive as to enact a law directly prohibiting or burdening a religious practice as such. Our free exercise cases have all concerned generally applicable laws that had the effect of significantly burdening a religious practice. * * *

To say that a person's right to free exercise has been burdened, of course, does not mean that he has an absolute right to engage in the conduct. Under our established First Amendment jurisprudence, we have recognized that the freedom to act, unlike the freedom to believe, cannot be absolute. *Cantwell, Reynolds*. Instead, we have respected both the First Amendment's express textual mandate and the governmental interest in regulation of conduct by requiring the Government to justify any substantial burden on religiously motivated conduct by a compelling state interest and by means narrowly tailored to achieve that interest. See *Hernandez v. Commissioner* (1987), *Hobbie* [1987], *United States v. Lee* (1982), *Thomas v. Review Board* (1981), *McDaniel v. Paty* (1978), *Yoder* [1972], *Gillette v. United States* (1971), *Sherbert v. Verner* (1963).The compelling interest test effectuates the First Amendment's command that religious liberty is an independent liberty, that it occupies a preferred position, and that the Court will not permit encroachments upon this liberty, whether direct or indirect, unless required by clear and compelling governmental interests "of the highest order." *Yoder*. * * *

The Court attempts to support its narrow reading of the Clause by claiming that "[w]e have never held that an individual's religious beliefs excuse him from compliance with an otherwise valid law prohibiting conduct that the State is free to regulate." But as the Court later notes, as it must, in cases such as *Cantwell* and *Yoder* we have in fact interpreted the Free Exercise Clause to forbid application of a generally applicable prohibition to religiously motivated conduct. Indeed, in *Yoder* we expressly rejected the interpretation the Court now adopts. * * *

The Court endeavors to escape from our decisions in *Cantwell* and *Yoder* by labeling them "hybrid" decisions, but there is no denying that both cases expressly relied on the Free Exercise Clause and that we have consistently regarded those cases as part of the mainstream of our free exercise jurisprudence. Moreover, in each of the other cases cited by the Court to support its categorical rule we rejected the particular constitutional claims before us only after carefully weighing the competing interests. * * * That we rejected the free exercise claims in those cases hardly calls into question the applicability of First Amendment doctrine in the first place. * * *

* * *

Moreover, we have not "rejected" or "declined to apply" the compelling interest test in our recent cases. Recent cases have instead affirmed that test as a fundamental part of our First Amendment doctrine. See, e.g., *Hernandez*, *Hobbie*. The cases cited by the Court signal no retreat from our consistent adherence to the compelling interest test. In both *Bowen v. Roy* and *Lyng v. Northwest Indian Cemetery Protective Assn.*, for example, we expressly distinguished *Sherbert* on the ground that the First Amendment does not "require the Government itself to behave in ways that the individual believes will further his or her spiritual development . . . ." *Roy*. * * *

Similarly, the other cases cited by the Court for the proposition that we have rejected application of the *Sherbert* test outside the unemployment compensation field are distinguishable because they arose in the narrow, specialized contexts in which we have not traditionally required the government to justify a burden on religious conduct by articulating a compelling interest. See *Goldman v. Weinberger* (1986), . . . military regulations. . . ; *O'Lone v. Estate of Shabazz* (1987), . . . prison regulations. . . . * * *

The Court today gives no convincing reason to depart from settled First Amendment jurisprudence. * * * The Court's parade of horribles not only fails as a reason for discarding the compelling interest test, it instead demonstrates just the opposite: that courts have been quite capable of applying our free exercise jurisprudence to strike sensible balances between religious liberty and competing state interests.

Finally, the Court today suggests that the disfavoring of minority religions is an "unavoidable consequence" under our system of government and that accommodation of such religions must be left to the political process. In my view, however, the First Amendment was enacted precisely to protect the rights of those whose religious practices are not shared by the majority and may be viewed with hostility. The history of our free exercise doctrine amply demonstrates the harsh impact majoritarian rule has had on unpopular or emerging religious groups such as the Jehovah's Witnesses and the Amish. * * * The compelling interest test reflects the First Amendment's mandate of preserving religious liberty to the fullest extent possible in a pluralistic society. For the Court to deem this command a "luxury" is to denigrate "[t]he very purpose of a Bill of Rights."

The Court's holding today not only misreads settled First Amendment precedent; it appears to be unnecessary to this case. I would reach the same result applying our established free exercise jurisprudence.

There is no dispute that Oregon's criminal prohibition of peyote places a severe burden on the ability of respondents to freely exercise their religion. * * *

There is also no dispute that Oregon has a significant interest in enforcing laws that control the possession and use of controlled substances by its citizens. * * * [R]espondents do not seriously dispute that Oregon has a compelling interest in prohibiting the possession of peyote by its citizens.

Thus, the critical question in this case is whether exempting respondents from the State's general criminal prohibition "will unduly interfere with fulfillment of the governmental interest." Although the question is close, I would conclude that uniform application of Oregon's criminal prohibition is "essential to accomplish" its overriding interest in preventing the physical harm caused by the use of a Schedule I controlled substance. Oregon's criminal prohibition represents that State's judgment that the possession and use of controlled substances, even by only one person, is inherently harmful and dangerous. Because the health effects caused by the use of controlled substances exist regardless of the motivation of the user, the use of such substances, even for religious purposes, violates the very purpose of the laws that prohibit them. Moreover, in view of the societal interest in preventing trafficking in controlled substances, uniform application of the criminal prohibition at issue is essential to the effectiveness of Oregon's stated interest in preventing any possession of peyote.

For these reasons, I believe that granting a selective exemption in this case would seriously impair Oregon's compelling interest in prohibiting possession of peyote by its citizens. Under such circumstances, the Free Exercise Clause does not require the State to accommodate respondents' religiously motivated conduct. * * *

* * *

I would therefore adhere to our established free exercise jurisprudence and hold that the State in this case has a compelling interest in regulating peyote use by its citizens and that accommodating respondents' religiously motivated conduct "will unduly interfere with fulfillment of the governmental interest." Accordingly, I concur in the judgment of the Court.

Justice Blackmun, with whom Justice Brennan and Justice Marshall join, dissenting.

This Court over the years painstakingly has developed a consistent and exacting standard to test the constitutionality of a state statute that burdens the free exercise of religion. Such a statute may stand only if the law in general, and the State's refusal to allow a religious exemption in particular, are justified by a compelling interest that cannot be served by less restrictive means.

Until today, I thought this was a settled and inviolate principle of this Court's First Amendment jurisprudence. The majority, however, perfunctorily dismisses it as a "constitutional anomaly." As carefully detailed in Justice O'Connor's concurring opinion, the majority is able to arrive at this view only by mischaracterizing this Court's precedents. The Court discards leading free exercise cases, such as *Cantwell v. Connecticut* (1940) and *Wisconsin v. Yoder* (1972) as "hybrids." * * * The Court cites cases in which, due to various exceptional circumstances, we found strict scrutiny inapposite, to hint that the Court has repudiated that standard altogether. In short, it effectuates a wholesale overturning of settled law concerning the Religion Clauses of our Constitution. One hopes that the Court is aware of the consequences, and that its result is not a product of overreaction to the serious problems the country's drug crisis has generated.

* * *

For these reasons, I agree with Justice O'Connor's analysis of the applicable free exercise doctrine. . . . * * * I do disagree, however, with her specific answer to that question.

* * *

The State's interest in enforcing its prohibition, in order to be sufficiently compelling to outweigh a free exercise claim, cannot be merely abstract or symbolic. The State cannot plausibly assert that unbending application of a criminal prohibition is essential to fulfill any compelling interest, if it does not, in fact, attempt to enforce that prohibition. In this case, the State actually has not evinced any concrete interest in enforcing its drug laws against religious users of peyote. Oregon has never sought to prosecute respondents, and does not claim that it has made significant enforcement efforts against other religious users of peyote. The State's asserted interest thus amounts only to the symbolic preservation of an unenforced prohibition. * * *

* * *

The State proclaims an interest in protecting the health and safety of its citizens from the dangers of unlawful drugs. It offers, however, no evidence that the religious use of peyote has ever harmed anyone. The factual findings of other courts cast doubt on the State's assumption that religious use of peyote is harmful. * * *

The fact that peyote is classified as a Schedule I controlled substance does not, by itself, show that any and all uses of peyote, in any circumstance, are inherently harmful and dangerous. The Federal Government, which created the classifications of unlawful drugs from which Oregon's drug laws are derived, apparently does not find peyote so dangerous as to preclude an exemption for religious use. * * *

The carefully circumscribed ritual context in which respondents used peyote is far removed from the irresponsible and unrestricted recreational use of unlawful drugs. The Native American Church's internal restrictions on, and supervision of, its members' use of peyote substantially obviate the State's health and safety concerns. * * *

Moreover, just as in *Yoder*, the values and interests of those seeking a religious exemption in this case are congruent, to a great degree, with those the State seeks to promote through its drug laws. * * * Not only does the Church's doctrine forbid nonreligious use of peyote; it also generally advocates self-reliance, familial responsibility, and abstinence from alcohol. * * * Far from promoting the lawless and irresponsible use of drugs, Native American Church members' spiritual code exemplifies values that Oregon's drug laws are presumably intended to foster.

The State also seeks to support its refusal to make an exception for religious use of peyote by invoking its interest in abolishing drug trafficking. There is, however, practically no illegal traffic in peyote. * * *

* * *

For these reasons, I conclude that Oregon's interest in enforcing its drug laws against religious use of peyote is not sufficiently compelling to outweigh respondents' right to the free exercise of their religion. Since the State could not constitutionally enforce its criminal prohibition against respondents,

the interests underlying the State's drug laws cannot justify its denial of unemployment benefits. Absent such justification, the State's regulatory interest in denying benefits for religiously motivated "misconduct" is indistinguishable from the state interests this Court has rejected in *Frazee*, *Hobbie*, *Thomas*, and *Sherbert*. The State of Oregon cannot, consistently with the Free Exercise Clause, deny respondents unemployment benefits.

I dissent.

Following *Smith*, the Court was quiet in the free exercise area for the next three terms until the 1993 case of *Church of the Lukumi Babalu Aye v. Hialeah*. In this decision the Court reaffirmed the *Smith* test, and Thomas added a sixth voice to the five-person majority in *Smith*. The Court issued a unanimous liberal decision, however, ruling that the city of Hialeah had violated the religious freedom of members of the Santeria religion.

The case arose because of the controversial practice of animal sacrifice associated with a religious sect known as the Santerians. In April of 1987, a Santerian group in Hialeah leased land and announced that they were going to build a church as well as a school, a cultural center, and a museum. The city council held an emergency public session to discuss these plans, and a set of ordinances regulating animal sacrifice was passed unanimously. These ordinances were upheld by the lower federal courts against challenges from the Santerians that their free exercise rights were being violated. The Supreme Court, however, ruled in favor of the Santerians.

Kennedy's majority opinion was based upon *Smith*, but he provided a further elaboration of how the Free Exercise Clause was to be interpreted under this new test. Citing *Smith*, Kennedy stated that the Court's free exercise cases ". . . establish the general proposition that a law that is neutral and of general applicability need not be justified by a compelling governmental interest even if the law has the incidental effect of burdening a particular religious practice . . ." (508 U.S. at 531). Any law that is not neutral and generally applicable, however, must be justified by a compelling government interest achieved by narrowly tailored means. In applying these standards to the animal sacrifice case, Kennedy argued that the Hialeah ordinances were not neutral and general but rather were directed toward suppressing the central element of the Santeria worship service. The city of Hialeah thus had to meet strict scrutiny standards, and Kennedy argued that the ordinances did not serve a compelling interest and also were not narrowly tailored. Thus, Kennedy concluded, the ordinances were unconstitutional.

Despite the unanimous vote of the Court, significant differences regarding the interpretation of the Free Exercise Clause arose in the separate, concurring opinions. Scalia, joined by Rehnquist, raised concerns about Kennedy's separate analyses of the concepts of neutrality and general applicability, which Scalia saw as very closely related terms. Blackmun, joined by O'Connor, wrote a separate opinion in which he repeated his opposition to the *Smith* test and advocated the strict scrutiny test as the appropriate one for free exercise cases.

Souter also wrote a separate opinion. Although no other member of the Court joined Souter, his opinion is nonetheless significant because it represents his first discussion of the Free Exercise Clause and because it is a well-balanced assessment of the Court's free exercise jurisprudence. Souter argued, quite correctly, that the Court's free exercise jurisprudence was in tension with itself. On the one hand, the *Reynolds*, *Gobitis*, *Braunfeld*, *Lyng*, and *Smith* line of decisions reject the idea that any exemptions should be made for general, neutral laws that interfere with religious practices. On the other hand, the *Barnette*, *Sherbert*, *Yoder*, *Thomas*, *Lee*, *Bob Jones*, *Hobbie*, *Hernandez*, and *Frazee* line of cases establish the principle that religious exemptions to general laws should be made unless the government can establish that it is pursuing a compelling interest through narrowly tailored means. Souter argued that the strict scrutiny approach was the most appropriate interpretation of the Free Exercise Clause, and he called for the Court to reexamine *Smith*.

Church of the Lukumi Babalu Aye v. Hialeah

508 U.S. 520, 124 L.Ed. 2d 472 (1993)

■ Santeria is a religion that has its origins with the Yoruba people of eastern Africa. When thousands of the Yoruba were brought from Africa to Cuba as slaves, their traditional African religion fused with elements of Roman Catholicism to create the Santeria religion. One of the principal forms of devotion in the religion is animal sacrifice, including various birds, chickens, goats, sheep, and turtles. Typically, the throats of the animals are cut, and then the animals are cooked and eaten during various religious rituals. Santeria was brought to Florida by exiles of the Cuban revolution. In 1987 a Santerian group, the Church of the Lukumi Babalu Aye, Inc., announced that it was going to build a worship center and other cultural buildings on land it had leased in Hialeah, Florida. When the Hialeah city council passed a series of ordinances that prohibited animal sacrifices, the Church filed suit in federal district court claiming a violation of their rights under the Free Exercise Clause. The district court ruled in favor of Hialeah, and the Eleventh Circuit Court of Appeals affirmed in a one-paragraph per curiam opinion.

This is an important case because it was the first free exercise of religion case decided by the Court following *Oregon v. Smith* (1990), the case in which the Court seemed to reject the *Sherbert* test and to adopt the *Smith* test. As you read this case, consider the following questions: (1) Does Justice Kennedy's majority opinion clarify when the Court will use the *Sherbert* test and when it will use the *Smith* test in free exercise cases? (2) What reasons might explain why the lower federal courts seemed to have little trouble finding the Hialeah ordinances constitutional but the United States Supreme Court ruled unanimously that they were unconstitutional? (3) Is Justice Souter correct in his separate opinion that the Court's free exercise jurisprudence is characterized by an "intolerable tension?" (4) What reasons does Souter offer for the Court to reexamine the *Smith* decision?

Vote:

The Court unanimously found the ordinances unconstitutional.

Justice Kennedy delivered the opinion of the Court.

The principle that government may not enact laws that suppress religious belief or practice is so well understood that few violations are recorded in our opinions. Concerned that this fundamental nonpersecution principle of the First Amendment was implicated here, however, we granted certiorari.

Our review confirms that the laws in question were enacted by officials who did not understand, failed to perceive, or chose to ignore the fact that their official actions violated the Nation's essential commitment to religious freedom. The challenged laws had an impermissible object; and in all events the principle of general applicability was violated because the secular ends asserted in defense of the laws were pursued only with respect to conduct motivated by religious beliefs. We invalidate the challenged enactments and reverse the judgment of the Court of Appeals.

In addressing the constitutional protection for free exercise of religion, our cases establish the general proposition that a law that is neutral and of general applicability need not be justified by a compelling governmental interest even if the law has the incidental effect of burdening a particular religious practice. [*Oregon v. Smith*, 1990] Neutrality and general applicability are interrelated, and, as becomes apparent in this case, failure to satisfy one requirement is a likely indication that the other has not been satisfied. A law failing to satisfy these requirements must be justified by a compelling governmental interest and must be narrowly tailored to advance that interest. These ordinances fail to satisfy the *Smith* requirements. We begin by discussing neutrality.

* * *

At a minimum, the protections of the Free Exercise Clause pertain if the law at issue discriminates against some or all religious beliefs or regulates or prohibits conduct because it is undertaken for religious reasons. * * *

* * *

In sum, the neutrality inquiry leads to one conclusion: The ordinances had as their object the suppression of religion. The pattern we have recited discloses animosity to Santeria adherents and their religious practices; the ordinances by their own terms target this religious exercise; the texts of the ordinances were gerrymandered with care to proscribe religious killings of animals but to exclude almost all secular killings; and the ordinances suppress much more religious conduct than is necessary in order to achieve the legitimate ends asserted in their defense. These ordinances are not neutral, and the court below committed clear error in failing to reach this conclusion.

We turn next to a second requirement of the Free Exercise Clause, the rule that laws burdening religious practice must be of general applicability. *Oregon v. Smith*. * * *

The principle that government, in pursuit of legitimate interests, cannot in a selective manner impose burdens only on conduct motivated by religious belief is essential to the protection of the rights guaranteed by the Free Exercise Clause. * * * In this case we need not define with precision the standard used to evaluate whether a prohibition is of general application, for these ordinances fall well below the minimum standard necessary to protect First Amendment rights.

Respondent claims that [the ordinances] advance two interests: protecting the public health and preventing cruelty to animals. The ordinances are underinclusive for those ends. They fail to prohibit nonreligious conduct that endangers these interests in a similar or greater degree than Santeria sacrifice does. The underinclusion is substantial, not inconsequential. Despite the city's proffered interest in preventing cruelty to animals, the ordinances are drafted with care to forbid few killings but those occasioned by religious sacrifice. Many types of animal deaths or kills for nonreligious reasons are either not prohibited or approved by express provision. For example, fishing—which occurs in Hialeah—is legal. Extermination of mice and rats within a home is also permitted. * * *

* * *

The ordinances are also underinclusive with regard to the city's interest in public health, which is threatened by the disposal of animal carcasses in open public places and the consumption of uninspected meat. Neither interest is pursued by respondent with regard to conduct that is not motivated by religious conviction. The health risks posed by the improper disposal of animal carcasses are the same whether Santeria sacrifice or some nonreligious killing preceded it. The city does not, however, prohibit hunters from bringing their kill to their houses, nor does it regulate disposal after their activity. Despite substantial testimony at trial that the same public health hazards result from improper disposal of garbage by restaurants, restaurants are outside the scope of the ordinances. Improper disposal is a general problem that causes substantial health risks, but which respondent addresses only when it results from religious exercise.

* * *

We conclude, in sum, that each of Hialeah's ordinances pursues the city's governmental interests only against conduct motivated by religious belief. The ordinances "ha[ve] every appearance of a prohibition that society is prepared to impose upon [Santeria worshipers] but not upon itself." * * * This precise evil is what the requirement of general applicability is designed to prevent.

A law burdening religious practice that is not neutral or not of general application must undergo the most rigorous of scrutiny. To satisfy the commands of the First Amendment, a law restrictive of religious practice must advance "interests of the highest order" and must be narrowly tailored in pursuit of those interests. * * * A law that targets religious conduct for distinctive treatment or advances legitimate governmental interests only against conduct with a religious motivation will survive strict scrutiny only in rare cases. It follows from what we have already said that these ordinances cannot withstand this scrutiny.

First, even were the governmental interests compelling, the ordinances are not drawn in narrow terms to accomplish those interests. As we have discussed, all four ordinances are overbroad or underinclusive in substantial respects. * * * The absence of narrow tailoring suffices to establish the invalidity of the ordinances. * * *

Respondent has not demonstrated, moreover, that, in the context of these ordinances, its governmental interests are compelling. Where government restricts only conduct protected by the First Amendment and fails to enact feasible measures to restrict other conduct producing substantial harm or alleged harm of the same sort, the interest given in justification of the restriction is not compelling. * * *

The Free Exercise Clause commits government itself to religious tolerance, and upon even slight suspicion that proposals for state intervention stem from animosity to religion or distrust of its practices, all officials must pause to remember their own high duty to the Constitution and to the rights it secures. Those in office must be resolute in resisting importunate demands and must ensure that the sole reasons for imposing the burdens of law and regulation are secular. Legislators may not devise mechanisms, overt or disguised, designed to persecute or oppress a religion or its practices. The laws here in question were enacted contrary to these constitutional principles, and they are void.

Reversed.

* * *

Justice Scalia, with whom the Chief Justice joins, concurring in part and concurring in the judgment. [omitted]

Justice Souter, concurring in part and concurring in the judgment.

This case turns on a principle about which there is no disagreement, that the Free Exercise Clause bars government action aimed at suppressing religious belief or practice. The Court holds that Hialeah's animal-sacrifice laws violate that principle, and I concur in that holding without reservation.

Because prohibiting religious exercise is the object of the laws at hand, this case does not present the more difficult issue addressed in our last free-exercise case, *Oregon v. Smith*, which announced the rule that a "neutral, generally applicable" law does not run afoul of the Free Exercise Clause even when it prohibits religious exercise in effect. The Court today refers to that rule in dicta, and despite my general agreement with the Court's opinion I do not join [that part] where the dicta appear, for I have doubts about whether the *Smith* rule merits adherence. I write separately to explain why the *Smith* rule is not germane to this case and to express my view that, in a case presenting the issue, the Court should re-examine the rule *Smith* declared.

According to *Smith*, if prohibiting the exercise of religion results from enforcing a "neutral, generally applicable" law, the Free Exercise Clause has not been offended. I call this the *Smith* rule to distinguish it from the noncontroversial principle, also expressed in *Smith* though established long before, that the Free Exercise Clause is offended when prohibiting religious exercise results from a law that is not neutral or generally applicable. It is this noncontroversial principle, that the Free Exercise Clause requires neutrality and general applicability, that is at issue here. * * *

* * *

The proposition for which the *Smith* rule stands, then, is that formal neutrality, along with general applicability, are sufficient conditions for constitutionality under the Free Exercise Clause. That proposition is not at issue in this case, however, for Hialeah's animal-sacrifice ordinances are not neutral under any definition, any more than they are generally applicable. This case, rather, involves the noncontroversial principle repeated in *Smith*, that formal neutrality and general applicability are necessary conditions for free-exercise constitutionality. It is only "this fundamental nonpersecution principle of the First Amendment [that is] implicated here," . . . and it is to that principle that the Court adverts when it holds that Hialeah's ordinances "fail to satisfy the *Smith* requirements." In applying that principle the Court does not tread on troublesome ground.

* * *

In being so readily susceptible to resolution by applying the Free Exercise Clause's "fundamental nonpersecution principle," this is far from a representative free-exercise case. While, as the Court observes, the Hialeah City Council has provided a rare example of a law actually aimed at suppressing religious exercise, *Smith* was typical of our free-exercise cases, involving as it did a formally neutral, generally applicable law. The rule *Smith* announced, however, was decidedly untypical of the cases involving the same type of law. Because *Smith* left those prior cases standing, we are left with a free-exercise jurisprudence in tension with itself, a tension that should be addressed, and that may legitimately be addressed, by reexamining the *Smith* rule in the next case that would turn upon its application.

In developing standards to judge the enforceability of formally neutral, generally applicable laws against the mandates of the Free Exercise Clause, the Court has addressed the concepts of neutrality and general applicability by indicating, in language hard to read as not foreclosing the *Smith* rule, that the Free Exercise Clause embraces more than mere formal neutrality, and that formal neutrality and general applicability are not sufficient conditions for free-exercise constitutionality. * * * Not long before the *Smith* decision, indeed, the Court specifically rejected the argument that "neutral and uniform" requirements for governmental benefits need satisfy only a reasonableness standard, in part because "[s]uch a test has no basis in precedent." *Hobbie v. Unemployment Appeals Comm'n of Florida* (1987). Rather, we have said, "[o]ur cases have established that '[t]he free exercise inquiry asks whether government has placed a substantial burden on the observation of a central religious belief or practice and, if so, whether a compelling governmental interest justifies the burden.'"

Thus we have applied the same rigorous scrutiny to burdens on religious exercise resulting from the enforcement of formally neutral, generally applicable laws as we have applied to burdens caused by laws that single out religious exercise: "only those interests of the highest order and those not otherwise served can overbalance legitimate claims to the free exercise of religion." *McDaniel v. Paty*, *Yoder*, *Hernandez v. Commissioner*, *Frazee v. Illinois Dept. of Employment Security*, *Hobbie v. Unemployment Appeals Comm'n*, *Bob Jones University v. United States*, *United States v. Lee*, *Thomas*, *Sherbert v.*

Verner, *Cantwell v. Connecticut*. Though *Smith* sought to distinguish the free-exercise cases in which the Court mandated exemptions from secular laws of general application, I am not persuaded. *Wisconsin v. Yoder* and *Cantwell v. Connecticut*, according to *Smith*, were not true free-exercise cases but "hybrid[s]" involving "the Free Exercise Clause in conjunction with other constitutional protections, such as freedom of speech and of the press, or the right of parents . . . to direct the education of their children." *Smith*. Neither opinion, however, leaves any doubt that "fundamental claims of religious freedom (were) at stake." *Yoder*. * * *

Smith sought to confine the remaining free-exercise exemption victories, which involved unemployment compensation systems, see *Frazee*, *Hobbie*, *Thomas*, and *Sherbert*, as "stand[ing] for the proposition that where the State has in place a system of individual exemptions, it may not refuse to extend that system to cases of 'religious hardship' without compelling reason." But prior to *Smith* the Court had already refused to accept that explanation of the unemployment compensation cases. * * *

As for the cases on which *Smith* primarily relied as establishing the rule it embraced, *Reynolds v. United States* (1879) and *Minersville School Dist. v. Gobitis* (1940), their subsequent treatment by the Court would seem to require rejection of the *Smith* rule. *Reynolds* . . . has been read as consistent with the principle that religious conduct may be regulated by general or targeting law only if the conduct "pose[s] some substantial threat to public safety, peace or order." And *Gobitis* . . . was explicitly overruled in *West Virginia Board of Education v. Barnette*.

Since holding in 1940 that the Free Exercise Clause applies to the States, the Court repeatedly has stated that the Clause sets strict limits on the government's power to burden religious exercise, whether it is a law's object to do so or its unanticipated effect. *Smith* responded to these statements by suggesting that the Court did not really mean what it said, detecting in at least the most recent opinions a lack of commitment to the compelling-interest test in the context of formally neutral laws. But even if the Court's commitment were that pallid, it would argue only for moderating the language of the test, not for eliminating constitutional scrutiny altogether. In any event, I would have trouble concluding that the Court has not meant what it has said in more than a dozen cases over several decades, particularly when in the same period it repeatedly applied the compelling-interest test to require exemptions, even in a case decided the year before *Smith*. In sum, it seems to me difficult to escape the conclusion that, whatever *Smith*'s virtues, they do not include a comfortable fit with settled law.

The *Smith* rule, in my view, may be reexamined consistently with principles of stare decisis. To begin with, the *Smith* rule was not subject to "full-dress argument" prior to its announcement. * * *

The *Smith* rule's vitality as precedent is limited further by the seeming want of any need of it in resolving the question presented in that case. * * * While I am not suggesting that the *Smith* Court lacked the power to announce its rule, I think a rule of law unnecessary to the outcome of a case, especially one not put into play by the parties, approaches without more the sort of "dicta . . . which may be followed if sufficiently persuasive but which are not controlling."

* * *

The considerations of full-briefing, necessity, and novelty thus do not exhaust the legitimate reasons for reexamining prior decisions, or even for reexamining the *Smith* rule. One important further consideration warrants mention here, however, because it demands the reexamination I have in mind. *Smith* presents not the usual question of whether to follow a constitutional rule, but the question of which constitutional rule to follow, for *Smith* refrained from overruling prior free-exercise cases that contain a free-exercise rule fundamentally at odds with the rule *Smith* declared. *Smith*, indeed, announced its rule by relying squarely upon the precedent of prior cases. ("Our decisions reveal that the . . . reading" of the Free Exercise Clause contained in the *Smith* rule "is the correct one"). Since that precedent is nonetheless at odds with the *Smith* rule, as I have discussed above, the result is an intolerable tension in free-exercise law which may be resolved, consistently with principles of stare decisis, in a case in which the tension is presented and its resolution pivotal.

While the tension on which I rely exists within the body of our extant case law, a rereading of that case law will not, of course, mark the limits of any enquiry directed to reexamining the *Smith* rule, which should be reviewed in light not only of the precedent on which it was rested but also of the text of the Free Exercise Clause and its origins. As for text, *Smith* did not assert that the plain language of the Free Exercise Clause compelled its rule, but only that the rule was "a permissible reading" of the Clause. Suffice it to say that a respectable argument may be made that the pre-*Smith* law comes closer to fulfilling the language of the Free Exercise Clause than the rule *Smith* announced. * * *

Nor did *Smith* consider the original meaning of the Free Exercise Clause, though overlooking the opportunity was no unique transgression. Save in a handful of passing remarks, the Court has not explored the history of the Clause since its early attempts in 1879 and 1890, attempts that recent scholarship makes clear were incomplete. The curious absence of history from our free-exercise decisions creates a stark contrast with our cases under the Establishment Clause, where historical analysis has been so prominent.

This is not the place to explore the history that a century of free-exercise opinions have overlooked, and it is enough to note that, when the opportunity to reexamine *Smith* presents itself, we may consider recent scholarship raising serious questions about the *Smith* rule's consonance with the original understanding and purpose of the Free Exercise Clause. * * *

* * *

Justice Blackmun, with whom Justice O'Connor joins, concurring in the judgment.

The Court holds today that the city of Hialeah violated the First and Fourteenth Amendments when it passed a set of restrictive ordinances explicitly directed at petitioners' religious practice. With this holding I agree. I write separately to emphasize that the First Amendment's protection of religion extends beyond those rare occasions on which the government explicitly targets religion (or a particular religion) for disfavored treatment, as is done in this case. In my view, a statute that burdens the free exercise of religion "may stand only if the law in general, and the State's refusal to allow a religious exemption in particular, are justified by a compelling interest that cannot be served by less restrictive means." *Oregon v. Smith*. The Court, however, applies a different test. It applies the test announced in *Smith*, under which "a law that is neutral and of general applicability need not be justified by a compelling governmental interest even if the law has the incidental effect of burdening a particular religious practice." I continue to believe that *Smith* was wrongly decided, because it ignored the value of religious freedom as an affirmative individual liberty and treated the Free Exercise Clause as no more than an antidiscrimination principle. Thus, while I agree with the result the Court reaches in this case, I arrive at that result by a different route.

When the State enacts legislation that intentionally or unintentionally places a burden upon religiously motivated practice, it must justify that burden by "showing that it is the least restrictive means of achieving some compelling state interest." * * *

* * *

When a law discriminates against religion as such, as do the ordinances in this case, it automatically will fail strict scrutiny under *Sherbert v. Verner* . . . . This is true because a law that targets religious practice for disfavored treatment both burdens the free exercise of religion and, by definition, is not precisely tailored to a compelling governmental interest.

Thus, unlike the majority, I do not believe that "[a] law burdening religious practice that is not neutral or not of general application must undergo the most rigorous of scrutiny." In my view, regulation that targets religion in this way, ipso facto, fails strict scrutiny. It is for this reason that a statute that explicitly restricts religious practices violates the First Amendment. * * *

* * *

Conclusion

The Rehnquist Court thus appears to have engaged in a conservative counterrevolution regarding the Free Exercise Clause. The Warren Court established the strict scrutiny test in *Sherbert v. Verner* in 1963, and this test became the applicable standard in most of the Court's subsequent free exercise cases. This test was undermined in a series of cases between 1986 and 1988, however, and then the *Smith* case of 1990 relegated the strict scrutiny test to the limited area of unemployment compensation denials in noncriminal cases or to cases in which laws are directed at particular religious groups. Under the new *Smith* test, free exercise claims will not be upheld if the law is valid, neutral, and generally applicable.

A judgment of the wisdom of the Court's decision in *Smith* perhaps ultimately depends on one's conception of the role of the Court in American society. The majority in *Smith* opted for a vastly reduced role for the Court in protecting and enforcing the Free Exercise Clause, preferring instead to leave these determinations largely in the hands of the majoritarian branches. The dissenters preferred a more activist role for the Court in holding the majoritarian branches to a strict standard of scruting if they interfere with religious freedom, which they view as a constitutional value of critical and fundamental importance.

The *Smith* test seems to be secure despite the constantly changing membership of the Court. In the 1993 *Hialeah* case, six justices—Scalia, Rehnquist, Kennedy, White, Stevens, and Thomas—accepted the *Smith* test. Even if Ginsburg's replacement of White should reduce this alignment, a five-person majority would still exist. The history of the Free Exercise Clause cautions against assuming too much permanency, however. Souter and O'Connor are clearly in favor of rejecting the *Smith* test and returning to the *Sherbert* test. Ginsburg and Breyer could certainly join Souter and O'Connor. A switch by any remaining justice in the *Hialeah* majority or the retirement and replacement of any of these justices could thus result in a further change in the Court's controlling precedents. Regardless of changing issues or personnel, however, the Court's interpretations of the Free Exercise Clause will generate continuing debates about the proper approach for interpreting this important provision of the First Amendment.

REFERENCES

Abraham, Henry. *Freedom and the Court*. 5th ed. New York: Oxford University Press, 1988.

Alderman, Ellen and Caroline Kennedy. *In Our Defense: The Bill of Rights in Action*. New York: Avon Books, 1991.

Alley, Robert S. *The Supreme Court on Church and State*. New York: Oxford University Press, 1988.

Barnum, David G. *The Supreme Court and American Democracy*. New York: St. Martin's Press, 1993.

Bartee, Alice Fleetwood. *Cases Lost, Causes Won: The Supreme Court and the Judicial Process*. New York: St. Martin's Press, 1984.

Bradley, Gerard V. "Beguiled: Free Exercise Exemptions and the Siren Song of Liberalism." *Hofstra Law Review* 20(1991): 245-319.

Durham, W. Cole. "Religious Liberty and the Call of Conscience." *DePaul Law Review* 42(1992): 71-88.

Hamburger, Phillip A. "A Constitutional Right of Religious Exemption: An Historical Perspective." *George Washington Law Review* 60(1992): 915-48.

Hentoff, Nat. "A Blow to Freedom of Religion." *The Progressive*, 54(1990): 16-17.

Irons, Peter. *The Courage of Their Convictions*. New York: Penguin Books, 1990.

Kairys, David. *With Liberty and Justice for Some: A Critique of the Conservative Supreme Court*. New York: The New Press, 1993.

Lindsay, Thomas. "James Madison on Religion and Politics: Rhetoric and Reality." *American Political Science Review* 85(1991): 1321-37.

McConnell, Michael W. "Free Exercise Revisionism and the *Smith* Decision." *University of Chicago Law Review* 57(1990a): 1109-1153.

________. "The Origins and Historical Understanding of Free Exercise of Religion." *Harvard Law Review* 103(1990b):1409-1517.

Neuhaus, Richard. "Church, State, and Peyote." *National Review,* 11 June 1990.

Schwartz, Herman. Ed. *The Burger Years*. New York: Penguin Books, 1987.

Urofsky, Melvin I. *The Continuity of Change: The Supreme Court and Individual Liberties, 1953-1986*. Belmont, Calif.: Wadsworth, 1991.

CHAPTER

Freedom of Expression

CASE STUDY

New York Times Co. v. Sullivan (1964)

On March 29, 1960, the *New York Times* ran a one-page advertisement entitled "Heed Their Rising Voices." The ad was financed by a civil rights group, the Committee to Defend Martin Luther King and the Struggle for Freedom in the South. The title for the ad was taken from a *Times* editorial of March 19, 1960, which was partially quoted in the right hand corner of the ad. The quote from the editorial read: "The growing movement of peaceful mass demonstrations by Negroes is something new in the South, something understandable. . . . Let Congress heed their rising voices, for they will be heard" (*New York Times Co. v. Sullivan*, 376 U.S. at 292). Following the quote were ten paragraphs of text. The ad began by describing the repression and terror facing Southern African American students who were protesting against the racial segregation of the South. It then focused on the efforts of Southern officials to silence the leader of the civil rights movement, Martin Luther King. In the concluding paragraph of the ad, an appeal was made for financial contributions to support the defense of Dr. King, to support the students' activities, and to assist the right-to-vote movement. Following the last paragraph of text, the ad listed sixty-four sponsors as well as the names of twenty ministers from the South.

Although this advertisement dealt with one of the major social concerns in American society, neither the ad sponsors nor the *Times* could have anticipated that it would trigger a series of actions leading to a Supreme Court decision in 1964 that would fundamentally alter the meaning of the First Amendment of the United States Constitution.

Reaction to the ad came quickly. On April 8, 1960, L.B. Sullivan, a commissioner of the city of Montgomery, Alabama, sent a registered letter to the *Times*. In the letter, Sullivan charged that the ad was libelous because it contained false and defamatory information about him, and he demanded that the paper print a full retraction.

The *Times'* initial response to Sullivan's letter came a week later. In the letter the *Times* indicated that they had investigated the statements in the ad and found them to be substantially correct. The central thrust of the letter, however, questioned how the ad could reflect on Sullivan when he was not even mentioned in the ad and asked Sullivan to explain further his concerns.

Sullivan never replied to the letter. Instead, he filed a libel action on April 19, 1960, in the Circuit Court of Montgomery County, Alabama, against the *New York Times*. The suit claimed that portions of the ad were false and defamatory, and Sullivan sought damages of $500,000.

Sullivan was not alone in seeking damages for libel. He was joined by the mayor of Montgomery, Earl James; another city commissioner, Frank Parks; and a former city commissioner, Clyde

Sellers. Each of these individuals also sought $500,000 in damages from the *Times*. Finally, Alabama Governor John Patterson also filed a libel suit, seeking $1 million in damages. Thus, the *Times* was faced with law suits totalling $3 million.

The attorneys for the *Times* faced formidable challenges in the Alabama court. The judge, Walter Burgwyn Jones, was a white supremacist. The jury was also racially biased, consisting of twelve white males. Finally, the United States Supreme Court had historically regarded libel as beyond constitutional protection, and thus the *Times* did not have a First Amendment defense.

The trial was conducted quickly, and a predictable decision was reached. The *Times* was found guilty of libeling Sullivan, and the jury awarded him the full $500,000 he had sought. The jury had little trouble finding that portions of the ad were false because the *Times* conceded that certain statements were inaccurate. A more contentious issue was whether Sullivan had been defamed, that is, whether his reputation had been harmed. The attorneys for the *Times* argued that the ad in no way referred to Sullivan. They also vigorously pursued a line of questioning with Sullivan regarding whether he had been ridiculed or shunned because of the ad, and Sullivan replied that he had not personally experienced any such action against him. Sullivan's attorneys, however, counteracted by bringing six witnesses to the stand who testified that the ads implicated Sullivan and would lower his reputation if people read and believed them. The jury took only two hours to find in favor of Sullivan.

The Alabama Supreme Court affirmed the lower court's decision two years later on August 30, 1962. The state high court upheld all aspects of Judge Jones's rulings and also ruled that the half-million dollar judgment was not excessive.

Both sides knew that the case was not finished with the state supreme court decision because too much was at stake. The case was a major victory for white officials in the South in their struggle against the civil rights movement. Libel actions could now be used as a threat and a weapon against the northern press. Just as the case represented a major legal and political victory for white southern officials, the state court decisions presented an enormous threat not only to the financial status of the *Times* and other media sources but also to their ability to report the news. The very survival of the *Times* was brought into question by the potential $3 million judgments facing them from the Sullivan and related cases, and by 1964 Southern officials had instituted libel actions against the press reaching nearly $300 million (Lewis 1991, p. 36). Facing these types of lawsuits, the press nationwide was forced into an extraordinary degree of self-censorship, especially in reporting on the struggle for racial equality in the South.

With the stakes so high and the odds seemingly so long, the *Times* faced a crucial choice in selecting an attorney to persuade the United States Supreme Court to hear the case and to rule in favor of the *Times*. The paper chose Herbert Wechsler, a professor at Columbia Law School. Wechsler was a seasoned veteran, having argued nearly a dozen cases before the Supreme Court, and he was an expert not only in civil rights and liberties but also in principles of American federalism, both of which were central to the case.

In his petition to the Court seeking a writ of certiorari, Wechsler was confronted with the basic problem of convincing the justices that they should enter into an area where they had never before ventured: state libel law. Wechsler chose to emphasize that the decisions of the Alabama courts in this case directly implicated the United States Constitution because their rulings struck at the very heart of the First Amendment by making it difficult if not impossible for the press to express criticisms of public officials on controversial issues.

Wechsler's appeal was successful. On January 7, 1963, the Court announced it would hear the case of *New York Times Co. v. L. B. Sullivan*. Although pleased, Wechsler knew that this was a victory in only one battle; the war had yet to be won. The high court's decision to grant certiorari simply meant that at least four justices had voted to hear the case. Wechsler still faced the formidable task of convincing the Court to alter 170 years of American libel law.

Wechsler decided to attack boldly, arguing that both history and the Court's own precedents required a decision in favor of the *Times*. In his historical analysis, Wechsler emphasized that the First Amendment guarantees of freedom of speech and of the press were created primarily to allow criticism of the government. He relied heavily upon the history of the Sedition Act of 1798, which made it a crime to express any false, scandalous, and malicious views against Congress or the president for the purpose of defaming them. Although the Supreme Court never ruled on the constitutionality of the law, Wechsler argued that history supported the position that it violated the First Amendment. Wechsler also argued that the Court's modern precedents strongly supported First Amendment protection for the *Times* ad. The Court had in recent decades continually expanded the meaning and scope of the First Amendment, recognizing its central importance for a democratic system of government. Furthermore, the Court's previous references to libel law had been in the context of civil suits involving private citizens. This case presented an entirely new issue, Wechsler argued, a libel suit involving public issues and public officials, thus directly implicating the First Amendment.

Wechsler had to draw a line, however. Although he would urge the Court to establish an absolute immunity of the press from libel suits by public officials, he feared that this position might be too extreme. He therefore suggested to the Court a variety of options for limiting libelous expression. One of these proposals was that public officials could win libel suits only if they established **actual malice,** publishing a damaging statement with the knowledge that it was false or with a reckless disregard of the truth.

Although Wechsler was presenting a variety of novel legal arguments to the Court, his views were supported in several important amicus curiae briefs. The *Washington Post*, the *Chicago Tribune*, the American Civil Liberties Union, and the New York Civil Liberties Union filed amicus briefs that supported and reinforced the arguments about the relevancy of the First Amendment in this case.

Roland Nachman of Montgomery, Alabama, who had represented Sullivan throughout the case, was the primary author of the Supreme Court brief for Sullivan. Nachman emphasized precedent, arguing that the Court had consistently viewed libel as outside the protection of the First Amendment. Nachman also argued that if the Court accepted the *Times'* radical new conception of libel law, then the press would have virtually absolute authority to print any type of false statements about public officials.

Oral arguments in the case occurred on January 6, 1964, and produced few surprises. Neither side emerged from oral argument as a clear winner, and thus both sides began the anxious wait for the Court's decision.

On March 9, 1964, just two months after oral argument, Wechsler was interrupted in the middle of one of his law classes. He was handed a note that said, "Judgment reversed. Decision unanimous." Wechsler read the note to his class, which burst into applause (Lewis 1991, p. 140). His arguments had convinced the Court to enter a new area of First Amendment law by redefining the requirements for establishing libel in regard to public officials. Justice Brennan wrote the six-person majority opinion, and Justices Black, Douglas, and Goldberg concurred in the judgment while writing separate opinions.

Brennan's majority opinion accepted most of the arguments advanced by Wechsler with one important exception: the press did not receive absolute immunity from libel suits involving public officials. Brennan began his opinion by stating that the case presented a new issue for the Court: "The extent to which the constitutional protections for speech and press limit a State's power to award damages in a libel action brought by a public official against critics of his official conduct" (376 U.S. at 256). Brennan's basic position on this issue was that libel laws have no automatic immunity from constitutional requirements but rather must be judged by First Amendment standards. These standards, Brennan argued, involve a ". . .profound national commitment to the principle that debate on public issues should be uninhibited, robust, and wide-open, and that it may well include vehement, caustic, and sometimes unpleasantly sharp attacks on government and public officials" (376 U.S. at 270). Brennan then turned to the traditional criteria in libel suits, falsity and defamation of character, to determine if these standards remove statements from constitutional protection. His answer was no. Erroneous statements, Brennan reasoned, are inevitable in free debate and must be tolerated if genuine freedom of expression is to exist in a democratic society. Defamation of public officials must also be tolerated, he continued; public officials in a democratic system must be ". . .men of fortitude, able to thrive in a hearty climate. . ." (376 U.S. at 273). Drawing heavily from Wechsler's brief, Brennan presented a detailed history of the Sedition Act of 1798 to support the basic argument that a central meaning of the First Amendment is that public officials should not be shielded from criticism of their official conduct. Brennan also gave substantial attention to a critical problem with current libel law, the extent to which the media engage in self-censorship out of fear of libel suits. Brennan refused to recognize an absolute immunity for the press, however: "The constitutional guarantees require, we think, a federal rule that prohibits a public official from recovering damages for a defamatory falsehood relating to his official conduct unless he proves that the statement was made with 'actual malice'—that is, with knowledge that it was false or with reckless disregard of whether it was false or not" (376 U.S. at 279–80).

In the final section of the opinion, Brennan applied the new standards for libel to the specific suit involving Sullivan and the *Times.* He argued that the facts of the case provided no basis that the *Times* had acted with actual malice, that is, with knowledge that the material in the ad was false or with a reckless disregard of the truth. In addition, Brennan rejected the argument of the Alabama courts that the ad could be interpreted as referring to Sullivan.

Black, Douglas, and Goldberg concurred in the judgment, ruling in favor of the *Times.* Each of these justices, however, argued an even more liberal position, stating that the protection of the press from libel suits by public officials should be absolute.

Although the Court's 9-0 decision in favor of the *Times* suggested a strong consensus on the Court over the issue, Anthony Lewis's (1991, pp. 164–182) research has established that the Court was badly fragmented over the reasoning behind the judgment and that Brennan had to exert extraordinary efforts to achieve a majority opinion. Brennan wrote eight different drafts of the opinion, trying to satisfy the divergent views of his colleagues.

Measuring the impact of Supreme Court decisions is an extremely difficult task, and the task is even more difficult in a multifaceted case like *New York Times Co. v. Sullivan.* The decision certainly made it easier for the national media to report on the civil rights movement and to affect the nation's attitude toward racial equality. The exact impact of the decision on the movement for racial equality is impossible to determine, but the dramatic successes of the civil rights movement in the sixties were certainly due in some part to the *New York Times* decision. The evidence regarding the effect of the decision on freedom of the press in American society is also difficult to measure. Although the decision established much more stringent standards for public officials to win libel suits, the *New York Times* decision did not end the filing of libel suits against the press. Lewis argues that "twenty years after *New York Times Co. v. Sullivan,* libel suits were a flourishing American industry" (1991, p. 205). This development may very well have occurred, however, in spite of *New York Times* rather than because of it.

One impact that is beyond debate is the increased caseload that the Court created in regard to libel law. The *New York Times* decision left numerous questions regarding libel law unanswered. Did these new standards apply to all public officials or just to major, elected officials? Did the *New York Times* rules apply only to comments regarding the official conduct of public officials? Would libel suits by nonpublic officials have to meet the same standards as set forth in *New York Times?* The Court has been faced with these and many other difficult questions since 1964, and we will examine these issues later in the chapter. We can conclude this case study by noting that the Court has remained committed to the ideas and ideals of the *New York Times* case in the three decades since it was decided.

Historical Origins and Contemporary Conflicts

Our case study of *New York Times Co. v. Sullivan* (1964) reveals that the contemporary Supreme Court frequently examines the history of the founding period of the Constitution for guidance. As we stress throughout this book, an understanding of history is important in all areas of civil rights and liberties, and thus we focus in this section on the historic origins of the First Amendment guarantees of freedom of expression. Using this historic backdrop, we will also provide an overview of some of the most important contemporary conflicts over freedom of expression that are confronting American society and the Supreme Court.

Pre-Colonial Background: Athens, Rome, and England

Although the American colonial period was influenced most directly by developments in England, freedom of expression had much earlier foundations in the democracies of ancient Athens and Rome. Scholars have not been successful in tracing direct linkages of freedom of expression from Athens to Rome to England to America, but interesting parallels do exist in the historical development of freedom of expression in each of these societies. Two especially important patterns can be found. First, the growth and expansion of freedom of expression has been gradual, beginning with the most elite members of society and slowly spreading to wider segments of society. Second, freedom of expression has never been treated as an absolute, that is, as beyond government regulation. Indeed, governments have historically exercised tight control over many forms of expression, especially that which is critical of existing governmental authority.

The birth of freedom of expression can be traced to the Greek city-state of Athens during the centuries from 800 B.C. to 400 B.C., where citizens could participate in debates in open forums. Although only limited classes of citizens were initially allowed to engage in free speech, gradually this liberty was expanded to all who had the status of citizens, which was approximately 40 percent of the population (Tedford 1985, p. 8). An extraordinary degree of freedom of expression existed in Athens, but it was nevertheless limited in many ways. Noncitizens, who were the majority of the populace, were denied the right to speak freely, and citizens could be punished for seditious speech against the government, defaming the reputation of another person, and a variety of other types of speech. Socrates, who was sentenced to death and died drinking a cup of hemlock, is perhaps the most famous example of a Greek citizen who was punished for exceeding the boundaries of accepted expression.

A somewhat similar pattern can be found in the period of the Roman Republic. Freedom of expression was initially sharply limited, with only members of the governing class being allowed to speak in the political bodies. Gradually, however, a substantial degree of toleration for freedom of expression spread to much broader segments of the population. As in Athens, however, substantial segments of the population did not enjoy the right of freedom of expression, and many forms of expression were subject to punishment regardless of who was the speaker.

The Roman Republic was replaced with the Roman Empire around 27 B.C., and freedom of expression declined as various forms of authoritarian government dominated the European continent and England for centuries. Given this long period of authoritarian rule, it is not surprising that historians can find no clear linkages between, on the one hand, the Athenian and Roman experiences with democratic government and freedom of expression and, on the other hand, the emergence of various forms of freedom of expression in England. Nonetheless, the two predominant themes of Athens and Rome—the gradual expansion of freedom of expression and its nonabsolute nature—also characterized English history.

Protection against government interference with freedom of expression developed slowly over many centuries in England. A critically important event in all of Western history was the signing of the **Magna Carta** or the "Great Charter" in 1215 by King John, whose tyrannical conduct stimulated the movement to limit the power of the monarchy and to assure basic rights for all free men. Although the Magna Carta made no specific reference to freedom of speech, the word liberty appeared in the document at several points. The seeds of the American Constitution had been planted.

Church and state authorities both resisted for centuries, however, the ideas and ideals associated with the Magna Carta. Monarchs and high church officials were the only persons who could speak without fear of government punishment during the Middle Ages. In 1689 another landmark document was signed, the English Bill of Rights. This enactment provided for only limited protection of freedom of speech, however, because it applied only to members of Parliament during legislative sessions. Criticism of the government by ordinary citizens was not protected, and frequent convictions occurred against those who spoke or wrote critically about the government.

English history reveals not only a lengthy process of many centuries for the development of freedom of expression but also a long history of severe punishments for those who exceeded the permissible boundaries of speech and press. Most prosecutions involved seditious speech, that which is critical of the government or governmental officials. Sedition was initially prohibited by an act of Parliament in 1275, and such laws remained for nearly six hundred years. For almost a century beginning in 1542, the English monarchs used the **Star Chamber** to prosecute those who criticized the government. Torture was frequently used to gain confessions, and victims were tried without benefit of a jury. Although the Star Chamber was abolished in 1641, the monarchs continued to punish seditious expression vigorously in the common law courts. Little attention was given to procedural fairness in these trials, and punishments were frequently brutal. For example, William Twyn was convicted of publishing a book that argued in favor of the right of revolution, and he was sentenced to death by hanging, emasculating, disemboweling, quartering, and beheading (Tedford 1985, p. 16).

What was the legacy that England provided the American colonies in regard to freedom of expression? This is a rather difficult judgment to make because of the changing patterns of many centuries, but we can offer some generalizations. One important contribution was the recognition of freedom of expression as an important human right. The Magna Carta, the Bill of Rights of 1689, and the writings of such British authors as John Milton and John Stuart Mill all played a significant role in the development of the Declaration of Independence and the Bill of Rights.

A somewhat contradictory legacy, however, was the significant degree of control exercised by the government over freedom of expression, especially spoken and written criticisms of government. Thus, American colonial societies found themselves confronted with precisely the same dilemma as England, the Roman Republic, and others faced: how to balance the frequently conflicting values of freedom of expression and the maintenance of public order. We turn now to the colonial period of American history and then to the Revolutionary War and development of the Constitution to learn how the United States initially dealt with this dilemma.

The American Colonial Experience

American mythology paints a picture of the early colonists escaping from the authoritarian rulers of Europe to establish new governments in the American colonies where freedom of expression was a cherished and widely respected liberty. While appealing, this view is simply not accurate. As Leonard Levy (1963, p. 34) has written: ". . . liberty of expression in principle or practice barely existed, if at all, in the American colonies during the seventeenth century." A much more accurate picture of the American colonial experience with freedom of expression prior to the Revolutionary War can be gained by looking at the historical experiences of Athens, the Roman Republic, and England. Like these societies, colonial America experienced a very slow and somewhat uneven expansion of freedom of expression from the elite few to a much broader segment of the population. American colonial governments were also frequently very harsh in repressing and punishing those who went beyond the established boundaries of freedom of expression.

The extension of the liberties of freedom of speech, press, and assembly to the common American took over two centuries to accomplish. Initially, colonial governments typically provided freedom of expression only for high government officials and important religious leaders. Directly paralleling historical developments in the Roman Republic and England during the monarchy, elected legislative officials in the American colonies gradually gained protection against prosecution for their statements made in their official capacities as legislators. Despite liberalizing tendencies in many colonies and the magnificent language of the Declaration of Independence, freedom of expression did not become a recognized protection against the government for all citizens until the First Amendment was ratified in 1791.

Government suppression of freedom of expression was also frequent and harsh throughout much of American colonial history. Most prosecutions occurred in regard to blasphemy and seditious speech. Thus, in early seventeenth century Virginia, the penalty of death could be imposed against someone speaking against established religious principles. Nor were citizens free to criticize government policies; for example, the Virginia government imprisoned a man in 1660 for criticizing a tax bill.

A pattern of gradual liberalizing of freedom of expression occurred throughout the American colonies in the eighteenth century prior to the Revolutionary War, but powerful government controls remained over the freedom of citizens to express themselves. The dominant conception of the law in colonial America was patterned after the authoritative interpretations of English common law provided by **Sir William Blackstone,** who published his *Commentaries on the Laws of England* between 1765 and 1796. In regard to freedom of expression, Blackstone wrote that this liberty simply meant that no prior restraint—censorship—should be exercised by the government. Sanctions could be imposed after ideas were communicated, however, and the government had few constraints in determining what forms of expression could be punished. Thus ". . . during the entire colonial period from the time of the first settlements to the Revolutionary War and the framing of the first bill of rights, America had very little experience with freedom of speech or press as a meaningful condition of life" (Cohen and Danelski 1994, p. 56).

The Revolutionary War and Founding Period

Although substantial agreement exists among scholars that a rather narrow view of freedom of expression existed throughout most of the colonial period of American history, strong disagreement can be found regarding the intentions and understanding of the freedom of expression guarantees when the First Amendment was written and ratified. One school of thought, associated most predominantly with Zechariah Chafee (1946), argues that the freedom of expression guarantees of the First Amendment represented a dramatic break with the past by providing much stronger protection for freedom of expression than had ever existed in colonial America. This viewpoint tends to be known as the Madisonian or libertarian approach, named after the primary author of the Bill of Rights, James Madison. In contrast, other scholars, with Leonard Levy (1960, 1963, 1985) as the most frequently cited, argue that the conception of freedom of expression associated with the Bill of Rights was fundamentally consistent with the view that had existed prior to the Revolutionary War. This view is typically referred to as the Blackstonian or conservative approach, representing Sir William Blackstone's interpretation of English common law that freedom of expression prevented only prior restraint by the government but not subsequent punishment.

We need to give some detailed attention to these dramatically different views of the meaning of the First Amendment because not only scholars but also Supreme Court justices have given substantial attention to this controversy. What evidence is offered for each side? Does one side have a stronger argument? Has the Supreme Court come down on one side or the other?

Professor Chafee provides a wide variety of historical evidence in support of his libertarian view. He argues that the Blackstone view of freedom of expression not only was largely irrelevant in the American context but also was not even accurate in England where Fox's Libel Act of 1792 dramatically liberalized English law. Chafee also argues that Madison's strongly libertarian views on freedom of expression were widely accepted, resulting in the absolutist language of the First Amendment—"Congress shall make no laws. . ."—and the strong support for the First Amendment in the ratification process. Chafee (1946, p. 18) also cites statements by many other prominent leaders during this period, concluding as follows:

> *The contemporaneous evidence in the passages just quoted shows that in the years before the First Amendment freedom of speech was conceived as giving a wide and genuine protection for all sorts of discussion of public matters. These various statements are, of course, absolutely inconsistent with any Blackstonian theory that liberty of the press forbids nothing except censorship. The men of 1791 went as far as Blackstone, and much farther.*

In contrast, Levy has strongly rejected this libertarian interpretation of the original meaning of the First Amendment's guarantees of freedom of expression. Levy argues that the Framers were products of the Blackstone tradition and adhered to it after the Revolutionary War. As an important piece of evidence, Levy states that in the decade from 1781 to 1791, the newly independent states did not change their English common law approach to seditious libel, allowing the states wide latitude to punish those who criticized government officials and policies. In Levy's words (1985, p. xv), "If the Revolution produced any radical libertarians on the meaning of freedom of speech and the press, they were not present at the Constitutional Convention or the First Congress, which drafted the Bill of Rights."

Which view is correct? Unfortunately, this question probably cannot be answered definitely. Disagreement still exists. Cohen and Danelski (1994, p. 58), for example, state that "the historical analysis provided by Chafee is widely, but not universally, accepted." In contrast, O'Brien (1995, p. 371) argues that ". . . the predominant view of freedom of speech and press was that the First Amendment incorporated traditional Blackstonian common-law principles, rather than broader libertarian principles." This debate will likely remain unresolved because so much critical information is missing. Insufficient evidence exists, for example, regarding debate in Congress over the First Amendment guarantees of freedom of expression as well as public debate in the states during the ratification process.

One definitive conclusion can be offered, however. Whatever the intention of the Framers of the First Amendment and whatever the original understanding among Americans involved in ratifying the First Amendment, the modern Supreme Court has strongly endorsed the libertarian, Madisonian view of freedom of expression. Even the most conservative current members of the Court—Rehnquist, Scalia, and Thomas—support the idea that the First Amendment goes beyond prohibiting censorship and provides extraordinarily strong protection to citizens who express ideas critical of government policies and officials.

Although this type of expression is given strong protection, it is not given absolute protection. Under some circumstances, the Court is willing to allow the government to arrest and punish citizens for expressing their ideas. Judicial lines can and must be drawn. This brings us to examination of the various tests or doctrines the Court has developed to deal with the difficult freedom of expression cases that it decides.

Before turning to these doctrines, however, we need to present some of the most important contemporary conflicts confronting the Court in the area of freedom of expression. Questions involving the closely related guarantees of freedom of speech and assembly have presented the Court with some of its most difficult and controversial cases. Should hate speech be given constitutional protection or is it beyond the scope of the First Amendment? Is burning the American flag in political protest a form of symbolic expression that comes within the First Amendment? How far can antiabortion protestors go in demonstrations outside abortion clinics in attempting to prevent women from obtaining abortions? The Court has also been confronted with numerous controversial issues involving freedom of the press. Do the libel law standards developed for public officials in *New York Times* also extend to public figures and to private persons? Can restrictions be placed on the press when their activities may threaten a defendant's right to a fair trial? Should commercial speech—advertising—be included within the meaning of the First Amendment? We will seek answers to these and other important First Amendment questions throughout this chapter. In dealing with these questions, the Court relies heavily on various doctrinal guidelines, and thus we now turn to a detailed consideration of the most important tests or doctrines the Court has developed in the area of freedom of expression.

Supreme Court Decision Making in Freedom of Expression Cases

We saw in the earlier chapters on the Establishment Clause and the Free Exercise of Religion Clause that judicial tests or doctrines play an important part in Supreme Court decision making, and this is also true in the area of freedom of expression. Useful and prevalent as these tests are, however, they certainly do not provide an easy means by which the justices can quickly reach a judgment and an opinion in a case.

Many reasons account for the ambiguity and confusion that characterize the Supreme Court's freedom of expression doctrines. First, as we saw in the previous section, history does not provide any clear guidance regarding the intention of the writers of these First Amendment guarantees or the original understanding of the freedom of expression guarantees when they were ratified. Second, American society has undergone dramatic changes in its basic cultural values regarding freedom of expression throughout history, and tests that were appropriate for one era have been rejected as inappropriate for later eras. A good example involves sexually explicit materials. Any such material that might fall into the hands of a young person could be suppressed in the last part of the nineteenth century and the early twentieth century; but American values and attitudes have changed, and now the Supreme Court uses tests that provide much greater protection for sexually oriented expression. A third reason involves changes in the Court's personnel. As a central theme of this book, we emphasize that newly appointed justices may bring very different judicial and political attitudes regarding freedom of expression to the Court than those possessed by their predecessors, and this can result in the new justices seeking to modify existing doctrines or introduce new doctrines more consistent with their values. Fourth, sitting justices have sometimes undergone dramatic changes in their views regarding freedom of expression as they have gained experience on the Court, and consequently they may modify or even reject their earlier adherence to particular doctrines. Fifth, new developments in technology can force the justices to modify old tests or to develop new tests. For example, the Court had to take a very different look at freedom of the press when radio and television joined newspapers as major forms of the media. A sixth reason for the ambiguity associated with freedom of expression doctrines is the huge diversity of activities associated with freedom of expression. Freedom of expression cases can involve such diverse activities as violent protests, burning the American flag, hate speech, libel, obscenity, press activities threatening a fair trial, and commercial advertisements. It should not be surprising that many tests are needed to deal with such diverse forms of expression. A seventh reason for the ambiguity and difficulty in understanding freedom of expression doctrines is that the Court has been active in this area longer than any other area of civil rights and liberties, and hence the justices have had the opportunity over time to develop more tests in this area. Finally, in this area, as well as in other areas, the justices are continually trying to improve the quality of constitutional interpretation they provide American society. As Justice O'Connor remarked in a recent freedom of expression case involving a woman who was fined for hanging an antiwar sign in a window of her home during the Gulf War, ". . . reexamination is part of the process by which our rules evolve and improve" (*Ladue v. Gilleo*, 62 L.W. at 4482, 1994).

Our task is to make some sense out of the rather vast and somewhat bewildering array of freedom of expression doctrines that the Court has developed throughout its history. To make this job somewhat more manageable, we will tend to emphasize the most recent doctrinal approaches of the Court, giving relatively less attention to doctrines that were once of central importance but that have become less important with the passage of time. A prime example involves the clear and present danger test, probably the most famous freedom of expression doctrine. Although many texts give substantial emphasis to this test, we will treat it in a relatively cursory manner because the Court has essentially abandoned this test for the past twenty-five years.

Two General Approaches: Balancing and Preferred Freedoms

The Court has tended to treat freedom of expression cases from either of two quite different general approaches, the **balancing approach** and the **preferred freedoms approach.** These are considered approaches rather than tests or doctrines because of their general nature. They involve differing perspectives on the importance of the freedom of expression guarantees. Thus, they do not provide specific guidelines for deciding particular cases in the manner that more specific tests or doctrines do. These approaches are important, however, because they structure the nature of the more precise tests. The balancing approach typically provides relatively low protection for claimed violations of freedom of expression, while the preferred freedoms approach gives strong support to claims of government interference with expression.

The basic idea associated with the balancing approach is that the First Amendment freedom of expression guarantees should not be given any special weight or importance in comparison with the government's competing interests in regulating expression. Thus, the literal image that the balancing approach suggests is that the Court uses a finely tuned scale to weigh an individual's First Amendment claims against the government's interests to see which side has the better argument. In actual practice, however, the balancing approach tends to favor strongly the government because the Court will typically find the broader interests of the government to outweigh those of the single person.

In recent years, the Rehnquist Court has tended to apply the **rational basis** or **minimal scrutiny test** as a specific doctrine embodying the philosophy of the balancing approach. Under this test in a freedom of expression case, the government simply has to show that it is pursuing a legitimate objective through means that bear some type of rational relationship to this objective. This is an easy standard for the government to meet. Justice White used the balancing approach and the rational basis test recently in his majority opinion in *Burdick v. Takushi* (1992). In this case involving a challenge to Hawaii's ban on write-in voting, a man wanted to write Donald Duck's name on the ballot to protest against all the candidates running for office. Arguing that this ban did not impose a severe restriction on First Amendment rights, White stated that ". . .when a state election law provision imposes only 'reasonable, nondiscriminatory restrictions' upon the First . . . Amendment rights of voters, . . . the State's . . . regulatory interests are generally sufficient to justify the restrictions" (504 U.S. at 434).

The balancing approach was used primarily by the Court in the years prior to 1937 before the Court's "switch-in-time-that-saved-nine," the period when the Court changed the focus of its agenda from protecting businesses from government economic regulation to protecting individuals from government violations of their civil rights and liberties. Although the balancing approach was dominant only before 1937, the approach continues to be used by the Court. Indeed, from 1946 to 1953, the Vinson Court frequently embraced the balancing approach to many First Amendment cases, especially those involving national security issues. Furthermore, the Rehnquist Court continues today to use the rational basis or minimal scrutiny test in several types of cases. These cases include ones involving students, prisoners, and government employees; speech-plus-conduct; nonpublic forums; radio and television broadcasting; content-neutral government regulations; conflicts with other constitutional rights; and challenges of vagueness and overbreadth. We will discuss each of these in greater detail in the next section of this chapter.

In contrast to the balancing approach, the preferred freedoms approach gives high priority to the guarantees of the First Amendment, viewing them as critically important to a democratic society and therefore deserving of special protection by the Court. The Court has developed a variety of specific tests for applying the preferred freedoms approach, but the Rehnquist Court has increasingly used the **strict scrutiny** or **compelling government interest test** to provide strong protection in First Amendment freedom of expression cases. Under the strict scrutiny approach, the Court requires the government to defend the challenged law or action by showing that a compelling government interest exists and that this interest is being achieved by narrowly tailored means. This places an extraordinary burden of proof on the government, although in some cases the government has been successful in convincing the Court that it meets this heavy burden.

Why has the Court accepted the preferred freedoms approach to interpreting the freedom of expression guarantees of the First Amendment? The primary reason involves the importance of freedom of expression for a democratic society. American democracy is based on the belief that ultimate authority resides with the people and that this authority is expressed through the ballot box in a representative democracy. Voting decisions must be made by an informed citizenry, and freedom of expression is critically important if voters are to make intelligent and informed decisions in elections. A second reason involves the belief that individual self-fulfillment and self-realization require freedom of expression; government censorship and regulation of expression deprive the individual of the opportunity to hear and evaluate the full range of ideas that influence personal growth and development. Implicit in both of these reasons for adherence to the preferred freedoms approach is a commitment to the idea that individual citizens will have the capacity to judge good ideas from bad ideas and to separate truth from falsehood.

The Court applies the strict scrutiny approach in a wide variety of cases, which will be discussed in greater detail in the next section of this chapter. These cases include ones involving pure speech, content-based government regulations, viewpoint-based government regulations, traditional or designated public forums, and censorship.

Before turning our attention to more specific freedom of expression doctrines, we need to acknowledge some ambiguities associated with the balancing and preferred freedoms approaches. First, even when the justices use the preferred freedoms approach, a certain type of balancing process does occur. Under the strict scrutiny test, for example, the government's interests may be sufficiently compelling to outweigh the individual's First Amendment protections. The only doctrine that avoids the necessity of balancing is an **absolutist** orientation, which maintains that the government can never interfere with First Amendment guarantees. Although Justices Black and Douglas frequently advanced this argument, the Court has never had a majority of justices who have adhered to the absolutist position.

Second, the Rehnquist Court has increasingly been using an **intermediate scrutiny** or **important government objective test** in freedom of expression cases. This level of protection falls between the low level provided by the minimum scrutiny test and the high protection associated with the strict scrutiny test. Under this intermediate scrutiny test, the government must be pursuing an "important government objective" through means that are "closely related" to these interests. We view this test as coming within the preferred freedoms approach because of the heightened protection it provides, but clearly this test provides less support for freedom of expression claims than the strict scrutiny test. Example areas where intermediate scrutiny is used include symbolic speech, commercial speech, and cable broadcasting.

Finally, some scholars do not view the approaches of balancing and preferred freedoms as useful concepts because of their general and somewhat ambiguous nature. Many other experts do find these concepts helpful, however, (e.g., Shapiro 1966; Witt 1988; and Abraham and Perry 1994), and we believe that they are valid and insightful.

Specific Freedom of Expression Doctrines

Helpful as these two general approaches are in understanding the Court's decision-making process in freedom of expression cases, they provide only limited guidance in resolving specific issues and cases before the Court. Under what circumstances does the Court use the balancing approach, and when is the preferred freedoms approach utilized? If the preferred freedoms approach is appropriate, then what specific criteria can be applied to determine if an individual's First Amendment rights have been violated?

Although these questions cannot be answered in any easy manner, the Court's general approach and more specific tests in freedom of expression cases seem to be influenced by two general considerations: (1) various characteristics associated with the *specific case* before the Court, and (2) various characteristics of the *specific government law or action* that is alleged to violate the individual's constitutional rights. Each of these general considerations needs to be discussed in some detail.

Case Characteristics

The general approach as well as the specific test used by the Court in any case is influenced strongly by the unique characteristics associated with each freedom of expression case that comes before it. These characteristics include *what* was expressed, *who* brings the case, *where* it was expressed, and *how* it was expressed.

What. One important concern for the Court involves the question of *what* was said or printed by the person alleging a First Amendment violation. This concern focuses on the content of the expression. Two categories of expression are important here: expression lacking social value and expression of a commercial nature.

The question of whether expression has **social value** has long been a fundamental concern to the Court in freedom of expression cases because the Court has continuously taken the position that the First Amendment applies only to expression that has social value. The Court's classic statement in this area came in *Chaplinsky v. New Hampshire* (1942). In this case, Chaplinsky was arrested under a law prohibiting the use in public of offensive or derisive language—fighting words—for calling a police officer a "God-damned racketeer" and a "damned Fascist." The Court unanimously upheld his conviction, providing the following dicta regarding expression lacking in social value:

> *There are certain well-defined and narrowly limited classes of speech, the prevention and punishment of which has never been thought to raise any constitutional questions. These include the lewd and the obscene, the profane, the libelous, and the insulting or "fighting words"—those which by their very utterance inflict injury or tend to incite an immediate breach of the peace. It has been observed that such utterances are no essential part of any exposition of ideas, and are of such slight social value as a step to truth that any benefit that may be derived from them is clearly outweighed by the social interests in law and order (315 U.S. at 574).*

Thus, a simple dichotomy seems to exist based on the idea of the social value of expression. Expression involving obscenity, profanity, libel, and fighting words is so lacking in social value as to be beyond constitutional protection; government can freely regulate in each of these areas. Expression that has social value, however, comes within the protection of the First Amendment and can be regulated only if government has a compelling interest in doing so. This dichotomy turns out to be anything but simple, however.

Two categories of expression identified in *Chaplinsky*, profanity and fighting words, have not generated much litigation before the Court and appear to be protected under the First Amendment. Profanity is so widespread in American popular culture that government prosecution is almost unthinkable except in regard to the broadcast media. The Court has also heard few cases involving expression labeled as fighting words, and the Court has not been willing to find even such language as "Fuck the Draft" in *Cohen v. California* (1971) to constitute fighting words. The Court continues to maintain that fighting words are beyond constitutional protection, but it is not clear what types of language would fit this category.

Libel has been a major concern of the Court since the landmark case of *New York Times Co. v. Sullivan* (1964), our case study that began this chapter. As we saw in our analysis of this landmark case, the Court significantly increased the protection of the press in regard to libel suits involving public figures by requiring not only the traditional criteria of falseness and defamation but also actual malice in order for a publisher to be found guilty of libel. This new test certainly embodied the preferred position approach to the First Amendment. As we will discover later in this chapter, the Court subsequently extended the preferred freedoms approach to libel regarding public figures as well as private persons. In the 1967 companion cases of *Associated Press v. Walker* and *Curtis Publishing Company v. Butts*, the Court extended the criteria of the *Sullivan* case—falseness, defamation, and actual malice—to public figures, those individuals who are well-known to the general public but do not hold public office, such as movie stars and famous athletes. In *Gertz v. Robert Welch*

(1973), the Burger Court further extended protection for the press against libel suits by private persons by requiring that falseness, defamation, and actual malice had to be established in order for a jury to award punitive damages; compensatory damages could be awarded, however, if falseness, defamation, and negligence were established.

Obscenity is the fourth type of expression identified in *Chaplinsky* as lacking in social value. As we observed in our introduction to the section of the book dealing with the First Amendment, the topic of obscenity is so complex and has generated so many cases before the Court that we are devoting an entire chapter to it (Chapter 8). We can note here, however, that the Court has defined obscenity in such a way that substantial constitutional protection is given to sexual expression.

In addition to paying close attention to what is being communicated in regard to social value, the Court also makes an important distinction in regard to what is being said in terms of commercial versus noncommercial speech. **Commercial speech** refers to communication involving the advertising of products, services, and companies. For most of the Court's history, commercial speech was considered to be outside the protection of the First Amendment. In *Bigelow v. Virginia* (1975), however, the Burger Court recognized commercial speech as falling within the parameters of the First Amendment because such expression involved the communication of ideas that were of public importance. The Court did not view commercial expression as deserving the same level of protection as other forms of expression, however, because commercial expression did not deal with ideas that were central to the effective functioning of a democratic society. Thus, the Court in *Central Hudson Gas and Electric Corporation v. Public Service Commission of New York* (1980) set forth a four-part test that involved an intermediate level of scrutiny between the rational basis and strict scrutiny tests. The **Central Hudson test** requires that (1) an advertisement must concern lawful activity and not be misleading, (2) the challenged government regulation must involve a substantial government interest, (3) the regulation must directly advance this government interest, and (4) the regulation must be no more extensive than necessary.

Who. In regard to *who* brings a case before the Court, at least three groups have historically been given less protection by the justices: government employees, students, and prisoners. As mentioned earlier in this section, the Court typically employs a balancing approach with freedom of expression claims by members of any of these groups. The Court only requires the government to establish that it is pursuing a legitimate objective through means that are rationally related to this objective.

In the situation of government employees, the Court has taken the position that the government as employer can exercise substantial control over the expression activities of its employees in order to promote the efficient performance of government services. The test used by the Court in this type of case is to rule against government control of expression only if the speech is on a matter of public concern and if the employee's interests outweigh any injury the speech could cause to the government's interests. Not surprisingly, government employees have fared poorly under this test, as seen most recently in *Waters v. Churchill* (1994), where the Court upheld the firing of a nurse in a public hospital who was terminated for criticizing hospital procedures.

Students have also been given only minimal protection by the Court, especially in recent decades. The Warren Court did rule in favor of students who were expelled for wearing black armbands in protest of the Vietnam War, stating: "It can hardly be argued that . . . students . . . shed their constitutional rights to freedom of speech or expression at the schoolhouse gate" (*Tinker v. Des Moines School District*, 393 U.S. at 509, 1969). Nonetheless, the Burger and Rehnquist Courts have been decidedly less generous in their protection of the freedom of expression rights of school children, taking a highly deferential balancing approach on the basis that a substantial amount of discretion should be given to school authorities in their efforts to maintain order and to promote an effective learning environment in the public schools. Thus, the Burger Court upheld the punishment of Matthew Fraser for making suggestive comments in a school assembly (*Bethel School District v. Fraser*, 1986), and the Rehnquist Court upheld a school official's censorship of articles scheduled to be published in a school newspaper in *Hazelwood v. Kuhlmeier* (1988).

Finally, the Court has used a minimal scrutiny balancing approach in cases involving prisoners. The rationale here is that correctional officials must be given substantial leeway to regulate freedom of expression because of heightened concerns about order and security in prisons. Thus, for example, prison officials can examine mail being sent to a prisoner (*Thornburgh v. Abbott*, 1989).

Where. The type of protection the Court provides to freedom of expression also depends on *where* the expression occurs. The primary issue for the Court in this regard has involved government-owned property. The Court has advanced the argument that the government, like a private property owner, has a substantial degree of authority to regulate activities on its own property. At the same time, the government is limited by the requirements of the First Amendment to observe citizens' rights to freedom of speech, press, and assembly. Given these conflicting interests, the Court has developed over time a **forum-based approach** for determining the appropriate restrictions which the government can establish regarding the exercise of freedom of expression on its property. The Court has recognized three types of public forums. The first is the **traditional public forum,** which involves such places as streets, parks, and sidewalks. A second category is the **designated public forum,** an area which the government specifically indicates can be used for the expression of ideas. An example of a designated public forum might be a particular room or facility at a public university which has been designated as an open forum to all students. The third category is simply all other remaining public property that is not a traditional or designated public forum.

If either a traditional or designated public forum is involved in a case, then the Court requires the government to meet the standards of strict scrutiny, i.e., to establish that a compelling government interest exists in regulating expression and that the means being utilized are narrowly tailored to achieve this compelling objective. Justice Kennedy has offered an excellent analysis of the logic behind applying strict scrutiny in cases involving traditional or designated public forums:

> *The liberties protected by our doctrine derive from the Assembly, as well as the Speech and Press Clause of the First Amendment, and are essential to a functioning democracy. Public forums are of necessity the locus of discussion for public issues, as well as protest against arbitrary government action. At the heart of our jurisprudence lies the principle that in a free nation citizens must have the right to gather and speak with other persons in public places. The recognition that certain government-owned property is a public forum provides open notice to citizens that their freedoms may be exercised there without fear of a censorial government, adding tangible reinforcement to the idea that we are a free people* (*International Society for Krishna Consciousness v. Lee*, 505 U.S. at 695, 1992).

If, however, the case involves government interference with freedom of expression on public property that is not a traditional or designated public forum, then the government needs only to meet the standards of minimal scrutiny, establishing that a rational basis exists for its action and that the regulation is viewpoint-neutral.

How. In our examination of specific case characteristics associated with the individual who is claiming a violation of his or her freedom of expression liberties, we have thus far examined three relevant queries that the Court may raise: *what* was expressed, *who* expressed it, and *where* it was expressed. Now we turn to the question of *how* it was expressed. This question is somewhat broader than the previous three questions because it refers to the general context of the communication; as Justice Brennan noted in the 1989 flag burning case of *Texas v. Johnson*, this type of concern requires ". . .careful consideration of the actual circumstances surrounding such expression. . ." (491 U.S. at 409). Also, Holmes's dissenting opinion in *Gitlow v. New York* seemed to make the same point: "The only difference between the expression of an opinion and an incitement in the narrower sense is the speaker's enthusiasm for the result" (286 U.S. at 660, 1925). This can be made more specific, however, by identifying three specific concerns raised by the Court in regard to the question of how a person engages in expressing ideas. The first concern recognizes that speech can occur in a variety of ways: **pure speech**, **symbolic speech,** and **speech-plus-conduct.** The second concern is whether the expression involves **incitement,** that is, directly encouraging others to immediate, lawless action. Yet a third concern is whether the expression is communicated through the means of broadcasting. We will now examine each of these areas of First Amendment law in greater detail.

In ruling on the First Amendment liberties of freedom of speech and assembly, the Court has recognized that one important circumstance in regard to how people express themselves is whether the communication involves pure speech, symbolic speech, or speech-plus-conduct. Although the Court has not found it possible to make completely clear distinctions among these three forms of expression, the justices have nonetheless recognized that differences do exist and that the differences justify differing levels of protection by the Court.

Pure speech involves direct oral communication. Because this form of expression poses little inherent threat to societal interests and presumably involves the type of debate over government that is at the core of the First Amendment, the Court will generally apply the strict scrutiny standard when pure speech is involved.

In contrast to pure speech is speech-plus-conduct, which typically involves not only speech but also assembly in the form of protests, demonstrations, marches, and other types of large-group activities. Speech-plus-conduct involves inherently greater threats to public order and safety because of the substantial numbers of people involved. The Court therefore allows the government substantially greater regulatory power over this type of expression. The general rule is that reasonable, content-neutral time, place, and manner regulations can be used by the government in regard to speech-plus-conduct. Thus, this form of expression tends to be treated from the balancing approach rather than the preferred freedoms orientation.

Falling between pure speech and speech-plus-conduct is symbolic speech, which involves using symbols of some type to communicate ideas. Burning the American flag is a dramatic example of symbolic speech. Although symbolic speech does not create the inherent concerns with public order and safety associated with speech-plus-conduct, symbolic speech activities are frequently highly emotional and potentially disruptive. The Court has had substantial difficulty in setting an appropriate standard by which to analyze symbolic speech, perhaps because such a wide variety of activities can be included in this category of expression. Despite some ambiguity, however, the Court seems to be committed to an intermediate level of scrutiny in regard to symbolic speech. This approach had its origins in the Vietnam War era case of *United States v. O'Brien* (1968), in which the Warren Court upheld the constitutionality of a federal law that prohibited burning or otherwise destroying one's draft card. The **O'Brien test** requires the government to meet four requirements: (1) the challenged regulation must be within the constitutional power of the government; (2) the law must further an important or substantial government interest; (3) this important government interest must be unrelated to the suppression of freedom of expression; and (4) the interference with First Amendment rights must be no greater than is needed to further the state's important interests. In applying this test in the *O'Brien* case, the Court ruled that the federal law prohibiting the burning of a draft card was not unconstitutional because the law met all four requirements of the test.

The second type of contextual concern that has confronted the Court in regard to how freedom of expression is exercised involves incitement, speech that leads directly to lawless action. This has been an area of freedom of expression in which numerous cases have arisen, typically involving seditious speech, for example, speech directed toward disobeying government laws, harming public officials, or even engaging in revolutionary activity. The difficult problem for the Court in this area has been to determine when government officials can interfere with such expression when illegal, violent activities are possible but have not yet occurred. The Court has used three different tests in this area. The **bad tendency test** involves a balancing approach in which the government's interests usually prevail over freedom of expression claims because the government can interfere with expression that has even a tendency to create threats to safety and security. The **incitement test** embodies a preferred freedoms approach, protecting expression from government interference until a direct incitement to imminent lawless action exists. The **clear and present danger test** is more difficult to classify in terms of the level of protection it provides for freedom of expression; it was originally intended to embody a preferred freedoms approach, but over time it came to be applied in a wide variety of confusing, and indeed contradictory, ways. Each of these tests will be discussed in greater detail in the next section of this chapter, but we can note that the Court has embraced the incitement test since the 1969 case of *Brandenburg v. Ohio*.

A third concern arising from the question of how expression is communicated involves broadcasting, communicating through the means of radio, television, or other forms of electronic media. This is an area of twentieth-century law because these technologies are of relatively recent development. Government regulation emerged quickly once these technologies developed because of two factors: (1) only a limited number of frequencies existed, and these had to be carefully allocated in order for any stations to be heard, and (2) these media came into the homes and could be heard and seen easily by young children. In a series of cases, the Court ruled that the broadcast media were distinctively different than the print media, and therefore the government needed to meet only minimal scrutiny standards in regard to radio and television (cf. *Red Lion Broadcasting v. FCC*, 1969). Recently, however, the Court has distinguished cable television from regular television, thus requiring the government to meet the higher level of intermediate scrutiny in regulating the cable industry (see *Turner Broadcasting System v. FCC*, 1994).

Characteristics of the Government Activity Being Challenged

Thus far in this section we have been examining tests associated with the *characteristics of the case* being brought by an individual against the government. Additional doctrines have been developed by the Court based upon the *characteristics of the government law or action* being challenged as violative of freedom of expression rights. We turn our attention now to a discussion of these doctrines. The relevant characteristics which we will examine include whether the government is engaged in censorship, whether the government is involved in regulating the content of expression, whether the government law is too vague, and whether a government law is too broad.

Censorship. **Censorship** is the strongest charge that can be leveled against the government in regard to violations of freedom of expression. Censorship, or **prior restraint,** involves laws or actions by the government that interfere with freedom of expression by regulating or prohibiting the expression *before it occurs.* Censorship has always been strongly opposed by the Court. One reason for this strong opposition involves historic practices that led to the inclusion of freedom of the press in the Bill of Rights. Both English authorities as well as American colonial officials attempted to exercise censorship over press activities, but they were met with strong resistance. Thus, when freedom of the press was written into the First Amendment, the Framers intended the guarantee to prevent official censorship. In addition to these historic reasons for opposing censorship, the justices have advanced more contemporary arguments against censorship. Most fundamentally, the Court has viewed the free flow of information as being critical to American democracy and an unrestricted press as essential to the exchanges of ideas that inform political debate. The history of modern totalitarian societies also reveals that censorship is a critical method of control for authoritarian governments. Thus, the Court has taken the position that abuses of freedom of the press must be dealt with through methods of subsequent punishment rather than through prior restraint.

Despite the clear consensus that has long existed within the Supreme Court over the impermissibility of government censorship, the justices have not developed a clear test to apply in censorship cases. The Court has come close to developing an absolutist approach, but most justices have acknowledged that certain circumstances could conceivably arise that would justify government censorship. The most famous case in recent history involving censorship was *New York Times Company v. United States* (1971), in which the United States government tried to prevent the publication of *The Pentagon Papers*, a history of American involvement in the Vietnam War that revealed that government officials had deceived the American public for decades about the extent of American involvement in the conflict. The Court ruled 6-3 against the government's attempt to prevent publication of the papers, but could not agree upon a controlling standard. In rejecting the government position in a brief per curiam statement, the justices said, "Any system of prior restraints of expression comes to this Court bearing a heavy presumption against its constitutional validity" (403 U.S. at 714). Although the justices could not agree upon a proper standard, consensus did exist that only the most extraordinary circumstances would justify government censorship; in Justice Stewart's words, the government would have to establish clearly that publication would cause the government "direct, immediate, and irreparable damage" (403 U.S. at 730).

Regulation of Content. In addition to censorship, another type of government activity that raises immediate concern for the Court involves laws or actions that affect the *content* of expression. The Court will generally use a balancing approach if the challenged government regulation is content-neutral, that is, it does not regulate expression based upon the content of the message being communicated. If the government is involved in content-based regulation, however, then the Court will apply the preferred freedoms approach using strict scrutiny. Justice O'Connor explained the justification for this concern with content-based regulations in *City of*

Ladue v. Gilleo (1994): ". . .content-based speech restrictions are especially likely to be improper attempts to value some forms of speech over others, or are particularly susceptible to being used by the government to distort public debate" (62 L.W. at 4482). *Boos v. Barry* (1988) illustrates these ideas. This case involved a challenge to a District of Columbia law that prohibited signs or displays critical of a foreign government from being displayed within five hundred feet of embassies. The Court viewed this legislation as being content-based, thus requiring strict scrutiny analysis. The majority held that regardless of whether the government had a compelling interest in this matter, the means chosen were not narrowly tailored to achieve the government's interests, and hence the law was unconstitutional.

Overbreadth and Vagueness. The final category of characteristics associated with the challenged government policy involves the closely related but distinct concepts of **overbreadth** and **vagueness.** Overbreadth refers to overly broad government regulations of expression that go beyond the legitimate authority of the government to regulate expression and infringe improperly upon constitutionally protected expression. A recent case involving an overbreadth challenge before the Supreme Court was *Forsyth County, Georgia v. The Nationalist Movement* (1992). The Nationalist Movement, a white supremacist group, wanted to hold a demonstration opposing the federal holiday recognizing the birthday of Martin Luther King, Jr. Forsyth County had an ordinance requiring the issuance of a permit for such a demonstration and allowed a county administrator to set the permit fee based upon the amount of hostility that would be created. In his majority opinion, Justice Blackmun argued that the ordinance was unconstitutional because it gave overly broad discretion to the administrator in setting the fee.

Vagueness refers to government regulations that are so ambiguous or vague that an individual does not know what expression is being regulated. The danger with vague laws is that they can create self-censorship by a person who chooses not to engage in constitutionally protected expression out of fear of being arrested under the vague law.

The Court has not developed specific tests for determining if particular laws are overly broad or vague. One reason for this is that issues of overbreadth and vagueness historically have arisen out of general concerns with due process and can be applied to all laws, not just laws affecting the First Amendment (Tedford 1985, p. 448). In freedom of expression cases, vagueness and overbreadth challenges are typically threshold or initial questions that an attorney might raise. The trial or appellate court will normally use a balancing approach to deal with these challenges, asking how a rational person would interpret the law. If the judgment is that a rational person would view the law as being either overly broad or so vague that constitutionally protected expression could be suppressed, then the law can be ruled unconstitutional.

The Emerging Three-Level Doctrinal Framework in Freedom of Expression Cases

We can summarize this lengthy discussion of Supreme Court approaches to decision making in freedom of expression cases by developing a table that summarizes much of the previous discussion. Table 7.1 presents the three-level doctrinal framework that seems to have emerged during the Rehnquist Court era.

The rational basis or minimal scrutiny test provides limited protection to individuals claiming First Amendment violations because the government needs only to establish that it is pursuing a legitimate objective through means that are rationally related to this objective. The minimal scrutiny test has been used in a wide variety of

TABLE 7.1: The Rehnquist Court's Three-Level Doctrinal Framework in Freedom of Expression Cases

Test	Rational Basis Test	Important Government Objective Test	Compelling Government Interest Test
Level of Scrutiny	Minimal	Intermediate	Strict
Types of Cases Where Applicable	Students Prisoners Government employees Conflicts with other rights Radio & TV broadcasting Nonpublic forums Content-neutral regulations Overbreadth Vagueness Speech-plus-conduct	Symbolic speech Commercial speech Cable broadcasting	Pure speech Content-based regulations Viewpoint-based regulations Traditional and designated public forums Censorship
Questions Asked by the Court	(1) Is the government pursuing a legitimate objective? (2) Are the means used by the government rationally related to the legitimate objective?	(1) Is the government pursuing an important objective? (2) Are the means used by the government closely related to the important objective?	(1) Is the government pursuing a compelling interest? (2) Are the means used by the government narrowly tailored to achieve the compelling interest?

cases: students, prisoners, government employees, conflicts with other constitutional rights, speech-plus-conduct, radio and television broadcasting, nonpublic forums, content-neutral regulations, overbreadth challenges, and vagueness challenges.

A heightened level of protection for the individual is provided by the intermediate scrutiny or important government objective test. In these cases involving symbolic speech, commercial speech, and cable broadcasting, the government must typically show that it is pursuing an important objective through means that are closely related to this objective.

The highest level of protection for the individual is provided by the strict scrutiny or compelling government interest test. This test is typically used in cases involving pure speech, content-based regulations, viewpoint-based regulations, traditional or designated public forums, and censorship. The government has a very difficult time prevailing in these cases because it must be shown that the government is pursuing compelling interests through narrowly tailored means.

Implicit in this framework is a fourth category of cases, those beyond the reach of the First Amendment. Thus, the Court has taken the position that obscenity, libel, fighting words, and incitement simply do not deserve any type of constitutional protection. The government is free to regulate these forms of expression and to punish those who engage in them.

A concluding word of caution is necessary regarding the doctrinal framework in Table 7.1. Although the justices of the Rehnquist Court have made frequent references to this three-level doctrinal system in their freedom of expression cases, this table is our construction rather than the Court's. Furthermore, the table oversimplifies a complex reality, and the Court continues to modify and develop this framework each term. Thus, the table should be treated as a tentative attempt to make sense out of the Court's complex freedom of expression jurisprudence.

The Supreme Court and Freedom of Expression: A Quantitative Analysis

Having completed an examination of the most important doctrines that the Court uses in freedom of expression cases, we can now undertake a quantitative analysis of the Supreme Court's expression cases during the eras of the Warren, Burger, and Rehnquist Courts. Quantitative techniques are employed throughout the book to aid us in analyzing the effects of membership change on the policies of the Supreme Court. Although quantitative techniques have important limitations, they can provide insights that are difficult to obtain through the more traditional analysis of the Court's written opinions.

Our quantitative analysis in this chapter will include all freedom of expression cases except for the area of obscenity. In undertaking our quantitative analysis of freedom of expression cases in this chapter, we will not be able to break the cases into separate categories because the United States Supreme Court Judicial Database does not classify freedom of expression cases into conventional groupings. For example, cases involving symbolic speech, speech-plus-conduct, censorship, the conflict between a free press and a fair trial, and broadcasting are all grouped together in a "miscellaneous" category. Despite this limitation, however, the quantitative analysis can provide us with important insights regarding Supreme Court decision making patterns in the important area of freedom of expression.

We will begin by comparing the three Court eras, and then we will examine each period in greater detail. Throughout the analysis, we define a liberal decision as one in which the Court rules in favor of the individual bringing a claim that the government unconstitutionally infringed upon a First Amendment freedom of expression liberty. Conversely, a conservative decision will be considered one in which the Court rules in favor of the government.

In comparing the voting records of the Warren, Burger, and Rehnquist Courts, we might expect to see sharp differences across the three eras. The Warren Court era is widely regarded as the most liberal period in Supreme Court history, whereas the Burger and Rehnquist Courts have frequently been viewed as far more conservative in regard to freedom of expression issues (e.g., Zion 1987; Halperin 1987; Kairys 1993). Other scholars, however, have argued that the Burger and Rehnquist Courts' freedom of expression decisions can best be characterized as involving continuity rather than conservative change (e.g., Dorsen and Gura 1983; Emerson 1983; and Friedelbaum 1994). Which view is most accurate?

The data in Table 7.2 provide some interesting insights into this question. The Warren Court was indeed strongly liberal, deciding 70 percent of its 127 cases in favor of the individual. With the changing personnel from the Warren Court era to the Burger Court period, the Court did become more conservative but not dramatically so. As can be seen in Table 7.2, the Burger Court justices decided a majority (53 percent) of their freedom of expression cases liberally. Furthermore, the Rehnquist Court has been more liberal than the Burger Court in regard to freedom of

TABLE 7.2: Liberal/Conservative Outcomes of Freedom of Expression Cases for the Warren, Burger, and Rehnquist Courts, 1953-94 Terms

	Outcomes		
Court Era	Liberal	Conservative	Totals
Warren Court, 1953-68 Terms	70% (89)	30% (38)	127
Burger Court, 1969-85 Terms	53% (78)	47% (69)	147
Rehnquist Court, 1986-94 Terms	57% (35)	43% (26)	61
Totals	60% (202)	40% (133)	335

expression, deciding 57 percent of these cases against the government. Thus, our preliminary conclusion based on these aggregate data is that the Burger and Rehnquist Courts have not engaged in a conservative counterrevolution in the area of freedom of expression.

We need to pursue the quantitative analysis further, however, because aggregate data can hide important differences and trends. Thus, we need to examine each of the three eras in greater detail, paying specific attention to the question of whether changes in the Court's personnel have been associated with shifts in the ideological direction of the Court's freedom of expression decisions. We begin by examining the Warren Court. Table 7.3 compares the Warren Court of the fifties with the Warren Court of the sixties. The table reveals that the Court became increasingly liberal over time. In the period from the 1953 term through the 1961 term, the Warren Court decided 63 percent of its freedom of expression cases in favor of the individual. The Court's liberal output was substantially higher during the sixties, with 78 percent of the decisions being decided liberally.

Changes in the Court's personnel played an important role in the substantial increase in liberal outcomes in the period from the 1962 to the 1968 terms. Table 7.4 provides insightful data regarding the voting records of individual justices and the importance of changes in the Court's membership. When Warren became chief justice in 1953, the Court was deeply divided across the ideological spectrum. Douglas and Black occupied one polar extreme. Their absolutist orientation to the First Amendment meant that they voted liberally in nearly every case. Read and Minton occupied the conservative end of the spectrum, with each voting liberally in only 8 percent of the Warren Court's freedom of expression cases. Warren frequently

TABLE 7.3: Liberal/Conservative Outcomes of Freedom of Expression Cases During the Warren Court Era, 1953-68 Terms

	Outcomes		
Court Era	Liberal	Conservative	Totals
1953-61 Terms	63% (42)	37% (25)	67
1962-68 Terms	78% (47)	22% (13)	60
Totals	70% (89)	30% (38)	127

joined Douglas and Black, but the remaining justices—Frankfurter, Whittaker, Burton, and Clark—were moderately conservative.

The Court's membership gradually changed during the fifties and early sixties, and each change brought to the Court a new member who was more liberal than his predecessor. Nine justices in Table 7.4 have liberal scores of 55 percent or higher, and all of these justices served on the Court in the sixties. From the 1962 term onward, the Court had at least five justices who were strongly committed to liberal freedom of expression values. Douglas, Black, Brennan, and Warren all served on the Court throughout the sixties, and they had liberal scores of 86 percent or higher. Goldberg joined the Court in 1962 and was replaced by Fortas in 1965; both justices were strongly supportive of freedom of expression claims, with Goldberg voting 87 percent liberally and Fortas favoring a liberal outcome in 79 percent of the cases. When Marshall joined the Court in 1967, the liberal coalition grew to six members. This was the pinnacle of liberal dominance of the Court in regard to freedom of expression.

Important as membership change is in explaining changes in the Court's decisional patterns, we need to guard against the simplistic idea that all changes in Supreme Court policies can be explained by changes in the Court's membership. Reality is much more complex. Societal changes and accompanying shifts in public opinion can have an effect on Court policies. American society experienced profound changes in the fifties and sixties, and the members of the Court were affected by these changes. In addition, different issues are continually presented to the Court. Various legal constraints also exist on the justices, and these may mitigate against changes in Court policy even if the Court's membership changes. We will see evidence of all of these factors as we examine specific areas of freedom of expression policy in the remainder of this chapter.

TABLE 7.4: Liberal/Conservative Voting Records of the Justices of the Warren Court in Freedom of Expression Cases, 1953-68 Terms

	Outcomes	
Justices	Liberal	Conservative
Douglas (1953-68)	98% (123)	2% (2)
Marshall (1967-68)	92% (12)	8% (1)
Black (1953-68)	90% (113)	10% (12)
Brennan (1956-68)	88% (99)	12% (14)
Goldberg (1962-65)	87% (20)	13% (3)
Warren (1953-68)	86% (106)	14% (18)
Fortas (1965-68)	79% (26)	21% (7)
Stewart (1958-68)	58% (56)	42% (40)
White (1962-68)	55% (31)	45% (25)
Frankfurter (1953-62)	48% (30)	52% (32)
Harlan (1955-68)	46% (55)	54% (65)
Whittaker (1957-62)	38% (17)	62% (28)
Burton (1953-58)	37% (10)	63% (17)
Clark (1953-67)	35% (38)	65% (70)
Jackson (1953-54)	33% (1)	67% (2)
Reed (1953-57)	8% (1)	92% (12)
Minton (1953-56)	8% (1)	92% (12)

Did further changes in the Court's personnel between the Warren Court and the Burger Court periods have an effect on the ideological outcomes of freedom of expression cases? The answer suggested by the data in Table 7.5 seems to be "yes, somewhat." The Burger Court was less liberal in freedom of expression cases than was the Warren Court. As can be seen in Table 7.5, the Burger Court justices reached liberal outcomes in 53 percent of their freedom of expression cases compared to a 70 percent liberal voting record of the Warren Court (see Table 7.2). The data in Table 7.5 suggest that changes in the Court's membership influenced the direction of the Court's decision making. The addition of Burger in 1969 and Blackmun in 1970 did not produce dramatic changes in the Court's liberal support in freedom of expression cases; during the 1969 and 1970 terms the Court voted liberally in 65 percent of these cases. The Court did shift rather sharply in a conservative direction, however, when Rehnquist and Powell joined the Court in the 1971 term. As can be seen in Table 7.5, the Burger Court's support for individuals claiming freedom of expression violations by the government declined to 46 percent for the terms from 1971 through 1975. This was the lowest level of First Amendment support during the Burger Court years. The Court was slightly more liberal during the periods when Stevens joined the Court in 1976 and O'Connor joined in 1981.

The impact of the appointment of conservative justices by Republican presidents can also be seen in Table 7.6, which shows the voting patterns of the individual justices of the Burger Court in freedom of expression cases. As we saw previously, the Warren Court was dominated in the last half of the sixties by six liberal justices: Warren, Fortas, Black, Douglas, Brennan, and Marshall. Only Brennan and Marshall served on the Court throughout the Burger Court years. The initial change from the Warren Court to the Burger Court involved the respective chief justices. Burger was far more conservative than his predecessor, Warren, whom he replaced in 1969; Burger voted liberally in only 36 percent of the freedom of expression cases compared to Warren's record of 86 percent liberal voting. The next year Blackmun replaced Fortas, further weakening the liberal bloc that had dominated the latter years of the Warren Court. Fortas had supported liberal outcomes in 79 percent of the freedom of expression cases compared to Blackmun's overall record of 51 percent liberalism, and Blackmun was much more conservative in his initial years on the Court.

Although the addition of Burger and Blackmun moved the Court in a somewhat less liberal direction in the 1969 and 1970 terms, it was the appointments of Rehnquist and Powell to replace Harlan and Black, respectively, that had the biggest impact on the Court. Rehnquist was the most conservative justice on the Burger Court in freedom of expression cases, voting conservatively 79 percent of the time.

TABLE 7.5: Liberal/Conservative Outcomes of the Burger Court Freedom of Expression Cases, 1969-85 Terms

	Outcomes		
Periods	Liberal	Conservative	Totals
1969-70 Terms	65% (17)	35% (9)	26
1971-75 Terms	46% (16)	54% (19)	35
1976-80 Terms	51% (22)	49% (21)	43
1981-85 Terms	53% (23)	47% (20)	43
Totals	53% (78)	47% (69)	147

TABLE 7.6: Liberal/Conservative Voting Records of the Justices of the Burger Court in Freedom of Expression Cases, 1969-85 Terms

	Outcomes	
Justices	Liberal	Conservative
Douglas (1969-75)	92% (55)	8% (5)
Marshall (1969-85)	81% (114)	19% (27)
Brennan (1969-85)	81% (116)	19% (27)
Black (1969-71)	73% (19)	27% (7)
Stevens (1975-85)	63% (48)	37% (28)
Stewart (1969-81)	61% (62)	39% (40)
Powell (1972-85)	52% (57)	48% (52)
Blackmun (1970-85)	51% (69)	49% (67)
O'Connor (1981-85)	42% (18)	58% (25)
White (1969-85)	42% (62)	58% (85)
Harlan (1969-71)	38% (10)	62% (16)
Burger (1969-85)	36% (52)	64% (93)
Rehnquist (1972-85)	21% (24)	79% (90)

Rehnquist's predecessor Harlan voted conservatively in 54 percent of his freedom of expression cases. Powell's replacement of Black also had an impact. Although Powell did vote liberally in 52 percent of the freedom of speech and press cases, Black supported the liberal position in 90 percent of the cases.

Richard Nixon thus had a significant impact on Supreme Court decision making in freedom of expression cases. Each of his four new appointments to the Court voted significantly more conservatively than the justices they replaced. Indeed, by replacing Warren, Fortas, and Black, Nixon was able to reduce dramatically the six-person liberal bloc that had controlled the Court through much of the sixties.

Once again, however, we need to exercise caution regarding our conclusions about the degree of impact of membership change on the Court's decision-making patterns in freedom of expression cases. First, the Burger Court can hardly be characterized as radically conservative; its overall record from the 1969 through the 1985 terms shows a 53 percent liberal voting pattern. In addition, the 1975 retirement of the Court's most liberal justice, Douglas, did not result in the Court becoming more conservative in freedom of expression cases even though his successor, Stevens, was less liberal than Douglas. Similarly, O'Connor's replacement of Stewart in 1981 did not have the effect of making the Court's outcome patterns more conservative in First Amendment freedom of speech and press cases. A final cautionary point involves recognizing the inherent limitations of quantitative analysis of Supreme Court decision making, for numbers alone do not allow us to consider such important factors as the relative importance of cases and the Court's treatment of existing precedents and doctrines.

The voting patterns of the Supreme Court during the Rehnquist Court era provide support for these cautions regarding the danger of assuming that membership change will produce policy change. As we observed earlier in Table 7.2, the efforts of Presidents Reagan and Bush to appoint more conservative justices to the Court did not result in the Court becoming more conservative in regard to the area of freedom of expression. Indeed, the Rehnquist Court has decided 57 percent of its freedom of expression cases liberally, an increase over the Burger Court's 53 percent

TABLE 7.7: Liberal/Conservative Outcomes of Freedom of Expression Cases for the Rehnquist Court, 1986-94 Terms

	Outcomes		
Court Term	Liberal	Conservative	Totals
1986-87	57% (4)	43% (3)	7
1987-88	70% (7)	30% (3)	10
1988-89	33% (3)	67% (6)	9
1989-90	54% (6)	46% (5)	11
1990-91	50% (2)	50% (2)	4
1991-92	71% (5)	29% (2)	7
1992-93	50% (2)	50% (2)	4
1993-94	50% (2)	50% (2)	4
1994-95	80% (4)	20% (1)	5
Totals	57% (35)	43% (26)	61

and a pattern not dramatically different than the 70 percent liberal record of the Warren Court.

We need to pursue this analysis further, however. The data presented in Table 7.7 cover each of the nine terms of the Rehnquist Court from the 1986–87 term through the 1994–95 term. No clear trend can be seen in the data, but we can certainly reject the idea that the Court has become increasingly conservative over time. Indeed, the most conservative term was in 1988 when the Court decided only 33 percent of the freedom of expression cases liberally, whereas the Court's most liberal term was the most recent one of 1994 when 80 percent of the cases were decided liberally.

The aggregate data thus provide strong evidence that the Supreme Court during the period of the chief justiceship of William Rehnquist has not become strongly conservative in regard to First Amendment freedom of expression issues. Indeed, the Court has been distinctively liberal, exceeding the liberal orientation of the Burger Court. Because these findings are somewhat surprising, we need to examine in detail the individual voting records of the justices of the Rehnquist Court to seek to understand why the Court has been more liberal than we might have expected.

A strong core of liberal justices can be observed from the data in Table 7.8, which shows the individual voting records of the justices of the Rehnquist Court in freedom of expression cases. Nine of the fourteen justices have liberal voting records; three justices—O'Connor, Scalia, and Thomas—have supported liberal outcomes at least 40 percent of the time; and only two justices—White and Rehnquist—have highly conservative records. Three of the leading liberals—Marshall, Brennan, and Blackmun—have retired from the Court; but new Court members Souter, Ginsburg, and Breyer have all established liberal records thus far in freedom of expression cases.

We can gain additional insights into the voting behavior of the Rehnquist Court justices in freedom of expression cases by undertaking bloc voting analysis, which is presented in Table 7.9. (Five justices—Powell, Souter, Thomas, Ginsburg, and Breyer—were omitted from the bloc voting analysis because they participated in less than one-half of the cases.) Two small voting blocs emerge. Marshall, Brennan, and Blackmun form a three-person liberal bloc with an interagreement score of 88 percent agreement, while Rehnquist and White constitute a two-person conservative bloc, also with an 88 percent agreement score. These results are certainly not

TABLE 7.8: Liberal/Conservative Voting Records of the Justices of the Rehnquist Court in Freedom of Expression Cases, 1986-94 Terms

	Outcomes	
Justices	Liberal	Conservative
Ginsburg	89% (8)	11% (1)
Marshall	88% (36)	12% (5)
Brennan	86% (32)	14% (5)
Breyer	80% (4)	20% (1)
Souter	75% (18)	25% (6)
Blackmun	73% (41)	27% (15)
Stevens	67% (41)	33% (20)
Kennedy	58% (28)	42% (20)
Powell	57% (4)	43% (3)
O'Connor	46% (28)	54% (33)
Thomas	44% (8)	56% (10)
Scalia	42% (25)	58% (35)
White	31% (16)	69% (36)
Rehnquist	24% (14)	76% (45)

TABLE 7.9: Bloc Voting Analysis of the Rehnquist Court Freedom of Expression Cases, 1986-94 Terms (numbers are percentages)

	MA	BR	BL	ST	KE	OC	SC	WH	RE
Marshall	—	100	83	68	61	44	45	41	31
Brennan	100	—	81	70	62	41	50	46	31
Blackmun	83	81	—	73	77	52	55	54	50
Stevens	68	70	73	—	75	62	53	63	56
Kennedy	61	62	77	75	—	75	77	69	66
O'Connor	44	41	52	62	75	—	72	65	71
Scalia	45	50	55	53	77	72	—	76	78
White	41	46	54	63	69	65	76	—	88
Rehnquist	31	31	50	56	66	71	78	88	—

Court mean = 63
Sprague Criterion = 81
Liberal bloc: Marshall, Brennan, Blackmun = 88
Conservative bloc: White, Rehnquist = 88

surprising because they reflect closely the individual voting records we observed in Table 7.8. It is important to note, however, that four of the five justices in these voting blocs are no longer on the Court. The liberal bloc has disappeared completely with the resignations of Brennan, Marshall, and Blackmun; White's retirement leaves Rehnquist as the lone strongly conservative justice.

We can conclude the quantitative analysis with a cautionary note regarding our findings about the liberal directions of the Rehnquist Court in freedom of expression cases. The Court has been surprisingly liberal in this area since 1986, and year-by-year trend analysis suggests this moderately liberal orientation will continue. Three of the Court's leading liberals—Marshall, Brennan, and Blackmun—have resigned, however, and thus the Court could move in different directions in the future. Several of the Court's newest members—Souter, Ginsburg, and Breyer—appear to have strong liberal commitments concerning freedom of expression issues, but it is too soon to offer this assessment with great confidence.

Analyzing the Rehnquist Court's Freedom of Expression Cases Through the Doctrinal Framework

Our quantitative analysis in the previous section has led us to conclude that the Rehnquist Court has not engaged in a conservative counterrevolution in the area of freedom of expression, but we are well aware of the limitations associated with quantitative techniques of analysis. We emphasize throughout this book that the quantitative analysis of Supreme Court decision making has both strengths and weaknesses. The examination of voting data allows us to offer generalizations and to make comparisons based upon reliable, systematic data, but these data fail to capture many important dimensions of Supreme Court decision making. We therefore have developed an alternative method of systematically analyzing the decisions of the Rehnquist Court by employing our framework for the doctrinal analysis of cases, and we now turn to this framework to examine the Rehnquist Court's freedom of expression cases from this alternative perspective. Based on this framework, the Rehnquist Court can only be considered to be engaged in a conservative counterrevolution if a significant number of cases are placed in the categories of major importance, majority opinion, and either the conservative modification of existing precedent or the creation of a new conservative precedent.

The information in Table 7.10 indicates clearly that the Rehnquist Court has not engaged in a conservative counterrevolution in the area of freedom of expression. In the thirteen cases classified as being of major importance and being decided by majority opinions, eight were liberal interpretations of existing precedent and five were conservative interpretations of existing precedents; none of these cases involved the modification of existing precedent or the creation of a new precedent. Interestingly, sixty of the sixty-one freedom of expression cases of the Rehnquist Court were classified as involving the application of existing precedent.

The only exception to this pattern was *Thornburgh v. Abbott* (1989), a case classified as a conservative modification of existing precedent, and this was classified as a case of minor importance. *Thornburgh* involved the constitutionality of a federal prison regulation that authorized prison officials to refuse to forward to prisoners incoming publications that were determined to be detrimental to prison security needs. In *Procunier v. Martinez* (1974) the Court set forth a heightened scrutiny standard regarding censorship of personal correspondence sent by prisoners to noninmates. In subsequent cases involving prisoners' mail, the Court ruled that a lower standard of reasonableness should be applied to incoming—as opposed to outgoing—mail. In *Thornburgh* a Court majority approved the federal prison regulation under a reasonableness standard and stated explicitly that *Martinez* was overruled insofar as it could be interpreted to apply to incoming mail. This was the only case, however, in which the author of the controlling opinion explicitly acknowledged either the modification or overturning of a Court precedent in the area of freedom of expression.

1986-94 Terms

Major or Minor Importance	Majority or Plurality Opinion	Treatment of Precedent: Creation of New Liberal Precedent	Liberal Modification of Existing Precedent	Liberal Interpretation of Existing Precedent	Conservative Interpretation of Existing Precedent	Conservative Modification of Existing Precedent	Creation of New Conservative Precedent
Major	Majority			Rankin v. McPherson (1987) Hustler v. Falwel (1988) Texas v. Johnso (1989) U.S. v. Eichman (1990) RAV v. St. Paul (1992) Madsen v. Center (1994) Hurley v. Irish-American (1995) McIntyre v. Ohio (1995)	Hazelwood v. Kuhlmeier (1988) Frisby v. Schultz (1988) Milkovich v. Journal (1990) Wisconsin v. Mitchell (1993) Florida Bar v. Went For It (1995)		
Major	Plurality						
Minor	Majority			Tashjian v. Republicans (1986) FEC v. Citizens for Life (1986) Turner v. Safley (1987) Houston v. Hill (1987) Commissioners v. Jews (1987) Meyer v. Grant (1988) Riley v. Federation (1988) Eu v. Democratic Comm. (1989) Florida Star v. BJF (1989) Butterworth v. Smith (1990) Keller v. State Bar (1990) Rutan v. Republican Party (1990) Gentile v. State Bar (1991) Simon & Schuster v. Board (1991) Norman v. Reed (1992) Dawson v. Delaware (1992) Forsyth Co. v. Movement (1992) Lee v. Krishnas (1992) Cincinnati v. Discovery (1993) Edenfield v. Fane (1993) Ladue v. Gilleo (1994) Ibanez v. Board (1994) Turner v. FCC (1994) Rubin v. Coors (1995) U.S. v. NTEU (1995)	Munro v. Socialist Party (1986) Meese v. Keene (1987) San Francisco Arts v. USOC (1987) Dallas v. Stanglin (1989) Ward v. Rock Against (1989) Harte-Hanks v. Connaughton (1989) Trustees v. Fox (1989) U of Penn v. EEOC (1990) FTC v. Trial Lawyers (1990) Austin v. Chamber (1990) Leathers v. Medlock (1991) Masson v. New Yorker (1991) Cohen v. Cowles Media (1991) Burdick v. Takushi (1992)	Thornburgh v. Abbott (1989)	
Minor	Plurality			Boos v. Barry (1988) Shapero v. Bar (1988) Lakewood v. Plain Dealer (1988) FW/PBS v. Dallas (1990) Peel v. Commission (1990)	U.S. v. Kokinda (1990) Burson v. Freeman (1992) Krishnas v. Lee (1992) U.S. v. Edge Broadcasting (1993) Waters v. Churchill (1994)		

Freedom of Speech

Having used both quantitative methods of analysis and our doctrinal framework to examine major trends in Supreme Court decision making, we can now engage in a more detailed study of the Court's major decisions in regard to the freedoms of speech and press. We turn initially to the subject of free speech, and we will examine the following topics: national security, symbolic speech, offensive speech and hate speech, speech-plus-conduct, and commercial speech. Then we will turn our attention to freedom of the press, examining the topics of press censorship, libel, the conflict between a free press and a fair trial, and broadcasting. As we examine each of these topics, we will follow the same approach we use throughout the book, organizing our discussion around the historical evolution of Supreme Court policy with special attention to the question of whether changes in the Court's personnel have been associated with changes in the Court's freedom of expression policies. Thus, each topic will be examined historically by looking at the pre-Warren Court era, the Warren Court period, the Burger Court years, and finally the current period of the Rehnquist Court.

National Security Cases

The Court did not issue any major freedom of expression cases during the late eighteenth century and the entire nineteenth century. Until the Civil War, the Court's primary attention was directed toward issues within the main body of the Constitution. Reflecting the new nation's struggle to make its experiment in democracy work effectively, the Court was called upon primarily to decide questions of government powers, such as the relationship of the states to the national government, the powers of the various branches of government, and the relationships among the various branches. Then, for many decades after the Civil War, the Court focused its attention on economic questions.

Events associated with World War I forced the Court to interpret the freedom of expression guarantees of the First Amendment. The country's long history of isolationism ended with American entry into World War I, and the country struggled with its new role in a world suddenly perceived to be threatening and hostile. In addition to the challenge presented by Germany and its allies, the United States also seemed directly threatened by the success of the Bolshevik Revolution in Russia, which introduced a communist system of government whose ideology was dedicated to the destruction of capitalist economic systems and their governments. In this environment, both the federal and state governments passed espionage and sedition laws that placed significant restrictions upon freedom of expression. Congress enacted the Espionage Act in 1917 and the Sedition Act in 1918. Most state governments also passed sedition laws during this period of time, which reinforced criminal anarchy laws that some states had passed at the beginning of the century in response to President McKinley's assassination by a self-proclaimed anarchist. Substantial variation existed among these state and federal laws, but they all shared the common characteristic of allowing government authorities substantial discretion to arrest persons for expressing criticism and opposition to the government.

The numerous prosecutions brought to the Court under these laws forced the justices for the first time to confront the meaning of the broad clauses of the First Amendment. What is the meaning of the words "Congress shall make no law . . . abridging the freedom of speech, or of the press. . . ?" Are these guarantees absolute, as the language suggests? If these liberties are not absolute, under what circumstances can the government limit them? What legal principles should guide the Court and the country in interpreting the guarantees of freedom of expression?

The Court's initial answer in a series of cases between 1919 and 1927 was a decidedly conservative one. The justices strongly rejected the idea that these guarantees were absolute. Instead the high court adopted a balancing approach in these cases, typically applying the bad tendency test in which the government's interests prevailed easily over the First Amendment claims of individuals arrested for advocating radical political ideas. A brief review of both the federal and state cases decided by the Court will illustrate these developments.

The Court was primarily concerned with freedom of expression cases arising under federal legislation, the 1918 Sedition Act and the 1917 Espionage Act. The initial case was *Schenck v. United States* (1919). Schenck, a socialist, was arrested and convicted under the Espionage Act for mailing fifteen thousand brochures condemning America's involvement in World War I and urging young American males to resist the draft. The Court upheld Schenck's arrest and conviction in a unanimous opinion by Justice Holmes. Holmes's opinion was a curious blend of the clear and present danger test and the bad tendency test. On the one hand, Holmes wrote, "The question in every case is whether the words are used in such circumstances and are of such a nature as to create a clear and present danger that they will bring about the substantive evils that Congress has a right to prevent" (249 U.S. at 51). This language would seem to require a conclusion that Schenck's conviction would be overturned because no evidence had been introduced regarding the success of his leaflets. But Holmes strongly undercut the effect of the clear and present danger test. He admitted that in "ordinary times" Schenck's expression would have been protected by the First Amendment, but his arrest and conviction did not occur in ordinary times. "When a nation is at war many things that might be said in time of peace are such a hindrance to its efforts that their utterance will not be endured as long as men fight, and that no court could regard them as protected by any constitutional right" (249 U.S. at 52). Holmes then concluded his opinion by setting forth the bad tendency standard: "If the act (speaking, or circulating a paper), its tendency and intent with which it is done, are the same, we perceive no ground for saying that success alone warrants making the act a crime" (249 U.S. at 52).

Schenck v. United States

249 U.S. 47, 39 S.Ct. 247, 63 L.Ed. 470 (1919)

■ Charles Schenck, secretary of the Socialist Party, was arrested for violating the Espionage Act of 1917. He was tried and convicted in the District Court of the United States for the Eastern District of Pennsylvania. The Espionage Act was passed in response to the communist scare and the fear of foreigners and aliens amid the Bolshevik Revolution in Russia. Schenck had printed and mailed fifteen thousand leaflets to men subject to the draft. In these documents, he encouraged opposition to American involvement in World War I. Schenck appealed his conviction to the United States Supreme Court, asserting that this particular act violated his First Amendment rights.

This case is significant because it was the first to challenge the constitutionality of the Espionage Act. Moreover, it was the Supreme Court's first case in a series that attempted to define tests, or standards, for interpreting the meaning of the freedom of expression guarantees of the First Amendment. In reading Justice Oliver Wendell Holmes's majority opinion for the Court, consider the following: (1) Did Schenck's distribution of the leaflets involve a "clear and present danger" to the war effort and the security of the country? (2) Did Holmes's opinion establish a strong or weak basis for subsequent cases involving freedom of expression guarantees? (3) Is it necessary to place stronger restrictions on personal liberty in times of war or crisis?

Vote:

The Court voted unanimously that Schenck's constitutional rights were not violated.

Justice Holmes delivered the opinion of the Court.

* * *

This is an indictment in three counts. The first charges a conspiracy to violate the Espionage Act of June 15, 1917, by causing and attempting to cause insubordination, etc., in the military and naval forces of the United States, and to obstruct the recruiting and enlistment service of the United States, when the United States was at war with the German Empire; to wit, that the defendant willfully conspired to have printed and circulated to men who had been called and accepted for military service a document set forth and alleged to be calculated to cause such insubordination and obstruction. The count alleges overt acts in pursuance of the conspiracy, ending in the distribution of the document set forth. The second count alleges a conspiracy to commit an offense against the United States; to wit, to use the mails for the transmission of matter declared to be nonmailable, to wit, the above-mentioned document, with an averment of the same overt acts. The third count charges an unlawful use of the mails for the transmission of the same matter and otherwise as above. The defendants were found guilty on all counts. * * *

* * *

The document in question, upon its first printed side, recited the 1st section of the 13th Amendment, said that the idea embodied in it was violated by the Conscription Act, and that a conscript is little better than a convict. In impassioned language it intimated that conscription was despotism in its worst form and a monstrous wrong against humanity, in the interest of Wall Street's chosen few. It said: "Do not submit to intimidation;" but in form at least confined itself to peaceful measures, such as a petition for the repeal of the act. The other and later printed side of the sheet was headed, "Assert Your Rights." It stated reasons for alleging that anyone violated the Constitution when he refused to recognize "your right to assert your opposition to the draft," and went on: "If you do not assert and support your rights, you are helping to deny or disparage rights which it is the solemn duty of all citizens and residents of the United States to retain." It described the arguments on the other side as coming from cunning politicians and a mercenary capitalist press, and even silent consent to the Conscription Law as helping to support an infamous conspiracy. It denied the power to send our citizens away to foreign shores to shoot up the people of other lands, and added that words could not express the condemnation such cold-blooded ruthlessness deserves, etc., etc., winding up, "You must do your share to maintain, support, and uphold the rights of the people of this country." Of course the document would not have been sent unless it had been intended to have some effect, and we do not see what effect it could be expected to have upon persons subject to the draft except to influence them to obstruct the carrying of it out. The defendants do not deny that the jury might find against them on this point.

But it is said, suppose that that was the tendency of this circular, it is protected by the 1st Amendment to the Constitution. Two of the strongest expressions are said to be quoted respectively from well-known public men. It well may be that the prohibition of laws abridging the freedom of speech is not confined to previous restraints, although to prevent them may have been the main purpose. . . . * * * We admit that in many places and in ordinary times the defendants, in saying all that was said in the circular, would have been within their constitutional rights. But the character of every act depends upon the circumstances in which it is done.

The most stringent protection of free speech would not protect a man in falsely shouting fire in a theater, and causing a panic. It does not even protect a man from an injunction against uttering words that may have all the effect of force. The question in every case is whether the words used are used in such circumstances and are of such a nature as to create a clear and present danger that they will bring about the substantive evils that Congress has a right to prevent. It is a question of proximity and degree. When a nation is at war many things that might be said in time of peace are such a hindrance to its effort that their utterance will not be endured so long as men fight, and that no court could regard them as protected by any constitutional right. It seems to be admitted that if an actual obstruction of the recruiting service were proved, liability for words that produced that effect might be enforced. The Statute of 1917, in § 4, punishes conspiracies to obstruct as well as actual obstruction. If the act (speaking, or circulating a paper), its tendency and the intent with which it is done, are the same, we perceive no ground for saying that success alone warrants making the act a crime. * * *

* * *

Judgments affirmed.

The Court heard five other major federal sedition and espionage cases in 1919 and 1920, affirming convictions in each case against claims that the First Amendment was being violated. In *Frohwerk v. United States* (1919) the Court unanimously upheld the conviction of a person who had written articles for a German-language newspaper critical of American involvement in World War I. The Court also unanimously affirmed the conviction of Eugene Debs, a prominent leader of the Socialist Party, for giving a speech advocating the beliefs of socialism and opposing United States intervention into the war. Similarly, in *Abrams v. United States* (1919), *Schafer v. United States* (1920), and *Pierce v. United States* (1920), the Court affirmed federal convictions under the espionage and sedition acts, using the bad tendency test to support its decisions.

The Court also heard important national security cases in the twenties involving state sedition laws, and the justices decided these state cases in a similar fashion to the earlier federal cases, voting to uphold arrests and convictions under the bad tendency doctrine. *Gitlow v. New York* (1925) was the first state case decided by the Court. Benjamin Gitlow, a member of the Socialist Party, was a political activist who was elected to the New York legislature in 1918 and was later to become the Communist Workers' Party presidential candidate in the 1928 election. He was arrested and convicted in 1919 under the New York Criminal Anarchy Act of 1902 for publishing a pamphlet entitled the *Left Wing Manifesto*, which called for action by the proletariat class to overthrow the ruling bourgeoisie class of American society. In an opinion by Justice Sanford, the Court acknowledged that no evidence existed that the publication had led to any type of violence. This was not required to sustain Gitlow's conviction, however. The Court rejected the idea that the government needed to wait to act until a clear and present danger existed; rather, government could act if expression had a tendency to threaten society.

The Court reaffirmed the *Gitlow* decision in *Whitney v. California* (1927), a case involving Anita Whitney who was the niece of a former justice of the Supreme Court, Stephen J. Field. She was arrested and convicted under a California law for participating in a convention establishing the Communist Labor Party of California. She had argued in favor of committing the party to seek change through electoral means, but the convention rejected this position and instead adopted a resolution in favor of revolutionary class struggle. The Court upheld her conviction, again using a balancing approach and the bad tendency test.

Justices Holmes and Brandeis were frequently in dissent in these national security cases of the twenties. They rejected the use of the bad tendency test, arguing instead that the clear and present danger test—interpreted liberally—should guide the Court's decision making.

The constitutional revolution of 1937 had a major impact on many areas of civil rights and liberties, including freedom of expression where the Court began to champion the preferred freedoms approach. This new philosophy had an important effect in national security cases, where the Court rejected the bad tendency test of the twenties and embraced the ideas associated with the clear and present danger test that Holmes and Brandeis had championed in dissent. In *DeJonge v. Oregon* (1937) the Court unanimously reversed DeJonge's conviction for holding a meeting to discuss the ideas of the Communist Party. Neither his membership in an organization advocating violent overthrow of the government nor his discussion of ideas associated with the communist ideology justified the government's arrest and conviction. The Court decided a second case in 1937 involving national security, *Herndon v. Lowry*. Herndon was an African American member of the Communist Party who had attempted to recruit African Americans in Atlanta, Georgia. In a 5-4 decision, the Court overturned his arrest and conviction. The Court majority rejected the bad tendency test advocated by the dissenting justices. In his majority opinion, Justice Roberts advanced a standard closer to the clear and present danger test: "The power of a state to abridge freedom of speech and of assembly is the exception rather than the rule and penalizing even of utterances of a defined character must find its justification in a reasonable apprehension of danger to organized government" (301 U.S. at 258).

The Court's commitment to the preferred freedoms approach in national security cases was short-lived, however. Immediately following World War II, the tenuous anti-German alliance that had existed during the war between the Soviet Union and the United States quickly transformed into an intense Cold War between these two ideological rivals. Both federal and state governments enacted legislation to confront the perceived threat to American values and security. These laws took a variety of forms, including statutes banning membership in groups advocating violence and requiring government employees to take loyalty oaths. Despite their differences, these laws had an important commonality—limitations on citizens' ability to express their viewpoints freely. Numerous cases reached the Court in the pre-Warren era, and the justices, reflecting dominant public opinion, upheld most government prosecutions under the balancing approach and the bad tendency test.

Numerous cases arose from the various federal and state loyalty programs that were written into law in the late forties and early fifties. Federal government programs extended to all civilian employees of the executive branch, who could be dismissed if "reasonable doubt" existed regarding a person's loyalty to the government. Although the Court never ruled directly on the constitutionality of the programs, the justices consistently upheld various activities under these programs, beginning with *Joint Anti-Fascist Refugee Committee v. McGrath* (1951). State loyalty programs were widespread, involving not only government workers but also other public employees, including teachers. Although some of the more liberal justices, especially Douglas and Black, dissented frequently, the Vinson Court typically sustained the constitutionality of state loyalty programs and the prosecutions that occurred under them.

The most famous national security case of the pre-Warren Court era involved the 1940 Smith Act. This Act was directed against the Communist Party and made it a criminal act to organize or join any group advocating violent revolution against the government. The constitutionality of this law was challenged in *Dennis v. United States* (1951). Eugene Dennis and ten other leaders of the Communist Party of the United States were arrested and convicted under the Smith Act, which they argued violated their First Amendment liberties. The Court upheld their convictions in a 6-2 decision, but the justices were sharply divided in terms of their reasoning. Chief Justice Vinson wrote the controlling opinion for a four-person plurality. Although mentioning the clear and present danger test, Vinson's reasoning embraced the philosophy of the bad tendency doctrine.

Justices Black and Douglas wrote impassioned dissents. Black viewed the case as ". . .a virulent form of prior censorship of speech and press, which I believe the First Amendment forbids" (341 U.S. at 579). Douglas argued strongly for the preferred freedoms approach and a strict application of the clear and present danger test.

DENNIS V. UNITED STATES

341 U.S. 494, 71 S. Ct. 857, 95 L.Ed. 1137 (1951)

■ In 1948, Eugene Dennis and ten other members of the American Communist Party were arrested for violation of the conspiracy provisions of the Smith Act of 1940. Dennis and the other party members were found guilty in the United States District Court for the Southern District of New York on a charge of conspiracy to promote the overthrow of the government through force or violent means. The defendants appealed their convictions to the United States Court of Appeals for the Second Circuit, but the convictions were upheld in an opinion by Judge Learned Hand that emphasized the "gravity of the evil" as an important consideration within the clear and present danger test. The attorneys for Dennis and the other party members appealed this Court of Appeals holding to the United States Supreme Court by arguing that the Smith Act violated the party members' First Amendment rights.

This case is significant because the Court used the clear and present danger test in a manner that interpreted the First Amendment freedom of expression guarantees very narrowly. As you read the plurality and dissenting opinions in this case, consider the following issues: (1) To what extent does this case reveal the impact of political events and public opinion on the decisions of the justices? (2) What does this case reveal about the utility of the clear and present danger test as a guideline for the justices in freedom of expression cases? (3) Is the "gravity of the evil" principle a defensible one in analyzing freedom of expressions cases? (4) Black concluded his opinion by recognizing that the Court's opinion was consistent with current public opinion, but he went on to state: "There is hope, however, that in calmer times, when present pressures, passions and fears subside, this or some later Court will restore the First Amendment liberties to the high preferred place where they belong in a free society." Have subsequent developments proven Black correct?

VOTE:

6 justices found the law to be constitutional (Burton, Frankfurter, Jackson, Minton, Reed, Vinson).

2 justices found the law to be unconstitutional (Black and Douglas).

Chief Justice Vinson announced the judgment of the Court and an opinion in which Justice Reed, Justice Burton, and Justice Minton join.

* * *

* * * We granted certiorari limited to the following two questions: (1) Whether either § 2 or § 3 of the Smith Act, inherently and applied in the instant case, violates the First Amendment and other provisions of the Bill of Rights; (2) whether either § 2 or § 3 of the Act, inherently or as construed and applied in the instant case, violates the First and Fifth Amendments because of indefiniteness.

* * *

The obvious purpose of the statute is to protect existing Government, not from change by peaceable, lawful and constitutional means, but from change by violence, revolution and terrorism. That it is within the *power* of the Congress to protect the Government of the United States from armed rebellion is a proposition which requires little discussion. Whatever theoretical merit there may be to the argument that there is a "right" to rebellion against dictatorial governments is without force where the existing structure of the government provides for peaceful and orderly change. We reject any principle of governmental helplessness in the face of preparation for revolution, which principle, carried to its logical conclusion, must lead to anarchy. No one could conceive that it is not within the power of Congress to prohibit acts intended to overthrow the Government by force and violence. The question with which we are concerned here is not whether Congress has such *power*, but whether the *means* which it has employed conflict with the First and Fifth Amendments to the Constitution.

One of the bases for the contention that the means which Congress has employed are invalid takes the form of an attack on the face of the statute on the grounds that by its terms it prohibits academic discussion of the merits of Marxism-Leninism, that it stifles ideas and is contrary to all concepts of a free speech and a free press. * * *

The very language of the Smith Act negates the interpretation which petitioners would have us impose on that Act. It is directed at advocacy, not discussion. Thus, the trial judge properly charged the jury that they could not convict if they found that petitioners did "no more than pursue peaceful studies and discussions or teaching and advocacy in the realm of ideas." He further charged that it was not unlawful "to conduct in an American college and university a course explaining the philosophical theories set forth in the books which have been placed in evidence." Such a charge is in strict accord with the statutory language, and illustrates the meaning to be placed on those words. Congress did not intend to eradicate the free discussion of political theories, to destroy the traditional rights of Americans to discuss and evaluate ideas without fear of governmental sanction. Rather Congress was concerned with the very kind of activity in which the evidence showed these petitioners engaged.

But although the statute is not directed at the hypothetical cases which petitioners have conjured, its application in this case has resulted in convictions for the teaching and advocacy of the overthrow of the Government by force and violence, which, even though coupled with the intent to accomplish that overthrow, contains an element of speech. For this reason, we must pay special heed to the demands of the First Amendment marking out the boundaries of speech.

* * *

The rule we deduce from these cases is that where an offense is specified by a statute in non-speech or nonpress terms, a conviction relying upon speech or press as evidence of violation may be sustained only when the speech or publication created a "clear and present danger" of attempting or accomplishing the prohibited crime, e.g., interference with enlistment. The dissents, we repeat, in emphasizing the value of speech, were addressed to the argument of the sufficiency of the evidence.

* * *

In this case we are squarely presented with the application of the "clear and present danger" test, and must decide what that phrase imports. We first note that many of the cases in which this Court has reversed convictions by use of this or similar tests have been based on the fact that the interest which the State was attempting to protect was itself too insubstantial to warrant restriction of speech. * * * Overthrow of the Government by force and violence is certainly a substantial enough interest for the Government to limit speech. Indeed, this is the ultimate value of any society, for if a society cannot protect its very structure from armed internal attack, it must follow that no subordinate value can be protected. If, then, this interest may be protected, the literal problem which is presented is what has been meant by the use of the phrase "clear and present danger" of the utterances bringing about the evil within the power of Congress to punish.

Obviously, the words cannot mean that before the Government may act, it must wait until the putsch is about to be executed, the plans have been laid and the signal is awaited. If Government is aware that a group aiming at its overthrow is attempting to indoctrinate its members and to commit them to a course whereby they will strike when the leaders feel the circumstances permit, action by the Government is required. The argument that there is no need for Government to concern itself, for Government is strong, it possesses ample powers to put down a rebellion, it may defeat the revolution with ease needs no answer. For that is not the question. Certainly an attempt to overthrow the Government by force, even though doomed from the outset because of inadequate numbers or power of the revolutionists, is a sufficient evil for Congress to prevent. The damage which such attempts create both physically and politically to a nation makes it impossible to measure the validity in terms of the probability of success, or the immediacy of a successful attempt. In the instant case the trial judge charged the jury that they could not convict unless they found that petitioners intended to overthrow the Government "as speedily as circumstances would permit." This does not mean, and could not properly mean, that they would not strike until there was certainty of success. What was meant was that the revolutionists would strike when they thought the time was ripe. We must therefore reject the contention that success or probability of success is the criterion.

* * *

Chief Judge Learned Hand, writing for the majority below, interpreted the phrase as follows: "In each case [courts] must ask whether the gravity of the 'evil,' discounted by its improbability, justifies such invasion of free speech as is necessary to avoid this danger." We adopt this statement of the rule. As articulated by Chief Judge Hand, it is as succinct and inclusive as any other we might devise at this time. It takes into consideration those factors which we deem relevant, and relates their significances. More we cannot expect from words.

* * * This analysis disposes of the contention that a conspiracy to advocate, as distinguished from the advocacy itself, cannot be constitutionally restrained, because it comprises only the preparation. It is the existence of the conspiracy which creates the danger. If the ingredients of the reaction are present, we cannot bind the Government to wait until the catalyst is added.

* * *

The question in this case is whether the statute which the legislature has enacted may be constitutionally applied. In other words, the Court must examine judicially the application of the statute to the particular situation, to ascertain if the Constitution prohibits the conviction. We hold that the statute may be applied where there is a "clear and present danger" of the substantive evil which the legislature had the right to prevent. Bearing, as it does, the marks of a "question of law," the issue is properly one for the judge to decide.

There remains to be discussed the question of vagueness—whether the statute as we have interpreted it is too vague, not sufficiently advising those who would speak of the limitations upon their activity. It is urged that such vagueness contravenes the First and Fifth Amendments. This argument is particularly nonpersuasive when presented by petitioners, who, the jury found, intended to overthrow the Government as speedily as circumstances would permit. * * *

We agree that the standard as defined is not a neat, mathematical formulary. Like all verbalizations it is subject to criticism on the score of indefiniteness. But petitioners themselves contend that the verbalization "clear and present danger" is the proper standard. We see no difference from the standpoint of vagueness, whether the standard of "clear and present danger" is one contained in haec verba within the statute, or whether it is the judicial measure of constitutional applicability. We have shown the indeterminate standard the phrase necessarily connotes. We do not think we have rendered that standard any more indefinite by our attempt to sum up the factors which are included within its scope. We think it well serves to indicate to those who would advocate constitutionally prohibited conduct that there is a line beyond which they may not go—a line which they, in full knowledge of what they intend and the circumstances in which their activity takes place, will well appreciate and understand. * * *

* * *

We hold that §§ 2 (a) (1), (2) (a) (3) and 3 of the Smith Act, do not inherently, or as construed or applied in the instant case, violate the First Amendment and other provisions of the Bill of Rights, or the First and Fifth Amendments because of indefiniteness. Petitioners intended to overthrow the Government of the United States as speedily as the circumstances would permit. Their conspiracy to organize the Communist Party and to teach and advocate the overthrow of the Government of the United States by force and violence created a "clear and present danger" of an attempt to overthrow the Government by force and violence. They were properly and constitutionally convicted for violation of the Smith Act. The judgments of conviction are

Affirmed.

Justice Frankfurter, concurring in affirmance of the judgment (omitted).

Justice Jackson, concurring (omitted).

Justice Black dissenting.

* * *

At the outset I want to emphasize what the crime involved in this case is, and what it is not. These petitioners were not charged with an attempt to overthrow the Government. They were not charged with overt acts of any kind designed to overthrow the Government. They were not even charged with saying anything or writing anything designed to overthrow the Government. The charge was that they agreed to assemble and to talk and publish certain ideas at a later date: The indictment is that they conspired to organize the Communist Party and to use speech or newspapers and other publications in the future to teach and advocate the forcible overthrow of the Government. No matter how it is worded, this is a virulent form of prior censorship of speech and press, which I believe the First Amendment forbids. I would hold § 3 of the Smith Act authorizing this prior restraint unconstitutional on its face and as applied.

. . .[T]he other opinions in this case show that the only way to affirm these convictions is to repudiate directly or indirectly the established "clear and present danger" rule. This the Court does in a way which greatly restricts the protections afforded by the First Amendment. The opinions for affirmance indicate that the chief reason for jettisoning the rule is the expressed fear that advocacy of Communist doctrine endangers the safety of the Republic. Undoubtedly, a governmental policy of unfettered communication of ideas does entail dangers. To the Founders of this Nation, however, the benefits derived from free expression were worth the risk. They embodied this philosophy in the First Amendment's command that Congress "shall make no law abridging. . .the freedom of speech, or of the press. . . ." I have always believed that the First Amendment is the keystone of our Government, that the freedoms it guarantees provide the best insurance against destruction of all freedom. At least as to speech in the realm of public matters, I believe that the "clear and present danger" test does not "mark the furthermost constitutional boundaries of protected expression" but does "no more than recognize a minimum compulsion of the Bill of Rights."

So long as this Court exercises the power of judicial review of legislation, I cannot agree that the First Amendment permits us to sustain laws suppressing freedom of speech and press on the basis of Congress' or our own notions of mere "reasonableness." Such a doctrine waters down the First Amendment so that it amounts to little more than an admonition to Congress. The Amendment as so construed is not likely to protect any but those "safe" or orthodox views which rarely need its protection. * * *

Public opinion being what it now is, few will protest the conviction of these Communist petitioners. There is hope, however, that in calmer times, when present pressures, passions and fears subside, this or some later Court will restore the First Amendment liberties to the high preferred place where they belong in a free society.

Justice Douglas, dissenting.

If this were a case where those who claimed protection under the First Amendment were teaching the techniques of sabotage, the assassination of the President, the filching of documents from public files, the planting of bombs, the art of street warfare, and the like, I would have no doubts. The freedom to speak is not absolute; the teaching of methods of terror and other seditious conduct should be beyond the pale along with obscenity and immorality. This case was argued as if those were the facts. The argument imported much seditious conduct into the record. That is easy and it has popular appeal, for the activities of Communists in plotting and scheming against the free world are common knowledge. But the fact is that no such evidence was introduced at the trial. There is a statute which makes a seditious conspiracy unlawful. Petitioners, however, were not charged with a "conspiracy to overthrow" the Government. They were charged with a conspiracy to form a party and groups and assemblies of people who teach and advocate the overthrow of our Government by force or violence and with a conspiracy to advocate and teach its overthrow by force and violence. It may well be that indoctrination in the techniques of terror to destroy the Government would be indictable under either statute. But the teaching which is condemned here is of a different character.

* * *

* * * The Act, as construed, requires the element of intent—that those who teach the creed believe in it. The crime then depends not on what is taught but on who the teacher is. That is to make freedom of speech turn not on *what is said*, but on the intent with which it is said. Once we start down that road we enter territory dangerous to the liberties of every citizen.

* * *

Intent, of course, often makes the difference in the law. An act otherwise excusable or carrying minor penalties may grow to an abhorrent thing if the evil intent is present. We deal here, however, not with ordinary acts but with speech, to which the Constitution has given a special sanction.

* * *

Free speech has occupied an exalted position because of the high service it has given our society. Its protection is essential to the very existence of a democracy. * * *

* * *

There comes a time when even speech loses its constitutional immunity. Speech innocuous one year may at another time fan such destructive flames that it must be halted in the interests of the safety of the Republic. That is the meaning of the clear and present danger test. When conditions are so critical that there will be no time to avoid the evil that the speech threatens, it is time to call a halt. Otherwise, free speech which is the strength of the Nation will be the cause of its destruction.

Yet free speech is the rule, not the exception. The restraint to be constitutional must be based on more than fear, on more than passionate opposition against the speech, on more than a revolted dislike for its contents. There must be some immediate injury to society that is likely if speech is allowed. * * *

* * * Free speech—the glory of our system of government—should not be sacrificed on anything less than plain and objective proof of danger that the evil advocated is imminent. On this record no one can say that petitioners and their converts are in such a strategic position as to have even the slightest chance of achieving their aims.

* * *

Our concern should be that we accept no such standard for the United States. Our faith should be that our people will never give support to these advocates of revolution, so long as we remain loyal to the purposes for which our Nation was founded.

The *Dennis* decision was a major precedent for the Warren Court, whose freedom of expression cases primarily concerned various issues of national security. These decisions typically involved government prosecutions of persons belonging to the American Communist Party or supporting their beliefs, thus presenting a possible threat to American security interests. Many of these prosecutions arose under federal acts passed during the 1940s and early 1950s before the beginning of the Warren Court. In addition, numerous congressional committees, especially the House Committee on Un-American Activities, conducted investigations into alleged subversive activities. State governments also became involved in passing laws and undertaking investigations to deal with the perceived threats to American security from communism.

The Warren Court found itself besieged by freedom of expression claims from individuals who argued that their First Amendment rights were being violated by these various laws and investigations. Although the decisions of the Warren Court fluctuated substantially in these national security cases, a distinctive trend can be discerned throughout the fifties and sixties as the Court increasingly ruled against both the federal and state governments. This liberal pattern can be attributed in part to the changing personnel of the Court, but it was also due to a significant degree to changing social conditions and attitudes related to the demise of the Cold War and fears of communism.

Yates v. United States (1957) was an early decision of the Warren Court that signaled a distinct break from the more conservative positions of the Vinson Court in national security cases. *Yates* presented the Court with facts remarkably similar to those of the *Dennis* decision of 1951. The *Yates* case involved Oleta Yates and thirteen other minor officials of the American Communist Party who had been convicted under the Smith Act following the *Dennis* decision. Writing for a six-person majority with only Justice Clark in dissent, Justice Harlan interpreted the Smith Act in a narrow fashion and argued that the First Amendment freedom of expression rights of Yates and her associates had been violated. Harlan stated that the Smith Act's provision making it illegal to organize a group that advocated the violent overthrow of the government applied to the founding of the American Communist Party in 1945, rejecting the government's argument that organizing was an ongoing, continuous process. Furthermore, because Yates and the other defendants were arrested in 1951, the three-year statute of limitations invalidated their indictments in regard to organizing the Communist Party. Most critically for First Amendment purposes, Harlan made a sharp distinction between advocating an abstract doctrine, which was constitutionally protected, and advocating unlawful action, which was not protected. In dissent, Clark argued that the logic of the *Dennis* precedent required upholding the convictions of Yates and the other Communists.

Clark was correct, but the majority implicitly rejected the underlying principles of the *Dennis* decision without formally overturning it. Vinson's opinion in *Dennis* stated that the government did not have to wait for direct and immediate threats, but Harlan in *Yates* rejected this position and argued that the government could limit seditious expression only when there was direct incitement to lawless action.

The *Yates* decision was more evolutionary than revolutionary, however. The Warren Court majority did not explicitly overturn *Dennis*, no new freedom of expression doctrine was introduced, and the Smith Act was not ruled unconstitutional. Nonetheless, a solid majority had signaled that the anti-Communist hysteria of the Cold War had subsided, and government prosecutions under the Smith Act were sharply curtailed.

Important as the *Yates* decision was in terms of marking a shift in the Court's interpretation of security-related cases, the Warren Court did give some important victories to the government. For example, in *Barenblatt v. United States* (1959), a majority of the justices rejected Barenblatt's argument that he could refuse to answer a congressional committee's questions about his political beliefs and associations because they infringed his First Amendment rights. In *Scales v. United States* (1961), the high court upheld a section of the Smith Act that prohibited membership in subversive organizations. A final example of the Warren Court's support of subversive legislation came in *Communist Party of the United States v. Subversives Activities Control Board (SACB)* (1961) in which the justices upheld the McCarren Act, which required the registration of all subversive organizations.

The Warren Court became increasingly supportive of freedom of expression claims in national security cases as new justices joined the Court in the sixties. Goldberg's replacement of Frankfurter in 1962 was an especially important membership shift, and White's appointment to Whittaker's seat in 1962 also added a more liberal voice to the Court. Fortas's replacement of Goldberg in 1965 involved two ideologically similar justices, but the liberal majority of the Warren Court was strengthened even further in 1967 when Marshall was named to replace Clark. The Warren Court dealt the McCarren Act severe blows in *Albertson v. Subversives Activities Control Board* (1965), where the Court ruled that individuals could not be required to register as members of subversive organizations, and in *United States v. Robel* (1967), when the Court ruled 6-2 that the McCarren Act violated the right of political association by denying all members of Communist-affiliated organizations the right to hold jobs in defense-related industries.

Loyalty oath programs also came under attack by the Warren Court in the sixties. For example, in *Elfbrandt v. Russell* (1966) the Court ruled in favor of a Quaker teacher in Arizona who challenged the state's laws that not only required state employees to take a loyalty oath to the United States and to Arizona but also declared that membership in the Communist Party constituted a violation of that oath. A year later in *Keyishian v. Board of Regents of the University of the State of New York* (1967), the Court also found the First Amendment to be violated by a New York law that allowed the board of regents to deny jobs to members of subversive organizations. The Warren Court heard a total of twelve First Amendment cases involving security issues during its last four terms from 1965 to 1968, deciding ten of them in favor of the individual claiming governmental interference with constitutionally protected freedom of expression.

The Court's long, fifty-year struggle with the issue of subversive speech, which had begun with the 1919 *Schenck* case, came to a conclusion in one of the last decisions of the Warren Court, *Brandenburg v. Ohio* (1969). Somewhat ironically, the *Brandenburg* case did not involve a member of the Communist Party but rather a leader of the Ku Klux Klan in southern Ohio. In a per curiam opinion, the Court embraced the incitement test to rule an Ohio law unconstitutional. The Court made no reference to the clear and present danger test, which virtually disappeared from the Court's opinions after *Brandenburg*. Interestingly, however, the Warren Court justices fully embraced the spirit of Justice Holmes's original formulation of the clear and present danger test even as they rejected the actual words "clear and present danger." This phrase apparently had been given too many varying interpretations and had been associated with too many contradictory outcomes to be of use any more to the high court. But the justices of the Warren Court fully embraced the philosophical position of Holmes that seditious speech must be given a high level of protection by the Court, with government interference permissible only when there is a direct incitement to imminent lawless action and the action is likely to occur.

BRANDENBURG V. OHIO

395 U.S. 444, 89 S. Ct. 1827, 23 L.Ed. 2d 430 (1969)

■ Clarence Brandenburg, a Ku Klux Klan leader, spoke at a Klan rally where he verbally attacked African Americans and Jews, declaring that revenge might be sought if the government proceeded to neglect the white race. At the rally, a large cross was burned and many of the group members carried pistols, rifles, and shotguns. A Cincinnati television staff filmed the demonstration and turned the evidence over to prosecutors. Under Ohio's criminal syndicalism law, Brandenburg was arrested and convicted for "advocating . . . violence or unlawful methods of terrorism as a means of accomplishing . . . political reform" and of "assembling with a . . . group or assemblage of persons formed to teach or advocate the doctrines of criminal syndicalism." He was fined $1,000 and sentenced to a maximum of ten years in jail. Brandenburg appealed the Ohio state court decision by challenging the constitutionality of the criminal syndicalism statute under the First and Fourteenth Amendments. The intermediate appellate court of Ohio upheld his conviction, and the Supreme Court of Ohio failed to grant review, citing lack of a constitutional issue. Brandenburg's case was granted review by the United States Supreme Court.

This case is significant because the Court set forth explicit guidelines for deciding cases involving seditious expression. In this case, the Court replaced the clear and present danger test with the incitement test. Consider the following questions as you read the opinions in this case: (1) What are the standards associated with the incitement test? (2) Why did the Court rule in favor of Brandenburg? (3) Why did the Court not explicitly reject the clear and present danger test in the per curiam opinion?

Vote:

The Court voted unanimously that Brandenburg's constitutional rights were violated.

Per Curiam.

The Ohio Criminal Syndicalism Statute was enacted in 1919. From 1917 to 1920, identical or quite similar laws were adopted by 20 States and two territories. * * * In 1927, this Court sustained the constitutionality of California's Criminal Syndicalism Act, the text of which is quite similar to that of the laws in Ohio. *Whitney v. California*. The Court upheld the statute on the ground that, without more, "advocating" violent means to effect political and economic change involves such danger to the security of the State that the State may outlaw it. But *Whitney* has been thoroughly discredited by later decisions. These later decisions have fashioned the principle that the constitutional guarantees of free speech and free press do not permit a State to forbid or proscribe advocacy of the use of force or of law violation except where such advocacy is directed to inciting or producing imminent lawless action and is likely to incite or produce such action. As we said in *Noto v. United States* (1961), "the mere abstract teaching. . .of the moral necessity for a resort to force and violence, is not the same as preparing a group for violent action and steeling it to such action." A statute which fails to draw this distinction impermissibly intrudes upon the freedoms guaranteed by the First and Fourteenth Amendments. It sweeps within its condemnation speech which our Constitution has immunized from governmental control.

Measured by this test, Ohio's Criminal Syndicalism Act cannot be sustained. The Act punishes persons who "advocate or teach the duty, necessity, or propriety" of violence "as a means of accomplishing industrial or political reform"; or who publish or circulate or display any book or paper containing such advocacy; or who "justify" the commission of violent acts "with intent to exemplify, spread or advocate the propriety of the doctrines of criminal syndicalism"; or who "voluntarily assemble" with a group formed "to teach or advocate the doctrines of criminal syndicalism." Neither the indictment nor the trial judge's instructions to the jury in any way refined the statute's bald definition of the crime in terms of mere advocacy not distinguished from incitement to imminent lawless action.

Accordingly, we are here confronted with a statute which, by its own words and as applied, purports to punish mere advocacy and to forbid, on pain of criminal punishment, assembly with others merely to advocate the described type of action. Such a statute falls within the condemnation of the First and Fourteenth Amendments. The contrary teaching of *Whitney v. California* cannot be supported, and that decision is therefore overruled.

Reversed.

Justice Black, concurring.

I agree with the views expressed by Mr. Justice Douglas in his concurring opinion in this case that the "clear and present danger" doctrine should have no place in the interpretation of the First Amendment. * * *

Justice Douglas, concurring.

While I join the opinion of the Court, I desire to enter a caveat.

* * *

* * * I see no place in the regime of the First Amendment for any "clear and present danger" test, whether strict and tight as some would make it, or free-wheeling as the Court in *Dennis* rephrased it.

When one reads the opinions closely and sees when and how the "clear and present danger" test has been applied, great misgivings are aroused. First, the threats were often loud but always puny and made serious only by judges so wedded to the status quo that critical analysis made them nervous. Second, the test was so twisted and perverted in *Dennis* as to make the trial of those teachers of Marxism an all-out political trial which was part and parcel of the cold war that has eroded substantial parts of the First Amendment.

* * *

The line between what is permissible and not subject to control and what may be made impermissible and subject to regulation is the line between ideas and overt acts.

The example usually given by those who would punish speech is the case of one who falsely shouts fire in a crowded theater.

This is, however, a classic case where speech is brigaded with action. They are indeed inseparable and a prosecution can be launched for the overt acts actually caused. Apart from rare instances of that kind, speech is, I think, immune from prosecution.

Freedom of expression cases involving national security issues have largely disappeared from the Court's agenda in recent decades. This does not mean that they will never reappear, however. History reveals a recurring pattern of the emergence of concerns about American security and the subsequent passage of legislation that seeks to promote national security by limiting freedom of expression. If this pattern should reoccur, the liberal *Brandenburg* test will be controlling doctrine. The high court's commitment to *Brandenburg* cannot be confidently predicted, however; rather, the Court's decision making in national security cases will depend not only on the force of precedent but also on such factors as the pressure of public opinion and the values of the justices making the decisions.

Symbolic Speech

Supreme Court cases involving symbolic speech frequently share some common characteristics with national security cases because both frequently originate in activities expressing opposition to American war efforts or to the American form of government. Symbolic expression involves the use of symbols to communicate ideas, for example destroying a flag to express hostility to the values the flag represents. Symbolic speech can be an extremely powerful way of expressing ideas, and reactions against symbolic speech are frequently intense because of the passions that are aroused by symbols.

The Court has long recognized that symbolic expression comes within the protection of the First Amendment, but the justices have frequently struggled with exactly how to treat such cases. One problem involves distinguishing symbolic expression from other forms of expression. For example, is a sit-in by a group of people protesting a government policy considered to be symbolic expression or a demonstration? How should the Court treat a case in which a person is arrested after organizing an antiwar demonstration, making a speech against American foreign policy, and then burning the American flag? In addition to the problem of classifying activities as involving symbolic speech, the Court has struggled with determining an appropriate test for judging the constitutionality of symbolic speech. Although the Court has vacillated somewhat in its approach to symbolic speech, the Warren Court ruled in *United States v. O'Brien* (1968) that symbolic speech deserves heightened but not strict scrutiny, and subsequent Courts have accepted this intermediate scrutiny approach.

The Warren Court certainly did not address the area of symbolic speech in a vacuum. In two important cases of the thirties and forties that we have already discussed, the Court recognized the importance of protecting symbolic speech from arbitrary government interference. In *Stromberg v. California* (1931), the Court overturned the conviction of Yetta Stromberg for displaying the flag of the Soviet Union each morning at a children's summer camp in violation of a California law prohibiting the display of a flag opposing organized government. A decade later, in *West Virginia State Board of Education v. Barnette* (1943), the Court ruled unconstitutional West Virginia's law compelling all public school children to stand and salute the American flag at the beginning of each school day.

The Warren Court's first major symbolic expression case, *United States v. O'Brien* (1968), arose from a protest against the Vietnam War. David O'Brien, joined by three other antiwar protestors, burned his draft card outside a courthouse in South Boston. O'Brien was arrested for violating a 1965 amendment to the Selective Service Act, which made it illegal to destroy one's draft card. The federal district court found O'Brien's actions to be protected by the First Amendment. The United States sought review by the Supreme Court, and Thurgood Marshall, the Warren Court justice with a 90 percent liberal voting record in freedom of expression cases, played a most unusual role in the case. Marshall was solicitor general when the United States appealed the case, and Marshall asked the Court to hear the case and to rule that O'Brien's protest activity was not protected by the First Amendment. Marshall was opposed by attorneys from the American Civil Liberties Union who were representing O'Brien. By the time the Court decided the case, Marshall was a sitting justice and did not participate in the decision.

The Court ruled 7-1 against O'Brien and set forth important standards, known as the **O'Brien test,** for assessing symbolic speech. In his majority opinion, Chief Justice Warren acknowledged the difficulty of determining if various forms of conduct intended to express ideas fall within the guarantees of the First Amendment. Even assuming that O'Brien's activities were within the First Amendment, however, Warren argued that government regulations were constitutionally permissible if each of four conditions was met: (1) the regulation is within the constitutional power of the government; (2) the regulation furthers an important or substantial interest of the government; (3) the regulation is not related to the suppression of expression; and (4) the restriction is no greater than is necessary to further the government's interest. In this case, Warren argued, the government met each of these requirements.

One year later the Warren Court was faced with another symbolic speech case arising from a protest against the Vietnam War. *Tinker v. Des Moines School District* (1969) involved children who were suspended from public school for wearing black armbands containing a peace symbol. Writing for a 7-2 Court, Justice Fortas, citing *Barnette*, ruled in favor of the Tinker children. Fortas argued that this type of symbolic act was within the protection of the First Amendment and, indeed, ". . .was closely akin to pure speech, which, we have repeatedly held, is entitled to comprehensive protection under the First Amendment" (393 U.S. at 505-506). No actual or potentially disruptive conduct occurred in the case, and thus school officials lacked a sufficient basis to interfere with constitutionally protected rights.

A third important symbolic speech case decided by the Warren Court involved the American flag. In *Street v. New York* (1968), a man was arrested because of his actions protesting the shooting of civil rights activist James Meredith. Street burned the American flag, declaring that the flag was not needed in a country such as the United States. He was arrested under a New York law that prohibited mutilating the flag or casting contempt on it by word or deed. The Court ruled that the prohibition on verbal condemnation of the flag was too broad and thus unconstitutional, but the justices divided 4-4 over the question of the constitutionality of the ban on the destruction of the flag. As we will see, this question was eventually decided by the Rehnquist Court.

The Burger Court also decided several important symbolic speech cases. The Vietnam War generated enormous controversy and conflict in American society, and various forms of protest activity were prevalent through the last half of the sixties and the first half of the seventies. The Burger Court was thus confronted with symbolic speech issues stemming from anti-Vietnam war protests, with the justices providing strong support for freedom of expression.

"Guerilla theatre" was a common form of antiwar protest activity, typically involving a short play acted out on a sidewalk or in a park. In *Schacht v. United States* (1970), Schacht was an actor who wore an army uniform in a play outside a Houston induction center. In this play, American soldiers were depicted killing Vietnamese women and children. Schacht was arrested and convicted of wearing a military uniform in a play unfavorable to the armed forces of the United States. The Burger Court unanimously overturned the verdict, arguing that the uniform was a part of the actor's speech, which was protected by the First Amendment.

The Burger Court also ruled in favor of two individuals who used the American flag in protest of the Vietnam War. In *Smith v. Goguen* (1974) the Court dealt with a case in which a protestor had placed a small flag on the rear of his pants. He was arrested and convicted under a Massachusetts law prohibiting the "contemptuous" treatment of the flag. The Court reversed the conviction, ruling that the statute was unconstitutionally vague. *Spence v. Washington* (1974) stemmed from the May 4, 1970, killing of four Kent State University students during an antiwar protest. Spence placed a peace symbol on the American flag and flew it upside down in his apartment window to protest the war and the killing of the students. He was arrested and convicted under a Washington state law prohibiting defacing of the flag. In a per curiam opinion, the Court recognized that Spence's activity was a form of symbolic expression protected by the First Amendment. The state could punish Spence only if some substantial government interest was threatened, and Washington failed to prove any such substantial interest was involved in this case.

The Burger Court did not always favor individual or group protestors in symbolic speech cases, however, as seen in the 1984 case of *Clark v. Community for Creative Non-Violence*. The CCNV wanted to call attention to the problem of homelessness in America, and the organization sought a permit from the National Park Services allowing them to construct two tent cities in Lafayette Park and in the Mall area in the heart of Washington, D.C. In addition, CCNV sought permission to sleep in the sixty tents it planned to erect. The Park Services granted permission to the group to set up the tents; however, relying on regulations prohibiting camping in these areas, the government denied the request of demonstrators to sleep in the tents. The Court voted 7-2 that the decision of the Park Services did not violate the freedom of expression rights of CCNV members. Although White's majority opinion waffled as to whether this was a case involving symbolic speech or expressive conduct subject to time, place, and manner restrictions, the four-part test from the 1968 *O'Brien* case was the framework used, and the government met each prong of the test.

The freedom of expression decisions of the Rehnquist Court that generated the most intense public controversy were symbolic speech cases involving burning the American flag in political protest. Despite the earlier cases of the Warren and Burger eras dealing with the flag, the Court had never dealt squarely with the question of whether burning the American flag is a form of expression protected by the First Amendment. In *Texas v. Johnson* (1989) and *United States v. Eichman* (1990), the Court by narrow 5-4 majorities ruled unconstitutional state and federal laws criminalizing flag burning. These decisions not only bitterly divided the members of the Court but also unleashed a torrent of public criticism of the Court and generated numerous threats to amend the Constitution.

Gregory Lee Johnson was a participant in a political demonstration in Dallas, Texas, at the 1984 Republican National Convention. During the protest activity, Johnson poured kerosene on an American flag and set it on fire. He was subsequently arrested under a Texas law for desecrating a venerated object. A trial court found him guilty, and this decision was affirmed by an initial state appellate court; a second appellate court reversed, however, ruling the state law unconstitutional.

Brennan wrote the majority opinion for the Court, which involved a surprising alignment. Marshall and Blackmun predictably supported Brennan's liberal opinion. Far less predictably, Kennedy and Scalia also joined Brennan to create a five-person majority. Brennan began his argument by establishing that Johnson's act was symbolic expression within the meaning of the First Amendment and that the *O'Brien* test might therefore apply. Brennan argued further, however, that one prong of the *O'Brien* test required that a government regulation must not be related to the suppression of expression. Because the Texas law was content-based, Brennan argued, Texas had to meet the Court's toughest standard of strict scrutiny, requiring the State to prove that the law served a compelling government interest. Texas offered as a justification its concern with preserving the flag as a symbol of nationhood and national unity, but Brennan rejected this argument. Brennan concluded his opinion with his preferred alternative to criminalizing flag burning: "The way to preserve the flag's special role is not to punish those who feel differently about these matters. It is to persuade them that they are wrong" (491 U.S. at 419).

Rehnquist answered Brennan in an impassioned dissent joined by White and O'Connor. Rehnquist began by tracing the unique position the flag has occupied for over two hundred years as the symbol of the American nation, citing songs and poems about the flag. Rehnquist also argued that the Court should exercise judicial self-restraint when Congress and forty-eight states had laws criminalizing the burning of the flag. The chief justice also argued that the Court's prior decisions regarding use of the flag for purposes of symbolic speech had left open the question of the constitutionality of laws banning flag burning. For Rehnquist, the proper approach to this case was to use the social value doctrine originally set forth in *Chaplinsky v. New Hampshire* (1942). In the current case, the burning of the American flag ". . .was no essential part of any exposition of ideas, and at the same time had a tendency to incite a breach of the peace" (491 U.S. at 430). Rehnquist concluded his dissent with a stinging criticism of Brennan's suggestion that the proper approach to this situation was to persuade flag burners that they were wrong: "The Court concludes its opinion with a regrettably patronizing civics lecture, presumably addressed to the members of both Houses of Congress, the members of the 48 state legislatures that enacted prohibitions against flag burning, and the troops fighting under that flag in Vietnam who objected to its being burned. . ." (491 U.S. at 434-35).

TEXAS V. JOHNSON

491 U.S. 397, 109 S. Ct. 2533, 105 L.Ed. 2d 342 (1989)

■ Gregory Johnson and other demonstrators marched through the streets of Dallas, Texas, to protest the nomination of President Ronald Reagan for reelection at the 1984 Republican National Convention. After the political demonstration, Johnson burned an American flag while others chanted, "America, the red, white, and blue, we spit on you." Johnson was convicted in a Texas trial court for violation of a state law that banned the desecration of state or national flags. Johnson appealed the trial court's ruling on the basis that the statute violated his freedom of speech. The state appeals court for the Fifth District held that the act of flag burning was symbolic speech deserving of First Amendment scrutiny; however, it also found the Texas statute to be constitutional because it safeguarded the public peace and preserved the flag as a symbol of unity for the United States. The Court of Criminal Appeals of Texas reversed the state appeals court ruling by declaring the desecration statute unconstitutional because it was too broad for free speech purposes concerning public peace. In addition, the state's interest in protecting the flag did not support the law. Texas appealed to the United States Supreme Court.

This is an important case because it was the first time the Court had directly considered the constitutionality of a law criminalizing the desecration of the American flag. It was also one of the most widely publicized and controversial decisions in recent American history. As you read the opinions in this case, reflect upon the following issues: (1) Why did the majority not use the *O'Brien* test in this case? (2) Why and how was the strict scrutiny test used by the majority? (3) Can evidence be found in the opinions in this case of each of the three models of judicial politics—the legal, the political, and the attitudinal—we discussed in Chapter 1?

VOTE:

5 justices found the law to violate Johnson's constitutional rights (Blackmun, Brennan, Kennedy, Marshall, Scalia).

4 justices found the law not to violate Johnson's constitutional rights (O'Connor, Rehnquist, Stevens, White).

Justice Brennan delivered the opinion of the Court.

After publicly burning an American flag as a means of political protest, Gregory Lee Johnson was convicted of desecrating a flag in violation of Texas law. This case presents the question whether his conviction is consistent with the First Amendment. We hold that it is not.

* * *

Johnson was convicted of flag desecration for burning the flag rather than for uttering insulting words. This fact somewhat complicates our consideration of his conviction under the First Amendment. We must first determine whether Johnson's burning of the flag constituted expressive conduct, permitting him to invoke the First Amendment in challenging his conviction. If his conduct was expressive, we next decide whether the State's regulation is related to the suppression of free expression. If the State's regulation is not related to expression, then the less stringent standard we announced in *United States v. O'Brien* (1968) for regulations of noncommunicative conduct controls. If it is then we are outside of *O'Brien*'s test, and we must ask whether this interest justifies Johnson's conviction under a more demanding standard. A third possibility is that the State's asserted interest is simply not implicated on these facts, and in that event the interest drops out of the picture.

The First Amendment literally forbids the abridgment only of "speech," but we have long recognized that its protection does not end at the spoken or written word. While we have rejected "the view that an apparently limitless variety of conduct can be labeled 'speech' whenever the person engaging in the conduct intends thereby to express an idea," we have acknowledged that conduct may be sufficiently imbued with elements of communication to fall within the scope of the First and Fourteenth Amendments.

In deciding whether particular conduct possesses sufficient communicative elements to bring the First Amendment into play, we have asked whether "a[n] intent to convey a particularized message was present, and [whether] the likelihood was great that the message would be understood by those who viewed it." Hence, we have recognized the expressive nature of students' wearing of black armbands to protest American military involvement in Vietnam, of a sit-in by blacks in a "whites only" area to protest segregation, of the wearing of American military uniforms in a dramatic presentation criticizing American involvement in Vietnam, and of picketing about a wide variety of causes.

Especially pertinent to this case are our decisions recognizing the communicative nature of conduct relating to flags. Attaching a peace sign to the flag, saluting the flag, and displaying a red flag, we have held, all may find shelter under the First Amendment. That we have had little difficulty identifying an expressive element in conduct relating to flags should not be surprising. The very purpose of a national flag is to serve as a symbol of our country. . . . * * *

We have not automatically concluded, however, that any action taken with respect to our flag is expressive. Instead in characterizing such action for First Amendment purposes, we have considered the context in which it occurred. * * *

The State of Texas conceded for purposes of its oral argument in this case that Johnson's conduct was expressive conduct. . . . Johnson burned an American flag as part—indeed, as the culmination—of a political demonstration that coincided with the convening of the Republican Party and its renomination of Ronald Reagan for President. The expressive, overtly political nature of this conduct was both intentional and overwhelmingly apparent. * * * In these circumstances, Johnson's burning of the flag was conduct "sufficiently imbued with elements of communication" to implicate the First Amendment.

The Government generally has a freer hand in restricting expressive conduct than it has in restricting the written or spoken word. It may not, however, proscribe particular conduct *because* it has expressive elements. * * * It is, in short, not simply the verbal or nonverbal nature of the expression, but the *governmental* interest at stake, that helps to determine whether a restriction on that expression is valid.

Thus, although we have recognized that where " 'speech' and 'nonspeech' elements are combined in the same course of conduct, a sufficiently important governmental interest in regulating the nonspeech element can justify incidental limitations on First Amendment freedoms," we have limited the applicability of *O'Brien*'s relatively lenient standard to those cases in which "the governmental interest is unrelated to the suppression of the free expression."

* * *

In order to decide whether *O'Brien*'s test applies here, therefore, we must decide whether Texas has asserted an interest in support of Johnson's conviction that is unrelated to the suppression of expression. If we find that an interest asserted by the State is simply not implicated on the facts before us, we need not ask whether *O'Brien*'s test applies. The State offers two separate interests to justify this conviction: preventing breaches of the peace, and preserving the flag as a symbol of nationhood and national unity. We hold that the first interest is not implicated on this record and that the second is related to the suppression of expression.

Texas claims that its interest in preventing breaches of the peace justifies Johnson's conviction for flag desecration. However, no disturbance of the peace actually occurred or threatened to occur because of Johnson's burning of the flag. * * *

The State's position, therefore, amounts to a claim that an audience that takes serious offense at particular expression is necessarily likely to disturb the peace and that the expression may be prohibited on this basis. Our precedents do not countenance such a presumption. On the contrary, they recognize that a principal "function of free speech under our system of government is to invite dispute. It may indeed best serve its high purpose when it induces a condition of unrest, creates dissatisfaction with conditions as they are, or even stirs people to anger." * * *

Thus, we have not permitted the Government to assume that every expression of a provocative idea will incite a riot, but have instead required careful consideration of the actual circumstances surrounding such expression, asking whether the expression "is directed to inciting or producing imminent lawless action and is likely to incite or produce such action." *Brandenburg v. Ohio* (1969). To accept Texas' arguments that it need only demonstrate "the potential for a breach of the peace," and that every flag-burning necessarily possesses that potential, would be to eviscerate our holding in *Brandenburg*. This we decline to do.

Nor does Johnson's expressive conduct fall within that small class of "fighting words" that are "likely to provoke the average person to retaliation, and thereby cause a breach of the peace." *Chaplinsky v. New Hampshire* (1942). No reasonable onlooker would have regarded Johnson's generalized expression of dissatisfaction with the policies of the Federal Government as a direct personal insult or an invitation to exchange fisticuffs. We thus conclude that the State's interest in maintaining order is not implicated on these facts.

The State also asserts an interest in preserving the flag as a symbol of nationhood and national unity. In *Spence*, we acknowledged that the Government's interest in preserving the flag's special symbolic value "is directly related to expression in the context of activity" such as affixing a peace symbol to a flag. We are equally persuaded that this interest is related to expression in the case of Johnson's burning of the flag. The State, apparently, is concerned that such conduct will lead people to believe either that the flag does not stand for nationhood and national unity, but instead reflects other, less positive concepts, or that the concepts reflected in the flag do not in fact exist, that is, we do not enjoy unity as a Nation. These concerns blossom only when a person's treatment of the flag communicates some message, and thus are related "to the suppression of free expression" within the meaning of *O'Brien*. We are thus outside of *O'Brien*'s test altogether.

It remains to consider whether the State's interest in preserving the flag as a symbol of nationhood and national unity justifies Johnson's conviction.

As in *Spence*, "[w]e are confronted with a case of prosecution for the expression of an idea through activity," and "[a]ccordingly, we must examine with particular care the interests advanced by [petitioner] to support its prosecution." Johnson was not, we add, prosecuted for the expression of just any idea; he was prosecuted for his expression of dissatisfaction with the policies of this country, expression situated at the core of our First Amendment values.

* * *

Whether Johnson's treatment of the flag violated Texas law thus depended on the likely communicative impact of his expressive conduct. Our decision in *Boos v. Barry* (1988) tells us that this restriction on Johnson's expression is content-based. In *Boos*, we considered the constitutionality of a law prohibiting "the display of any sign within 50 feet of a foreign embassy if that sign tends to bring that foreign government into 'public odium' or 'public disrepute.' " Rejecting the argument that the law was content-neutral because it was justified by "our international law obligation to shield diplomats from speech that offends their dignity," we held that a "[t]he emotive impact of speech on its audience is not a 'secondary effect' " unrelated to the content of the expression itself.

According to the principles announced in *Boos*, Johnson's political expression was restricted because of the content of the message he conveyed. We must therefore subject the State's asserted interest in preserving the special symbolic character of the flag to "the most exacting scrutiny."

Texas argues that its interest in preserving the flag as a symbol of nationhood and national unity survives this close analysis. * * * According to Texas, if one physically treats the flag in a way that would tend to cast doubt on either the idea that nationhood and national unity are the flag's referents or that national unity actually exists, the message conveyed thereby is a harmful one and therefore may be prohibited.

If there is a bedrock principle underlying the First Amendment, it is that the Government may not prohibit the expression of an idea simply because society finds the idea itself offensive or disagreeable.

We have not recognized an exception to this principle even where our flag has been involved. In

Street v. New York (1969), we held that a State may not criminally punish a person for uttering words critical of the flag. * * * Nor may the Government, we have held, compel conduct that would evince respect for the flag. [*Barnette*, 1943.] * * *

In *Spence* [1974], we held that the same interest asserted by Texas here was insufficient to support a criminal conviction under a flag-misuse statute for the taping of a peace sign to an American flag. * * *

In short, nothing in our precedents suggests that a State may foster its own view of the flag by prohibiting expressive conduct relating to it. * * *

* * *

There is, moreover, no indication—either in the text of the Constitution or in our cases interpreting it—that a separate juridical category exists for the American flag alone. Indeed, we would not be surprised to learn that the persons who framed our Constitution and wrote the Amendment that we now construe were not known for their reverence for the Union Jack. The First Amendment does not guarantee that other concepts virtually sacred to our Nation as a whole—such as the principle that discrimination on the basis of race is odious and destructive—will go unquestioned in the market-place of ideas. We decline, therefore, to create for the flag an exception to the joust of principles protected by the First Amendment.

* * *

The way to preserve the flag's special role is not to punish those who feel differently about these matters. It is to persuade them that they are wrong. * * * And precisely because it is our flag that is involved, one's response to the flag-burner may exploit the uniquely persuasive power of the flag itself. We can imagine no more appropriate response to burning a flag than waving one's own, no better way to counter a flag-burner's message than by saluting the flag that burns, no surer means of preserving the dignity even of the flag that burned than by—as one witness here did—according its remains a respectful burial. We do not consecrate the flag by punishing its desecration, for in doing so we dilute the freedom that this cherished emblem represents.

Johnson was convicted for engaging in expressive conduct. The State's interest in preventing breaches of the peace does not support his conviction because Johnson's conduct did not threaten to disturb the peace. Nor does the State's interest in preserving the flag as a symbol of nationhood and national unity justify his criminal conviction for engaging in political expression. The judgment of the Texas Court of Criminal Appeals is therefore affirmed.

Justice Kennedy, concurring.

I write not to qualify the words Justice Brennan chooses so well, for he says with power all that is necessary to explain our ruling. I join this opinion without reservation, but with a keen sense that this case, like others before us from time to time, exacts its personal toll. This prompts me to add to our pages these few remarks.

* * *

The hard fact is that sometimes we must make decisions we do not like. We make them because they are right, right in the sense that the law and the Constitution, as we see them, compel the result. And so great is our commitment to the process that, except in the rare case, we do not pause to express distaste for the result, perhaps for fear of undermining a valued principle that dictates the decision. This is one of those rare cases.

* * *

With all respect to those views, I do not believe the Constitution gives us the right to rule as the dissenting members of the Court urge, however painful this judgment is to announce. Though symbols often are what we ourselves make of them, the flag is constant in expressing beliefs Americans share, beliefs in law and peace and that freedom which sustains the human spirit. The case here today forces recognition of the costs to which those beliefs commit us. It is poignant but fundamental that the flag protects those who hold it in contempt.

* * *

Chief Justice Rehnquist, with whom Justice White and Justice O'Connor join, dissenting.

In holding this Texas statute unconstitutional, the Court ignores Justice Holmes' familiar aphorism that "a page of history is worth a volume of logic." For more than 200 years, the American flag has occupied a unique position as the symbol of our Nation, a uniqueness that justifies a governmental prohibition against flag burning in the way respondent Johnson did here.

* * *

The American flag, then, throughout more than 200 years of our history, has come to be the visible symbol embodying our Nation. It does not represent the views of any particular political party, and it does not represent any particular political philosophy. The flag is not simply another "idea" or "point of view" competing for recognition in the marketplace of ideas. Millions and millions of Americans regard it with an almost mystical reverence regardless of what sort of social, political, or philosophical beliefs they may have. I cannot agree that the First Amendment invalidates the Act of Congress, and the laws of 48 of the 50 States, which make criminal the public burning of the flag.

* * *

But the Court insists that the Texas statute prohibiting the public burning of the American flag infringes on respondent Johnson's freedom of expression. In *Chaplinsky v. New Hampshire*, a unanimous Court said:

> Allowing the broadest scope to the language and purpose of the Fourteenth Amendment, it is well understood that the right of free speech is not absolute at all times and under all circumstances. There are certain well-defined and narrowly limited classes of speech, the prevention and punishment of which have never been thought to raise any Constitutional problem. These include the lewd and obscene, the profane, the libelous, and the insulting or "fighting" words—those which by their very utterance inflict injury or tend to incite an immediate breach of the peace. It has been well observed that such utterances are no essential part of any exposition of ideas, and are of such slight social value as a step to truth that any benefit that may be derived from them is clearly outweighed by the social interest in order and morality.

The Court upheld Chaplinsky's conviction under a state statute that made it unlawful to "address any offensive, derisive or annoying word to any person who is lawfully in any street or other public place." Chaplinsky had told a local marshal, "You are a God-damned racketeer" and a "damned Fascist and the whole government of Rochester are Fascists or agents of Fascists."

Here it may equally be said that the public burning of the American flag by Johnson was no essential part of any exposition of ideas, and at the same time it had a tendency to incite a breach of the peace. Johnson was free to make any verbal denunciation of the flag that he wished; indeed, he was free to burn the flag in private. He could publicly burn other symbols of the Government or effigies of political leaders. He did lead a march through the streets of Dallas, and conducted a rally in front of the Dallas City Hall. He engaged in a "die-in" to protest nuclear weapons. He shouted out various slogans during the march, including: "Reagan, Mondale which will it be? Either one means World War III"; "Ronald Reagan, killer of the hour, Perfect example of U.S. power"; and "red, white and blue, we spit on you, you stand for plunder, you will go under." For none of these acts was he arrested or prosecuted; it was only when he proceeded to burn publicly an American flag stolen from its rightful owner that he violated the Texas statute.

* * *

The result of the Texas statute is obviously to deny one in Johnson's frame of mind one of many means of "symbolic speech." Far from being a case of "one picture being worth a thousand words," flag burning is the equivalent of an inarticulate grunt or roar that, it seems fair to say, is most likely to be indulged in not to express any particular idea, but to antagonize others. * * *

* * *

Our Constitution wisely places limits on powers of legislative majorities to act, but the declaration of such limits by this Court "is, at all times, a question of much delicacy, which ought seldom, if ever, to be decided in the affirmative, in a doubtful case." Uncritical extension of constitutional protection to the burning of the flag risks the frustration of the very purpose for which organized governments are instituted. The Court decides that the American flag is just another symbol, about which not only must opinions pro and con be tolerated, but for which the most minimal public respect may not be enjoined. The government may conscript men into the Armed Forces where they must fight and perhaps die for the flag, but the government may not prohibit the public burning of the banner under which they fight. I would uphold the Texas statute as applied in this case.

Justice Stevens, dissenting. [omitted]

Public reaction to the Court's decision was immediate, intense, and hostile. President Bush, who had successfully used the symbolic value of the flag in his 1988 presidential campaign, called for a constitutional amendment to prohibit flag burning and to overturn *Johnson*. After intense lobbying by civil liberties groups against a constitutional amendment, Congress instead passed the Flag Protection Act of 1989. Supporters of the law hoped that it would receive approval from the Supreme Court. This hope was based on the more precise language of the federal statute and the intense public outcry against the *Johnson* decision. These hopes were dashed in *United States v. Eichman* (1990).

Immediately following the passage of the 1989 Flag Protection Act, Shawn Eichman and others were arrested for burning the American flag on the steps of the United States Capitol. The United States District Court for the District of Columbia ruled the law unconstitutional based on *Johnson,* and the Supreme Court found itself once again confronting the controversial issue of flag burning.

Eichman was a replay of *Johnson*. Brennan again wrote the majority opinion, which was joined by Marshall, Blackmun, Kennedy, and Scalia. Brennan's argumentation was virtually identical in the two cases, although he did explicitly reject the government's argument that the Court should reconsider the *Johnson* decision based on the strong public reaction against it. Stevens, who had written a separate dissent in *Johnson,* wrote a dissenting opinion joined by Rehnquist, O'Connor, and White. Stevens repeated the arguments of the dissenters in *Johnson,* but he used less impassioned language.

Substantial continuity can thus be seen in the treatment of symbolic speech by the Supreme Court throughout the Warren, Burger, and Rehnquist Court eras. Despite some ambiguity, the justices have generally viewed symbolic speech as requiring an intermediate level of scrutiny with the four-part *O'Brien* test providing the specific questions in analyzing these cases. The application of this test has generally resulted in liberal outcomes despite the criticism that these decisions have generated.

Offensive Speech and Hate Speech

As with many other concepts associated with the First Amendment guarantees of freedom of expression, the closely related terms of offensive speech and hate speech are somewhat ambiguous ones. Offensive speech cases have typically involved nonobscene sexual expression as well as fighting words, especially those directed toward law enforcement personnel. Hate speech cases are a recent development, stemming from challenges to laws that prohibit hostile, discriminatory expression directed toward persons based on their race, sexual orientation, or other similar types of characteristics. Both offensive speech and hate speech are frequently analyzed under the social value doctrine because they can be viewed as forms of expression that are so lacking in social value as to be beyond constitutional protection.

Despite the arguments that can be made that offensive speech and hate speech do not deserve constitutional protection, the Supreme Court has generally taken a preferred freedoms approach to rule against government efforts to prohibit or punish these types of expression. The major exception where the Court has supported the government has been in cases involving minors and students.

The Burger and Rehnquist Courts have heard most of the major cases involving offensive speech and hate speech. Two early cases that can be mentioned briefly, however, are *Cantwell v. Connecticut* (1940) and *Chaplinsky v. New Hampshire* (1942). In *Cantwell* the Court overturned a breach of the peace conviction of Jessie Cantwell, a Jehovah's Witness, who had stopped two men on a sidewalk and played a record that attacked their Catholic religion. The men expressed their opposition to the record and to Cantwell's activities; although they found his views to be highly offensive, no violence occurred. Nonetheless, Cantwell was arrested. The Court used both the clear and present danger test and the vagueness doctrine in ruling that his First Amendment rights had been violated. In *Chaplinsky* the Court set forth the social value doctrine in upholding the conviction of Chaplinsky for calling a police officer a "God-damned racketeer" and a "damned Fascist." According to a unanimous Court, these were fighting words that lacked social value and thus were beyond the protection of the First Amendment.

The decade of the fifties was a quiet one for the Court in regard to the area of offensive speech, perhaps because of cultural values that mitigated against this type of expression. The tumultuous decade of the sixties created a dramatically different cultural environment, however, and the increase in offensive forms of expression in American society led to arrests, convictions, and ultimately appeals to the Supreme Court. Given the lengthy process of appealing such cases, it was the Burger Court justices who were confronted with a variety of cases involving offensive speech. Individuals who had been arrested for their offensive expression typically found a sympathetic audience with the Burger Court.

The leading case in this area was *Cohen v. California* (1971). The case began one evening in the late sixties when Paul Robert Cohen attended an antiwar meeting. During the meeting someone painted the words "Fuck the Draft" on Cohen's jacket. The next day he wore the jacket with the sign into the Los Angeles County Courthouse, and he was arrested and convicted under a California breach of the peace statute for engaging in offensive conduct.

Justice John Marshall Harlan wrote the majority opinion, which used extensively many of the freedom of expression doctrines developed by the Warren Court justices. Harlan began by asserting that the case dealt solely with offensive speech and not with any type of conduct. Harlan acknowledged that freedom of speech is not absolute, but he also recognized that the government could interfere with speech only under limited conditions. These conditions did not exist in this case. Cohen was not trying to incite disruption of the draft. Cohen's expression was not obscene because the word "fuck" was not being used in a sexual manner. Cohen's message also did not constitute fighting words because they were not directed toward any particular person and nobody reacted violently to Cohen. In addition, Cohen's message did not infringe on the rights of anyone else, specifically any right to privacy regarding unwelcome views or words. Against this background, Harlan continued, California's case came down to its concerns either that this expression would inherently cause a violent reaction or that public morality required punishing this expression. For Harlan and the Court majority, these reasons were insufficient. In Harlan's words,

> *The constitutional right of free expression is powerful medicine in a society as diverse and populous as ours. It is designed and intended to remove governmental restraints from the arena of public discussion, putting the decision as to what views shall be voiced largely into the hands of each of us, in the hope that use of such freedom will ultimately produce a more capable citizenry and more perfect polity and in the belief that no other approach would comport with the premise of individual dignity and choice upon which our political system rests* (403 U.S. at 24).

Cohen v. California

403 U.S. 15, 91 S. Ct. 1780, 29 L.Ed. 2d 284 (1971)

■ Paul Robert Cohen entered the Los Angeles County Courthouse wearing a jacket displaying the words "Fuck the Draft" to demonstrate his opposition to the Vietnam conflict and draft. Cohen was arrested, tried, and convicted in the Los Angeles Municipal Court for violating a California breach of the peace statute. Under the California law, he was sentenced to thirty days in jail. The Court of Appeals for the Second Appellate District in California affirmed his conviction. On appeal to the United States Supreme Court, Cohen asserted that the First Amendment protected his right to use certain four-letter words to express his political ideas.

This is a significant case because it was one of the Burger Court's earliest freedom of expression cases and indicated that the Court would be committed to many of the same liberal approaches and doctrines utilized by the Warren Court. In reading this decision, consider these questions: (1) What freedom of expression doctrines does Harlan use in his majority opinion? (2) Would the Court have reached a different decision if Cohen had been physically attacked in the courthouse because of the message on his jacket?

Vote:

5 justices voted that Cohen's constitutional rights were violated (Brennan, Douglas, Harlan, Marshall, Stewart).

4 justices voted that Cohen's constitutional rights were not violated (Black, Blackmun, Burger, White).

Justice Harlan delivered the opinion of the Court.

This case may seem at first blush too inconsequential to find its way into our books, but the issue it presents is of no small constitutional significance.

* * *

In order to lay hands on the precise issue which this case involves, it is useful first to canvass various matters which this record does *not* present.

The conviction quite clearly rests upon the asserted offensiveness of the *words* Cohen used to convey his message to the public. The only "conduct" which the State sought to punish is the fact of communication. Thus, we deal here with a conviction resting solely upon "speech. . . ." * * * The State certainly lacks power to punish Cohen for the underlying content of the message the inscription conveyed. At least so long as there is no showing of an intent to incite disobedience to or disruption of the draft, Cohen could not, consistently with the First and Fourteenth Amendments, be punished for asserting the evident position on the inutility or immorality of the draft his jacket reflected.

Appellant's conviction, then, rests squarely upon his exercise of the "freedom of speech" protected from arbitrary governmental interference by the Constitution and can be justified, if at all, only as valid regulation of the manner in which he exercised that freedom, not as a permissible prohibition on the substantive message it conveys. This does not end the inquiry, of course, for the First and Fourteenth Amendments have never been thought to give absolute protection to every individual to speak whenever or wherever he pleases, or to use any form of address in any circumstances that he chooses. In this vein, too, however, we think it important to note that several issues typically associated with such problems are not presented here.

In the first place, Cohen was tried under a statute applicable throughout the entire State. Any attempt to support this conviction on the ground that the statute seeks to preserve an appropriately decorous atmosphere in the courthouse where Cohen was arrested must fail in the absence of any language in the statute that would have put appellant on notice that certain kinds of otherwise permissible speech or conduct would nevertheless, under California law, not be tolerated in certain places. No fair reading of the phrase "offensive conduct" can be said sufficiently to inform the ordinary person that distinctions between certain locations are thereby created.

In the second place, as it comes to us, this case cannot be said to fall within those relatively few categories of instances where prior decisions have established the power of government to deal more comprehensively with certain forms of individual expression simply upon a showing that such a form was employed. This is not, for example, an obscenity case. Whatever else may be necessary to give rise to the State's broader power to prohibit obscene expression, such expression must be, in some significant way, erotic. It cannot plausibly be maintained that this vulgar allusion to the Selective Service System would conjure up such psychic stimulation in anyone likely to be confronted with Cohen's crudely defaced jacket.

This Court has also held that the States are free to ban the simple use, without a demonstration of additional justifying circumstances, of so-called "fighting words," those personally abusive epithets which, when addressed to the ordinary citizen, are, as a matter of common knowledge, inherently likely to provoke violent reaction. While the four-letter word displayed by Cohen in relation to the draft is not uncommonly employed in a personally provocative fashion, in this instance it was clearly not "directed to the person of the hearer." No individual actually or likely to be present could reasonably have regarded the words on appellant's jacket as a direct personal insult. Nor do we have here an instance of the exercise of the State's police power to prevent a speaker from intentionally provoking a given group to hostile reaction. * * *

Finally, in arguments before this Court much has been made of the claim that Cohen's distasteful mode of expression was thrust upon unwilling or unsuspecting viewers, and that the State might therefore legitimately act as it did in order to protect the sensitive from otherwise unavoidable exposure to appellant's crude form of protest. Of course, the mere presumed presence of unwitting listeners or viewers does not serve automatically to justify curtailing all speech capable of giving offense. While this Court has recognized that government may properly act in many situations to prohibit intrusion into the privacy of the home of unwelcome views and ideas which cannot be totally banned from the public dialogue, we have at the same time consistently stressed that "we are often 'captives' outside the sanctuary of the home and subject to objectionable speech." The ability of government, consonant with the Constitution, to shut off discourse solely to protect others from hearing it is, in other words, dependent upon a showing that substantial privacy interests are being invaded in an essentially intolerable manner. Any broader view of this authority would effectively empower a majority to silence dissidents simply as a matter of personal predilections.

In this regard, persons confronted with Cohen's jacket were in a quite different posture than, say, those subjected to the raucous emissions of sound trucks blaring outside their residences. Those in the Los Angeles courthouse could effectively avoid further bombardment of their sensibilities simply by averting their eyes. And, while it may be that one has a more substantial claim to a recognizable privacy interest when walking through a courthouse corridor than, for example, strolling through Central Park, surely it is nothing like the interest in being free from unwanted expression in the confines of one's own home. * * *

Against this background, the issue flushed by this case stands out in bold relief. It is whether California can excise, as "offensive conduct," one particular scurrilous epithet from the public discourse, either upon the theory of the court below that its use is inherently likely to cause violent reaction or upon a more general assertion that the States, acting as guardians of public morality, may properly remove this offensive word from the public vocabulary.

The rationale of the California court is plainly untenable. At most it reflects an "undifferentiated fear or apprehension of disturbance [which] is not enough to overcome the right to freedom of expression." We have been shown no evidence that substantial numbers of citizens are standing ready to strike out physically at whoever may assault their sensibilities with execrations like that uttered by Cohen. There may be some persons about with such lawless and violent proclivities, but that is an insufficient base upon which to erect, consistently with constitutional values, a governmental power to force persons who wish to ventilate their dissident views into avoiding particular forms of expression. * * *

Admittedly, it is not so obvious that the First and Fourteenth Amendments must be taken to disable the States from punishing public utterance of this unseemly expletive in order to maintain what they regard as a suitable level of discourse within the body politic. We think, however, that examination and reflection will reveal the shortcomings of a contrary viewpoint.

At the outset, we cannot overemphasize that, in our judgment, most situations where the State has a justifiable interest in regulating speech will fall within one or more of the various established exceptions, discussed above but not applicable here, to the usual rule that governmental bodies may not prescribe the form or content of individual expression. Equally important to our conclusion is the constitutional backdrop against which our decision must be made. The constitutional right of free expression is powerful medicine in a society as diverse and populous as ours. It is designed and intended to remove governmental restraints from the arena of public discussion, putting the decision as to what views shall be voiced largely into the hands of each of us, in the hope that use of such freedom will ultimately produce a more capable citizenry and more perfect polity and in the belief that no other approach would comport with the premise of individual dignity and choice upon which our political system rests.

To many, the immediate consequence of this freedom may often appear to be only verbal tumult, discord, and even offensive utterance. These are, however, within established limits, in truth necessary side effects of the broader enduring values which the process of open debate permits us to achieve. That the air may at times seem filled with verbal cacophony is, in this sense not a sign of weakness but of strength. We cannot lose sight of the fact that, in what otherwise might seem a trifling and annoying instance of individual distasteful abuse of a privilege, these fundamental societal values are truly implicated. * * *

Against this perception of the constitutional policies involved, we discern certain more particularized considerations that peculiarly call for reversal of this conviction. First, the principle contended for by the State seems inherently boundless. How is one to distinguish this from any other offensive word? Surely the State has no right to cleanse public debate to the point where it is grammatically palatable to the most squeamish among us. Yet no readily ascertainable general principle exists for stopping short of that result were we to affirm the judgment below. For, while the particular four-letter word being litigated here is perhaps more distasteful than most others of its genre, it is nevertheless often true that one man's vulgarity is another's lyric. Indeed, we think it is largely because governmental officials cannot make principled distinctions in this area that the Constitution leaves matters of taste and style so largely to the individual.

Additionally, we cannot overlook the fact, because it is well illustrated by the episode involved here, that much linguistic expression serves a dual communicative function: it conveys not only ideas capable of relatively precise, detached explication, but otherwise inexpressible emotions as well. In fact, words are often chosen as much for their emotive as their cognitive force. We cannot sanction the view that the Constitution, while solicitous of the cognitive content of individual speech, has little or no regard for that emotive function which, practically speaking, may often be the more important element of the overall message sought to be communicated. * * *

Finally, and in the same vein, we cannot indulge the facile assumption that one can forbid particular words without also running a substantial risk of suppressing ideas in the process. Indeed, governments might soon seize upon the censorship of particular words as a convenient guise for banning the expression of unpopular views. We have been able, as noted above, to discern little social benefit that might result from running the risk of opening the door to such grave results.

It is, in sum, our judgment that, absent a more particularized and compelling reason for its actions, the State may not, consistently with the First and Fourteenth Amendments, make the simple public display here involved of this single four-letter expletive a criminal offense. Because that is the only arguably sustainable rationale for the conviction here at issue, the judgment below must be

Reversed.

Justice Blackmun, with whom The Chief Justice and Justice Black join.

I dissent. . . .

. . . Cohen's absurd and immature antic, in my view, was mainly conduct and little speech. Further, the case appears to me to be well within the sphere of *Chaplinsky v. New Hampshire*, where Mr. Justice Murphy, a known champion of First Amendment freedoms, wrote for a unanimous bench. As a consequence, this Court's agonizing over First Amendment values seems misplaced and unnecessary.

* * *

The Burger Court handed down a number of other liberal decisions in cases involving various types of offensive speech. In *Gooding v. Wilson* (1972), the Court overturned the conviction of an African American who called a white police officer a "son-of-a-bitch" and threatened to kill him. In a somewhat related case, *Lewis v. New Orleans* (1974), the Burger Court justices ruled unconstitutional a law prohibiting cursing at a police officer. Yet another case involving offensive expression raised the question of First Amendment protection for the owner of a drive-in theater, where movies were shown containing nudity that could be seen by homeowners and from cars passing the drive-in. In a 6-3 decision in *Erzoznick v. City of Jacksonville* (1975), the Burger Court ruled that freedom of expression concerns outweighed the limited privacy interests that arose in this case.

Despite a record that generally found offensive speech to be within the protection of the First Amendment, the Burger Court made exceptions in some areas, including broadcasting and public schools. In *Federal Communications Commission v. Pacifica Foundation* (1976), the Court upheld the FCC's ban on indecent expression over the radio in a case stemming from comedian George Carlin's monologue on "seven dirty words" that could not be used in radio or television. We will examine this case in greater detail when we analyze the area of broadcasting. The Burger Court also ruled conservatively in the controversial decision of *Bethel School District No. 403 v. Fraser* (1986). This case arose out of a speech given at a high school assembly by Matthew Fraser, who was nominating another student, Jeff Kuhlman, for elective office. Fraser used sexually suggestive language at several points in his speech, e.g., "'I know a man who is firm—he's firm in his pants, he's firm in his shirt, his character is firm—but most of all, his belief in you, the students of Bethel, is firm'" (478 U.S. at 687). Fraser was subsequently suspended from school for several days for his "indecent, lewd, and offensive" speech. Writing for a five-person majority, Chief Justice Burger used a balancing approach, concluding that Fraser's First Amendment interests were outweighed by ". . . society's countervailing interest in teaching students the boundaries of socially appropriate behavior" (478 U.S. at 681).

The Rehnquist Court has dealt with cases involving both offensive speech and hate speech. Although hate speech cases have been the most widely publicized and controversial, the Rehnquist Court has ruled on two interesting cases involving offensive speech. *Rankin v. McPherson* (1987), a case we classify as being of major importance, involved a public employee who was fired for making a remark that she hoped that President Reagan would be assassinated. *Houston v. Hill* (1987) involved a gay rights activist who was arrested for interrupting a police officer in the performance of his duties. In both cases the Rehnquist Court ruled that the individual's First Amendment freedom of speech rights had been violated.

Ardith McPherson, an African American woman, was a clerical worker in the office of Walter Rankin, the constable of Harris County, Texas. In March of 1981 McPherson and other employees heard over the radio that an assassination attempt had been made on President Reagan. McPherson speculated that the attempt might have been made by an African American person because Reagan was cutting back on many welfare programs that benefitted African Americans, and then she stated, "If they go for him again, I hope they get him" (483 U.S. at 381). The conversation was reported to Rankin, who fired McPherson for her remarks.

In ruling in favor of McPherson, the Court divided 5-4 along familiar liberal/conservative lines. Marshall wrote the five-person majority opinion and was joined by Brennan, Blackmun, Stevens, and Powell. Scalia authored the dissent, supported by Rehnquist, White, and O'Connor.

Marshall recognized that the Court's earlier precedents involving free speech and public employees (*Pickering v. Board of Education*, 1968 and *Connick v. Meyers*, 1983) had established a balancing approach in such cases. The threshold question in this balancing test was whether the speech involved a matter of public concern, and Marshall argued that McPherson's statement was made in the context of discussing the public policies of the Reagan administration. Marshall then weighed the interests of the government in promoting the efficient operation of its public services against the employee's First Amendment interest. He concluded that McPherson's free speech rights outweighed the government's interest because her comments presented only the most minimal threat to the effective functioning of the constable's office.

Scalia agreed with Marshall that the two-pronged approach of *Pickering* and *Connick* should be used in this case, but he came to very different conclusions than Marshall reached. Scalia rejected the argument that McPherson's statement involved matters of public concern and was much closer to statements beyond all First Amendment protection, such as fighting words or threats to assassinate the president. Scalia further contended that even if her comments involved matters of public concern, the constable's interest in running an effective law enforcement office outweighed McPherson's First Amendment interests. In Scalia's view, ". . .no law enforcement agency is required by the First Amendment to permit one of its employees to 'ride with the cops and cheer for the robbers. . .' " (483 U.S. at 394).

The Rehnquist Court also reached a liberal decision in *Houston v. Hill.* Raymond Hill was a gay rights activist in Houston, Texas, living in a neighborhood that was the center of the gay community in Houston. Hill observed a friend of his stopping traffic on a busy street in the neighborhood, seeking to permit a vehicle to enter the traffic. Two police officers approached Hill's friend, and after a short period of time Hill began shouting at the officers, asking them, "Why don't you pick on somebody your own size?" (482 U.S. at 454). Hill had a long history of confrontations with local police, and he testified that he challenged the officers because he was afraid they were about to hit his friend. He was arrested under a city ordinance for ". . .willfully or intentionally interrupting a city policeman . . . by verbal challenge during an investigation" (482 U.S. at 454).

The Court ruled 8-1 in favor of Hill on the basis that the ordinance was overbroad and therefore in violation of the First Amendment. Brennan wrote the majority opinion for the Court. In characterizing the ordinance as overly broad, Brennan argued, "It is not limited to fighting words nor even to obscene or opprobrious language, but prohibits speech that in any manner . . . interrupt[s] an officer. The Constitution does not allow such speech to be made a crime. The freedom of individuals verbally to oppose or challenge police action without thereby risking arrest is one of the principal characteristics by which we distinguish a free nation from a police state" (482 U.S. at 462–63).

The Rehnquist Court confronted a new topic of freedom of expression in the nineties when it ruled on two cases involving hate speech, *R.A.V. v. City of St. Paul* (1992) and *Wisconsin v. Mitchell* (1993). These cases, as well as many other state and lower federal cases, had their origins in the enactment of numerous hate speech laws by state legislatures, city councils, and college and university governing boards in the 1980s and 1990s. These laws have taken a wide variety of forms, but they typically prohibit hostile and discriminatory expression directed toward another person based on such characteristics as race, gender, sexual orientation, ethnicity, or religion.

The controversy over the need and the constitutionality of hate speech laws has created unusual tensions and alignments for liberals and conservatives both on and off the Court. Liberals typically oppose government efforts to regulate expression, favoring freedom over order, while conservatives are more likely to support order over freedom and thus support various forms of government regulation of speech and press. Hate speech laws create a conflict between a different set of values—freedom and equality. Liberals are more likely to support equality when these two values come into conflict, and thus liberals can find themselves in the unusual and uncomfortable position of favoring government regulation of freedom of expression when hate speech is involved. Conservatives also feel some ambiguity about hate speech laws because this area can constitute an exception to their general approach of supporting government interference with expression; many conservatives view hate speech laws as liberal attempts to impose "politically correct" speech on society.

The Supreme Court had few direct precedents upon which to draw when hate speech cases began to emerge in the early 1990s in response to the development of laws regulating hate speech. The famous case of *Brandenburg v. Ohio* (1969) involved a racist speech by a member of the Ku Klux Klan, but this case involved a law that dealt with subversive activities rather than hate speech. The Court also dealt briefly with a controversy which arose in Skokie, Illinois, in the 1970s when a neo-Nazi group, the National Socialist party, sought to hold a march in Skokie, a community with a substantial Jewish population that included survivors of German concentration camps. The Supreme Court in a brief per curiam opinion ruled that Skokie's refusal to allow the march raised serious First Amendment issues and that the decision had to be reviewed by state courts. Thus, the Skokie case, like *Brandenburg*, did not directly involve the issue of hate speech, but in both cases the Court came down against government attempts to control various forms of hate speech.

In the Court's first case, *R.A.V. v. St. Paul* (1992), the justices voted unanimously that a city ordinance directed at hate speech was unconstitutional, but the unanimous vote masked sharp disagreements among the members of the high court. The case arose from the actions of Robert A. Viktora and other teenage companions who burned a crudely-made cross inside the fenced yard of an African American family that lived across the street from Viktora. A Minnesota trial court ruled the ordinance under which Viktora was convicted was unconstitutional because it was overbroad as well as impermissibly content-based, but the Minnesota Supreme Court reversed and upheld the law as constitutional.

Justice Scalia authored the five-person majority opinion for the Court, joined by Rehnquist, Thomas, Kennedy, and Souter. Scalia began by stating that it was not necessary to consider the overbreadth issue. Instead, he argued, the case should be approached from the social value doctrine originally set forth in *Chaplinsky v. New Hampshire* (1942). *Chaplinsky* established that certain forms of expression—that is, fighting words, obscenity, the libelous—are so lacking in social value as to be beyond the protection of the First Amendment. Scalia accepted the Minnesota Supreme Court's view that the St. Paul ordinance dealt only with fighting words within the meaning of *Chaplinsky*, but he argued that the government does not have complete power to regulate such expression. Specifically, it is impermissible to regulate this expression based upon the underlying content of the message being conveyed. Applying these principles to the St. Paul ordinance, Scalia argued that the law was invalid because it embodied content as well as viewpoint discrimination.

Justice White authored a lengthy concurring opinion joined by O'Connor, Kennedy, and Stevens. White's opinion, which read more like a dissent than a concurrence, agreed with Scalia's majority opinion on only one point—the unconstitutionality of the St. Paul ordinance. On every other major point, White harshly criticized the majority opinion for ". . .cast[ing] aside long-established First Amendment doctrine. . ." and engaging in reasoning that was ". . .transparently wrong" (505 U.S. at 398). White argued that the case should have easily been decided on overbreadth grounds, the only issue upon which certiorari had been granted and therefore the focus of the briefs and oral argument. In regard to the majority's interpretation of the *Chaplinsky* doctrine and fighting words, White accused his colleagues of misreading the Court's clear position that fighting words are categorically outside of First Amendment protection. The majority's approach, according to White, ". . . legitimates hate speech as a form of public discussion" (505 U.S. at 402).

R.A.V. v. St. Paul

505 U.S. 377, 112 S.Ct. 2538, 20 L.Ed. 2d 305 (1992)

■ The 1989 St. Paul Bias-Motivated Crime Ordinance stated: "Whoever places on public or private property a symbol, object, appellation, characterization or graffiti, including, but not limited to, a burning cross or a Nazi swastika, which one knows or has reasonable grounds to know causes anger, alarm, or resentment in others on the basis of race, color, creed, religion, or gender commits disorderly conduct and shall be guilty of a misdemeanor." On June 21, 1990, several teenagers burned a homemade cross on the yard of the only African American family in a St. Paul neighborhood. One teenager, Robert Viktora, was arrested and charged with violating the St. Paul ordinance. In a Minnesota state trial court, the complaint against the youth was dismissed, but on appeal the Minnesota Supreme Court reversed. The United States Supreme Court granted certiorari.

This case is important because it was the first time the Supreme Court had confronted the constitutionality of "hate-speech" laws. As you read the opinions in this case, give thought to the following questions: (1) What does Scalia mean in his majority opinion when he speaks of a "limited categorical approach" to the First Amendment? (2) On what basis does White argue in his concurrence that the Court majority "casts aside long-established First Amendment doctrine?" (3) Why do you think the justices were in unanimous agreement on the outcome of the case but were in such sharp disagreement regarding their reasoning?

Vote:

The justices voted unanimously that the law was unconstitutional.

Justice Scalia delivered the opinion of the Court.

* * *

The First Amendment generally prevents government from proscribing speech, e.g., *Cantwell v. Connecticut*, or even expressive conduct, see, e.g., *Texas v. Johnson*, because of disapproval of the ideas expressed. Content-based regulations are presumptively invalid. From 1791 to the present, however, our society, like other free but civilized societies, has permitted restrictions upon the content of speech in a few limited areas, which are "of such slight social value as a step to truth that any benefit that may be derived from them is clearly outweighed by the social interest in order and morality." *Chaplinsky*. We have recognized that "the freedom of speech" referred to by the First Amendment does not include a freedom to disregard these traditional limitations. Our decisions since the 1960's have narrowed the scope of the traditional categorical exceptions for defamation and for obscenity, but a limited categorical approach has remained an important part of our First Amendment jurisprudence.

We have sometimes said that these categories of expression are "not within the area of constitutionally protected speech," or that the "protection of the First Amendment does not extend" to them. . . . Such statements must be taken in context, however, and are no more literally true than is the occasionally repeated shorthand characterizing obscenity "as not being speech at all." What they mean is that these areas of speech can, consistently with the First Amendment, be regulated *because of their constitutionally proscribable content* (obscenity, defamation, etc.)—not that they are categories of speech entirely invisible to the Constitution, so that they may be made the vehicles for content discrimination unrelated to their distinctively proscribable content. Thus, the government may proscribe libel; but it may not make the further content discrimination of proscribing *only* libel critical of the government. * * *

Our cases surely do not establish the proposition that the First Amendment imposes no obstacle whatsoever to regulation of particular instances of such proscribable expression, so that the government "may regulate [them] freely." * * *

The proposition that a particular instance of speech can be proscribable on the basis of one feature (e.g., obscenity) but not on the basis of another (e.g., opposition to the city government) is commonplace, and has found application in many contexts. We have long held, for example, that nonverbal expressive activity can be banned because of the action it entails, but not because of the ideas it expresses—so that burning a flag in violation of an ordinance against outdoor fires could be punishable, whereas burning a flag in violation of an ordinance against dishonoring the flag is not. * * *

In other words, the exclusion of "fighting words" from the scope of the First Amendment simply means that, for purposes of that Amendment, the unprotected features of the words are, despite their verbal character, essentially a "nonspeech" element of communication. Fighting words are thus analogous to a noisy sound truck: Each is, as Justice Frankfurter recognized, a "mode of speech," both can be used to convey an idea; but neither has, in and of itself, a claim upon the First Amendment. As with the sound truck, however, so also with fighting words: The government may not regulate use based on hostility—or favoritism—towards the underlying message expressed. * * *

* * *

Even the prohibition against content discrimination that we assert the First Amendment requires is not absolute. It applies differently in the context of proscribable speech than in the area of fully protected speech. The rationale of the general prohibition, after all, is that content discrimination "rais[es] the specter that the Government may effectively drive certain ideas or viewpoints from the marketplace." * * *

When the basis for the content discrimination consists entirely of the very reason the entire class of speech at issue is proscribable, no significant danger of idea or viewpoint discrimination exists. Such a reason, having been adjudged neutral enough to support exclusion of the entire class of speech from the First Amendment protection, is also neutral enough to form the basis of distinction within the class. To illustrate: A State might choose to prohibit only that obscenity which is the most patently offensive in its prurience—i.e., that which involves the most lascivious displays of sexual activity. But it may not prohibit, for example, only that obscenity which includes offensive political messages. * * *

Another valid basis for according differential treatment to even a content-defined subclass of proscribable speech is that the subclass happens to be associated with particular "secondary effects" of the speech, so that the regulation is "justified without reference to the content of the. . .speech." *Renton v. Playtime Theatres, Inc.* * * *

* * *

Applying these principles to the St. Paul ordinance, we conclude that, even as narrowly construed by the Minnesota Supreme Court, the ordinance is facially unconstitutional. Although the phrase in the ordinance, "arouses anger, alarm, or resentment in others," has been limited by the Minnesota Supreme Court's construction to reach only those symbols or displays that amount to "fighting words," the remaining, unmodified terms make clear that the ordinance applies only to "fighting words" that insult, or provoke violence, "on the basis of race, color, creed, religion or gender." Displays containing abusive invective, no matter how vicious or severe, are permissible unless they are addressed to one of the specified disfavored topics. Those who wish to use "fighting words" in connection with other ideas—to express hostility, for example, on the basis of political affiliation, union membership, or homosexuality—are not covered. The First Amendment does not permit St. Paul to impose special prohibitions on those speakers who express views on disfavored subjects.

In its practical operation, moreover, the ordinance goes even beyond mere content discrimination, to actual viewpoint discrimination. Displays containing some words—odious racial epithets, for example—would be prohibited to proponents of all views. But "fighting words" that do not themselves invoke race, color, creed, religion, or gender—aspersions upon a person's mother, for example—would seemingly be usable *ad libitum* in the placards of those arguing in favor of racial, color, etc. tolerance and equality, but could not be used by that speaker's opponents. One could hold up a sign saying, for example, that all "anti-Catholic bigots" are misbegotten; but not that all "papists" are, for that would insult and provoke violence "on the basis of religion." St. Paul has no such authority to license one side of a debate to fight freestyle, while requiring the other to follow Marquis of Queensbury Rules.

What we have here, it must be emphasized, is not a prohibition of fighting words that are directed at certain persons or groups (which would be *facially* valid if it met the requirements of the Equal Protection Clause); but rather, a prohibition of fighting words that contain (as the Minnesota Supreme Court repeatedly emphasized) messages of "bias-motivated" hatred and in particular, as applied to this case, messages "based on virulent notions of racial supremacy."
* * *

* * *

The content-based discrimination reflected in the St. Paul ordinance comes within neither any of the specific exceptions to the First Amendment prohibition we discussed earlier, nor within a more general exception for content discrimination that does not threaten censorship of ideas. It assuredly does not fall within the exception for content discrimination based on the very reasons why the particular class of speech at issue (here, fighting words) is proscribable. As explained earlier, the reason why fighting words are categorically excluded from the protection of the First Amendment is not that their content communicates any particular idea, but that their content embodies a particularly intolerable (and socially unnecessary) *mode* of expressing *whatever* idea the speaker wishes to convey. St. Paul has not singled out one especially offensive mode of expression—it has not, for example, selected for prohibition only those fighting words that communicate ideas in a threatening (as opposed to a merely obnoxious) manner. Rather, it has proscribed fighting words of whatever manner that communicate messages of racial, gender, or religious intolerance. Selectivity of this sort creates the possibility that the city is seeking to handicap the expression of particular ideas. That possibility would alone be enough to render the ordinance presumptively invalid, but St. Paul's comments and concessions in this case elevate the possibility to a certainty.

* * *

Let there be no mistake about our belief that burning a cross in someone's front yard is reprehensible. But St. Paul has sufficient means at its disposal to prevent such behavior without adding the First Amendment to the fire.

The judgment of the Minnesota Supreme Court is reversed, and the case is remanded for proceedings not inconsistent with this opinion.

It is so ordered.

Justice White, with whom Justice Blackmun and Justice O'Connor join, and with whom Justice Stevens joins except as to Part I(A), concurring in the judgment.

I agree with the majority that the judgment of the Minnesota Supreme Court should be reversed. However, our agreement ends there.

This case could easily be decided within the contours of established First Amendment law by holding, as petitioner argues, that the St. Paul ordinance is fatally overbroad because it criminalizes not only unprotected expressions but expressions protected by the First Amendment. Instead, "find[ing] it unnecessary" to consider the questions upon which we granted review, the Court holds the ordinance facially unconstitutional on a ground that was never presented to the Minnesota Supreme Court, a ground that requires serious departures from the teaching of prior cases and is inconsistent with the plurality opinion in *Burson v. Freeman*, which was joined by two of the five Justices in the majority in the present case.

* * *

In the present case, the majority casts aside long-established First Amendment doctrine without the benefit of briefing and adopts an untried theory. This is hardly a judicious way of proceeding, and the Court's reasoning in reaching its result is transparently wrong.

* * *

Today, the Court announces that earlier Courts did not mean their repeated statements that certain categories of expressions are "not within the area of constitutionally protected speech." The present Court submits that such clear statements "must be taken in context" and are not "literally true."

To the contrary, those statements meant precisely what they said: The categorical approach is a firmly entrenched part of our First Amendment jurisprudence. * * *

In its decision today, the Court points to "[n]othing. . .in this Court's precedents warrant[ing] disregard of this longstanding tradition." Nevertheless, the majority holds that the First Amendment protects those narrow categories of expression long held to be undeserving of First Amendment protection—at least to the extent that lawmakers may not regulate some fighting words more strictly than others because of their content. The Court announces that such content-based distinctions violate the First Amendment because "the government may not regulate use based on hostility—or favoritism—towards the underlying message expressed." Should the government want to criminalize certain fighting words the Court now requires it to criminalize all fighting words.

It is inconsistent to hold that the government may proscribe an entire category of speech because the content of that speech is evil, but that the government may not treat a subset of that category differently without violating the First Amendment; the content of the subset is by definition worthless and undeserving of constitutional protection.

The majority's observation that fighting words are "quite expressive indeed," is no answer. Fighting words are not a means of exchanging views, rallying supporters, or registering a protest; they are directed against individuals to provoke violence or to inflict injury. Therefore, a ban on all fighting words or on a subset of the fighting words category would restrict only the social evil of hate speech, without creating the danger of driving viewpoints from the marketplace.

Therefore, the Court's insistence on inventing its brand of First Amendment underinclusiveness puzzles me. The overbreadth doctrine has the redeeming virtue of attempting to avoid the chilling of protected expressions, but the Court's new "underbreadth" creation serves no desirable function. Instead, it permits, indeed invites, the continuation of expressive conduct that in this case is evil and worthless in First Amendment terms, until the city of St. Paul cures the underbreadth by adding to its ordinance a catch-all phrase such as "and all other fighting words that may constitutionally be subject to this ordinance."

Any contribution of this holding to First Amendment jurisprudence is surely a negative one, since it necessarily signals that expressions of violence, such as the message of intimidation and racial hatred conveyed by burning a cross on someone's lawn, are of sufficient value to outweigh the social interests in order and morality that has traditionally placed such fighting words outside the First Amendment. Indeed, by characterizing fighting words as a form of "debate," the majority legitimates hate speech as a form of public discussion.

Furthermore, the Court obscures the line between speech that could be regulated freely on the basis of content (i.e., the narrow categories of expression falling outside the First Amendment) and that which could be regulated on the basis of content only upon a showing of a compelling state interest (i.e., all remaining expressions). By placing fighting words, which the Court has long held to be valueless, on at least equal constitutional footing with political discourse and other forms of speech that we have deemed to have the greatest social value, the majority devalues the latter category.

In a second break with precedent, the Court refuses to sustain the ordinance even though it would survive under the strict scrutiny applicable to other protected expression. Assuming, arguendo, that the St. Paul ordinance is a content-based regulation of protected expression, it nevertheless would pass First Amendment review under settled law upon a showing that the regulation " 'is necessary to serve a compelling state interest and is narrowly drawn to achieve that end.' " St. Paul has urged that its ordinance, in the words of the majority, "help[s] to ensure the basic human rights of members of groups that have historically been subjected to discrimination. . . ."

The Court expressly concedes that this interest is compelling and is promoted by the ordinance. Nevertheless, the Court treats strict scrutiny analysis as irrelevant to the constitutionality of the legislation. * * *

* * *

As with its rejection of the Court's categorical analysis, the majority offers no reasoned basis for discarding our firmly established strict scrutiny analysis at this time. The majority appears to believe that its doctrinal revisionism is necessary to prevent our elected lawmakers from prohibiting libel against members of one political party but not another and from enacting similarly preposterous laws. The majority is misguided.

Although the First Amendment does not apply to categories of unprotected speech, such as fighting words, the Equal Protection Clause requires that the regulation of unprotected speech be rationally related to a legitimate government interest. A defamation statute that drew distinctions on the basis of political affiliation or "an ordinance prohibiting only those legally obscene works that contain criticism of the city governments," would unquestionably fail rational basis review.

Turning to the St. Paul ordinance and assuming arguendo, as the majority does, that the ordinance is not constitutionally overbroad, there is no question that it would pass equal protection review. The ordinance proscribes a subset of "fighting words," those that injure "on the basis of race, color, creed, religion, or gender." This selective regulation reflects the City's judgment that harms based on race, color, creed, religion, or gender are more pressing public concerns than the harms caused by other fighting words. In light of our Nation's long and painful experience with discrimination, this determination is plainly reasonable. Indeed, as the majority concedes, the interest is compelling.

* * *

Although I disagree with the Court's analysis, I do agree with its conclusion: The St. Paul ordinance is unconstitutional. However, I would decide the case on overbreadth grounds.

* * *

In the First Amendment context, "[c]riminal statutes must be scrutinized with particular care; those that make unlawful a substantial amount of constitutionally protected conduct may be held facially invalid even if they also have legitimate application." The St. Paul antibias ordinance is such a law. Although the ordinance reaches conduct that is unprotected, it also makes criminal expressive conduct that causes only hurt feelings, offense, or resentment, and is protected by the First Amendment. The ordinance is therefore fatally overbroad and invalid on its face.

Justice Blackmun, concurring in the judgment. [omitted]

Justice Stevens, with whom Justice White and Justice Blackmun join as to Part I, concurring in the judgment.

* * *

. . . [M]y colleagues today wrestle with two broad principles: first, that certain "categories of expression [including 'fighting words'] are 'not within the area of constitutionally protected speech' " and second, that "[c]ontent-based regulations [of expression] are presumptively invalid." Although in past opinions the Court has repeated both of these maxims, it has—quite rightly—adhered to neither with the absolutism suggested by my colleagues. Thus, while I agree that the St. Paul ordinance is unconstitutionally overbroad for the reasons stated in Justice White's opinion, I write separately to suggest how the allure of absolute principles has skewed the analysis of both the majority and concurring opinions.

* * *

As an initial matter, the Court's revision of the categorical approach seems to me something of an adventure in a doctrinal wonderland, for the concept of "obscene antigovernment" speech is fantastical. The category of the obscene is very narrow; to be obscene, expression must be found by the trier of fact to "appea[l] to the prurient interests, . . . depic[t] or describ[e], in a patently offensive way, sexual conduct, [and] taken as a whole, lac[k] serious literary, artistic, political or scientific value." *Miller v. California* (1973). "Obscene antigovernment" speech, then, is a contradiction in terms: If expression is antigovernment, it does not "lac[k] serious . . . political . . . value" and cannot be obscene.

* * *

I am, however, even more troubled by the second step of the Court's analysis—namely, its conclusion that the St. Paul ordinance is an unconstitutional content-based regulation of speech. Drawing on broadly worded dicta, the Court establishes a near-absolute ban on content-based regulations of expression and holds that the First Amendment prohibits the regulation of fighting words by subject matter. Thus, while the Court rejects the "all-or-nothing-at-all" approach, it promptly embraces an absolutism of its own: within a particular "proscribable" category of expression, the Court holds, a government must either proscribe all speech or no speech at all. This aspect of the Court's ruling fundamentally misunderstands the role and constitutional status of content-based regulations on speech, conflicts with the very nature of First Amendment jurisprudence, and disrupts well-settled principles of First Amendment law.

* * *

Our First Amendment decisions have created a rough hierarchy in the constitutional protection of speech. Core political speech occupies the highest, most protected position; commercial speech and nonobscene, sexually explicit speech are regarded as a sort of second-class expression; obscenity and fighting words receive the least protection of all. Assuming that the Court is correct that this last class of speech is not wholly "unprotected," it certainly does not follow that fighting words and obscenity receive the same sort of protections afforded core political speech. Yet in ruling that proscribable speech cannot be regulated based on subject matter, the Court does just that. Perversely, this gives fighting words greater protection than is afforded commercial speech. * * *

* * *

In sum, the central premise of the Court's ruling—that "[c]ontent-based regulations are presumptively invalid"—has simplistic appeal, but lacks support in our First Amendment jurisprudence. To make matters worse, the Court today extends this overstated claim to reach categories of hitherto unprotected speech and, in doing so, wreaks havoc in an area of settled law. Finally, although the Court recognizes exceptions to its new principle, those exceptions undermine its very conclusions that the St. Paul ordinance is unconstitutional. Stated directly, the majority's position cannot withstand scrutiny.

* * *

As the foregoing suggests, I disagree with both the Court's and part of Justice White's analysis of the constitutionality of the St. Paul ordinance. Unlike the Court, I do not believe that all content-based regulations are equally infirm and presumptively invalid; unlike Justice White, I do not believe that fighting words are wholly unprotected by the First Amendment. To the contrary, I believe our decisions establish a more complex and subtle analysis, one that considers the content and context of the regulated speech, and the nature and scope of the restriction on speech. Applying this analysis and assuming arguendo (as the Court does) that the St. Paul ordinance is not overbroad, I conclude that such a selective, subject-matter regulation on proscribable speech is constitutional.

* * *

In sum, the St. Paul ordinance (as construed by the Court) regulates expressive activity that is wholly proscribable and does so not on the basis of viewpoint, but rather in recognition of the different harms caused by such activity. Taken together, these several considerations persuade me that the St. Paul ordinance is not an unconstitutional content-based regulation on speech. Thus, were the ordinance not overbroad, I would vote to uphold it.

The justices were able to achieve a much higher level of consensus in the second hate speech case they decided, *Wisconsin v. Mitchell* (1993). This case involved a quite different law, one providing for an enhanced prison sentence when a crime was racially motivated. The case arose from an ugly incident in Kenosha, Wisconsin, in 1989 where a group of African American youths were discussing a scene from the movie "Mississippi Burning" in which a white man had beaten an African American youth who was praying. When a white youth happened to walk by the area where the African American youths had congregated, Todd Mitchell led an attack on the boy. The group beat him severely, and he remained in a coma for days. Mitchell was convicted in a jury trial for aggravated battery, which normally carried a maximum two-year sentence, but the jury increased the sentence to a maximum of seven years under a Wisconsin law providing for sentence enhancement when a defendant ". . .intentionally selects the person against whom the crime . . . is committed. . .because of race, religion, color, disability, sexual orientation, national origin or ancestry of that person. . ." (508 U.S. at 480).

Rehnquist wrote for a unanimous Court in upholding the Wisconsin law against a First Amendment challenge. Rehnquist argued that the statute was aimed at criminal conduct and that sentencing authorities have traditionally had wide discretion in considering factors relevant to imposing a sentence. This case could thus be distinguished from *R.A.V.*, according to Rehnquist, because that case dealt with an ordinance which focused on expression, whereas ". . .the statute in this case is aimed at conduct unprotected by the First Amendment" (508 U.S. at 487). The Court's decision was widely supported, for forty-nine states as well as the United States government had urged the Court in amicus briefs to uphold the law.

The Court certainly has not heard its final case regarding hate speech laws. The question of sentence enhancement for race-based crimes does seem settled by the Court's unanimous decision in *Mitchell.* The *R.A.V.* case shows, however, that the Court and the country will probably experience a long and difficult struggle over the wisdom and constitutionality of hate speech laws. A wide consensus exists in American society against various forms of hate speech, but should laws be written criminalizing this type of expression? Is such expression within or beyond the protection of the First Amendment? Even if such laws are desirable, can they be written narrowly and precisely enough that they do not infringe upon constitutionally protected expression? The Supreme Court will eventually have to provide answers to these questions.

Speech-Plus-Conduct

Speech-plus-conduct is another major category of cases that we need to examine under the heading of freedom of speech. Speech-plus-conduct refers to activities such as demonstrations, rallies, and protests, which typically involve a substantial number of people. Three freedom of expression guarantees of the First Amendment can be involved in speech-plus-conduct cases: speech, assembly, and petition.

Speech-plus-conduct cases have come before the Court frequently and have often involved the major social-political issues in American society. For example, the Warren Court considered several decisions involving demonstrations associated with the civil rights movement of the sixties, the Burger Court confronted several cases stemming from protests over the Vietnam War, and the Rehnquist Court has had to deal with protest demonstrations involving the abortion controversy.

The justices of the Supreme Court have struggled to find guiding doctrinal principles in speech-plus-conduct cases. This struggle seems to stem from the conflict between the competing values of freedom and order, which tend to stand in particularly sharp contrast in regard to speech-plus-conduct. The justices are well aware that important First Amendment values are at stake in these cases, which frequently involve debate over the most controversial public policy issues in American society. At the same time, protest and demonstration activities frequently involve large numbers of people who can create direct threats to public order and safety. In our examination of the Court's speech-plus-conduct cases, we will pay particular attention to the justices' search for doctrinal guidelines that can adequately balance the competing values of freedom and order.

The Warren Court heard more than a dozen cases involving protest demonstrations, but speech-plus-conduct cases had arisen in earlier decades as well. In *DeJonge v. Oregon* (1937), the Court not only nationalized the guarantee of freedom of assembly but also recognized it as being of equal importance with freedom of speech and freedom of the press. *Hague v. Committee for Industrial Organization* (1939) was an important case because the Court introduced the concept of the public forum. In rejecting efforts by Jersey City, New Jersey's mayor, Frank Hague, to prevent union organizers from using public facilities, the Court recognized that public forums like streets and parks had always been considered open for purposes of assembling to discuss public issues. The Court also recognized in *Hague*, however, that the government had legitimate interests to protect, and this idea was developed more fully in *Cox v. New Hampshire* (1941). Cox was one of sixty-eight Jehovah's Witnesses arrested for parading without a permit. The high court unanimously agreed that activities like a parade or demonstration posed significant potential problems to public order and safety. Thus, a governmental unit could legitimately require a group seeking to engage in such an activity to obtain a permit; also, reasonable time, place, and manner restrictions could be imposed on the activity, but such regulations must be precisely drawn and must not discriminate based on the viewpoint being expressed.

The Warren Court used these guidelines in a series of cases in the sixties involving civil rights demonstrations, but the justices frequently found it difficult to resolve the competing interests in these cases despite the predominance of liberals on the Court. Most members of the Court were highly sympathetic to First Amendment claims. In addition, these speech-plus-conduct cases of the sixties typically involved white segregationist authorities in suppressing civil rights demonstrators, and the liberal Warren Court justices supported efforts to eliminate all vestiges of racial discrimination. Nonetheless, the justices also recognized the necessity for government officials to provide for public order and safety, which could easily be threatened by protest demonstrations. Thus, the Warren Court was closely divided in its outcomes in protest demonstration cases, deciding eight liberally and six conservatively. This 57 percent liberal pattern was the lowest degree of liberalism in any category of free expression cases for the Warren Court.

The Warren Court justices did hand down several major liberal decisions involving speech-plus-conduct, with *Edwards v. South Carolina* (1963) being one of the most important. The *Edwards* case involved a peaceful protest demonstration in 1961 by African American students at the state capital in Columbia, South Carolina. When the demonstrators refused to obey an order to disperse, they were arrested and subsequently found guilty of disturbing the peace. On appeal, the United States Supreme Court ruled 8-1 that the demonstrators' First Amendment rights were violated. Writing for the majority, Justice Stewart viewed the case as involving the guarantees of speech, assembly, and petition. He recognized that under some circumstances the demonstrators could have been arrested, for example, if they had blocked traffic or protested during a time clearly prohibited by law. In this case, however, the demonstrators were peacefully protesting and were arrested under a law that was so vague and general that it was "'not susceptible of exact definition'" (372 U.S. at 237).

EDWARDS V. SOUTH CAROLINA

372 U.S. 229, 83 S.Ct. 680, 9 L.Ed. 2d 697 (1963)

■ On March 2, 1961, 187 African Americans from the Zion Baptist Church in Columbia, South Carolina, peaceably assembled at the South Carolina State House to protest policies of racial discrimination. After singing patriotic and religious songs and listening to a religious lecture by one of their leaders, the demonstrators were arrested by police for violation of the common law crime of breach of the peace. Even though the assembly was peaceful with no threat of violence, the protestors were convicted in a magistrate's court in Columbia, South Carolina. On appeal, the South Carolina Supreme Court upheld their convictions. In petitioning the United States Supreme Court, the defendants argued that their convictions were unconstitutional in view of the record showing a nonviolent and peaceful expression of their grievances. Using the First and Fourteenth Amendments, they asserted that the arrests and convictions were infringements upon their rights of freedom of expression.

This is a significant case because the Court interpreted the First Amendment to provide protection for peaceful civil rights demonstrators during the turbulent period of the 1960s. As you read this decision, consider the following questions: (1) Under what circumstances, if any, would the Court have upheld the convictions as constitutional? (2) Is the clear and present danger test used in an unambiguous manner in this case? (3) Was the Court's decision based on concerns for racial equality as well as freedom of expression?

VOTE:

8 justices found the convictions to be unconstitutional (Black, Brennan, Douglas, Goldberg, Harlan, Stewart, Warren, White).

1 justice found the convictions to be constitutional (Clark).

Justice Stewart delivered the opinion of the Court.

* * *

* * * It is clear to us that in arresting, convicting, and punishing the petitioners under the circumstances disclosed by this record, South Carolina infringed the petitioners' constitutionally protected rights of free speech, free assembly, and freedom to petition for redress of their grievances.

It has long been established that these First Amendment freedoms are protected by the Fourteenth Amendment from invasion by the States. The circumstances in this case reflect an exercise of these basic constitutional rights in their most pristine and classic form. The petitioners felt aggrieved by laws of South Carolina which allegedly "prohibited Negro privileges in this State." They peaceably assembled at the site of the State Government and there peaceably expressed their grievances "to the citizens of South Carolina, along with the Legislative Bodies of South

Carolina." Not until they were told by police officials that they must disperse on pain of arrest did they do more. Even then, they but sang patriotic and religious songs after one of their leaders had delivered a "religious harangue." There was no violence or threat of violence on their part, or on the part of any member of the crowd watching them. Police protection was "ample."

* * *

We do not review in this case criminal convictions resulting from the evenhanded application of a precise and narrowly drawn regulatory statute evincing a legislative judgment that certain specific conduct be limited or proscribed. If, for example, the petitioners had been convicted upon evidence that they had violated a law regulating traffic, or had disobeyed a law reasonably limiting the periods during which the State House grounds were open to the public, this would be a different case. These petitioners were convicted of an offense so generalized as to be, in the words of the South Carolina Supreme Court, "not susceptible of exact definition." And they were convicted upon evidence which showed no more than that the opinions which they were peaceably expressing were sufficiently opposed to the views of the majority of the community to attract a crowd and necessitate police protection.

The Fourteenth Amendment does not permit a State to make criminal the peaceable expression of unpopular views. "[A] function of free speech under our system of government is to invite dispute. It may indeed best serve its high purpose when it induces a condition of unrest, creates dissatisfaction with conditions as they are, or even stirs people to anger. Speech is often provocative and challenging. It may strike at prejudices and preconceptions and have profound unsettling effects as it presses for acceptance of an idea. That is why freedom of speech . . . is . . . protected against censorship or punishment, unless shown likely to produce a clear and present danger of a serious substantive evil that rises far above public inconvenience, annoyance, or unrest. . . . There is no room under our Constitution for a more restrictive view. For the alternative would lead to standardization of ideas either by legislatures, courts, or dominant political or community groups." *Terminiello v. Chicago*. As in the *Terminiello* case, the courts of South Carolina have defined a criminal offense so as to permit conviction of the petitioners if their speech "stirred people to anger, invited public dispute, or brought about a condition of unrest. A conviction resting on any of those grounds may not stand."

As Chief Justice Hughes wrote in *Stromberg v. California*, "The maintenance of the opportunity for free political discussion to the end that government may be responsive to the will of the people and that changes may be obtained by lawful means, an opportunity essential to the security of the Republic, is a fundamental principle of our constitutional system. A statute which upon its face, and as authoritatively construed, is so vague and indefinite as to permit the punishment of the fair use of this opportunity is repugnant to the guaranty of liberty contained in the Fourteenth Amendment. . . ."

For these reasons we conclude that these criminal convictions cannot stand.

Reversed.

Justice Clark, dissenting.

The convictions of the petitioners, Negro high school and college students, for breach of the peace under South Carolina law are accepted by the Court "as binding upon us to that extent" but are held violative of "petitioners' constitutionally protected rights of free speech, free assembly, and freedom to petition for redress of their grievances." Petitioners, of course, had a right to peaceable assembly, to espouse their cause and to petition, but in my view the manner in which they exercised those rights was by no means the passive demonstration which this Court relates; rather, as the City Manager of Columbia testified, "a dangerous situation was really building up" which South Carolina's courts expressly found had created "an actual interference with traffic and an imminently threatened disturbance of the peace of the community." Since the Court does not attack the state courts' findings and accepts the convictions as "binding to the extent that the petitioners' conduct constituted a breach of the peace," it is difficult for me to understand its understatement of the facts and reversal of the convictions.

* * * . . .[I]t is our duty to consider the context in which the arrests were made. Certainly the city officials would be constitutionally prohibited from refusing petitioners access to the State House grounds merely because they disagreed with their views. * * * It is undisputed that the city official specifically granted petitioners permission to assemble, imposing only the requirement that they be "peaceful." * * *

* * *

* * * The question thus seems to me whether a State is constitutionally prohibited from enforcing laws to prevent breach of the peace in a situation where city officials in good faith believe and the record shows, that disorder and violence are imminent, merely because the activities constituting that breach contain claimed elements of constitutionally protected speech and assembly. To me the answer under our cases is clearly in the negative.

* * *

The Warren Court also ruled in favor of protesting demonstrators in *Cox v. Louisiana* (1965) and *Brown v. Louisiana* (1966). The *Cox* case stemmed from the arrest and conviction of Reverend B. Elton Cox, who in 1961 led approximately two thousand black college students from Southern University in a march from the state capitol to a courthouse to protest the arrest and jailing of twenty-three students who had attempted to integrate lunch counters serving only whites. The march and demonstration at the courthouse were orderly, and at the conclusion of the demonstration Cox urged the demonstrators to seek service at the lunch counter. Police then ordered the demonstrators to disperse and fired tear gas into the crowd. Cox was subsequently arrested and convicted of violating state laws regarding breach of the peace, interference with public passage, and interference with the administration of justice. Writing for the majority, Justice Goldberg acknowledged again the principles that the government can set reasonable time, place, and manner restrictions on demonstrations and furthermore that police can interfere with a peaceful assembly that becomes violent. In this case, however, like *Edwards*, the laws in question were too broad, and the demonstration had been a peaceful one.

Brown v. Louisiana (1966) was yet another case in which the Court ruled in favor of the right of peaceful protest. In this case, five African American men refused to leave a public library reserved only for whites, and they were arrested under a breach of the peace statute. Once again, the Warren Court ruled that this type of activity came within the protection of the First Amendment, and the facts of the case did not justify government interference with freedom of expression.

We can discuss one additional liberal decision of the Warren Court involving speech-plus-conduct, a case concerning protest activities on private property as opposed to being in a public forum. In general, the First Amendment does not extend to expression on private property, but the Warren Court justices carved out an exception to this rule in *Amalgamated Food Employees Union Local 590 v. Logan Valley Plaza* (1968). In this case, members of a food employees union picketed a store that did not use union workers in a private mall near Altoona, Pennsylvania. The store owner and the mall owner won an injunction prohibiting the picketing, but the high court reversed. Writing for a 6-3 majority, Justice Marshall argued that the mall was open to the public and served as the area's business center, and therefore the mall could be considered public property for First Amendment purposes.

Despite this line of decisions supporting various forms of demonstrations, the Warren Court also issued several decisions in which the Court gave constitutional approval to government arrests of peaceful protestors. We will examine two of these cases, *Adderley v. Florida* (1966) and *Walker v. City of Birmingham* (1967).

Harriett Adderley was among approximately two hundred Florida A & M students who marched from their university to a county jail to protest the arrests of several students who had tried to integrate a theater that prohibited blacks from attendance. The county sheriff informed them they would have to leave the jail grounds or be arrested for trespass. Although some of the students left, Adderley and others remained. They were subsequently arrested and convicted under a Florida trespass statute. Writing for a narrow five-person majority, Justice Black ruled that the students' First Amendment rights were not violated. Black recognized that this case presented similarities to the *Edwards* and *Cox* cases, but, he argued, critical differences distinguished this case. Unlike the laws in *Edwards* and *Cox*, the law in this case did not suffer from vagueness or overbreadth. Furthermore, Black argued, jail grounds are much different than state capitol or courthouse grounds. Jails are built for security purposes, and the sheriff was within his legitimate authority to order the demonstrators off the grounds because of his concern over security issues.

The Court was sharply split in *Adderley*. Douglas wrote a strong dissent joined by Warren, Brennan, and Fortas. Citing *Hague* and *Edwards* as controlling precedents, Douglas argued that a jailhouse was a government place and that the Constitution protected peaceful protest in a case like this.

Adderley v. Florida

385 U.S. 39, 875 S.Ct. 242, 17 L.Ed. 2d 149 (1966)

■ Harriet Louise Adderley and thirty-one other students from Florida A & M University in Tallahassee, Florida, were arrested for violating a Florida law that prohibited trespassing "with a malicious and mischievous intent." According to the statute, the protesters were subject to a maximum of three months in prison and $100 fine. The students had been demonstrating on the grounds of the Leon County jail grounds to protest the arrest of other protesting students the previous day. More generally, they also were protesting the state and local practices of racial segregation, including segregation of the prison. The students appealed but the convictions were upheld by the Florida Circuit Court and, subsequently, by the Florida District Court of Appeals, the highest state court of appeal. Adderley and the demonstrators appealed to the United States Supreme Court, contending that their rights of free speech, assembly, petition, due process of law, and equal protection of the laws were denied as provided by the First and Fourteenth Amendments.

This case is important because it represents one of the more conservative freedom of expression decisions of the Warren Court and illustrates the difficult task of drawing lines in speech-plus-conduct cases. As you read the opinions in this case, think about the following questions: (1) Did Justice Black make a convincing argument in distinguishing this case from *Edwards v. South Carolina* (1963)? (2) Justice Marshall replaced Justice Clark following the *Adderley* decision. Would this case have been decided differently if Marshall had been on the Court?

Vote:

5 justices voted that the demonstrators' constitutional rights were not violated (Black, Clark, Harlan, Stewart, White).

4 justices voted the demonstrators' constitutional rights were violated (Brennan, Douglas, Fortas, Warren).

Justice Black delivered the opinion of the Court.

* * *

Petitioners have insisted from the beginning of this case that it is controlled by and must be reversed because of our prior cases of *Edwards v. South Carolina* and *Cox v. Louisiana*. We cannot agree.

The *Edwards* case, like this one, did come up when a number of persons demonstrated on public property against their State's segregation policies. * * * In *Edwards*, the demonstrators went to the South Carolina State Capitol grounds to protest. In this case, they went to the jail. Traditionally, state capitol grounds are open to the public. Jails, built for security purposes, are not. The demonstrators at the South Carolina Capitol went in through a public driveway and as they entered they were told by state officials there that they had a right as citizens to go through the State House grounds as long as they were peaceful. Here the demonstrators entered the jail grounds through a driveway used only for jail purposes and without warning to or permission from the sheriff. More importantly, South Carolina sought to prosecute its State Capitol demonstrators by charging them with the common-law crime of breach of the peace. This Court in *Edwards* took pains to point out at length the indefinite, loose, and broad nature of this charge; indeed, this Court pointed out that the South Carolina Supreme Court had itself declared that the "breach of the peace" charge is "not susceptible of exact definition." South Carolina's power to prosecute, it was emphasized, would have been different had the State proceeded under a "precise and narrowly drawn regulatory statute evincing a legislative judgment that certain specific conduct be limited or proscribed" such as, for example, "limiting the periods during which the State House grounds were open to the public. . . ." The South Carolina breach-of-the-peace statute was thus struck down as being too broad and all-embracing as to jeopardize speech, press, assembly and petition, under the constitutional doctrine enunciated in *Cantwell v. Connecticut* and followed in many subsequent cases. And it was on this same ground of vagueness that in *Cox v. Louisiana*, the Louisiana breach-of-the-peace law used to prosecute Cox was invalidated.

The Florida trespass statute under which these petitioners were charged cannot be challenged on this ground. It is aimed at conduct of one limited kind, that is, for one person or persons to trespass upon the property of another with malicious and mischievous intent. There is no lack of notice in this law, nothing to entrap or fool the unwary.

* * *

* * * [The only remaining question is] whether conviction of the state offense, thus defined, unconstitutionally deprives petitioners of their rights to freedom of speech, press, assembly, or petition. We hold it does not. * * * Nothing in the Constitution of the United States prevents Florida from even-handed enforcements of its general trespass statute against those refusing to obey the sheriff's order to remove themselves from what amounted to the curtilage of the jailhouse. The State, no less than a private owner of property, has power to preserve the property under its control for the use to which it is lawfully dedicated. For this reason there is no merit to the petitioners' argument that they had a constitutional right to stay on the property, over the jail custodian's objections, because this "area chosen for the peaceful civil rights demonstration was not only 'reasonable' but also particularly appropriate. . . ." The United States Constitution does not forbid a State to control the use of its own property for its own lawful nondiscriminatory purpose.

These judgments are

Affirmed.

Justice Douglas, with whom the Chief Justice, Justice Brennan, and Justice Fortas concur, dissenting.

The First Amendment, applicable to the States by reason of the Fourteenth (*Edwards v. South Carolina*), provides that "Congress shall make no law . . . abridging . . . the right of the people peaceably to assemble, and to petition the Government for a redress of grievances." * * * With all respect, . . . the Court errs in treating the case as if it were an ordinary trespass case or an ordinary picketing case.

* * * Conventional methods of petitioning may be, and often have been, shut off to large groups of our citizens. Legislators may turn deaf ears; formal complaints may be routed endlessly through a bureaucratic maze; courts may let the wheels of justice grind very slowly. Those who do not control television and radio, those who cannot afford to advertise in newspapers or circulate elaborate pamphlets may have only a more limited type of access to public officials. Their methods should not be condemned as tactics of obstruction and harassment as long as the assembly and petition are peaceable, as these were.

* * *

We do violence to the First Amendment when we permit this "petition for redress of grievances" to be turned into a trespass action. It does not help to analogize this problem to the problem of picketing. Picketing is a form of protest usually directed against private interests. I do not see how rules governing picketing in general are relevant to this express constitutional right to assemble and to petition for redress of grievances. In the first place the jailhouse grounds were not marked with "NO TRESPASSING!" signs, nor does respondent claim that the public was generally excluded from the grounds. Only the sheriff's fiat transformed lawful conduct into an unlawful trespass. To say that a private owner could have done the same if the rally had taken place on private property is to speak of a different case, as an assembly and a petition for redress of grievances run to government, not to private proprietors.

* * *

* * * When we allow Florida to construe her "malicious trespass" statute to bar a person from going on property knowing it is not his own and to apply that prohibition to public property, we discard *Cox* and *Edwards*. Would the case be any different if, as is common, the demonstration took place outside a building which housed both the jail and the legislative body? I think not.

* * *

Today a trespass law is used to penalize people for exercising a constitutional right. Tomorrow a disorderly conduct statute, a breach-of-the-peace statute, a vagrancy statute will be put to the same end. It is said that the sheriff did not make the arrests because of the views which petitioners espoused. That excuse is usually given, as we know from the many cases involving arrests of minority groups for breaches of the peace, unlawful assemblies, and parading without a permit. * * * . . . [S]uch arrests are usually sought to be justified by some legitimate function of government. Yet by allowing these orderly and civilized protests against injustice to be suppressed, we only increase the forces of frustration which the convictions of second-class citizenship are generating amongst us.

The Warren Court was also sharply divided in *Walker v. City of Birmingham* (1967), voting 5-4 to uphold the arrest and conviction of Martin Luther King and seven others who violated a court injunction against parading without a permit. King and other leaders of the Southern Christian Leadership Conference had engaged in a number of demonstrations against racial discrimination in Birmingham, Alabama, and city officials refused to issue parade permits for further demonstrations. When the civil rights activists decided to parade without a permit, a state court issued an injunction ordering them not to parade, but the planned demonstrations were held despite the injunction. Justice Stewart wrote the majority opinion upholding the contempt of court finding against King and the other civil rights leaders. Warren, Douglas, Brennan, and Fortas were again in dissent as they had been in *Adderley.*

The Burger Court also heard a substantial number of cases involving speech-plus-conduct, and, like the Warren Court, the Burger Court justices struggled to find a proper balance between the values of freedom and order. The Burger Court's decisions in this area tended to be closely associated with the developing doctrine of public forum analysis. Rallies, demonstrations, and other forms of speech-plus-conduct were given heightened protection if they occurred in public forums, that is, places like streets and parks, which were traditionally available for public expression. If these activities occurred in nonpublic forums, however, then relatively low protection was given by the Court to First Amendment rights.

In a series of cases in the seventies and eighties, the Burger Court justices ruled in favor of various types of protest activities because they occurred in public forums. These decisions were consistent with the Warren Court decisions in *Edwards v. South Carolina* (1963) and *Cox v. Louisiana* (1965). In *Police Department of City of Chicago v. Mosley* (1972), the Burger Court ruled in favor of demonstrators using the sidewalk and street in front of a public school. Peaceful demonstrations in Lafayette Park in Washington, D.C., were upheld in *Chief of the Capitol Police v. Jeanette Rankin Brigade* in 1972. Municipal auditoriums were brought within the category of public forums in the 1975 case of *Southeastern Promotions v. Conrad.* And the Supreme Court itself was the cite of a demonstration giving rise to the case of *United States v. Grace* (1982); the justices ruled that the sidewalks surrounding the Court are a public forum where freedom of expression enjoys a high degree of protection.

The Burger Court also found, however, that several areas were not public forums. Just as the Warren Court had ruled in *Adderley v. Florida* (1966) that the area surrounding jails was not appropriate for protest demonstrations, so too the Burger Court ruled in *Flower v. United States* (1972) and *Greer v. Spock* (1976) that military bases are not public forums, and therefore protest activities can be tightly regulated by base commanders.

The cases we have just examined involved the Burger Court in drawing difficult distinctions between public forums and nonpublic forums on *public land.* The justices had even more difficulty in determining appropriate standards regarding speech-plus-conduct activities on *private property.* Does the First Amendment provide protection in such cases? We can recall that the Warren Court answered this question affirmatively in *Amalgamated Food Employees Union v. Logan Valley Plaza* (1968), but the answer was not so clear to the justices who constituted the Burger Court. In *Lloyd Corporation, Ltd. v. Tanner* (1972) the Court ruled in favor of the owners of a private shopping mall who prohibited the distribution of handbills by opponents of the Vietnam War. Writing for a five-person majority that included the four Nixon appointees, Justice Powell distinguished the *Lloyd* decision from the *Logan Valley Plaza* case because the former involved a purely private mall whereas the latter involved a company town in which private and public distinctions were blurred. The Burger Court seemed to reinforce the *Lloyd* precedent four years later in *Hudgens v. National Labor Relations Board* (1976), ruling in favor of mall owners who prohibited striking employees of a shoe warehouse from picketing a retail store of the company located in the mall. A majority of the Burger Court justices ruled that this type of picketing was not even protected by the First Amendment, and three justices maintained that the *Lloyd* decision had the effect of overruling the Warren Court's *Logan Valley Plaza* precedent.

Although these cases made it appear that the Burger Court justices were not going to provide any degree of First Amendment protection to speech-plus-conduct activities on private property, the 1980 case of *PruneYard Shopping Center v. Robins* saw the Court support expressive conduct in a private mall. Michael Robins and several of his high school friends set up a card table in the central courtyard of PruneYard Shopping Center, a privately owned shopping mall in Campbell, California, and sought signatures on a petition opposing a United Nations resolution condemning Zionism. A security guard forced them to leave, however, based upon the mall's policy of prohibiting public expressive activities unrelated to the mall's commercial purposes. The California Supreme Court ruled in favor of Robins on the basis of the State constitution's guarantee of freedom of expression. The shopping center appealed to the U.S. Supreme Court on the basis of *Lloyd* and *Hudgens*, but the Burger Court unanimously rejected their argument. In the Court's majority opinion, Justice Rehnquist stated that California could adopt in its own constitutional guarantees of freedom of expression more extensive than those of the Federal Constitution.

First Amendment cases involving speech-plus-conduct have occupied a prominent place on the agenda of the Rehnquist Court, which has developed further the public forum analysis of previous Court eras. Under this forum-based approach, the Rehnquist Court recognizes that speech-plus-conduct activities frequently occur on government property, which is divided into three categories: (1) the traditional public forum such as "streets and parks [which] have immemorially been held in trust for the use of the public and, time out of mind, have been used for purposes of assembly, communicating thoughts between citizens, and discussing public questions" (*Hague v. CIO*, 307 U.S. at 515–16); (2) the designated public forum, government property that has been specifically opened for expressive activity; and (3) the nonpublic forum, which includes all other government property. If a case involves either a traditional or designated public forum, then some type of heightened scrutiny is applicable, depending on whether the government regulation is content-neutral or content-based. If the law is content-based, then the highest level of scrutiny applies, requiring the government to show that the regulation is necessary to serve a compelling government interest and is narrowly drawn to achieve that interest. If the government action is a content-neutral regulation involving time, place, or manner, then an intermediate level of scrutiny applies; the government must establish that it is pursuing significant interests through narrowly tailored means and that ample alternative channels of communication are available. Finally, if the case involves a nonpublic forum, then the government needs only to satisfy a minimal scrutiny test of reasonableness.

The Rehnquist Court's decisions in this area of freedom of speech have been predominantly conservative, even when the strict scrutiny test has been used. These cases have generated substantial disagreement among the justices, with the liberals frequently writing forceful dissenting opinions. We will focus attention on the two speech-plus-conduct cases that are classified as being of major importance—*Frisby v. Schultz* (1988) and *Madsen v. Women's Health Center* (1994)—but several other cases deserve some attention as well.

Sandra Schultz held strong views against abortion and was actively involved in organizing several peaceful picketing demonstrations in April and May of 1985 on a public street by the residence of a Brookfield, Wisconsin, physician who performed abortions. In response to complaints about these demonstrations, the governing

Board of the city passed an ordinance banning all picketing of residential homes in the city. Schultz and others filed suit in federal district court and won a preliminary injunction. A closely divided circuit court upheld the district court decision, and the Supreme Court granted cert.

O'Connor wrote a majority opinion, joined by Rehnquist, Scalia, Kennedy, and Blackmun, which upheld the ordinance as constitutional. She began by reasoning that this case involved a traditional public forum, the public streets of a city. In the next step of the analysis, O'Connor concluded that the ordinance was content-neutral because it prohibited all forms of picketing. Given this finding, the government only had to show that it was pursuing a significant interest through narrowly tailored means and left open ample alternative channels of communication. O'Connor argued that the city met each element. The significant interest was the protection of residential privacy, the ordinance was narrowly tailored because it could be interpreted to prohibit only picketing directed at a single residence, and the demonstrators had many other alternative means to protest against the doctor.

Brennan, Marshall, and Stevens dissented in the case, presenting a somewhat ironic situation in which three justices who supported the abortion decision of *Roe v. Wade* (1973) took a position in favor of the antiabortion protestors. Brennan and Marshall found the ordinance unconstitutional because it was not narrowly tailored, banning all picketing in residential areas. Stevens's dissent was based on his view that the ordinance was unconstitutional because it was overly broad.

The Rehnquist Court's other speech-plus-conduct case of major importance, *Madsen v. Women's Health Center* (1994), also involved demonstrations over the abortion controversy. Judy Madsen and other antiabortion protestors had been demonstrating at a Florida abortion clinic as well as at the homes of doctors and clinic workers. In response to complaints that these activities were impeding access to the clinic and physically abusing some patients, a state court issued a series of strong injunction orders against the demonstrators. These included prohibiting the demonstrators from a 36-foot buffer zone around the clinic; restricting excessive noise-making; prohibiting demonstrators from approaching clinic clients within a 300-foot zone around the clinic if they did not consent to talk; and creating a 300-foot buffer zone around the residences of staff members of the clinic. The Florida Supreme Court upheld all provisions of the injunction.

Madsen was a difficult and divisive case for the Rehnquist Court. The Court ruled that portions of the 36-foot buffer zone and the noise regulation did not violate the First Amendment, but the other key provisions of the injunctions were determined to be unconstitutional. Rehnquist wrote a five-person majority opinion, and the chief justice was joined by four liberals and moderates: Blackmun, Ginsburg, Souter, and O'Connor. Scalia, joined by Kennedy and Thomas, wrote a lengthy opinion dissenting on the 36-foot buffer zone, accusing the majority of undermining basic First Amendment values. *Madsen*, then, presents an important case that cautions us about making automatic assumptions about the voting alignments of the Rehnquist Court justices in freedom of expression cases.

In his majority opinion, Rehnquist argued that this case was different than normal public forum cases because it involved a court injunction rather than a legislative ordinance. He argued that the injunction was content-neutral because it was directed at a group that had violated a previous court order. While this finding would normally trigger an intermediate level of scrutiny, Rehnquist reasoned that injunctions, that are imposed by judicial decree, must be reviewed under a somewhat more demanding standard: "We must ask . . . whether the challenged provisions of the injunction burden no more speech than is necessary to serve a significant government interest" (129 L.Ed.2d at 608). In applying this unusual standard,

Rehnquist drew some very fine judicial lines, arguing that the only two aspects of the injunction that did not burden more speech than was necessary were (1) the 36-foot buffer zone around the clinic entrances and driveway (but not the 36-foot zone as applied to private property adjacent to the clinic) and (2) the noise restriction. The other parts of the injunction, in contrast, burdened more speech than was necessary and were unconstitutional.

Scalia, joined by Kennedy and Thomas, argued that the Court should have applied the strict scrutiny approach to find all aspects of the injunction unconstitutional. He accused the majority of creating a new standard of "intermediate-intermediate scrutiny" (129 L.Ed.2d at 623) and of departing from other First Amendment principles as well. Scalia went even further and offered an explanation for the majority's alleged deviation from precedent. The explanation was the abortion controversy, which had resulted in the Court disregarding and nullifying various Court doctrines in the past. "Today," Scalia wrote, "the ad hoc nullification machine claims its latest, greatest, and most surprising victim—the First Amendment" (129 L.Ed.2d at 620).

Madsen v. Women's Health Center

114 S.Ct. 2516, 129 L.Ed. 2d 593 (1994)

■ In 1993, in Melbourne, Florida, the administrators of the Aware Woman Center for Choice attempted to obtain an injunction against Judy Madsen and other members of the organization Operation Rescue. The injunction would deny the antiabortion demonstrators access to the driveway and a nearby street as well as prevent them from bothering patients and physicians entering the clinic. Trial judge Robert McGregor issued the injunction that created a "buffer zone" around the clinic. The court order prohibited demonstrations within thirty-six feet of the clinic and also established a three hundred foot zone around the homes of all clinic employees that disallowed any approaching or demonstrating by the Operation Rescue followers. Furthermore, Judge McGregor forbade any loud noises by the protestors in the morning "during surgical procedures and recovery periods" for the purpose of protecting the women's physical and mental health.

On appeal to the state supreme court, the leaders of Operation Rescue argued that the injunction violated their First Amendment rights. The Florida Supreme Court upheld Judge McGregor's injunction. After a separate appeal was filed in federal court, the United States Court of Appeals for the Eleventh Circuit concluded that the injunction was unconstitutional. Operation Rescue appealed the state supreme court ruling to the United States Supreme Court. The Supreme Court agreed to review the case in order to settle the dispute between the Florida State Supreme Court and the Court of Appeals for the Eleventh Circuit.

This case is significant because the Court set forth guidelines regarding the activities of antiabortion groups engaged in protest demonstrations outside of abortion clinics and the residences of abortion providers. As you read the opinions in this case, think about these questions: (1) What are the various standards advocated in the justices' opinions, and what effect do these varying standards have on the justices' answers to the specific issues in this case? (2) To what extent did the justices seem to be affected by their perceptions of the facts of the case, specifically the protest activities of the antiabortion demonstrators? (3) Is Scalia correct that the majority's opinion nullifies important First Amendment principles because of the underlying issue of abortion?

Vote:

6 justices ruled that certain portions of the injunction were constitutional and other portions were unconstitutional (Blackmun, Ginsburg, O'Connor, Rehnquist, Souter, Stevens).

3 justices ruled that all portions of the injunction were unconstitutional (Kennedy, Scalia, Thomas).

Chief Justice Rehnquist delivered the opinion of the Court.

Petitioners challenge the constitutionality of an injunction entered by a Florida state court which prohibits antiabortion protesters from demonstrating in certain places and in various ways outside of a health clinic that performs abortions. We hold that the establishment of a 36-foot buffer zone on a public street from which demonstrators are excluded passes muster under the First Amendment, but that several other provisions of the injunction do not.

* * *

We begin by addressing petitioners' contention that the state court's order, because it is an injunction that restricts only the speech of antiabortion protesters, is necessarily content or viewpoint based. Accordingly, they argue, we should examine the entire injunction under the strictest standard of scrutiny. We disagree. To accept petitioners' claim would be to classify virtually every injunction as content or viewpoint based. An injunction, by its very nature, applies only to a particular group (or individuals) and regulates the activities, and perhaps the speech, of that group. It does so, however, because of the group's past actions in the context of a specific dispute between real parties. The parties seeking the injunction assert a violation of their rights; the court hearing the action is charged with fashioning a remedy for a specific deprivation, not with the drafting of a statute addressed to the general public.

The fact that the injunction in the present case did not prohibit activities of those demonstrating in favor of abortion is justly attributable to the lack of any similar demonstrations by those in favor of abortion, and of any consequent request that their demonstrations be regulated by injunction. There is no suggestion in this record that Florida law would not equally restrain similar conduct directed at a target having nothing to do with abortion; none of the restrictions imposed by the court were directed at the contents of petitioner's message.

Our principal inquiry in determining content neutrality is whether the government has adopted a regulation of speech "without reference to the content of the regulated speech." *Ward v. Rock Against Racism* (1989). We thus look to the government's purpose as the threshold consideration. Here, the state court imposed restrictions on petitioners incidental to their antiabortion message because they repeatedly violated the court's original order. That petitioners all share the same viewpoint regarding abortion does not in itself demonstrate that some invidious content- or viewpoint-based purpose motivated the issuance of the order. It suggests only that those in the group *whose conduct* violated the court's order happen to share the same opinion regarding abortions being performed at the clinic. In short, the fact that the injunction covered people with a particular viewpoint does not itself render the injunction content or viewpoint based. Accordingly, the injunction issued in this case does not demand the level of heightened scrutiny set forth in *Perry Education Assn*. And we proceed to discuss the standard which does govern.

If this were a content-neutral, generally applicable statute, instead of an injunctive order, its constitutionality would be assessed under the standard set forth in *Ward v. Rock Against Racism*, and similar cases. Given that the forum around the clinic is a traditional public forum, we would determine whether the time, place, and manner regulations were "narrowly tailored to serve a significant governmental interest."

There are obvious differences, however, between an injunction and a generally applicable ordinance. Ordinances represent a legislative choice regarding the promotion of particular societal interests. Injunctions, by contrast, are remedies imposed for violations (or threatened violations) of a legislative or judicial decree. * * *

We believe that these differences require a somewhat more stringent application of general First Amendment principles in this context. * * * . . .[W]hen evaluating a content-neutral injunction, we think that our standard time, place, and manner analysis is not sufficiently rigorous. We must ask instead whether the challenged provisions of the injunction burden no more speech than necessary to serve a significant government interest. * * *

Both Justice Stevens and Justice Scalia disagree with the standard we announce, for policy reasons. Justice Stevens believes that "injunctive relief should be judged by a more lenient standard than legislation," because injunctions are imposed on individuals or groups who have engaged in illegal activity. Justice Scalia, by contrast, believes that content-neutral injunctions are "*at least* as deserving of strict scrutiny as a statutory, content-based restriction." Justice Scalia bases his belief on the danger that injunctions, even though they might not "attack content *as content*," may be used to suppress particular ideas; that individual judges should not be trusted to impose injunctions in this context; and that an injunction is procedurally more difficult to challenge than a statute. We believe that consideration of *all* of the differences and similarities between statutes and injunctions supports, as a matter of policy, the standard we apply here.

* * *

We begin with the 36-foot buffer zone. The state court prohibited petitioners from "congregating, picketing, patrolling, demonstrating or entering" any portion of the public right-of-way or private property within 36 feet of the property line of the clinic as a way of ensuring access to the clinic. This speech-free buffer zone requires that petitioners move to the other side of Dixie Way and away from the driveway of the clinic, where the state court found that they repeatedly had interfered with the free access of patients and staff. * * *

* * *

The 36-foot buffer zone protecting the entrances to the clinic and the parking lot is a means of protecting unfettered ingress to and egress from the clinic, and ensuring that petitioners do not block traffic on Dixie Way. * * *

The need for a complete buffer zone near the clinic entrances and driveway may be debatable, but some deference must be given to the state court's familiarity with the facts and the background of the dispute between the parties even under our heightened review. Moreover, one of the petitioners' witnesses during the evidentiary hearing before the state court conceded that the buffer zone was narrow enough to place petitioners at a distance of no greater than 10 to 12 feet from cars approaching and leaving the clinic. Protesters standing across the narrow street from the clinic can still be seen and heard from the clinic parking lots. We also bear in mind the fact that the state court originally issued a much narrower injunction, providing no buffer zone, and that this order did not succeed in protecting access to the clinic. The failure of the first order to accomplish its purpose may be taken into consideration in evaluating the constitutionality of the broader order. On balance, we hold that the 36-foot buffer zone around the clinic entrance and driveway burdens no more speech than necessary to accomplish the governmental interest at stake.

Justice Scalia's dissent argues that a videotape made of demonstrations at the clinic represents "what one must presume to be the worst of the activity justifying the injunction." This seems to us a gratuitous assumption. The videotape was indeed introduced by respondents, presumably because they thought it supported their request for the second injunction. But witnesses also testified as to relevant facts in a 3-day evidentiary hearing, and the state court was therefore not limited to Justice Scalia's rendition of what he saw on the videotape to make its findings in support of the second injunction. Indeed, petitioners themselves studiously refrained from challenging the factual basis for the injunction both in the state courts and here.

The inclusion of private property on the back and side of the clinic in the 36-foot buffer zone raises different concerns. The accepted purpose of the buffer zone is to protect access to the clinic and to facilitate the orderly flow of traffic on Dixie Way. Patients and staff wishing to reach the clinic do not have to cross the private property abutting the clinic property on the north and west, and nothing in the record indicates that petitioners' activities on the private property have obstructed access to the clinic. Nor was evidence presented that protestors located on the private property blocked vehicular traffic on Dixie Way. Absent evidence that petitioners standing on the private property have obstructed access to the clinic, blocked vehicular traffic, or otherwise unlawfully interfered with the clinic's operation, this portion of the buffer zone fails to serve the significant government interests relied on by the Florida Supreme Court. We hold that on the record before us the 36-foot buffer zone as applied to the private property to the north and west of the clinic burdens more speech than necessary to protect access to the clinic.

In response to high noise levels outside the clinic, the state court restrained the petitioners from "singing, chanting, whistling, shouting, yelling, use of bullhorns, auto horns, sound amplification equipment or other sounds or images observable to or within earshot of the patients inside the [c]linic" during the hours of 7:30 a.m. through noon on Mondays through Saturdays. We must, of course, take account of the place to which the regulations apply in determining whether these restrictions burden more speech than necessary. We have upheld similar noise restrictions in the past, and as we noted in upholding a local noise ordinance around public schools, "the nature of a place, 'the pattern of its normal activities, dictate the kinds of regulations . . . that are reasonable.'" * * *

We hold that the limited noise restrictions imposed by the state court order burden no more speech than necessary to ensure the health and well-being of the patients at the clinic. The First Amendment does not demand that patients at a medical facility undertake Herculean efforts to escape the cacophony of political protests. "If overamplified loudspeakers assault the citizenry, government may turn them down." That is what the state court did here, and we hold that its action was proper.

The same, however, cannot be said for the "images observable" provision of the state court's order. Clearly, threats to patients or their families, however communicated, are proscribable under the First Amendment. But rather than prohibiting the display of signs that could be interpreted as threats or veiled threats, the state court issued a blanket ban on all "images observable." This broad prohibition on all "images observable" burdens more speech than necessary to achieve the purpose of limiting threats to clinic patients or their families. Similarly, if the blanket ban on "images observable" was intended to reduce the level of anxiety and hypertension suffered by the patients inside the clinic, it would still fail.

The only plausible reason a patient would be bothered by "images observable" inside the clinic would be if the patient found the expression contained in such images disagreeable. But it is much easier for the clinic to pull its curtains than for a patient to stop up her ears, and no more is required to avoid seeing placards through the windows of the clinic. This provision of the injunction violates the First Amendment.

The state court ordered that petitioners refrain from physically approaching any person seeking services of the clinic "unless such person indicates a desire to communicate" in an area within 300 feet of the clinic. The state court was attempting to prevent clinic patients and staff from being "stalked" or "shadowed" by the petitioners as they approached the clinic. * * *

But it is *difficult*, indeed, to justify a prohibition on *all* uninvited approaches of persons seeking the services of the clinic, regardless of how peaceful the contact may be, without burdening more speech than necessary to prevent intimidation and to ensure access to the clinic. Absent evidence that the protesters' speech is independently proscribable (i.e., "fighting words" or threats), or is so infused with violence as to be indistinguishable from a threat of physical harm, this provision cannot stand. * * *

The final substantive regulation challenged by petitioners relates to a prohibition against picketing, demonstrating, or using sound amplification equipment within 300 feet of the residences of clinic staff. The prohibition also covers impeding access to streets that provide the sole access to streets on which those residences are located. The same analysis applies to the use of sound amplification equipment here as that discussed above: the government may simply demand that petitioners turn down the volume if the protests overwhelm the neighborhood.

As for the picketing, our prior decision upholding a law banning targeted residential picketing remarked on the unique nature of the home, as " 'the last citadel of the tired, the weary, and the sick.' " *Frisby*. We stated that "[t]he State's interest in protecting the well-being, tranquility, and privacy of the home is certainly of the highest order in a free and civilized society."

* * * By contrast, the 300-foot zone would ban "[g]eneral marching through residential neighborhoods, or even walking a route in front of an entire block of houses." The record before us does not contain sufficient justification for this broad a ban on picketing; it appears that a limitation on the time, duration of picketing, and number of pickets outside a smaller zone could have accomplished the desired result.

* * *

In sum, we uphold the noise restrictions and the 36-foot buffer zone around the clinic entrances and driveway because they burden no more speech than necessary to eliminate the unlawful conduct targeted by the state court's injunction. We strike down as unconstitutional the 36-foot buffer zone as applied to the private property to the north and west of the clinic, the "images observable" provision, the 300-foot no-approach zone around the residences, because these provisions sweep more broadly than necessary to accomplish the permissible goals of the injunction. Accordingly, the judgment of the Florida Supreme Court is *affirmed in part, and reversed in part*.

Justice Souter, concurring. [omitted]

Justice Stevens, concurring in part and dissenting in part.

The certiorari petition presented three questions, corresponding to petitioners' three major challenges to the trial court's injunction. The Court correctly and unequivocally rejects petitioners' argument that the injunction is a "content-based restriction on free speech," as well as their challenge to the injunction on the basis that it applies to persons acting "in concert" with them. I therefore join [these parts] of the Court's opinion, which properly dispose of the first and third questions presented. I part company with the Court, however, on its treatment of the second question presented, including its enunciation of the applicable standard of review.

I agree with the Court that a different standard governs First Amendment challenges to generally applicable legislation than the standard that measures such challenges to judicial remedies for proven wrongdoing. Unlike the Court, however, I believe that injunctive relief should be judged by a more lenient standard than legislation. As the Court notes, legislation is imposed on an entire community regardless of individual culpability. By contrast, injunctions apply solely to an individual or a limited group of individuals who, by engaging in illegal conduct, have been judicially deprived of some liberty—the normal consequence of illegal activity. Given this distinction, a statute provision prohibiting demonstrations within 36 feet of an abortion clinic would probably violate the First Amendment, but an injunction directed at a limited group of persons who have engaged in unlawful conduct in a similar zone might well be constitutional.

* * *

Justice Scalia, with whom Justice Kennedy and Justice Thomas join, concurring in the judgment in part and dissenting in part.

The judgment in today's case has an appearance of moderation and Solomonic wisdom, upholding as it does some portions of the injunction while disallowing others. That appearance is deceptive. The entire injunction in this case departs so far from the established course of our jurisprudence that in any other context it would have been regarded as a candidate for summary reversal.

But the context here is abortion. A long time ago, in dissent from another abortion-related case, Justice O'Connor . . . wrote: "This Court's abortion decisions have already worked a major distortion in the Court's constitutional jurisprudence. Today's decision goes further, and makes it painfully clear that no legal rule or doctrine is safe from ad hoc nullification by this Court when an occasion for its application arises in a case involving state regulation of abortion." * * * Today the ad hoc nullification machine claims its latest, greatest, and most surprising victim: the First Amendment.

Because I believe that the judicial creation of a 36-foot zone in which only a particular group, which had broken no law, cannot exercise its rights of speech, assembly, and association, and the judicial enactment of a noise prohibition, applicable to that group and that group alone, are profoundly at odds with our First Amendment precedents and traditions, I dissent.

The record of this case contains a videotape, with running caption of time and date, displaying what one must presume to be the worst of the activity justifying the injunction issued by Judge McGregor and partially approved today by this Court. The tape was shot by employees of, or volunteers at, the Aware Woman Clinic on three Saturdays in February and March 1993. * * *

Anyone seriously interested in what this case was about must view that tape. And anyone doing so who is familiar with run-of-the-mine labor picketing, not to mention some other social protests, will be aghast at what it shows we have today permitted an individual judge to do. * * *

* * *

The videotape and the rest of the record, including the trial court's findings, show that a great many forms of expression and conduct occurred in the vicinity of the clinic. These include singing, chanting, praying, shouting, the playing of music both from the clinic and from handheld boom boxes, speeches, peaceful picketing, communication of familiar political messages, handbilling, persuasive speech directed at opposing groups on the issue of abortion, efforts to persuade individuals not to have abortions, personal testimony, interviews with the press, and media efforts to report on the protest. What the videotape, the rest of the record, and the trial court's findings do not contain is any suggestion of violence near the clinic, nor do they establish any attempt to prevent entry or exit.

Under this Court's jurisprudence, there is no question that this public sidewalk area is a "public forum," where citizens generally have a First Amendment right to speak. The parties to this case invited the Court to employ one or the other of the two well established standards applied to restrictions upon this First Amendment right. Petitioners claimed the benefit of so-called "strict scrutiny," the standard applied to content-based restrictions: the restriction must be "necessary to serve a compelling state interest and . . . narrowly drawn to achieve that end." Respondents, on the other hand, contended for what has come to be known as "intermediate scrutiny" (midway between the "strict scrutiny" demanded for content-based regulation of speech, and the "rational-basis" standard that is applied—under the Equal Protection Clause—to government regulation of non-speech activities).

That standard, applicable to so-called "time, place, manner regulations" of speech, provides that the regulations are permissible so long as they "are content-neutral, are narrowly tailored to serve a significant government interest, and leave open ample alternative channels of communication." The Court adopts neither of these, but creates, brand-new for this abortion-related case, an additional standard that is (supposedly) "somewhat more stringent" than intermediate scrutiny, yet not as "rigorous" as strict scrutiny. The Court does not give this new standard a name, but perhaps we could call it intermediate-intermediate scrutiny. The difference between it and intermediate scrutiny (which the Court acknowledges is inappropriate for injunctive restrictions on speech) is frankly too subtle for me to describe, so I must simply recite it: whereas intermediate scrutiny requires that the restriction be "narrowly tailored to serve a significant government interest," the new standard requires that the restriction "burden no more speech than necessary to serve a significant government interest."

* * *

* * * The danger of content-based statutory restrictions upon speech is that they may be designed and used precisely to suppress the ideas in question

rather than to achieve any other proper governmental aim. But that same danger exists with injunctions. Although a speech-restricting injunction may not attack content *as content* (in the present case, as I shall discuss, even that is not true), it lends itself just as readily to the targeted suppression of particular ideas. When a judge, on the motion of an employer, enjoins picketing at the site of a labor dispute, he enjoins (and he *knows* he is enjoining) the expression of pro-union views. Such targeting of one or the other side of an ideological dispute cannot readily be achieved in speech-restricting general legislation except by making content the basis of the restriction; it is achieved in speech-restricting injunctions almost invariably. The proceedings before us here illustrate well enough what I mean. The injunction was sought against a single-issue advocacy group by persons and organizations with a business or social interest in suppressing that group's point of view.

The second reason speech-restricting injunctions are at least as deserving of strict scrutiny is obvious enough: they are the product of individual judges rather than of legislatures—and often of judges who have been chagrined by prior disobedience of their orders. The right to free speech should not lightly be placed within the control of a single man or woman. And the third reason is that the injunction is a much more powerful weapon than a statute, and so should be subjected to greater safeguards. * * *

* * *

* * * The proposition that injunctions against speech are subject to a standard indistinguishable from (unless perhaps more lenient in its application than) the "intermediate scrutiny" standard we have used for "time, place, and manner" legislative restrictions; the notion that injunctions against speech need not be closely tied to any violation of law, but may simply implement sound social policy; and the practice of accepting trial-court conclusions permitting injunctions without considering whether those conclusions are supported by any findings of fact—these latest byproducts of our abortion jurisprudence ought to give all friends of liberty great concern.

For these reasons, I dissent from that portion of the judgment upholding parts of the injunction.

* * *

Although he was disturbed by the majority's opinion in *Madsen*, Scalia joined the majority opinions in the Rehnquist Court's other significant speech-plus-conduct cases, most of which upheld various forms of government regulations. In *Boos v. Barry* (1988) challenges arose to a District of Columbia law regulating demonstrations in front of foreign embassies. The Court ruled unconstitutional by a 5-3 vote a regulation prohibiting the display of any sign within 500 feet of an embassy if the sign could bring the embassy into "public odium or disrepute." Applying strict scrutiny, the majority found the regulation to lack narrowly tailored means. In the same case, however, the justices gave unanimous approval to a regulation that prohibited the congregation of three or more people within 500 feet of a foreign embassy.

The Rehnquist Court also approved government regulation of various forms of speech-plus-conduct in *Ward v. Rock Against Racism* (1989), *United States v. Kokinda* (1990), and *International Society for Krishna Consciousness v. Lee* (1992). In *Ward*, the Court ruled the First Amendment was not violated by New York City guidelines requiring the sponsors of concerts in Central Park to use sound-amplification equipment and sound technicians provided by the city. The justices in *Kokinda* upheld against a First Amendment challenge a United States Postal Service prohibition on in-person soliciting of funds on sidewalks adjoining a post office. Finally, the *Krishna* case found a Court majority declaring that an airport terminal operated by a public authority was a nonpublic forum, and, under the reasonableness standard, the terminal officials could ban face-to-face solicitations. In a companion case, however, a 5-4 majority ruled that a ban on literature distribution did violate the First Amendment.

The Supreme Court has thus had a long history of deciding cases involving speech-plus-conduct. The Court's decisions have tended to be more conservative in this area than other freedom of expression categories because of the inherent threats to public order and safety associated with protest and demonstration activities. Nonetheless, the Court has also recognized the important First Amendment values at stake in these cases. The Rehnquist Court justices have attempted to balance these competing interests through an intricate doctrinal system combining considerations of public forum analysis and content regulation. Consensus remains elusive, however. The justices are frequently in disagreement regarding appropriate standards and even more frequently in regard to the application of the standards in particular cases.

Commercial Speech

The final category of speech activities we will examine is commercial speech, which involves the advertising of goods and services. The Court's approach to commercial speech has undergone dramatic changes in the past half-century. When the Court was first called upon to analyze commercial speech in the early forties, the justices ruled that this form of expression did not come within the meaning of the First Amendment. The Court adhered to this position for several decades, but in the mid-seventies the Burger Court ruled that commercial speech was protected under the First Amendment. Eventually the Burger Court developed a four-part, intermediate scrutiny test for commercial speech, and the Rehnquist Court has adhered to this approach. Despite the consensus by the justices regarding the proper doctrinal test in commercial speech cases, however, this has been another controversial area of freedom of expression.

When the Court first confronted the issue of commercial speech in a 1942 case, the justices ruled that this form of expression was not protected under the First Amendment. In *Valentine v. Chrestensen*, the justices unanimously upheld an ordinance that prohibited the circulation of commercial handbills, even though one side of the handbill contained a message protesting that the ordinance violated the First Amendment. *Chrestensen* remained controlling precedent for over three decades because the Warren Court did not decide any cases directly involving commercial speech.

The Burger Court was actively involved in commercial speech cases, however, and indeed the Burger Court's most dramatic departure from past precedent in freedom of expression cases occurred in the area of commercial speech. *Bigelow v. Virginia* (1975) was the case in which the Burger Court first brought advertising within the protection of the First Amendment. Jeffrey Bigelow was managing editor of the *Virginia Weekly* when the paper ran an advertisement in 1971, two years before *Roe v. Wade* (1973), regarding legal abortions in New York. Bigelow was charged with violating an 1878 Virginia law that made it a criminal act to advertise abortion services. Bigelow did not contest that he had violated the law; instead, he argued that the law was an unconstitutional infringement of the First Amendment. The Virginia state courts rejected his argument, but the Burger Court agreed with him in a 7-2 decision. Blackmun wrote the seven-person majority opinion, with Rehnquist and White in dissent. Without explicitly overturning *Chrestensen*, Blackmun stated that ". . .speech is not stripped of First Amendment protection merely because it appears in [commercial] form" (421 U.S. at 818). The basic rationale supporting this position was that the ad ". . .contained factual material of clear 'public interest'" (421 U.S. at 822). Blackmun's majority opinion did leave the door open for government regulation, however, for he advocated a general balancing approach in commercial speech cases: "to the extent that commercial activity is subject to regulation, the relationship of speech to that activity may be one factor, among others, to be considered in weighing the First Amendment interest against the government interest alleged" (421 U.S. at 826).

Rehnquist wrote a dissenting opinion, joined by White, in which he advanced a series of arguments he would continue to champion in a long series of commercial speech cases. Rehnquist argued that the Court's precedents had established that purely commercial speech does not fall within the protection of the First Amendment. In this particular case, he continued, the ad was ". . .classic commercial proposition directed toward the exchange of services rather than the exchange of ideas" (421 U.S. at 831). Furthermore, Rehnquist argued, even if the First Amendment was somehow implicated, the appropriate test would be the minimal scrutiny of the rational basis test, requiring Virginia to show only that it was pursuing a legitimate purpose by reasonable means. Virginia's purposes were clearly legitimate to Rehnquist: ". . .to maintain high ethical standards in the medical profession and to protect the public from unscrupulous practices" (421 U.S. at 832).

BIGELOW V. VIRGINIA

421 U.S. 809, 95 S.Ct. 2222, 44 L.Ed. 2d 600 (1975)

■ As a newspaper editor of the *Virginia Weekly,* Jeffery C. Bigelow was held responsible for publishing an advertisement that offered out-of-state services related to legal abortions. Bigelow was convicted in the County Court of Albemarle County, Virginia, for violating a state law that prohibited the circulation of any publication that promoted abortions. The editor appealed to the Circuit Court of Albemarle County, but his conviction was upheld. The Supreme Court of Virginia also affirmed the county court judgment. Bigelow appealed to the United States Supreme Court, asserting that the Virginia statute violated his First Amendment rights.

This case is significant because the Court for the first time explicitly brought commercial speech—advertising—within the protection of the First Amendment. As you read the opinions in this case, think about the following questions: (1) Is the decision consistent with the Court's past precedents or a departure from them? (2) What arguments are advanced by the majority for giving First Amendment protection to commercial speech? (3) What test did the Court set forth to evaluate the constitutionality of commercial speech? (4) Based on this decision, does the First Amendment extend to all forms of commercial speech?

VOTE:

7 justices found the law to violate Bigelow's constitutional rights (Blackmun, Brennan, Burger, Douglas, Marshall, Stewart, Powell).

2 justices found the law to be constitutional (Rehnquist, White).

Justice Blackmun delivered the opinion of the Court.

An advertisement carried in appellant's newspaper led to his conviction for a violation of a Virginia statute that made it a misdemeanor, by the sale or circulation of any publication, to encourage or prompt the procuring of an abortion. The issue here is whether the editor appellant's First Amendment rights were unconstitutionally abridged by the statute.

The central assumption made by the Supreme Court of Virginia was that the First Amendment guarantees of speech and press are inapplicable to paid commercial advertisements. Our cases, however, clearly establish that speech is not stripped of First Amendment protection merely because it appears in that form.

The fact that the particular advertisement in appellant's newspaper had commercial aspects or reflected the advertiser's commercial interests did not negate all First Amendment guarantees. * * *

Although other categories of speech—such as fighting words, *Chaplinsky v. New Hampshire*, or obscenity, *Roth v. United States*, or incitement, *Brandenburg v. Ohio*—have been held unprotected, no contention has been made that the particular speech embraced in the advertisement in question is within any of these categories.

The appellee, as did the Supreme Court of Virginia, relies on *Valentine v. Chrestensen* (1942), where a unanimous Court, in a brief opinion, sustained an ordinance which had been interpreted to ban the distribution of a handbill advertising the exhibition of a submarine. The handbill solicited customers to tour the ship for a fee. The promoter-advertiser had first attempted to distribute a single-faced handbill consisting only of the advertisement, and was denied permission to do so. He then had printed, on the reverse side of the handbill, a protest against official conduct refusing him to use the wharfage facilities. The Court found that the message of asserted "public interest" was appended solely for the purpose of evading the ordinance and therefore did not constitute an "exercise of the freedom of communicating information and disseminating opinion." * * * But the holding is distinctly a limited one: the ordinance was upheld as a reasonable regulation of the manner in which commercial advertising could be distributed. The fact that it had the effect of banning a particular handbill does not mean that *Chrestensen* is authority for the proposition that all statutes regulating commercial advertising are immune from constitutional challenge. The case obviously does not support any sweeping proposition that advertising is unprotected per se.

This Court's cases decided since *Chrestensen* clearly demonstrate as untenable any reading of that case that would give it so broad an effect. In *New York Times Co. v. Sullivan*, a city official instituted a civil libel action against four clergymen and the New York Times. The suit was based on an advertisement carried in the newspaper criticizing police action against members of the civil rights movement and soliciting contributions for the movement. The Court held that this advertisement, although containing factually erroneous defamatory content, was entitled to the same degree of constitutional protection as ordinary speech. * * *

The principle that commercial advertising enjoys a degree of First Amendment protection was reaffirmed in *Pittsburgh Press Co. v. Human Rel. Comm'n* (1973). There, the Court, although divided, sustained an ordinance that had been construed to forbid newspapers to carry help-wanted advertisements in sex-designated columns except where based upon a bona fide occupational exemption. The Court did describe the advertisements at issue as "classic examples of commercial speech," for each was "no more than a proposal of possible employment." But the Court indicated that the advertisements would have received some degree of First Amendment protection if the commercial proposal had been legal. * * *

The legitimacy of appellant's First Amendment claim in the present case is demonstrated by the important differences between the advertisement presently at issue and those involved in *Chrestensen* and in *Pittsburgh Press*. The advertisement published in appellant's newspaper did more than simply propose a commercial transaction. It contained factual material of clear "public interest." Portions of its message, most prominently the lines, "Abortions are now legal in New York. There are no residency requirements," involve the exercise of the freedom of communicating information and disseminating opinion.

Viewed in its entirety, the advertisement conveyed information of potential interest and value to a diverse audience—not only to readers possibly in need of the services offered, but also to those with a general curiosity about, or genuine interest in, the subject matter or the law of another State and its development, and to readers seeking reform in Virginia. * * * Thus, in this case, appellant's First Amendment interests coincided with the constitutional interests of the general public.

* * *

We conclude, therefore, that the Virginia courts erred in their assumptions that advertising, as such, was entitled to no First Amendment protection and that appellant Bigelow had no legitimate First Amendment interest. * * *

Advertising, like all public expression, may be subject to reasonable regulation that serves a legitimate public interest. To the extent that commercial activity is subject to regulation, the relationship of speech to that activity may be one factor, among others, to be considered in weighing the First Amendment interest against the governmental interest alleged. Advertising is not thereby stripped of all First Amendment protection. The relationship of speech to the marketplace of products or of services does not make it valueless in the marketplace of ideas.

* * *

If application of this statute were upheld under these circumstances, Virginia might exert the power sought here over a wide variety of national publications or interstate newspapers carrying advertisements similar to the one that appeared in Bigelow's newspaper or containing articles on the general subject matter to which the advertisement referred. Other States might do the same. The burdens thereby imposed on publications would impair, perhaps severely, their proper functioning. We know from experience that "liberty of the press is in peril as soon as the government tries to compel what is to go into a newspaper." The policy of the First Amendment favors dissemination of information and opinion, and "[t]he guarantees of freedom of speech and press were not designed to prevent the censorship of the press merely, but any action of the government by means of which it might prevent such free and general discussion of public matters as seems absolutely essential. . . ."

We conclude that Virginia could not apply [this law], as it read in 1971, to appellant's publication of the advertisement in question without unconstitutionally infringing upon his First Amendment rights. The judgment of the Supreme Court of Virginia is therefore reversed.

It is so ordered.

Justice Rehnquist, with whom Justice White joins, dissenting.

* * *

As a threshold matter the advertisement appears to me, as it did to the courts below, to be a classic commercial proposition directed toward the exchange of services rather than the exchange of ideas. * * * Whatever slight factual content the advertisement may contain and whatever expression of opinion may be laboriously drawn from it does not alter its predominantly commercial content. "If that evasion were successful, every merchant who desires to broadcast. . .need only append a civic appeal, or a moral platitude, to achieve immunity from the law's command." I am unable to perceive any relationship between the instant advertisement and that for example in issue in *New York Times Co. v. Sullivan*. Nor am I able to distinguish this commercial proposition from that held to be purely commercial in *Pittsburgh Press Co. v. Human Rel. Comm'n*. As the Court recognizes, a purely commercial proposal is entitled to little constitutional protection.

Assuming arguendo that this advertisement is something more than a normal commercial proposal, I am unable to see why Virginia does not have a legitimate public interest in its regulation. The Court apparently concedes that the States have a strong interest in the prevention of commercial advertising in the health field—both in order to maintain high ethical standards in the medical profession and to protect the public from unscrupulous practices. * * *

* * *

Without denying the power of either New York or Virginia to prohibit advertising such as that in issue where both publication of the advertised activity and the activity itself occur in the same State, the Court instead focuses on the multistate nature of this transaction concluding that a State "may not, under the guise of exercising internal police powers, bar a citizen of another State from disseminating information about an activity that is legal in that State." * * *

The source of this rigid territorial limitation on the power of the States in our federal system to safeguard the health and welfare of their citizens is not revealed. It is surely not to be found in cases from this Court. . . .[W]e have consistently recognized that irrespective of a State's power to regulate extraterritorial commercial transactions in which its citizens participate it retains an independent power to regulate the business of commercial solicitation and advertising within its borders. * * *

Were the Court's statements taken literally, they would presage a standard of the lowest common denominator for commercial ethics and business conduct. * * *

Since the Court saves harmless from its present opinion our prior cases in this area, it may be fairly inferred that it does not intend the results which might otherwise come from a literal reading of its opinion. But solely on the facts before it, I think the Court today simply errs in assessing Virginia's interest in its statute because it does not focus on the impact of the practices in question on the State. * * *

Since the statute in question is a "reasonable regulation that serves a legitimate public interest," I would affirm the judgment of the Supreme Court of Virginia.

Bigelow opened the flood gates for First Amendment cases concerned with commercial speech because Blackmun's opinion had left many questions unanswered. Was all advertising protected by the First Amendment or just advertising that involved matters of public interest? Did the justices intend to apply the minimal scrutiny of the rational basis test in commercial speech cases, or was a higher level of judicial scrutiny to be used? The Burger Court dealt with these and other questions in a series of cases in the seventies and eighties, generally providing liberal answers over the strong objections of Justice Rehnquist.

Several cases decided shortly after *Bigelow* established the principle that the First Amendment applied broadly to commercial speech, including advertisements that were purely commercial, that is, without political or social content. *Virginia State Board of Pharmacy v. Virginia Citizens Consumer Council, Inc.* (1976) involved a challenge to a Virginia law which prohibited pharmacies from advertising the prices of their prescription drugs. The Burger Court ruled 7-1 that the law violated the First Amendment. Blackmun's majority opinion acknowledged that the advertisement was purely economic, but this did not remove it from First Amendment protection. The next year the Burger Court justices faced the issue of whether a state could ban attorneys from advertising their fees in newspapers. Writing for a narrow 5-4 majority in *Bates v. State Bar of Arizona* (1977), Justice Blackmun argued that such advertising was protected by the First Amendment.

Two additional decisions involving commercial speech by attorneys revealed the willingness of the Burger Court to draw lines beyond which First Amendment protection did not extend. The case of *In re Primus* (1977) involved an American Civil Liberties Union attorney, Edna Primus; working in a *pro bono* capacity, she contacted a potential client to inquire about serving as a plaintiff in a suit being pursued by the ACLU. *Ohralik v. Ohio State Bar* (1977) involved an attorney named Albert Ohralik who had followed two accident victims to a hospital where he offered them his legal services. Perhaps not surprisingly, the Court found the First Amendment to provide protection for Primus but not for Ohralik because Primus's activity was passive and was not motivated by personal monetary gain.

Although these decisions in the seventies helped to clarify the Burger Court's views regarding commercial speech, the justices still had not articulated a specific doctrinal approach in this area. In *Central Hudson Gas and Electric Corporation v. Public Service Commission of New York* (1980), however, a four-part test was developed to adjudicate commercial speech cases. In this case, Central Hudson had developed promotional advertisements that ran afoul of a law that prohibited utility companies from advertising. The Court ruled the regulation unconstitutional by a vote of 8-1, with only Justice Rehnquist in dissent. Justice Powell set forth the following four-part test in commercial speech cases: (1) Is the speech truthful and concerned with lawful activity? (2) Is the asserted government interest a substantial one? (3) Does the regulation directly advance the government interest? and (4) Is the regulation no more extensive than necessary?

This test provides an intermediate level of judicial scrutiny between the highest scrutiny of the compelling government interest test and the minimal scrutiny of the rational basis test. The underlying assumption behind the test is that commercial speech is not of the same level of significance as political and social expression but is nonetheless deserving of substantial protection because of the public's interest in economic information. This test continues to guide the Rehnquist Court in commercial speech cases, but, as we will see, the test does not automatically yield easy, clear answers to constitutional questions.

The Rehnquist Court has given a substantial amount of attention to commercial speech cases, although few of the cases qualify under our criteria as being of major importance. The Court has ruled on eleven commercial speech cases since the 1986 term, ruling liberally—against the government regulations—in seven of the decisions.

Consensus has generally characterized these cases. Nine of the eleven decisions have been by majority opinion, and the intermediate scrutiny test of *Hudson* enjoys wide support. The degree of consensus should not be overstated, however. As in other areas of freedom of expression, the justices of the Rehnquist Court do not hold a uniform perspective on commercial speech cases. An examination of three leading commercial speech cases of the Rehnquist Court—*Board of Trustees, S.U.N.Y. v. Fox* (1989), *Cincinnati v. Discovery Network* (1993), and *Florida Bar v. Went For It* (1995)—reveals that important differences exist among the justices regarding not only the details of the *Hudson* test but also the degree of protection that commercial speech should receive under the First Amendment.

The *Fox* case, sometimes referred to as the "Tupperware Bust Case," involved a First Amendment challenge to a regulation of the State University of New York prohibiting private commercial companies from holding demonstrations in students' dormitory rooms. A representative of American Future Systems, Inc., a company that sells housewares such as china and silverware to college students, was conducting a demonstration in a student dorm room on the Cortland campus of SUNY in October of 1982. Campus police informed her that she was in violation of the regulation prohibiting such demonstrations, and when she refused to leave the police arrested her.

The central issue before the Court in this case involved the proper interpretation of the fourth prong of the *Hudson* test. In his majority opinion joined by five other justices, Scalia argued that the case involved commercial speech and that both parties to the case agreed that the first three prongs of the *Hudson* test were met: (1) the speech involved in the case concerned lawful activity and was not misleading, (2) the government interests advanced were substantial, including preventing commercial exploitation of students and preserving tranquility and an educational environment, and (3) the regulation directly advanced the asserted government interest. The critical question thus involved the proper interpretation of the fourth prong, whether the regulation was more extensive than necessary to serve the government's interests. The circuit court had interpreted this to mean that the regulation had to be the "least restrictive means" to achieve these interests, but Scalia rejected this standard. He admitted that some confusion existed on this issue; but he argued that the least restrictive means test was associated with the Court's strict scrutiny approach to political speech, and thus it would be an inappropriate standard to use with commercial speech, which had a subordinate position under the First Amendment. The proper standard, Scalia wrote, is a "reasonable fit" between the legislative goals and the means chosen to achieve those goals. For Scalia and the majority, a reasonable fit did exist.

Blackmun wrote the dissenting opinion and was joined by Brennan and Marshall. He accused the majority of ". . .recasting a good bit of contrary language in our past cases" (492 U.S. at 486) and argued that the Court should have ruled the regulation unconstitutional on overbreadth grounds.

Cincinnati v. Discovery Network (1993) is an interesting case that not only provides an excellent example of the Court's application of the *Hudson* test, as modified by *Fox*, but also shows the strong disagreements that exist among the justices regarding the protection commercial speech should receive under the First Amendment. The case stemmed from a 1990 decision by the city of Cincinnati to revoke the permits of two companies, Discovery Network and Harmon Publishing, to distribute their commercial publications through freestanding newsracks, which were located on public streets. The city justified its decision on the basis of its concern for safety and beauty. The companies appealed the decision on First Amendment grounds, and the district and circuit courts ruled on behalf of the companies using the *Hudson* test.

A six-person Supreme Court majority, with Stevens writing the opinion, agreed with the lower courts that the companies' First Amendment rights had been violated. Stevens's analysis was a straightforward application of the *Hudson* test using the "reasonable fit" criterion of *Fox*. Stevens argued that substantial agreement existed on most prongs of the *Hudson* test. The case involved commercial speech, the publications were not unlawful or misleading, and the city had a substantial interest in promoting safety and esthetics. Thus, the critical question was whether a reasonable fit existed between the city's interests and the means selected to achieve those interests. Stevens and the Court majority answered negatively, primarily because only 62 of the 1,500–2,000 newsracks would be removed, a "paltry" amount.

The separate opinions in the case presented sharply divergent viewpoints on the degree of protection commercial speech should be given under the First Amendment. In a concurring opinion, Blackmun argued that ". . .the analysis set forth in

Central Hudson and refined in *Fox* affords insufficient protection for truthful, noncoercive commercial speech concerning lawful activities" (507 U.S. at 431). Blackmun argued that commercial speech should be given the Court's highest level of protection under the strict scrutiny test. In a dissent joined by Thomas and White, Rehnquist took strong exception to Blackmun's position. Rehnquist argued that commercial speech should have a subordinate position under the First Amendment for several reasons; commercial speech is supported strongly by economic self-interest, it is less central to the core values of the democratic process which underlie the First Amendment, and the importance of noncommercial speech could be diminished by giving commercial speech equal status. Rehnquist agreed that the *Hudson* test was appropriate, but he saw a reasonable fit between Cincinnati's interests and the means they chose.

The justices' divergent perspectives in applying the *Hudson* test can also be seen in a recent 1995 commercial speech case. *Florida Bar v. Went For It* involved a challenge to the constitutionality of Florida Bar regulations that prohibited attorneys from sending direct-mail solicitations to accident victims or their families until thirty days after the accident had occurred. A five-person majority composed of O'Connor, Rehnquist, Scalia, Thomas, and Breyer found the regulation to be constitutional, meeting each prong of the *Hudson* test. In sharp contrast, Kennedy, Stevens, Souter, and Ginsburg argued that the regulation failed each prong of *Hudson.*

Commercial speech thus appears to be a relatively settled area of freedom of expression in regard to the proper doctrinal approach. The justices seem committed to the *Hudson* test and the principles underlying it. Commercial speech is regarded as communicating important ideas and is thus deserving of heightened First Amendment protection against government control. Commercial speech is not viewed as being as important as political expression, however, and thus receives intermediate rather than strict scrutiny. Despite their consensus on general principles, however, the Rehnquist Court justices are frequently in disagreement on the application of these principles to specific cases.

Freedom of the Press

Having analyzed in detail the major topics within freedom of speech, we now shift our focus to the major areas of freedom of the press. The specific topics we shall examine are censorship, libel, the conflict between a free press and a fair trial, and broadcasting. Our approach in analyzing these issues will be the same as we followed in examining freedom of speech; we will organize our analysis historically, focusing upon the pre-Warren, Warren, Burger, and Rehnquist Court eras, and we will give special attention to the question of whether changes in the Court's membership have produced changes in the Court's policies regarding freedom of the press.

Censorship

Although much disagreement exists regarding the intent of the writers and the country's original understanding of the guarantee of freedom of the press, a widespread consensus does exist that at a minimum this constitutional guarantee prevents government censorship or prior restraint of the press. As we saw in the earlier historical section of this chapter, a primary grievance of the colonists was against press censorship, and even the conservative Blackstone approach to law was adamantly opposed to government censorship. The Supreme Court has frequently been called upon to decide cases in which government censorship has been alleged, and the Court has been consistent in placing a heavy burden of proof on the government to justify any form of prior restraint.

The Court's first major decision involving press censorship came in *Near v. Minnesota* in 1931. We initially encountered this case in Chapter 4, Incorporation of the Bill of Rights, because *Near* is the case in which the Court is considered to have nationalized freedom of the press. *Near* is also a major case, however, because the Court set forth important principles regarding the topic of press censorship.

J. M. Near was the publisher of *The Saturday Press*, a Minneapolis newspaper that was published on a weekly basis. Near's publication contained frequent attacks on minority and labor groups, and he also accused local law enforcement officials of corruption. The county attorney sought to halt publication of the periodical and to prosecute Near under a 1925 Minnesota law. Near unsuccessfully challenged the constitutionality of the law in the Minnesota courts, but then the United States Supreme Court agreed to hear his case.

The Court ruled 5-4 that the law was unconstitutional because it allowed government the power of censorship over the press, and censorship is prohibited by the First Amendment: "In determining the extent of the constitutional protection, it has been generally, if not universally, considered that it is the chief purpose of the guaranty to prevent previous restraints upon publication" (283 U.S. at 713). The Court majority did recognize, however, that censorship might be permissible under a few exceptional circumstances: publishing information about the size and location of troops during war, publishing obscene material, publishing incitements to violence, and publishing statements that invade privacy rights.

Near v. Minnesota

283 U.S. 697, 51 S.Ct. 625, 75 L.Ed. 1357 (1931)

■ As editor of a tabloid periodical, the *Saturday Press*, Jay Near was prevented from publishing under a 1925 Minnesota public nuisance statute. Under this law, a newspaper was prohibited from publishing "malicious, scandalous and defamatory" material. Near used the publication for the expression of his anti-Semitic, anti-Catholic, anti-labor, and anti-black viewpoints. In addition, in a series of articles Near charged that Minneapolis police and prosecutors were in collusion with Jewish gangsters involved in gambling, bootlegging, and racketeering. The Hennepin County Attorney brought action to ban the publication and proceeded to prosecute Near. The District Court for Hennepin County as well as the State Supreme Court of Minnesota upheld the constitutionality of the Minnesota statute. Arguing that the law violated First Amendment rights of free speech and press, Near appealed to the United States Supreme Court with the support of Robert McCormick, publisher of the *Chicago Tribune*.

This case is significant for two reasons: (1) the Court explicitly stated that the First Amendment guarantees of freedom of speech and the press were applicable to the states through the Due Process Clause of the Fourteenth Amendment, and (2) the Court provided a strong argument against government censorship of the press. As you read this opinion, analyze the following questions: (1) Why did Chief Justice Hughes make a strong distinction between censorship and subsequent punishment? (2) Should exceptions be made to the general principle that the government is prohibited by the First Amendment from censoring the press?

Vote:

5 justices voted that Near's constitutional rights were violated (Brandeis, Holmes, Hughes, Roberts, Stone).

4 justices voted that Near's constitutional rights were not violated (Butler, McReynolds, Sutherland, Van Devanter).

Chief Justice Hughes delivered the opinion of the Court.

Chapter 285 of the Session Laws of Minnesota for the year 1925 provides for the abatement, as a public nuisance, of a "malicious, scandalous and defamatory newspaper, magazine or other periodical."

* * *

Under this statute, (section one, clause (b)), the county attorney of Hennepin county brought this action to enjoin the publication of what was described as a "malicious, scandalous, and defamatory newspaper, magazine and periodical," known as "The Saturday Press," published by the defendants in the city of Minneapolis. * * *

Without attempting to summarize the contents of the voluminous exhibits attached to the complaint, we deem it sufficient to say that the articles charged in substance that a Jewish gangster was in control of gambling, bootlegging and racketeering in Minneapolis, and that law enforcing officers and agencies were not energetically performing their duties. * * *

* * *

This statute, for the suppression as a public nuisance of a newspaper or periodical, is unusual, if not unique, and raises questions of grave importance transcending the local interests involved in the particular action. It is no longer open to doubt that the liberty of the press and of speech is within the liberty safeguarded by the due process clause of the 14th Amendment from invasions by state action. It was found impossible to conclude that this essential personal liberty of the citizen was left unprotected by the general guaranty of fundamental rights of person and property. *Gitlow v. New York*. In maintaining this guaranty, the authority of the State to enact laws to promote the health, safety, morals and general welfare of its people is necessarily admitted. The limits of this sovereign power must always be determined with appropriate regard to the particular subject of its exercise. * * *

* * *

It is thus important to note precisely the purpose and effect of the statute as the state court has construed it.

* * *

If we cut through mere details of procedure, the operation and effect of the statute in substance is that public authorities may bring the owner or publisher of a newspaper or periodical before a judge upon a charge of conducting a business of publishing scandalous and defamatory material—in particular that the matter consists of charges against public officers of official dereliction—and unless the owner or publisher is able and disposed to bring competent evidence to satisfy the judge that the charges are true and are published with good motives and for justifiable ends, his newspaper or periodical is suppressed and further publication is made punishable as a contempt. This is the essence of censorship.

The question is whether a statute authorizing such proceedings in restraint of publication is consistent with the conception of liberty of the press as historically conceived and guaranteed. In determining the extent of the constitutional protection, it has been generally, if not universally, considered that it is the chief purpose of the guaranty to prevent previous restraints upon publication. The struggle in England, directed against the legislative power of the licenser, resulted in renunciation of the censorship of the press. The liberty deemed to be established was thus described by Blackstone: "The liberty of the press is indeed essential to the nature of a free state; but this consists in laying no *previous* restraints upon publications, and not in freedom from censure for criminal matter when published. Every freeman has an undoubted right to lay what sentiments he pleases before the public; to forbid this, is to destroy the freedom of the press; but if he publishes what is improper, mischievous or illegal, he must take the consequences of his own temerity."

* * *

The criticism upon Blackstone's statement has not been because immunity from previous restraint upon publication has been regarded as deserving of special emphasis, but chiefly because that immunity cannot be deemed to exhaust the conception of the liberty guaranteed by state and Federal constitutions. The point of criticism has been "that the mere exemption from previous restraints cannot be all that is secured by the constitutional provisions;" and that "the liberty of the press might be rendered a mockery and a delusion, and the phrase itself a by-word, if, while every man was at liberty to publish what he pleased, the public authorities might nevertheless punish him for harmless publications." But it is recognized that punishment for abuse of the liberty accorded to the press is essential to the protection of the public, and that the common law rules that subject the libeler to responsibility for the public offense, as well as for the private injury, are not abolished by the protection extended in our constitutions. * * * In the present case, we have no occasion to inquire as to the permissible scope of subsequent punishment. For whatever wrong the appellant has committed or may commit, by his publications, the state appropriately affords both public and private redress by its libel laws. As has been noted, the statute in question does not deal with punishments; it provides for no punishment, except in case of contempt for violation of the court's order, but for suppression and injunction, that is, for restraint of publication.

The objection has also been made that the principle as to immunity from previous restraint is stated too broadly, if every such restraint is deemed to be prohibited. That is undoubtedly true; the protection even as to previous restraint is not absolutely unlimited. * * * No one would question but that a government might prevent actual obstruction to its recruiting service or the publication of the sailing dates of transports or the number and location of troops. On similar grounds, the primary requirements of decency may be enforced against obscene publications. The security of the community life may be protected against incitements to acts of violence or the overthrow by force of orderly government. * * *

* * *

The fact that for approximately one hundred fifty years there has been an almost entire absence of attempts to impose previous restraints upon publications relating to the malfeasance of public officers is significant of the deep-seated conviction that such restraints would violate constitutional rights. Public officers, whose character and conduct remain open to debate and free discussion in the press, find their remedies for false accusations in actions under libel laws providing for redress and punishment, and not in proceedings to restrain the publication of newspapers and periodicals. The general principle that the constitutional guaranty of the liberty of the press gives immunity from previous restraints has been approved in many decisions under the provisions of state constitutions.

* * *

In attempted justification of the statute, it is said that it deals not with publication per se, but with the "business" of publishing defamation. If, however, the publisher has a constitutional right to publish, without previous restraint, an edition of his newspaper charging official derelictions, it cannot be denied that he may publish subsequent editions for the same purpose. If his right exists, it may be exercised in publishing nine editions, as in this case, as well as in one edition. If previous restraint is permissible, it may be imposed at once; indeed, the wrong may be as serious in one publication as in several. Characterizing the publication as a business, and the business as a nuisance, does not permit an invasion of the constitutional immunity against restraint. * * *

* * *

For these reasons we hold the statute, so far as it authorized the proceedings in this action . . ., to be an infringement of the liberty of the press guaranteed by the Fourteenth Amendment. We should add that this decision rests upon the operation and effect of the statute, without regard to the question of the truth of the charges contained in the particular periodical. The fact that the public officers named in this case, and those associated with the charges of official dereliction, may be deemed to be impeccable, cannot affect the conclusion that the statute imposes an unconstitutional restraint upon publication.

Judgment reversed.

Justice Butler, dissenting.

The decision of the court in this case . . . gives to freedom of the press a meaning and a scope not heretofore recognized and construes "liberty" in the due process clause of the 14th Amendment to put upon the states a Federal restriction that is without precedent.

* * *

It is of the greatest importance that the states shall be untrammeled and free to employ all just and appropriate measures to prevent abuses of the liberty of the press.

* * *

The Minnesota statute does not operate as a previous restraint on publication within the proper meaning of the phrase. It does not authorize administrative control in advance such as was formerly exercised by the licensers and censors but prescribes a remedy to be enforced by a suit in equity. In this case there was previous publication made in the course of the business of regularly producing malicious, scandalous and defamatory periodicals. The business and publications unquestionably constitute an abuse of the right of free press. The statute denounces the things done as a nuisance on the ground, as stated by the state supreme court, that they threatened morals, peace and good order. There is no question of the power of the state to denounce such transgressions. The restraint authorized is only in respect of continuing to do what has been duly adjudged to constitute a nuisance. * * * There is nothing in the statute purporting to prohibit publications that have not been adjudged to constitute a nuisance. * * *

* * *

It is well known, as found by the state supreme court, that existing libel laws are inadequate effectively to suppress evils resulting from the kind of business and publications that are shown in this case. The doctrine that measures such as the one before us are invalid because they operate as previous restraints to infringe freedom of press exposes the peace and good order of every community and the business and private affairs of every individual to the constant and unprotected false and malicious assaults of any insolvent publisher who may have purpose and sufficient capacity to contrive and put into effect a scheme or program for oppression, blackmail or extortion.

The judgment should be affirmed.

Justice Van Devanter, Justice McReynolds, and Justice Sutherland concur in this opinion.

Although the Warren Court heard few cases involving press censorship, the principles set forth in *Near* were reaffirmed in a 1966 decision, *Mills v. Alabama*. This case involved an Alabama law that prohibited the solicitation of votes on the day of an election. The editor of an Alabama newspaper was convicted under this law because he had printed an editorial on election day urging his readers to vote in a particular way on a ballot proposal. Writing for the Court majority in striking down the law, Justice Black stated, "It is difficult to conceive of a more obvious and flagrant abridgment of the constitutionally guaranteed freedom of the press" (384 U.S. at 219).

Unlike the Warren Court, the Burger Court issued a number of important decisions involving press censorship. Following in the tradition of earlier precedents, the justices of the Burger Court provided strong protection for the press against a variety of forms of prior restraint.

The Pentagon Papers Case (*New York Times Company v. United States*, 1971) was the Burger Court's most important decision regarding prior restraint. In June of 1971 the *New York Times* and the *Washington Post* began publishing materials from a top secret document entitled "History of U.S. Decision-Making Process on Vietnam Policy," a 7,000 page analysis of how the United States became involved in the Vietnam War. The U.S. government sought injunctions against both newspapers in federal district court to prevent the publication of the document, arguing that these articles could do serious damage to national security. The lower courts that heard the case came to different conclusions, and in an extraordinarily speedy fashion the Burger Court justices heard the case and ruled against the government. The justices had already finished their 1970–71 term, but they extended the term to rule on this important case. Oral arguments were made on June 26, and the Court issued a brief per curiam opinion four days later on June 30. In this unsigned opinion supported by six justices, the Court cited earlier precedents, which stated that the government bears a heavy burden in justifying any type of prior restraint and in this case ". . . the government had not met the burden" (402 U.S. at 714).

All nine justices wrote separately to express their individual views regarding the case, undoubtedly reflecting the lack of time to achieve a broader consensus. Black, Douglas, and Brennan, the Court's leading liberals in interpreting the First Amendment, argued strongly in favor of the *Times* and *Post*, taking an absolutist approach. In Black's words, "Both the history and language of the First Amendment support the view that the press must be left free to publish news, whatever the source, without censorship, injunctions, or prior restraints" (403 U.S. at 717).

Justices Stewart, White, and Marshall also voted in favor of the newspapers, but they saw the case from a less absolutist perspective. Stewart and White saw two great constitutional principles in conflict: the freedom of the press from government censorship and the extensive authority of the executive branch in the area of foreign affairs. Although acknowledging that prior restraint may be permitted under certain circumstances, they did not think that the government had established that disclosure of all of these materials would result in ". . . direct, immediate, and irreparable damage to our Nation or its people" (403 U.S. at 731). Marshall took a unique perspective, arguing that the executive branch was violating the Constitution's separation of powers principle; by asking the courts to enjoin the papers from publishing, the executive branch and the courts would be making law without regard for Congress, which holds the law-making function.

Chief Justice Burger and Justices Harlan and Blackmun filed dissents. The three dissenters did share their colleagues' concern about the dangers of prior restraint on the press. As Chief Justice Burger noted at the outset of his opinion, "There is . . . little variation among the members of the Court in terms of resistance to prior restraints against publication" (403 U.S. at 748). The dissenting justices expressed their deep concerns, however, about the haste in which the case had been decided, leaving not only the lower courts but also the Supreme Court insufficient time to analyze the complex and important questions presented. Burger, Blackmun, and Harlan therefore argued that the cases should be remanded to the lower courts for expeditious but careful resolution of all the issues that had been raised.

New York Times Co. v. United States

403 U.S. 713, 91 S.Ct. 2140, 29 L.Ed. 2d 822 (1971)

■ In 1971, the Nixon administration attempted to prevent the *New York Times* and the *Washington Post* from printing a sequence of articles based on the forty-seven volume study entitled "*History of U.S. Decision-Making Process on Vietnam Policy.*" The study, also known as "The Pentagon Papers," was produced in 1968 and classified as "Top Secret." Daniel Ellsberg had supplied the *New York Times* with the document after secretly copying it.

After the printing of three articles by the *New York Times* and two items by the *Washington Post* detailing selected portions, the federal government sought an injunction to prohibit the newspapers from publishing the study. Federal district courts in New York and the District of Columbia denied injunctive relief. The Court of Appeals for the District of Columbia agreed with the D.C. District Court, but the Second Circuit Court of Appeals remanded the case to the New York District Court. On appeal to the United States Supreme Court, the *New York Times* argued that the stay of publication and the government's attempt at an injunction abridged the freedom of press guarantee of the First Amendment.

This case is significant because the Court took a strong position regarding censorship, even when the government was making a case that national security required it. As you read this decision, give attention to the following questions: (1) Why did the Court resort to a brief, per curiam opinion in such an important case? (2) Why is it ambiguous to state that three justices dissented in this case? (3) Under what circumstances, if any, might the Court have ruled in favor of the government?

Vote:

6 justices voted against granting an injunction on publishing the articles (Black, Brennan, Douglas, Marshall, Stewart, White).

3 justices voted to place restraints on publication pending further hearings by the federal district courts (Blackmun, Burger, Harlan).

Per Curiam.

We granted certiorari in these cases in which the United States seeks to enjoin the *New York Times* and the *Washington Post* from publishing the contents of a classified study entitled "History of U.S. Decision-Making Process on Vietnam Policy."

"Any system of prior restraints of expression comes to this Court bearing a heavy presumption against its constitutional validity." [*Near*] The Government "thus carries a heavy burden of showing justification for the imposition of such a restraint." The District Court for the Southern District of New York in the *New York Times* case and the District Court for the District of Columbia and the Court of Appeals for the District of Columbia Circuit in the *Washington Post* case held that the Government had not met that burden. We agree.

The judgment of the Court of Appeals for the District of Columbia Circuit is therefore affirmed. The order of the Court of Appeals for the Second Circuit is reversed and the case is remanded with directions to enter a judgment affirming the judgment of the District Court for the Southern District of New York. The stays entered June 25, 1971, by the Court are vacated. The judgments shall issue forthwith.

So ordered.

Justice Black, with whom Justice Douglas joins, concurring.

I adhere to the view that the Government's case against the Washington Post should have been dismissed and that the injunction against the *New York Times* should have been vacated without oral argument when the cases were first presented to the Court. I believe that every moment's continuance of the injunctions against these newspapers amounts to a flagrant, indefensible, and continuing violation of the First Amendment. * * * In my view it is unfortunate that some of my Brethren are apparently willing to hold that the publication of news may sometimes be enjoined. Such a holding would make a shambles of the First Amendment.

* * *

In seeking injunctions against these newspapers and in its presentation to the Court, the Executive Branch seems to have forgotten the essential purpose and history of the First Amendment. * * *Madison and other Framers of the First Amendment, able men that they were, wrote in language they earnestly believed could never be misunderstood: "Congress shall make no law . . . abridging the freedom . . . of the press. . . ." Both the history and language of the First Amendment support the view that the press must be left free to publish news, whatever the source, without censorship, injunctions, or prior restraints.

In the First Amendment the Founding Fathers gave the free press the protection it must have to fulfill its essential role in our democracy. The press was to serve the governed, not the governors. The Government's power to censor the press was abolished so that the press would remain forever free to censure the Government. The press was protected so it could bare the secrets of government and inform the people. Only a free and unrestrained press can effectively expose deception in government. And paramount among the responsibilities of a free press is the duty to prevent any part of the government from deceiving the people and sending them off to distant lands to die of foreign fevers and foreign shot and shell. In my view, far from deserving condemnation for their courageous reporting, the *New York Times*, the *Washington Post*, and other newspapers should be commended for serving the purpose that the Founding Fathers saw so clearly. In revealing the workings of government that led to the Vietnam war, the newspapers nobly did precisely that which the Founders hoped and trusted they would do.

The Government's case here is based on premises entirely different from those that guided the Framers of the First Amendment. * * *

. . .[W]e are asked to hold that despite the First Amendment's emphatic command, the Executive Branch, the Congress, and the Judiciary can make laws enjoining the publication of current news and abridging freedom of the press in the name of "national security." The Government does not even attempt to rely on any act of Congress. Instead, it makes the bold and dangerously far-reaching contention that the courts should take it upon themselves to "make" a law abridging freedom of the press in the name of equity, presidential power, and national security. * * * To find that the President has "inherent power" to halt the publication of news by resort to the courts would wipe out the First Amendment and destroy the fundamental liberty and security of the very people the Government hopes to make "secure." No one can read the history of the adoption of the First Amendment without being convinced beyond any doubt that it was injunctions like those sought here that Madison and his collaborators intended to outlaw in this Nation for all time.

Justice Douglas, with whom Justice Black joins, concurring [omitted].

Justice Brennan, concurring.

I write separately in these cases only to emphasize what should be apparent: that our judgments in the present cases may not be taken to indicate the propriety, in the future, of issuing temporary stays and restraining orders to block the publication of material sought to be suppressed by the Government. So far as I can determine, never before has the United States sought to enjoin a newspaper from publishing information in its possession. The relative novelty of the questions presented, the necessary haste with which decisions were reached, the magnitude of the interests asserted, and the fact that all the parties have concentrated their arguments upon the question whether permanent restraints were proper may have justified at least some of the restraints heretofore imposed in these cases. * * * But even if it be assumed that some of the interim restraints were proper in the two cases before us, that assumption has no bearing upon the propriety of similar judicial action in the future. To begin with, there has now been ample time for reflection and judgment; whatever value there may be in the preservation of novel questions for appellate review may not support any restraints in the future. More important, the First Amendment stands as an absolute bar to the imposition of judicial restraints in circumstances of the kind presented by these cases.

The error that has pervaded these cases from the outset was the granting of any injunctive relief whatsoever, interim or otherwise. The entire thrust of the Government's claim throughout these cases has been that publication of the material sought to be enjoined "could," or "might," or "may" prejudice the national interest in various ways. But the First Amendment tolerates absolutely no prior judicial restraints of the press predicated upon surmise or conjecture that untoward consequences may result. * * *

Justice Stewart, with whom Justice White joins, concurring.

In the governmental structure created by our Constitution, the Executive is endowed with enormous power in the two related areas of national defense and international relations. This power, largely unchecked by the Legislative and Judicial branches, has been pressed to the very hilt since the advent of the nuclear missile age. For better or for worse, the simple fact is that a President of the United States possesses vastly greater constitutional independence in these two vital areas of power than does, say, a prime minister of a country with a parliamentary form of government.

In the absence of the governmental checks and balances present in other areas of our national life, the only effective restraint upon executive policy and power in the areas of national defense and international affairs may lie in an enlightened citizenry—in an informed and critical public opinion which alone can here protect the values of democratic government. For this reason, it is perhaps here that a free press that is alert, aware, and free most vitally serves the basic purpose of the First Amendment. For without an informed and free press there cannot be an enlightened people.

Yet it is elementary that the successful conduct of international diplomacy and the maintenance of an effective national defense require both confidentiality and secrecy. Other nations can hardly deal with this Nation in an atmosphere of mutual trust unless they can be assured that their confidences will be kept. And within our own executive departments, the development of considered and intelligent international policies would be impossible if those charged with their formulation could not communicate with each other freely, frankly, and in confidence. In the area of basic national defense the frequent need for absolute secrecy is, of course, self-evident.

I think there can be but one answer to this dilemma, if dilemma it be. The responsibility must be where the power is. If the Constitution gives the Executive a large degree of unshared power in the conduct of foreign affairs and the maintenance of our national defense, then under the Constitution the Executive must have the largely unshared duty to determine and preserve the degree of internal security necessary to exercise that power successfully. It is an awesome responsibility, requiring judgment and wisdom of a high order. I should suppose that moral, political, and practical considerations would dictate that a very first principle of that wisdom would be an insistence upon avoiding secrecy for its own sake. For when everything is classified, then nothing is classified, and the system becomes one to be disregarded by the cynical or the careless, and to be manipulated by those intent upon self-protection or self-promotion. I should suppose, in short, that the hallmark of a truly effective internal security system would be the maximum possible disclosure, recognizing that secrecy can best be preserved only when credibility is truly maintained. But be that as it may, it is clear to me that it is the constitutional duty of the Executive—as a matter of sovereign prerogative and not as a matter of law as the courts know law—through the promulgation and enforcement of executive regulations, to protect the confidentiality necessary to carry out its responsibilities in the fields of international relations and national defense.

This is not to say that Congress and the courts have no role to play. Undoubtedly Congress has the power to enact specific and appropriate criminal laws to protect government property and preserve government secrets. * * * Moreover, if Congress should pass a specific law authorizing civil proceedings in this field, the courts would likewise have the duty to decide the constitutionality of such a law as well as its applicability to the facts proved.

But in the cases before us we are asked neither to construe specific regulations nor to apply specific laws. We are asked, instead, to perform a function that the Constitution gave to the Executive, not the Judiciary. We are asked, quite simply, to prevent the publication by two newspapers of material that the Executive Branch insists should not, in the national interest, be published. I am convinced that the Executive is correct with respect to some of the documents involved. But I cannot say that disclosure of any of them will surely result in direct, immediate, and irreparable damage to our Nation or its people. That being so, there can under the First Amendment be but one judicial resolution of the issues before us. I join the judgments of the Court.

Justice White, with whom Justice Stewart joins, concurring.

I concur in today's judgments, but only because of the concededly extraordinary protection against prior restraints enjoyed by the press under our constitutional system. I do not say that in no circumstances would the First Amendment permit an injunction against publishing information about governmental plans or operations. Nor, after examining the materials the Government characterizes as the most sensitive and destructive, can I deny that revelation of these documents will do substantial damage to public interests. Indeed, I am confident that their disclosure will have that result. But I nevertheless agree that the United States has not satisfied the very heavy burden that it must meet to warrant an injunction against publication in these cases, at least in the absence of express and appropriately limited congressional authorization for prior restraint in circumstances such as these.

The Government's position is simply stated: The responsibility of the Executive for the conduct of foreign affairs and for the security of the Nation is so basic that the President is entitled to an injunction against publication of a newspaper story whenever he can convince a court that the information to be revealed threatens "grave and irreparable" injury to the public interest; and the injunction should issue whether or not the material to be published is classified, whether or not publication would be lawful under relevant criminal statutes enacted by Congress, and regardless of the circumstances by which the newspaper came into possession of the information.

At least in the absence of legislation by Congress, based on its own investigations and findings, I am quite unable to agree that the inherent powers of the Executive and the courts reach so far as to authorize remedies having such sweeping potential for inhibiting publications by the press. Much of the difficulty inheres in the "grave and irreparable danger" standard suggested by the United States. If the United States were to have judgment under such a standard in these cases, our decisions would be of little guidance to other courts in other cases, for the material at issue here would not be available from the court's opinion or from public records, nor would it be published by the press. Indeed, even today where we hold that the United States has not met its burden, the material remains sealed in court records and it is properly not discussed in today's opinions. Moreover, because the material poses substantial dangers to national interests and because of the hazards of criminal sanctions, a responsible press may choose never to publish the more sensitive materials. To sustain the Government in these cases would start the courts down a long and hazardous road that I am not willing to travel, at least without congressional guidance and direction.

* * *

Justice Marshall, concurring [omitted].

Chief Justice Burger, dissenting.

So clear are the constitutional limitations of prior restraint against expression, that from the time of *Near v. Minnesota* (1931) . . . we have had little occasion to be concerned with cases involving prior restraints against news reporting on matters of public interest. There is, therefore, little variation among the members of the Court in terms of resistence to prior restraint against publication. Adherence to this basic constitutional principle, however, does not make these cases simple. In these cases, the imperative of a free and unfettered press comes into collision with another imperative, the effective functioning of a complex modern government and specifically the effective exercise of certain constitutional powers of the Executive. Only those who view the First Amendment as an absolute—a view I respect, but reject—can find such cases as these to be simple or easy.

These cases are not simple for another and more immediate reason. We do not know the facts of the cases. * * *

* * *

I suggest . . . these cases have been conducted in unseemly haste.* * *

. . .[T]he frenetic haste is due in large part to the manner in which the *Times* proceeded from the date it obtained the purloined documents. It seems reasonably clear now that the haste precluded reasonable and deliberate judicial treatment of these cases and was not warranted. The precipitate action of this Court aborting trials not yet completed is not the kind of judicial conduct that ought to attend the disposition of a great issue.

The newspapers make a derivative claim under the First Amendment; they denominate this right as the public "right to know"; by implication, the *Times* asserts a sole trusteeship of that right by virtue of its journalistic "scoop." The right is asserted as an absolute. Of course, the First Amendment right itself is not an absolute, as Justice Holmes so long ago pointed out in his aphorism concerning the right to shout "fire" in a crowded theater if there was no fire. There are other exceptions, some of which Chief Justice Hughes mentioned by way of example in *Near v. Minnesota*. There are no doubt other exceptions no one has had occasion to describe or discuss.

* * *

It is not disputed that the *Times* has had unauthorized possession of the documents for three to four months, during which it has had its expert analysts studying them, presumably digesting them and preparing the material for publication. During all of this time, the *Times*, presumably in its capacity as trustee of the public's "right to know," has held up publication for purposes it considered proper and thus public knowledge was delayed. No doubt this was for a good reason; the analysis of 7,000 pages of complex material drawn from a vastly greater volume of material would inevitably take time and the writing of good news stories takes time. But why should the United States Government, from whom this information was illegally acquired by someone, along with all the counsel, trial judges, and appellate judges be placed under needless pressure? After these months of deferral, the alleged "right to know" has somehow and suddenly become a right that must be vindicated instanter.

Would it have been unreasonable, since the newspaper could anticipate the Government's objections to release of secret material, to give the Government an opportunity to review the entire collection and determine whether agreement could be reached on publication? Stolen or not, if security was not in fact jeopardized, much of the material could no doubt have been declassified, since it spans a period ending in 1968. With such an approach—one that great newspapers have in the past practiced and stated editorially to be the duty of an honorable press—the newspapers and Government might well have narrowed the area of disagreement as to what was and what was not publishable, leaving the remainder to be resolved in orderly litigation, if necessary. To me it is hardly believable that a newspaper long regarded as a great institution in American life would fail to perform one of the basic and simple duties of every citizen with respect to the discovery or possession of stolen property or secret government documents. That duty, I had thought—perhaps naively—was to report forthwith, to responsible public officers. This duty rests on taxi drivers, Justices, and the *New York Times*. The course followed by the *Times*, whether so calculated or not, removed any possibility of orderly litigation of the issues. If the action of the judges up to now has been correct, that result is sheer happenstance.

* * *

I would affirm the Court of Appeals for the Second Circuit and allow the District Court to complete the trial aborted by our grant of certiorari. . . . I would direct that the District Court on remand give priority to the *Times* case to the exclusion of all other business of that court but I would not set arbitrary deadlines.

* * *

Justice Harlan, with whom The Chief Justice and Justice Blackmun join, dissenting.

* * * With all respect, I consider that the Court has been almost irresponsibly feverish in dealing with these cases.

* * *

This frenzied train of events took place in the name of the presumption against prior restraints created by the First Amendment. Due regard for the extraordinarily important and difficult questions involved in these litigations should have led the Court to shun such a precipitate timetable. In order to decide the merits of these cases properly, some or all of the following questions should have been faced:

1. Whether the Attorney General is authorized to bring these suits in the name of the United States.

* * *

2. Whether the First Amendment permits the federal courts to enjoin publication of stories which would present a serious threat to national security.

3. Whether the threat to publish highly secret documents is of itself a sufficient implication of national security to justify an injunction on the theory that regardless of the contents of the documents harm enough results simply from the demonstration of such a breach of secrecy.

4. Whether the unauthorized disclosure of any of these particular documents would seriously impair the national security.

5. What weight should be given to the opinion of high officers in the Executive Branch of the Government with respect to question 3 and 4.

6. Whether the newspapers are entitled to retain and use the documents notwithstanding the seemingly uncontested facts that the documents, or the originals of which they are duplicates, were purloined from the Government's possession and that the newspapers received them with knowledge that they had been feloniously acquired.

7. Whether the threatened harm to the national security or the Government's possessory interest in the documents justifies the issuance of an injunction against publication in light of—

a. The strong First Amendment policy against prior restraints on publication;

b. The doctrine against enjoining conduct in violation of criminal statutes;

c. The extent to which the materials at issue have apparently already been otherwise disseminated.

These are difficult questions of fact, of law, and of judgment; the potential consequences of erroneous decisions are enormous. The time which has been available to us, to the lower courts, and to the parties has been wholly inadequate for giving these cases the kind of consideration they deserve. It is a reflection on the stability of the judicial process that these great issues—as important as any that have arisen during my time on the Court—should have been decided under the pressures engendered by the torrent of publicity that has attended these litigations from their inception.

Forced as I am to reach the merits of these cases, I dissent from the opinion and judgments of the Court. Within the severe limitations imposed by the time constraints under which I have been required to operate, I can only state my reasons in telescoped form, even though in different circumstances I would have felt constrained to deal with the cases in the fuller sweep indicated above.

* * *

* * * It is plain to me that the scope of the judicial function in passing upon the activities of the Executive Branch of the Government in the field of foreign affairs is very narrowly restricted. This view is, I think, dictated by the concept of separation of powers upon which our constitutional system rests.

* * *

Pending further hearings in each case conducted under the appropriate ground rules, I would continue the restraints on publication. I cannot believe that the doctrine prohibiting prior restraints reaches to the point of preventing courts from maintaining the status quo long enough to act responsibly in matters of such national importance as those involved here.

Justice Blackmun, dissenting.

* * *

The First Amendment, after all, is only one part of an entire Constitution. Article II of the great document vests in the Executive Branch primary power over the conduct of foreign affairs and places in that branch the responsibility for the Nation's safety. Each provision of the Constitution is important, and I cannot subscribe to a doctrine of unlimited absolutism at the cost of downgrading other provisions. First Amendment absolutism has never commanded a majority of this Court. * * * What is needed here is a weighing, upon properly developed standards, of the broad right of the press to print and of the very narrow right of the Government to prevent. Such standards are not yet developed. The parties here are in disagreement as to what those standards should be. * * *

I therefore would remand these cases to be developed expeditiously, of course, but on a schedule permitting the orderly presentation of evidence from both sides, with the use of discovery, if necessary, as authorized by the rules, and with the preparation of briefs, oral argument, and court opinions of a quality better than has been seen to this point. * * * . . .[T]hese cases and the issues involved and the courts, including this one, deserve better than has been produced thus far.

In addition to the Pentagon Papers Case, the Burger Court issued a substantial number of other decisions opposing various forms of prior restraint over the press. In *Miami Herald Publishing Co. v. Tornillo* (1974), the Court ruled unanimously against a Florida law that allowed a political candidate who was assailed by a newspaper the right to demand the printing of a reply free of charge. Pat Tornillo, a candidate for the Florida House of Representatives, had been attacked in a series of editorials by the *Miami Herald*, telling voters that it would be inexcusable if not illegal to elect Tornillo. When he sought to have the paper print his reply, the *Herald* refused. Writing for the Court, Chief Justice Burger likened this law to a form of prior restraint and argued that it could lead to self-censorship by newspaper editors.

Another case that illustrates the Burger Court's strong opposition to prior restraint of the press is *Cox Broadcasting Corporation v. Cohn* (1975). Cynthia Cohn was a seventeen-year-old girl who attended a high school drinking party, became intoxicated, was raped by six young males, and died from suffocation. Charges of rape and murder were brought against all six of the teenage males. During the process of investigating the case, a reporter for a Cox Broadcasting station discovered Cynthia's name in public documents and reported her name in a broadcast. Cynthia's father filed suit against the Cox Corporation, charging that this was a violation of his right to privacy as well as a violation of a Georgia law prohibiting any news media from making known the name of any rape victim. Despite their sympathy for the father, the Burger Court justices ruled 8-1, with only Rehnquist in dissent, that the First Amendment protects the media in reporting truthful information contained in public records.

The Burger Court also ruled against various forms of prior restraint in the cases of *Southeastern Promotions v. Conrad* (1975), *Landmark Communications, Inc. v. Virginia* (1978), and *Smith v. Daily Mail Publishing Company* (1979). In *Southeast Promotions*, the issue involved the decision of Chattanooga, Tennessee, to deny the use of its municipal auditorium for a stage production of the musical *Hair,* which featured nudity and strong sexual content. The Court viewed this as a form of censorship and thus a violation of the First Amendment. The Burger Court justices unanimously struck down in *Landmark Communications* a Virginia law that prohibited the press from publishing information about the activities of the state's Judicial Inquiry and Review Commission, which reviewed complaints about the disability or misconduct of state judicial officials. And in the *Daily Mail* case, the Burger Court justices ruled as an unconstitutional prior restraint a law that prohibited the publishing of the names of juveniles arrested by the police.

In concluding our analysis of the Burger Court and censorship, we need to recognize that the Supreme Court has long recognized that prior restraint of the press may be constitutionally permissible under some circumstances, and the Burger Court did rule in favor of governmental prior control in a few cases. In *Pittsburgh Press Co. v. Human Relations Commission* (1973), the justices gave approval to a Pittsburgh ordinance prohibiting ads that classified jobs based on male and female interest. The Court in *Snepp v. United States* (1980) approved a rule of the Central Intelligence Agency that required employees to submit manuscripts to the agency for approval prior to publication. These cases were rather narrowly based decisions dealing with forms of commercial speech, however, and they do not undermine our argument that the Burger Court gave strong support to press claims involving prior restraint by the government.

The Rehnquist Court has maintained this tradition. Two important exceptions do exist, however. The Rehnquist Court upheld a school principal's censorship of articles that were to appear in a school newspaper, and it also rejected a First Amendment challenge by a reporter who was sued for revealing the name of an informant who had been promised confidentiality. We will examine these two cases before turning to a series of cases in which the Rehnquist Court upheld freedom of the press claims against various forms of prior restraint.

In *Hazelwood School District v. Kuhlmeier* (1988), Robert Reynolds was the principal of Hazelwood East High School in St. Louis County, Missouri. Reynolds reviewed page proofs of the school newspaper, *Spectrum*, and he objected to two articles that were scheduled to appear in a May, 1983 issue. One article dealt with three Hazelwood East students' experiences with pregnancy, and the other article discussed the impact of divorce on Hazelwood students. Operating under time deadlines, Reynolds decided to withhold the two articles from publication. Three students who worked on *Spectrum* filed suit in federal district court alleging a violation of their First Amendment rights. The district court ruled against the students, but a circuit court of appeals reversed and found in favor of the students.

White wrote a five-person majority opinion, joined by Rehnquist, Scalia, O'Connor, and Stevens, which found no First Amendment violation. White paid little attention to the censorship issue. He began his opinion by arguing that school boards rather than federal courts have primary authority in assessing students' First Amendment rights. White then turned to public forum analysis. He argued that *Spectrum* was a nonpublic forum, which meant that school officials only had to justify their actions by a reasonableness standard. In White's view, Reynolds' action "...was reasonable under the circumstances as he understood them" (484 U.S. at 276).

Brennan authored a strongly libertarian dissent, which was joined by Marshall and Blackmun. Brennan saw this as an obvious case of censorship that could only be justified on the basis of serving a substantial government interest achieved by narrowly tailored means, and neither feature existed in this case. Brennan concluded his opinion with a harsh rebuke of Reynolds's decision: "Such unthinking contempt for individual rights is intolerable from any state official. It is particularly insidious from one to whom the public entrusts the task of inculcating in its youth an appreciation for the cherished democratic liberties that our Constitution guarantees" (484 U.S. at 290).

The Rehnquist Court also gave approval to a form of indirect prior restraint in *Cohen v. Cowles Media Co.* (1991). Dan Cohen was working for a candidate in a 1982 Minnesota gubernatorial race, and he made available to reporters from Cowles

Media unfavorable information about the lieutenant governor candidate of an opposition party. Cohen had been promised confidentiality, but an editorial decision was made to publish his name in the story. When the story appeared, Cohen was immediately fired from his job. Cohen sued Cowles Media under Minnesota law, and a jury awarded him $200,000 in compensatory damages and $500,000 in punitive damages. Both awards were overturned on appeal, however, with the Minnesota Supreme Court ruling that enforcement of the law in this case would violate the First Amendment.

The Supreme Court overturned the Minnesota high court in a five-person majority opinion authored by White. As in *Kuhlmeier*, White did not view the case as involving any type of prior restraint on the press, explicitly rejecting this line of precedent. Instead, White viewed the case as one involving breach of contract. In such cases, White argued, "the First Amendment does not forbid its application to the press" (501 U.S. at 670).

The dissenting justices viewed the case as involving fundamental First Amendment values, specifically the protection for the publication of truthful information. The government can prevent this only when a state interest of the highest order is being served, and Minnesota's interest in this case was far from compelling according to Blackmun, Marshall, and Souter.

Kuhlmeier and *Cohen* notwithstanding, the overall record of the Rehnquist Court was one of ruling against various forms of prior restraint on the press. We will briefly discuss four of these cases.

Lakewood v. Plain Dealer (1988) involved a First Amendment challenge by the *Cleveland Plain Dealer* to an ordinance passed by the city of Lakewood, Ohio, which gave the city's mayor complete authority to grant or deny applications to place newsracks on public property. Although the Court could not achieve a majority opinion with only seven justices participating, the ordinance was ruled unconstitutional by a 4-3 vote. Brennan authored the plurality opinion. He began his opinion by citing numerous precedents that had at their root ". . .the time-tested knowledge that in the area of free expression a licensing statute placing unbridled discretion in the hands of a government official or agency constitutes a prior restraint and may result in censorship" (486 U.S. at 757). In this particular case, Brennan argued, the lack of any explicit limits on the mayor's discretion created such serious threats of censorship as to violate the First Amendment.

The next year the Court handed down another narrow decision affirming the freedom of the press over governmental prior restraints in *The Florida Star v. B.J.F.* A Florida law prohibited publishing the name of the victim of any sexual offense, but a reporter obtained the name of a rape victim from a report available in the pressroom of the local sheriff's department. The newspaper published the story with the victim's name. She sued and won both compensatory and punitive damages.

Marshall wrote a 5-4 majority opinion, joined by Brennan, Blackmun, Stevens, and Kennedy, arguing that imposing these damages violated the First Amendment. Although recognizing the important personal privacy rights involved in the case, Marshall argued that a newspaper can be punished for publishing lawfully obtained, truthful information only when a state interest of the highest order is pursued through narrowly tailored means. Given the facts of this case, Marshall concluded, the state did not meet these requirements.

The justices found themselves in unanimous agreement in the 1990 case of *Butterworth v. Smith*, another case involving a form of prior restraint. Michael Smith was a reporter for the *Charlotte Herald-News* in Charlotte County, Florida. He had obtained information relevant to a grand jury investigation, and he was called to testify. He was told that Florida law forbade him to reveal his testimony in any manner, but he wanted to publish some of his testimony after the grand jury had finished its investigation. He therefore filed suit in federal district court to have the law declared unconstitutional; the district court upheld the law, but a circuit court ruled the law unconstitutional.

Writing for a unanimous Court, Chief Justice Rehnquist agreed that the law violated the First Amendment. In a rather narrowly based opinion, Rehnquist argued that the law placed a dramatic burden on a reporter's freedom of expression. In this case, Florida's interests were not sufficiently strong to overcome the First Amendment right, especially when the investigation of the grand jury had ended.

Simon and Schuster v. Crime Victims Board (1991) is the fourth and final example of the Rehnquist Court ruling against an indirect prior restraint on the press. The issue in this case was the constitutionality of New York's "Son of Sam" law. A serial killer who called himself the Son of Sam terrorized New York in the summer of 1977. In the aftermath of this murder case, New York passed a law that required that any income from a criminal's book about the crime should be put into escrow and used to assist the victims of the crime. In 1981, Simon and Schuster Publishing Company entered into a publishing agreement with an author, Nicholas Pileggi, to do a book about the life of a notorious crime figure, Henry Hill. Pileggi and Hill produced a best-selling book called *Wiseguy: Life in a Mafia Family*, and both men were to receive royalties. The New York Crime Victims Board notified Simon and Schuster that they had violated the Son of Sam law because they had not provided the Board with the contract and had made advanced royalty payments to Hill. In addition, all money owed to Hill had to be turned over to the Board to be placed in escrow for victims of Hill's crimes. Simon and Schuster filed a suit claiming that the law violated the First Amendment, but both a federal district and a circuit court found the law to be constitutional.

The Rehnquist Court unanimously reversed, finding the law unconstitutional. O'Connor wrote the majority opinion, arguing that the Son of Sam law was a content-based government regulation, which triggers the Court's strictest scrutiny because under such laws ". . .the Government may effectively drive certain ideas or viewpoints from the marketplace" (502 U.S. at 116). In applying the two-pronged strict scrutiny test, O'Connor argued that New York did have a compelling interest in assisting victims to be compensated by those who harm them, but she stated that New York's law was not narrowly tailored to that interest. As the law was written, O'Connor reasoned, books written on such figures as Malcolm X, Martin Luther King, and Jesse Jackson could be forced to comply with the law, but the government's purpose of assisting victims harmed by crime would not be served.

The Supreme Court has thus taken a consistent position for more than half a century on the issue of censorship. Changing membership patterns on the Court have thus not produced discernible changes in the Court's policy in this area of constitutional law. Although the Court has not accepted the absolutist position advocated by Black and Douglas, it has taken a preferred freedoms approach in censorship cases, placing a heavy burden on the government to justify all forms of prior restraint. The Court has not developed a consistent test in censorship cases, but the justices have implicitly and explicitly stated that the strict scrutiny standards of a compelling interest achieved through narrowly tailored means must be met to justify any form of prior censorship.

Libel

We have already had an introduction to the next freedom of the press topic—libel—through our introductory case study of *New York Times Co. v. Sullivan* (1964). In this section we will place *New York Times* into a broader historical context, tracing the Court's libel decisions from their origins through the most recent decisions of the Rehnquist Court.

Prior to *New York Times*, libel was considered to be beyond the protection of the First Amendment based upon the social value doctrine articulated in *Chaplinsky v. New Hampshire* (1942). Although *Chaplinsky* was a case involving fighting words, the Court in dicta stated that several forms of expression—fighting words, obscenity, profanity, incitement, and libel—had long been considered to be so lacking in social value in terms of communicating ideas that they could be regulated by the government without any constraints in terms of the First Amendment. Thus, throughout American history, states enforced libel laws based on the standards of printed words that were false and defamatory.

The Warren Court made its most important contribution to strengthening freedom of the press in the area of libel law, with *New York Times Co. v. Sullivan* (1964) as the leading case. Because we examined *New York Times* in detail to begin this chapter, only the highlights of the decision need to be discussed here. In his majority opinion, Justice Brennan established for the first time that the First Amendment guarantees of freedom of speech and press do place limits on a state's authority to impose monetary damages in a libel action brought by public officials regarding criticism of their official conduct. Specifically, damages could be awarded only if the public official could prove that a defamatory falsehood was made with actual malice, i.e., " . . . with knowledge that it was false or with reckless disregard of whether it was false or not" (376 U.S. at 279–80). In this particular case, although the advertisement did contain some false statements, the evidence did not support a finding of actual malice. For Brennan and the other justices of the Warren Court, the underlying philosophy of the decision involved " . . . a profound national commitment to the principle that debate on public issues should be uninhibited, robust, and wide open, and that it may well include vehement, caustic and sometimes unpleasantly sharp attacks on government and public officials" (376 U.S. at 270).

The Court's vote in *New York Times* was unanimous, but both Black and Goldberg wrote concurring opinions, both of which Douglas joined. Despite the precedent-setting nature of the decision, the majority opinion did not go far enough for these three justices. In Goldberg's words, " . . . the First and Fourteenth Amendments to the Constitution afford to the citizen and to the press an absolute, unconditioned privilege to criticize official conduct despite the harm which may flow from excesses and abuses" (376 U.S. at 298).

NEW YORK TIMES CO. V. SULLIVAN

376 U.S. 254, 84 S.Ct. 710, 11 L.Ed. 2d 687 (1964)

[The facts of the case are omitted because they were presented in the introductory case study.]

■ This is an important case because the Court introduced new principles into libel law regarding the conduct of public officials. Prior to the *New York Times* case, public officials could win libel suits by establishing falseness and defamation. In *New York Times,* the Court ruled that actual malice also had to be established. In reading this case, consider the following questions: (1) Does it seem surprising that the Court voted unanimously to make such a sweeping change in constitutional law? (2) What were the reasons why the Court introduced the additional criterion of actual malice for libel suits involving public officials? (3) In what ways can this decision be considered somewhat conservative? (4) What questions regarding libel law were left unresolved by this decision?

VOTE:

The justices voted unanimously that the constitutional rights of the* New York Times *were violated.

Justice Brennan delivered the opinion of the Court.

We are required in this case to determine for the first time the extent to which the constitutional protections for speech and press limit a State's power

to award damages in a libel action brought by a public official against critics of his official conduct.

* * *

Because of the importance of the constitutional issues involved, we granted the separate petitions for certiorari of the individual petitioners and of the *Times*. We reverse the judgment. We hold that the rule of law applied by the Alabama courts is constitutionally deficient for failure to provide the safeguards for freedom of speech and of the press that are required by the First and Fourteenth Amendments in a libel action brought by a public official against critics of his official conduct. We further hold that under the proper safeguards the evidence presented in this case is constitutionally insufficient to support the judgment for respondent.

We may dispose at the outset of two grounds asserted to insulate the judgment of the Alabama courts from constitutional scrutiny. The first is the proposition relied on by the State Supreme Court—that "The Fourteenth Amendment is directed against State action and not private action." That proposition has no application to this case. Although this is a civil lawsuit between private parties, the Alabama courts have applied a state rule of law which petitioners claim to impose invalid restrictions on their constitutional freedoms of speech and press. * * *

The second contention is that the constitutional guarantees of freedom of speech and of the press are inapplicable here, at least so far as the *Times* is concerned, because the allegedly libelous statements were published as part of a paid, "commercial" advertisement. * * *

The publication here was not a "commercial" advertisement in the sense in which the word was used in *Chrestensen*. It communicated information, expressed opinion, recited grievances, protested claimed abuses, and sought financial support on behalf of a movement whose existence and objectives are matters of the highest public interest and concern. That the *Times* was paid for publishing the advertisement is as immaterial in this connection as is the fact that newspapers and books are sold. Any other conclusion would discourage newspapers from carrying "editorial advertisements" of this type, and so might shut off an important outlet for the promulgation of information and ideas by persons who do not themselves have access to publishing facilities—who wish to exercise their freedom of speech even though they are not members of the press. * * *

* * *

Respondent relies heavily, as did the Alabama courts, on statements of this Court to the effect that the Constitution does not protect libelous publications. Those statements do not foreclose our inquiry here. None of the cases sustained the use of libel laws to impose sanctions upon expression critical of the official conduct of public officials. * * *

In deciding the question now, we are compelled by neither precedent nor policy to give any more weight to the epithet "libel" than we have to other "mere labels" of state law. Like insurrection, contempt, advocacy of unlawful acts, breach of the peace, obscenity, solicitation of legal business, and the various other formulae for the repression of expression that have been challenged in this Court, libel can claim no talismanic immunity from constitutional limitations. It must be measured by standards that satisfy the First Amendment.

The general proposition that freedom of expression upon public questions is secured by the First Amendment has long been settled by our decisions. The constitutional safeguard, we have said, "was fashioned to assure unfettered interchange of ideas for the bringing about of political and social changes desired by the people." * * *

* * *

Thus, we consider this case against the background of a profound national commitment to the principle that debate on public issues should be uninhibited, robust, and wide-open, and that it may well include vehement, caustic, and sometimes unpleasantly sharp attacks on government and public officials. The present advertisement, as an expression of grievance and protest on one of the major public issues of our time, would seem clearly to qualify for the constitutional protection. The question is whether it forfeits that protection by the falsity of some of its factual statements and by its alleged defamation of respondent.

Authoritative interpretations of the First Amendment guarantees have consistently refused to recognize an exception for any test of truth—whether administered by judges, juries, or administrative officials—especially one that puts the burden of proving truth on the speaker. The constitutional protection does not turn upon "the truth, popularity, or social utility of the ideas and beliefs which are offered." * * *

* * *

Injury to official reputation affords no more warrant for repressing speech that would otherwise be free than does factual error. Where judicial officers are involved, this Court has held that concern for the dignity and reputation of the courts does not justify the punishment as criminal contempt of criticism of the judge or his decision. This is true even though the utterance contains "half-truths" and "misinformation." Such repression can be justified, if at all, only by a clear and present danger of the obstruction of justice. If judges are to be treated as "men of fortitude, able to thrive in a hardy climate," surely the same must be true of other government officials, such as elected city commissioners. * * *

If neither factual error nor defamatory content suffices to remove the constitutional shield from criticism of official conduct, the combination of the two elements is no less inadequate. This is the lesson to be drawn from the great controversy over the Sedition Act of 1798, which first crystallized a national awareness of the central meaning of the First Amendment. That statute made it a crime, punishable by a $5,000 fine and five years in prison, "if any person shall write, print, utter or publish. . . any false, scandalous and malicious writings or writings against the government of the United States, or either house of the Congress. . ., or the President. . ., with intent to defame. . .or to bring them, or either of them, into contempt or disrepute; or to excite against them, or either or any of them, the hatred of the good people of the United States." * * *

* * *

Although the Sedition Act was never tested in this Court, the attack upon its validity has carried the day in the court of history. Fines levied in its prosecution were repaid by Act of Congress on the ground that it was unconstitutional. * * * Jefferson, as President, pardoned those who had been convicted and sentenced under the Act and remitted their fines. * * *

* * *

What a State may not constitutionally bring about by means of a criminal statute is likewise beyond the reach of its civil law of libel. The fear of damage awards under a rule such as that invoked by the Alabama courts here may be markedly more inhibiting than the fear of prosecution under a criminal statute. * * *

The state rule of law is not saved by its allowance of the defense of truth. * * *

* * *

A rule compelling the critic of official conduct to guarantee the truth of all his factual assertions—and to do so on pain of libel judgments virtually unlimited in amount—leads to "self-censorship." Allowance of the defense of truth, with the burden of proving it on the defendant, does not mean that only false speech will be deterred. Even courts accepting this defense as an adequate safeguard have recognized the difficulties of adducing legal proofs that the alleged libel was true in all its factual particulars. Under such a rule, would-be critics of official conduct may be deterred from voicing their criticism, even though it is believed to be true, because of doubt whether it can be proved in court or fear of the expense of having to do so. They tend to make only statements which "steer far wider of the unlawful zone." The rule thus dampens the vigor and limits the variety of public debate. It is inconsistent with the First and Fourteenth Amendments.

The constitutional guarantees require, we think, a federal rule that prohibits a public official from recovering damages for a defamatory falsehood relating to his official conduct unless he proves that the statement was made with "actual malice"—that is, with knowledge that it was false or with reckless disregard of whether it was false or not. * * *

* * *

Such a privilege for criticism of official conduct is appropriately analogous to the protection accorded to a public official when he is sued for libel by a private citizen. In *Barr v. Matteo*, this Court held the utterance of a federal official to be absolutely privileged if made "within the outer perimeter" of his duties. The States accord the same immunity to statements of their highest officers, although some differentiate their lesser officials and qualify the privilege they enjoy. But all hold that all officials are protected unless actual malice can be proved. The reason for the official privilege is said to be that the threat of damage suits would otherwise "inhibit the fearless, vigorous, and effective administration of policies of government" and "dampen the ardor of all but the most resolute, or the most irresponsible, in their unflinching discharge of their duties." Analogous considerations support the privilege for the citizen-critic of government. It is as much his duty to criticize as it is the official's duty to administer. As Madison said, "the censorial power is in the people over the Government, and not in the Government over the people." It would give public servants an unjustified preference over the public they serve, if critics of official conduct did not have a fair equivalent of the immunity granted to the officials themselves.

We conclude that such a privilege is required by the First and Fourteenth Amendments.

We hold today that the Constitution delimits a State's power to award damages for libel in actions brought by public officials against critics of their official conduct. Since this is such an action, the rule requiring proof of actual malice is applicable. While Alabama law apparently requires proof of actual malice for an award of punitive damages, where general damages are concerned malice is "presumed." Such a presumption is inconsistent with the federal rule. * * *

Since respondent may seek a new trial, we deem that considerations of effective judicial administration require us to review the evidence in the present record to determine whether it could constitutionally support a judgment for respondent. This Court's duty is not limited to the elaboration of constitutional principles; we must also in proper cases review the evidence to make certain that those principles have been constitutionally applied. This is such a case, particularly since the question is one of alleged trespass across "the line between speech unconditionally guaranteed and speech which may legitimately be regulated." * * *

Applying these standards, we consider that the proof presented to show actual malice lacks the convincing clarity which the constitutional standard demands, and hence that it would not constitutionally sustain the judgment for respondent under the proper rule of law. The case of the individual petitioners requires little discussion. Even assuming that they could constitutionally be found to have authorized the use of their names on the advertisement, there was no evidence whatever that they were aware of any erroneous statements or were in any way reckless in that regard. The judgment against them is thus without constitutional support.

As to the *Times*, we similarly conclude that the facts do not support a finding of actual malice. The statement by the *Times*' Secretary that ... he thought the advertisement was "substantially correct," affords no constitutional warrant for the Alabama Supreme Court's conclusion that it was a "cavalier ignoring of the falsity of the advertisement [from which] the jury could not have but been impressed with the bad faith of the *Times*, and its maliciousness inferable therefrom." The statement does not indicate malice at the time of the publication; even if the advertisement was not "substantially correct"—although respondent's own proofs tend to show that it was—that opinion was at least a reasonable one, and there was no evidence to impeach the witness' good faith in holding it. * * *

Finally, there is evidence that the *Times* published the advertisement without checking its accuracy against the news stories in the *Times*' own files. The mere presence of the stories in the files does not, of course, establish that the *Times* "knew" the advertisement was false, since the state of mind required for actual malice would have to be brought home to the persons in the *Times*' organization having responsibility for the publication of the advertisement. * * *

We think the evidence against the *Times* supports at most a finding of negligence in failing to discover the misstatements, and is constitutionally insufficient to show the recklessness that is required for a finding of actual malice.

We also think the evidence was constitutionally defective in another respect: it was incapable of supporting the jury's finding that the allegedly libelous statements were made "of and concerning" respondents. * * *

* * *

There was no reference to respondent in the advertisement, either by name or official position. * * *

* * *

The judgment of the Supreme Court of Alabama is reversed and the case is remanded to that court for further proceedings not inconsistent with this opinion.

Reversed and remanded.

Justice Black, with whom Justice Douglas joins, concurring.

I concur in reversing this half-million-dollar judgment against the New York Times Company and the four individual defendants. In reversing the Court holds that "the Constitution delimits a State's power to award damages for libel in actions brought by public officials against critics of their official conduct." I base my vote to reverse on the belief that the First and Fourteenth Amendments not merely "delimit" a State's power to award damages to "public officials against critics of their official conduct" but completely prohibit a State from exercising such a power. The Court goes on to hold that a State can subject such critics to damages if "actual malice" can be proved against them. "Malice," even as defined by the Court, is an elusive, abstract concept, hard to prove and hard to disprove. The requirement that malice be proved provides at best an evanescent protection for the right critically to discuss public affairs and certainly does not measure up to the sturdy safeguard embodied in the First Amendment. Unlike the Court, therefore, I vote to reverse exclusively on the ground that the *Times* and the individual defendants had an absolute, unconditional constitutional right to publish in the *Times* advertisement their criticisms of the Montgomery agencies and officials. * * *

* * *

Justice Goldberg, with whom Justice Douglas joins, concurring in the result.

* * *

In my view, the First and Fourteenth Amendments to the Constitution afford to the citizen and to the press an absolute, unconditional privilege to criticize official conduct despite the harm which may flow from excesses and abuses. The prized American right "to speak one's mind" about public officials and affairs needs "breathing space to survive." The right should not depend upon a probing by the jury of the motivation of the citizen or press. The theory of our Constitution is that every citizen may speak his mind and every newspaper express its view on matters of public concern and may not be barred from speaking or publishing because those in control of government think that what is said or written is unwise, unfair, false, or malicious. In a democratic society, one who assumes to act for the citizens in an executive, legislative, or judicial capacity must expect that his official acts will be commented upon and criticized. Such criticism cannot, in my opinion, be muzzled or deterred by the courts at the instance of public officials under the label of libel.

* * *

The *New York Times* decision resolved some important First Amendment issues, but the case also left unresolved many questions regarding libel law. One important issue was the boundary of official conduct. Do all activities of public officials come within the rule of the *New York Times* decision? Another important issue involved the definition of a public official. Do all government employees fall under the rule? Yet another major, unresolved matter was the application of the *New York Times* guidelines to private persons.

Two cases decided by the Warren Court in 1967 provided a partial answer to this last question. In *Curtis Publishing Company v. Butts* and *Associated Press v. Walker*, the justices were faced with the issue of libel law as applied to "public figures," persons who were not government officials but who were well-known to the general public. In the former case, Wally Butts, then the athletic director at the University of Georgia, was accused in an article in the *Saturday Evening Post* of fixing a 1962 football game between Georgia and Alabama. Butts was the head football coach at Georgia in 1962, and the story alleged that he provided Bear Bryant, the Alabama coach, with critical information regarding Georgia's game plan. In the latter case, Edwin Walker, a retired army general, was alleged in a 1962 Associated Press story to have led a riot against federal marshals who were attempting to assure the admission of James Meredith, a black student, at the University of Mississippi. Both Butts and Walker were successful in their libel suits at the trial court level, Butts winning a judgment of $3,060,000 and Walker being awarded $800,000.

In these cases, the Court ruled that the actual malice standard of *New York Times* should apply to public figures as well as public officials. The Court was closely divided over this issue, however. A five-person majority led by Chief Justice Warren argued that the same principles supporting the actual malice rule for public officials also applied in regard to public figures; but Harlan, Clark, Stewart, and Fortas argued that a somewhat lower standard should apply to public figures because their activities were not as significant to a democratic system of government.

Interestingly, the Court introduced a further consideration into libel law in these cases—the concept of "hot news"—which directly affected the outcome of the two cases. The idea of hot news is that fast-breaking events require immediate reporting and cannot be subjected to the same careful scrutiny as regular news. The Walker case involved hot news, and thus the Court overturned the libel judgment in this case. In contrast, the Butts case was not hot news; and because the *Saturday Evening Post* had shown a reckless disregard for the truth in investigating the story, the Warren Court upheld the libel award to Butts.

The Burger Court heard nearly two dozen libel suits in which they had to interpret the legacies of the Warren court's decisions, and substantial disagreement exists regarding the direction of the Burger Court's decision making regarding this important aspect of freedom of the press. Some commentators have been harshly critical of the Burger Court. Zion (1987, p. 45) has referred to the " . . . awesome trashing. . ." of the freedom of the press guarantee generally and libel law specifically by the Burger Court, and Denniston (1987, p. 24) concludes that the decisions of the Burger Court ". . .mean that the press's protection against damages for libel has been narrowed significantly." Urofsky (1991, p. 138), in contrast, sees much more continuity between the Warren and Burger Courts in regard to libel law: "The basic principles and fundamental political theory remained intact."

Which view is correct? Did the Burger Court depart dramatically from the principles of the Warren Court in its libel decisions, or did the justices of the Burger Court adhere to the basic ideas established by the Warren Court justices? In order to answer these questions, we need to examine two major areas of libel law. First, we will analyze a series of cases involving the standards to be used in libel suits brought by private persons. Second, we can look at how actual malice is to be established.

The most difficult and important issue that confronted the Burger Court in the area of libel law was what standards to apply to private persons. *Sullivan, Walker,* and *Butts* had established that both public officials and public figures had to prove falseness, defamation, and actual malice to win damages, but the Warren Court did not rule in a case involving private figures. When the Burger Court confronted this question, the justices faced a complicating issue as well—does it make a difference if the subject matter of the suit involves topics of public concern rather than private matters? The Burger Court's first attempt to resolve these difficult issues came in *Rosenbloom v. Metromedia* (1971). George Rosenbloom was a distributor of adult magazines in Philadelphia, and a radio station broadcast a story that he was a primary source of obscene materials in the city. Rosenbloom sued on the grounds that he had been acquitted of obscenity charges, and a jury awarded him damages of $750,000 on the basis of falseness and defamation. The Court reversed the decision by a 5-3 vote, ruling that the actual malice standard of the *New York Times* case should apply to private persons if the story involved a matter of public concern. The justices were sharply split in their reasoning, however. Brennan's plurality opinion was joined by Blackmun and Burger; but Black thought the opinion did not go far enough in protecting the press against libel suits, and White wanted a more narrow ruling. Marshall, Stewart, and Harlan were in dissent, arguing that the actual malice standard should not apply in libel cases brought by private persons.

Rosenbloom generated as much controversy off the Court as it did among the justices, and three years later in *Gertz v. Robert Welch* (1974) a five-person majority rejected the actual malice standard for private persons bringing libel suits even if the suit involved a controversy over matters of public affairs. Elmer Gertz was a Chicago attorney in a civil case against a police officer who had shot to death an African American youth. Gertz was attacked in an article in a publication of the ultraconservative John Birch Society, and Gertz filed a libel suit against the publisher, Robert Welch. The federal district court ruled in favor of Welch under the actual malice standard, and the United States Supreme Court agreed to review the case.

A five-person majority rejected the argument of the lower court, ruling instead that private persons like Gertz did not have to establish actual malice to win damages in a libel suit, even if the topic dealt with a public issue. Powell wrote the opinion and was joined by Marshall, Stewart, Blackmun, and Rehnquist, a somewhat unusual alliance. Powell recognized that extensive disagreements had divided the Court in libel cases, and he identified the three basic approaches that various justices had advocated. The first was Black's absolutist approach, which would provide total immunity for the media from libel suits. A second approach would apply the *New York Times* test to all situations, thereby permitting libel suits to be filed but awarding damages only if actual malice was proven. The third option would ". . .vary the level of constitutional privilege for defamatory falsehood with the status of the person defamed" (418 U.S. at 333). Under this third option, Powell wrote, public officials and public figures would have to prove actual malice to win damages, but private persons would not have to meet this stringent standard. Although the Court did not specify exactly what standards states should use in libel cases brought by private persons, the majority did state clearly that only compensatory damages—not punitive damages—could be imposed if actual malice was not established.

GERTZ v. WELCH

418 U.S. 323, 94 S.Ct. 2997, 41 L.Ed. 2d 789 (1974)

■ Elmer Gertz was a well-known Chicago attorney who was hired by an African American family whose son had been shot and killed by a white Chicago police officer. The officer had been found guilty in a criminal trial of second degree murder, and Gertz had been hired subsequently to pursue civil litigation against the officer. Gertz was attacked in a magazine, *American Opinion,* which was published by Robert Welch for the John Birch Society. The magazine had been warning its readers of a nationwide communist plot to discredit local law enforcement agencies as part of a revolutionary strategy; and in a March 1969 article entitled "Frame-up," Gertz was accused of being a communist who masterminded the frame-up of the police officer in the criminal trial. Gertz filed a libel suit against the periodical. Initially, the attorney was awarded $50,000 in damages after the United States District Court for the Northern District of Illinois submitted the dispute to a jury. However, upon further consideration, the District Court ruled that the "actual malice" standard must apply to this action and overturned the jury's award. The United States Court of Appeals for the Seventh Circuit affirmed this ruling. Gertz appealed his case to the United States Supreme Court.

This case is significant because the Court set forth standards that juries should use in libel suits brought by private persons in matters involving public concerns. As you read this case, consider this series of inquiries: (1) What new standards for libel law were introduced in this case? (2) Why did the Court argue that different standards should apply to private persons than to public officials and public figures? (3) Were the dissenting justices in agreement? (4) What important questions regarding libel law were left unanswered by the *Gertz* decision?

VOTE:

5 justices voted in favor of Gertz on the basis that the strict* New York Times *standard should not apply to private persons (Blackmun, Marshall, Powell, Rehnquist, Stewart).

4 justices dissented from the majority opinion (Brennan, Burger, Douglas, White).

Justice Powell delivered the opinion of the Court.

This Court has struggled for nearly a decade to define the proper accommodation between the law of defamation and the freedoms of speech and press protected by the First Amendment. With this decision we return to that effort. * * *

* * *

The principal issue in this case is whether a newspaper or broadcaster that publishes defamatory falsehoods about an individual who is neither a public official nor a public figure may claim a constitutional privilege against liability for the injury inflicted by those statements. The Court considered this question on the rather different set of facts presented in *Rosenbloom v. Metromedia, Inc.* (1971). * * *

* * * The eight Justices who participated in *Rosenbloom* announced their views in five separate opinions, none of which commanded more than three votes. The several statements not only reveal disagreement about the appropriate result in that case; they also reflect divergent traditions of thought about the general problem of reconciling the law of defamation with the First Amendment. One approach has been to extend the *New York Times* test to an expanding variety of situations. Another has been to vary the level of constitutional privilege for defamatory falsehood with the status of the person defamed. And a third view would grant to the press and broadcast media absolute immunity from liability for defamation. * * *

* * *

We begin with the common ground. Under the First Amendment there is no such thing as a false idea. However pernicious an opinion may seem, we depend for its correction not on the conscience of judges and juries but on the competition of other ideas. But there is no constitutional value in false statements of fact. Neither the intentional lie nor the careless error materially advances society's interest in "uninhibited, robust, and wide open" debate on public issues. They belong to that category of utterances which "are no essential part of any exposition of ideas, and are of such slight social value as a step to truth that any benefit that may be derived from them is clearly outweighed by the social interest in order and morality." *Chaplinsky v. New Hampshire*.

Although the erroneous statement of fact is not worthy of constitutional protection, it is nevertheless inevitable in free debate. * * * And punishment of error runs the risk of inducing a cautious and restrictive exercise of the constitutionally guaranteed freedoms of speech and press. Our decisions recognize that a rule of strict liability that compels a publisher or broadcaster to guarantee the accuracy of his factual assertions may lead to intolerable self-censorship. * * * The First Amendment requires that we protect some falsehood in order to protect speech that matters.

The need to avoid self-censorship by the news media is, however, not the only societal value at issue. If it were, this Court would have embraced long ago the view that publishers and broadcasters enjoy an unconditional and indefeasible immunity from liability for defamation. * * *

The legitimate state interest underlying the law of libel is the compensation of individuals for the harm inflicted on them by defamatory falsehood. We would not lightly require the State to abandon this purpose, for, as Mr. Justice Stewart has reminded us, the individual's right to the protection of his own good name "reflects no more than our basic concept of the essential dignity and worth of every human being—a concept at the root of any decent system of ordered liberty." * * *

Some tension necessarily exists between the need for a vigorous and uninhibited press and the legitimate interest in redressing wrongful injury. * * * In our continuing effort to define the proper accommodation between these competing concerns, we have been especially anxious to assure the freedoms of speech and press that "breathing space" essential to their fruitful exercise. To that end this Court has extended a measure of strategic protection to defamatory falsehood.

The *New York Times* standard defines the level of constitutional protection appropriate to the context of defamation of a public person. Those who, by reason of the notoriety of their achievements or the vigor and success with which they seek the public's attention, are properly classed as public figures and those who hold governmental office may recover for injury to reputation only on clear and convincing proof that the defamatory falsehood was made with knowledge of its falsity or with reckless disregard for the truth. * * * Despite this substantial abridgment of the state law right to compensate for wrongful hurt to one's reputation, the Court has concluded that the protection of the *New York Times* privilege should be available to publishers and broadcasters of defamatory falsehood concerning public officials and public figures. * * * We believe that the *New York Times* rule states an accommodation between this concern and the limited state interest present in the context of libel actions brought by public persons. For the reasons stated below, we conclude that the state interest in compensating injury to the reputation of private individuals requires that a different rule should obtain with respect to them.

* * *

* * * . . .[W]e have no difficulty in distinguishing among defamation plaintiffs. The first remedy of any victim of defamation is self-help—using available opportunities to contradict the lie or correct the error and thereby to minimize its adverse impact on reputation. Public officials and public figures usually enjoy significantly greater access to the channels of effective communication and hence have a more realistic opportunity to counteract false statements than private individuals normally enjoy. Private individuals are therefore more vulnerable to injury, and the state interest in protecting them is correspondingly greater.

More important than the likelihood that private individuals will lack effective opportunities for rebuttal, there is a compelling normative consideration underlying the distinction between public and private defamation plaintiffs. An individual who decides to seek governmental office must accept certain necessary consequences of that involvement in public affairs. He runs the risk of closer public scrutiny than might otherwise be the case. And society's interest in the officers of government is not strictly limited to the formal discharge of official duties. * * *

Those classed as public figures stand in a similar position. Hypothetically, it may be possible for someone to become a public figure through no purposeful action of his own, but the instances of truly involuntary public figures must be exceedingly rare. For the most part those who attain this status have assumed roles of especial prominence in the affairs of society. * * *

Even if the foregoing generalities do not obtain in every instance, the communications media are entitled to act on the assumption that public officials and public figures have voluntarily exposed themselves to increased risk of injury from defamatory falsehood concerning them. No such assumption is justified with respect to a private individual. He has not accepted public office or assumed an "influential role in ordering society." He has relinquished no part of his interest in the protection of his own good name, and consequently he has a more compelling call on the courts for redress of injury inflicted by defamatory falsehood. Thus, private individuals are not only more vulnerable to injury than public officials and public figures; they are also more deserving of recovery.

For these reasons we conclude that the States should retain substantial latitude in their efforts to enforce a legal remedy for defamatory falsehood injurious to the reputation of a private individual. The extension of the *New York Times* test proposed by the *Rosenbloom* plurality would abridge this legitimate state interest to a degree that we find unacceptable. And it would occasion the additional difficulty of forcing state and federal judges to decide on an ad hoc basis which publications address issues of "general or public interest" and which do not—to determine, in the words of Mr. Justice Marshall, "what information is relevant to self-government." We doubt the wisdom of committing this task to the conscience of judges. Nor does the Constitution require us to draw so thin a line between the drastic alternatives of the *New York Times* privilege and the common law of strict liability for defamatory error. The "public or general interest" test for determining the applicability of the *New York Times* standard to private defamation actions inadequately serves both of the competing values at stake. On the one hand, a private individual whose reputation is injured by defamatory falsehood that does concern an issue of public or general interest has no recourse unless he can meet the rigorous requirements of *New York Times*. This is true despite the factors that distinguish the state interest in compensating private individuals from the analogous interest involved in the context of public persons. On the other hand, a publisher or broadcaster of a defamatory error which a court deems unrelated to an issue of public or general interest may be held liable in damages even if it took every reasonable precaution to ensure the accuracy of its assertion. And liability may far exceed compensation for any actual injury to the plaintiff, for the jury may be permitted to presume damages without proof of loss and even to award punitive damages.

We hold that, so long as they do not impose liability without fault, the States may define for themselves the appropriate standard of liability for a publisher or broadcaster of defamatory falsehood injurious to a private individual. This approach provides a more equitable boundary between the competing concerns involved here. It recognizes the strength of the legitimate state interest in compensating private individuals for wrongful injury to reputation. * * * We hold that the States may not permit recovery of presumed or punitive damages, at least when liability is not based on a showing of knowledge of falsity or reckless disregard for the truth.

* * *

* * * In short, the private defamation plaintiff who establishes liability under a less demanding standard than that stated by *New York Times* may recover only such damages as are sufficient to compensate him for actual injury.

Notwithstanding our refusal to extend the *New York Times* privilege to defamation of private individuals, respondent contends that we should affirm the judgment below on the ground that petitioner is either a public official or a public figure. There is little basis for the former assertion. Several years prior to the present incident, petitioner had served briefly on housing committees appointed by the mayor of Chicago, but at the time of publication he had never held any remunerative governmental position. Respondent admits this but argues that petitioner's appearance at the coroner's inquest rendered him a "de facto public official." Our cases recognize no such concept. Respondent's suggestion would sweep all lawyers under the *New York Times* rule as officers of the court and distort the plain meaning of the "public official" category beyond all recognization. We decline to follow it.

Respondent's characterization of petitioner as a public figure raises a different question. That designation may rest on either of two alternative bases. In some instances an individual may achieve such pervasive fame or notoriety that he becomes a public figure for all purposes and in all contexts. More commonly, an individual voluntarily injects himself or is drawn into a particular public controversy and thereby becomes a public figure for a limited range of issues. In either case such persons assume special prominence in the resolution of public questions.

* * *

In this context it is plain that petitioner was not a public figure. He played a minimal role at the coroner's inquest, and his participation related solely to his representation of a private client. He took no part in the criminal prosecution of Officer Nuccio. Moreover, he never discussed either the criminal or civil litigation with the press and was never quoted as having done so. He plainly did not thrust himself in the vortex of this public issue, nor did he engage the public's attention in an attempt to influence its outcome. We are persuaded that the trial court did not err in refusing to characterize petitioner as a public figure for the purpose of this litigation.

We therefore conclude that the *New York Times* standard is inapplicable to this case and that the trial court erred in entering judgment for respondent. Because the jury was allowed to impose liability without fault and was permitted to presume damages without proof of injury, a new trial is necessary. We reverse and remand for further proceedings in accord with this opinion.

It is so ordered.

Justice Blackmun, concurring [omitted].

Chief Justice Burger, dissenting.

* * *

Agreement or disagreement with the law as it has evolved to this time does not alter the fact that it has been orderly development with a consistent basic rationale. In today's opinion the court abandons the traditional thread so far as the ordinary private citizen is concerned and introduces the concept that the media will be liable for negligence in publishing defamatory statements with respect to such persons. * * * I am frank to say I do not know the parameters of a "negligence" doctrine as applied to the news media. Conceivably this new doctrine could inhibit some editors, as the dissents of Mr. Justice Douglas and Mr. Justice Brennan suggest. But I would prefer to allow this area of law to continue to evolve as it has up to now with respect to private citizens rather than embark on a new doctrinal theory which has no jurisprudential ancestry.

* * *

Justice Douglas, dissenting.

The Court describes this case as a return to the struggle of "defin[ing] the proper accommodation between the law of defamation and the freedoms of speech and press protected by the First Amendment." It is indeed a struggle, once described by Mr. Justice Black as "the same quagmire" in which the Court "is now helplessly struggling in the field of obscenity." I would suggest that the struggle is a quite hopeless one, for, in light of the command of the First Amendment, no "accommodation" of its freedoms can be "proper" except those made by the Framers themselves.

* * * I have stated before my view that the First Amendment would bar Congress from passing any libel law. This was the view held by Thomas Jefferson and it is one Congress has never challenged through enaction of a civil libel statute. * * *

* * *

* * * The standard announced today leaves the States free to "define for themselves the appropriate standard of liability for a publisher or broadcaster" in the circumstances of this case. This of course leaves the simple negligence standard as an option, with the jury free to impose damages upon a finding that the publisher failed to act as "a reasonable man." With such continued erosion of First Amendment protection, I fear that it may well be the reasonable man who refrains from speaking.

Since in my view the First and Fourteenth Amendments prohibit the imposition of damages upon respondent for this discussion of public affairs, I would affirm the judgment below.

Justice Brennan, dissenting.

* * * I cannot agree ... that free and robust debate—so essential to the proper functioning of our system of government—is permitted adequate "breathing space," when as the Court holds, the States may impose all but strict liability for defamation if the defamed party is a private person and "the substance of the defamatory statement 'makes substantial danger to reputation apparent.'" I adhere to my view expressed in *Rosenbloom v. Metromedia, Inc.*, that we strike the proper accommodation between avoidance of media self-censorship and protection of individual reputations only when we require States to apply the *New York Times Co. v. Sullivan*, knowing-or-reckless-falsity standard in civil libel actions concerning media reports of the involvement of private individuals in events of public or general interest.

* * *

Justice White, dissenting.

For some 200 years—from the very founding of the Nation—the law of defamation and right of the ordinary citizen to recover for false publication injurious to his reputation have been almost exclusively the business of state courts and legislatures. Under typical state defamation law, the defamed private citizen had to prove only a false publication that would subject him to hatred, contempt, or ridicule. Given such publication, general damage to reputation was presumed, while punitive damages required proof of additional facts. * * *

But now using the First Amendment as the chosen instrument, the Court, in a few printed pages, has federalized major aspects of libel law by declaring unconstitutional in important respects the prevailing defamation law in all or most of the 50 States. * * *

I assume these sweeping changes will be popular with the press, but this is not the road to salvation for a court of law. As I see it, there are wholly insufficient grounds for scuttling the libel laws of the States in such wholesale fashion, to say nothing of deprecating the reputation interest of ordinary citizens and rendering them powerless to protect themselves. I do not suggest that the decision is illegitimate or beyond the bounds of judicial review, but it is an ill-considered exercise of the power entrusted to this Court, particularly when the Court has not had the benefit of briefs and argument addressed to most of the major issues which the Court now decides. I respectfully dissent.

* * *

Although the *Gertz* decision answered some important questions about the distinctions between private and public persons, the Burger Court continued to be confronted with cases raising the issue of how courts should determine who is a private person and who is a public figure. In *Gertz*, the majority had provided some guidelines for determining who is a public figure. A person could become a public figure under all circumstances through the achievement of ". . .general fame or notoriety in the community, and pervasive involvement in the affairs of society. . ." (418 U.S. at 352). Alternatively, a person could become a public figure in regard to just a particular public controversy, in which case a court must examine ". . .the nature and extent of an individual's participation in the particular controversy giving rise to the defamation" (418 U.S. at 352).

In a series of subsequent cases, the Burger Court justices interpreted these definitions in a manner that made it difficult for the media to establish that someone was a public figure who needed to prove actual malice. In *Time, Inc. v. Firestone* (1976), the Court ruled that Mary Alice Sullivan was not a public figure although she was involved in a sensationalized divorce case against her husband, tire magnate Russell Firestone. The Burger Court reaffirmed the principle that a person does not become a public figure by being involuntarily thrust into the public spotlight in *Hutchinson v. Proxmire* (1979) and *Wolston v. Reader's Digest Association, Inc.* (1979).

In addition to being confronted with cases involving who should be considered a public figure, the Burger Court was also forced to clarify another aspect of the *Gertz* decision, the distinction between matters of public and private concern. Although the Court had seemed to discard this distinction in *Gertz*, two cases at the end of the Burger Court era brought new life to this concern. In *Dun and Bradstreet, Inc. v. Greenmoss Builders* (1985), the Court ruled 5-4 that the *New York Times* standards did not apply in libel cases involving purely private matters. The Court ruled that the concerns over the importance of a free and robust press in a democracy were not present in cases involving only private issues. This importance of public issues, however, was reinforced a year later in *Philadelphia Newspapers v. Hepps* (1986) where the Court ruled that the press did not have to prove the truth of stories dealing with matters of public concern.

The *Gertz* decision thus gave rise to a complex set of cases involving distinctions not only between public figures and private persons but also between public concerns and private concerns. In addition, the question of standards of proof regarding actual malice also arose in the aftermath of *Gertz*, although this issue goes back to *Sullivan*. The Burger Court's most provocative case involving actual malice was *Herbert v. Lando* (1979), a case that arose out of a story on the CBS show *60 Minutes*. Lieutenant Colonel Anthony Herbert had gained substantial publicity when he accused his superior officers of engaging in cover-ups of war crimes in Vietnam. When *60 Minutes*, as well as an article in *Atlantic Magazine*, implied that he had fabricated the charges to explain his being relieved of his command, Herbert brought a libel suit. He acknowledged that he was a public figure who had to prove actual malice, and he argued that those seeking to establish actual malice should be able to inquire into the thoughts, opinions, and conclusions of the media members being charged with libel. In a decision strongly condemned by the press, the Court ruled 6-3 in favor of Herbert.

What conclusions can we reach regarding the Burger Court's libel cases? Certainly this was a busy and difficult area for the justices. They decided twenty-one full opinion cases and split nearly evenly in liberal and conservative outcomes, with ten decisions favoring the press and eleven decisions going against the press. Furthermore, the decisions typically were closely divided and involved multiple concurring and dissenting opinions. The Burger Court clearly did not engage in a liberal expansion of the Warren Court's libel decisions; but the judgment that the Burger

Court "trashed" or significantly narrowed press protection against libel suits seems too strong. The Burger Court maintained the strong protection of the actual malice standard in cases brought by public officials and public figures. Although this actual malice standard was not extended to private persons, convincing arguments exist for giving private persons greater protection against libel. The Burger Court's emphasis on protecting private matters is also consistent with the underlying philosophy of Brennan's majority opinion in *New York Times* (Brennan 1965). Thus, the Burger Court struggled with the difficult subject of the compatibility of freedom of the press and libel law, and its decisions can be characterized as moderate and reasonable, even if the press was not always pleased with the results.

The Rehnquist Court has also been active in this controversial area of constitutional law. Two of the three freedom of press cases classified as being of major importance in Table 7.10 involve libel law, and the Rehnquist Court has heard additional interesting libel cases as well.

The justices of the Rehnquist Court have adhered to the basic guidelines set forth in the major libel cases of the Warren and Burger Courts. When lower courts have clearly deviated from these standards, the Rehnquist Court has overturned the lower courts and reaffirmed the existing guidelines. When confronted with novel issues about the meaning of ambiguous ideas in earlier precedents, however, the Rehnquist Court has tended to provide conservative interpretations going against the press.

The most widely publicized decision of the Rehnquist Court involving libel was *Hustler Magazine v. Falwell* (1988). *Hustler* printed an advertisement parody that involved an "interview" with Jerry Falwell, a nationally known televangelist minister, about his first sexual experience, which was supposedly with his mother in the family outhouse after a drinking episode. Falwell sued *Hustler*, charging libel, the invasion of privacy, and the intentional infliction of emotional distress. Although the lower federal courts rejected Falwell's libel claim because the ad was a parody, the courts did award him both compensatory and punitive damages on the basis of his tort claim of the intentional infliction of emotional distress using an "outrageous conduct" standard.

In a rare unanimous decision in the area of libel law, the high court overturned the circuit court and ruled in favor of *Hustler*. Chief Justice Rehnquist wrote the majority opinion. In a relatively brief opinion, Rehnquist agreed with the lower courts that *Hustler* could not be found guilty of libel because the ad was a parody that could not be taken as describing actual facts. Rehnquist rejected, however, the circuit court's argument that an outrageous conduct standard should apply to the charge of the intentional infliction of emotional distress. Because of the important First Amendment concerns involved, the *New York Times* standard should apply, requiring the showing of a false statement of fact made with actual malice. This could not be done in this case, and thus the judgment against *Hustler* was reversed.

Hustler Magazine v. Falwell

485 U.S. 46, 108 S.Ct. 876, 99 L.Ed. 2d 41 (1988)

■ *Hustler* magazine is a national publication containing sexually explicit pictures and articles. In a November 1983 issue in a section labeled "Fiction: Ad and Personal Parody," the magazine featured Jerry Falwell in a parody of a Campari Liqueur advertisement. Campari had developed a famous series of ads in which they interviewed celebrities about their "first time," which seemed to refer to their first sexual experience but really involved their first taste of Campari. Using a similar form and layout, *Hustler* created a parody of the ad in which they interviewed Falwell about his first time, which they reported as a drunken sexual encounter with his mother in the family outhouse after they had both been drinking Campari. At the bottom of the page was a statement: "Ad parody—not to be taken seriously."

Falwell brought suit against *Hustler* and its publisher, Larry Flynt. Falwell sought damages for libel, privacy invasion, and the intentional infliction of emotional distress. The jury rejected Falwell's libel claim but awarded him both compensatory and punitive damages on the basis of his claim of the intentional infliction of emotional distress. A federal circuit court affirmed. The circuit court ruled that the guidelines set forth in *New York Times* and *Walker* did not apply in this case. Instead, the circuit court ruled that the standard of outrageous conduct should be applied in judging the tort claim of the intentional infliction of emotional distress, and *Hustler*'s conduct was sufficiently outrageous in this case. Hustler appealed to the Supreme Court, which granted cert.

This is an important case because the Rehnquist Court affirmed the basic principles of libel law—particularly the actual malice standard—in regard to public figures and used the standard in regard to the charge of the intentional infliction of emotional distress. In reading Chief Justice Rehnquist's opinion, think about the following questions: (1) Why did Rehnquist call the issue raised in this case a "novel" one? (2) Why did the Court argue that false statements of fact are "valueless" but are still protected by the First Amendment? (3) Why did Rehnquist reject the argument that outrageous conduct which inflicts emotional distress should not receive First Amendment protection?

VOTE:
The Court ruled unanimously that the* Hustler *ad parody was within the protection of the First Amendment (Kennedy did not participate).

Chief Justice Rehnquist delivered the opinion of the Court.

* * *

This case presents us with a novel question involving First Amendment limitations upon a State's authority to protect its citizens from the intentional infliction of emotional distress. We must decide whether a public figure may recover damages for emotional harm caused by the publication of an ad parody offensive to him, and doubtless gross and repugnant in the eyes of most. Respondent would have us find that a State's interest in protecting public figures from emotional distress is sufficient to deny First Amendment protection to speech that is patently offensive and is intended to inflict emotional injury, even when that speech could not reasonably have been interpreted as stating actual facts about the public figure involved. This we decline to do.

At the heart of the First Amendment is the recognition of the fundamental importance of the free flow of ideas and opinions on matters of public interest and concern. "The freedom to speak one's mind is not only an aspect of individual liberty—and thus a good unto itself—but also is essential to the common quest for truth and the vitality of society as a whole." We have therefore been particularly vigilant to ensure that individual expressions of ideas remain free from governmentally imposed sanctions. The First Amendment recognizes no such thing as a "false" idea.

* * *

The sort of robust political debate encouraged by the First Amendment is bound to produce speech that is critical of those who hold public office or those public figures who are "intimately involved in the resolution of important public questions or, by reason of their fame, shape events in areas of concern to society at large." Such criticism, inevitably, will not always be reasoned or moderate; public figures as well as public officials will be subject to "vehement, caustic, and sometimes unpleasantly sharp attacks." *New York Times.*

* * *

Of course, this does not mean that any speech about a public figure is immune from sanctions in the form of damages. Since *New York Co. v. Sullivan*, we have consistently ruled that a public figure may hold a speaker liable for the damage to reputation caused by publication of a defamatory falsehood, but only if the statement was made "with knowledge that it was false or with reckless disregard of whether it was false or not." False statements of fact are particularly valueless; they interfere with the truth-seeking function of the marketplace of ideas, and they cause damages to an individual's reputation that cannot easily be repaired by counterspeech, however persuasive or effective. But even though falsehoods have little value in and of themselves, they are "nevertheless inevitable in free debate," and a rule that would impose strict liability on a publisher for false assertions would have an undoubted "chilling" effect on speech relating to public figures that does have constitutional value. "Freedoms of expression require 'breathing space.'" This breathing space is provided by a constitutional rule that allows public figures to recover for libel or defamation only when they can prove both that the statement was false and that the statement was made with the requisite level of culpability.

Respondent argues, however, that a different standard should apply in this case because here the State seeks to prevent not reputational damage, but the severe emotional distress suffered by the person who is the subject of an offensive publication. In respondent's view, and in the view of the Court of Appeals, so long as the utterance was intended to inflict emotional distress, was outrageous, and did in fact inflict serious emotional distress, it is of no constitutional import whether the statement was a fact or an opinion, or whether it was true or false. It is the intent to cause injury that is the gravamen of the tort, and the State's interest in preventing emotional harm simply outweighs whatever interest a speaker may have in speech of this type.

Generally speaking the law does not regard the intent to inflict emotional distress as one which should receive much solicitude, and it is quite understandable that most if not all jurisdictions have chosen to make it civilly culpable where the conduct in question is sufficiently "outrageous." But in the world of debate about public affairs, many things done with motives that are less than admirable are protected by the First Amendment. In *Garrison v. Louisiana* (1964), we held that even when a speaker or writer is motivated by hatred or ill-will his expression was protected by the First Amendment. * * * Thus while such a bad motive may be deemed controlling for purposes of tort liability in other areas of the law, we think the First Amendment prohibits such a result in the area of public debate about public figures.

Were we to hold otherwise, there can be little doubt that political cartoonists and satirists would be subjected to damages awards without any showing that their work falsely defamed its subject. Webster's defines a caricature as "the deliberately distorted picturing or imitating of a person, literary style, etc. by exaggerating features or mannerisms for satirical effect." The appeal of the political cartoon or caricature is often based on exploitation of unfortunate physical traits or politically embarrassing events—an exploitation often calculated to injure the feelings of the subject of the portrayal. The art of the cartoonist is often not reasoned or evenhanded, but slashing and one-sided.

* * *

Despite their sometimes caustic nature, from the early cartoon portraying George Washington as an ass down to the present day, graphic depictions and satirical cartoons have played a prominent role in public and political debate. Nast's castigation of the Tweed Ring, Walt McDougall's characterization of Presidential candidate James G. Blaine's banquet with the millionaires at Delmonico's as "The Royal Feast of Belshazzar," and numerous other efforts have undoubtedly had an effect on the course and outcome of contemporaneous debate. * * * From the viewpoint of history it is clear that our political discourse would have been considerably poorer without them.

Respondent contends, however, that the caricature in question here was so "outrageous" as to distinguish it from more traditional political cartoons. There is no doubt that the caricature of respondent and his mother published in *Hustler* is at best a distant cousin of the political cartoons described above, and a rather poor relation at that. If it were possible by laying down a principled standard to separate the one from the other, public discourse would probably suffer little or no harm. But we doubt that there is any such standard, and we are quite sure that the pejorative description "outrageous" does not supply one. "Outrageousness" in the area of political and social discourse has an inherent subjectiveness about it which would allow a jury to impose liability on the basis of the jurors' tastes or views, or perhaps on the basis of their dislike of a particular expression. An "outrageousness" standard thus runs afoul of our long-standing refusal to allow damages to be awarded because the speech in question may have an adverse emotional impact on the audience. * * *

Admittedly, these oft-repeated First Amendment principles, like other principles, are subject to limitations. We recognized in *FCC v. Pacifica Foundation* that speech that is " ' vulgar,' 'offensive,' and 'shocking'" is "not entitled to absolute constitutional protection under all circumstances." In *Chaplinsky v. New Hampshire*, we held that a State could lawfully punish an individual for the use of insulting " 'fighting' words—those which by their very utterance inflict injury or tend to incite an immediate breach of the peace." These limitations are but recognition . . .that this Court has "long recognized that not all speech is of equal First Amendment importance." But the sort of expression involved in this case does not seem to us to be governed by any exception to the general First Amendment principles stated above.

We conclude that public figures and public officials may not recover for the tort of intentional infliction of emotional distress by reason of publications such as the one here at issue without showing in addition that the publication contains a false statement of fact which was made with "actual malice," i.e., with knowledge that the statement was false or with reckless disregard as to whether or not it was true. This is not merely a "blind application" of the *New York Times* standard; it reflects our considered judgment that such a standard is necessary to give adequate "breathing space" to the freedoms protected by the First Amendment.

Here it is clear that respondent Falwell is a "public figure" for purposes of First Amendment law. The jury found against respondent on his libel claim when it decided that the *Hustler* ad parody could not "reasonably be understood as describing actual facts about [respondent] or actual events in which [he] participated." The Court of Appeals interpreted the jury's finding to be that the ad parody "was not reasonably believable," and in accordance with our custom we accept this finding. Respondent is thus relegated to his claim for damages awarded by the jury for the intentional infliction of emotional distress by "outrageous" conduct. But for reasons heretofore stated this claim cannot, consistently with the First Amendment, form a basis for the award of damages when the conduct in question is the publication of a caricature such as the ad parody involved here. The judgment of the Court of Appeals is accordingly reversed.

Justice Kennedy took no part in the consideration or decision of this case.

Justice White concurs in the judgment [omitted].

Milkovich v. Lorain Journal Co. (1990) was another libel decision of major importance decided by the Rehnquist Court. This case involved a reporter who accused a high school wrestling coach of lying in testimony before a state court. Michael Milkovich coached the Maple Heights, Ohio, wrestling team, which became involved in a fight during a match with a rival school that left several people injured. The Ohio High School Athletic Association conducted a hearing at which Milkovich testified, and following the hearing the OHSAA placed the Maple Heights wrestling team on a year's probation and censured Milkovich. Maple Heights parents and wrestlers then sued OHSAA on the grounds that they had been denied due process in the hearings. Milkovich testified again, and the court ruled against the OHSAA. In a story the next day in a local newspaper, a sportswriter wrote that Milkovich had lied in his sworn testimony.

Milkovich lost in a state libel suit that lasted nearly fifteen years. The Ohio courts eventually ruled that the statements made in the newspaper involved opinion rather than fact and that libel suits could not be brought against opinion.

In a 7-2 decision, Rehnquist rejected the Ohio courts' interpretation of libel law, refusing to recognize a separate constitutional protection for statements of opinion. Rehnquist provided a detailed history of American libel law and argued that existing constitutional doctrine provided a proper balance between freedom of expression and protection of a person's reputation. The key concern under existing libel law, Rehnquist stated, is whether a statement on matters of public concern can be proven false. If it cannot be proven false, then no liability can be established under libel law. If it can be proven false, however, a person can be found guilty of libel. Applying these principles to this case, Rehnquist argued that the statements did imply that Milkovich had perjured himself by lying in the state court trial and that this statement was sufficiently factual to be proven true or false. In taking the position that statements of opinion can be challenged as libelous, Rehnquist concluded, the Court was seeking to balance properly two important values, the First Amendment's ". . .vital guarantee of free and uninhibited discussion of public issues. . ." and the ". . .pervasive and strong interest in preventing and redressing attacks upon reputation" (497 U.S. at 22).

Although Brennan and Marshall were in dissent, they agreed with the majority's interpretation of the guiding principles. Their disagreement came in applying the principles to the particular case, for they did not think that the challenged statements could be interpreted as stating or implying any defamatory facts. Thus, because the statements could not be proven false, they could not be found to be libelous.

Masson v. New Yorker Magazine (1991) is another libel decision of the Rehnquist Court that deserves attention. In this case, Janet Malcolm, an author, interviewed a prominent Freudian psychologist, Jeffery Masson, who had become disillusioned with the Freudian approach. In her article, Malcolm used a substantial number of direct quotes from Masson that he claimed he had not made and that were both false and defamatory. Masson sued Malcolm and the *New Yorker Magazine*, in which the article appeared. He acknowledged that he was a public figure, but he also argued that the attribution of quotes to him that he did not make constituted actual malice. A federal district court granted summary judgment in favor of Malcolm and the *New Yorker Magazine*, and a court of appeals affirmed.

In a 7-2 decision, the Court reversed the lower court decisions, ruling in favor of Masson. The central issue was the standards to be used in determining when the alteration of quotations constitutes actual malice. In the majority opinion, Kennedy wrote that the concept of falseness was the key to resolving this issue. His review of the history of libel law and the Court's precedents led him to conclude that the mere alteration of words in a quote is not sufficient to establish falseness. Rather, the key is whether ". . .the alteration results in a material change in the meaning conveyed by the statement" (501 U.S. at 517). In this particular case, Kennedy concluded, sufficient evidence existed that Malcolm had materially changed the meaning of several quotes, and hence the case was remanded for further consideration by the lower courts.

What conclusions can we draw regarding the Supreme Court's decisions involving libel? Certainly the Warren Court can be considered to have engaged in a liberal revolution in this area of freedom of the press. The Warren Court heard ten libel cases, deciding nine of them liberally. More importantly, the Warren Court justices dramatically changed the standards for finding the press guilty of libel in regard to public officials and public figures. By adding actual malice to the requirements of falseness and defamation, the Warren Court provided far greater protection for the press than had existed previously in American society.

Although the Burger Court and the Rehnquist Court have been less generous to the press in the area of libel law than the Warren Court, the Burger and Rehnquist Courts have remained committed to the general principles of the Warren Court. The Burger Court decided eleven of twenty-one libel decisions conservatively, but the Burger Court justices in *Gertz* did extend the common law requirements for a private person to win a libel suit, thus providing greater First Amendment protection for the press. The Rehnquist Court has been less active in the area of libel law, handing down only five decisions, with three of those being decided liberally. *Hustler* is an especially noteworthy case because the Rehnquist Court justices extended the *New York Times* standards into tort law involving the intentional infliction of emotional distress. The Supreme Court will undoubtedly continue to confront difficult issues in this highly technical area of freedom of the press, but the justices seem to be committed to the basic principle that the needs of a democratic society are best served by a press that is given a substantial degree of freedom in reporting on matters involving public officials and public figures.

The Conflict Between a Free Press and a Fair Trial

Another important topic under freedom of the press involves the potential conflict between the First Amendment guarantee of freedom of the press and the Sixth Amendment guarantee of the right to a trial by an impartial jury. Ideally, these two constitutional guarantees would not come into conflict but rather would be complementary. For example, a free press can help to assure a fair trial for a criminal defendant through reporting on any improprieties by judges, prosecutors, or other officials involved in judicial proceedings. Press activities can also undermine a defendant's guarantee of a fair trial, however. This can occur in several ways. Most frequently, the problem arises in pretrial publicity, which makes selection of an unbiased jury a difficult task, or in press reports during a trial, which can reach the members of a jury and influence them improperly. The conflict between the constitutional guarantees of a free press and an unbiased jury most frequently arise in sensationalized murder cases or in cases involving famous people. The O. J. Simpson murder case is a notable recent example of this conflict.

The free press/fair trial conflict is a relatively recent development in American constitutional law. The Supreme Court had heard relatively few cases involving press coverage of trials before the sixties, and most of these cases involved contempt rulings by judges against newspapers that were critical of their handling of cases. In a series of cases in the forties—*Bridges v. California* (1941), *Pennekamp v. Florida* (1946), and *Craig v. Harney* (1947)—the Court ruled against judicial contempt citations of the press. *Bridges* was the leading case. It involved the constitutionality of a contempt citation issued by a trial court judge over published criticisms of his handling of a trial. Justice Black's majority opinion took a strong position opposing judicial use of contempt power against the press in coverage of a pending case. Black applied the clear and present danger test, finding no evidence that any such danger to the court's interests were created by the press publication. The Court has never wavered from the *Bridges* principle, but the justices have had to confront many other difficult cases involving the conflict between the guarantees of a free press and a fair trial.

The Warren Court directly confronted this conflict in a series of cases in the sixties. The basic principle that the Court established in these cases was that a defendant's Sixth Amendment rights must be safeguarded with the least possible restrictions imposed on the press. This principle meant that the right to an unbiased jury prevailed over freedom of the press because the person's freedom—and possibly life—was at stake, but press freedom was to be observed as fully as possible. Finding the precise methods to achieve this balance was not an easy task, however.

The Warren Court's most important decision was *Sheppard v. Maxwell* (1966), but several prior decisions established the foundations for *Sheppard.* In *Irvin v. Dowd* (1961), for example, the justices for the first time overturned a state conviction because of the adverse effects of pretrial publicity. In the *Irvin* case, the defendant confessed to committing six murders, and press coverage was extensive. Although the trial was moved to another county, eight of the twelve jurors indicated before the trial began that they believed the defendant was guilty. The Court unanimously found this to violate the guarantee of an unbiased jury, although the justices did note that preconceived ideas about guilt or innocence of a defendant did not automatically disqualify a juror. Similarly, in *Rideau v. Louisiana* (1963) and *Estes v. Texas* (1964) the Warren Court justices ruled that extensive media coverage had interfered with the right to a fair trial of the defendants in these cases.

The Warren Court's most thorough treatment of the conflict between the guarantees of a free press and a fair trial came in the 1966 *Sheppard* decision. This case arose from the 1954 murder of Marilyn Sheppard, the wife of a prominent Cleveland osteopath, Dr. Sam Sheppard. Mrs. Sheppard, who was pregnant, was bludgeoned to death in her bedroom. Dr. Sheppard claimed that he had fallen asleep on the couch and was awakened by his wife's screams; when he ran to her bedroom, he was knocked unconscious by the killer. Sheppard became the primary suspect immediately, and Cleveland newspapers began a month-long campaign pressuring officials to arrest him. The press coverage grew in intensity after his arrest and during his trial. As described by Justice Clark in his majority opinion, the trial had a " . . . carnival atmosphere. . ." in which ". . .bedlam reigned at the courthouse . . . and newsmen took over practically the entire courtroom, hounding most of the participants in the trial, especially Sheppard. . ." (384 U.S. at 345).

In addressing the free press/fair trial conflict, Clark acknowledged the important role the press had played throughout history in promoting fairness in criminal trials; but he also recognized that in some cases press coverage can undermine a fair trial, and he emphasized that " . . . trial courts must take strong measures to ensure that the balance is never weighed against the accused" (384 U.S. at 352). Clark specified a variety of measures that could be used to avoid adverse pretrial publicity: delaying the trial until publicity dies down, transferring the case to another jurisdiction where the publicity is much less intense, and careful questioning of potential jurors about their views. Clark also specified a variety of measures that could be used at the trial stage. These included strict rules regarding the number of press members in the courtroom, their location, and their conduct; sequestering the jury; insulating witnesses from the press; and even ordering a new trial if press publicity threatened the fairness of the trial. The most controversial proposal advanced by Clark was the suggestion that " . . . the trial court might well have proscribed extrajudicial statements by any lawyer, party, witness, or court official which divulged prejudicial matters" (384 U.S. at 365). This approval of judicial "gag orders" was to raise serious issues that the Burger Court was subsequently forced to address.

The Burger Court heard a substantial number of important cases involving the conflict between freedom of the press and the right to a trial by an unbiased jury. Three major issues arose during this period: the constitutionality of court-ordered "gag rules," the question of whether the press has a constitutionally protected right of access to trials, and the issue of cameras in the courtroom. Although the Burger Court justices struggled with these issues and frequently found themselves in sharp disagreement, the overall pattern of their decisions was one of protecting the right of the criminally accused to a fair and impartial trial while placing the fewest restrictions necessary on the press.

One important question that the Burger Court confronted was whether judicial gag orders violate the First Amendment. The high court's answer in *Nebraska Press Association v. Stuart* (1976) was "yes," but the 9-0 vote in this case masked a variety of views among the justices. The case arose out of a grisly murder case in which Erwin Simants was arrested for the 1975 deaths of six members of the Henry Kellie family in the rural town of Sutherland, Nebraska, population 850. Because of the sensationalized nature of the murders in a small town, the judge issued a gag order on the press on the first day of the preliminary hearing, barring the media from reporting on confessions or admissions until the jury was selected.

Chief Justice Burger wrote the opinion for the Court, arguing that less drastic means could have been used to assure the selection of an unbiased jury. Burger argued that the order involved a severe form of prior restraint on the press that could be justified only under the most exceptional circumstances, and such circumstances did not exist in this case. No majority consensus emerged, however, regarding the constitutionality of all gag orders. Justices Brennan, Stewart, and Marshall were the only members of the Court who took the position that all gag rules were impermissible prior restraints on the press.

Nebraska Press Association v. Stuart

427 U.S. 539, 96 S. Ct. 2791, 49 L.Ed. 2d 683 (1976)

■ On October 18, 1975, in the small rural community of Sutherland, Nebraska, six members of the Kellie family were found murdered in their home. At the crime scene, police released a description of the suspect to news reporters. The next day, Erwin Charles Simants was arrested for the murders. The Lincoln County attorney and Simants's attorney both requested that the trial judge issue a restraining order on material that could become public because of the widespread coverage by the media and the possibility that prejudicial news would prevent a fair trial.

The State District Judge, Hugh Stuart, entered an order restraining the Nebraska Press Association from publishing or broadcasting reports concerning five topics: (1) Simants's confessions or statements made to police, (2) confessions or statements made to third parties, (3) a note Simants had written prior to the crime, (4) medical evidence revealed at the preliminary hearing, and (5) the identity of the family members who were assaulted sexually as well as other information related to the assault. The Nebraska Press Association appealed the order to the Nebraska Supreme Court. The state supreme court affirmed the trial judge's ruling but altered the order to prohibit publishing or broadcasting reports related to only three issues: (a) confessions or statements made to police officers, (b) confessions or statements made to third parties, not including the press, and (c) other information "strongly implicative" of Simants. The Nebraska Press Association contested the constitutionality of these orders by appealing to the United States Supreme Court.

This case is significant because the Court provided its first detailed analysis of the constitutionality of judicial gag orders on the press, ruling in this case that these orders were unconstitutional. In reading the opinions in this case, give consideration to the following questions: (1) Why did the justices view gag orders as a serious First Amendment concern? (2) Under what circumstances, if any, might the Court approve judicial gag orders? (3) What actions should the trial judge have taken in this case to assure the defendant a fair trial?

VOTE:
The Court voted unanimously that the judicial gag order violated the First Amendment.

Chief Justice Burger delivered the opinion of the Court.

The respondent State District Judge entered an order restraining the petitioners from publishing or broadcasting accounts of confessions or admissions made by the accused or facts "strongly implicative" of the accused in a widely reported murder of six persons. We granted certiorari to decide whether the entry of such an order on the showing made before the state court violated the constitutional guarantee of freedom of the press.

* * *

The Sixth Amendment in terms guarantees "trial, by an impartial jury. . ." in federal criminal prosecutions. Because "trial by jury in criminal cases is fundamental to the American scheme of justice," the Due Process Clause of the Fourteenth Amendment guarantees the same right in state criminal prosecutions. * * *

In the overwhelming majority of criminal trials, pretrial publicity presents few unmanageable threats to this important right. But when the case is a "sensational" one tensions develop between the right of the accused to trial by an impartial jury and the rights guaranteed others by the First Amendment. The relevant decisions of the Court, even if not dispositive, are instructive by way of background.

In *Irvin v. Dowd* (1961) the defendant was convicted of murder following intensive and hostile news coverage. The trial judge had granted a defense motion for a change of venue, but only to an adjacent county, which had been exposed to essentially the same news coverage. * * * On review the Court vacated the conviction and death sentence and remanded to allow a new trial for, "[w]ith his life at stake, it is not requiring too much that petitioner be tried in an atmosphere undisturbed by so huge a wave of public passion. . .."

* * *

In *Sheppard v. Maxwell* (1966) the Court focused sharply on the impact of pretrial publicity and a trial court's duty to protect the defendant's constitutional right to a fair trial. * * * The Court ordered a new trial for the petitioner, even though the first trial had occurred 12 years before. * * *

* * *

Taken together, these cases demonstrate that pretrial publicity—even pervasive, adverse publicity—does not inevitably lead to an unfair trial. The capacity of the jury eventually impaneled to decide the case fairly is influenced by the tone and extent of the publicity, which is in part, and often in large part, shaped by what attorneys, police, and other officials do to precipitate news coverage. The trial judge has a major responsibility. What the judge says about a case, in or out of the courtroom, is likely to appear in newspapers and broadcasts. More important, the measures a judge takes or fails to take to mitigate the effects of pretrial publicity may well determine whether the defendant receives a trial consistent with the requirements of due process. * * *

* * *

The state trial judge in the case before us acted responsibly, out of a legitimate concern, in an effort to protect the defendant's right to a fair trial. What we must decide is not simply whether the Nebraska courts erred in seeing the possiblility of real danger to the defendant's rights, but whether in the circumstances of this case the means employed were foreclosed by another provision of the Constitution.

The First Amendment provides that "Congress shall make no law. . .abridging the freedom. . .of the press. . .." The Court has interpreted these guarantees to afford special protection against orders that prohibit the publication or broadcast of particular information or commentary—orders that impose a "previous" or "prior" restraint on speech. * * *

* * *

The thread running through all these cases is that prior restraints on speech and publication are the most serious and the least tolerable infringement on First Amendment rights. A criminal penalty or a judgment in a defamation case is subject to the whole panoply of protections afforded by deferring the impact of the judgment until all avenues of appellate review have been exhausted. Only after judgment has become final, correct or otherwise, does the law's sanction become fully operative.

A prior restraint, by contrast and by definition, has an immediate and irreversible sanction. If it can be said that a threat of criminal or civil sanctions after publication "chills" speech, prior restraint "freezes" it at least for the time.

* * *

Of course, the order at issue . . . does not prohibit but only postpones publication. Some news can be delayed and most commentary can even more readily be delayed without serious injury, and there often is a self-imposed delay when responsible editors call for verification of information. * * *

* * *

We turn now to the record in this case to determine whether, as Learned Hand put it, "the gravity of the 'evil,' discounted by its improbability, justifies such invasion of free speech as is necessary to avoid the danger." To do so, we must examine the evidence before the trial judge when the order was entered to determine (a) the nature and extent of pretrial news coverage; (b) whether other measures would be likely to mitigate the effects of unrestrained pretrial publicity; and (c) how effectively a restraining order would operate to prevent the threatened danger. The precise terms of the restraining order are also important. We must then consider whether the record supports the entry of a prior restraint on publication, one of the most extraordinary remedies known to our jurisprudence.

In assessing the probable extent of publicity, the trial judge had before him newspapers demonstrating that the crime had already drawn intensive news coverage, and the testimony of the County Judge, who had entered the initial restraining order based on the local and national attention the case had attracted. * * *

Our review of the pretrial record persuades us that the judge was justified in concluding that there would be intense and pervasive pretrial publicity concerning this case. He could also reasonably conclude, based on common human experience, that publicity might impair the defendant's right to a fair trial. He did not purport to say more, for he found only "a clear and present danger that pre-trial publicity *could* impinge upon the defendant's right to a fair trial." * * *

We find little in the record that goes to another aspect of our task, determining whether measures short of an order restraining all publication would have insured the defendant a fair trial. * * *

Most of the alternatives to prior restraint of publication in these circumstances were discussed with obvious approval in *Sheppard v. Maxwell:* (a) a change of trial venue to a place less exposed to the intense publicity that seemed imminent in Lincoln County; (b) postponement of the trial to allow public attention to subside; (c) searching questioning of prospective jurors. . . ; (d) the use of emphatic and clear instructions on the sworn duty of each juror to decide the issues only on evidence presented in open court. Sequestration of jurors is, of course, always available. Although that measure insulates jurors only after they are sworn, it also enhances the likelihood of dissipating the impact of pretrial publicity and emphasizes the elements of the jurors' oath.

* * *

We have noted earlier that pretrial publicity, even if pervasive and concentrated, cannot be regarded as leading automatically and in every kind of criminal case to an unfair trial. * * *

We have therefore examined this record to determine the probable efficacy of the measures short of prior restraint on the press and speech. There is no finding that alternative measures would not have protected Simants' rights, and the Nebraska Supreme Court did no more than imply that such measures might not be adequate. Moreover, the record is lacking in evidence to support such a finding.

We must also assess the probable efficacy of prior restraint on publication as a workable method of protecting Simants' right to a fair trial, and we cannot ignore the reality of the problems of managing and enforcing pretrial restraining orders. The territorial jurisdiction of the issuing court is limited by concepts of sovereignty. * * *

The Nebraska Supreme Court narrowed the scope of the restrictive order, and its opinion reflects awareness of the tensions between the need to protect the accused as fully possible and the need to restrict publication as little as possible. The dilemma posed underscores how difficult it is for trial judges to predict what information will in fact undermine the impartiality of jurors, and the difficulty of drafting an order that will effectively keep prejudicial information from prospective jurors. When a restrictive order is sought, a court can anticipate only part of what will develop that may injure the accused. But information not so obviously prejudicial may emerge, and what may properly be published in these "gray zone" circumstances may not violate the restrictive order and yet be prejudicial.

Finally, we note that the events disclosed by the record took place in a community of 850 people. It is reasonable to assume that, without any news accounts being printed or broadcast, rumors would travel swiftly by word of mouth. One can only speculate on the accuracy of such reports, given the generative propensities of rumors; they could well be more damaging than reasonably accurate news accounts. But plainly a whole community cannot be restrained from discussing a subject intimately affecting life within it.

Given these practical problems, it is far from clear that prior restraint on publication would have protected Simants' rights.

* * *

The record demonstrates, as the Nebraska courts held, that there was indeed a risk that pretrial news accounts, true or false, would have some adverse impact on the attitudes of those who might be called as jurors. But on the record now before us it is not clear that further publicity, unchecked, would so distort the views of potential jurors that 12 could not be found who would, under proper instructions, fulfill their sworn duty to render a just verdict exclusively on the evidence presented in open court. We cannot say on this record that alternatives to a prior restraint on petitioners would not have sufficiently mitigated the adverse effects of pretrial publicity so as to make prior restraint unnecessary. Nor can we conclude that the restraining order actually entered would serve its intended purpose. * * *

Of necessity our holding is confined to the record before us. But our conclusion is not simply a result of assessing the adequacy of the showing made in this case; it results in part from the problems inherent in meeting the heavy burden of demonstrating, in advance of trial, that without prior restraint a fair trial will be denied. The practical problems of managing and enforcing restrictive orders will always be present. In this sense, the record now before us is illustrative rather than exceptional. It is significant that when this Court has reversed a state conviction because of prejudicial publicity, it has carefully noted that some course of action short of prior restraint would have made a critical difference. However difficult it may be, we need not rule out the possibility of showing the kind of threat to fair trial rights that would possess the requisite degree of certainty to justify restraint. This Court has frequently denied that First Amendment rights are absolute and has consistently rejected the proposition that a prior restraint can never be employed.

Our analysis ends as it began, with a confrontation between prior restraint imposed to protect one vital constitutional guarantee and the explicit command of another that the freedom to speak and publish shall not be abridged. We reaffirm that the guarantees of freedom of expression are not an absolute prohibition under all circumstances, but the barriers to prior restraint remain high and the presumption against its use continues intact. We hold that, with respect to the order entered in this case prohibiting reporting or commentary on judicial proceedings held in public, the barriers have not been overcome; to the extent that this order restrained publication of such material, it is clearly invalid. To the extent that it prohibited publication based on information gained from other sources, we conclude that the heavy burden imposed as a condition to securing a prior restraint was not met and the judgment of the Nebraska Supreme Court is therefore reversed.

Justice White, concurring [omitted].

Justice Powell, concurring.

* * *

In my judgment a prior restraint properly may issue only when it is shown to be necessary to prevent the dissemination of prejudicial publicity that otherwise poses a high likelihood of preventing, directly and irreparably, the impaneling of a jury meeting the Sixth Amendment requirement of impartiality. This requires a showing that (i) there is a clear threat to the fairness of trial, (ii) such a threat is posed by the actual publicity to be restrained, and (iii) no less restrictive alternatives are available. * * *

* * *

Justice Brennan, with whom Justice Stewart and Justice Marshall join, concurring in the judgment.

The question presented in this case is whether, consistently with the First Amendment, a court may enjoin the press, in advance of publication, from reporting or commenting on information acquired from public court proceedings, public court records, or other sources about the pending judicial proceedings. The Nebraska Supreme Court upheld such a direct prior restraint on the press, issued by the judge presiding over a sensational state murder trial, on the ground there existed a "clear and present danger that pretrial publicity could substantially impair the right of the defendant [in the murder trial] to a trial by an impartial jury unless restraints were imposed." * * *

* * *

I unreservedly agree with Mr. Justice Black that "free speech and fair trials are two of the most cherished policies of our civilization, and it would be a trying task to choose between them." But I would reject the notion that a choice is necessary, that there is an inherent conflict that cannot be resolved without essentially abrogating one right or the other. To hold that courts cannot impose any prior restraints on the reporting of or commentary upon information revealed in open court proceedings, disclosed in public documents, or divulged by other sources with respect to the criminal justice system is not, I must emphasize, to countenance the sacrifice of precious Sixth Amendment rights on the altar of the First Amendment. For although there may in some instances be tension between uninhibited and robust reporting by the press and fair trials for criminal defendants, judges possess adequate tools short of injunctions against reporting for relieving that tension. To be sure, these alternatives may require greater sensitivity and effort on the part of judges conducting criminal trials than would the stifling of publicity through the simple expedient of issuing a restrictive order on the press; but that sensitivity and effort is required in order to ensure the full enjoyment and proper accommodation of both First and Sixth Amendment rights.

There is, beyond peradventure, a clear and substantial damage to freedom of the press whenever even a temporary restraint is imposed on reporting of material concerning the operations of the criminal justice system, an institution of such pervasive influence in our constitutional scheme. And the necessary impact of reporting even confessions can never be so direct, immediate, and irreparable that I would give credence to any notion that prior restraints may be imposed on that rationale. It may be that such incriminating material would be of such slight news value or so inflammatory in particular cases that responsible organs of the media, in an exercise of self-restraint, would choose not to publicize that material, and not make the judicial task of safeguarding precious rights of criminal defendants more difficult. Voluntary codes such as the Nebraska Bar-Press Guidelines are a commendable acknowledgment by the media that constitutional prerogatives bring enormous responsibilities, and I would encourage continuation of such voluntary cooperative efforts between the bar and the media. However, the press may be arrogant, tyrannical, abusive, and sensationalist, just as it may be incisive, probing, and informative. But at least in the context of prior restraints on publication, the decision of what, when, and how to publish is for editors, not judges.

Every restrictive order imposed on the press in this case was accordingly an unconstitutional prior restraint on the freedom of the press, and I would therefore, reverse the judgment of the Nebraska Supreme Court and remand for further proceedings not inconsistent with this opinion.

* * *

Justice Stevens, concurring in the judgment.

For the reasons eloquently stated by Mr. Justice Brennan, I agree that the judiciary is capable of protecting the defendant's right to a fair trial without enjoining the press from publishing information in the public domain, and that it may not do so.

Most trial court judges read *Nebraska Press Association* to mean that gag orders could not be used to prevent adverse pretrial publicity, and many judges turned to the alternative of barring the press from pretrial hearings in order to limit publicity that could affect the selection of an unbiased jury. Not surprisingly, this gave rise to court challenges by the press, and the Burger Court was confronted by numerous cases raising the question of whether the First Amendment guarantees access of the press to criminal court proceedings. After initially answering this question negatively in *Gannett Co. v. DePasquale* (1979), the Burger Court found itself under sharp attack and recognized a First Amendment right of access of the press to criminal court activities.

Gannett was one of the Burger Court's most controversial decisions. The case involved the suspected murder of Wayne Clapp on a fishing trip by two men who were in a conspiracy with Clapp's wife. A great deal of media publicity arose concerning the case, and the defendants requested at a pretrial hearing that the press and public be excluded from the courtroom. Judge DePasquale granted the motion, ruling that the right of the defendants to receive a fair trial outweighed the interests of the press and public in attending the pretrial hearings. A bitterly divided

Court ruled 5-4 in support of Judge DePasquale, but Stewart's majority opinion raised far more questions than it answered. He seemed to argue that the case only involved the Sixth Amendment, but he made frequent references to a First Amendment right of access of the press and the public to criminal court proceedings. Stewart also referred frequently to criminal trials as well as to pretrial hearings, leaving it unclear as to the scope of the ruling.

The *Gannett* decision immediately triggered an extraordinary amount of reaction in the summer of 1979. Numerous trial court judges throughout the country read this case as a green light to close both pretrial hearings and criminal trials. The press launched vigorous attacks on the *Gannett* decision and on the subsequent closing of courthouse doors to the press. Four members of the Court, apparently alarmed over reactions to the case, took the highly unusual approach of explaining the decision in public speeches. The justices only added to the confusion, however, because they explained the decision in contradictory ways! For example, Burger stated that the case applied only to pretrial hearings, but Blackmun contradicted the chief justice in a speech before a group of federal district judges.

The Court thus found itself in the position of needing to bring clarity to an important area of First Amendment law that was clouded in uncertainty. *Richmond Newspapers, Inc. v. Virginia* (1980) provided that opportunity. This case also involved a murder trial, one in which a defendant was standing trial for the fourth time. The defendant moved to have the trial closed, the prosecutor raised no objection to the request, and the trial judge granted the motion. Richmond Newspapers challenged the action. Although the Court ruled 7-1 against closing the trial, the justices could not achieve a majority opinion. Chief Justice Burger wrote the plurality opinion, joined by White and Stevens, distinguishing this case from *Gannett*, which he argued involved only the Sixth Amendment and only pretrial proceedings. This case, in contrast, raised the issue of First Amendment rights at the trial stage of the criminal justice process. In his analysis, Burger concluded, "We hold that the right to attend criminal trials is implicit in the guarantees of the First Amendment; without the freedom to attend such trials, which people have exercised for centuries, important aspects of freedom of speech and of the press could be eviscerated. . ." (448 U.S. at 580). Burger's opinion did not go as far as the Court's more liberal justices desired, however. Brennan, joined by Marshall, wrote a concurring opinion arguing for the explicit rejection of *Gannett* and the recognition of a right of access to both pretrials and trials.

Brennan eventually prevailed. In *Globe Newspaper Company v. Superior Court for the County of Norfolk* (1982), the specific issue was the constitutionality of a Massachusetts law that required trial judges to bar the press and public when all young victims of sex crimes were testifying. Writing for a six-person majority, Brennan stated that the First Amendment guarantees the press and the public access to both pretrial hearings and regular trials. Brennan acknowledged that this right was not absolute, but in this case the total prohibition on access was impermissible prior restraint. The Burger Court justices reinforced in subsequent cases the principle of a First Amendment right of access to criminal proceedings. In *Press-Enterprise Co. v. Superior Court of California* (1984), the Court unanimously supported the constitutional principle of open access in ruling against a judge who had barred the press and public from attending the *voir dire* examination of potential jurors in a case involving the rape and murder of a teenage girl. Finally, in the 1986 case of *Press-Enterprise Co. v. Superior Court of California*, the Court strongly reaffirmed the First Amendment's guarantee of access to court proceedings in ruling against a judge's decision to close preliminary hearings in a case based on a request by the accused, with Chief Justice Burger writing the majority opinion.

A final issue that the Burger Court confronted in the conflict between a free press and a fair trial involved cameras in the courtroom, specifically the televising of criminal trials. Historically, the broadcast media had been viewed as a threat to the fair conduct of criminal trials. The American Bar Association had long taken a position against all broadcast coverage of criminal trials, and the Supreme Court in *Estes v. Texas* (1964) seemed to support this position. As television became both more common and less intrusive because of technological developments, however, attitudes began to change. The ABA began to relax its opposition, and in 1978 the Conference of State Chief Justices voted to give each state the freedom to develop guidelines regarding the broadcasting of criminal trials (Witt 1989, p. 171). The Burger Court was confronted with this issue in *Chandler v. Florida* (1981). Noel Chandler was a former Miami Beach police officer who had been charged with burglary, and his criminal trial was televised under an experimental Florida program. Chandler argued that his right to a fair trial was violated by the television coverage, citing *Estes* as controlling precedent. Writing for the Court, Chief Justice Burger rejected Chandler's arguments, ruling that states must be free to experiment with television coverage of criminal trials while being alert to possible dangers to a defendant's right to a fair trial.

Although the Burger Court was actively involved in deciding numerous controversial cases over the conflict between a free press and a fair trial, the Rehnquist Court has not decided any cases directly involving this topic. Thus, the precedents of the Burger Court embody the contemporary policies regarding limitations on the press in covering criminal trials. The legacy is distinctively liberal. The Burger Court took a strong position against gag orders, recognized a First Amendment right of access of the press and public to attend criminal trials, and gave support to the idea of limited televising of trials. Despite the pattern of recognizing the importance of freedom of the press, however, the Court has maintained that the press must not compromise an individual's right to a fair trial.

Broadcasting

The last topic under freedom of the press is the newest one that the Court has faced: broadcasting. The press topics we have thus far examined have all involved primarily the print media, but twentieth-century technology has created various forms of electronic media, including radio, television, and cable communication.

This is a topic where the historic analysis of the founding period cannot provide guidance, for at the time of the writing of the First Amendment radio and television did not exist. Indeed, the issue of government regulation of the broadcast media did not become a matter of public policy concern until the 1920s when numerous radio stations began broadcasting. The result was chaotic because the stations were interfering with each other, making it difficult for any station to be heard. In response, Congress created the Federal Communications Commission in 1934 under its general power to regulate interstate commerce. The FCC was granted broad authority to regulate the broadcast media for the public interest. These powers included issuing licenses, requiring equal time for opposing political candidates, banning indecent and obscene language, and providing for fair coverage of both sides of public issues. The regulatory power of the FCC over broadcasting was justified primarily on the grounds that only a limited number of radio, and later television, frequencies existed, and therefore government regulation was required. In addition, the broadcast media were also viewed as different from the print media because radio and television were primarily concerned with providing entertainment rather than news.

The Court's first major broadcasting case did not occur until 1969 in *Red Lion Broadcasting v. Federal Communications Commission. Red Lion* involved a challenge to the constitutionality of the FCC's "fairness doctrine," which required radio and television stations to give both sides of a public issue the opportunity to be heard. The Court had little precedent upon which to draw in *Red Lion.* In one of the few cases testing the powers of the FCC before *Red Lion,* the Court in *NBC v. United States* (1943) rejected challenges to the FCC by viewing their regulations not as a First Amendment issue but rather as a matter of permissible government economic regulation.

Writing for a unanimous Court in *Red Lion,* Justice White provided a strong defense for both the general authority of the FCC over the broadcast media as well as the specific fairness doctrine. Although acknowledging that " . . . broadcasting is clearly a medium affected by a First Amendment interest. . .," White also argued that " . . . differences in the characteristics of news media justify differences in the First Amendment standards applied to them" (395 U.S. at 386). These standards included not only licensing requirements but also more specific requirements such as the fairness doctrine. Given the unique characteristics of the broadcast media, government regulations serve to further " . . . the purpose of the First Amendment to preserve an uninhibited marketplace of ideas in which truth will ultimately prevail. . ." (395 U.S. at 390).

Red Lion Broadcasting v. Federal Communications Commission

395 U.S. 367, 89 S.Ct. 1794, 23 L.Ed. 2d 371 (1969)

■ The Federal Communications Commission established a fairness doctrine that imposed requirements upon radio and television broadcast stations. Under this FCC doctrine, the debate of public issues on broadcast stations must allow each side of a public controversy to be granted fair coverage. On November 27, 1964, a Pennsylvania radio station licensed to the Red Lion Broadcasting Company aired a program by the Reverend Billy James Hargis. In this particular show, Hargis attacked Fred J. Cook, author of a book entitled *Goldwater—Extremist on the Right.* During his fifteen-minute broadcast, Hargis referred to Cook as a Communist, a supporter of Alger Hiss, and an enemy of the Central Intelligence Agency. Cook demanded free reply time, but Red Lion refused. Cook then wrote to the FCC stating that Red Lion had violated the fairness doctrine. The FCC agreed with Cook and, subsequently, the Court of Appeals for the District of Columbia Circuit found in favor of Cook and ruled that the fairness doctrine was constitutional. The broadcasters appealed to the United States Supreme Court, arguing that the fairness doctrine abridged their freedom of speech and press. *Red Lion* was heard along with a companion case, *United States v. Radio Television News Directors Association* (1969).

This case is significant because it was the Court's first extended analysis of the relationship of the First Amendment freedom of expression guarantees to broadcasting. As you read the opinion, think about the following questions: (1) How does the broadcast media differ from the print media to justify greater control over the former? (2) Does the fairness doctrine create a serious problem of self-censorship? (3) Have technological developments undercut the rationale of the *Red Lion* decision?

Vote:

The Court voted unanimously (Douglas did not participate) that the FCC regulations did not violate the First Amendment.

Justice White delivered the opinion of the Court.

* * * The two cases before us now, which were decided separately below, challenge the constitutional and statutory bases of the [fairness] doctrine and component rules. Red Lion involves the application of the fairness doctrine to a particular broadcast, and RTNDA arises as an action to review the FCC's 1967 promulgation of the personal attack and political editorializing regulations, which were laid down after the *Red Lion* litigation had begun.

* * *

The broadcasters challenge the fairness doctrine and its specific manifestations in the personal attack and political editorial rules on conventional First Amendment grounds, alleging that the rules abridge their freedom of speech and press. Their contention is that the First Amendment protects their desire to use their allotted frequencies continuously to broadcast whatever they choose, and to exclude whomever they choose from ever using that frequency. No man may be prevented from saying or publishing what he thinks, or from refusing in his speech or other utterances to give equal weight to the views of his opponents. This right, they say, applies equally to broadcasters.

Although broadcasting is clearly a medium affected by a First Amendment interest, differences in the characteristics of news media justify differences in the First Amendment standards applied to them. * * *

* * *

Where there are substantially more individuals who want to broadcast than there are frequencies to allocate, it is idle to posit an unabridgeable First Amendment right to broadcast comparable to the right of every individual to speak, write, or publish. If 100 persons want broadcast licenses but there are only 10 frequencies to allocate, all of them may have the same "right" to a license; but if there is to be any effective communication by radio, only a few can be licensed and the rest must be barred from the airwaves. It would be strange if the First Amendment, aimed at protecting and furthering communications, prevented the Government from making radio communication possible by requiring licenses to broadcast and by limiting the number of licenses so as not to overcrowd the spectrum.

This has been the consistent view of the Court. Congress unquestionably has the power to grant and deny licenses and to eliminate existing stations. No one has a First Amendment right to a license or to monopolize a radio frequency; to deny a station license because "the public interest" requires it "is not a denial of free speech."

By the same token, as far as the First Amendment is concerned those who are licensed stand no better than those to whom licenses are refused. A license permits broadcasting, but the licensee has no constitutional right to be the one who holds the license or to monopolize a radio frequency to the exclusion of his fellow citizens. There is nothing in the First Amendment which prevents the Government from requiring a licensee to share his frequency with others and to conduct himself as a proxy or fiduciary with obligations to present those views and voices which are representative of his community and which would otherwise, by necessity, be barred from the airwaves.

* * *

In terms of constitutional principles, and as enforced sharing of a scarce resource, the personal attack and political editorial rules are indistinguishable from the equal-time provision of § 315, a specific enactment of Congress requiring stations to set aside reply time under specified circumstances and to which the fairness doctrine and these constituent regulations are important complements. That provision, which has been part of the law since 1927, has been held valid by this Court as an obligation of the licensee relieving him of any power in any way to prevent or censor the broadcast, and thus insulating him from liability for defamation. The constitutionality of the statute under the First Amendment was unquestioned.

Nor can we say that it is inconsistent with the First Amendment goal of producing an informed public capable of conducting its own affairs to require a broadcaster to permit answers to personal attacks occurring in the course of discussing controversial issues, or to require that the political opponents of those endorsed by the station be given a chance to communicate with the public. Otherwise, station owners and a few networks would have unfettered power to make time available only to the highest bidders, to communicate only their own views on public issues, people and candidates, and to permit on the air only those with whom they agreed. There is no sanctuary in the First Amendment for unlimited private censorship operating in a medium not open to all. * * *

It is strenuously argued, however, that if political editorials or personal attacks will trigger an obligation in broadcasters to afford the opportunity for expression to speakers who need not pay for time and whose views are unpalatable to the licenses, then broadcasters will be irresistibly forced to self-censorship and their coverage of controversial public issues will be eliminated or at least rendered wholly ineffective. Such a result would indeed be a serious matter, for should licensees actually eliminate their coverage of controversial issues, the purposes of the doctrine would be stifled.

At this point, however, as the Federal Communications Commission has indicated, that possibility is at best speculative. The communications industry, and in particular the networks, have taken pains to present controversial issues in the past, and even now they do not assert that they intend to abandon their efforts in this regard. It would be better if the FCC's encouragement were never necessary to induce the broadcasters to meet their responsibility. And if experience with the administration of these doctrines indicates that they have the net effect of reducing rather than enhancing the volume and quality of coverage, there will be time enough to reconsider the constitutional implications. The fairness doctrine in the past has had no such overall effect.

That this will occur now seems unlikely, however, since if present licenses should suddenly prove timorous, the Commission is not powerless to insist that they give adequate and fair attention to public issues. It does not violate the First Amendment to treat licensees given the privilege of using scarce radio frequencies as proxies for the entire community, obligated to give suitable time and attention to matters of great public concern. To condition the granting or renewal of licenses on a willingness to present representative community views on controversial issues is consistent with the ends and purposes of those constitutional provisions forbidding the abridgment of freedom of speech and freedom of the press. Congress need not stand idly by and permit those with licenses to ignore the problems which beset the people or exclude from the airways anything but their own views of fundamental questions. * * *

* * *

In view of the scarcity of broadcast frequencies, the Government's role in allocating those frequencies, and the legitimate claims of those unable without governmental assistance to gain access to those frequencies for expression of their views, we hold the regulations and ruling at issue here are both authorized by statute and constitutional. * * *

It is so ordered.

The fairness doctrine remained a controversial policy for two decades after *Red Lion,* and in 1987 the FCC abandoned the doctrine. The elimination of the fairness doctrine was part of a much broader pattern of government deregulation in the eighties, but the argument was also made that the doctrine had inhibited rather than promoted freedom of expression.

The Burger Court also handed down a number of First Amendment decisions involving the broadcast media. The Burger Court justices supported the basic principle of *Red Lion* that government regulation of radio and television could be substantially more extensive than regulation of the traditional press, but the high court found itself confronted by changing technology and novel issues that raised difficult First Amendment questions.

Comedian George Carlin's radio monologue entitled "Filthy Words" triggered the Burger Court's most controversial decision involving the broadcast media in the case of *Federal Communications Commission v. Pacifica Foundation* (1978). Carlin's monologue, recorded before a live audience in a California theater, was a twelve-minute satire on seven words that could not be said on the airwaves: shit, piss, fuck, cunt, cocksucker, motherfucker, and tits. A New York radio station owned by Pacifica Foundation broadcast Carlin's comedy routine during an afternoon program, and a father who heard the recording while in a car with his young son filed a complaint with the FCC. The Commission, ruling that it had the power to regulate obscene broadcasting, condemned the station and warned that the station could lose its license if future complaints were filed. A federal court of appeals ruled against the FCC, which appealed to the Supreme Court.

Although the justices were in sharp disagreement over the case, a five-person majority did emerge which found that the FCC actions did not violate the First Amendment and therefore reversed the judgment of the circuit court. In the critical portion of Justice Stevens's opinion, which was joined by Powell, Blackmun, Burger, and Rehnquist, the justices cited *Red Lion* to argue that broadcasting receives the most limited First Amendment protection of all forms of communication. Stevens offered two reasons to justify the reduced protection, which were especially important in this case. First, the broadcast media have a unique and pervasive presence in the lives of Americans, and the right of individuals to be left alone in the privacy of their own homes outweighs First Amendment rights to present indecent material over the airways. A second concern involved the unique accessibility of broadcasting to young children, for the Court in many contexts has allowed the government to regulate expression to protect the young.

The Burger Court justices were confronted with a variety of additional interesting broadcast cases raising the general question of whether government regulation in this unique area is compatible with or contradictory to freedom of expression. The 1973 case of *Columbia Broadcasting System v. Democratic National Committee* presented an excellent example of the difficulties confronting the Court. CBS refused to broadcast certain paid political advertisements by the Democratic National Committee, which argued that the fairness doctrine required that CBS give them access to the air. A majority of the Court, in an opinion by Chief Justice Burger, reasoned that the fairness doctrine did require broadcasters to present various views in a fair manner but did not guarantee a right of access for all individuals and groups wishing to express an opinion. According to the majority, substantial discretion can be left in the hands of broadcasters, thus reinforcing the principles of freedom of expression. In dissent, Brennan and Marshall saw the case in a completely different manner; these justices saw freedom of expression being denied to those who wanted to purchase air time.

The Warren and Burger Courts thus provided somewhat conservative interpretations in the area of government regulation of radio and television broadcasting. Operating on the premise that these forms of electronic communication were substantially different than the print media, the high court adopted a minimal scrutiny approach to these cases, requiring the government to show only that the regulations were rationally related to a legitimate government interest.

The Rehnquist Court has been confronted with two cases involving an important new form of technology, cable television. A majority of the justices has viewed cable television as being sufficiently different from conventional radio and television that it deserves a higher level of constitutional protection under the intermediate scrutiny approach.

Leathers v. Medlock (1991) involved a First Amendment challenge by cable television operators to an Arkansas law that exempted newspapers and magazines from a sales tax but required cable television services to pay the tax. The Court ruled 7-2 that the law did not violate the First Amendment, with O'Connor authoring the majority opinion. O'Connor began her opinion by recognizing that cable television is engaged in press and speech within the meaning of the First Amendment. She then cited a series of cases in which the Court had established the principle that differential taxation applied to those protected by the First Amendment must be closely examined if the taxation could suppress the expression of specific viewpoints or ideas. In this case, however, O'Connor concluded, the Arkansas tax on cable television does not involve any type of unconstitutional viewpoint discrimination. Marshall, joined by Blackmun, dissented: "Under the First Amendment, government simply has no business interfering with the process by which citizens' preferences for information formats evolves" (499 U.S. at 465).

The Rehnquist Court's most fully developed analysis of the applicability of the First Amendment to cable television came in *Turner Broadcasting System v. FCC* (1994). This case arose from a 1992 congressional law, the Cable Television Consumer Protection and Competition Act. The specific sections that were challenged by various cable programmers and operators were the "must-carry" provisions, which mandated that cable operators carry the signals of a specified number of local stations, both commercial and educational. The United States District Court for the District of Columbia granted summary judgment in favor of the federal government, thus ruling against the First Amendment challenge of the cable television interests.

In vacating the judgment of the district court and remanding the case back for further proceedings, the Rehnquist Court justices achieved agreement on some general principles regarding cable television and the First Amendment but could not achieve a majority consensus on how these principles applied to this particular case. Despite the ambiguity and uncertainty surrounding the decision, however, this case represented a significant victory for cable television.

The most important issue in the case was the appropriate level of scrutiny to apply. The federal government argued that the Court should treat cable television in the same manner as broadcast television and radio, thus applying the minimal scrutiny standard set forth in *Red Lion.* In sharp contrast, attorneys for the cable television interests argued that the Court should use the tough standards of strict scrutiny in this case. The Court rejected both of these extreme positions and accepted instead an intermediate level of scrutiny. Writing for an eight-person majority, Kennedy argued that the technology associated with cable television is significantly different from radio and television broadcasting because there is no inherent limitation to the number of speakers who can be carried on cable television nor is there a problem in cable television regarding interference between speakers attempting to use the same channel. Thus, Kennedy reasoned, the justifications allowing substantial government regulation over broadcast radio and television under a reasonable basis standard do not exist in regard to cable television. Instead, Kennedy stated that the key consideration is whether the cable television regulation is content-based or content-neutral; a content-based regulation would trigger strict scrutiny, whereas a content-neutral regulation would be evaluated under intermediate scrutiny.

Kennedy's support shrank to a bare five-person majority when he took the position that the must-carry provisions of the federal law were content-neutral, thus triggering intermediate scrutiny. Blackmun, Stevens, Souter, and—surprisingly—Rehnquist joined Kennedy in arguing that the appropriate intermediate test had been established in the *O'Brien* case of 1968. In applying this test, the five justices concluded that Congress was pursuing several important government interests, including preserving the benefits of free, local broadcast television. In applying the means standard of *O'Brien,* which requires that no greater burden be placed on speech than is necessary, a four-person plurality thought that the federal government had not satisfied this concern; Stevens believed, in contrast, that the government had met the standard.

O'Connor, joined by Scalia, Ginsburg, and Thomas, took a far different view of the case. They argued that the law was not content-neutral, and therefore strict scrutiny should be used to evaluate the regulation. For O'Connor, even if the government's interests were compelling, a point she did not concede, the means used were not sufficiently tailored to be constitutional. Thus, these four justices would have reversed the district court's judgment.

The topic of broadcasting thus provides us with another area where we can reject the idea of the Rehnquist Court engaging in a conservative counterrevolution. The Warren Court took an essentially conservative stance in *Red Lion,* its major case involving the broadcast media, and the Burger court also embraced a minimal scrutiny approach in radio and television broadcasting cases. The Rehnquist Court, however, appears to have adopted the more liberal intermediate scrutiny test in regard to cable broadcasting.

Broadcasting cases are likely to occupy a significant place on the court's future agenda because of the dramatic technological changes occurring in the communications industry. One example involves the Internet, the global computer communication system. Government regulation of this system is being considered in regard to such concerns as fraud and indecency. Will the Court view the Internet as similar to the print media, to radio and television, or to cable communication? Alternatively, will the Internet be viewed as something unique, requiring a new approach by the court? Whatever the answer, it seems likely that the Court will eventually face the question of permissible government regulation of the internet.

Conclusion

The Supreme Court has been remarkably consistent in the area of freedom of expression during the Warren, Burger, and Rehnquist Court eras, with the justices of the Burger and Rehnquist Courts generally upholding the liberal precedents of the Warren Court era and even extending liberal policies in some fields. This is a dramatically different pattern than we saw in the previous two chapters on the Establishment Clause (Chapter 5) and the Free Exercise Clause (Chapter 6). In both of these chapters we observed major doctrinal changes in the Court's policies as the Court's membership changed during the Warren, Burger, and Rehnquist Court eras. In contrast, continuity rather than change has characterized the Court in the area of freedom of expression. Both quantitative and qualitative analyses support this conclusion.

A systematic comparison of the voting records of the three Court eras has shown that the Court reached its liberal apex when Warren was chief justice, deciding 70 percent of its freedom of expression cases liberally. This declined to 53 percent during the Burger Court era, but the Rehnquist Court justices have decided 57 percent of their cases liberally. Thus, recent membership changes on the Court—especially the series of conservative appointments by Presidents Reagan and Bush—do not appear to have had direct, major effects on the Court's decision making in freedom of expression cases.

The doctrinal analysis presented in this chapter reinforces the conclusions drawn from the quantitative analysis. Throughout both the Burger and Rehnquist Court periods, we have observed an essential continuity with freedom of expression approaches and doctrines of the Warren Court era. The Burger Court not only remained committed to the leading freedom of expression precedents of the Warren Court but also moved in a more liberal direction than its predecessor by extending First Amendment protection to advertising. The Rehnquist Court justices have also been committed to maintaining the liberal freedom of expression doctrines inherited from the Warren and Burger Courts. In most areas of freedom of expression, the Rehnquist Court has shown strong support for the preferred freedoms approach, increasingly using the strict scrutiny test as a technique to protect freedom of expression values. This test appears to be the standard in cases involving pure, political speech in public forums as well as in situations where government regulations are not content or viewpoint neutral. A somewhat lower standard of intermediate scrutiny tends to be used with certain forms of expression such as symbolic and commercial speech, but this level of scrutiny still provides heightened protection for freedom of expression. The Rehnquist Court justices have also maintained the traditionally strong opposition to prior restraint on the press and the commitment to the actual malice standard in libel cases.

A belief in freedom of expression is deeply ingrained in American culture. The liberties of speech, press, assembly, and petition are viewed as vital to our democratic society and to our individual development. The deep human yearning for these freedoms spans both time and cultures. We examined in this chapter the inexorable expansion of freedom of expression in Greece, Rome, England, and colonial America. Recent events throughout the world in Eastern Europe, South

Africa, and the People's Republic of China attest to the human desire for freedom of expression. In the United States, the Supreme Court has played a profound role as the guardian of these freedoms. Social conditions change, issues before the Court evolve, and new justices replace old justices. Despite the constancy of change, however, the strong and continuing commitment of the country and the Court to freedom of expression values has been impressive.

REFERENCES

Abraham, Henry J., and Barbara A. Perry. *Freedom and the Court*. 6th ed. New York: Oxford University Press, 1994.

Brennan, William J., Jr. "The Supreme Court and the Meiklejohn Interpretation of the First Amendment," *Harvard Law Review* 79 (1965):1-20.

Chafee, Zechariah. *Free Speech in the United States*. Cambridge: Harvard University Press, 1946.

Cohen, William, and Danelski, David J. *Constitutional Law: Civil Liberty and Individual Rights*. 3rd ed. Westbury, New York: The Foundation Press, 1994.

Denniston, Lyle. "The Burger Court and the Press." In *The Burger Years,* edited by Herman Schwartz, 23-44. New York: Penguin Books, 1987.

Dorsen, Norman, and Gura, Joel. "The Burger Court and Freedom of Speech." In *The Burger Court: The Counter-Revolution That Wasn't*, edited by Vincent Blasi, 28-45. New Haven: Yale University Press, 1983.

Emerson, Thomas I. "Freedom of the Press Under the Burger Court." In *The Burger Court: The Counter-Revolution That Wasn't,* edited by Vincent Blasi, 1-27. New Haven,Connecticut: Yale University Press, 1983.

Friedelbaum, Stanley. *The Rehnquist Court: In Pursuit of Judicial Conservatism*. Westport, Connecticut: Greenwood Press, 1994.

Halperin, Morton H. "The National Security State: Never Question the President." In *The Burger Years,* edited by Herman Schwartz, 50-55. New York: Penguin Books, 1987.

Kairys, David. *With Liberty and Justice for Some*. New York: The New Press, 1993.

Levy, Leonard. *Emergence of a Free Press*. New York: Oxford, 1985.

________. *Freedom of Speech and Press in Early American History*. New York: Harper & Row, 1963.

________. *Legacy of Suppression*. Cambridge: Harvard University Press, 1960.

Lewis, Anthony. *Make No Law: The Sullivan Case and the First Amendment*. New York: Random House, 1991.

O'Brien, David M. *Constitutional Law and Politics: Civil Rights and Civil Liberties*. 2nd ed. New York: W. W. Norton, 1995.

Shapiro, Martin. *Freedom of Speech: The Supreme Court and Judicial Review*. Englewood Cliffs, New Jersey: Prentice-Hall, 1966.

Tedford, Thomas L. *Freedom of Speech in the United States*. New York: Random House, 1985.

Urofsky, Melvin I. *The Continuity of Change*. Belmont, California: Wadsworth, 1991.

Witt, Elder. *The Supreme Court and Individual Rights*. 2nd ed. Washington, D.C.: Congressional Quarterly Press, 1988.

Zion, Sidney. "Freedom of the Press: A Tale of Two Libel Theories." In *The Burger Years,* edited by Herman Schwartz, 45-49. New York: Penguin Books, 1987.

CHAPTER 8 OBSCENITY

CASE STUDY

CASE STUDY: ROTH V. UNITED STATES (1957)

Samuel Roth did not always pick his enemies wisely. In testifying in 1955 before a Senate subcommittee investigating the relationship between pornography and juvenile delinquency, Roth challenged and antagonized the subcommittee chair, Senator Estes Kefauver, and shortly thereafter he was arrested for sending obscene material through the mail. Roth was found guilty and received the maximum sentence under the law, a fine of $5,000 and five years in a federal penitentiary. Roth's case eventually reached the United States Supreme Court, but the Court upheld Roth's conviction in the first majority ruling on obscenity handed down by the high court.

Roth was a New York publisher as well as a distributor of erotic literature. Roth believed that he was involved with works that had significant literary value and that his activities were therefore protected from government censorship and punishment by the freedom of expression guarantees of the First Amendment. Government officials took a sharply different view of the materials published and distributed by Roth, however, and he continually found himself being prosecuted during the 1930s, 1940s, and 1950s. In 1930, for example, he received a sixty-day jail sentence for distributing James Joyce's *Ulysses*. In 1935 he received a three-year jail sentence for mailing obscene books, two of which were Boccaccio's *The Perfumed Garden* and D. H. Lawrence's *Lady Chatterley's Lover*. Similar prosecutions recurred in subsequent decades (Cohen and Danelski 1994, p. 135).

Roth had thus obtained substantial notoriety when he was subpoenaed to appear before Kefauver's committee in 1955. Kefauver was hostile toward Roth, accusing him of dealing with "slime," being a "reprehensible" person, and contributing to the problem of juvenile delinquency in American society. Roth remained calm throughout his appearance before the subcommittee. He argued that he was publishing and distributing materials with significant literary value and that his own children had worked in his office and had not become delinquents. At the conclusion of his testimony, Roth directly challenged Kefauver: " 'I believe the people who have criticized me are wrong. I believe you [Kefauver] are a great deal more wrong than they are, because you are sitting in judgment on me, and I believe that I will someday within the very near future convince you that you are wrong' " (Cohen and Danelski 1994, p. 136).

Roth was not successful in fulfilling his promise. Shortly after his Senate testimony, the federal government indicted him under the Comstock Act of 1873 on twenty-six counts of sending obscene materials through the mail. Roth's trial was before District Judge John M. Cashin and a jury in the United States District Court for the Southern District of New York. Roth and his attorney, Philip Wittenberg, carefully prepared his defense because of the serious penalties under the law, which included a maximum fine of $5,000 and a maximum jail sentence of five years. Following nine days of trial and twelve hours of deliberation, the jury found Roth guilty on four of the twenty-six counts. One count involved mailing a quarterly magazine entitled *An American Aphrodite*, and three counts were for mailing advertising circulars that were sexually suggestive. Roth did not expect a severe sentence, but his attorney warned him that Justice Department officials were seeking the maximum penalties: "'You are an old offender . . . [a]nd your enemies include a member of the United States Senate'" (Cohen and Danelski 1994, p. 137). The prediction of Roth's attorney was accurate. On February 5, 1956, Judge Cashin imposed a five-year, $5,000 punishment. Roth appealed the decision to the United States Court of Appeals for the Second Circuit, but a three-judge panel upheld his conviction against challenges that the Comstock Act was unconstitutional and that the trial judge had improperly instructed the jury.

Roth's final appeal was to the United States Supreme Court. By this time, the case had attracted a substantial amount of national attention. Roth's new attorneys—David Von Albrecht and O. John Rogge—were supported by amicus curiae briefs filed by numerous groups, including the American Civil Liberties Union, the Author's League of America, the American Book Publishers Council, and various publishing companies. These organizations viewed this case as one of critical importance to freedom of expression, but the federal government also viewed this as an important test of the power of the government to regulate obscenity. Roger Fisher of the Justice Department, supported by Solicitor General J. Lee Ranken, argued the case for the government.

The central issue before the Court in *Roth* and a companion case from California, *Alberts v. California* (1957), was whether the obscenity statutes violated the First Amendment guarantees of freedom of speech and the press. The Court also considered two additional questions: whether the Comstock Act was unconstitutional because it was too vague, and whether it was unconstitutional because it encroached upon the powers of the states under the Ninth and Tenth Amendments. Justice Brennan wrote a five-person majority opinion for the Court, upholding Roth's convictions and finding the Comstock Act constitutional on all grounds (case excerpt on p. 382). Brennan began his opinion by stating that "[t]he dispositive question is whether obscenity is utterance within the area of protected speech and press" (354 U.S. at 481). His answer to this question was "no." Although he acknowledged that this was the first time the question had been put directly before the Court, numerous opinions of the Court had always assumed that the obscene was not protected by the First Amendment. The key concept emphasized by Brennan was "social value:"

> All ideas having even the slightest redeeming social importance—unorthodox ideas, controversial ideas, even ideas hateful to the prevailing climate of opinion—have the full protection of the guarantees, unless excludable because they encroach upon the limited area of more important interests. But implicit in the history of the First Amendment is the rejection of obscenity as utterly without redeeming social importance. This rejection for that reason is mirrored in the universal judgment that obscenity should be restrained, reflected in the international agreement of over 50 nations, in the obscenity laws of all of the 48 states, and in the 20 obscenity laws enacted by the Congress from 1842 to 1956. This is the same judgment expressed by this Court in *Chaplinsky v. New Hampshire* (1942) . . . .
>
> We hold that obscenity is not within the area of constitutionally protected speech or press (354 U.S. at 485–86).

Brennan then turned to the difficult challenge of defining obscenity. He stated that the traditional standard had been the *Hicklin* test developed originally in England in the nineteenth century, which allowed the government to criminalize any sexually oriented materials that could have a tendency to affect the most susceptible persons, particularly the young. This test, Brennan argued, was not sufficiently protective of freedom of speech and press because it could easily result in the suppression of expression dealing legitimately with matters of sex. Instead, Brennan reasoned, obscenity should be viewed through a more modern test that is appropriately protective of First Amendment values: ". . . whether to the average person, applying contemporary community standards, the dominant theme of the material taken as a whole appeals to prurient interest" (354 U.S. at 489). In Roth's case, Brennan's majority opinion stated, the trial judge had properly used this standard in his instructions to the jury.

Brennan also rejected the arguments of Roth's attorneys concerning the vagueness issue and the question of federal authority to pass obscenity laws. In regard to vagueness, Brennan argued that the Constitution does not require impossibly precise language but only requires words that give adequate warning about proscribed conduct judged by common understanding and practice, and the Comstock Act met this standard. Turning to the argument of Roth's attorneys that federal laws regulating obscenity infringed upon the rights reserved to the states by the Ninth and Tenth Amendments, Brennan quickly disposed of this contention by stating that obscenity had no protection under the First Amendment and therefore Congress could regulate its distribution through the mail under the postal power granted Congress in Article 1, Section 8 of the Constitution.

Justice Douglas issued a strong dissenting opinion, which was joined by Black. Douglas's dissent was based on his view that the First Amendment, which is expressed in absolute language, places freedom of expression in a preferred position deserving strong judicial protection. Free speech and free press can only be restricted, therefore, if they are closely and clearly associated with illegal action. For Douglas and Black, the available evidence failed to demonstrate that obscene literature was a significant factor in producing illegal or even deviant behavior. Furthermore, the dissenters argued, the obscenity test set forth in the majority opinion ". . . is too loose, too capricious, too destructive of freedom of expression to be squared with the First Amendment" (354 U. S. at 512).

The *Roth* decision remains a landmark, controversial decision in American constitutional law. The Warren Court struggled with the obscenity question throughout the late fifties and the sixties. Despite hearing a substantial number of cases, the justices were in sharp disagreement over the definition of obscenity and how to apply it to the rapidly changing values and attitudes of American society. In general, however, the Warren Court used the *Roth* decision to provide substantial protection to freedom of expression, rarely upholding federal or state obscenity convictions. Ironically, Sam Roth was one of the few individuals the Warren Court ever found to violate the *Roth* standard of obscenity.

The Burger Court substantially modified the *Roth* test in the 1973 case of *Miller v. California*. In the Court's first majority opinion since the 1957 *Roth* case, the four new Nixon appointees were joined by Justice White in giving state and local governments substantially greater authority to control obscene materials. The *Miller* decision did not succeed, however, in ending the confusion and disagreement surrounding the obscenity issue, nor did the *Miller* case have the effect of reducing the growth of sexually explicit materials in American society.

The obscenity controversy continues to embroil the Rehnquist Court, which has been called upon to elaborate the meaning of the *Miller* test for obscenity as well as to deal with related questions of pornography, indecency, and nudity. Answers remain elusive. It does seem clear, however, that Sam Roth's materials would not be found obscene in contemporary American society; they would most likely be greeted by yawns rather than raised eyebrows, and they certainly would not trigger federal prosecution.

Historical Origins and Contemporary Conflicts

Our case study of *Roth* shows that the issue of obscenity is a highly controversial and rapidly changing area of constitutional law. This has not always been true, however. Intense controversy over the constitutional limitations of sexually oriented expression is a relatively recent development, dating to the 1950s. Throughout most of American history, sexually explicit materials were relatively rare, few people were concerned with the issue, and the courts were rarely called upon to adjudicate in this area. Nonetheless, it is instructive to give some attention to the historic origins of obscenity legislation.

Obscenity was simply not an issue of relevant concern during the writing and ratification of the First Amendment guarantees of freedom of speech and freedom of the press. Massachusetts was the only colony that had any laws dealing with obscenity, but no evidence exists of any prosecutions in Massachusetts during the colonial period. Indeed, the first obscenity case in the United States did not occur until 1815 in Pennsylvania. (*Report of the Commission on Obscenity and Pornography*, 1970, pp. 296–300, hereafter *Report.*) In light of this historic record, it can be argued that the First Amendment was intended to protect all forms of sexual expression because of the absolute language of the First Amendment and because obscenity was not criminalized in most of the American colonies. A more accurate characterization seems to be, however, that it is impossible to discern authoritatively the intentions of those who wrote and ratified the First Amendment regarding the issue of obscenity. Sexually explicit materials were rare, they were not considered to be a pressing social issue, and they were not discussed during the drafting and ratifying of the Constitution.

Obscenity legislation developed slowly throughout the nineteenth century until Anthony Comstock's efforts led to the dramatic growth of obscenity laws in the latter part of the century. Vermont was the first state to pass an obscenity law in 1821, Connecticut adopted a law in 1834, and a year later Massachusetts expanded its colonial obscenity law. The first federal law dealing with obscenity was passed by Congress in 1842 as part of a customs law, apparently focusing on French postcards, and in 1865 Congress passed the first law dealing with the mailing of obscene materials. Around this time, Comstock began a crusade to enact and enforce legislation dealing with obscene materials. Supported by the Young Men's Christian Association, Comstock became the chief Washington lobbyist for the Committee for the Suppression of Vice, and Congress responded to these efforts in 1873 by passing the Comstock Act, an amendment to the 1865 mail act, which established criminal penalties for mailing obscene materials. (This was the law under which Sam Roth was to be charged.) Following the lead of Congress, state obscenity legislation increased dramatically, and by the end of the nineteenth century at least thirty states had passed laws regulating obscene materials (*Report*, pp. 300–1).

Despite the growth of obscenity laws and Comstock's personal efforts to enforce them, obscenity remained a relatively minor social and legal issue throughout the first half of the twentieth century. This was to change dramatically in the last half of the century, however. We therefore turn our attention now to a brief overview of some of the major current controversies surrounding the issue of obscenity, controversies that we will explore in greater detail later in this chapter.

Contemporary American society seems to be besieged by conflicts over government regulation, censorship, and punishment of persons who produce and distribute sexually oriented materials. Two examples from 1990 are illustrative of these controversies.

Robert Mapplethorpe was a critically acclaimed but highly controversial photographer who died in 1989. Following his death, an extensive exhibition of his work was compiled and shown at museums throughout the country. The exhibition was shown without controversy until it reached Cincinnati, Ohio, where Cincinnati's Contemporary Arts Center and its director, Dennis Barrie, were charged with pandering obscenity and violating child pornography laws. The charges involved seven photographs out of the 175 in the exhibit. One of the photographs charged with being obscene showed a male urinating into the mouth of another male, and one of the pictures seized for violating child pornography legislation showed a toddler with her dress raised and her genitals exposed. After a lengthy and controversial trial, a jury found the museum and its director innocent on all counts.

During the same period of the Mapplethorpe controversy, Luther Campbell and his rap group 2 Live Crew were facing obscenity charges in Florida for their album "As Nasty As They Wanna Be." The album was reported to contain " . . . 87

descriptions of oral sex, 116 mentions of male and female genitalia and other lyrical passages referring to male ejaculation . . . " (*New York Times*, 12 June 1990, p. A10). In June of 1990, a federal district judge in Southern Florida ruled that the album was obscene. Subsequently, a Florida record-store owner was arrested and convicted on obscenity charges for selling a copy of the album.

These are two of numerous examples of controversies over obscenity in contemporary American society. Obscenity questions are associated with virtually every form of communication. Are sexually explicit movies and videocassettes obscene or constitutional? Are magazines and books featuring explicit sexual materials constitutionally protected under the First Amendment? To what extent can government control the sexual content of television and radio programs? Is dial-a-porn constitutionally protected? Can commercial establishments offer nude dancing? These and numerous other questions divide the American public and confound the American courts.

Two particularly difficult questions characterize the contemporary controversy over obscenity: (1) Is obscenity harmful? and (2) How is obscenity to be defined? We need to examine each of these questions because they are important recurring themes in the Supreme Court's obscenity decisions.

The question of the harmful effects of obscene materials is at the heart of the controversy. If widespread agreement existed that obscenity was not harmful, then presumably little reason would exist to have the government regulate or prohibit obscenity, and the Supreme Court would not be called upon to adjudicate in this area. No such agreement exists, however. Indeed, scholars and Supreme Court justices are in sharp disagreement regarding the harmful effects of obscenity. The Commission on Obscenity and Pornography in its 1970 *Report* issued a strong statement that the existing scholarly literature revealed no casual link between exposure to obscene or pornographic materials and the undertaking of sex crimes: "Research to date thus provides no substantial basis for the belief that erotic materials constitute a primary or significant cause of the development of character deficit or that they operate as a significant determinative factor in causing crime and delinquency" (*Report* 1970, p. 243). This conclusion was certainly not unanimous, however, among the Commission members. For example, in a separate minority report, two commission members, Morton Hill and Winfrey Link, called the majority report " . . . a Magna Carta for the pornographer" (p. 385) and characterized the research supporting the majority report as " . . . a shoddy piece of scholarship that will be quoted ad nauseam by cultural polluters and their attorneys within society" (p. 385).

This debate over the harm caused by obscenity has continued and indeed intensified since 1970. A second federal commission—The Attorney General's Commission on Pornography—was created in 1985 to study and make policy recommendations on pornography, and its *Final Report* (1986) reached dramatically different conclusions than were advanced in the 1970 report. The 1986 Commission examined four categories of sexually related materials: (1) sexually violent materials, (2) nonviolent materials depicting degradation, domination, subordination, or humiliation, (3) nonviolent and nondegrading material, and (4) nudity. Except for nudity, the Commission argued that definite harm could be causally linked to each of these forms of pornography (*Final Report* 1986, pp. 322–50). Predictably strong reactions arose from all directions to the Commission's report, including the American Civil Liberties Union, many psychologists, and a report issued by the Surgeon General's Workshop on Pornography and Public Health (see Zillmann 1989). The controversy over the harm caused by obscenity and pornography has been intensified even further in recent years as feminist scholars have argued strongly about the harmful effects of pornography on women (e.g., Itzin 1992, and MacKinnon 1993).

These sharp divisions among scholars regarding the harm caused by obscenity and pornography have been reflected in the opinions of Supreme Court justices. For example, in *Stanley v. Georgia* (1969), in which the Court upheld the right of a person to possess obscene materials in his home, Justice Marshall in his majority opinion rejected Georgia's argument that exposure to obscene materials could cause sex crimes or deviant sexual behavior: "There appears to be little empirical basis for that assertion" (394 U.S. at 566). However, Chief Justice Burger in *Miller v. California* (1973) offered a very different perspective, citing favorably the Hill-Link minority report in the 1970 *Report* that " . . . there is at least an arguable correlation between obscene materials and crime" (413 U.S. at 58).

In addition to the deep division over the issue of whether obscenity is harmful, a second major source of disagreement involves the issue of how to define obscenity. The problem of defining obscenity has been one of the most troublesome and enduring issues to confront the Supreme Court. As we will examine in detail in the next section, the Court has advanced several different definitions of obscenity, but all of them have been surrounded by ambiguity, confusion, and controversy. Justice Stewart in *Jacobellis v. Ohio* (1964) expressed his frustration about the difficulty of defining obscenity by stating that the Court was " . . . faced with the task of trying to define what may be indefinable" (378 U.S. at 197). Stewart's frustration was epitomized in his well-known statement that he could not define the obscene, but "I know it when I see it" (*Jacobellis*, 378 U.S. at 197).

The inherently difficult problem of defining obscenity is compounded by the term's close association with an equally elusive word, pornography. Ambiguity surrounds the term pornography in both scholarly writings and in the opinions of the Court. Catherine Itzin (1992, pp. 435–36) argues that the legal definition originally formulated by Andrea Dworkin and Catherine MacKinnon (1985) marked a major breakthrough in defining pornography:

> *Pornography means the graphic sexually explicit subordination of women through pictures and/or words that also includes one or more of the following: (i) women are presented dehumanized as sexual objects, things, or commodities; or (ii) women are presented as sexual objects who enjoy humiliation or pain; or (iii) women are presented as sexual objects experiencing sexual pleasure in rape, incest or other sexual assault; or (iv) women are presented as sexual objects tied up, cut up or mutilated or bruised or physically hurt; or (v) women are presented in postures or positions of sexual submission, servility, or display; or (vi) women's body parts—including but not limited to vaginas, breasts, or buttocks—are exhibited such that women are reduced to those parts; or (vii) women are presented being penetrated by objects or animals; or (viii) women are presented in scenarios of degradation, humiliation, injury, torture, shown as filthy or inferior, bleeding, bruised, or hurt in a context that makes these conditions sexual.*

Precise and detailed as this definition is, it has not come to be widely accepted. Versions of this definition were incorporated into local ordinances in Minneapolis, Minnesota, and Indianapolis, Indiana, but they did not survive legal challenge. The problems of defining pornography have been summarized by Donald Downs (1989, pp. xxii–xxiii): "Pornography comes in many forms, conveys different messages, and, depending on the situation, has a range of effects. This point applies to those who wish to censor pornography as well as jealous libertarians who refuse to acknowledge the potential harms of pornography."

Not surprisingly, the Supreme Court has been no more successful in defining pornography than have scholars. Indeed, the Court's opinions provide a bewildering array of references to the term pornography. In the landmark decision of *Miller v. California* (1973), Chief Justice Burger at one point in his majority opinion equated obscenity and pornography when he stated that the Court had struggled unsuccessfully since the *Roth* case in determining " . . . what constitutes obscene, pornographic material subject to regulation under the State's police power" (413 U.S. at 22). Later in his *Miller* opinion, however, Burger stated that obscenity and pornography are not the same, because obscenity involves " . . . 'hard core' pornography . . . " (413 U.S. at 29). Justice Stevens in *Fort Wayne Books v. Indiana* (1989) also suggested that obscenity and pornography were different because obscenity was not protected by the First Amendment while pornography could be protected, but the line between the two was " 'dim and uncertain' " (498 U.S. at 79).

We will largely ignore the term pornography in this chapter. One reason involves the complex definition problems we have just discussed. More fundamentally, however, the Supreme Court has not focused its attention on the term pornography. Instead the Court has concentrated on the word obscenity, and this will be our primary concentration as well.

Supreme Court Decision Making in Obscenity Cases

Just as the Court has used various doctrines or tests to guide and facilitate its decision making in other areas of freedom of speech and freedom of the press, so too has the Court developed judicial tests in its obscenity cases. The tests developed in the area of obscenity have been unique, however, because the Court has never viewed the obscene as coming within the protection of the First Amendment. Thus, the Court has tried to develop precise definitions of obscenity in order that determinations could be made by everyone concerned—producers and distributors of sexual materials, legislators, police and prosecutors, and judges—as to what was permissible and what was prohibited. As we saw in the previous section of this chapter, this has not been an easy task for the Court. In this section we will examine the major definitional tests the Court has used throughout history, and then in the remainder of this chapter we will examine the historical evolution of these tests in greater detail.

The initial standard for judging obscenity was the ***Hicklin test,*** developed in the nineteenth century. This case—*Regina v. Hicklin* (1868)—was an English case rather than an American case, involving a pamphlet that was antireligious and had sexual content. The test set forth in *Hicklin* was " . . . whether the tendency of the matter charged as obscenity is to deprave and corrupt those whose minds are open to such immoral influences, and into whose hands a publication of this sort may fall" (*Report* 1970, p. 299). This test obviously provided little protection for sexually oriented expression because the effect of the test was to make obscene any material that could conceivably have a negative influence on the very young. The *Hicklin* test was generally used in both state and federal prosecutions of obscene materials throughout the last half of the nineteenth century and the first half of the twentieth century, including the 1878 Supreme Court case of *Ex parte Jackson,* which upheld the Comstock Act.

The *Hicklin* test was explicitly rejected in 1957 in *Roth v. United States,* our case study that began this chapter. In his majority opinion in *Roth,* Justice Brennan argued that the *Hicklin* test was much too sweeping in scope because it resulted in materials being declared obscene that were clearly within the protection of the First Amendment. The proper test of obscenity, Brennan argued, was one that had been gradually emerging in the state and federal courts: " . . . whether to the average person, applying contemporary community standards, the dominant theme of the material taken as a whole appeals to prurient interest" (354 U.S. at 489). Brennan sought with this test to provide substantially greater protection to freedom of expression involving sexual matters; for under the new test the reference point was the normal adult rather than a young child, the entire work had to be considered rather than an isolated portion of the work, and the material had to appeal to "lustful"—or "shameful or morbid"—thoughts (354 U.S. at 487).

Although the ***Roth* test** dramatically strengthened the constitutional protection for sexually-oriented expression, Brennan nonetheless emphasized that obscenity was not within the meaning of the First Amendment under the social value doctrine of *Chaplinsky v. New Hampshire* (1942), which we discussed in Chapter 7. Under the ***Chaplinsky* test,** ideas that are lacking in social value are not protected from government regulation and control, and " . . . implicit in the history of the First Amendment is the rejection of obscenity as utterly without redeeming social importance" (354 U.S. at 484–85).

The Warren Court struggled continuously in the late fifties and sixties with the *Roth* test, attempting to expand and clarify its meaning. In *Jacobellis v. Ohio* (1964), for example, the Court ruled that the community standards of the *Roth* test were national in scope, thus preventing more conservative states and cities from controlling sexually related materials based on their more localized standards.

Finally, in *Memoirs v. Massachusetts* (1966), the Court set forth an expanded, three-part test of obscenity. Under the ***Memoirs* test,** " . . . three elements must coalesce: it must be established that (a) the dominant theme of the material taken as a whole appeals to a prurient interest in sex; (b) the material is patently offensive because it affronts contemporary community standards relating to the description or representation of sexual matters; and (c) the material is utterly without redeeming social value" (388 U.S. at 418). Under this test, something could be found obscene only if all three of these characteristics were present, thus providing extraordinarily strong protection for sexually oriented expression. This opinion was, however, a plurality opinion supported by only three justices, and the justices were sharply divided as to whether the *Memoirs* test was a logical extension of the *Roth* test or a dramatic departure from it. Justice Douglas, for example, characterized the *Memoirs* case as simply one in which " . . . the *Roth* test was elaborated . . . " (*Miller v. California*, 413 U.S. at 38, 1973). For Chief Justice Burger, however, the *Memoirs* decision " . . . produced a drastically altered test . . . " (*Miller v. California*, 413 U.S. at 22, 1973).

The Burger Court substantially modified the *Roth/Memoirs* test in the landmark 1973 case of *Miller v. California* and its companion case of *Paris Adult Theatre v. Slaton*. The impact of membership change on the policies of the Court is crystal clear here, for Richard Nixon's four appointees—Burger, Blackmun, Rehnquist, and Powell—joined White to create a majority opinion that altered the *Roth* test in several significant ways. In his majority opinion, Burger set forth the new ***Miller* test** as follows: "The basic guidelines for the trier of fact must be: (a) whether 'the average person, applying contemporary community standards' would find the work, taken as a whole, appeals to the prurient interest . . . ; (b) whether the work depicts or describes in a patently offensive way, sexual conduct specifically defined by the applicable state law; and (c) whether the work, taken as a whole, lacks serious literary, artistic, political or scientific value" (413 U.S. at 24).

The *Miller* test represented an effort by the Court to give state and local governments substantially greater authority to control obscenity than they had possessed under the *Roth/Memoirs* test. The most important difference involved the third prong, the social value component. Under *Roth/Memoirs*, a work could be found obscene only if it was "utterly without redeeming social value," which Burger correctly characterized in *Miller* as being a burden that government prosecutors found virtually impossible to prove. Any isolated reference to Shakespeare, for example, could conceivably establish the "social value" of a work under the *Roth* test. Under the *Miller* test, however, the work must be viewed as a whole, and furthermore, it must possess "serious" value. This prong of the *Miller* test is so central to the definition of obscenity that the *Miller* test is sometimes referred to as the **LAPS test**, emphasizing the centrality of the serious *l*iterary, *a*rtistic, *p*olitical, or *s*cientific value. The *Miller* test also differed sharply from the *Roth* test in emphasizing applicable state laws in the second prong, for under the *Roth* line of cases the Court had established that national standards were to be used in assessing obscenity.

The *Miller* test remains controlling precedent, but the Court has provided further refinement of the test. One important elaboration occurred in 1987 in *Pope v. Illinois.* In this case the Court faced the issue of whether state or national standards should be used in evaluating the third or social value prong of the obscenity test. The Court ruled unanimously that a national standard was to be employed with the third prong of the *Miller* test, even though the first two prongs were to be analyzed by state criteria.

Pre-Warren Court Period

Having completed an examination of the historic origins, some major contemporary conflicts, and the major tests associated with the issue of obscenity, we now have the foundation for a detailed examination of the Supreme Court's obscenity cases. The Court's decisions are not characterized by consistency, coherence, and agreement. Instead, as the justices of the Court have acknowledged, we are embarking on a study of the Court's single most contentious area of civil rights and liberties. Justice Harlan referred to this as " . . . the intractable obscenity problem" (*Interstate Circuit, Inc. v. Dallas*, 390 U.S. at 704, 1968), and in the same case Harlan characterized the Court's obscenity cases as involving " . . . a variety of views among the members of the Court unmatched in any other course of constitutional adjudication" (390 U.S. at 704–5). Chief Justice Burger in *Miller* referred to the " . . . somewhat tortured history of the Court's obscenity decisions" (413 U.S. at 20). In *Paris Adult Theatre v. Slaton* (1973), the companion case to *Miller*, Justice Brennan rejected Burger's *Miller* test as an effective approach to the issue of obscenity, but he did agree with the Chief Justice about the difficult nature of this area of constitutional law: "No other aspect of the First Amendment has, in recent years, demanded so substantial a commitment of our time, generated such disharmony of views, and remained so resistant to the formulation of stable and manageable standards" (413 U.S. at 73).

The intractable problem of obscenity is of relatively recent vintage, however. During the long period of Court history before Earl Warren became chief justice in 1953, the Court heard very few cases dealing with obscenity and was never directly confronted with the question of the relationship of obscenity to the First Amendment. Nonetheless, the Warren Court did not operate on a blank slate. The high court had issued a few rulings relevant to the obscenity question, and both state and federal courts had been involved in a substantial amount of obscenity litigation.

The Supreme Court's decisions prior to the Warren era that had the greatest impact on modern obscenity law were not cases that dealt directly with sexually oriented expression. Instead, these cases dealt with other issues of freedom of expression and address obscenity only in *dicta.* Two key cases were *Near v. Minnesota* (1931) and *Chaplinsky v. New Hampshire* (1942), both of which we have discussed in detail in previous chapters. The Court took the position that the obscene was beyond constitutional protection. In *Near*, the Court stated that "the primary requirements of decency may be enforced against obscene publications"

(283 U.S. at 716). The Court developed this position more fully in *Chaplinsky*, where the Court argued that the First Amendment protected only expression that has social value, and the obscene was among those forms of expression lacking such social value: "There are certain well-defined and narrowly limited classes of speech, the prevention and punishment of which have never been thought to raise any constitutional problem. These include the lewd and obscene. . . . It has been well observed that such utterances are no essential part of any exposition of ideas, and are of such slight social value as a step to truth that any benefit that may be derived from them is clearly outweighed by the social interest in order and morality . . . " (315 U.S. at 571–72).

Although the Supreme Court prior to the Warren Court era did not have to confront directly the issue of the relationship of the First Amendment and obscenity and consequently did not have to deal with the problem of defining obscenity, the lower federal courts as well as the state courts did have to confront these matters. During the last half of the nineteenth century and the first half of the twentieth century, two divergent approaches to obscenity emerged. The *Hicklin* test was the more restrictive standard, providing the government with an extraordinarily wide range of control over sexually oriented materials. Gradually, however, challenges arose to the *Hicklin* test, and more liberal ideas emerged, which found ultimate acceptance in the 1957 *Roth* test.

As was discussed in the previous section, the *Hicklin* test originated in the English case of *Regina v. Hicklin* (1868), but this test became widely incorporated into American law during the late nineteenth and early twentieth centuries (Schauer 1976, pp. 15–24). The test placed extraordinarily tight restrictions on freedom of expression because of several specific standards associated with the test. Any portion of a publication could be examined in isolation to determine if the entire work was obscene. In addition, obscenity was to be judged by its possible effect on the least susceptible members of a community, which meant children or " . . . the mentally weak or immature . . . " (Schauer 1976, p. 16).

Challenges arose throughout the first half of the twentieth century to the restrictive features of the *Hicklin* test. One of the most important cases involved the question of whether James Joyce's *Ulysses* could be imported into the United States. In *United States v. One Book Called "Ulysses"* (1933), New York federal district judge Woolsey rejected two major facets of the *Hicklin* test by inquiring into the intent of the author and by viewing the work as a whole rather than focusing on isolated portions of the book. Woolsey ruled that the intent of the author was to produce a serious literary work; furthermore, the sexual content of the book was an important and integral part of the entire work. The *Hicklin* focus on the least susceptible mind also came under sharp attack in the first half of the twentieth century, with most cases adopting instead a "reasonable" or "average" person standard for judging obscenity (Schauer 1976, p. 28). Finally, the twentieth-century courts began to recognize the importance of evolving community standards in evaluating sexually oriented forms of expression.

The Warren Court Era

The Warren Court, unlike its predecessors, could not avoid the obscenity issue. The conflict between the restrictive *Hicklin* test and the emerging liberal standards of many state and federal courts required an ultimate resolution by the Supreme Court. Furthermore, the post-World War II decade in American society had experienced a dramatic proliferation of sexually oriented materials. This development led to attempts by local, state, and federal officials to control allegedly obscene materials, and these efforts were frequently challenged by lawsuits claiming interference with the First Amendment.

The Warren Court's approach to the obscenity issue was one of declaring obscenity beyond the protection of the First Amendment but also defining it in a narrow manner that provided a substantial amount of constitutional protection to sexually oriented forms of expression. The Court's initial formulation came in *Roth*, and in a series of cases in the sixties the Court elaborated and expanded the *Roth* definition, culminating in the three-part test of *Memoirs*. These cases were characterized by an enormous amount of confusion and disagreement among the justices, but the overall trend was one in which the Court defined obscenity so narrowly that it was difficult to find anything obscene.

Writing for a five-person majority in the *Roth* case, Justice Brennan began his opinion by arguing that the Court had always assumed that obscenity was not protected as freedom of expression. The First Amendment was intended to protect ideas having some degree of social importance, but the obscene was a form of expression " . . . utterly without redeeming social importance" (354 U.S. at 484–85).

Having declared obscenity to be outside of the First Amendment, Brennan was thus forced to provide a definition of it. Brennan emphasized that sex and obscenity were not the same thing, and he rejected the *Hicklin* test as an improper standard. Instead, Brennan reasoned, obscenity should be defined by the test that had been emerging to challenge and replace the *Hicklin* standard: " . . . whether to the average person, applying contemporary community standards, the dominant theme of the material taken as a whole appeals to prurient interest" (354 U.S. at 489). Applying this test to the *Roth* case and the companion *Alberts* case, Brennan argued that the trial courts had used the proper standards, and therefore the convictions were affirmed.

Roth v. United States

354 U.S. 476, 77 S.Ct. 1304, 1 L. Ed. 2d 1498 (1957)

[The facts of the case are omitted because they were presented in the case study at the beginning of this chapter.]

■ This is an important case because it was the first time the Court dealt directly with the obscenity issue, ruling the obscene as beyond constitutional protection and also setting forth a definition of obscenity. As you read this case, consider the following questions: (1) Did Brennan in his majority opinion present a convincing argument that obscene expression does not come within the protection of the First Amendment? (2) What is the Court's definition of obscenity, and how satisfactory is the definition for those affected by it, including producers and distributors of sexually oriented materials as well as police, prosecutors, and lower court judges?

Vote:

6 justices voted to uphold Roth's obscenity conviction (Brennan, Burton, Clark, Frankfurter, Warren, Whittaker).

3 justices voted to overturn Roth's obscenity conviction (Black, Douglas, Harlan).

Justice Brennan delivered the opinion of the Court.

* * *

The dispositive question is whether obscenity is utterance within the area of protected speech and press. Although this is the first time the question has been squarely presented to this Court, either under the First Amendment or under the Fourteenth Amendment, expressions found in numerous opinions indicate that this Court has always assumed that obscenity is not protected by the freedoms of speech and press.

The guaranties of freedom of expression in effect in 10 of the 14 states which by 1792 had ratified the Constitution, gave no absolute protection for every utterance. Thirteen of the 14 States provided for the prosecution of libel, and all of those States made either blasphemy or profanity, or both, statutory crimes. As early as 1712, Massachusetts made it criminal to publish "any filthy, obscene, or profane song, pamphlet, libel or mock sermon" in imitation or mimicking of religious services. Thus, profanity and obscenity were related offenses.

In light of this history it is apparent that the unconditional phrasing of the First Amendment was not intended to protect every utterance. This phrasing did not prevent this Court from concluding that libelous utterances are not within the area of constitutionally protected speech. At the time of the adoption of the First Amendment, obscenity law was not as fully developed as libel law, but there is sufficiently contemporaneous evidence to show that obscenity, too, was outside the protection intended for speech and press.

The protection given speech and press was fashioned to assure unfettered interchange of ideas for the bringing about of political and social changes desired by the people. * * *

* * *

All ideas having even the slightest redeeming social importance—unorthodox ideas, controversial ideas, even ideas hateful to the prevailing climate of opinion—have the full protection of the guaranties, unless excludable because they encroach upon the limited area of more important interests. But implicit in the history of the First Amendment is the rejection of obscenity as utterly without redeeming social importance. This rejection for that reason is mirrored in the universal judgment that obscenity should be restrained, reflected in the international agreement of over 50 nations, in the obscenity laws of all of the 48 States, and in the 20 obscenity laws enacted by the Congress from 1842-1956. This is the same judgment expressed by this Court in *Chaplinsky v. New Hampshire* [1942]: "There are certain well-defined and narrowly limited classes of speech, the prevention and punishment of which have never been thought to raise any Constitutional problem. These include the lewd and obscene. . . . It has been well observed that such utterances are no essential part of any exposition of ideas, and are of such slight social value as a step to truth that any benefit that may be derived from them is clearly outweighed by the social interest in order and morality . . . ."

We hold that obscenity is not within the area of constitutionally protected speech or press.

* * *

However, sex and obscenity are not synonymous. Obscene material is material which deals with sex in a manner appealing to prurient interest. The portrayal of sex, e.g., in art, literature and scientific works, is not itself sufficient reason to deny material the constitutional protection of freedom of speech and press. Sex, a great and mysterious motive force in human life, has indisputably been a subject of absorbing interest to mankind through the ages; it is one of the vital problems of human interest and public concern. * * *

* * *

The fundamental freedoms of speech and press have contributed greatly to the development and well-being of our free society and are indispensable to its continued growth. Ceaseless vigilance is the watchword to prevent their erosion by Congress or by the States. The door barring federal and state intrusion into this area cannot be left ajar; it must be kept tightly closed and opened only the slightest crack necessary to prevent encroachment upon more important interests. It is therefore vital that the standards for judging obscenity safeguard the protection of freedom of speech and press for material which does not treat sex in a manner appealing to prurient interest.

The early leading standard of obscenity allowed material to be judged merely by the effect of an isolated excerpt upon particularly susceptible persons. *Regina v. Hicklin* (1868). Some American courts adopted this standard but later decisions have rejected it and substituted this test: whether to the average person, applying contemporary community standards, the dominant theme of the material taken as a whole appeals to prurient interest. The *Hicklin* test, judging obscenity by the effect of isolated passages upon the most susceptible persons, might well encompass material legitimately treating with sex, and so it must be rejected as unconstitutionally restrictive of the freedoms of speech and press. On the other hand, the substituted standard provides safeguards adequate to withstand the charge of constitutional infirmity.

Both trial courts below sufficiently followed the proper standard. Both courts used the proper definition of obscenity.

* * *

Many decisions have recognized that these terms of obscenity statutes are not precise. This Court, however, has consistently held that lack of precision is not itself offensive to the requirements of due process. " . . . [T]he Constitution does not require impossible standards"; all that is required is that the language "conveys sufficiently definite warning as to the proscribed conduct when measured by common understanding and practices . . . ." * * *

In summary, then, we hold that these statutes, applied according to the proper standard for judging obscenity, do not offend constitutional safeguards against convictions based upon protected material, or fail to give men in acting adequate notice of what is prohibited.

* * *

The judgments are Affirmed.

* * *

Justice Harlan dissenting.

* * *

We are faced here with the question whether the federal obscenity statute, as construed and applied in this case, violates the First Amendment to the Constitution. To me, this question is of quite a different order than one where we are dealing with state legislation under the Fourteenth Amendment. I do not think it follows that state and federal powers in this area are the same, and that just because the State may suppress a particular utterance, it is automatically permissible for the Federal Government to do the same. * * *

The Constitution differentiates between those areas of human conduct subject to the regulation of the States and those subject to the powers of the Federal Government. The substantive powers of the two governments, in many instances, are distinct. * * *

The Federal Government has, for example, power to restrict seditious speech directed against it, because that Government certainly has the substantive authority to protect itself against revolution. But in dealing with obscenity we are faced with the converse situation, for the interests which obscenity statutes purportedly protect are primarily entrusted to the care, not of the Federal Government, but of the States. Congress has no substantive power over sexual morality. Such powers as the Federal Government has in this field are but incidental to its other powers, here the postal power, and are not of the same nature as those possessed by the States, which bear direct responsibility for the protection of the local moral fabric. * * *

* * *

Not only is the federal interest in protecting the Nation against pornography attenuated, but the dangers of federal censorship in this field are far greater than anything the States may do. It has often been said that one of the great strengths of our federal system is that we have, in the forty-eight States, forty-eight experimental social laboratories. * * * Different States will have different attitudes toward the same work of literature. The same book which is freely read in one State might be classed as obscene in another. And it seems to me that no overwhelming danger to our freedom to experiment and to gratify our tastes in literature is likely to result from the suppression of a borderline book in one of the States, so long as there is no uniform nation-wide suppression of the book, and so long as other States are free to experiment with the same or bolder books.

Quite a different situation is presented, however, where the Federal Government imposes the ban. The danger is perhaps not great if the people of one State, through their legislature, decide that "Lady Chatterley's Lover" goes so far beyond the acceptable standards of candor that it will be deemed offensive and non-sellable, for the State next door is still free to make its own choice. At least we do not have one uniform standard. But the dangers to free thought and expression are truly great if the Federal Government imposes a blanket ban over the Nation on such a book. The prerogative of the States to differ on their ideas of morality will be destroyed, the ability of the States to experiment will be stunted. The fact that the people of one state cannot read some of the works of D. H. Lawrence seems to me, if not wise or desirable, at least acceptable. But that no person in the United States should be allowed to do so seems to me to be intolerable, and violative of both the letter and spirit of the First Amendment.

I judge this case, then, in view of what I think is the attenuated federal interest in this field, in view of the very real danger of a deadening uniformity which can result from nation-wide federal censorship, and in view of the fact that the constitutionality of this conviction must be weighed against the First and not the Fourteenth Amendment. So viewed, I do not think that this conviction can be upheld. * * *

* * *

Justice Douglas, with whom Justice Black concurs, dissenting.

When we sustain these convictions, we make the legality of a publication turn on the purity of thought which a book or tract instills in the mind of the reader. I do not think we can approve that standard and be faithful to the command of the First Amendment, which by its terms is a restraint on Congress and which by the Fourteenth is a restraint on the States.

* * *

The test of obscenity the Court endorses today gives the censor free range over a vast domain. To allow the State to step in and punish mere speech or publication that the judge or the jury thinks has an *undesirable* impact on thoughts but that is not shown to be a part of unlawful action is drastically to curtail the First Amendment. * * *

If we were certain that impurity of sexual thoughts impelled to action, we would be on less dangerous ground in punishing the distributors of this sex literature, But it is by no means clear that obscene literature, as so defined, is a significant factor in influencing substantial deviations from the community standards.

* * *

The absence of dependable information on the effect of obscene literature on human conduct should make us wary. It should put us on the side of protecting society's interest in literature, except and unless it can be said that the particular publication has an impact on action that the government can control.

* * *

The standard of what offends "the common conscience of the community" conflicts, in my judgment, with the command of the First Amendment that "Congress shall make no law . . . abridging the freedom of speech, or of the press." Certainly that standard would not be an acceptable one if religion, economics, politics, or philosophy were involved. How does it become a constitutional standard when literature treating with sex is concerned?

Any test that turns on what is offensive to the community's standard is too loose, too capricious, too destructive of freedom of expression to be squared with the First Amendment. * * *

* * *

* * * I reject too the implication that problems of freedom of speech and of the press are to be resolved by weighing against the values of free expression, the judgment of the Court that a particular form of that expression has "no redeeming social importance." The First Amendment, its prohibition in terms absolute, was designed to preclude courts as well as legislatures from weighing the values of speech against silence. The First Amendment puts free speech in the preferred position.

Freedom of expression can be suppressed if, and to the extent that, it is so closely brigaded with illegal action as to be an inseparable part of it. * * * I would give the broad sweep of the First Amendment full support. I have the same confidence in the ability of our people to reject noxious literature as I have in their capacity to sort out the true from the false in theology, economics, politics, or any other field.

The *Roth* decision was an attempt by the Court to bring clarity to a novel and controversial area of constitutional law, but the decision was more successful in raising questions than in providing answers. One major question was what did it mean that obscenity was to be determined by an "average person" using "contemporary community standards." Were these community values to be based on local, state, or national standards? Another unresolved question centered around the idea that the "dominant theme" of the work was to be considered. Did a work have to focus primarily or exclusively on sex to be obscene? Finally, what did the Court mean by a "prurient interest" in sex? Brennan offered a definition of this phrase in a footnote, but the use of the words "lustful," "longing," and "itching" did not bring much clarity to the concept of prurience.

Given these ambiguities, the Court was inevitably confronted with a series of cases in which it was forced to develop further the definition of obscenity set forth in *Roth*. Among the most important of these cases were *Kingsley International Corporation v. Regents of University of New York* (1959), *Manual Enterprises, Inc. v. Day* (1962), *Jacobellis v. Ohio* (1964), and *A Book Named "John Cleland's Memoirs of a Woman of Pleasure" v. Massachusetts* (1966). In *Kingsley*, the Court considered whether the government could prohibit the showing of the movie *Lady Chatterley's Lover*, and the Court ruled that works could not be banned on the basis that the dominant theme dealt with sexuality. *Manual Enterprises* expanded the idea of prurient interest by requiring that obscene materials must appeal to prurient interest in a patently offensive manner. The *Jacobellis* case was important because the Court ruled that community standards were to be national rather than state or local in scope. In addition, in *Jacobellis* Justice Brennan elaborated further on the concept of the dominant theme of a work by arguing that it had to be utterly without redeeming social value in order to be obscene. These ideas were incorporated into a three-part test of obscenity in the *Memoirs* case, all three of which had to be present: (1) the material's dominant theme taken as a whole appealed to a prurient interest in sex; (2) the material presented sex in a patently offensive manner based upon national standards; and (3) the material was utterly without redeeming social value.

The evolution of the *Roth* test into the *Memoirs* test was characterized by intense disagreement and confusion among the members of the Court. This was seen most vividly in the fact that no majority agreement emerged regarding the definition of obscenity in any Warren Court case after *Roth*. In *Memoirs*, for example, only Warren, Fortas, and Brennan subscribed to the three-part test, and Warren had serious reservations about the use of a national standard. Another example of the Court's divisions over the issue of obscenity can be seen in three companion cases in 1966 dealing with the question of how sexually oriented materials can be advertised; in these three cases, seven justices wrote fourteen opinions, but no opinion was joined by a majority of the Court.

Deeply frustrated over the difficulty of achieving consensus regarding a workable definition of obscenity, the Court took a different path toward obscenity in the 1967 case of *Redrup v. New York*. Redrup was employed by the owner of a New York newstand that sold books and magazines of a sexually explicit nature. A plainclothes police officer bought two books entitled *Lust Pool* and *Shame Agent*, determined that they were obscene, and arrested Redrup for pandering obscenity. Redrup was convicted, but the Supreme Court overturned his conviction as well as two other convictions in companion cases to *Redrup*. In a brief per curiam opinion joined by seven justices, the Court acknowledged that they were deeply divided over the proper definition of obscenity but said that the convictions in all three cases could not stand regardless of which definition was used.

Although seemingly a minor case at the time, *Redrup* can be viewed historically as an important turning point in the obscenity cases of the Warren Court. Beginning with *Redrup*, the Court backed away from deriving a definition of obscenity that could command the support of a majority of the Court, apparently viewing this as an exercise in futility. Instead, the justices, using their various definitions of obscenity, took the approach between 1967 and 1969 of summarily reversing thirty-two lower court obscenity convictions by simply citing *Redrup* (Kobylka 1991, p. 6).

The *Redrup* decision and the numerous reversals of obscenity convictions that followed *Redrup* clearly revealed that the Warren Court was willing to provide broad protection for expression related to sexual matters in American society. In *Redrup*, however, the Court did identify three areas where governments could exercise substantial control over sexually explicit materials: (1) juveniles, (2) privacy, and (3) pandering. In *Redrup* the Court indicated that government could pass legislation which " . . . reflected a specific and limited concern for juveniles" (386 U.S. at 786), and a majority strongly affirmed this principle a year later in *Ginsberg v. New York* (1968) where the Court upheld the conviction of Samuel Ginsberg who was charged with selling to a sixteen-year-old boy two magazines that featured female nudity but were not legally obscene. The *Redrup* opinion also stated that governments could regulate sexually oriented publications to prevent " . . . an assault upon individual privacy by publication in a manner so obtrusive as to make it impossible for an unwilling individual to avoid exposure to it" (386 U.S. at 768). The primary practical effect of this principle was to restrict the sexual explicitness of magazine and book covers as well as motion picture advertisements. Finally, in *Redrup* the Court reaffirmed its earlier decision in *Ginzburg v. United States* (1966) against "pandering" sexually oriented materials. In *Ginzburg*, a five-person majority had upheld the conviction of Ralph Ginzburg, publisher of *Eros* magazine; although the Court did not find the material to be legally obscene, the federal convictions under the Comstock Act were upheld because advertisements involved " . . . an exploitation of interest in titillation by pornography . . . " (383 U.S. at 475).

The liberal thrust of the Warren Court's obscenity decisions culminated in the Court's last major case in this area, *Stanley v. Georgia* (1969), in which the Court ruled unanimously that a person has the constitutionally protected right to possess obscene materials in the privacy of one's own home. Marshall wrote a forceful majority opinion, arguing that Georgia could not constitutionally make the mere private possession of obscene materials a criminal activity. Marshall relied on both the explicit guarantees of free expression of the First Amendment and the implicit constitutional guarantee of privacy. In a frequently quoted passage, Marshall stated: "If the First Amendment means anything, it means that a State has no business telling a man, sitting alone in his own house, what books he may read or what films he may watch. Our whole constitutional heritage rebels at the thought of giving government the power to control men's minds" (394 U.S. at 565). Marshall emphasized that this decision did not undermine the *Roth* case; the states still possessed broad powers to regulate obscenity, but those powers did not extend into the private possession of obscene materials in one's home.

Stanley v. Georgia

394 U.S. 557, 89 S.Ct. 1243, 22 L.Ed. 2d 542 (1969)

■ Robert Stanley was suspected of engaging in illegal bookmaking activities, and federal and state agents obtained a warrant to search his home. Although the agents found little evidence of bookmaking activity, they did find three reels of eight-millimeter film in a desk drawer in an upstairs bedroom. Using a projector and screen found in Stanley's residence, the officers viewed the films and determined they were obscene. Stanley was arrested and convicted of possessing obscene materials by a Georgia jury, and the Georgia Supreme Court affirmed the conviction. Stanley appealed his case to the United States Supreme Court.

This case is important because the Warren Court made a sharp distinction between the production/distribution of obscene material and the private possession of obscene materials in one's own home. As you read this case, consider the following questions: (1) How did Marshall's majority opinion establish a relationship between freedom of expression and the right of privacy? (2) Is it logically consistent for the Court to hold that the production and distribution of obscene materials is beyond constitutional protection but that the private possession of such materials is protected? Can the same logic be applied to other areas, for example, illegal drugs? (3) Does the logic of the *Stanley* decision extend to consensual, homosexual relations in the privacy of one's own home?

Vote:

The Court voted unanimously that Stanley's constitutional rights were violated.

Justice Marshall delivered the opinion of the Court.

* * *

* * * Appellant argues here, and argued below, that the Georgia obscenity statute, insofar as it punishes mere private possession of obscene matter, violates the First Amendment, as made applicable to the States by the Fourteenth Amendment. For reasons set forth below, we agree that the mere private possession of obscene matter cannot constitutionally be made a crime.

* * *

* * * We do not believe that this case can be decided simply by citing *Roth*. *Roth* and its progeny certainly do mean that the First and Fourteenth Amendments recognize a valid governmental interest in dealing with the problem of obscenity. But the assertion of that interest cannot, in every context, be insulated from all constitutional protections. * * * That holding cannot foreclose an examination of the constitutional implications of a statute forbidding mere private possession of such material.

It is now well established that the Constitution protects the right to receive information and ideas. * * * This right to receive information and ideas, regardless of their social worth, is fundamental to our free society. Moreover, in the context of this case—a prosecution for mere possession of printed or filmed matter in the privacy of a person's own home—that right takes on an added dimension. For also fundamental is the right to be free, except in very limited circumstances, from unwanted governmental intrusions into one's privacy.

* * *

These are the rights that appellant is asserting in the case before us. He is asserting the right to read or observe what he pleases—the right to satisfy his intellectual and emotional needs in the privacy of his own home. He is asserting the right to be free from state inquiry into the contents of his library. Georgia contends that appellant does not have these rights, that there are certain types of materials that the individual may not read or even possess. Georgia justifies this assertion by arguing that the films in the present case are obscene. But we think that mere categorization of these films as "obscene" is insufficient justification for such a drastic invasion of personal liberties guaranteed by the First and Fourteenth Amendments. Whatever may be the justifications for other statutes regulating obscenity, we do not think they reach into the privacy of one's own home. If the First Amendment means anything, it means that a State has no business telling a man, sitting alone in his own house, what books he may read or what films he may watch. Our whole constitutional heritage rebels at the thought of giving government the power to control men's minds.

And yet, in the face of these traditional notions of individual liberty, Georgia asserts the right to protect the individual's mind from the effects of obscenity. We are not certain that this argument amounts to anything more than the assertion that the State has the right to control the moral content of a person's thoughts. To some, this may be a noble purpose, but it is wholly inconsistent with the philosophy of the First Amendment. * * *

Perhaps recognizing this, Georgia asserts that exposure to obscene materials may lead to deviant sexual behavior or crimes of sexual violence. There appears to be little empirical basis for that assertion. * * * Given the present state of knowledge, the State may no more prohibit possession of obscene matter on the ground that it may lead to antisocial conduct than it may prohibit possession of chemistry books on the ground that they may lead to the manufacture of homemade spirits.

It is true that in *Roth* this Court rejected the necessity of proving that exposure to obscene material would create a clear and present danger of antisocial conduct or would probably induce its recipients to such conduct. But that case dealt with public distribution of obscene materials, and such distribution is subject to different objections. For example, there is always the danger that obscene material might fall into the hands of children or that it might intrude upon the sensibilities or privacy of the general public. No such dangers are present in this case.

* * *

We hold that the First and Fourteenth Amendments prohibit making mere private possession of obscene material a crime. *Roth* and the cases following that decision are not impaired by today's holding. As we have said, the States retain broad power to regulate obscenity; that power simply does not extend to mere possession by the individual in the privacy of his own home. Accordingly, the judgment of the court below is reversed and the case is remanded for proceedings not inconsistent with this opinion.

It is so ordered.

As the Warren Court era came to an end in the spring of 1969, obscenity remained an unsettled and controversial area of constitutional law. Despite the admitted confusion and disagreement, however, the Warren Court had clearly handed down a series of decisions that provided strong protection for sexually oriented expression in all of its manifest forms. The Court had explicitly rejected the highly restrictive *Hicklin* test, substituting instead the much more liberal *Roth* test. Furthermore, in a series of subsequent decisions, the Court expanded the criteria of the *Roth* test to provide even greater protection for freedom of sexual expression by requiring national standards and by requiring a work to be utterly without redeeming social value in order to be obscene. Using these liberal criteria, the Court's decisional patterns strongly favored individuals claiming government interference with First Amendment guarantees. As can be seen in Table 8.1, the Warren Court ruled liberally in 73 percent of its full opinion obscenity cases. Furthermore, as was noted previously, following the *Redrup* decision the Court summarily reversed thirty-two lower court obscenity convictions.

The obscenity decisions of the Warren Court certainly had an effect on society. The decade of the sixties saw an explosion of sexually oriented materials in American society. The primary causes of this development can probably be linked most closely to changing societal values, because the decade of the sixties was one of massive cultural change, including the sexual revolution, which was closely associated with the advent of the birth control pill. While the decisions of the Supreme Court were probably not the primary factor explaining the dramatic growth in sexually oriented materials, the Court's policies certainly contributed to this development.

The Report of the Commission on Obscenity and Pornography in 1970 can be viewed as the final chapter of the Warren Court's history because the Commission's findings and conclusions provided strong support for the thrust of the Court's obscenity rulings. The Commission concluded that little evidence existed that obscenity and pornography caused harm to adults and recommended ". . . that federal, state, and local legislation prohibiting the sale, exhibition, or distribution of sexual materials to consenting adults should be repealed" (*Report* 1970, p. 51). The Commission had been created in 1968 by a Democratic Congress and appointed by a Democratic president, Lyndon Johnson. By the time the Commission issued its report in 1970, however, American society had changed dramatically. Republican Richard Nixon occupied the White House, and he was in the process of remaking the Supreme Court through the appointment of four new justices. These changes produced a significantly different approach to obscenity.

The Burger Court Era

The area of obscenity provides one of the clearest examples of the impact of changing Court membership on constitutional law. Richard Nixon had made the Court's obscenity decisions an important issue in the 1968 presidential campaign, and his 1969 nominee for chief justice—Warren Burger—shared Nixon's views in opposition to the liberal direction of the Warren Court's obscenity decisions as well as to the conclusions and recommendations of the 1970 *Report* on obscenity and pornography. With the addition of three more Nixon appointees to the Court—Blackmun, Rehnquist, and Powell—a new majority was now in place that significantly changed the Court's interpretation of obscenity law. The Burger Court's *Miller* test altered the *Roth/Memoirs* standards in several important ways, and it was much more supportive of government control of sexually oriented materials. Nonetheless, the Burger Court was continually confronted with vexing questions regarding the definition of obscenity, and the growth of sexually oriented materials continued throughout the seventies and eighties.

The new chief justice played a major role in altering the Court's approach to obscenity. Burger was initially unsuccessful as the remaining members of the Warren Court adhered to their liberal orientation in a series of 1970 cases, forcing Burger to attack the *Roth/Memoirs* test from dissent. By 1973, however, Burger was able to forge a new, conservative majority when White joined the four Nixon appointees in *Miller v. California*.

In upholding Marvin Miller's conviction for mailing advertisements for obscene materials, the Burger Court by a 5-4 vote explicitly modified the *Roth/Memoirs* test with a new, three-pronged test for judging obscenity. Burger began the majority opinion by reviewing " . . . the somewhat tortured history of the Court's obscenity decisions" (413 U.S. at 20), and he acknowledged that the Court had been unable since the 1957 *Roth* decision to achieve a majority consensus on the definition of obscenity. Consensus did exist, however, on the principle that obscene material was not protected by the First Amendment, and now, Burger announced, a Court majority had agreed upon a new, three-pronged test for obscenity: " . . . (a) whether 'the average person, applying contemporary community standards' would find the work, taken as a whole, appeals to the prurient interest . . .; (b) whether the work depicts or describes, in a patently offensive way, sexual conduct specifically defined by the applicable state law; and (c) whether the work, taken as a whole, lacks serious literary, artistic, political, or scientific value" (413 U.S. at 24).

Burger recognized that the two major innovations in this new test were the replacement of national standards with local standards and the alteration of the social value criterion from being utterly without redeeming social value to possessing serious social value. He therefore gave substantial attention to justifying these new definitional innovations. Burger rejected as unrealistic, unnecessary, and futile the national standard approach to determining the meaning of the key phrases of "prurient interest" and "patently offensive." The chief justice argued, "It is neither realistic nor constitutionally sound to read the First Amendment as requiring that the people of Maine or Mississippi accept public depiction of conduct found tolerable in Las Vegas or New York City. People in different States vary in their tastes and attitudes, and this diversity is not to be strangled by the absolutism of imposed uniformity" (413 U.S. at 32). In justifying the substitution of the much more demanding LAPS criterion (*l*iterary, *a*rtistic, *p*olitical, *s*cientific value) for the *Memoirs* standard of utterly without social value, Burger argued that the historic purpose of the First Amendment was to provide protection for the exchange of ideas relating to political and social change. Thus, Burger reasoned, the new social value test was much more consistent with the true meaning and intent of the First Amendment.

Miller v. California

413 U.S. 15, 93 S.Ct. 2607, 37 L.Ed. 2d 419 (1973)

■ Marvin Miller had conducted a mass mailing to advertise the sale of four illustrated books entitled "Intercourse," "Man-Woman," "Sex Orgies Illustrated," and "An Illustrated History of Pornography," as well as a film entitled "Marital Intercourse." These advertising brochures contained various explicit pictures and drawings that showed men and women in groups of two or more engaging in various sexual activities. A restaurant in Newport Beach, California, was on the mailing list, and the manager of the restaurant and his mother were offended by the unsolicited mail and complained to the local police. Miller was arrested and convicted under California law of knowingly distributing obscene material, and his conviction was upheld by a California appellate court. The United States Supreme Court agreed to review the case.

This case is important because the Burger Court set forth new definitional guidelines for obscenity, allowing state and local governments substantially more authority to regulate obscene materials. As you read the justices' opinions, consider the following questions: (1) Why did the Court majority modify the previous obscenity standards stemming from *Roth v. United States* (1957)? (2) Does the new definition of obscenity in *Miller* provide clearer guidelines than existed under *Roth* and its progeny? (3) Does Douglas in his dissent offer a reasonable solution to the obscenity question when he suggests that the people should decide the issue through a constitutional amendment?

Vote:

5 justices found Miller's conviction to be constitutional (Burger, Blackmun, Powell, Rehnquist, White).

4 justices found Miller's conviction to be unconstitutional (Brennan, Douglas, Marshall, Stewart).

Chief Justice Burger delivered the opinion of the Court.

This is one of a group of "obscenity-pornography" cases being reviewed by the Court in a re-examination of standards enunciated in earlier cases involving what Mr. Justice Harlan called "the intractable obscenity problem." * * *

* * *

This case involves the application of a State's criminal obscenity statute to a situation in which sexually explicit materials have been thrust by aggressive sales action upon unwilling recipients who had in no way indicated any desire to receive such materials. This Court has recognized that the States have a legitimate interest in prohibiting dissemination or exhibition of obscene material when the mode of dissemination carries with it a significant danger of offending the sensibilities of unwilling recipients or of exposure to juveniles. It is in this context that we are called on to define the standards which must be used to identify obscene material that a State may regulate without infringing on the First Amendment as applicable to the States through the Fourteenth Amendment.

* * * Since the Court now undertakes to formulate standards more concrete than those in the past, it is useful for us to focus on two of the landmark cases in the somewhat tortured history of the Court's obscenity decisions. In *Roth v. United States* (1957), the Court sustained a conviction under a federal statute punishing the mailing of "obscene, lewd, lascivious or filthy . . . " materials. The key to that holding was the Court's rejection of the claim that obscene materials were protected by the First Amendment. * * *

* * *

Nine years later, in *Memoirs v. Massachusetts* (1966), the Court veered sharply away from the *Roth* concept and, with only three justices in the plurality opinion, articulated a new test of obscenity. The plurality held that under the *Roth* definition

> "as elaborated in subsequent cases, three elements must coalesce: it must be established that (a) the dominant theme of the material taken as a whole appeals to a prurient interest in sex; (b) the material is patently offensive because it affronts contemporary community standards relating to the description or representation of sexual matters; and (c) the material is utterly without redeeming social value."

* * *

While *Roth* presumed "obscenity" to be "utterly without redeeming social importance," *Memoirs* required that to prove obscenity it must be affirmatively established that the material is "*utterly* without redeeming social value"—a burden virtually impossible to discharge under our criminal standards of proof.

* * *

Apart from the initial formulation in the *Roth* case, no majority of the Court has at any given time been able to agree on a standard to determine what constitutes obscene, pornographic material subject to regulation under the States' police power. We have seen "a variety of views among the members of the Court unmatched in any other course of constitutional adjudication." This is not remarkable, for in the area of freedom of speech and press the courts must always remain sensitive to any infringement of genuinely serious literary, artistic, political or scientific expression. This is an area in which there are few eternal verities.

The case we now review was tried on the theory that the California Penal Code approximately incorporates the three-stage *Memoirs* test. But now the *Memoirs* test has been abandoned as unworkable by its author, and no Member of the Court today supports the *Memoirs* formulation.

This much has been categorically settled by the Court, that obscene material is unprotected by the First Amendment. We acknowledged, however, the inherent dangers of undertaking to regulate any form of expression. State statutes designed to regulate obscene materials must be carefully limited. As a result, we now confine the permissible scope of such regulation to works which depict or describe sexual conduct. That conduct must be specifically defined by the applicable state law, as written or authoritatively construed. A state offense must also be limited to works which, taken as a whole, appeal to prurient interest in sex, which portray sexual conduct in a patently offensive way, and which, taken as a whole, do not have serious literary, artistic, political or scientific value.

The basic guidelines for the trier of fact must be: (a) whether "the average person, applying contemporary community standards" would find that the work, taken as a whole, appeals to the prurient interest; (b) whether the work depicts or describes, in a patently offensive way, sexual conduct specifically defined by the applicable state law; and (c) whether the work, taken as a whole, lacks serious literary, artistic, political, or scientific value. We do not adopt as a constitutional standard the "*utterly* without redeeming social value" test of *Memoirs v. Massachusetts*; that concept has never commanded the adherence of more than three Justices at one time. If a state law that regulates obscene material is thus limited, as written or construed, the First Amendment values applicable to the States through the Fourteenth Amendment are adequately protected by the ultimate power of appellate courts to conduct an independent review of constitutional claims when necessary.

We emphasize that it is not our function to propose regulatory schemes for the States. That must await their concrete legislative efforts. It is possible, however, to give a few plain examples of what a state statute could define for regulation under part (b) of the standard announced in this opinion:

(a) Patently offensive representations or descriptions of ultimate sexual acts, normal or perverted, actual or simulated.

(b) Patently offensive representations or descriptions of masturbation, excretory functions, and lewd exhibition of the genitals.

Sex and nudity may not be exploited without limit by films or pictures exhibited or sold in places of public accommodation any more than live sex and nudity can be exhibited or sold without limit in such public places. At a minimum, prurient, patently offensive depiction or description of sexual conduct must have serious literary, artistic, political, or scientific value to merit First Amendment protection. * * * In resolving the inevitably sensitive questions of fact and law, we must continue to rely on the jury system, accompanied by the safeguards that judges, rules of evidence, presumptive features provide, as we do with rape, murder, and a host of other offenses against society and its individual members.

* * *

Under the holdings announced today, no one will be subject to prosecution for the sale or exposure of obscene materials unless these materials depict or describe patently offensive "hard core" sexual conduct specifically defined by the regulating state law, as written or construed. We are satisfied that these specific prerequisites will provide fair notice to a dealer in such materials that his public and commercial activities may bring prosecution.

* * *

It is certainly true that the absence, since *Roth*, of a single majority view of this Court as to proper standards for testing obscenity has placed a strain on both state and federal courts. But today, for the first time since *Roth* was decided in 1957, a majority of this Court has agreed on concrete guidelines to isolate "hard core" pornography from expression protected by the First Amendment. Now we may abandon the casual practice of *Redrup v. New York* (1967) and attempt to provide positive guidance to the federal and state courts alike.

This may not be an easy road, free from difficulty. But no amount of "fatigue" should lead us to adopt a convenient "institutional" rationale—an absolutist, "anything goes" view of the First Amendment—because it will lighten our burdens.

* * *

Under a national Constitution, fundamental First Amendment limitations on the powers of the States do not vary from community to community, but this does not mean that there are, or should or can be, fixed, uniform national standards of precisely what appeals to the "prurient interest" or is "patently offensive." These are essentially questions of fact, and our nation is simply too big and too diverse for this Court to reasonably expect that such standards could be articulated for all 50 States in a single formulation, even assuming the prerequisite consensus exists. When triers of fact are asked to decide whether "the average person, applying contemporary standards" would consider certain materials "prurient," it would be unrealistic to require that the answer be based on some abstract formulation. The adversary system, with lay jurors as the usual ultimate factfinders in criminal prosecutions, has historically permitted triers-of-fact to draw on the instructions of the law. To require a State to structure obscenity proceedings around evidence of a *national* "community standard" would be an exercise in futility.

As noted before, this case was tried on the theory that the California obscenity statute sought to incorporate the tripartite test of *Memoirs*. This, a "national" standard of First Amendment protection enumerated by a plurality of this Court, was correctly regarded at the time of trial as limiting state prosecution under the controlling case law. The jury, however, was explicitly instructed that, in determining whether the "dominant theme of the material as a whole . . . appeals to the prurient interest" and in determining whether the material "goes substantially beyond customary limits of candor and affronts contemporary community standards of decency" it was to apply "contemporary community standards of the State of California."

During the trial, both the prosecution and the defense assumed that the relevant "community standards" in making the factual determination of obscenity were those of the State of California, not some hypothetical standard of the entire United States of America. Defense counsel at trial never objected to the testimony of the State's expert on community standards or to the instructions of the trial judge on "state-wide" standards. On appeal to the Appellant Department, Superior Court of California, County of Orange, appellate for the first time contended that application of state, rather than national, standards violated the First and Fourteenth Amendments.

We conclude that neither the State's alleged failure to offer evidence of "national standards," nor the trial court's charge that the jury consider state community standards, were constitutional errors. Nothing in the First Amendment requires that a jury must consider hypothetical and unascertainable "national standards" when attempting to determine whether certain materials are obscene as a matter of fact. * * *

It is neither realistic nor constitutionally sound to read the First Amendment as requiring that the people of Maine or Mississippi accept public depiction of conduct found tolerable in Las Vegas, or New York City. People in different States vary in their tastes and attitudes, and this diversity is not to be strangled by the absolutism of imposed uniformity. * * * We hold the requirement that the jury evaluate the materials with reference to "contemporary standards of the State of California" serves this protective purpose and is constitutionally adequate.

* * *

The dissenting Justices sound the alarm of repression. But, in our view, to equate the free and robust exchange of ideas and political debate with commercial exploitation of obscene material demeans the grand conception of the First Amendment and its high purposes in the historic struggle for freedom. It is a "misuse of the great guarantees of free speech and free press . . . ." The First Amendment protects works which, taken as a whole, have serious literary, artistic, political, or scientific value, regardless of whether the government or a majority of the people approve of the ideas these works represent. "The protection given speech and press was fashioned to assure unfettered interchange of *ideas* for the bringing about of political and social changes desired by the people," *Roth v. United States*. But the public portrayal of hard core sexual conduct for its own sake, and for ensuing commercial gain, is a different matter.

* * *

In sum, we (a) reaffirm the *Roth* holding that obscene material is not protected by the First Amendment; (b) hold that such material can be regulated by the States, subject to the specific safeguards enunciated above without a showing that the material is "*utterly* without redeeming social value"; and (c) hold that obscenity is to be determined by applying "contemporary community standards" not "national standards." The judgment of the Appellate Department of the Superior Court, Orange County, California, is vacated and the case remanded to that court for further proceedings not inconsistent with the First Amendment standards established by this opinion.

Vacated and remanded.

Justice Douglas, dissenting.

Today we leave open the way for California to send a man to prison for distributing brochures that advertise books and a movie under freshly written standards defining obscenity which until today's decision were never the part of any law. The Court has worked hard to define obscenity and concededly has failed. * * *

* * *

Today the Court retreats from the earlier formulations of the constitutional test and undertakes to make new definitions. This effort, like the earlier ones, is earnest and well intentioned. The difficulty is that we do not deal with constitutional terms, since "obscenity" is not mentioned in the Constitution or Bill of Rights. And the First Amendment makes no such exception from "the press" which it undertakes to protect nor, as I have said on other occasions, is an exception necessarily implied, for there was no recognized exception to the free press at the time the Bill of Rights was adopted which treated "obscene" publications differently from other types of papers, magazines, and books. So there are no constitutional guidelines for deciding what is and what is not "obscene." The Court is at large because we deal with tastes and standards of literature. What shocks me may be sustenance for my neighbor. What causes one person to boil up in rage over one pamphlet or movie may reflect only his neurosis, not shared by others. We deal here with a regime of censorship which, if adopted, should be done by constitutional amendment after full debate by the people.

* * *

The idea that the First Amendment permits government to ban publications that are "offensive" to some people puts an ominous gloss on freedom of the press. That test would make it possible to ban any paper or any journal or magazine in some benighted place. The First Amendment was designed "to invite dispute," to induce "a condition of unrest," to "create dissatisfaction with conditions as they are," and even to stir "people to anger." The idea that the First Amendment permits punishment for ideas that are "offensive" to the particular judge or jury sitting in judgment is astounding. No greater leveler of speech or literature has ever been designed. To give the power to the censor, as we do today, is to make a sharp and radical break with the traditions of a free society. The First Amendment was not fashioned as a vehicle for dispensing tranquilizers to the people. * * *

* * *

We deal with highly emotional, not rational, questions. To many the Song of Solomon is obscene. I do not think we, the judges, were ever given the constitutional power to make definitions of obscenity. If it is to be defined, let the people debate and decide by a constitutional amendment what they want to ban as obscene and what standards they want the legislatures and the courts to apply. Perhaps the people will decide that the path towards a mature, integrated society requires that all ideas competing for acceptance must have no censor. Perhaps they will decide otherwise. Whatever the choice, the courts will have some guidelines. Now we have none except our own predilections.

In *Paris Adult Theatre v. Slaton* (1973), a companion case to *Miller*, Burger, writing for the same five-person majority, provided further justification for tightening government control over obscenity by focusing on the harm issue, a subject that was not addressed in *Miller*. Burger argued that the guidelines in *Miller* should be applied to this case by Georgia, and he strongly attacked the theory that the state could not regulate obscene films if they were shown to consenting adults. This case differed sharply from *Stanley v. Georgia* (1969), Burger argued, because *Stanley* involved a person's home whereas the *Paris* case involved a place of public accommodation. In such public places, the government has a strong interest in controlling obscene materials because of the various harms they can inflict on a community, including eroding the moral quality of life, undermining the commercial tone of urban centers, and possibly threatening public safety. Burger gave direct consideration to the argument raised in the 1970 *Report* and in Marshall's majority opinion in *Stanley* (1969) that no scientific evidence established a causal link between exposure to obscene materials and deviant or criminal behavior. Although acknowledging that no conclusive proof of this relationship existed, Burger nonetheless argued that the legislature of Georgia could reasonably pass legislation based on the assumption that such a relationship does or might exist.

Brennan led the dissenters' attack on Burger's reasoning in *Miller* and *Paris*. Brennan had authored the Court's last majority opinion defining obscenity in *Roth*, and he also was the author of the three-part plurality test in *Memoirs*. After sixteen years of experimentation and debate, Brennan concluded in his dissent in *Paris* that it was impossible to define the concept of obscenity with sufficient clarity to make distinctions between protected and unprotected sexual expression. The Court's efforts to draw such lines through elaborate definitional guidelines had created three major problems, according to Brennan: (1) a lack of fair notice to producers and distributors of sexually oriented materials, (2) a chilling effect on protected expression because of the fear of prosecution, and (3) a high degree of institutional stress on the courts, which had to commit an enormous amount of time viewing "miserable stuff" with only the vaguest of guidelines for assistance. Weighing these concerns along with the lack of clear evidence of harm done to adults by exposure to obscene materials, Brennan therefore concluded that the First Amendment should be read to prohibit the state and the federal governments from suppressing allegedly obscene materials except in regard to juveniles and unconsenting adults.

Paris Adult Theatre v. Slaton

413 U.S. 49, 93 S.Ct. 2628, 37 L.Ed. 2d 446 (1973)

■ In a companion case to *Miller v. California* (1973), the owners and managers of two Atlanta, Georgia, adult movie theaters—Paris Adult Theatre I and Paris Adult Theatre II—were arrested for showing allegedly obscene films entitled "Magic Mirror" and "It All Comes Out in the End," which depicted simulated scenes of oral sex and group sexual intercourse. The trial judge dismissed the charges, arguing that the showing of the films was constitutionally protected—even if they were obscene—because the theaters had posted signs prohibiting minors and warning customers of the content of the films. The Georgia Supreme Court unanimously reversed the lower court, however, ruling that the films were obscene and without First Amendment protection.

This case is important not only because the Court applied the new *Miller* standards but also because the Court rejected the argument that consenting adults should be able to view obscene movies in commercial theaters. In reading Chief Justice Burger's majority opinion and Justice Brennan's dissenting opinion, think about the following questions: (1) What is the view of the majority regarding the question of whether obscenity is harmful? (2) Why does the majority opinion reject the argument that consenting adults should be able to view what they want? (3) Does Brennan in his dissent offer convincing reasons why the government should not be allowed to suppress obscene materials?

VOTE:

5 justices found the government action to be constitutional (Burger, Blackmun, Powell, Rehnquist, White).

4 justices found the government action to be unconstitutional (Brennan, Douglas, Marshall, Stewart).

Chief Justice Burger delivered the opinion of the Court.

* * *

We categorically disapprove the theory, apparently adopted by the trial judge, that obscene, pornographic films acquire constitutional immunity from state regulation simply because they are exhibited for consenting adults only. This holding was properly rejected by the Georgia Supreme Court. Although we have often pointedly recognized the high importance of the state interest in regulating the exposure of obscene materials to juveniles and unconsenting adults, this Court has never declared these to be the only legitimate state interests permitting regulation of obscene material. The States have long-recognized legitimate interest in regulating the use of obscene material in local commerce and in all places of public accommodation, as long as these regulations do not run afoul of specific constitutional prohibitions. * * *

In particular, we hold that there are legitimate state interests at stake in stemming the tide of commercialized obscenity, even assuming it is feasible to enforce effective safeguards against exposure to juveniles and to passersby. Rights and interests "other than those of the advocates are involved," *Breard v. Alexandria* (1951). These include the interest of the public in the quality of life and the total community environment, the tone of commerce in the great city centers, and, possibly, the public safety, itself. The Hill-Link Minority Report of the Commission on Obscenity and Pornography indicates that there is at least an arguable correlation between obscene material and crime. Quite apart from sex crimes, however, there remains one problem of large proportions aptly described by Professor Bickel: "It concerns the tone of the society, the mode, or to use terms that have perhaps greater currency, the style and quality of life, now and in the future." * * *

As Mr. Chief Justice Warren stated, there is a "right of the Nation and of the States to maintain a decent society . . . " *Jacobellis v. Ohio* (1964).

But, it is argued, there are no scientific data which conclusively demonstrate that exposure to obscene material adversely affects men and women or their society. It is urged on behalf of the petitioners that, absent such a demonstration, any kind of state regulation is "impermissible." We reject this argument. It is not for us to resolve empirical uncertainties underlying state legislation, save in the exceptional case where that legislation plainly impinges upon rights protected by the Constitution itself. * * * Although there is no conclusive proof of a connection between antisocial behavior and obscene material, the legislature of Georgia could quite reasonably determine that such a connection does or might exist. In deciding *Roth*, this Court implicitly accepted that a legislature could legitimately act on such a conclusion to protect *"the social interest in order and morality."*

* * *

* * * The sum of experience, including that of the past two decades, affords an ample basis for legislatures to conclude that a sensitive, key relationship of human existence, central to family life, community welfare, and the development of human personality, can be debased and distorted by crass commercial exploitation of sex. Nothing in the Constitution prohibits a State from reaching such a conclusion and acting on it legislatively simply because there is no conclusive evidence or empirical data.

* * *

The States, of course, may follow such a "laissez-faire" policy and drop all controls on commercialized obscenity, if that is what they prefer, just as they can ignore consumer protection in the marketplace, but nothing in the Constitution *compels* the States to do so with regard to matters falling within state jurisdiction. * * *

It is asserted, however, that standards for evaluating state commercial regulations are inapposite in the present context, as state regulation of access by consenting adults to obscene material violates the constitutionally protected right to privacy enjoyed by petitioners' customers. * * *

Our prior decisions recognizing a right to privacy guaranteed by the Fourteenth Amendment included "only personal rights that can be deemed 'fundamental' or 'implicit' in the concept of ordered liberty." This privacy right encompasses and protects the personal intimacies of the home, the family, marriage, motherhood, procreation, and child rearing. Nothing, however, in this Court's decisions intimates that there is any "fundamental" privacy right "implicit in the concept of ordered liberty" to watch obscene movies in places of public accommodation.

* * *

Finally, petitioners argue that conduct which directly involves "consenting adults" only has, for that sole reason, a special claim to constitutional protection. Our Constitution establishes a broad range of conditions on the exercise of power by the States, but for us to say that our Constitution incorporates the proposition that conduct involving consenting adults only is always beyond state regulation, is a step we are unable to take. Commercial exploitation of depictions, descriptions, or exhibitions of obscene conduct on commercial premises open to the adult public falls within a State's broad power to regulate commerce and protect the public environment. The issue in this context goes beyond whether someone, or even the majority, considers the conduct depicted as "wrong" or "sinful." The States have the power to make a morally neutral judgment that public exhibition of obscene material has a tendency to injure the community as a whole, to endanger the public safety, or to jeopardize, in Mr. Chief Justice Warren's words, the States' "right . . . to maintain a decent society."

To summarize, we have today reaffirmed the basic holding of *Roth v. United States* that obscene material has no protection under the First Amendment. * * * In this case we hold that the States have a legitimate interest in regulating commerce in obscene material and in regulating exhibition of obscene material in places of public accommodation, including so-called "adult" theaters from which minors are excluded. In light of these holdings, nothing precludes the State of Georgia from the regulation of the allegedly obscene material exhibited in Paris Adult Theatre I or II, provided that the applicable Georgia law, as written or authoritatively interpreted by the Georgia courts, meets the First Amendment standards set forth in *Miller v. California*. * * *

Vacated and remanded.

Justice Douglas, dissenting [omitted].

* * *

Justice Brennan, with whom Justice Stewart and Justice Marshall join, dissenting.

This case requires the Court to confront once again the vexing problem of reconciling state efforts to suppress sexually oriented expression with the protections of the First Amendment, as applied to the States through the Fourteenth Amendment. No other aspect of the First Amendment has, in recent years, demanded so substantial a commitment of our time, generated such disharmony of views, and remained so resistant to the formulation of stable and manageable standards. I am convinced that the approach initiated 16 years ago in *Roth v. United States* (1957), and culminating in the Court's decision today, cannot bring stability to this area of the law without jeopardizing fundamental First Amendment values, and I have concluded that the time has come to make a significant departure from that approach.

* * *

* * * After 16 years of experimentation and debate I am reluctantly forced to the conclusion that none of the available formulas, including the one announced today, can reduce the vagueness to a tolerable level while at the same time striking an acceptable balance between the protection of the First and Fourteenth Amendments, on the one hand, and on the other the asserted state interest in regulating the dissemination of certain sexually oriented materials. Any effort to draw a constitutionally acceptable boundary on state power must resort to such indefinite concepts as "prurient interest," "patent offensiveness," "serious literary value," and the like. The meaning of these concepts necessarily varies with the experience, outlook, and even idiosyncrasies of the person defining them. Although we have assumed that obscenity does exist and that we "know it when (we) see it," *Jacobellis v. Ohio* (1964), we are manifestly unable to describe it in advance except by reference to concepts so elusive that they fail to distinguish clearly between protected and unprotected speech.

* * *

The vagueness of the standards in the obscenity area produces a number of separate problems, and any improvement must rest on an understanding that the problems are to some extent distinct. First, a vague statute fails to provide adequate notice to persons who are engaged in the type of conduct that the statute could be thought to proscribe. * * *

In addition to problems that arise when any criminal statute fails to afford fair notice of what it forbids, a vague statute in the areas of speech and press creates a second level of difficulty. We have indicated that "stricter standards of permissible statutory vagueness may be applied to a statute having a potentially inhibiting effect on speech; a man may the less be required to act at his peril here, because the free dissemination of ideas may be the loser" *Smith v. California* (1959). * * *

* * *

The problems of fair notice and chilling protected speech are very grave standing alone. But it does not detract from their importance to recognize that a vague statute in this area creates a third, although admittedly more subtle, set of problems. These problems concern the institutional stress that inevitably results where the line separating protected from unprotected speech is excessively vague. In *Roth* we conceded that "there may be marginal cases in which it is difficult to determine the side of the line on which a particular fact situation falls . . . ." Our subsequent experience demonstrates that almost every case is "marginal." And since the "margin" marks the point of separation between protected and unprotected speech, we are left with a system in which almost every obscenity case presents a constitutional question of exceptional difficulty. * * *

* * *

But the sheer number of cases does not define the full extent of the institutional problem. For, quite apart from the number of cases involved and the need to make a fresh constitutional determination in each case, we are tied to the "absurd business of perusing and viewing the miserable stuff that pours into the Court . . . ." While the material may have varying degrees of social importance, it is hardly a source of edification to the members of this Court who are compelled to view it before passing on its obscenity.

* * *

The severe problem arising from the lack of fair notice, from the chill on protected expression, and from the stress imposed on the state and federal judicial machinery persuade me that a significant change in direction is urgently required. I turn therefore, to the alternatives that are now open.

* * *

In short, while I cannot say that the interests of the State—apart from the question of juveniles and unconsenting adults—are trivial or nonexistent, I am compelled to conclude that these interests cannot justify the substantial damage to constitutional rights and to this Nation's judicial machinery that inevitably results from the state efforts to bar the distribution even of unprotected material to consenting adults. I would hold, therefore, that at least in the absence of distribution to juveniles or obtrusive exposure to unconsenting adults, the First and Fourteenth Amendments prohibit the State and Federal Governments from attempting wholly to suppress sexually oriented materials on the basis of their allegedly "obscene" contents. Nothing in this approach precludes those governments from taking action to serve what may be strong and legitimate interests through regulation of the manner of distribution of sexually oriented material.

The majority decision in *Miller* assured that the Supreme Court would continue to be confronted with numerous obscenity cases. The vast majority of the states accepted the Court's invitation in *Miller* to formulate obscenity laws consistent with the three-prong test; within a decade thirty-seven states and the District of Columbia had passed such laws (see *New York v. Ferber*, 458 U.S. at 1122, 1982). These laws gave rise to strong efforts in many states to prosecute those involved in producing and distributing sexually oriented materials, and many of these cases eventually reached the Supreme Court.

The Burger Court took a strongly conservative stance in these cases, contrasting sharply with the approach of the Warren Court. Typically, the Court would simply refuse to grant certiorari in cases where obscenity convictions were being appealed, which had the effect of upholding the lower court decision in favor of the government. The Burger Court did grant cert and issue full opinions in a substantial number of cases, however, and these decisions typically favored the government's obscenity prosecutions. As can be seen in Table 8.1, the Burger Court heard thirty-three obscenity cases and decided seventy percent of them conservatively. These results were almost exactly the opposite of the Warren Court, thus illustrating the dramatically different approaches of the two Courts.

The Burger Court was certainly not willing to give state and local governments complete control over sexual expression, however. For example, in the 1974 case of *Jenkins v. Georgia* involving a mainstream Hollywood film entitled *Carnal Knowledge,* which starred Jack Nicholson and Ann Margaret, the Court ruled unanimously that the film was not obscene under the *Miller* test and thus could not be banned by Georgia.

Although the Burger Court took a much more conservative approach to the obscenity issue than did the Warren Court, the two Courts did share one important

TABLE 8.1: Liberal/Conservative Outcomes of First Amendment Obscenity Cases for the Warren, Burger, and Rehnquist Courts, 1953-94 Terms

	Outcomes		
Court Era	Liberal	Conservative	Totals
Warren Court, 1953-68 Terms	73% (16)	27% (6)	22
Burger Court, 1969-85 Terms	30% (10)	70% (23)	33
Rehnquist Court, 1986-94 Terms	20% (2)	80% (8)	10
Totals	43% (28)	57% (37)	65

feature in common: a struggle to deal effectively with defining obscenity. As Melvin Urofsky (1991, p. 102) has noted: "The Burger Court, for better or worse, never repudiated that definitional approach, and its efforts proved no more successful in establishing an objective obscenity test." Given the long and unsuccessful definitional struggle of the Warren Court, it was inevitable that the Burger Court would also encounter numerous, difficult problems with the *Miller* test. The terms "prurient interest" and "patently offensive" were carried over from the *Roth* test, and these terms were as vague to jurors in the seventies and eighties as they had been in the fifties and sixties. In addition, the new *Miller* requirement that a work must have "serious literary, artistic, political, or scientific value" was even more difficult to apply than the *Roth* standard of "utterly without redeeming social value." As Burger correctly pointed out in *Miller*, it was virtually impossible for the government to prove a work had absolutely no social value. In contrast, juries found it much more difficult to weigh whether a work had serious social value. Finally, the amorphous concept of "community standards" continued to perplex judges and juries alike.

One area of general agreement did emerge, however, during the Burger Court era: the illegality of sexual materials involving minors. The lead case was *New York v. Ferber* (1982), in which the Court unanimously upheld a New York law that prohibited persons from distributing any materials that depicted sexual performances by children under the age of sixteen. Ferber was arrested for selling in his store two films involving young boys. Although the Court ruled that the films were not obscene under the *Miller* standards, White's majority opinion stated that a state has substantially greater freedom to regulate sexually oriented materials involving minors. Because of the widely accepted evidence of the harm associated with child pornography, White argued, states may pass specifically defined laws that prohibit ". . . works that visually depict sexual conduct by children below a specified age" (458 U.S. at 764). O'Connor, Brennan, and Stevens each wrote short, concurring opinions, but they all agreed in the judgment upholding the constitutionality of the law and Ferber's conviction.

NEW YORK V. FERBER

485 U.S. 747, 102 S.Ct. 3348, 73 L.Ed. 2d 1113

■ Paul Ferber was the proprietor of a Manhattan store that sold sexually oriented products. Ferber was arrested for selling to an undercover police officer two films that involved young boys masturbating. Ferber was convicted by a state jury of violating a New York law that prohibited anyone from distributing materials depicting sexual activities by children under the age of sixteen. An intermediate appellate court upheld the conviction, but the New York Court of Appeals reversed the conviction on the grounds that the law in question violated the First Amendment.

This decision is important because the Court ruled that the government has substantially greater authority to regulate sexually oriented materials involving minors than in regard to adults. As you read the Court's decision, consider the following questions: (1) Why does the Court believe that child pornography should be much more closely regulated than pornography involving adults? (2) Is the *Ferber* decision consistent with the *Miller* obscenity guidelines?

VOTE:

The Court ruled unanimously that the New York law was constitutional.

Justice White delivered the opinion of the Court.

At issue in this case is the constitutionality of a New York criminal statute which prohibits persons from knowingly promoting sexual performances by children under the age of 16 by distributing material which depicts such performances.

In recent years, the exploitive use of children in the production of pornography has become a serious national problem. The Federal Government and 47 States have sought to combat the problem with statutes specifically directed at the production of child pornography. At least half of such statutes do not require that the materials produced be legally obscene. Thirty-five States and the United States Congress have also passed legislation prohibiting the distribution of such materials; 20 States prohibit the distribution of material depicting children engaged in sexual conduct without requiring that the material be legally obscene.

* * *

This case constitutes our first examination of a statute directed at and limited to depictions of sexual activity involving children. We believe our inquiry should begin with the question of whether a State has somewhat more freedom in proscribing works which portray sexual acts or lewd exhibitions of genitalia by children.

* * *

The *Miller* standard, like its predecessors, was an accommodation between the State's interests in protecting the "sensibilities of unwilling recipients" from exposure to pornographic material and the dangers of censorship inherent in unabashedly content-based laws. Like obscenity statutes, laws directed at the dissemination of child pornography run the risk of suppressing protected expression by allowing the hand of the censor to become unduly heavy. For the following reasons, however, we are persuaded that the States are entitled to greater leeway in the regulation of pornographic depiction of children.

First. It is evident beyond the need for elaboration that a State's interest in "safeguarding the physical and psychological well-being of a minor" is "compelling." * * *

The prevention of sexual exploitation and abuse of children constitutes a government objective of surpassing importance. * * *

* * *

* * * Suffice it to say that virtually all of the States and the United States have passed legislation proscribing the production or otherwise combating "child pornography." The legislative judgment, as well as the judgment found in the relevant literature, is that the use of children as subjects of pornographic materials is harmful to the physiological, emotional, and mental health of the child. That judgment, we think, easily passes muster under the First Amendment.

Second. The distribution of photographs and films depicting sexual activity by juveniles is intrinsically related to the sexual abuse of children in at least two ways. First, the materials produced are a permanent record of the children's participation and the harm to the child is exacerbated by their circulation. Second, the distribution network for child pornography must be closed if the production of material which requires the sexual exploitation of children is to be effectively controlled. Indeed, there is no serious contention that the legislature was unjustified in believing that it is difficult, if not impossible, to halt the exploitation of children by pursuing only those who produce the photographs and movies. While the production of pornographic materials is a low-profile, clandestine industry, the need to market the resulting products requires a visible apparatus of distribution. The most expeditious if not the only practical method of law enforcement may be to dry up the market for this material by imposing severe criminal penalties on persons selling, advertising, or otherwise promoting the product. Thirty-five States and Congress have concluded that restraints on the distribution of pornographic materials are required in order to effectively combat the problem, and there is a body of literature and testimony to support these legislative conclusions.

* * *

Third. The advertising and selling of child pornography provide an economic motive for and are thus an integral part of the production of such materials, an activity illegal throughout the Nation. * * *

Fourth. The value of permitting live performances and photographic reproductions of children engaged in lewd sexual conduct is exceedingly modest, if not de minimis. We consider it unlikely that visual depictions of children performing sexual acts or lewdly exhibiting their genitals would often constitute an important and necessary part of a literary performance or scientific or educational work. As a state judge in this case observed, if it were necessary for literary or artistic value, a person over the statutory age who perhaps looked younger could be utilized. Simulation outside of the prohibition of the statute could provide another alternative. Nor is there any question here of censoring a particular literary theme or portrayal of sexual activity. The First Amendment interest is limited to that of rendering the portrayal somewhat more "realistic" by utilizing or photographing children.

Fifth. Recognizing and classifying child pornography as a category of material outside the protection of the First Amendment is not incompatible with our earlier decisions.

* * *

There are, of course, limits on the category of child pornography which, like obscenity, is unprotected by the First Amendment. As with all legislation in this sensitive area, the conduct to be prohibited must be adequately defined by the applicable state law, as written or authoritatively construed. Here the nature of the harm to be combated requires that the state offense be limited to works that *visually* depict sexual conduct by children below a specified age. The category of "sexual conduct" proscribed must also be suitably limited and described.

The test for child pornography is separate from the obscenity standard enunciated in *Miller*, but may be compared to it for purpose of clarity. The *Miller* formulation is adjusted in the following respects: A trier of fact need not find that the material appeals to the prurient interest of the average person; it is not required that sexual conduct portrayed be done so in a patently offensive manner; and the material at issue need not be considered as a whole. We note that the distribution of descriptions or other depictions of sexual conduct, not otherwise obscene, which do not involve live performances, retains First Amendment protection. * * *

* * *

* * * As applied to Paul Ferber and to others who distribute similar material, the statute does not violate the First Amendment as applied to the States through the Fourteenth. The decision of the New York Court of Appeals is reversed, and the case is remanded to that court for further proceedings not inconsistent with this opinion.

So ordered.

Justice Blackmun concurs in the result.

Justice O'Connor, concurring [omitted].

* * *

Justice Brennan, with whom Justice Marshall joins, concurring in the judgment [omitted].

* * *

Justice Stevens, concurring in the judgment [omitted].

What was the practical effect of the *Miller* test in terms of the availability of sexually explicit materials in American society and the success of governments in instituting successful obscenity prosecutions? Despite the efforts and intentions of the Burger Court, sexually oriented materials proliferated in American society throughout the seventies and early eighties, the materials became substantially more explicit and oriented toward violence, and the number of prosecutions for obscenity declined between 1973 and 1985. Donald Downs (1989, pp. 20–21) offers seven reasons why the *Miller* decision has not been effective in controlling obscene materials in American society. First, prosecutors have given low priority to obscenity cases because of limited resources and higher priority to other types of crime. Second, public attitudes, reflected by judges and juries, are tolerant of sexually oriented expression. Third, criminal convictions, requiring proof beyond a reasonable doubt, are difficult to obtain when the concepts of the *Miller* test are so confusing and complex. Fourth, political pressure to prosecute is inconsistent. Fifth, a reinforcing pattern can be found of relatively few complaints, relatively few police investigators, and relatively few tough sentences. Sixth, frequently jury members are aroused by materials they must review, and they are consequently reluctant to admit that it appeals to "prurient interests" or is "patently offensive." Finally, producers and distributors of sexually oriented materials have well-paid, experienced attorneys who are skilled at defending their clients.

A final topic involving the Burger Court that needs to be discussed is a series of decisions involving various forms of sexually oriented expression that were nonobscene but that nonetheless were possibly subject to government regulation. These included such things as nude dancing, adult bookstores, and adult theaters. The Burger Court did not provide any clear doctrinal guidelines in this area, but the Court during this time period did give substantial power to state and local governments to regulate—but not to prohibit—these types of sexually oriented activities. In *Schad v. Borough of Mount Ephraim* (1981), for example, the Burger Court ruled unconstitutional a law that prohibited nude dancing in an adult entertainment establishment, arguing that nude dancing is expression within the meaning of the First Amendment. The Burger Court did allow, however, states to prohibit nude dancing in businesses that served liquor, arguing that this power could be found within the Twenty-first Amendment, which repealed Prohibition. The Burger Court also gave approval to various zoning laws that restricted where adult-entertainment businesses could be located. In *Young v. American Mini Theatres, Inc*, (1976), for example, the Court approved a Detroit zoning ordinance that prohibited adult theaters from being within one thousand feet of other adult theaters or within five hundred feet of a residential area. Similarly, in *City of Renton v. Playtime Theatres, Inc*, (1986) the Burger Court upheld Renton, Washington's prohibition on adult theaters being within one thousand feet of residential, apartment, church, park, or school areas based on the government's concern with the secondary effects of crime, prostitution, and economic deterioration that can accompany the establishment of sexually oriented businesses.

The Rehnquist Court Era

Our analysis of the Burger Court era has revealed clearly that the changes in the Court's membership produced dramatic alterations in the Court's obscenity decisions. The Burger Court significantly modified the definition of obscenity, allowing state and local governments substantially greater authority to control sexually oriented materials, and the Court's decisions were far more supportive of the government than were the decisions of the Warren Court.

We turn now to an analysis of the Rehnquist Court's obscenity decisions, focusing on the question of whether the changes in the Court's personnel have produced significant alterations in either the doctrinal guidelines or the patterns of liberal/conservative outcomes regarding sexually oriented freedom of expression cases. As in previous chapters, we will employ both quantitative and qualitative methods of analysis. We begin with quantitative analysis of the voting patterns of the Rehnquist Court in obscenity decisions. In this analysis, liberal outcomes are those in which the Court rules in favor of the individual or organization bringing a claim that government regulation or punishment of sexually oriented expression has violated the guarantees of the First Amendment. Conversely, conservative outcomes are those that favor government control of sexual expression, finding no First Amendment violation. When we complete the quantitative analysis of the Rehnquist Court, we will then use our doctrinal framework to examine in detail the legal reasoning of the Rehnquist Court's obscenity cases to determine if substantial changes have occurred in the Court's policies in this area.

Our initial inquiry involves a comparison of the Warren, Burger, and Rehnquist Courts. Has the Rehnquist Court been significantly more conservative than either the Warren or Burger Courts? The data in Table 8.1 reveal that the Rehnquist Court's decision making in the area of obscenity has been similar to the Burger Court's; both Courts have been decidedly conservative, with the Burger Court deciding 70 percent of its cases conservatively and the Rehnquist Court reaching a conservative outcome in 80 percent of its cases. These results are in sharp contrast to the decisional outcomes of the Warren Court, which voted conservatively in only 27 percent of its obscenity cases. Thus, the Court has undergone a dramatic shift in voting patterns in the area of obscenity, but this shift occurred between the Warren and Burger Courts; the Rehnquist Court has followed closely the conservative pattern of decision making by the Burger Court.

The data in Table 8.2 allow us to examine the voting records of the individual justices of the Rehnquist Court. A sharp division among the justices of the Rehnquist Court can be observed in Table 8.2, although Powell, Souter, Thomas, Ginsburg, and Breyer have participated in too few decisions for meaningful analysis. Three justices—Brennan, Stevens, and Marshall—have voted consistently liberal; Brennan and Marshall voted liberally 100 percent of the time and Stevens's liberal record is 90 percent. Conversely, five of the justices—Rehnquist, Scalia, Kennedy, O'Connor, and White—have been predominantly conservative in their voting behavior, although each of these justices has voted liberally on occasion. Justice Blackmun appears to be the lone moderate on the Court in this area, splitting his votes equally between liberal and conservative outcomes.

The data in Table 8.3 confirm that two strong blocs have indeed emerged in the area of obscenity. The conservative coalition of Rehnquist, O'Connor, Scalia, Kennedy, and White has an average interagreement score of 88 percent, substantially above the threshold level of the Sprague Criterion. The three liberal justices—Marshall, Brennan, and Stevens—have perfect interagreement scores of 100 percent. Blackmun is not aligned with either bloc, a somewhat surprising result given Blackmun's generally strong and consistent liberal voting record in other areas of civil rights and liberties. Blackmun and Kennedy form a two-person bloc, however.

What do these results suggest regarding the future of the Rehnquist Court? The most obvious point to make is that Brennan and Marshall have left the Court, thus

TABLE 8.2: Liberal/Conservative Voting Records of Justices of the Rehnquist Court in First Amendment Obscenity Cases, 1986-94 Terms

Justice	Liberal Votes	Conservative Votes
Marshall	100% (8)	0% (0)
Brennan	100% (7)	0% (0)
Stevens	90% (9)	10% (1)
Blackmun	56% (5)	44% (4)
Thomas	50% (1)	50% (1)
White	33% (3)	67% (6)
Souter	33% (1)	67% (2)
Kennedy	33% (3)	67% (6)
Scalia	30% (3)	70% (7)
O'Connor	22% (2)	78% (7)
Rehnquist	20% (2)	80% (8)
Powell	0% (0)	100% (1)
Ginsburg	0% (0)	100% (1)
Breyer	0% (0)	100% (1)

TABLE 8.3: Bloc Voting Analysis of the Rehnquist Court First Amendment Obscenity Cases, 1986-94 Terms (Percent Agreement Rates)

	BR	MA	ST	BL	KE	RE	OC	SC	WH
Brennan	—	100	100	43	33	29	33	29	29
Marshall	100	—	100	50	29	25	29	25	38
Stevens	100	100	—	56	44	30	33	20	33
Blackmun	43	50	56	—	88	67	62	67	78
Kennedy	33	29	44	88	—	89	88	78	75
Rehnquist	29	25	30	67	89	—	100	90	89
O'Connor	33	29	33	62	88	100	—	89	88
Scalia	29	25	20	67	78	90	89	—	89
White	29	38	33	78	75	89	88	89	—

Court Mean = 60
Sprague Criterion = 80
Liberal bloc: Brennan, Marshall, Stevens = 100
Conservative bloc: Kennedy, Rehnquist, O'Connor, Scalia, White = 88
Additional bloc: Blackmun, Kennedy = 88

leaving Stevens as the lone liberal remaining member of the bloc in the area of obscenity. In contrast, four members of the conservative bloc remain on the Court: Rehnquist, O'Connor, Scalia, and Kennedy. Souter, Thomas, Ginsburg, and Breyer have participated in such a small number of obscenity decisions that it is premature to predict with confidence how they will align. Thomas does seem likely to join the conservative coalition, however, thus providing the conservative bloc with the five votes needed to control decision making in this area. If Thomas joins the conservative bloc, a majority coalition of conservative justices would exist to control the Court's obscenity decisions even if Ginsburg and Breyer should take a liberal approach in this area.

The quantitative analysis provides only part of the picture, however. We need to examine the written opinions of the Rehnquist Court to gain a more complete understanding of the directions and policies of the current Court in the area of obscenity. Table 8.4 provides a framework for the doctrinal analysis of the Rehnquist Court's obscenity decisions, and the information in the table reveals that the Rehnquist Court has not been involved in modifying or creating new conservative precedents in regard to obscenity. All of the conservative decisions of the Rehnquist Court are classified as conservative interpretations of existing precedent, thus showing substantial continuity with the decisions of the Burger Court. The justices of the Rehnquist Court have maintained a commitment to the *Miller* test, they have maintained the strong opposition to child pornography, and they have generally been supportive of government efforts to control both obscene and certain forms of nonobscene sexual expression. Like the Burger Court, however, the Rehnquist Court has on occasion drawn the line in favor of freedom of expression values.

The first obscenity case to confront the Rehnquist Court involved an interpretation of the third prong of the *Miller* test, the requirement that an obscene work, taken as a whole, must lack serious literary, artistic, political, or scientific value. In *Pope v. Illinois* (1987), the issue before the Court was whether the LAPS test was to be determined by statewide community standards or a broader standard of a reasonable person," that is, a national standard. Richard Pope and Charles Morrison, attendants at two adult bookstores, were charged separately with selling

TABLE 8.4: A Framework for the Doctrinal Analysis of the Rehnquist Court's First Amendment Obscenity Cases, 1986-94 Terms

Major or Minor Importance	Majority or Plurality Opinion	Treatment of Precedent					
		Creation of New Liberal Precedent	Liberal Modification of Existing Precedent	Liberal Interpretation of Existing Precedent	Conservative Interpretation of Existing Precedent	Conservative Modification of Existing Precedent	Creation of New Conservative Precedent
Major	Majority			FCC v. Sable (1989)	Sable v. FCC (1989) Osborne v. Ohio (1990)		
	Plurality				Barnes v. Glen Theatre (1991)		
Minor	Majority			Fort Wayne Books v. Indiana (1989)	Pope v. Illinois (1987) Sappenfield v. Indiana (1989) Alexander v. US (1993) US v. X-Citement Video (1995)		
	Plurality				Massachusetts v. Oakes (1989)		

allegedly obscene magazines in violation of an Illinois obscenity law. The juries were instructed to judge the obscenity of the magazines under the three-part *Miller* test, approaching each of the three questions from the perspective of ordinary adults in the state of Illinois. Both Pope and Morrison were found guilty, and their convictions were upheld on appeal. The United States Supreme Court granted certiorari to determine if the third prong of the *Miller* test should have been interpreted under the community standards of the state of Illinois or whether a more objective, national standard should have been used.

Justice White wrote the majority opinion for the Court, and he was joined by Rehnquist, Scalia, O'Connor, and Powell. In a very brief analysis, White argued that this case was controlled by the 1977 case of *Smith v. United States*, in which the Burger Court had ruled that the first two prongs of the *Miller* test were to be determined by "contemporary community standards," that is, state or local, but the third prong dealing with the value of a work was to be based upon " . . . whether a reasonable person would find such value in the material, taken as a whole" (481 U.S. 501). This interpretation, White argued, was consistent with language of the *Miller* test, which specified the application of contemporary community standards only for the first two prongs.

This liberal interpretation of the *Miller* test was supported by every member of the Court, but substantial disagreement nonetheless arose among the justices. One area of contention involved the disposition of the case. The five-person majority remanded the case back to the Illinois appellate court, stating that the convictions could stand if the error was determined to be harmless. The four liberal dissenters called for the direct reversal of the convictions. The second area of disagreement was even more fundamental because the liberal bloc of Brennan, Stevens, and Marshall opposed the entire *Miller* approach to obscenity, arguing that " . . . government may not constitutionally criminalize mere possession or sale of obscene literature, absent some connection to minors or obtrusive display to unconsenting adults" (481 U.S. at 513).

An especially interesting development in the *Pope* case involved the views of Justice Scalia. We have seen that Scalia is a member of the conservative bloc of the Rehnquist Court in obscenity cases, and he joined White's opinion in this decision. Nevertheless, Scalia distanced himself somewhat from his fellow conservatives by writing a concurring opinion in which he called for a reexamination of the *Miller* test because " . . . in my view it is quite impossible to come to an objective assessment of (at least) literary and artistic value, there being many accomplished people who have found literature in Dada, and art in the replication of a soup can" (481 U.S. at 504). Thus, Scalia established himself in his initial obscenity case as a potential ally with his liberal colleagues, but thus far this alliance has remained only a potentiality.

The Court's next personnel change involved Kennedy replacing Powell after the 1986–87 term. Because of the intense confirmation struggle over Powell's replacement, Kennedy's first full term on the Court was in 1988–89, when the Court decided five obscenity cases. Although Kennedy took a distinctively conservative position in the area of obscenity, his record was not significantly different than Powell's, and thus Kennedy had little impact on the Court's decision making regarding obscenity.

The two major obscenity cases that the Court decided during the 1988–89 term—*Sable Communications v. F.C.C.* and *F.C.C. v. Sable Communications*—involved a relatively new phenomenon, "dial-a-porn." Dial-a-porn involves companies providing either prerecorded telephone messages or live telephone conversations dealing with sex. Dial-a-porn became a lucrative business in the eighties; one estimate placed the number of calls in New York City alone at one million per month in 1985 (*Sable Communications v. F.C.C.*, 492 U.S. at 119). Numerous complaints were made to government officials about dial-a-porn, especially by parents who had received extraordinary phone bills as a result of their children's calls. Congress responded in 1988 by amending the Communications Act of 1934 to impose a ban on both obscene and indecent interstate commercial telephone messages. Sable Communications of California, a company providing sexually oriented telephone messages, brought suit in federal district court, alleging that this ban violated the First Amendment. The district court ruled that the ban on obscene messages was constitutionally permissible but that the ban on indecent messages violated the First Amendment. Both decisions were appealed to the United States Supreme Court.

The Rehnquist Court affirmed the lower court decisions, ruling unanimously that the ban on indecent communications was a violation of freedom of speech but deciding 6-3 that the obscenity ban did not violate the First Amendment. In regard to the indecency ban, White wrote an opinion joined by every member of the Court, an extraordinary rare occurrence in this area of constitutional law. White argued that "sexual expression which is indecent but not obscene is protected by the First Amendment . . . " (492 U.S. at 126), and government can regulate such expression only if it meets strict scrutiny standards of promoting a compelling government interest by narrowly tailored means. The government did have a compelling interest of protecting minors from indecent messages, White argued, but the means employed—a total ban—were not sufficiently narrow to meet First Amendment requirements.

The Court's consensus disappeared regarding the ban on obscene dial-a-porn. On this issue, White wrote for a six-person majority, which included Rehnquist, O'Connor, Scalia, Kennedy, and Blackmun. White disposed of this question rather quickly, asserting that the First Amendment does not protect obscene speech and therefore Congress was free to prohibit completely obscene telephone messages. Brennan wrote a dissent in this case and was joined by his liberal bloc colleagues, Marshall and Stevens. Brennan repeated his frequently stated argument that the Constitution prohibited the government from imposing criminal penalties for distributing obscene materials or messages to consenting adults; furthermore, Brennan argued, although the government does have a strong interest in protecting children from obscene materials, a complete ban like this one is overbroad and therefore unconstitutional.

The 1988–89 term was an exceptionally busy one for the Court in the area of obscenity because the justices handed down three other decisions in addition to the dial-a-porn opinions. None of the other three decisions are classified as being of major importance, however.

Massachusetts v. Oakes (1989) involved the criminal prosecution of Donald Oakes, who had taken several color photographs of his fourteen-year-old stepdaughter, who was attending modeling school at the time. The pictures showed her around a bar, wearing only a bikini panty and a scarf with her breasts fully exposed in all the photographs. The central issue before the Court was whether the Massachusetts statute criminalizing the taking of nude pictures of minors was overly broad, as the Massachusetts Supreme Court ruled. As is typical in obscenity cases, the high court was severely fractured in its reasoning. O'Connor's plurality opinion, which was joined by Rehnquist, White, and Kennedy, argued that the Court did not have to consider the overbreadth argument because the statute had already been amended to add a lascivious intent requirement to the nudity law, thus making the law specific enough to be constitutional. Scalia, joined by Blackmun, argued that the original statute was not overbroad. Finally, Brennan again penned a dissenting opinion, joined by Marshall and Stevens, arguing that the statute was indeed overbroad. The end result of the case was that Massachusetts' Supreme Court's decision was vacated, and the case was remanded for further proceedings.

The cases of *Fort Wayne Books v. Indiana* (1989) and *Sappenfield v. Indiana* (1989) were separate obscenity cases from Indiana that the Court consolidated because they both involved the state of Indiana using its RICO (Racketeer Influenced and Corrupt Organizations) statute against operators of adult bookstores. In *Sappenfield*, the issue before the Court was whether the RICO statute could constitutionally be applied to obscenity violations. *Fort Wayne Books* confronted the Court with a different question, the constitutionality of a trial court decision that probable cause existed that the bookstore was violating the RICO statute and therefore that the bookstore could be padlocked and all of its contents could be seized and hauled away by law enforcement officials. As in the dial-a-porn cases, the Court decided one case liberally and one case conservatively, ruling in the *Sappenfield* case that the RICO statute could be applied to the distribution of obscene materials but holding in the Fort Wayne Books case that the state had far exceeded its authority.

The Court's conservative coalition remained solidified in the only obscenity case of the 1989–90 term, *Osborne v. Ohio* (1990). Clyde Osborne was convicted under an Ohio child pornography statute of possessing in his home four photographs that showed a nude, fourteen-year-old male posed in sexually explicit positions. This case presented the Court with a conflict between two major precedents, *Stanley v. Georgia* (1969) and *New York v. Ferber* (1982). *Stanley* established that a person has a constitutional right to possess obscene materials in the privacy of one's own home, whereas *Ferber* provided the government with broad powers over child pornography. Writing for a six-person majority, White argued that the interests of the government in combatting the evils of child pornography are so great that the *Stanley* decision should not be extended to include the possession of sexual materials involving children. Thus, White concluded, Ohio could constitutionally ban the possession and viewing of child pornography. Brennan, joined by Marshall and Stevens, wrote his final obscenity case dissent in *Osborne*, arguing that the law was overbroad and, much more fundamentally, that *Stanley* rather than *Ferber* should control this case. According to Brennan, *Ferber* involved the production and distribution of child pornography but did not extend to its private possession. Stanley, however, prohibited the government from criminalizing the private possession of obscene materials, and this was exactly what Ohio's law did, thus violating the First Amendment.

With Brennan's resignation from the Court at the end of the 1989–90 term, the liberal bloc became even smaller, shrinking from three justices to two, Marshall and Stevens. Brennan's successor, Souter, voted with the Court's conservative justices in a major 1991 sexual expression case, *Barnes v. Glen Theatre*. It is probably premature to assess Souter's views on obscenity, however, because *Barnes* involved the subject of public indecency rather than obscenity, and Souter wrote a separate concurring opinion in the case.

This case involved two establishments in South Bend, Indiana—The Kitty Kat Lounge and Glen Theatre—which wished to offer totally nude dancing. This was prohibited, however, by an Indiana statute that required female dancers to wear pasties and a g-string when they performed. Both establishments as well as individual dancers brought suit against Indiana, arguing that the law prohibiting complete nudity violated their First Amendment rights.

Although the Court ruled 5-4 in favor of Indiana, the justices could not agree on a majority opinion. Rehnquist wrote the plurality opinion, but he was joined only by O'Connor and Kennedy. Rehnquist acknowledged that nude dancing as entertainment did come within the protection of the First Amendment, although "only marginally so" (501 U.S. at 566). Rehnquist argued that nude dancing was a form of symbolic expression and that therefore the four-prong test for symbolic expression set forth in *United States v. O'Brien* (1968), the draft card burning case, should be used. Applying this test, Rehnquist found Indiana's law to meet each requirement: (1) the public indecency statute was within the constitutional power of the state, (2) the law furthered substantial government interests of protecting societal order and morality, (3) the government interest was unrelated to suppressing freedom of expression, and (4) the infringement on expression was a limited one essential to furthering the government's substantial interests.

Scalia and Souter both agreed with the judgment in favor of the Indiana law, but they did so for different reasons than the Court plurality. Scalia did not view the law as even implicating the First Amendment freedom of speech guarantee; he saw it as a general law regulating a form of conduct, public nudity, and for Scalia this was clearly within the state's legitimate power. Souter agreed with the plurality on two key points: nude dancing as entertainment was expression within the meaning of the First Amendment, and the four-part *O'Brien* test was the appropriate approach. He disagreed with the plurality, however, regarding Indiana's interests in the law. Souter rejected the viewpoint that the state was promoting societal morality; instead, he argued that the law promoted the state's interests in combatting the harmful secondary effects associated with adult entertainment establishments, including prostitution, sexual assault, and other similar types of crimes.

White wrote a dissenting opinion that was joined by Blackmun, Stevens, and Marshall. Souter's replacement of Brennan was thus a critical development in regard to this case, because Brennan would undoubtedly have sided with the four dissenters to create a majority finding the law unconstitutional. White argued that the Indiana law was not a general law but was directed at protected expression under the First Amendment, requiring the state to meet the strict scrutiny test requiring a compelling government interest achieved by narrowly tailored means. According to White, Indiana could not satisfy either requirement of the strict scrutiny approach.

Barnes v. Glen Theatre

501 U.S. 560, 111 S.Ct. 2456, 115 L.Ed. 2d. 504

■ Two adult establishments in South Bend, Indiana—The Kitty Kat Lounge and Glen Theatre—wanted to provide totally nude dancing as entertainment for paying customers, but an Indiana law regulating public nudity required that the dancers wear pasties and a G-string when dancing. The owners of these businesses and various dancers at the establishments brought suit in federal district court alleging that the Indiana law violated their First Amendment guarantee of freedom of expression. In an exceptionally involved set of cases in the lower federal courts, the Seventh Circuit Court of Appeals eventually ruled in a divided decision that the Indiana law did violate the First Amendment.

This case is important because it illustrates the Court's involvement with legislation regulating sexual expression that is not obscene. As you read this decision, consider the following questions: (1) Should nonobscene nude dancing be included within the meaning of the First Amendment? (2) Is it logical to apply the *O'Brien* test to this case when *O'Brien* involved an antiwar protestor burning his draft card? (3) What decision would the Court have reached if the strict scrutiny test had been used?

Vote:

5 justices voted that the law was constitutional (Kennedy, O'Connor, Rehnquist, Scalia, Souter).

4 justices voted that the law was unconstitutional (Blackmun, Marshall, Stevens, White).

Chief Justice Rehnquist announced the judgment of the Court and delivered an opinion, in which Justice O'Connor and Justice Kennedy join.

* * *

Several of our cases contain language suggesting that nude dancing of the kind involved here is expressive conduct protected by the First Amendment. *Doran v. Salem Inn, Inc.* (1975), *California v. LaRue* (1972), *Schad v. Borough of Mount Ephram* (1981). These statements support the conclusion of the Court of Appeals that nude dancing of the kind sought to be performed here is expressive conduct within the outer perimeters of the First Amendment, though we view it as only marginally so. This, of course, does not end our inquiry. We must determine the level of protection to be afforded to the expressive conduct at issue, and must determine whether the Indiana statute is an impermissible infringement of that protected activity.

* * * Respondents contend that while the state may license establishments such as the ones involved here, and limit the geographical area in which they do business, it may not in any way limit the performance of the dances within them without violating the First Amendment. The petitioner contends, on the other hand, that Indiana's restriction on nude dancing is a valid "time, place, or manner" restriction under cases such as *Clark v. Community for Creative Non-Violence* (1984).

The "time, place, or manner" test was developed for evaluating restrictions on expression taking place on public property which had been dedicated as a "public forum," *Ward v. Rock Against Racism* (1989), although we have on at least one occasion applied it to conduct occurring on private property. See *Renton v. Playtime Theatres, Inc.* (1986). In *Clark* we observed that this test has been interpreted to embody much the same standards as those set forth in *United States v. O'Brien* (1968), and we turn, therefore, to the rule enunciated in *O'Brien*.

O'Brien burned his draft card on the steps of the South Boston courthouse in the presence of a sizable crowd, and was convicted of violating a statute that prohibited the knowing destruction or mutilation of such a card. He claimed that his conviction was contrary to the First Amendment because his act was "symbolic speech"—expressive conduct. The court rejected his contention that symbolic speech is entitled to full First Amendment protection, saying:

> [E]ven on the assumption that the alleged communicative element in O'Brien's conduct is sufficient to bring into play the First Amendment, it does not necessarily follow that the destruction of a registration certificate is constitutionally protected activity. This Court has held that when "speech" and "nonspeech" elements are combined in the same course of conduct, a sufficiently important governmental interest in regulating the nonspeech element can justify incidental limitations on First Amendment freedoms. To characterize the quality of the governmental interest which must appear, the Court has employed a variety of descriptive terms: compelling; substantial; subordinating; paramount; cogent; strong. Whatever imprecision inheres in these terms, we think it clear that a government regulation is sufficiently justified if it is within the constitutional power of the Government; if it furthers an important or substantial governmental interest; if the governmental interest is unrelated to the suppression of free expression; and if the incidental restriction on alleged First Amendment freedoms is no greater than is essential to the furtherance of that interest.

Applying the four-part *O'Brien* test enunciated above, we find that Indiana's public indecency statute is justified despite its incidental limitations on some expressive activity. The public indecency statute is clearly within the constitutional power of the State and furthers substantial governmental interests. * * * The statute's purpose of protecting societal order and morality is clear from its text and history. * * *

* * *

This interest is unrelated to the suppression of free expression. * * *

* * * The requirement that the dancers don pasties and a G-string does not deprive the dance of whatever erotic message it conveys; it simply makes the message slightly less graphic. * * * Public nudity is the evil the state seeks to prevent, whether or not it is combined with expressive activity.

* * *

The fourth part of the O'Brien test requires that the incidental restriction on First Amendment freedom be no greater than is essential to the furtherance of the governmental interest. * * * It is without cavil that the public indecency statute is "narrowly tailored;" Indiana's requirement that the dancers wear at least pasties and a G-string is modest, and the bare minimum necessary to achieve the state's purpose.

The judgment of the Court of Appeals accordingly is reversed.

Justice Scalia, concurring in the judgment.

I agree that the judgment of the Court of Appeals must be reversed. In my view, however, the challenged regulation must be upheld, not because it survives some lower level of First Amendment scrutiny, but because, as a general law regulating conduct and not specifically directed at expression, it is not subject to First Amendment scrutiny at all.

* * *

Indiana's statute is in the line of a long tradition of laws against public nudity, which have never been thought to run afoul of traditional understanding of "the freedom of speech." * * *

* * *

Since the Indiana regulation is a general law not specifically targeted at expressive conduct, its application to such conduct does not in my view implicate the First Amendment.

The First Amendment explicitly protects "the freedom of speech [and] of the press"—oral and written speech—not "expressive conduct." When any law restricts speech, even for a purpose that has nothing to do with the suppression of communication, we insist that it meet the high, First Amendment standard of justification. But virtually *every* law restricts conduct, and virtually *any* prohibited conduct can be performed for an expressive purpose—if only expressive of the fact that the actor disagrees with the prohibition. It cannot reasonably be demanded, therefore, that every restriction of expression incidentally produced by a general law regulating conduct pass normal First Amendment scrutiny, or even—as some of our cases have suggested, e.g., *United States v. O'Brien* (1968)—that it be justified by an "important or substantial" government interest. Nor do our holdings require such justification: we have never invalidated the application of a general law simply because the conduct that it reached was being engaged in for expressive purposes and the government could not demonstrate a sufficiently important state interest.

This is not to say that the First Amendment affords no protection to expressive conduct. Where the government prohibits conduct *precisely because of its communicative attributes,* we hold the regulation unconstitutional. Where that has not been the case, however—where suppression of communicative use of the conduct was merely the incidental effect of forbidding the conduct for other reasons—we have allowed the regulation to stand. *O'Brien.* * * *

* * *

While I do not think the plurality's conclusions differ greatly from my own, I cannot entirely endorse its reasoning. The plurality purports to apply to this general law, insofar as it regulates this allegedly expressive conduct, an intermediate level of First Amendment scrutiny: the government interest in the regulation must be "important or substantial." As I have indicated, I do not believe such a heightened standard exists. I think we should avoid wherever possible, moreover, a method of analysis that requires judicial assessment of the "importance" of government interests—and especially of government interests in various aspects of morality.

* * * In *Bowers* [1986], we held that since homosexual behavior is not a fundamental right, a Georgia law prohibiting private homosexual intercourse needed only a rational basis in order to comply with the Due Process Clause. Moral opposition to homosexuality, we said, provided that rational basis. I would uphold the Indiana statute on precisely the same ground: moral opposition to nudity supplies a rational basis for its prohibition, and since the First Amendment has no application to this case no more than that is needed.

Indiana may constitutionally enforce its prohibition of public nudity even against those who choose to use public nudity as a means of communication. The State is regulating conduct, not expression, and those who choose to employ conduct as a means of expression must make sure that the conduct they select is not generally forbidden. For these reasons, I agree that the judgment should be reversed.

Justice Souter, concurring in the judgment.

* * *

* * * I agree with the plurality and the dissent that an interest in freely engaging in the nude dancing at issue here is subject to a degree of First Amendment protection.

I also agree with the plurality that the appropriate analysis to determine the actual protection is the four-part enquiry described in *United States v. O'Brien* (1968). * * * I nonetheless write separately to rest my concurrence in the judgment, not on the possible sufficiency of society's moral views to justify the limitations at issue, but on the State's substantial interest in combating the secondary effects of adult entertainment establishments of the sort typified by respondents' establishments.

* * *

In *Renton v. Playtime Theatres* (1986), we upheld a city's zoning ordinance designed to prevent the occurrence of harmful secondary effects, including the crime associated with adult entertainment. * * *

* * * In light of *Renton*'s recognition that legislation seeking to combat the secondary effects of adult entertainment need not await localized proof of those effects, the State of Indiana could reasonably conclude that forbidding nude entertainment of the type offered at the Kitty Kat Lounge and the Glen Theatre's "bookstore" furthers its interest in preventing prostitution, sexual assault, and associated crimes. * * *

* * *

Accordingly, I find *O'Brien* satisfied and concur in the judgment.

Justice White, with whom Justice Marshall, Justice Blackmun, and Justice Stevens join, dissenting.

* * *

The Court's analysis is erroneous in several respects. Both the Court and Justice Scalia in his concurring opinion overlook a fundamental and critical aspect of our cases upholding the State's exercise of their police powers. None of the cases they rely upon, including *O'Brien* and *Bowers v. Hardwick*, involved anything less than truly *general* proscriptions on individual conduct. * * * By contrast, in this case Indiana does not suggest that its statute applies to, or could be applied to, nudity wherever it occurs, including the home. * * *

We are told by the Attorney General of Indiana that, in *State v. Baysinger* (1979), the Indiana Supreme Court held that the statute at issue here cannot and does not prohibit nudity as a part of some larger form of expression meriting protection when the communication of ideas is involved. Petitioners also state that the evils sought to be avoided by applying the statute in this case would not obtain in the case of theatrical productions, such as Salome or Hair. Neither is there any evidence that the State has attempted to apply the statute to nudity in performances such as plays, ballets, or operas. * * *

Thus, the Indiana statute is not a *general* prohibition of the type we have upheld in prior cases. As a result, the Court's and Justice Scalia's simple references to the State's general interest in promoting societal order and morality is not sufficient justification for a statute which concededly reaches a significant amount of protected expressive activity. Instead, in applying the *O'Brien* test we are obligated to carefully examine the reasons the State has chosen to regulate this expressive conduct in a less than general statute. In other words, when the State enacts a law which draws a line between expressive conduct which is regulated and nonexpressive conduct of the same type which is not regulated, *O'Brien* places the burden on the State to justify the distinctions it has made. Closer inquiry as to the purpose of the statute is surely appropriate.

* * *

The Court holds that the third requirement of the *O'Brien* test, that the governmental interest be unrelated to the suppression of free expression, is satisfied because in applying the statute to nude dancing, the State is not "proscribing nudity because of the erotic message conveyed by the dancers." * * *

In arriving at its conclusion, the Court concedes that nude dancing conveys an erotic message and concedes that the message would be muted if the dancers wore pasties and G-strings. * * * The nudity is itself an expressive component of the dance, not merely incidental "conduct." * * *

This being the case, it cannot be that the statutory prohibition is unrelated to expressive conduct. Since the State permits the dancers to perform if they wear pasties and G-strings but forbids nude dancing, it is precisely because of the distinctive, expressive content of the nude dancing performances at issue in this case that the State seeks to apply the statutory prohibition. * * *

That fact dictates the level of First Amendment protection to be accorded the performances at issue here. In *Texas v. Johnson* (1989) the Court observed: "Whether Johnson's treatment of the flag violated Texas law thus depended on the likely communicative impact of his expressive conduct. . . . We must therefore subject the State's asserted interest in preserving the special symbolic character of the flag to 'the most exacting scrutiny.' " Content based restrictions "will be upheld only if narrowly drawn to accomplish a compelling governmental interest." Nothing could be clearer from our cases.

That the performances in the Kitty Kat Lounge may not be high art, to say the least, and may not appeal to the Court, is hardly an excuse for distorting and ignoring settled doctrine. * * *

The Court and Justice Souter do not go beyond saying that the state interests asserted here are important and substantial. But even if there were compelling interests, the Indiana statute is not narrowly drawn. If the State is genuinely concerned with prostitution and associated evils, as Justice Souter seems to think, or the type of conduct that was occurring in *California v. LaRue* (1972), it can adopt restrictions that do not interfere with the expressiveness of nonobscene nude dancing performances. For instance, the State could perhaps require that, while performing, nude performers remain at all times a certain minimum distance from spectators, that nude entertainment be limited to certain hours, or even that establishments providing such entertainment be dispersed throughout the city. Likewise, the State clearly has the authority to criminalize prostitution and obscene behavior. Banning an entire category of expressive activity, however, generally does not satisfy the narrow tailoring requirement of strict First Amendment scrutiny. Furthermore, if nude dancing in barrooms, as compared with other establishments, is the worrisome problem, the State could invoke its Twenty-First Amendment powers and impose appropriate regulation.

As I see it, our cases require us to affirm absent a compelling state interest supporting the statute. Neither the Court nor the State suggest that the statute could withstand scrutiny under that standard.

* * *

Accordingly, I would affirm the judgment of the Court of Appeals, and dissent from this Court's judgment.

The Rehnquist Court has heard few obscenity cases since *Barnes*, deciding only two cases in the four terms from 1991–1994. In both *Alexander v. United States* (1993) and *United States v. X-Citement Video* (1995), the Court upheld the constitutionality of laws that were being challenged as violating the First Amendment. Both cases are classified as being of minor importance, but they provide important insight into the conservative direction of the Rehnquist Court in the area of obscenity.

Alexander involved the Court in supporting the constitutionality of forfeiting provisions of the federal Racketeer Influenced and Corrupt Organizations Act (RICO). Ferris Alexander was the owner of over a dozen stores and theaters in Minnesota dealing in sexually explicit materials, and he was convicted by a Minnesota Federal District Court jury of seventeen obscenity counts. Based on these obscenity convictions, Alexander was also convicted of three racketeering offenses under the RICO statute. He was sentenced to six years in prison and fined $100,000 on the obscenity charges. Applying the RICO laws, the district court determined that Alexander had acquired a vast business empire through his racketeering activities, and the Court ordered Alexander to forfeit all his businesses and assets as well as nearly $9,000,000 in moneys he had acquired through the businesses. The decision was affirmed by the court of appeals.

In a 5-4 decision, the Supreme Court upheld the forfeiture order against Alexander's claims that his First Amendment freedom of expression rights were violated on several grounds. He argued that the forfeiture provisions of the RICO statute constituted a form of prior restraint, were overbroad, and had a chilling effect on freedom of expression. Writing for a majority that included White, O'Connor, Scalia, and Thomas, Chief Justice Rehnquist rejected all of these claims. The Court did, however, remand the case to the court of appeals to analyze the forfeiture under the Eighth Amendment excessive fines clause.

The *X-Citement Video* case saw the Court upholding the constitutionality of the 1977 Protection of Children Against Sexual Exploitation Act. This law provided among its features that no person should distribute any visual depiction of anyone under eighteen years of age engaged in sexually explicit conduct. In this case, Ruben Gottesman owned and operated a company named X-Citement Video, which produced sexually explicit films. Gottesman's company made a number of films featuring Traci Lords, who had represented herself as over eighteen but was actually younger. Gottesman was convicted in district court of violating the child pornography statute, but the Ninth Circuit Court of Appeals reversed the conviction. The circuit court ruled that the First Amendment requires that a criminal defendant in a case like this must possess knowledge that a performer was a minor, and the 1977 Act violated this requirement because the law did not require a showing of such knowledge.

Rehnquist wrote the seven-person majority opinion, which consisted of an unusual coalition of Stevens, Souter, O'Connor, Kennedy, Ginsburg, and Breyer.

Rehnquist conceded that the language of the statute was somewhat ambiguous, but he argued that the law could ultimately be interpreted to require proof that a defendant has knowledge of the age of a performer. Thus, Rehnquist concluded, the law does not violate the requirements of the First Amendment.

The Rehnquist Court appears to be removing itself to some extent from the area of obscenity. The Court has heard only two obscenity cases in its four most recent terms, and both of these cases involved federal law. Given the Court's careful control over its agenda, this evidence suggests that the Court may be consciously seeking to extricate itself from this contentious area of constitutional law. If this is a conscious path the Court is seeking to pursue, however, the justices are not likely to be completely successful. The pervasiveness of sexually oriented materials in American society coupled with the dramatic changes occurring in technology are likely to keep obscenity and pornography issues before the Court. For example, the 1996 Communications Decency Act imposes criminal penalties upon individuals who send "indecent" material over the Internet to persons younger than eighteen years of age, and a federal district court has found this law to be unconstitutional.

Conclusion

The Rehnquist Court has taken a generally conservative position in its obscenity cases, but the Court has not engaged in a conservative counterrevolution in this area of constitutional law. Instead, the Rehnquist Court has essentially followed the path established by the Burger Court, which set forth the *Miller* test as a more conservative approach to the obscenity question than the Warren Court had established in *Roth* and its successor cases. Furthermore, the Rehnquist Court has established a voting record remarkably similar to that of the Burger Court, favoring the government in roughly three-fourths of its obscenity decisions, whereas the Warren Court ruled liberally in three-fourths of its cases.

Despite these important differences between the Warren Court on the one hand and the Burger and Rehnquist Courts on the other hand, important continuities can also be seen. First, the Court during all three eras has consistently maintained the position that obscenity is beyond constitutional protection because it is lacking in social value. Second, despite all the time and effort given to this area by the Court, relatively little in the way of consensus and clarity has emerged among the justices. Third, American society has seen a dramatic and continuous growth since the 1950s in the availability and explicitness of sexually oriented materials despite the more conservative approach to obscenity introduced by the Burger Court and supported by the Rehnquist Court.

Obscenity is going to remain a highly contentious issue in American society. Liberal critics of the Court will continue to argue that the Court should abandon its efforts to define obscenity and should include it within the protection of the First Amendment. Similarly, conservative critics of the Court—as well as many people who are liberals on other issues—will continue to argue that the Court should permit much tighter government control on sexually oriented materials because obscenity, and pornography more generally, are harmful to individuals and to society. The justices will remain in the eye of the storm and seem unlikely to satisfy anyone, including themselves.

REFERENCES

Cohen, William, and David S. Danelski *Constitutional Law: Civil Liberty and Individual Rights*. 3d ed. Westburg, New York: The Foundation Press, 1994.

Downs, Donald A. *The New Politics of Pornography*. Chicago: University of Chicago Press, 1989.

Dworkin, Andrea, and Catherine A. MacKinnon *Pornography and Civil Rights: A New Day for Women's Equality*. Minneapolis, Minnesota: Organizing Against Pornography, 1988.

Final Report: Attorney General's Commission on Pornography. Washington, D.C.: U.S. Department of Justice, 1986.

Itzen, Catherine. "A Legal Definition of Pornography." Chap. 22 in *Pornography: Women, Violence, and Civil Liberties*, edited by Catherine Itzen. New York: Oxford University Press, 1992.

Kobylka, Joseph F. *The Politics of Obscenity*. Westport, Conn.: Greenwood Press, 1991.

MacKinnon, Catherine A. *Only Words*. Cambridge, Massachusetts: Harvard University Press, 1993.

The Report of the Commission on Obscenity and Pornography. Washington, D.C.: U.S. Government Printing Office, 1970.

Schauer, Frederick F. *The Law of Obscenity*, Washington, D.C.: The Bureau of National Affairs, 1976.

Urofsky, Melvin I. *The Continuity of Change: The Supreme Court and Individual Liberties, 1953-1986*. Belmont, California: Wadsworth Publishing Co., 1991.

Zillman, Dolf. "Pornography Research and Public Policy." Chap. 15 in *Pornography: Research Advances and Policy Considerations*, edited by Dolf Zillman and Jennings Bryant. Hillsdale, New Jersey: Lawrence Erlbaum Associates, 1989.

Constitutional Guarantees for the Criminally Accused

Introduction and Overview

OVERVIEW

In the next four chapters, we will examine the constitutional guarantees that protect people who are suspects or defendants in criminal proceedings. In fact, these guarantees, such as the prohibition against unreasonable searches and seizures contained in the Fourth Amendment, protect everyone against certain governmental intrusions. Few Americans would want to see law enforcement officials have the authority to search people and their property without proper justification because of the risk that such activities would violate our privacy and freedom. Despite the applicability of these constitutional provisions to all Americans, most of the cases in which the Supreme Court has analyzed and defined these constitutional guarantees concern instances in which people are suspected or accused of criminal activity.

The Fourth Amendment deals with government searches and seizures:

> *The right of the people to be secure in their persons, houses, papers, and effects, against unreasonable searches and seizures, shall not be violated, and no Warrants shall issue, but upon probable cause, supported by Oath or affirmation, and particularly describing the place to be searched, and the persons or things to be seized.*

The basic purpose of the Fourth Amendment is to guarantee citizens the right to be free from arbitrary actions by law enforcement officials. Thus, the Fourth Amendment indicates that a law enforcement officer should not engage in a search or an arrest unless a warrant—a judicial order—has been obtained by the officer. This officer must have convinced a judicial official that probable cause indicates the existence of a crime and supports the requested permission to search or arrest. Despite the explicit wording of the Fourth Amendment, however, the Court has long recognized that warrants cannot be obtained in all situations if we are to enjoy an orderly society in which criminal activity is controlled. To take an obvious example, a police officer could make an immediate arrest without a warrant if a masked man was observed robbing a convenience store. Warrantless searches and arrests can thus be constitutional and are, in fact, quite common. The Supreme Court has devoted significant attention to the question of the circumstances under which warrantless searches are permissible.

A major area of controversy associated with the Fourth Amendment deals with the exclusionary rule, a judicial principle that any evidence obtained in violation of a person's Fourth (or Fifth) Amendment rights must be excluded from use by the prosecution. The exclusionary rule is not mentioned in the words of the Fourth Amendment, but the Supreme Court developed this rule in the early twentieth century as a way of deterring police misconduct and assuring greater fairness in the criminal justice process. The Court and the country continue to debate the wisdom of the exclusionary rule.

The Fifth Amendment contains numerous guarantees, including the Grand Jury Clause, the Double Jeopardy Clause, the Self-Incrimination Clause, the Due Process Clause, and the Just Compensation Clause. Although several states use grand juries, the right to indictment by a grand jury is limited to certain kinds of charges in the federal courts and therefore will not be a focus of Chapter 10. The Double Jeopardy Clause means that a person can be tried only once for the same crime, but, as we shall see, the exact meaning of the clause has raised many complex questions for the Court. The Fifth Amendment's privilege against compelled self-incrimination is intended to prevent government officials from using their coercive powers—including torture and beatings—to gain confessions from arrested suspects. This clause has generated a large number of cases and is the foundation for the *Miranda* warnings.

The Sixth Amendment contains numerous guarantees applicable to the criminal justice process, especially during the trial stage. These constitutional provisions include: (1) the right to a speedy trial; (2) the right to a public trial; (3) the right to a jury trial; (4) the right of the accused to be informed of the charges being pursued by the prosecution; (5) the right of the accused to confront witnesses against him or her; (6) the right to have compulsory process for obtaining witnesses in one's favor through the use of a court order, called a subpoena; and (7) the right to have the assistance of defense counsel. All of these specific guarantees are focused on the overriding purpose of assuring a defendant a fair trial, which is part of the even broader guarantee of due process of law. Although these Sixth Amendment guarantees may appear to be specific and clear, we will discover that the Court has been confronted with numerous complex and intriguing cases in which it has had to interpret the meaning of these clauses.

The Eighth Amendment contains prohibitions against excessive bail, excessive fines, and cruel and unusual punishments. The Court has given relatively little attention either to the excessive bail or to the excessive fines clause, and neither clause has been nationalized (see Chapter 4). By contrast, the Court has given extensive attention to the guarantee against cruel and unusual punishments. Many of these cases have involved the death penalty, but other cases have focused on other kinds of punishments and prison conditions.

Relationships among the Guarantees

We now turn to a brief discussion of how the Fourth, Fifth, Sixth, and Eighth Amendments relate to each other. We want to suggest two ways of viewing the relationships among these four amendments, recognizing that the following generalizations are oversimplified. They are presented in an attempt to provide a basis for organizing and analyzing the Supreme Court's actions and impact on the criminal justice process.

One way of thinking about the relationship of these four amendments is to view them as roughly parallel to the four stages of the criminal justice process. Thus, the Fourth Amendment generally deals with the initial investigatory stage where a crime has been reported, the search for evidence occurs, and an arrest is made. The Fifth Amendment can be viewed as corresponding to the pretrial stage of the criminal justice process. Although the Double Jeopardy Clause does not fit this characterization, the Self-Incrimination Clause and the Grand Jury Clause concern suspects identified during the criminal investigation who are drawn into contact with prosecutorial officials in the justice system. The Sixth Amendment guarantees apply at the third stage of the criminal justice process, the trial stage. One of the Sixth Amendment's protections, the right to counsel, also extends into the earlier pretrial stages of the process. Finally, the Eighth Amendment clauses dealing with excessive fines as well as cruel and unusual punishments correspond to the fourth and final stage of the criminal justice process, the sentencing and punishment stage for those found guilty.

A different approach to thinking about the relationships of the four criminal justice amendments involves the relative balancing by the Court of the individual's asserted constitutional right versus the interests of government and society. Recognizing again that we are oversimplifying, one can arguably say the Court gives increasingly greater weight to the individual's interests as it moves from Fourth Amendment issues through the stages of the justice process to the final-stage Eighth Amendment issues. With respect to Fourth Amendment issues, law enforcement personnel are faced with the difficult realities of investigating criminal cases, many of which will never be solved. In striking a balance between the individual and society, the Court is often willing to give law enforcement personnel substantial leeway in conducting searches and seizures as part of the difficult investigatory process. In emphasizing the societal interests in law enforcement and criminal investigations, the justices may appear to minimize the burdens placed on people in certain search and seizure situations.

After an individual is arrested and the potentially awesome power of government is brought to bear in questioning a person held in custody, the Court may demonstrate greater concern for protecting the individual in striking its balance between individuals' asserted rights and societal interests. During the trial stage, the individual defendant has moved closer to the possibility of punishment and loss of liberty. Thus the Sixth and Eighth Amendments spur the Court to place even greater weight on individuals' asserted constitutional rights and develop clearer rules for appropriate conduct by justice system officials. In sum, the Court frequently appears to minimize the adverse effects of governmental intrusions on individuals' autonomy and privacy in deciding Fourth Amendment cases; at the opposite extreme, the Court often expresses grave concerns about the care with which the justice system decides death penalty cases that involve the Eighth Amendment.

This is not to say that the government wins all Fourth Amendment cases or that individuals win all Sixth and Eighth Amendment cases. As we will see, the outcomes of cases depend on the nature of the issues and the views of the justices who are on the Court when a case is presented for decision. The foregoing generalizations are merely a rough, imprecise effort to identify underlying patterns in the Court's decisions. As you read the text and cases in the following chapters, you can assess for yourself whether you agree that the Court's balancing of societal law enforcement interests versus individuals' interests in constitutional rights varies as the justices confront issues arising from different constitutional amendments.

As we move from considering the First Amendment in the preceding section to this section's examination of the Fourth, Fifth, Sixth, and Eighth Amendment rights, we are omitting coverage of several provisions in the Bill of Rights. These amendments, the Second, Third, and Seventh, were sufficiently important to the framers of the Bill of Rights to deserve inclusion in the Constitution. However, the Supreme Court has devoted scant attention to their interpretation as compared to other provisions of the Bill of Rights and the Fourteenth Amendment. The Second Amendment refers to "the right of the people to keep and bear Arms." These words have provided the basis for significant political debates about the government's authority to regulate or ban the possession, sale, and ownership of firearms. This issue spurs debate, in part, because the so-called right to keep and bear arms is presented in the Second Amendment's words as related to the need for a "well-regulated Militia" rather than as an explicit, unequivocal guarantee for every individual citizen. While the public debates continue to rage about the meaning of the Second Amendment, the Supreme Court has never interpreted it to provide a constitutional right to own firearms and, moreover, the Court has not incorporated the amendment to apply it to the states.

The Third Amendment, concerning the quartering of troops in people's homes, was intended to prevent a British practice that essentially never materialized as a problem for Americans as they governed their own country. The Supreme Court has had occasion to interpret the Seventh Amendment's right to a jury trial in civil cases, but the amendment was never incorporated for application to the states so the relevant cases primarily concern judicial proceedings arising under federal statutes. Because these amendments have received so little attention from the Supreme Court, we will omit them and move ahead to the amendments concerning criminal proceedings.

Organization 

This section of the book is organized around the four constitutional amendments associated with the guarantees affecting people drawn into contact with the criminal justice system. Chapter 9 analyzes the Fourth Amendment, focusing on the topics of warrantless searches and the exclusionary rule. The Fifth Amendment is examined in Chapter 10, and the focus is on the *Miranda* warnings. Chapter 11 analyzes the various provisions of the Sixth Amendment. Finally, Chapter 12 examines the Eighth Amendment, focusing primarily on the death penalty.

CHAPTER

THE FOURTH AMENDMENT GUARANTEE AGAINST UNREASONABLE SEARCHES AND SEIZURES

CASE STUDY

MAPP V. OHIO (1961)

On May 23, 1957, three police officers in Cleveland, Ohio, came to the home of Dollree Mapp. The police had received a confidential tip that a bombing suspect was hiding in Ms. Mapp's house. They also had information indicating that gambling paraphernalia was in Mapp's home. When the officers knocked on the door, Mapp, who had telephoned her lawyer upon their arrival, told them they could not enter unless they showed her their search warrant. The officers called their headquarters and remained on the scene keeping the house under surveillance. Three hours later, more officers arrived and demanded entrance to the home. When Mapp would not answer the door, the officers forced their way into the house. Mapp met the officers on the stairway and demanded to see their search warrant. One officer waved a piece of paper in the air. When Mapp grabbed the paper and placed it inside her blouse, the officers wrestled with her and retrieved it. Mapp was then placed in handcuffs for being, according to the officers, "belligerent" and for resisting their efforts to retrieve the piece of paper. Mapp's attorney, Walter Green, arrived on the scene, but the police barred him from entering the house or seeing his client (Barker and Barker 1972, p. 261). According to the U.S. Supreme Court's later description of the scene, "[r]unning roughshod over [Mapp], a policeman 'grabbed' her, 'twisted [her] hand,' and she 'yelled [and] pleaded with him' because 'it was hurting' " (*Mapp v. Ohio,* 367 U.S. at 645).

The police officers went upstairs and searched a dresser, chest of drawers, a closet, and some suitcases. They also looked through a photo album and Mapp's personal papers. The police officers found a brown paper bag containing several books. Mapp yelled at the police officers, "Better not look at those. They might excite you." When asked if the bag belonged to her, Mapp replied "No." The bag contained books with such titles as *The Affairs of the Troubadour, London Stage Affairs, Little Darlings,* and *Memories of Hotel Man.* The officers proceeded to search the bedroom of Mapp's teenage daughter as well as the living room, kitchen, and dinette. They also searched the basement and a trunk in the basement. Although the officers did not find the bombing suspect or any gambling materials, they charged Mapp with possession of obscene materials because the books were found in her home (Barker and Barker 1972, p. 262).

Mapp's chief attorney, A. L. Kearns, made a motion on September 3, 1958, to suppress the evidence against her on the grounds that it had been seized illegally. Judge Donald Lybarger of the Cuyahoga County Common Pleas Court rejected the motion and Mapp's trial began. Gertrude Bauer Mahon, the assistant county prosecutor, sought to prove that the books, which the state had labeled as "obscene," belonged to Mapp. The prosecution did not present any search warrant into evidence nor was there an explanation for the whereabouts of the search warrant that the police had claimed justified their search. Mapp took the witness stand and testified that the books belonged to a boarder who had recently moved out and left many of his possessions behind. Her other attorney, Walter Green, testified about the nature of the search and asserted that the police conduct had been unlawful. Mapp's attorneys also argued that the Ohio obscenity statute under which she was charged violated the First Amendment's protections for free expression and should be declared unconstitutional (Barker and Barker 1972, pp. 262–63).

Judge Lybarger did not accept the arguments presented by Mapp's attorneys. At the conclusion of the trial, he told the jury that Ohio law permitted illegally obtained evidence to be used in criminal proceedings. Mapp was given an indeterminate sentence of from one to seven years in prison. She was released on bail pending her appeal, but she lost her first appeal in the state court of appeals on March 31, 1959. Mapp's attorneys immediately pursued her appeal in the Ohio Supreme Court. Her attorneys made three arguments. First, they argued that the materials were not in her "possession" under the terms of the obscenity statute. Second, they argued that the evidence was taken by the police during an illegal search and seizure. Third, they argued that the statute was an unconstitutional infringement of the First Amendment. On March 23, 1960, the Ohio Supreme Court issued its opinion. Justice Kingsley Taft's majority opinion acknowledged that there was considerable doubt about whether the police actually had a search warrant, which meant that the police officers had violated state statutes and the state constitution, which both required that warrants support searches and describe the objects of the search. However, the Ohio Supreme Court cited both state case law and the U.S. Supreme Court's decision in *Wolf v. Colorado* (1949) to justify their conclusion that illegally seized items are admissible as evidence in criminal trials. When it examined Mapp's First Amendment claim, the state justices decided by a four-to-three vote that the Ohio statute infringed freedom of speech and press. Unfortunately for Mapp, because the Ohio Constitution required that state supreme court decisions invalidating state statutes must have unanimity or near unanimity (i.e., no more than one dissenter), the justices' opinion could not invalidate the statute and therefore Mapp's conviction remained undisturbed (Barker and Barker 1972, pp. 263–68).

Mapp's attorneys immediately sought to have the U.S. Supreme Court review her conviction. They were joined by Bernard Berkman, a Cleveland lawyer who submitted an *amicus* brief for Mapp on behalf of the American Civil Liberties Union and who participated in oral arguments. The brief and oral arguments presented by Mapp's attorney, A. L. Kearns, focused exclusively on the First Amendment issue and sought to have the Ohio obscenity statute invalidated. Berkman's brief for the ACLU focused on First Amendment arguments, but also included one paragraph asserting that the high court should reconsider its *Wolf* precedent that permitted state courts to admit evidence obtained during the course of illegal searches and seizures (Barker and Barker 1972, pp. 268–70).

When the U.S. Supreme Court issued its decision on June 29, 1961, the majority focused on the Fourth Amendment search and seizure issue rather than on the First Amendment free expression issue that had been the focus of the attorneys' arguments (case excerpt on p. 432). In writing for five of the six justices in the majority, Justice Tom Clark declared that Ms. Mapp's Fourth Amendment rights had been violated by the illegal search and, perhaps more importantly, the evidence obtained through the illegal search could not be used against her in court. The "exclusionary rule" concerning the inadmissibility of illegally obtained evidence had applied against federal law enforcement officers since 1914. The effect of the *Mapp* decision was to apply this rule to state and local police too. Clark declared that "the exclusionary rule is an essential part of both the Fourth and Fourteenth Amendments" (367 U.S. at 657). According to Clark, "To hold otherwise is to grant the right [against unreasonable searches and seizures] but in reality to withhold its privilege and enjoyment" (367 U.S. at 656). A central premise of the majority opinion was that there were no alternative remedies short of exclusion of evidence that would protect people's Fourth Amendment rights against violation by the police. In Clark's words, "The experience of California that such other remedies have been worthless and futile is buttressed by the experience of other

States" (367 U.S. at 652). This conclusion about the inadequacies of other possible remedies was reiterated by Justice William O. Douglas in a concurring opinion.

Justice Potter Stewart was the sixth member of the majority by virtue of his vote to reverse Mapp's conviction. However, Stewart based his vote on the First Amendment issue argued by the attorneys. He believed that the Ohio obscenity statute that served as the basis for Mapp's conviction violated the First Amendment. Stewart explicitly declined to rule on the Fourth Amendment issue.

In a concurring opinion, Justice Hugo Black expressed doubts about whether the Fourth Amendment required that improperly obtained evidence be barred from use against a defendant at trial. According to Black, "[T]he Fourth Amendment does not itself contain any provision expressly precluding the use of such evidence, and I am extremely doubtful that such a provision could properly be inferred from nothing more than the basic command against unreasonable searches and seizures" (367 U.S. at 661–62). However, Black agreed that the exclusionary rule was applicable to Mapp's case and other cases of illegal searches because he saw such cases as raising both Fourth *and* Fifth Amendment issues. In Black's eyes, evidence obtained through improper searches constituted a violation against compelled self-incrimination. Thus, according to Black, "when the Fourth Amendment's ban against unreasonable searches and seizures is considered together with the Fifth Amendment's ban against compelled self-incrimination, a constitutional basis emerges which not only justifies but actually requires the exclusionary rule" (367 U.S. at 662).

In dissent, Justice John Harlan, joined by Justices Felix Frankfurter and Charles Whittaker, complained that the Supreme Court should not impose such a significant new rule on police departments throughout the country without the benefit of briefs and oral arguments focused exclusively on the issue of search and seizure. They did not believe that the Court should make such an important Fourth Amendment decision in a case that was argued on the First Amendment issue of obscenity. The dissenters also argued that the Supreme Court should respect the autonomy of states and permit them to develop their own solutions to criminal justice problems without imposing a single search and seizure rule on every police department in the nation.

Although more than half of the states had already developed their own exclusionary rule, the *Mapp* decision produced a storm of controversy when the Supreme Court made exclusion of illegally obtained evidence a requirement for law enforcement officials in every state (Walker 1994, p. 125). Underlying the *Mapp* decision is a value choice that is not shared universally by justices, commentators, or citizens, many of whom are most concerned about ensuring that guilty offenders receive criminal punishment (see, e.g., Schlesinger 1977). By contrast, *Mapp* is based on the idea that society should be willing to see some guilty criminals go free, through the exclusion of relevant but illegally obtained evidence, rather than endure improper conduct by police officers that violates people's constitutional rights and that jeopardizes the integrity of judicial proceedings through the use of tainted evidence. Although a majority of members of the Warren Court believed that this choice represented the proper effectuation of the Fourth Amendment's purposes, other justices have disagreed. The controversial *Mapp* decision was one of the Warren Court cases that became a symbol to critics of the Supreme Court's active policy making and its alleged inclination to provide excessively broad constitutional protections for criminal defendants. Presidents Nixon, Reagan, and Bush sought to appoint justices who would view criminal defendants' rights more narrowly. As a result, in many of the Supreme Court's Fourth Amendment cases after *Mapp*, the Burger and Rehnquist Court justices questioned, refined, and narrowed the scope of the exclusionary rule imposed on law enforcement officers by the Warren Court.

Historical Origins and Contemporary Conflicts

Like other amendments, the Fourth Amendment finds its origins in historical developments in England. Search and seizure law does not have documented historical origins in any particular event or year. Instead, according to Edward Fisher

(1970, p. 2), "The inception and development of legally authorized search and seizure is shrouded in the semi-obscurity of the early English common law. Search warrants appear not to have been known as such at this remote period but crept gradually into the law by almost imperceptible practice, their use at first having been confined to searches for stolen goods." Eventually governments of various English kings began to use general warrants in abusive ways. Such warrants did not specify places to be searched or the items being sought. Instead, these general warrants authorized law enforcement officers to search when and where they pleased. In addition, the warrants were no longer used simply to search for stolen goods, but instead were used to seek any books and pamphlets that were critical of the king and his government (Fisher 1970, p. 3). In the mid-eighteenth century, Parliament passed resolutions condemning the use of such warrants, and English courts began to limit their use. In 1766, William Pitt, the Earl of Chatham, gave a speech before Parliament that included a classic declaration about the importance of protecting the sanctity of people's homes and effects from the intrusion of government searches. In Pitt's words,

> *Every man's house is called his castle. Why? Because it is surrounded by a moat, or defended by a wall? No. It may be a straw-built hut, the wind may whistle around it, the rain may enter it, but the King cannot.* * * *
>
> *The poorest man may, in his cottage, bid defiance to all the forces of the Crown. It may be frail; its roof may shake; the wind may blow through it; the storm may enter; the rain may enter; but the King of England may not enter; all his forces dare not cross the threshold of the ruined tenement.* (Fisher 1970, p. 3)

The American colonists drew from the lessons of English practice and expressed their concerns about these matters in the Fourth Amendment. The Fourth Amendment embodies the skepticism and fears of the authors of the Bill of Rights concerning the government's power to enter people's homes and businesses in pursuit of evidence. The framers of the Constitution felt abused by British officials' search practices, and they wanted to be sure that the new American government would respect the privacy and security of people's homes and property. American colonists had been victimized by "writs of assistance," general warrants used by the British to conduct exploratory searches (Alderman and Kennedy 1991, p. 135). These searches had been used primarily by British officials who wanted to inspect ships, cellars, warehouses, and other locations to be certain that proper taxes and duties were paid to the King for all goods. Because disputes over taxation were a key issue in the colonists' disputes with Britain that led to the Revolutionary War, the abuses from British search and seizure practices helped to inflame the anger of many Americans. The authors of the Bill of Rights were aware of famous English judicial decisions seeking to protect the goods and papers of British subjects from discretionary searches (e.g., Lord Camden's opinion in *Entick v. Carrington,* 1765). They drew from the underlying principles of such English precedents in order to protect themselves against abusive practices by the new government that they were creating, and they wrote into the Bill of Rights provisions requiring specific warrants supported by probable cause and prohibiting unreasonable searches and seizures. Thus, the Fourth Amendment provides limitations on the government's search and seizure powers.

According to the words of the Fourth Amendment, "The right of the people to be secure in their persons, houses, papers and effects, against unreasonable searches and seizures, shall not be violated, and no Warrants shall issue, but upon probable cause, supported by Oath or affirmation, and particularly describing the place to be searched, and the persons or things to be seized." The Amendment contains two primary components. First, the amendment provides protection against "unreasonable searches and seizures." Although this right is stated categorically, the Supreme Court often finds itself faced with the difficult task of defining what police behavior constitutes a "search" or a "seizure," and whether such behavior was "reasonable" within the meaning of the Constitution. The inherent ambiguity of these terms gives the justices significant ability to define and change the definition of permissible searches and seizures.

Second, the amendment prescribes rules for warrants that apply both to search warrants, for searching places, and arrest warrants, for seizing people. The purpose of the warrant requirement is to prevent police from using their own uncontrolled discretion to determine when a search or seizure is proper and appropriate. By requiring the police to demonstrate to a neutral third party (judge or magistrate) that sufficient evidence exists ("probable cause") to justify a search, the warrant requirement seeks to protect people from unsubstantiated, vindictive, and exploratory searches. Because the two halves of the amendment are independent, the second component of the Fourth Amendment does not require that *all* searches be conducted with warrants in order to fulfill the first component's reasonableness requirement. A search may require a warrant in order to be reasonable in some circumstances, but warrantless searches may be proper in other situations.

For example, if police officers are pursuing a suspect in a chase after a robbery has been reported, it would make little sense to require the officers to obtain an arrest warrant before apprehending the subject. In the time that it takes to present evidence to a judge in order to obtain a warrant, the perpetrator will escape and valuable evidence carried on his or her person will be lost. On the other hand, if the police plan a search or arrest after a lengthy undercover investigation and the suspect does not know that he or she is the object of a police investigation, there is little reason to give police the discretionary authority to conduct searches or make arrests whenever they choose. If there is time for the police to present evidence to a judge so that the judge can ensure that the evidence fulfills the Fourth Amendment's "probable cause" requirement, then it makes sense to require a warrant.

Approaches to Fourth Amendment Decision Making

As indicated by the foregoing examples, innumerable situations may arise which produce Fourth Amendment questions. Such questions include: whether a "search" was conducted; whether a "seizure" of person or property was undertaken; whether the police activity was "reasonable"; whether a warrant was required; whether a warrant was supported by "probable cause"; and whether the search was limited to the areas and objects specified in the warrant. The limitless variations of search and seizure contexts as well as the disagreements among the justices about the meaning of the Fourth Amendment have precluded the development and maintenance of consistent legal theories. An indication of the case-by-case development of decision making on Fourth Amendment issues is shown by the sheer number of such cases decided during the Warren, Burger, and Rehnquist Court eras. The Supreme Court decided 212 Fourth Amendment cases from 1953 through 1995. Thus the Court's interpretation of the Fourth Amendment involves the justices' assessment of and reaction to large numbers of varying circumstances under which police conduct searches and make arrests.

With respect to some constitutional rights, especially the First Amendment's protections for free speech and free press, the justices emphasize the importance of the right in our constitutional democracy. As we saw in the chapter on the freedom of speech, by treating such rights as preferred freedoms, the justices accept some unpleasant consequences for society because the paramount emphasis is placed on free expression as a highly prized and constitutionally protected value. By contrast, the Supreme Court's decisions on the Fourth Amendment are characterized by a balancing approach that favors protection of the defendant's rights in some situations but favors aggressive law enforcement practices by the police in others. This balancing approach reflects the difficulties facing the justices in determining whether society should endure costs, such as letting guilty defendants go free, in order to protect the principles of the Fourth Amendment. The justices have frequently disagreed with each other about how to strike the appropriate balance between Fourth Amendment rights and society's interest in crime control.

Although there is no dominant theory of the Fourth Amendment discernible in the cases, one matter of principle has been a consistent issue for debate among the justices for decades: the necessity of the exclusionary rule. The Court has been divided between justices who believe that the Fourth Amendment requires exclusion of illegally obtained evidence and those who believe that other remedies can adequately prevent abusive police practices without risking the release of guilty criminals. Justices who see the exclusionary rule as an essential component of the Constitution have been very consistent in seeking exclusion of evidence from unreasonable or otherwise improper searches. However, even these justices do not always agree about the circumstances under which exclusion is required. For example, Justice Black, a member of the *Mapp* majority, dissented against his Warren Court colleagues' decision to exclude evidence obtained through warrantless electronic eavesdropping at a public telephone booth (*Katz v. United States,* 1967). Black accused the majority of using the Fourth Amendment improperly to expand the concept of the right to privacy.

Other justices believe that the exclusionary rule is a judicially created requirement that should be applied only in circumstances in which it is necessary to prevent abusive police practices. Justice O'Connor, for example, was a member of the majority in *United States v. Leon* (1984) in which the Court declared that "[t]he [exclusionary] rule . . . operates as 'a judicially created remedy designed to safeguard Fourth Amendment rights generally through its deterrent effect, rather than a personal constitutional right of the party aggrieved' " (468 U.S. at 906). Justice O'Connor's identification of the exclusionary rule as merely a judge-created rule rather than a constitutionally mandated principle did not mean that she would never support the rule's application. Three years after the *Leon* decision, O'Connor wrote a dissenting opinion joined by Justices Brennan, Marshall, and Stevens that urged exclusion of evidence obtained in a warrantless search of a business (*Illinois v. Krull,* 1987).

For those justices who do not endorse the exclusionary rule as a matter of constitutional principle, as was true of most justices on the Burger and Rehnquist Courts, Fourth Amendment decisions are often based on balancing the costs and benefits of excluding the evidence in the circumstances of each case. These justices make a subjective assessment of whether the benefit of exclusion (i.e., the potential for deterring police misconduct and preventing the violation of rights) outweighs the cost to society from exclusion (i.e., the risk that a guilty person will go free). In the *Leon* case, for example, Justice White's majority opinion asserted that "[w]e conclude that the marginal or nonexistent benefits produced by suppressing evidence obtained in objectively reasonable reliance on a subsequently invalidated search warrant cannot justify the substantial costs of exclusion" (468 U.S. at 922). There is nothing systematic about the balances struck by the individual justices. The justices do not quantify the value of the costs and benefits in order to explain how they weigh conflicting interests in a case. To a substantial degree, it is simply a matter of how individual justices react to the factual circumstances of each case. In a case concerning a police officer's movement of stereo equipment in order to locate its serial numbers during a warrantless search of an apartment, Justice Scalia's majority opinion supporting exclusion explicitly acknowledged the balancing process as the source of disagreement among the justices in these cases concerning the Fourth Amendment: "It may well be that, in [some] circumstances, no effective means short of a search exist [to determine whether criminal activity has occurred]. But there is nothing new in the realization that the Constitution sometimes insulates the criminality of a few in order to protect the privacy of us all. Our disagreement with the dissenters pertains to where the proper balance should be struck; we choose to adhere to the textual and traditional standard of probable cause [in this case]" (*Arizona v. Hicks,* 480 U.S. at 329, 1987).

Pre-Warren Court Period

The Supreme Court's Fourth Amendment decisions prior to the beginning of the Warren Court era in 1953 were dominated by the issue of incorporation. To what extent should the Court require the states to abide by the same rules as the federal government? The Court's application of the exclusionary rule against the federal government created an incentive for defendants in states that lacked their own exclusionary rules to seek a ruling that the Fourth Amendment rule should protect citizens from state and local police. As with other rights, the incorporation of the exclusionary rule was not completed until the 1960s (i.e., *Mapp v. Ohio,* 1961). However, unlike some other rights in which incorporation took place in a single, sudden judicial decision, an evolutionary quality is evident in the Court's Fourth Amendment decisions. In other words, the Court made several intermediate decisions both prior to and during the early Warren Court era that set the stage for the application of the Fourth Amendment on equal terms for both federal and state law enforcement officials.

In 1914, the Supreme Court laid the groundwork for the exclusionary rule debates that would dominate its Fourth Amendment decisions for the remainder of the century. In *Weeks v. United States,* a defendant was arrested, charged, and convicted for violating a federal law prohibiting the use of the mails to transport lottery tickets. Police officers and a U.S. marshal went to the defendant's home and were told by a neighbor where to find a key. They proceeded to enter, search the house, and seize papers that they found. The defendant challenged the warrantless search as a violation of his Fourth Amendment rights. The Supreme Court decided in favor of Weeks and declared that the illegally seized evidence could not be used against him. According to Justice William Day's opinion, "If letters and private documents can thus be seized and held and used in evidence against a citizen accused of an offense, the protection of the 4th Amendment, declaring his right to be secure against such searches and seizures, is of no value, and, so far as those thus placed are concerned, might as well be stricken from the Constitution" (232 U.S. at 393). The exclusionary rule created by the Court in the *Weeks* case applied only against the federal government in its investigations of federal offenses. As we will see in Chapter 10, the Court later also applied the exclusionary rule to violations of the Fifth Amendment right against compelled self-incrimination when police officers improperly question suspects arrested for crimes.

WEEKS V. UNITED STATES

232 U.S. 383, 34 S. Ct. 341, 58 L. Ed. 652 (1914)

■ The defendant was arrested by police, acting without a warrant, at the train station in Kansas City, Missouri, where he was employed by a freight company. He was charged and eventually convicted of using the mails to transport lottery tickets. At the time of his arrest, police officers and a U.S. marshal went to his home, learned the location of the key from a neighbor, entered the house, and conducted a thorough search. The U.S. marshal seized letters and papers found in a drawer. Both before and after his trial, the defendant challenged the warrantless search of his home and the seizure of his personal papers.

The *Weeks* case is important because it contains an early broad statement about the meaning and purpose of the Fourth Amendment. The Supreme Court's decision also mandated the application of the exclusionary rule to federal law enforcement officials, and this precedent served as the basis for the Court's subsequent cases concerning whether the rule should also apply against the states. As you read this opinion, consider the following questions: (1) Why did the Court impose the exclusionary rule? (2) Did the Court consider alternative remedies other than exclusion of evidence to ensure fulfillment of citizens' Fourth Amendment rights? (3) Did the Court consider the impact of the exclusionary rule on crime control and law enforcement effectiveness?

VOTE:

The Court unanimously found the U.S. marshal's actions to be unconstitutional.

Justice Day delivered the opinion of the Court.

* * *

The history of [the Fourth] Amendment is given with particularity in the opinion of Mr. Justice Bradley, speaking for the court in *Boyd v. United States* [1886]. As was there shown, it took its origin in the determination of the framers of the Amendments to the Federal Constitution to provide for that instrument a Bill of Rights, securing to the American people, among other things, those safeguards which had grown up in England to protect the people from unreasonable searches and seizures, such as were permitted under the general warrants issued under authority of the government, by which there had been invasions of the home and privacy of the citizens, and seizure of their private papers in support of charges, real or imaginary, made against them. Such practices had also received sanction under warrants and seizures under the so-called writs of assistance, issued in the American colonies. . . . Resistance to these practices had established the principle which was enacted into the fundamental law in the [Fourth] Amendment, that a man's house was his castle, and not to be invaded by a general authority to search and seize his goods and papers. . . . In *Ex parte Jackson* [1878], this court recognized the principle of protection as applicable to letters and sealed packages in the mail, and held that, consistent with this guaranty of the right of the people to be secure in their papers against unreasonable searches and seizures, such matter could only be opened and examined upon warrants issued on oath or affirmation, particularly describing the thing to be seized, "as is required when papers are subjected to search in one's own household."

* * *

The effect of the [Fourth] Amendment is to put the courts of the United States and Federal officials, in the exercise of their power and authority, under limitations and restraints as to the exercise of such power and authority, and to forever secure the people, their persons, houses, papers, and effects, against all unreasonable searches and seizures under the guise of law. This protection reaches all alike, whether accused of crime or not, and the duty of giving to it force and effect is obligatory upon all [e]ntrusted under our Federal system with the enforcement of the laws. The tendency of those who execute the criminal laws of the country to obtain conviction by means of unlawful seizures and enforced confessions, the latter often obtained after subjecting accused persons to unwarranted practices destructive of rights secured by the Federal Constitution, should find no sanction in the judgments of the courts, which are charged at all times with the support of the Constitution, and to which people of all conditions have a right to appeal for the maintenance of such fundamental rights.

* * *

The case in the aspect of which we are dealing with it involves the right of the court in a criminal prosecution to retain for the purposes of evidence the letters and correspondence of the accused, seized in his house in his absence and without his authority, by a United States marshal holding no warrant for his arrest and none for the search of his premises. The accused, without awaiting his trial, made timely application to the court for an order for the return of these letters, as well [as for] other property. This application was denied, the letters retained and put in evidence, after a further application at the beginning of the trial, both applications asserting the rights of the accused under the 4th and

5th Amendments to the Constitution. If letters and private documents can thus be seized and held and used in evidence against a citizen accused of an offense, the protection of the [Fourth] Amendment, declaring his right to be secure against such searches and seizures, is of no value, and, so far as those thus placed are concerned, might as well be stricken from the Constitution. The efforts of the courts and their officials to bring the guilty to punishment, praiseworthy as they are, are not to be aided by the sacrifice of those great principles established by years of endeavor and suffering which have resulted in their embodiment in the fundamental law of the land. The United States marshal could only have invaded the house of the accused when armed with a warrant issued as required by the Constitution, upon sworn information, and describing with reasonable particularity the thing for which the search was to be made. Instead, he acted without sanction of law, doubtless prompted by the desire to bring further proof to the aid of the government, and under color of his office undertook to make a seizure of private papers in direct violation of the constitutional prohibition against such action. Under such circumstances, without sworn information and particular description, not even an order of the court would have justified such procedure; much less was it within the authority of the United States marshal to thus invade the house and privacy of the accused. . . . To sanction such proceedings would be to affirm by judicial decision a manifest neglect, if not an open defiance, of the prohibitions of the Constitution, intended for the protection of the people against such unauthorized action.

* * *

We therefore reach the conclusion that the letters in question were taken from the house of the accused by an official of the United States, acting under color of his office, in direct violation of the constitutional rights of the defendant; that having made a reasonable application for their return, which was heard and passed upon by the court, there was involved in the order refusing the application a denial of the constitutional rights of the accused, and that the court should have restored these letters to the accused. In holding them and permitting their use upon the trial, we think prejudicial error was committed. As to the papers and property seized by the [local] policemen [who accompanied the U.S. marshal], it does not appear that they acted under any claim of Federal authority such as would make the amendment applicable to such unauthorized seizures. The record shows that what they did by way of arrest and search and seizure was done before the finding of the indictment in the Federal court; under what supposed right or authority does not appear. What remedies the defendant may have against them, we need not inquire, as the [Fourth] Amendment is not directed to individual misconduct of such officials. Its limitations reach the Federal government and its agencies. . . .

It results that the judgment of the court below must be reversed, and the case remanded for further proceedings in accordance with this opinion.

Reversed.

The Supreme Court expanded the impact of the exclusionary rule in *Silverthorne Lumber Co. v. United States* (1920) by declaring that the government could not use information gained from an illegal search in order to secure a subpoena for the documents it had illegally viewed. This decision provided the basis for the "fruit of the poisonous tree" doctrine in which the Court excluded evidence indirectly discovered through illegal methods rather than through some independent, legal source. Thus, for example, in later cases, statements obtained during legal interrogation of a suspect could be excluded from evidence if the interrogation was preceded by an improper warrantless arrest (see *Wong Sun v. United States,* 1963). The suspect's statements could be excluded as the "fruit" of the original warrantless search.

In 1928, the Court considered the question of whether wiretapping amounted to search and seizure. In *Olmstead v. United States,* a five-member majority rejected the defendant's claim that the Fourth Amendment provided protection against the government's use of discretionary wiretapping to obtain criminal evidence. On behalf of the majority, Chief Justice William Taft declared that the Fourth Amendment was limited to searches of material things, such as houses, papers, and personal effects. In a famous dissent, Justice Louis Brandeis bemoaned the use of wiretapping as an instrument of tyranny and oppression in violation of individuals' right to privacy.

As we discussed in Chapter 4 concerning the incorporation of the Bill of Rights, criminal defendants brought cases to the Supreme Court throughout the early decades of the twentieth century seeking to have specific provisions of the Bill of Rights applied to the states. Prior to the 1960s, with the exception of two Sixth Amendment cases (see Chapter 11 for *Powell v. Alabama,* 1932 and *In re Oliver,* 1948), the Supreme Court was not generally receptive to arguments favoring the incorporation of rights for criminal defendants. The Court's incorporation decisions during the 1920s, 1930s, and 1940s primarily concerned First Amendment rights. However, unlike most other rights affecting criminal justice, the Fourth Amendment right against unreasonable search and seizure was addressed and incorporated by the Court prior to the Warren Court era.

In *Wolf v. Colorado* (1949), the Supreme Court considered whether states should be bound by the Fourth Amendment exclusionary rule requirements that had governed federal law enforcement since the *Weeks* decision in 1914. Justice Felix Frankfurter's majority opinion made a powerful statement about the right against unreasonable search and seizure when he incorporated the Fourth Amendment and applied it against the states:

> *The security of one's privacy against arbitrary intrusion by the police—which is at the core of the Fourth Amendment—is basic to a free society. It is therefore implicit in the "concept of ordered liberty" and as such enforceable against the States through the Due Process Clause [of the Fourteenth Amendment]. The knock at the door, whether by day or by night, as a prelude to search, without authority of law but solely on the authority of the police, did not need the commentary of recent history to be condemned as inconsistent with the conception of human rights enshrined in the history and the basic constitutional documents of English-speaking peoples* (338 U.S. at 27-28).

Despite Frankfurter's emphatic assertion that the Fourth Amendment was applicable to the states, he and the other justices in the majority declined to require the states to adhere to the *Weeks* exclusionary rule. Frankfurter was a strong supporter of states' authority to handle their own affairs as much as possible without interference of federal courts. He indicated that the states should be able to apply their own remedies to problems of police conduct, such as disciplining officers who violate rights and permitting lawsuits against officers, and he expressed confidence that local public opinion would serve as an important check against abusive police practices. In dissenting opinions, Justices Rutledge, Murphy, and Douglas agreed that the Fourth Amendment should be incorporated and applied to the states, but they asserted that the exclusionary rule must also be applied to the states in order to prevent lawlessness by the police.

Three years later, the Court confronted the case of *Rochin v. California* (1952) in which sheriff's deputies entered a home at night without a warrant. When the deputies entered the homeowner's bedroom and saw him swallow some capsules that had been on the nightstand, they attempted through the application of sheer physical force to retrieve the capsules from the man's throat. Their efforts failed so they took the homeowner to the hospital and ordered a doctor to force a substance into the man's stomach to induce vomiting. After the man's stomach was thus emptied, the capsules were recovered and determined to be morphine. The homeowner challenged his conviction on narcotics charges by claiming that the deputies had obtained the evidence through an illegal search and seizure. Justice

Frankfurter again wrote the majority opinion for the Court. This time, however, he ordered that the evidence against Rochin be excluded from use at trial. Frankfurter continued to believe that the exclusionary rule should not be imposed on the states, but the *Rochin* case forced him to recognize that some actions by state law enforcement officials were so abusive that they required clear, strong remedies. According to Frankfurter, "we are compelled to conclude that the proceedings by which this conviction was obtained do more than offend some fastidious squeamishness or private sentimentalitism about combatting crime too energetically. This is conduct that shocks the conscience. Illegally breaking into the privacy of the petitioner, the struggle to open his mouth and remove what was there, the forcible extraction of his stomach's contents—this course of proceeding by agents of government to obtain evidence is bound to offend even hardened sensibilities. They are methods too close to the rack and the screw to permit of constitutional differentiation" (342 U.S. at 172). After the *Rochin* case, police officers knew that federal courts might order the exclusion of evidence in "conscience-shocking" circumstances, but the officers had no way of knowing which circumstances would produce exclusion. Frankfurter endorsed exclusion in the *Rochin* case because the officers' actions "shock[ed] the conscience." Such a test, however, leaves it up to individual judges to determine when police officers have gone too far in violating individuals' Fourth Amendment rights and thereby provides little guidance to police about the consequences of various actions they may choose to take in conducting searches and seizures.

Because the issue of the exclusionary rule's applicability to federal law enforcement had been settled in *Weeks* (1914), subsequent federal cases raised additional issues, such as the permissibility of warrantless searches in various contexts. In *Carroll v. United States* (1925), for example, the Court approved the actions of federal agents who ripped open the seats of an automobile while searching for illegal liquor during Prohibition. The previous year, the Court had established the "open fields" exception to the warrant requirement by permitting law enforcement officers to search open fields and other grounds around houses and buildings (*Hester v. United States,* 1924). In 1947, the Court approved warrantless searches of the premises in conjunction with lawful arrests. In *United States v. Rabinowitz,* federal agents conducted a general ransacking of the arrestee's office in a search for forged U.S. postage stamps. In *Harris v. United States,* law enforcement officers searched an entire four-room apartment after the suspect was arrested in the living room (Fisher 1970, p. 204). The Warren Court later narrowed the permissible scope of warrantless searches conducted in conjunction with lawful arrests to areas within a suspect's immediate control (*Chimel v. California,* 1969).

The Warren Court Era

By the beginning of the Warren Court era in 1953, the Supreme Court had already created the exclusionary rule (*Weeks*) and incorporated the Fourth Amendment for application against the states (*Wolf*). Although the Court had not applied the exclusionary rule systematically to all state and local law enforcement practices, the *Rochin* decision clearly indicated that the rule applied to some state and local practices when officers' conduct violated the ill-defined test of "shock[ing] the conscience[s]" of judges. Thus the Warren Court justices did not develop and initiate the Fourth Amendment principles and policies that would later produce such great political controversy and backlash. Instead, the Warren Court expanded and made systematic the application of Fourth Amendment concepts, especially the exclusionary rule, that had been developed by its predecessors. When the Warren Court era ended in 1969, common rules applied to law enforcement officers throughout the country and officers were given clear indications that violations of citizens' Fourth Amendment rights would automatically produce exclusion of evidence.

The Warren Court justices did not immediately impose the *Weeks* exclusionary rule on state and local officials. As we described in the opening case study, it was not until 1961 that the justices nationalized the exclusionary rule in their decision in *Mapp v. Ohio*.

MAPP V. OHIO

367 U.S. 644, 81 S. Ct. 1684, 6 L. Ed. 2d 1081 (1961)
[The facts of this case are omitted because they were presented in the case study at the beginning of the chapter.]

■ The case is important because the Supreme Court used its decision to impose the exclusionary rule on state and local law enforcement officers. The decision generated political controversy and became a focal point for opposition to the Warren Court's decisions. As you read the opinion, consider the following questions: (1) Why did the Court no longer permit the use of remedies other than exclusion of evidence for violations of search and seizure rights? (2) Should the Court have decided the Fourth Amendment issue in a case in which the competing attorneys had not researched, briefed, and argued that issue? (3) Does this decision violate the principle of federalism that permits states to determine their own public policies with respect to criminal justice and other issues?

VOTE:

5 justices found that the Constitution required nationalization of the exclusionary rule (Black, Brennan, Clark, Douglas, Warren).

1 justice found that the obscenity statute violated the First Amendment (Stewart).

3 justices found that states could develop their own remedies for Fourth Amendment violations (Frankfurter, Harlan, Whittaker).

Justice Clark delivered the opinion of the Court.

* * *

The State says that even if the search were made without authority, or otherwise unreasonably, it is not prevented from using the unconstitutionally seized evidence at trial, citing *Wolf v. Colorado* [1949], in which this Court did indeed hold "that in a prosecution in a State court for a State crime the Fourteenth Amendment does not forbid the admission of evidence obtained by unreasonable search and seizure." On this appeal, of which we have noted probable jurisdiction, . . . it is urged once again that we review that holding.[3]

* * *

There are in the cases of this Court some passing references to the *Weeks* [exclusionary] rule as being one of evidence. But the plain and unequivocal language of *Weeks*—and its later paraphrase in *Wolf*—to the effect that the *Weeks* rule is of constitutional origin, remains entirely undisturbed. * * *

In 1949, 35 years after *Weeks* was announced, this Court, in *Wolf v. People of the State of Colorado*, . . . again for the first time, discussed the effect of the Fourth Amendment upon the States through the operation of the Due Process Clause of the Fourteenth Amendment. * * * [T]he Court decided that the *Weeks* exclusionary rule would not then be imposed upon the States as "an essential ingredient of the right [against unreasonable search and seizure]." . . . The Court's reasons for not considering essential to the right to privacy, as a curb imposed upon the States by the Due Process Clause, that which decades before had been posited as part and parcel of the Fourth Amendment's limitation upon federal encroachment of individual privacy, were bottomed on several factual considerations.

While they are not basically relevant to a decision that the exclusionary rule is an essential ingredient of the Fourth Amendment as the right it embodies is vouchsafed against the States by the Due Process Clause, we will consider the current validity of the factual grounds upon which *Wolf* was based.

* * * While in 1949, prior to the *Wolf* case, almost two-thirds of the States were opposed to the use of the exclusionary rule, now, despite the *Wolf* case, more than half of those since passing upon it, by their own legislative or judicial decision, have wholly or partly adopted or adhered to the *Weeks* rule. . . . Significantly, among those now following the rule is California, which, according to its highest courts, was "compelled to reach that conclusion

[3]Other issues have been raised on this appeal but, in the view we have taken of the case, they need not be decided. Although appellant chose to urge what may have appeared to be the surer ground for favorable disposition and did not insist that *Wolf* be overruled, the *amicus curiae* [American Civil Liberties Union], who was also permitted to participate in oral argument, did urge the Court to overrule *Wolf*.

because other remedies have completely failed to secure compliance with the constitutional provisions". . . . In connection with this California case, we note that the second basis elaborated in *Wolf* in support of its failure to enforce the exclusionary doctrine against the States was that "other means of protection" have been afforded "the right to privacy.". . . The experience of California that such other remedies have been worthless and futile is buttressed by the experience of other States. The obvious futility of relegating the Fourth Amendment to the protection of other remedies has, moreover, been recognized by this Court since *Wolf.* See *Irvine v. People of State of California* [1954]. . . .

* * *

It, therefore, plainly appears that the factual considerations supporting the failure of the *Wolf* Court to include the *Weeks* exclusionary rule when it recognized the enforceability of the right to privacy against the States in 1949, while not basically relevant to the constitutional consideration, could not, in any analysis, now be deemed to be controlling.

* * *

Since the Fourth Amendment's right of privacy has been declared enforceable against the States through the Due Process Clause of the Fourteenth, it is enforceable against them by the same sanction of exclusion as is used against the Federal Government. Were it otherwise, then just as without the *Weeks* rule the assurance against unreasonable federal searches and seizures would be "a form of words," valueless and undeserving of mention in a perpetual charter of inestimable human liberties, so too, without that rule the freedom from state invasions of privacy would be so ephemeral and so neatly severed from its conceptual nexus with the freedom from all brutish means of coercing evidence as not to merit this Court's high regard as a freedom "implicit in 'the concept of ordered liberty.' " At the time that the Court held in *Wolf* that the Amendment was applicable to the States through the Due Process Clause, the cases of this Court, as we have seen, had steadfastly held that as to federal officers the Federal Amendment included the exclusion of the evidence seized in violation of its provision. Even *Wolf* "stoutly adhered" to that proposition. The right to privacy, when conceded operatively enforceable against the States, was not susceptible of destruction by avulsion of the sanction upon which its protection and enjoyment had always been deemed dependent under the *Boyd, Weeks,* and *Silverthorne* [*Lumber Co. v. United States* (1920)] cases. Therefore, in extending the substantive protections of due process to all constitutionally unreasonable searches—state or federal—it was logically and constitutionally necessary that the exclusion doctrine—an essential part of the right to privacy—be also insisted upon as an essential ingredient of the right newly recognized by the *Wolf* case. In short, the admission of the new constitutional right by *Wolf* could not consistently tolerate denial of its most important constitutional privilege, namely, the exclusion of the evidence which an accused had been forced to give by reason of the unlawful seizure. To hold otherwise is to grant the right but in reality to withhold its privilege and enjoyment. Only last year the Court itself recognized that the purpose of the exclusionary rule "is to deter—to compel respect for the constitutional guaranty in the only effectively available way—by removing the incentive to disregard it." *Elkins v. United States,* 364 U.S. at 217. . . .

* * * This Court has not hesitated to enforce as strictly against the States as it does against the Federal Government the rights of free speech and of free press, the rights to notice and to a fair, public trial, including, as it does, the right not to be convicted by use of a coerced confession, however logically relevant it be, and without regard to its reliability. . . . And nothing could be more certain than that when a coerced confession is involved, "the relevant rules of evidence" are overridden without regard to "the incidence of such conduct by the police," slight or frequent. Why should not the same rule apply to what is tantamount to coerced testimony by way of unconstitutional seizure of goods, papers, effects, documents, etc.? We find that, as to the Federal Government, the Fourth and Fifth Amendments and, as to the State, the freedom from unconscionable invasions of privacy and the freedom from convictions based upon coerced confessions do enjoy an "intimate relation" in their perpetuation of "principles of humanity and civil liberty [secured] . . . only after years of struggle." * * * The philosophy of each Amendment and of each freedom is complementary to, although not dependent upon, that of the other in its sphere of influence—the very least that together they assure in either sphere is that no man is to be convicted on unconstitutional evidence. . . .

Moreover, our holding that the exclusionary rule is an essential part of both the Fourth and Fourteenth Amendments is not only the logical dictate of prior cases, but it also makes very good sense. There is no war between the Constitution and common sense. Presently, a federal prosecutor may make no use of evidence illegally seized, but a State's attorney across the street may, although he supposedly is operating under the enforceable prohibitions of the same

Amendment. Thus the State, by admitting evidence unlawfully seized, serves to encourage disobedience to the Federal Constitution which it is bound to uphold. * * *

Federal-state cooperation in the solution of crime under constitutional standards will be promoted, if only by recognition of their now mutual obligation to respect the same fundamental criteria in their approaches. * * *

* * *

The ignoble shortcut to conviction left open to the States tends to destroy the entire system of constitutional restraints on which the liberties of the people rest. Having once recognized that the right to privacy embodied in the Fourth Amendment is enforceable against the States, and that the right to be secure against rude invasions of privacy by state officers is, therefore, constitutional in origin, we can no longer permit the right to remain an empty promise. Because it is enforceable in the same manner and to like effect as other basic rights secured by the Due Process Clause, we can no longer permit it to be revocable at the whim of any police officer who, in the name of law enforcement itself, chooses to suspend its enjoyment. Our decision, founded on reason and truth, gives to the individual no more than that which the Constitution guarantees him, to the police officer no less than that to which honest law enforcement is entitled, and, to the courts, that judicial integrity so necessary in the true administration of justice.

The judgment of the Supreme Court of Ohio is reversed and the cause remanded for further proceedings not inconsistent with this opinion.

Reversed and remanded.

[Concurring opinions by Justices Black and Douglas are omitted.]

Memorandum of Justice Stewart.

. . . I express no view as to the merits of the constitutional issue which the Court today decides. I would, however, reverse the judgment in this case, because I am persuaded that the [Ohio obscenity statute], upon which the petitioner's conviction was based, is, in the words of Mr. Justice Harlan, not "consistent with the rights of free thought and expression assured against state action by the Fourteenth Amendment."

Justice Harlan, with whom Justice Frankfurter and Justice Whittaker join, dissenting.

In overruling the *Wolf* case the Court, in my opinion, has forgotten the sense of judicial restraint which, with due regard for *stare decisis,* is one element that should enter into deciding whether a past decision of this Court should be overruled. Apart from that I also believe that the *Wolf* rule represents sounder Constitutional doctrine than the new rule which now replaces it.

* * * [T]he new and pivotal issue brought to the Court by this appeal is whether [the Ohio obscenity statute] . . . under which appellant has been convicted, is consistent with the rights of free thought and expression assured against state action by the Fourteenth Amendment. That was the principal issue which was decided by the Ohio Supreme Court, which was tendered by appellant's Jurisdictional Statement, and which was briefed and argued in this Court.

Given this posture of things, I think it fair to say that five members of this Court have simply "reached out" to overrule *Wolf.* With all respect for the views of the majority, and recognizing that *stare decisis* carries different weight in constitutional adjudication than it does in nonconstitutional decision, I can perceive no justification for regarding this case as an appropriate occasion for reexamining *Wolf.*

* * *

It cannot be too much emphasized that what was recognized in *Wolf* was not that the Fourth Amendment *as such* is enforceable against the States as a facet of due process. . . . It would not be proper to expect or impose any precise equivalence, either as regards the scope of the right or the means of its implementation, between the requirements of the Fourth and Fourteenth Amendments. For the Fourth, unlike what was said in *Wolf* of the Fourteenth, does not state a general principle only; it is a particular command, having its setting in a pre-existing legal context on which both interpreting decisions and enabling statutes must build.

* * *

I would not impose upon the States this federal exclusionary remedy. The reasons given by the majority for now suddenly turning its back on *Wolf* seem to me notably unconvincing.

* * *

The preservation of the proper balance between state and federal responsibility in the administration of criminal justice demands patience on the part of those who might like to see things move faster among the States in this respect. Problems of criminal law enforcement vary widely from State to State. One State, in considering the totality of its legal picture, may conclude that the need for embracing the *Weeks* rule is pressing because other remedies are unavailable or inadequate to secure compliance with the substantive Constitutional principle involved. Another, though equally solicitous of Constitutional rights, may choose to pursue one purpose at a time, allowing all evidence relevant to guilt to be brought into a criminal trial, and dealing with Constitutional infractions by other means. Still another may consider the exclusionary rule too rough-and-ready a remedy, in that it reaches only unconstitutional intrusions which eventuate in criminal prosecution of the victims. Further, a State after experimenting with the *Weeks* rule for a time may, because of unsatisfactory experience with it, decide to revert to a non-exclusionary rule. And so on. * * * In my view this Court should forbear from fettering the States with an adamant rule which may embarrass them in coping with their own peculiar problems in criminal law enforcement.

* * *

I regret that I find so unwise in principle and so inexpedient in policy a decision motivated by the high purpose of increasing respect for Constitutional rights. But in the last analysis I think this Court can increase respect for the Constitution only if it rigidly respects the limitations which the Constitution places upon it, and respects as well the principles inherent in its own processes. In the present case I think we exceed both, and that our voice becomes only a voice of power, not a voice of reason.

After the *Mapp* decision, the Court faced many new cases requiring it to define when searches and seizures are "unreasonable" so that police officers would know when their actions would produce exclusion. In *Katz v. United States* (1967), the Supreme Court rejected the earlier decision in *Olmstead v. United States* (1928) by applying the Fourth Amendment to governmental electronic eavesdropping at a public phone booth. The *Olmstead* opinion had declared that the Fourth Amendment only protects against unreasonable searches of material objects, such as houses, papers, and personal effects. In *Katz,* however, the Court expanded the coverage of the Fourth Amendment by declaring that the Fourth Amendment protects people and not places, and that coverage extends to that which people intend to keep private, such as telephone conversations, even when conducted in a public area. The *Katz* decision forced the government to adhere to the Fourth Amendment's warrant requirement when seeking to use wiretaps as the means to obtain evidence.

In other cases, the Warren Court limited the potential expansion of the exclusionary rule by defining contexts in which warrantless searches were reasonable. In *Terry v. Ohio* (1968), for example, a police officer with thirty years of experience observed several men repeatedly walking back and forth in front of a store and peering into the window. Their behavior aroused the police officer's suspicions because he believed that they could be preparing to commit a robbery. The officer approached the men, identified himself as a police officer, and patted down the exterior clothing of one man. When he found a revolver in the man's coat pocket, he ordered the other two men to stand against a wall and he discovered a weapon in the coat pocket of one of the other men. The two men sought to have the handguns excluded from evidence in their trial on the charge of carrying a concealed weapon. They asserted that the officer's patdown search of their outer clothing was not justified by probable cause because the officer had no evidence to indicate that they had committed any crime. In an eight-to-one decision, the Warren Court endorsed the officer's actions. According to Chief Justice Warren's opinion, such "stop and frisk" actions by police officers constitute searches and seizures which are governed by the Fourth Amendment. In Warren's words, "it is simply fantastic to urge that such a procedure performed in public by a policeman while the citizen stands helpless, perhaps facing a wall with his hands raised, is a 'petty indignity.' It is a serious intrusion upon the sanctity of the person, which may inflict great indignity and arouse strong resentment, and it is not to be undertaken lightly" (392 U.S. at 16-17). However, Warren concluded that such a search may be reasonable under the Fourth

Amendment because "there must be a narrowly drawn authority to permit a reasonable search for weapons for the protection of the police officer, where he has reason to believe that he is dealing with an armed and dangerous individual, regardless whether he has probable cause to arrest the individual for a crime" (392 U.S. at 27). By reaching this conclusion, the Warren Court demonstrated that its concerns about the safety of police officers and the public could outweigh arguments favoring the protection of individuals' rights.

Terry v. Ohio

392 U.S. 1, 88 S. Ct. 1868, 20 L. Ed. 2d 889 (1968)

■ Prior to trial, the defendants sought to have handguns excluded from evidence against them as the products of an improper search as a result of the officer stopping and frisking them. The trial court rejected the defense motion and the state appellate courts upheld the men's convictions. In the U.S. Supreme Court, the defendants claimed that the evidence should be excluded because the police officer lacked a sufficient basis to conduct a search. Thus, they argued that his search was unreasonable under the terms of the Fourth Amendment.

The case is important because it set the standard for the circumstances and scope of warrantless searches based on police officers' observations of suspicious behavior. The case is also important because it shows the Warren Court justices' efforts to strike an appropriate balance between protecting Fourth Amendment rights and permitting law enforcement officers to have sufficient authority to investigate suspicious activities in order to prevent the commission of crimes and to protect police officers and the public. As you read the opinion, consider the following questions: (1) Does the Court's decision respect or violate the literal words of the Fourth Amendment? (2) Under what precise circumstances are police permitted to undertake pat-down searches? (3) Is Justice Douglas correct in declaring that this decision moves the United States "down the totalitarian path?"

Vote:

8 justices found the police officer's action constitutional (Black, Brennan, Fortas, Harlan, Marshall, Stewart, Warren, White).

1 justice found the police officer's action unconstitutional (Douglas).

Chief Justice Warren delivered the opinion of the Court.

* * *

The Fourth Amendment provides . . . [t]his inestimable right of personal security [that] belongs as much to the citizen on the streets of our cities as to the homeowner closeted in his study to dispose of his secret affairs. * * *

We would be less than candid if we did not acknowledge that this question thrusts to the fore difficult and troublesome issues regarding a sensitive area of police activity—issues which have never before been squarely presented to this Court. Reflective of the tensions involved are the practical and constitutional arguments pressed with great vigor on both sides of the public debate over the power of the police to "stop and frisk"—as it is sometimes euphemistically termed—suspicious persons.

On the one hand, it is frequently argued that in dealing with the rapidly unfolding and often dangerous situations on city streets the police are in need of an escalating set of flexible responses, graduated in relation to the amount of information they possess. For this purpose it is urged that distinctions should be made between a "stop" and an "arrest" (or a "seizure" of a person), and between a "frisk" and a "search." Thus, it is argued, the police should be allowed to "stop" a person and detain him briefly for questioning upon suspicion that he may be connected with criminal activity. Upon suspicion that the person may be armed, the police should have the power to "frisk" him for weapons. If the "stop" and the "frisk" give rise to probable cause to believe that the suspect has committed a crime, then the police should be empowered to make a formal "arrest," and a full incident "search" of the person. This scheme is justified in part upon the notion that a "stop" and a "frisk" amount to a mere "minor inconvenience" and petty indignity, which can properly be imposed upon the citizen in the interest of effective law enforcement on the basis of a police officer's suspicion.

On the other side the argument is made that the authority of the police must be strictly circumscribed by the law of arrest and search as it has developed to date in the traditional jurisprudence of the Fourth Amendment. It is contended with some force that there is not—and cannot be—a variety of police activity which does not depend solely upon the voluntary cooperation of the citizen and yet which stops short of an arrest based upon probable cause to make such an arrest. The heart of the Fourth Amendment, the argument runs, is a severe requirement of specific justification for any intrusion upon protected personal security, coupled with a highly developed system of judicial controls to enforce upon the agents of the State the commands of the Constitution. Acquiescence by the courts in the compulsion inherent in the field interrogation practices at issue here, it is urged, would constitute an abdication of judicial control over, and indeed an encouragement of, substantial interference with liberty and personal security by police officers whose judgment is necessarily colored by their primary involvement in "the often competitive enterprise of ferreting out crime." * * * This, it is argued, can only serve to exacerbate police-community tensions in the crowded centers of our Nation's cities.

In this context we approach the issues in this case mindful of the limitations of the judicial function in controlling the myriad daily situations in which policemen and citizens confront each other on the street. The State has characterized the issue here as "the right of a police officer . . . to make an on-the-street stop, interrogate, and pat down for weapons (known in street vernacular as 'stop and frisk')." But this is only partly accurate. For the issue is not the abstract propriety of the police conduct, but the admissibility against petitioner of the evidence uncovered by the search and seizure. Ever since its inception, the rule excluding evidence seized in violation of the Fourth Amendment has been recognized as a principal mode of discouraging lawless police conduct . . . , and experience has taught that it is the only effective deterrent to police misconduct in the criminal context, and that without it the constitutional guarantee against unreasonable searches and seizures would be a mere "form of words." * * * Courts which sit under our Constitution cannot and will not be made party to lawless invasions of the constitutional rights of citizens by permitting unhindered governmental use of the fruits of such invasions. Thus in our system evidentiary rulings provide the context in which the judicial process of inclusion and exclusion approves some conduct as comporting with constitutional guarantees and disapproves other actions by state agents. A ruling admitting evidence in a criminal trial, we recognize, has the necessary effect of legitimizing the conduct which produced the evidence, while an application of the exclusionary rule withholds the constitutional imprimatur.

* * * Street encounters between citizens and police officers are incredibly rich in diversity. They range from wholly friendly exchanges of pleasantries or mutually useful information to hostile confrontations of armed men involving arrests, or injuries, or loss of life. Moreover, hostile confrontations are not all of a piece. Some of them begin in a friendly enough manner, only to take a different turn upon the injection of some unexpected element into the conversation. Encounters are initiated by police for a wide variety of purposes, some of which are wholly unrelated to a desire to prosecute for crime. Doubtless some police "field interrogation" conduct violates the Fourth Amendment. But a stern refusal by this Court to condone such activity does not necessarily render it responsive to the exclusionary rule. Regardless of how effective the rule may be where obtaining convictions is an important objective of the police, it is powerless to deter invasions of constitutionally guaranteed rights where the police either have no interest in prosecuting or are willing to forgo successful prosecution in the interest of serving some other goal.

Proper adjudication of cases in which the exclusionary rule is invoked demands a constant awareness of these limitations. The wholesale harassment by certain elements of the police community, of which minority groups, particularly Negroes, frequently complain, will not be stopped by the exclusion of evidence from any criminal trial. Yet a rigid and unthinking application of the exclusionary rule, in futile protest against practices which it can never be used effectively to control, may exact a high toll in human injury and frustration of efforts to prevent crime. * * * And, of course, our approval of legitimate and restrained investigative conduct undertaken on the basis of ample factual justification should in no way discourage the employment of other remedies than the exclusionary rule to curtail abuses for which that sanction may prove inappropriate.

* * *

* * * It is quite plain that the Fourth Amendment governs "seizures" of the person which do not eventuate in a trip to the station house and prosecution for crime—"arrests" in traditional terminology. It must be recognized that whenever a police officer accosts an individual and restrains his freedom to walk away, he has "seized" that person. And it is nothing less than sheer torture of the English language to suggest that a careful exploration of the outer surfaces of a person's clothing all over his or her body in an attempt to find weapons is not a "search." Moreover, it is simply fantastic to urge that such a procedure performed in public by a policeman while the citizen stands helpless, perhaps facing a wall with his hands raised, is a "petty indignity." It is a serious intrusion upon the sanctity of the person,

which may inflict great indignity and arouse strong resentment, and it is not to be undertaken lightly.

* * *

* * * We therefore reject the notion that the Fourth Amendment does not come into play at all as a limitation upon police conduct if the officers stop short of something called a "technical arrest" or a "full-blown search."

In this case there can be no question, then, that Officer McFadden "seized" petitioner and subjected him to a "search" when he took hold of him and patted down the outer surfaces of his clothing. We must decide whether at that point it was reasonable for Officer McFadden to have interfered with petitioner's personal security as he did. And in determining whether the seizure and search were "unreasonable" our inquiry is a dual one—whether the officer's action was justified at its inception, and whether it was reasonably related in scope to the circumstances which justified the interference in the first place.* * *

* * * [I]n justifying the particular intrusion the police officer must be able to point to specific and articulatable facts which, taken together with rational inferences from those facts, reasonably warrant that intrusion. The scheme of the Fourth Amendment becomes meaningful only when it is assured that at some point the conduct of those charged with enforcing the laws can be subjected to the more detached, neutral scrutiny of a judge who must evaluate the reasonableness of a particular search or seizure in light of the particular circumstances. And in making that assessment it is imperative that the facts be judged against an objective standard: would the facts available to the officer at the moment of the seizure or the search "warrant a man of reasonable caution in the belief" that the action taken was appropriate? . . . Anything less would invite intrusions upon constitutionally guaranteed rights based on nothing more substantial than inarticulate hunches, a result this Court has consistently refused to sanction. . . . And simple " 'good faith on the part of the arresting officer is not enough.' * * * If subjective good faith alone were the test, the protections of the Fourth Amendment would evaporate, and the people would be 'secure in their persons, houses, papers, and effects,' only in the discretion of the police." . . .

Applying these principles to this case, we consider first the nature and extent of the governmental interests involved. One general interest is of course that of effective crime prevention and detection; it is this interest which underlies the recognition that a police officer may in appropriate circumstances and in an appropriate manner approach a person for purposes of investigating possibly criminal behavior even though there is no probable cause to make an arrest. It was this legitimate investigative function Officer McFadden was discharging when he decided to approach petitioner and his companions. He had observed Terry, Chilton, and Katz go through a series of acts, each of them perhaps innocent in itself, but which taken together warranted further investigation . . . . It would have been poor police work indeed for an officer of 30 years' experience in the detection of thievery from stores in this same neighborhood to have failed to investigate this behavior further.

The crux of this case, however, is not the propriety of Officer McFadden's taking steps to investigate petitioner's suspicious behavior, but rather, whether there was justification for McFadden's invasion of Terry's personal security by searching him for weapons in the course of that investigation. We are now concerned with more than the governmental interest in fighting crime; in addition, there is the more immediate interest of the police officer in taking steps to assure himself that the person with whom he is dealing is not armed with a weapon that could unexpectedly and fatally be used against him. Certainly it would be unreasonable to require that police officers take unnecessary risks in the performance of their duties. American criminals have a long tradition of armed violence, and every year in this country many law enforcement officers are killed in the line of duty, and thousands more are wounded. Virtually all of these deaths and a substantial portion of the injuries are inflicted with guns and knives.

In view of these facts, we cannot blind ourselves to the need for law enforcement officers to protect themselves and other prospective victims of violence in situations where they may lack probable cause for an arrest. When an officer is justified in believing that the individual whose suspicious behavior he is investigating at close range is armed and presently dangerous to the officer or to others, it would appear to be clearly unreasonable to deny the officer the power to take necessary measures to determine whether the person is in fact carrying a weapon and to neutralize the threat of physical harm.

* * *

Our evaluation of the proper balance that has to be struck in this type of case leads us to conclude that there must be a narrowly drawn authority to permit a reasonable search for weapons for the protection of the police officer, where he has reason to believe that he is dealing with an armed and dangerous individual, regardless of whether he has probable cause to arrest the individual for a crime.

The officer need not be absolutely certain that the individual is armed; the issue is whether a reasonably prudent man in the circumstances would be warranted in the belief that his safety or that of others was in danger. . . . And in determining whether the officer acted reasonably in such circumstances, due weight must be given, not to his inchoate and unparticularized suspicion or "hunch," but to the specific reasonable inferences which he is entitled to draw from the facts in light of his experience. . . .

* * * [W]hen Officer McFadden approached the three men gathered before the display window at Zucker's store he had observed enough to make it quite reasonable to fear that they were armed; and nothing in their response to his hailing them, identifying himself as a police officer, and asking their names served to dispel that reasonable belief. We cannot say his decision at that point to seize Terry and pat his clothing for weapons was the product of a volatile or inventive imagination, or was undertaken simply as an act of harassment; the record evidences the tempered act of a policeman who in the course of an investigation had to make a quick decision as to how to protect himself and others from possible danger, and took limited steps to do so.

* * *

The scope of the search in this case presents no serious problem in light of these standards. Officer McFadden patted down the outer clothing of petitioner and his two companions. He did not place his hands in their pockets or under the outer surface of their garments until he had felt weapons, and then he merely reached for and removed the guns. He never did invade Katz' person beyond the outer surfaces of his clothes, since he discovered nothing which might have been a weapon. Officer McFadden confined his search strictly to what was minimally necessary to learn whether the men were armed and to disarm them once he discovered the weapons. He did not conduct a general exploratory search for whatever evidence of criminal activity he might find.

We conclude that the revolver seized from Terry was properly admitted in evidence against him. At the time he seized petitioner and searched him for weapons, Officer McFadden had reasonable grounds to believe that petitioner was armed and dangerous, and it was necessary for the protection of himself and others to take swift measures to discover the true facts and neutralize the threat of harm if it materialized. The policeman carefully restricted his search to what was appropriate to the discovery of the particular items which he sought. Each case of this sort will, of course, have to be decided on its own facts. We merely hold today that where a police officer observes unusual conduct which leads him reasonably to conclude in light of his experience that criminal activity may be afoot and that the persons with whom he is dealing may be armed and presently dangerous, where in the course of investigating this behavior he identifies himself as a policeman and makes reasonable inquiries, and where nothing in the initial stages of the encounter serves to dispel his reasonable fear for his own or others' safety, he is entitled for the protection of himself and others in the area to conduct a carefully limited search of the outer clothing of such persons in an attempt to discover weapons which might be used to assault him.

Such a search is a reasonable search under the Fourth Amendment, and any weapons seized may properly be introduced in evidence against the person from whom they were taken.

Affirmed.

[*The concurring opinions of Justices Black, Harlan, and White are omitted.*]

Justice Douglas dissenting.

I agree that petitioner was "seized" within the meaning of the Fourth Amendment. I also agree that frisking petitioner and his companions for guns was a "search." But it is a mystery how that "search" and that "seizure" can be constitutional by Fourth Amendment standards, unless there was probable cause to believe that (1) a crime had been committed or (2) a crime was in the process of being committed or (3) a crime was about to be committed.

The opinion of the Court disclaims the existence of "probable cause." If loitering were in issue and that was the offense charged, there would be "probable cause" shown. But the crime here is carrying concealed weapons; and there is no basis for concluding that the officer had "probable cause" for believing that that crime was being committed. Had a warrant been sought, a magistrate would, therefore, have been unauthorized to issue one, for he can act only if there is a showing of "probable cause." We hold today that the police have greater authority to make a "seizure" and conduct a "search" than a judge has to authorize such action. We have said precisely the opposite over and over again.

In other words, police officers up to today have been permitted to effect arrests and searches without warrants only when the facts within their knowledge would satisfy the constitutional standard of *probable cause.* At the time of their "seizure" without a warrant they must possess facts concerning the person arrested that would have satisfied a magistrate that "probable cause" was indeed present.

* * *

The infringement on personal liberty of any "seizure" of a person can only be "reasonable" under the Fourth Amendment if we require the police to possess "probable cause" before they seize him. Only that line draws a meaningful distinction between an officer's mere inkling and the presence of facts within the officer's personal knowledge which would convince a reasonable man that the person seized has committed, is committing, or is about to commit a particular crime. * * *

To give the police greater power than a magistrate is to take a long step down the totalitarian path. Perhaps such a step is desirable to cope with modern forms of lawlessness. But if it is taken, it should be the deliberate choice of the people through a constitutional amendment.

Until the Fourth Amendment, which is closely allied with the Fifth, is rewritten, the person and the effects of the individual are beyond the reach of all government agencies until there are reasonable grounds to believe (probable cause) that a criminal venture has been launched or is about to be launched.

There have been powerful hydraulic pressures throughout our history that bear heavily on the Court to water down constitutional guarantees and give the police the upper hand. That hydraulic pressure has probably never been greater than it is today.

Yet if the individual is no longer to be sovereign, if the police can pick him up whenever they do not like the cut of his jib, if they can "seize" and "search" him in their discretion, we enter a new regime. The decision to enter it should be made after a full debate by the people of this country.

In the companion case of *Sibron v. New York* (1968), the Court rejected a stop and frisk search in which an officer discovered heroin in a suspect's pocket, but lacked a sufficient basis to conduct a *Terry*-type search. The heroin was declared to be inadmissible in court as evidence against the suspect. This second decision underscored the fact that the Court would not endorse stop and frisk searches unless such searches were triggered by a factual situation that supported an officer's suspicions that someone might be carrying a weapon with the intent to commit a crime. If there was an insufficient basis for the officer to be suspicious, then the officer should not conduct the stop and frisk.

The following year, the Court clarified the permissible scope of a search incident to a lawful arrest. In *Chimel v. California* (1969), the police arrived at a man's home with a warrant for his arrest on burglary charges. The officers incorrectly stated to the suspect's wife that they had the authority to search the home on the basis of their arrest warrant. They proceeded to search the entire house, including drawers in the bedroom and sewing room. In concluding that the officers' search of the house was unreasonable, Justice Stewart's majority opinion clarified the permissible scope of a search conducted in conjunction with an arrest:

> *When an arrest is made, it is reasonable for the arresting officer to search the person arrested in order to remove any weapons that the latter might seek to use in order to resist arrest or effect his escape. Otherwise, the officer's safety might well be endangered, and the arrest itself frustrated. In addition, it is entirely reasonable for the arresting officer to search for and seize any evidence on the arrestee's person in order to prevent its concealment and destruction. And the area into which an arrestee might reach in order to grab a weapon or evidentiary items must, of course, be governed by a like rule. A gun on a table or in a drawer in front of one who is arrested can be as dangerous to the arresting officer as one concealed in the clothing of the person arrested. There is ample justification, therefore, for a search of the arrestee's person and the area "within his immediate control"—construing that phrase to mean the area from within which he might gain possession of a weapon or destructible evidence* (395 U.S. at 762–63).

The *Chimel* decision effectively reduced the free rein granted to law enforcement officers in *Rabinowitz* (1947) and *Harris* (1947) to conduct warrantless searches of premises after arrests. Although the Court limited the scope of officers' authority to conduct searches incident to lawful arrests, it did not curtail such authority. Instead, the Court demonstrated its concern about police officers' safety and the preservation of evidence by attempting to strike an appropriate balance between these interests and the rights of individual arrestees.

In considering other warrantless search contexts, the Court approved seizing evidence that would otherwise be lost, such as administering a blood test to a driver in a motor vehicle accident whose blood alcohol level would diminish during the time it would take to obtain a warrant (*Schmerber v. California,* 1966). The Court also approved warrantless searches undertaken in "hot pursuit" of a suspect, such as in response to a victim's screams (*Warden v. Hayden,* 1967). The Court disapproved other warrantless searches, however. For example, although a person can consent to a warrantless search, the justices would not permit a hotel clerk to grant permission for police to search a resident's room (*Stoner v. California,* 1964). The Warren Court was concerned about violations of an individual's reasonable expectation of privacy if other people were granted the authority to give consent for searches of places and belongings not directly under their ownership and control.

As illustrated by these examples, although the Warren Court expanded the reach of the Fourth Amendment (*Katz*) and imposed the exclusionary rule on all law enforcement officers (*Mapp*), the justices sought to protect the law enforcement interests of society. In *Terry* and *Chimel,* the Court recognized that the safety of police officers and the public as well as the preservation of evidence required that officers be given the authority to conduct limited warrantless searches tailored to protect those interests.

The Burger Court Era

President Nixon's four appointees to the Supreme Court altered the Court's approach to criminal justice issues, including those raised in Fourth Amendment cases. When assessing the impact of Nixon's appointees and other justices who eventually replaced Warren Court holdovers, scholars have concluded that "the Burger Court significantly chipped away at Warren Court precedents in . . . criminal procedure" (Lamb and Halpern 1991, p. 434). However, even though a majority of justices gave greater weight to law enforcement interests in striking a new balance that defined the scope of Fourth Amendment rights, the justices did not reverse *Mapp* and the other Warren Court precedents. Instead, they reshaped and limited the nature and extent of rights defined by their predecessors. This process of reshaping the Fourth Amendment involved a significant increase in the percentage of decisions favoring the government over individual claimants (see Table 9.1). As a consequence, the Burger Court diminished the strength and clarity of the exclusionary rule for both the Fourth and Fifth Amendments (see Chapter 10).

Nixon's first appointment, that of Warren Burger to replace retiring Chief Justice Earl Warren, clearly reflected Nixon's desire to reduce the scope of rights for criminal defendants. According to Henry Abraham, "Mr. Nixon . . . deliberately selected an individual who would presumably act favorably on his often-expressed plaint that courts, led by the Warren Court, 'have gone too far in weakening the peace forces as against the criminal forces' " (Abraham 1985, p. 298). At the very beginning of his tenure on the Court, Burger issued a stinging attack on the exclusionary rule. In *Bivens v. Six Unknown Named Agents of Federal Bureau of Narcotics* (1971), a majority decided that a man could file a civil rights lawsuit against the federal government after federal agents violated his Fourth Amendment rights in the course of searching his home and arresting him. In a dissenting opinion, Burger seized the opportunity to criticize the exclusionary rule. Burger elaborated on the claims made by Justice Frankfurter twenty-one years earlier in *Wolf* by arguing that alternatives other than the exclusion of evidence could best protect both law enforcement interests and the rights of individuals. Burger claimed that the exclusionary rule punished society rather than the individual police officer by barring the use of improperly obtained evidence. Burger complained that the exclusionary rule improperly treated honest mistakes by police officers with the same harshness as intentional actions to violate citizens' rights. The Chief Justice also asserted that states could develop their own remedies to prevent or remedy police misbehavior without excluding relevant evidence from use at trials. One critic of the exclusionary rule has called Burger's dissent "the most eloquent and comprehensive statement of opposition to the exclusionary rule to emerge from the Supreme Court" (Schlesinger 1977, p. 36). Burger never succeeded in abolishing the exclusionary rule, but he eventually saw his ideas applied to weaken the rule when the Supreme Court's composition continued to change in a conservative direction.

Although conservative critics have argued that the exclusionary rule effectively facilitates the release of many guilty defendants, research on the rule's effect casts doubt on such assertions. Studies have shown that exclusionary issues are raised in relatively few cases and most defendants' efforts to have evidence excluded are rejected by judges. In one study, for example, only 0.9 percent of search warrant cases generated successful defense motions to exclude evidence (Uchida and Bynum 1991). Even if defendants succeed in having evidence excluded, police and prosecutors frequently have enough other evidence to gain convictions anyway. Exclusionary rule issues arise most frequently in drug and weapons possession cases in which the prosecution's case rests primarily on the seizure of physical evidence. One review of the studies on the exclusionary rule's impact concluded that "[t]he exclusionary rule does not let 'thousands' of dangerous criminals loose on the streets and it has almost no effect on violent crime. Warren Burger and other critics of the exclusionary rule are guilty of reacting to a few celebrated cases. Yes, some convictions are overturned and some of those defendants are guilty. But these are fairly rare events" (Walker 1994, p. 128). Despite the limited adverse impact of the exclusionary rule, some critics, including Warren Burger, adopted the position that it is too great of a burden on society to permit even a single guilty offender to go free because of the exclusionary rule. Moreover, the exclusionary rule, like *Miranda* warnings, became a symbol of the Warren Court's liberal judicial activism, and conservative critics could use this symbol as a focus in expressing their dissatisfaction with the percentage of Warren Court decisions favoring criminal defendants (Alexander 1990). Thus, Chief Justice Burger and other appointees to the Burger and Rehnquist Courts sought to use their judicial decisions to reduce the coverage of the exclusionary rule.

Early in the Burger era, the Court clarified the "plain view" doctrine, which permits police officers to seize incriminating items not named in their warrant when those items are in plain view (*Coolidge v. New Hampshire,* 1971). The "plain view" doctrine represents an important exception to the Fourth Amendment's warrant requirement. According to Justice Stewart's majority opinion, "Where, once an otherwise lawful search is in progress, the police inadvertently come upon a piece of evidence, it would often be a needless inconvenience, and sometimes dangerous—to the evidence or to the police themselves—to require them to ignore it until they have obtained a warrant particularly describing it" (403 U.S. at 467–68).

Stewart emphasized that the discovery must be inadvertent and that any evidence specifically sought by the police must be described in the warrant. In essence, the police need not ignore any evidence sitting in the open when they are lawfully present in any location, whether or not they are there to conduct a search for some other items.

The Burger Court's decisions narrowed the range of Fourth Amendment protections. For example, in *United States v. Caceres* (1979), the majority diminished the impact of the *Katz* precedent by permitting Internal Revenue Service (IRS) officials to use evidence obtained in violation of the IRS's own regulations governing electronic surveillance. In another case, the Court effectively avoided the limitations of the *Terry* decision by deciding that police officers' questioning of a drug suspect at an airport did not constitute a "seizure" that would be governed by Fourth Amendment limitations (*Florida v. Royer,* 1983). The Court declared that a "seizure" did not occur unless a reasonable person would not have felt free to leave the scene of the police officers' questioning. According to law professor Wayne LaFave, the leading expert on search and seizure, only a person with "the hide of an elephant" would feel free to walk away from such encounters because "a reasonable person with just average dermatological characteristics would, in the language of *Royer,* ordinarily feel that he was 'not free to leave' when under police inquiry regarding criminal activity" (LaFave 1991, p. 227).

In *Illinois v. Gates* (1983), the Burger Court eliminated the Warren Court's previous requirement that police show the basis and veracity of their informers' tips in order to support probable cause for issuing a warrant. In this case, an anonymous letter to the police providing information about a married couple's drug trafficking activities served as the basis for a search warrant after the letter accurately predicted that the couple would fly to Florida and drive back to Illinois within a few days. Instead of requiring police to show that their informants were of proven reliability, judges after the *Gates* decision could simply take the existence (or lack thereof) of informers' proven reliability into consideration as one factor in deciding whether probable cause for the warrant was supported by the "totality of circumstances." In effect, the Court made it easier for police to seek and judges to issue warrants for searches.

The Burger Court made it significantly easier for police officers to search automobiles. Automobiles always received less protection than houses under the Fourth Amendment because motor vehicles are mobile and could disappear if police were required to seek warrants before every search. Moreover, most justices have assumed that people have diminished expectations of privacy in their automobiles as compared to their homes. During the first decade of the Burger Court, the justices had issued several decisions that limited police officers' ability to conduct warrantless searches of containers found inside automobiles once those containers or vehicles had been seized (e.g., *United States v. Chadwick,* 1977; *Arkansas v. Sanders,* 1979; *Robbins v. California,* 1981). However, the Court claimed that its next case presented a different fact situation and thereby sidestepped its own recent precedents by relying on the *Carroll* precedent from 1925 to justify its loosened restrictions on automobile searches (*United States v. Ross,* 1982). In *Ross,* after receiving a tip about a suspect selling drugs out of his car, officers searched the entire car, including a zippered pouch inside the trunk, after arresting the suspect and finding a bullet on the floor of the vehicle. The majority declared that police officers could search any containers or areas within the automobile for which they had probable cause to justify the search. In dissent, Justices Marshall and Brennan complained that the Court was permitting the police to avoid the Fourth Amendment's warrant requirement by allowing officers rather than neutral judges to determine whether probable cause exists, even when the cars and drivers have been seized and therefore there is time for the police to seek a judicial warrant.

In *New York v. Belton* (1981), the Court permitted a search of an automobile interior and containers inside the interior *after* the driver and passengers had been arrested and the automobile was completely within the custody of the police. The majority claimed that the search was justified by the *Chimel* precedent concerning warrantless searches incident to lawful arrests. However, Justices Brennan and Marshall noted in dissent that the *Chimel* search was justified by the officers' need to locate weapons or evidence quickly that might be within reach of the arrestee. By contrast, the automobile search in *Belton* occurred after the arrestees were in custody outside of the car and therefore could not reach any weapons or evidence within the vehicle. According to the dissenters, the police had the opportunity to seek a warrant from a judge since the automobile had been seized.

In *California v. Ciraolo* (1986), the Court approved aerial observation of a backyard surrounded by a ten-foot fence. The surveillance revealed that marijuana was growing in the backyard. To some observers, this was an expansion of the "open fields" exception to the warrant requirement that had been enunciated in *Hester* (1924). Professor LaFave views the Court's decision as a reduction in scope of privacy previously protected by the Warren Court's *Katz* decision: "[A] defendant cannot get by even the first *Katz* hurdle unless he has taken steps to ensure against all conceivable efforts at scrutiny, so that it is not enough (as the dissenters put it) that 'he had taken steps to shield those activities from the view of passersby' [by building a high fence around the yard]. To assert that such extraordinary precautions are necessary cannot be squared with *Katz,* for in that case, 'there was no suggestion that the defendant in the phone booth took any precautions against the wiretapping at issue in that case' " (LaFave 1991, p. 225).

Burger Court decisions produced expansions of police powers with respect to other contexts in which warrantless searches were permissible. For example, although the Warren Court had indicated that hotel clerks, landlords, and others could not give permission for searches of a suspect's domicile or property, the Burger Court indicated that roommates could give permission to search a shared bedroom (*United States v. Matlock,* 1974).

The Burger Court's direct reduction of the exclusionary rule occurred in *United States v. Leon* (1984). After receiving a tip from a confidential informant of unproven reliability about people selling and storing drugs at certain houses five months earlier, police initiated an investigation of people living at and visiting the named addresses. The police obtained a search warrant from a judge, and they discovered large quantities of illegal narcotics when they conducted their searches. On appeal, the defendants challenged the validity of the search warrant, and the U.S. Court of Appeals determined that the police lacked an adequate basis for obtaining a warrant. The information used to gain the warrant was not sufficiently current because it relied on events from five months earlier. Moreover, the police did not establish the credibility of their confidential informant. Thus the Court of Appeals reversed the conviction and ordered a new trial. The U.S. Supreme Court, however, reversed the Court of Appeals and reinstated the convictions. The justices established a "good faith" exception to the exclusionary rule that would permit the admission of improperly obtained evidence as long as the police believed that they were acting properly and attempted to follow proper procedures. In this case, it was the judge's error in issuing the warrant based on faulty information that produced the defect in the warrant, not the police officers' errors in preparing the application for the warrant. In effect, the Burger Court majority shifted the balance of interests in favor of law enforcement rather than in favor of defendants whose rights were violated.

UNITED STATES V. LEON

468 U.S. 897, 104 S. Ct. 3405, 82 L. Ed. 2d 677 (1984)
[The facts of this case are described in the chapter's text.]

■ This case is important because the Supreme Court created a "good faith" exception to the exclusionary rule. The police officers acted in good faith in presenting evidence to the magistrate to establish probable cause for issuance of a search warrant. However, the magistrate erred in issuing the warrant based on stale information: an informant's dated tip about activities that occurred five months earlier at the house in question. In addition, the opinions provide excellent illustrations of the justices' use of the language of cost-benefit analysis in determining the proper balance between law enforcement interests and individuals' rights. As you read the case, consider the following questions: (1) Does Justice White give adequate consideration to the protection of Fourth Amendment rights when he balances the competing costs and benefits? (2) Does the decision encourage police officers to be careful about applying for warrants only when they are confident that "probable cause" exists to justify the search? (3) How does an appellate court know whether the police officers acted in "good faith?"

VOTE:

6 justices found the police officers' actions constitutional (Blackmun, Burger, O'Connor, Powell, Rehnquist, White).

3 justices found the police officers' actions unconstitutional (Brennan, Marshall, Stevens).

Justice White delivered the opinion of the Court.

This case presents the question whether the Fourth Amendment exclusionary rule should be modified so as not to bar the use in the prosecution's case in chief of evidence obtained by officers acting in reasonable reliance on a search warrant issued by a detached and neutral magistrate but ultimately found to be unsupported by probable cause. To resolve this question, we must consider once again the tension between the sometimes competing goals of, on the one hand, deterring official misconduct and removing inducements to unreasonable invasions of privacy and, on the other, establishing procedures under which criminal defendants are "acquitted or convicted on the basis of all the evidence which exposes the truth." * * *

* * *

Language in opinions of this Court and of individual Justices has sometimes implied that the exclusionary rule is a necessary corollary of the Fourth Amendment, *Mapp v. Ohio* (1961); *Olmstead v. United States* (1928), or that the rule is required by the conjunction of the Fourth and Fifth Amendments. *Mapp v. Ohio* (Black, J., concurring); *Agnello v. United States* (1925). These implications need not detain us long. The Fifth Amendment theory has not withstood critical analysis or the test of time, see *Andresen v. Maryland* (1976), and the Fourth Amendment "has never been interpreted to proscribe the introduction of illegally seized evidence in all proceedings or against all persons." *Stone v. Powell,* 428 U.S. at 486 (1976).

The Fourth Amendment contains no provision expressly precluding the use of evidence obtained in violation of its commands, and an examination of its origin and purposes makes clear that the use of fruits of a past unlawful search or seizure "work[s] no new Fourth Amendment wrong." *United States v. Calandra,* 414 U.S. at 354 (1974). The wrong condemned by the Amendment is "fully accomplished" by the unlawful search or seizure itself, and the exclusionary rule is neither intended nor able to "cure the invasion of the defendant's rights which he has already suffered."... The rule thus operates as "a judicially created remedy designed to safeguard Fourth Amendment rights generally through its deterrent effect, rather than a personal constitutional right of the party aggrieved." *United States v. Calandra,* 414 US. at 348.

Whether exclusionary sanction is appropriately imposed in a particular case, our decisions make clear, is "an issue separate from the question whether the Fourth Amendment rights of the party seeking to invoke the rule were violated by police conduct." * * * Only the former question is currently before us, and it must be resolved by weighing the costs and benefits of preventing the use in the prosecution's case in chief of inherently trustworthy tangible evidence in reliance on a search warrant issued by a detached and neutral magistrate that ultimately is found to be defective.

The substantial social costs exacted by the exclusionary rule for the vindication of Fourth Amendment rights have long been a source of concern. * * * An objectionable collateral consequence of this interference with the criminal justice system's truth-finding function is that some guilty defendants may go free or receive reduced sentences as a result of favorable plea bargains. Particularly when law enforcement officers have acted in objective good faith or their transgressions have been minor, the magnitude of the benefit conferred on such guilty defendants offends basic concepts of the criminal justice system.... Indiscriminate application of the exclusionary rule, therefore, may well "generat[e] disrespect for the law and administration of justice." * * * Accordingly, "[a]s with any remedial device, the application of the rule has been restricted to those areas where its remedial objectives are thought most efficaciously served." * * *

* * *

As yet, we have not recognized any form of good-faith exception to the Fourth Amendment exclusionary rule. But the balancing approach that has evolved during the years of experience with the rule provides strong support for the modification currently urged upon us. As we discuss below our evaluation of the costs and benefits of suppressing reliable physical evidence seized by an officer reasonably relying on a warrant issued by a detached and neutral magistrate leads to the conclusion that such evidence should be admissible in the prosecution's case in chief.

* * *

. . .[W]e discern no basis, and are offered none, for believing that exclusion of evidence seized pursuant to a warrant will have a significant deterrent effect on the issuing judge or magistrate. Many of the factors that indicate that the exclusionary rule cannot provide an effective "special" or "general" deterrent for individual offending law enforcement officers apply as well to judges or magistrates. And, to the extent that the rule is thought to operate as a "systemic" deterrent on a wider audience, it clearly can have no such effect on individuals empowered to issue search warrants. Judges and magistrates are not adjuncts to the law enforcement team; as neutral judicial officers, they have no stake in the outcome of particular criminal prosecutions. The threat of exclusion thus cannot be expected significantly to deter them. Imposition of the exclusionary sanction is not necessary meaningfully to inform judicial officers of their errors, and we cannot conclude that admitting evidence obtained pursuant to a warrant while at the same time declaring that the warrant was somehow defective will in any way reduce judicial officers' professional incentives to comply with the Fourth Amendment, encouraging them to repeat their mistakes, or lead to the granting of all colorable warrant requests.

* * *

We have frequently questioned whether the exclusionary rule can have any deterrent effect when the offending officers acted in the objectively reasonable belief that their conduct did not violate the Fourth Amendment. "No empirical researcher, proponent or opponent of the rule, has yet been able to establish with any assurance whether the rule has a deterrent effect." * * * But even assuming that the rule effectively deters some police misconduct and provides incentives for the law enforcement profession as a whole to conduct itself in accord with the Fourth Amendment, it cannot be expected, and should not be applied, to deter objectively reasonable law enforcement activity.

* * *

. . .[W]hen an officer acting with objective good faith has obtained a search warrant from a judge or magistrate and acted within its scope[,] . . . [i]n most such cases, there is no police illegality and thus nothing to deter. It is the magistrate's responsibility to determine whether the officer's allegations establish probable cause and, if so, to issue a warrant comporting in form with the requirements of the Fourth Amendment. In the ordinary case, an officer cannot be expected to question the magistrate's probable-cause determination or his judgment that the form of the warrant is technically sufficient. * * * Penalizing the officer for the magistrate's error, rather than his own, cannot logically contribute to the deterrence of Fourth Amendment violations.

We conclude that the marginal or nonexistent benefits produced by suppressing evidence obtained in objectively reasonable reliance on a subsequently invalidated search warrant cannot justify the substantial costs of exclusion. We do not suggest, however, that exclusion is always inappropriate in cases where an officer has obtained a warrant and abided by its terms. * * * [T]he officer's reliance on the magistrate's probable-cause determination and on the technical sufficiency of the warrant he issues must be objectively reasonable, . . . and it is clear that in some circumstances the officer will have no reasonable grounds for believing that the warrant was properly issued.

Suppression therefore remains an appropriate remedy if the magistrate or judge in issuing a warrant was misled by information in an affidavit that the affiant knew was false or would have known was false except for his reckless disregard of the truth . . . . The exception we recognize today will also not apply in cases where the issuing magistrate wholly abandoned his judicial role. . . . [I]n such circumstances, no reasonably well trained officer should rely on the warrant. Nor would an officer manifest objective good faith in relying on a warrant based on an affidavit "so lacking in indicia of probable cause as to render official belief in its existence entirely unreasonable." * * * Finally, depending on the circumstances of the particular case, a warrant may be so facially deficient,—*i.e.,* in failing to particularize the place to be searched or the things to be seized—that the executing officers cannot reasonably presume it to be valid.* * *

* * * The good-faith exception for searches conducted pursuant to warrants is not intended to signal our unwillingness strictly to enforce the requirements of the Fourth Amendment, and we do not believe that it will have this effect. As we have already suggested, the good-faith exception, turning as it does on objective reasonableness, should not be difficult to apply in practice. When officers have acted pursuant to a warrant, the prosecution should ordinarily be able to establish objective good faith without a substantial expenditure of judicial time.

* * *

In the absence of an allegation that the magistrate abandoned his detached and neutral role, suppression is appropriate only if the officers were dishonest or reckless in preparing their affidavit or could not have harbored an objectively reasonable belief in the existence of probable cause. * * *

Accordingly, the judgment of the Court of Appeals is

Reversed.

Justice Blackmun concurring.

* * * [B]ecause I believe that the rule announced today advances the legitimate interests of the criminal justice system without sacrificing the individual rights protected by the Fourth Amendment[,] I write separately . . . to underscore what I regard as the unavoidable provisional nature of today's decisions.

* * *

* * * If it should emerge from experience that, contrary to our expectations, the good-faith exception to the exclusionary rule results in a material change in police compliance with the Fourth Amendment, we shall have to reconsider what we have undertaken here. The logic of a decision that rests on untested predictions about police conduct demands no less.

If a single principle may be drawn from this Court's exclusionary rule decisions from *Weeks* through *Mapp v. Ohio* . . . to the decisions handed down today, it is that the scope of the exclusionary rule is subject to change in light of changing judicial understanding about the effects of the rule outside the confines of the courtroom. It is incumbent on the Nation's law enforcement officers, who must continue to observe the Fourth Amendment in the wake of today's decisions, to recognize the double-edged nature of that principle.

Justice Brennan, with whom Justice Marshall joins, dissenting.

* * *

The Court seeks to justify this result on the ground that the "costs" of adhering to the exclusionary rule in cases like those before us exceed the "benefits." But the language of deterrence and cost/benefit analysis, if used indiscriminantly, can have a narcotic effect. It creates an illusion of technical precision and ineluctability. It suggests that not only constitutional principle but also empirical data support the majority's result. When the Court's analysis is examined carefully, however, it is clear that we have not been treated to an honest assessment of the merits of the exclusionary rule, but have instead been drawn into a curious world where the "costs" of excluding illegally obtained evidence loom to exaggerated heights and where the "benefits" of such exclusion are made to disappear with a mere wave of the hand.

* * *

. . .[I]n this bit of judicial stagecraft, while the sets sometimes change, the actors always have the same lines. Given this well-rehearsed pattern, one might have predicted with some assurance how the present case would unfold. First there is the ritual incantation of the "substantial social costs" exacted by the exclusionary rule, followed by the virtually foreordained conclusion that, given the marginal benefits, application of the rule in the circumstances of these cases is not warranted. Upon analysis, however, such a result cannot be justified even on the Court's own terms.

At the outset, the Court suggests that society has been asked to pay a high price—in terms either of setting guilty persons free or of impeding the proper functioning of trials—as a result of excluding relevant physical evidence in cases where the police, in conducting searches and seizing evidence, have made only an "objectively reasonable" mistake concerning the constitutionality of their actions. . . . But what evidence is there to support such a claim?

Significantly, the Court points to none, and indeed, as the Court acknowledges [in a footnote], recent studies have demonstrated that the "costs" of the exclusionary rule—calculated in terms of dropped prosecutions and lost convictions—are quite low. Contrary to the claims of the rule's critics that exclusion leads to "the release of countless guilty criminals," . . .these studies have demonstrated that federal and state prosecutors very rarely drop cases because of potential search and seizure problems. For example, a 1979 study prepared at the request of Congress by the General Accounting Office [GAO] reported that only 0.4% of all cases actually declined for prosecution by federal prosecutors were declined primarily because of illegal search problems. . . . If the GAO data are restated as a percentage of *all* arrests, the study shows only 0.2% of all felony arrests are declined for prosecution because of potential exclusionary rule problems. * * * Of course, these data describe only the costs attributable to the exclusion of evidence in all cases; the costs that are due to the exclusion of evidence in the narrower category of cases where police have made objectively reasonable mistakes must necessarily be even smaller. The Court, however, ignores this distinction and mistakenly weighs the aggregated costs of exclusion in *all* cases, irrespective of the circumstances that led to exclusion . . . against the potential benefits associated with only those cases in which evidence is excluded because police reasonably but mistakenly believe that their conduct does not violate the Fourth Amendment. . . . When such faulty scales are used, it is little wonder that the balance tips in favor of restricting the application of the rule.

* * *

If the overall educational effect of the exclusionary rule is considered, application of the rule to even those situations in which individual police officers have acted on the basis of a reasonable but mistaken belief that their conduct was authorized can still be expected to have a considerable long-term deterrent effect. If evidence is consistently excluded in these circumstances, police departments will surely be prompted to instruct their officers to devote greater care and attention to providing sufficient information to establish probable cause when applying for a warrant, and to review with some attention the form of the warrant that they have been issued, rather than automatically assuming that whatever document the magistrate has signed will necessarily comport with Fourth Amendment requirements.

After today's decisions, however, that institutional incentive will be lost. Indeed, the Court's "reasonable mistake" exception to the exclusionary rule will tend to put a premium on police ignorance of the law. Armed with the assurance provided by today's decisions that evidence will always be admissible whenever an officer has reasonably relied upon a warrant, police departments will be encouraged to train officers that if a warrant has simply been signed, it is reasonable, without more, to rely on it. Since in close cases there will no longer be any incentive to err on the side of constitutional behavior, police would have every reason to adopt a "let's-wait-until-it's decided" approach in situations in which there is a question about a warrant's validity or the basis of its issuance.* * *

Although the Court brushes these concerns aside, a host of grave consequences can be expected to result from its decision to carve this new exception out of the exclusionary rule. A chief consequence of today's decisions will be to convey a clear and unambiguous message to magistrates that their decisions to issue warrants are now insulated from subsequent judicial review. Creation of this new exception for good-faith reliance upon a warrant implicitly tells magistrates that they need not take much care in reviewing warrant applications, since their mistakes will from now on have virtually no consequence: If their decision to issue a warrant was correct, the evidence will be admitted; if their decision to issue the warrant was incorrect but the police relied in good faith on the warrant, the evidence will also be admitted. Inevitably, the care and attention devoted to such an inconsequential chore will dwindle. * * *

* * *

When the public, as it quite properly has done in the past as well as in the present, demands that those in government increase their efforts to combat crime, it is all too easy for those in government to seek expedient solutions. In contrast to such costly and difficult measures as building more prisons, improving law enforcement methods, or hiring more prosecutors and judges to relieve the overburdened court systems in the country's metropolitan areas, the relaxation of Fourth Amendment standards seems a tempting, costless means of meeting the public's demand for better law enforcement. In the long run, however, we as a society pay a heavy price for such expediency, because as Justice Jackson observed, the rights guaranteed in the Fourth Amendment "are not mere second-class rights but belong in the catalog of indispensable freedoms." * * * Once lost, such rights are difficult to recover. There is hope, however, that in time this or some later Court will restore these precious freedoms to their rightful place as a primary protection for our citizens against overreaching officialdom.

I dissent.

Justice Stevens dissenting.

* * *

The notion that a police officer's reliance on a magistrate's warrant is automatically appropriate is one the Framers of the Fourth Amendment would have vehemently rejected. The precise problem that the Amendment was intended to address was *the unreasonable issuance of warrants.* As we have often observed, the Amendment was actually motivated by the practice of issuing general warrants—warrants which did not satisfy the particularity and probable-cause requirements. * * *

In short, the Framers of the Fourth Amendment were deeply suspicious of warrants; in their minds the paradigm of an abusive search was the execution of a warrant not based on probable cause. The fact that colonial officers had magisterial authorization for their conduct when they engaged in general searches surely did not make their conduct "reasonable." The Court's view that it is consistent with our Constitution to adopt a rule that it is presumptively reasonable to rely on a defective warrant is the product of constitutional amnesia.

* * *

As we discussed earlier, Fourth Amendment cases tend to be decided by the justices' reactions to the facts in individual cases and their subjective balancing of the competing values at issue. These cases are not decided according to any grand theory or principle, except when a majority of justices take a principled position on the exclusionary rule as they did during the Warren Court era. In his majority opinion in *Leon,* Justice White explicitly acknowledged the Court's need to weigh the costs and benefits of the exclusionary rule: "[T]he . . . question . . . before us . . . must be resolved by weighing the costs and benefits of preventing the use in the prosecution's case in chief of inherently trustworthy tangible evidence obtained in reliance on a search warrant issued by a detached and neutral magistrate that ultimately is found to be defective" (468 U.S. at 906–7). In answering the question he posed about the appropriate balance, White also used the language of costs and benefits. White's opinion declared that "the marginal or nonexistent benefits produced by suppressing evidence obtained in objectively reasonable reliance on a subsequently invalidated search warrant cannot justify the substantial costs of exclusion" (468 U.S. at 922). Moreover, he asserted that "when law enforcement officers have acted in objective good faith or their transgressions have been minor, the magnitude of the benefit conferred on such guilty defendants offends basic concepts of the criminal justice system" (468 U.S. at 908).

Justice Brennan's dissenting opinion, joined by Justice Marshall, took issue with White's use of the language of cost-benefit analysis to justify his subjective value judgments. Brennan noted that in previous exclusionary rule cases his conservative colleagues had claimed that the costs to society of the exclusionary rule outweigh the rule's benefits without giving any indication of how they are measuring costs and benefits. According to Brennan, "Given this well-rehearsed pattern, one might have predicted with some assurance how the present case would unfold. First there is the ritual incantation of the 'substantial social costs' exacted by the exclusionary rule, followed by the virtually foreordained conclusion that, given the marginal benefits, application of the rule in the circumstances of these cases is not warranted" (468 U.S. at 949). Brennan then proceeded to discuss the social science studies of the exclusionary rule, which indicated that the rule is seldom raised by defendants, even less frequently successful, and often offset by other kinds of evidence that ensures the conviction of the offender. Brennan worried that the Court was sending the wrong message to police officers by permitting them to take insufficient care in preparing warrant applications. After *Leon,* any deficiencies in approved warrants would be blamed on errant judges and thus improperly obtained evidence could be used at trial.

The *Leon* decision, as well as its companion case, *Massachusetts v. Sheppard* (1984), concerning police officers' good faith use of an improper warrant form, represented the fulfillment of one of Chief Justice Burger's criticisms of the exclusionary rule from his *Bivens* dissent thirteen years earlier. Burger complained that honest mistakes were treated as harshly as intentional rights violations, and the Burger Court acted to differentiate those two categories of actions. From the perspective of the individual whose Fourth Amendment rights were violated, it makes little difference whether the violation occurs intentionally or inadvertently. However, the *Leon* decision made clear that a majority on the Court viewed some rights violations from the perspective of law enforcement officers rather than from the perspective of individual claimants. As we will discuss in Chapter 10, the justices created additional exceptions to the exclusionary rule in Fifth Amendment cases. Thus the composition changes on the Supreme Court during the Burger Court era led to a significant reshaping and diminution of the Fourth and Fifth Amendment principles enunciated by the Warren Court. The exclusionary rule was not eliminated and thus the *Mapp* precedent remained as a symbol detested by the Warren Court's conservative critics. However, the landmark precedent had begun to experience a "swiss cheese" effect as the Burger Court created exceptions that increasingly permitted improperly obtained evidence to be used against criminal defendants. At the same time, the clarity of the rule disappeared, and police officers had more trouble knowing precisely which situations and actions would lead to exclusion of evidence.

The Rehnquist Court Era

During the Rehnquist Court era, the Supreme Court decided cases affecting nearly every aspect of Fourth Amendment issues, and in most cases the Court either favored government by interpreting precedents in a conservative manner or created new conservative interpretations of existing precedents. Although a few decisions favored individuals, these cases preserved but did not enlarge specific protections for individuals. The Rehnquist Court's impact on the Fourth Amendment has been much more consistent than its impact on other criminal justice rights. As we will see in Chapters 10, 11, and 12, the Rehnquist Court issued at least a few decisions expanding liberal principles in its cases concerning the Fifth, Sixth, and Eighth Amendments. By contrast, the Rehnquist Court's Fourth Amendment decisions have generally made it easier for law enforcement officers to conduct warrantless searches in various contexts and to make use of evidence that was obtained through improper means.

As indicated in Table 9.1, the Burger Court favored the government in Fourth Amendment cases much more frequently than did the Warren Court (69 percent vs. 39 percent). In addition, the Rehnquist Court has been even less favorable to Fourth Amendment claims by individuals, ruling for the government in 77 percent of the

TABLE 9.1: Liberal/Conservative Outcomes of Fourth Amendment Cases for the Warren, Burger, and Rehnquist Courts, 1953-94 Terms

	Outcomes		
Court Era	Liberal	Conservative	Totals
Warren Court 1953-68 Terms	61% (35)	39% (22)	57
Burger Court 1969-85 Terms	31% (36)	69% (80)	116
Rehnquist Court 1986-94 Terms	23% (9)	77% (30)	39
Totals	38% (80)	62% (132)	212

cases involving the Fourth Amendment. This shift is not surprising since the exclusionary rule and Fourth Amendment rights were specific targets of the conservative presidents who selected justices during the Burger and Rehnquist Court eras.

The individual voting records presented in Table 9.2 show that most justices opposed constitutional rights claims in two-thirds or more of Fourth Amendment cases. Only four justices during the Rehnquist Court era favored individuals in most cases (Brennan, Marshall, Stevens, Ginsburg). Justice Blackmun, whose liberal voting record on many other issues is illustrated in other chapters' tables, favored the government in nearly two-thirds of Fourth Amendment cases. Ten justices supported the government in nearly two-thirds or more of Fourth Amendment cases, with Chief Justice Rehnquist ranking as the most consistently conservative member of the Court.

Not surprisingly, the strong support for the government in Fourth Amendment cases produced a dominant conservative voting bloc. As indicated in Table 9.3, Chief Justice Rehnquist and Justices Kennedy, O'Connor, White, and Scalia voted together at a rate (87) that far exceeded even the stringent Sprague Criterion (79). Justices Brennan and Marshall formed a unified liberal bloc, but a two-justice bloc is obviously less influential than a five-justice bloc.

The distribution of decisions by term in Table 9.4 does not indicate that any specific appointments during the Rehnquist era had a noticeable effect on case outcomes. Conservative outcomes were prevalent from the outset of the Rehnquist Court era as the justices continued and strengthened the patterns established during the Burger Court era. The strongest conservative performance (5-0) came with the retirement of Justice Brennan and the appointment of Justice Souter for the 1990 term. However, the Court had consistently favored conservative outcomes in the terms prior to Brennan's retirement. The 1992 term stands out as an unusual term because of its two out of three decisions favorable to individuals. Because the most liberal justices (Brennan and Marshall) had retired before this term, it appears that the particular cases decided by the Court must have raised different kinds of issues than those presented in previous terms. Indeed, one of the decisions was

TABLE 9.2: Liberal/Conservative Voting Records of Justices of the Rehnquist Court in Fourth Amendment Cases, 1986-94 Terms

Justices	Liberal Votes	Conservative Votes
Powell	0% (0)	100% (9)
Rehnquist	10% (4)	90% (35)
Kennedy	20% (5)	80% (20)
White	22% (8)	78% (28)
Scalia	26% (10)	74% (29)
O'Connor	28% (11)	72% (28)
Thomas	33% (2)	67% (4)
Breyer	33% (1)	67% (2)
Souter	36% (4)	64% (7)
Blackmun	39% (14)	61% (22)
Ginsburg	67% (2)	33% (1)
Stevens	69% (27)	31% (12)
Brennan	96% (26)	4% (1)
Marshall	97% (32)	3% (1)

TABLE 9.3: Bloc Voting Analysis of the Rehnquist Court's Fourth Amendment Cases, 1986-94 Terms (Percent Agreement Rates)

	Ken	OCon	Scal	Rehn	Whit	Blkm	Stev	Bren	Mar
Kennedy	—	96	93	93	92	68	46	23	18
O'Connor	96	—	82	82	81	58	54	26	24
Scalia	93	82	—	85	83	69	56	26	24
Rehnquist	93	82	85	—	86	69	41	11	9
White	92	81	83	86	—	67	56	22	21
Blackmun	68	58	69	69	67	—	61	44	42
Stevens	46	54	56	41	56	61	—	63	70
Brennan	23	26	26	11	22	44	63	—	100
Marshall	18	24	24	9	21	42	70	100	—

Court mean = 57
Sprague Criterion = 79
Liberal bloc: Marshall, Brennan = 100
Conservative bloc: Kennedy, O'Connor, White, Scalia, Rehnquist = 87

TABLE 9.4: Liberal/Conservative Outcomes of Fourth Amendment Cases During the Rehnquist Court Era by Term, 1986-94 Terms

	Outcomes		
Term	Liberal	Conservative	Totals
1986	22% (2)	78% (7)	9
1987	0% (0)	100% (3)	3
1988	20% (1)	80% (4)	5
1989	27% (3)	73% (8)	11
1990	0% (0)	100% (5)	5
1991	—	—	0
1992	67% (2)	33% (1)	3
1993	—	—	0
1994	33% (1)	67% (2)	3
Totals	23% (9)	77% (30)	39

unanimous (*Soldal v. Cook County,* 1993) in defining the eviction of a trailer home with sheriff's deputies present as a "seizure" under the Fourth Amendment. The other case presented an opportunity for the Court to weaken the Warren Court precedent from *Terry v. Ohio* (1968), but a six-member majority decided to retain some limits on the scope of police patdown searches that are characteristic of the stop and frisk situation (*Minnesota v. Dickerson,* 1993). After officers have determined that the suspect has no weapons, they are not free to continue searching small containers that they feel in the suspect's pocket simply because they believe such containers might be used to carry drugs.

Table 9.5 shows the doctrinal breakdown of Fourth Amendment cases. The Rehnquist Court's activity in Fourth Amendment cases has attracted the attention of observers, as indicated by the relatively large number of decisions classified as "important" by both the *New York Times* and the *Lawyers Edition* Supreme Court reports. Not surprisingly, all but one of these important decisions favored the

TABLE 9.5: A Framework for the Doctrinal Analysis of the Rehnquist Court's Cases on the Fourth Amendment, 1986-94 Terms

Major or Minor Importance	**Majority or Plurality Opinion**	**Treatment of Precedent**					
		Creation of New Liberal Precedent	Liberal Modification of Existing Precedent	Liberal Interpretation of Existing Precedent	Conservative Interpretation of Existing Precedent	Conservative Modification of Existing Precedent	Creation of New Conservative Precedent
Major	Majority			Minnesota v. Dickerson (1993)	California v. Greenwood (1988) U.S. v. Sokolow (1989) Michigan v. Sitz (1990) Florida v. Bostick (1991)	Skinner v. Railway Labor (1989) NTEU v. Von Raab (1989) Co. of Riverside v. McLaughlin (1991) Vernonia School Dist. v. Acton (1995)	
	Plurality						
Minor	Majority		Wilson v. Arkansas (1995)	Arizona v. Hicks (1987) Brower v. Co. of Inyo (1989) James v. Illinois (1990) Minnesota v. Olson (1990) Florida v. Wells (1990) Soldal v. Cook Co. (1992)	Maryland v. Garrison (1987) U.S. v. Dunn (1987) Illinois v. Krull (1987) New York v. Burger (1987) Colorado v. Bertine (1987) Michigan v. Chesternut (1988) Murray v. U.S. (1988) Florida v. Riley (1989) Maryland v. Buie (1990) New York v. Harris (1990) Alabama v. White (1990) Florida v. Jimeno (1991) California v. Acevedo (1991) California v. Hodari D. (1991) U.S. v. Padilla (1993)	O'Connor v. Ortega (1987) Griffin v. Wisconsin (1987) U.S. v. Verdugo-Urquidez (1990) Horton v. California (1990) Illinois v. Rodriguez (1990) Arizona v. Evans (1995)	
	Plurality						

{Excluded Cases: California v. Rooney (1987) [not a decision on the merits]; U.S. v. Ojeda-Ross (1990) [statutory issue]} government. The lone exception was the case of *Minnesota v. Dickerson* in which a majority of justices preserved the *Terry* rule.

Four of the Court's important decisions constituted conservative modifications of existing precedent that directly reduced the scope of protections previously presumed to exist under the Fourth Amendment. In *Skinner v. Railway Labor Executives' Association* (1989), a seven-member majority approved Federal Railroad Administration regulations mandating drug and alcohol tests of railway employees without warrants or individualized suspicion of wrongdoing after the occurrence of an accident. The majority concluded that the government's interest in protecting public safety by monitoring the conduct of certain railway employees (e.g., engineers) justified the endorsement of an exception to the Fourth Amendment's warrant requirement. In dissent, Justices Marshall and Brennan agreed that there may be an immediate need to obtain blood samples of relevant personnel after an accident without obtaining a warrant because evidence might otherwise be lost if alcohol or drug evidence fades from the bloodstream over time. However, once the government had the samples in its possession and thereby preserved the potential evidence, the dissenters argued that the government should be required to establish probable cause for individualized suspicion before obtaining a warrant authorizing testing of the samples.

In a related case decided the same day, five members of the Court approved random drug testing for U.S. Customs Service personnel (*National Treasury Employees Union v. Von Raab,* 1989). Critics of the Court regarded these two decisions as significantly expanding the government's ability to conduct searches without any evidence or basis for suspecting wrongdoing by a particular individual. Again, the majority justified abandonment of the warrant requirement on the grounds that government interests, in this case, crime control, outweighed individuals' privacy interests protected by the Fourth Amendment. Because Customs Service employees have special responsibilities for searching and seizing people who attempt to bring illegal drugs into the United States, there are arguably strong reasons to make certain that they do not become connected to drug abuse and drug trafficking. Justices Scalia and Stevens joined Brennan and Marshall in dissent against what Scalia described as "a kind of immolation of privacy and human dignity in symbolic opposition to drug use" (489 U.S. at 681). Scalia viewed the two drug testing cases differently because there was a history of substance abuse factors involved in railway accidents but there was no indication of employee drug problems affecting the work of the Customs Service.

In the third "major" modification of precedent, the Court clarified the requirement that a preliminary hearing be held promptly after a person has been "seized" in a warrantless arrest. When officers obtain a search warrant, they have already demonstrated to a judge that they possess sufficient evidence to justify an arrest. When there is a warrantless arrest, however, there is a risk that an officer may use his or her discretionary authority to deprive an innocent person of freedom without any basis. A five-member majority declared that a probable cause determination must be made in court within forty-eight hours after an arrest. Justice O'Connor's opinion claimed that the forty-eight-hour rule balanced the competing interests of law enforcement officials and citizens. Law enforcement officials need some period of time to go through all of the administrative steps involved in processing an arrest. However, citizens should not be deprived of their freedom for an excessive period of time without the police providing evidence to justify warrantless arrests. In establishing the forty-eight-hour rule, O'Connor's opinion actually shortened the amount of time that Riverside County had applied in many cases when, for example, someone arrested on a Thursday prior to a holiday weekend would not appear in court until the following Tuesday. Three dissenters (Marshall, Blackmun, and Stevens) endorsed the Court of Appeals' determination that probable cause hearings must be held within thirty-six hours because it did not take more than thirty-six hours to complete administrative processing of an arrest. In a strong dissent, Justice Scalia argued that nearly every previous federal and state court decision on this issue had regarded twenty-four hours as an adequate time period to process an arrest before holding a hearing. Scalia argued that the Court should set a twenty-four-hour rule but permit the police to justify the need for longer periods of time in individual cases. Scalia's dissent concluded with one of his characteristically strident criticisms of the detrimental result produced by the majority's decision:

> *While in recent years we have invented novel applications of the Fourth Amendment to release the unquestionably guilty, we today repudiate one of its core applications so that the presumptively innocent may be left in jail. Hereafter a law-abiding citizen wrongfully arrested may be compelled to await the grace of a Dickensian bureaucratic machine, as it churns its cycle for up to two days—never once given the opportunity to show a judge that there is absolutely no reason to hold him, that a mistake has been made. In my view, this is an image of a system of justice that has lost its ancient sense of priority, a system that few Americans would recognize as their own.* (111 S. Ct. at 1677)

In the fourth case, a 6-3 majority approved an Oregon school district's rule requiring urinalysis drug testing of students who participate on school sports teams (*Vernonia School District v. Acton,* 1995). The school district's rule had been challenged by a seventh-grade student and his parents who refused to sign the mandatory testing consent form when the student sought to join the junior high school football team. In writing for the majority, Justice Scalia endorsed the school policy as one imposing a relatively unobtrusive search (urinalysis) as a means to protect students from a severe social and medical problem (drug abuse). In dissent, Justice O'Connor, joined by Justices Stevens and Souter, objected to the use of mass suspicionless searches. They viewed such suspicionless searches as unreasonable under the Fourth Amendment unless the school district could demonstrate that its objectives could not be achieved by limiting searches to students whose behavior raised reasonable suspicions about their use of illegal drugs. Interestingly, President Clinton's two Democratic appointees, Justices Ginsburg and Breyer, joined the Court's conservatives in supporting the policy, while three Republican appointees dissented on behalf of the student's constitutional rights claim.

In the other major cases, the Supreme Court made conservative interpretations of existing precedents that effectively provided police with greater flexibility in investigating suspected criminal conduct. In *United States v. Sokolow* (1989), the Court endorsed the use of "drug courier profiles" as the basis for law enforcement officers to stop and question people at airports. The police were at the airport watching for people who had several specific characteristics: flying to or from Miami; not checking any luggage; round-trip ticket with a very short stay at Miami; paid cash for plane tickets; and name on ticket did not match name under which telephone number was listed. A seven-member majority supported Chief Justice Rehnquist's view that courts must consider a totality of circumstances to decide whether or not police officers have a reasonable basis to stop people. Justices Brennan and Marshall disagreed and questioned the use of stereotypical profiles as the basis for police stops. In other decisions concerning the basis for police stops, a six-member majority approved the use of highway sobriety checkpoints in which police stop all vehicles to assess whether drivers show signs of intoxication (*Michigan Department of State Police v. Sitz,* 1990). In *Florida v. Bostick* (1991), a six-member majority approved the practice of police officers entering interstate buses, questioning passengers, and requesting to search various passengers' luggage. For the majority, Justice O'Connor expressed the view that reasonable persons would know that they could decline to answer questions and refuse to agree to searches. Justice Marshall, however, argued on behalf of the three dissenters that the police were exploiting a coercive technique by approaching passengers within the confined space of a bus during the course of a sweep not based on any reasonable suspicion of wrongdoing.

Florida v. Bostick

501 U.S. 429, 111 S.Ct. 2382, 115 L Ed. 2d 389 (1991)

■ At a stop in Fort Lauderdale, Florida, two police officers boarded a bus bound from Miami to Atlanta. Without an articulable basis for suspicion, they picked out the defendant and asked to see his ticket and his identification. The identification matched the name on the ticket. The officer persisted in questioning the defendant and requested permission to search his luggage. The officers claimed that they informed the defendant of his right to refuse, but the defendant claimed that they had not informed him of this right and that they searched one of his bags without permission. The bag contained illegal narcotics. The trial court found that the officers had advised the defendant of his right to refuse and that the search had been conducted with his permission. After he was convicted, the defendant challenged the police officers' authority to question people randomly and seek to conduct searches without any grounds for suspicion.

The case is important because it shows how the Rehnquist Court justices possess less skepticism about police motives and actions than their predecessors on the Warren Court. The Court also relies on a presumption that people are well aware of their constitutional rights, a presumption that the Warren Court justices may well have rejected. As you read the opinion, consider the following questions: (1) Was the atmosphere of the police questioning "coercive," when even the majority acknowledges that the defendant was not entirely free to leave? (2) Do people know that they are free to refuse to answer questions posed to them by police officers? (3) Was the majority's view affected by the highly publicized "war on drugs" declared at the time of the decision by the Bush administration?

Vote:

6 justices found the police officers' actions constitutional (Kennedy, O'Connor, Rehnquist, Scalia, Souter, White).

3 justices found the police officers' actions unconstitutional (Blackmun, Marshall, Stevens).

Justice O'Connor delivered the opinion of the Court.

We have held that the Fourth Amendment permits police officers to approach individuals at random in airport lobbies and other public places to ask them questions and request consent to search their luggage, so long as a reasonable person would understand that he or she could refuse to cooperate. This case requires us to determine whether the same rule applies to police encounters that take place on a bus.

Drug interdiction efforts have led to the use of police surveillance at airports, train stations, and bus depots. Law enforcement officers stationed at such locations routinely approach individuals, either randomly or because they suspect in some vague way that the individuals may be engaged in criminal activity, and ask them potentially incriminating questions. Broward County has adopted such a program. County Sheriff's Department officers routinely board buses at scheduled stops and ask passengers for permission to search their luggage.

In this case, two officers discovered cocaine when they searched a suitcase belonging to Terrance Bostick. The underlying facts of the search are in dispute, but the Florida Supreme Court, whose decision we review here, stated explicitly the factual premise for its decision:

> Two officers, complete with badges, insignia and one of them holding a recognizable zipper pouch, containing a pistol, boarded a bus bound from Miami to Atlanta during a stopover in Fort Lauderdale. Eyeing the passengers, the officers admittedly without articulable suspicion, picked out the defendant passenger and asked to inspect his ticket and identification. The ticket, from Miami to Atlanta, matched the defendant's identification and both were immediately returned to him as unremarkable. However, the two police officers persisted and explained their presence as narcotics agents on the lookout for illegal drugs. In pursuit of that aim, they then requested the defendant's consent to search his luggage. Needless to say, there is a conflict in the evidence about whether the defendant consented to the search of the second bag in which the contraband was

found and as to whether he was informed of his right to refuse consent. However, any conflict must be resolved in favor the state, it being a question of fact decided by the trial judge. * * *

Two facts are particularly worth noting. First, the police specifically advised Bostick that he had the right to refuse consent. Bostick appears to have disputed the point, but, as the Florida Supreme Court noted explicitly, the trial court resolved this evidentiary conflict in the State's favor. Second, at no time did the officers threaten Bostick with a gun. The Florida Supreme Court indicated that one officer carried a zipper pouch containing a pistol—the equivalent of carrying a gun in a holster—but the court did not suggest that the gun was ever removed from its pouch, pointed at Bostick, or otherwise used in a threatening manner. The dissent's characterization of the officers as "gun-wielding inquisitor[s]" . . . is colorful, but lacks any basis in fact.

* * *

The sole issue presented for our review is whether a police encounter on a bus of the type described above necessarily constitutes a "seizure" within the meaning of the Fourth Amendment. The State concedes, and we accept for purposes of this decision, that the officers lacked the reasonable suspicion required to justify a seizure and that, if a seizure took place, the drugs found in Bostick's suitcase must be suppressed as tainted fruit.

Our cases make it clear that a seizure does not occur simply because a police officer approaches an individual and asks a few questions. So long as a reasonable person would feel free "to disregard the police and go about his business," . . . the encounter is consensual and no reasonable suspicion is required. The encounter will not trigger Fourth Amendment scrutiny unless it loses its consensual nature. The Court made precisely this point in *Terry v. Ohio* (1968). . . . "Only when the officer, by means of physical force or show of authority, has in some way restrained the liberty of a citizen may we conclude that a 'seizure' has occurred."

* * *

There is no doubt that if this same encounter had taken place before Bostick had boarded the bus or in the lobby of the bus terminal, it would not rise to the level of a seizure. * * *

Bostick insists that this case is different because it took place in the cramped confines of a bus. A police encounter is much more intimidating in this setting, he argues, because the police tower over a seated passenger and there is little room to move around. Bostick claims to find support in language from *Michigan v. Chesternut* (1988) . . . and other cases, indicating that a seizure occurs when a reasonable person would believe that he or she is not "free to leave." Bostick maintains that a reasonable bus passenger would not feel free to leave under the circumstances of this case because there is nowhere to go on a bus. Also, the bus was about to depart. Had Bostick disembarked, he would have risked being stranded and losing whatever baggage he had locked away in the luggage compartment.

The Florida Supreme Court found this argument persuasive, so much so that it adopted a *per se* rule prohibiting the police from randomly boarding buses as a means of drug interdiction. The state court erred, however, in focusing on whether Bostick was "free to leave" rather than on the principle that those words were intended to capture. When police attempt to question a person who is walking down the street or through an airport lobby, it makes sense to inquire whether a reasonable person would feel free to continue walking. But when the person is seated on a bus and has no desire to leave, the degree to which a reasonable person would feel that he or she could leave is not an accurate measure of the coercive effect of the encounter.

Here, for example, the mere fact that Bostick did not feel free to leave the bus does not mean that the police seized him. Bostick was a passenger on a bus that was scheduled to depart. He would not have felt free to leave the bus even if the police had not been present. Bostick's movements were "confined" in a sense, but this was the natural result of his decision to take the bus; it says nothing about whether or not the police conduct at issue was coercive.

* * *

* * * Accordingly, the "free to leave" analysis on which Bostick relies is inapplicable. In such a situation, the appropriate inquiry is whether a reasonable person would feel free to decline the officers' requests or otherwise terminate the encounter. This formulation follows logically from prior cases and breaks no new ground. We have said before that the crucial test is whether, taking into account all of the circumstances surrounding the encounter, the police conduct would "have communicated to a reasonable person that he was not at liberty to ignore the police presence and go about his business." * * * Where the encounter takes place is one factor, but only one factor. And, as the Solicitor General correctly observes, an individual may decline an officer's request without fearing prosecution. . . . We have consistently held that a refusal to cooperate, without more, does not furnish the minimal level of objective justification needed for a detention or seizure. . . .

* * *

The dissent characterizes our decision as holding that police may board buses and by an "*intimidating* show of authority," . . . demand of passengers their "voluntary" cooperation. That characterization is incorrect. Clearly, a bus passenger's decision to cooperate with law enforcement officers authorizes the police to conduct a search without first obtaining a warrant *only* if the cooperation is voluntary. "Consent" that is the product of official intimidation or harassment is not consent at all. Citizens do not forfeit their constitutional rights when they are coerced to comply with a request that they would prefer to refuse. The question to be decided by the Florida courts on remand is whether Bostick chose to permit the search of his luggage.

The dissent also attempts to characterize our decision as applying a lesser degree of constitutional protection to those individuals who travel by bus, rather than by other forms of transportation. This, too, is an erroneous characterization. Our Fourth Amendment inquiry in this case—whether a reasonable person would have felt free to decline the officers' request or otherwise terminate the encounter—applies equally to police encounters that take place on trains, planes, and city streets. It is the dissent that would single out this particular mode of travel for differential treatment by adopting a *per se* rule that random bus searches are unconstitutional.

The dissent reserves its strongest criticism for the proposition that police officers can approach individuals as to whom they have no reasonable suspicion and ask them potentially incriminating questions. But this proposition is by no means novel; it has been endorsed by the Court any number of times. *Terry [v. Ohio,* 1968], [*Florida v.] Royer* [1983], [*Florida v.] Rodriguez* [1984], and [*Immigration and Naturalization Service v.] Delgado* [1984] are just a few examples. As we have explained, today's decision follows logically from those decisions and breaks no new ground. Unless the dissent advocates overruling a long, unbroken line of decisions dating back more than 20 years, its criticism is not well taken.

* * *

Justice Marshall, with whom Justice Blackmun and Justice Stevens join, dissenting.

Our Nation, we are told, is engaged in a "war on drugs." No one disputes that it is the job of law-enforcement officials to devise effective weapons for fighting this war. But the effectiveness of a law-enforcement technique is not proof of its constitutionality. The general warrant, for example, was certainly an effective means of law enforcement. Yet it is one of the primary aims of the Fourth Amendment to protect citizens from the tyranny of being singled out for search and seizure without particularized suspicion *notwithstanding* the effectiveness of this method. . . . In my view, the law-enforcement technique with which we are confronted in this case—the suspicionless police sweep of buses in intrastate or interstate travel—bears all of the indicia of coercion and unjustified intrusion associated with the general warrant. Because I believe that the bus sweep issue in this case violates the core values of the Fourth Amendment, I dissent.

* * *

To put it mildly, these sweeps "are inconvenient, intrusive, and intimidating." * * * They occur within cramped confines, with officers typically placing themselves in between the passenger selected for an interview and the exit of the bus. * * * Because the bus is only temporarily stationed at a point short of its destination, the passengers are in no position to leave as a means of evading the officers' questioning. Undoubtedly, such a sweep holds up the progress of the bus. . . . Thus, this "new and increasingly common tactic," . . . burdens the experience of traveling by bus with a degree of governmental interference to which, until now, our society was proudly unaccustomed. * * *

This aspect of the suspicionless sweep has not been lost on many of the lower courts called upon to review the constitutionality of this practice. Remarkably, the courts located at the heart of the "drug war" have been the most adamant in condemning this technique. * * *

* * *

I have no objection to the manner in which the majority frames the test for determining whether a suspicionless bus sweep amounts to a Fourth Amendment "seizure." I agree that the appropriate question is whether a passenger who is approached during such a sweep "would feel free to decline the officers' requests or otherwise terminate the encounter." * * * What I cannot understand is how the majority can possibly suggest an affirmative answer to this question.

* * *

As far as is revealed by facts on which the Florida Supreme Court premised its decision, the officers did not advise respondent that he was free to break off this "interview." Inexplicably, the majority repeatedly stresses the trial court's implicit finding that the police officers advised the respondent that he was free to refuse permission to search his travel bag. . . . This aspect of the exchange between respondent and the police is completely irrelevant to the issue before us. For as the State concedes, and as the majority purports to "accept," . . . *if* respondent was unlawfully seized when the officers approached him and initiated questioning, the resulting search was likewise unlawful no matter how well advised respondent was of his right to refuse it. . . . Consequently, the issue is not whether a passenger in respondent's position would have felt free to deny consent to the search of his bag, but whether such a passenger—without being apprised of his rights—would have felt free to terminate the antecedent encounter with the police.

Unlike the majority, I have no doubt that the answer to this question is no. Apart from trying to accommodate the officers, respondent had only two options. First, he could have remained seated while obstinately refusing to respond to the officers' questioning. But in light of the intimidating show of authority that the officers made upon boarding the bus, respondent reasonably could have believed that such behavior would only arouse the officers' suspicions and intensify their interrogation. Indeed, officers who carry out bus sweeps like the one at issue here frequently admit that this is the effect of a passenger's refusal to cooperate. . . . The majority's observation that a mere refusal to answer questions, "without more," does not give rise to a reasonable basis for seizing a passenger, . . . is utterly beside the point, because a passenger unadvised of his rights and otherwise unversed in constitutional law *has no reason to know* that the police cannot hold his refusal to cooperate against him.

Second, respondent could have tried to escape the officers' presence by leaving the bus altogether. But because doing so would have required respondent to squeeze past the gun-wielding inquisitor who was blocking the aisle of the bus, this hardly seems like a course that respondent reasonably would have viewed as available to him. The majority lamely protests that nothing in the stipulated facts shows that the questioning officer "*point[ed]* [his] gu[n] at [respondent] or otherwise *threatened* him" with the weapon. . . . (emphasis added). Our decisions recognize the obvious point, however, that the choice of the police to "display" their weapons during an encounter exerts significant coercive pressure on the confronted citizen. . . . We have never suggested that the police must go so far as to put a citizen in immediate apprehension of *being shot* before a court can take account of the intimidating effect of being questioned by an officer with weapon in hand.

Even if respondent had perceived that the officers would *let* him leave the bus, moreover, he could not reasonably have been expected to resort to this means of evading their intrusive questioning. For so far as respondent knew, the bus's departure from the terminal was imminent. Unlike a person approached by the police on the street . . . or at a bus or airport terminal after reaching his destination, . . . a passenger approached by the police at an intermediate point in a long bus journey cannot simply leave the scene and repair to a safe haven to avoid unwanted probing by law-enforcement officials. The vulnerability that an intrastate or interstate traveler experiences when confronted by police outside of "his own familiar territory" surely aggravates the coercive quality of such an encounter. . . .

* * *

Rather than requiring the police to justify the coercive tactics employed here, the majority blames respondent for his own sensation of constraint. The majority concedes that respondent "did not feel free to leave the bus" as a means of breaking off the interrogation by the Broward County officers. * * * But this experience of confinement, the majority explains, "was the natural result of *his* decision to take the bus." (emphasis added). * * * Thus, in the majority's view, because respondent's "freedom of movement was restricted by a factor independent of police conduct—*i.e.*, by his being a passenger on a bus," . . . respondent was not seized for purposes of the Fourth Amendment.

This reasoning borders on sophism and trivializes the values that underlie the Fourth Amendment. Obviously, a person's "voluntary decision" to place himself in a room with only one exit does not authorize the police to force an encounter upon him by placing themselves in front of the exit. It is no more acceptable for the police to force an encounter on a person by exploiting his "voluntary decision" to expose himself to perfectly legitimate personal or social constraints. By consciously deciding to single out persons who have undertaken interstate or intrastate travel, officers who conduct suspicionless, dragnet-style sweeps put passengers to the choice of cooperating or of exiting their buses and their possibly being stranded in unfamiliar locations. It is exactly because this "choice" is no "choice" at all that police engage this technique.

In my view, the Fourth Amendment clearly condemns the suspicionless, dragnet-style sweep of intrastate and interstate buses. Withdrawing this particular weapon from the government's drug-war arsenal would hardly leave the police without any means of combatting the use of buses as instrumentalities of the drug trade. The police would remain free, for example, to approach passengers whom they have a reasonable, articulable basis to suspect of criminal wrongdoing.[4] Alternatively, they could continue to confront passengers without suspicion so long as they took simple steps, like advising passengers confronted of their right to decline to be questioned, to dispel the aura of coercion and intimidation that pervades such encounters. There is no reason to expect that such requirements would render the Nation's buses law-enforcement-free zones.

The majority attempts to gloss over the violence that today's decision does to the Fourth Amendment with empty admonitions. "If th[e] [war on drugs] is to be fought," the majority intones, "those who fight it must respect the rights of individuals, whether or not those individuals are suspected of having committed a crime." * * * The majority's actions, however, speak louder than its words.

I dissent.

[4]Insisting that police officers explain their decision to single out a particular passenger for questioning would help prevent their reliance on impermissible criteria such as race. . . .

In the lone remaining major decision, *California v. Greenwood* (1988), a 6–2 majority declared that the Fourth Amendment does not prohibit a warrantless search of garbage that is left on the curb for collection. This decision was consistent with the Burger Court's view that people have protected privacy expectations in only limited contexts (see *California v. Ciraolo,* 1986). This theme was reinforced in other Rehnquist Court decisions. Police officers were permitted to peer into the door of a barn after entering private property without a warrant (*United States v. Dunn,* 1987) and to undertake aerial surveillance from a helicopter (*Florida v. Riley,* 1989).

Other Rehnquist Court decisions further reduced the coverage of Fourth Amendment rights and gave law enforcement officials more freedom to conduct searches. In *Griffin v. Wisconsin* (1987), a five-member majority supported the warrantless search of a probationer's home with the minimal requirement that law enforcement officials have reasonable grounds for suspicion that contraband or illegal activities may be present. This provides people on probation with less Fourth Amendment protection than other citizens for whom the amendment requires that police establish "probable cause" and obtain a warrant. The Court also created a "good faith" exception to situations in which officers conduct warrantless searches with the permission of the resident of a house or apartment. In *Illinois v. Rodriguez* (1990), the police obtained entry into an apartment based on the mistaken belief that the suspect's ex-girlfriend, who granted permission for the search and supplied the key to gain entry, resided at the apartment.

Illinois v. Rodriguez

110 S. Ct. 2793 (1990)

■ A woman summoned police officers to her home and presented her daughter, who showed signs of a severe beating. The daughter told officers that she had been assaulted by a man at an apartment elsewhere in the city. The daughter stated that the man was presently asleep at the apartment. She agreed to travel with the police to the apartment and unlock the apartment door with her key so that officers could enter. During the conversation with the police, she referred to the premises as "our" apartment and indicated that she had personal belongings there. When she unlocked the door to the apartment, officers discovered white powder in "plain view" in the living room which later proved to be cocaine. The defendant was charged with possession of narcotics with intent to deliver. He sought to suppress all evidence obtained by the police during their entry into the apartment on the grounds that his girlfriend, who had opened the door, lacked the authority to give consent to have the apartment entered and searched. The girlfriend did not reside at the apartment, she did not contribute to paying rent at the apartment, and the trial court concluded that she was merely an "infrequent visitor."

This case is important because it illustrates the Rehnquist Court's consistent pattern of reducing the coverage of the Fourth Amendment, creating exceptions to the exclusionary rule, and expanding exceptions to the warrant requirement. As you the read the opinion, ask yourself the following questions: (1) Did the police officers' actions violate the defendant's Fourth Amendment rights? (2) What effect will the decision have on the care taken by police officers to investigate which individuals have the authority to grant permission for searches of homes and apartments?

VOTE:

6 justices found the police officers' actions constitutional (Blackmun, Kennedy, O'Connor, Rehnquist, Scalia, White).

3 justices found the police officers' actions unconstitutional (Brennan, Marshall, Stevens).

Justice Scalia delivered the opinion of the Court.

* * *

The Fourth Amendment generally prohibits the warrantless entry of a person's home, whether to make an arrest or to search for specific objects.... The prohibition does not apply, however, to situations in which voluntary consent has been obtained, either from the individual whose property is searched, . . . or from a third party who possesses common authority over the premises. . . . The State of Illinois contends that that exception applies in the present case.

As we stated in [*United States v.*] *Matlock* [1974] . . . "[c]ommon authority" rests "on mutual use of the property by persons generally having joint access or control for most purposes. . . ." The burden of establishing that common authority rests upon the State. On the basis of this record, it is clear that burden was not sustained [in the state's effort to show the girlfriend's authority to give consent for the search]. The evidence showed although [the girlfriend], with her two small children, had lived with Rodriguez beginning in December 1984, she had moved out on July 1, 1985, almost a month before the search at issue here, and had gone to live with her mother. She took her and her children's clothing with her, though leaving behind some furniture and household effects. During the period after July 1 she sometimes spent the night at Rodriguez's apartment, but never invited her friends there, and never went there herself when he was not home. Her name was not on the lease nor did she contribute to the rent. She had a key to the apartment, which she said at trial she had taken without Rodriguez's knowledge (though she testified at the preliminary hearing that Rodriguez had given her the key). On these facts the State had not established that, with respect to the South California [Street] apartment, [the girlfriend] had "joint access or control for most purposes." To the contrary, the Appellate Court's determination of no common authority over the apartment was obviously correct.

* * *

* * * It is apparent that in order to satisfy the "reasonableness" requirement of the Fourth Amendment, what is generally demanded of the many factual determinations that must regularly be made by agents of the government—whether the magistrate issuing a warrant, the police officer executing a warrant, or the police officer conducting a search or seizure under one of the exceptions to the warrant requirement—is not that they always be correct, but that they always be reasonable. * * *

We see no reason to depart from this general rule with respect to facts bearing on the authority to consent to a search. Whether the basis for such authority exists is the sort of recurring factual question to which law enforcement officials must be expected to apply their judgment; and all the Fourth Amendment requires is that they answer it reasonably. The Constitution is no more violated when officers enter without a warrant because they reasonably (though erroneously) believe that the person who has consented to their entry is a resident of the premises, than it is violated when they enter without a warrant because they reasonably (though erroneously) believe they are in pursuit of a violent felon who is about to escape.* * *

* * *

. . .[W]hat we hold today does not suggest that law enforcement officers may always accept a person's invitation to enter premises. Even when the invitation is accompanied by an explicit assertion that the person lives there, the surrounding circumstances could conceivably be such that a reasonable person would doubt its truth and not act upon it without further inquiry. As with other factual determinations bearing upon search and seizure, determination of consent to enter must "be judged against an objective standard: would the facts available to the officer at the moment...'warrant a man of reasonable caution in the belief' " that the consenting party had authority over the premises. * * * If not, then warrantless entry without further inquiry is unlawful unless authority actually exists. But if so, the search is valid.

* * *

Justice Marshall, with whom Justice Brennan and Justice Stevens join, dissenting.

* * *

The majority agrees with the Illinois appellate court's determination that [the girlfriend] did not have authority to consent to the officers' entry of Rodriguez's apartment. * * * The Court holds that the warrantless entry into Rodriguez's home was nonetheless valid if the officers reasonably believed that [the girlfriend] had authority to consent. * * *

The majority's defense of this position rests on a misconception of the basis for third-party consent searches. That such searches do not give rise to claims of constitutional violations rests not on the premise that they are "reasonable" under the Fourth Amendment, . . . but on the premise that a person may voluntarily limit his expectation of privacy by allowing others to exercise authority over his possessions. * * * Thus, an individual's decision to permit another "joint access [to] or control [over the property] for most purposes," . . . limits that individual's reasonable expectation of privacy and to that extent limits his Fourth Amendment protections. . . . If an individual has not so limited his expectation of privacy, the police may not dispense with the safeguards established by the Fourth Amendment.

The baseline for the reasonableness of a search or a seizure in the home is the presence of a warrant. * * * Indeed, "searches and seizures inside a home without a warrant are presumptively unreasonable." * * * Exceptions to the warrant requirement must therefore serve "compelling" law enforcement goals. * * * Because the sole law enforcement purpose underlying the third-party consent searches is avoiding the inconvenience of securing a warrant, a departure from the warrant requirement is not justified simply because an officer reasonably believes a third party has consented to a search of the defendant's home. In holding otherwise, the majority ignores our longstanding view that "the informed and deliberate determinations of magistrates . . . as to what searches and seizures are permissible under the Constitution are to be preferred over the hurried action of officers and others who may happen to make arrests."* * *

* * *

The Court has tolerated departures from the warrant requirement only when an exigency makes a warrantless search imperative to the safety of the police and of the community. . . . The Court has often heard, and steadfastly rejected, the invitation to carve out further exceptions to the warrant requirement for searches of the home because of the burdens on police investigation and prosecution of crime. Our rejection of such claims is not due to a lack of appreciation of the difficulty and importance of effective law enforcement, but rather to our firm commitment to "the view of those who wrote the Bill of Rights that the privacy of a person's home and property may not be totally sacrificed in the name of maximum simplicity in enforcement of the criminal law." . . .

In the absence of an exigency, then, warrantless home searches and seizures are unreasonable under the Fourth Amendment. The weighty constitutional interest in preventing unauthorized intrusions into the home overrides any law enforcement interest in relying on the reasonable but potentially mistaken belief that a third party has authority to consent to such a search or seizure. Indeed, as the present case illustrates, only the minimal interest in avoiding the inconvenience of obtaining a warrant weighs in on the law enforcement side.

* * *

Unlike searches conducted pursuant to the recognized exceptions to the warrant requirement, . . . third-party consent searches are not based on an exigency and therefore serve no compelling social goal. Police officers, when faced with the choice of relying on consent by a third party or securing a warrant, should secure a warrant, and must therefore accept the risk of error should they instead choose to rely on consent.

* * *

The majority's assertion . . . is premised on the erroneous assumption that third-party consent searches are generally reasonable. The cases the majority cites thus provide no support for its holding. * * * Because reasonable factual errors by law enforcement officers will not validate unreasonable searches, the reasonableness of the officer's mistaken belief that the third party had authority to consent is irrelevant.

* * *

Our cases demonstrate that third-party consent searches are free from constitutional challenge only to the extent that they rest on consent by a party empowered to do so. The majority's conclusion to the contrary ignores the legitimate expectations of privacy on which individuals are entitled to rely. That a person who allows another joint access over his property thereby limits his expectation of privacy does not justify trampling the rights of a person who has not similarly relinquished any of his privacy expectation.

* * * Where this free-floating creation of "reasonable" exceptions to the warrant requirement will end, now that the Court has departed from the balancing approach that has long been part of our Fourth Amendment jurisprudence, is unclear. But by allowing a person to be subjected to a warrantless search in his home without his consent and without exigency, the majority has taken away some of the liberty that the Fourth Amendment was designed to protect.

The Court diminished the effect of the traditional "fruit of the poisonous tree" doctrine by permitting the police to use statements made by a defendant at the police station after law enforcement officers had illegally entered his home without a warrant to arrest him (*New York v. Harris,* 1990). The Court also declared that the Fourth Amendment does not apply to American law enforcement officials' actions overseas when U.S. officials cooperated with Mexican police in apprehending a suspect in Mexico, searching his home without a warrant, and delivering him to the United States for prosecution (*United States v. Verdugo-Urquidez,* 1990). Justices Brennan and Marshall argued in dissent that if a defendant is to be prosecuted and held accountable under American criminal law, then that defendant is also entitled to the protections of the U.S. Constitution.

In other cases, the Court relied on a "good faith" justification when officers with a search warrant for a third-floor apartment searched *the wrong apartment* but were still able to use evidence found there against the resident (*Maryland v. Garrison,* 1987). In addition, the Court weakened a major premise of the "plain view" doctrine articulated by the Burger Court in *Coolidge v. New Hampshire* (1971) by permitting police to use evidence obtained during a warrantless search even when the discovery of the "plain view" evidence was *not* inadvertent (*Horton v. California,* 1990). In *Horton,* officers had a warrant to search the suspect's home for three rings that had been stolen during an armed robbery. The officers knew that the robbers had used certain kinds of weapons during the robbery, and they kept an eye out for those weapons during the search even though the magistrate had limited the warrant to a search for stolen jewelry. Thus, when they found the weapons and other evidence in "plain view," the discovery was not inadvertent.

The Rehnquist Court also expanded the ability of police officers to conduct warrantless searches of containers within automobiles, even when the officers lack probable cause for searching the automobile itself. As long as officers have probable cause to support a search of the container within the automobile, they may proceed with the search and make use of the evidence (*California v. Acevedo,* 1991). In addition, the Court approved the warrantless search of a closed backpack during an inventory of items contained in an impounded vehicle (*Colorado v. Bertine,* 1987). These decisions reinforced and expanded the Burger Court's diminution of the warrant and "probable cause" requirements for Fourth Amendment searches when automobiles and their contents are the objects of the searches.

While the Rehnquist Court's conservative decisions had the effect of narrowing the coverage of the Fourth Amendment, the few liberal decisions did little to expand any aspect of Fourth Amendment protections. *Minnesota v. Dickerson* (1993) preserved but did not expand the patdown rules established in *Terry v. Ohio* (1968). *Arizona v. Hicks* (1987) preserved but did not change the "plain view" doctrine. The Court did not permit police to assert that the evidence indicating that a stereo was stolen property was in "plain view" when, in fact, the officers had to move the stereo in order to locate the serial numbers. Among the remaining six liberal decisions, four were unanimous decisions and two of these merely clarified the definition of a "seizure" rather than produced a final outcome that would necessarily favor individuals when all of the litigation in each case was completed in the lower court (*Soldal v. Cook County,* 1992; *Brower v. County of Inyo,* 1989). The one case that expanded Fourth Amendment protections was *Wilson v. Arkansas* (1995). In this case, a unanimous Court rejected "no-knock" searches by declaring that the traditional practice, dating back to English common law, of police officers knocking on the door and announcing their identities before entering was indeed a constitutional requirement during the execution of search warrants.

Conclusion

The Burger Court's efforts to reduce the scope of Fourth Amendment protections and expand law enforcement officers' opportunities to gather and use evidence were continued and strengthened by the decisions of the Rehnquist Court. The Rehnquist Court majority consistently endorsed police practices that diminished the Fourth Amendment requirements for demonstrating "probable cause" and obtaining warrants before conducting searches. According to one scholar, the Burger and Rehnquist Courts' tilt in favor of law enforcement is such that "[i]n virtually every case, [the Rehnquist Court] will state that the warrant requirement and probable cause test is the standard that normally is to be employed in assessing the propriety of a police search and seizure and, thereafter, as it suits the Court's convenience, invoke this or that exception or doctrine in order to conclude that all was fair and reasonable [in deciding in favor of the government]" (Decker 1992, p. 52). Despite the departures of the final two Warren Court holdovers (Brennan and Marshall) who strongly supported expansive interpretations of the Fourth Amendment, the Rehnquist Court has not eliminated the exclusionary rule. The impact of the rule has been significantly diminished through the creation of exceptions (e.g., "good faith") and through relaxed standards for searches of automobiles and property other than personal residences. Thus a majority of Rehnquist Court justices may believe that they have struck the appropriate balance for giving police officers freedom to investigate crimes while also preserving a measure of protection, albeit reduced since the Warren Court era, against unreasonable searches and seizures. The Fourth Amendment represents one area of constitutional law in which the conservative justices have consistently controlled case outcomes, especially in major cases, since the final years of the Burger Court. Thus we can expect to see further incremental reductions in the coverage of the Fourth Amendment, although there is no indication that a majority of justices is inclined to take dramatic actions, such as abolishing the exclusionary rule in all situations.

The appointments of new justices to the Supreme Court during the Rehnquist Court era have not had a discernible impact on Fourth Amendment decisions. When Justices Brennan and Marshall provided consistent votes in favor of individuals' claims during the initial years of the Rehnquist Court, the liberals still were able to prevail in only a handful of cases. Even if President Clinton's appointees, Justices Ginsburg and Breyer, prove to be as consistent as Brennan and Marshall in supporting expansive Fourth Amendment rights (and it is not at all clear that they will be), they will still find themselves dissenting against the solid conservative majority unless more substantial changes take place in the Court's composition.

References

Abraham, Henry J. *Justices and Presidents: A Political History of Appointments to the Supreme Court.* 2d ed. New York: Oxford University Press, 1985.

Alderman, Ellen, and Caroline Kennedy. *In Our Defense: The Bill of Rights in Action.* New York: William Morrow, 1991.

Alexander, Rudolph Jr. "The Mapp, Escobedo, and Miranda Decisions: Do They Serve a Liberal or a Conservative Agenda?" *Criminal Justice Policy Review* 4 (1990): 39–52.

Barker, Lucius J., and Twiley W. Barker, Jr. *Freedoms, Courts, Politics: Studies in Civil Liberties.* Rev. ed. Englewood Cliffs, N. J.: Prentice-Hall, 1972.

Decker, John F. *Revolution to the Right: Criminal Procedure Jurisprudence during the Burger-Rehnquist Court Era.* New York: Garland Publishing, 1992.

Fisher, Edward C. *Search and Seizure.* Evanston, Ill.: Traffic Institute of Northwestern University, 1970.

LaFave, Wayne. "The Fourth Amendment: A Bicentennial 'Checkup.' " *Valparaiso University Law Review* 26 (1991): 223-41.

Lamb, Charles M., and Stephen C. Halpern. "The Burger Court and Beyond." In *The Burger Court: Political and Judicial Profiles,* edited by Charles M. Lamb and Stephen C. Halpern. Urbana, Ill.: University of Illinois Press, 1991.

Schlesinger, Steven R. *Exclusionary Injustice.* New York: Marcel Dekker, 1977.

Uchida, Craig, and Timothy Bynum. "Search Warrants, Motions to Suppress and 'Lost Cases': The Effects of the Exclusionary Rule in Seven Jurisdictions." *Journal of Criminal Law and Criminology* 81 (1991): 1034-66.

Walker, Samuel. *Sense and Nonsense about Crime and Drugs.* 3d ed. Belmont, Calif.: Wadsworth, 1994.

CHAPTER

10 The Fifth Amendment Guarantees Against Compelled Self-Incrimination and Double Jeopardy

CASE STUDY

Miranda v. Arizona (1966)

Shortly before midnight on March 2, 1963, an eighteen-year-old woman left her job at a movie theater in downtown Phoenix and headed home by bus. Just after twelve o'clock, she got off the bus and began to walk the short distance toward her house. Without any warning, a man got out of a car parked in front of an apartment house, grabbed the young woman, dragged her to the car, tied her hands behind her, and sped away. The man drove his victim out into the desert, raped her, and then drove her back to a spot just four blocks from her home. After her family called the police and took her to the hospital, the victim described her attacker and the car he had been driving. Police initially had concerns about inconsistencies in the victim's description of events, and they subsequently were told by her family that she was mentally retarded (Baker 1983, pp. 3–9).

One week later, the victim's brother-in-law saw a car that matched the general description given by the victim. He gave the license plate number to the police who tracked down and arrested Ernesto Miranda. Upon examination, Miranda's car contained a rope strung along the back seat, just as the victim had described, and he fit the victim's description of her assailant's ethnicity and age. Miranda was a twenty-three-year-old laborer with an eighth-grade education who worked at a produce warehouse. He had a long police record and a history of sexual problems, including convictions for being a "peeping Tom" and for assault with intent to commit rape. He had served sentences in juvenile institutions in California and Arizona, military stockades during a brief stint in the Army, and two federal prisons (Baker 1983, pp. 8–11).

Phoenix detectives immediately placed Miranda in a lineup for the victim, who thought he might be her attacker. After the lineup, the detectives indicated to Miranda that the victim had identified him as her assailant. The detectives took their suspect into an interrogation room and later emerged with Miranda's signed confession. Miranda also confessed to the robbery of a woman in a downtown parking lot and to an additional attempted rape. The robbery victim identified him in a later police lineup, but the second rape victim could not be located. A few days later, as required under Arizona law, a local lawyer was appointed to represent Miranda in court. Miranda's attorney was Alvin Moore, a seventy-three-year-old private practitioner who had agreed only one month earlier to accept criminal appointments in the midst of a strike by other attorneys seeking higher pay for representing indigent defendants. Moore sought to use the insanity defense on Miranda's behalf. However, although two psychiatrists diagnosed Miranda as suffering from serious psychological and sexual problems, they both agreed that he was not legally insane (Baker 1983, pp. 12–21).

Miranda's trial on kidnapping and rape charges began on June 20, 1963. He had already been convicted of the robbery charge. The primary evidence against Miranda was his signed confession, which, having been typed by the detectives before he signed it in the interrogation room, matched the details in the victim's testimony. Moore, who had no witnesses to present on Miranda's behalf, attacked the testifying detectives during cross-examination for not informing Miranda that he had a right to have an attorney present during questioning. Moore entered a formal objection into the record to note his opposition to the admission of the confession into evidence. Moore mistakenly believed that the U.S. Supreme Court had ruled that defendants are entitled to be represented by counsel from the moment of their arrest. The judge, Yale McFate, denied Moore's objection but subsequently gave careful instructions to the jury that they could disregard the confession if they believed that it had been involuntary or otherwise produced as a result of police coercion. After five hours of deliberation, the jury of nine men and three women found Miranda guilty, and he was given a sentence of twenty to thirty years in prison (Baker 1983, pp. 21–24).

Moore pursued an appeal on Miranda's behalf in the Arizona Supreme Court by claiming that the confession should be inadmissible because Miranda had not been informed by the police that he had the right to be represented by an attorney. On April 22, 1965, the five justices on the state supreme court rejected Moore's argument and unanimously affirmed Miranda's conviction (Baker 1983, pp. 24–25, 49–50).

The Arizona Supreme Court's decision caught the eye of Robert Corcoran, a volunteer attorney for the Phoenix office of the American Civil Liberties Union. The U.S. Supreme Court had recently decided that suspects who are represented by counsel cannot be denied the opportunity to have their attorneys present during police questioning (*Escobedo v. Illinois,* 1964). Corcoran believed that Miranda's case might be attractive to the Supreme Court as a vehicle to expand the *Escobedo* principle to obligate police officers to inform suspects of their right to be represented by counsel. The case raised issues concerning the Fifth Amendment because the failure of suspects to understand their constitutional rights during questioning created risks that their privilege against compelled self-incrimination could be violated. The Fifth Amendment says, in part, "No person . . . shall be compelled in any criminal case to be a witness against himself." Unfortunately for Miranda, the ACLU could only offer to help Moore prepare the case; they could not compensate the attorney for his work. At that point, Moore had already received the maximum available payment from the state for his work on Miranda's behalf: $100 for conducting the trial and $100 for presenting an appeal in the state courts. Moore declined to pursue Miranda's case in the Supreme Court, citing a lack of funds and, given his age, a lack of physical stamina (Baker 1983, pp. 61–62).

Corcoran turned to one of Phoenix's largest law firms, Lewis, Roca, Scoville, Beauchamps, and Linton, which had a standing agreement to handle two cases each year for the ACLU. John Flynn, the law firm's chief trial attorney, agreed to take the case with the law firm absorbing the expenses and the lawyers working without compensation. Flynn's cocounsel from the firm was John Frank, a scholar who had taught at Indiana University and Yale before moving to the dry Arizona climate because of problems with chronic asthma. Frank was the author of several books on the Supreme Court and had established a solid reputation in Arizona as an appellate lawyer. By the time the firm presented Miranda's case to the Supreme Court, Frank estimated that it had expended in excess of $50,000 in lawyers' time and other expenses (Baker 1983, pp. 62–66).

The Supreme Court accepted Miranda's case for hearing in November 1965, and the case was argued before the Supreme Court on February 28, 1966, with John Flynn making the oral arguments for Miranda. Miranda's case was heard at the same time as five other cases concerning confessions, but the Court had instructed that Miranda's case be argued first on that day. In response to a question from Justice Potter Stewart, Flynn presented the essence of his argument: "I simply say that that stage of the proceeding, under the facts and circumstances in *Miranda* of a man of limited education, of a man who certainly is mentally abnormal, and who is, certainly, an indigent, that when that adversary process came into being, that the police at the very least had an obligation to extend to this man, not only his clear Fifth Amendment right, but to accord him the right to counsel" (Baker 1983, p. 137).

Although Flynn had presented Miranda's case as concerning the Fifth Amendment privilege against compelled self-incrimination and the Sixth Amendment right to counsel, his adversary, Gary Nelson, an Arizona assistant attorney general, treated the case as concerning the Sixth Amendment right to counsel. In subsequent arguments concerning the other confessions cases, the justices asked questions that indicated their individual concerns about both the Fifth Amendment and Sixth Amendment implications produced by police questioning of suspects who have not been informed of their rights to remain silent and to be represented by counsel during questioning (Baker 1983, pp. 138–150).

The Supreme Court's decision in *Miranda v. Arizona* was announced on June 13, 1966 (case excerpt on p. 477). Chief Justice Earl Warren, the author of the majority opinion, took a full hour to read the entire opinion from the bench (Baker 1983, p. 166). Warren spoke for a slim five-member majority that included Justices Hugo Black, William O. Douglas, William Brennan, and Abe Fortas when he reversed Miranda's conviction and declared that the police must follow new procedures to protect the rights of criminal suspects: "[W]e hold that an individual held for interrogation must be clearly informed that he has the right to consult with a lawyer and to have the lawyer with him during interrogation. . . [and a right to] warnings of the right to remain silent and that anything stated can be used in evidence against him. . . . The privilege against self-incrimination secured by the Constitution applies to all individuals. The need for counsel in order to protect the privilege exists for the indigent as well as the affluent" (384 U.S. at 471–72). Warren supported his opinion by describing the risks of police abusing and coercing suspects into confessing, and by reviewing the strategies described in police interrogation manuals, which recommended the application of psychological pressure on suspects kept in isolation during questioning. As a former prosecutor, Warren was keenly aware of the techniques employed by law enforcement officials in their efforts to obtain confessions. The Chief Justice flatly rejected arguments put forth by many police chiefs and prosecutors that society's need for confessions as a means to solve crimes should outweigh the Fifth Amendment privilege against compelled self-incrimination. Warren noted that the Federal Bureau of Investigation (FBI) had remained an exceptionally effective law enforcement agency even as it had followed for two decades the practice of informing suspects of their rights before questioning. He suggested that "[t]he practice of the FBI can readily be emulated by state and local enforcement agencies" (384 U.S. at 486).

With respect to the facts in Miranda's case and companion cases raising similar issues, Warren noted that "[i]n each of the cases, the defendant was thrust into an unfamiliar atmosphere and run through menacing police interrogation procedures. The potentiality for compulsion is forcefully apparent, for example, in *Miranda,* where the indigent Mexican defendant was a seriously disturbed individual with pronounced sexual fantasies" (384 U.S. at 457).

In dissent Justice Tom Clark complained that the majority unfairly characterized police interrogation practices as coercive. He argued for a case-by-case determination of whether confessions were voluntary or coerced: "In the absence of warnings [given to the suspect by the police about the right to remain silent and to be represented by counsel], the burden would be on the State to prove that counsel was knowingly and intelligently waived or that in the totality of the circumstances, including the failure to give the necessary warnings, the confession was clearly voluntary" (U.S. 384 at 503). Applying his standard to Miranda's case, Clark concluded that Miranda's conviction should be affirmed.

Justice John Harlan's dissent on behalf of Justices Potter Stewart and Byron White questioned the applicability of the Fifth Amendment to the police station context and instead advocated a case-by-case examination of the voluntariness of confessions under the Fourteenth Amendment right to due process of law. Harlan also presented a detailed discussion of the policy considerations raised by the Court's new rules for police conduct. Harlan argued that the Court's decisions favored too strongly the interests of criminal defendants over those of society: "There can be little doubt that the Court's new code would markedly decrease the number of confessions. . . . We do know that some crimes cannot be solved without confessions, that ample expert testimony attests to their importance in crime control, and that the Court is taking a real risk with society's welfare in imposing its new regime on the country. The social costs of crime are too great to call the new rules anything but a hazardous experimentation" (384 U.S. at 516–17). Justice White reiterated these views in an additional dissenting opinion in which he added this stark warning: "In some unknown number of cases the Court's rule will return a killer, a rapist or other criminal to the streets and to the environment which produced him, to repeat his crime whenever it pleases him" (384 U.S. at 542).

Miranda's victory in the Supreme Court did not win his release from prison. Arizona held Miranda in prison as it prepared to retry him on the rape charge. This time, however, Arizona would not be able to use the improperly obtained confession against him. In the second trial, John Flynn, Miranda's Supreme Court advocate from the prominent Phoenix law firm, handled the defense. At first it appeared that Miranda would go free because his original conviction rested almost entirely on his now-inadmissible confession. However, the prosecution gained new evidence when Miranda's common-law wife, who had taken up with another man during Miranda's imprisonment, came forward to testify that Miranda had admitted to her that he committed the crime. The nine-day trial which began on February 15, 1967, included only one day of testimony presented to the jury because the lawyers spent most of their time making arguments to the judge about the admissibility of the new evidence. The judge ultimately permitted the common-law wife's testimony to be presented to the jury, and Miranda was once again convicted of the crime and returned to prison. Miranda's legal victory in the U.S. Supreme Court, which expanded rights for all criminal suspects, had not changed the outcome of his case. Miranda was later released from prison on parole in December 1972. He had difficulty obtaining a job and resorted to standing on the steps of the Phoenix courthouse selling autographed copies of *Miranda* warning cards that police read to inform suspects of their rights. In January 1975 Miranda was returned to prison briefly for parole violations when he was caught with amphetamines and a loaded pistol. One year later, on January 31, 1976, Miranda was stabbed to death in a Phoenix bar after a fistfight stemming from a poker game dispute (Baker 1983, pp. 192–94, 381–83, 408).

The Supreme Court's *Miranda* decision created significant political backlash from law enforcement officials who believed that it would interfere with their ability to convict criminals (Walker 1994, p. 130). This backlash was a component of the political forces that eventually led Presidents Nixon, Reagan, and Bush to appoint justices to the Supreme Court who would diminish the scope of rights for criminal defendants established by the high court during the Warren Court era. As we will see in this chapter, the changes in the Supreme Court's composition produced new decisions that reduced the scope of Fifth Amendment rights.

Historical Origins and Contemporary Conflicts

The Fifth Amendment provides protection for several rights, not all of which are limited to the context of criminal justice. The amendment reads:

> *No person shall be held to answer for a capital, or otherwise infamous crime, unless on a presentment or indictment of a grand jury, except in cases arising in the land or naval forces, or in the militia, when in actual service in time of war or public danger; nor shall any person be subject for the same offense to be twice put in jeopardy of life or limb; nor shall be compelled in any criminal case to be a witness against himself, nor be deprived of life, liberty, or property, without due process of law; nor shall private property be taken for public use without just compensation.*

The Due Process Clause provides a useful tool for the justices to use in limiting actions by government that offend their conceptions of individual rights but do not violate any specific provisions of the Bill of Rights. For example, the Court was forced to use the Fifth Amendment's Due Process Clause to forbid discrimination by the federal government because the Equal Protection Clause in the Fourteenth Amendment is applicable specifically to states (*Bolling v. Sharpe*, 1954). Although a general right to due process has been applied by the Court to some criminal cases, we will focus our attention primarily on the specific rights against compelled self-incrimination and double jeopardy in this chapter's discussion of the Fifth Amendment's applicability to criminal proceedings.

Grand Jury

Like other rights contained in the Bill of Rights, the provisions of the Fifth Amendment have their origins in the traditions and practices of English law. The requirement that suspects accused of committing serious offenses be indicted by grand juries developed from the English practice. As described by Leonard Levy (1968, pp. 10–11),

> *[King Henry II in 1166] instructed the royal judges on circuit, or eyre, to take jurisdiction over certain serious crimes or felonies presented to them by sworn inquests, the representative juries of the various localities. Twelve men from each . . . county and four from each township, or vill, . . . were to be summoned by the sheriff to attend the public eyre. They were enjoined to inquire into all crimes committed since the beginning of Henry II's reign, and to report under oath all persons accused or suspected. . . . The parties who were thus presented, if not already in custody, would be arrested and put to the ordeal of cold water.*

As the accusatory system of criminal justice gained further development in England and later in America, the grand jury became the mechanism to check the prosecution and assure that evidence of wrongdoing existed before formally charging defendants and bringing them to trial. Rather than permit a government official (i.e., the prosecutor) to use his or her own discretion to determine when someone should be prosecuted for a serious crime, a group of citizens listens to a description of the preliminary evidence and decides whether formal charges are warranted. This protection against abusive prosecutions was enshrined in the Fifth Amendment by the founders of the United States who, after their experiences in clashing with British authorities, sought to provide a mechanism to prevent the government from using its power improperly to prosecute and punish citizens who had committed no crimes. Because the right to indictment by grand jury is one of the few rights in the Bill of Rights that has never been incorporated and applied to the states through the Fourteenth Amendment (see Chapter 4 on Incorporation of the Bill of Rights), it exists only in the federal courts and in those states that have chosen to employ this method for initiating prosecution. Thus it has received relatively little attention from the Supreme Court (see *Hurtado v. California* [1884] in Chapter 4), and we will not examine the right to indictment by a grand jury. Instead, we will examine two other Fifth Amendment rights that have been the primary focus of the Supreme Court's attention, the privilege against compelled self-incrimination and the right against double jeopardy.

Self-Incrimination

The privilege against compelled self-incrimination developed in English ecclesiastical courts that investigated clergymen and other people who were suspected of deviating from orthodox religious or political viewpoints. Initially these tribunals pressured people into admitting that their religious or political beliefs were at odds with those required by the king. Over time, suspects resisted this procedure and asserted that they were not required to provide testimony against themselves. The statute that abolished the ecclesiastical courts in 1641 indicated that the principle of avoiding compelled self-incrimination had gained acceptance and legitimacy because Parliament forbade church tribunals from compelling suspects to answer questions. Although these processes initially had nothing to do with the common law courts that handled regular criminal cases, according to Stephen Schulhofer, the practices in religious tribunals had produced a situation in which "compulsory examination of the accused had acquired a bad name" (1991, p. 312). Thus by the late 1600s it was accepted in English common law courts that defendants could not be forced to testify against themselves. The Americans adopted this English principle by placing it first into several state constitutions in 1776 and then eventually imposing it against the national government in the Fifth Amendment of the Bill of Rights (Levy 1968, pp. 405–32).

In modern times, the Supreme Court has decided many cases concerning the issue of self-incrimination. For the most part, these cases concern the permissibility of police practices in questioning and obtaining confessions or other incriminating statements from criminal suspects. The Court must regularly determine the circumstances in which incriminating statements can be admitted into evidence or used to contradict testimony presented by a defendant at trial. In addressing the privilege against compelled self-incrimination, the Court has often linked the Fifth Amendment with the Sixth Amendment's right to counsel. By requiring suspects to be informed about their right to counsel and by making attorneys available during questioning, the Court has sought to diminish the risk that police officers would compel people to incriminate themselves during questioning. Although the *Miranda* decision established a relatively clear rule instructing law enforcement officers about how they must warn and, if requested, provide representation for suspects prior to questioning, new justices appointed during the Burger and Rehnquist Court eras weakened *Miranda*'s impact and clarity by identifying situations in which the Fifth Amendment did not bar the use of improperly obtained incriminating statements by suspects.

Double Jeopardy

The right against double jeopardy was established in American colonies long before the Bill of Rights was authored. Like other rights concerning the criminal justice process, this right reflected both the idealistic principles embodied in English common law practices and the colonists' distrust of authorities who, in England, did not always apply criminal processes and punishments fairly and consistently. The right against double jeopardy appeared in one of the colonies' earliest legal documents concerning rights, the Massachusetts Body of Liberties in 1641 (Bodenhamer 1992, pp. 14–16). The policy objective underlying the right against double jeopardy is clear:

> *Without a double jeopardy prohibition, the state would possess almost limitless power to disrupt the lives and fortune of the citizenry. A citizen could be subjected to perpetual prosecution for any act whatsoever, leading at best to the squandering of a person's assets [in repeatedly fighting criminal charges] and at worst to multiple punishments for the same offense. Without a double jeopardy prohibition, in short, a citizen could have no clear and settled expectation concerning liability to criminal prosecution and punishment.* (Allen, Ferrall, and Ratnaswamy 1991, p. 281)

Although they are less numerous than self-incrimination cases, double jeopardy cases have regularly appeared on the Supreme Court's docket. The classic incorporation case, *Palko v. Connecticut* (1937), was a double jeopardy case decided before the Court had applied this right to the states through the Fourteenth Amendment (see Chapter 4 on Incorporation). Double jeopardy issues arise in a number of ways, but they frequently concern whether or not multiple criminal charges may be pursued when they are based on the same action by the defendant. Cases also arise when seemingly settled cases are reopened and produce different results after guilty pleas are withdrawn or invalidated.

Approaches to Fifth Amendment Decision Making

As in other cases concerning rights in the criminal justice process, Supreme Court justices are generally not applying grand legal theories to determine the outcomes of cases. Instead, most justices seem to react on a case-by-case basis to individual situations that arise in either police questioning of suspects or multiple criminal charges and proceedings based on a single event. It is apparent that the justices' decisions are shaped by balancing policy interests in specific factual contexts. For example, as indicated by the foregoing discussion of the *Miranda* case, the justices in the majority were very concerned about the adverse consequences for individuals who might be subjected to police pressure, both blatant and subtle, to make incriminating statements. By contrast, the dissenters placed greater emphasis on their policy preference for giving law enforcement officers the opportunity to catch and punish lawbreakers as long as the officers' did not take actions which clearly indicated that suspects' confessions were involuntary.

The competing policy concerns of protecting individuals from even subtle police pressure versus freeing the police to gain evidence from lawbreakers are weighed differently by different justices. They are also weighed inconsistently by individual justices in specific cases in which these justices believe new factual circumstances have arisen. For example, in 1977 Justice Stewart wrote an opinion for the Court finding a violation of a suspect's right when police officers directed comments to the suspect as they drove in a police car. The officers said to the suspect that it would be a shame if the victim's body could not be located because the victim and her family deserved to have a Christian funeral at Christmastime. These comments elicited incriminating statements from the suspect whose attorneys had not been permitted to ride in the car in order to monitor interrogation and prevent improper questioning (*Brewer v. Williams,* 1977). Three years later, Justice Stewart authored another opinion for a different majority coalition in a similar situation that approved the police officers' actions when, as they traveled in a police car with the suspect in the backseat, one officer said to the other, it would be too bad if a child found the missing shotgun that had been used in the robbery and had apparently been thrown away in the vicinity of a school for handicapped children. The comment elicited an incriminating statement from the suspect (*Rhode Island v. Innis,* 1980). Justices Stewart and Powell, alone among the Court's members, saw these two situations as different based on the person to whom the comments were directed. When directed to the suspect, Stewart and Powell regarded such comments as improper questioning. When directed to a fellow officer within earshot of the suspect, Stewart and Powell did not regard these comments as constituting police questioning. By contrast, Chief Justice Burger and Justices Rehnquist, Blackmun, and White viewed the police officers' actions as proper in both circumstances, and they would have admitted both incriminating statements into evidence. Meanwhile, Justices Brennan, Marshall, and Stevens were skeptical of the officers' actions in both cases because they believed that the police were using subtle methods to elicit incriminating statements from suspects outside of the presence of those criminal suspects' attorneys. Although some justices are exceptionally consistent in either voting to exclude questionable confessions (e.g., Brennan and Marshall) or in voting to declare such incriminating statements admissible (e.g., Rehnquist and Burger), the case-by-case reactions of justices such as Stewart and Powell determined the outcomes of many cases and thereby made the Court's decisions on Fifth Amendment and other criminal justice issues seem somewhat inconsistent.

Pre-Warren Court Period

Prior to the incorporation of the Fifth Amendment, the Court had little reason to decide Fifth Amendment cases. Most crimes are defined by state law, and the vast majority of defendants are prosecuted in state courts. During this period, the Court established an influential test for double jeopardy cases, but did relatively little with respect to self-incrimination.

Double Jeopardy

Early double jeopardy cases in which the Supreme Court actually defined and applied the right were limited to those in federal court. For example, a basic enduring test for determining whether two criminal offenses are the same for double jeopardy purposes was established in *Blockburger v. United States* (1932). The *Blockburger* rule precludes a second prosecution when both offenses require the prosecution to prove the same elements of the crime. As we will see, this "same-elements" test continued to be a relevant issue for analysis and discussion in cases addressed by the Rehnquist Court (*Grady v. Corbin,* 1990; *United States v. Dixon,* 1993).

The most prominent double jeopardy case prior to the Warren Court era was *Palko v. Connecticut* (1937). As we discussed in Chapter 4, Palko was tried for first-degree capital murder, but the jury found him guilty only of second degree murder and he was given a life sentence. The state successfully sought to retry Palko based on alleged errors that occurred during the first trial and, with the blessing of the state appellate courts, the second trial took place and resulted in Palko's conviction for first degree and a death sentence. In an influential decision affecting numerous subsequent cases concerning the issue of incorporation, Justice Benjamin Cardozo wrote that the Fifth Amendment right against double jeopardy was *not* a fundamental right that was "of the very essence of a scheme of ordered liberty" (*Palko,* 302 U.S. at 325–26), and therefore the double jeopardy right applied only against the federal government and not against the states. This decision precluded the Supreme Court's active consideration of most double jeopardy claims until the Warren Court justices acted to incorporate the protection against double jeopardy.

Self-Incrimination

During the early and mid-twentieth century, the Court rejected efforts to have the Fifth Amendment privilege against compelled self-incrimination incorporated and applied against the states. The issue arose in courtroom contexts when judges or prosecutors made negative comments to juries about defendants' unwillingness to take the witness stand (e.g., *Twining v. New Jersey,* 1908). In *Adamson v. California* (1947), for example, which we discussed in Chapter 4, Adamson was on trial for murder; but he knew that if he took the witness stand in his own behalf, he would open the door for the prosecutor to ask him questions that would reveal to the jury his prior, unrelated criminal convictions. When he did not take the stand, arguments were made to the jurors that they should infer Adamson's guilt from the fact that he did not testify. Such comments by prosecutors and judges clashed with the concept of a privilege against compelled self-incrimination, but prior to incorporation the right applied only against the federal government unless individual states had their own rules barring such comments in court.

Prior to the incorporation of the Fifth Amendment privilege against compelled self-incrimination, the Supreme Court established a basis for examining whether police officers, including state and local officers, were using improper methods to obtain confessions from suspects. In *Brown v. Mississippi* (1936), for example, the Court invalidated confessions that local police officers obtained by hanging suspects by their necks from trees and whipping them with leather straps. The Court declared that the application of such tortures violated the suspects' Fourteenth Amendment right to due process of law. The use of such techniques for questioning does not simply collide with traditional notions of fairness concerning the privilege against compelled self-incrimination inherited from Britain; these methods also make the confessions obtained by police inherently unreliable. When someone is tortured into confessing, there is no way to know whether they are actually guilty. Although the Court favored the defendants in the *Brown* case, abusive police practices remained widespread, especially when applied to poor and African American suspects. Because these abuses took place prior to the application of the right to counsel for indigent defendants, most victims of police abuse had no way to use the judicial process in order to seek the help of a higher court to prevent improper police conduct.

Prior to the 1960s, police officers in many places were merely untrained political patronage appointees whose primary qualification for office was loyalty to a particular public official or political "machine" organization. These officers, who were exclusively white and male, often misused their authority in harassing political opponents, racial minorities, and other social out-groups. The justices on the Warren Court who comprised the majority for *Miranda* and other cases expanding rights for criminal defendants possessed great skepticism about police motives and behavior. Their desire to create clear-cut rules for police behavior stemmed from personal knowledge and experience about abusive police practices. These justices were already adults during the 1930s when the Wickersham Commission's investigations and several highly publicized cases brought national public attention to the problems of abusive police practices. Moreover, several justices had personal experiences that exposed them to coercive police tactics aimed at producing confessions. For example, Hugo Black had been a local judge in Alabama and Earl Warren had been a prosecutor in California. William Brennan's father was a labor leader in New Jersey who was beaten by police when he tried to organize workers. In addition, William O. Douglas and Thurgood Marshall had experienced direct police harassment in their younger years by virtue of their personal characteristics. Douglas came from an extremely poor family, and Marshall was an African American. Thus the near-absence of judicial action to curb police abuses prior to the Warren Court era, in effect, contributed to the education of several future high court justices who observed abusive practices and gained skepticism about police behavior while coming of age as young lawyers (Smith 1990). By contrast, several justices on the Rehnquist Court came of age *after* Court decisions and police professionalization trends had curbed many of the worst police abuses. These younger justices lacked personal experiences that would cause them to be skeptical about the behavior of police officers.

Shortly before Earl Warren's appointment as chief justice, Justices Black and Douglas seized the opportunity to advocate the incorporation of the Fifth Amendment in concurring opinions in *Rochin v. California* (1952). As described in Chapter 9, sheriff's deputies entered Rochin's home without a warrant and eventually ordered a doctor to force a vomit-inducing substance into Rochin's stomach through a tube. When Rochin vomited, capsules were recovered and tests revealed that they contained morphine. In a majority opinion written by Justice Felix Frankfurter, the Supreme Court threw out Rochin's conviction by declaring that the conscience-shocking behavior of the police officers violated Rochin's Fourteenth Amendment right to due process of law. Black and Douglas concurred in the result, but they argued that the forcible extraction of the capsules violated Rochin's Fifth Amendment privilege against compelled self-incrimination and that the Fifth Amendment should be made applicable against the states.

The Warren Court Era

In many ways, the Supreme Court's decisions during the Warren Court era activated the Fifth Amendment and made it a meaningful limitation on the actions of law enforcement officials, especially with respect to self-incrimination. The Warren era justices applied their expansive views on individuals' rights to the Fifth Amendment and began to identify particular police and prosecution tactics that would no longer be permitted. The Warren Court's decisions on the Fifth Amendment contributed to a significant redefinition of the relationships between police and suspects as law enforcement officers were required to follow specific rules and procedures that would protect suspects' rights against compelled self-incrimination.

Self-Incrimination

In a case in 1957 that raised the identical issue to that in *Rochin,* the Warren Court justices had an opportunity to address the Fifth Amendment. The unconscious driver of a vehicle involved in a fatal accident smelled of liquor. Police officers took him to a hospital and instructed a doctor to take an involuntary blood sample from the unconscious suspect. Blood tests showed that his blood alcohol level exceeded legal limits. When the driver sought to challenge the blood test, Black and Douglas again saw the police actions as constituting a violation of the privilege against compelled self-incrimination, but a majority of justices distinguished the case from *Rochin* and found no violation of due process because, unlike in *Rochin,* the officer's behavior did not "shock the conscience" (*Breihaupt v. Abram,* 1957). In effect, a blood test was viewed as less invasive than the pummeling and "stomach pumping" applied to Rochin. A majority of justices also declined to incorporate the Fifth Amendment for application against the states. Thus the case was characterized as concerning the right to due process of law rather than the privilege against compelled self-incrimination. Subsequently, even after the Warren Court justices had incorporated the Fifth Amendment in the 1960s, a majority remained opposed to the argument advanced by Black and Douglas that blood samples and other kinds of physical evidence (e.g., photographs) should be included in the Fifth Amendment's privilege against compelled self-incrimination (e.g., *Schmerber v. California,* 1966). The Court limited the concept of self-incrimination to personal communications or testimony (Abraham 1988, p. 142).

In 1964, the Supreme Court issued several significant decisions affecting the privilege against compelled self-incrimination. In *Malloy v. Hogan* (1964), the Court incorporated the privilege against compelled self-incrimination and applied it against the states through the Due Process Clause of the Fourteenth Amendment. Connecticut had threatened Malloy with a contempt of court citation for refusing to testify about gambling activities when he declined to testify by asserting his right not to incriminate himself. The 5–4 split within the Court was consistent with the Court's polarization on other cases, such as *Miranda,* because Justices Harlan and

Clark opposed nationalization of the Fifth Amendment and Justices White and Stewart objected to broad judicial rulings that limited the ability of law enforcement officials to obtain information from suspects (Abraham 1988, p. 88). The companion case of *Murphy v. Waterfront Commission of New York Harbor* (1964) produced a decision permitting assertions of the privilege against compelled self-incrimination in state proceedings when the suspect fears that the testimony might generate federal criminal charges.

Two additional cases in 1964 had implications for the privilege against compelled self-incrimination even though the Court's decisions focused primarily on the Sixth Amendment right to counsel. Both cases concerned the circumstances under which law enforcement officers can question defendants outside of the presence of counsel. In *Escobedo v. Illinois* (1964), police officers prevented the defendant and his attorney from meeting together, even though they saw each other in the corridor of the police station, until the police had questioned the defendant for more than fourteen hours and arranged a damaging confrontation between codefendants that produced incriminating statements. The Court's holding specified that defendants have a right to counsel when "the investigation is no longer a general inquiry into an unsolved crime, but has begun to focus on a particular suspect, the suspect has been taken into police custody, [and] the police carry out a process of interrogations that lends itself to eliciting incriminating statements" (378 U.S. at 491–92). In effect, the justices expanded the Sixth Amendment right to counsel to apply to an earlier point in the criminal justice process as a means to guard against law enforcement officers' actions that might violate the Fifth Amendment privilege against compelled self-incrimination.

Similarly, in *Massiah v. United States* (1964), the Supreme Court linked the rights contained in the Fifth and Sixth Amendments. In *Massiah,* a defendant who had been indicted and was already represented by counsel was lured into an automobile containing a radio transmitter by a codefendant who was working for the police. Discussions in the car initiated by the codefendant produced incriminating statements that were recorded by the police. A 6-3 majority opinion by Justice Stewart, who often disagreed with decisions favoring criminal defendants in other cases, declared that the questioning of the defendant by a police agent outside of the presence of defense counsel violated both the Fifth Amendment privilege against compelled self-incrimination and the Sixth Amendment right to counsel.

The Court's decisions in *Escobedo* and *Massiah* were regarded as extremely harmful by law enforcement officials throughout the country who were accustomed to relying on interrogations and confessions as the means to solve crimes. According to Henry Abraham (1988, p. 158), "To interrogate a suspect behind closed doors in order to secure a confession not only was a concept based on the custom and usage of centuries, but it had become a deeply entrenched police practice, strongly supported by both 'traditional' and 'reform' elements in the ranks of those charged with the administration of criminal justice." The unhappiness that law enforcement officers felt about the Warren Court's criminal justice decisions, including *Mapp v. Ohio* (1961) on the exclusionary rule and the 1964 cases on self-incrimination, became inflamed by the *Miranda* decision in 1966. As we discussed at the beginning of the chapter, the *Miranda* decision imposed a new set of rules on law enforcement officers that forced them to inform arrestees of Fifth and Sixth Amendment rights before any questioning was initiated. Because the *Miranda* decision clashed so strongly with customary police investigative procedures, it has been called "the most bitterly criticized, most contentious, and most diversely analyzed criminal procedure decision by the Warren Court" (Abraham 1988, p. 159).

MIRANDA V. ARIZONA

384 U.S. 436, 86 S. Ct. 1602, 16 L. Ed. 2d 694 (1966)
[The facts of this case are omitted because they were presented in the case study at the beginning of this chapter.]

■ The case is important because it constituted a landmark decision in which the Supreme Court imposed controversial obligations on law enforcement officers to warn people about their Fifth and Sixth Amendment rights before questioning them when they are taken into custody. As you read the case, consider the following questions: (1) What are the reasons for the majority's decision to require police officers to inform suspects about their constitutional rights? (2) Precisely what are police officers required to do when they arrest a suspect? (3) Are the dissenters correct in arguing that this decision significantly diminishes the ability of law enforcement officials to gather needed evidence for criminal cases?

VOTE:

Five justices found the police officers' actions to be unconstitutional (Black, Brennan, Douglas, Fortas, Warren).

Four justices found the police officers' actions to be constitutional (Clark, Harlan, Stewart, White).

Chief Justice Warren delivered the opinion of the Court:

* * *

Our holding will be spelled out with some specificity in the pages which follow but briefly stated it is this: the prosecution may not use statements, whether exculpatory or inculpatory, stemming from custodial interrogation of the defendant unless it demonstrates the use of procedural safeguards effective to secure the privilege against self-incrimination. By custodial interrogation, we mean questioning initiated by law enforcement officers after a person has been taken into custody or otherwise deprived of his freedom of action in any significant way. As for the procedural safeguards to be employed, unless other fully effective means are devised to inform accused persons of their right to silence and to assure a continuous opportunity to exercise it, the following measures are required. Prior to any questioning, the person must be warned that he has a right to remain silent, that any statement he does make may be used as evidence against him, and that he has the right to the presence of an attorney, either retained or appointed. The defendant may waive effectuation of these rights, provided the waiver is made voluntarily, knowingly, and intelligently. If, however, he indicates in any manner and at any stage of the process that he wishes to consult with an attorney before speaking there can be no questioning. Likewise, if the individual is alone and indicates in any manner that he does not wish to be interrogated, the police may not question him. The mere fact that he may have answered some questions or volunteered some statements on his own does not deprive him of the right to refrain from answering any further inquiries until he has consulted with an attorney and thereafter consents to be questioned.

The constitutional issue we decide in each of these cases is the admissibility of statements obtained from a defendant questioned while in custody or otherwise deprived of his freedom of action in any significant way. In each, the defendant was questioned by police officers, detectives, or a prosecuting attorney in a room in which he was cut off from the outside world. In none of these cases was the defendant given a full and effective warning of his rights at the outset of the interrogation process. In all the cases, the questioning elicited oral admissions, and in all three of them, signed statements as well which were admitted at their trials. They all thus share salient features—incommunicado interrogation of individuals in a police-dominated atmosphere, resulting in self-incriminating statements without full warnings of constitutional rights.

An understanding of the nature and setting of this in-custody interrogation is essential to our decisions today. The difficulty in depicting what transpires at such interrogations stems from the fact that in this country they have largely taken place incommunicado. From extensive factual studies undertaken in the early 1930's, including the famous Wickersham Report to Congress by a Presidential Commission, it is clear that police violence and the "third degree" flourished at that time.

In a series of cases decided by this Court long after these studies, the police resorted to physical brutality—beatings, hanging, whipping—and to sustained and protracted questioning incommunicado in order to extort confessions. The Commission on Civil Rights in 1961 found much evidence to indicate that "some policemen still resort to physical force to obtain confessions." . . .The use of physical brutality and violence is not, unfortunately, relegated to the past or to any part of the country. Only recently in Kings County, New York, the police brutally beat, kicked, and placed lighted cigarette butts on the back of a potential witness under interrogation for the purpose of securing a statement incriminating a third party. . . .

The examples given above are undoubtedly the exception now, but they are sufficiently widespread to be the object of concern. Unless a proper limitation upon custodial interrogation is achieved—such as these decisions will advance—there can be no assurance that practices of this nature will be eradicated in the foreseeable future. . . .

* * *

Again we stress that the modern practice of in-custody interrogation is psychologically oriented rather than physically oriented. . . . Interrogation still takes place in privacy. Privacy results in secrecy and this in turn results in a gap in our knowledge as to what in fact goes on in the interrogation rooms. A valuable source of information about present police practices, however, may be found in various police manuals and texts which document procedures employed with success in the past, and which recommend various other effective tactics. These texts are used by law enforcement agencies as guides. . . .

* * *

To highlight the isolation and unfamiliar surroundings, the manuals instruct the police to display an air of confidence in the suspect's guilt and from outward appearance to maintain an interest in confirming certain details. The guilt of the subject is to be posited as a fact. The interrogator should direct his comments toward the reasons why the subject committed the act, rather than court failure by asking the subject whether he did it. Like other men, perhaps the subject has had a bad family life, had an unhappy childhood, had too much to drink, had an unrequited desire for women. The officers are instructed to minimize the moral seriousness of the offense, to place blame on the victim or on society. These tactics are designed to put the subject in a psychological state where his story is but an elaboration of what the police purport to know already—that he is guilty. Explanations to the contrary are dismissed and discouraged.

* * *

The interrogators sometimes are instructed to induce a confession out of trickery [by falsely telling the defendant that he was positively identified by a witness in a line-up]. . . .

* * *

Even without employing brutality, the "third degree" or the specific stratagems described above, the very fact of custodial interrogation exacts a heavy toll on individual liberty and trades on the weakness of individuals. . . .

In the cases before us today, given this background, we concern ourselves primarily with this interrogation atmosphere and the evils it can bring. . . . [I]n No. 584, *California v. Stewart,* the local police held the defendant for five days in the station and interrogated him on nine separate occasions before they secured his inculpatory statement.

In these cases, we might not find the defendants' statements to have been involuntary in traditional terms. Our concern for adequate safeguards to protect precious Fifth Amendment rights is, of course, not lessened in the slightest. In each of these cases, the defendant was thrust into an unfamiliar atmosphere and run through menacing police interrogation procedures. The potentiality for compulsion is forcefully apparent, for example, in *Miranda,* where the indigent Mexican defendant was a seriously disturbed individual with pronounced sexual fantasies, and in *Stewart,* in which the defendant was an indigent Los Angeles Negro who had dropped out of school in the sixth grade. To be sure, the records do not evince overt physical coercion or patent psychological ploys. The fact remains that in none of these cases did the officers undertake to afford appropriate safeguards at the outset of the interrogation to insure that the statements were truly the product of free choice.

It is obvious that such an interrogation environment is created for no purpose other than to subjugate the individual to the will of his examiner. This atmosphere carries its own badge of intimidation. To be sure, this is not physical intimidation, but it is equally destructive of human dignity. The current practice of incommunicado interrogation is at odds with one of our Nation's most cherished principles—that the individual may not be compelled to incriminate himself. Unless adequate protective devices are employed to dispel the compulsion inherent in custodial surroundings, no statement obtained from the defendant can truly be the product of his free choice.

* * *

Today, then, there can be no doubt that the Fifth Amendment privilege is available outside of criminal court proceedings and serves to protect persons in all settings in which their freedom of action is curtailed in any significant way from being compelled to incriminate themselves. We have concluded that without proper safeguards the process of in-custody interrogation of persons suspected or accused of crime contains inherently compelling pressures which work to undermine the individual's will to resist and to compel him to speak where he would not otherwise do so freely. In order to combat these pressures and to permit a full opportunity to exercise the privilege against self-incrimination, the accused must be adequately and effectively apprised of his rights and exercise of those rights must be fully honored.

* * *

If the interrogation continues without the presence of an attorney and a statement is taken, a heavy burden rests on the government to demonstrate that the defendant knowingly and intelligently waived his privileges against self-incrimination and his right to retained or appointed counsel. . . . This Court has always set high standards of proof for the waiver of constitutional rights, and we reassert these standards as applied to in-custody interrogation. Since the State is responsible for establishing the isolated circumstances under which the interrogation takes place and has the only means of making available corroborated evidence of warnings given during incommunicado interrogation, the burden is rightly on its shoulders.

An express statement that the individual is willing to make a statement and does not want an attorney followed closely by a statement could constitute a waiver. But a valid waiver will not be presumed simply from the silence of the accused after warnings are given or simply from the fact that a confession was in fact eventually obtained. . . .

* * *

Our decision is not intended to hamper the traditional function of police officers investigating crime. . . . When an individual is in custody on probable cause, the police may, of course, seek out evidence in the field to be used at trial against him. Such investigation may include inquiry of persons not under restraint. General on-the-scene questioning as to the facts surrounding a crime or other general questioning of citizens in the fact-finding process is not affected by our holding. It is an act of good citizenship for individuals to give whatever information they may have to aid in law enforcement. In such situations the compelling atmosphere inherent in the process of in-custody interrogation is not necessarily present.

In dealing with statements obtained through interrogation, we do not purport to find all confessions inadmissible. Confessions remain a proper element in law enforcement. Any statement given freely and voluntarily without any compelling influences is, of course, admissible in evidence. . . .There is no requirement that police stop a person who enters a police station and states that he wishes to confess to a crime, or a person who calls the police to offer a confession or any other statement he desires to make. Volunteered statements of any kind are not barred by the Fifth Amendment and their admissibility is not affected by our holding today.

* * *

A recurrent argument made in these cases is that society's need for interrogation outweighs the privilege [against self-incrimination]. This argument is not unfamiliar to this Court. . . . The whole thrust of our foregoing discussion demonstrates that the Constitution has prescribed the rights of the individual when confronted with the power of government when it provided in the Fifth Amendment that an individual cannot be compelled to be a witness against himself. That right cannot be abridged. . . .

* * *

In announcing these principles, we are not unmindful of the burdens which law enforcement officials must bear, often under trying circumstances. We also fully recognize the obligation of all citizens to aid in enforcing the criminal laws. This Court, while protecting individual rights, has always given ample latitude to law enforcement agencies in the legitimate exercise of their duties. The limits we have placed on the interrogation process should not constitute an undue interference with a proper system of law enforcement. . . .

* * *

Over the years the Federal Bureau of Investigation has compiled an exemplary record of effective law enforcement while advising any suspect or arrested person, at the outset of an interview, that he is not required to make a statement, that any statement may be used against him in court, that the individual may obtain the services of an attorney of his own choice, and, more recently, that he has a right to free counsel if he is unable to pay. . . .

* * *

The practice of the FBI can readily be emulated by state and local enforcement agencies. The argument that the FBI deals with different crimes than are dealt with by state authorities does not mitigate the significance of the FBI experience.

* * *

It is also urged upon us that we withhold decision on this issue until state legislative bodies and advisory groups have had an opportunity to deal with these problems by rule making. . . . Congress and the states are free to develop their own safeguards for the privilege [against self-incrimination], so long as they are fully as effective as those described above in informing accused persons of their right of silence and in affording continuous opportunity to exercise it. In any event, however, the issues presented are of constitutional dimensions and must be determined by the courts. The admissibility of a statement in the face of a claim that it was obtained in violation of the defendant's constitutional rights is an issue the resolution of which has long since been undertaken by this Court. . . . Judicial solutions to problems of constitutional dimension have evolved decade by decade.

As courts have been presented with the need to enforce constitutional rights, they have found means of doing so. That was our responsibility when *Escobedo* was before us and it is our responsibility today. Where rights secured by the Constitution are involved, there can be no rule making or legislation which would abrogate them.

* * *

We reverse [Miranda's conviction]. From the testimony of the officers and by the admission of respondent, it is clear that Miranda was not in any way apprised of his right to consult with an attorney and to have one present during the interrogation, nor was his right not to be compelled to incriminate himself effectively protected in any other manner. Without these warnings the statements were inadmissible. The mere fact that he signed a statement which contained a typed-in clause stating that he had "full knowledge" of his "legal rights" does not approach the knowing and intelligent waiver required to relinquish constitutional rights. . . .

Justice Clark dissenting.

It is with regret that I find it necessary to write in these cases. However, I am unable to join the majority because its opinion goes too far on too little, while my dissenting brethren do not go quite far enough. Nor can I join in the Court's criticism of the present practices of police and investigatory agencies as to custodial interrogation. The materials it refers to as "police manuals" are, as I read them, merely writings in this field by professors and some police officers. Not one is shown by the record here to be the official manual of any police department, much less in universal use in crime detection. Moreover the examples of police brutality mentioned by this Court are rare exceptions to the thousands of cases that appear every year in the law reports. The police agencies—all the way from municipal and state forces to the federal bureaus—are responsible for law enforcement and public safety in this country. I am proud of their efforts, which in my view are not fairly characterized by the Court's opinion.

* * *

The rule prior to today . . . depended upon a "totality of circumstances evidencing an involuntary . . . admission of guilt." . . . I would continue to follow that rule. . . .

Rather than employing the arbitrary Fifth Amendment rule which the Court lays down I would follow the more pliable dictates of the Due Process Clauses of the Fifth and Fourteenth Amendments which we are accustomed to administering and which we know from our cases are effective instruments in protecting persons in police custody. In this way we would not be acting in the dark nor in one full sweep changing the traditional rules of custodial interrogation which this Court has for so long recognized as a justifiable and proper tool in balancing individual rights against the rights of society. . . .

Justice Harlan, with whom Justice Stewart and Justice White join, dissenting.

* * *

Without at all subscribing to the generally black picture of police conduct painted by the Court, I think it must be frankly recognized at the outset that police questioning allowable under due process precedents may inherently entail some pressure on the suspect and may seek advantage in his ignorance or weakness. . . . Until today, the role of the Constitution has been only to sift out *undue* pressure, not to assure spontaneous confessions.

The Court's new rules aim to offset these minor pressures and disadvantages intrinsic to any kind of police interrogation. The rules do not serve due process interests in preventing blatant coercion since, as I noted earlier, they do nothing to contain the policeman who is prepared to lie from the start. . . .

What the Court largely ignores is that its rules impair, if they will not eventually serve to frustrate, an instrument of law enforcement that has long and quite reasonably been thought worth the price paid for it. There can be little doubt that the Court's new code would markedly decrease the number of confessions. . . .

How much harm this decision will inflict on law enforcement cannot fairly be predicted with accuracy. . . . We do know that some crimes cannot be solved without confessions, that ample expert testimony attests to their importance in crime control, and that the Court is taking a real risk with society's welfare in imposing its new regime on the country. The social costs of crime are too great to call the new rules anything but a hazardous experiment. . . .

Justice White, with whom Justice Harlan and Justice Stewart join, dissenting.

The proposition that the privilege against self-incrimination forbids in-custody interrogation without the warnings specified in the majority opinion and without a clear waiver of counsel has no significant support in the history of the privilege or in the language of the Fifth Amendment. As for the English authorities and the common-law history, the privilege, firmly established in the second half of the seventeenth century, was never applied except to prohibit compelled judicial interrogations. . . .

* * *

Criticism of the Court's opinion, however, cannot stop with a demonstration that the factual and textual bases for the rule it propounds are, at best, less than compelling. Equally relevant is an assessment of the rule's consequences measured against community values. . . . More than the human dignity of the accused is involved; the human personality of others in society must also be preserved. Thus the values reflected by the privilege are not the sole desideratum; society's interest in the general security is of equal weight.

The obvious underpinning of the Court's decision is a deep-seated distrust of all confessions. . . . This is the not so subtle overtone of the opinion—that it is inherently wrong for the police to gather evidence from the accused himself. And this is precisely the nub of this dissent. I see nothing wrong or immoral, and certainly nothing unconstitutional, in the police's asking a suspect whom they have reasonable cause to arrest whether or not he killed his wife or in confronting him with the evidence on which the arrest was based, at least where he has been plainly advised that he may remain completely silent. . . .

* * *

The rule announced today will measurably weaken the ability of the criminal law to perform [its] tasks. It is a deliberate calculus to prevent interrogations, to reduce the incidence of confessions and pleas of guilty and to increase the number of trials. Criminal trials, no matter how efficient the police are, are not sure bets for the prosecution, nor should they be if the evidence is not forthcoming. Under the present law, the prosecution fails to prove its case in about 30% of the criminal cases actually tried in the federal courts. . . . But it is something else again to remove from the ordinary criminal case all those confessions which heretofore have been held to be free and voluntary acts of the accused and to thus establish a new constitutional barrier to the ascertainment of truth by the judicial process. There is, in my view, every reason to believe that a good many criminal defendants who otherwise would have been convicted on what this Court has previously thought to be the most satisfactory kind of evidence will now under this new version of the Fifth Amendment, either not be tried at all or will be acquitted if the State's evidence, minus the confession, is put to the test of litigation.

I have no desire whatsoever to share the responsibility for any such impact on the present criminal process.

In some unknown number of cases the Court's rule will return a killer, a rapist or other criminal to the streets and to the environment which produced him, to repeat his crime whenever it pleases him. As a consequence, there will not be a gain, but a loss, in human dignity. . . .

In *Miranda,* the justices' knowledge and skepticism about police interrogation procedures were underlying factors in the majority's decision. According to Chief Justice Warren (*Miranda,* 384 U.S. at 445–47),

> *An understanding of the nature and setting of this in-custody interrogation is essential to our decisions today. The difficulty in depicting what transpires at such interrogations stems from the fact that in this country they have largely taken place incommunicado. From extensive factual studies undertaken in the 1930s, including the famous Wickersham Report to Congress by a Presidential Commission, it is clear that police violence and the "third degree" flourished at that time. In a series of cases decided by this Court long after these studies, the police resorted to physical brutality—beatings, hangings, whipping—and to sustained and protracted questioning incommunicado in order to extort confessions. . . . The use of physical brutality and violence is not, unfortunately, relegated to the past or to any part of the country. Only recently in Kings County, New York, the police brutally beat, kicked, and placed lighted cigarette butts on the back of a potential witness under interrogation. . . .*
>
> *The examples given above are undoubtedly the exception now, but they are sufficiently widespread to be the object of concern. . . .*

Although many critics took issue with Warren's negative characterization of police methods, Warren and the other members of the majority clearly relied on their knowledge and experience to declare that the protection of individual rights is far more important than enabling the police to obtain confessions freely.

Studies of the impact of *Miranda* have found that the decision has not significantly impaired the ability of law enforcement officials to solve crimes. For example, a study in Pittsburgh shortly after the *Miranda* decision found a reduction in the number of confessions obtained from suspects, but the conviction rate remained the same after the introduction of *Miranda* because evidence other than confessions can provide the basis for convictions (Seeburger and Wettick 1967).

Double Jeopardy

In its final incorporation decision, the Warren Court applied the Fifth Amendment right against double jeopardy to the states in 1969. A man tried in Maryland for larceny and burglary was acquitted on the larceny charge but convicted of burglary and sentenced to ten years in prison. His conviction was set aside by a Maryland Court of Appeals decision concerning the nature of the oaths that jurors must swear as a component of jury service. In the second trial, the state gained convictions against him for both larceny and burglary, and he received a fifteen-year sentence. The U.S. Supreme Court invalidated his larceny conviction by applying the Fifth Amendment right against double jeopardy to the states (*Benton v. Maryland,* 1969).

The Warren Court's decisions concerning the Fifth Amendment, especially *Miranda v. Arizona,* helped to generate political controversy. According to Bodenhamer (1992, pp. 122–23), "Police officers, prosecutors, commentators, and politicians were quick to denounce the *Miranda* warnings. Critics charged that recent Court decisions, culminating with *Escobedo* and *Miranda,* had 'handcuffed' police efforts to fight crime. This claim found a receptive audience among a majority of the general public worried about rising crimes rates, urban riots, racial conflict, and the counterculture's challenge to middle-class values." The Court's decisions and the unfavorable image of those decisions in the eyes of the police and the public helped to motivate President Nixon to replace retiring Warren Court justices with new appointees who would favor the government more frequently in cases concerning the rights of criminal defendants.

The Burger Court Era

The Burger Court majority began the process of narrowing the definition of Fifth Amendment rights and weakening the rules that applied to police officers' questioning of suspects. The Court did not undo the activation of the Fifth Amendment undertaken by the Warren Court, but the Burger era justices reduced the scope of the privilege against compelled self-incrimination, in particular, when deciding several cases.

Self-Incrimination

Because *Miranda* and other Warren Court decisions were decided by close votes on the Supreme Court, it is not surprising that decisions began to go against individual claimants when President Nixon had the opportunity to appoint four new justices who were selected, in part, for their conservatism on the issue of rights for criminal defendants. In 1971, the Burger Court began to limit the impact of the *Miranda* rules on law enforcement officers' ability to use confessions and other incriminating statements against defendants. A man charged with selling heroin to an undercover officer made incriminating statements to the police when they questioned him without giving him proper *Miranda* warnings. Although the *Miranda* decision made those statements inadmissible as direct evidence against the defendant, a 5–4 majority limited the reach of *Miranda* by permitting the use of improperly obtained statements to impeach the defendant's testimony. Thus when the defendant testified during trial that he had never sold heroin, the prosecution was allowed to tell the jury about how his improperly obtained statements contradicted his in-court testimony (*Harris v. New York,* 1971). The Court subsequently expanded the opportunities for police to seek incriminating statements that could be used for impeachment purposes. After a defendant was advised of his *Miranda* rights and he requested the presence of an attorney, the police refused to honor his request and instead kept questioning him. When they elicited incriminating statements from him, they were still permitted to use these statements to impeach his trial testimony despite their violation of his *Miranda* rights (*Oregon v. Hass,* 1975). In a dissenting opinion, Justice Brennan complained, "Under today's holding, however, once the [*Miranda*] warnings are given, police have almost no incentive for following *Miranda*'s requirement that '[i]f the individual states that he wants an attorney, the interrogation must cease until the attorney is present' " (420 U.S. at 725).

In 1974, the Court directly undercut the basis for *Miranda* warnings. A defendant was questioned without being informed of his rights. As a result of his incriminating statements, a witness was identified who subsequently testified against the defendant. Although the defendant's incriminating statements could not be used against him, the witness, whose identity and testimony were a product of the improper questioning, was permitted to testify (*Michigan v. Tucker,* 1974). The most significant aspect of the decision was the Court's declaration that *Miranda* warnings were not mandated by the Constitution, but were merely useful rules created by judges in an effort to prevent improper police activities. As John Decker has noted, "[T]he Court's characterization of the *Miranda* provisions as mere prophylactic devices not necessarily mandated by the Constitution provided the Court with a mechanism for one day asserting that *Miranda* violations do not implicate *constitutional* violations and, accordingly, should not be subject to the exclusionary rule" (Decker 1992, p. 65).

The Court further limited the contours of the protection against compelled self-incrimination in several cases. For example, it decided that witnesses appearing before grand juries do not need to be warned that their statements can be used against them (*United States v. Mandujano,* 1976) and that a juvenile who asked to be accompanied by his probation officer during questioning was not invoking his *Miranda* right to representation during interrogation (*Fare v. Michael C.,* 1979). The Court also placed greater emphasis on warning only suspects who are "in custody" by determining that the Internal Revenue Service need not provide *Miranda* warnings to people questioned in their homes (*Beckwith v. United States,* 1976) and that the police need not warn people about their privilege against compelled self-incrimination when they are stopped for traffic violations (*Berkemer v. McCarty,* 1984). While these decisions limited the contexts in which *Miranda* principles were applicable, it was not until the mid-1980s that the Burger Court made major decisions that narrowed *Miranda* itself in the context of questioning suspects who have been placed under arrest and using their statements against them as direct evidence rather than merely as impeachment evidence.

The Burger Court carved out a major exception to the *Miranda* rule in *New York v. Quarles* (1984). A woman approached two police officers on patrol and told them that she had been sexually assaulted by a man with a gun who had just run into a grocery store. She gave a description of her assailant, and a man matching that description was spotted by the officers when they entered the store. The officers apprehended the man and, while frisking him, found he was wearing an empty shoulder holster. Upon placing handcuffs on the suspect, instead of immediately reading him his *Miranda* rights, the officers asked him where he had put the gun.

The suspect told them that they could find the gun by some nearby boxes within the store. Because the suspect's incriminating statement was elicited before the *Miranda* warnings were given, the New York state courts excluded from use at trial the suspect's statement and the gun, which was the product of the improperly obtained statements. However, the U.S. Supreme Court reversed the state courts' decisions by creating a "public safety" exception to the *Miranda* rule, which permitted both the statement and the gun to be admitted into evidence. Justice Rehnquist's majority opinion declared "[w]hatever the motivation of individual officers in such a situation, we do not believe that the doctrinal underpinnings of *Miranda* require that it be applied in all its rigor to a situation in which police officers ask questions reasonably prompted by a concern for the public safety. . . . We conclude that the need for answers to questions in a situation posing a threat to the public safety outweighs the need for the prophylactic rule protecting the Fifth Amendment's privilege against self-incrimination" (467 U.S. at 656–57).

Because "public safety" is a broad, undefined concept, it was not clear from the decision exactly when officers may ask questions and use incriminating statements against suspects without informing them of their *Miranda* rights. In an opinion concurring in part and dissenting in part, Justice O'Connor argued that the incriminating statement should be excluded but that the gun could be admitted into evidence. O'Connor also raised a concern about the impact of the Court's opinion in "blurring [*Miranda*'s] . . . clear strictures" (467 U.S. at 660) and thereby making police officers less certain about when they may ask questions without first informing suspects of their rights.

In dissent, Justice Marshall, joined by Justices Brennan and Stevens, complained that the Court had created a broad "public safety" exception in a case in which there was no risk to the public. At the time the police asked the suspect about the gun, the suspect was already in handcuffs and therefore could not seize the weapon to endanger the officers or other members of the public. Moreover, the store was nearly deserted in the middle of the night, so that there was little risk that some member of the public would come upon the weapon before officers had the opportunity to search the store and find it. Marshall argued that if police officers choose to question suspects without complying with the requirements of *Miranda,* then they should not be able to use the evidence obtained from such questioning against the suspect.

New York v. Quarles

467 U.S. 649, 104 S. Ct. 2626, 81 L.Ed.2d 550(1984)

■ After placing handcuffs on a suspect, the officers asked him where he had put his gun. The suspect responded "the gun is over there" and nodded toward some boxes. The officers retrieved the gun from under the boxes. The suspect sought to have his statement and the gun excluded from evidence because they were obtained through an incriminating statement in response to police questioning prior to being given his *Miranda* warnings. The trial court excluded the statement and the gun because they were obtained in violation of *Miranda,* and the Appellate Division of the New York Supreme Court and the New York Court of Appeals affirmed the trial judge's ruling. The U.S. Supreme Court considered whether the statement and gun should be admissible as evidence despite the officers' failure to provide *Miranda* warnings prior to questioning the handcuffed suspect.

The case is important because the Burger Court used it to establish an important exception to the exclusionary rule that had applied to violations of *Miranda* rights. As you read the case, consider the following questions: (1) Did the Supreme Court have a compelling reason in this case to create an exception to the Miranda rule? (2) How do the justices characterize the costs and benefits of excluding relevant evidence in order to prevent improper actions by police officers? (3) After this decision, do police officers know exactly when and how they can question a suspect prior to providing *Miranda* warnings?

VOTE:

Six justices found the admission of the evidence to be constitutional (Blackmun, Burger, O'Connor, Powell, Rehnquist, White).

Three justices found the admission of the evidence to be unconstitutional (Brennan, Marshall, Stevens).

[O'Connor concurred in part and dissented in part]

Justice Rehnquist delivered the opinion of the Court.

Respondent Benjamin Quarles was charged in the New York trial court with criminal possession of a weapon. The trial court suppressed the gun in question, and a statement made by respondent, because the statement was obtained by police before they read respondent his "*Miranda* rights." That ruling was affirmed on appeal through the New York Court of Appeals. We granted certiorari, . . . and we now reverse. We conclude that under the circumstances involved in this case, overriding considerations of public safety justify the officer's failure to provide *Miranda* warnings before he asked questions devoted to locating the abandoned weapon.

* * *

[The New York Court of Appeals] concluded that respondent was in "custody" within the meaning of *Miranda* during all questioning and rejected the State's argument that the exigencies of the situation justified Officer Kraft's failure to read respondent his *Miranda* rights until after he had located the gun. The court declined to recognize an exigency exception to the usual requirements of *Miranda* because it found no indication from Officer Kraft's testimony at the suppression hearing that his subjective motivation in asking the question was to protect his own or the safety of the public. . . . For the reasons which follow, we believe that this case presents a situation where concern for public safety must be paramount to adherence to the literal language of the prophylactic rules enunciated in *Miranda.*[3]

The Fifth Amendment guarantees that "[n]o person . . . shall be compelled in any criminal case to be a witness against himself." In *Miranda* this Court for the first time extended the Fifth Amendment privilege against compulsory self-incrimination to individuals subjected to custodial interrogation by the police. . . . The *Miranda* Court, however, presumed that interrogation in certain custodial circumstances is inherently coercive and held that statements made under those circumstances are inadmissible unless the suspect is specifically informed of his *Miranda* rights and freely decides to forgo those rights. The prophylactic *Miranda* warnings therefore are "not themselves rights protected by the Constitution but [are] instead measures to insure that the right against compulsory self-incrimination [is] protected." *Michigan v. Tucker,* 417 U.S. . . . 444 (1974). Requiring *Miranda* warnings before custodial interrogation provides "practical reinforcement" for the Fifth Amendment right. . . .

In this case we have before us no claim that respondent's statements were actually compelled by police conduct which overcame his will to resist. . . . Thus the only issue before us is whether Officer Kraft was justified in failing to make available to respondent the procedural safeguards associated with the privilege against compulsory self-incrimination since *Miranda.*

The New York Court of Appeals was undoubtedly correct in deciding that the facts of this case come within the ambit of the *Miranda* decision as we have subsequently interpreted it. We agree that respondent was in custody. . . . Here Quarles was surrounded by at least four police officers and was handcuffed when the questioning at issue took place. . . . The New York Court of Appeals' majority declined to express an opinion as to whether there might be an exception to the *Miranda* rule if the police had been acting to protect the public, because the lower courts in New York had made no factual determination that the police had acted with that motive.

We hold that on these facts there is a "public safety" exception to the requirement that *Miranda* warnings be given before a suspect's answers may be admitted into evidence, and that the availability of that exception does not depend upon the motivation of the individual officers involved. In a kaleidoscopic situation such as the one confronting these officers, where spontaneity rather than adherence to a police manual is necessarily the order of the day, the application of the exception which we recognize today should not be made to depend on *post hoc* findings at a suppression hearing concerning the subjective motivation of the arresting officer. Undoubtedly most police officers, if placed in Officer

[3]We have long recognized an exigent-circumstances exception to the warrant requirement in the Fourth Amendment context. See, *e.g., Michigan v. Tyler* . . . (1978). . . . We have found the warrant requirement of the Fourth Amendment inapplicable in cases where the " 'exigencies of the situation' make the needs of law enforcement so compelling that the warrantless search is objectively reasonable under the Fourth Amendment." *Mincey v. Arizona,* 437 U.S. . . . 394 (1978). . . . Although "the Fifth Amendment's strictures, unlike the Fourth's, are not removed by showing reasonableness," . . . we conclude today that there are limited circumstances where the judicially imposed strictures of *Miranda* are inapplicable.

Kraft's position, would act out of a host of different, instinctive, and largely unverifiable motives—their own safety, the safety of others, and perhaps as well the desire to obtain incriminating evidence from the suspect.

Whatever the motivation of individual officers in such a situation, we do not believe that the doctrinal underpinnings of *Miranda* require that it be applied in all its rigor to a situation in which police officers ask questions reasonably prompted by a concern for the public safety. . . . The *Miranda* majority . . . apparently felt that whatever the cost to society in terms of fewer convictions of guilty suspects, that cost would simply have to be borne in the interest of enlarged protection for the Fifth Amendment privilege.

The police in this case, in the very act of apprehending a suspect, were confronted with the immediate necessity of ascertaining the whereabouts of a gun which they had every reason to believe the suspect had just removed from his empty holster and discarded in the supermarket. So long as the gun was concealed somewhere in the supermarket, with its actual whereabouts unknown, it obviously posed more than one danger to the public safety: an accomplice might make use of it, a customer or employee might later come upon it.

In such a situation, if the police are required to recite the familiar *Miranda* warnings before asking the whereabouts of the gun, suspects in Quarles' position might well be deterred from responding. Procedural safeguards which deter a suspect from responding were deemed acceptable in *Miranda* in order to protect the Fifth Amendment privilege; when the primary social cost of those added protections is the possibility of fewer convictions, the *Miranda* majority was willing to bear that cost. Here, had the *Miranda* warnings deterred Quarles from responding to Officer Kraft's question about the whereabouts of the gun, the cost would have been something more than merely the failure to obtain evidence useful in convicting Quarles. Officer Kraft needed an answer to his question not simply to make his case against Quarles but to insure that further danger to the public did not result from the concealment of the gun in a public area.

We conclude that the need for answers to questions in a situation posing a threat to the public safety outweighs the need for the prophylactic rule protecting the Fifth Amendment's privilege against self-incrimination. We decline to place officers such as Officer Kraft in the untenable position of having to consider, often in a matter of seconds, whether it best serves society for them to ask the necessary questions without the *Miranda* warnings and render whatever probative evidence they uncover inadmissible, or for them to give the warnings in order to preserve the admissibility of evidence they might uncover but possibly damage or destroy their ability to obtain that evidence and neutralize the volatile situation confronting them.

In recognizing a narrow exception to the *Miranda* rule in this case, we acknowledge that to some degree we lessen the desirable clarity of that rule. . . . We think police officers can and will distinguish almost instinctively between questions necessary to secure their own safety or the safety of the public and questions designed solely to elicit testimonial evidence from a suspect.

The facts of this case clearly demonstrate that distinction and an officer's ability to recognize it. Officer Kraft asked only the question necessary to locate the missing gun before advising respondent of his rights. It was only after securing the loaded revolver and giving the warnings that he continued with investigatory questions about ownership and place of purchase of the gun. The exception which we recognize today, far from complicating the thought processes and the on-the-scene judgments of police officers, will simply free them to follow their legitimate instincts when confronting situations presenting a danger to the pubic safety. . . .

Justice O'Connor, concurring in the judgment in part and dissenting in part.

In *Miranda v. Arizona,* . . . the Court held unconstitutional, because inherently compelled, the admission of statements derived from in-custody questioning not preceded by an explanation of the privilege against self-incrimination and the consequences of forgoing it. Today, the Court concludes that overriding considerations of public safety justify the admission of evidence—oral statements and a gun—secured without the benefit of such warnings. . . . In so holding, the Court acknowledges that it is departing from prior precedent, . . . and that it is "lessen[ing] the desirable clarity of [the *Miranda*] rule". . . . Were the Court writing from a clean slate, I could agree with its holding. But *Miranda* is now the law and, in my view, the Court has not provided sufficient justification for departing from it or blurring its now clear strictures. Accordingly, I would require suppression of the initial statement taken from respondent in this case. On the other hand, nothing in *Miranda* or the privilege itself requires exclusion of nontestimonial evidence derived from informal custodial interrogation, and I therefore agree with the Court that admission of the gun in evidence is proper.

* * *

Since the time *Miranda* was decided, the Court has repeatedly refused to bend the literal terms of that decision. To be sure, the Court has been sensitive to the substantial burden the *Miranda* rules place on local law enforcement efforts, and consequently has refused to extend the decision or to increase its strictures on law enforcement agencies in almost any way. . . . Similarly, where "statements taken in violation of the *Miranda* principles [have] not be[en] used to prove the prosecution's case at trial," the Court has allowed evidence derived from those statements to be admitted. . . . But wherever an accused has been taken into "custody" and subjected to "interrogation" without warnings, the Court has consistently prohibited the use of his responses for prosecutorial purposes at trial. . . . As a consequence, the "meaning of *Miranda* has become reasonably clear and law enforcement practices have adjusted to its strictures."

* * *

In my view, a "public safety" exception unnecessarily blurs the edges of the clear line heretofore established and makes *Miranda*'s requirements more difficult to understand. In some cases, police will benefit because a reviewing court will find that an exigency excused their failure to administer required warnings. But in other cases, police will suffer because, though they thought an exigency excused their noncompliance, a reviewing court will view the "objective" circumstances differently and require exclusion of admissions thereby obtained. The end result will be a finespun new doctrine on public safety exigencies incident to custodial interrogation, complete with the hair-splitting distinctions that currently plague our Fourth Amendment jurisprudence. . . .

The justification the Court provides for upsetting the equilibrium that has finally been achieved—that police cannot and should not balance considerations of public safety against the individual's interest in avoiding compulsory testimonial self-incrimination—really misses the critical question to be decided. . . . *Miranda* has never been read to prohibit police from asking questions to secure the public safety. Rather, the critical question *Miranda* addresses is who shall bear the cost of securing the public safety when such questions are asked and answered: the defendant or the State. *Miranda,* for better or worse, found the resolution of that question implicit in the prohibition against compulsory self-incrimination and placed the burden on the State. When police ask custodial questions without administering required warnings, *Miranda* quite clearly requires that the answers received be presumed compelled and they be excluded from evidence at trial. . . .

The Court concedes, as it must, both that respondent was in "custody" and subject to "interrogation" and that his statement "the gun is over there" was compelled within the meaning of our precedent. . . . In my view, since there is nothing about an exigency that makes custodial interrogation any less compelling, a principled application of *Miranda* requires that respondent's statement be suppressed.

The Court below assumed, without discussion, that the privilege against self-incrimination required that the gun derived from respondent's statement also be suppressed, whether or not the State could independently link it to him. That conclusion was, in my view, incorrect.

* * *

Only the introduction of a defendant's own *testimony* is proscribed by the Fifth Amendment's mandate that no person "shall be compelled in any criminal case to be a witness against himself." That mandate does not protect an accused from being compelled to surrender *nontestimonial* evidence against himself.

* * *

[This] case is problematic because police compelled respondent not only to provide the gun but also to admit that he knew where it was and that it was his.

* * *

The values underlying the privilege [against self-incrimination] may justify exclusion of an unwarned person's out-of-court statements, as perhaps they may justify exclusion of statements and derivative evidence compelled under the threat of contempt. But when the only evidence to be admitted is derivative evidence such as a gun—derived not from actual compulsion but from a statement taken in the absence of *Miranda* warnings—those values simply cannot require suppression, at least no more so than they would for other such nontestimonial evidence.

* * *

[W]hen the *Miranda* violation consists of a deliberate and flagrant abuse of the accused's constitutional rights, amounting to a denial of due process, application of a broader exclusionary rule is warranted. Of course, "a defendant raising [such] a coerced-confession claim . . . must first prevail in a voluntariness hearing before his confession and evidence derived from it [will] become inadmissible." . . . By contrast, where the accused proves only that the police failed to administer the *Miranda* warnings, exclusion of the statement itself is all that will and should be required. Limitation of the *Miranda* prohibition to testimonial use of the statements themselves adequately serves the purposes of the privilege against self-incrimination. . . .

Justice Marshall, with whom Justice Brennan and Justice Stevens join, dissenting.

* * *

The majority's entire analysis rests on the factual assumption that the public was at risk during Quarles' interrogation. This assumption is completely in conflict with the facts as found by New York's highest court. Before the interrogation began, Quarles had been "reduced to a condition of physical powerlessness." . . . Contrary to the majority's speculations, . . . Quarles was not believed to have, nor did he in fact have, an accomplice to come to his rescue. When the questioning began, the arresting officers were sufficiently confident of their safety to put away their guns. As Officer Kraft acknowledged at the suppression hearing, "the situation was under control." . . . Based on Officer Kraft's own testimony, the New York Court of Appeals found: "Nothing suggests that any of the officers was by that time concerned for his own physical safety." . . . The Court of Appeals also determined that there was no evidence that the interrogation was prompted by the arresting officers' concern for the public safety. . . .

The majority attempts to slip away from these unambiguous findings of New York's highest court by proposing that danger be measured by objective facts rather than the subjective intentions of arresting officers. . . . Though clever, this ploy was anticipated by the New York Court of Appeals: "[T]here is no evidence in the record before us that there were exigent circumstances posing a risk to the public safety. . . ."

* * *

The New York court's conclusion that neither Quarles nor his missing gun posed a threat to the public's safety is amply supported by the evidence presented at the suppression hearing. Again, contrary to the majority's intimations, . . . no customers or employees were wandering about the store in danger of coming across Quarles' discarded weapon. Although the supermarket was open to the public, Quarles' arrest took place during the middle of the night when the store was apparently deserted except for the clerks at the check-out counter. The police could easily have cordoned off the store and searched for the missing gun. Had they done so, they would have found the gun forthwith. The police were well aware that Quarles had discarded his weapon somewhere near the scene of the arrest. As the State acknowledged before the New York Court of Appeals: "After Officer Kraft had handcuffed and frisked the defendant in the supermarket, *he knew with a high degree of certainty that the defendant's gun was within the immediate vicinity of the encounter.* He undoubtedly would have searched for it in the carton a few feet away without the defendant having looked in that direction and saying that it was there." Brief of the Appellant [State of New York] . . . (emphasis added).

Earlier this Term, four Members of the majority joined an opinion stating: "[Q]uestions of historical fact . . . must be determined, in the first instance, by state courts and deferred to, in the absence of 'convincing evidence' to the contrary, by the federal courts." . . . In this case, there was convincing evidence, indeed almost overwhelming, evidence to support the New York court's conclusion that Quarles' hidden weapon did not pose a risk either to the arresting officers or to the public. The majority ignores this evidence and sets aside the factual findings of the New York Court of Appeals. More cynical observers might well conclude that a state court's findings of fact "deserv[e] a 'high measure of deference,' " . . . only when deference works against the interests of a criminal defendant.

The majority's treatment of the legal issues presented in this case is no less troubling than its abuse of the facts. Before today's opinion, the Court had twice concluded that, under *Miranda v. Arizona* . . . police officers conducting custodial interrogations must advise suspects of their rights before any questions concerning the whereabouts of incriminating weapons can be asked. *Rhode Island v. Innis* . . . (1980) (dicta); *Orozco v. Texas* . . . (1969) (holding). Now the majority departs from these cases and rules that police may withhold *Miranda* warnings whenever custodial interrogations concern matters of public safety.

* * *

In a chimerical quest for public safety, the majority has abandoned the rule that brought 18 years of tranquility to the field of custodial interrogations. As the majority candidly concedes, . . . a public-safety exception destroys forever the clarity of *Miranda* for both law enforcement officers and members of the judiciary. The Court's candor cannot mask what a serious loss the administration of justice has incurred.

This case is illustrative of the chaos the "public-safety" exception will unleash. The circumstances of Quarles' arrest have never been in dispute. After the benefit of briefing and oral argument, the New York Court of Appeals, as previously noted, concluded that there was "no evidence in the record before us that there were exigent circumstances posing a risk to the public safety." . . . Upon reviewing the same facts and hearing the same arguments, a majority of this Court has come to precisely the opposite conclusion. . . .

If after plenary review two appellate courts so fundamentally differ over the threat to public safety presented by the simple and uncontested facts of this case, one must seriously question how law enforcement officers will respond to the majority's new rule in the confusion and haste of the real world. . . . Disagreements of the scope of the "public-safety" exception and mistakes in its application are inevitable.

* * *

In fashioning its "public-safety" exception to *Miranda,* the majority makes no attempt to deal with the constitutional presumption established by that case. The majority does not argue that police questioning about issues of public safety is any less coercive than custodial interrogations into other matters. The majority's only contention is that police officers could more easily protect the public if *Miranda* did not apply to custodial interrogations concerning the public's safety. But *Miranda* was not a decision about public safety; it was a decision about coerced confessions. Without establishing that interrogations concerning the public's safety are less likely to be coercive than other interrogations, the majority cannot endorse the "public-safety" exception and remain faithful to the logic of *Miranda v. Arizona.*

* * *

The majority should not be permitted to elude the [Fifth] Amendment's absolute prohibition simply by calculating special costs that arise when the public's safety is at issue. Indeed, were constitutional adjudication always conducted in such an ad hoc manner, the Bill of Rights would be a most unreliable protector of individual liberties. . . .

In 1984, the Court revisited a case it had previously decided in order to create another exception to the exclusionary rule's applicability to statements elicited through improper police questioning. In *Brewer v. Williams* (1977), the Court had excluded incriminating statements (as well as the victim's body discovered as a result of those statements) when police officers exploited their knowledge that a psychologically disturbed defendant was deeply religious after having agreed not to question the defendant outside of the presence of his attorney. The police officers' statements to the defendant as they drove in the police car included the following: "I want to give you something to think about while we're traveling down the road. . . . I feel that you yourself are the only person that knows where this little girl's body is. . . . I feel that we could stop and locate the body, that the parents of this little girl should be entitled to a Christian burial for the little girl who was snatched away from them on Christmas [Eve] and murdered" (430 U.S. at 392–93). This so-called "Christian Burial Speech" caused the defendant to lead the police to the victim's body. The majority of justices held that the defendant's right to counsel was violated by the interrogation outside of the presence of defense attorneys and ordered that the conviction be overturned. When Iowa was subsequently successful in gaining a second conviction of the defendant for murdering the girl, the defendant again challenged his conviction based on the use of improperly obtained incriminating statements. This time, however, a majority of justices held that the defendant could be convicted even without the incriminating statements because the state would have discovered the girl's body eventually anyway (*Nix v. Williams,* 1984). Thus, the Burger Court created an "inevitable discovery" exception to the exclusionary rule, which permits the prosecution to use evidence obtained through unlawful questioning on the theory that the police would have discovered the evidence inevitably anyway. In dissent, Justices Brennan and Marshall complained that the Court had never required the police to show that they would indeed have found the body based on the searches that were underway at the time.

The following year, the Court further reduced the protective power of *Miranda* through its decision in *Oregon v. Elstad* (1985). Police officers brought an arrest warrant to the home of an eighteen-year-old suspect to arrest him on burglary charges. The suspect's mother invited the police into the home. Without telling the youth that they had a warrant for his arrest or reading him his *Miranda* rights, one officer sat down with the suspect in the living room and told the suspect that the officer had a feeling that the suspect was involved in the burglary. The suspect immediately admitted, "I was there." The police transported the suspect to the police station, informed him of his *Miranda* rights, and gained a confession from the suspect. The Oregon Court of Appeals reversed the subsequent conviction for burglary. However, the U.S. Supreme Court reinstated the conviction. The Supreme Court found that the post-*Miranda* warning confession was not tainted by the earlier improper questioning. Justices Brennan and Marshall complained that defendants, after having made inadmissible incriminating statements prior to the delivery of *Miranda* warnings, will go ahead and confess again after *Miranda* warnings are given because they will believe that "the cat is out of the bag." According to John Decker, the Court's decision in *Oregon v. Elstad* produced a significant reduction in *Miranda*'s protections: "[T]he Court has created a mechanism where police easily circumvent *Miranda*. Simply put: interrogate the defendant without reference to the *Miranda* litany, extract an incriminating statement, and now, 'with the cat out of the bag,' instruct him pursuant to *Miranda* and have him repeat what he has already reported" (1992, pp. 72–73).

In 1986, the majority of justices further demonstrated their lack of skepticism about police tactics in seeking to gain incriminating information from defendants. An attorney obtained by a murder defendant's sister telephoned the police station to inquire whether the police intended to interrogate the defendant during the night and to insist on being present whenever questioning was to occur. The attorney was informed that the police would not interrogate the defendant or place him in a line-up until the following morning. Less than an hour later, the defendant was brought to an interrogation room for the first of a series of questioning sessions. The police did not inform the defendant that the attorney had called, and the defendant waived his right to have an attorney present. Eventually, the defendant confessed to the murder. The majority on the Court found no violation of the defendant's Fifth Amendment privilege against compelled self-incrimination or Sixth Amendment right to counsel. While Justice O'Connor's majority opinion said that it was "distaste[ful]" that the police deliberately misled the attorney, the Court found that lying to an attorney was not relevant to the defendant's privilege against compelled self-incrimination. As conservative justices often do in criminal justice cases, O'Connor used a balancing approach that compared the protection of individual's rights with society's desire to apprehend criminals: "Because, as *Miranda* holds, full comprehension of the rights to remain silent and request an attorney are sufficient to dispel whatever coercion is inherent in the interrogation process, a rule requiring the police to inform the suspect of an attorney's efforts to contact him would contribute to the protection of the Fifth Amendment privilege only incidentally, if at all. This minimal benefit, however, would come at a substantial cost to society's legitimate and substantial interest in securing admissions of guilt" (475 U.S. at 412). By contrast, Justice Stevens' dissenting opinion, joined by Justices Brennan and Marshall, raised grave concerns about police interference with communications between lawyers and clients and about the Court's endorsement of incommunicado questioning of suspects by the police: "Until today, incommunicado questioning has been viewed with the strictest scrutiny by this Court; today, incommunicado questioning is embraced as a societal goal of the highest order that justifies police deception of the shabbiest kind" (475 U.S. at 438–39). It was obvious from this decision that changes in the Court's composition had reduced the level of skepticism among Supreme

Court justices about police tactics in seeking confessions. While Chief Justice Warren had emphasized the dangers of permitting police to conduct incommunicado interrogations, the Burger Court majority was obviously more concerned about permitting police to seek incriminating statements from suspects during questioning.

Moran v. Burbine

475 U.S. 412, 106 S. Ct. 1135, 89 L. Ed. 2d 410 (1986)

■ After Cranston, Rhode Island, police arrested Brian Burbine for burglary, they realized that information previously obtained from a confidential informant indicated that Burbine might be the person responsible for an unsolved murder in Providence, Rhode Island, the previous year. Providence police officers came to the Cranston station at about 7 P.M. to question Burbine. Meanwhile, Burbine's sister, who was unaware that her brother was a murder suspect, telephoned the public defender's office to secure representation for Burbine on the burglary charge. At 8:15 P.M. a public defender telephoned the Cranston detective bureau at the police station to inform the police that she would represent Burbine and to inquire whether the police intended to question him that evening. The attorney was told that Burbine would not be questioned until the following morning. The attorney was not informed that Burbine was a murder suspect or that the Providence police had arrived in Cranston to question him. Shortly thereafter, Burbine was taken to an interrogation room for the first of a series of questioning sessions. He was given his *Miranda* warnings prior to each session, and he signed statements waiving his rights prior to signing a murder confession. The police did not inform Burbine that his sister had secured an attorney to represent him or that the attorney had offered to come to the station to advise Burbine if the police wished to question him. After being convicted of first degree murder, Burbine unsuccessfully filed an appeal with the Rhode Island Supreme Court alleging that his Fifth Amendment rights were violated. After losing his state appeals, Burbine filed a habeas corpus petition in the federal courts. He lost his claim in a U.S. district court, but a U.S. court of appeals ruled that the police had violated his privilege against compelled self-incrimination and his right to counsel by not informing him of the attorney's call on his behalf before he waived his Fifth and Sixth Amendment rights. The U.S. Supreme Court faced the issue of whether Burbine's confession should be rendered inadmissible because of a violation of his Fifth and Sixth Amendment rights.

The case is important because it clearly illustrates that the Burger Court justices were much less skeptical about police officers' motives and actions than were their predecessors on the Warren Court. As you read the case, consider the following questions: (1) Could Burbine make a "knowing and intelligent" waiver of his rights without being informed that he already had an attorney ready to represent him? (2) Does the Supreme Court's decision endorse and encourage dishonesty on the part of law enforcement officers?

Vote:

Six justices found the police officers' actions to be constitutional (Blackmun, Burger, O'Connor, Powell, Rehnquist, White).

Three justices found the police officers' actions to be unconstitutional (Brennan, Marshall, Stevens).

Justice O'Connor delivered the opinion of the Court.

* * *

We granted certiorari to decide whether a prearraignment confession preceded by an otherwise valid waiver must be suppressed either because the police misinformed an inquiring attorney about their plans concerning the suspect or because they failed to inform the suspect of the attorney's efforts to reach him.... We now reverse [the Court of Appeals decision upholding Burbine's claim].

* * *

[W]e have no doubt that the respondent validly waived his right to remain silent and to the presence of counsel. The voluntariness of the waiver is not at issue.... Nor is there any question about respondent's comprehension of the full panoply of rights set out in the *Miranda* warnings and of the potential consequences of a decision to relinquish them. Nonetheless, the Court of Appeals believed that the "[d]eliberate or reckless" conduct of the police, in particular their failure to inform respondent of the telephone call, fatally undermined the validity of an otherwise proper waiver.... We find this conclusion untenable as a matter of both logic and precedent.

Events occurring outside of the presence of the suspect and entirely unknown to him surely can have no bearing on the capacity to comprehend and knowingly relinquish a constitutional right.... No doubt the additional information would have been useful to respondent; perhaps even it might have affected his decision to confess. But we have never read the Constitution to require that the police supply a suspect with a flow of information to help him to calibrate his self-interest in deciding whether to speak or stand by his rights. . . . Once it is determined that a suspect's decision not to rely on his rights was uncoerced, that he at all times knew he could stand mute and request a lawyer, and that he was aware of the State's intention to use his statements to secure a conviction, the analysis is complete and the waiver is valid as a matter of law. The Court of Appeals' conclusion to the contrary was in error.

Nor do we believe that the level of the police's culpability in failing to inform respondent of the telephone call [from the attorney] has any bearing on the validity of the waivers. . . . [W]hether intentional or inadvertent, the state of mind of the police is irrelevant to the question of the intelligence and voluntariness of respondent's election to abandon his rights. Although highly inappropriate, even deliberate deception of an attorney could not possibly affect a suspect's decision to waive his *Miranda* rights unless he were at least aware of the incident. . . . Nor was the failure to inform respondent of the telephone call the kind of "trick[ery]" [discussed in the *Miranda* opinion] that can vitiate the validity of a waiver. . . . Granting that the "deliberate or reckless" withholding of information is objectionable as a matter of ethics, such conduct is only relevant to the constitutional validity of a waiver if it deprives a defendant of knowledge essential to his ability to understand the nature of his rights and the consequences of abandoning them. Because respondent's voluntary decision to speak was made with the full awareness and comprehension of all the information *Miranda* requires the police to convey, the waivers were valid.

* * *

At the outset, while we share respondent's distaste for the deliberate misleading of an officer of the court, reading *Miranda* to forbid police deception of an *attorney* "would cut [the decision] completely loose from its own explicitly stated rationale." . . . As is now well established, "[t]he . . . *Miranda* warnings are 'not themselves rights protected by the Constitution but [are] instead measures to insure that the [suspect's] right against compulsory self-incrimination [is] protected.' " . . . Their objective is not to mold police conduct for its own sake. Nothing in the Constitution vests in us the authority to mandate a code of behavior for state officials wholly unconnected to any federal right or privilege. The purpose of the *Miranda* warnings instead is to dissipate the compulsion inherent in custodial interrogation and, in so doing, guard against abridgement of the suspect's Fifth Amendment rights. Clearly, a rule that focused on how the police treat an attorney—conduct that has no relevance at all to the degree of compulsion experienced by the defendant during interrogation—would ignore both *Miranda*'s mission and its only source of legitimacy.

Nor are we prepared to adopt a rule requiring that the police inform a suspect of an attorney's efforts to reach him. While such a rule might add marginally to *Miranda*'s goal of dispelling the compulsion inherent in custodial interrogation, overriding practical considerations counsel against its adoption. As we have stressed on numerous occasions, "[o]ne of the principal advantages" of *Miranda* is the ease and clarity of its application. . . . We have little doubt that the approach urged by respondent and endorsed by the Court of Appeals would have the inevitable consequence of muddying *Miranda*'s otherwise relatively clear waters. The legal questions it would spawn are legion: To what extent should the police be held accountable for knowing that the accused has counsel? Is it enough that someone in the station house know of counsel's efforts to contact the suspect? Do counsel's efforts to talk to the suspect concerning one criminal investigation trigger the obligation to inform the defendant before interrogation may proceed on a wholly separate matter? We are unwilling to modify *Miranda* in a manner that would so clearly undermine the decision's central "virtue of informing police and prosecutors with specificity . . . what they may do in conducting [a] custodial interrogation, and of informing courts under what circumstances statements obtained during such interrogation are not admissible."

* * *

Moreover, problems of clarity to one side, reading *Miranda* to require the police in each instance to inform a suspect of an attorney's efforts to reach him would work a substantial and, we think, inappropriate shift in the subtle balance struck in that decision. Custodial interrogations implicate two competing concerns. On the one hand, "the need for police questioning as a tool for effective enforcement of criminals laws" cannot be doubted. . . . Admissions of guilt are more than merely "desirable[;]" . . . they are essential to society's compelling interest in finding, convicting, and punishing those who violate the law. On the other hand, the Court has recognized that the interrogation process is "inherently coercive" and that, as a consequence, there exists a substantial risk that the police will inadvertently traverse the fine line between legitimate efforts to elicit admissions and constitutionally impermissible compulsion. . . . *Miranda* attempted to reconcile these opposing concerns by giving the *defendant* the power to exert some control over the course of the interrogation. . . .

The position urged by respondent would upset this carefully drawn approach in a manner that is both unnecessary for the protection of the Fifth Amendment privilege and injurious to legitimate law enforcement. Because, as *Miranda* holds, full comprehension of the rights to remain silent and request an attorney are sufficient to dispel whatever coercion is inherent in the interrogation process, a rule requiring the police to inform the suspect of an attorney's efforts to contact him would contribute to the protection of the Fifth Amendment privilege only incidentally, if at all. This minimal benefit, however, would come at a substantial cost to society's legitimate and substantial interest in securing admissions of guilt. . . .

We acknowledge that a number of state courts have reached a contrary conclusion. . . . We recognize also that our interpretation of the Federal Constitution . . . is at odds with the policy recommendations embodied in the American Bar Association Standards of Criminal Justice. . . . Nothing we say today disables the States from adopting different requirements for the conduct of its employees and officials as a matter of state law. We hold only that the Court of Appeals erred in construing the Fifth Amendment to the Federal Constitution to require the exclusion of respondent's three confessions.

[Justice O'Connor's discussion and rejection of Burbine's Sixth Amendment arguments are omitted.]

Justice Stevens, with whom Justice Brennan and Justice Marshall join, dissenting.

This case poses fundamental questions about our system of justice. As this Court has long recognized, and reaffirmed only weeks ago, "ours is an accusatorial and not an inquisitorial system." . . . The Court's opinion today represents a startling departure from that basic insight.

The Court concludes that the police may deceive an attorney by giving her false information about whether her client will be questioned, and that the police may deceive a suspect by failing to inform him of his attorney's communications and efforts to represent him. For the majority, this conclusion, though "distaste[ful]," . . . is not even debatable. The deception of the attorney is irrelevant because the attorney has no right to information, accuracy, honesty, or fairness in the police response to her questions about her client. The deception of the client is acceptable, because, although the information would affect the client's assertion of his rights, the client's actions in ignorance of the availability of his attorney are voluntary, knowing, and intelligent; additionally society's interest in apprehending, prosecuting, and punishing criminals outweighs the suspect's interest in information regarding his attorney's efforts to communicate with him. Finally, even mendacious police interference in the communications between a suspect and his lawyer does not violate any notion of fundamental fairness because it does not shock the conscience of the majority.

* * *

The murder of Mary Jo Hickey was a vicious crime, fully meriting a sense of outrage and a desire to find and prosecute the perpetrator swiftly and effectively. . . .

The recognition that ours is an accusatorial, and not an inquisitorial system nevertheless requires that the government's actions, even in responding to this brutal crime, respect those liberties and rights that distinguish this society from most others. As Justice Jackson observed shortly after his return from Nuremberg, cases of this kind present "a real dilemma in a free society . . . for the defendant is shielded by such safeguards as no system of law except the Anglo-American concedes to him."

* * *

The Court's holding focuses on the period after a suspect has been taken into custody and before he has been charged with an offense. The core of the Court's holding is that police interference with an attorney's access to her client during that period is not unconstitutional. The Court reasons that a State has a compelling interest, not simply in custodial interrogation, but in lawyer-free, incommunicado custodial interrogation. Such incommunicado interrogation is so important that a lawyer may be given false information that prevents her presence and representation; it is so important that police may refuse to inform a suspect of his attorney's communications and immediate availability. This conclusion flies in the face of this Court's repeated expressions of deep concern about incommunicado questioning. Until today, incommunicado questioning has been viewed with the strictest scrutiny by this Court; today, incommunicado questioning is embraced as a societal goal of the highest order that justifies police deception of the shabbiest kind.

It is not only the Court's ultimate conclusion that is deeply disturbing; it is also its manner of reaching that conclusion. The Court completely rejects an entire body of law on the subject—the many carefully reasoned state decisions that have come to precisely the opposite conclusion. The Court similarly dismisses the fact that the police deception which it sanctions quite clearly violates the American Bar Association's Standards for Criminal Justice—Standards which the Chief Justice has described as "the single most comprehensive and probably the most monumental undertaking in the field of criminal justice ever attempted by the American legal profession in our national history," and which this Court frequently finds helpful. And, of course, the Court dismisses the fact that the American Bar Association has emphatically endorsed the prevailing state-court position and expressed its serious concern about the effect that a contrary view—a view, such as the Court's, that exalts incommunicado interrogation, sanctions police deception, and demeans the right to consult with an attorney—will have in police stations and courtrooms throughout this Nation. Of greatest importance, the Court misapprehends or rejects the central principles that have, for several decades, animated this Court's decisions concerning incommunicado interrogation.

Police interference with communications between an attorney and his client is a recurrent problem. The factual variations in the many state-court opinions condemning this interference as a violation of the Federal Constitution suggest the variety of contexts in which the problem emerges. In Oklahoma, police led a lawyer to several different locations while they interrogated the suspect; in Oregon, police moved a suspect to a new location when they learned that his lawyer was on his way; in Illinois, authorities failed to tell a suspect that his lawyer had arrived at the jail and asked to see him; in Massachusetts, police did not tell suspects that their lawyers were at or near the police station. In all these cases, the police not only failed to inform the suspect, but also misled the attorneys. The scenarios vary, but the core problem of police interference remains. . . .

The near-consensus of state courts and the legal profession's Standards about this recurrent problem lends powerful support to the conclusion that police may not interfere with communications between an attorney and the client whom they are questioning. Indeed, at least two opinions from this Court seemed to express precisely that view [citing *Miranda v. Arizona,* 1966 and *Escobedo v. Illinois,* 1964]. The Court today flatly rejects that widely held view and responds to this recurrent problem by adopting the most restrictive interpretation of the federal constitutional restraints on police deception, misinformation, and interference with attorney-client communications.

* * *

Well-settled principles of law lead inexorably to the conclusion that the failure to inform Burbine of the call from his attorney makes the subsequent waiver of his constitutional rights invalid. Analysis should begin with an acknowledgement that the burden of proving the validity of a waiver of constitutional rights is always on the *government.* When such a waiver occurs in a custodial setting, that burden is an especially heavy one because custodial interrogation is inherently coercive, because disinterested witnesses are seldom available to describe what actually happened, and because history has taught us that the danger of overreaching during incommunicado interrogation is so real.

* * *

[T]he Court's truncated analysis, which relies in part on a distinction between deception accomplished by means of an omission of a critically important fact and deception by means of a misleading statement, is simply untenable. If, as the Court asserts, "the analysis is at an end" as soon as the suspect is provided with enough information to have the *capacity* to understand and exercise his rights, I see no reason why the police should not be permitted to make the same kind of misstatements to the suspect that they are apparently allowed to make to his lawyer. *Miranda,* however, clearly establishes that both kinds of deception vitiate the suspect's waiver of his right to counsel.

* * *

The Court's balancing approach is profoundly misguided. The cost of suppressing evidence of guilt will always make the value of a procedural safeguard appear "minimal," "marginal," or "incremental." Indeed, the value of any trial at all seems like a "procedural technicality" when balanced against the interest in administering prompt justice to a murderer or a rapist caught redhanded. The individual interest in procedural safeguards that minimize the risk of error is easily discounted when the fact of guilt appears certain beyond doubt.

What is the cost of requiring the police to inform a suspect of his attorney's call? It would decrease the likelihood that custodial interrogation will enable the police to obtain a confession. This is certainly a real cost, but it is the same cost that this Court has repeatedly found necessary to preserve the character of our free society and our rejection of an inquisitorial system. . . .

* * *

If the court's cost-benefit analysis were sound, it would justify repudiation of a right to a warning about counsel itself. There is only a difference in degree between a presumption that advice about the immediate availability of a lawyer would not affect the voluntariness of a decision to confess, and a presumption that every citizen knows that he has a right to remain silent and therefore no warnings of any kind are needed. In either case, the withholding of information serves precisely the same law enforcement interests. And in both cases, the cost can be described as nothing more than an incremental increase in the risk that an individual will make an unintelligent waiver of his rights. . . .

* * *

The possible reach of the Court's opinion is stunning. For the majority seems to suggest that police may deny counsel all access to a client who is being held. At least since *Escobedo v. Illinois,* it has been widely accepted that police may not simply deny attorneys access to their clients who are in custody. This view has survived the recasting of *Escobedo* from a Sixth Amendment to a Fifth Amendment case that the majority finds so critically important. That this prevailing view is shared *by the police* can be seen in the state-court opinions detailing various forms of police deception of attorneys. For, if there were no obligation to give attorneys access, there would be no need to take elaborate steps to avoid access, such as shuttling the suspect to a different location, or taking the lawyer to different locations; police could simply refuse to allow the attorneys to see the suspect. But the law enforcement profession has apparently believed, quite rightly in my view, that denying lawyers access to their clients is impermissible. The Court today seems to assume that this view was error. . . .

* * *

This case turns on a proper appraisal of the role of the lawyer in our society. If a lawyer is seen as a nettlesome obstacle to the pursuit of wrongdoers—as in an inquisitorial society—then the Court's decision makes a good deal of sense. If a lawyer is seen as an aid to the understanding and protection of constitutional rights—as in an accusatorial society—then today's decision makes no sense at all.

Like the conduct of the police in the Cranston station on the evening of June 29, 1977, the Court's opinion today serves the goal of insuring that the perpetrator of a vile crime is punished. Like the police on that June night as well, however, the Court has trampled on well-established legal principles and flouted the spirit of our accusatorial system of justice.

I respectfully dissent.

The Burger Court never overturned *Miranda,* but it created exceptions to the rules requiring suspects to be informed of their rights and it created opportunities for police to use incriminating statements by suspects that were obtained through improper or questionable means. Although the Burger Court majority frequently indicated that society's interest in obtaining evidence against lawbreakers outweighed concerns about guarding against infringements on the privilege against compelled self-incrimination, there was little evidence that *Miranda* had actually reduced the number of convictions obtained by prosecutors. Studies conducted in several cities indicated that police officers did not always fully comply with the *Miranda* rules and that there was no discernible difference in conviction rates as a result of the *Miranda* requirement that arrestees be informed of their rights (Berger 1980, p. 131). In fact, many suspects continue to confess voluntarily despite being informed of their right to remain silent and to be represented by an attorney during questioning. Some suspects are overcome by guilt, but many others seek to obtain a more favorable plea bargain by cooperating with the police. Moreover, "[t]he typical felony suspect is young, poorly educated, and in many instances functionally illiterate" (Walker 1994, pp. 130–31) and thus many suspects possess little actual understanding of the fact that they need not respond to police officers' questions.

Double Jeopardy

The Burger Court made several decisions concerning the issue of double jeopardy. Although most people think of double jeopardy as barring a second prosecution after a final judgment is entered in a first proceeding, various rules have been used to activate double jeopardy claims in cases that never reached a verdict or judgment. As leading legal scholars have noted, "Under the rule traditionally applied in the federal courts, jeopardy attaches in jury trials when the jury is 'empaneled or sworn' and it attaches in bench trials [i.e., trial before a judge but not a jury] when the 'first witness is sworn' " (Kamisar, LaFave, and Israel 1990, p. 1418). Thus questions arise about whether there can be a renewed prosecution if a mistrial is declared during the course of the initial proceeding. The Burger Court's inclination to narrow the scope of double jeopardy protection is best illustrated by comparing two cases. In *United States v. Jenkins* (1975), reprosecution was barred by the Double Jeopardy Clause after a trial judge dismissed charges against a defendant before a verdict was reached during a trial. The dismissal was based on the judge's interpretation of the criminal elements necessary to prove the charge against the defendant. In *United States v. Scott* (1978), the Court reversed the *Jenkins* precedent. The Court permitted a second prosecution after dismissal of initial charges during trial. In *Scott,* the defendant had successfully sought dismissal because of the government's delay in initiating the first prosecution. This decision placed greater emphasis on double jeopardy as a right to protect against reprosecution of cases that had received final judgments rather than as a bar to reprosecution of uncompleted cases. Four dissenters, in an opinion by Justice White, disagreed and declared that "[t]he purpose of the [Double Jeopardy] Clause, which the Court today fails sufficiently to appreciate, is to protect the accused against the agony and risks attendant upon undergoing more than one criminal trial for any single offense" (437 U.S. at 105). In other words, the justices were divided over whether it is unconstitutionally burdensome for defendants to face new trials, even when their first trial never came to completion.

The Court also faced questions concerning whether or not defendants could be subjected to multiple prosecutions for a single action or set of actions. In *Heath v. Alabama* (1985), the conservative justices' concerns about federalism and the need to respect the authority of states to handle their own affairs appeared to take precedence over concerns about double jeopardy. Heath hired two men from Georgia to kill his girlfriend in Alabama. The men abducted the woman in Alabama and took her to Georgia where they killed her. Heath was indicted for murder in Georgia in November 1981 and entered a guilty plea in February 1982 in exchange for a life sentence with parole eligibility. In May 1982, Alabama indicted Heath for the offense of murder during kidnapping, and in January 1983 Heath was convicted by an Alabama jury and sentenced to death. Heath sought to invalidate his Alabama conviction on double jeopardy grounds because he had already been convicted for his actions in the Georgia court before he was even charged by Alabama. The Supreme Court, however, rejected Heath's double jeopardy claim. According to Justice O'Connor's majority opinion, "A State's interest in vindicating its sovereign authority through enforcement of its laws by definition can never be satisfied by another State's enforcement of its own laws" (474 U.S. at 93). In dissent, Justices Marshall and Brennan argued that "[w]hether viewed as a violation of the Double Jeopardy Clause or simply as an affront to the due process guarantee of fundamental fairness, Alabama's prosecution of petitioner cannot survive constitutional scrutiny" (474 U.S. at 103).

The Rehnquist Court Era

The changing composition of the Supreme Court has apparently had a significant impact on the high court's Fifth Amendment decisions. Table 10.1 indicates that the Burger and Rehnquist Courts were considerably less supportive of individuals' Fifth Amendment claims than was the Warren Court. The Warren Court supported individuals in more than half of its decisions (56%) while the Burger (31%) and Rehnquist Courts (21%) moved the Court increasingly toward decisions favorable to

TABLE 10.1: Liberal/Conservative Outcomes of Fifth Amendment Criminal Justice Cases for the Warren, Burger, and Rehnquist Courts, 1953-94 Terms

	Outcomes		
Court Era	Liberal	Conservative	Totals
Warren Court, 1953-68 Terms	57% (42)	43% (32)	74
Burger Court, 1969-85 Terms	31% (32)	69% (70)	102
Rehnquist Court, 1986-94 Terms	21% (6)	79% (23)	29
Totals	39% (80)	61% (125)	205

the government. Table 10.2 shows that the differences between the Court eras were most pronounced with respect to self-incrimination cases. The Warren Court's liberal percentage (66%) far exceeded those of the succeeding Court eras (Burger, 26%; Rehnquist, 19%). With respect to double jeopardy claims, it is clear from Table 10.3 that the Court has been consistently conservative across all three eras. In fact, the Burger Court was more liberal (38%) in double jeopardy cases than were either the Warren (28%) or Rehnquist Courts (23%). Unlike with other civil rights and liberties issues, the Warren Court had its lowest percentage of liberal decisions for any issue area in double jeopardy cases. All three tables indicate that the Rehnquist Court produced a lower percentage of liberal decisions than its immediate predecessor, the Burger Court.

Table 10.4 indicates the differences in the individual justices' decision-making patterns concerning the Fifth Amendment during the Rehnquist Court years. As in cases concerning other civil rights and liberties issues (described in other chapters), Chief Justice Rehnquist and Justices Thomas, O'Connor, Scalia, White, Powell, and Kennedy supported the government in more than three-quarters of Fifth Amendment cases, with Powell (100%), Thomas (100%), Rehnquist (97%), and O'Connor (93%) supporting conservative outcomes in every or nearly every case. Justice Breyer, who was appointed by Democratic President Clinton in 1994, also had a 100 percent pro-government record, but because he participated in only one Fifth

TABLE 10.2: Liberal/Conservative Outcomes of Fifth Amendment Self-Incrimination Cases for the Warren, Burger, and Rehnquist Courts, 1953-94 Terms

	Outcomes		
Court Era	Liberal	Conservative	Totals
Warren Court, 1953-68 Terms	66% (37)	34% (19)	56
Burger Court, 1969-85 Terms	26% (15)	74% (42)	57
Rehnquist Court, 1986-94 Terms	19% (3)	81% (13)	16
Totals	43% (55)	57% (74)	129

TABLE 10.3: Liberal/Conservative Outcomes of Fifth Amendment Double Jeopardy Cases for the Warren, Burger, and Rehnquist Courts, 1953-94 Terms

	Outcomes		
Court Era	Liberal	Conservative	Totals
Warren Court, 1953-68 Terms	28% (5)	72% (13)	18
Burger Court, 1969-85 Terms	38% (17)	62% (28)	45
Rehnquist Court, 1986-94 Terms	23% (3)	77% (10)	13
Totals	33% (25)	67% (51)	76

TABLE 10.4: Liberal/Conservative Voting Records of Justices of the Rehnquist Court in Fifth Amendment Criminal Justice Cases, 1986-94 Terms

Justices	Liberal Votes	Conservative Votes
Powell	0% (0)	100% (6)
Thomas	0% (0)	100% (6)
Breyer	0% (0)	100% (1)
Rehnquist	3% (1)	97% (28)
O'Connor	7% (2)	93% (26)
Scalia	17% (5)	83% (24)
Kennedy	18% (4)	82% (18)
White	24% (6)	76% (19)
Ginsburg	25% (1)	75% (3)
Souter	29% (2)	71% (5)
Blackmun	54% (15)	46% (13)
Stevens	59% (17)	41% (12)
Brennan	76% (16)	24% (5)
Marshall	95% (21)	5% (1)

Amendment case, it is too early to know how his decision-making pattern will develop. Justices Souter and Ginsburg each supported the government in nearly three-fourths of the small number of cases in which they participated after appointment to the Court. Justices Blackmun and Stevens supported the government in virtually half of the Fifth Amendment cases during the Rehnquist Court era. On many other issues, such as criminal punishment (see Chapter 12, Table 12.2), they supported the government much less frequently. In addition, Justice Brennan, usually a consistent supporter of individuals' claims, endorsed conservative outcomes in almost one-quarter of the Fifth Amendment cases. Only Justice Marshall, who supported a conservative outcome in just one case, supported Fifth Amendment rights claims as frequently as he supported liberal outcomes in the civil rights and liberties cases described in other chapters (95%).

The bloc voting analysis in Table 10.5 shows that a strong conservative voting bloc existed among the justices who participated in at least half of the Rehnquist Court's Fifth Amendment cases. Chief Justice Rehnquist and Justices O'Connor,

TABLE 10.5: Bloc Voting Analysis of the Rehnquist Court's Fifth Amendment Cases, 1986-94 Terms (Percent Agreement Rates)

	Scal	Whit	Rehn	OCon	Ken	Stev	Blkm	Bren	Mar
Scalia	—	84	83	82	77	57	54	43	27
White	84	—	80	88	78	79	64	38	27
Rehnquist	83	80	—	97	82	54	50	29	9
O'Connor	82	88	97	—	86	59	56	30	14
Kennedy	77	78	82	86	—	59	52	43	25
Stevens	57	79	54	59	59	—	70	50	41
Blackmun	54	64	50	56	52	70	—	76	64
Brennan	43	38	29	30	43	50	76	—	85
Marshall	27	27	9	14	25	41	64	85	—

Court mean = 58
Sprague Criterion = 79
Conservative bloc: Scalia, White, Rehnquist, O'Connor, Kennedy = 84
Liberal bloc: Brennan, Marshall = 85

Table 10.6: Liberal/Conservative Outcomes of Fifth Amendment Criminal Justice Cases During the Rehnquist Court Era by Term, 1986-94 Terms

	Outcomes		
Term	Liberal	Conservative	Totals
1986	0% (0)	100% (6)	6
1987	25% (1)	75% (3)	4
1988	17% (1)	83% (5)	6
1989	33% (2)	67% (4)	6
1990	100% (1)	0% (0)	1
1991	0% (0)	100% (1)	1
1992	0% (0)	100% (1)	1
1993	33% (1)	67% (2)	3
1994	0% (0)	100% (1)	1
Totals	21% (6)	79% (23)	29

Scalia, Kennedy, and White formed a highly cohesive voting bloc that had an average interagreement score of 84 percent. Justices Brennan and Marshall, who had both retired by 1992, formed the only liberal voting bloc.

The term-by-term presentation of liberal versus conservative decisions in Table 10.6 does not indicate that any individual retirements and new appointments directly altered the outcomes in Fifth Amendment cases. Most of the Rehnquist Court's self-incrimination and double jeopardy cases were accepted and decided prior to Justice Brennan's retirement in 1990. After Justice Brennan's retirement, the Court accepted very few of such cases for decision. One can only speculate about whether Brennan's departure removed a vote for granting certiorari in Fifth Amendment cases and therefore affected the Court's willingness to accept such cases. The addition of Justice Ginsburg during the 1993 term coincided with an increase in Fifth Amendment decisions. After deciding only one case during each of the preceding three terms, the Court decided three cases. Again, we can only speculate on whether Ginsburg added a new vote for granting certiorari in such cases during that term, although her presence and that of newcomer Justice Breyer in the 1994 term had no noticeable impact on the number of cases accepted. Only two liberal outcomes were produced after Brennan's retirement. The lone liberal self-incrimination decision came in a five-to-four decision in *Arizona v. Fulminante* (1991), in which the Court found that a confession was coerced when an undercover police officer posing as a prisoner encouraged another prisoner to make self-incriminating statements by pretending to be an organized crime boss who could protect the other prisoner. However, commentators do not regard that case as a liberal victory because Scalia deserted the majority on a separate issue in the same case. He helped to form a different five-member majority to establish a new conservative rule that coerced confessions could be regarded as "harmless errors" that need not necessarily lead to reversals of convictions (Smith 1992–93, pp. 208–9). In double jeopardy cases, the only liberal decision was a five-to-four opinion finding a violation of double jeopardy in the imposition of a state tax for storing marijuana when the individuals involved had already received criminal punishments for their possession of the controlled substance (*Department of Revenue of Montana v. Kurth Ranch,* 1994).

The Rehnquist Court's inclination to produce conservative outcomes in Fifth Amendment cases is illustrated by Table 10.7. Nearly 80 percent of the Court's decisions favored the government, including one of the two "major" cases (*Pennsylvania v. Muniz,* 1990) and the lone decision that created a new conservative precedent (*United States v. Dixon,* 1993).

Self-Incrimination

Like the self-incrimination decisions during the Burger Court era, the Rehnquist Court limited the scope of *Miranda* rights without overturning the landmark precedent. For example, in *Colorado v. Connelly* (1986), a mentally ill suspect waived his *Miranda* rights and confessed to committing murder. A psychiatrist testified that the suspect was capable of understanding his *Miranda* rights even though he suffered from "command hallucinations," a psychotic condition in which he believed that he was following "the voice of God" in confessing to the murder. A six-member majority on the Court found the confession to be voluntary and admissible because there had been no coercive actions by the police. The dissenters, Justices Brennan, Marshall, and Stevens, argued that whether coercive police action was involved in the questioning, the suspect could not voluntarily waive his *Miranda* rights when his waiver was produced as the result of mental illness.

In another example, *Braswell v. United States* (1988), a five-member majority ruled that the president of a corporation could not resist a subpoena to produce corporate records based on the Fifth Amendment claim that the records would incriminate him. Chief Justice Rehnquist's majority opinion asserted, among other things, that the recognition of a Fifth Amendment right in this context would impede the government's ability to investigate and prosecute white-collar crime. The case produced an unusual split among the justices as consistent conservatives Kennedy and Scalia, joined by the most liberal justices, Brennan and Marshall, argued that the subpoena violated the corporate officer's privilege against compelled self-incrimination.

One of the Court's few major decisions on the Fifth Amendment clarified the admissibility of evidence when drunk-driving suspects are arrested by the police. A suspect was taken to the police station where he was videotaped responding to questions about his name, address, date of birth, and other personal matters. He was also taped doing various sobriety tests, including counting, performing simple tasks,

TABLE 10.7: A Framework for the Doctrinal Analysis of the Rehnquist Court's Fifth Amendment Criminal Justice Cases, 1986–94 Terms

Major or Minor Importance	Majority or Plurality Opinion	Treatment of Precedent: Creation of New Liberal Precedent	Liberal Modification of Existing Precedent	Liberal Interpretation of Existing Precedent	Conservative Interpretation of Existing Precedent	Conservative Modification of Existing Precedent	Creation of New Conservative Precedent
Major	Majority		Dept of Rev. Mont. v. Kurth Ranch (1994)		Penn. v. Muniz (1990)		
	Plurality						
Minor	Majority		Ariz. v. Roberson (1988) Grady v. Corbin (1990)	U.S. v. Halper (1989) Minnick v. Miss. (1990) Ariz. v. Fulminante (1991)	Colorado v. Connelly (1986) Colorado v. Spring (1987) Conn. v. Barrett (1987) Greer v. Miller (1987) Ricketts v. Adamson (1987) Ariz. v. Mauro (1987) U.S. v. Robinson (1988) Braswell v. U.S. (1988) Lockhart v. Nelson (1988) Doe v. U.S. (1988) U.S. v. Brace (1989) Ala. v. Smith (1989) Illinois v. Perkins (1989) Dowling v. U.S. (1990) U.S. v. Felix (1992) U.S. v. Davis (1994) Schiro v. Farley (1994)	Jones v. Thomas (1989 Duckworth v. Eagan (1989) Baltimore v. Bouknight (1990)	U.S. v. Dixon (1993)
	Plurality						

and refusing a request to take a breathalyzer test. Afterward, the suspect was read his *Miranda* rights. The suspect sought to have the videotape excluded as a violation of his privilege against compelled self-incrimination because he was asked questions and instructed to perform tasks before being informed of his rights. A slim majority of justices excluded the suspect's response to one question about whether he could calculate the date of his sixth birthday, but all of the justices except Marshall regarded the remainder of the videotape as admissible because it presented nontestimonial evidence. In other words, it showed his condition and did not rely on him incriminating himself through his own testimony (*Pennsylvania v. Muniz,* 1990).

The Rehnquist Court produced liberal outcomes in only three self-incrimination cases. These three decisions had only a modest impact on criminal defendants' rights, but they clearly reinforced the Rehnquist Court's commitment to preserve *some* aspects of the *Miranda* principles and the exclusionary rule for certain kinds of Fifth Amendment violations. As previously mentioned, the Court's decision in *Arizona v. Fulminante* (1991) had both liberal and conservative implications when the prisoner's confession to an undercover officer posing as an inmate was deemed coerced. The Court had clearly established in another case that undercover officers need not give *Miranda* warnings to other prisoners when posing as convicted offenders in correctional institutions because inmates generally cannot be coerced when they do not know that they are being questioned by law enforcement officers (*Illinois v. Perkins,* 1989). However, the undercover officer in *Arizona v. Fulminante* coerced the confession in the eyes of five justices because he told the prisoner that he, in playing a role as an imprisoned organized crime boss, would protect the prisoner from other inmates if he made a full confession.

In *Minnick v. Mississippi* (1990), over the dissents of Scalia and Rehnquist, the Court declared that law enforcement officers cannot reinitiate questioning outside of the presence of counsel after an arrestee has asserted his right to counsel and consulted with his attorney. Scalia complained that the "Court today establishes an irrebuttable presumption that a criminal suspect, after invoking his *Miranda* right to counsel, can *never* validly waive that right during any police-initiated encounter, even after the suspect has been provided multiple *Miranda* warnings and has actually consulted with his attorney" (498 U.S. at 156). Scalia and Rehnquist argued that the Court should simply examine the voluntariness of individual confessions rather than enforce a rule barring reinitiation of questioning.

In its only liberal modification of existing precedent involving self-incrimination (*Arizona v. Roberson,* 1988), the Court expanded the rule from *Edwards v. Arizona* (1981) that officers must cease questioning when a suspect requests to communicate exclusively through an attorney. In an expansion of the principle, the majority applied the *Edwards* rule to situations in which police wish to question the suspect about a crime other than the one for which the suspect has already secured representation. Chief Justice Rehnquist and Justice Kennedy dissented because they believed that the Court was depriving law enforcement officers of a legitimate investigative technique.

The justices' conservative modifications of precedent and creation of a new conservative precedent had a more significant effect on constitutional law and public policy regarding self-incrimination than did their liberal decisions. In *Duckworth v. Eagan* (1989), the majority of justices permitted police to change the content of *Miranda* warnings in a way that could diminish suspects' awareness of their rights. A suspect was arrested for attempted murder after stabbing a woman. When the police officers informed the suspect of his rights to remain silent and to be represented by an attorney during questioning, they added an additional statement:

"We have no way of giving you a lawyer, but one will be appointed for you, if you wish, if and when you go to court" (492 U.S. at 198). The suspect subsequently confessed to the stabbing, but later sought to have his confession excluded based on the improper and confusing *Miranda* warnings delivered by the police prior to questioning. In approving the police officers' actions, Chief Justice Rehnquist asserted that "[w]e have never insisted that *Miranda* warnings be given in the exact form described in that decision. . . . The inquiry [for reviewing courts] is simply whether the warnings reasonably 'conve[y] to [a suspect] his rights as required by *Miranda*.' We think the initial warnings given to respondent touched all of the bases required by *Miranda*" (492 U.S. at 203). In a strident dissenting opinion joined by Justices Brennan, Stevens, and Blackmun, Justice Marshall accused the five-member majority of "disemboweling *Miranda* directly" (492 U.S. at 221). According to the dissenters, the majority had defeated the fundamental purpose of *Miranda* by inviting police officers to confuse suspects:

> *In concluding that the first warning given to respondent Eagan . . . satisfies the dictates of* Miranda, *the majority makes a mockery of that decision. . . . What goes wholly overlooked in the Chief Justice's analysis is that the recipients of police warnings are often frightened suspects unlettered in the law, not lawyers or judges or others schooled in interpreting legal or semantic nuance. . . . [A] warning qualified by an "if and when" caveat still fails to give a suspect any indication of* when *he will be taken to court. Upon hearing the warnings given in this case, a suspect would likely conclude that no lawyer would be provided until trial* (492 U.S. at 215–17).

Commentators feared that the *Duckworth* decision would encourage police officers to experiment with various forms of phrasing for *Miranda* warnings with the hope of confusing suspects enough to elicit incriminating statements (Kamisar 1989).

Duckworth v. Eagan

492 U.S. 195, 109 S. Ct. 2875, 106 L. Ed. 2d 166 (1989)

The defendant was identified by a woman as her attacker who had stabbed her nine times and left her for dead. Before being questioned by police, the defendant signed a waiver form that included the following statement among the usual elements of the *Miranda* warnings: "We have no way of giving you a lawyer, but one will be appointed for you, if you wish, if and when you go to court." The defendant maintained that he was innocent during initial questioning. The following day, however, after being read the traditional *Miranda* rights by officers, he confessed to the crime. At trial, the defendant challenged the first *Miranda* warnings as defective, but the judge permitted the confession to be used against him. He was convicted and state appellate courts upheld his conviction. When he challenged his conviction through a habeas corpus petition in the federal courts, the U.S. Court of Appeals reversed his conviction by deciding that the initial *Miranda* warnings did not clearly indicate to him that he was entitled to representation by an attorney during questioning. The U.S. Supreme Court considered whether the phrasing of the *Miranda* warnings fulfilled the requirements of the Constitution.

The case is important because it demonstrated the Rehnquist Court majority's view that the *Miranda* precedent did not impose precise requirements on police for how they must treat criminal suspects. As you read the case, consider the following questions: (1) Did the warning given to the defendant fulfill the objective of *Miranda* or did the phrasing create the potential for confusion? (2) How will police officers inform suspects of their *Miranda* rights in the aftermath of this decision? (3) How capable are criminal suspects of understanding the scope of the Fifth and Sixth Amendment rights based on the warnings they receive from the police?

Vote:

Five justices found the police officers' actions to be constitutional (Kennedy, O'Connor, Rehnquist, Scalia, White).

Four justices found the police officers' actions to be unconstitutional (Blackmun, Brennan, Marshall, Stevens).

Chief Justice Rehnquist delivered the opinion of the Court.

Respondent confessed to stabbing a woman nine times after she refused to have sexual relations with him, and he was convicted of attempted murder. Before confessing, respondent was given warnings by the police, which included the advice that a lawyer would be appointed "if and when you go to court." The United States Court of Appeals for the Seventh Circuit held that such advice did not comply with the requirements of *Miranda v. Arizona* . . . (1966). We disagree and reverse.

* * *

We have never insisted that *Miranda* warnings be given in the exact form described in that decision. In *Miranda* itself, the Court said that "[t]he warnings required and the waiver necessary in accordance with our opinion today are, *in the absence of a fully effective equivalent,* prerequisites to the admissibility of any statement made by a defendant." 384 U.S. at 476 (emphasis added). * * *

* * *

We think the initial warnings given to respondent touched all of the bases required by *Miranda.* The police told respondent that he had the right to remain silent, that anything he said could be used against him in court, that he had the right to speak to an attorney before and during questioning, that he had "this right to the advice and presence of a lawyer even if [he could] not afford to hire one," and that he had the "right to stop answering at any time until [he] talked to a lawyer." . . . As noted, the police also added that they could not provide respondent with a lawyer, but that one would be appointed "if and when you go to court." The Court of Appeals thought this "if and when you go to court" language suggested that "only those accused who can afford an attorney have the right to have one present before answering any questions," and "implie[d] that if the accused does not 'go to court,' *i.e.*[,] the government does not file charges, the accused is not entitled to counsel at all."

* * *

In our view, the Court of Appeals misapprehended the effect of the inclusion of "if and when you go to court" language in *Miranda* warnings. First, this instruction accurately described the procedure for the appointment of counsel in Indiana. Under Indiana law, counsel is appointed at the defendant's initial appearance in court, . . . and formal charges must be filed at or before that hearing. . . . We think it must be relatively commonplace for a suspect after receiving *Miranda* warnings, to ask *when* he will obtain counsel. The "if and when you go to court" advice simply anticipates that question. Second, *Miranda* does not require that attorneys be producible on call, but only that the suspect be informed, as here, that he has the right to an attorney before and during questioning, and that an attorney would be appointed for him if he could not afford one. The Court in *Miranda* emphasized that it was not suggesting that "each police station must have a 'station house lawyer' present at all times to advise prisoners." . . . If the police cannot provide appointed counsel, *Miranda* requires only that the police not question a suspect unless he waives his right to counsel. . . . Here, respondent did just that. . . .

[*Justice O'Connor's concurring opinion, joined by Justice Scalia, is omitted.*]

Justice Marshall, with whom Justice Brennan, Justice Blackmun, and Justice Stevens join, dissenting.

The majority holds today that a police warning advising a suspect that he is entitled to an appointed lawyer only "if and when he goes to court" satisfies the requirements of *Miranda v. Arizona* . . . . The majority reaches this result by seriously mischaracterizing that decision. Under *Miranda,* a police warning must *"clearly infor[m]"* a suspect taken into custody "that if he cannot afford an attorney one will be appointed for him *prior to any questioning* if he so desires." . . . (emphasis added). A warning qualified by an "if and when you go to court" caveat does nothing of the kind; instead, it leads the suspect to believe that a lawyer will not be provided until some indeterminate time in the future *after questioning.* I refuse to acquiesce in the continuing debasement of this historic precedent [citing *Oregon v. Elstad,* 1985 and *New York v. Quarles,* 1984], . . . and therefore I dissent.

* * *

In concluding that the first warning given to respondent Eagan, . . . satisfies the dictates of *Miranda,* the majority makes a mockery of that decision. Eagan was initially advised that he had the right to the presence of counsel before and during questioning. But in the very next breath, the police informed Eagan that, if he could not afford a lawyer, one would be appointed to represent him only "if and when" he went to court. As the Court of Appeals found, Eagan could easily have concluded from the "if and when" caveat that only "those accused who can afford an attorney have the right to have one present before answering any questions; those who are not so fortunate must wait." . . . Eagan was, after all, never told that questioning would be *delayed* until a lawyer was appointed "if and when" Eagan did, in fact, go to court. Thus, the "if and when" caveat may well have had the effect of negating the initial promise that counsel could be present. At best, a suspect like Eagan "would not know . . . whether or not he had a right to the services of a lawyer."

* * *

In lawyerlike fashion, the Chief Justice parses the initial warnings given Eagan and finds that the most plausible interpretation is that Eagan would not be questioned until a lawyer was appointed when he later appeared in court. What goes wholly overlooked in the Chief Justice's analysis is that the recipients of police warnings are often frightened suspects unlettered in law, not lawyers or judges or others schooled in interpreting legal or semantic nuance. Such suspects can hardly be expected to interpret, in as facile a manner as the Chief Justice, "the pretzel-like warnings here—intertwining, contradictory, and ambiguous as they are." . . . The majority thus refuses to recognize that "[t]he warning of a right to counsel would be hollow if not couched in terms that would convey to the indigent—the person most often subjected to interrogation—the knowledge that he too has the right to have counsel present."

* * *

Even if the typical suspect could draw the inference the majority does—that questioning will not commence until a lawyer is provided at a later court appearance—a warning qualified by an "if and when" caveat still fails to give a suspect any indication of *when* he will be taken to court. Upon hearing the warnings given in this case, a suspect would likely conclude that no lawyer would be provided until trial. In common parlance, "going to court" is synonymous with "going to trial." Furthermore, the negative implication of the caveat is that, if the suspect is never taken to court, he "is not entitled to an attorney at all." . . . An unwitting suspect harboring uncertainty on this score is precisely the sort of person who may feel compelled to talk "voluntarily" to the police, without the presence of counsel, in an effort to extricate himself from his predicament:

> "The suspect is effectively told that he can talk now or remain in custody—in an alien, friendless, harsh world—for an indeterminate length of time. To the average accused, still hoping at this stage to be home on time, the implication that his choice is to answer questions right away or remain in custody until that nebulous time 'if and when' he goes to court is a coerced choice of the most obvious kind." *Dickerson v. State* . . . (1972) [Indiana state court opinion].

* * *

But if a suspect does not understand that a lawyer will be made available within a reasonable period of time after he has been taken into custody and advised of his rights, the suspect may decide to talk to the police *for that reason alone.* The threat of an indefinite deferral of interrogation, in a system like Indiana's, thus constitutes an effective means by which the police can pressure a suspect to speak without the presence of counsel. Sanctioning such police practices simply because the warnings given do not misrepresent state law does nothing more than let the state-law tail wag the federal constitutional dog.

* * *

It poses no great burden on law enforcement officers to eradicate the confusion stemming from the "if and when" caveat. Deleting the sentence containing the offending language is all that needs to be done. . . . Purged of this language, the warning tells the suspect in a straightforward fashion that he has the right to the presence of a lawyer before and during questioning, and that a lawyer will be appointed if he cannot afford one. The suspect is given no reason to believe that the appointment of an attorney may come after interrogation. To the extent one doubts that it is the "if and when" caveat that is the source of the confusion, compare the initial warning given Eagan, . . . and the crystal-clear warning currently used by the FBI. . . . The majority's claim that the two are indistinguishable in the message conveyed to a suspect defies belief. I dissent.

Not content with disemboweling *Miranda* directly, Justice O'Connor seeks to do so indirectly as well, urging that federal courts be barred from considering *Miranda* claims on habeas corpus review. . . .

* * *

It is not only disapprobation for federal habeas review that pervades Justice O'Connor's concurring opinion, but also a profound distaste for *Miranda.* How else to explain the remarkable statement that "*no* significant federal values are at stake" when *Miranda* claims are raised in federal habeas corpus proceedings?

* * *

In any event, I vehemently oppose the suggestion that it is for the Court to decide, based on our own vague notions of comity, finality, and the intrinsic value of particular constitutional rights, which claims are worthy of collateral federal review and which are not. . . . The federal courts have been reviewing *Miranda* claims on federal habeas for 23 years, and Congress has never even remotely indicated that they have been remiss in doing so. To the extent Justice O'Connor is unhappy with *Miranda,* she should address the decision head on. But an end run through the habeas statute is judicial activism at its worst. ■

In *Baltimore City Department of Social Services v. Bouknight* (1990), a mother, who was under special child custody restrictions because of evidence that she had abused her child, was jailed for contempt of court for failing to produce or provide the whereabouts of the child whom government officials believed she may have killed. The mother asserted that the order to produce or provide information about the child violated her privilege against compelled self-incrimination. The case presented the justices with a new issue that the Court had never before faced. A majority of justices found no violation of the mother's rights by analogizing her situation to that of corporate officials who are ordered to produce documents that may be incriminating. According to Justice O'Connor's opinion, "The Court has on several occasions recognized that the Fifth Amendment privilege may not be invoked to resist compliance with a regulatory regime constructed to effect the State's public purposes unrelated to the enforcement of its criminal laws" (110 S.Ct. at 905). Justices Marshall and Brennan dissented because they thought that a court order issued to an individual who faced a criminal investigation was not the same as a general civil regulation, such as one governing corporations and their financial documents.

In the self-incrimination cases that it accepted for hearing, the Rehnquist Court issued decisions that reduced the scope of Fifth Amendment protections for individuals. In the *Duckworth* and *Bouknight* decisions, for example, the Court relaxed guidelines that might have limited the ability of authorities to gain information from a defendant. Throughout this period, the justices had many opportunities to reverse *Miranda*. However, they declined to do so. In a few cases, they decided in favor of individuals, and in so doing, the justices indicated that the essence of *Miranda* would remain in effect, although law enforcement officers would have much greater flexibility in investigating cases and questioning suspects in many situations.

Double Jeopardy

The Rehnquist Court's double jeopardy decisions consistently rejected claims of individuals. One of the Court's three liberal decisions supporting the claim of an individual (*Grady v. Corbin,* 1990) was later overturned by a subsequent conservative decision (*United States v. Dixon,* 1993). Another liberal outcome was a unanimous decision in which the entire Court declared that the government could not pursue punitive civil fines against an individual who had already been convicted and received criminal punishment for the same acts of filing false Medicare claims (*United States v. Halper,* 1988). The most recent liberal decision concerned a similar issue of a state tax imposed on people who had already received criminal punishments for growing marijuana (*Department of Revenue of Montana v. Kurth Ranch,* 1994).

In favoring the government with its decisions, the Rehnquist Court identified a variety of situations in which defendants can be subjected to new prosecutions and punishments. For example, in *Ricketts v. Adamson* (1987), a five-member majority on the Court permitted reprosecution of a defendant on first-degree murder charges after the prosecution invalidated his plea agreement for second-degree murder by claiming that he had failed to fulfill the agreement. The state claimed that the agreement included a waiver of any potential double jeopardy claims. The defendant had agreed to testify against codefendants as part of his plea agreement, and he did so. However, he refused to testify in a second set of trials when his codefendants' convictions were overturned because he believed that he had fulfilled his plea agreement by testifying at the initial trials. While Justice White's majority opinion approved the state's decision to retry the defendant on first-degree murder charges and sentence him to death, the four dissenters (Brennan, Marshall, Stevens, and

Blackmun) questioned the prosecution's assertion that the defendant had indeed violated his plea agreement and asserted that the defendant needed to violate the agreement knowingly in order to waive his double jeopardy rights. In *Dowling v. United States* (1990), the Court permitted the admission of witness testimony against a defendant concerning a separate criminal charge for which he had already been acquitted.

The Court's lone conservative modification of existing precedent arose out of a complicated factual situation in which a defendant was sentenced to fifteen years for robbery and a subsequent life sentence for felony-murder arising out of the same robbery, which was to be served after completion of the sentence for robbery. When the Missouri Supreme Court determined in separate cases that an offender could not be given two sentences for a felony-murder and the underlying felony, the prisoner claimed that when he fulfilled his punishment by completing the robbery sentence the state could not continue his imprisonment on the claim that he was actually serving his life sentence for felony-murder all along. A five-member majority endorsed the state's actions vacating the robbery conviction and resentencing him to life in prison for felony-murder by declaring that the years he served on his original now-invalid robbery conviction were actually applied toward his felony-murder conviction (*Jones v. Thomas,* 1989). However, a strong dissenting opinion by Justice Scalia, joined by Justices Brennan, Marshall, and Stevens, noted that this case was indistinguishable from prior precedents dating back to 1874 in which the Supreme Court had declared that the state's power to punish wrongdoers ceases when the offenders fulfill one of the alternative punishments provided by law for a criminal act and imposed upon them by the trial court.

The Rehnquist Court's most notable and controversial double jeopardy decisions concerned the *Blockburger* issue of when a second criminal charge can be pursued based on a single criminal act or set of actions. In *Grady v. Corbin* (1990), a motorist crossed the centerline on a highway and smashed into an oncoming car, resulting in one person's death and another person's serious injury. The motorist was immediately charged with driving while intoxicated, and an assistant prosecutor began gathering evidence for a homicide prosecution. This assistant prosecutor did not inform the prosecutors in traffic court about his investigation. The defendant appeared in traffic court two weeks after the accident and, with no prosecutors present, entered a guilty plea to the traffic citations. At the sentencing hearing three weeks later, neither the judge nor the prosecutor in attendance knew that the traffic accident had produced a fatality because the traffic court prosecutor could not locate the file for the case. Thus the judge fined the defendant and temporarily revoked his license as punishment for the traffic citations. Two months later, a grand jury indicted the defendant for reckless manslaughter, and the defendant challenged the indictment as a violation of the Double Jeopardy Clause. A five-member majority of the Supreme Court supported the defendant's claim and extended the *Blockburger* rule by holding that "the Double Jeopardy Clause bars subsequent prosecution if, to establish an essential element of an offense charged in that prosecution, the government will prove conduct that constitutes an offense for which the defendant has already been prosecuted" (495 U.S. at 510). The case attracted attention and criticism from interested members of the public and legal community because of the unpopular outcome of an apparently guilty offender escaping punishment for a homicide simply because the prosecutor's office did not coordinate its case-processing procedures effectively. Justice Scalia's dissenting opinion castigated the majority's opinion and declared "[e]ven if we had no constitutional text and no prior case law to rely upon, rejection of today's opinion is adequately supported by the modest desire to protect our criminal justice system from ridicule" (495 U.S. at 542). Although Scalia's sarcastic characterization of the Court's opinion is questionable, he was correct in his prediction about what would happen in subsequent cases: "A limitation that is so unsupported in reason and so absurd in application is unlikely to survive" (495 U.S. at 543). The *Grady* precedent did not survive, but its demise is directly attributable to a change in the Court's composition rather than to any inherent deficiencies in the majority opinion's reasoning.

The Court revisited the double jeopardy issue in 1993 after two members of the *Grady* majority, Warren Court holdovers Brennan and Marshall, had been replaced by President Bush's appointees, Justices Souter and Thomas. In *United States v. Dixon* (1993), two defendants violated the conditions of their pretrial release for a pending criminal charge by being arrested, respectively, for assault and possession of narcotics. When they were convicted of criminal contempt for violating their bail conditions, they sought dismissal of their narcotics and assault indictments based on double jeopardy claims from the *Grady* decision. They argued that their criminal contempt convictions for violating release conditions precluded their prosecution for other charges arising out of the same incidents because the government would have to prove conduct that constituted an offense for which they had already been prosecuted. However, the four *Grady* dissenters, Scalia, Rehnquist, Kennedy, and O'Connor, had gained the fifth vote that they needed through Justice Thomas's replacement of Justice Marshall. Thus a slim five-member majority reversed the liberal *Grady* decision and returned to using the "same-elements" test from *Blockburger*. Thus, although the Court barred the narcotics prosecution, the majority found that the assault charges were not barred by the *Blockburger* test because of the differing knowledge and intent requirements for criminal contempt and assault. As often happens when a precedent is overturned in a few short years due to a change in the Court's composition, the dissenters complained about the propriety of the majority's actions. As expressed by Justice Blackmun, "I also share both [Justice Souter's] and Justice White's dismay that the Court so cavalierly has overruled a precedent that is barely three years old and that has proved neither unworkable nor unsound" (113 S.Ct. at 2880).

United States v. Dixon

509 U.S. 688, 113 S.Ct. 2849, 125 L. Ed. 2d 556 (1993)

■ The Supreme Court considered jointly the cases of two separate defendants, Dixon and Foster. The title to the case reflected merely an alphabetical listing of defendants, although most of the opinion actually discussed Foster's case. Dixon was arrested for second-degree murder and was released on bail. His release conditions specified that he was not to commit any other crime. While awaiting trial, however, he was arrested for narcotics possession. Because he had violated his pretrial release conditions, he was quickly convicted of contempt of court and sentenced to jail for six months. He later claimed his right against double jeopardy meant that this contempt conviction precluded his further prosecution on the narcotics charge. Dixon won his double jeopardy claim in the trial court and that ruling was upheld by the court of appeals. Foster's wife had obtained a court order to prevent him from coming near her because of his abusive behavior. In violation of the order, on several occasions he came to his wife's home and assaulted her. After he was convicted of violating the court order and sentenced to 600 days in prison, he claimed that his double jeopardy right barred his prosecution on the assault charge. Foster's claim was rejected by the trial court, but the court of appeals reversed in his favor. The U.S. Supreme Court accepted the cases to consider whether the convictions for contempt of court and for violating a court order precluded further prosecution of the underlying felonies because of the defendants' rights against double jeopardy.

The case is important because the Rehnquist Court reversed its own three-year-old precedent and thereby made it more difficult for defendants to assert double jeopardy claims successfully. As you read the case, consider the following questions: (1) Is it damaging to the Supreme Court and/or constitutional law to overturn a precedent that was established only a few years earlier? (2) What is the Court's reason for overturning the precedent? (3) If the precedent had been preserved, what administrative difficulties would prosecutors face in seeking to make certain that prosecution of serious felonies was not precluded by related prosecutions?

VOTE:

Five justices found no constitutional violation in Foster's case (Kennedy, O'Connor, Rehnquist, Scalia, Thomas).

Four justices found a violation of double jeopardy in Foster's case (Blackmun, Souter, Stevens, White).

Justice Scalia announced the judgment of the Court and delivered the opinion of the Court with respect to Parts I, II, and IV and an opinion with respect to Parts III and V, in which Justice Kennedy joins.

* * *

II

* * *

The Double Jeopardy Clause, whose application to this new context we are called upon to consider, provides that no person shall "be subject for the same offence to be twice put in jeopardy of life or limb." U.S. Const., Amdt. 5. This protection applies both to successive punishments and to successive prosecutions for the same criminal offense. . . .

* * *

In both the multiple punishment and multiple prosecution contexts, this Court has concluded that where the two offenses for which the defendant is punished or tried cannot survive the "same-elements" test, the double jeopardy bar applies. . . . The same-elements test, sometimes referred to as the "*Blockburger*" test, inquires whether each offense contains an element not contained in the other; if not, they are the "same offence" and double jeopardy bars additional punishment and successive prosecution. . . .

We recently held in *Grady* [*v. Corbin,* 1990] that in addition to passing the *Blockburger* test, a subsequent prosecution must satisfy a "same-conduct" test to avoid the double jeopardy bar. The *Grady* test provides that, "if, to establish an essential element of an offense charged in that prosecution, the government will prove conduct that constitutes an offense for which the defendant has already been prosecuted," a second prosecution may not be had. . . .

III

[In Part III of the opinion, Scalia, joined by Kennedy, found that all of Dixon's prosecutions and some of Foster's charges met the *Blockburger* "same-elements" test and therefore were barred by the Double Jeopardy Clause. Justices Blackmun, Souter, Stevens, and White concurred in this aspect of the judgment.]

* * *

The remaining four counts in *Foster,* assault with intent to kill . . . and threats to injure or kidnap. . ., are not barred under *Blockburger.* . . . On the basis of the same episode, Foster was then indicted for violation of . . . assault with intent to kill. Under governing law, that offense requires proof of specific intent to kill, simple assault does not. . . . Similarly, the contempt offense [for violating the court order] required proof of knowledge of the [Civil Protective Order], which assault with intent to kill does not. Applying the *Blockburger* elements test, the result is clear: These crimes were different offenses and the subsequent prosecution did not violate the Double Jeopardy Clause. . . .

Counts II, III, and IV of Foster's indictment are likewise not barred. . . . Conviction of the contempt required willful violation of the [Civil Protective Order]—which conviction under [threatening to injure or kidnap] did not; and conviction under [threatening to injure or kidnap] required that the threat be a threat to kidnap, to inflict bodily injury, or to damage property—which conviction of the contempt [for violating the Civil Protective Order] did not. Each offense therefore contained a separate element, and the *Blockburger* test for double jeopardy was not met.

IV

Having found that at least some of the counts [against Foster] at issue here are not barred by the *Blockburger* test, we must consider whether they are barred by the new, additional double jeopardy test we announced three Terms ago in *Grady v. Corbin* [1990]. They undoubtedly are, since *Grady* prohibits "a subsequent prosecution if, to establish an essential element of an offense charged in that prosecution [here, assault as an element of assault with intent to kill, or threatening as an element of threatening bodily injury], the government will prove conduct that constitutes an offense for which the defendant has already been prosecuted [here, the assault and the threatening, which conduct constituted the offense of violating the [Civil Protective Order]].". . .

We have concluded, however, that *Grady* must be overruled. Unlike *Blockburger* analysis, whose definition of what prevents two crimes from being the "same offence," U.S. Const., Amdt. 5, has deep historical roots and has been accepted in numerous precedents of this Court, *Grady* lacks constitutional roots. The "same-conduct" rule it announced is wholly inconsistent with earlier Supreme Court precedent and with the clear common-law understanding of double jeopardy. . . . We need not discuss the many proofs of these statements, which were set forth at length in the *Grady* dissent. See 495 U.S. at 526 . . . (Scalia, J., dissenting). . . .

* * *

But *Grady* was not only wrong in principle; it has already proved unstable in application. Less than two years after it came down, in *United States v. Felix* . . . (1992), we were forced to recognize a large exception to it. There we concluded that a subsequent prosecution for conspiracy to manufacture, possess, and distribute methamphetamine was not barred by a previous conviction for attempt to manufacture the same substance. We offered as a justification for avoiding a "literal" (*i.e.*, faithful) reading of *Grady* "longstanding authority" to the effect that prosecution for conspiracy is not precluded by prior prosecution for the substantive offense. . . . Of course the very existence of such a large and longstanding "exception" to the *Grady* rule gave cause for concern that the rule was not an accurate expression of the law. This "past practice" excuse is not available to support the ignoring of *Grady* in the present case, since there is no Supreme Court precedent even discussing this fairly new breed of successive prosecution (criminal contempt for violation of a court order prohibiting a crime, followed by prosecution for the crime itself).

A hypothetical based on the facts in *Harris* [*v. Oklahoma,* 1977] reinforces the conclusion that *Grady* is a continuing source of confusion and must be overruled. Suppose the State first tries the defendant for felony-murder, based on robbery, and then indicts the defendant for robbery with a firearm in the same incident. Absent *Grady,* our cases provide a clear answer to the double-jeopardy claim in this situation. Under *Blockburger,* the second prosecution is not barred—as it clearly was not barred at common law, as a famous case establishes. In *King v. Vandercomb* . . .[1796], the government abandoned, midtrial, prosecution of defendant for burglary by breaking and entering and stealing goods, because it turned out that no property had been removed on the date of the alleged burglary. The defendant was then prosecuted for burglary by breaking and entering with intent to steal. That second prosecution was allowed, because "these two offences are so distinct in their nature, that evidence of one of them will not support an indictment for the other."

* * *

Having encountered today yet another situation in which the pre-*Grady* understanding of the Double Jeopardy Clause allows a second trial, though the "same-conduct" test would not, we think it time to acknowledge what is now, three years after *Grady,* compellingly clear: the case was a mistake. We do not lightly reconsider a precedent, but, because *Grady* contradicted an "unbroken line of decisions," contained "less than accurate" historical analysis, and has produced "confusion," we do so here. . . . Although *stare decisis* is the "preferred course" in constitutional adjudication, "when governing decisions are unworkable or are badly reasoned, 'this Court has never felt constrained to follow precedent.' " [citing *Payne v. Tennessee,* 1991]. . . . We would mock *stare decisis* and only add chaos to our double jeopardy jurisprudence by pretending that *Grady* survives when it does not. We therefore accept the Government's invitation to overrule *Grady,* and Counts II, III, IV, and V of Foster's subsequent prosecution are not barred. . . .

[*Chief Justice Rehnquist's opinion concurring in part and dissenting in part, joined by Justice O'Connor and Justice Thomas, is omitted.* Rehnquist argued that none of the prosecutions against Dixon and Foster were barred by double jeopardy. He dissented against Scalia's conclusion that the *Blockburger* test barred the prosecutions against Dixon.]

[*Justice White's opinion concurring in the judgment in part and dissenting in part, joined by Justice Stevens and joined as to Part I by Justice Souter, is omitted.* White argued that all further prosecutions against Dixon and Foster are barred by double jeopardy, and that the Court should not have overruled *Grady*.]

[*Justice Blackmun's opinion concurring in the judgment in part and dissenting in part is omitted.* Blackmun agreed with White's conclusions but sought to emphasize additional reasons.]

Justice Souter, with whom Justice Stevens joins, concurring in the judgment in part and dissenting in part.

While I agree with the Court as far as it goes in holding that a citation for criminal contempt and an indictment for violating a substantive criminal statute may amount to charges of the "same offence" for purposes of the Double Jeopardy Clause. . ., I cannot join the Court in restricting the Clause's reach and dismembering the protection against successive prosecution that the Constitution was meant to provide. The Court has read our precedents so narrowly as to leave them bereft of the principles animating that protection, and has chosen to overrule the most recent of the relevant cases, *Grady v. Corbin* . . ., decided three years ago. Because I think that *Grady* was correctly decided, amounting merely to an expression of just those animating principles, . . . I respectfully dissent. . . .

* * *

An example will show why [*Blockburger* provides insufficient protection against successive prosecutions] . . . . Assume three crimes: robbery with a firearm, robbery in a dwelling and simple robbery. The elements of the three crimes are the same, except that robbery with a firearm has the element that a firearm be used in the commission of the robbery while the other two crimes do not, and robbery in dwelling has the element that the robbery occur in a dwelling while the other two crimes do not.

If a person committed a robbery in a dwelling with a firearm and was prosecuted for simple robbery, all agree that he could not be prosecuted subsequently for either of the greater offenses of robbery with a firearm or robbery in a dwelling. Under the lens of *Blockburger,* however, if that same person were prosecuted first for robbery with a firearm, he could be prosecuted subsequently for robbery in a dwelling, even though he could not be prosecuted on the basis of that same robbery for simple robbery. This is true simply because neither of the crimes, robbery with a firearm and robbery in a dwelling, is either identical to or a lesser-included offense of the other. But since the purpose of the Double Jeopardy Clause's protection against successive prosecutions is to prevent repeated trials in which a defendant will be forced to defend against the same charge again and again, and in which the government may perfect its presentation with dress rehearsal after dress rehearsal, it should be irrelevant that the second prosecution would require the defendant to defend himself not only from the charge that he committed the robbery, but also from the charge of some additional fact, in this case, that the scene of the crime was a dwelling. If, instead, protection against successive prosecution were as limited as it would be by *Blockburger* alone, the doctrine would be as striking for its anomalies as for the limited protection it would provide. Thus, in the relatively few successive prosecution cases we have had over the years, we have not held that the *Blockburger* test is the only hurdle the government must clear. . . .

* * *

Grady simply applied a rule with roots in our cases going back over 100 years. . . . Overruling *Grady* cannot remove this principle from our constitutional jurisprudence. . . .

Conclusion

The Rehnquist Court consistently supported conservative outcomes in Fifth Amendment cases concerning both self-incrimination and double jeopardy. Although a few liberal decisions kept essential aspects of the *Miranda* rules intact, the majority of justices gradually identified an ever-increasing number of situations in which incriminating statements can be used as evidence even though these statements were obtained during questioning conducted without defense attorneys present. In addition, the Court's decision in *Duckworth v. Eagan* (1989) creates the possibility that police officers may be free to change the form of *Miranda* warnings and thereby, intentionally or inadvertently, confuse criminal suspects about the nature of their rights.

As indicated by Table 10.4, one factor enhancing the high percentage of outcomes favoring the government in Fifth Amendment cases was the relatively conservative performance of several justices who support individual claimants more frequently in cases concerning other civil rights and liberties issues. For example, Justices Stevens and Blackmun, who supported liberal outcomes in 100 percent and 90 percent, respectively, of Eighth Amendment cases (see Chapter 12), both supported liberal outcomes in barely half of the Fifth Amendment cases. Moreover, the replacement of the most liberal justices (Brennan and Marshall) by justices (Souter and Thomas) who support individuals' claims infrequently tilted the Court even further in a conservative direction on Fifth Amendment issues. Thus the presence of President Clinton's recent Democratic appointees, Ruth Bader Ginsburg and Stephen Breyer, are likely to have little noticeable impact on the conservative direction of Fifth Amendment jurisprudence.

REFERENCES

Abraham, Henry J. *Freedom and the Court.* 5th ed. New York: Oxford University Press, 1988.

Allen, Ronald J., Bard Ferrall, and John Ratnaswamy. "The Double Jeopardy Clause, Constitutional Interpretation and the Limits of Formal Logic." *Valparaiso University Law Review* 26(1991): 281-310.

Baker, Liva. *Miranda: Crime, Law and Politics.* New York: Atheneum, 1983.

Bodenhamer, David J. *Fair Trial: Rights of the Accused in American History.* New York: Oxford University Press, 1992.

Berger, Mark. *Taking the Fifth: The Supreme Court and the Privilege Against Self-Incrimination.* Lexington, Mass: Lexington Books, 1980.

Decker, John F. *Revolution to the Right: Criminal Procedure Jurisprudence during the Burger-Rehnquist Court Era.* New York: Garland Publishing, 1992.

Kamisar, Yale. "*Duckworth v. Eagan*: A Little-Noticed *Miranda* Case that May Cause Much Mischief." *Criminal Law Bulletin* 25(1989): 550-56.

Kamisar, Yale, Wayne LaFave, and Jerold Israel. *Modern Criminal Procedure.* 7th ed. St. Paul, Minn.: West Publishing, 1992.

Levy, Leonard. *Origins of the Fifth Amendment: The Right against Self-Incrimination.* New York: Oxford University Press, 1968.

Schulhofer, Stephen. "Some Kind Words for the Privilege against Self-Incrimination." *Valparaiso University Law Review* 26(1991): 311-36.

Seeburger, Richard H., and R. Stanton Wettick, Jr., "*Miranda* in Pittsburgh—A Statistical Study." *University of Pittsburgh Law Review* (1967). Excerpted in *Law and Society: Readings on the Social Study of Law,* edited by Stewart Macaulay, Lawrence M. Friedman, and John Stookey. New York: W.W. Norton, 1995.

Smith, Christopher E. "Police Professionalism and the Rights of Criminal Defendants." *Criminal Law Bulletin* 26(1990): 155-66.

________. "Justice Antonin Scalia and Criminal Justice Cases." *Kentucky Law Journal* 81(1992-93): 187-212.

Walker, Samuel. *Sense and Nonsense about Crime and Drugs.* 3d ed. Belmont, Calif.: Wadsworth Publishing, 1994.

CHAPTER 11

The Sixth Amendment and Fair Trial Guarantees

CASE STUDY

Gideon v. Wainwright (1963)

On the night of June 3, 1961, someone broke into the Bay Harbor Poolroom in Panama City, Florida. The burglar had smashed a window, entered the building, broken into a cigarette machine and a jukebox, and stolen an undetermined amount of money in coins as well as a small amount of beer and wine. A police officer had discovered the break-in during the course of a routine patrol. Based on the statement of a witness who claimed he could identify the person he had seen inside the closed Poolroom, Clarence Earl Gideon was arrested and charged with felonious breaking and entering and misdemeanor petty larceny (Lewis 1964, pp. 57–62).

Gideon was a fifty-one-year-old white man with an eighth grade education. He ran away from home at age fourteen and had spent most of his life shuttling back and forth between unskilled jobs, gambling activities, and prison. He had served a total of eighteen years in prisons in Missouri, Kansas, and Texas for a series of convictions for burglary, robbery, and larceny. He suffered from tuberculosis and his family had disintegrated as welfare officials periodically placed his children in foster homes when he was in jail and his wife struggled with alcohol problems (Lewis 1964, pp. 65–78).

On August 4, 1961, Gideon was tried in the Bay County Circuit Court by Judge Robert McCrary, Jr., and a jury of six men. As the trial began, Gideon immediately requested that the judge appoint an attorney to represent him and asserted that he possessed a constitutional right to be represented by appointed counsel (Lewis 1964, pp. 9–10, 57):

JUDGE McCRARY: Now tell us what you said again, so we can understand you, please.

GIDEON: Your Honor, I said: I request this Court to appoint counsel to represent me in this trial.

JUDGE McCRARY: Mr. Gideon, I am sorry, but I cannot appoint counsel to represent you in this case. Under the laws of the State of Florida, the only time the court can appoint counsel to represent a Defendant is when that person is charged with a capital offense. I am sorry, but I will have to deny your request to appoint counsel to defend you in this case.

GIDEON: The United States Supreme Court says I am entitled to be represented by counsel.

JUDGE McCRARY: Let the record show that the defendant has asked the court to appoint counsel to represent him in this trial and the court denied the request and informed the defendant that the only time the court could appoint counsel to represent a defendant was in cases where the defendant was charged with a capital offense. The defendant stated to the court that the United States Supreme Court said he was entitled to it.

Judge McCrary sought to be fair to Gideon. At the start of the trial, he invited Gideon to exclude any of the jurors by saying "just look them over and if you don't like their looks that's all it takes to get them excused" (Lewis 1964, p. 58). The judge also invited Gideon to make an opening statement to the jury. McCrary did not, however, provide assistance to Gideon. Gideon was on his own in cross-examining prosecution witnesses and eliciting testimony from his own witnesses through questioning. The prosecution's case rested on the testimony of Henry Cook, an acquaintance of Gideon's who testified that he saw Gideon coming out of the Poolroom carrying a bottle of wine at 5:30 A.M. and that he saw that someone had broken into the cigarette machine. Gideon's cross-examination of Cook was ineffective. Gideon's presentation of his own witnesses was also ineffective. The testimony presented in court provided a basis for Gideon to cast doubt upon his guilt, but he lacked the knowledge and skill necessary to ask appropriate follow-up questions that would highlight for the jury the possibility that someone other than Gideon committed the crime. After brief closing arguments, the jury found Gideon guilty and Judge McCrary sentenced him to the maximum term of five years in prison (Lewis 1964, pp. 57–62).

From his cell in the Florida State Prison, Gideon prepared petitions to challenge his conviction. Gideon had attempted to educate himself in law by reading books during his time spent in prisons. Gideon's petitions "were written in pencil. They were done in carefully formed printing, like a schoolboy's, on lined sheets" that had prison postal regulations printed at the top of each page (Lewis 1964, p. 4). After the Florida Supreme Court declined to review his case, Gideon submitted a petition to the U.S. Supreme Court requesting that the nation's highest court examine his case and vindicate his asserted right to have a lawyer appointed to represent him during his trial. At the time Gideon filed his petition, the Supreme Court had ruled that indigent defendants are entitled to appointed representation only when judges make discretionary determinations that the individual defendants suffer from "special circumstances" such as illiteracy or mental retardation (*Betts v. Brady*, 1942). Gideon did not claim that his ability to represent himself was hindered by any special circumstances. Instead, he asserted that he, and by implication everyone else, possessed an absolute constitutional right to be represented by counsel in criminal cases based on the Sixth Amendment's statement that "[i]n all criminal prosecutions, the accused shall enjoy the right . . . to have the Assistance of Counsel for his defence" (Lewis 1964, pp. 4–9).

The justices of the Supreme Court agreed to hear Gideon's case, and they appointed Abe Fortas, a prominent Washington, D.C. attorney who would later become a Supreme Court justice, to prepare and present Gideon's case. Fortas relied upon junior attorneys at his law firm to research Sixth Amendment issues and formulate promising arguments on Gideon's behalf. Fortas received additional assistance from outside sources. Prominent law professors supplied their research to Fortas and helped to prepare an amicus brief for the American Civil Liberties Union. In response to Florida's request for support from other states, Minnesota Attorney General Walter Mondale helped to organize twenty-three states to file an amicus brief providing arguments in *support of* Gideon's claim rather than to assist Florida as requested. At the time of Gideon's case, thirty-seven states already had their own formal rules requiring the appointment of attorneys to represent indigent defendants, and judges in eight other states normally made such appointments as a matter of informal practice (Lewis 1964, pp. 48, 132, 151).

By contrast, Florida's arguments in opposition to Gideon's claim were prepared by a young assistant state attorney general, Bruce Jacob, a twenty-six year old who had been a lawyer for less than three years. The Florida Attorney General gave Jacob permission to retain responsibility for the case's preparation even when Jacob left government service to join a law firm in a small town. Thus, unlike the experienced Fortas, who had a small army of associates and outside experts to assist in case preparation, the inexperienced Jacob drove sixty miles to the nearest law library on weekends to prepare the case by himself with clerical assistance from his wife. Jacob found himself even more outnumbered when only two states, Alabama and North Carolina, agreed to file an amicus brief with the Court in opposition to Gideon's claim (Lewis 1964, pp. 140, 152–156).

The progress of events leading to oral arguments in the Supreme Court indicated that developments were moving in Gideon's favor. When Justice Felix Frankfurter retired from the Supreme

Court in August 1962 and was subsequently replaced by Justice Arthur Goldberg, Jacob concluded that he had little chance of prevailing on Florida's behalf. With Frankfurter's departure, the Court lost one of its foremost advocates of judicial deference to policies and practices instituted by individual state governments (Lewis 1964, p. 155). Goldberg, who was appointed by President John F. Kennedy, was much more inclined than Frankfurter to interpret the Constitution broadly to expand the rights of individuals, including criminal defendants.

The oral argument occurred on January 15, 1963. Fortas argued Gideon's case along with J. Lee Rankin, a former solicitor general of the United States, who appeared as amicus curiae representing the American Civil Liberties Union. Jacob was joined in oral arguments by George Mentz from the Alabama attorney general's office who argued in support of the amicus brief filed by Alabama and North Carolina (Irons and Guitton 1993, p. 192). Following oral argument, the attorneys for each side had a relatively short wait for the Court's decision because Justice Hugo Black announced the opinion in the case just two months later on March 18, 1963.

The Court ruled unanimously in Gideon's favor and thereby established a national rule that states must provide attorneys for indigent defendants facing incarceration for serious crimes (case excerpt on p. 524). Justice Black, the author of the majority opinion, had been a dissenter in the prior case of *Betts v. Brady* (1942), in which the Court had declined to incorporate the Sixth Amendment guarantee of right to counsel into the Fourteenth Amendment's Due Process Clause in order to apply it to all state courts (see Chapter 4 on Incorporation of the Bill of Rights). Because Black was one of the Court's most ardent advocates of incorporation, he was happy to seize the opportunity to overrule the *Betts* precedent and expand the right to counsel to the states. Black declared: "We accept *Betts v. Brady*'s assumption, based as it was on our prior cases, that a provision of the Bill of Rights which is 'fundamental and essential to a fair trial' is made obligatory upon the States by the Fourteenth Amendment. We think the Court in *Betts* was wrong, however, in concluding that the Sixth Amendment's guarantee of counsel was not one of these fundamental rights" (*Gideon v. Wainwright*, 372 U.S. at 342). Black concluded that "[The] noble ideal [of fair trials before impartial tribunals] cannot be realized if the poor man charged with crime has to face his accusers without a lawyer to assist him" (372 U.S. at 344).

Three justices supported Gideon's claim in individual concurring opinions. Justice William O. Douglas wrote a concurring opinion to emphasize that people should enjoy the same rights against infringement by states that they enjoy against infringement by the federal government. Justice Tom Clark's concurring opinion argued that there was no basis for the Court's previous decisions that distinguished between capital and noncapital cases in granting attorneys to those facing execution but not those facing incarceration. Justice Harlan's concurring opinion reiterated his consistent opposition to the concept of incorporation but acknowledged that the right to counsel should now be regarded as a fundamental right that should be considered a component of people's Fourteenth Amendment right to due process.

The direct effect of the decision was to reverse Gideon's conviction and remand his case to the Florida courts for action consistent with the U.S. Supreme Court's new decision on the right to counsel. The Florida Supreme Court ordered a new trial for Gideon and on August 5, 1963, Gideon's second trial began. Fortas had suggested to Gideon that he accept representation from a lawyer from the Florida Civil Liberties Union. Gideon initially agreed but later began to talk about representing himself. Judge McCrary was relieved when Gideon accepted his suggestion to select a local attorney who could be appointed as defense counsel. In the second trial, the local attorney proved that his familiarity with trial tactics and the personalities within the local community could provide significant benefits in presenting an effective defense. Gideon's attorney, Fred Turner, was acquainted with Henry Cook, the prosecution's prime witness, and he managed to poke holes in Cook's testimony during cross-examination. Ultimately, Turner argued to the jury that the evidence pointed most convincingly to Cook as the actual culprit in the breaking and entering at the Bay Harbor Poolroom. After deliberating for one hour, the jury found Gideon to be *not guilty* of the crime for which he had already served two years behind bars (Lewis 1964, pp. 223–238).

For most criminal defendants in the United States, the *Gideon* decision had little impact. Most states already provided defense counsel for defendants facing serious charges. Defendants in the minority of states that did not previously provide representation experienced the direct benefits of the decision. Because the *Gideon* decision primarily endorsed and accelerated a practice that already existed in most of the country, its most important impact was in laying a foundation for a series of subsequent Sixth Amendment cases throughout the Warren, Burger, and Rehnquist Court eras. By declaring that the Sixth Amendment right to counsel applied to the states, the Court set the stage for additional decisions defining the timing of appointment of counsel during the criminal justice process and the stages and circumstances in the process in which the right did and did not apply. We shall also see in subsequent sections of this chapter that, as the Court's first case formally incorporating a right from the Sixth Amendment, the *Gideon* case broke ground for subsequent decisions recognizing and applying other Sixth Amendment rights, including the right to trial by jury, right to speedy trial, and right to confront witnesses.

Historical Origins and Contemporary Conflicts

The fair trial guarantees of the Sixth Amendment find their origins in the English development of trials as the means to determine the guilt or innocence of people accused of crimes. Prior to the thirteenth century, the Angles, Saxons, and their conquerors, the Normans, determined criminal guilt by seeking divine decisions through the processes of battle, ordeal, and compurgation. Trial by battle, which has been described as a combination of a prize fight and a religious ceremony, was based on the presumption that divine intervention would insure that the innocent combatant would not be killed. The value and attractiveness of trial by battle diminished in the twelfth century when accused persons began to have the opportunity to hire professional champions to fight in their stead. Trial by ordeal presented accused persons with a very undesirable situation. For example, criminal defendants had their hands and feet tied, and they were then thrown into a pond. If they managed to swim, they were judged guilty and executed. They were presumed to be able to swim in such a situation because they possessed (or were possessed by) some evil power. If they sank and drowned, then they were regarded as innocent and they received a respectful burial. There were other forms of trial by ordeal, such as lifting and carrying red-hot iron weights or placing human limbs into kettles of boiling water. Compurgation involved determining guilt by having people swear oaths attesting to an accused's honesty and innocence. These forms of "trials" began to give way to more legalistic trials when Pope Innocent III forbade clergy from performing religious ceremonies in conjunction with ordeals in 1215. This declaration removed the religious sanction that had provided the basis for believing that divine intervention produced correct outcomes (Heller 1951, pp. 3–5).

The early English jury differed significantly from modern juries because the jurors acted as witnesses to the alleged crime rather than merely as judges of evidence: "[Jurors] were expected to be already familiar with the facts when the trial began and to announce the verdict based on their own personal knowledge of crime and defendant. It was the jurors' duty, upon being summoned for jury service, to make inquiry into the facts of the case to be tried, to sift the information and then, in court, to state their conclusion in terms of guilt or innocence" (Heller 1951, p. 8). The shift toward jurors as judges rather than witnesses was gradual. Until the early seventeenth century, however, defendants had no assurances that they would be permitted to present evidence on their own behalf in opposition to the evidence presented by the prosecutor. Criminal defendants did not have the opportunity to be represented by counsel at trials until the end of the seventeenth century. The late seventeenth century was also the time when jurors gained independence and no longer risked fines if they failed to obey a judge's orders in determining the verdict. The English colonists who came to North America regarded the jury trial as a fundamental component of their judicial processes. The American colonies used juries, although they did not always use uniform practices with respect to the size of juries and the population from which jurors were drawn. Early colonial laws and state constitutions, as well as the later Bill of Rights, contained declarations about the right to trial by jury (Heller 1951, pp. 13–34).

The Sixth Amendment contains several specific guarantees designed to insure that criminal defendants receive fair trials. The Sixth Amendment says:

> *In all criminal prosecutions, the accused shall enjoy the right to a speedy and public trial, by an impartial jury of the State and district wherein the crime shall have been committed, which district shall have been previously ascertained by the law, and to be informed of the nature and cause of the accusation; to be confronted with the witnesses against him; to have compulsory process for obtaining witnesses in his favor, and to have the Assistance of Counsel for his defence.*

Because most provisions of the Bill of Rights were regarded as applying only against the federal government until the mid-twentieth century (see Chapter 4 on Incorporation of the Bill of Rights), the Sixth Amendment's list of protections had little impact on the vast majority of criminal cases. Most criminal cases arise under state statutes, and only a relatively small number are processed by the federal courts. Many states provided some of these rights through their own constitutions and statutes, but the application of these rights varied from state to state (Bodenhamer 1992). It was not until the Supreme Court began applying Sixth Amendment rights against the states that the justices' interpretations of the specific provisions of the amendment began to have broad impact on all American criminal justice systems.

Obviously, one major historical controversy concerned the Sixth Amendment's applicability to the states. As we will see, the justices applied individual pieces of the Sixth Amendment against the states beginning slowly with a single decision in the 1930s and ending with a flurry of decisions by the Warren Court in the 1960s. The incorporation questions concerning the applicability of the Sixth Amendment to the states were not the only matters of controversy concerning the amendment. The justices have also had to interpret the individual provisions of the Sixth Amendment to determine the timing, nature, and scope of the rights it provides.

Approaches to Sixth Amendment Decision Making

As in cases concerning other criminal justice issues, the justices' interpretations are guided by a number of factors when they interpret the Sixth Amendment. As with other provisions of the Constitution, justices may use the Framers' intentions or historical evidence about trial practices in 1791 to determine the original intent of the Sixth Amendment. However, debates about historical practices seem to have had less importance in interpreting the meaning of trial rights than in interpreting many other rights. Perhaps this is because the literal words of the Sixth Amendment are less ambiguous than those of some other amendments. While historical debates remain important for interpretations of the Eighth Amendment's inherently ambiguous phrase "cruel and unusual punishments," the Sixth Amendment's phrasing of rights to trial by jury and to confront adverse witnesses seems less uncertain. This is not to say that the justices do not engage in significant disagreements about the meaning and applicability of Sixth Amendment rights. They certainly do. It merely means that the justices place much greater reliance on policy considerations and on their individual conceptions of the elements necessary to produce a "fair" trial. For example, the Court has been deeply divided about Confrontation Clause issues concerning whether child victims of sexual abuse should be forced to come face-to-face with their alleged abusers when giving testimony during a trial. Some justices have endorsed the use of devices such as one-way mirror/screens and closed-circuit television by arguing, as Justice Harry Blackmun did in *Coy v. Iowa* (1988), that the Court should strike a balance between the competing policy interests of the defendant's right to confront adverse witnesses and the child-victim's need to avoid psychological trauma. By contrast, other justices have taken the literal words of the Constitution as providing a clear statement of the Sixth Amendment's required policy. Thus, in a case in which a narrow majority approved the use of a child's testimony via closed-circuit television, Justice Antonin Scalia wrote in dissent: "Seldom has this Court failed so conspicuously to sustain a categorical guarantee of the Constitution against the tide of prevailing opinion. The Sixth Amendment provides, with unmistakable clarity, that '[i]n all criminal prosecutions, the accused shall enjoy the right . . . to be confronted with the witnesses against him'" (*Maryland v. Craig*, 497 U.S. at 860-861, 1990).

Justices have also considered the issue of federalism and the extent to which all states should follow precisely the same procedures. New judicially imposed requirements for providing jury trials and appointing defense attorneys for indigents can potentially add great expense to a state court system that possesses limited resources. Justice Harlan frequently argued that the Court should give individual states the freedom to develop criminal justice procedures that are tailored to their own peculiar situations, resources, and problems. In the case of *Duncan v. Louisiana* (1968), which we discussed in Chapter 4, the majority of justices concluded that the states must provide jury trials for criminal defendants in exactly the same circumstances in which the federal courts provide jury trials: when defendants face the possibility of six months or more of incarceration. In dissent, however, Justice Harlan emphasized the desirability of permitting states to develop their own policies: "The jury system . . . is a cumbersome process, . . . imposing great cost in time and money on both the State and the jurors themselves . . . . Exactly why the States should not be allowed to make continuing adjustments, based on the state of their criminal dockets and the difficulty of summoning jurors, simply escapes me" (391 U.S. at 188, 192–93).

Justices' individual conceptions of fairness in trial procedures have emerged in Sixth Amendment cases concerning such issues as acceptable methods for selecting jurors. Justice Thurgood Marshall, for example, showed great concern about preventing racial considerations from diminishing the fairness of trials by affecting any aspect of jury selection. In a case in which a white defendant unsuccessfully objected to the systematic exclusion of African Americans from his jury through the use of discretionary peremptory challenges, Marshall argued: "Racially motivated peremptory challenges are as destructive of the public's perception that our system of criminal justice is fair as are exclusions of certain racial groups from the [jury pool]" (*Holland v. Illinois*, 493 U.S. at 497, 1990). By contrast, Justice Scalia and the other justices in the majority did not view racially motivated exclusion of jurors as affecting the fairness of the trial for Sixth Amendment purposes when the defendant was of a different race than the excluded juror. The Court's conclusions later changed, however, in an equal protection case raising jury issues.

Conceptions of fairness have also shaped the justices' decisions concerning the scope and timing of the right to counsel. How early in the process should the right to counsel apply? Immediately upon arrest? When a suspect is placed in a line-up? How far into the process does the right apply with respect to posttrial appeals? For example, the Court was deeply divided and thereby demonstrated the justices' differing conceptions of fairness when a narrow five-member majority concluded that indigent defendants were not entitled to attorneys in trials that resulted in fines or punishments other than actual confinement (*Scott v. Illinois*, 1979). As we examine the Supreme Court's cases in the remainder of this chapter, notice how frequently the justices' conceptions of fairness or assessments of policy consequences, rather than disagreements about the interpretation of a phrase within the Sixth Amendment, appear to guide their decisions and reasoning.

Pre-Warren Court Period

The Sixth Amendment's applicability, like that of rights contained in other amendments, was initially limited by the Supreme Court's decision in *Barron v. Baltimore* (1833) declaring that the Bill of Rights applied only against actions by the federal government (see Chapter 4). The Supreme Court confirmed the limited applicability of the Sixth Amendment thirty-five years later in *Twitchell v. Pennsylvania* (1868) by declaring that the *Barron* decision still controlled the interpretation of the Bill of Rights.

Right to Counsel

Until the twentieth century, the right to counsel expressed by the Sixth Amendment applied only against the federal government and merely meant that defendants could hire an attorney if they had sufficient funds. The Court's first alteration in the limited definition of defendants' right to representation occurred in the case of *Powell v. Alabama* (1932). Like many other Depression era youths, a number of young African American men were riding freight trains from city to city in Alabama looking for work. There was a fight between nine African American youths and seven white young men in an open gondola car on a freight train. All of the white men except one were thrown off the train, leaving behind the African American men, two young white women, and one white youth. Word of the fight reached Scottsboro, Alabama, before the train pulled into town. Upon arrival, the two women claimed that they had been sexually assaulted by the African American men in the gondola car. One of the women recanted and the other's testimony was shown to be riddled with inconsistencies (Carter 1969). However, the nine young men were arrested and the Scottsboro sheriff called for military assistance to protect the defendants from a gathering mob of angry whites. The defendants, who were illiterate, were put on trial twelve days after the occurrence of the alleged crime. Under Alabama state law, the defendants were entitled to be represented by appointed counsel as they faced the possibility of the death penalty. Although the judge announced that he had appointed all of the attorneys in town collectively to represent the defendants against the capital rape charges, no attorneys actually represented the youths in court. On the morning of the trial, a lawyer from Tennessee, who was unfamiliar with Alabama's laws and legal procedures, volunteered to provide assistance to any local attorney who represented the defendants. However, no defense attorney had investigated the case or prepared any evidence and arguments on behalf of the youths. Thus, not surprisingly, the defendants were swiftly convicted by the all-white jury and most were sentenced to death.

By a 7–2 vote, the Supreme Court decided that the so-called "Scottsboro boys" should have received meaningful representation from appointed defense counsel.

The Court did not, however, base its decision on the Sixth Amendment. In the preceding years, the Court had just begun the process of incorporation with the rights to freedom of speech and press, and it was apparently not yet ready to incorporate rights on behalf of criminal defendants. Instead, the Court declared that Alabama's actions violated the defendants' right to due process under the Fourteenth Amendment. According to Justice George Sutherland:

> *[U]nder the circumstances . . . , the necessity of counsel was so vital and imperative that the failure of the trial court to make an effective appointment of counsel was likewise a denial of due process within the meaning of the Fourteenth Amendment. Whether this would be so in other criminal prosecutions, or under other circumstances, we need not determine. All that it is necessary now to decide, is that in a capital case, where the defendant is unable to employ counsel, and is incapable adequately of making his own defense because of ignorance, feeble mindedness, illiteracy, or the like, it is the duty of the court, whether requested or not, to assign counsel for him as a necessary requisite of due process of law; and that duty is not discharged by an assignment at such a time or under such circumstances as to preclude the giving of effective aid in the preparation and trial of the case. (Powell v. Alabama,* 287 U.S. at 71 [1932])

Although the Court's decision was applicable only to capital cases involving indigent defendants who had limited capacity to present arguments on their own behalf, it represented the first time that the Supreme Court identified any affirmative obligations for government with respect to the right to counsel.

Powell v. Alabama

287 U.S. 45, 53 S.Ct. 55, 77 L. Ed. 158 (1932)

■ Several African American youths were charged with the capital offense of raping two white women. Although Alabama state law required that the defendants be represented by counsel, no attorneys actually prepared a defense for the defendants. During a brief trial, the young African American men were quickly convicted of rape and sentenced to death. The trial was conducted in such a hostile environment that the sheriff requested military assistance in guarding the prisoners to keep them safe from angry mobs of whites. The Alabama Supreme Court affirmed the convictions over the dissent of its chief justice who believed that the defendants had not received a fair trial. The U.S. Supreme Court considered whether they were denied due process of law and a fair trial because they were not represented by counsel.

The case is important because it represents the first time that the Supreme Court imposed an affirmative constitutional obligation on the states to provide defense attorneys for a specific category of indigent defendants. As you read the case, consider the following questions: (1) What provision of the U.S. Constitution does the Supreme Court believe was violated during the defendants' trial? (2) After this decision, which indigent defendants were entitled to free representation by attorneys? (3) How does this case fit into the historical development of incorporation?

Vote:

Seven justices found the trial judge's actions to be unconstitutional (Brandeis, Cardozo, Hughes, Roberts, Stone, Sutherland, Van Devanter).

Two justices found the trial judge's actions to be constitutional (Butler, McReynolds).

Justice Sutherland delivered the opinion of the Court:

* * *

The indictment was returned in a state court of first instance on March 31, 1931, and the record recites that on the same day the defendants were arraigned and entered pleas of not guilty. There is a further recital to the effect that upon the arraignment they were represented by counsel. But no counsel had been employed, and aside from a statement made by the trial judge several days later during a colloquy immediately preceding the trial, the record does not disclose when, or under what circumstances, an appointment of counsel was made, or who was appointed. During the colloquy referred to, the trial judge, in response to a question, said that he had appointed all the members of the bar for the purpose of arraigning the defendants and then of course anticipated that the members of the bar would continue to help the defendants if no counsel appeared. Upon the argument here both sides accepted that as a correct statement of the facts concerning the matter.

* * *

The record shows that immediately upon the return of the indictment defendants were arraigned and pleaded not guilty. Apparently they were not asked whether they had, or were able to employ, counsel, or wished to have counsel appointed; or whether they had friends or relatives who might assist in that regard if communicated with.

* * *

It is hardly necessary to say that, the right to counsel [under Alabama state law] being conceded, a defendant should be afforded a fair opportunity to secure counsel of his own choice. Not only was that not done here, but such designation of counsel as was attempted was either so indefinite or so close upon the trial as to amount to a denial of effective and substantial aid in that regard.

* * *

[U]ntil the very morning of the trial no lawyer had been named or definitely designated to represent the defendants. Prior to that time, the trial judge had "appointed all the members of the bar" for the limited "purpose of arraigning the defendants." Whether they would represent the defendants thereafter if no counsel appeared in their behalf, was a matter of speculation only, or, as the judge indicated, of mere anticipation on the part of the court. Such a designation, even if made for all purposes, would, in our opinion, have fallen far short of meeting, in any proper sense, a requirement of appointment of counsel.

* * *

In any event, the circumstance lends emphasis to the conclusion that during perhaps the most critical period of the proceedings against these defendants, that is to say, from the time of their arraignment until the beginning of their trial, when consultation, thoroughgoing investigation and preparation were vitally important, the defendants did not have the aid of counsel in any real sense, although they were as much entitled to such aid during that period as at the trial itself.

* * *

The question, however, which it is our duty, and within our power, to decide, is whether the denial of assistance of counsel contravenes the due process clause of the Fourteenth Amendment to the federal Constitution.

* * *

It thus appears that in at least twelve of the thirteen colonies the rule of the English common law [against a right to counsel for criminal defendants], in the respect now under consideration, had been definitely rejected and the right to counsel fully recognized in all criminal prosecutions, save that in one or two instances the right was limited to capital offenses or to the more serious crimes . . . . * * *

We do not overlook the case of *Hurtado v. California*, 110 U.S. 516 [1884], where this court determined that due process of law does not require an indictment by a grand jury. * * * In support of that conclusion the court referred to the fact that the Fifth Amendment, in addition to containing the due process of law clause, provides in explicit terms [a right to indictment by grand jury for capital and other "infamous" offenses], and said that since no part of this important amendment could be regarded as superfluous, the obvious inference is that in the sense of the Constitution due process of law was not intended to include . . . the institution and procedure of a grand jury in any case; and that the same phrase, employed in the Fourteenth Amendment to restrain the action of the states, was to be interpreted as having been used in the same sense and with no greater extent; and that if it had been the purpose of that Amendment to perpetuate the institution of the grand jury in the states, it would have embodied, as did the Fifth Amendment, an express declaration to that effect.

The Sixth Amendment, in terms, provides that in all criminal prosecutions the accused shall enjoy the right "to have the assistance of counsel for his defense." In the face of the reasoning of the *Hurtado* case, if it stood alone, it would be difficult to justify the conclusion that the right to counsel, being thus specifically granted by the Sixth Amendment, was also within the intendment of the due process of law clause. But the *Hurtado* case does not stand alone. In the later case of *Chicago, Burlington & Quincy R. Co. v. Chicago* [1897], this court held that a judgment of a state court, even though authorized by statute, by which private property was taken for public use without just compensation, was in violation of the due process of law required by the Fourteenth Amendment, notwithstanding that the Fifth Amendment explicitly declares that private property shall not be taken for public use without just compensation . . . . * * *

Likewise, this court has considered that freedom of speech and of the press are rights protected by the due process clause of the Fourteenth Amendment, although in the First Amendment, Congress is prohibited in specific terms from abridging the right. *Gitlow v. New York* [1925]; *Stromberg v. California* [1931]; *Near v. Minnesota* [1931].

These later cases establish that notwithstanding the sweeping character of the language in the *Hurtado* case, the rule laid down is not without exceptions. The rule is an aid to construction, and in some instances may be conclusive; but it must yield to more compelling considerations whenever such considerations exist. The fact that the right involved is of such a character that it cannot be denied without violating those "fundamental principles of liberty and justice which lie at the base of all our civil and political institutions" (*Hebert v. Louisiana* [1926]), is obviously one of those compelling considerations which must prevail in determining whether it is embraced within the due process clause of the Fourteenth Amendment, although it be specifically dealt with in another part of the federal Constitution. * * * While this question has never been categorically determined by this court, a consideration of the nature of the right and a review of the expressions of this and other courts, makes it clear that the right to the aid of counsel is of this fundamental character.

* * *

In light of the facts outlined in the forepart of this opinion — the ignorance and illiteracy of the defendants, their youth, the circumstances of public hostility, the imprisonment and the close surveillance of the defendants by military forces, the fact that their friends and families were all in other states and communication with them [was] necessarily difficult, and above all that they stood in deadly peril of their lives — we think the failure of the trial court to give them reasonable time and opportunity to secure counsel was a clear denial of due process.

But passing that, and assuming their inability, even if the opportunity had been given, to employ counsel, as the trial court evidently did assume, we are of opinion that, under the circumstances just stated, the necessity of counsel was so vital and imperative that the failure of the trial court to make an effective appointment of counsel was likewise a denial of due process within the meaning of the Fourteenth Amendment. Whether this would be so in other criminal prosecutions, or under other circumstances, we need not determine. All that it is necessary now to decide, as we do decide, is that in a capital case, where the defendant is unable to employ counsel, and is incapable adequately of making his own defense because of ignorance, feeble mindedness, illiteracy, or the like, it is the duty of the court, whether requested or not, to assign counsel for him as a necessary requisite of due process of law; and that duty is not discharged by an assignment at such a time or under such circumstances as to preclude the giving of effective aid in the preparation and trial of the case . . . .

The judgments must be reversed and the causes remanded for further proceedings not inconsistent with this opinion.

Judgments reversed.

[The dissenting opinion of Justice Butler is omitted.]

The Scottsboro case attracted national attention. It was viewed by many northerners as a prime example of the injustice produced by racial discrimination in southern courts. When the cases were retried with northern attorneys providing representation, four defendants were convicted in prejudicial proceedings before an overtly biased judge. One was sentenced to death and the others received long prison terms. The state dropped the rape charges against a fifth defendant when he received a sentence of twenty years in prison for assaulting a deputy while in jail. Despite the fact that the same alleged evidence applied to all of the defendants, Alabama subsequently dropped the rape charges against the other four defendants after holding them in jail for six years. One was virtually blind, one suffered from severe venereal disease, and the two others were ages twelve and thirteen when the alleged crime took place. All of the convicted defendants eventually gained their freedom. Four were paroled between 1943 and 1950, and one escaped from an Alabama prison in 1948 and was protected from extradition by the Governor of Michigan when he was later discovered in Detroit (Carter 1969, pp. 376–377, 411–413).

Six years after the *Powell* decision, the Court used the Sixth Amendment to place affirmative obligations on the federal government. In *Johnson v. Zerbst* (1938), the Court declared that defendants in the federal courts who face the prospect of imprisonment are entitled to have an attorney appointed to represent them if they could not afford to hire their own counsel. The decision was based squarely on the dictates of the Sixth Amendment but applied only to the relatively small number of defendants who are prosecuted for federal crimes. A few short years later, the Court had the opportunity to consider the incorporation of the Sixth Amendment in order to apply the right to counsel to the states.

In *Betts v. Brady* (1942), the defendant was indicted for robbery and prosecuted in the Maryland state courts. Because he was unable to afford an attorney, he requested that the judge appoint an attorney to represent him. The judge declined and informed him that attorneys were only provided to indigent defendants facing rape or murder charges. In a six-to-three decision, the Supreme Court decided that states are not obligated to provide counsel for indigent defendants in all cases. Appointed attorneys were required only in cases in which representation was justified by special circumstances.

In the majority opinion, Justice Owen Roberts emphasized that the Sixth Amendment is only applicable against the federal government and he declined to apply the *Johnson* rule to the states. Justice Roberts relied on a historical examination of judicial practices in colonial America and England to conclude that "it is evident that the constitutional provisions to the effect that a defendant should be 'allowed' counsel or should have a right 'to be heard by himself and his counsel,' or that he might be heard by 'either or both,' at his election, were intended to do away with the rules which denied representation, in whole or in part, by counsel in criminal prosecutions, but were not aimed to compel the State to provide counsel for a defendant" (316 U.S. at 466). Roberts also emphasized the trial judge's conclusion that the defendant did not suffer from any special circumstances that would require representation by an attorney in order to achieve a fair trial: "[T]he accused was not helpless, but was a man forty-three years old, of ordinary intelligence, and ability to take care of his own interests on the trial of that narrow issue. He had once before been in a criminal court, pleaded guilty to larceny and served a sentence and was not wholly unfamiliar with criminal procedure" (316 U.S. at 472). The majority opinion placed an indigent defendant's entitlement to representation in the hands of judges' subjective assessments concerning whether the concept of a "fair" trial would be violated if a particular defendant did not have an attorney: "[T]he Fourteenth Amendment prohibits the conviction and incarceration of one whose trial is offensive to the common and fundamental ideas of fairness and right . . . [but] we cannot say that the Amendment embodies an inexorable command that no trial . . . can be fairly conducted and justice accorded a defendant who is not represented by counsel" (316 U.S. at 473).

In a dissenting opinion, Justice Black, joined by Justices Douglas and Murphy, argued that the Court should incorporate the Sixth Amendment in order to apply the right to counsel against the states. Black also noted that the defendant in question was a poor farmhand who lacked the education necessary to have any hope of defending himself effectively. Black concluded his opinion by noting that most states had developed practices "which assure that no man shall be deprived of counsel merely because of his poverty. Any other practice seems to me to defeat the promise of our democratic society to provide equal justice under law" (316 U.S. at 477). Black's dissenting opinion, as well as his continued presence on the Court during the Warren Court era, helped to establish the basis for subsequent decisions expanding the definition and application of the right to counsel.

Trial Rights

Sixth Amendment cases have raised a variety of issues concerning the right to a jury trial, the "speediness," "fairness," and "publicness" of trials, and the appropriate composition of juries. In addition, Sixth Amendment cases have examined the rights to compulsory process and to confront witnesses. Although the words of the Sixth Amendment have presented the opportunity for judicial examination of these issues since 1791, most of the Supreme Court's cases defining the contours of trial rights have been decided since 1960. Relatively few cases concerning these issues arose for most of American history, in part because the Sixth Amendment had not been incorporated to apply against the states.

An early important case concerning juries, *Strauder v. West Virginia* (1880), decided that a West Virginia statute that permitted only white males to serve as jurors violated the right to equal protection of the laws. In subsequent decades, however, various states still applied various means to exclude both women and African Americans from juries. The *Strauder* decision had limited impact on discrimination in jury service "because the defendant was required to show a definite purpose to discriminate by jury officials; [thus] the state action was presumed constitutional and the lower court findings were presumed to be true unless the defendant proved the contrary" (Kamisar, LaFave, and Israel 1990, p. 1304).

With respect to the proper size and voting criteria for juries, the Court stated in 1898 that it adopted the traditional view of the need for twelve-member juries rendering unanimous verdicts: "[t]he wise men who framed the Constitution . . . [believed that] in criminal prosecutions, [justice] would not be adequately secured except through the unanimous verdict of twelve jurors" (*Thompson v. Utah*, 170 U.S. at 353). This view was based on the historical traditions in England, especially the Magna Carta's statement that juries would have twelve members, and understandings of the common law practices used in American courts in 1789 when the Bill of Rights was drafted (Heller 1951, p. 64). This dominant view did not, however, prevent a five-member majority on the Court from upholding a criminal conviction produced by a 9–3 jury vote in the Hawaiian Islands Territory (*Hawaii v. Mankichi*, 1903). The Court claimed that it was deferring to congressional intentions to maintain Hawaiian court practices as they existed prior to American acquisition of the territory in 1898.

Similar reasoning led the justices to conclude not merely that juries could render nonunanimous verdicts, but that the right to trial by jury did not exist at all in the American territories of the Philippines, Puerto Rico, and the Virgin Islands. Because the Sixth Amendment right to trial by jury was not regarded as "fundamental," that right was not thought to be sufficiently important to impose on territories that did not use juries because they drew their judicial traditions from Spain (i.e., the Philippines, Puerto Rico) and Denmark (i.e., Virgin Islands). The Court rejected the Alaska Territory's use of six-person juries (*Rasmussen v. United States*, 1905), but only because of the justices' interpretation of the treaty that acquired Alaska, not because of the Sixth Amendment (Heller 1951, pp. 48–50).

In a decision rendered in 1930 concerning a trial in which an eleven-member jury reached a verdict after one juror became ill, the Court reiterated the traditional view that the jury should contain twelve members who reach a unanimous decision. However, the justices said that defendants could waive their right to a constitutional jury (*Patton v. United States*, 1930). This decision effectively cast jury trials as an elective right of defendants rather than as a constitutional requirement of government as indicated by the Jury Clause of Article III, Section 2 of the original Constitution (Heller 1951, p. 68). According to Article III: "The Trial of all Crimes, except in cases of Impeachment, shall be by Jury; and such Trial shall be held in the State where the said Crimes shall have been committed . . . ." This language in the Constitution concerning government obligations has received little attention since being overshadowed by the focus in subsequent Supreme Court cases on defendants' Sixth Amendment right to trial by jury.

The Supreme Court's seminal incorporation case, *Palko v. Connecticut* (1937), used the Sixth Amendment right to trial by jury as an example of a right that is *not* fundamental and therefore not applicable to the states (see Chapter 4). However, in 1948 the Court invalidated the Michigan practice of secret sentencing procedures and thereby effectively incorporated the "public trial" provision of the Sixth Amendment (*In re Oliver*, 1948). This implicit incorporation of a portion of the Sixth Amendment did not apply the right to jury trials to the states, but it provided a Sixth Amendment precedent that later cases would use in expanding the applicability of the Sixth Amendment to the states (Abraham 1988, p. 78).

The Compulsory Process Clause of the Sixth Amendment is designed to enable defendants to gather information and evidence necessary to present an effective defense. The right to compulsory process gained importance in the decades immediately following the ratification of the Bill of Rights. In the treason case against Vice President Aaron Burr, Chief Justice John Marshall declared that "the right given by this article must be deemed sacred by the courts" (*United States v. Burr*, 25 F. Cas. at 33, [1807]) and must be applied even against the president of the United States who allegedly possessed two letters that had been used as key evidence to bring charges against Burr (Garcia 1992, p. 115).

The Confrontation Clause of the Sixth Amendment seeks to assure that defendants have the opportunity to cross-examine witnesses against them in order to illuminate inconsistencies in their testimony. Thus the right to confront witnesses seeks to avoid the possibility that a court will accept testimony from an absent witness who has not been tested by cross-examination or hear testimony outside of the presence of the defendant. Several nineteenth-century Supreme Court cases laid the groundwork for later Confrontation Clause cases (Garcia 1992, pp. 73-74). In *Reynolds v. United States* (1879), the Court upheld the admission of witness testimony from a previous trial because the defendant was responsible for the witness' absence at the later trial. In *Mattox v. United States* (1895), the Court relied on "considerations of public policy and the necessities of the case" (153 U.S. at 243) to conclude that previous trial testimony from now-deceased witnesses could be used at a later trial. Finally, in *Motes v. United States* (1900), the Court barred introduction of preliminary hearing testimony from a prosecution witness when the witness was absent due to the prosecutor's negligence. According to Alfredo Garcia (1992, p. 74), "If a pattern is to be discerned from the interpretive analysis of the confrontation doctrine by the Court in these early cases, it is that the critical right to confrontation accorded to a defendant under the Sixth Amendment is constrained by a rule of '[witness] availability.' This doctrine, in turn, chiefly meant to prevent manifest injustice in the sense of tying the prosecutor's hand when events beyond the control of the government adversely affected the prosecution's case."

The Warren Court Era

The justices on the Supreme Court during the Warren era expanded greatly the constitutional rights provided to criminal defendants, including rights under the Sixth Amendment. Prior to the Warren Court era, the Court's decisions provided modest protections for defendants in limited circumstances. By contrast, the Warren Court justices issued broad rulings that applied the right to counsel and other rights to criminal courts throughout the country at the state and federal levels.

Right to Counsel

As we saw in the introduction to this chapter, the *Betts* case remained in force for twenty-one years until the Warren Court justices unanimously overruled it, incorporated the Sixth Amendment, and applied the *Johnson* rule to the states in *Gideon v. Wainwright* (1963). The *Gideon* case is one of the most famous and popular decisions in Supreme Court history (Garcia 1992, p. 9). Because relatively few states did not appoint counsel for indigent defendants by 1963, the *Gideon* case represented the final nationalization of a policy that had gradually spread from state to state.

GIDEON V. WAINWRIGHT

372 U.S. 335, 835 S.Ct. 792, 9 L. Ed. 2d 799 (1963)
[The facts of this case are omitted because they were presented in the case study at the beginning of this chapter.]

■ The case is important because it applied the right to counsel to the criminal trial courts in all fifty states. As you read the case, consider the following questions: (1) How does Justice Black characterize the existence, or lack thereof, of Supreme Court precedents supporting the recognition of the Sixth Amendment right to counsel as a fundamental right? (2) Because six of the justices who supported Gideon were on the Court together as far back as 1956 and could have formed a majority to nationalize the right to counsel, why did they wait until 1963 to make this decision?

VOTE:

Nine justices found Florida's denial of appointed counsel to be unconstitutional (Black, Brennan, Clark, Douglas, Goldberg, Harlan, Stewart, Warren, White).

No justices found Florida's practice to be constitutional.

Justice Black delivered the opinion of the Court.

* * *

We think the Court in *Betts* [*v. Brady*, 1942] had ample precedent for acknowledging that those guarantees of the Bill of Rights which are fundamental safeguards of liberty immune from federal abridgment are equally protected against state invasion by the Due Process Clause of the Fourteenth Amendment. This same principle was recognized, explained, and applied in *Powell v. Alabama* . . ., a case upholding the right of counsel, where the Court held that despite sweeping language to the contrary in *Hurtado v. California*, . . . the Fourteenth Amendment "embraced" those "fundamental principles of liberty and justice which lie at the base of all our civil and political institutions," even though they had been "specifically dealt with in another part of the federal Constitution." [*Powell*,] 287 U.S. at 67. In many cases other than *Powell* and *Betts*, this Court has looked to the fundamental nature of the original Bill of Rights guarantees to decide whether the Fourteenth Amendment makes them obligatory on the States. Explicitly recognized to be of this "fundamental nature" and therefore made immune from state invasion by the Fourteenth, or some part of it, are the First Amendment's freedoms of speech, press, religion, assembly, association, and petition for redress of grievances. For the same reason, though not always in precisely the same terminology, the Court has made obligatory on the States the Fifth Amendment's command that private property shall not be taken for public use without just compensation, the Fourth Amendment's prohibition of unreasonable searches and seizures, and the Eighth's ban on cruel and unusual punishment. On the other hand, this Court in *Palko v. Connecticut* (1937), refused to hold that the Fourteenth Amendment made the double jeopardy provision of the Fifth Amendment obligatory on the States. In so refusing, however, the Court, speaking through Mr. Justice Cardozo, was careful to emphasize that "immunities that are valid as against the federal government by force of the specific pledges of particular amendments have been found to be implicit in the concept of ordered liberty, and thus, through the Fourteenth Amendment, have become valid as against the states" and that guarantees "in their origin . . . effective against the federal government alone" had by prior cases "been taken over from the earlier articles of the federal bill of rights and brought within the Fourteenth Amendment by a process of absorption." [*Palko*], 302 U.S. at 324-325, 326.

We accept *Betts v. Brady*'s assumption, based as it was on our prior cases, that a provision of the Bill of Rights which is "fundamental and essential to a fair trial" is made obligatory upon the States by the Fourteenth Amendment. We think the Court in *Betts* was wrong, however, in concluding that the Sixth Amendment's guarantee of counsel is not one of these fundamental rights. Ten years before *Betts v. Brady*, this Court, after full consideration of all the historical data examined in *Betts*, had unequivocally declared that "the right to the aid of counsel is of this fundamental character." *Powell v. Alabama*, 287 U.S. 45, 68 (1932). While the Court at the close of its *Powell* opinion did by its language, as this Court frequently does, limit its holding to the particular facts and circumstances of that case, its conclusions about the fundamental nature of the right to counsel are unmistakable. Several years later, in 1936, the Court reemphasized what it had said about the fundamental nature of the right to counsel in this language:

> "We concluded that certain fundamental rights, safeguarded by the first eight amendments against federal action, were also safeguarded against state action by the due process of law clause of the Fourteenth Amendment, and among them the fundamental right of the accused to the aid of counsel in a criminal prosecution." *Grosjean v. American Press Co.*, 297 U.S. 233, 243-44 (1936).

And again in 1938 this Court said:

> "[The assistance of counsel] is one of the safeguards of the Sixth Amendment deemed necessary to insure fundamental human rights of life and liberty . . . . The Sixth Amendment stands as a constant admonition that if the constitutional safeguards it provides be lost, justice will not 'still be done'." *Johnson v. Zerbst,* 304 U.S. 458, 462 (1938). To the same effect, see *Avery v. Alabama* (1940), *Smith v. O'Grady* (1941).

In light of these and many other prior decisions of this Court, it is not surprising that the *Betts* Court, when faced with the contention that "one charged with crime, who is unable to obtain counsel, must be furnished counsel by the State," conceded that "[e]xpressions in the opinions of this court lend color to the argument . . . ." 316 U.S. at 462-463. The fact is that in deciding as it did — that "appointment of counsel is not a fundamental right, essential to a fair trial" — the Court in *Betts v. Brady* made an abrupt break with its own well-considered precedents. In returning to these old precedents, sounder we believe than the new, we but restore constitutional principles established to achieve a fair system of justice. Not only these precedents but also reason and reflection require us to recognize that in our adversary system of criminal justice, any person haled into court, who is too poor to hire a lawyer, cannot be assured a fair trial unless counsel is provided to him. This seems to us to be an obvious truth. Governments, both state and federal, quite properly spend vast sums of money to establish machinery to try defendants accused of crime. Lawyers to prosecute are everywhere deemed essential to protect the public's interest in an orderly society. Similarly, there are few defendants charged with crime, few indeed, who fail to hire the best lawyers they can get to prepare and present their defenses. That government hires lawyers to prosecute and defendants who have the money hire lawyers to defend are the strongest indications of the widespread belief that lawyers in criminal courts are necessities, not luxuries. The right of one charged with crime to counsel may not be deemed fundamental and essential to fair trials in some countries, but it is in ours. From the very beginning, our state and national constitutions and laws have laid great emphasis on procedural and substantive safeguards designed to assure fair trials before impartial tribunals in which every defendant stands equal before the law. This noble ideal cannot be realized if the poor man charged with crime has to face his accusers without a lawyer to assist him . . . . The Court in *Betts v. Brady* departed from the sound wisdom upon which the Court's holding in *Powell v. Alabama* rested. Florida, supported by two other States, has asked that *Betts v. Brady* be left intact. Twenty-two States, as friends of the Court, argue that *Betts* was "an anachronism when handed down" and that it should now be overruled. We agree.

The judgment is reversed and the cause is remanded to the Supreme Court of Florida for further action not inconsistent with this opinion.

Reversed.

[The concurring opinions of Justices Douglas, Clark, and Harlan are omitted.]

Although the *Gideon* decision had little impact except in those states which did not provide attorneys for indigents, it provided the basis for further decisions in which the Supreme Court could interpret and apply the Sixth Amendment in creating additional rules for all state court systems to follow. For example, on the very day that the Court's decision in *Gideon* was announced, the justices also decided *Douglas v. California* (1963), which required all states to extend the right to appointed counsel beyond the trial stage by also supplying representation for indigent offenders for their first postconviction appeal granted as a matter of right under state law. Justice Douglas's opinion in the *Douglas* case did not rest on the

Sixth Amendment. Instead, he talked generally about fair procedures and equality for rich and poor defendants. However, the impact of the decision effectively expanded the scope of the right to counsel as contained in the Sixth Amendment.

The Warren Court's most significant impact on right to counsel came through a series of cases that defined *when* a person is entitled to representation in the criminal justice process. These cases were discussed in Chapter 10 because they concern a suspect's Fifth Amendment right to be free from self-incrimination. However, they also affect the Sixth Amendment right to counsel. For example, when the Court required police officers to inform arrestees of their rights in *Miranda v. Arizona* (1966), it also effectively required that indigent defendants who wished to receive appointed representation immediately be provided with attorneys before any police questioning occurs. Similarly, *Escobedo v. Illinois* (1964) established that incriminating statements made by defendants could not be used against them if the police had refused to accommodate the defendants' requests to speak to an attorney. *Massiah v. United States* (1964) established that the police could not use agents, such as codefendants, to question indicted defendants who were represented by counsel and had already asserted their right to be represented by counsel during police questioning. In *Mempa v. Rhay* (1967) the Court required the availability of representation for proceedings concerning probation revocation and resentencing.

In effect, the Warren Court drastically altered the protections for criminal defendants, not by establishing a right to counsel at trial in *Gideon*, because that practice already existed in most states, but rather by requiring states to make attorneys available at earlier stages in the criminal process. After the Warren Court era, indigent defendants could receive legal advice and assistance that disrupted the customary interrogation practices of police departments and potentially diminished the ability of police to obtain incriminating information directly from suspects. Although the criminal justice process was significantly altered by the expanded availability and role of defense counsel, it is difficult to determine precisely how the outcomes of criminal cases have been affected. Even after defendants received the benefits of the expanded Sixth Amendment right to counsel, many defendants continued either to waive their right to counsel during questioning or to provide incriminating information to police with the advice of counsel in order to gain more favorable plea bargain agreements.

Trial Rights

The Warren Court justices did not limit themselves to the expansion of the right to counsel when they interpreted and applied the Sixth Amendment during the 1960s. These justices also applied the other provisions of the Sixth Amendment to the states.

In 1965, the Supreme Court incorporated the Confrontation Clause in *Pointer v. Texas.* The Court unanimously reversed the conviction of a man after the prosecution used at trial a transcript of preliminary hearing testimony given by an absent codefendant. Justice Black emphasized that the confrontation right requires that the defendant have the opportunity to cross-examine witnesses. Although Pointer was convicted at a second trial when the absent witness returned to Texas, his case helped to broaden the application of Sixth Amendment rights (Abraham 1988, pp. 89–90).

The following year the Court incorporated the right to an "impartial jury" by overturning the conviction of a defendant because of prejudicial remarks made to the sequestered jury by a bailiff (*Parker v. Gladden*, 1966). In 1967, the Court decided two more cases that expanded the application of the Sixth Amendment. In *Klopfer v. North Carolina* the Court incorporated the right to a speedy trial after North Carolina had attempted to assert the authority to wait indefinitely before initiating the trial of a college professor who had participated in a civil rights protest. In *Washington v. Texas* the justices extended the confrontation right to enable defendants to confront favorable witnesses as well as adverse witnesses.

The *Washington* case also "gave new impetus to the right to compulsory process by equating it with the right to present a defense and by characterizing compulsory process as a 'fundamental element of due process' " (Garcia 1992, p. 116). Texas rules had barred a codefendant from testifying on Washington's behalf in a murder case, but the Court declared that the state could not prevent a capable witness from presenting testimony that was relevant to the defendant's defense.

In 1968, the Warren Court completed its incorporation of the Sixth Amendment by declaring in *Duncan v. Louisiana* that the right to trial by jury was applicable to the states in the same manner that it was applicable to the federal government. Thus, as we saw in Chapter 4, the states were obligated to provide jury trials for defendants accused of "serious" crimes that could produce penalties of six months or more in prison. The Court dramatically reshaped the meaning and applicability of the Sixth Amendment in the short five-year span from *Gideon* (1963) to *Duncan* (1968). These decisions expanded and standardized the protections for arrestees and defendants who were drawn into criminal courts throughout the nation.

The Burger Court Era

The changing composition of the Supreme Court during the Burger era produced new decisions that expanded some aspects of Sixth Amendment rights but, more frequently, limited or reduced the application of rights defined by Warren Court decisions. The Burger Court did not eliminate the decisions of the Warren Court, but it narrowed the scope of the rights established by those decisions.

Right to Counsel

The Burger Court's composition was significantly different from that of the Warren Court because President Nixon had the opportunity to appoint four new justices to the Court between 1969 and 1972. Despite Nixon's intention to appoint justices who would restrict the scope of criminal defendants' rights recognized in the Warren Court's decisions, the Burger Court justices did not uniformly restrict the right to counsel. In some cases they actually expanded the availability of representation for defendants. In *Argersinger v. Hamlin* (1972), the Court expanded the Sixth Amendment protection by declaring that indigent defendants were entitled to representation for petty offenses if they faced the possibility of incarceration as a punishment. The *Gideon* decision had focused on nonpetty offenses with possible punishments of six months or more in prison. According to Justice Douglas's majority opinion in *Argersinger*, "Under the rule we announce today, every judge will know when the trial of a misdemeanor starts that no imprisonment may be imposed, even though local law permits it, unless the accused is represented by counsel" (407 U.S. at 40). In *Gagnon v. Scarpelli* (1973), the justices stated that with respect to probation and parole revocation hearings "[i]n some cases, these modifications in the nature of the revocation hearing must be endured and the costs borne [by the state] because [the] probationer's or parolee's version of a disputed issue can fairly be represented only by a trained advocate" (411 U.S. at 788). Although the *Gagnon* decision represented an expansion of the right to counsel to new posttrial stages in the criminal process, Justice Lewis Powell's emphasis that the right to appointed counsel existed only "[i]n *some* cases" (emphasis supplied) accurately indicated that the Burger Court majority was intent on limiting the continuing expansion of the right to counsel that had begun in the Warren Court era.

The Burger Court curtailed the expansion of the right to counsel in *Ross v. Moffitt* (1974) by limiting the application of the Warren Court's decision in *Douglas v. California* (1963). The *Douglas* decision had granted a right to appointed counsel for first appeals as a matter of right, but the *Ross* decision declared that no such right exists for subsequent discretionary appeals, such as an appeal to a state supreme court after losing an appeal in an intermediate appellate court. Like the *Douglas* opinion, Justice William Rehnquist's opinion in *Ross* made no mention of the Sixth Amendment but instead asserted that neither the Equal Protection Clause nor the Due Process Clause was violated by a failure to supply representation for discretionary appeals.

A further restriction on the right to counsel appeared in a subsequent Rehnquist-authored majority opinion, *Scott v. Illinois* (1979). Scott was charged with shoplifting, and he did not receive an appointed attorney because the prosecutor announced prior to trial that he would ask for only a fine and not a jail sentence if Scott were convicted. In a narrow 5–4 decision, Justice Rehnquist declined to extend the *Argersinger* principle to cases in which incarceration is not imposed as a punishment. The implicit premise of the majority's decision was that punishments other than imprisonment are not so serious as to require full adversarial proceedings through the clash of contending attorneys. Critics of the Court's decision charge, however, that criminal convictions, even for minor offenses, can produce social stigma and a criminal record that may interfere with employment and other opportunities for people convicted of petty offenses. If unrepresented people are wrongly convicted in the manner of Clarence Earl Gideon, they may bear life-long burdens even though they are not required to serve time in a jail or prison (Smith 1991, p. 101). In the *Scott* decision, Rehnquist also relied on concerns about federalism and the policy impact on the states when he asserted that "*Argersinger* has proved reasonably workable, whereas any extension would create confusion and impose unpredictable, but necessarily substantial, costs on 50 quite diverse states" (440 U.S. at 373). This kind of concern about imposing uncertain costs on the states had not been emphasized by the Warren Court majority, but such arguments found a more receptive audience among Nixon's appointees to the Burger Court.

The Burger Court also began to alter the requirements for the timing of appointment of counsel. The Supreme Court's emphasis has been on insuring representation when criminal investigations move to a "critical stage" of focusing the mechanisms of arrest and prosecution at particular defendants. The Warren Court had ruled that defendants are entitled to representation at line-ups, in which victims and witnesses identify suspects (*United States v. Wade*, 1967). However, the Burger Court majority narrowly revised the definition of "critical stage" by deciding that counsel is not required at either pre-indictment line-ups (*Kirby v. Illinois*, 1972) or photo-identification sessions at which the accused is not present (*United States v. Ash*, 1973). The Warren Court decisions were based on the majority's concerns about eyewitness errors, suggestive presentations by the police and prosecutor, and difficulties in discerning other prejudicial elements that may occur if no defense attorney is present to object and raise questions. According to critics of the Burger Court, "the *Kirby* Court ignored the policy considerations supporting the [Warren Court decisions] and rested their affirmance of Kirby's conviction entirely on the fact that he had been neither indicted or formally charged nor subject to the 'initiation of adversary judicial criminal proceedings' " (Decker 1992, p. 89).

The Supreme Court's decisions during the Burger era clarified issues about the quality of representation to be provided to defendants, but this clarification ultimately provided little protection for individual defendants. In *Morris v. Slappy* (1983), one week before trial, the defendant's court-appointed attorney who had handled the investigation and preliminary hearing was hospitalized. A second public defender took over the case and, over the objections of the defendant who claimed that the second attorney had insufficient time to prepare, the new public defender claimed that he was adequately prepared after one week. The Supreme Court rejected the federal appellate court's ruling that defendants have a right to a meaningful relationship with their attorneys. Therefore, the justices found no violation of the defendant's rights when his new attorney had relatively little time to become familiar with the case. In *Strickland v. Washington* (1984), the Court established criteria for determining whether a defendant received "ineffective assistance of counsel" that was so inadequate as to violate the Sixth Amendment (Garcia 1992, p. 33). However, because the Court established a presumption in favor of the effectiveness of attorneys and clearly did not wish for judges to second-guess attorneys' trial tactics, defendants bear a difficult burden of proof in seeking to demonstrate their attorneys' constitutionally deficient ineffectiveness. Defendants must demonstrate not only that their attorneys were ineffective but also that such ineffectiveness affected the outcome of the case. In practice, it is extremely difficult to present sufficient proof (Decker 1992, p. 95).

Trial Rights

The Burger Court's decisions demonstrated a different vision of the jury than that portrayed in early cases such as *Thompson v. Utah* (1898) and *Patton v. United States* (1930) in which the justices envisioned twelve members rendering unanimous verdicts. In *Williams v. Florida* (1970), the Court endorsed Florida's use of six-member juries in criminal cases. The decision was not the result of changes in the Court's composition. Only one Nixon appointee, Chief Justice Burger, participated in the case, yet only one justice, Justice Thurgood Marshall, dissented from the Court's holding. The 7–1 decision was essentially produced by Warren Court holdovers.

Two years later, the Court further altered the traditional view of the American jury. In *Apodaca v. Oregon* (1972), a deeply divided Court endorsed Oregon's use of less-than-unanimous criminal jury verdicts. Five justices approved Oregon's rule permitting a minimum of ten jurors to produce a verdict of guilty over the disagreement of the remaining two jurors. In this case, the Court's composition may have been a major factor in the outcome because the four new Nixon appointees (Burger, Blackmun, Rehnquist, and Powell) were joined by only one Warren Court holdover (Justice Byron White) in producing what Justice William O. Douglas labeled a "radical departure from American traditions" (406 U.S. at 381).

Apodaca v. Oregon

406 U.S. 404, 92 S.Ct 1628, 32 L.Ed. 2d 184 (1972)

■ Robert Apodaca, Henry Cooper, and James Madden were tried on charges of assault with a deadly weapon, burglary, and larceny. Under Oregon law, juries can convict defendants on less-than-unanimous votes. Apodaca and Madden were convicted by 11–1 votes and Cooper was convicted by a 10–2 vote, the minimum requisite vote under state law for sustaining a conviction. Their convictions were sustained by the Oregon Court of Appeals and the Oregon Supreme Court. They petitioned the U.S. Supreme Court to assert their claim that less-than-unanimous verdicts in criminal cases violate the Sixth Amendment right to trial by jury. The case was decided simultaneously with a companion case, *Johnson v. Louisiana*, concerning Louisiana's comparable split-verdict rules that permitted 9–3 decisions as the minimum standard to convict defendants at trial.

This case is important because it illustrates the Burger Court's inclination to give states greater flexibility to govern criminal trials with their own practices and procedures. The decision also deviated from the Warren Court's usual practice of requiring state courts to follow the same procedures as federal courts with respect to defining and protecting the rights of criminal defendants. As you read the case, consider the following questions: (1) Which justices are in the majority and which components of the opinions constitute binding precedential reasoning for other courts to follow? (2) To what extent are the opinions based on policy considerations rather than on legal reasoning? (3) What are the consequences of having different jury voting practices utilized in the criminal courts of different states?

VOTE:

Five justices found the less-than-unanimous criminal jury verdicts to be constitutional (Blackmun, Burger, Powell, Rehnquist, White).

Four justices found the less-than-unanimous criminal jury verdicts to be unconstitutional (Brennan, Douglas, Marshall, Stewart).

Justice White announced the judgment of the Court in an opinion in which Chief Justice Burger, Justice Blackmun, and Justice Rehnquist joined.

* * *

In *Williams v. Florida* [1970], . . . we had occasion to consider a related issue: whether the Sixth Amendment's right to trial by jury requires that all juries consist of 12 men. After considering the history of the 12-man requirement and the functions it performs in contemporary society, we concluded that it was not of constitutional stature. We reach the same conclusion today with regard to the requirement of unanimity.

Like the requirement that juries consist of 12 men, the requirement of unanimity arose during the Middle Ages and had become an accepted feature of the common-law jury by the 18th century. But, as we observed in *Williams*, "the relevant constitutional history casts considerable doubt on the easy assumption . . . that if a given feature existed in a jury at common law in 1789, then it was necessarily preserved in the Constitution" [399 U.S. at 92-93]. . . .

As we observed in *Williams*, one can draw conflicting inferences from the legislative history . . . . Surely one fact that is absolutely clear from this history is that, after a proposal had been made to specify precisely which of the common-law requisites of the jury were to be preserved by the Constitution, the Framers explicitly rejected the proposal and instead left such specification for the future. As in *Williams*, we must accordingly consider what is meant by the concept of "jury" and determine whether a feature commonly associated with it is constitutionally required. And, as in *Williams*, our inability to divine "the intent of the Framers" when they eliminated references to the "accustomed requisites" requires that in determining what is meant by a jury we must turn to other than purely historical considerations.

Our inquiry must focus upon the function served by the jury in contemporary society . . . ."[T]he essential feature of a jury obviously lies in the interposition between the accused and his accuser of the commonsense judgment of a group of laymen . . . ."[*Williams*, 399 at 100] . . . . A requirement of unanimity, however, does not materially contribute to the exercise of this commonsense judgment . . . . Requiring unanimity would obviously produce hung juries in some situations where non-unanimous juries will convict or acquit. But in either case, the interest of the defendant in having the judgment of his peers interposed between himself and the officers of the State who prosecute and judge him is equally well served.

Petitioners nevertheless argue that unanimity serves other purposes constitutionally essential to the continued operation of the jury system. Their principal contention is that a Sixth Amendment "jury trial" made mandatory on the States by virtue of the Due Process Clause of the Fourteenth Amendment [in *Duncan v. Louisiana*] should be held to require a unanimous jury verdict in order to give substance to the reasonable-doubt standard otherwise mandated by the Due Process Clause. See [*In re Winship* (1970) that required the reasonable-doubt standard for convictions in juvenile proceedings].

We are quite sure, however, that the Sixth Amendment itself has never been held to require proof beyond a reasonable doubt in criminal cases. The reasonable-doubt standard developed separately from both the jury trial and the unanimous verdict. As the Court noted in the *Winship* case, the rule requiring proof of crime beyond a reasonable doubt did not crystallize in this country until after the Constitution was adopted . . . . And in [*Winship*], which held such a burden of proof to be constitutionally required, the Court purported to draw no support from the Sixth Amendment.

* * *

Petitioners also cite quite accurately a long line of decisions of this Court upholding the principle that the Fourteenth Amendment requires jury panels to reflect a cross section of the community . . . . They then contend that unanimity is a necessary precondition for effective application of the cross-section requirement, because a rule permitting less than unanimous verdicts will make it possible for convictions to occur without the acquiescence of minority elements within the community.

There are two flaws in this argument. One is petitioners' assumption that every distinct voice in the community has a right to be represented on every jury and a right to prevent conviction of a defendant in any case. All that the Constitution forbids, however, is systematic exclusion of identifiable segments of the community from jury panels and from the juries ultimately drawn from those panels; a defendant may not, for example, challenge the makeup of a jury merely because no members of his race are on the jury, but must prove that his race has been systematically excluded . . . . No group, in short, has the right to block convictions; it has only the right to participate in the overall legal processes by which criminal guilt and innocence are determined.

We also cannot accept petitioners' second assumption—that minority groups, even when they are represented on a jury, will not adequately represent the viewpoint of those groups simply because they may be outvoted in the final result. They will be present during all deliberations, and their views will be heard. We cannot assume that the majority of the jury will refuse to weigh the evidence and reach a decision upon rational grounds, just as it must now do in order to obtain unanimous verdicts, or that a majority will deprive a man of his liberty on the basis of prejudice when a minority is presenting a reasonable argument in favor of acquittal. We simply find no proof for the notion that a majority will disregard its instructions and cast its votes for guilt or innocence based on prejudices rather than the evidence.

We accordingly affirm the judgment of the Court of Appeals of Oregon.

It is so ordered.

Judgment affirmed.

Justice Blackmun concurring.

I join the Court's opinion and judgment in each of these cases. I add only the comment, which should be obvious and should not need saying, that in so doing I do not imply that I regard a State's split-verdict system as a wise one. My vote means only that I cannot conclude that the system is constitutionally offensive. Were I a legislator, I would disfavor it as a matter of policy. Our task here, however, is not to pursue and strike down what happens to impress us as undesirable legislative policy.

I do not hesitate to say, either, that a system employing a 7-5 standard, rather than a 9-3 or 75% minimum, would afford me great difficulty. As Mr. Justice White points out, . . . "a substantial majority of the jury" are to be convinced. That is all that is before us in each of these cases.

Justice Powell concurring.

I concur in the judgment of the Court that conviction based on less-than-unanimous jury verdicts in these cases did not deprive criminal defendants of due process of law under the Fourteenth Amendment. As my reasons for reaching this conclusion in the Oregon case differ from those expressed in the plurality opinion of Mr. Justice White, I will state my views separately.

* * *

[The plurality opinion's] premise is that the concept of jury trial, as applicable to the States under the Fourteenth Amendment, must be identical in every detail to the concept required in federal courts by the Sixth Amendment. I do not think that all of the elements of jury trial within the meaning of the Sixth Amendment are necessarily embodied in or incorporated into the Due Process Clause of the Fourteenth Amendment . . . . * * *

In an unbroken line of cases reaching back into the late 1800's, the Justices of this Court have recognized, virtually without dissent, that unanimity is one of the indispensable features of *federal* jury trial . . . . In these cases, the Court has presumed that unanimous verdicts are essential in federal jury trials, not because unanimity is necessarily fundamental to the function performed by the jury, but because that result is mandated by history. The reasoning that runs throughout this Court's Sixth Amendment precedents is that, in amending the Constitution to guarantee the right to jury trial, the framers desired to preserve the jury safeguard as it was known to them at common law. At the time the Bill of Rights was adopted, unanimity had long been established as one of the attributes of a jury conviction at common law. It therefore seems to me, in accord both with history and precedent, that the Sixth Amendment requires a unanimous jury verdict to convict in a federal criminal trial.

But it is the Fourteenth Amendment, rather than the Sixth, that imposes upon the States the requirement that they provide jury trials to those accused of serious crimes. This Court has said, in cases decided when the intendment of that Amendment was not as clouded by the passage of time, that due process does not require that the States apply the federal jury-trial right with all its gloss.

* * *

Viewing the unanimity controversy as one requiring a fresh look at the question of what is fundamental in jury trial, I see no constitutional infirmity in the provision adopted by the people of Oregon. It is the product of a constitutional amendment, approved by a vote of the people in the State, and appears to be patterned on a provision of the American Law Institute's Code of Criminal Procedure. A similar decision has been echoed more recently in England where the unanimity requirement was abandoned by statutory enactment. Less-than-unanimous verdict provisions also have been viewed with approval by the American Bar Association's Criminal Justice Project . . . .

Justice Stewart, with whom Justice Brennan and Justice Marshall join, dissenting.

In *Duncan v. Louisiana* [1968] . . ., the Court squarely held that the Sixth Amendment right to trial by jury in a federal criminal case is made wholly applicable to state criminal trials by the Fourteenth Amendment. Unless *Duncan* is to be overruled, therefore, the only relevant question here is whether the Sixth Amendment's guarantee of trial by jury embraces a guarantee that the verdict of the jury be unanimous. The answer to that question is clearly "yes," as my Brother Powell has cogently demonstrated in that part of his concurring opinion that reviews almost a century of Sixth Amendment adjudication.

Until today, it had been universally understood that a unanimous verdict is an essential element of a Sixth Amendment jury trial . . . [citations to five cases].

I would follow these settled Sixth Amendment precedents and reverse the judgment before us.

Justice Douglas, with whom Justice Brennan and Justice Marshall join, dissenting.

* * *

With due respect to the majority, I dissent from this radical departure from American tradition.

* * *

Do today's decisions mean that States may apply a "watered down" version of the Just Compensation Clause [or other rights contained in the Bill of Rights]? Or are today's decisions limited to a paring down of civil rights protected by the Bill of Rights and up until now as fully applicable to the States as to the Federal Government?

These civil rights—whether they concern speech, searches and seizures, self-incrimination, criminal prosecutions, bail, or cruel and unusual punishments extend, of course, to everyone, but in cold reality touch mostly the lower castes in our society. I refer, of course, to the blacks, the Chicanos, the one-mule farmers, the agricultural workers, the off-beat students, the victims of the ghetto. Are we giving the States the power to experiment in diluting their civil rights? It has long been thought that "thou shall nots" in the Constitution and Bill of Rights protect everyone against governmental intrusion or overreaching. The idea has been obnoxious that there are some who can be relegated to second-class citizenship. But if we construe the Bill of Rights and the Fourteenth Amendment to permit States to "experiment" with the basic rights of people, we open a veritable Pandora's box. For hate and prejudice are versatile forces that can degrade the constitutional scheme.

* * *

I would construe the Sixth Amendment, when applicable to the States, precisely as I would when applied to the Federal Government.

The plurality approves a procedure which diminishes the reliability of a jury . . . .

The diminution of verdict reliability flows from the fact that nonunanimous juries need not debate and deliberate as fully as must unanimous juries. As soon as the requisite majority is attained, further consideration is not required either by Oregon or by Louisiana even though the dissident jurors might, if given the chance, be able to convince the majority. Such persuasion does in fact occasionally occur in States where the unanimous requirement applies: "In roughly one case in ten, the minority eventually succeeds in reversing an initial majority, and these may be cases of special importance" [quoted from a study of juries conducted by psychologists]. One explanation for this phenomenon is that because jurors are often not permitted to take notes and because they have imperfect memories, the forensic process of forcing jurors to defend their conflicting recollections and conclusions flushes out many nuances which otherwise would go overlooked. This collective effort to piece together the puzzle of historical truth, however, is cut short as soon as the requisite majority is reached in Oregon and Louisiana. Indeed, if a necessary majority is immediately obtained, then no deliberation at all is required in these States. (There is a suggestion that this may have happened in the 10-2 verdict rendered in only 41 minutes in Apodaca's case.) . . .The Court now extracts from the jury room this automatic check against hasty fact-finding by relieving jurors of the duty to hear out fully the dissenters.

* * *

Proof beyond a reasonable doubt and unanimity of criminal verdicts and the presumption of innocence are basic features of the accusatorial system. What we do today is not in that tradition but more in the tradition of the inquisition. Until new [constitutional] amendments are adopted setting new standards, I would let no man be fined or imprisoned in derogation of what up to today was indisputably the law of the land.

Justice Brennan, with whom Justice Marshall joins, dissenting.

* * *

It is in this context that we must view the constitutional requirement that all juries be drawn from an accurate cross section of the community. When verdicts must be unanimous, no member of the jury may be ignored by the others. When less than unanimity is sufficient, consideration of minority views may become nothing more than a matter of majority grace. In my opinion, the right of all groups in this Nation to participate in the criminal process means the right to have their voices heard. A unanimous verdict vindicates that right. Majority verdicts could destroy it.

Justice Marshall, with whom Justice Brennan joins, dissenting.

Today the Court cuts the heart out of two of the most important and inseparable safeguards the Bill of Rights offers a criminal defendant: the right to submit his case to a jury, and the right to proof beyond a reasonable doubt. Together, these safeguards occupy a fundamental place in our constitutional scheme, protecting the individual defendant from the awesome power of the State. After today, the skeleton of these safeguards remains, but the Court strips them of life and of meaning. I cannot refrain from adding my protest to that of my Brothers Douglas, Brennan, and Stewart, whom I join.

* * *

More distressing still than the Court's treatment of the right to jury trial is the cavalier treatment the Court gives to proof beyond a reasonable doubt. The Court asserts that when a jury votes nine to three for conviction [in Louisiana], the doubts of the three do not impeach the verdict of the nine . . . . But . . . we know what has happened: the prosecutor has tried and failed to persuade those [three] jurors of the defendant's guilt. In such circumstances, it does violence to language and logic to say that the government has proved the defendant's guilt beyond a reasonable doubt.

* * *

Each time this Court has approved a change in the familiar characteristics of the jury, we have reaffirmed the principle that its fundamental characteristic is its capacity to render a commonsense, laymen's judgment, as a representative body drawn from the community. To fence out dissenting jurors fences out a voice from the community, and undermines the principle on which our whole notion of the jury now rests . . . . The doubts of a single juror are in my view evidence that the government has failed to carry its burden of proving guilt beyond a reasonable doubt. I dissent.

Critics questioned the *Williams* and *Apodaca* decisions because of the possibility that small juries and nonunanimous juries might be more easily influenced by improper biases or might be less able to evaluate evidence thoroughly. Moreover, small juries may be less representative of the various segments of the community, and nonunanimous juries may permit dissenting jurors to be ignored.

Subsequently, in cases decided in 1978 and 1979, the Court resolved lingering questions about the size and unanimity requirements for criminal juries by setting constitutional minimum standards. Juries must have at least six members (*Ballew v. Georgia*, 1978), and juries containing only six members must render unanimous verdicts (*Burch v. Louisiana*, 1979). Justice Blackmun's majority opinion in *Ballew* relied on an examination of social science studies on jury decision making in determining the need for minimum constitutional standards (Levine 1992, p. 28). Ultimately, the line of decisions from *Williams* to *Burch* permitted states to develop their own jury procedures, as long as they did not violate the Court's minimum constitutional standards, rather than adhere to the federal court practice of twelve-member unanimous juries in criminal cases.

Although the Supreme Court increased the flexibility of states' choices about the size and voting requirements for juries, the Burger-era justices imposed requirements concerning jury composition to attempt to reduce discrimination in jury selection. In 1975, the Court emphasized that the Sixth Amendment contains a requirement that juries be selected from a fair cross section of the community. The Court used this requirement to invalidate Louisiana's statute which provided that women would not be selected for jury duty unless they filed a written declaration asking to be considered, thus barring mechanisms that systematically exclude women from jury service (*Taylor v. Louisiana*, 1975). In order to advance its desire to preclude discrimination in jury selection, the Court used the Equal Protection Clause in 1986 to bar prosecutors from using peremptory challenges in a systematic way to exclude potential jurors from particular racial groups (*Batson v. Kentucky*, 1986). Peremptory challenges normally permit lawyers to exclude potential jurors without giving any reason. Studies have shown that prosecutors often use their challenges to exclude potential jurors who are poor, young, or members of minority groups (Hans and Vidmar 1986, p. 75). Thus the unrestricted use of peremptory challenges creates risks that lawyers can manipulate the composition of the jury in discriminatory ways or in a manner to produce rather than eliminate bias among the jurors. With this decision at the close of the Burger era, the Supreme Court began to pay closer attention to the use of racially motivated peremptory challenges by various parties in criminal and civil cases to manipulate the composition of juries.

The Burger Court also relied on examinations of defendants' right to due process of law under the Fourteenth Amendment to issue important decisions concerning the processing of guilty pleas. The definition of such due process rights is especially important because the vast majority of criminal convictions are produced through negotiated guilty pleas rather than through trials. Only 6 percent of the more than 1.5 million criminal cases completed in state courts each year are decided through jury trials (Smith 1993, p. 179). Plea bargaining advances the interests of all parties involved, including the prosecutor, defense attorney, and defendant, by speeding up case processing and eliminating the unpredictability produced for both sides by jury trials. Thus due process rights as well as the Sixth Amendment right to counsel, both of which affect negotiated guilty pleas, actually impact far larger numbers of cases than do Sixth Amendment rights concerning jury trials.

The Supreme Court effectively endorsed the practice of plea bargaining as a means to secure defendants' guilty pleas when it required prosecutors to fulfill the promises they made regarding sentence recommendations when inducing a defendant to plead guilty (*Santobello v. New York*, 1971). Later, in *Bordenkircher v. Hayes* (1978), the Court approved the prosecutor's ability to pressure the defendant in plea negotiations by threatening to pursue more serious charges at trial if the defendant chose not to enter a guilty plea. This practice did not violate the defendant's right to due process of law. In effect, the Burger Court justices provided legitimacy and guidance for plea bargaining practices that had already developed throughout the United States for many decades.

Bordenkircher v. Hayes

434 U.S. 357, 98 S.Ct. 663, 54 L.Ed. 2d 604 (1978)

■ Hayes was charged with forging a check, an offense punishable by a sentence of two to ten years in prison. During plea negotiations between his attorney and the prosecutor, the prosecutor offered to recommend a sentence of five years if Hayes would agree to plead guilty. The prosecutor also said that if Hayes chose not to plead guilty, the prosecutor would seek a new indictment against him under the state's habitual offender statute, which could lead to a mandatory life sentence because Hayes had already been convicted twice before on other felony charges. Hayes chose not to plead guilty. The prosecutor obtained the habitual offender indictment, and Hayes was sentenced to life in prison as a habitual criminal after being convicted for forging the check. The Kentucky Court of Appeals rejected Hayes' appeal. When Hayes initiated a habeas corpus action in the federal courts, the district court found no constitutional violations in his case. However, the federal circuit court of appeals found that the prosecutor's actions during plea bargaining had violated the principle from *Blackledge v. Perry* (1974), which forbids "vindictive" actions by prosecutors. The Supreme Court accepted the case to consider whether a prosecutor violates the right to due process of law when his or her charging decisions are influenced by the expectation of gaining advantages in the course of plea negotiations.

The case is important because the Supreme Court found no constitutional impediments to prevent prosecutors from putting pressure on defendants during plea bargaining. As you read the case, consider the following questions: (1) Should plea bargaining be considered a constitutionally acceptable means to process criminal cases when the Constitution does not mention the procedure but instead emphasizes the right to trial? (2) Does the Supreme Court's decision unfairly give prosecutors extra power in the adversarial face-off against defendants in criminal cases? (3) Does the result in the case produce improper pressures on defendants to surrender their right to seek a jury trial?

VOTE:

Five justices found the prosecutor's actions to be constitutional (Burger, Rehnquist, Stevens, Stewart, White).

Four justices found the prosecutor's actions to be unconstitutional (Blackmun, Brennan, Marshall, Powell).

Justice Stewart delivered the opinion of the Court.

* * *

We have recently had occasion to observe: "[W]hatever might be the situation in an ideal world, the fact is that the guilty plea and the often concomitant plea bargain are important components of this country's criminal justice system. Properly administered, they can benefit all concerned." *Blackledge v. Allison*, 431 U.S. 63, 71 (1974) . . . . The open acknowledgement of this previously clandestine practice has led this Court to recognize the importance of counsel during plea negotiations, . . . the need for a public record indicating that a plea was knowingly and voluntarily made, . . . and the requirement that a prosecutor's plea-bargaining promise be kept . . . . The decision of the Court of Appeals in the present case, however, did not deal with considerations such as these, but held that the substance of the plea offer itself violated the limitations imposed by the Due Process Clause of the Fourteenth Amendment. * * * For the reasons that follow, we have concluded that the Court of Appeals was mistaken in so ruling.

* * *

In those cases [of improper prosecutorial vindictiveness,] the Court was dealing with the State's unilateral imposition of a penalty upon a defendant who had chosen to exercise a legal right to attack his original conviction—a situation "very different from the give-and-take negotiation common in plea bargaining between prosecution and defense, which arguably possess relatively equal bargaining power." * * * The Court emphasized that the due process violation in [prosecutorial vindictiveness] cases . . . lay not in the possibility that a defendant might be deterred from the exercise of a legal right, . . . but rather in the danger that the State might be retaliating against the accused for lawfully attacking his conviction. * * *

Plea bargaining flows from "the mutuality of advantage" to defendants and prosecutors, each with his own reasons for wanting to avoid trial . . . . Defendants advised by competent counsel and protected by other procedural safeguards are presumptively capable of intelligent choice in response to prosecutorial persuasion, and unlikely to be driven to false self-condemnation. * * * Indeed, acceptance of the basic legitimacy of plea bargaining necessarily implies rejection of any notion that a guilty plea is involuntary in a constitutional sense simply because it is the end result of the bargaining process. * * *

* * *

[B]y tolerating and encouraging the negotiation of pleas, this Court has necessarily accepted as constitutionally legitimate the simple reality that the prosecutor's interest at the bargaining table is to persuade the defendant to forego his right to plead not guilty.

* * *

To hold that the prosecutor's desire to induce a guilty plea is an "unjustifiable standard," which, like race or religion, may play no part in his charging decision, would contradict the very premises that underlie the concept of plea bargaining itself. Moreover, a rigid constitutional rule that would prohibit a prosecutor from acting forthrightly in his dealings with the defense would only invite unhealthy subterfuge that would drive the practice of plea bargaining back into the shadows from which it has so recently emerged . . . .

There is no doubt that the breadth of discretion that our country's legal system vests in prosecuting attorneys carries with it the potential for both individual and institutional abuse. And broad though that discretion may be, there are undoubtedly constitutional limits upon its exercise. We hold only that the course of conduct engaged in by the prosecutor in this case, which no more than openly presented the defendant with the unpleasant alternatives of forgoing trial or facing charges on which he was plainly subject to prosecution, did not violate the Due Process Clause of the Fourteenth Amendment.

Accordingly, the judgment of the Court of Appeals is

Reversed.

Justice Blackmun, with whom Justice Brennan and Justice Marshall join, dissenting.

* * *

The Court now says, however, that this concern with [prosecutorial] vindictiveness is of no import in the present case, despite the difference [in the defendant's sentence] between five years in prison and a life sentence, because we are here concerned with plea bargaining where there is give-and-take negotiation, and where, it is said [by the majority opinion] "there is no such element of punishment or retaliation so long as the accused is free to accept or reject the prosecution's offer." Yet in this case vindictiveness is present to the same extent as it was thought to be [in prior cases]; the prosecutor here admitted . . . that the sole reason for the new indictment was to discourage the respondent from exercising his right to a trial. Even had such an admission not been made, when plea negotiations, conducted in the face of the less serious charge under the first indictment, fail, charging by a second indictment a more serious crime for the same conduct creates "a strong inference" of vindictiveness. As then Judge McCree aptly observed, in writing for a unanimous panel of the Sixth Circuit [U.S. Court of Appeals], the prosecutor initially "makes a discretionary determination that the interests of the state are served by not seeking more serious charges." . . . I therefore do not understand why, as in [prior cases], due process does not require that the prosecution justify its action on some basis other than discouraging respondent from the exercise of his right to trial.

Prosecutorial vindictiveness, it seems to me, in the present narrow context, is the fact against which the Due Process Clause ought to protect. I perceive little difference between vindictiveness after what the Court describes . . . as the exercise of a "legal right to attack his original conviction" [in previous cases that found impermissible vindictiveness] and [permissible] vindictiveness in the "give-and-take negotiation common in plea bargaining." Prosecutorial vindictiveness in any context is still prosecutorial vindictiveness. The Due Process Clause should protect an accused against it, however it asserts itself. The Court of Appeals rightly so held, and I would affirm the judgment.

It might be argued that it really makes little difference how this case, now that it is here, is decided. The Court's holding gives plea bargaining full sway despite vindictiveness. A contrary result, however, merely would prompt the aggressive prosecutor to bring the greater charge initially in every case, and only thereafter to bargain. The consequences to the accused would still be adverse, for then he would bargain against a greater charge, face the likelihood of increased bail, and run the risk that the court would be less inclined to accept a bargained plea. Nonetheless, it is far preferable to hold prosecution to the charge it was originally content to bring and to justify in the eyes of the public.

[Justice Powell's dissenting opinion is omitted.]

The Rehnquist Court Era

As we saw in previous chapters, the composition changes that shaped the Supreme Court during the Rehnquist Court era contributed to an increased disinclination for the high court to support claims by criminal defendants. The data in Table 11.1 indicate that the Rehnquist Court produced a percentage of liberal outcomes (29%) lower than that produced by the Burger Court (32%). In both of these Supreme Court eras, justices were significantly less supportive of constitutional claims than were the Warren Court justices (76%).

Table 11.2 shows that the Rehnquist Court's conservatism has been most pronounced when deciding cases concerning the right to counsel. The Rehnquist Court's support for liberal outcomes in such cases (9%) is markedly lower than both the Burger (45%) and Warren Courts (81%). By contrast, Table 11.3 indicates that the Rehnquist Court has been more supportive of individuals' claims in other Sixth Amendment trial right cases (39%) than was the Burger Court (23%). By splitting the Sixth Amendment cases into two categories, Tables 11.2 and 11.3 make clear that the Rehnquist Court era has not been more conservative than the Burger Court on all aspects of the guarantees for the criminally accused.

Table 11.4 shows the voting records of individual Rehnquist Court justices on Sixth Amendment cases. Nine justices supported the government in nearly two-thirds or more of all cases (Thomas, Rehnquist, White, Scalia, O'Connor, Kennedy, Powell,

TABLE 11.1: Liberal/Conservative Outcomes of Sixth Amendment Right to Counsel and Trial Rights Cases for the Warren, Burger, and Rehnquist Courts, 1953-94 Terms

Court Era	Outcomes		
	Liberal	Conservative	Totals
Warren Court, 1953-68 Terms	76% (31)	24% (9)	40
Burger Court, 1969-85 Terms	32% (24)	68% (51)	75
Rehnquist Court, 1986-94 Terms	29% (10)	71% (24)	34
Totals	44% (65)	56% (84)	149

TABLE 11.2: Liberal/Conservative Outcomes of Sixth Amendment Right to Counsel Cases for the Warren, Burger, and Rehnquist Courts, 1953-94 Terms

Court Era	Outcomes		
	Liberal	Conservative	Totals
Warren Court, 1953-68 Terms	81% (17)	19% (4)	21
Burger Court, 1969-85 Terms	45% (14)	55% (17)	31
Rehnquist Court, 1986-94 Terms	9% (1)	91% (10)	11
Totals	51% (32)	49% (31)	63

TABLE 11.3: Liberal/Conservative Outcomes of Sixth Amendment Trial Rights Cases for the Warren, Burger, and Rehnquist Courts, 1953-94 Terms

Court Era	Outcomes		
	Liberal	Conservative	Totals
Warren Court, 1953-68 Terms	74% (14)	26% (5)	19
Burger Court, 1969-85 Terms	23% (10)	77% (34)	44
Rehnquist Court, 1986-94 Terms	39% (9)	61% (14)	23
Totals	38% (33)	62% (53)	86

TABLE 11.4: Liberal/Conservative Voting Records of Justices of the Rehnquist Court in Sixth Amendment and Trial Rights Cases, 1986-94 Terms

Justices	Liberal Votes	Conservative Votes
Thomas	12% (1)	88% (7)
Rehnquist	15% (5)	85% (29)
White	23% (7)	77% (24)
Scalia	24% (8)	76% (26)
O'Connor	24% (8)	76% (26)
Kennedy	25% (6)	75% (18)
Powell	33% (2)	67% (4)
Ginsburg	33% (1)	67% (2)
Souter	38% (5)	62% (8)
Blackmun	71% (24)	29% (10)
Stevens	82% (28)	18% (6)
Brennan	100% (21)	0% (0)
Marshall	100% (25)	0% (0)
Breyer	—	—

Ginsburg, and Souter). Because Justice Ginsburg was appointed by Democratic President Bill Clinton, her presence among the Republican conservatives on Sixth Amendment issues may seem surprising. It remains to be seen whether the three Sixth Amendment cases in which Ginsburg participated during her initial term provide an accurate indication of how she will decide such issues in later terms. By contrast, Marshall and Brennan always supported the defendant, and Stevens and Blackmun supported the government in less than one-third of such cases.

These stark divisions between the justices who usually supported individuals and those that nearly always supported the government are reflected in the voting bloc analysis in Table 11.5. A very strong liberal voting bloc composed of Justices Marshall, Brennan, and Stevens was essentially overwhelmed by a strong *majority*

TABLE 11.5: Bloc Voting Analysis of the Rehnquist Court's Sixth Amendment Cases, 1986-94 Terms (Percent Agreement Rate)

	Mar	Bren	Stev	Blkm	Scal	OCon	Ken	Whit	Rehn
Marshall	—	100	84	68	28	20	20	16	12
Brennan	100	—	81	67	29	19	9	14	10
Stevens	84	81	—	65	41	41	38	39	32
Blackmun	68	67	65	—	35	35	50	48	44
Scalia	28	29	41	35	—	88	79	84	85
O'Connor	20	19	41	35	88	—	83	90	91
Kennedy	20	9	38	50	79	83	—	95	92
White	16	14	39	48	84	90	95	—	94
Rehnquist	12	10	32	44	85	91	92	94	—

Court mean = 54
Sprague Criterion = 77
Liberal bloc: Marshall, Brennan, Stevens = 88
Conservative bloc: Rehnquist, White, Kennedy, O'Connor, Scalia = 88

conservative bloc containing five justices (Rehnquist, White, Kennedy, O'Connor, and Scalia) that could effectively control outcomes in favor of the government for most Sixth Amendment cases.

The term-by-term presentation of liberal versus conservative decisions in Table 11.6 does not indicate that any individual retirements and new appointments immediately changed the Court's outcomes in Sixth Amemdment and trial rights cases. The only term in which a substantial change in the outcome patterns can be observed is in 1993, the only term in which the Court did not favor individuals in any cases, ruling conservative in the three cases decided that term. This was the term in which Justice Ginsburg replaced Justice White, but we cannot conclude that Ginsburg's replacement of White resulted in the Court becoming more conservative. Table 11.4 shows that White has a more conservative ranking in these cases than Ginsburg, and thus it seems likely that White would have voted at least as conservatively as Ginsburg in the cases in the 1993 term. The Court's conservative rulings in these cases thus seems most likely to be due to the particular circumstances of the cases, which led to consistently conservative outcomes.

Right to Counsel

As indicated by Table 11.7, the Rehnquist Court seldom favored an individual's claim concerning the Sixth Amendment right to counsel. Furthermore, all of these cases were decided by majority opinions, showing a strong consensus among the justices. In the Rehnquist Court's first right to counsel case, a narrow five-member majority rejected Sixth Amendment claims concerning a defense attorney's failure to present available mitigating evidence at a capital sentencing hearing (*Burger v. Kemp*, 1987). The following year, over the objections of four dissenters, the five-member majority determined that providing *Miranda* warnings to a defendant during postindictment questioning can provide the basis for a defendant's knowing and intelligent waiver of counsel without any additional explanations to the defendant of the potential pitfalls of continuing to answer questions without a defense attorney present (*Patterson v. Illinois*, 1988). Critics of the Court's decision argued that the *Miranda* warnings given to arrestees are inadequate sources of information for indicted defendants who are clearly the focus of criminal proceed-

TABLE 11.6: Liberal/Conservative Outcomes of Sixth Amendment and Trial Rights Cases During the Rehnquist Court Era by Term, 1986–94 Terms

	Outcomes		
Term	Liberal	Conservative	Totals
1986	33% (2)	67% (4)	6
1987	29% (2)	71% (5)	7
1988	25% (1)	75% (3)	4
1989	25% (1)	75% (3)	4
1990	25% (1)	75% (3)	4
1991	50% (2)	50% (2)	4
1992	50% (1)	50% (1)	2
1993	0% (0)	100% (3)	3
1994	— (0)	— (0)	0
Totals	29% (10)	71% (24)	34

TABLE 11.7: A Framework for the Doctrinal Analysis of the Rehnquist Court's Cases on the Sixth Amendment, Right to Counsel, 1986–94 Terms

		Treatment of Precedent					
Major or Minor Importance	**Majority or Plurality Opinion**	Creation of New Liberal Precedent	Liberal Modification of Existing Precedent	Liberal Interpretation of Existing Precedent	Conservative Interpretation of Existing Precedent	Conservative Modification of Existing Precedent	Creation of New Conservative Precedent
Major	Majority					U.S. v. Monsanto (1989)	
	Plurality						
Minor	Majority			Satterwhite v. Texas (1988)	Burger v. Kemp (1987) Wheat v. U.S. (1988) Patterson v. Illinois (1988) McNeil v. Wisconsin (1991) Lockhart v. Fretwell (1993)	Perry v. Leake (1989) Caplin & Drysdale v. U.S. (1989) Michigan v. Harvey (1990)	Nichols v. U.S. (1994)
	Plurality						

ings and therefore require the legal representation necessary for a fair adversarial process (Garcia 1992, p. 26).

The following year, in a pair of 5–4 decisions that included the Court's lone "major" right-to-counsel case, the Court decided that government rules concerning forfeiture of drug proceeds could be used to prevent defendants from hiring the defense attorneys of their own choosing (*United States v. Monsanto*, 1989; *Caplin & Drysdale v. United States*, 1989). In effect, prior to convicting a defendant of any crime, the government can freeze potential forfeitable assets. Defendants unsuccessfully sought to assert a Sixth Amendment right to bar the government from freezing assets that could be used to hire defense counsel. Once again, harsh criticism was leveled at the majority. According to Garcia (1992, p. 37), "the Court profoundly altered the balance of forces between the government and the accused in the criminal process . . . . [The] majority succeeded not only in undermining the essence of the adversary system but it also gave the government virtually unfettered discretion to deter and disqualify talented or aggressive defense counsel from representing defendants in complex drug-related cases." Other commentators noted that the Court's reasoning could permit states to find ways to freeze assets of defendants charged with other kinds of crimes, and thus these decisions were characterized as "literally dropp[ing] a bomb on the right to *retained* counsel" (Decker 1992, p. 98).

In the same term, a six-member majority approved a trial judge's actions in barring a defendant from consulting with his attorney during a brief trial recess (*Perry v. Leake*, 1989). This decision appeared to clash with a 1976 precedent (*Geders v. United States*), which had determined that defendants cannot be barred from consulting with their attorneys during an overnight trial recess. However, Justice Stevens' majority opinion declared that a brief recess is different than an overnight recess, and thus he asserted that the two decisions were not in conflict.

In 1990, a five-member majority further narrowed the meaning of the Sixth Amendment's right to counsel. In *Michigan v. Harvey* (1990), the state admitted that police officers had improperly initiated questioning of a defendant outside of the presence of his attorney. However, the prosecution still sought to use the defendant's improperly obtained statements at trial for the purpose of impeaching his testimony. The divided Supreme Court endorsed the use of such statements by the prosecution. According to the Court, the prosecution cannot use improperly obtained statements to prove its case, but it can use such statements to show contradictions and inconsistencies in a defendant's subsequent trial testimony.

With the exception of one unanimous decision supporting a defendant when the prosecution failed to provide proper advance notice to a defense attorney about a psychiatric examination of the defendant (*Satterwhite v. Texas*, 1988), all of the Rehnquist Court's right-to-counsel decisions supported the government. The Court was deeply divided on right-to-counsel cases as the conservative justices sought to steer decisions toward narrower definitions of the Sixth Amendment. In fact, prior to Justice Brennan's retirement in 1990, six of the seven right-to-counsel decisions favoring government were decided by 5–4 votes. Subsequent cases reflected the same disagreements within the Court, but the conservatives prevailed by more comfortable margins. A 1991 right-to-counsel decision favored the government by a 6–3 margin when Justice Souter replaced Justice Brennan (*McNeil v. Wisconsin*). The 1993 decision of *Lockhart v. Fretwell* produced a 7–2 score favoring the government when Justice Thomas replaced Justice Marshall and Justices Stevens and Blackmun were left as the only remaining justices who sought to preserve a broad right to counsel. Thus, more so than with other issues, the Rehnquist Court's right-to-counsel decisions have reflected the anticipated consequences of replacing holdover liberal justices from the Warren Court era with appointees named by conservative Republican presidents.

Justice Ginsburg's lone liberal vote came in a right to counsel case (*Nichols v. United States*, 1994), so her appointment to the Court in place of Justice White may have strengthened the liberal wing for some right to counsel cases. However, even if Justice Breyer adopts the relatively liberal stance of his predecessor Justice Blackmun, the conservative justices will still maintain a strong majority on this issue.

Trial Rights

Table 11.8 shows that the Rehnquist Court has favored the government more frequently than defendants (14 decisions v. 9 decisions) in cases concerning trial rights, but the Court regularly decided cases in favor of individuals. Actually, the Court's performance would appear even more balanced if the table included the Rehnquist Court's equal protection cases rejecting the systematic use of racial and gender considerations in jury selection (*Georgia v. McCollum*, 1992; *J.E.B. v. Alabama ex rel. T.B.*, 1994). These cases will be included in the framework for doctrinal analysis of equal protection decisions. In *Georgia v. McCollum*, the Court declared that in the jury selection process, neither defendants nor prosecutors can use race as the basis for excluding jurors through the use of peremptory challenges. Traditionally, both sides in a trial are allotted a set number of peremptory challenges that they can use to exclude potential jurors without providing any reason. In *J.E.B. v. Alabama ex rel T.B.*, the Court expanded its rationale to bar the use of gender-based peremptory challenges.

The Court's "major" cases on trial rights in Table 11.8 all concerned the Confrontation Clause. In *Coy v. Iowa* (1988), Justice Scalia authored the majority opinion for a six-member majority that rejected Iowa's effort to place a screen in the courtroom between a defendant and two juvenile girls who testified that the defendant sexually assaulted them. Scalia emphasized "the literal irreducible meaning of the [Confrontation] Clause: 'a right to *meet face to face* all those who appear and give evidence *at trial*' " (457 U.S. at 1021). In dissent, Justice Blackmun argued that the state's public policy interest in protecting child-victims from the trauma of facing their victimizers ought to outweigh a literal interpretation of the confrontation right. Scalia's authorship of the *Coy* opinion was indicative of his special interest in the Confrontation Clause, a provision of the Sixth Amendment in which his interpretive approach of emphasizing the Constitution's text led him to support several liberal outcomes. During his first term on the Court, Scalia had joined the four most liberal justices to author an opinion on behalf of the five-member majority that rejected the prosecution's use against the defendant of a pretrial confession from a nontestifying codefendant (*Cruz v. New York*, 1987). Scalia also provided a pivotal vote in another major Confrontation Clause case in which a five-member majority barred the use at trial of hearsay statements made by a child sexual abuse victim to a pediatrician (*Idaho v. Wright*, 1990).

In other cases, however, majorities on the Court issued conservative decisions concerning confrontation rights. For example, in *Kentucky v. Stincer* (1987), a six-member majority rejected a Confrontation Clause claim when a defendant was barred from attending a hearing to determine whether a child witness was competent to testify in court. In a subsequent major decision, a five-member majority adopted Justice Blackmun's argument from *Coy v. Iowa* (1988) about the need to place the welfare of child witnesses above the defendant's confrontation rights (*Maryland v. Craig*, 1990). The majority approved the use of child-victims' testimony via closed circuit television because, according to Justice O'Connor's opinion, "face-to-face confrontation is not an absolute constitutional requirement [and] it may

TABLE 11.8: A Framework for the Doctrinal Analysis of the Rehnquist Court's Cases on the Sixth Amendment, Trial Rights, 1986-94 Terms

		Treatment of Precedent					
Major or Minor Importance	**Majority or Plurality Opinion**	Liberal Creation of New Liberal Precedent	Liberal Modification of Existing Precedent	Interpretation of Existing Precedent	Conservative Interpretation of Existing Precedent	Conservative Modification of Existing Precedent	Creation of New Conservative Precedent
Major	Majority			Coy v. Iowa (1988) Idaho v. Wright (1990)		Maryland v. Craig (1990)	
	Plurality						
Minor	Majority		Riggins v. Nevada (1992)	Cruz v. New York (1987) Rock v. Arkansas (1987) Carella v. Calif. (1989) Yates v. Evatt (1991) Doggett v. U.S. (1992) Sullivan v. Louisiana (1993)	Calif. v. Brown (1987) Richardson v. Marsh (1987) Kentucky v. Stincer (1987) U.S. v. Owens (1988) U.S. v. Taylor (1988) Holland v. Illinois (1990) Mu'min v. Virginia (1991) Michigan v. Lucas (1991) Estelle v. McGuire (1991) White v. Illinois (1992) Victor v. Nebraska (1994)	Taylor v. Illinois (1988) Shannon v. U.S. (1994)	
	Plurality						

be abridged . . . where there is a 'case-specific finding of necessity' " (497 U.S. at 858). This reformulation of the confrontation right was at odds with Scalia's description in *Coy v. Iowa* (1988) of the Confrontation Clause as requiring literal, face-to-face contact between witnesses and defendants. Thus, the Court held that "where necessary to protect a child witness from trauma that would be caused by testifying in the physical presence of the defendant, at least where such trauma would impair the child's ability to communicate, the Confrontation Clause does not prohibit the use of a procedure, that despite the absence of face-to-face confrontation, ensures the reliability of the evidence by subjecting it to rigorous adversarial testing and thereby preserves the essence of effective confrontation" (497 U.S. at 857). In a strong dissent on behalf of Justices Brennan, Marshall, and Stevens, Justice Scalia declared that "[s]eldom has this Court failed so conspicuously to sustain a categorical guarantee of the Constitution against the tide of prevailing public opinion . . . . The purpose of enshrining [the confrontation right] in the Constitution was to assure that none of the many policy interests from time to time pursued by statutory law could overcome a defendant's right to face his or her accusers in court" (497 U.S. at 860).

Maryland v. Craig

497 U.S. 836, 110 S.Ct. 3157, 111 L.Ed. 2d 666 (1990)

Mrs. Craig, the operator of a preschool program, was accused of child abuse and sexual misconduct. Under Maryland state law, if the trial judge determined that face-to-face contact between a child-victim and alleged victimizer "will result in the child suffering serious emotional distress such that the child cannot reasonably communicate," then the judge can permit the child to testify via closed-circuit television. A judge permitted four children to testify against Mrs. Craig through the use of closed-circuit television, and she was convicted at trial. The Maryland Court of Special Appeals affirmed the conviction, but the Maryland Court of Appeals ordered a new trial. The Maryland Court of Appeals rejected Craig's claim that the Confrontation Clause always requires face-to-face encounters between defendants and witnesses. However, this state appellate court ordered a new trial because the trial judge had not adequately fulfilled the statutory requirements for demonstrating the need for the television testimony. According to the Maryland Court of Appeals, the Confrontation Clause always requires face-to-face encounters unless such encounters would prevent the child from testifying. The U.S. Supreme Court accepted the case to decide whether or not the Confrontation Clause always requires face-to-face contact in the courtroom.

The case is important because it represented a new, more flexible interpretation of the Confrontation Clause's requirements. As you read the case, consider the following questions: (1) Is the Court's decision consistent with prior precedents? (2) How does the majority justify its interpretation of the Confrontation Clause? (3) Should policy considerations be given greater emphasis than the literal words of the Constitution?

VOTE:

Five justices found Maryland's statute constitutional (Blackmun, Kennedy, O'Connor, Rehnquist, White).

Four justices found Maryland's statute unconstitutional (Brennan, Marshall, Scalia, Stevens).

Justice O'Connor delivered the opinion of the Court.

This case requires us to decide whether the Confrontation Clause of the Sixth Amendment categorically prohibits a child witness in a child abuse case from testifying against a defendant at trial, outside the defendant's physical presence, by one-way closed circuit television.

* * *

We observed in *Coy v. Iowa* [1988] that "the Confrontation Clause guarantees the defendant a face-to-face meeting with witnesses appearing before the trier of fact . . . ." [citing seven cases from 1895 to 1987]. This interpretation derives not only from the literal text of the Clause, but also from our understanding of its historical roots . . . .

We have never held, however, that the Confrontation Clause guarantees criminal defendants the *absolute* right to a face-to-face meeting with witnesses against them at trial. Indeed, in *Coy v. Iowa*, we expressly "le[ft] for another day . . . the question whether any exceptions exist" to the "irreducible literal meaning of the Clause["] . . . . We concluded [in *Coy*] that "[s]ince there ha[d] been no individualized findings that these particular witnesses needed special protection, the judgment [in *Coy*] could not be sustained by any conceivable exception." . . . Because the trial court in [*Craig*] made individualized findings that each of the child witnesses needed special protection, this case requires us to decide the question reserved in *Coy*.

* * *

The combined effect of these elements of confrontation—physical presence, oath, cross-examination, and observation of demeanor by the trier of fact—serves the purposes of the Confrontation Clause by ensuring that evidence admitted against an accused is reliable and subject to the rigorous adversarial testing that is the norm of Anglo-American criminal proceedings . . . .

* * *

Although face-to-face confrontation forms "the core of the values furthered by the Confrontation Clause," . . . we have nevertheless recognized that it is not the *sine qua non* of the confrontation right . . . . see also [*Kentucky v.*] *Stincer* [1987] . . . (confrontation right is not violated by exclusion of the defendant from competency hearing of child witnesses, where defendant had opportunity for full and effective cross-examination at trial) . . . .

For this reason, we have never insisted on an actual face-to-face encounter at trial in *every* instance in which testimony is admitted against a defendant. Instead, we have repeatedly held that the Clause permits, where necessary, the admission of certain hearsay statements against a defendant despite the defendant's inability to confront the declarant at trial . . . . In *Mattox* [*v. United States*, 1895], for example, we held that the testimony of a government witness at a former trial against the defendant, where the witness was fully cross-examined but had died after the first trial, was admissible in evidence against the defendant at his second trial . . . . Thus, in certain narrow circumstances, "competing interests, if 'closely examined,' may warrant dispensing with confrontations at trial." . . . We have recently held, for example, that hearsay statements of nontestifying co-conspirators may be admitted against a defendant despite the lack of any face-to-face encounter with the accused. See *Bourjaily v. United States* [1987] . . . . Given our hearsay cases, the word "confront," as used in the Confrontation Clause, cannot simply mean face-to-face confrontation, for the Clause would then, contrary to our cases, prohibit the admission of any accusatory hearsay statement made by an absent declarant—a declarant who is undoubtedly as much a "witness against" a defendant as one who actually testifies at trial.

In sum, our precedents establish that "the Confrontation Clause reflects a *preference* for face-to-face confrontation at trial." * * *

* * *

The critical inquiry in this case, therefore, is whether use of the [closed circuit television] procedure is necessary to further an important state interest. The State contends that it has a substantial interest in protecting children who are allegedly victims of child abuse from the trauma of testifying against the alleged perpetrator and that its statutory procedure for receiving testimony from such witnesses is necessary to further that interest.

We have of course recognized that a State's interest in "the protection of minor victims of sex crimes from further trauma and embarrassment" is a "compelling" one [citations to four cases] . . . . In *Globe Newspaper* [*Co. v Superior Court*, 1982], for example, we held that a State's interest in the physical and psychological well-being of a minor victim was sufficiently weighty to justify depriving the press and public of their constitutional right to attend criminal trials, where the trial court makes a case-specific finding that closure of the trial is necessary to protect the welfare of the minor. * * *

We likewise conclude today that a State's interest in the physical and psychological well-being of child abuse victims may be sufficiently important to outweigh, at least in some cases, a defendant's right to face his or her accusers in court. That a significant majority of States has enacted statutes to protect child witnesses from the trauma of giving testimony in child abuse cases attests to the widespread belief in the importance of such a public policy . . . . Thirty-seven States, for example, permit the use of videotaped testimony of sexually abused children; 24 States have authorized the use of one-way closed circuit television testimony in child abuse cases; and 8 States authorize the use of a two-way system in which the child-witness is permitted to see the courtroom and the defendant on a video monitor and in which the jury and judge are permitted to view the child during the testimony.

* * *

Given the State's traditional and "transcendent interest in protecting the welfare of children," . . . and buttressed by the growing body of academic literature documenting the psychological trauma suffered by child abuse victims who must testify in court [citations to psychology research] . . . , we will not second-guess the considered judgment of the Maryland Legislature regarding the importance of its interest in protecting child abuse victims from the emotional trauma of testifying. Accordingly, we hold that, if the State makes an adequate showing of necessity, the state interest in protecting child witnesses from the trauma of testifying in a child abuse case is sufficiently important to justify the use of a special procedure that permits a child witness in such cases to testify at trial against a defendant in the absence of face-to-face confrontation with the defendant.

The requisite finding of necessity must of course be a case-specific one: the trial court must hear evidence and determine whether use of the one-way closed circuit television procedure is necessary to protect the welfare of the particular child witness who seeks to testify. * * *

* * *

Because there is no dispute that the child witnesses in this case testified under oath, were subject to full cross-examination, and were able to be observed by the judge, jury, and defendant as they testified, we conclude that, to the extent that a proper finding of necessity has been made, the admission of such testimony would be consonant with the Confrontation Clause.

* * *

We therefore vacate the judgment of the Court of Appeals of Maryland and remand the case for further proceedings not inconsistent with this opinion.

It is so ordered.

Justice Scalia, with whom Justice Brennan, Justice Marshall, and Justice Stevens join, dissenting.

Seldom has this Court failed so conspicuously to sustain a categorical guarantee of the Constitution against the tide of prevailing current opinion. The Sixth Amendment provides, with unmistakable clarity, that "[i]n all criminal prosecutions, the accused shall enjoy the right . . . to be confronted with the witnesses against him." The purpose of enshrining this protection in the Constitution was to assure that none of the many policy interests from time to time pursued by statutory law could overcome a defendant's right to face his or her accusers in Court . . . .

Because of this subordination of explicit constitutional text to currently favored public policy, the following scene can be played out in an American courtroom for the first time in two centuries: A father whose young daughter has been given over to the exclusive custody of his estranged wife, or a mother whose young son has been taken into custody by the State's child welfare department, is sentenced to prison for sexual abuse on the basis of testimony by a child the parent has not seen or spoken to for many months; and the guilty verdict is rendered without giving the parent so much as the opportunity to sit in the presence of the child, and to ask, personally or through counsel, "it is really not true, is it, that I — your father (or mother) whom you see before you — did these terrible things?" Perhaps that is a procedure today's society desires; perhaps (though I doubt it) it is even a fair procedure; but it is assuredly not a procedure permitted by the Constitution.

Because the text of the Sixth Amendment is clear, and because the Constitution is meant to protect against, rather than conform to, current "widespread belief," I respectfully dissent.

* * *

The Court characterizes the State's interest which "outweigh[s]" the explicit text of the Constitution as an "interest in the physical and psychological well-being of child abuse victims," . . . and "interest in protecting" such victims "from the emotional trauma of testifying," . . . . This is not so. A child who meets the Maryland statute's requirement of suffering such "serious emotional distress" from confrontation that he "cannot reasonably communicate" would seem entirely safe. Why would a prosecutor want to call a witness who cannot reasonably communicate? And if he did, it would be the State's own fault. Protection of the child's interest — as far as the Confrontation Clause is concerned — is entirely within Maryland's control [by simply not calling on such children to be witnesses]. The State's interest here is in fact no more and no less than what the State's interest always is when it seeks to get a class of evidence admitted in criminal proceedings: more convictions of guilty defendants. That is not an unworthy interest, but it should not be dressed up as a humanitarian one.

And the interest on the other side is also what it usually is when the State seeks to get a new class of evidence admitted: fewer convictions of innocent defendants — specifically, in the present context, innocent defendants accused of particularly heinous crimes. The "special" reasons that exist for suspending one of the usual guarantees of reliability in the case of children's testimony are perhaps matched by "special" reasons for being particularly insistent upon it in the case of children's testimony. Some studies show that children are substantially more vulnerable to suggestion than adults, and often unable to separate recollected fantasy (or suggestion) from reality [citations to academic studies] . . . .

* * *

The Court today has applied "interest balancing" analysis where the text of the Constitution simply does not permit it. We are not free to conduct a cost-benefit analysis of clear and explicit constitu-

tional guarantees, and then to adjust their meaning to comport with our findings. The Court has convincingly proved that the Maryland procedure serves a valid interest, and gives the defendant virtually everything the Confrontation Clause guarantees (everything, that is, except confrontation). I am persuaded, therefore, that the Maryland procedure is virtually constitutional. Since it is not, however, actually constitutional I would affirm the judgment of the Maryland Court of Appeals reversing judgment of conviction.

A five-member majority on the Court also made a major alteration in the right to compulsory process in its controversial decision in *Taylor v. Illinois* (1988). In *Taylor*, a defense attorney failed to provide a complete list of defense witnesses to the prosecution prior to trial. When the defense attorney produced a new, unlisted witness on the second day of the attempted murder trial, the judge barred the witness from testifying as a punishment against the defense attorney for not abiding by state procedural rules. In the majority opinion, Justice Stevens stated that "[t]he State's interest in the orderly conduct of a criminal trial is sufficient to justify the imposition and enforcement of firm, though not always inflexible, rules relating to the identification and presentation of evidence" (484 U.S. at 411). Stevens also rejected the argument that the defendant should not be penalized through the exclusion of plausible, relevant testimony just because the defense attorney violated court procedures. In dissent, Justice Brennan noted that the jury was deprived of the opportunity to hear that the victim brought a gun to the altercation with the defendant that resulted in the victim being wounded by a gunshot. Brennan also noted the irony inherent in a decision applying an "exclusionary rule" for violations of court procedures by the very same justices who sought to reduce or eliminate the exclusionary rule as a penalty for police violations of defendants' Fourth and Fifth Amendment rights (see Chapters 9 and 10): "It seems particularly ironic that the Court should approve the exclusion of evidence in this case at a time when several of its Members have expressed serious misgivings about the evidentiary costs of exclusionary rules in other contexts. Surely the deterrence of constitutional violations [in the Fourth and Fifth Amendment contexts] cannot be less important than the deterrence of discovery violations [in state trial court procedures]" (484 U.S. at 437).

TAYLOR V. ILLINOIS

484 U.S. 400, 108 S.Ct. 646, 98 L.Ed. 2d 798 (1988)

■ Prior to the start of a murder trial, the prosecutor filed a discovery motion requesting a list of defense witnesses. The list submitted by the defense attorney did not contain the name of Mr. Wormley. A later witness list submitted by the defense attorney on the first day of trial also did not contain Mr. Wormley's name. On the second day of the trial, the defense attorney asked for permission to amend his list in order to call Mr. Wormley as a witness. The attorney claimed that he did not previously list Mr. Wormley's name as a witness because he had been unable to locate Mr. Wormley. Prior to permitting Mr. Wormley to testify, the judge learned from the potential witness that he had actually met with the defense attorney two weeks prior to trial. The judge refused to permit Mr. Wormley to testify. The exclusion of the witness was the judge's sanction against the attorney for a blatant and willful violation of discovery rules by not listing a known witness on the list submitted on the first day of trial and then subsequently being untruthful in stating that he had not been able to locate the witness until the second day of trial. Discovery rules govern the sharing of information between attorneys for each side in a case. The defendant was convicted of attempted murder at the conclusion of the trial. The Illinois Appellate Court affirmed the defendant's conviction. The Illinois Supreme Court declined to hear the defendant's appeal. The U.S. Supreme Court accepted the case to consider whether the judge's action in excluding the witness violated the defendant's Sixth Amendment right to compulsory process in producing and submitting relevant evidence.

The case is important because it represented a conservative modification of compulsory process legal doctrines by permitting judges to sanction defense attorneys through the exclusion of evidence relevant to the client's criminal case. As you read the case, consider the following questions: (1) What is the majority's view of the meaning of the Compulsory Process Clause? (2) Is exclusion of evidence a proper sanction for attorney misbehavior or does it create an excessively detrimental effect on the defendant's right to produce evidence for a fair and complete trial? (3) How does the decision to exclude evidence in this case compare with "exclusionary rule" doctrines in Fourth and Fifth Amendment cases?

VOTE:

Five justices found the trial judge's action to be constitutional (O'Connor, Rehnquist, Scalia, Stevens, White).

Three justices found the trial judge's action to be unconstitutional (Blackmun, Brennan, Marshall).

[Justice Kennedy did not participate]

Justice Stevens delivered the opinion of the Court.

* * *

In this Court petitioner makes two arguments. He first contends that the Sixth Amendment bars a court from ever ordering the preclusion of evidence as a sanction for violating a discovery rule. Alternatively, he contends that even if the right to present witnesses is not absolute, on the facts of this case the preclusion of Wormley's testimony was constitutional error. Before addressing these contentions, we consider the State's argument that the Compulsory Process Clause of the Sixth Amendment is merely a guarantee that the accused shall have the power to subpoena witnesses and simply does not apply to rulings on the admissibility of evidence.

In the State's view, no Compulsory Process concerns are even raised by authorizing preclusion as a discovery sanction .... We have, however, consistently given the Clause the broader reading reflected in contemporaneous state constitutional provisions.

* * *

Few rights are more fundamental than that of an accused to present witnesses in his own defense .... Indeed, this right is an essential attribute of the adversary system itself .... The right to compel a witness' presence in the courtroom could not protect the integrity of the adversary process if it did not embrace the right to have the witness' testimony heard by the trier of fact. The right to offer testimony is thus grounded in the Sixth Amendment even though it is not expressly described in so many words ....

The right of the defendant to present evidence "stands on no lesser footing than the other Sixth Amendment rights that we have previously held applicable to the States." ... We cannot accept the State's argument that this constitutional right may never be offended by the imposition of a discovery sanction that entirely excludes the testimony of a material defense witness.

Petitioner's claim that the Sixth Amendment creates an absolute bar to the preclusion of the testimony of a surprise witness is just as extreme and just as unacceptable as the State's position that the Amendment is simply irrelevant. The accused does not have an unfettered right to offer testimony that is incompetent, privileged, or otherwise inadmissible under standard rules of evidence. The Compulsory Process Clause provides him with an effective weapon, but it is a weapon that cannot be used irresponsibly.

* * *

The principle that undergirds the defendant's right to present exculpatory evidence is also the source of essential limitations on the right. The adversary process could not function effectively without adherence to rules of procedure that govern the orderly presentation of facts and arguments to provide each party with a fair opportunity to assemble and submit evidence to contradict or explain the opponent's case. The trial process would be a shambles if either party had an absolute right to control the time and content of his witnesses' testimony. Neither may insist on the right to interrupt the opposing party's case, and obviously there is no absolute right to interrupt the deliberations of the jury to present newly discovered evidence. The State's interest in the orderly conduct of a criminal trial is sufficient to justify the imposition and enforcement of firm, though not always inflexible, rules relating to the identification and presentation of evidence.

* * *

The "State's interest in protecting itself against an eleventh-hour defense" is merely one component of the broader public interest in a full and truthful disclosure of critical facts.

* * *

It may well be true that alternative sanctions are adequate and appropriate in most cases, but it is equally clear that they would be less effective than the preclusion sanction and that there are instances in which they would perpetuate rather than limit the prejudice to the State and the harm to the adversary process . . . .

It would demean the high purpose of the Compulsory Process Clause to construe it as encompassing an absolute right to an automatic continuance or mistrial to allow presumptively perjured testimony to be presented to a jury. We reject petitioner's argument that a preclusion sanction is never appropriate no matter how serious the defendant's discovery violation may be.

Petitioner argues that the preclusion sanction was unnecessarily harsh in this case because the [questioning] of Wormley [by the judge prior to his opportunity to testify before the jury] adequately protected the prosecution from any possible prejudice resulting from surprise. Petitioner also contends that it is unfair to visit the sins of the lawyer upon his client. Neither argument has merit.

More is at stake than possible prejudice to the prosecution. We are also concerned with the impact of this kind of conduct on the integrity of the judicial process itself. The trial judge found that the discovery violation in this case was both willful and blatant . . . . Regardless of whether prejudice to the prosecution could have been avoided in this particular case, it is plain that the case fits into the category of willful misconduct in which the severest sanction is appropriate . . . .

The argument that the client should not be held responsible for his lawyer's misconduct strikes at the heart of the attorney-client relationship. Although there are basic rights that the attorney cannot waive without the fully informed and publicly acknowledged consent of the client, the lawyer has — and must have — full authority to manage the conduct of the trial. The adversary process could not function effectively if every tactical decision required client approval. Moreover, given the protections afforded by the attorney-client privilege and the fact that extreme cases may involve unscrupulous conduct by both the client and the lawyer, it would be highly impracticable to require an investigation into their relative responsibilities before applying the sanction of preclusion . . . . Whenever a lawyer makes use of the sword provided by the Compulsory Process Clause, there is some risk that he may wound his own client.

The judgment of the Illinois Appellate Court is *Affirmed.*

Justice Brennan, with whom Justice Marshall and Justice Blackmun join, dissenting.

* * *

The question in this case . . . is not whether discovery rules should be enforced, but whether the need to correct and deter discovery violations requires a sanction that itself distorts the truthseeking process by excluding material evidence of innocence in a criminal case . . . . I would hold that, absent evidence of the defendant's personal involvement in a discovery violation, the Compulsory Process Clause *per se* bars discovery sanctions that exclude criminal defense evidence.

* * *

The Compulsory Process Clause and the Due Process Clause . . . require courts to conduct a searching inquiry whenever the government seeks to exclude criminal defense evidence. After all, "[f]ew rights are more fundamental than that of an accused to present witnesses in his own defense." . . . The exclusion of criminal defense evidence undermines the central truthseeking aim of our criminal justice system, . . . because it deliberately distorts the record at the risk of misleading the jury into convicting an innocent person. Surely the paramount value our criminal justice system places on acquitting the innocent, see, *e.g.*, *In re Winship* . . . (1970), demands close scrutiny of any law preventing the jury from hearing evidence favorable to the defendant. On the other hand, the Compulsory Process Clause does not invalidate every restriction on the presentation of evidence. The Clause does not, for example, require criminal courts to admit evidence that is irrelevant, . . . testimony by persons who are mentally infirm, . . . or evidence that represents half-truth . . . . That the inquiry required under the Compulsory Process Clause is sometimes difficult does not, of course, justify abandoning the task altogether.

* * *

[P]recluding witness testimony is clearly arbitrary and disproportionate to the purpose discovery intended to serve — advancing the quest for truth. Alternative sanctions — namely, granting the prosecution a continuance and allowing the prosecutor to comment [to the jury] on the witness concealment — can correct for any adverse impact the discovery violation would have on the truthseeking process. Moreover, the alternative sanctions, unlike the preclusion sanction, do not distort the truthseeking process by excluding material evidence of innocence.

* * *

Witness preclusion . . . punishes discovery violations in a way that is both disproportionate — it might result in a defendant charged with a capital offense being convicted and receiving a death sentence he would not have received but for the discovery violation — and arbitrary — it might, in another case involving an identical discovery violation, result in a defendant suffering no change in verdict, or if charged with a lesser offense, being convicted and receiving a light or suspended sentence. In contrast, direct punitive measures (such as contempt sanctions or, if the attorney is responsible, disciplinary proceedings) can gradate the punishment to correspond to the severity of the discovery violation.

The arbitrary and disproportionate nature of the preclusion sanction is highlighted where the penalty falls on the defendant even though he bore no responsibility for the discovery violation. In this case, although there was ample evidence that the defense attorney willfully violated [the discovery rule concerning listing all known witnesses], there was no evidence that the defendant played any role in that violation. Nor did the trial court make any effort to determine whether the defendant bore any responsibility for the discovery violation. Indeed, reading the record leaves the distinct impression that the main reason the trial court excluded Wormley's testimony was a belief that the defense counsel had purposefully lied about when he had located Wormley.

Worse yet, the trial court made clear that it was excluding Wormley's testimony not only in response to the defense counsel's actions in this case but also in response to the actions of other defense attorneys in other cases. The trial court stated:

> ". . . All right, I am going to deny Wormley the opportunity to testify here. He is not going to testify. I find this a blatent [*sic*] violation of the discovery rules, willful violation of the rules. I also feel that defense attorneys have been violating discovery in this courtroom in the last three or four cases blatently [*sic*] and I am going to put a stop to it and this is one way to do so."

Although the [Supreme Court's majority opinion] recognizes this problem, it offers no response other than the cryptic statement that "[u]nrelated discovery violations . . . would not . . . normally provide a proper basis for curtailing the defendant's constitutional right to present a complete defense." . . . We are left to wonder either why this case is abnormal or why an exclusion founded on an improper basis should be upheld.

* * *

The situation might be different if the defendant willfully caused the discovery violation . . . . But that is no explanation for allowing defense witness preclusion where there is no evidence that the defendant bore any responsibility for the discovery violation. At a minimum, we would be obligated to remand for further factfinding to establish the defendant's responsibility. Deities may be able to visit the sins of the father on the son, but I cannot agree that courts should be permitted to visit the sins of the lawyer on the innocent client.

* * *

In this case there is no doubt that willfully concealing the identity of witnesses one intends to call at trial is attorney misconduct, that the government seeks to deter such behavior in all instances, and that the attorney knows such behavior is misconduct and not a legitimate tactical decision at the time it occurs. Direct punitive sanctions against the attorney are available [under state court rules] . . . .

* * *

It seems particularly ironic that the Court should approve the exclusion of evidence in this case at a time when several of its Members have expressed serious misgivings about the evidentiary costs of exclusionary rules in other contexts. Surely the deterrence of constitutional violations cannot be less important than the deterrence of discovery violations. Nor can it be said that the evidentiary costs are more significant when they are imposed on the prosecution. For that would turn on its head what Justice Harlan termed the "fundamental value determination of our society that it is far worse to convict an innocent man than to let a guilty man go free." *In re Winship*, 397 U.S. at 372 (concurring opinion).

Discovery rules are important, but only as a means for helping the criminal justice system convict the guilty and acquit the innocent. Precluding defense witnesses' testimony as a sanction for a defense counsel's willful discovery violation not only directly subverts criminal justice by basing convictions on a partial presentation of facts, . . . but is also arbitrary and disproportionate to any of the purposes served by discovery rules or discovery sanctions. The Court today thus sacrifices the paramount values of the criminal justice system in a misguided and unnecessary effort to preserve the sanctity of discovery. We may never know for certain whether the defendant or [the victim's] brother fired the shot for which the defendant was convicted. We do know, however, that the jury that convicted the defendant was not permitted to hear evidence that would have both placed a gun in [the victim's] brother's hands and contradicted the testimony of [the victim] and his brother that they possessed no weapons that evening — and that, because of the defense counsel's 5-day delay in identifying a witness, an innocent man may be serving 10 years in prison. I dissent.

[The dissenting opinion of Justice Blackmun is omitted.]

The Rehnquist Court had opportunities to address issues involving other aspects of the Sixth Amendment. These decisions showed mixed results regarding support for government versus support for constitutional claims by defendants. For example, in a case concerning the right to a speedy trial, a five-member majority including Justices Souter, Kennedy, and White made a liberal decision in finding a constitutional violation in the federal government's negligent eight-year delay between the indictment and arrest of an individual sought for drug offenses (*Doggett v. United States*, 1992). With respect to trial judges' discretionary decisions in overseeing criminal trials, a five-member majority found no fault with a judge's failure to question potential jurors about their exposure to news media reports about the murder case before them (*Mu'min v. Virginia*, 1991). Meanwhile, a different seven-member majority overruled a judge's action in permitting forcible administration of psychiatric medications to a defendant to control his behavior during trial (*Riggins v. Nevada*, 1992). The justices' reactions to individual issues brought before them created shifting majorities and both liberal and conservative outcomes for cases concerning various trial rights.

The Rehnquist Court moved constitutional law in a liberal direction with respect to the use of peremptory challenges in jury selection. After initially rejecting a claim by a white defendant that the exclusion of African Americans from his jury constituted a violation of his Sixth Amendment right to a jury drawn from a fair cross section of the community (*Holland v. Illinois*, 1990), the Court began to apply the Equal Protection Clause instead to bar the use of racial and gender motivations in peremptory challenges. In 1991, the Court decided the same issue — a white defendant contesting the exclusion of African American jurors — and concluded that the Equal Protection Clause, unlike the Sixth Amendment, barred such racially motivated use of peremptory challenges (*Powers v. Ohio*, 1991). The Court also applied the Equal Protection Clause to place a similar limitation on the use of challenges in civil trials (*Edmonson v. Leesville Concrete Co.*, 1991). In 1992, the Court extended the Equal Protection reasoning from *Batson v. Kentucky* (1986), which had prohibited prosecutors from using racial motivations for the systematic exclusion of potential jurors, and placed the identical limitation on defense attorneys in criminal cases (*Georgia v. McCollum*, 1992).

Georgia v. McCollum

505 U.S. 42, 112 S.Ct. 2348, 120 L.Ed. 2d 33 (1992)

■ A white couple was charged with committing assault and battery against an African-American couple. Before jury selection began, the prosecutor made a motion to preclude the defense from exercising peremptory challenges in a discriminatory manner. The prosecutor intended to show that the victims' race was a factor in the assault. Because the defense had twenty peremptory challenges at its disposal, the prosecutor was worried that these challenges could be used to exclude African American jurors and thereby create an all-white jury. The trial judge ruled that criminal defendants are not subject to case precedents barring the racially motivated use of peremptory challenges. The Supreme Court of Georgia affirmed the trial court's ruling. The U.S. Supreme Court accepted the case to determine whether or not the Equal Protection Clause bars the racially motivated use of peremptory challenges by criminal defendants.

The case is important because it shows how the Rehnquist Court has expanded the application of the Equal Protection Clause in jury selection to limit the use of peremptory challenges. As you read the case, consider the following questions: (1) If the Equal Protection Clause governs only discriminatory *state* action, how could the Supreme Court apply the Clause to regulate actions by private defense attorneys? (2) What is the substance of the concurring opinions by Chief Justice Rehnquist and Justice Thomas? (3) Because this case was decided in favor of the prosecution, should it be classified as a "liberal" decision that expanded the constitutional rights of individuals?

Vote:

Seven justices found the trial judge's ruling to be unconstitutional (Blackmun, Kennedy, Rehnquist, Souter, Stevens, Thomas, White).

Two justices found the trial judge's ruling to be constitutional (O'Connor, Scalia).

Justice Blackmun delivered the opinion of the Court.

For more than a century, this Court consistently and repeatedly has reaffirmed that racial discrimination by the State in jury selection offends the Equal Protection Clause. See, *e.g., Strauder v. West Virginia* [1880] .... Last Term, this Court held that racial discrimination in a civil litigant's exercise of peremptory challenges also violates the Equal Protection Clause. See *Edmonson v. Leesville Concrete Co.* [1991], ... Today, we are asked to decide whether the Constitution prohibits a *criminal defendant* from engaging in purposeful racial discrimination in the exercise of peremptory challenges.

* * *

"[T]he harm from discriminatory jury selection extends beyond that inflicted on the defendant and the excluded juror to touch the entire community." *Batson* [*v. Kentucky*, 1986], 476 U.S. at 87.... One of the goals of our jury system is "to impress upon the criminal defendant and the community as a whole that a verdict of conviction or acquittal is given in accordance with the law by persons who are fair." ... Selection procedures that purposefully exclude African Americans from juries undermine that public confidence — as well they should ....

The need for public confidence is especially high in cases involving race-related crimes. In such cases, emotions in the affected community will inevitably be heated and volatile. Public confidence in the integrity of the criminal justice system is essential for preserving community peace in trials involving race-related crimes ....

Be it at the hands of the State or the defense, if a court allows jurors to be excluded because of group bias, it is a willing participant in a scheme that could only undermine the very foundation of our system of justice — our citizens' confidence in it. Just as public confidence in criminal justice is undermined by a conviction in a trial where racial discrimination has occurred in jury selection, so is public confidence undermined where a defendant, assisted by racially discriminatory peremptory strikes, obtains an acquittal.

* * *

[T]he second question that must be answered is whether a criminal defendant's exercise of a peremptory challenge constitutes state action for purposes of the Equal Protection Clause.

* * *

As in *Edmonson*, a Georgia [criminal] defendant's right to exercise peremptory challenges and the scope of that right are established by a provision of state law ....

* * *

[T]he Court in *Edmonson* found that peremptory challenges perform a traditional function of government. "Their sole purpose is to permit litigants to assist the government in the selection of an impartial trier of fact." ... And, as the *Edmonson* Court recognized, the jury system in turn, "performs the critical governmental functions of guarding the rights of litigants and insur[ing] continued acceptance of the laws by all of the people" .... These same conclusions apply with even greater force in the criminal context because the selection of a jury in a criminal case fulfills a unique and constitutionally compelled governmental function ....

Finally, the *Edmonson* Court indicated that the courtroom setting in which the peremptory challenge is exercised intensifies the harmful effects of the private litigant's discriminatory act and contributes to its characterization as state action. These concerns are equally present in the context of a criminal trial. Regardless of who precipitated the jurors' removal, the perception and reality in a criminal trial will be that the court has excused jurors based on race, an outcome that will be attributed to the State.

* * *

Nor does a prohibition of the exercise of discriminatory peremptory challenges violate a defendant's Sixth Amendment right to the effective assistance of counsel. Counsel can ordinarily explain the reasons for peremptory challenges without revealing anything about trial strategy or any confidential client communications. In the rare case in which the explanation for a challenge would entail confidential communications or reveal trial strategy, an *in camera* discussion can be arranged .... In any event, neither the Sixth Amendment right nor the attorney-client privilege gives a criminal defendant the right to carry out through counsel an unlawful course of conduct ....

Lastly, a prohibition of the discriminatory exercise of peremptory challenges does not violate a defendant's Sixth Amendment right to a trial by an impartial jury. The goal of the Sixth Amendment is "jury impartiality with respect to both contestants." *Holland v. Illinois*, 493 U.S. 474, 483 ... (1990).

* * *

We hold that the Constitution prohibits a criminal defendant from engaging in purposeful discrimination on the ground of race in the exercise of peremptory challenges. Accordingly, if the State demonstrates a prima facie case of racial discrimination by the defendants, the defendants must articulate a racially neutral explanation for the peremptory challenges. The judgment of the Supreme Court of Georgia is reversed and the case is remanded for further proceedings not inconsistent with this opinion.

It is so ordered.

Chief Justice Rehnquist concurring.

I was in dissent in *Edmonson v. Leesville Concrete Co.*, . . . and continue to believe that case to have been wrongly decided. But so long as it remains the law, I believe that it controls the disposition of this case on the issue of "state action" under the Fourteenth Amendment. I therefore join the opinion of the Court.

Justice Thomas concurring in the judgment.

As a matter of first impression, I think I would have shared the view of the dissenting opinions. A criminal defendant's use of peremptory strikes cannot violate the Fourteenth Amendment because it does not involve state action. Yet, I agree with the Court and the Chief Justice that our decision last term in *Edmonson v. Leesville Concrete Co.*, . . . governs this case and requires the opposite conclusion. Because the respondents do not question *Edmonson*, I believe that we must accept its consequences. I therefore concur in the judgment reversing the Georgia Supreme Court.

I write separately to express my general dissatisfaction with our continuing attempts to use the Constitution to regulate peremptory challenges . . . . In my view, by restricting a criminal defendant's use of such challenges, this case takes us further from the reasoning and the result in *Strauder v. West Virginia* [1880] . . . . I doubt that this departure will produce favorable consequences. On the contrary, I am certain that black criminal defendants will rue the day that this court ventured down this road that inexorably will lead to the elimination of peremptory strikes.

* * *

Our departure from *Strauder* has two negative consequences. First, it produces a serious misordering of our priorities. In *Strauder*, we put the rights of defendants foremost. Today's decision, while protecting jurors, leaves defendants with less means of protecting themselves. Unless jurors actually admit prejudice during *voir dire*, defendants generally must allow them to sit and run the risk that racial animus will affect the verdict . . . . In effect, we have exalted the right of citizens to sit on juries over the rights of the criminal defendant, even though it is the defendant, not the jurors, who faces imprisonment or even death. At a minimum, I think that this inversion of priorities should give us pause.

Second, our departure from *Strauder* has taken us down a slope of inquiry that has no clear stopping point . . . . Next will come the question whether defendants can exercise peremptories on the basis of sex . . . . The consequences for defendants of our decision and of these future cases remain to be seen. But whatever the benefits were that this Court perceived in a criminal defendant's having members of his class on the jury, see *Strauder*, 100 U.S. at 309-10, they have evaporated.

Justice O'Connor dissenting.

The Court reaches the remarkable conclusion that criminal defendants being prosecuted by the State act on behalf of their adversary when they exercise peremptory challenges during jury selection. The Court purports merely to follow precedents, but our cases do not compel this perverse result. To the contrary, our decisions specifically establish that criminal defendants and their lawyers are not government actors when they perform traditional trial functions.

* * *

Considered in purely pragmatic terms, moreover, the Court's holding may fail to advance nondiscriminatory criminal justice. It is by now clear that conscious and unconscious racism can affect the way white jurors perceive minority defendants and the facts presented at their trials, perhaps determining the verdict of guilt or innocence . . . . Using peremptory challenges to secure minority representation on the jury may help to overcome such racial bias, for there is substantial reason to believe that the distorting influence of race is minimized on a racially mixed jury . . . . In a world where the outcome of a minority defendant's trial may turn on the misconceptions or biases of white jurors, there is reason to question the implications of this Court's good intentions.

That the Constitution does not give federal judges the reach to wipe all marks of racism from every courtroom in the land is frustrating, to be sure. But such limitations are the necessary and intended consequence of the Fourteenth Amendment's state action requirement. Because I cannot accept the Court's conclusion that government is responsible for decisions criminal defendants make while fighting state prosecution, I respectfully dissent.

Justice Scalia dissenting.

I agree with the Court that its judgment follows logically from *Edmonson v. Leesville Concrete Co.* . . . . For the reasons given in the *Edmonson* dissents, however, I think that case was wrongly decided. Barely a year later, we witness its reduction to the terminally absurd: A criminal defendant, in the process of defending himself against the state, is held to be acting on behalf of the state. Justice O'Connor demonstrates the sheer inanity of this proposition (in case the mere statement of it does not suffice), and the contrived nature of the Court's justification. I see no need to add to her discussion, and differ from her views only in that I do not consider *Edmonson* distinguishable in principle — except in the principle that a bad decision should not be followed logically to its illogical conclusion.

Today's decision gives the lie, once again to the belief that an activist, "evolutionary" constitutional jurisprudence always evolves in the direction of greater individual rights. In the interest of promoting the supposedly greater good of race relations in the society as a whole (make no mistake that that is what underlies all of this), we use the Constitution to destroy the ages-old right of criminal defendants to exercise peremptory challenges as they wish, to secure a jury that they consider fair. I dissent.

The Court later extended this limitation on peremptory challenges to prohibit systematic exclusion of jurors by gender (*J.E.B. v. Alabama ex rel. T.B.*, 1994). Throughout this series of decisions, Justice Scalia objected strenuously to what he considered to be the "vandalizing of our people's traditions" by the majority's imposition of limitations on the use of peremptory challenges (62 U.S.L.W. at 4230).

Although these decisions ostensibly expanded the protection of equal protection rights during jury trials, a little-noticed decision in 1995 revealed that these liberal decisions may have more symbolic value than substance. The Court decided *Purkett v. Elem* (1995) based on attorneys' written submissions without accepting the case for complete briefing and oral argument, and therefore the case is not included in our database. In *Purkett*, a prosecutor had excluded African Americans from the jury pool and when challenged to justify his actions as not based on race, the prosecutor said:

> *I struck [juror] number twenty-two because of his long hair. He had long curly hair. He had the longest hair of anybody on the panel by far. He appeared to not be a good juror for that fact, the fact that he had long hair hanging down shoulder length, curly, unkempt hair. Also, he had a mustache and a goatee type beard. And juror number twenty-four also has a mustache and a goatee type beard. Those are the only two people on the jury . . . with any facial hair . . . and I don't like the way they looked, with the way the hair is cut, both of them. And the mustaches and the beards look suspicious to me.* (Purkett v. Elem, 115 S.Ct. at 1770).

Although the defendant's attorney claimed that the prosecutor's excuses were clearly a pretext for making improper race-based exclusions from the jury pool, the Supreme Court, in a 7–2 decision supporting the trial judge's ruling in the prosecutor's favor, said that reasons for exclusion can be silly, superstitious, implausible, or fantastic. In other words, the Supreme Court gave trial judges the discretionary authority to accept any reasons for excluding jurors, including the systematic exclusion of jurors by race or gender, as long as prosecutors and defense attorneys do not admit that they are making the exclusions based on race or gender. If the Supreme Court permits attorneys to freely manufacture justifications, including implausible justifications, the equal protection message underlying *Batson, Powers, Leesville, McCollum* and *J.E.B.* will have little actual impact on jury selection unless individual trial judges, on their own, take a tough stance against discrimination in jury selection (Smith and Ochoa 1996).

Conclusion

The Rehnquist Court moved constitutional law in a generally conservative direction with respect to the Sixth Amendment and trial rights. The Court was deeply divided over right to counsel issues in a series of cases prior to the retirements of liberal Justices Brennan and Marshall, but justices who favored conservative outcomes consistently gained sufficient votes to control the outcomes of cases and thereby narrow the definition of this Sixth Amendment right. Table 11.2 shows quite clearly the frequency with which the Court's decisions favored the government in controversies concerning the right to counsel. By contrast, there was greater balance between liberal and conservative decisions when the Court addressed other trial rights. Although many commentators believe that the Court's decisions ultimately diminished defendants' rights, especially with respect to the confrontation of witnesses (*Maryland v. Craig*, 1990) and compulsory process (*Taylor v. Illinois*, 1988), other decisions concerning such issues as peremptory challenges (*Powers v. Ohio*, 1991) and speedy trial rights (*Doggett v. United States*, 1992) clearly favored liberal outcomes.

There were relatively few major decisions on the Sixth Amendment and trial rights. Fundamentally, these decisions favored the government. In the right to counsel context, *United States v. Monsanto* (1989), along with its companion case *Caplin & Drysdale v. United States* (1989), broke new ground in permitting the government to freeze assets of accused, but as-yet-unconvicted drug suspects in a manner that prevented such defendants from selecting and hiring their own attorneys. The other three major cases all concerned the Confrontation Clause. Although two of these cases produced liberal outcomes (*Coy v. Iowa*, 1989; *Idaho v. Wright*, 1990), the most significant and recent of these major Confrontation Clause decisions modified the nature of the confrontation right by permitting it to be balanced against policy interests, such as the protection of child witnesses (*Maryland v. Craig*, 1990). This conservative modification of Sixth Amendment precedent significantly weakened the liberal interpretation that had been presented in *Coy*, the earliest of these major decisions in the Rehnquist Court era.

References

Abraham, Henry J. *Freedom and the Court*. 5th ed. New York: Oxford University Press, 1988.

Bodenhamer, David. *Fair Trial*. New York: Oxford University Press, 1992.

Carter, Dan T. *Scottsboro: A Tragedy of the American South*. Baton Rouge, La.: Louisiana State University Press, 1969.

Decker, John F. *Revolution to the Right*. New York: Garland, 1992.

Garcia, Alfredo. *The Sixth Amendment in Modern American Jurisprudence*. New York: Greenwood Press, 1992.

Hans, Valerie P., and Neil Vidmar. *Judging the Jury*. New York: Plenum Press, 1986.

Heller, Francis H. *The Sixth Amendment to the Constitution of the United States*. New York: Greenwood Press, 1951.

Irons, Peter, and Stephanie Guitton, eds. *May It Please the Court*. New York: The New Press, 1993.

Kamisar, Yale, Wayne R. LaFave, and Jerold H. Israel. *Modern Criminal Procedure*. 7th ed. St. Paul, Minn.: West Publishing, 1990.

Levine, James P. *Juries and Politics*. Pacific Grove, Calif: Brooks/Cole Publishing, 1992.

Lewis, Anthony. *Gideon's Trumpet*. New York: Random House, 1964.

Smith, Christopher E. *Courts and the Poor*. Chicago: Nelson-Hall, 1991.

_________. *Courts, Politics, and the Judicial Process*. Chicago: Nelson-Hall, 1993.

Smith, Christopher E., and Roxanne Ochoa. "The Peremptory Challenge in the Eyes of the Trial Judge." *Judicature* 79 (1996):185-189.

CHAPTER

12 The Eighth Amendment Guarantee Against Cruel and Unusual Punishments

CASE STUDY

Furman v. Georgia (1972)

On the night of August 10, 1967, William Micki, an active duty member of the U.S. Coast Guard, returned to his small house in Savannah, Georgia, from his first night moonlighting in a second job as a waiter. Some time shortly after 1 A.M., Micki and his wife thought they heard their son Jimmy sleepwalking. Micki got out of bed, went into the hallway, and said, "Come on, Jimmy, let's go back to bed." Instead of seeing Jimmy in the hallway, Micki saw an intruder by the kitchen door. He rushed toward the intruder and ran into the door when it swung closed as the intruder fled onto the back porch. As the door shut, a gunshot rang out and a bullet cut through the door, striking Micki in the chest. Micki died in a pool of blood, lying on his kitchen floor (Stevens 1978, pp. 15–22).

Shortly thereafter, a police officer observed a man emerging from a wooded area near the Micki house. Police officers chased the man and followed his tracks to a hole next to a nearby house. The police found William Furman hiding underneath the house. Furman had a .22 caliber pistol, and laboratory tests later showed that it matched the gun that had been used to kill William Micki. At the police station, Furman admitted that he had broken into Micki's house and that he had fired a shot through the kitchen door, although he later claimed that the gun discharged accidently when he tripped and fell while leaving the house (Stevens 1978, pp. 23–31).

Furman was a twenty-four-year-old African American man who had dropped out of school in the sixth grade to help support his family. He worked regularly as an unskilled laborer. At the time of the shooting, he was on parole after serving a jail sentence for his fourth burglary conviction. Because Furman was poor and could not afford to hire an attorney, Chatham County Superior Court Judge Dunbar Harrison appointed B. Clarence Mayfield, one of only three African American attorneys in Savannah, to represent Furman. Georgia paid appointed counsel only $150 in capital cases, despite the fact that private counsel in such cases would charge thousands of dollars in fees and would need hundreds more to pay investigators and secretaries and to hire expert witnesses. Mayfield effectively used his own time and money to pursue Furman's case vigorously (Stevens 1978, pp. 25, 33).

As a civil rights activist, Mayfield was keenly aware that Furman was likely to receive the death penalty because, in Georgia, capital punishment was most frequently applied when African Americans were accused of killing white people. Because Micki was white, Mayfield had little doubt about what penalty would await Furman if he were convicted of murder. Since Georgia began using the electric chair in 1924, 83 percent of the four hundred people sentenced to death had been African Americans. When Mayfield visited Furman in jail, he quickly concluded that his client's mental capacity was very low. He decided to argue that Furman lacked the mental capability to assist in his own defense, and indeed psychiatrists at the state's mental hospital found that Furman suffered from a mild to moderate mental deficiency as well as psychotic episodes associated with a convulsive disorder. Although the psychiatrists initially concluded that Furman was incapable of assisting in the preparation of his own defense, after treating Furman at the hospital for a few months, they decided that he was not suffering from psychosis at that moment and therefore could assist with his defense. Thus Mayfield had to proceed with the trial without being able to use the insanity defense on Furman's behalf (Stevens 1978, pp. 41, 52, 70).

On September 20, 1968, after a brief half-day trial, a jury of eleven whites and one African American deliberated for one hour and thirty-five minutes before finding Furman guilty of murder and sentencing him to death. After the conviction, Mayfield appealed to Judge Harrison to overturn the conviction. Mayfield claimed several grounds, including the lack of African Americans on the grand jury that had indicted Furman. Mayfield also claimed that the death penalty was inherently "cruel and unusual" in violation of the Eighth Amendment to the U.S. Constitution, and that the Eighth Amendment was violated because the penalty was applied so selectively and therefore was arbitrary and unfair. Judge Harrison rejected Mayfield's arguments, and on April 24, 1969, the Georgia Supreme Court unanimously upheld Furman's conviction (Stevens 1978, pp. 79–81).

Near the end of the 1960s, states abided by an informal moratorium on executions as they waited for the Supreme Court to rule clearly on the constitutionality of capital punishment. Several legal interest groups, including the NAACP Legal Defense Fund (LDF) and the American Civil Liberties Union (ACLU), had been bringing cases to court to challenge capital punishment. The LDF was the same organization that Thurgood Marshall headed for many years before he became a federal judge, and it was well known for its success in school desegregation cases, including the famous case of *Brown v. Board of Education* (1954). Mayfield was acquainted with LDF lawyers from his civil rights work, and he began working with LDF lawyers to take Furman's case to the U.S. Supreme Court. In 1971, the Supreme Court selected Furman's case, along with those of convicted rapists in Texas and Georgia and a convicted murderer in California, as the means through which to consider whether capital punishment violates the Eighth Amendment's prohibition on cruel and unusual punishments.

The arguments on behalf of Furman were prepared by LDF lawyers along with leading law professors and Mayfield. The brief on Furman's behalf made two arguments. First, it argued that the death penalty was cruel and unusual because it was imposed infrequently and in an arbitrary way. Second, it argued that the death penalty never should have been imposed on someone as mentally unstable and incompetent as Furman. The briefs on behalf of the other condemned men made further arguments about the barbaric nature of executions and the discriminatory application of death sentences to poor people and members of racial minority groups. In opposition to the arguments on behalf of Furman and the others, Georgia argued that capital punishment is supported by the public and is not applied in a discriminatory fashion (Stevens 1978, p. 109–23).

Furman's case and those of the other death row inmates were originally scheduled to be argued on the first day of the Court's 1971 term, October 12, 1971. However, two elderly justices from the Warren Court era, Hugo Black and John Harlan, resigned for health reasons. Thus, Furman's case was rescheduled for January 17, 1972, so that President Nixon's two new appointees, Lewis Powell and William Rehnquist, could participate in the Court's decisions about the death penalty issue (Stevens 1978, p. 113).

Professor Anthony Amsterdam of the Stanford Law School argued the case for Furman and one of the other death row prisoners. Jack Greenberg, the lawyer who had succeeded Thurgood Marshall as the head of LDF in the early 1960s, argued for another prisoner. Melvin Bruder, a Dallas attorney, made arguments for the Texas prisoner. Arguing in opposition were Dorothy Beasley, an assistant attorney general of Georgia; Ronald George, the California deputy attorney general; and Charles Alan Wright, a professor from the University of Texas. A few months after the oral arguments, the California case was dismissed, and the prisoner no longer faced execution because California's Supreme Court had declared that the death penalty violated the state's constitution. Thus, Furman's name came first alphabetically among the remaining death row cases, so the Supreme Court's decision would bear his name in its title (Stevens 1978, pp. 124–36).

On June 29, 1972, Chief Justice Warren Burger announced the Supreme Court's decision in *Furman v. Georgia* and the two remaining death penalty cases (case excerpt on p. 569). By a vote of five to four, the Supreme Court decided the death penalty was unconstitutional as it was being applied by Georgia and the other states. The dissenters were the four justices appointed to the Court by President Nixon between 1969 and 1971—Warren Burger, Harry Blackmun, Lewis Powell, and William Rehnquist. All nine justices wrote separate opinions, including the five justices in the majority who could not agree on the proper reasoning for the decision. The opinion for the Court was a brief per curiam opinion that simply stated: "The Court holds that the imposition and carrying out of the death penalty in these cases constitute cruel and unusual punishment in violation of the Eighth and Fourteenth Amendments" (408 U.S. at 239, 240).

Among the five justices in the majority, two justices, William Brennan and Thurgood Marshall, argued that the death penalty always constitutes a violation of the Eighth Amendment's prohibition on cruel and unusual punishments. Brennan argued that capital punishment is inherently unconstitutional because "[i]t is a denial of human dignity for the State arbitrarily to subject a person to an unusually severe punishment that society has indicated it does not regard as acceptable, and that cannot be shown to serve any penal purpose more effectively than a significantly less drastic punishment" (408 U.S. at 286). Justice Marshall examined the history of American capital punishment and the purposes of capital punishment. He concluded that "the death penalty is an excessive and unnecessary punishment that . . . serves no purpose that life imprisonment could not serve equally well" (408 U.S. at 358, 359). Moreover, because the Warren Court justices had declared in the 1950s that "[t]he [Eighth] Amendment must draw its meaning from evolving standards of decency that mark the progress of a maturing society" (*Trop v. Dulles,* 356 U.S. at 101, 1958), Marshall argued that the American people "would find [capital punishment] to be [barbarously cruel] in the light of all information presently available" (408 U.S. at 362).

By contrast, the other concurring opinions of Justices William O. Douglas, Potter Stewart, and Byron White presented other bases for finding the *application* of capital punishment, rather than the concept itself, in violation of the Eighth Amendment. Douglas's opinion focused on the arbitrary application and discriminatory consequences of discretionary death penalty decisions that are left to the whim of a judge or twelve jurors: "We know that the discretion of judges and juries in imposing the death penalty enables the penalty to be selectively applied, feeding prejudices against the accused if he is poor and despised, and lacking in political clout, or if he is a member of a suspect or unpopular minority, and saving those who by social position may be in a more protected position" (408 U.S. at 255).

Justice Stewart also emphasized the arbitrariness of capital punishment by declaring that "[t]hese death sentences are cruel and unusual in the same way that being struck by lightening is cruel and unusual. . . . [T]he petitioners are among a capriciously selected random handful upon whom the sentence of death has in fact been imposed" (408 U.S. at 309). Justice White agreed that because of juries' discretionary authority "the death penalty is exacted with great infrequency even for the most atrocious crimes and . . . there is no meaningful basis for distinguishing the few cases in which it is imposed from the many cases in which it is not" (408 U.S. at 313).

A common theme ran through the opinions of Douglas, Stewart, and White: "They each suggested that the death-sentencing systems under scrutiny in *Furman* were unconstitutional because of two factors: the infrequency with which juries actually imposed the death penalty, and the lack of any legitimate explanation of why some persons among those convicted of atrocious crimes received life sentences, while others convicted of atrocious crimes were sentenced to death" (Baldus, Woodworth, and Pulaski 1990, pp. 12–13).

The four dissenters were much more unified than the five justices in the majority. Although they each wrote separate opinions, they joined each other's opinions in a show of support against the majority's decision. The dissenters emphasized their belief that the majority was substituting its judgment opposing capital punishment for the policy decision favoring the death penalty by the citizens' duly elected representatives in state legislatures. The dissenters also questioned whether capital punishment offended contemporary society's standards and whether infrequent application of the death penalty constituted cruel and unusual punishment.

After the Supreme Court's decision, death row prisoners all over the country had their sentences commuted to life imprisonment. Meanwhile, state legislatures went back to the drawing board to attempt to create statutes that would meet the concerns expressed by Douglas, Stewart, and White about discrimination, excess discretion, and arbitrariness. When Mayfield went to Georgia Central Hospital to tell Furman about the legal victory in the Supreme Court, he found a man ravaged by mental illness, tuberculosis, and other ailments who did not even recognize his attorney or understand what had occurred (Stevens 1978, p. 146).

As we will discover in subsequent sections of this chapter, the *Furman* decision did not represent the Court's final word on the issue of capital punishment. It did, however, serve to raise many of the same questions that would face the modern Court in case after case concerning the death penalty. For example, how should the Court define the term "cruel and unusual punishment"? How much discretion should judges and juries possess in determining the sentences for criminal offenders? Should discriminatory consequences of sentencing practices provide the basis for invalidating those practices?

In addition, the *Furman* case demonstrated how the Court's composition can affect its decisions. During the 1968 election, President Nixon won the presidency while promising to appoint judges who would be tough on crime. The four dissenters in *Furman* were all Nixon appointees who supported the continuation of capital punishment and opposed the holdover Warren Court justices. When the Court is deeply divided over an issue, such as capital punishment, new appointees can determine case outcomes by casting their votes with one faction or the other on the divided Court. As the years passed, Republican presidents had the opportunity to appoint replacements for four of the five Warren Court holdovers in the *Furman* majority (Douglas, Stewart, Brennan, and Marshall). As a result, the Court's later decisions concerning the death penalty and other aspects of criminal punishment during the Burger Court and Rehnquist Court eras often favored the arguments advanced by the *Furman* dissenters.

Approaches to Eighth Amendment Decision Making

The Eighth Amendment in the Bill of Rights is the constitutional provision concerned most directly with the punishment imposed by government upon convicted criminals. Many Americans often wonder why convicted criminals have any rights at all. A popular view of criminals is that they should forfeit all of their constitutional rights because they did not abide by society's rules. Such a view is premised on a "social contract" theory of rights that regards individuals' constitutional protections as dependent on a cooperative, reciprocal relationship between society and the individual. Under this theory, if an individual violates the social contract, then the government is no longer obligated to provide the individual with the benefits, privileges, and protections of a member of society. The Eighth Amendment is not, however, written in "social contract" terms. Instead, it is written in "natural law" terms which indicate that everyone possesses certain rights against the government no matter what. The words of the Eighth Amendment do not focus on the behavior of the individual. The Amendment says,

> *"Excessive bail shall not be required, nor excessive fines imposed, nor cruel and unusual punishments inflicted."*

The Eighth Amendment focuses on the risk of the abusive application of government power against individuals. Thus, although the precise meaning of the amendment is unclear and must be interpreted by the Supreme Court, the Eighth

Amendment clearly intends to place limits on what the government can do in punishing individuals, including individuals convicted of crimes.

When interpreting the Eighth Amendment, the Supreme Court's justices face the difficult task of giving meaning to the term "cruel and unusual." In the Supreme Court's decisions, the justices often talk about four different methods for determining the meaning of this ambiguous term. First, when considering whether a punishment is "cruel and unusual," justices often examine whether a particular punishment was applied at the time that the Eighth Amendment was drafted and enacted. The obvious presumption under an original intent approach to interpreting the amendment is that any punishment that was used in 1791 must not have been considered "cruel and unusual" by the framers of the Bill of Rights.

Although the history of punishment presumably provides a clearer basis for inferring the originally intended meaning of the Eighth Amendment than that provided by historical material for the meanings of other constitutional provisions, contemporary justices show particular discomfort in adhering too closely to original intent as the iron-clad rule for interpreting the amendment. Justice Scalia, for example, who is one of the Rehnquist Court justices most inclined to look to the original meaning of constitutional provisions, has explicitly disclaimed strict adherence to original intent with respect to the Eighth Amendment. In a speech that was later published, Scalia argued that the Constitution should be interpreted according to the original intentions of its authors. However, Scalia pointed to the Eighth Amendment as the one provision of the Constitution to which he would not apply originalism in every case:

> *What if some state should enact a new law providing for public lashing, or branding of the right hand, as punishment for certain criminal offenses? Even if it could be demonstrated unequivocally that these were not cruel and unusual measures in 1791, and even though no prior Supreme Court decision has specifically disapproved them, I doubt whether any federal judge—even among the many who consider themselves originalists—would sustain them against an [E]ighth [A]mendment challenge. . . .*
>
> *Having made that endorsement [of original intent], I hasten to confess that in a crunch I may prove a faint-hearted originalist. I cannot imagine myself, any more than any other federal judge, upholding a statute that imposes the punishment of flogging.* (Scalia 1989, p. 864)

The second approach to interpreting the Eighth Amendment is to assess punishments for cruelty and unusualness in light of contemporary standards of human dignity in modern society. As expressed by the Warren Court justices during the late 1950s, "The [Eighth] Amendment must draw its meaning from evolving standards of decency that mark the progress of a maturing society" (*Trop v. Dulles*, 356 U.S. at 101, 1958). Although this vague formulation provides little concrete guidance about the Eighth Amendment's meaning, it has become the dominant test for assessing the constitutionality of criminal punishments. Because the justices do not agree with each other when assessing contemporary social values, majority and dissenting opinions frequently debate each other by making references to public opinion polls, enactments by state legislatures, and state court decisions as evidence of current standards.

The third approach involves assessing whether a punishment is disproportionate to the crime for which the offender was convicted. As Justice Powell declared in an opinion concerning a life sentence imposed for a series of relatively minor offenses, the prohibition on "cruel and unusual" punishments contained in the Eighth Amendment "prohibits not only barbaric punishments, but also sentences that are disproportionate to the crime committed" (*Solem v. Helm*, 463 U.S. at 277, 1983). While most contemporary justices agree that proportionality in sentencing is mandated by the Eighth Amendment, the justices have always had difficulty articulating clear tests to guide lower courts' examinations of this issue. In some cases, justices appeared to decide cases based on whether or not the sentence shocked their consciences. As we will see later in the chapter, this proportionality principle has served as the basis for invalidating both capital and noncapital sentences.

The fourth approach, which is not entirely separable from the second and third, is for the justices to apply their own personal values in determining the meaning of "cruel and unusual" punishments. No justices ever admit that they are merely applying their own values. They always claim that they are applying evolving standards of contemporary society. However, when they disagree about whether specific situations constitute cruel and unusual punishment, they accuse each other of applying personal values rather than societal standards. Because of the difficulty, if not impossibility, of determining a precise, single standard for the contemporary standards of American society, it would be very difficult for justices to separate their own views from the views that they attribute to American society.

Although it is difficult in most cases to know whether a justice's assessment of current societal standards is shaped by the justice's own views, some justices will adopt a restrained judicial role by explicitly overriding their personal preferences in favor of deference to the decisions of elected officials. Justice Harry Blackmun's dissenting opinion in *Furman* demonstrated a conscious effort to subordinate his personal views to his limited conception of his proper authority as a judicial officer: "I yield to no one in the depth of my distaste, antipathy, and, indeed, abhorrence, for the death penalty. . . . Were I a legislator, I would vote against the death penalty. . . . [However, in our] sole task [as] judges[,] [w]e should not allow our personal preferences as to the wisdom of legislative and congressional action, or our distaste for such action . . . to guide our judicial decision in cases such as these" (408 U.S. at 405, 406, 411). As this chapter's discussions of individual justices' views will reveal, Blackmun later began to interpret criminal punishment issues in favor of criminal defendants' and offenders' rights. Thus, during the Rehnquist Court era, one could wonder whether Blackmun believed societal standards had changed or whether Blackmun's role orientation changed to permit his personal distaste for the death penalty to affect his decisions.

The Eighth Amendment is not the only constitutional provision applied by the Supreme Court to determine the permissibility of criminal punishments. The Equal Protection Clause of the Fourteenth Amendment also provides a basis for judicial action. If a state's application of punishment improperly discriminated against specific categories of people, the Court could have grounds to invalidate the state's punishments or the procedures that produced those punishments. However, as we will see in *McCleskey v.Kemp* (1987), some justices are not eager to apply the Equal Protection Clause, even when there is evidence of racial discrimination.

The Court may also examine issues affecting criminal punishment through cases that raise questions about the procedures applied during a trial or appeal. For example, the Supreme Court has decided several capital punishment cases by considering whether the trial judge gave proper instructions to the jury when they began to deliberate about whether to impose the death penalty. After Chief Justice Rehnquist sought unsuccessfully to have Congress limit the opportunities for death row inmates to have their convictions reviewed by the federal courts (Smith 1992, pp. 94–95), the Supreme Court made decisions that advanced Rehnquist's policy goal without any legislative action. For example, the Court decided that attorney errors that result in violations of state court procedural rules, such as filing court papers a few days late, will result in forfeiture of the convicted offender's opportunity to have federal courts review a conviction (*Coleman v. Thompson,* 1991). The Rehnquist Court's emphasis on procedural decisions affecting capital punishment has led one legal scholar to remark that "the Court is not yet prepared to hop off the endless merry-go-round that it boarded when it first chose to interpret the Eighth Amendment in death-penalty cases primarily in procedural, rather than substantive, terms" (Hoffmann 1993, p. 832).

Some cases that might appear to implicate the Eighth Amendment are actually decided on other grounds. For example, in *Brown v. Mississippi* (1936), the Supreme Court's opinion described how police officers tortured African American suspects until they confessed: "[T]hey hanged [Ellington] by a rope to the limb of a tree, and having let him down, they hung him again, and when he . . . still protested his innocence, he was tied to a tree and whipped . . . signs of the rope on his neck were plainly visible. . . . [Brown and Shields] were made to strip and they were laid over chairs and their backs were cut to pieces with a leather strap with buckles on it . . ." (297 U.S. at 281-82). The Court overturned the defendants' convictions because the use of torture violated their Fourteenth Amendment right to due process of law. The Court did not apply the Eighth Amendment because the right against cruel and unusual punishment only applies to sentencing and treatment of an offender *after* he or she has been convicted of a crime. The use of torture in the *Brown* case came *prior* to the conviction as the means to obtain confessions for the purpose of gaining convictions. Thus the torture of suspects in the *Brown* case did not constitute punishment of convicted criminals.

Historical Development Prior to the Warren Court Era

The wording of the Eighth Amendment is drawn almost directly from the English Bill of Rights of 1689. The English prohibition against cruel and unusual punishments was aimed at excessive punishments (i.e., those disproportionate to the crime) and not at torturous punishments because England continued to apply such punishments as burning at the stake as well as drawing and quartering until the beginning of the nineteenth century. By the time the Americans first adopted the same language prohibiting cruel and unusual punishments in the Virginia Declaration of Rights in 1776, according to one scholar, "the concept of cruel and unusual punishment was clearly interpreted much more broadly. There is no doubt whatsoever that . . . our founding fathers intended to prohibit torture and other cruel punishments" (Berkson 1975, pp. 3, 5). By modern standards, however, the punishments imposed on offenders were harsh and painful: "Fines, stocks, flogging, branding, and maiming were the primary means to control deviancy and to maintain public safety" (Cole 1992, pp. 545–46). The death penalty was imposed for a wide range of offenses, including burglary, robbery, and horse stealing. The development of incarceration as a punishment began at the dawn of the nineteenth century as the states of Pennsylvania and New York took the lead in developing prisons that would isolate offenders from society. Conditions in these early prisons were harsh as Pennsylvania initially kept offenders in complete isolation except for a weekly visit from a clergyman. New York differed only by making its prisoners work in complete silence in workshops during the day (Cole 1992, pp. 549–50).

Because every state except Connecticut and Vermont has a prohibition against cruel and unusual punishments in its state constitution, a variety of state courts decided cases concerning criminal punishment beginning in 1811 (Berkson 1975, p. 9). However, the U.S. Supreme Court had little reason to examine the Eighth Amendment because, prior to incorporation during the Warren Court era, the Amendment applied only against the federal government. The Court first faced the issue of interpreting the Eighth Amendment when prisoners in the late nineteenth century unsuccessfully attempted to have Eighth Amendment rights applied against the states. In *Wilkerson v. Utah* (1879), the Court rejected a condemned prisoner's claim and thereby effectively endorsed a sentence of public execution by shooting applied to an offender convicted of premeditated murder. Although the Supreme Court's holding concerned the territorial court's power to determine a mode of execution despite the absence of statutory language specifying how condemned convicts would be put to death, the unanimous Court added a comment about the meaning of cruel and unusual punishment in its opinion: "Difficulty would attend the effort to define with exactness the extent of the constitutional provision which provides that cruel and unusual punishments shall not be inflicted; but it is safe to affirm that punishments of torture . . . and all others in the same line of unnecessary cruelty, are forbidden by that amendment to the Constitution" (99 U.S. at 135–36).

In 1890, the Supreme Court decided the case of William Kemmler, the first of many offenders sentenced to die in the newly invented electric chair. Because the Eighth Amendment was not yet applied to the states through incorporation, Kemmler asked the Supreme Court to declare that the execution would violate the privileges and immunities clause of the Fourteenth Amendment (Berkson 1975, p. 25). In rejecting Kemmler's claim, the Court decided that even if a punishment is unusual, as electrocution was when first developed, it did not constitute cruel and unusual punishment if it was adopted by the legislature for a humane purpose (*In re Kemmler*, 1890).

Two years later, an Eighth Amendment claim arose when a Vermont man convicted of illegal liquor sales was sentenced to a fine of $6,140 and court costs of $498. He was to be held in prison until the fines were paid; and if they were not paid by a certain date, his sentence was to be raised to three days per dollar of the fine, which effectively constituted a sentence of fifty-four years at hard labor. The U.S. Supreme Court rejected the claim because the Eighth Amendment did not apply against the states (*O'Neil v. Vermont*, 1892). In dissent, Justice Field argued that cruel and unusual punishment should not be reserved as a label for torturous punishments but should also apply to "all punishments which by their excessive lengths and severity are greatly disproportioned to the offences charged" (144 U.S. at 339–40).

The first landmark decision in which the Supreme Court applied the Eighth Amendment to overturn a sentence was *Weems v. United States* (1910). Weems was a disbursing officer in the Bureau of the Coast Guard and Transportation of the United States Government of the Philippine Islands. He was convicted of falsifying an official document by falsely recording that a total of 618 pesos had been paid to lighthouse workers. He was sentenced to fifteen years incarceration and hard labor with chains on his ankles and loss of his civil rights. Because the Philippines Islands were under the control of the U.S. government, there was no incorporation issue in the case. The Supreme Court struck down the sentence by adopting Justice Fields's rationale in *O'Neil* that disproportionate sentences violated the Eighth Amendment. The Court compared the sentence imposed on Weems with the lesser sentences mandated by law for more serious offenses such as homicide, rebellion, conspiracy, and robbery in concluding that Weems's sentence was unconstitutionally cruel and unusual by virtue of its excessiveness.

Although the *Weems* decision represented a breakthrough for the application of cruel and unusual punishment to excessive sentences, state and federal courts rarely took the *Weems* approach of comparing sentences for various crimes. Because the Eighth Amendment was not incorporated into the Due Process Clause of the Fourteenth Amendment until 1962, state courts did not feel obligated to follow the *Weems* approach in interpreting their own state constitutional provisions forbidding cruel and unusual punishment. In addition, many judges were reluctant to substitute their own judgments about appropriate punishments for the judgments made by elected legislators. Thus, according to one scholar, "the method of imposing the [*Weems* excessiveness] principle remained to a large degree abstract if not ambiguous. Lacking effective guidelines, courts simply reverted to the idea that any sentence within statutory limits was constitutional unless so disproportionate to the offense that it shocked the moral sense of all reasonable men" (Berkson 1975, p. 71).

Although the Court did not review many Eighth Amendment claims, in one particular case in 1947 the Court assumed, without making a formal decision, that the Eighth Amendment should be incorporated and applied to the states (Abraham 1988, p. 82 n. 153). Louisiana's first attempt to execute Willie Francis for murder went horribly wrong when the electric shock failed to kill him after he writhed in agony for two minutes. Before the state could repair the electric chair to make a second attempt to deliver a lethal dose of electrical current, lawyers petitioned the Supreme Court on behalf of Francis to claim that a second attempted electrocution would constitute cruel and unusual punishment. In a narrow 5–4 decision, the Court rejected the claim that facing a second execution would constitute cruel and unusual mental anguish and physical pain (*Louisiana ex rel. Francis v. Resweber*, 1947). The formal incorporation of the Eighth Amendment for application to the states came later during the Warren Court era.

The Warren Court Era

With the exception of the *Weems* decision in 1910, the Supreme Court essentially left criminal punishment under the authority of state and federal officials until the 1950s. During the Warren Court era, the justices became more receptive to individuals' challenges to the exercise of governmental authority. As indicated in other chapters, the Warren-era justices' concerns about civil rights and liberties led to controversial decisions affecting racial segregation, freedom of religion, and criminal defendants' rights. Not surprisingly, these justices also reconsidered the definition and application of the Eighth Amendment in response to petitions from individuals who believed that their punishments violated the Constitution.

The major case that helped to develop the definition of "cruel and unusual punishments" was *Trop v. Dulles* (1958). Trop was a native-born American citizen who served in the U.S. Army during World War II. In May of 1944, he was confined to a military stockade in French Morocco for a breach of military disciplinary rules. He escaped from the stockade and was missing for less than a day when he willingly surrendered himself to the occupants of a passing Army vehicle while he was walking back toward the stockade. A general court-martial convicted Trop of desertion and sentenced him to three years hard labor and a dishonorable discharge. After he served his sentence and the war ended, Trop applied for a passport in 1952. His application was denied because under the Nationality Act of 1940 he had lost his American citizenship by virtue of his conviction and dishonorable discharge for wartime desertion. Seven thousand other American servicemen lost their citizenship during World War II for committing the same offense. Trop challenged the forfeiture of citizenship as an unconstitutional cruel and unusual punishment.

In a 5–4 decision, the Supreme Court supported Trop's claim. In his plurality opinion that announced the judgment of the Court, Chief Justice Warren declared that the Eighth Amendment "must draw its meaning from the evolving standards of decency that mark the progress of a maturing society" (356 U.S. at 101). This famous statement became the primary standard that the Supreme Court would subsequently quote and apply in Eighth Amendment cases. Except for occasional criticisms during the Rehnquist Court era by Justices Scalia and Thomas, the search for contemporary values as the means to define the Eighth Amendment has enjoyed support from both liberal and conservative justices.

In explaining why Trop's punishment violated the contemporary standards of the Eighth Amendment, Warren emphasized that the prohibition on cruel and unusual punishments did not merely apply to physical torture:

> *[U]se of denationalization as a punishment is barred by the Eighth Amendment. There may be involved no physical mistreatment, no primitive torture. There is instead the total destruction of the individual's status in organized society. It is a form of punishment more primitive than torture, for it destroys for the individual the political existence that was centuries in the development. The punishment strips the citizen of his status in the national and international political community. His very existence is at the sufferance of the country in which he happens to find himself.* (356 U.S. at 101)

The Warren Court justices formally incorporated the Eighth Amendment into the Due Process Clause of the Fourteenth Amendment in 1962. The case of *Robinson v. California* (1962) made the Eighth Amendment fully applicable against the states. Robinson was convicted of violating a California statute that made it a crime to "be addicted to the use of narcotics." Robinson was convicted based on a police officer's testimony about the presence of needle marks and scars on Robinson's arm. Robinson challenged the constitutionality of the law that made it a crime to be a drug addict.

In writing the Court's opinion, Justice Stewart applied the contemporary standards test established in *Trop* to declare that states cannot create "status" crimes. Robinson was not convicted of buying, selling, possessing, or using drugs. Thus he was not convicted of taking any "action" with respect to drug use, possession, or trafficking. Instead, he was convicted for his "status," that of being a drug addict. Stewart compared the status offense applied to Robinson to hypothetical criminal laws that might target people for having a particular condition or disease: "It is unlikely that any State at this moment in history would attempt to make it a criminal offense for a person to be mentally ill, or a leper, or to be afflicted with venereal disease. . . . [I]n light of contemporary human knowledge, a law which made a criminal offense of such a disease would doubtless be universally thought to be an infliction of cruel and unusual punishment in violation of the Eighth Amendment" (370 U.S. at 666).

Stewart again made reference to contemporary standards of society in concluding the opinion by declaring that "[w]e would forget the teachings of the Eighth Amendment if we allowed sickness to be made a crime and permitted sick people to be punished for being sick. This age of enlightenment cannot tolerate such barbarous action" (370 U.S. at 678).

In dissent, Justice White accused the majority of applying their own personal values improperly in the place of the policy decisions made by the California legislature: "I deem this application of 'cruel and unusual punishment' so novel that I suspect the Court was hard put to find a way to ascribe to the Framers of the Constitution the result reached today rather than to its own notions of ordered liberty. . . . I fail to see why the Court deems it more appropriate to write into the Constitution its own abstract notions of how best to handle the narcotics problem, for it obviously cannot match either the States or Congress in expert understanding" (370 U.S. at 689).

Robinson v. California

370 U.S. 660, 82 S.Ct. 1417, 8 L.Ed 2d 758 (1962)

■ California had a statute that made it a criminal offense to "be addicted to the use of narcotics." Lawrence Robinson was arrested for violating this statute after an officer examined his arm and observed scar tissue and "what appeared to be numerous needle marks and a scab which was approximately three inches below the crook of the elbow." The officer also testified that Robinson admitted that he used narcotics. After a jury convicted Robinson of the offense, he appealed unsuccessfully to the Appellate Department of the Los Angeles County Superior Court, the highest court available in California's system to hear his appeal. In the U.S. Supreme Court, Robinson's case raised the issue of whether the California statute criminalizing the status rather than the actions of narcotics addicts violated the Eighth and Fourteenth Amendments.

The case is important because it represents the moment when the Warren Court officially (albeit implicitly) incorporated the Eighth Amendment's prohibition against cruel and unusual punishments into the Due Process Clause of the Fourteenth Amendment for application against the states. As you read the case, consider the following questions: (1) Does Justice Stewart's effort to compare narcotics addiction to other illnesses make sense when narcotics addiction frequently involves illegal activities initiated and perpetuated by the addict? (2) Does this opinion give useful guidance to other courts about the meaning of the Eighth Amendment? (3) How would the eighteenth-century authors of the Eighth Amendment have viewed the Court's application of the concept of cruel and unusual punishment to Robinson?

Vote:

6 justices found the law unconstitutional (Black, Brennan, Douglas, Harlan, Stewart, Warren) [Harlan concurred in the judgment but did not join Stewart's majority opinion].

2 justices found the law constitutional (Clark, White).

[Justice Frankfurter did not participate]

Justice Stewart delivered the opinion of the Court:

* * *

The broad power of a State to regulate the narcotic drugs traffic within its borders is not here in issue. . . . Such regulation, it can be assumed, could take a variety of valid forms. A State might impose criminal sanctions, for example, against the unauthorized manufacture, prescription, sale, purchase, or possession of narcotics within its borders. In the interest of discouraging the violation of such laws, or in the interest of the general health or welfare of its inhabitants, a State might establish a program of compulsory treatment for those addicted to narcotics. Such a program of treatment might require periods of involuntary confinement. And penal sanctions might be imposed for failure to comply with established compulsory procedures. . . . Or a state might choose to attack the evils of narcotics traffic on broader fronts also—through public health education, for example, or by efforts to ameliorate the economic and social conditions under which those evils might be thought to flourish. In short, the range of valid choices which a State might make in this area is undoubtedly a wide one, and the wisdom of any particular choice within the allowable spectrum is not for us to decide. Upon that premise we turn to the California law in issue here.

It would be possible to construe the statute under which the appellant was convicted as one which is operative only upon proof of the actual use of narcotics. But the California courts have not so construed this law. Although there was evidence in the present case that the appellant had used narcotics in Los Angeles, the jury were instructed that they could convict him even if they disbelieved that evidence. The appellant could be convicted, they were told, if they found simply that the appellant's "status" or "chronic condition" was that of being "addicted to the use of narcotics." And it is impossible to know from the jury's verdict that the defendant was not convicted upon precisely such a finding.

* * *

The statute, therefore, is not one which punishes a person for the use of narcotics, for their purchase, sale or possession, or for antisocial or disorderly behavior resulting from their administration. It is not a law which even purports to provide or require medical treatment. Rather we deal with a statute which makes the "status" of narcotics addiction a criminal offense, for which the offender may be prosecuted "at any time before he reforms." California has said that a person can be continuously guilty of this offense, whether or not he has ever used or possessed any narcotics within the State, and whether or not he has been guilty of any antisocial behavior there.

It is unlikely that any State at this moment in history would attempt to make it a criminal offense for a person to be mentally ill, or a leper, or to be afflicted with a venereal disease. A State might determine that the general health and welfare require that the victims of these and other human afflictions be dealt with by compulsory treatment, involving quarantine, confinement, or sequestration. But, in the light of contemporary human knowledge, a law which made a criminal offense of such disease would doubtless be universally thought to be an infliction of cruel and unusual punishment in violation of the Eighth and Fourteenth Amendments. See *Louisiana ex rel. Francis v. Resweber*. . . .

We cannot but consider the statute before us as of the same category. In this Court counsel for the State recognized that narcotic addiction is an illness. Indeed, it is apparently an illness which may be contracted innocently or involuntarily.[9] We hold that a state law which imprisons a person thus afflicted as a criminal, even though he had never touched any narcotic drug within the State or been guilty of any irregular behavior there, inflicts a cruel and unusual punishment in violation of the Fourteenth Amendment. To be sure, imprisonment for ninety days is not, in the abstract, a punishment which is either cruel or unusual. But the question cannot be considered in the abstract. Even one day in prison would be a cruel and unusual punishment for the "crime" of having a common cold.

We are not unmindful that the vicious evils of the narcotics traffic have occasioned the grave concern of government. There are, as we have said, countless fronts on which those evils may be legitimately attacked. We deal in this case only with an individual provision of a particularized local law as it has so far been interpreted by the California courts.

Reversed.

Justice Douglas, concurring.

While I join the Court's opinion, I wish to make more explicit the reasons why I think it is "cruel and unusual" punishment in the sense of the Eighth Amendment to treat as a criminal a person who is a drug addict.

* * *

The impact that an addict has on a community causes alarm and often leads to punitive measures. Those measures are justified when they relate to acts of transgression. But I do not see how under our system *being an addict* can be punished as a crime. If addicts can be punished for their addiction, then the insane can also be punished for their insanity. Each has a disease and each must be treated as a sick person.

* * *

The addict is a sick person. He may, of course, be confined for treatment or for the protection of society. Cruel and unusual punishment results not from confinement, but from convicting the addict of a crime. . . . A prosecution for addiction, with its resulting stigma and irreparable damage to the good name of the accused, cannot be justified as a means of protecting society, where civil commitment would do as well. . . . We would forget the teachings of the Eighth Amendment if we allowed sickness to be made a crime and permitted sick people to be punished for being sick. This age of enlightenment cannot tolerate such barbarous action.

Justice Harlan, concurring.

I am not prepared to hold that on the present state of medical knowledge it is completely irrational and hence unconstitutional for a State to conclude that narcotics addiction is something other than an illness, nor that it amounts to cruel and unusual punishment for the State to subject narcotics addicts to its criminal law. . . . But in this case the trial court's instructions permitted the jury to find the appellant guilty on no more proof than that he was present in California while he was addicted to narcotics. Since addiction alone cannot reasonably be thought to amount to more than a compelling propensity to use narcotics, the effect of this instruction was to authorize criminal punishment for a bare desire to commit a criminal act.

If the California statute reaches this type of conduct, and for present purposes we must accept the trial court's construction as binding, . . . it is an arbitrary imposition which exceeds the power that a State may exercise in enacting its criminal law. Accordingly, I agree that the application of the California statute was unconstitutional in this case and join the judgment of reversal.

Justice Clark, dissenting.

* * *

The majority strikes down the conviction primarily on the grounds that the petitioner was denied due process by the imposition of criminal penalties for nothing more than being in a status. This viewpoint is premised upon the theme that [the California statute] is a "criminal" provision authorizing a punishment, for the majority admits that "a State might establish a program of compulsory treatment for those addicted to narcotics" which "might require periods of involuntary confinement." I submit that California has done exactly that. The majority's error is in instructing the California Legislature that hospitalization is the *only treatment* for narcotics addiction—that anything less is a punishment denying due process. California has found otherwise after

9Not only may addiction innocently result from the use of medically prescribed narcotics, but a person may even be a narcotics addict from the moment of his birth. . . .

a study which I suggest was more extensive than that conducted by the Court. . . . The test is the overall purpose and effect of a State's act, and I submit that California's program relative to narcotic addicts—including both the "criminal" and "civil" provisions—is inherently one of treatment and lies well within the power of a State. . . .

Justice White, dissenting.

* * *

Finally, I deem this application of "cruel and unusual punishment" so novel that I suspect the Court was hard put to find a way to ascribe to the Framers of the Constitution the result reached today rather than to its own notions of ordered liberty. If this case involved economic regulation, the present Court's allergy to substantive due process would surely save the statute and prevent the Court from imposing its own philosophical predilections upon state legislatures or Congress. I fail to see why the Court deems it more appropriate to write into the Constitution its own abstract notions of how best to handle the narcotics problem, for it obviously cannot match either the States or Congress in expert understanding.

I respectfully dissent.

The Warren Court's lasting contributions to the development of Eighth Amendment jurisprudence were the contemporary standards test for "cruel and unusual punishments" enunciated in *Trop* and the incorporation of the Eighth Amendment and ban on "status" crimes in *Robinson.* These cases were cited regularly in Eighth Amendment cases that came to the Supreme Court during later eras.

In addition to supplying these enduring precedents, the Supreme Court also helped to lay the groundwork for Eighth Amendment issues that would confront the high court in subsequent eras. First, several Warren Court justices raised the question of whether the death penalty should be considered cruel and unusual. Although the Supreme Court did not face the issue during the Warren Court era, it faced this very issue in *Furman* during the early years of the Burger Court era. The issue was initially raised most starkly by Justice Goldberg in 1963. The Court was asked to review the case of *Rudolph v. Alabama,* (1963), an interracial rape case in which the defendant received a death sentence but claimed that his confession had not been voluntary. The case came to the Court on an issue of criminal procedure, but Justice Goldberg circulated a memo to his colleagues suggesting that they accept the case to examine the question whether "the evolving standards of decency that mark the progress of [our] maturing society now condemn as barbaric and inhumane the deliberate institutionalized taking of human life by the state" (quoted in Epstein and Kobylka 1992, p. 43). Many justices objected to Goldberg's attempt to raise a controversial issue on his own that was not presented by the parties in the case. When the Court declined to hear the case, Justice Goldberg wrote an unusual dissent from the denial of certiorari that was joined by Justices Douglas and Brennan. Goldberg urged the Court to consider the issue of whether capital punishment violated the Eighth Amendment. Goldberg's law clerk mailed copies of the dissenting opinions to lawyers throughout the country and thereby helped to signal to interested lawyers and interest groups that some justices were ready to receive cases challenging capital punishment. Goldberg's memo helped to encourage LDF and the ACLU to work toward challenging capital punishment in court (Epstein and Kobylka 1992, pp. 43-45).

Second, in *Cooper v. Pate* (1964), the Supreme Court decided that prisoners can use the Civil Rights Act of 1871 (42 U.S. Code section 1983) to initiate federal lawsuits to challenge conditions in correctional institutions. Prior to the Warren Court justices' decision, courts had traditionally applied a "hands off" policy to prisons. The Supreme Court's decision eventually provided the basis for thousands of legal actions each year against state and local authorities. Although most prisoner civil rights suits are dismissed for lack of a valid constitutional claim, many such legal actions have led federal judges to issue rulings defining the scope of prisoners' rights and supervising the administration of correctional facilities. The Warren Court decision provided the legal basis for later decisions that applied the Eighth Amendment to conditions inside jails and prisons (Smith 1993, pp. 93–109).

The Burger Court Era

One of President Nixon's primary goals when he nominated Warren Burger to replace retiring Chief Justice Earl Warren in 1969 was to appoint federal judges, including Supreme Court justices, who would be tough on crime. Nixon had made "law and order" an issue in his presidential campaign, and he viewed judicial appointments as an opportunity to show the public that he meant what he said. Burger had a reputation as a "law and order" judge, and Nixon's other Supreme Court appointees also proved to be less supportive of individuals' claims in criminal justice cases than were their predecessors from the Warren Court. However, with respect to criminal punishment issues, the Nixon appointees did not cause the Court to narrow constitutional protections for convicted offenders. In fact, individual Nixon appointees joined Warren Court holdovers to establish precedents that narrowed the discretion of decision makers in capital cases and endorsed judicial supervision of conditions inside prisons.

Capital Punishment

In its initial decisions on capital punishment, the Burger Court maintained the status quo by permitting states to impose the death penalty after criminal trials without any special procedures or standards for sentencing (*McGautha v. California*, 1971; *Crampton v. Ohio*, 1971). Because of an informal moratorium on executions, no prisoners had been executed since 1968 while the death row populations climbed to five hundred. The LDF hoped that the number of prisoners on death row "would weigh heavily on the minds of the justices, since in essence their decisions could result in mass executions" when they considered the issue of capital punishment in subsequent cases (Epstein and Kobylka 1992, p. 66).

In 1971, the Court accepted the cases of William Furman and three others for hearing, and in 1972 the justices issued their famous decision in *Furman v. Georgia*.

Furman v. Georgia

408 U.S. 238, 92 S.Ct. 2726, 33 L.Ed. 2d 346 (1972) [decided simultaneously with *Jackson v. Georgia* and *Branch v. Texas*]

[The facts of this case are omitted because they were presented in the case study at the beginning of this chapter.]

■ The case is important because it began the process of setting limits and standards for the application of capital punishment. As you read the case, consider the following questions: (1) Why were the justices in the majority unable to agree on the reasoning for the decision? (2) Which justices had the most accurate view of how the death penalty should be evaluated in light of contemporary society's values? (3) What is the proper interpretive approach for determining whether or not capital punishment is permissible under the Constitution?

VOTE:

5 justices found the death penalty to be unconstitutional in these cases (Brennan, Douglas, Marshall, Stewart, White).

4 justices found the death penalty to be constitutional (Blackmun, Burger, Powell, Rehnquist).

Per Curiam.

Petitioner in No. 69-5003 was convicted of murder in Georgia and was sentenced to death pursuant to [Georgia's statute]. . . . Petitioner No. 69-5030 was convicted of rape in Georgia and sentenced to death pursuant to [Georgia's statute]. . . . Petitioner No. 69-5031 was convicted of rape in Texas and was sentenced to death pursuant to [Texas's statute]. . . . Certiorari was granted limited to the following question: "Does the imposition and carrying out of the death penalty in [these cases] constitute cruel and unusual punishment in violation of the Eighth and Fourteenth Amendments?". . . . The Court holds that the imposition and carrying out of the death penalty in these cases constitute cruel and unusual punishment in violation of the Eighth and Fourteenth Amendments. The judgment in each case is therefore reversed insofar as it leaves undisturbed the death sentences imposed, and the cases are remanded for further proceedings. So ordered.

Judgment in each case reversed in part and cases remanded.

Justice Douglas, concurring.

In these three cases the death penalty was imposed, one of them for murder, and two for rape. In each the determination of whether the penalty should be death or a lighter punishment was left by the State to the discretion of the judge or of the jury. . . . I vote to vacate each judgment, believing that the exaction of the death penalty does violate the Eighth and Fourteenth Amendments.

* * *

In a Nation committed to equal protection of the laws there is no permissible "caste" aspect of law enforcement. Yet we know that the discretion of judges and juries in imposing the death penalty enables the penalty to be selectively applied, feeding prejudices against the accused if he is poor and despised, and lacking political clout, or if he is a member of a suspect or unpopular minority, and saving those who by social position may be in a more protected position. In ancient Hindu law a Brahman was exempt from capital punishment, and under that law, "[g]enerally, in the law books, punishment increased in severity as social status diminished." We have, I fear, taken in practice the same position, partially as a result of making the death penalty discretionary and partially as a result of the ability of the rich to purchase the services of the most respected and most resourceful legal talent in the Nation.

The high service rendered by the "cruel and unusual" punishment clause of the Eighth Amendment is to require legislatures to write penal laws that are evenhanded, nonselective, and nonarbitrary, and to require judges to see to it that general laws are not applied sparsely, selectively, and spottily to unpopular groups. . . .

Justice Brennan, concurring.

The question presented in these cases is whether death is today a punishment for crime that is "cruel and unusual" and consequently, by virtue of the Eighth and Fourteenth Amendments, beyond the power of the State to inflict.

* * *

Ours would indeed be a simple task were we required merely to measure a challenged punishment against those that history has long condemned. That narrow and unwarranted view of the [Cruel and Unusual Punishments] Clause, however, was left behind with the 19th century. Our task today is more complex. We know "that the words of the [Clause] are not precise, and that their scope is not static." We know, therefore, that the Clause "must draw its meaning from the evolving standards of decency that mark the progress of a maturing society."

* * *

At bottom, then, the Cruel and Unusual Punishments Clause prohibits the infliction of uncivilized and inhuman punishments. The State, even as it punishes, must treat its members with respect for their intrinsic worth as human beings. A punishment is "cruel and unusual," therefore, if it does not comport with human dignity.

* * *

The primary principle is that a punishment must not be so severe as to be degrading to the dignity of human beings. Pain, certainly, may be a factor in that judgment. . . .

* * *

In determining whether a punishment comports with human dignity, we are aided also by a second principle inherent in the Clause—that the State must not arbitrarily inflict a severe punishment. This principle derives from the notion that the State does not respect human dignity when, without reason, it inflicts upon some people a severe punishment that it does not inflict upon others. . . .

* * *

A third principle inherent in the Clause is that a severe punishment must not be unacceptable to contemporary society. Rejection by society, of course, is a strong indication that a severe punishment does not comport with human dignity. . . .

* * *

The final principle inherent in the Clause is that a severe punishment must not be excessive. A punishment is excessive under this principle if it is unnecessary: The infliction of a severe punishment by the State cannot comport with human dignity when it is nothing more than the pointless infliction of suffering. If there is a significantly less severe punishment adequate to achieve the purposes for which the punishment is inflicted, . . . the punishment inflicted is unnecessary and therefore excessive.

* * *

The only explanation for the uniqueness of [the] death [penalty] is its extreme severity. Death is today an unusually severe punishment, unusual in its pain, in its finality, and in its enormity. No other existing punishment is comparable to death in terms of physical and mental suffering. Although our information is not conclusive, it appears that there is no method available that guarantees an immediate and painless death. Since the discontinuance of flogging as a constitutionally permissible punishment, *Jackson v. Bishop,* 404 F. 2d 571 (CA 8 1968), death remains as the only punishment that may involve the conscious infliction of physical pain. In addition, we know that mental pain is an inseparable part of our practice of punishing criminals by death, for the prospect of pending execution exacts a frightful toll during the inevitable long wait between the imposition of sentence and actual infliction of death. . . . As the California Supreme Court pointed out, "the process of carrying out a verdict of death is often so degrading and brutalizing to the human spirit as to constitute psychological torture."* * *

* * *

Death is truly an awesome punishment. The calculated killing of a human being by the State involves, by its very nature, a denial of the executed person's humanity. The contrast with the plight of a person punished by imprisonment is evident. An individual in prison does not lose "the right to have rights." . . . A prisoner remains a member of the human family. . . .

In comparison to all other punishments today, then, the deliberate extinguishment of human life by the State is uniquely degrading to human dignity. I would not hesitate to hold, on that ground alone, that death is today a "cruel and unusual" punishment, were it not that death is a punishment of long-standing usage and acceptance in this country. I therefore turn to the second principle—that the State may not arbitrarily inflict an unusually severe punishment.

The outstanding characteristic of our present practice of punishing criminals by death is the infrequency with which we resort to it. The evidence is conclusive that death is not the ordinary punishment for any crime.

* * *

. . . Juries, "express[ing] the conscience of the community on the ultimate question of life or death," . . . have been able to bring themselves to vote for death in a mere 100 or so cases among the thousands tried each year where the punishment is available. Governors, elected by and acting for us, have regularly commuted a substantial number of those sentences. And it is our society that insists upon due process of law to the end that no person will be unjustly put to death, thus ensuring that many more of those sentences will not be carried out. In sum, we have made death a rare punishment today. . . .

The progressive decline in, and the current rarity of, the infliction of death demonstrate that our society seriously questions the appropriateness of this punishment today. . . .

* * *

In sum, the punishment of death is inconsistent with all four principles: Death is an unusually severe and degrading punishment; there is a strong probability that it is inflicted arbitrarily; its rejection by contemporary society is virtually total; and there is no reason to believe that it serves any penal purpose more effectively than the less severe punishment of imprisonment. The function of these principles is to enable a court to determine whether a punishment comports with human dignity. Death, quite simply, does not.

* * *

. . . When examined by the principles applicable under the Cruel and Unusual Punishments Clause, death stands condemned as fatally offensive to human dignity. The punishment of death is therefore "cruel and unusual," and the States may no longer inflict it as a punishment for crimes. . . .

Justice Stewart, concurring.

* * *

[T]he death sentences now before us are the product of a legal system that brings them, I believe, within the very core of the Eighth Amendment's guarantee against cruel and unusual punishments, a guarantee applicable against the States through the Fourteenth Amendment. *Robinson v. California*. . . . In the first place, it is clear that these sentences are "cruel" in the sense that they excessively go beyond, not in degree but in kind, the punishments that the state legislatures have determined to be necessary. *Weems v. United States*. . . . In the second place, it is equally clear that these sentences are "unusual" in the sense that the penalty of death is infrequently imposed for murder, and that its imposition for rape is extraordinarily rare. But I do not rest my conclusion upon these two propositions alone.

These death sentences are cruel and unusual in the same way that being struck by lightning is cruel and unusual. For, of all the people convicted of rapes and murders in 1967 and 1968, many just as reprehensible as these, the petitioners are among a capriciously selected random handful upon whom the sentence of death has in fact been imposed. My concurring Brothers have demonstrated that, if any basis can be discerned for the selection of these few to be sentenced to die, it is the constitutionally impermissible basis of race. . . . But racial discrimination has not been proved and I put it to one side. I simply conclude that the Eighth and Fourteenth Amendments cannot tolerate the infliction of a sentence of death under legal systems that permit this unique penalty to be so wantonly and freakishly imposed.

For these reasons I concur in the judgments of the Court.

Justice White, concurring.

* * *

I need not restate the facts and figures that appear in the opinions of my Brethren. Nor can I "prove" my conclusion from these data. But, like my Brethren, I must arrive at judgment; and I can do no more than state a conclusion based on 10 years of almost daily exposure to the facts and circumstances of hundreds and hundreds of federal and state criminal cases involving crimes for which death is the authorized penalty. That conclusion, as I have said, is that the death penalty is exacted with great infrequency even for the most atrocious crimes and that there is no meaningful basis for distinguishing the few cases in which it is imposed from the many cases in which it is not. The short of it is that the policy of vesting sentencing authority primarily in juries—a decision largely motivated by the desire to mitigate the harshness of the law and to bring community judgment to bear on the sentence as well as guilt or innocence—has so effectively achieved its aims that capital punishment within the confines of the statutes now before us has for all practical purposes run its course.

* * *

In this respect, I add only that past and present legislative judgment with respect to the death penalty loses much of its force when viewed in light of the recurring practice of delegating sentencing authority to the jury and the fact that a jury, in its own discretion and without violating its trust or any statutory policy, may refuse to impose the death penalty no matter what the circumstances of the crime. Legislative "policy" is thus necessarily defined not by what is legislatively authorized but by what juries and judges do in exercising the discretion so regularly conferred upon them. In my judgment what was done in these cases violated the Eighth Amendment.

I concur in the judgments of the Court.

Justice Marshall, concurring.

* * *

[H]istory demonstrates that capital punishment was carried from Europe to America but, once here, was tempered considerably. At times in our history, strong abolitionist movements have existed. But, they have never been completely successful, as no more than one-quarter of the States of the Union have, at any one time, abolished the death penalty. They have had partial success, however, especially in reducing the number of capital crimes, replacing mandatory death sentences with jury discretion, and developing more humane methods of conducting executions.

This is where our historical foray leads us. The question now to be faced is whether American society has reached a point where abolition is not dependent on a successful grass roots movement in particular jurisdictions, but is demanded by the Eighth Amendment. . . .

* * *

There is but one conclusion that can be drawn from [a review of studies on the deterrent effects of capital punishment]—*i.e.*, the death penalty is an excessive and unnecessary punishment. The statistical evidence is not convincing beyond all doubt, but it is persuasive. It is not improper at this point to take judicial notice of the fact that for more than 200 years men have labored to demonstrate that capital punishment serves no purpose that life imprisonment could not serve equally well. And they have done so with great success. Little, if any, evidence has been adduced to prove the contrary. The point has now been reached at which deference to the legislatures is tantamount to abdication of our judicial roles as factfinders, judges, and ultimate arbiters of the Constitution. We know that at some point the presumption of constitutionality accorded legislative acts gives way to a realistic assessment of those acts. This point comes when there is sufficient evidence available so that judges can determine, not whether the legislature acted wisely, but whether it had any rational basis whatsoever for acting. We have this evidence before us now. There is no rational basis for concluding that capital punishment is not excessive. It therefore violates the Eighth Amendment.

* * *

. . . I believe that the following facts would serve to convince even the most hesitant of citizens to condemn death as a sanction: capital punishment is imposed discriminatorily against certain identifiable classes of people; there is evidence that innocent people have been executed before their innocence can be proved; and the death penalty wreaks havoc with our entire criminal justice system. . . .

* * *

Assuming knowledge of all the facts presently available regarding capital punishment, the average citizen would in my opinion, find it shocking to his conscience and sense of justice. For this reason alone capital punishment cannot stand.

* * *

Chief Justice Burger, with whom Justice Blackmun, Justice Powell, and Justice Rehnquist join, dissenting.

At the outset it is important to note that only two members of the Court, Mr. Justice BRENNAN and Mr. Justice MARSHALL, have concluded that the Eighth Amendment prohibits capital punishment for all crimes and under all circumstances. Mr. Justice DOUGLAS has also determined that the death penalty contravenes the Eighth Amendment, although I do not read his opinion as necessarily requiring final abolition of the penalty. . . . Mr. Justices STEWART and WHITE have concluded that petitioners' death sentences must be set aside because prevailing sentencing practices do not comply with the Eighth Amendment. . . .

* * *

In the 181 years since the enactment of the Eighth Amendment, not a single decision of this Court has cast the slightest shadow of doubt on the constitutionality of capital punishment. In rejecting Eighth Amendment attacks on particular modes of execution, the Court has more than once implicitly denied that capital punishment is impermissibly "cruel" in a constitutional sense. . . . It is only fourteen years since Mr. Chief Justice Warren, speaking for four members of the Court, stated without equivocation:

> "Whatever the arguments may be against capital punishment, both on moral grounds and in terms of accomplishing the purposes of punishment—and they are forceful—the death penalty has been employed throughout our history, and, in a day when it is still widely accepted, it cannot be said to violate the constitutional concept of cruelty." *Trop v. Dulles,* 356 U.S. at 99. . . .

* * *

. . . Punishments such as branding and cutting off of ears, which were commonplace at the time of the adoption of the Constitution, passed from the penal scene without judicial intervention because they became basically offensive to the people and the legislatures responded to this sentiment. . . .

* * *

. . . [T]he primacy of the legislative role narrowly confines the scope of judicial inquiry. Whether or not provable, and whether or not true at all times, in a democracy the legislative judgment is presumed to embody the basic standards of decency prevailing in society. This presumption can only be negated by unambiguous and compelling evidence of legislative default.

There are no obvious indications that capital punishment offends the conscience of society to such a degree that our traditional deference to the legislative judgment must be abandoned. It is not a punishment such as burning at the stake that everyone would ineffably find to be repugnant to all civilized standards. Nor is it a punishment so roundly condemned that only a few aberrant legislatures have retained it on the statute books. Capital punishment is authorized by statute in 40 States, the District of Columbia, and in the federal courts for the commission of certain crimes. On four occasions in the last 11 years Congress has added to the list of federal crimes punishable by death. In looking for reliable indicia of contemporary attitude, none more trustworthy has been advanced.

* * *

It would, of course, be unrealistic to assume that juries have been perfectly consistent in choosing the cases where the death penalty is to be imposed, for no human institution performs with perfect consistency. There are doubtless prisoners on death row who would not be there had they been tried before a different jury or in a different State. In this sense their fate has been controlled by fortuitous circumstance. However, this element of fortuity does not stand as an indictment either of the general functioning of juries in capital cases or of the integrity of jury decisions in individual cases. There is no empirical basis for concluding that juries have generally failed to discharge in good faith the responsibility described in *Witherspoon [v. Illinois* (1968)]—that of choosing between life and death in individual cases according to the dictates of community values.

* * *

The critical factor in the concurring opinions of both Mr. Justice STEWART and Mr. Justice WHITE is the infrequency with which the penalty is imposed. This factor is taken not as evidence of society's abhorrence of capital punishment—the inference that petitioners would have the Court draw—but as the earmark of a deteriorated system of sentencing. It is concluded that petitioners' sentences must be set aside, not because the punishment is impermissibly cruel, but because juries and judges have failed to exercise their sentencing discretion in acceptable fashion.

* * *

. . . The decisive grievance of these [concurring] opinions—not translated into Eighth Amendment terms—is that the present system of discretionary sentencing in capital cases has failed to produce evenhanded justice; the problem is not that too few have been sentenced to die, but that the selection process has followed no rational pattern. This claim of arbitrariness is not only lacking in empirical support, but also it manifestly fails to establish that the death penalty is a "cruel and unusual" punishment. The Eighth Amendment was included in the Bill of Rights to assure that certain types of punishments would never be imposed, not to channelize the sentencing process. The approach of these concurring opinions has no antecedent in the Eighth Amendment cases. It is essentially and exclusively a procedural due process argument.

* * *

While I would not undertake to make a definitive statement as to the parameters of the Court's ruling, it is clear that if state legislatures and the Congress wish to maintain the availability of capital punishment, significant statutory changes will have to be made. Since the two pivotal concurring opinions turn on the assumption that the punishment of death is now meted out in a random and unpredictable manner, legislative bodies may seek to bring their laws into compliance with the Court's ruling by providing standards for juries and judges to follow in determining the sentence in capital cases or by more narrowly defining the crimes for which the penalty is to be imposed. . . .

[The individual dissenting opinions of Justices Blackmun, Powell, and Rehnquist are omitted.]

The decision in *Furman* ended the death penalty, but only temporarily. Two of the justices in the majority (White and Stewart) believed that the death penalty violated the Constitution in the way that it was being applied. They did not rule out the possibility that new sentencing procedures designed to reduce the capriciousness of capital punishment would correct the constitutional flaws in the application of the death penalty. From 1972 to 1974, twenty-seven states followed Florida's lead in designing new capital sentencing procedures, and nine more states followed suit in subsequent years. In the new procedures, states sought mechanisms to guide the discretion of judges and juries in deciding who would receive the death penalty. For example, many states created "bifurcated" proceedings in which a first trial was held to determine guilt or innocence and a second proceeding focused exclusively on the issue of punishment. States also required the sentencers to identify aggravating factors that made the crime especially brutal or heinous, and some states required consideration of mitigating factors, such as a perpetrator's youthful age or difficult family life, that made the offender less worthy of receiving a death sentence. Other states sought to make the death penalty mandatory for specific crimes in order to avoid capriciousness in the sentencers' discretionary sentencing decisions. The speed and intensity of the political backlash against the *Furman* decision, as indicated by the many state legislatures acting quickly to pass new capital punishment laws, appeared to undercut the LDF's argument that the values and standards of contemporary American society no longer accepted capital punishment as an appropriate criminal penalty (Epstein and Kobylka 1992, pp. 85–94).

The Supreme Court examined these new death penalty statutes in a series of cases in 1976. By this time, the opponents of capital punishment had lost one dependable ally on the Court through the retirement of Justice Douglas, and they were unsure of the views of President Gerald Ford's new appointee, Justice John Paul Stevens. The lead case, *Gregg v. Georgia* (1976), considered Georgia's new capital sentencing procedures.

Gregg and a companion were hitchhiking in Florida. They were convicted of robbing and murdering the two men who gave them a ride from Florida through Georgia. Georgia used a bifurcated proceeding in which the same jury that convicted Gregg of the crimes heard separate arguments from the prosecutor and the defense attorney about whether Gregg should receive the death penalty. The judge instructed the jury that they could not impose the death penalty unless they found beyond a reasonable doubt the existence of at least one of three aggravating factors: that the murder occurred during the commission of armed robbery; that the murder was committed for the purpose of robbing the victims; or that the murder was outrageously and wantonly vile, horrible, and inhuman. The jury concluded that the first two aggravating factors existed and sentenced Gregg to death.

In a 7–2 decision, the Supreme Court approved Georgia's capital sentencing procedures and effectively renewed its endorsement of the constitutionality of the death penalty. Although the seven justices could not agree on a single opinion, they all believed that Georgia's new procedures satisfied the concerns expressed in *Furman* about preventing the sentencers' discretion from producing arbitrary and capricious applications of capital punishment. In a plurality opinion, joined by Justices Powell and Stevens, expressing the judgment of the Court, Justice Stewart wrote:

> *Left unguided, [under the* Furman *procedures] juries imposed the death sentence in a way that could only be called freakish. The new Georgia sentencing procedures, by contrast, focus the jury's attention on the particularized nature of the crime and the particularized characteristics of the individual defendant. While the jury is permitted to consider any aggravating or mitigating circumstances, it must find and identify at least one statutory aggravating factor before it may impose a penalty of death. No longer can a jury wantonly and freakishly impose the death sentence; it is always circumscribed by the legislative guidelines* (428 U.S. at 206–7).

Not surprisingly, Justices Brennan and Marshall were the lone dissenters based on their consistent view that the death penalty is always "cruel and unusual."

GREGG V. GEORGIA

428 U.S. 153, 96 S.Ct. 2909, 49 L.Ed. 2d 859 (1976)

■ In the aftermath of *Furman v. Georgia,* Georgia and other states enacted new capital punishment statutes. Georgia's statute mandated new procedures: a bifurcated trial with a separate sentencing hearing after a determination of guilt; the consideration of aggravating and mitigating factors during the sentencing phase; the requirement of finding beyond a reasonable doubt of the existence of at least one of ten specified aggravating factors before a death sentence may be imposed; and automatic appellate review by the state supreme court. Troy Gregg was convicted of armed robbery and murder after he and a companion killed the men who gave them a ride when they were hitchhiking. Gregg challenged the imposition of the death penalty as a violation of the Eighth Amendment's prohibition on cruel and unusual punishments.

This case is important because the Supreme Court reactivated the death penalty after the *Furman* decision had placed the status of capital punishment in limbo. As you read the case, consider the following questions: (1) Did any justices change their views from the opinions expressed in the *Furman* case? (2) What elements of Georgia's sentencing law provide the basis for the Court's approval of the new capital punishment procedures? (3) Do Georgia's new procedures solve the problems that provided the basis for the Court's rejection of capital punishment in *Furman*?

VOTE:

7 justices found the law constitutional (Blackmun, Burger, Powell, Rehnquist, Stevens, Stewart, White).

2 justices found the law unconstitutional (Brennan, Marshall).

Justice Stewart announced the judgment of the Court and an opinion joined by Justices Powell and Stevens.

The issue in this case is whether the imposition of the sentence of death for the crime of murder under the law of Georgia violates the Eighth and Fourteenth Amendments.

* * *

. . . [Under the Georgia statute,] [t]he capital defendant's guilt or innocence is determined in the traditional manner, either by a trial judge or a jury, in the first stage of a bifurcated trial.

. . . After a verdict, finding, or plea of guilty to a capital crime, a presentence hearing is conducted before whoever made the determination of guilt. The sentencing procedures are essentially the same in both bench and jury trials. At the hearing:

> "[T]he judge [or jury] shall hear additional evidence in extenuation, mitigation, and aggravation

of punishment, including the record of any prior criminal convictions and pleas of guilty or pleas of nolo contendere of the defendant, or the absence of any prior conviction and pleas: Provided, however, that only such evidence in aggravation as the State has made known to the defendant prior to his trial shall be admissible. The judge [or jury] shall also hear argument by the defendant or his counsel and the prosecuting attorney . . . regarding the punishment to be imposed."

The defendant is accorded substantial latitude as to the types of evidence that he may introduce. . . .

. . . Before a convicted defendant may be sentenced to death, however, except in cases of treason or aircraft hijacking, the jury, or the trial judge in cases tried without a jury, must find beyond a reasonable doubt one of the 10 aggravating circumstances specified in the statute. The sentence of death may be imposed only if the jury (or judge) finds one of the statutory aggravating circumstances and then elects to impose that sentence. . . .

* * *

. . . [In *Furman*,] [f]our Justices would have held that capital punishment is not unconstitutional *per se*; two Justices would have reached the opposite conclusion; and three Justices, while agreeing that the statutes then before the Court were invalid as applied, left open the question whether such punishment may ever be imposed. We now hold that the punishment of death does not invariably violate the Constitution.

* * *

[I]n assessing a punishment selected by a democratically elected legislature against the constitutional measure, we presume [the statute's] validity. We may not require the legislature to select the least severe penalty possible so long as the penalty selected is not cruelly inhumane or disproportionate to the crime involved. And a heavy burden rests on those who would attack the judgment of the representatives of the people.

* * *

The imposition of the death penalty for the crime of murder has a long history of acceptance both in the United States and in England. . . . It is apparent from the text of the Constitution itself that the existence of capital punishment was accepted by the Framers. . . . For nearly two centuries, this Court, repeatedly and often expressly, has recognized that capital punishment is not invalid *per se*. . . .

The petitioners in the capital cases before the Court today renew the "standards of decency" argument, but developments during the four years since *Furman* have undercut substantially the assumptions upon which their argument rested. Despite the continuing debate, dating back to the 19th century, over the morality and utility of capital punishment, it is now evident that a large proportion of American society continues to regard it as an appropriate and necessary criminal sanction.

The most marked indication of society's endorsement of the death penalty for murder is the legislative response to *Furman*. The legislatures of 35 States have enacted new statutes that provide for the death penalty for at least some crimes that result in the death of another person. . . .

* * *

[T]he concerns expressed in *Furman* that the penalty of death not be imposed in an arbitrary or capricious manner can be met by a carefully drafted statute that ensures that the sentencing authority is given adequate information and guidance. As a general proposition these concerns are best met by a system that provides for a bifurcated proceeding at which the sentencing authority is apprised of the information relevant to the imposition of sentence and provided with standards to guide its use of the information.

* * *

In short, Georgia's new sentencing procedures require as a prerequisite to the imposition of the death penalty, specific jury findings as to the circumstances of the crime or the character of the defendant. Moreover, to guard further against a situation comparable to that presented in *Furman*, the Supreme Court of Georgia compares each death sentence with the sentences imposed on similarly situated defendants to ensure that the sentence of death in a particular case is not disproportionate. On their face these procedures seem to satisfy the concerns of *Furman*. . . .

* * *

The basic concern of *Furman* centered on those defendants who were being condemned to death capriciously and arbitrarily. Under the procedures before the Court in that case, sentencing authorities were not directed to give attention to the nature or circumstances of the crime committed or to the character or record of the defendant. Left unguided, juries imposed the death sentence in a way that could only be called freakish. The new Georgia sentencing procedures, by contrast, focus the jury's attention on the particularized nature of the crime and the particularized characteristics of the individual defendant. While the jury is permitted to consider any aggravating or mitigating circumstances, it must find and identify at least one statutory aggravating factor before it may impose a penalty of death. In this way the jury's discretion is channeled. No longer can a jury wantonly and freakishly impose the death sentence; it is always circumscribed by the legislative guidelines. In addition, the review function of the Supreme Court of Georgia affords additional assurance that the concerns that prompted our decision in *Furman* are not present to any significant degree in the Georgia procedure applied here.

For the reasons expressed in this opinion, we hold that the statutory system under which Gregg was sentenced to death does not violate the Constitution. Accordingly, the judgment of the Georgia Supreme Court is affirmed.

Justice White, with whom Chief Justice Burger and Justice Rehnquist join, concurring in the judgment.

* * *

Petitioner's argument that prosecutors behave in a standardless fashion in deciding which cases to try as capital felonies is unsupported by any facts. Petitioner simply asserts that since prosecutors have the power not to charge capital felonies they will exercise that power in a standardless fashion. This is untenable. Absent facts to the contrary it cannot be assumed that prosecutors will be motivated in their charging decision by factors other than the strength of the case and the likelihood that a jury would impose the death penalty if it convicts. . . .

Petitioner's argument that there is an unconstitutional amount of discretion in the system which separates those suspects who receive the death penalty from those who receive life imprisonment, a lesser penalty or are acquitted or never charged seems to be in the final analysis an indictment of our entire system of justice. Petitioner has argued in effect that no matter how effective the death penalty may be as a punishment, government, created and run as it must be by humans, is inevitably incompetent to administer it. This cannot be accepted as a proposition of constitutional law. Imposition of the death penalty is surely an awesome responsibility for any system of justice and those who participate in it. Mistakes will be made and discriminations will occur which will be difficult to explain. However, one of society's most basic tasks is that of protecting the lives of its citizens and one of the most basic ways in which it achieves the tasks is through criminal laws against murder. I decline to interfere with the manner in which Georgia has chosen to enforce such laws on what is simply an assertion of lack of faith in the ability of the system of justice to operate in a fundamentally fair manner. . . .

[The statement of Chief Justice Burger and the concurring opinion of Justice Blackmun are omitted.]

Justice Brennan, dissenting.

* * *

The fatal constitutional infirmity in the punishment of death is that it treats "members of the human race as nonhumans, as objects to be toyed with and discarded. [It is] thus inconsistent with the fundamental premise of the [Cruel and Unusual Punishments] Clause that even the vilest criminal remains a human being possessed of common human dignity." [quoting his own opinion in *Furman*] . . . As such it is a penalty that "subjects the individual to a fate forbidden by the principle of civilized treatment guaranteed by the [Eighth Amendment]." I therefore would hold on that ground alone, that death is today a cruel and unusual punishment prohibited by the Clause. "Justice of this kind is obviously no less shocking than the crime itself, and the new 'official' murder, far from offering redress for the offense committed against society, adds instead a second defilement to the first."* * *

Justice Marshall, dissenting.

* * *

Since the decision in *Furman*, the legislatures of 35 States have enacted new statutes authorizing the imposition of the death sentence for certain crimes, and Congress has enacted a law providing for the death penalty for air piracy resulting in death. . . . I would be less than candid if I did not acknowledge that these developments have a significant bearing on a realistic assessment of the moral acceptability of the death penalty to the American people. But if the constitutionality of the death penalty turns, as I have urged, on the opinion of an *informed* citizenry, then even the enactment of new death statutes cannot be viewed as conclusive. In *Furman*, I observed that the American people are largely unaware of the information critical to a judgment on the morality of the death penalty, and concluded that if they were better informed they would consider it shocking, unjust, and unacceptable. . . . A recent study, conducted after the enactment of the post-*Furman* statutes, has confirmed that the American people know little about the death penalty, and that the opinions of an informed public would differ significantly from those of a public unaware of the consequences and effects of the death penalty. [citing Sarat and Vidmar, "Public Opinion, the Death Penalty, and the Eighth Amendment: Testing the Marshall Hypothesis," *Wisconsin Law Review* (1976): 171].

* * *

The death penalty, unnecessary to promote the goal of deterrence or to further any legitimate notion of retribution, is an excessive penalty forbidden by the Eighth and Fourteenth Amendments. I respectfully dissent from the Court's judgment upholding the sentences of death imposed upon the petitioners in these cases.

The Court's decision in *Gregg* clearly indicated that the LDF and other opponents of capital punishment had not won a decisive victory in *Furman*. The *Gregg* decision contributed to the end of the moratorium on executions as Gary Gilmore, a convicted murderer in Utah, was executed by firing squad in 1977 after he decided not to pursue any further legal actions to contest his conviction. The pace of executions remained slow as prisoners challenged their convictions through appeals and habeas corpus petitions (White 1991, pp. 33-34). By 1995, nearly three thousand prisoners were on death row but only 290 had been executed since the *Gregg* decision (Kaplan 1995, pp. 24-25).

At the same time that the Court reactivated the death penalty with the *Gregg* decision, 5–4 majorities on the Court struck down laws that mandated the death penalty for specific crimes (*Roberts v. Louisiana*, 1976; *Woodson v. North Carolina*, 1976). Justices Stewart, Stevens, and Powell joined Justices Brennan and Marshall in declaring that mandatory death penalty statutes are unconstitutional. Although the Court had sought since *Furman* to insure that death penalty decisions were not capricious, a majority of justices believed that each capital case deserved individualized attention and a careful decision by the sentencers. Thus the Court approved bifurcated proceedings that focused the sentencers' attention on mitigating and aggravating factors. Mandatory sentences sought to avoid capriciousness by eliminating the sentencers' discretion, but the Court's decisions indicated that discretion should be guided and channeled rather than eliminated.

In a series of subsequent decisions, the Burger-era justices developed further limits on capital punishment. Historically, capital punishment for rape had been applied to African American defendants in southern states in a grossly disproportionate and discriminatory manner. It was relatively rare for a white defendant to receive the death penalty for rape, yet hundreds of African Americans were sentenced to death row and executed for this crime. In 1977, the Supreme Court decided by a 7–2 vote that capital punishment could not be imposed for the crime of rape (*Coker v. Georgia*, 1977). The Court later added a further limitation to capital punishment by ruling 5–4 that insane prisoners could not be executed (*Ford v. Wainwright*, 1986).

The Court reinforced its view that the imposition of the death penalty requires individualized decisions in which judges and juries examine each crime and individual defendant carefully. Thus the Court refined its conception of channeled discretion by barring limitations on the jury's consideration of mitigating factors. For example, in *Lockett v. Ohio* (1978), the Court declared that the jury may "not be precluded from considering, as a mitigating factor, any aspect of a defendant's character or record and any of the circumstances of the offense that the defendant proffers as a basis for a sentence less than death" (438 U.S. at 605). While giving the defendant broad latitude to present evidence of mitigating circumstances, the Court also limited the state's ability to define aggravating factors so broadly that they fail to limit and guide the jury's discretion (e.g., *Godfrey v. Georgia*, 1980).

Noncapital Punishment

The Warren Court justices created the opportunity for prisoners to file lawsuits claiming that practices and conditions inside correctional institutions violated specific provisions of the Constitution (*Cooper v. Pate*, 1964). As a result, prisoners sought judicial recognition and protection for a variety of rights. For example, prisoners gained rights to practice their religious beliefs while incarcerated and to have access to legal materials in order to prepare their appeals and habeas corpus petitions. When prisoners filed lawsuits alleging that living conditions and disciplinary practices in correctional institutions violated the prohibition on cruel and unusual punishments, the Burger Court justices began to set Eighth Amendment standards for conditions inside prisons.

In *Estelle v. Gamble* (1976), a prisoner's back was injured when a 600-pound bale of cotton fell on him while he worked at a prison job. After receiving intermittent treatments from prison medical personnel for several months, he filed a lawsuit against the prison claiming that inadequate medical care constituted cruel and unusual punishment. The Supreme Court accepted the idea that a prisoner could sue for deprivation of medical care, but determined that this prisoner's case did not meet the standards for a successful claim. In an 8–1 decision, Justice Marshall's majority opinion established the standard by which prisoners' medical claims should be evaluated under the Eighth Amendment: "We therefore conclude that deliberate indifference to serious medical needs of prisoners constitutes the 'unnecessary and wanton infliction of pain' . . . proscribed by the Eighth Amendment" (429 U.S. at 104).

Justice Stevens dissented because he believed that the Court's standard was too lax. Stevens argued that the Court should look at the prison conditions and practices themselves rather than examine the thoughts and motivations (i.e., "deliberate indifference") of prison officials: "[T]he Court improperly attaches significance to the subjective motivation of the defendant [prison officials] as a criterion for determining whether cruel and unusual punishment has been inflicted. . . . [W]hether the constitutional standard has been violated should turn on the character of the punishment rather than the motivation of the individual who inflicted it" (429 U.S. at 285).

The Court's most important decision concerning the conditions of confinement in prisons came in *Hutto v. Finney* (1978). The *Hutto* case came to the Supreme Court after years of litigation concerning the Arkansas prison system. The prison in question in this litigation was known as Cummins Farm. Most of the guards at the institution were simply prisoners, known as "trusties," who had been issued guns and given free rein to victimize and control the other prisoners. Only eight nonconvict guards were employed to supervise one thousand prisoners. The trusties beat and even shot other prisoners with impunity. Prisoners were subjected to beatings with leather straps and "a hand-cranked device was used to administer electrical shocks to various sensitive parts of an inmate's body" (437 at 682 n.5). Although the National Academy of Sciences recommends that the average male consume 2,700 calories per day and an inactive person will expend 2,000 calories in a day just lying, sitting, and standing, "[p]risoners in isolation received fewer than 1,000 calories a day; their meals consisted primarily of a 4-inch square of 'grue,' a substance created by mashing meat, potatoes, oleo, syrup, vegetables, eggs, and seasoning into a paste and baking the mixture in a pan" (437 U.S. at 683).

In *Hutto*, the Supreme Court considered whether the lower courts had issued permissible remedial orders in setting the number of prisoners per cell, maximum duration of confinement in isolation, and minimum diet for prisoners confined to punitive isolation. The conditions in the isolation cells were found by the lower courts to violate the Eighth Amendment's prohibition on cruel and unusual punishments:

> *Confinement in punitive isolation was for an indeterminate period of time. An average of 4, and sometimes as many as 10 or 11 prisoners were crowded into windowless 8' by 10' cells containing no furniture other than a source of water and a toilet that could only be flushed from outside the cell. . . . At night the prisoners were given mattresses to spread on the floor. Although some prisoners suffered from infectious diseases such as hepatitis and venereal disease, mattresses*

were removed and jumbled together each morning, then returned to the cells at random in the evening. . . . Prisoners were sometimes left in isolation for months, their release depending on "their attitudes as appraised by prison personnel" (437 U.S. at 682, 684).

Although the justices were deeply divided concerning the separate issue of whether the prisoners' lawyers were entitled to have their attorneys' fees paid by the State of Arkansas, eight justices supported the lower courts' decisions and remedial orders concerning the unconstitutionality of the conditions in the prison. The tests listed in Justice Stevens' majority opinion for finding prison conditions to be cruel and unusual did not rely on the subjective standard used in *Estelle v. Gamble* (1976) to assess prison medical treatment. Instead, the tests for unconstitutional conditions of confinement effectively echoed Stevens' dissent in *Estelle* by applying an objective standard that examined the conditions themselves rather than the correctional officials' motivations: "The Eighth Amendment's ban on inflicting cruel and unusual punishments, made applicable to the States by the Fourteenth Amendment, 'proscribe[s] more than physically barbarous punishments.' . . . It prohibits penalties that are grossly disproportionate to the offense, . . . as well as those that transgress today's 'broad and idealistic concepts of dignity, civilized standards, humanity, and decency' " (437 U.S. at 685).

Justice Rehnquist dissented because he claimed that the lower court judges were unduly interfering with the administration of prisons in Arkansas by mandating such specific remedies "against a prison practice which has not been shown to violate the Constitution" (437 U.S. at 710).

The Supreme Court decision in *Hutto* effectively endorsed an accelerating nationwide trend of federal judges intervening into the administration of state correctional institutions. By the late 1980s, virtually every state had some prisons or jails that were under court order to improve conditions and practices, and some states had their entire correctional systems placed under judicial supervision. As a result, many states were forced to either raise taxes or divert resources from other programs in order to improve conditions inside their prisons and jails (Smith 1993, pp. 93–109).

Although the Burger Court justices had endorsed judicial intervention to remedy unconstitutional conditions of confinement in correctional institutions, the justices clearly signaled in 1981 that lower court judges must not be too aggressive in identifying and remedying constitutional violations in correctional institutions. In *Rhodes v. Chapman* (1981), the Court reversed a lower court decision that had found unconstitutional the practice of placing two prisoners into cells that were designed and constructed to hold only one prisoner. The majority opinion reiterated the objective Eighth Amendment standard for finding conditions cruel and unusual if they violate "contemporary standard[s] of decency," involve "wanton and unnecessary infliction of pain," or result in "unquestioned and serious deprivations of basic human needs" (452 U.S. at 347). However, the Court declined to endorse a finding that the degree of overcrowding inherent in double celling constitutes an unconstitutional condition of confinement.

The Burger Court also addressed the issue of whether harsh sentences violate the Eighth Amendment by being disproportionate to the crime. In *Rummel v. Estelle* (1980), a man was sentenced to life in prison under a statute requiring such sentences for anyone who has been convicted of three felonies. Mr. Rummel's three felonies that resulted in a life sentence were fraudulent use of a credit card for $80 in 1964, passing a forged check for $28.36 in 1969, and obtaining $120.75 under false pretenses in 1973. Thus Rummel received a life sentence for stealing a total of

$229.11 in three separate offenses over a nine-year period. In a 5–4 decision, the Supreme Court upheld the application of the mandatory repeat offender statute to Rummel by finding that the sentence did not violate the Eighth Amendment. Although Justice Rehnquist's majority opinion argued that the principle of proportionality is most applicable to death penalty cases, Justice Powell's dissenting opinion argued that the Eighth Amendment's prohibition on cruel and unusual punishments extends to any punishments that are grossly disproportionate to the crime. Powell argued that Texas's law was especially harsh when compared to laws in other states. Three-quarters of the states had never adopted a habitual offender statute and, unlike Texas, the few states that had such laws required the commission of more than three offenses, required the commission of at least one violent crime, limited the penalty to less than a life sentence, or made the life sentence optional rather than mandatory. By emphasizing contemporary society's evolving values as the basis for defining the Eighth Amendment, Powell concluded that Rummel's sentence "would be viewed as grossly unjust by virtually every layman and lawyer" (445 U.S. at 307).

Rummel v. Estelle

445 U.S. 263, 100 S.Ct. 1133, 63 L.Ed. 2d 382 (1980)

■ Texas had a "recidivist statute" mandating that anyone convicted three times of felonies shall be imprisoned for life. For three felonies in which he stole a total of $229.11 over a nine-year period, Rummel was sentenced to life imprisonment. He challenged his sentence as grossly disproportionate to his crimes and therefore a violation of the Eighth Amendment's prohibition on cruel and unusual punishments.

The case is important because it illustrates the Burger Court justices' analysis of the proportionality element of the Eighth Amendment. As you read the case, consider the following questions: (1) Do the justices treat the Eighth Amendment as requiring sentences that are proportionate to the crimes committed? (2) How do the justices in the majority justify the outcome of the case? (3) What does this decision tell states about the constitutional limits on their ability to mandate harsh punishments for repeat offenders?

Vote:

Five justices found the law constitutional (Blackmun, Burger, Rehnquist, Stewart, White).

Four justices found the law unconstitutional (Brennan, Marshall, Powell, Stevens).

Justice Rehnquist delivered the opinion of the Court.

* * *

This Court has on occasion stated that the Eighth Amendment prohibits the imposition of a sentence that is grossly disproportionate to the severity of the crime. . . . In recent years this proposition has appeared most frequently in opinions dealing with the death penalty. . . . Rummel cites these . . . opinions dealing with capital punishment as compelling the conclusion that his sentence is disproportionate to his offenses. But as Mr. Justice STEWART noted in *Furman*:

> "The penalty of death differs from all other forms of criminal punishment, not in degree but in kind. It is unique in its total irrevocability. It is unique in the rejection of rehabilitation of the convict as a basic purpose of criminal justice. And it is unique, finally, in its absolute renunciation of all that is embodied in our concept of humanity" [408 U.S.] at 306.

This theme, the unique nature of the death penalty for purposes of Eighth Amendment analysis, has been repeated time and time again in our opinions. . . . Because a sentence of death differs in kind from any sentence of imprisonment, no matter how long, our decisions applying the prohibition on cruel and unusual punishments to capital cases are of limited assistance in deciding the constitutionality of the punishment meted out to Rummel.

Outside the context of capital punishment, successful challenges to the proportionality of particular sentences have been exceedingly rare. . . .

* * *

In an attempt to provide us with objective criteria against which we might measure the proportionality of his life sentence, Rummel points to certain characteristics of his offenses that allegedly render them "petty." He cites, for example, the absence of violence in his crimes. But the presence or absence of

violence does not always affect the strength of society's interest in deterring a particular crime or in punishing a particular criminal. A high official in a large corporation can commit undeniably serious crimes in the area of antitrust, bribery, or clean air or water standards without coming close to engaging in any "violent" or short-term "life-threatening" behavior. Additionally, Rummel cites the "small" amount of money taken in each of his crimes. But to recognize that the State of Texas could have imprisoned Rummel for life if he had stolen $5,000, $50,000, or $500,000, rather than the $120.75 that a jury convicted him of stealing, is virtually to concede that the lines to be drawn are indeed "subjective," and therefore properly within the province of legislatures, not courts. . . .

* * *

Undaunted by earlier cases [in which the Supreme Court rejected Eighth Amendment claims for severe prison sentences], Rummel attempts to ground his proportionality attack on an alleged "nationwide" trend away from mandatory life sentences and toward "lighter, discretionary sentences." . . . According to Rummel, "[n]o jurisdiction in the United States or the Free World punishes habitual offenders as harshly as Texas." . . . In support of this proposition, Rummel offers detailed charts and tables documenting the history of recidivist statutes in the United States since 1776.

* * *

Rummel's charts and tables do appear to indicate that he might have received more lenient treatment in almost any State other than Texas, West Virginia, or Washington. The distinctions, however, are subtle rather than gross. A number of States impose a mandatory life sentence upon conviction of four felonies rather than three. Other States require one or more of the felonies to be "violent" to support a life sentence. Still other States leave the imposition of a life sentence after three felonies within the discretion of a judge or jury. It is one thing for a court to compare those States that impose capital punishment for a specific offense with those States that do not. . . . It is quite another thing for a court to attempt to evaluate the position of any particular recidivist scheme within Rummel's complex matrix.

Nor do Rummel's extensive charts even begin to reflect the complexity of the comparison he asks this Court to make. Texas, we are told, has a relatively liberal policy of granting "good time" credits to its prisoners, a policy that historically has allowed a prisoner serving a life sentence to become eligible for parole in as little as 12 years. . . . We agree with Rummel that his inability to enforce any "right" to parole precludes us from treating his life sentence as if it were equivalent to a sentence of 12 years. Nevertheless, because parole is "an established variation on imprisonment of convicted criminals," *Morrissey v. Brewer*, 408 U.S. 471 . . . (1972), a proper assessment of Texas' treatment of Rummel could hardly ignore the possibility that he will not actually be imprisoned for the rest of his life. If nothing else, the possibility of parole, however slim, serves to distinguish Rummel from a person sentenced under a recidivist statute like Mississippi's, which provides for a sentence of life without parole upon conviction of three felonies including at least one violent felony. . . .

* * *

Perhaps, as asserted in *Weems*, "time works changes" upon the Eighth Amendment, bringing into existence "new conditions and purposes." . . . We all, of course, would like to think that we are "moving down the road toward human decency." *Furman v. Georgia*, 408 U.S. at 410 . . . (BLACKMUN, J., dissenting). Within the confines of this judicial proceeding, however, we have no way of knowing in which direction the road lies. Penologists themselves have been unable to agree whether sentences should be light or heavy, discretionary or determinate. This uncertainty reinforces our conviction that any "nationwide trend" toward lighter, discretionary sentences must find its source and its sustaining force in the legislatures, not in the federal courts.

* * *

. . . Like the line dividing felony theft from petty larceny, the point at which a recidivist will be deemed to have demonstrated the necessary propensities and the amount of time that the recidivist will be isolated from society are matters largely within the discretion of the punishing jurisdiction.

We therefore hold that the mandatory life sentence imposed upon this petitioner does not constitute cruel and unusual punishment under the Eighth and Fourteenth Amendments. The judgment of the Court of Appeals is *Affirmed*.

Justice Stewart, concurring.

I am moved to repeat the substance of what I had to say on another occasion about the recidivist legislation of Texas:

> "If the Constitution gave me a roving commission to impose upon the criminal courts of Texas my own notions of enlightened policy, I would not join the Court's opinion. For it is clear to me that the recidivist procedures adopted in recent years by many other States . . . are far superior to those utilized [here]. But the question for decision

is not whether we applaud or even whether we personally approve the procedures followed in [this case]. The question is whether those procedures fall below the minimum level the [Constitution] will tolerate. Upon that question I am constrained to join the opinion and judgment of the Court." *Spencer v. Texas,* 385 U.S. 554. . . .

Justice Powell, with whom Justice Brennan, Justice Marshall, and Justice Stevens join, dissenting.

* * *

This Court today affirms the Fifth Circuit's decision. I dissent because I believe that (i) the penalty for a noncapital offense may be unconstitutionally disproportionate, (ii) the possibility of parole should not be considered in assessing the nature of the punishment, (iii) a mandatory life sentence is grossly disproportionate as applied to petitioner, and (iv) the conclusion that this petitioner has suffered a violation of his Eighth Amendment rights is compatible with principles of judicial restraint and federalism.

* * *

The scope of the Cruel and Unusual Punishments Clause extends not only to barbarous methods of punishment, but also to punishments that are grossly disproportionate. Disproportionality analysis measures the relationship between the nature and number of offenses committed and the severity of the punishment inflicted upon the offender. The inquiry focuses on whether a person deserves such punishment, not simply whether the punishment would serve a utilitarian goal. A statute that levied a mandatory life sentence for overtime parking might well deter vehicular lawlessness, but it would offend our felt sense of justice. The Court concedes today that the principle of disproportionality plays a role in the review of sentences imposing the death penalty, but suggests that the principle may be less applicable when a noncapital sentence is challenged. Such a limitation finds no support in the history of Eighth Amendment jurisprudence.

* * *

A holding that the possibility of parole discounts a prisoner's sentence for the purposes of the Eighth Amendment would be cruelly ironic. The combined effect of our holdings under the Due Process Clause of the Fourteenth Amendment and the Eighth Amendment would allow a State to defend an Eighth Amendment claim by contending that parole is probable even though the prisoner cannot enforce that expectation. Such an approach is inconsistent with the Eighth Amendment. The Court has never before failed to examine a prisoner's Eighth Amendment claim because of speculation that he might be pardoned before the sentence was carried out.

* * *

Examination of the objective factors traditionally employed by the Court to assess the proportionality of a sentence demonstrates that petitioner suffers a cruel and unusual punishment. . . . A comparison of petitioner to other criminal[s] sentenced in Texas shows that he has been punished for three property-related offenses with a harsher sentence than that given to first-time or two-time offenders convicted of far more serious offenses. The Texas system assumes that all three-time offenders deserve the same punishment whether they commit three murders or cash three fraudulent checks.

The petitioner has committed criminal acts for which he may be punished. He has been given a sentence that is not inherently barbarous. But the relationship between the criminal acts and the sentence is grossly disproportionate. For having defrauded others of about $230, the State of Texas has deprived petitioner of his freedom for the rest of his life. The State has not attempted to justify the sentence as necessary either to deter other persons or to isolate a potentially violent individual. Nor has petitioner's status as a habitual offender been shown to justify a mandatory life sentence. . . .

* * *

We are construing a living Constitution. The sentence imposed upon the petitioner would be viewed as grossly unjust by virtually every layman and lawyer. In my view, objective criteria clearly establish that a mandatory life sentence for defrauding persons of about $230 crosses any rationally drawn line separating punishment that lawfully may be imposed from that which is proscribed by the Eighth Amendment. I would reverse the decision of the Court of Appeals.

In 1982, the Court applied the proportionality principle to a capital case by finding that a felony-murder accomplice who did not participate in the killing and did not intend for a life to be taken could not be sentenced to death (*Enmund v. Florida,* 1982). Enmund was convicted of driving the getaway car after two of his associates shot and killed an elderly couple during a robbery. In a 5–4 decision, Justice White's majority opinion concluded that the offender's punishment must be tailored to fit his personal responsibility and moral guilt. Thus, Enmund could be punished for his participation in the fatal robbery that came under the felony-murder law but could not be executed for a killing that he did not commit and did not intend to commit.

In 1983, the Supreme Court revisited the proportionality issue with respect to noncapital sentences (*Solem v. Helm*, 1983). Helm was sentenced to life imprisonment without possibility of parole when he was convicted of issuing a "no account" check for $100. His sentence was based on South Dakota's habitual offender statute because during the preceding fifteen years Helm had been convicted six times of burglary, grand larceny, and driving while intoxicated. Unlike the *Rummel* case three years earlier, *Solem* produced a 5–4 decision invalidating Helm's sentence. Justice Powell's majority opinion clearly stated that the Eighth Amendment's prohibition on cruel and unusual punishments "prohibits not only barbaric punishments, but also sentences that are disproportionate to the crime committed" (463 U.S. at 284) and that this disproportionality principle is applicable to noncapital cases. The majority did not overturn the previous decision in *Rummel*, but distinguished *Solem* by observing that Rummel was eligible for parole consideration after serving in prison for twelve years in Texas. By contrast, under South Dakota's law, Helm was ineligible for parole. Although the possibility existed that Helm could have his sentence commuted by the governor, the majority viewed commutation as much more difficult to attain than parole. Although the Court placed great weight on the difference between parole eligibility as the basis for distinguishing the *Solem* case from *Rummel*, as a practical matter, it was only Justice Blackmun's vote that hinged on that distinction. The other members of the *Rummel* majority, with Justice O'Connor replacing Justice Stewart, dissented in *Solem* and believed that the life sentences were permissible in both cases. In essence, the issue of parole eligibility provided a sufficient basis to persuade Justice Blackmun to join the *Rummel* dissenters in order to invalidate the application of South Dakota's habitual offender statute to Helm.

Although the Burger Court's decisions defeated the efforts of capital punishment opponents to interpret the Eighth Amendment to ban the death penalty, the Court narrowed the application of the death penalty, initiated procedures to channel capital sentencers' discretion, and expanded Eighth Amendment protections in prison and other noncapital cases.

The Rehnquist Court Era

As discussed in previous chapters, the Supreme Court's composition changed during the Rehnquist Court era as conservative Republican presidents appointed five new members to the Court between 1981 and 1991. The changes in the Court's composition raised questions about whether the new justices led the Court to decide cases in a more conservative manner than during the Warren and Burger Court eras. This is the central question for commentators who debate whether the Rehnquist Court justices have initiated a conservative counterrevolution. Consistent with the other chapters in the book, a conservative decision is regarded as one favoring the government and a liberal decision is one favoring the individual in a civil rights and liberties case.

Has the Rehnquist Court become more distinctively conservative than the Burger and Warren Courts in deciding Eighth Amendment and capital punishment cases? The empirical data from the Supreme Court Judicial Database provide some surprising results. The data in the tables combine the Rehnquist Court cases classified as death penalty, noncapital Eighth Amendment, and jury issues in capital cases. Although the Rehnquist Court produced a higher percentage of conservative outcomes than the Warren Court, Table 12.1 indicates that the Rehnquist Court produced a higher percentage of liberal decisions than the Burger Court. The Rehnquist Court's liberal margin over the Burger Court, 46 percent to 42 percent, is certainly modest, but it raises questions about whether the perceived degree of conservatism of the Rehnquist Court on Eighth Amendment and capital punishment issues is accurate.

As indicated by Table 12.2, the justices of the Rehnquist era were deeply divided on Eighth Amendment and capital punishment issues. Four justices always or almost always supported the individual (Marshall, Brennan, Stevens, Blackmun), three justices supported the government in three-fourths or more of the cases (Thomas, Scalia, Rehnquist), and the remaining justices supported conservative or liberal outcomes depending on the particular issues of each case. Because there were two clearly defined "wings" of the Court on these issues, the justices in the middle effectively controlled the outcomes in each case depending on how many of them joined the liberal or conservative wing in a decision.

In addition, the table indicates that the justices who were appointed to the Court during the Rehnquist era were each more conservative on Eighth Amendment and capital punishment issues than were the justices that they replaced. Justice Thomas's 85 percent support for conservative outcomes was diametrically opposed to the 100 percent support that his predecessor, Justice Marshall, gave to liberal outcomes. Justice Kennedy's 66 percent support for conservative outcomes exceeded the 43 percent support of the justice he replaced, Justice Powell. In addition, Justice Souter's 44 percent support for conservative outcomes was different than retired Justice Brennan's 100 percent support for liberal outcomes.

Table 12.3 shows the bloc voting analysis for Eighth Amendment and death penalty cases. A strong liberal voting bloc was evident that included Justices Stevens, Marshall, Brennan, and Blackmun. The conservative justices who participated in at least half of these decisions were less united and, with the exception of Scalia, their decisions were not as consistently in one direction as those of the liberal justices. Two overlapping conservative blocs can be seen in Table 12.3. Scalia, Rehnquist, and White formed the most conservative voting bloc; a second bloc consisted of Rehnquist, White, Kennedy, and O'Connor. Rehnquist and White were thus members of both blocs. Scalia's agreement rates with O'Connor (73 percent) and Kennedy (75 percent) were not high enough to create a five-person conservative

TABLE 12.1: Liberal/Conservative Outcomes of Eighth Amendment and Capital Punishment Cases for the Warren, Burger, and Rehnquist Courts, 1953–94 Terms

	Outcomes		
Court Era	Liberal	Conservative	Totals
Warren Court 1953–68 Terms	67% (4)	33% (2)	6
Burger Court 1969–85 Terms	42% (18)	58% (25)	43
Rehnquist Court 1986–94 Terms	46% (19)	54% (22)	41
Totals	46% (41)	54% (49)	90

TABLE 12.2: Liberal/Conservative Voting Records of Justices of the Rehnquist Court in Eighth Amendment and Capital Punishment Cases, 1986-94 Terms

Justices	Liberal Votes	Conservative Votes
Breyer	0% (0)	100% (1)
Scalia	10% (4)	90% (37)
Thomas	15% (2)	85% (11)
Rehnquist	20% (8)	80% (33)
Kennedy	34% (11)	66% (21)
White	36% (13)	64% (23)
O'Connor	37% (15)	63% (26)
Ginsburg	40% (2)	60% (3)
Souter	56% (10)	44% (8)
Powell	57% (4)	43% (3)
Blackmun	90% (36)	10% (4)
Stevens	95% (39)	5% (2)
Brennan	100% (23)	0% (0)
Marshall	100% (28)	0% (0)

TABLE 12.3: Bloc Voting Analysis of the Rehnquist Court's Eighth Amendment and Capital Punishment Cases, 1986-94 Terms (Percent Agreement Rate)

	Stev	Mar	Bren	Blkm	OCon	Ken	Whit	Rhen	Scal
Stevens	—	100	100	90	41	41	36	24	15
Marshall	100	—	100	89	25	21	29	11	11
Brennan	100	100	—	87	22	21	26	13	13
Blackmun	90	89	87	—	48	42	44	30	20
O'Connor	41	25	22	48	—	91	69	83	73
Kennedy	41	21	21	42	91	—	78	88	75
White	36	29	26	44	69	78	—	83	75
Rehnquist	24	11	13	30	83	88	83	—	90
Scalia	15	11	13	20	73	75	75	90	—

Court mean = 53
Sprague Criterion = 77
Liberal bloc: Stevens, Marshall, Brennan, Blackmun = 94
Conservative blocs: White, Rehnquist, Scalia = 83
O'Connor, Kennedy, White, Rehnquist = 82

bloc. These results are in contrast to the bloc voting analyses we saw in Chapters 9 (Fourth Amendment), 10 (Fifth Amendment), and 11 (Sixth Amendment) where five-person conservative blocs did exist. This provides further evidence of the more moderate voting patterns of the Rehnquist Court in Eighth Amendment and death penalty cases.

It is possible that the data in Table 12.1 obscure the picture of the Rehnquist Court's conservatism by aggregating the era's nine terms into a single percentage. Because each new appointee was more distinctively conservative than the retiring justices who were being replaced, it is possible that the Court's decisions became increasingly conservative as the Rehnquist Court era developed. By breaking the Court's decisions into individual terms, it is possible to tell if the Rehnquist Court gradually became more conservative than the Burger Court. As indicated in Table 12.4, the Court's level of support for liberal outcomes dropped significantly during the 1988 term. This drop coincided with Justice Kennedy's first full term on the Court and moved the Rehnquist Court's support for liberal outcomes below the average support level of the Burger Court. The Court's support for liberal outcomes dropped even farther the following year without any change in the Court's composition and then rose again with the successive appointments of Justices Souter and Thomas. Because the Court decides relatively few Eighth Amendment and capital punishment cases each term, the percentages can fluctuate easily if the Court decides only one or two cases in a different direction. It is interesting to note, however, that when Justice Thomas was appointed to the Court and the Court reached the pinnacle of its conservative composition, the Court supported *liberal* outcomes in every Eighth Amendment case during the 1991 term, despite the fact that Thomas supported the government in each case. By contrast, the addition of Democratic-appointee Justice Ginsburg in the 1993 term coincided with a modest drop in the percentage of liberal outcomes as did the addition of Democratic-appointee Justice Breyer in 1994. Obviously, the Court's decisions are not controlled by a simple count of the number of "liberals" and "conservatives" on the Court in a given term. Instead, some justices' support for liberal or conservative outcomes depends on the nature of the issue presented in each case rather than on any automatic, ideological outcome preference.

As we noted in previous chapters, quantitative methods of analysis have their limitations. Most importantly, they do not take into account the relative importance of cases or the legal reasoning supporting the Court's judgments. Thus, written opinions of the justices must be examined to assess whether the Court has engaged in dramatic modification or rejection of existing precedents and doctrines and the creation of new conservative precedents and doctrines.

Table 12.5 provides the analytical framework for assessing doctrinal developments during the Rehnquist Court era. As indicated by the table, the Court's overall decisions were divided almost evenly between liberal and conservative outcomes, but the Court's doctrinal changes and major decisions moved more frequently in a conservative direction.

TABLE 12.4: Liberal/Conservative Outcomes of Eighth Amendment and Capital Punishment Cases During the Rehnquist Court Era by Term, 1986-94 Terms

	Outcomes		
Term	Liberal	Conservative	Totals
1986	57% (4)	43% (3)	7
1987	57% (4)	43% (3)	7
1988	33% (1)	67% (2)	3
1989	17% (1)	83% (5)	6
1990	40% (2)	60% (3)	5
1991	100% (3)	0% (0)	3
1992	60% (3)	40% (2)	5
1993	25% (1)	75% (3)	4
1994	0% (0)	100% (1)	1
Totals	46% (19)	54% (22)	41

TABLE 12.5: A Framework for the Doctrinal Analysis of the Rehnquist Court's Cases on the Eighth Amendment and Capital Punishment, 1986-94 Terms

		Treatment of Precedent					
Major or Minor Importance	**Majority or Plurality Opinion**	Creation of New Liberal Precedent	Liberal Modification of Existing Precedent	Liberal Interpretation of Existing Precedent	Conservative Interpretation of Existing Precedent	Conservative Modification of Existing Precedent	Creation of New Conservative Precedent
Major	Majority				Stanford v. Kentucky (1989) Penry v. Lynaugh (1989) Blystone v. Pennsylvania (1990)	Tison v. Arizona (1987) McCleskey v. Kemp (1987)	Payne v. Tennessee (1991)
	Plurality				Harmelin v. Michigan (1991)		
Minor	Majority	Austin v. U.S. (1993)	Booth v. Maryland (1987) Johnson v. Mississippi (1988) Lankford v. Idaho (1991)	Hitchcock v. Dugger (1987) Gray v. Mississippi (1987) Sumner v. Schuman (1987) Mills v. Maryland (1988) Maynard v. Cartwright (1988) South Carolina v. Gathers (1989) McKoy v. North Carolina (1990) Parker v. Dugger (1991) Richmond v. Lewis (1992) Hudson v. McMillian (1992) Sochor v. Florida (1992) Morgan v. Illinois (1992) Helling v. McKinney (1993) Simmons v. South Carolina (1994)	Buchanan v. Kentucky (1987) Lowenfield v. Phelps (1988) Lewis v. Jeffers (1990) Boyde v. California (1990) Walton v. Arizona (1990) Johnson v. Texas (1993) Arave v. Creech (1993) Tuilaepa v. California (1994) Romano v. Oklahoma (1994) Farmer v. Brennan (1994) Harris v. Alabama (1995)	Ross v. Oklahoma (1988) Clemmons v. Mississippi (1990)	Wilson v. Seiter (1991)
	Plurality		Thompson v. Oklahoma (1988)		Franklin v. Lynaugh (1988)		

Capital Punishment

The Rehnquist Court made two major decisions affecting capital punishment during its initial term. In *Tison v. Arizona* (1987), the Supreme Court revisited the issue of the death penalty for felony-murder accomplices that had been decided in *Enmund v. Florida* (1982). Raymond and Ricky Tison were teenage boys who helped their family smuggle guns into an Arizona prison in order to free their father, a convicted murderer. The boys joined their father, an older brother, and their father's convicted murderer cellmate in fleeing from the prison. When their getaway car broke down in the desert, the boys helped to flag down a passing car containing a young couple and two children. While the boys were pushing one car into the desert and moving items from one car to another, their father and his cellmate executed all four good Samaritans who had stopped to help, including a two-year old boy. When the escapees later encountered a police roadblock, the older brother was killed in the shootout, the father escaped into the desert and died from exposure, and Ricky, Raymond, and their father's cellmate were captured. All three were tried and sentenced to death for the murders. The Tisons relied on the *Enmund* precedent to claim that they could not be sentenced to death because they did not plan or participate in the murders. In a 5–4 decision, however, the Supreme Court revised the *Enmund* precedent in order to affirm the Tisons' death sentences.

Justice O'Connor's majority opinion did not reverse *Enmund*. Instead, it claimed to refine *Enmund* by declaring that even those who do not plan or participate in a killing may receive the death penalty if they demonstrate "reckless indifference to human life" as participants in a felony-murder. Although O'Connor purported to make a modest clarification of *Enmund*'s meaning, her opinion virtually nullified *Enmund* without formally overruling it. The *Enmund* decision had established a "bright-line rule" for the death penalty by stating that only those who plan or participate in a killing can receive the death penalty as felony-murder accomplices. It was clear from the accomplice's participation whether he or she could be subject to the death penalty. The *Tison* decision destroyed the bright-line rule. In the aftermath of *Tison*, capital punishment decisions concerning accomplices became determined by the discretion of prosecutors and jurors. Prosecutors may use their judgment—and biases—to seek a death sentence for some felony-murder accomplices, but not seek it for others. Jurors may use their discretion—and biases—to find some murders so despicable that they place the label of "reckless indifference" on accomplices who did not participate directly in the killings.

At first glance, it may appear odd that O'Connor did not seek to reverse *Enmund* because she had written such a strong dissenting opinion in the 1982 case. However, an examination of the Court's composition suggests why she chose to nullify *Enmund* with her reasoning without admitting that she was doing so. The Court's composition was unchanged since 1982, except for Justice Scalia's vote replacing Chief Justice Burger's vote in support of the death penalty for accomplices. Thus, O'Connor needed to persuade one member of the *Enmund* majority to join her in order to gain a five-member majority for the *Tison* decision. Justice White, who was often conservative on criminal justice issues, was persuaded to provide the fifth vote for O'Connor's *Tison* majority. Because White was the author of the *Enmund* majority, he may have been unwilling to join a *Tison* opinion that reversed his own *Enmund* opinion. That would have been tantamount to admitting that he had made a mistake in *Enmund*. Thus, by claiming that her opinion merely clarified the precedent even though her reasoning effectively nullified the principle in *Enmund*, O'Connor seems to have attracted White's vote without forcing him to admit that he had been mistaken in *Enmund* (Smith 1992). Because O'Connor's opinion significantly altered *Enmund* without overruling the precedent, it has been classified as a conservative modification of existing precedent.

In another capital case during the same initial term, the Court faced what many death penalty opponents considered to be the last "best" chance to have capital punishment declared unconstitutional in *McCleskey v. Kemp* (1987). Warren McCleskey was among four persons convicted of robbing a furniture store in Georgia. A police officer was killed by the robbers, and McCleskey was sentenced to death because the jury held him responsible for the shooting. McCleskey was African American and the police officer was white. McCleskey challenged his death sentence in the Supreme Court based on a study conducted by several scholars under the leadership of Professor David Baldus of the University of Iowa College of Law. The "Baldus study," as it was called, examined more than two thousand murder cases that occurred in Georgia during the 1970s. Using sophisticated social science techniques and 230 variables, the Baldus study found that the race of defendants and victims was highly associated with the application of the death penalty in Georgia. The study found that: "[T]he death penalty was assessed in 22% of the death cases involving black defendants and white victims; 8% of cases involving white defendants and white victims; 1% of the cases involving black defendants and black victims; and 3% of the cases involving white defendants and black victims. . . . [D]efendants charged with killing whites were 4.3 times as likely to receive a death sentence as defendants charged with killing blacks" (481 U.S. at 286, 287). Based on the study, McCleskey argued that Georgia's death penalty was infused with racial discrimination in violation of the Equal Protection Clause and that the existence of such widespread discrimination also violated the Eighth Amendment.

In a 5–4 decision that split the Court exactly as it was split in *Tison,* the majority rejected McCleskey's claim. Although the Court had accepted the use of statistical proof of discrimination in employment discrimination and jury discrimination cases, the majority rejected the use of such statistical proof to demonstrate discrimination in death penalty cases. The Court established a rule that a death row inmate claiming discrimination "must prove that the decisionmakers in *his* case acted with discriminatory purpose" (481 U.S. at 292). Thus they precluded the use of studies showing that the entire criminal justice system was infected with discriminatory decisions. This new rule led to the classification of the case as a conservative modification of precedent because the Court had not previously ruled on this issue.

The majority also rejected McCleskey's Eighth Amendment claim by determining that his sentence was neither arbitrary nor disproportionate. Justice Powell's majority opinion explicitly accepted that "[a]pparent disparities in sentencing are an inevitable part of our criminal justice system" (481 U.S. at 312). This conclusion reflected the shift in the Court's composition with the departure of Warren Court era justices who had believed that it was their responsibility to guard against rather than accept discriminatory disparities.

Justice Powell's opinion declared that the Court must respect the existence of discretion in sentencing, but Justice Brennan argued in dissent that "[d]iscretion is a means, not an end" and that the discriminatory application of discretion in Georgia "reflects a devaluation of the lives of black persons" (481 U.S. at 336). Justice Stevens's dissenting opinion accused the majority of fearing that if it opened its eyes to the strong social science evidence of racial discrimination it might be forced to eliminate capital punishment: "The Court's decision appears to be based on a fear that the acceptance of McCleskey's claim would sound the death knell for capital punishment in Georgia. If society were indeed forced to choose between a racially discriminatory death penalty . . . and no death penalty at all, the choice [against capital punishment] mandated by the Constitution would be plain" (481 U.S. at 367).

McCleskey v. Kemp

481 U.S. 279, 107 S.Ct. 1756, 95 L.Ed. 2d 262 (1987)

■ McCleskey, an African American defendant, was convicted of shooting and killing a white police officer in the course of robbing a furniture store along with several accomplices. McCleskey challenged his death sentence by using a sophisticated social science study that indicated that defendants convicted of killing white victims were much more likely to be sentenced to death than defendants convicted of killing black victims. He sought to invalidate his death sentence by claiming that racial discrimination was pervasive in Georgia's system for determining which defendants would receive capital punishment.

The case is important because it was regarded by opponents of capital punishment as the final "best chance" to win a judicial declaration that the death penalty violates the Constitution. As you read the case, consider the following questions: (1) What proof does the majority opinion demand to establish the existence of unconstitutional racial discrimination? (2) In what contexts will the Supreme Court accept statistical proof of discrimination? (3) What consequences do the majority fear from a decision favoring the defendant? Are these fears justified?

Vote:

5 justices found the practices constitutional (O'Connor, Powell, Rehnquist, Scalia, White).

4 justices found the practices unconstitutional (Blackmun, Brennan, Marshall, Stevens).

Justice Powell delivered the opinion of the Court.

This case presents the question whether a complex statistical study that indicates a risk that racial considerations enter into capital sentencing determinations proves that petitioner McCleskey's capital sentence is unconstitutional under the Eighth or Fourteenth Amendment.

McCleskey, a black man, was convicted of two counts of armed robbery and one count of murder in the Superior Court of Fulton County, Georgia, on October 12, 1978. . . . During the course of [a furniture store] robbery, a police officer, answering a silent alarm, entered the store through the front door. As he was walking down the center aisle of the store, two shots were fired. Both struck the officer. One hit him in the face and killed him.

Several weeks later, McCleskey was arrested in connection with an unrelated offense. He confessed that he participated in the furniture store robbery, but denied that he had shot the police officer. At trial, the State introduced evidence that at least one of the bullets that struck the officer was fired from a .38 caliber Rossi revolver. This description matched the description of the gun that McCleskey had carried during the robbery. The State also introduced the testimony of two witnesses who had heard McCleskey admit to the shooting.

The jury convicted McCleskey of murder. . . . The jury recommended that he be sentenced to death on the murder charge and to consecutive life sentences on the armed robbery charges. The court followed the jury's recommendation and sentenced McCleskey to death. . . .

McCleskey . . . filed a petition for a writ of habeas corpus in [federal court]. . . . His petition raised 18 claims, one of which was that the Georgia capital sentencing process is administered in a racially discriminatory manner in violation of the Eighth and Fourteenth Amendments to the United States Constitution. In support of his claim, McCleskey proffered a statistical study performed by Professors David C. Baldus, George Woodworth, and Charles Pulaski (the Baldus study) that purports to show disparity in the imposition of the death sentence in Georgia based on the race of the murder victim and, to a lesser extent, the race of the defendant. The Baldus study is actually two sophisticated statistical studies that examine over 2,000 murder cases that occurred in Georgia during the 1970s. The raw numbers collected by Professor Baldus indicate that defendants charged with killing white persons received the death penalty in 11% of cases, but defendants charged with killing blacks received the death penalty in only 1% of cases. The raw numbers also indicate a reverse racial disparity according to the race of the defendant: 4% of the black defendants received the death penalty, as opposed to 7% of the white defendants.

Baldus also divided the cases according to the combination of the race of the defendant and the race of the victim. He found that the death penalty was assessed in 22% of the cases involving black defendants and white victims; 8% of the cases involving white defendants and white victims; 1% of the cases involving black defendants and black victims; and 3% of the cases involving white defendants and black victims. Similarly, Baldus found that prosecutors sought the death penalty in 70% of the cases involving black defendants and white victims; 32% of the cases involving white defendants and white victims; 15% of the cases involving black defendants and black victims; and 19% of the cases involving white defendants and black victims.

Baldus subjected his data to an extensive analysis, taking account of 230 variables that could have explained the disparities on nonracial grounds. One of his models concludes that, even after taking account of 39 nonracial variables, defendants charged with killing white victims were 4.3 times as likely to receive a death sentence as defendants charged with killing blacks. According to this model, black defendants were 1.1 times as likely to receive a death sentence as other defendants. Thus, the Baldus study indicates that black defendants, such as McCleskey, who kill white victims have the greatest likelihood of receiving the death penalty.[5]

The District Court . . . concluded that McCleskey's "statistics do not demonstrate a prima facie case in support of the contention that the death penalty was imposed upon him because of his race, because of the race of the victim, or because of any Eighth Amendment concern." . . . As to McCleskey's Fourteenth Amendment claim, the court found that the methodology of the Baldus study was flawed in several respects. . . .

* * *

. . . As a black defendant who killed a white victim, McCleskey claims that the Baldus study demonstrates that he was discriminated against because of the race of his victim. In its broadest form, McCleskey's claim of discrimination extends to every actor in the Georgia capital sentencing process, from the prosecutor who sought the death penalty and the jury that imposed the sentence, to the State itself that enacted the capital punishment statute and allows it to remain in effect despite its allegedly discriminatory application. We agree with the [lower courts] . . . that this claim must fail.

. . . [T]o prevail under the Equal Protection Clause, McCleskey must prove that the decisionmakers in *his* case acted with discriminatory purpose. He offers no evidence specific to his own case that would support an inference that racial considerations played a part in his sentence. Instead, he relies solely on the Baldus study. McCleskey argues that the Baldus study compels an inference that his sentence rests on purposeful discrimination. . . .

[5]Baldus's 230-variable model divided cases into eight different ranges, according to the estimated aggravation level of the offense. Baldus argued in his testimony to the District Court that the effects of racial bias were most striking in the mid-range cases. "[W]hen the cases become tremendously aggravated so that everybody would agree that if we're going to have a death sentence, these are the cases that should get it, the race effects go away. It's only in the mid-range of cases where the decision makers have a real choice as to what to do. If there's room for the exercise of discretion, then [racial] factors begin to play a role." . . . Under this model, Baldus found that 14.4% of the black-victim mid-range cases received the death penalty, and 34.4% of the white-victim cases received the death penalty. . . . According to Baldus, the facts of McCleskey's case placed it within the mid-range.

The Court has accepted statistics as proof of intent to discriminate in certain limited contexts. First, this Court has accepted statistical disparities as proof of an equal protection violation in the selection of the jury venire in a particular district. . . . Second, this Court has accepted statistics in the form of multiple regression analysis to prove statutory violations under Title VII [regarding employment discrimination]. . . .

But the nature of the capital sentencing decision, and the relationship of the statistics to that decision, are fundamentally different from the corresponding elements in the venire-selection or Title VII cases. Most importantly, each particular decision to impose the death penalty is made by a petit jury selected from a properly constituted venire. Each jury is unique in its composition, and the Constitution requires that its decision rest on consideration of innumerable factors that vary according to the characteristics of the individual defendant and the facts of the particular capital offense. . . . Thus, the application of an inference drawn from the general statistics to a specific decision in a trial and sentencing simply is not comparable to the application of an inference drawn from general statistics to a specific venire-selection or Title VII case. In those cases, the statistics relate to fewer entities, and fewer variables are relevant to the challenged decisions.

Another important difference between the cases in which we have accepted statistics as proof of discriminatory intent and this case is that, in the venire-selection and Title VII contexts, the decision-maker has an opportunity to explain the statistical disparity. . . .

Finally, McCleskey's statistical proffer must be viewed in the context of his challenge . . . at the heart of the State's criminal justice system. . . . Implementation of [criminal justice] laws necessarily requires discretionary judgments. Because discretion is essential to the criminal justice process, we would demand exceptionally clear proof before we would infer that the discretion has been abused. . . . [W]e hold that the Baldus study is clearly insufficient to support an inference that any of the decisionmakers in McCleskey's case acted with discriminatory purpose. . . .

* * *

. . . As legislatures necessarily have wide discretion in the choice of criminal laws and penalties, and as there were legitimate reasons for the Georgia Legislature to adopt and maintain capital punishment, . . . we will not infer a discriminatory purpose on the part of the State of Georgia. . . .

* * *

... McCleskey argues that the sentence in his case is disproportionate to the sentences in other murder cases. ...

* * *

... [A]bsent a showing that the Georgia capital punishment system operates in an arbitrary and capricious manner, McCleskey cannot prove a constitutional violation by demonstrating that other defendants who may be similarly situated did *not* receive the death penalty. ...

Because McCleskey's sentence was imposed under Georgia sentencing procedures that focus discretion "on the particularized nature of the crime and the particularized characteristics of the individual defendant," ... we lawfully may presume that McCleskey's death sentence was not "wantonly and freakishly" imposed, ... and thus that the sentence is not disproportionate within any recognized meaning under the Eighth Amendment.

... McCleskey further contends that the Georgia capital punishment system is arbitrary and capricious in *application*, and therefore his sentence is excessive, because racial considerations may influence capital sentencing decisions in Georgia. ...

... Even Professor Baldus does not contend that his statistics *prove* that race enters into any capital sentencing decisions or that race was a factor in McCleskey's particular case. Statistics at most show only a likelihood that a particular factor entered into some decisions. There is, of course, some risk of racial prejudice influencing a jury's decision in a criminal case. There are similar risks that other kinds of prejudice will influence other criminal trials. ... The question "is at what point that risk becomes constitutionally unacceptable. ..." McCleskey asks us to accept the likelihood allegedly shown by the Baldus study as the constitutional measure of unacceptable risk of racial prejudice influencing capital sentencing decisions. This we decline to do. ...

* * *

McCleskey's argument that the Constitution condemns the discretion allowed decisionmakers in the Georgia capital sentencing system is antithetical to the fundamental role of discretion in our criminal justice system. Discretion in the criminal justice system offers substantial benefits to the criminal defendant. Not only can a jury decline to impose the death sentence, it can decline to convict. ...

At most, the Baldus study indicates a discrepancy that appears to correlate with race. Apparent disparities in sentencing are an inevitable part of our criminal justice system. ...

* * *

... McCleskey's claim, taken to its logical conclusion, throws into serious question the principles that underlie our entire criminal justice system. The Eighth Amendment is not limited in application to capital punishment, but applies to all penalties. ... Thus, if we accepted McCleskey's claim that racial bias has impermissibly tainted the capital sentencing decision, we could soon be faced with similar claims as to other types of penalty. ...

... McCleskey's arguments are best presented to legislative bodies. ... Legislatures ... are better qualified to weigh and "evaluate the results of statistical studies in terms of their own local conditions."* * *

Justice Brennan, with whom Justice Marshall, joins, and with whom Justice Blackmun and Justice Stevens join in all but Part I, dissenting.

I

... [M]urder defendants in Georgia with white victims are more than four times as likely to receive the death sentence as are defendants with black victims. ... Nothing could convey more powerfully the intractable reality of the death penalty: "that the effort to eliminate arbitrariness in the infliction of that ultimate sanction is so plainly doomed to failure that it—and the death penalty—must be abandoned altogether."

* * *

II

At some point in this case, Warren McCleskey doubtless asked his lawyer whether a jury was likely to sentence him to die. A candid reply to this question would have been disturbing. First, counsel would have to tell McCleskey that few of the details of the crime or of McCleskey's past criminal conduct were more important than the fact that his victim was white. ... Furthermore, counsel would feel bound to tell McCleskey that defendants charged with killing white victims in Georgia are 4.3 times as likely to be sentenced to death as defendants charged with killing blacks. ... In addition, frankness would compel the disclosure that it was more likely than not that the race of McCleskey's victim would determine whether he received a death sentence: 6 of every 11 defendants convicted of killing a white person would not have received the death penalty if their victims had been black. ...

The Court today ... finds no fault in a system in which lawyers must tell their clients that race casts a large shadow on the capital sentencing process. The Court arrives at this conclusion by stating that the Baldus Study cannot "*prove* that race enters into any capital sentencing decisions." ... [W]e can identify only "a likelihood that a particular factor entered into some decisions," ... and "a discrepancy that appears to correlate to race." . . . This "likelihood" and "discrepancy," holds the Court, is insufficient to establish a constitutional violation. The Court reaches this conclusion by placing four factors on the scales opposite McCleskey's evidence: the desire to encourage sentencing discretion, the existence of "statutory safeguards" in the Georgia scheme, the fear of encouraging widespread challenges to other sentencing decisions, and the limits of the judicial role. The Court's evaluation of the significance of petitioner's evidence is fundamentally at odds with our consistent concern for rationality in capital sentencing, and the considerations that the majority invokes to discount that evidence cannot justify its force.

It is important to emphasize at the outset that the Court's observation that McCleskey cannot prove the influence of race on any particular sentencing decision is irrelevant in evaluating his Eighth Amendment claim. Since *Furman v. Georgia* [1972], . . . the Court has been concerned with the *risk* of the imposition of an arbitrary sentence, rather than the proven fact of one. *Furman* held that the death penalty "may not be imposed under sentencing procedures that create a substantial risk that the punishment will be inflicted in an arbitrary and capricious manner."* * *

* * *

Defendants challenging their death sentences thus never have had to prove that impermissible considerations have actually infected sentencing decisions. We have required instead that they establish that the system under which they were sentenced posed a significant risk of such an occurrence. McCleskey's claim does differ, however, in one respect from these earlier cases: it is the first to base a challenge not on speculation about how a system *might* operate, but empirical documentation of how it *does* operate.

The Court assumes the statistical validity of the Baldus study, . . . and acknowledges that McCleskey has demonstrated a risk that racial prejudice plays a role in capital sentencing in Georgia. . . . Nevertheless, it finds the probability of prejudice insufficient to create constitutional concern. . . . Close analysis of the Baldus study, however, in light of both statistical principles and human experience, reveals that the risk that race influenced McCleskey's sentence is intolerable by an imaginable standard. . . .

* * *

. . . [B]lacks who kill whites are sentenced to death at nearly *22 times* the rate of blacks who kill blacks, and more than *7 times* the rate of whites who kill blacks. . . . Since our decision upholding the Georgia capital-sentencing system in *Gregg*, the State has executed 7 persons. All of the 7 were executed for killing whites, and 6 of the 7 executed were black. Such execution figures are especially striking in light of the fact that, during the period encompassed by the Baldus study, only 9.2% of Georgia homicides involved black defendants and white victims, while 60.7% involved black victims.

McCleskey's statistics have particular force because most of them are the product of sophisticated multiple-regression analysis. Such analysis is designed precisely to identify patterns in the aggregate, even though we may not be able to reconstitute with certainty any individual decision that goes to make up that pattern. Multiple-regression analysis is particularly well-suited to identify the influence of impermissible considerations in sentencing, since it is able to control for permissible factors that may explain an apparent arbitrary pattern. . . . In this case, Professor Baldus in fact conducted additional regression analyses in response to criticisms and suggestions by the District Court, all of which confirmed, and some of which even strengthened, the study's original conclusions.

The statistical evidence in this case thus relentlessly documents the risk that McCleskey's sentence was influenced by racial considerations. . . .

. . . We must also ask whether the conclusion suggested by those numbers [in the Baldus study] is consonant with our understanding of history and human experience. Georgia's legacy of a race-conscious criminal justice system, as well as this Court's own recognition of the persistent danger that racial attitudes may affect criminal proceedings, indicate that McCleskey's claim is not a fanciful product of mere statistical artifice. . . .

* * *

The Court maintains that petitioner's claim "is antithetical to the fundamental role of discretion in our criminal justice system."* * *

Reliance on race in imposing capital punishment, however, is antithetical to the very rationale for granting sentencing discretion. Discretion is a means, not an end. It is bestowed in order to permit the sentencer to "trea[t] each defendant in a capital case with that degree of respect due the uniqueness of the individual."* * *

Considering the race of the defendant or victim in deciding if the death penalty should be imposed is completely at odds with this concern that an individual be evaluated as a unique human being. . . . Enhanced willingness to impose the death sentence on black defendants, or diminished willingness to render such a sentence when blacks are victims, reflects a devaluation of the lives of black persons. . . .

* * *

The Court . . . states that its unwillingness to regard the petitioner's evidence as sufficient is based in part on the fear that recognition of McCleskey's claim would open the door to widespread challenges to all aspects of criminal sentencing. . . . Taken on its face, such a statement seems to suggest a fear of too much justice. Yet surely the majority would acknowledge that if striking evidence indicated that other minority groups, or women, or even persons with blond hair, were disproportionately sentenced to death, such a state of affairs would be repugnant to deeply rooted conceptions of fairness. . . .

Justice Blackmun, with whom Justice Marshall and Justice Stevens join and with whom Justice Brennan joins in all but Part IV-B, dissenting.

* * *

IV

A

One of the final concerns discussed by the Court may be the most disturbing aspect of its opinion. Granting relief to McCleskey in this case, it is said, could lead to further constitutional challenges. . . . That, of course, is no reason to deny McCleskey his rights under the Equal Protection Clause. If a grant of relief to him were to lead to a closer examination of the effects of racial considerations throughout the criminal-justice system, the system, and hence society, might benefit. Where no such factors come into play, the integrity of the system is enhanced. Where such considerations are shown to be significant, efforts can be made to eradicate their impermissible influence and to ensure an evenhanded application of criminal sanctions. . . .

Justice Stevens, with whom Justice Blackmun joins, dissenting.

* * *

The Court's decision appears to be based on a fear that the acceptance of McCleskey's claim would sound the death knell for capital punishment in Georgia. If society were indeed forced to choose between a racially discriminatory death penalty (one that provides heightened protection against murder "for whites only") and no death penalty at all, the choice mandated by the Constitution would be plain. . . . But the Court's fear is unfounded. One of the lessons of the Baldus study is that there exist certain categories of extremely serious crimes for which prosecutors consistently seek, and juries consistently impose, the death penalty without regard to the race of the victim or the race of the offender. If Georgia were to narrow the class of death-eligible defendants to those categories, the danger of arbitrary and discriminatory imposition of the death penalty would be significantly decreased, if not eradicated. As Justice BRENNAN has demonstrated in his dissenting opinion, such a restructuring of the sentencing scheme is surely not too high a price to pay.

Although the slim majorities produced significant conservative decisions affecting capital punishment during the Rehnquist Court's 1986–87 term, all of its decisions affecting capital punishment during that term were not conservative. As indicated in Table 12.5, the Court produced three minor decisions applying liberal interpretations of precedent (*Hitchcock v. Dugger*, 1987; *Gray v. Mississippi*, 1987; *Sumner v. Schuman*, 1987). These decisions favored defendants in deciding issues concerning capital juries and rejected a mandatory death penalty for people who commit murders in prison while serving life sentences. An additional 1987 decision produced a liberal modification of precedent in *Booth v. Maryland* (1987) when Justice Powell deserted the conservative justices to provide the critical fifth vote for a decision favoring an individual. In *Booth*, the 5–4 majority decided that "victim impact statements" were impermissible during the sentencing phase of capital cases. Prosecutors attempted to use victim impact statements to inform jurors about how a particular homicide had devastated surviving family members or had eliminated a valued and admired member of society. According to Justice Powell's majority opinion, victim impact statements are irrelevant to a capital sentencing decision, and their introduction creates the risk of capricious application of capital punishment. Such testimony was regarded as creating a risk that capital punishment would be imposed based upon how much society values a particular victim's life rather than based on the viciousness of the defendant's actions. Thus the murderer of a town's doctor might be more likely to receive the death penalty than the murderer of a janitor, or the murderer of a white person might receive the penalty more freely than the murderer of an African American person, if the jurors valued whites' lives more highly. In dissent, Justice White characterized victim impact statements as "counteracting the mitigating evidence which the defendant is entitled to put in . . . by reminding the sentencer that just as the murderer should be considered as an individual, so too the victim is an individual whose death represents a unique loss to society and in particular to his family" (482 U.S. at 517).

During the Rehnquist Court's 1987–88 term, the justices again produced both liberal and conservative decisions affecting capital punishment. In *Thompson v. Oklahoma* (1988), a 5–3 majority decided that states could not apply the death penalty to offenders who were younger than sixteen years of age at the time that they committed their capital offense. Because only a plurality of justices (Brennan, Marshall, and Blackmun) supported Justice Stevens' reasoning, the case did not produce a clear precedent. The case was argued before Justice Kennedy's confirmation as the replacement for retiring Justice Powell. Although Justice O'Connor provided the fifth vote for the majority, she did not agree with Justice Stevens' conclusion that execution of juveniles violates the Eighth Amendment by offending civilized standards of decency. O'Connor expressed the belief that a national consensus probably existed against execution for those who commit acts while under the age of sixteen, but she declined to agree with any firm rule about the minimum age for execution.

Justice Kennedy participated in all of the Court's cases during the 1988–89 term. Just as Kennedy provided the crucial fifth vote for a series of narrow conservative precedents affecting abortion (e.g., *Webster v. Reproductive Health Services* [1989], see Chapter 17) and racial discrimination (e.g., *Patterson v. McLean Credit Union* [1989], see Chapter 13), he also had an immediate impact on capital punishment cases. In the major case of *Stanford v. Kentucky* (1989), Kennedy's vote, along with that of O'Connor, provided a five-vote majority for a conservative interpretation of *Thompson v. Oklahoma* (1988). The new interpretation established that the imposition of the death penalty for those who commit capital crimes at ages sixteen and seventeen does not violate the Eighth Amendment. The members of Stevens' plurality during the previous term suddenly found themselves dissenting on the issue of capital punishment for juveniles. In another major case, *Penry v. Lynaugh* (1989), the same five-member majority approved the application of the death penalty to mentally retarded murder defendants. In the case, the defendant had the "mental age" (i.e., ability to learn) of a six-and-a-half-year-old child and the "social maturity" (i.e., ability to function in the world) of a nine or ten year old. Like all of the Rehnquist Court era's other major cases on criminal punishment, these cases advanced conservative outcomes.

In a reaffirmation of liberal precedent, Justice White parted company with his usual conservative allies to provide the fifth vote necessary to continue the exclusion of victim impact statements (*South Carolina v. Gathers*, 1989). Justice Scalia's dissenting opinion foretold that the conservative justices were waiting for additional conservative appointees in order to overrule the precedent established in *Booth*: "I doubt that overruling *Booth* will so shake the citizenry's faith in the Court. Overrulings of precedent rarely occur without a change in the Court's personnel. The only distinctive feature here is that the overruling would follow not long after the original decision. But that is hardly unprecedented" (482 U.S. at 824).

There were no changes in the Court's composition the following year during the 1989–90 term. As indicated by Table 12.4, the pivotal fifth vote provided by Justice Kennedy produced five 5–4 decisions favoring conservative outcomes out of the six capital punishment cases decided by the Court that term. The Court was deeply divided between a consistent bloc of justices supporting the government (Rehnquist, Scalia, O'Connor, White, and Kennedy) and a consistent bloc of justices favoring individuals for these issues (Brennan, Marshall, Blackmun, and Stevens). The Court produced several conservative interpretations of precedents concerning instructions for juries considering death penalty cases. The only major case during the term was a 5–4 decision endorsing a Pennsylvania statute that mandated the death penalty if a jury finds at least one aggravating factor and no mitigating circumstances in a case (*Blystone v. Pennsylvania*, 1990). The dissenters argued that even in the absence of mitigating factors, the jury should be able to weigh the aggravating factors to make a decision about whether to impose a death sentence.

In 1990, Justice Brennan, a Warren Court holdover, retired and was replaced by President Bush's first appointee, Justice David Souter. In his initial term on the Court during 1990–91, Souter supported the government much more frequently than had Justice Brennan in civil rights and liberties cases. In particular, Souter cast a decisive fifth vote favoring conservative outcomes in seven criminal justice cases that would have been decided in favor of individuals if Justice Brennan had remained on the Court (Smith and Johnson 1992). The Court's major capital punishment decision during Souter's initial term produced a new conservative precedent by permitting the introduction of victim impact statements at capital sentencing hearings. In *Payne v. Tennessee* (1991), a new majority fulfilled Justice Scalia's prophecy about the effects of additional changes in the Court's composition by overruling precedents established just two and four years earlier (*South Carolina v. Gathers*, 1989 and *Booth v. Maryland*, 1987). Despite the two earlier precedents barring the use of victim impact statements during the sentencing phase of capital cases, *Payne* permitted prosecutors to present testimony from family members about the impact of the victim's death upon their lives. The *Payne* decision provided a clear example of a quick and unusually complete doctrinal switch produced by the preferences of the justices appointed by Presidents Reagan and Bush who formed the nucleus of the Court's new dominant majority.

The retirement of Justice Marshall, one of the Court's strongest supporters of individuals in criminal punishment cases, and Marshall's replacement by President Bush's second appointee, Justice Clarence Thomas, did not produce any major new decisions on the issue of capital punishment and capital jury procedures. In two cases, the Court corrected errors by trial judges in capital cases who improperly selected jurors (*Morgan v. Illinois*, 1992) or improperly weighed aggravating factors (*Sochor v. Florida*, 1992).

When Justice Ginsburg replaced Justice White in 1993, many observers speculated that Ginsburg might provide a new vote against capital punishment and thereby provide additional strength to the remaining liberal bloc members, Stevens and Blackmun. Speculation about Ginsburg intensified when she resisted efforts by Republican senators to question her about her views on the legality of the death penalty during the Senate confirmation hearings. Ultimately, Ginsburg revealed that she apparently accepts the constitutionality of the death penalty by joining an eight-member majority that endorsed California's death penalty procedures (*Tuilaepa v. California*, 1994). Ginsburg joined the liberals in other cases that challenged the evidence considered by juries during capital cases (*Simmons v. South Carolina*, 1994; *Romano v. Oklahoma*, 1994). In 1995, after President Clinton's second appointee, Justice Breyer, had joined the Court, both Ginsburg and Breyer joined the conservatives in upholding an Alabama capital punishment statute (*Harris v. Alabama*, 1995). Without giving guidance on how a trial judge is supposed to weigh a jury recommendation of imprisonment instead of execution, the statute permitted judges to go against a jury's recommendation by imposing a death sentence. Justice Stevens was the lone dissenter.

As we mentioned previously in this chapter, much of the Rehnquist Court's impact on capital cases did not come through the interpretation of Eighth Amendment and other constitutional issues. Instead, the justices interpreted habeas corpus procedures in ways that limited opportunities for prisoners on death row to challenge the validity of their convictions. Habeas corpus provides the traditional process through which incarcerated people challenge the basis for their detention by asserting that constitutional rights violations occurred in the proceedings that led to their convictions. Through habeas corpus proceedings, inmates in state prisons have been able to have *federal judges* review their cases for constitutional violations, even though the crimes, convictions, and appeals were under state law and handled by state courts. Many critics of habeas corpus, including several justices on the Rehnquist Court, view the process as a means of federal judicial interference with states' control of their own criminal cases and a means by which death row inmates unnecessarily delay their executions. Habeas corpus cases, which generally concern the procedures for federal courts' postappeal reviews of state criminal cases, are not represented in this chapter's tables illustrating decisions classified as capital punishment, Eighth Amendment, and capital jury issues. Most habeas corpus petitions are not from death penalty cases.

Although habeas corpus cases do not focus on Eighth Amendment issues and capital punishment, they have a significant impact on death row inmates facing execution. For example, in 1991, the Court rejected a second case from Warren McCleskey, the defendant who lost his claim in 1987 concerning systemic racial discrimination in Georgia. McCleskey claimed that the police and prosecutors violated his rights when they planted an informant in his cell and then hid from McCleskey, his attorney, and the jury the fact that the informant-witness was working for the police and testifying against McCleskey in exchange for favors. Rather than consider whether the informant's activities violated McCleskey's Sixth Amendment right to be represented by counsel when questioned by police agents, a 6–3 majority on the Court simply created a new procedural rule to block McCleskey's claim. The Court ruled that a prisoner must normally use a single habeas corpus petition to present all claims (*McCleskey v. Zant*, 1991). Thus McCleskey exhausted his opportunity to bring claims to the federal court when he brought his action using statistics to show the existence of racial discrimination. McCleskey's claim about the unconstitutional use of a police informant was barred despite the fact the prosecutors allegedly hid relevant information from McCleskey's attorney until long after he had filed McCleskey's first challenge. In another case, the Court set an extremely difficult standard for condemned prisoners to meet if they discover evidence to demonstrate their actual innocence after trial (*Herrera v. Collins*, 1993). In a comment indicative of a strong desire to eliminate judicial interference with the death penalty, Justice Scalia declared that actual innocence is not a sufficient basis for judges to review and reverse capital convictions: "There is no basis in text, tradition, or even in contemporary practice (if that were enough), for finding in the Constitution a right to demand judicial consideration of newly discovered evidence of innocence brought forward after conviction" (506 U.S. at 427, 428). Because of the use of procedural issues to affect capital punishment in these and other cases, the Rehnquist Court's impact on the death penalty is greater than it appears from the discussion of constitutional issues in this chapter.

Justice Ginsburg's presence on the Court during the 1993 term in place of Justice White shifted the outcome on one habeas case. In *McFarland v. Scott* (1994), a five-member majority decided that federal district judges can order delays in executions until death-row inmates obtain legal representation for the final habeas challenges to their convictions and sentences. The *New York Times* speculated that the outcome of the *McFarland* case "suggested that a new majority had emerged [on the Court] that is unwilling to cut back the [habeas corpus] process much further" (Labaton 1994). It remains to be seen whether Ginsburg's and Breyer's participation in decisions will make a significant impact on the conservative direction of the Rehnquist Court's decisions affecting habeas corpus.

Noncapital Punishment

The Rehnquist Court's first decisions concerning the Eighth Amendment in contexts other than capital punishment were produced after Justice Souter replaced Justice Brennan in 1990. By this time, the justices who usually supported the government's position in criminal justice cases constituted a majority on the Court. In the first case, the justices unanimously rejected an Ohio prisoner's claim that the conditions inside his correctional institution violated the Eighth Amendment's prohibition on cruel and unusual punishments (*Wilson v. Seiter*, 1991). Justice Scalia could gain the support of only four other justices, however, for his majority opinion. Four justices (White, Marshall, Blackmun, and Stevens) used a concurring opinion to express strong disagreement with Scalia's reasoning. Scalia's majority opinion claimed to be following established precedents in declaring that prisoners must show deliberate indifference by responsible officials before they can prevail in a claim concerning unconstitutional conditions of confinement. Although Scalia did not purport to establish a new conservative precedent, his opinion is classified as a new precedent because the principle established is so different from those contained in the precedents that Scalia claimed to follow.

Scalia took the "deliberate indifference" test that the Burger Court had previously applied to claims concerning deprivations of medical care (*Estelle v. Gamble*, 1976) and declared that the test applied to all Eighth Amendment challenges to conditions of confinement in correctional institutions. Although the Court had previously focused on an objective examination of the totality of conditions inside prisons, Scalia's majority opinion dictated that judges henceforth apply a subjective test by asking what the corrections officials were thinking when the challenged conditions developed. As Justice White noted in his concurring opinion: "The majority's approach also is unwise. It leaves open the possibility, for example, that prison officials will be able to defeat a [civil rights] action challenging inhumane prison conditions simply by showing that the conditions are caused by insufficient funding from the state legislature rather than by any deliberate indifference on the part of the prison officials" (501 U.S. at 311). White then quoted the Bush administration's amicus brief that *opposed* Scalia's reasoning. The Bush administration argued that "seriously inhumane, pervasive conditions should not be insulated from constitutional challenge [simply] because the officials managing the institution have exhibited a conscientious concern for ameliorating its problems, and have made efforts (albeit unsuccessful) to that end" (115 L.Ed.2d at 287). Thus, the new precedent established by Scalia's majority opinion may permit inhumane conditions to exist in prisons as long as correctional officials exhibit concern about those conditions.

In a major case during that same term, Scalia wrote a majority opinion endorsing Michigan's mandatory sentence of life without possibility of parole for a first offender convicted of possessing more than 650 grams of cocaine (*Harmelin v. Michigan*, 1991). Harmelin had argued that the sentence was cruel and unusual because it was disproportionate to the crime. The sentence was more severe than that imposed by Michigan on murderers and other offenders who commit acts of violence. Because Michigan does not have the death penalty, the mandatory life sentence was the stiffest possible sentence in Michigan's criminal justice system. The same 5–4 majority endorsed Michigan's law that had established the new precedent for conditions of confinement in prisons. Portions of Scalia's opinion advocated complete abandonment of any proportionality principle for noncapital cases, but only Chief Justice Rehnquist joined those sections of Scalia's opinion. According to Scalia, because punishments must be cruel *and* unusual in order to violate the Eighth Amendment, the justices should dispense with considering whether any punishment is cruel and focus their attention on whether or not punishments are unusual. Thus Scalia concluded that "[s]evere, mandatory penalties may be cruel, but they are not unusual in the constitutional sense, having been employed in various forms throughout our Nation's history" (501 U.S. at 994, 995). Taken to its logical conclusion, Scalia's reasoning might render the Eighth Amendment meaningless as a limitation on government officials. In Scalia's eyes, if government officials choose to impose a punishment that has been used previously in Anglo-American history, it is apparently, ipso facto, not unusual and therefore constitutionally acceptable. Scalia's reasoning was at odds, for example, with his published speech expressing opposition to the reintroduction of public flogging as a constitutional means of criminal punishment (Scalia 1989).

Justices Kennedy, O'Connor, and Souter supported Michigan's statute, and they joined only the final section of Scalia's opinion, which declined to invalidate the statute. However, they also advocated maintaining a proportionality principle within the Eighth Amendment for noncapital cases. These three justices provide the basis for classifying the case as a plurality's conservative interpretation of existing precedent. Scalia's effort to establish a new precedent that would abolish proportionality lacked sufficient support. In dissent, Justice White found Scalia's ideas sufficiently disturbing that he implicitly raised the possibility in his opinion that Scalia's reasoning could lead to the judicial endorsement of life imprisonment as a punishment for parking tickets.

HARMELIN V. MICHIGAN

501 U.S. 957, 111 S.Ct. 2680, 115 L.Ed. 2d 836 (1991)

■ Harmelin was convicted of possessing 672 grams of cocaine and was sentenced to a mandatory term of life imprisonment without possibility of parole pursuant to a Michigan statute requiring such sentences for persons convicted of possessing more than 650 grams of cocaine. The severe mandatory punishment even applied to first-time offenders. Harmelin claimed that his sentence was cruel and unusual because it was disproportionate to the crime and because the mandatory sentence did not permit the judge to take into account the particularized circumstances of the crime.

The case is important because it illustrates the competing arguments among justices on the Rehnquist Court concerning the proportionality requirement of the Eighth Amendment. As you read the case, consider the following questions: (1) What is Justice Scalia's position on the Eighth Amendment's proportionality requirement? (2) Is Scalia's opinion creating a new precedent? (3) Which justice presents the most accurate view of the Eighth Amendment's meaning?

VOTE:

5 justices found the law constitutional (Kennedy, O'Connor, Rehnquist, Scalia, Souter).

4 justices found the law unconstitutional (Blackmun, Marshall, Stevens, White).

Justice Scalia announced the judgment of the Court and delivered the opinion of the Court with respect to Part V, and an opinion with respect to Parts I, II, III, and IV, in which Chief Justice Rehnquist joins.

I

* * *

. . . *Solem v. Helm*, 463 U.S. 277 . . . (1983), set aside under the Eighth Amendment, because it was disproportionate, a sentence of life imprisonment without possibility of parole, imposed under a South Dakota recidivist statute for successive offenses that included three convictions of third-degree burglary, one of obtaining money by false pretenses, one of grand larceny, one of third-offense driving while

intoxicated, and one of writing a "no account" check with intent to defraud. . . .

. . . [O]ur 5–4 decision eight years ago in *Solem* was scarcely the expression of clear and well accepted constitutional law. We have long recognized, of course, that the doctrine of *stare decisis* is less rigid in its application to constitutional precedents . . ., and we think that to be especially true of a constitutional precedent that is both recent and in apparent tension with other decisions. Accordingly, we have addressed anew, and in greater detail, the question whether the Eighth Amendment contains a proportionality guarantee. . . . We conclude from this examination that *Solem* was wrong; the Eighth Amendment contains no proportionality guarantee.

* * *

In sum, we think it most unlikely that the English Cruel and Unusual Punishment Clause [which served as the foundation for the Clause incorporated into the American Bill of Rights,] was meant to forbid "disproportionate" punishments. There is even less likelihood that proportionality of punishment was one of the traditional "rights and privileges of Englishmen" apart from the Declaration of Rights which happened to be included in the Eighth Amendment. Indeed, even those scholars who believe the [proportionality] principle to have been included within the Declaration of Rights do not contend that such a prohibition was reflected in English practice—nor could they. . . . [I]n 1791, England punished over 200 crimes with death. . . .

* * *

The Eighth Amendment received little attention during the proposal and adoption of the Federal Bill of Rights. However, what evidence exists from debates at the state ratifying conventions that prompted the Bill of Rights as well as the Floor debates in the First Congress which proposed it "confirm[s] the view that the cruel and unusual punishments clause was directed at prohibiting certain *methods* of punishment." * * *

* * *

We think it is enough that those who framed and approved the Federal Constitution chose, for whatever reason, not to include within it the guarantee against disproportionate sentences that some State Constitutions contained. It is worth noting, however, that there was good reason for that choice—a reason that reinforces the necessity of overruling *Solem*. While there are relatively clear historical guidelines and accepted practices that enable judges to determine which *modes* of punishment are "cruel and unusual," *proportionality* does not lend itself to such analysis. Neither Congress nor any state legislature has ever set out with the objective of crafting a penalty that is "disproportionate," yet as some of the examples . . . indicate, many enacted dispositions seem to be [disproportionate]—because they were made for other times or other places, with different social attitudes, different criminal epidemics, different public fears, and different prevailing theories of penology. This is not to say that there are no absolutes; one can imagine extreme examples that no rational person, in no time or place, could accept. But for the same reason these examples are easy to decide, they are certain never to occur. . . .

* * *

The first holding of this Court unqualifiedly applying a requirement of proportionality to criminal penalties was issued 185 years after the Eighth Amendment was adopted. In *Coker v. Georgia* [1977], the Court held that, because of the disproportionality, it was a violation of the Cruel and Unusual Punishments Clause to impose capital punishment for rape of an adult woman. Four years later, in *Enmund v. Florida* . . . (1982), we held that it violates the Eighth Amendment, because of disproportionality, to impose the death penalty upon a participant in a felony that results in murder, without any inquiry into the participant's intent to kill. *Rummel* . . . treated this line of authority as an aspect of our death penalty jurisprudence, rather than a generalizable aspect of Eighth Amendment law. We think that is an accurate explanation, and we reassert it. Proportionality review is one of several respects on which we have held that "death is different," and have imposed protections that the Constitution nowhere else provides. . . . We would leave it there, but will not extend it further.

V

. . . [Petitioner] apparently contends that the Eighth Amendment requires Michigan to create a sentencing scheme whereby life in prison without possibility of parole is simply the most severe of a range of available penalties that the sentencer may impose after hearing evidence in mitigation and aggravation.

As our earlier discussion should make clear, this claim has no support in the text and history of the Eighth Amendment. Severe, mandatory penalties may be cruel, but they are not unusual in the constitutional sense, having been employed in various forms throughout our Nation's history. As noted earlier, mandatory death sentences abounded in our first Penal Code. They were also common in the several States—both at the time of the founding and throughout the 19th century. . . . There can be no serious contention, then, that a sentence which is not otherwise cruel and unusual becomes so simply because it is "mandatory."* * *

* * *

Our cases creating and clarifying the "individualized capital sentencing doctrine" have repeatedly suggested that there is no comparable requirement outside the capital context, because of the qualitative difference between death and all other penalties. . . .

Justice Kennedy, with whom Justice O'Connor and Justice Souter join, concurring in part and concurring in the judgment.

. . . Regardless of whether Justice SCALIA or the dissent has the best of the historical argument . . . , *stare decisis* counsels our adherence to the narrow proportionality principle that has existed in our Eighth Amendment jurisprudence for 80 years. Although our proportionality decisions have not been clear or consistent in all respects, they can be reconciled, and they require us to uphold petitioner's sentence.

Our decisions recognize that the Cruel and Unusual Punishments Clause encompasses a narrow proportionality principle. We first interpreted the Eighth Amendment to prohibit " 'greatly disproportioned' " sentences in *Weems v. United States* . . . (1910), quoting *O'Neil v. Vermont* . . . (1892), (Field, J., dissenting). Since *Weems*, we have applied the principle in different Eighth Amendment contexts. Its most extensive application has been in death penalty cases. . . .

The Eighth Amendment proportionality principle also applies to noncapital sentences. In *Rummel v. Estelle* . . . (1980), we acknowledged the existence of the proportionality rule for both capital and noncapital cases, . . . but we refused to strike down a sentence of life imprisonment, with possibility of parole, for recidivism based on three underlying felonies. . . .

* * *

All of [the relevant] principles—the primacy of the legislature, the variety of legitimate penological schemes, the nature of our federal system, and the requirement that proportionality review be guided by objective factors—inform the final one: the Eighth Amendment does not require strict proportionality between crime and sentence. Rather, it forbids only extreme sentences that are "grossly disproportionate" to the crime. . . .

* * *

A penalty as severe and unforgiving as the one imposed here would make this a most difficult and troubling case for any judicial officer. Reasonable minds may differ about the efficacy of Michigan's sentencing scheme, and it is far from certain that Michigan's bold experiment [in applying harsh sentences] will succeed [in reducing drug trafficking]. The accounts of pickpockets at Tyburn hangings [in England] are a reminder of the limits of the law's deterrent force, but we cannot say the law before us has no chance of success and is on that account so disproportionate as to be cruel and unusual punishment. The dangers flowing from drug offenses and the circumstances of the crime committed here demonstrate that the Michigan penalty does not surpass constitutional bounds. . . .

Justice White, with whom Justice Blackmun and Justice Stevens join, dissenting.

* * *

The language of the [Eighth] Amendment does not refer to proportionality in so many words, but it does forbid "excessive" fines, a restraint that suggests that a determination of excessiveness should be based at least in part on whether the fine imposed is disproportionate to the crime committed. Nor would it be unreasonable to conclude that it would be both cruel and unusual to punish overtime parking by life imprisonment . . . , or, more generally, to impose any punishment that is grossly disproportionate to the offense for which the defendant has been convicted. . . .

* * *

. . . Justice SCALIA argues that all of the available evidence of the day indicated that those who drafted and approved the Amendment "chose . . . not to include within it the guarantee against disproportionate sentences that some State Constitutions contained." . . . Even if one were to accept the argument that the First Congress did not have in mind the proportionality issue, the evidence would hardly be strong enough to come close to proving an affirmative decision against the proportionality component. Had there been an intention to exclude it from the reach of the words that otherwise could reasonably be construed to include it, perhaps as plain-speaking Americans, the Members of the First Congress would have said so. And who can say with confidence what the members of the state ratifying conventions had in mind when they voted in favor of the Amendment? * * *

* * *

. . . The Court's capital punishment cases requiring proportionality reject Justice SCALIA's notion that the Amendment bars only cruel and unusual modes or methods of punishment. Under that view, capital punishment—a mode of punishment—would either be completely barred or left to the discretion of the legislature. Yet neither is true. The death penalty is appropriate in some cases and not in others. The same should be true of punishment by imprisonment.

* * *

[C]ontrary to Justice SCALIA's suggestion, . . . the fact that a punishment has been legislatively mandated does not automatically render it "legal" or "usual" in the constitutional sense. Indeed, . . . if this were the case, then the prohibition against cruel and unusual punishments would be devoid of any meaning. . . .

* * *

The first *Solem* factor requires a reviewing court to assess the gravity of the penalty. . . .

* * *

Mere possession of drugs—even in such large quantity—is not so serious an offense that it will always warrant, much less mandate, life imprisonment without possibility of parole. . . .

* * *

The second prong of the *Solem* analysis is an examination of "the sentences imposed on other criminals in the same jurisdiction." . . . [T]here is no death penalty in Michigan; consequently, life without parole, the punishment mandated here, is the harshest punishment available. . . . Crimes directed against the persons and property of others—such as second-degree murder, . . . rape, . . . and armed robbery, . . . do not carry such a harsh mandatory sentence, although they do provide for the possibility of a life sentence in the exercise of judicial discretion. It is clear that petitioner "has been treated in the same manner as, or more severely than, criminals who have committed far more serious crimes."* * *

The third factor set forth in *Solem* examines "the sentences imposed for commission of the same crime in other jurisdictions." . . . No other jurisdiction imposes a punishment nearly as severe as Michigan's for possession of the amount of drugs at issue here. Of the remaining 49 States, only Alabama provides for a mandatory sentence of life imprisonment without possibility of parole for a first-time drug offender, and then only when a defendant possesses *ten kilograms* or more of cocaine. . . . Possession of the amount at issue here would subject an Alabama defendant to a mandatory minimum sentence of only five years in prison. . . .

Application of *Solem's* proportionality analysis leaves no doubt that the Michigan statute at issue fails constitutional muster. The statutorily mandated penalty of life without possibility of parole for possession of narcotics is unconstitutionally disproportionate in that it violates the Eighth Amendment's prohibition against cruel and unusual punishment. . . .

[The separate dissenting opinions of Justice Marshall and Justice Stevens are omitted.]

After Justice Thomas replaced Justice Marshall in 1991, the Court decided three Eighth Amendment noncapital cases during Thomas's first two terms (1991–92 and 1992–93). Despite the Court's apparent dominance by conservative justices appointed by Presidents Reagan and Bush, all three cases were decided in favor of the individual claimants.

In *Hudson v. McMillian* (1992), two corrections officers placed handcuffs on a prisoner's wrists and shackles on his legs and then beat him while he was held in restraints: "McMillian punched Hudson in the mouth, eyes, chest, and stomach, while Woods held the inmate in place and kicked and punched him from behind. He further testified that Mezo, the [corrections] supervisor on duty, watched the beating but merely told the officers 'not to have too much fun' " (503 U.S. at 4). Because Hudson's beating produced only bruises, bleeding, loose teeth, and a cracked partial dental plate, the Court of Appeals rejected his civil rights lawsuit for damages by concluding that the injuries were merely "minor." According to the appellate court, Hudson would have to demonstrate "significant injury" in order to proceed with a lawsuit alleging violations of his Eighth Amendment rights.

In a 7–2 decision, Justice O'Connor's majority opinion overruled the appellate court's "significant injury" requirement and held that Eighth Amendment cases concerning physical force require courts to ask "whether force was applied in a good-faith effort to maintain or restore discipline, or [applied] maliciously and sadistically to cause harm" (503 U.S. at 7). The majority opinion also sought to reaffirm an objective test for physical force cases that makes such cases distinguishable from the conditions of confinement case at issue in *Wilson v. Seiter*. Thus O'Connor declared that the test for excessive force did not rest solely on the subjective intentions of corrections officers. Instead, judges could apply the Burger Court's Eighth Amendment standard of examining physical punishments to see if they comport with evolving standards of decency and avoid the unnecessary and wanton infliction of pain.

The two dissenters, Thomas and Scalia, accused their colleagues, including their usual allies Rehnquist, O'Connor, and Kennedy, of using judicial power to interfere with legislative and executive authority over correctional institutions:

> *Today's expansion of the Cruel and Unusual Punishment Clause beyond all bounds of history and precedent is, I suspect, yet another manifestation of the pervasive view that the Federal Constitution must address all ills in our society. Abusive behavior by prison guards is deplorable conduct that properly evokes outrage and contempt. But that does not mean that it is invariably unconstitutional. The Eighth Amendment is not, and should not be turned into, a National Code of Prison Regulation. . . . . [P]rimary responsibility for preventing and punishing such conduct rests not with the Federal Constitution but with the laws and regulations of the various states* (503 U.S. at 28).

The following year, the Court divided in an identical manner in a 7–2 decision that endorsed a nonsmoking prisoner's right to pursue an Eighth Amendment claim when he was placed in a cell with another inmate who smoked five packs of cigarettes each day (*Helling v. McKinney*, 1993). Justice White's majority opinion applied Scalia's subjective standard from *Wilson v. Seiter* to find that a prisoner could allege the existence of cruel and unusual punishment if he or she could show that corrections officials were deliberately indifferent to the exposure of the prisoner to potentially harmful levels of environmental tobacco smoke. A subsequent decision reinforced this point in the case of a transsexual prisoner who was assaulted after he was placed in the general population of a maximum security institution. The prisoner claimed that the prison officials were deliberately indifferent to his risk of injury (*Farmer v. Brennan*, 1994). The dissenters in *Helling v. McKinney*, Thomas and Scalia, reiterated their call for a "significant injury" requirement for Eighth Amendment cases and objected strongly to the Court's recognition of the *risk* of injury as a basis for an Eighth Amendment claim. Thomas's opinion, joined by Scalia, went even further by asserting that the Eighth Amendment should not apply at all to claims made by prisoners concerning conditions of confinement, excessive force, or other incarceration issues. According to the dissent, the Eighth Amendment should apply only to the sentencing decision itself (i.e., the judge's decision about the nature and duration of punishment) and not to the imposition of the punishment. Thomas and Scalia questioned the validity of the Burger Court's original prison case, *Estelle v. Gamble* (1976), and thereby issued a challenge to all of the Court's precedents concerning prisoners' Eighth Amendment rights.

In *Austin v. United States* (1993), the Court exhibited unusual unanimity in support of an individual's claim. The Court decided unanimously that the Eighth Amendment's Excessive Fines Clause applies to drug-related forfeitures of property imposed by the federal government. In another case decided the same day, the Court similarly declared that the Excessive Fines Clause of the Eighth Amendment applies to property forfeitures under the Racketeer Influenced and Corrupt Organizations Act (RICO) (*Alexander v. United States*, 1993). These cases call into the question the accuracy of classifying certain cases as "liberal" or "conservative" based on whether the justices support the individual or the government. In these cases, the government's actions impinged upon a right that is strongly supported by political conservatives, the right to hold and control private property. Thus, these cases presented an unusual situation in which the government's strongest supporters, Justice Thomas, Scalia, and Rehnquist, placed a higher value on the right in question (i.e., the right to private property) than on their normal support for the government's criminal justice policies and practices. As indicated by these cases, some issues strike the justices differently than other issues and thereby create unusual majority coalitions that seldom exist in other criminal justice cases.

Conclusion

The Rehnquist Court has moved in a conservative direction with respect to the Eighth Amendment and capital punishment. During the Rehnquist Court era, the justices were frequently deeply divided when considering such issues, and thus nearly equal numbers of decisions supported individuals and government. This apparent equality in the numbers of liberal and conservative decisions is deceptive, however, because it overstates the Court's support for individuals. As we see in Table 12.5, all of the Court's major decisions reinforced conservative precedents or moved constitutional principles in a conservative direction. There were no major decisions that favored an expansion of constitutional rights or supported claims by individuals. Moreover, the conservative nature of the Court's overall trend is especially apparent when one remembers that two of the Court's liberal decisions, *Booth v. Maryland* (1987) and *South Carolina v. Gathers* (1989), were reversed in 1991 by the decision in *Payne v. Tennessee* and therefore had no lasting impact.

With one exception (*Harmelin v. Michigan,* 1991), the Court's uniformly conservative major decisions concerned capital punishment. Although these decisions, along with the procedural habeas corpus decisions mentioned in this chapter, broadened and expedited the application of capital punishment, the Court also made decisions that broadened constitutional protections in noncapital cases. The Court expanded Eighth Amendment protections for individuals in cases concerning excessive fines, physical force applied to prisoners, and environmental health risks in correctional institutions.

It is difficult to predict the Court's doctrinal trends with respect to criminal punishment because future decisions are likely to be shaped by as-yet-unknown changes in the Court's composition. The addition of Justice Ruth Bader Ginsburg in place of Justice White in 1993 should not dramatically alter Eighth Amendment jurisprudence, but it is likely to provide a new vote favoring individuals' claims in many of the Court's closely divided decisions. Justice Harry Blackmun's 1994 announcement that he would oppose the imposition of the death penalty in all future capital cases created the opportunity for more debates about Eighth Amendment issues in justices' opinions (Kaplan 1994). However, the crystallization of his views in opposition to capital punishment had no discernible impact on case outcomes. Blackmun retired shortly thereafter and was replaced by Justice Stephen Breyer, a Clinton appointee. Although Breyer is more liberal than most of his colleagues, his presence on the Court has not altered the numerical dominance of conservative justices whose decisions have supported the maintenance and expansion of capital punishment.

REFERENCES

Abraham, Henry J. *Freedom and the Court*. 5th ed.New York: Oxford University Press, 1988.

Baldus, David C., George Woodworth, and Charles A. Pulaski, Jr. *Equal Justice and the Death Penalty.* Boston: Northeastern University Press, 1990.

Berkson, Larry Charles. *The Concept of Cruel and Unusual Punishment*. Lexington, Mass.: Lexington Books, 1975.

Cole, George F. *The American System of Criminal Justice*, 6th ed. Pacific Grove, Calif.: Brooks/Cole, 1992.

Epstein, Lee, and Joseph F. Kobylka. *The Supreme Court and Legal Change: Abortion and the Death Penalty*. Chapel Hill, N.C.: University of North Carolina Press, 1992.

Hoffmann, Joseph L. "Is Innocence Enough? An Essay on the U.S. Supreme Court's Continuing Problems with Federal Habeas Corpus and the Death Penalty." *Indiana Law Journal* 68 (1993): 817-34.

Kaplan, David A. "Death Be Not Proud at the Court." *Newsweek*, 17 March, 1994: 52.

_________. "Anger and Ambivalence." *Newsweek*, 7 August, 1995: 24-29.

Labaton, David. "U.S. Judges Can Delay Executions to Allow Habeas Reviews, Justices Rule." *New York Times*. 1 July 1994: A9.

Scalia, Antonin. "Originalism: The Lesser Evil." *Cincinnati Law Review* 57 (1989): 849-65.

Smith, Christopher E. *Courts and Public Policy*. Chicago: Nelson-Hall, 1993.

_________. *Politics in Constitutional Law: Cases and Questions*. Chicago: Nelson-Hall, 1992.

Smith, Christopher E. and Scott P. Johnson. "Newcomer on the High Court: Justice Souter and the Supreme Court's 1990 Term." *South Dakota Law Review* 37 (1992): 21-43.

Stevens, Leonard A. *Death Penalty: The Case of Life vs. Death in the United States.* New York: Cowan, McCann & Geoghegan, 1978.

White, Welsh S. *The Death Penalty in the Nineties*. Ann Arbor, Mich.: University of Michigan Press, 1991.

Equal Protection and Privacy: *Introduction, Overview, and Doctrinal Framework*

Introduction to Equal Protection

The Equal Protection Clause of the Fourteenth Amendment declares that "*No state shall . . . deny to any person within its jurisdiction the equal protection of the laws.*" The precise meaning of this phrase has evoked considerable controversy and different interpretations since its ratification in 1868.

The Background of the Equal Protection Clause

The Equal Protection Clause is a central provision of the Fourteenth Amendment, one of three amendments often referred to collectively as the Civil War or Reconstruction Amendments. The Thirteenth Amendment, ratified in 1865, abolished slavery "except as a punishment for crime," and the Fifteenth Amendment, ratified in 1870, prohibited states from denying the right to vote based upon race. The Fourteenth Amendment, ratified in 1868, was the most extensive of the three. It guaranteed the rights of citizenship to African Americans, particularly the newly freed slaves. In addition, the Fourteenth contained three major provisions: 1) the Privileges and Immunities Clause; 2) the Due Process Clause; and 3) the Equal Protection Clause. There has been considerable controversy over whether these provisions, particularly the Equal Protection Clause, were meant to apply only to African Americans, or whether the framers intended them to apply more broadly, to protect the rights of all persons in the United States. The Court originally adopted a narrow interpretation of equal protection in *The Slaughter–House Cases* (1873), when it ruled that "the one pervading purpose" of the Reconstruction Amendments was to secure the "freedom of the slave race" (16 Wall. at 71). Despite this language, it took about seventy-five years before the Equal Protection Clause was actually interpreted to protect the rights of African Americans. The Court's decisions in *The Civil Rights Cases* (1883) and *Plessy v. Ferguson* (1896) (discussed more fully in Chapter 13) permitted racial discrimination in public accommodations and ensured that African Americans would remain second-class citizens. More specifically, ***Plessy's* "separate but equal" doctrine, which sanctioned de jure segregation (by law), was not overturned until 1954 in the famous** *Brown v. Board of Education* decision.

Over time, however, the broader view of the Equal Protection Clause has prevailed. That is, the clause is not limited to protecting individuals from racial discrimination. It has been construed by the Court also to limit gender discrimination, as well as discrimination on the basis of alienage and illegitimacy. In addition, the high court has held that deprivations of certain "fundamental rights" constitute violations of the Equal Protection Clause.

Doctrines, Tests, and Standards in Equal Protection Analysis

Laws or government policies by their nature create classifications of people and actions, so the question for the Court becomes whether certain classifications are permissible or prohibited. To answer this question, the justices have employed several standards or tests. The accompanying table contains a doctrinal framework for the Court's equal protection analysis.

The traditional doctrine, the **rational basis test** was summarized by the Court as follows:

> *The equal protection clause of the Fourteenth Amendment does not take from the State the power to classify in the adoption of police laws, but admits of the exercise of a wide scope of discretion in that regard, and avoids what is done only when it is without any reasonable basis, and therefore is purely arbitrary.*
>
> *A classification having some reasonable basis does not offend against the clause merely because it is not made with mathematical nicety, or because in practice it results in some inequality.*
>
> *When the classification in such a law is called in question, if any state of facts reasonably can be conceived that would sustain it, the existence of that state of facts at the time the law was enacted must be assumed.*
>
> *One who assails the classification in such a law must carry the burden of showing that it does not rest upon any reasonable basis, but is essentially arbitrary. (Lindsley v. Natural Carbonic Gas Co.*, 220 U.S. at 78–79, 1911).

Doctrinal Framework for Equal Protection Analysis

	Test			
	Rational Basis	**Important Government Objective**	**Fundamental Rights**	**Suspect Classification**
Type of Issues/Cases	cases not falling under any of the other 3 tests, e.g., • alienage (some matters of public employment) • age • economic & social classifications	• gender • illegitimacy • alienage (public education)	violation of recognized implicit right: • Marriage & procreation • interstate travel • right to vote • access to justice	• race • alienage • affirmative action programs
Questions	1. Is there a legitimate government interest? 2. Are the means rationally related to the interest?	1. Is there an important governmental objective? 2. Is the classification substantially related to the achievement of the objective?	1. Is there a compelling state interest? 2. Are the means absolutely necessary or narrowly tailored to achieve that interest?	1. Is there a compelling state interest? 2. Are the means absolutely necessary or narrowly tailored to achieve that interest?
Burden of Proof	on individuals	on government	on government	on government
Level of Scrutiny	minimal	intermediate	strict	strict

With this test, the Court first asks whether there is a legitimate government interest. If so, the state must demonstrate that the classification is rationally related to that interest. Under the rational basis test, therefore, the Court provides only **minimal scrutiny** of the classification, requiring simply that the policy or classification being challenged is reasonable and not arbitrary or capricious. Moreover, because the Court defers to the judgments of policymakers, a classification examined under the rational basis test is normally upheld. For example, in *San Antonio v. Rodriguez* (1973) a narrow majority upheld a state's property tax system of school financing as a rational method of promoting local control of public education. "While assuring a basic education for every child in the State, it permits and encourages a large measure of participation in and control of each district's schools at the local level" (411 U.S. at 49).

In *Korematsu v. United States* (1944), the Court adopted a more stringent test for examining equal protection claims. The justices ruled that there are **suspect classifications,** specifically regarding race, which require a higher level of scrutiny by the Court. "[A]ll legal restrictions which curtail the civil rights of a single racial group are immediately suspect. That is not to say that all such restrictions are unconstitutional. It is to say that courts must subject them to the most rigid scrutiny. Pressing public necessity may sometimes justify the existence of such restrictions; racial antagonism never can" (323 U.S. at 216). The Court also declared alienage a suspect classification in *Graham v. Richardson* (1971). Subsequently, the Court explained that in order to fall into the suspect category, the class must possess "an immutable characteristic determined solely by the accident of birth," and it must have been "saddled with such disabilities, or subjected to such a history of purposeful unequal treatment, or relegated to such political powerlessness as to command extraordinary protection from the majoritarian political process" (*Johnson v. Robinson,* 415 U.S. at 375, n. 14). When a classification affects a suspect class, the government must first demonstrate a compelling interest for the classification. In addition, it must show that the classification is absolutely necessary or is narrowly tailored to achieve that interest. Consequently, classifications examined under this **strict scrutiny** approach are more likely to be declared unconstitutional.

Given the similarities between racial and gender discrimination, many people hoped that the Court would place gender in the suspect category. In *Frontiero v. Richardson* (1973), however, only four justices were willing to accord gender-based classifications the same level of scrutiny applied to classifications based on race or alienage. Writing for the plurality, Justice Brennan likened the history of discrimination against women to that against African Americans. He continued, "[S]ince sex, like race and national origin, is an immutable characteristic determined solely by the accident of birth, the imposition of special disabilities upon the members of a particular sex because of their sex would seem to violate 'the basic concept of our system that legal burdens should bear some relationship to individual responsibility . . .' " (411 U.S. at 686). Thus, Brennan concluded, "classifications based upon sex, like classifications based upon race, alienage, or national origin, are inherently suspect, and must therefore be subjected to strict judicial scrutiny" (411 U.S. at 688). Because his opinion did not command a majority, questions remained about whether lower courts were obligated to apply strict scrutiny to gender discrimination cases.

Three years after *Frontiero,* however, the Court adopted a new standard for examining gender-based classifications—the **important government objective test.** In *Craig v. Boren* (1976) the majority held that "classifications by gender must serve important governmental objectives and must be substantially related to the achievement of those objectives" (429 U.S. at 197). Under this **intermediate**

scrutiny approach, the burden of proof falls on the government to justify its gender distinctions. As the table illustrates, the important government objective test, which involves intermediate scrutiny, has been applied to classifications on the basis of illegitimacy (e.g., *Trimble v. Gordon,* 1977 and *Clark v. Jeter,* 1988) as well as to some claims involving discrimination against noncitizens (e.g., *Plyler v. Doe,* 1982).

Finally, the strict scrutiny approach has been applied in one additional area—to cases involving claims of violations of **fundamental rights.** As the table indicates, when a case involves an alleged infringement of four categories of implicit constitutional rights—marriage and procreation, interstate travel, the right to vote, and access to justice—the burden falls on the state to demonstrate that the classification employed is necessary or is narrowly tailored to achieve a compelling interest.

The Constitutional Right of Privacy

Neither the Constitution nor its amendments refer explicitly to a right of privacy. Some argue that such a right is implicitly contained in the Fourth Amendment protection against unreasonable searches and seizures. It reads, "The right of the people to be secure in their persons, houses, papers, and effects against unreasonable searches and seizures, shall not be violated." Because the Fourth Amendment is concerned primarily with criminal law, this provision has not been viewed as having broad application beyond the criminal arena. Privacy concerns were implicated in noncriminal rights cases in the 1920s, 1930s, and 1940s, but the Court did not establish an independent right of privacy until 1965. In that year, in *Griswold v. Connecticut,* the Court held that the right of privacy stemmed from the combination of various provisions of the Bill of Rights. Justice Douglas wrote, "[S]pecific guarantees in the Bill of Rights have penumbras, formed by emanations from those guarantees that help give them life and substance. Various guarantees create zones of privacy" (381 U.S. at 484). This right of privacy has primarily involved matters of reproductive freedom, specifically the use of contraceptives (*Griswold*) and abortion (*Roe v. Wade* and its progeny).

Although the right of privacy does not fall under equal protection, the Court's treatment of privacy is similar to its equal protection analysis, specifically the fundamental rights approach. Because privacy is an implicit right, government policies restricting it generally are examined using strict scrutiny (the compelling interest test). On occasion, however, the Court has used minimal scrutiny—the rational basis test—to determine the constitutionality of laws or regulations that allegedly restricted the right of privacy (e.g., *Kelley v. Johnson,* 1976 and *Bowers v. Hardwick,* 1986).

Organization of This Section

Chapters 13 and 14 discuss the Court's treatment of racial and gender discrimination, respectively. Chapter 15 examines the Court's treatment of the complex and controversial issue of affirmative action, while Chapter 16 focuses on equal protection cases that do not involve racial or gender discrimination claims. Chapter 17 examines the right of privacy, particularly the vexing issue of abortion.

CHAPTER

13

EQUAL PROTECTION AND RACE

CASE STUDY

CASE STUDY: LOVING V. VIRGINIA (1967)

In the early hours of the morning in mid-July of 1958, Richard and Mildred Loving were dragged from their beds by County Sheriff Garnett Brooks. The Lovings' were being arrested for violating Virginia's antimiscegenation statutes. Virginia was not the only state to have such laws. At the time of the Loving's arrest, fifteen other states had laws prohibiting interracial marriage—Alabama, Arkansas, Delaware, Florida, Georgia, Kentucky, Louisiana, Mississippi, Missouri, North Carolina, Oklahoma, South Carolina, Tennessee, Texas, and West Virginia. Fifteen nonsouthern and border states had only recently repealed their laws: Arizona, California, Colorado, Idaho, Indiana, Maryland, Michigan, Montana, Nebraska, Nevada, North Dakota, Oregon, South Dakota, Utah, and Wyoming. The Lovings' decision to challenge the constitutionality of the antimiscegenation statutes led to a landmark Supreme Court decision striking down the last of the "Jim Crow" laws.

Richard Loving and Mildred Jeter, white and African American, respectively, grew up in Caroline County, a rural area in Virginia, north of the state capital of Richmond. Loving and Jeter knew each other as children and later began dating. After a long courtship, they decided to get married, although they knew that this was forbidden by Virginia law. The legal prohibition against interracial marriage went back to 1691, and the original statutes were revised in 1924 by amendments entitled "A Bill to Preserve the Integrity of the White Race." The laws made it a felony for "white persons to intermarry with colored persons" and vice versa and subjected violators of the law to a prison term of up to five years. In addition, the person who performed the marriage ceremony, if discovered by the authorities, would be subject to a two hundred dollar fine. The informer would receive one-half of the fine for providing the incriminating information (Sickels 1972; Ginger 1974; and Irons and Guitton, 1993).

Because of the Virginia laws, Loving and Jeter traveled to Washington, D.C., where they were married on June 2, 1958. After a brief honeymoon, the Lovings returned to Virginia. About six weeks later, their troubles with the legal authorities began. After their arrest by Sheriff Brooks, they appeared before a justice of the peace, where they pled not guilty to the charge of violating the antimiscegenation statutes. The justice of the peace determined that there was probable cause for charging the Lovings with this felony and ordered them to appear before the grand jury. A couple of months later, the grand jury indicted them, and they were presented for trial before Judge Leon Bazile in Caroline County court. At this point, the Lovings decided to waive their right to a jury trial. The facts very clearly indicated that they had violated the statutes, and they hoped that a single judge would be more sympathetic in dealing with them. After each side presented its arguments, the Lovings changed their original pleas to guilty. Their strategy was somewhat successful. On January 6, 1959, Judge Bazile sentenced them each to a jail sentence of one year, rather than five, and, in addition, he suspended the sentence upon their willingness to meet certain conditions. Unfortunately, the conditions were that they leave the state and not return to it together or at the same time for twenty-five years. With no better alternatives, the Lovings accepted Judge Bazile's sentence and returned to Washington, D.C., to live (Sickels 1972).

The Lovings remained in Washington for about four years but were not very happy living there. In the summer of 1963, they and their three children returned to Virginia to visit relatives and friends. After being arrested again and let out on bail, Richard Loving sought assistance from higher government officials. He wrote a letter to U.S. Attorney General Robert Kennedy explaining his family's predicament and pleading for Kennedy's assistance. Believing that he could do nothing to help the Lovings, Kennedy sent the letter to the local chapter of the American Civil Liberties Union (ACLU), knowing that the public interest organization often took cases such as this. This proved to be a critical decision, because the ACLU appointed two Virginia attorneys, Bernard Cohen and Philip Hirschkop, to assist the Lovings in challenging the antimiscegenation statutes (Sickels 1972; Ginger 1974).

Cohen and Hirschkop decided to pursue a dual strategy by challenging the laws in both state and federal courts. On November 6, 1963, they filed a motion in state court to vacate Judge Bazile's decision and set aside the sentence he imposed on the Lovings (Ginger 1974). They alleged that the antimiscegenation statutes violated the Equal Protection Clause and unlawfully burdened interstate commerce. They alleged further that the sentence was cruel and unusual and that it violated the Due Process Clause. Judge Bazile did not act on this motion for over a year. He finally denied it on December 22, 1965, rejecting all of the arguments put forth by the ACLU attorneys. He said that the Lovings' sentence was not cruel and unusual, pointing to such punishments as burning at the stake, drawing and quartering, and crucifixion as more horrendous. Interstate commerce was not implicated, according to Bazile, because marriage is a purely domestic matter, and if the federal government can regulate it, it might move to regulate all sorts of things within the proper purview of state and local governments (Sickels 1972). Finally, Bazile concluded that interracial marriages violated the laws of God.

During the delay in obtaining a ruling from Bazile, Cohen and Hirschkop filed a class action suit on behalf of the Lovings in federal district court in late October of 1964. A three-judge panel was called to determine the constitutionality of the antimiscegenation statutes, and arguments were heard on December 28, 1964. On February 11, 1965, the panel refused to rule on the statutes, pending resolution of the issue in state courts. The panel did agree, however, to free the Lovings on bail if they were arrested or imprisoned while the court proceedings continued (Sickels 1972).

Following Judge Bazile's adverse ruling, Cohen and Hirschkop appealed to the Virginia Supreme Court of Appeals, arguing that the statutes clearly violated the Equal Protection and Due Process Clauses of the Fourteenth Amendment and that the sentence imposed on the Lovings deprived them of due process of law. The Virginia Supreme Court upheld the antimiscegenation laws, relying on its own precedent of *Naim v. Naim* (1955). In *Naim*, the court had upheld the state's laws against interracial marriage, and the U.S. Supreme Court had refused to hear an appeal. In *Loving*, however, the state supreme court did find the sentence imposed by Judge Bazile to be unreasonable. It said that the Lovings' marriage could have been forbidden without banishing them from Virginia; they could simply have been prohibited from cohabitation within the state (Sickels 1972).

Although the state supreme court modified the Lovings' original sentence, the ruling obviously was still unsatisfactory to the Lovings and their attorneys because the antimiscegenation laws were sustained. Therefore, the ACLU attorneys filed an appeal to the U.S. Supreme Court on May 31, 1966, and the Court noted jurisdiction on December 12 of that year. By this time, the case had attracted national attention, and the Court received several amicus briefs, most on behalf of the Lovings. Urging the Court to strike down the laws were the National Association for the Advancement of Colored People (NAACP) and its Legal Defense and Educational Fund, several Catholic organizations (in a joint brief), and the Japanese American Citizens League. The latter was also permitted to present oral arguments before the Court as amicus curiae. The only brief filed on behalf of the state of Virginia was from another southern state, North Carolina.

The Court heard oral arguments in the case on April 10, 1967. Attorneys Cohen and Hirschkop represented the Lovings; R. D. McIlwaine, the assistant attorney general, presented arguments for the state of Virginia; and William Marutani argued on behalf of the Japanese American Citizens League. Cohen and Hirschkop presented the Lovings' case first. Discussing the history of the Virginia antimiscegenation statutes and especially the revisions in 1924, Hirschkop noted that the laws were encouraged by such racist groups as the Ku Klux Klan, and he compared the laws requiring racial classification and forbidding interracial marriages to practices from Nazi Germany and South Africa. He went on to say that the state was determined to keep African Americans in their place and that the antimiscegenation statutes were the "most odious laws to come before the Court" (Irons and Guitton p. 280). In his arguments, Marutani focused on the possible application of the Virginia laws to marriages between Japanese persons and whites. He contended that the terms used in the statutes—"of pure white race," "white person," and "colored person"—were vague and could be applied by judges, juries, and law enforcement officials to all types of interracial marriages, not just to those between whites and African Americans.

McIlwaine first responded to Marutani's contentions, declaring that the terms used in the statutes were not vague. He claimed that the statutes clearly were meant to apply to marriages between African Americans and whites, given that these two groups "constitute[d] more than ninety-nine percent of the Virginia population" (Irons and Guitton p. 281). He then moved to his defense of the statutes in question. McIlwaine alleged that there was no violation of the Fourteenth Amendment because the history of that amendment demonstrated that it was not intended to interfere with the power of states to pass laws prohibiting interracial marriage. Even if the Fourteenth Amendment was applicable, however, McIlwaine continued, the state had a legitimate objective in prohibiting interracial marriages. The purpose was "preventing the sociological and psychological evils which attend interracial marriages," and he cited "scientific evidence" which he claimed illustrated that "intermarried families are subjected to much greater pressures and problems than are those of the intramarried" (Irons and Guitton p. 282). Furthermore, McIlwaine suggested that the prohibition on interracial marriage was no different from state laws against polygamous or incestuous marriages or from laws requiring minimum ages for marriage and those that prevent mentally incompetent people from being married.

Having heard oral arguments, the issue was left to the Court to decide. On June 12, 1967, ten days after the Lovings celebrated their ninth anniversary, the Court found the Virginia antimiscegenation laws in violation of both the Equal Protection and Due Process Clauses of the Fourteenth Amendment (case excerpt on p. 640). Writing for a unanimous Court, Chief Justice Warren rejected the state's contention that the Fourteenth Amendment was inapplicable to its antimiscegenation statutes. "The clear and central purpose of the Fourteenth Amendment was to eliminate all official state sources of invidious racial discrimination in the States" (388 U.S. at 10). After subjecting the statutes to strict scrutiny, Warren said there was no compelling justification for them, concluding that the state's only purpose was to maintain white supremacy. In addition, the justices held that the laws deprived the Lovings of liberty in violation of the Due Process Clause because the right to liberty includes the fundamental freedom to marry whom one chooses.

The decision made it possible for the Lovings (and other interracial couples) openly to acknowledge their marriage and love for each other without fear of prosecution. In a press conference following the announcement of the Court's ruling, Richard Loving proclaimed, "It feels so great . . . For the first time I can put my arm around her and publicly call her my wife" (Sickels pp. 1-2).

Historical Origins and Contemporary Conflicts

The controversy over interracial marriage is but one example of the problem of race in American society. Despite the lofty language in the Declaration of Independence declaring "All men are created equal," the United States was built on the principle of racial inequality, particularly with respect to African Americans. The language in the Constitution itself, as well as the history of the making of this document, reflects this fact (Jordan 1968; Berry 1971; Wiecek 1977; Nieman 1991; and Lively 1992). For example, in Article I, Section 2, a slave was characterized as three-fifths of a person for taxation and representation purposes, while Section 9 of that same article prohibited any congressional action to limit the slave trade until 1808. Also, the fugitive slave clause in Article IV required escaped slaves to be returned.

In 1857, the Supreme Court affirmed the inequality of Africans and their descendants in the landmark *Dred Scott v. Sandford* decision. Writing for the Court, Chief Justice Taney declared that people of African descent, whether slave or free, never were intended to be included as citizens of this country, that they were regarded as "beings of an inferior order," and that "they had no rights which the white man was bound to respect" (19 How. at 407). While this decision alone certainly did not cause the Civil War, most scholars believe that it was a major contributing factor. At the very least, the decision placed the Supreme Court of the United States on the side of pro-slavery forces at a moment in history when the American public was divided about the issue of slavery.

The legal status of African Americans did not change until the ratification of the Thirteenth Amendment after the Civil War. This amendment abolished slavery, "except as a punishment for crime," and authorized Congress to pass appropriate legislation to enforce it. President Lincoln earlier had issued the Emancipation Proclamation, but this document did not end slavery, because it only abolished slavery in the territory held at that time by the Confederacy. In reaction to the Thirteenth Amendment, southern states enacted laws to keep African Americans in the lowly status that they occupied prior to emancipation. These "**Black Codes,**" as they were known, "attempted to guarantee whites a cheap and tractable labor force and to compel African Americans to remain on plantations and farms where they would live and work under close supervision by whites" (Nieman 1991, p. 60). Various provisions of these Codes forbade African Americans from pursuing certain occupations; excluded them from jury service, public office, and voting; prevented them from living in certain areas; imposed harsher penalties on African Americans than on whites for comparable crimes; and subjected unemployed African Americans to vagrancy laws, which often resulted in their being sentenced to labor without compensation for a year at a time. "In sum," Lively noted, "the codes preserved slavery in fact after it had been abolished in theory" (1992, p. 43).

In order to counteract these measures, Congress passed the Civil Rights Act of 1866, which provided that "there shall be no discrimination in civil rights or immunities . . . on account of race . . . but the inhabitants of every race . . . shall have the same rights to make and enforce contracts, to sue, be parties, and give evidence, to inherit, purchase, lease, sell, hold, and convey real and personal property, and to full and equal benefit of all laws and proceedings for the security of persons and property, and shall be subject to like punishment" (Lively 1992, pp. 46–47).

Some members of Congress, however, were not satisfied that this act would secure legal rights and privileges for African Americans, so they pushed for passage of a constitutional amendment to do so. Thus the Fourteenth Amendment was ratified in 1868. Its most important provisions are sections 1 and 5. Section 1 reads, "All persons born or naturalized in the United States and subject to the jurisdiction thereof, are citizens of the United States and of the State wherein they reside. No State shall make or enforce any law which shall abridge the privileges or immunities of citizens of the United States; nor shall any State deprive any person of life, liberty, or property, without due process of law; nor deny to any person within its jurisdiction the equal protection of the laws." Section 5 empowers Congress to pass appropriate legislation to enforce these provisions. Disagreement remains over what the framers of the Fourteenth Amendment intended it to do, that is, how broad or narrow its reach was to be. Because the Thirteenth and Fourteenth Amendments and the Civil Rights Act of 1866 did not include voting rights, the Fifteenth Amendment was added in 1870. This amendment prohibited states from denying the right to vote based on race, but that right, for the most part, was frustrated by southern legislatures for nearly a century until Congress passed the Voting Rights Act of 1965. Through poll taxes, literacy tests, and the "white primary," southern states assured that most of their African American residents could not vote.

These three amendments, often referred to collectively as the Civil War or Reconstruction Amendments, have been subject to interpretation by the Supreme Court. The primary focus of this chapter is limited to the Equal Protection Clause of the Fourteenth Amendment as it relates to claims of racial discrimination. A number of important racial discrimination cases have involved the Thirteenth Amendment and the Due Process Clause of the Fourteenth Amendment, but the most significant cases have been concerned with the Equal Protection Clause. In addition, the Supreme Court has issued important decisions involving interpretations of civil rights statutes rather than the Equal Protection Clause, and these will be discussed where appropriate.

The cases have concerned such matters as racial segregation and discrimination in education, housing, and public accommodations; prohibitions against interracial marriage and cohabitation; and the right to a fair trial. The pre-Warren and Warren Courts heard cases regarding the constitutionality of segregation and discrimination, while cases heard by the Burger and Rehnquist Courts primarily have concerned the types and scope of remedies for discrimination.

One final note: the overwhelming majority of racial discrimination cases under the Equal Protection Clause involved African Americans, but a few decisions have resulted from people of Asian or Latin American ancestry bringing charges of discrimination. Significant cases involving these latter two groups also will be discussed.

Supreme Court Decision Making in Racial Discrimination Cases under the Equal Protection Clause

As we noted in the general introduction to this section, the traditional test or doctrine used to examine claims of unlawful discrimination under the Equal Protection Clause is the rational basis test. Under this standard, laws and government actions are presumed to be valid if they are rational, that is, not arbitrary or capricious. The burden is on the individual challenging the classification to prove that the law or government action is irrational.

In *Korematsu v. United States* (1944), the Court introduced a different and more stringent test for examining claims of racial discrimination. Justice Black wrote, "all legal restrictions which curtail the civil rights of a single racial group are immediately suspect. That is not to say that all such restrictions are unconstitutional. It is to say that courts must subject them to the most rigid scrutiny. Pressing public necessity may sometimes justify the existence of such restrictions; racial antagonism never can" (323 U.S. at 216). Under this strict scrutiny approach, the burden of proof shifts to the government, which must demonstrate that the classification is "narrowly tailored" to achieve a "compelling interest." Unfortunately, although the Court used the strict scrutiny approach in *Korematsu*, the government order requiring Japanese Americans to move to relocation centers during World War II ultimately was upheld. The public necessity here was deemed to be the prevention of espionage and sabotage by "disloyal" citizens of Japanese ancestry. It did not matter that the excessively harsh order applied to all Japanese Americans, without requiring the government to prove disloyalty. As a result, the Supreme Court endorsed the imposition of a grave injustice that caused Congress to apologize and pay compensation decades later to the people victimized by this discriminatory policy.

Despite the narrow (and misguided) application of strict scrutiny in *Korematsu*, this test has been used to strike down many racial classifications. It continues to be the standard employed in the Court's analysis of nearly all racial discrimination cases under the Equal Protection Clause.

The Pre-1937 Period

The Court's landmark pre-Civil War decision regarding race was *Dred Scott v. Sandford* (1857). The case arose when Dred Scott, a slave, filed suit in federal court seeking his freedom in an unusual set of circumstances following the death of his master. Because he had traveled with his master into a free state and free territory, he alleged that he was made free by reason of his residence on free soil. When the case reached the Supreme Court, the justices ruled by a vote of 7-2 that Scott still was a slave with no right to sue in federal courts. Speaking for the majority, Chief Justice Taney said that African Ameicans, whether slave or free, never were meant to be included as citizens of this country. Scott's suit was dismissed because only United States citizens had the privilege of suing in the federal courts. In one of the most infamous passages of the opinion, Taney wrote of Africans and their descendants, "They had for more than a century been regarded as beings of an inferior order, and altogether unfit to associate with the white race, either in social or political relations; and so far inferior, that they had no rights which the white man was bound to respect . . ." (16 How. at 407). In addition to determining that Scott was not entitled to sue in the federal courts, Taney also ruled that the Missouri Compromise was an unconstitutional exercise of congressional power. He said that Congress had no legal authority to forbid slavery in the territories of the United States, and therefore slaves were property protected by the Constitution in territories as well as in states.

Dred Scott v. Sandford

60 U.S. (19 How.) 393, 51 L.Ed. 691 (1857)

■ Dred Scott, a slave, had traveled with his master into a free state (Illinois) as well as to territory that was free under the Missouri Compromise. After returning to Missouri, a slave state, Scott contended that he no longer was a slave by virtue of having resided on free soil. The Missouri Supreme Court disagreed, holding that he remained a slave under state law. Scott then sued for his freedom in federal court, but the court dismissed the suit on the grounds that he was a slave, not a U.S. citizen with the privilege of suing in federal court. The case went to the Supreme Court on a writ of error.

This case is important primarily because the Court's ruling restricted the power of Congress to regulate slavery in the territories and became a factor contributing to the Civil War. As you read the case, consider these questions: 1) Why did the Court rule on the constitutionality of the Missouri Compromise when it was not necessary in deciding Scott's claims?

2) How is the concept of federalism implicated here? That is, what is the relationship between Missouri law and the Supremacy Clause of the U.S. Constitution?

VOTE:

7 justices held that African Americans, slave or free, could not be citizens of the United States and struck down the Missouri Compromise (Taney, Wayne, Catron, Daniel, Nelson, Grier, and Campbell).

2 justices dissented on the grounds that free African Americans were citizens of the United States and that the Missouri Compromise was constitutional (Curtis and McLean).

Chief Justice Taney delivered the opinion of the Court.

* * *

The question is simply this: Can a negro, whose ancestors were imported into this country, and sold as slaves, become a member of the political community formed and brought into existence by the Constitution of the United States, and as such become entitled to all the rights, and privileges, and immunities, guarantied by that instrument to the citizen? One of which rights is the privilege of suing in a court of the United States in the cases specified in the Constitution.

* * *

In discussing this question, we must not confound the rights of citizenship which a State may confer within its own limits, and the rights of citizenship as a member of the Union. It does not by any means follow, because he has all the rights and privileges of a citizen of a State, that he must be a citizen of the United States. He may have all of the rights and privileges of the citizen of a State, and yet not be entitled to the rights and privileges of a citizen in any other State. For previous to the adoption of the Constitution of the United States, every State had the undoubted right to confer on whomsoever it pleased the character of citizen, and to endow him with all its rights. * * *

* * *

The question then arises, whether the provisions of the Constitution, in relation to the personal rights and privileges to which the citizen of a State should be entitled, embraced the negro African race, at that time in this country, or who might afterwards be imported, who had then or should afterwards be made free in any State; and to put it in the power of a single State to make him a citizen of the United States, and endue him with the full rights of citizenship in every other State without their consent? Does the Constitution of the United States act upon him whenever he shall be made free under the laws of a State, and raised there to the rank of a citizen, and immediately clothe him with all the privileges of a citizen in every other State, and in its own courts?

The court think[s] the affirmative of these propositions cannot be maintained. And if it cannot, the plaintiff in error could not be a citizen of the State of Missouri, within the meaning of the Constitution of the United States, and, consequently, was not entitled to sue in its courts.

* * *

In the opinion of the court, the legislation and histories of the times, and the language used in the Declaration of Independence, show, that neither the class of persons who had been imported as slaves, nor their descendants, whether they had become free or not, were then acknowledged as a part of the people, nor intended to be included in the general words used in that memorable instrument.

* * *

They had for more than a century before been regarded as beings of an inferior order, and altogether unfit to associate with the white race, either in social or political relations; and so far inferior, that they had no rights which the white man was bound to respect; and that the negro might justly and lawfully be reduced to slavery for his benefit. He was bought and sold, and treated as an ordinary article of merchandise and traffic, whenever a profit could be made by it. This opinion was at that time fixed and universal in the civilized portion of the white race. It was regarded as an axiom in morals as well as in politics, which no one thought of disputing, or supposed to be open to dispute; and men in every grade and position in society daily and habitually acted upon it in their private pursuits, as well as in matters of public concern, without doubting for a moment the correctness of this opinion.

* * *

. . . [U]pon a full and careful consideration of the subject, the court is of opinion, that, upon the facts stated in the plea in abatement, Dred Scott was not a citizen of Missouri within the meaning of the Constitution of the United States, and not entitled as such to sue in its courts. . . .

* * *

We proceed, therefore, to inquire whether the facts relied on by the plaintiff entitled him to his freedom.

* * *

In considering this part of the controversy, two questions arise: 1st. Was he, together with his family, free in Missouri by reason of the stay in the territory of the United States hereinbefore mentioned? And

2nd. If they were not, is Scott himself free by reason of his removal to Rock Island, in the State of Illinois, as stated in the above admission?

We proceed to examine the first question.

The act of Congress, upon which the plaintiff relies, declares that slavery and involuntary servitude, except as a punishment for crime, shall be forever prohibited in all that part of the territory ceded by France, under the name of Louisiana, which lies north of thirty-six degrees thirty minutes north latitude, and not included within the limits of Missouri. And the difficulty which meets us at the threshold of this part of the inquiry is, whether Congress was authorized to pass this law under any of the powers granted to it by the Constitution; for if the authority is not given by that instrument, it is the duty of this court to declare it void and inoperative, and incapable of conferring freedom upon any one who is held as a slave under the laws of any one of the States.

The counsel for the plaintiff has laid much stress upon that article in the Constitution which confers on Congress the power "to dispose of and make all needful rules and regulations respecting the territory or other property belonging to the United States;" but, in the judgment of the court, that provision has no bearing on the present controversy, and the power there given, whatever it may be, is confined, and was intended to be confined, to the territory which at that time belonged to, or was claimed by, the United States, and was within their boundaries as settled by the treaty with Great Britain, and can have no influence upon a territory afterwards acquired from a foreign Government. It was a special provision for a known and particular territory, and to meet a present emergency, and nothing more.

* * *

The language used in the clause, the arrangement and combination of the powers, and the somewhat unusual phraseology it uses, when it speaks of the political power to be exercised in the government of the territory, all indicate the design and meaning of the clause to be such as we have mentioned. It does not speak of any territory, nor of Territories, but uses language which, according to its legitimate meaning, points to a particular thing. The power is given in relation only to the territory of the United States—that is, to a territory then in existence, and then known or claimed as the territory of the United States. * * *

* * *

Now, as we have already said in an earlier part of this opinion, upon a different point, the right of property in a slave is distinctly and expressly affirmed in the Constitution. The right to traffic in it, like an ordinary article of merchandise and property, was guaranteed to the citizens of the United States, in every State that might desire it, for twenty years. And the Government in express terms is pledged to protect it in all future time, if the slave escapes from his owner. This is done in plain words—too plain to be misunderstood. And no word can be found in the Constitution which gives Congress a greater power over slave property, or which entitles property of that kind to less protection than property of any other description. The only power conferred is the power coupled with the duty of guarding and protecting the owner in his rights.

Upon these considerations, it is the opinion of the court that the act of Congress which prohibited a citizen from holding and owning property of this kind in the territory of the United States north of the line therein mentioned, is not warranted by the Constitution, and is therefore void; and that neither Dred Scott himself, nor any of his family, were made free by being carried into this territory; even if they had been carried there by the owner, with the intention of becoming a permanent resident.

* * *

But there is another point in the case which depends on state power and state law. And it is contended, on the part of the plaintiff, that he is made free by being taken to Rock Island, in the State of Illinois, independently of his residence in the territory of the United States; and being so made free he was not again reduced to a state of slavery by being brought back to Missouri.

Our notice of this part of the case will be very brief; for the principle on which it depends was decided in this court, upon much consideration, in the case of *Strader v. Graham.* In that case, the slaves had been taken from Kentucky to Ohio, with the consent of the owner, and afterwards brought back to Kentucky. And this court held that their status or condition, as free or slave, depended upon the laws of Kentucky, when they were brought back into that State, and not of Ohio; and that this court had no jurisdiction to revise the judgment of a state court upon its own laws. This was the point directly before the court, and the decision that this court had not jurisdiction, turned upon it, as will be seen by the report of the case.

So in this case: as Scott was a slave when taken into the State of Illinois by his owner, and was there held as such, and brought back in that character, his status, as free or slave, depended on the laws of Missouri, and not of Illinois.

* * *

[*The concurring opinions of Justices Wayne, Nelson, Grier, Daniel, Campbell, and Catron each have been omitted.*]

Justice McLean dissented.

* * *

The prohibition of slavery north of thirty-six degrees thirty minutes, and of the State of Missouri, contained in the act admitting that State into the Union, was passed by a vote of 134, in the House of Representatives, to 42. Before Mr. Monroe signed the act, it was submitted by him to his Cabinet, and they held the restriction of slavery in a Territory to be within the constitutional powers of Congress. It would be singular, if in 1804 Congress had power to prohibit the introduction of slaves in Orleans Territory from any other part of the Union, under the penalty of freedom to the slave, if the same power, embodied in the Missouri compromise, could not be exercised in 1820.

But this law of Congress, which prohibits slavery north of Missouri and of thirty-six degrees thirty minutes, is declared to have been null and void by my brethren. And this opinion is founded mainly, as I understand, on the distinction drawn between the [Northwest] ordinance of 1787 and the Missouri compromise line. In what does the distinction consist? The ordinance, it is said, was a compact entered into by the confederated States before the adoption of the Constitution; and that in the cession of territory authority was given to establish a Territorial Government.

It is clear that the ordinance did not go into operation by virtue of the authority of the Confederation, but by reason of its modification and adoption by Congress under the Constitution. It seems to be supposed, in the opinion of the court, that the articles of cession placed it on a different footing from territories subsequently acquired. I am unable to perceive the force of this distinction. That the ordinance was intended for the government of the Northwestern Territory, and was limited to such Territory, is admitted. It was extended to Southern Territories, with modifications, by acts of Congress, and to some Northern Territories. But the ordinance was made valid by the act of Congress, and without such act could have been of no force. It rested for its validity on the act of Congress, the same, in my opinion, as the Missouri compromise line.

If Congress may establish a Territorial Government in the exercise of its discretion, it is a clear principle that a court cannot control that discretion. This being the case, I do not see on what ground the act is held to be void. It did not purport to forfeit property, or take it for public purposes. It only prohibited slavery; in doing which, it followed the ordinance of 1787.

* * *

Justice Curtis dissented.

* * *

It has been often asserted that the Constitution was made exclusively by and for the white race. It has already been shown that in five of the thirteen original States, colored persons then possessed the elective franchise, and were among those by whom the Constitution was ordained and established. If so, it is not true, in point of fact, that the Constitution was made exclusively by the white race. And that it was made exclusively for the white race is, in my opinion, not only an assumption not warranted by anything in the Constitution, but contradicted by its opening declaration, that it was ordained and established by the people of the United States, for themselves and their posterity. And as free colored persons were then citizens of at least five States, and so in every sense part of the people of the United States, they were among those for whom and whose posterity the Constitution was ordained and established.

* * *

The conclusions at which I have arrived on this part of the case are:

First. That the free native-born citizens of each State are citizens of the United States.

Second. That as free colored persons born within some of the States are citizens of those States, such persons are also citizens of the United States.

Third. That every such citizen, residing in any State, has the right to sue and is liable to be sued in the federal courts, as a citizen of that State in which he resides.

* * *

I dissent, therefore, from that part of the opinion of the majority of the court, in which it is held that a person of African descent cannot be a citizen of the United States; and I regret I must go further, and dissent both from what I deem their assumption of authority to examine the constitutionality of the act of Congress commonly called the Missouri Compromise act, and the grounds and conclusions announced in their opinion.

* * *

The Court's invalidation of the Missouri Compromise, many scholars contend, contributed to the hostilities that ultimately resulted in the Civil War. Moreover, legal scholars and historians view the *Dred Scott* decision as a factor contributing to the decreased legitimacy and prestige of the Court during the latter part of the nineteenth century.

The Supreme Court's next major decisions regarding race involved interpretations of the Reconstruction Amendments, particularly the Fourteenth Amendment's Equal Protection Clause. While there was agreement that the Fourteenth Amendment granted citizenship rights to the former slaves, some contended that the framers of the Amendment intended it to have broader application in protecting the rights of all citizens. In 1873, the Court addressed this latter claim in *The Slaughterhouse Cases,* which involved a challenge to a Louisiana statute that basically had granted a monopoly to a slaughterhouse company in New Orleans. A group of independent butchers argued that the state-created monopoly violated the Thirteenth Amendment and three clauses of the Fourteenth Amendment—Privileges and Immunities, Equal Protection, and Due Process. In ruling against the butchers, the Court said that the "one pervading purpose" of the Reconstruction Amendments was to secure the "freedom of the slave race" (16 Wall. at 71). The Court specifically rejected a broad application of the Privileges and Immunities Clause in this case, an interpretation that stands today.

Seven years later, the Court applied the Equal Protection Clause to prohibit states from excluding African Americans from jury service. In *Strauder v. West Virginia* (1880), the justices granted the request of an African American defendant to move his murder trial to the federal courts because West Virginia law prohibited African Americans from serving on juries. In applying the Fourteenth Amendment, Justice Strong wrote, "The words of the amendment . . . contain a necessary implication of a positive immunity, or right, most valuable to the colored race,—the right to exemption from unfriendly legislation against them distinctively as colored . . ." (100 U.S. at 307–8).

Three years after *Strauder,* a case arose concerning congressional authority to enforce the Reconstruction Amendments, particularly the Fourteenth. The Court's decision here would have major ramifications well into the twentieth century. In *The Civil Rights Cases* (1883), the Court invalidated provisions of the Civil Rights Act of 1875, passed by the Reconstruction Congress to protect African Americans from discrimination in various public accommodations. The act made it illegal to practice racial discrimination in inns, theaters, public transportation, and other places of public amusement. By an 8-1 vote, the Court said that the Fourteenth Amendment did not empower Congress to legislate against private discrimination but was limited to discrimination involving "**state action.**" The Amendment reads "No State shall . . . deny to any person within its jurisdiction the equal protection of the laws." This led Justice Bradley to declare, "It is state action of a particular character that is prohibited. Individual invasion of individual rights is not the subject-matter of the Amendment" (109 U.S. at 11).

The Civil Rights Cases

109 U.S. 3, 3 S.Ct. 18, 27 L.Ed. 835 (1883)

■ Utilizing its power to enforce the guarantees of the Fourteenth Amendment, Congress passed the Civil Rights Act of 1875. The statute prohibited racial discrimination in inns, public conveyances, theaters, and other "places of public amusement." The ***Civil Rights Cases*** actually are a group of five cases decided together. Four of the cases involved action brought by the U.S. government against proprietors of various public accommodations for violating the act, and the fifth concerned two individuals bringing suit against a railroad company for deprivation of their rights under the act. After decisions in the U.S. Circuit Courts, the cases went to the Supreme Court for review.

This case is important because it provided the Court's first interpretation of the extent of congressional power in enforcing the Fourteenth Amendment to protect African Americans from private discrimination. As you read the case, consider these questions: 1) Is the majority's reliance on the concept of "state action" well founded? That is, could one argue that the government acts to regulate what is thought to be private conduct in a number of areas of life? 2) If the Court had upheld the Civil Rights Act of 1875, would segregation have become so pervasive in American society?

VOTE:

8 justices voted to strike down the act (Bradley, Waite, Miller, Field, Woods, Matthews, Gray, and Blatchford).

1 justice voted to uphold the statute (Harlan).

Justice Bradley delivered the opinion of the Court.

* * *

The first section of the Fourteenth Amendment,—which is the one relied on,—after declaring who shall be citizens of the United States, and of the several states, is prohibitory in its character, and prohibitory upon the states. It declares that "no state shall make or enforce any law which shall abridge the privileges or immunities of citizens of the United States; nor shall any state deprive any person of life, liberty, or property without due process of law; nor deny to any person within its jurisdiction the equal protection of the laws." It is state action of a particular character that is prohibited. Individual invasion of individual rights is not the subject-matter of the amendment. It has a deeper and broader scope. It nullifies and makes void all state legislation, and state action of every kind, which impairs the privileges and immunities of citizens of the United States, or which injures them in life, liberty, or property without due process of law, or which denies to any of them the equal protection of the laws. . . . [T]he last section of the amendment invests Congress with power to enforce it by appropriate legislation. To enforce what? To enforce the prohibition. To adopt appropriate legislation for correcting the effects of such prohibited state law and state acts, and thus to render them effectually null, void, and innocuous. * * * It does not invest Congress with power to legislate upon subjects which are within the domain of state legislation. . . . It does not authorize Congress to create a code of municipal law for the regulation of private rights; but to provide modes of redress against the operation of state laws, and the action of state officers, executive or judicial, when these are subversive of the fundamental rights specified in the Amendment. * * *

* * *

An inspection of the law shows that it makes no reference whatever to any supposed or apprehended violation of the Fourteenth Amendment on the part of the states. * * * It proceeds *ex directo* to declare that certain acts committed by individuals shall be deemed offenses, and shall be prosecuted and punished by proceedings in the courts of the United States. It does not profess to be corrective of any constitutional wrong committed by the states. . . . * * * [I]t steps into the domain of local jurisprudence, and lays down rules for the conduct of individuals in society towards each other, and imposes sanctions for the enforcement of those rules, without referring in any manner to any supposed action of the state or its authorities.

If this legislation is appropriate for enforcing the prohibitions of the amendment, it is difficult to see where it is to stop. Why may not Congress, with equal show of authority, enact a code of laws for the enforcement and vindication of all rights of life, liberty, and property? If it is supposable that the states may deprive persons of life, liberty, and property without due process of law, (and the amendment itself does suppose this,) why should not Congress proceed at once to prescribe due process of law for the protection of every one of these fundamental rights, in every possible case, as well as to prescribe equal privileges in inns, public conveyances, and theaters. The truth is that the implication of a power to legislate in this manner is based upon the assumption that if the states are forbidden to legislate or act in a particular way on a particular subject, and power is conferred upon Congress to enforce the prohibition, this gives Congress power to legislate generally upon that subject, and not merely power to provide modes of redress against such state legislation or action. The assumption is certainly unsound. It is repugnant to the Tenth Amendment of the Constitution, which declares that powers not delegated to the United States by the Constitution, nor prohibited by it to the states, are reserved to the states respectively or to the people.

* * *

. . . [I]t is proper to state that civil rights, such as are guarantied by the constitution against state aggression, cannot be impaired by the wrongful acts of individuals, unsupported by state authority in the shape of laws, customs, or judicial or executive proceedings. The wrongful act of an individual, unsupported by any such authority, is simply a private wrong, or a crime of that individual; an invasion of the rights of the injured party, it is true, whether they affect his person, his property, or his reputation; but if not sanctioned in some way by the state, or not done under state authority, his rights remain in full force, and may presumably be vindicated by resort to the laws of the state for redress. * * *

* * *

. . . [T]he power of Congress to adopt direct and primary, as distinguished from corrective, legislation on the subject in hand, is sought, in the second place, from the Thirteenth Amendment, which abolishes slavery. * * * [A]nd it gives Congress power to enforce the Amendment by appropriate legislation.

* * *

. . . [W]e are forced to the conclusion that such an act of refusal [of accommodations] has nothing to do with slavery or involuntary servitude, and that if it is violative of any right of the party, his redress is to be sought under the laws of the state; or, if those laws are adverse to his rights and do not protect him, his remedy will be found in the corrective legislation which Congress has adopted, or may adopt, for counteracting the effect of state laws, or state action, prohibited by the Fourteenth Amendment. It would be running the slavery argument into the ground to make it apply to every act of discrimination which a person may see fit to make as to the guests he will entertain, or as to the people he will take into his coach or cab or car, or admit to his concert or theater, or deal with in other matters of intercourse or business. * * *

* * *

On the whole, we are of opinion that no countenance of authority for the passage of the law in question can be found in either the Thirteenth or Fourteenth Amendment of the constitution; and no other ground of authority for its passage being suggested, it must necessarily be declared void, at least so far as its operation in the several states is concerned.

* * *

Justice Harlan dissented.

The opinion in these cases proceeds, as it seems to me, upon grounds entirely too narrow and artificial. The substance and spirit of the recent amendments of the constitution have been sacrificed by a subtle and ingenious verbal criticism. * * *

* * *

The Thirteenth Amendment, it is conceded, did something more than to prohibit slavery as an *institution,* resting upon distinctions of race, and upheld by positive law. They admit that it established and decreed universal *civil freedom* throughout the United States. But did the freedom thus established involve nothing more than exemption from actual slavery? Was nothing more intended than to forbid one man from owning another as property? * * *

That there are burdens and disabilities which constitute badges of slavery and servitude, and that the express power delegated to Congress to enforce, by appropriate legislation, the Thirteenth Amendment, may be exerted by legislation of a direct and primary character, for the eradication, not simply of the institution, but of its badges and incidents, are propositions which ought to be deemed indisputable. * * *

* * *

[After examining the nature of public conveyances, inns, and places of public amusement, Harlan characterizes them as public or quasi-public businesses, subject to government regulation. Quoting from *Munn v. Illinois* (1877), Harlan wrote, "Property does become clothed with a public interest when used in a manner to make it of public consequence and affect the community at large."]

* * *

I am of the opinion that such discrimination practiced by corporations and individuals in the exercise of their public or *quasi* public functions is a badge of servitude, the imposition of which Congress may prevent under its power, by appropriate legislation, to enforce the Thirteenth Amendment; and, consequently, without reference to its enlarged power under the Fourteenth Amendment, the Act of March 1, 1875, is not, in my judgment, repugnant to the Constitution.

It remains now to consider these cases with reference to the power Congress has possessed since the adoption of the Fourteenth Amendment. Much that has been said as to the power of Congress under the Thirteenth Amendment is applicable to this branch of the discussion, and will not be repeated.

* * *

. . . [W]hat was secured to colored citizens of the United States—as between them and their respective states—by the grant to them of state citizenship? With what rights, privileges, or immunities did this grant from the nation invest them? There is one, if there be no others—exemption from race discrimination in respect of any civil right belonging to citizens of the white race in the same state. That, surely, is their constitutional privilege when within the jurisdiction of other states. And such must be their constitutional right, in their own state, unless the recent amendments be "splendid baubles," thrown out to delude those who deserved fair and generous treatment at the hands of the nation. Citizenship in this country necessarily imports equality of civil rights among citizens of every race in the same state. It is fundamental in American citizenship that, in respect of such rights, there shall be no discrimination by the state, or its officers, or by individuals, or corporations exercising public functions or authority, against any citizen because of his race or previous condition of servitude. * * *

* * *

* * * With all respect for the opinion of others, I insist that the national legislature may, without transcending the limits of the Constitution, do for human liberty and the fundamental rights of American citizenship, what it did, with the sanction of this court, for the protection of slavery and the rights of the masters of fugitive slaves. If fugitive slave laws, providing modes and prescribing penalties, whereby the master could seize and recover his fugitive slave, were legitimate exertions of an implied power to protect and enforce a right recognized by the Constitution, why shall the hands of Congress be tied, so that—under an express power, by appropriate legislation, to enforce a constitutional provision granting citizenship—it may not, by means of direct legislation, bring the whole power of this nation to bear upon States and their officers, and upon such individuals and corporations exercising public functions as assume to abridge, impair or deny rights confessedly secured by the supreme law of the land?

* * *

* * * I agree that government has nothing to do with social, as distinguished from technically legal, rights of individuals. * * * The rights which Congress, by the Act of 1875, endeavored to secure and protect are legal, not social rights. The right, for instance, of a colored citizen to use the accommodations of a public highway, upon the same terms as are permitted to white citizens, is no more a social right than his right, under the law, to use the public streets of a city or a town, or a turnpike road, or a public market, or a post office. . . . * * *

* * *

My brethren say, that when a man has emerged from slavery, and by the aid of beneficent legislation has shaken off the inseparable concomitants of that state, there must be some stage in the progress of his elevation when he takes the rank of a mere citizen, and ceases to be the special favorite of the laws, and when his rights as a citizen, or a man, are to be protected in the ordinary modes by which other men's rights are protected. It is, I submit, scarcely just to say that the colored race has been the special favorite of the laws. The statute of 1875, now adjudged to be unconstitutional, is for the benefit of citizens of every race and color. What the nation, through Congress, has sought to accomplish in reference to that race, is—what had already been done in every State of the Union for the white race—to secure and protect rights belonging to them as freemen and citizens; nothing more. It was not deemed enough "to help the feeble up, but to support him after." The one underlying purpose of congressional legislation has been to enable the black race to take the rank of mere citizens. The difficulty has been to compel a recognition of the legal right of the black race to take the rank of citizens, and to secure the enjoyment of privileges belonging, under the law, to them as a component part of the people for whose welfare and happiness government is ordained. At every step, in this direction, the nation has been confronted with class tyranny. . . . Today, it is the colored race which is denied, by corporations and individuals wielding public authority, rights fundamental in their freedom and citizenship. At some future time, it may be that some other race will fall under the ban of race discrimination. If the constitutional amendments be enforced, according to the intent with which, as I conceive, they were adopted, there cannot be, in this republic, any class of human beings in practical subjection to another class, with power in the latter to dole out to the former just such privileges as they may choose to grant. The supreme law of the land has decreed that no authority shall be exercised in this country upon the basis of discrimination, in respect of civil rights, against freemen and citizens because of their race, color, or previous condition of servitude. To that decree—for the due enforcement of which, by appropriate legislation, Congress has been invested with express power—every one must bow, whatever may have been, or whatever now are, his individual views as to the wisdom or policy, either of the recent changes in the fundamental law, or of the legislation which has been enacted to give them effect.

* * *

This "state action" doctrine legalized racial discrimination and subsequently helped to perpetuate it for six decades. Not until the Civil Rights Act of 1964 was passed was there an effective tool for combatting racial discrimination in public accommodations. The Court's decisions interpreting the 1964 act, however, relied upon the Commerce Clause rather than the Fourteenth Amendment (*Heart of Atlanta Motel v. U.S.*, 1964 and *Katzenbach v. McClung*, 1964). Congress had used its power to regulate commerce as a basis for passage of the act.

The Court's interpretation of the Fourteenth Amendment and its Equal Protection Clause was broadened in a case from California in 1886. First, the Court's decision made it clear that the Clause did not apply only to African Americans or to U.S. citizens. In addition, the Court developed the principle that, although a law may be facially neutral or nondiscriminatory, it may have a discriminatory effect that is unconstitutional. In *Yick Wo v. Hopkins* (1886), the Court examined a San Francisco laundry ordinance. The law required that applications for laundry licenses be approved by the city's board of supervisors and subjected those who operated laundries without such licenses to fines and imprisonment for up to six months. The ordinance excluded laundries that were operated in brick buildings. Given that the overwhelming number of Chinese laundries in the city were located in wooden buildings, it was clear that the ordinance was directed at businesses operated by the Chinese. The San Francisco ordinance was not an isolated law but was one of several attempts to coerce Chinese people into leaving major cities and to prevent more of them from migrating there. This case arose when Yick Wo, an operator of a laundry in the city for twenty-two years, was denied a license and was fined for continuing to operate his business. After refusing to pay the fine, he was sentenced to jail for ten days. The California Supreme Court denied his petition for a writ of habeas corpus, and he appealed to the U.S. Supreme Court. By a unanimous vote, the high court struck down the laundry ordinance as a violation of the Equal Protection Clause, ruling that the clause applied to all persons, citizens or not. Moreover, the fact that the ordinance was facially neutral did not save it from being unconstitutional. "Though the law itself be fair on its face and impartial in appearance, yet if it is applied and administered by public authority with an evil eye and an unequal hand, so as practically to make unjust and illegal discrimination between persons in similar circumstances, material to their rights, the denial of equal justice is still within the prohibition of the Constitution" (118 U.S. at 373–74).

As we saw earlier, even after passage of the Reconstruction Amendments, southern states continued their attempts to keep African Americans in an inferior status. One such effort involved laws requiring racial segregation in various aspects of life. One of these so-called **Jim Crow** laws was examined by the Court in the infamous case of *Plessy v. Ferguson* (1896). At issue in *Plessy* was a Louisiana statute that required "equal but separate" accommodations for African Americans and whites in railcars. Homer Plessy was arrested for violating the statute when he refused to move to the "colored" section of a train after being ordered to do so by railroad authorities. He alleged that the statute was unconstitutional under both the Thirteenth and Fourteenth Amendments. By a 7-1 vote, the Court rejected both of his arguments. The majority held that the Thirteenth Amendment was inapplicable because it was meant solely to forbid actions that reintroduced slavery. Neither did the Louisiana law violate the Equal Protection Clause because that clause was not meant to abolish all distinctions based on color or to guarantee social equality. Writing for the majority, Justice Brown relied upon prior decisions of state and federal courts upholding segregation in public schools and forbidding interracial marriages. In one of the opinion's strangest passages, he contended that the law did not "stamp the colored race with a badge of inferiority," but if it were so, it was "because the colored race cho[se] to put that construction upon it" (163 U.S. at 551). In general, the decision created the **separate but equal** doctrine, which permitted states to require separate facilities for African Americans and whites as long as they were equal. In most places, though, facilities for African Americans and whites were far from equal.

Justice John Marshall Harlan—whose grandson, John Marshall Harlan II, served on the Court from 1955–71—was the lone dissenter. He criticized the majority for affirming the power of states to deny civil rights to citizens because of their race. In the most quoted passage of his dissent, the elder Harlan wrote, "Our constitution is color-blind, and neither knows nor tolerates classes among citizens. In respect of civil rights, all citizens are equal before the law" (163 U.S. at 559). He argued further, "The destinies of the two races in this country are indissolubly linked together, and the interests of both require that the common government of all shall not permit the seeds of race hate to be planted under the sanction of law" (163 U.S. at 560).

Plessy v. Ferguson

163 U.S. 537, 16 S.Ct. 1138, 41 L.Ed. 256 (1896)

■ An 1890 Louisiana statute mandated racial segregation in railroad accommodations. Individuals who refused to sit in their designated railcars were subject to criminal penalties. This particular case arose after Homer Plessy, classified as "colored" although he was seven-eighths white, was arrested for refusing to move to the "colored" section of a coach. At his trial, Plessy requested the state supreme court to discontinue the proceedings against him. After the Louisiana court rejected his petition, Plessy sought review in the U.S. Supreme Court.

This case is important because the Court established the separate but equal doctrine that helped to maintain state-supported racial segregation for nearly fifty years. As you read the case, consider these questions: 1) Would the outcome have been any different had the Court used the "state action" doctrine from the *Civil Rights Cases*? 2) Would this statute be upheld or invalidated under the strict scrutiny test? 3) Is there any basis in constitutional history for rejecting Justice Harlan's statement that "our Constitution is color-blind?"

Vote:

7 justices agreed to uphold the statute (Brown, Fuller, Field, Gray, Shiras, White, and Peckham).

1 justice voted to invalidate the statute (Harlan).

1 justice did not participate in the case (Brewer).

Justice Brown delivered the opinion of the court.

* * *

That [the statute] does not conflict with the Thirteenth Amendment, which abolished slavery and involuntary servitude, except as a punishment for crime, is too clear for argument. Slavery implies involuntary servitude,—a state of bondage; the ownership of mankind as a chattel, or, at least, the control of the labor and services of one man for the benefit of another, and the absence of a legal right to the disposal of his own person, property, and services. * * *

* * *

By the Fourteenth Amendment, all persons born or naturalized in the United States, and subject to the jurisdiction thereof, are made citizens of the United States and of the state wherein they reside; and the states are forbidden from making or enforcing any law which shall abridge the privileges or immunities of citizens of the United States, or shall deprive any person of life, liberty, or property without due process of law, or deny to any person within their jurisdiction the equal protection of the laws.

* * *

The object of the amendment was undoubtedly to enforce the absolute equality of the two races before the law, but, in the nature of things, it could not have been intended to abolish distinctions based upon color, or to enforce social, as distinguished from political, equality, or a commingling of the two races upon terms unsatisfactory to either. Laws permitting, and even requiring, their separation, in places where they are liable to be brought into contact, do not necessarily imply the inferiority of either race to the other, and have been generally, if not universally, recognized as within the competency of the state legislatures in the exercise of their police power. The most common instance of this is connected with the establishment of separate schools for white and colored children, which have been held to be a valid exercise of the legislative power even by courts of states where the political rights of the colored race have been longest and most earnestly enforced.

One of the earliest of these cases is that of *Roberts v. Boston*, in which the supreme judicial court of Massachusetts held that the general school committee of Boston had power to make provision for the instruction of colored children in separate schools established exclusively for them, and to prohibit their attendance upon the other schools. * * *

Laws forbidding the intermarriage of the two races may be said in a technical sense to interfere with the freedom of contract, and yet have been universally recognized as within the police power of the state.

The distinction between laws interfering with the political equality of the negro and those requiring the separation of the two races in schools, theaters, and railway carriages has been frequently drawn by this court. * * *

* * *

So far, then, as a conflict with the Fourteenth Amendment is concerned, the case reduces itself to the question whether the statute of Louisiana is a reasonable regulation, and with respect to this there must necessarily be a large discretion on the part of the legislature. In determining the question of reasonableness, it is at liberty to act with reference to the established usages, customs, and traditions of the people, and with a view to the promotion of their comfort, and the preservation of the public peace and good order. Gauged by this standard, we cannot say that a law which authorizes or even requires the separation of the two races in public conveyances is unreasonable, or more obnoxious to the Fourteenth Amendment than the acts of Congress requiring separate schools for colored children in the District of Columbia, the constitutionality of which does not seem to have been questioned, or the corresponding acts of state legislatures.

We consider the underlying fallacy of the plaintiff's argument to consist in the assumption that the enforced separation of the two races stamps the colored race with a badge of inferiority. If this be so, it is not by reason of anything found in the act, but solely because the colored race chooses to put that construction upon it. The argument necessarily assumes that if, as has been more than once the case, and is not unlikely to be so again, the colored race should become the dominant power in the state legislature, and should enact a law in precisely similar terms, it would thereby relegate the white race to an inferior position. We imagine that the white race, at least, would not acquiesce in this assumption. The argument also assumes that social prejudices may be overcome by legislation, and that equal rights cannot be secured to the negro except by an enforced commingling of the two races. We cannot accept this proposition. If the two races are to meet upon terms of social equality, it must be the result of natural affinities, a mutual appreciation of each other's merits, and a voluntary consent of individuals. * * * Legislation is powerless to eradicate racial instincts, or to abolish distinctions based upon physical differences, and the attempt to do so can only result in accentuating the difficulties of the present situation. If the civil and political rights of both races be equal, one cannot be inferior to the other civilly or politically. If one race be inferior to the other socially, the constitution of the United States cannot put them upon the same plane.

* * *

The judgment of the court below is therefore affirmed.

Justice Brewer did not hear the argument or participate in the decision of this case.

Justice Harlan dissented.

* * *

In respect of civil rights, common to all citizens, the constitution of the United States does not, I think, permit any public authority to know the race of those entitled to be protected in the enjoyment of such rights. Every true man has pride of race, and under appropriate circumstances, when the rights of others, his equals before the law, are not to be affected, it is his privilege to express such pride and to take such action based upon it as to him seems proper. But I deny that any legislative body or judicial tribunal may have regard to the race of citizens when the civil rights of those citizens are involved. Indeed, such legislation as that here in question is inconsistent not only with that equality of rights which pertains to citizenship, national and state, but with the personal liberty enjoyed by every one within the United States.

The Thirteenth Amendment does not permit the withholding or the deprivation of any right necessarily inhering in freedom. It not only struck down the institution of slavery as previously existing in the United States, but it prevents the imposition of any burdens or disabilities that constitute badges of slavery or servitude. It decreed universal civil freedom in this country. This court has so adjudged. But, that amendment having been found inadequate to the protection of the rights of those who had been in slavery, it was followed by the Fourteenth Amendment, which added greatly to the dignity and glory of American citizenship, and to the security of personal liberty. * * * Finally, and to the end that no citizen should be denied, on account of his race, the privilege of participating in the political control of his country, it was declared by the Fifteenth Amendment that "the right of citizens of the United States to vote shall not be denied or abridged . . . on account of race, color, or previous condition of servitude."

These notable additions to the fundamental law were welcomed by the friends of liberty throughout the world. They removed the race line from our governmental systems. * * *

* * *

The white race deems itself to be the dominant race in this country. And so it is, in prestige, in achievements, in education, in wealth and in power. So, I doubt not, it will continue to be for all time, if it remains true to its great heritage and holds fast to the principles of constitutional liberty. But in view of the Constitution, in the eye of the law, there is in this country no superior, dominant, ruling class of citizens. There is no caste here. Our Constitution is color-blind, and neither knows nor tolerates classes among citizens. In respect of civil rights, all citizens are equal before the law. The humblest is the peer of the most powerful. The law regards man as man, and takes no account of his surroundings or of his color when his civil rights as guarantied by the supreme law of the land are involved. It is therefore to be regretted that this high tribunal, the final expositor of the fundamental law of the land, has reached the conclusion that it is competent for a state to regulate the enjoyment by citizens of their civil rights solely upon the basis of race.

In my opinion, the judgment this day rendered will, in time, prove to be quite as pernicious as the decision made by this tribunal in the *Dred Scott case.* * * *

* * *

I am of opinion that the statute of Louisiana is inconsistent with the personal liberty of citizens, white and black, in that state, and hostile to both the spirit and letter of the Constitution of the United States. * * *

* * *

* * * The destinies of the two races in this country, are indissolubly linked together, and the interests of both require that the common government of all shall not permit the seeds of race hate to be planted under the sanction of law. * * *

Whether or not Harlan was overreacting, the *Plessy* ruling encouraged states to maintain and pass laws requiring racial segregation in transportation, schools, housing, hospitals, and a host of other public facilities.

Three years after *Plessy,* the Court heard its first case regarding segregation in public schools, *Cumming v. Board of Education* (1899). The Court did not apply its own "separate but equal" doctrine, however. The justices refused to invalidate a Georgia school board decision closing a public high school for African Americans, although the board's action conflicted with a state law requiring "separate but equal" school facilities for African Americans and whites. Writing for a unanimous Court, Justice Harlan said the plaintiffs had not proven that the board decision was based solely on race, and, absent such evidence, federal authorities could not interfere with the power of the states to maintain their schools. In a subsequent decision, the Court upheld racial segregation in higher education as well. In *Berea College v. Kentucky* (1908), the Court refused to invalidate a state law that required separate classes for African Americans and whites in institutions teaching members of both races. Responding to the college's claim that the state illegally impaired the school's charter because the law required African Americans and whites to be taught separately, the justices said that, because the state did not prevent the college from teaching both races altogether, there was no significant injury to the school's charter. Finally, in *Gong Lum v. Rice* (1927), the Court upheld a Mississippi law that excluded children of Chinese descent from all-white public schools and required them to attend all-black schools instead.

The New Deal Era Until the Warren Court

Supreme Court decisions interpreting the Equal Protection Clause in the nineteenth and early twentieth centuries indicate that this constitutional provision was of limited use in eradicating racial discrimination in our society. In the period following President Franklin Roosevelt's introduction of his ill-fated court-packing plan, however, the Court began to take a more critical look at racial classifications and to view such classifications as violations of the Equal Protection Clause. It is important to note, moreover, that many of the cases heard by the Court during this time period were part of a legal strategy developed by the NAACP Legal Defense and Educational Fund. This litigation strategy was the brainchild of Charles Hamilton Houston, a professor of law at Howard University and mentor to Thurgood Marshall, who later became solicitor general of the United States and the first African American to sit on the U.S. Supreme Court. After Houston's resignation due to illness, Marshall became the chief litigator for the NAACP Legal Defense Fund. He and several other NAACP attorneys, including William Hastie, James Nabrit, and Leon Ransom, carried out this incremental approach to challenge segregation, particularly in education, with the ultimate goal being the overturning of *Plessy*'s separate but equal doctrine. They decided to focus initially on segregation in graduate and professional schools for two reasons. First, many states provided no opportunities for African Americans in these areas. Second, they assumed that entrance to these institutions by a small number of African American students would be less threatening to whites than would be the wholesale desegregation of primary and secondary schools (Carson et al. 1987).

The first case brought to the Supreme Court by the NAACP, *Missouri Ex Rel. Gaines v. Canada* (1938), involved Lloyd Gaines, an African American who had been denied entry to Missouri's all-white law school because of his race. The state, however, agreed to pay his tuition to any law school located in neighboring states that would admit African Americans. After state courts ruled in favor of Missouri, Charles Houston appealed to the Supreme Court to compel Missouri to admit Gaines to its law school. By a 6-2 vote, the Court held that Missouri's denial of Gaines's admission to the law school was unconstitutional and its willingness to pay his tuition for legal training elsewhere was not sufficient to provide him with equal protection of the laws. "By the operation of the laws of Missouri," Chief Justice Hughes wrote, "a privilege has been created for white law students which is denied to negroes by reason of their race" (305 U.S. at 349). The Court reaffirmed this decision ten years later in a brief per curiam opinion in *Sipuel v. Board of Regents* (1948), ruling that Oklahoma could not deny an African American applicant admission to its law school simply because of her race.

Six years after *Gaines v. Canada,* as the country was embroiled in World War II, the Court sent a mixed message regarding its willingness to tolerate racial discrimination in our society. In *Korematsu v. United States* (1944), the justices by a 6-3 vote decided that executive orders forcing Japanese Americans into relocation camps during the war did not deny them equal protection of the laws. At the same time, however, the Court adopted a new standard for examining racial classifications and restrictions under the Equal Protection Clause. Justice Black asserted that "all legal restrictions which curtail the civil rights of a single racial group are immediately suspect," and "courts must subject them to the most rigid scrutiny" (323 U.S. at 216). This new suspect classification or strict scrutiny approach was an important development because it would make it very difficult in future cases for racial classifications by the government to pass constitutional muster. Unfortunately, in *Korematsu,* the Court applied strict scrutiny in a way that allowed these exclusion orders to be upheld. In a remarkable passage, Justice Black insisted that Fred Korematsu (and other Japanese Americans) were not being sent to relocation centers because of racial hostility but "because we [were] at war with the Japanese Empire, because the properly constituted military authorities . . . decided that the military urgency of the situation demanded that all citizens of Japanese ancestry be segregated from the West Coast temporarily" (323 U.S. at 223). This decision never has been overturned, but four decades later Congress passed legislation providing reparations to still-living former detainees and their families.

Encouraged by their earlier success in *Gaines,* the NAACP attorneys directed their efforts toward racial segregation in housing. The objects of their attacks, however, were not laws requiring segregation but contracts known as restrictive covenants, which had the same effects. Restrictive covenants had become a popular tool for whites who wanted to prevent African Americans from moving into their neighborhoods after the Court struck down a municipal ordinance requiring residential segregation in *Buchanan v. Warley* (1917). That decision was based not on equal protection analysis but on the right of property owners to dispose of their property as they saw fit. Under the terms of restrictive covenants, white property owners entered into agreements not to sell their property to African Americans and members of other races for a designated period of time. Such restrictive covenants came to the Court for review in *Shelley v. Kraemer* (1948). The Shelleys, an African American couple, bought a house in a white neighborhood of St. Louis, Missouri, in 1945. The home was covered by a restrictive covenant that restricted it from being sold to African Americans or to persons of the "Mongolian race" for a period of fifty years. A Missouri trial court found the covenant to be technically flawed, but the state supreme court upheld it and ordered the trial court to enforce it.

By a vote of 6-0, with three justices not participating, the U.S. Supreme Court decided in favor of the Shelleys. Returning to the "state action" doctrine, the justices did not invalidate the restrictive covenants themselves but instead ruled that state judicial enforcement of such agreements was state action in violation of the Equal Protection Clause. "So long as the purposes of those agreements are effectuated by voluntary adherence to their terms," Chief Justice Vinson wrote, "there has been no action by the State and the provisions of the [Fourteenth] Amendment have not been violated" (334 U.S. at 13). Here, because the covenant was enforced by the state judiciary, "the States ha[d] denied petitioners the equal protection of the laws and . . . therefore, the action of the state courts cannot stand" (334 U.S. at 20). Thus the Court had limited the use (at least in theory) of one of the most effective tools of residential segregation.

Shelley v. Kraemer

334 U.S. 1, 68 S.Ct. 836, 92 L.Ed. 1161 (1948)

■ J.D. and Ethel Shelley, an African American couple, purchased a home in a white neighborhood in St. Louis, Missouri. They did not know that their new house, like others in the community, was covered by a restrictive covenant that had been in operation since 1911. Under the terms of the covenant, property owners agreed not to sell to African Americans or to persons of the "Mongolian race." The covenant applied to persons who originally signed the contract as well as to subsequent owners. Two months after the Shelleys purchased their home, the Kraemers and other homeowners in the community sued to prevent them from possessing the property. The trial court refused to enforce the covenant because it had not been signed by all of the property owners in the community. The Missouri Supreme Court ruled that it was a valid agreement and ordered its enforcement. The Shelleys sought review in the Supreme Court. Similar cases from Michigan (*McGhee v. Sipes*) and the District of Columbia (*Hurd v. Hodge*) were consolidated with *Shelley*.

This case is important because it provided a tool for African Americans (and other groups) to fight discrimination in housing. After the Court struck down state laws requiring housing segregation in *Buchanan v. Warley* (1917), whites increasingly turned to private agreements to prevent African Americans from moving into their neighborhoods. As you read the case, consider the following questions: 1) Is there any basis for a conclusion that the restrictive covenants themselves violate the constitutional guarantee of equal protection? 2) If the Fourteenth Amendment Equal Protection Clause applies only to "state action," how effective a tool is it for achieving racial equality in our society?

Vote:

6 justices ruled that judicial enforcement of restrictive covenants violates the Equal Protection Clause (Vinson, Black, Frankfurter, Douglas, Murphy, and Burton).

3 justices did not participate in the case (Reed, Jackson, and Rutledge).

Chief Justice Vinson delivered the opinion of the Court.

* * *

Whether the equal protection clause of the Fourteenth Amendment inhibits judicial enforcement by state courts of restrictive covenants based on race or color is a question which this Court has not heretofore been called upon to consider. * * *

* * *

* * * Here the particular patterns of discrimination and the areas in which the restrictions are to operate, are determined, in the first instance, by the terms of agreements among private individuals. Participation of the State consists in the enforcement of the restrictions so defined. The crucial issue with which we are here confronted is whether this distinction removes these cases from the operation of the prohibitory provisions of the Fourteenth Amendment.

Since the decision of this Court in the Civil Rights Cases, 1883, the principle has become firmly embedded in our constitutional law that the action inhibited by the first section of the Fourteenth Amendment is only such action as may fairly be said to be that of the States. That Amendment erects no shield against merely private conduct, however discriminatory or wrongful.

We conclude, therefore, that the restrictive agreements standing alone cannot be regarded as a violation of any rights guaranteed to petitioners by the Fourteenth Amendment. So long as the purposes of those agreements are effectuated by voluntary adherence to their terms, it would appear clear that there has been no action by the State and the provisions of the Amendment have not been violated.

But here there was more. These are cases in which the purposes of the agreements were secured only by judicial enforcement by state courts of the restrictive terms of the agreements. The respondents urge that judicial enforcement of private agreements does not amount to state action; or, in any event, the participation of the State is so attenuated in character as not to amount to state action within the meaning of the Fourteenth Amendment. * * *

That the action of state courts and of judicial officers in their official capacities is to be regarded as action of the State within the meaning of the Fourteenth Amendment, is a proposition which has long been established by decisions of this Court. * * *

* * *

The short of the matter is that from the time of the adoption of the Fourteenth Amendment until the present, it has been the consistent ruling of this Court that the action of the States to which the Amendment has reference, includes action of state courts and state judicial officials. Although, in construing the terms of the Fourteenth Amendment, differences have from time to time been expressed as to whether particular types of state action may be said to offend the Amendment's prohibitory provisions, it has never been suggested that state court action is immunized from the operation of those provisions simply because the act is that of the judicial branch of the state government.

* * *

We have no doubt that there has been state action in these cases in the full and complete sense of the phrase. The undisputed facts disclose that petitioners were willing purchasers of properties upon which they desired to establish homes. The owners of the properties were willing sellers; and contracts of sale were accordingly consummated. It is clear that but for the active intervention of the state courts, supported by the full panoply of state power, petitioners would have been free to occupy the properties in question without restraint.

* * *

We hold that in granting judicial enforcement of the restrictive agreements in these cases, the States have denied petitioners the equal protection of the laws and that, therefore, the action of the state courts cannot stand. We have noted that freedom from discrimination by the States in the enjoyment of property rights was among the basic objectives sought to be effectuated by the framers of the Fourteenth Amendment. That such discrimination has occurred in these cases is clear. * * *

* * *

Reversed.

Justice Reed, Justice Jackson, and Justice Rutledge took no part in the consideration or decision of these cases.

After the *Shelley* decision, the NAACP continued to press for an end to racial segregation in education. Two cases handed down on the same day in 1950 indicated that the separate but equal doctrine was on shaky ground. In *Sweatt v. Painter,* Heman Sweatt, an African American postal worker from Houston, applied for admission to the University of Texas Law School. As might be expected, he was denied admission solely on account of his race. A state court agreed that the law school's action denied him equal protection, but the court would not order his admission because the state was in the midst of establishing a separate law school for African Americans. After the school was established, Sweatt refused to apply, alleging that the education to be provided by the black school would be inferior to that offered at the University of Texas. When the state courts ruled that the two law schools were essentially equal, Sweatt sought review in the U.S. Supreme Court.

In a unanimous decision, the high court reversed the lower courts, ruling that the law school for African Americans was by no means equal to the University of Texas Law School. The facilities available at the latter, for example, the number of faculty, variety of courses, availability of law review, and volumes in the library, were far superior. In addition to examining these tangible factors, the Court addressed the inequality of intangible factors. "What is more important, the University of Texas Law School possesses to a far greater degree those qualities which are incapable of objective measurement but which make for greatness in a law school. Such qualities . . . include reputation of the faculty, experience of the administration, position and influence of the alumni, standing in the community, traditions and prestige" (339 U.S. at 634). The justices remarked that, given a choice between these two law schools, there is no question that an individual would choose the University of Texas. The Court, however, refused to reexamine the separate but equal doctrine, despite being encouraged to do so by Thurgood Marshall, Sweatt's attorney. Nonetheless, the focus here on intangible factors made it appear that the doctrine was imperiled.

In the second case, *McLaurin v. Oklahoma State Regents* (1950), the Court was faced with a different situation. After he previously had been denied admission, George McLaurin entered the all-white University of Oklahoma for graduate studies in education at the order of a federal court. Although admitted to the university, every aspect of his life there was segregated because state law required that, when African Americans and whites attended the same graduate school, the instruction must be provided "upon a segregated basis." In the classroom he was required to sit behind a rail with the sign, "For Coloreds Only"; in the library he had to study at a separate desk; and in the university cafeteria he had to eat at a separate table. McLaurin requested the district court to end this treatment, but that court found no constitutional violation. Thus McLaurin looked to the Supreme Court for help.

In a brief, unanimous opinion, the high court held that the treatment accorded McLaurin was an obvious violation of the Fourteenth Amendment. Although the state permitted him to attend the school, the restrictions it imposed on him "impair[ed] and inhibit[ed] his ability to study, to engage in discussion and exchange views with other students, and, in general, to learn his profession" (339 U.S. at 641). In placing these conditions upon McLaurin, the state "deprive[d] him of his personal and present right to the equal protection of the laws" (339 U.S. at 642). This case, like *Sweatt v. Painter,* cast serious doubts as to whether the "separate but equal" doctrine could continue to withstand constitutional challenges.

The Warren Court Era

The decisions of the Warren Court in the 1950s and 1960s contributed significantly to the civil rights revolution in this country. Under the leadership of Chief Justice Earl Warren, the Court reversed the separate but equal doctrine and made decisions that abolished legal segregation and discrimination in a number of areas including education, public accommodations, housing, marriage and family matters, and the right to trial by an impartial jury. In many of these cases, the Court extended the application of the Equal Protection Clause, although in some areas it continued to rely on the "state action" doctrine.

Racial Segregation in Education

By far the most well-known decision of the Warren Court with respect to racial equality was *Brown v. Board of Education of Topeka, Kansas I* (1954). As noted earlier, the decisions in the higher education cases paved the way for the *Brown I* ruling. *Brown I* actually was one of five consolidated cases that dealt with laws requiring or permitting segregation in public schools. The other cases came from South Carolina, Virginia, Delaware, and the District of Columbia. Although all five cases were argued together, the Court issued a separate ruling in the District of Columbia case, because the Equal Protection Clause of the Fourteenth Amendment applies only to states, and the segregation in the District of Columbia was challenged on Fifth Amendment due process grounds.

In *Brown,* a policy of the school board of Topeka, Kansas required local schools to be segregated by race. In a suit filed in federal court, the Reverend Oliver Brown challenged this policy on behalf of his daughter Linda and other African American school children. The case was handled by the NAACP Legal Defense and Educational Fund, under the direction of Thurgood Marshall. The lower court did not find a violation of the Equal Protection Clause, and the case was appealed to the U.S. Supreme Court. The cases were argued twice, first in December of 1952 and again in December of 1953. At the time of reargument, Earl Warren had replaced Fred Vinson as chief justice, Vinson having died unexpectedly in the summer of 1953. The justices moved very carefully in deciding these cases, knowing full well that their decision would have enormous implications. In attacking racial segregation in public schools, the plaintiffs were threatening the entire southern way of life.

In a brief, unanimous opinion written by Chief Justice Warren, the Court ruled that the laws regarding segregation in public schools violated the Fourteenth Amendment's Equal Protection Clause. First, Warren contended that the history of the amendment was inconclusive as to whether the framers intended it to prohibit school segregation. He said that the debates over the scope of the amendment did not answer this question, and he noted that public education at that time was quite different than in 1954. "In the South, the movement toward free common schools, supported by general taxation, had not yet taken hold. . . . Even in the North, the conditions of public education did not approximate those existing today. The curriculum was usually rudimentary; ungraded schools were common in rural areas; the school term was but three months a year in many states; and compulsory school attendance was virtually unknown" (347 U.S. at 490). In turning to the "separate but equal" doctrine, the Court was forced to determine whether segregation itself was unconstitutional, because in these cases the schools were basically equal (or soon to be) in terms of such tangible factors as buildings, curricula, and teacher qualifications and salaries. Warren emphasized that in deciding this case the justices could not return to 1868 when the Fourteenth Amendment was adopted or to 1896 when *Plessy* was decided. "[P]ublic education," declared Warren, must be considered "in the light of its full development and its present place in American life throughout the Nation" (347 U.S. at 492–93). He asserted that education probably was the "most important function of state and local government" because it was the "foundation of good citizenship" and prepared children for "later professional training" (347 U.S. at 493). He said that a good education was considered to be necessary for success in life, and if the state provides educational opportunity for its citizens, it must be provided to all on an equal basis.

Warren then examined the question of whether racial segregation deprived the African American students of equal protection. In the most criticized portion of the opinion, he turned to social science evidence in concluding that such segregation did amount to a deprivation of the minority children's rights to an equal education.

"To separate them from others of similar age and qualifications solely because of their race generates a feeling of inferiority as to their status in the community that may affect their hearts and minds in a way unlikely ever to be undone" (347 U.S. at 494). In making this conclusion, he relied to some extent on sociological studies regarding the negative effects of enforced racial segregation. In concluding, Warren wrote, "Separate educational facilities are inherently unequal" (347 U.S. at 495). The high court extended this ruling in *Bolling v. Sharpe* (1954), holding that the segregation of public schools in the District of Columbia was unconstitutional under the Due Process Clause of the Fifth Amendment. "In view of our decision that the Constitution prohibits the states from maintaining racially segregated public schools, it would be unthinkable that the same Constitution would impose a lesser duty on the Federal Government" (347 U.S. at 500).

Brown v. Board of Education of Topeka I

347 U.S. 483, 74 S.Ct. 686, 98 L.Ed. 873 (1954)

■ Linda Brown lived only a short distance from a white elementary school, but a Topeka school board policy required her to attend a school reserved for African American children, which was quite a distance away. Her father, the Reverend Oliver Brown, filed suit in federal district court on behalf of his daughter and other African American children similarly situated. After losing there, the Browns took their case to the U.S. Supreme Court. They and the plaintiffs from four other cases—*Briggs v. Elliot, Davis v. County School Board of Prince Edward County, Gebhart v. Belton,* and *Bolling v. Sharpe*—were represented by the NAACP Legal Defense Fund, with Thurgood Marshall acting as chief counsel.

This case is important because it marked the end of the separate but equal doctrine in equal protection analysis and paved the way for the Court to strike down laws mandating racial segregation in other aspects of life. As you read the case, consider the following questions: 1) Is it appropriate for the Court to use social science evidence in examining the validity of laws and government actions? 2) Which do you think was more critical to the justices as they decided the case, the higher education precedents or the social science evidence? 3) Why do you think Chief Justice Warren did not apply (or even mention) the strict scrutiny test?

Vote:

The Court unanimously voted to strike down the laws (Warren, Black, Burton, Clark, Douglas, Frankfurter, Jackson, Minton, Reed).

Chief Justice Warren delivered the opinion of the Court.

* * *

In each of the cases, minors of the Negro race, through their legal representatives, seek the aid of the courts in obtaining admission to the public schools of their community on a nonsegregated basis. In each instance, they have been denied admission to schools attended by white children under laws requiring or permitting segregation according to race. This segregation was alleged to deprive the plaintiffs of the equal protection of the laws under the Fourteenth Amendment. * * *

The plaintiffs contend that segregated public schools are not "equal" and cannot be made "equal," and that hence they are deprived of the equal protection of the laws. Because of the obvious importance of the question presented, the Court took jurisdiction. Argument was heard in the 1952 Term, and reargument was heard this Term on certain questions propounded by the Court.

Reargument was largely devoted to the circumstances surrounding the adoption of the Fourteenth Amendment in 1868. It covered exhaustively consideration of the Amendment in Congress, ratification by the states, then existing practices in racial segregation, and the views of proponents and opponents of the Amendment. This discussion and our own investigation convince us that, although these sources cast some light, it is not enough to resolve the problem with which we are faced. At best, they are inconclusive. The most avid proponents of the post-War Amendments undoubtedly intended them to remove all legal distinctions among "all persons born or naturalized in the United States." Their opponents, just as certainly, were antagonistic to both the letter and the spirit of the Amendments and wished them to have the most limited effect. What others in Congress and the state legislatures had in mind cannot be determined with any degree of certainty.

An additional reason for the inconclusive nature of the Amendment's history, with respect to segregated schools, is the status of public education at that time. In the South, the movement toward free common schools, supported by general taxation, had not yet taken hold. Education of white children was largely in the hands of private groups. Education of Negroes was almost nonexistent, and practically all of the race were illiterate. In fact, any education of Negroes was forbidden by law in some states. Today, in contrast, many Negroes have achieved outstanding success in the arts and sciences as well as in the business and professional world. It is true that public school education at the time of the Amendment had advanced further in the North, but the effect of the Amendment on Northern States was generally ignored in the congressional debates. Even in the North, the conditions of public education did not approximate those existing today. The curriculum was usually rudimentary; ungraded schools were common in rural areas; the school term was but three months a year in many states; and compulsory school attendance was virtually unknown. As a consequence, it is not surprising that there should be so little in the history of the Fourteenth Amendment relating to its intended effect on public education.

In the first cases in this Court construing the Fourteenth Amendment, decided shortly after its adoption, the Court interpreted it as proscribing all state-imposed discriminations against the Negro race. The doctrine of "separate but equal" did not make its appearance in this Court until 1896 in the case of *Plessy v. Ferguson,* involving not education but transportation. American courts have since labored with the doctrine for over half a century. * * *

* * *

In approaching this problem, we cannot turn the clock back to 1868 when the Amendment was adopted, or even to 1896 when *Plessy v. Ferguson* was written. We must consider public education in the light of its full development and its present place in American life throughout the Nation. Only in this way can it be determined if segregation in public schools deprives these plaintiffs of the equal protection of the laws.

Today, education is perhaps the most important function of state and local governments. Compulsory school attendance laws and the great expenditures for education both demonstrate our recognition of the importance of education to our democratic society. It is required in the performance of our most basic public responsibilities, even service in the armed forces. It is the very foundation of good citizenship. Today it is a principal instrument in awakening the child to cultural values, in preparing him for later professional training, and in helping him to adjust normally to his environment. In these days, it is doubtful that any child may reasonably be expected to succeed in life if he is denied the opportunity of an education. Such an opportunity, where the state has undertaken to provide it, is a right which must be made available to all on equal terms.

We come then to the question presented: Does segregation of children in public schools solely on the basis of race, even though the physical facilities and other "tangible" factors may be equal, deprive the children of the minority group of equal educational opportunities? We believe that it does.

In *Sweatt v. Painter* [1950], in finding that a segregated law school for Negroes could not provide them equal educational opportunities, this Court relied in large part on "those qualities which are incapable of objective measurement but which make for greatness in a law school." In *McLaurin v. Oklahoma State Regents* [1950], the Court, in requiring that a Negro admitted to a white graduate school be treated like all other students, again resorted to intangible considerations: ". . . his ability to study, to engage in discussions and exchange views with other students, and, in general, to learn his profession." Such considerations apply with added force to children in grade and high schools. To separate them from others of similar age and qualifications solely because of their race generates a feeling of inferiority as to their status in the community that may affect their hearts and minds in a way unlikely ever to be undone. The effect of this separation on their educational opportunities was well stated by a finding in the Kansas case by a court which nevertheless felt compelled to rule against the Negro plaintiffs:

> Segregation of white and colored children in public schools has a detrimental effect upon the colored children. The impact is greater when it has the sanction of the law; for the policy of separating the races is usually interpreted as denoting the inferiority of the Negro group. A sense of inferiority affects the motivation of a child to learn. Segregation with the sanction of law, therefore, has a tendency to [retard] the educational and mental development of Negro children and to deprive them of some of the benefits they would receive in a racial[ly] integrated school system.

Whatever may have been the extent of psychological knowledge at the time of *Plessy v. Ferguson,* this finding is amply supported by modern authority. [At this point in the opinion, Chief Justice Warren included the famous "footnote 11," which cited several social scientific studies regarding the negative effects of enforced racial segregation, most prominently Dr. Kenneth Clark's studies of the detrimental effects of segregation on the self-image and achievement of black children.] Any language in *Plessy v. Ferguson* contrary to this finding is rejected.

We conclude that in the field of public education the doctrine of "separate but equal" has no place. Separate educational facilities are inherently unequal. Therefore, we hold that the plaintiffs and others similarly situated for whom the actions have been brought are, by reason of the segregation complained of, deprived of the equal protection of the laws guaranteed by the Fourteenth Amendment. * * *

* * *

It is so ordered.

Thus the NAACP strategy finally had come to fruition. The infamous separate but equal doctrine no longer was a valid precedent. Unfortunately, this decision was only half of the battle; questions remained about the conditions under which public schools would be desegregated. The initial answer was given one year later in *Brown v. Board of Education II* (1955) after attorneys from both sides presented arguments to the Court. The NAACP attorneys encouraged the justices to implement desegregation immediately or, at the very least, to set firm deadlines by which the states must comply. On the other hand, the states' attorneys contended that proceeding in such a fashion was not feasible, and they pressed the Court to delay implementation indefinitely.

In another unanimous opinion, the Court attempted to find a middle ground between the two sides. The justices remanded the cases to the district courts that originally had heard them, directing those courts to supervise the implementation process; the justices' rationale was that each school system would have problems unique to it that best would be solved by a court in close proximity. In determining whether there was good faith implementation, the district courts were to consider problems related to administration, physical facilities, transportation, personnel, and the drawing of school district boundaries and attendance zones. While these problems were to be taken into consideration by the district courts, the school boards were to be required to make a "prompt and reasonable start" toward full compliance. Although the Court was attempting to establish a feasible, reasonable implementation strategy, resistance by state and local officials was inevitable. Moreover, four words in the opinion—"with all deliberate speed"—gave these officials an excuse for dragging their feet in implementing *Brown*. The opinion also ensured that the issue of school desegregation would return to the Court time and time again.

As was expected, the reaction to the two *Brown* decisions was intense and hostile, particularly in the South. Southern governors and legislators vowed to fight desegregation efforts and to preserve their way of life. They engaged in a number of tactics, including passage of "interposition" and "nullification" statutes, claiming that state laws requiring segregation took precedence over federal court decisions. Some legislatures repealed their compulsory education laws, while others adopted "freedom of choice" plans, which were doomed to failure because the hostility that existed guaranteed that few African Americans would opt to attend all-white schools and vice versa. Another tactic used by some states was to close their public schools rather than desegregate them and then to provide public funding for white children to attend segregated private schools.

Thus, in the decade or so after the *Brown* cases, the Court's decisions in this area primarily were attempts to keep in line those school districts intent on disobeying the orders to desegregate. In the first case, *Cooper v. Aaron* (1958), the justices refused to allow claims of ensuing violence to permit delay in the implementation of a plan to desegregate Central High School in Little Rock, Arkansas. The school board had developed the plan to allow for nine African American students to attend the school beginning in 1957. Governor Orval Faubus ordered the state national guard to prevent the students from entering Central High, claiming that violence was imminent. A district court decision forced Faubus to withdraw the guard. After his initial reluctance to become involved, President Eisenhower agreed to send in federal troops to protect the "Little Rock Nine." At the end of the school year, because of the tension that existed, the school board requested that the district court withdraw the African American students from Central High and delay further desegregation for two and a half years. The district court granted the request, but the court of appeals reversed, and the school board appealed to the Supreme Court.

The Court called a special summer term in late August in order to make a decision before the beginning of the school year. On September 12, a brief per curiam opinion affirmed the appeals court decision denying the implementation delay, and the Court issued its formal opinion on September 29. While sympathizing with the plight of the school board and acknowledging the board's good faith efforts at desegregation, the Court held "the constitutional rights of [the African American children] are not to be sacrificed or yielded to the violence and disorder which have followed upon the actions of the Governor and Legislature" (358 U.S. at 16). The justices insisted that they would not permit government officials to evade the command to desegregate, whether directly or indirectly. Despite this rebuke, government officials in various states continued developing schemes to avoid desegregating their schools.

By 1964, ten years after the initial *Brown* ruling, the Court was fed up with these evasive tactics. In *Griffin v. School Board of Prince Edward County* (1964), the Court said that there had been "entirely too much deliberation and not enough speed" in school desegregation efforts (377 U.S. at 229). Here, the county had closed its public schools in 1959 and had provided financial assistance for white children to attend all-white private schools. The county board offered to set up a similar scheme for African American children, but the African American community refused, preferring to fight for integrated schools. In 1961 a federal district court ordered the county to discontinue financial assistance to the all-white private schools, and in 1962 it ordered the county to reopen the public schools. The county sought review in the Supreme Court, and the Court unanimously affirmed the district court ruling. "Whatever nonracial grounds might support a State's allowing a county to abandon public schools, the object must be a constitutional one, and grounds of race and opposition to desegregation do not qualify as constitutional" (377 U.S. at 231).

Four years after *Griffin,* in its last major school desegregation case, the Warren Court ordered school districts to develop plans that would meaningfully desegregate public schools and would result in unitary, rather than dual, school systems. The issue in *Green v. School Board of New Kent County* (1968) was a rural Virginia county's "freedom of choice" plan adopted in 1965 that permitted students to decide which school within their district they would attend. Because of segregated housing, the Kent County schools continued to be racially segregated. In fact, when the case reached the Supreme Court, the justices noted that only 15 percent of African American students attended the previously all-white school, and, even more noticeable, no white students chose to enroll in an all-black school. Speaking for a unanimous Court, Justice Brennan concluded that the "freedom of choice" plan adopted by the school board was inadequate to bring about meaningful desegregation of the county's schools, and he ordered the board "to come forward with a plan that promises realistically to work, and promises realistically to work *now* [emphasis in original]" (391 U.S. at 439). Brennan did not say that "freedom of choice" plans automatically were invalid, but he noted that they usually were ineffective, and the

Kent County plan was clearly so. While not promoting a specific type of desegregation plan, preferring that individual school districts develop plans to meet their particular needs, the Court offered guidance to district courts in their supervisory role. "It is incumbent upon the district court to weigh that claim [of plan effectiveness] in light of the facts at hand and . . . any alternatives which may be shown as feasible and more promising in their effectiveness. Where the court finds the board to be acting in good faith and the proposed plan to have real prospects for dismantling the state-imposed dual system 'at the earliest practicable date,' then the plan may be said to provide effective relief" (391 U.S. at 439). The Court identified six factors relevant in assessing whether a school system has achieved unitary status: student assignments, transportation, physical facilities, extracurricular activities, faculty assignments, and resource allocation.

Public Accommodations

During the Warren era the Court continued to be confronted with the question of whether private discrimination was prohibited by the Constitution. The Warren Court's first attempt at providing an answer was *Burton v. Wilmington Parking Authority* (1961). The case arose when Burton, an African-American man, was refused service by the Eagle Restaurant, an establishment located in a city-owned parking garage in Wilmington, Delaware. Burton filed suit charging a violation of his right to equal protection under the Fourteenth Amendment. The Delaware Supreme Court ruled that Eagle was acting in a "purely private capacity" and that it "[wa]s not required [under Delaware law] to serve any and all persons entering its place of business" (365 U.S. at 717). Burton sought review in the U.S. Supreme Court. By a 6-3 vote, the Court decided in Burton's favor, concluding that state action was involved in Eagle's denial of service. The majority focused on the fact that the municipal parking garage and the restaurant were located on publicly owned land and that the city leased the space to the restaurant in order to provide funds for maintaining the public parking facility. This was deemed sufficient to establish that the state was involved in private conduct. "The State has so far insinuated itself into a position of interdependence with Eagle that it must be recognized as a joint participant in the challenged activity, which on that account cannot be considered to have been so 'purely private' as to fall without the scope of the Fourteenth Amendment" (365 U.S. at 725). The dissenters argued that the case should have been remanded to the state supreme court for clarification of its interpretation of the state law in relation to the action of the restaurant.

As we pointed out earlier, the Civil Rights Act of 1875, which prohibited discrimination in places of public accommodations, was struck down by the Court on the basis of the state action doctrine (*The Civil Rights Cases,* 1883). Nearly a century later, Congress passed a similar statute. Title II of the Civil Rights Act of 1964 prohibits racial discrimination in places of public accommodations that affect interstate commerce. These accommodations include inns, hotels, restaurants, movie theaters, and the like. The Court unanimously upheld Title II in the companion cases of *Heart of Atlanta Motel v. United States* and *Katzenbach v. McClung* (1964), but they were not decided on Fourteenth Amendment grounds. The justices ruled that this prohibition against racial discrimination in public accommodations was consistent with Congress's power to regulate interstate commerce. The legislative history of the act indicated that discrimination against African Americans impeded interstate travel and thus placed a burden on interstate commerce. Justices Douglas and Goldberg concurred in the decision, but they argued that the statute also was sanctioned by Section 5 of the Fourteenth Amendment authorizing congressional action to enforce equal protection.

Personal and Family Matters

A major aspect of racial segregation in this country has included laws preventing romantic involvements between whites and nonwhites, particularly between whites and African Americans. For example, a nineteenth-century Supreme Court decision, *Pace v. Alabama* (1883), upheld a state law that punished interracial adultery and fornication more severely than intraracial adultery and fornication. In the mid-1950s, the Warren Court refused to hear cases involving Alabama and Virginia laws that prohibited interracial marriage. Scholars have speculated that, after *Brown,* the Court was reluctant to tackle another issue certain to stimulate considerable controversy. By the 1960s, however, the justices were willing to examine these types of laws.

The Court ruled first on a Florida law that prohibited unmarried interracial couples from living together. In *McLaughlin v. Florida* (1964), by a unanimous vote, the Court held this cohabitation statute to constitute a denial of equal protection of the laws. Although encouraged to decide on the validity of antimiscegenation statutes as well, the Court declined this opportunity. Three years later, the high court met this issue head-on. In *Loving v. Virginia* (1967), (see the case study at the beginning of this chapter), a unanimous Court held that antimiscegenation statutes violated both the Equal Protection and Due Process Clauses.

LOVING V. VIRGINIA

388 U.S. 1, 87 S.Ct. 1817, 18 L.Ed.2d 1010 (1967)
[The facts of this case are omitted because they were presented in the case study at the beginning of the chapter.]

■ This case is important because the Court struck down the last of the Jim Crow laws that had existed in a number of states for a long time. As you read the case, consider these questions: 1) Would the antimiscegenation statutes be upheld or struck down using the rational basis test? 2) Is marriage a "purely domestic" matter not within the purview of the federal courts? 3) Is there any connection between state laws prohibiting interracial marriages and those maintaining racial segregation in public schools?

VOTE:
9 justices voted to strike down the antimiscegenation statutes (Warren, Black, Douglas, Clark, Harlan, Brennan, Stewart, White, and Fortas).

Chief Justice Warren delivered the opinion of the Court.

This case presents a constitutional question never addressed by this Court: whether a statutory scheme adopted by the State of Virginia to prevent marriages between persons solely on the basis of racial classifications violates the Equal Protection and Due Process Clauses of the Fourteenth Amendment. For reasons which seem to us to reflect the central meaning of those constitutional commands, we conclude that these statutes cannot stand consistently with the Fourteenth Amendment.

* * *

While the state court is no doubt correct in asserting that marriage is a social relation subject to the State's police power, the State does not contend in its argument before this Court that its powers to regulate marriage are unlimited notwithstanding the commands of the Fourteenth Amendment. Instead, the State argues that the meaning of the Equal Protection Clause, as illuminated by the statements of the Framers, is only that state penal laws containing an interracial element as part of the definition of the offense must apply equally to whites and Negroes in the sense that members of each race are punished to the same degree. Thus, the State contends that, because its miscegenation statutes punish equally both the white and the Negro participants in an interracial marriage, these statutes, despite their reliance on racial classifications do not constitute an invidious discrimination based upon race. The second argument advanced by the State assumes the validity of its equal application theory. The argument is that, if the Equal Protection Clause does not outlaw miscegenation statutes because of their reliance on racial classifications, the question of constitutionality would thus become whether there was any rational basis for a State to treat interracial marriages differently from other marriages. On this question, the State argues, the scientific evidence is substantially in doubt and, consequently, this Court should defer to the wisdom of the state legislature in adopting its policy of discouraging interracial marriages.

Because we reject the notion that the mere "equal application" of a statute containing racial classifications is enough to remove the classifications from the Fourteenth Amendment's proscription of all invidious racial discriminations, we do not accept the State's contention that these statutes should be upheld if there is any possible basis for concluding that they serve a rational purpose. * * * In the case at bar, we deal with statutes containing racial classifications, and the fact of equal application does not immunize the statute from the very heavy burden of justification which the Fourteenth Amendment has traditionally required of state statutes drawn according to race.

* * *

The State finds support for its "equal application" theory in the decision of the Court in *Pace v. State of Alabama* (1883). In that case, the Court upheld a conviction under an Alabama statute forbidding adultery or fornication between a white person and a Negro which imposed a greater penalty than that of a statute proscribing similar conduct by members of the same race. The Court reasoned that the statute could not be said to discriminate against Negroes because the punishment for each participant in the offense was the same. However, as recently as the 1964 Term, in rejecting the reasoning of that case, we stated "*Pace* represents a limited view of the Equal Protection Clause which has not withstood analysis in the subsequent decisions of this Court." As we there demonstrated, the Equal Protection Clause requires the consideration of whether the classifications drawn by any statute constitute an arbitrary and invidious discrimination. The clear and central purpose of the Fourteenth Amendment was to eliminate all official state sources of invidious racial discrimination in the States.

There can be no question but that Virginia's miscegenation statutes rest solely upon distinctions drawn according to race. The statutes proscribe generally accepted conduct if engaged in by members of different races. Over the years, this Court has consistently repudiated "[d]istinctions between citizens solely because of their ancestry" as being "odious to a free people whose institutions are founded upon the doctrine of equality." At the very least, the Equal Protection Clause demands that racial classifications, especially suspect in criminal statutes, be subjected to the "most rigid scrutiny," *Korematsu v. United States* (1944), and, if they are ever to be upheld, they must be shown to be necessary to the accomplishment of some permissible state objective, independent of the racial discrimination which it was the object of the Fourteenth Amendment to eliminate. * * *

There is patently no legitimate overriding purpose independent of invidious racial discrimination which justifies this classification. The fact that Virginia prohibits only interracial marriages involving white persons demonstrates that the racial classifications must stand on their own justification, as measures designed to maintain White Supremacy. We have consistently denied the constitutionality of measures which restrict the rights of citizens on account of race. There can be no doubt that restricting the freedom to marry solely because of racial classifications violates the central meaning of the Equal Protection Clause.

These statutes also deprive the Lovings of liberty without due process of law in violation of the Due Process Clause of the Fourteenth Amendment. The freedom to marry has long been recognized as one of the vital personal rights essential to the orderly pursuit of happiness by free men.

Marriage is one of the "basic civil rights of man," fundamental to our very existence and survival. To deny this fundamental freedom on so unsupportable a basis as the racial classifications embodied in these statutes, classifications so directly subversive of the principle of equality at the heart of the Fourteenth Amendment, is surely to deprive all the State's citizens of liberty without due process of law. The Fourteenth Amendment requires that the freedom of choice to marry not be restricted by invidious racial discriminations. Under our Constitution, the freedom to marry a person of another race resides with the individual and cannot be infringed by the State.

These convictions must be reversed. It is so ordered. Reversed.

[*The concurring opinion of Justice Stewart is omitted.*]

Racial Discrimination and the Right to Trial by Jury

In *Strauder v. West Virginia* (1880), the Supreme Court held that state laws excluding African Americans from jury duty violated the Equal Protection Clause. Beginning with *Hernandez v. Texas* in 1954, the Warren Court extended application of the clause in jury matters to include the grand jury stage, discrimination in jury selection, and discrimination involving other racial groups. In *Hernandez,* the Court said that to exclude systematically or arbitrarily any substantial racial group from jury duty was to violate the Fourteenth Amendment. Here, in a Texas county where 14 percent of the population was of Mexican or Latin American descent, no one from this group had ever served on a jury in the preceding 25 years. This was deemed a clear denial of equal protection. "Circumstances or chance may well dictate that no persons in a certain class will serve on a particular jury or during some particular period. But it taxes our credulity to say that mere chance resulted in there being no members of this class among the over six thousand jurors called in the past 25 years. The result bespeaks discrimination . . ." (347 U.S. at 482).

Statutory Cases

A major civil rights case decided during the last term of the Warren Court, although not involving interpretation of the Fourteenth Amendment, deserves mention here. *Jones v. Alfred H. Mayer Co.* (1968), a housing discrimination case, concerned the applicability of an 1866 civil rights law. A portion of that statute provided that "the inhabitants of every race . . . shall have the same rights to . . . inherit, purchase, lease, sell, hold, and convey real and personal property." Joseph Lee Jones, an African American man, alleged that the Alfred Mayer Company practiced discrimination in violation of the 1866 law when it refused to sell him a home in a particular community in St. Louis, Missouri. His suit was dismissed by a federal district court and court of appeals on the grounds that the act did not apply to actions of private individuals. The Supreme Court reversed the lower courts by a 7-2 vote. Justice Stewart, writing for the majority, asserted that the legislative history of the 1866 act indicated Congress's desire to prohibit both private and state-supported racial discrimination. On the question of the validity of the 1866 act itself, Stewart held that the Thirteenth Amendment was intended to remove "the badges and incidents of slavery," and Congress was empowered by section 2 of that amendment to pass legislation for this purpose. "[W]hen racial discrimination herds men into ghettos and makes their ability to buy property turn on the color of their skin, then it too is a relic of slavery" (392 U.S. at 443). Justices Harlan and White disagreed with the majority's construction of the legislative history, arguing that the 1866 act was directed only at state-imposed discrimination.

The Impact of the Warren Court

These decisions of the Warren Court marked a true revolution in the Court's analysis of racial segregation and discrimination under the Constitution. They contributed significantly to the civil rights movement, and many credit the Court with spurring congressional action to guarantee civil rights. Another interesting and important development near the end of the Warren era was the appointment to the Court of Thurgood Marshall, the first African American justice, in 1967. Marshall, the former chief litigator for the NAACP Legal Defense Fund, served the final two terms of the Warren Court, but his major impact would be felt during the Burger and Rehnquist eras.

The Burger Court Era

Chief Justice Earl Warren's retirement in 1968 led many to speculate about the direction the Court would move in examining claims of racial discrimination and attempts to remedy such discrimination. President Nixon had campaigned on a pledge to appoint conservative justices who would curb the excesses of the Warren era, particularly regarding the due process rights of criminal defendants. What this meant in terms of the Court's equal protection jurisprudence remained to be seen, but it appeared that eradicating racial discrimination in American society was not one of Nixon's top priorities. His first two appointees to the Court did not have particularly strong backgrounds in civil rights, but they were not considered to be strict conservatives in this area. Even so, however, they replaced two justices who had been liberal on civil rights issues. In 1969, Warren Burger replaced Warren as chief justice, and a year later Harry Blackmun succeeded Abe Fortas. In 1972 Nixon made two more appointments to the Court, Lewis Powell, a Virginian regarded as moderate in civil rights matters, and William Rehnquist, an outspoken opponent of civil rights laws and desegregation. Powell and Rehnquist succeeded Hugo Black and John Marshall Harlan, respectively, both considered to be moderate on civil rights issues.

The overall effect of these four Nixon appointments was to make the Burger Court more conservative on civil rights issues than the Warren Court. The Burger Court continued to grapple with such issues as desegregation of public schools, housing, and public accommodations, as well as questions regarding racial discrimination in jury selection. In addition, the Burger era justices were faced with more questions regarding the interpretation and application of civil rights statutes.

Desegregation of Public Schools

In its very first term, the Burger Court issued an important rebuke to school districts still attempting to evade the mandate of *Brown*. In *Alexander v. Holmes County Board of Education* (1969), a federal appeals court had permitted thirty-three Mississippi school districts to postpone desegregating their schools indefinitely. Over the objections of the Nixon administration, in a per curiam opinion the Court reversed the appeals court, calling for the end of the "all deliberate speed" standard and for the immediate operation of unitary school systems. "[T]he obligation of every school district is to terminate dual school systems at once and to operate now and hereafter only unitary schools" (396 U.S. at 20).

Alexander posed a fairly straightforward question: Is it permissible for federal judges to delay implementation of school desegregation plans? Yet a major issue remained regarding the scope of such desegregation plans. What methods of desegregation were appropriate and within the authority of the federal courts? *Swann v. Charlotte-Mecklenburg Board of Education* (1971) presented the Burger Court with the opportunity to answer this question. Here, a federal district judge supervising the desegregation efforts in Charlotte, North Carolina, ordered several remedies, the most controversial of which was busing African American children to schools in white neighborhoods and vice versa. In one sense, busing was not a new concept. Transporting children to and from school by means of school buses had existed for quite some time. In fact, by 1970, nearly 40 percent of the nation's public school children rode buses to get to school. North Carolina earlier had proclaimed itself "the schoolbusingest state in the Union" (Wilkinson 1979, p. 135). Therefore, the resistance by whites to busing for desegregation purposes prompted many African Americans to declare, "It's not the bus, it's us."

In Charlotte, the federal judge was influenced strongly by the fact that 29 percent of Charlotte's school children were black and they were concentrated in mostly African American schools. His plan was to reach a 71:29 percent white to African American ratio in the various Charlotte schools, and the busing program was designed to help achieve this goal. In a unanimous decision, the Court, speaking through Chief Justice Burger, upheld the district court order in light of the constitutional violations that had occurred. The evidence indicated that the school board had taken discriminatory actions and that segregated residential patterns were the result of actions of federal, state, and local governments. Furthermore, the federal judge had taken over the desegregation efforts only after the school board's repeated failure to develop a plan that would be effective. Acknowledging that meaningful desegregation did not mean that every school in a community had to reflect the racial composition of the school system, Burger wrote, "the very limited use of mathematical ratios was within the equitable remedial discretion of the District Court" (402 U.S. at 25). In addition, noting that "bus transportation has been an integral part of the public education system for years," the justices held that "the remedial techniques [including busing] used in the District Court's order were within that court's power to provide relief . . ." (402 U.S. at 30).

At the time of *Swann,* the Court had dealt only with southern school districts and with **de jure segregation,** that is, segregation required or permitted by statutory law. The Court had not viewed the Fourteenth Amendment to be implicated by **de facto segregation,** segregation created by the private decisions of individuals. In many nonsouthern states, schools also were segregated, although not because of formal state laws. De facto segregation of schools frequently occurred because of segregated residential patterns. It is important to note, however, that residential segregation did not occur by accident. Governmental housing programs, real estate practices, and banking policies contributed significantly to housing segregation. In addition to the restrictive covenants discussed earlier, realtors used steering and blockbusting to maintain racial separation. Steering, the act of refusing to show homes in white neighborhoods to people of color (and vice versa), became part of the National Association of Real Estate Boards' Code of Ethics in 1924. "A Realtor should never be instrumental in introducing into a neighborhood . . . members of any race or nationality, or any individuals whose presence will be clearly detrimental to property values in that neighborhood" (Anderson and Pickering 1986, p. 464, n. 10). Although this part of the Code of Ethics was amended in 1950, with the specific reference to race or nationality deleted, it was clear that the meaning was the same. With blockbusting, realtors would help an African American family move into a white neighborhood and then would inform the white families that their property values would decrease. Having created a panic, the realtors then could buy homes from white families at low prices and sell those same homes to African American families for significantly higher prices. In addition, many banks refused to grant mortgages to people of color attempting to move into predominantly white neighborhoods and also engaged in a practice called redlining. Redlining refers to the activity of drawing a (red) line around certain communities and refusing to grant loans for purchasing or improving homes there. The red-lined communities typically were those where significant numbers of people of color lived or sought to live. Policies and practices of government housing programs also contributed to residential segregation.

The decisions of local school boards also contributed to the creation and maintenance of racially segregated schools outside the southern states. For example, school boards often made discriminatory decisions in drawing district lines, building schools, assigning faculty and staff members, and allocating resources to schools. (See Chapters 8 and 9 in J. Harvie Wilkinson's *From Brown to Bakke: The Supreme Court and School Integration: 1954-1978* (1979).) These actions of the real estate and banking industries, coupled with school board decisions, often guaranteed that white and minority children, especially African Americans, would attend separate and often unequal schools. The question then became whether the Supreme Court would require desegregation of schools in states where segregation was not imposed explicitly by state law. A partial answer was provided in *Keyes v. School District #1, Denver* (1973). *Keyes,* a rather complicated case, involved two different sets of schools in the Denver school system. A lower court found that the school board deliberately had taken actions to segregate the first set of schools (Park Hill), but although the core city schools (the second set) were also segregated, school board action was not involved. The Court had to decide whether citywide busing was appropriate in these circumstances.

By a 7-1 vote, the Court provided a complex answer. First, the district court was to allow the school board to demonstrate that the Park Hill schools were in a "separate, identifiable and unrelated section of the school district that should be treated as isolated from the rest of the district" (413 U.S. at 213). If the board failed, the court was to examine whether the school board actions regarding the Park Hill schools affected the core city schools in such a way that Denver was operating a dual system. If this were the case, the board had "the affirmative duty to desegregate the entire system 'root and branch' " (413 U.S. at 213). If not, the school board had to prove that the core city schools were not intentionally segregated. Absent such proof, the lower court was authorized to "decree all-out desegregation of the core city schools" (413 U.S. at 214).

In effect, the Court included school board decisions in its definition of de jure segregation and emphasized that the intent to segregate was the problem. In a separate opinion, Justice Powell warned his colleagues that distinguishing between de jure and de facto segregation was inappropriate and would result in future decision-making problems. He argued, "where segregated public schools exist within a school district to a substantial degree, there is a prima facie case that the duly constituted public authorities . . . are sufficiently responsible to warrant imposing upon them a nationally applicable burden to demonstrate they nevertheless are operating a genuinely integrated school system" (413 U.S. at 224). Despite these reservations, Powell agreed with the outcome of this case. Many proponents of school desegregation also expressed concern about the majority's distinction between de jure and de facto segregation. They feared that because de facto segregation rather than de jure segregation had become the primary problem in many metropolitan areas, the Court's distinction between the two would result in the maintenance of racial segregation in an overwhelming number of school districts around the country.

Their concerns were well founded. One year later the Court, drawing upon the de jure-de facto distinction, severely limited the authority of federal judges to develop and implement comprehensive desegregation plans, particularly busing remedies. In *Milliken v. Bradley* (1974), the issue was a plan involving urban and suburban public schools in Detroit, Michigan. Because the Detroit city schools were overwhelmingly African American and a busing plan involving only those schools would not result in meaningful desegregation, a federal district judge ordered a multidistrict busing remedy involving fifty-four school districts in three counties. The court of appeals affirmed the order, but the Supreme Court, by a 5-4 vote, held that the district court had overstepped its remedial authority.

Writing for the majority, Chief Justice Burger said that although the inner city schools were segregated because of discriminatory actions by state and local officials, the suburban districts were not responsible for the segregation and therefore could not be part of the remedy. "[A]n interdistrict remedy might be in order where the racially discriminatory acts of one or more school districts caused racial segregation in an adjacent district, or where district lines have been deliberately drawn on the basis of race. In such circumstances an interdistrict remedy would be appropriate to eliminate the interdistrict segregation caused by the constitutional violation. Conversely, without an interdistrict violation and interdistrict effect, there is no constitutional wrong calling for an interdistrict remedy" (418 U.S. at 745).

The dissenters, led by Justice Marshall, the Court's lone African American, criticized the majority for ensuring that meaningful desegregation would not occur in the Detroit public schools. Marshall emphasized that the multidistrict remedy was appropriate, given the actions of state officials—including the governor, the attorney general, the state board of education, and the state superintendent of public instruction—in creating and maintaining segregated schools. "The constitutional violation found here was not some *de facto* racial imbalance, but rather the purposeful, intentional, massive, *de jure* segregation of the Detroit city schools, which under our decision in *Keyes,* forms 'a predicate for a finding of the existence of a dual system,' and justifies 'all-out desegregation' " (418 U.S. at 785–86).

MILLIKEN V. BRADLEY

418 U.S. 717, 94 S.Ct. 3112, 41 L.Ed.2d 1069 (1974)

■ Ronald Bradley, a student in the Detroit public schools, filed a class action suit in federal district court charging Governor William Milliken and other state and local officials with practicing segregation in the operation of the Detroit public schools. After finding that these officials did engage in such practices, the court authorized a multidistrict busing plan to desegregate the schools. Believing that a plan involving only the Detroit city schools would be ineffective because those schools were overwhelmingly African American, the court order included fifty-three additional school districts in the three-county metropolitan area. After this urban-suburban busing plan was upheld by the court of appeals, Governor Milliken and other officials sought review in the U.S. Supreme Court.

This case is important primarily because it significantly limited the power of federal judges to use cross-district busing to desegregate schools. As you read the case, consider these questions: 1) Although the suburban school districts allegedly were "innocent" of discrimination, is the situation here similar to that in *Keyes v. Denver School District #1,* decided a year earlier? That is, did the segregation by state and local officials with respect to the Detroit city schools have a significant impact on the suburban schools? 2) How much of a role do you think white resistance to busing for desegregation played in the majority's decision to strike down the plan here?

VOTE:

5 justices voted to invalidate the multidistrict busing plan (Burger, Stewart, Blackmun, Powell, and Rehnquist).

4 justices voted to uphold the multidistrict remedy (Douglas, Brennan, White, and Marshall).

Chief Justice Burger delivered the opinion of the Court.

We granted certiorari in these consolidated cases to determine whether a federal court may impose a multidistrict, areawide remedy to a single district *de jure* segregation problem absent any finding that the other included school districts have failed to operate unitary school systems within their districts, absent any claim or finding that the boundary lines of any affected school district were established with the purpose of fostering racial segregation in public schools, absent any finding that the included districts committed acts which effected segregation within the other districts, and absent a meaningful opportunity for the included neighboring school districts to present evidence or be heard on the propriety of a multidistrict remedy or on the question of constitutional violations by those neighboring districts.

* * *

Viewing the record as a whole, it seems clear that the District Court and the Court of Appeals shifted the primary focus from a Detroit remedy to the metropolitan area only because of their conclusion that total desegregation of Detroit would not produce the racial balance which they perceived as desirable. Both courts proceeded on an assumption that the Detroit schools could not be truly desegregated—in their view of what constituted desegregation—unless the racial composition of the student body of each school substantially reflected the racial composition of the population of the metropolitan area as a whole. The metropolitan area was then defined as Detroit plus 53 of the outlying school districts. * * *

* * *

The record before us, voluminous as it is, contains evidence of *de jure* segregated conditions only in the Detroit schools; indeed, that was the theory on which the litigation was initially based and on which the District Court took evidence. With no showing of significant violation by the 53 outlying school districts and no evidence of any inter-district violation or effect, the court went beyond the original theory of the case as framed by the pleadings and mandated a metropolitan area remedy. To approve the remedy ordered by the court would impose on the outlying districts, not shown to have committed any constitutional violation, a wholly impermissible remedy based on a standard not hinted at in *Brown I* and *II* or any holding of this Court.

In dissent Mr. Justice White and Mr. Justice Marshall undertake to demonstrate that agencies having statewide authority participated in maintaining the dual school system found to exist in Detroit. They are apparently of the view that once such participation is shown, the District Court should have a relatively free hand to reconstruct school districts outside of Detroit in fashioning relief. Our assumption . . . that state agencies did participate in the maintenance of the Detroit system, should make it clear that it is not on this point that we part company. The difference between us arises instead from established doctrine laid down by our cases. *Brown, Green, Swann, Scotland Neck* and *Emporia* each addressed the issue of constitutional wrong in terms of an established geographic and administrative school system populated by both Negro and White children. In such a context, terms such as "unitary" and "dual" systems, and "racially identifiable schools," have meaning, and the necessary federal authority to remedy the constitutional wrong is firmly established. But the remedy is necessarily designed, as all remedies are, to restore the victims of discriminatory conduct to the position they would have occupied in the absence of such conduct. Disparate treatment of White and Negro students occurred within the Detroit school system, and not elsewhere, and on this record the remedy must be limited to that system.

The constitutional right of the Negro respondents residing in Detroit is to attend a unitary school system in that district. Unless petitioners drew the district lines in a discriminatory fashion, or arranged for White students residing in the Detroit district to attend schools in Oakland and Macomb Counties, they were under no constitutional duty to make provisions for Negro students to do so. The view of the dissenters, that the existence of a dual system in Detroit can be made the basis for a decree requiring cross-district transportation of pupils, cannot be supported on the grounds that it represents merely the devising of a suitably flexible remedy for the violation of rights already established by our prior decisions. It can be supported only by drastic expansion of the constitutional right itself, an expansion without any support in either constitutional principle or precedent.

* * *

* * * Accepting . . . the correctness of [the lower courts'] finding of State responsibility for the segregated conditions within the city of Detroit, it does not follow that an interdistrict remedy is constitutionally justified or required. With a single exception, . . . there has been no showing that either the State or any of the 85 outlying districts engaged in activity that had a cross-district effect. The boundaries of the Detroit School District, which are coterminous with the boundaries of the city of Detroit, were established over a century ago by neutral legislation when the city was incorporated; there is no evidence in the record, nor is there any suggestion by the respondents, that either the original boundaries of the Detroit School District, or any other school district in Michigan, were established for the purpose of creating, maintaining or perpetuating segregation of races. There is no claim and there is no evidence hinting that petitioners and their predecessors, or the 40-odd other school districts in the tri-county area—but outside the District Court's "desegregation area"—have ever maintained or operated anything but unitary school systems. Unitary school systems have been required for more than a century by the Michigan Constitution as implemented by state law. Where the schools of only one district have been affected, there is no constitutional power in the courts to decree relief balancing the racial composition of that district's schools with those of the surrounding districts.

* * *

We conclude that the relief ordered by the District Court and affirmed by the Court of Appeals was based upon an erroneous standard and was unsupported by record evidence that acts of the outlying districts affected the discrimination found to exist in the schools of Detroit. Accordingly, the judgment of the Court of Appeals is vacated and the case is remanded for further proceedings consistent with this opinion leading to prompt formulation of a decree directed to eliminating the segregation found to exist in Detroit city schools, a remedy which has been delayed since 1970.

Reversed and remanded.

[*The concurring opinion of Justice Stewart is omitted.*]

[*The dissenting opinion of Justice Douglas is omitted.*]

Justice White, with whom Justice Douglas, Justice Brennan, and Justice Marshall joined, dissented.

* * *

Regretfully, and for several reasons, I can join neither the Court's judgment nor its opinion. The core of my disagreement is that deliberate acts of segregation and their consequences will go unremedied, not because a remedy would be infeasible or unreasonable in terms of the usual criteria governing school desegregation cases, but because an effective remedy would cause what the Court considers to be undue administrative inconvenience to the State. The result is that the State of Michigan, the entity at which the Fourteenth Amendment is directed, has successfully insulated itself from its duty to provide effective desegregation remedies by vesting sufficient power over its public schools in its local school districts. If this is the case in Michigan, it will be the case in most States.

* * *

I am surprised that the Court, sitting at this distance from the State of Michigan, claims better insight than the Court of Appeals and the District Court as to whether an interdistrict remedy for equal protection violations practiced by the State of Michigan would involve undue difficulties for the State in the management of its public schools. In the area of what constitutes an acceptable desegregation plan, "we must of necessity rely to a large extent, as this Court has for more than 16 years, on the informed judgment of the district courts in the first instance and on courts of appeals." * * *

I am even more mystified how the Court can ignore the legal reality that the constitutional violations, even if occurring locally, were committed by governmental entities for which the State is responsible and that it is the State that must respond to the command of the Fourteenth Amendment. An interdistrict remedy for the infringements that occurred in this case is well within the confines and powers of the State, which is the governmental entity ultimately responsible for desegregating its schools. * * *

* * *

Justice Marshall, with whom Justice Douglas, Justice Brennan, and Justice White joined, dissented.

* * *

I cannot subscribe to this emasculation of our constitutional guarantee of equal protection of the laws and must respectfully dissent. Our precedents, in my view, firmly establish that where, as here, state-imposed segregation has been demonstrated, it becomes the duty of the State to eliminate root and branch all vestiges of racial discrimination and to achieve the greatest possible degree of actual desegregation. I agree with both the District Court and the Court of Appeals that, under the facts of this case, this duty cannot be fulfilled unless the State of Michigan involves outlying metropolitan area school districts in its desegregation remedy. Furthermore, I perceive no basis either in law or in the practicalities of the situation justifying the State's interposition of school district boundaries as absolute barriers to the implementation of an effective desegregation remedy. Under established and frequently used Michigan procedures, school district lines are both flexible and permeable for a wide variety of purposes, and there is no reason why they must now stand in the way of meaningful desegregation relief.

* * *

Nowhere in the court's opinion does the majority confront, let alone respond to, the District Court's conclusion that a remedy limited to the city of Detroit would not effectively desegregate the Detroit city schools. * * *

* * *

Under a Detroit-only decree, Detroit's schools will clearly remain racially identifiable in comparison with neighboring schools in the metropolitan community. Schools with 65% and more Negro students will stand in sharp and obvious contrast to schools in neighboring districts with less than 2% Negro enrollment. Negro students will continue to perceive their schools as segregated educational facilities and this perception will only be increased when whites react to a Detroit-only decree by fleeing to the suburbs to avoid integration. School district lines, however innocently drawn, will surely be perceived as fences to separate the races when, under a Detroit-only decree, white parents withdraw their children from the Detroit city schools and move to the suburbs in order to continue them in all-white schools. * * *

Nor can it be said that the State is free from any responsibility for the disparity between the racial makeup of Detroit and its surrounding suburbs. The State's creation, through *de jure* acts of segregation, of a growing core of all-Negro schools inevitably acted as a magnet to attract Negroes to the areas served by such schools and to deter them from settling either in other areas of the city or in the suburbs. By the same token, the growing core of all-Negro schools inevitably helped drive whites to other areas of the city or to the suburbs. * * *

The State must also bear part of the blame for the white flight to the suburbs which would be forthcoming from a Detroit-only decree and would render such a remedy ineffective. Having created a system where whites and Negroes were intentionally kept apart so that they could not become accustomed to learning together, the State is responsible for the fact that many whites will react to the dismantling of that segregated system by attempting to flee to the suburbs. Indeed, by limiting the District Court to a Detroit-only remedy and allowing that flight to the suburbs to succeed, the Court today allows the State to profit from its own wrong and to perpetuate for years to come the separation of the races it achieved in the past by purposeful state action.

* * *

Desegregation is not and was never expected to be an easy task. Racial attitudes ingrained in our Nation's childhood and adolescence are not quickly thrown aside in its middle years. But just as the inconvenience of some cannot be allowed to stand in the way of the rights of others, so public opposition, no matter how strident, cannot be permitted to divert this Court from the enforcement of the constitutional principles at issue in this case. Today's holding, I fear, is more a reflection of a perceived public mood that we have gone far enough in enforcing the Constitution's guarantee of equal justice than it is the product of neutral principles of law. In the short run, it may seem to be the easier course to allow our great metropolitan areas to be divided up each into two cities—one white, the other black—it is a course, I predict, our people will ultimately regret. I dissent.

The decision in *Milliken v. Bradley* (1974), for all practical purposes, marked the limits of busing as a means to desegregate the nation's metropolitan school systems, because while busing continued to be utilized within major cities, the suburban communities surrounding them remained outside of the scope of busing plans. This was particularly true in nonsouthern states not tainted by laws requiring segregation. In addition, in *Pasadena City Board of Education v. Spangler* (1976), decided by a 6-2 vote, the Court held that, once a school system was desegregated, school authorities were not required to make annual adjustments in the composition of student bodies in order to maintain racial balance, even if immediate resegregation might occur. On the other hand, in *Columbus Board of Education v. Penick* and *Dayton Board of Education v. Brinkman,* both decided in 1979, the Court upheld systemwide remedies in situations where earlier discriminatory actions of school boards had systemwide effects. Because the school systems in Dayton and Columbus were determined to have been officially segregated at the time *Brown I* was decided, the Court said that the school boards had a constitutional obligation to end that segregation. Despite the rulings here, the *Penick* and *Brinkman* cases demonstrated that the Court truly was divided on this issue. *Penick* was decided by a 7-2 vote, with Justices Powell and Rehnquist in dissent; Chief Justice Burger and Justice Stewart also joined them in dissent in *Brinkman.*

By the time the Court heard another important busing case three years later, Sandra Day O'Connor had been appointed by President Reagan to succeed Potter Stewart. Not surprisingly, she joined Chief Justice Burger and Justices Powell and Rehnquist to dissent from the ruling in *Washington v. Seattle School District #1* (1982), in which the Court struck down a statute aimed at ending busing for desegregation. The statute, which had been adopted by referendum, prohibited students from being assigned to schools outside of their neighborhoods. Because the statute permitted such assignments for purposes other than school desegregation, the majority viewed it as a clear violation of the Equal Protection Clause.

Public Accommodations

In its two major cases involving racial discrimination in public accommodations, the Burger Court, unlike its predecessor, took a more restrictive view of the applicability of the Equal Protection Clause in forbidding such discrimination. First, in *Palmer v. Thompson* (1971), the Court permitted a city government to take official action to avoid desegregating its public facilities. City officials in Jackson, Mississippi, closed the public swimming pools, claiming that they would encounter safety problems and financial difficulties in operating them on an integrated basis. A five-member majority led by Justice Black ruled that there was no violation of the Equal Protection Clause because the pools were closed to everyone, not just to one race. Black said that neither the Fourteenth Amendment nor federal law required states to operate public swimming pools and that there was "no state action affecting blacks differently from whites" (403 U.S. at 225). In a sharp dissent, Justice White maintained that the action of closing the public swimming pools was consistent with the city's official policy against desegregation and was therefore a violation of the Fourteenth Amendment. He insisted that "closing the pools [wa]s an expression of public policy that Negroes are unfit to associate with whites" (403 U.S. at 240–41).

In the second case, *Moose Lodge v. Irvis* (1972), the state action doctrine was implicated. In Harrisburg, Pennsylvania, Leroy Irvis, an African American guest of a member of the Moose Lodge, was denied service. He filed suit in federal court charging that the lodge's action in refusing to serve him violated his rights to equal protection of the laws. Irvis said that the state was involved in the club's racially discriminatory policy because the state's liquor control board had issued a liquor license to the Moose Lodge. He sought an injunction to require the liquor control board to suspend the liquor license as long as the lodge continued its policy of racial discrimination. A federal court granted the injunction, but the Supreme Court reversed that decision by a 6-3 vote. Writing for the majority, Justice Rehnquist held that the liquor board's action in issuing the license and enforcing various liquor trade regulations did not amount to state action in violation of the Equal Protection Clause. "The Court has never held . . . that discrimination by an otherwise private entity would be violative of the Equal Protection Clause if the private entity receives any sort of benefit or service at all from the State, or if it is subject to state regulation in any degree whatever. Since state-furnished services include such necessities of life as electricity, water, and police and fire protection, such a holding would utterly emasculate the distinction between private as distinguished from State conduct set forth in *The Civil Rights Cases* and adhered to in subsequent decisions" (407 U.S. at 173). Moreover, Rehnquist insisted that the circumstances in *Moose Lodge* were different from those in *Burton v. Wilmington Parking Authority* (1961) in that the lodge was located on privately owned rather than publicly owned land. In dissent, Justice Brennan argued that the liquor licensing laws were "pervasive regulatory schemes under which the State dictates and continually supervises virtually every detail of the operation of the licensee's business" (407 U.S. at 185). In his view, this was sufficient to establish that state action supported the discrimination that occurred. This case, therefore, substantially limited the application of the state action doctrine in subjecting private acts of discrimination to the requirements of the Fourteenth Amendment. In general, the Burger Court was less willing than the Warren Court to find a nexus to state action in cases involving "private" discrimination.

Jury Selection and Housing Discrimination Cases

The Burger Court, like its predecessor, heard several cases involving discrimination in jury selection, both at the grand and petit levels. For example, in *Batson v. Kentucky* (1986), the Court ruled that in criminal trials prosecutors cannot use peremptory challenges to exclude potential jurors from particular racial groups.

In a case related to housing discrimination, *Hunter v. Erickson* (1969), the Court invalidated a provision of a city charter which required voters to approve any ordinance prohibiting discrimination on the basis of race, religion, or ancestry. By requiring a referendum for this issue but not for other housing matters such as building codes, public housing, and rent control, the city unconstitutionally singled out a particular class of people. In *Hills v. Gautreaux* (1976) the Court authorized a federal court to adopt a metropolitanwide remedy for segregated public housing in the city of Chicago. One year later, the justices ruled that a government's refusal to rezone property to permit the building of racially integrated housing for low- and moderate-income individuals did not violate the Equal Protection Clause, unless there was proof of discriminatory intent (*Village of Arlington Heights v. Metropolitan Housing Development Corporation*, 1977).

Statutory Cases

By the early 1970s, the Burger Court began to hear a number of cases involving racial discrimination in employment. These cases primarily involved the interpretation of Title VII of the Civil Rights Act of 1964 rather than the Fourteenth Amendment. For example, in *Griggs v. Duke Power Co.* (1971), the Court held that Title VII prohibited the use of job qualification requirements not significantly related to job performance if they had discriminatory effects. Under this so-called **disparate impact analysis,** the Court held that an employment practice, although neutral on its face, may have discriminatory effects that would violate Title VII. Five years later, however, the Court ruled that in disparate impact cases brought on constitutional, rather than statutory grounds, there must be evidence of an *intent* to discriminate (*Washington v. Davis,* 1976). Finally, the Court used a section of the Civil Rights Act of 1866 that forbade discrimination in the making of contracts to prohibit a private school from discriminating on the basis of race in their admissions decisions. *Runyon v. McCrary* (1976) extended the precedent established in *Jones v. Alfred H. Mayer Co.* (1968), which applied the 1866 act to prohibit private racial discrimination in housing.

Impact of the Burger Court

As these decisions indicate, the Burger Court did not overturn any of the major liberal precedents of the Warren Court. In fact, the Burger Court extended the prohibition against racial discrimination in jury selection, and it approved the use of busing for school desegregation. At the same time, however, the Burger Court limited the use of busing to cases involving de jure segregation. The effect of this was to perpetuate racial segregation in schools in major metropolitan areas. In addition, the Court limited the application of the state action doctrine, and it was more likely to require clear proof of an intent to discriminate, rather than the mere fact of discrimination, before finding violations of the Equal Protection Clause or civil rights statutes.

The Rehnquist Court Era

By the end of the Burger era, the Court was subject to increased criticism by some for its alleged insensitivity to the problems of racial discrimination in American society. In contrast, some observers praised the Court's efforts to make the judicial branch less actively involved in discrimination issues. Civil rights activists maintained that the Court's insensitivity was demonstrated by some of the Burger Court's decisions regarding school desegregation, public accommodations, employment discrimination, and affirmative action (see Chapter 15). Thus it was not surprising that they expressed similar concerns about the Rehnquist Court, given Chief Justice Rehnquist's conservative record in this area and Justice Scalia's writings regarding racial discrimination, particularly his opposition to affirmative action.

The Rehnquist Court has not heard many cases involving racial discrimination under the Equal Protection Clause. The cases heard primarily have involved school desegregation and jury selection. The Rehnquist Court also has issued a few important decisions regarding interpretation of civil rights statutes. In general, the Rehnquist Court's record in this area is similar to that of its predecessor. Like the Burger Court, the Rehnquist Court has been moderately liberal in race discrimination cases, but the Rehnquist Court has been substantially less liberal than the Warren

Court. Following the pattern of previous chapters, these cases will be examined from both quantitative and doctrinal perspectives.

The data for the decisions of the Warren, Burger, and Rehnquist Courts are presented in Table 13.1. As the table illustrates, the Rehnquist Court has been less liberal (56%) than the Burger Court (64%) or especially the Warren Court (92%). While these data do provide us with some insight into the Rehnquist Court, it has heard substantially fewer cases (9) than either the Warren (40) or Burger (42) Courts.

With respect to individual justices of the Rehnquist Court era (Table 13.2), civil rights activists were correct in their predictions about Justice Scalia and Chief Justice Rehnquist. These two, along with Justice O'Connor, were the most conservative justices, as they voted for conservative outcomes 100%, 78%, and 78%, respectively. At the other end of the spectrum, the most liberal justices were Marshall (100%), Stevens (89%), and Blackmun (88%). Justices Brennan, Ginsburg, and Breyer also cast liberal votes 100% of the time, but each participated in only one case. While Justice Brennan was one of the most liberal justices in racial discrimination cases during his long tenure on the Court, Justices Ginsburg and Breyer have participated in too few cases for their scores to be very meaningful at this point. Justice Kennedy's reputation as an increasingly moderate member of the Court seems to be supported by the data, as his conservative and liberal votes were nearly evenly divided. Finally, Justices Souter, Thomas, and White generally were more liberal than conservative, having voted for liberal outcomes 71%, 67%, and 62%, respectively. Thomas, however, has participated in only three cases.

The bloc voting analysis of the Rehnquist Court shown in Table 13.3 also produced some interesting results. During the 1986 through 1994 terms, two overlapping blocs existed. Justices Marshall, Blackmun, Stevens, and Souter formed one bloc, a liberal coalition with an average interagreement rate of 89 percent. Justice Souter also joined with Justices White and Kennedy to form another cohesive bloc with a mean agreement rate of 91 percent, and this bloc was more moderate in its support of racial equality claims. An especially noteworthy feature of Table 13.3 is the absence of a conservative voting bloc. Although Scalia, Rehnquist, and O'Connor were all decidedly conservative in terms of their individual voting records, they did not vote similarly in enough cases to form a cohesive conservative bloc.

The doctrinal analysis presented in Table 13.4 reflects the fact that neither the liberal nor the conservative justices have prevailed in racial discrimination cases.

TABLE 13.1: Liberal/Conservative Outcomes of Racial Discrimination Cases for the Warren, Burger, and Rehnquist Courts, 1953-94 Terms

	Outcomes		
Court Era	Liberal	Conservative	Totals
Warren Court, 1953-68 Terms	92% (37)	8% (3)	40
Burger Court, 1969-85 Terms	64% (27)	36% (15)	42
Rehnquist Court, 1986-94 Terms	56% (5)	44% (4)	9*
Totals	76% (69)	24% (22)	91

**Shaw v. Reno* (1993) and *Miller v. Johnson* (1995) are not included in this table. There were coded in a separate voting rights category in the United States Court Judical Database.

TABLE 13.2 Liberal/Conservative Voting Records of Justices of the Rehnquist Court in Racial Discrimination Cases, 1986–94 Terms

Justices	Liberal Votes	Conservative Votes
Marshall	100% (5)	0% (0)
Brennan	100% (1)	0% (0)
Ginsburg	100% (1)	0% (0)
Breyer	100% (1)	0% (0)
Stevens	89% (8)	11% (1)
Blackmun	88% (7)	12% (1)
Souter	71% (5)	29% (2)
Thomas	67% (2)	33% (1)
White	63% (5)	37% (3)
Kennedy	44% (4)	56% (5)
O'Connor	22% (2)	78% (7)
Rehnquist	22% (2)	78% (7)
Scalia	0% (0)	100% (9)
Powell	Did not Participate	

TABLE 13.3: Bloc Voting Analysis of the Rehnquist Court in Racial Discrimination Cases, 1986–94 Terms (Percent Agreement Rate)

	MA	BL	ST	SO	WH	KE	OC	RE	SC
Marshall	—	100	100	67	60	40	20	0	0
Blackmun	100	—	100	83	75	63	38	38	13
Stevens	100	100	—	86	75	56	33	33	11
Souter	67	83	86	—	100	86	57	57	29
White	60	75	75	100	—	88	63	63	38
Kennedy	40	63	56	86	88	—	78	78	56
O'Connor	20	38	33	57	63	78	—	78	78
Rehnquist	0	38	33	57	63	78	78	—	78
Scalia	0	13	11	29	38	56	78	78	—

Court mean = 59
Sprague Criterion = 79
Liberal bloc: Marshall, Blackmun, Stevens, Souter = 89
Moderate bloc: Souter, White, Kennedy = 91

Five of the nine cases were decided by a liberal interpretation of existing precedent (*Missouri v. Jenkins I, Powers v. Ohio, Edmonson, McCollum,* and *Fordice*), and four involved a conservative interpretation of existing precedent (*Dowell, Freeman, Hernandez,* and *Missouri v. Jenkins II*). Thus, none of the cases involved the modification of existing precedent or the creation of new precedent, revealing that the Rehnquist Court has not engaged in a conservative counterrevolution in this area of constitutional law. We now turn to a detailed discussion of these cases.

School Desegregation Cases

The Rehnquist Court heard no cases involving school desegregation until the early 1990s, when it addressed questions regarding the scope of remedies available to

Table 13.4: A Framework for the Doctrinal Analysis of the Rehnquist Court's Racial Discrimination Cases, 1986-94 Terms

		Treatment of Precedent					
Major or Minor Importance	**Majority or Plurality Opinion**	Creation of New Liberal Precedent	Liberal Modification of Existing Precedent	Liberal Interpretation of Existing Precedent	Conservative Interpretation of Existing Precedent	Conservative Modification of Existing Precedent	Creation of New Conservative Precedent
Major	Majority			Missouri v. Jenkins I (1990)	Bd of Ed of OK Schools v. Dowell (1991) Freeman v. Pitts (1992) Missouri v. Jenkins II (1995)		
	Plurality						
Minor	Majority			Powers v. Ohio (1991) Edmonson v. Leesville Concrete (1991) Georgia v. McCollum (1992) U.S. v. Fordice (1992)	Hernandez v. New York (1991)		
	Plurality						

federal judges in dismantling segregated school systems and the duration of federal court supervision over school desegregation activities. By this time, Justice Kennedy had succeeded Justice Powell, who was generally considered to be a moderate on school desegregation issues. In the first case, *Missouri v. Jenkins I* (1990), a sharply divided Court upheld a federal court order to school board officials in Kansas City, Missouri, to increase taxes to help pay for a "magnet school" plan that would promote integration by attracting suburban students back to the inner-city schools. The order required the school board to levy taxes higher than the limits set by the state. Writing for a five-member majority, Justice White said, "The KCMSD [Kansas City, Missouri, School District] may be ordered to levy taxes despite the statutory limitations on its authority in order to compel the discharge of an obligation imposed on KCMSD by the Fourteenth Amendment" (495 U.S. at 57). The dissenters, led by Justice Kennedy, argued that federal courts had no authority to impose state taxes, whether directly or indirectly.

In *Board of Education of Oklahoma City Public Schools v. Dowell* (1991), the issue was how long federal courts are required to maintain their jurisdiction over school districts under orders to desegregate because of de jure segregation. In a 5-3 decision with David Souter, William Brennan's successor, not yet on the Court, the justices indicated that such supervision was not required for an unlimited period of time. The majority authorized school districts to end busing in favor of neighborhood schools, despite the fact that this would likely result in a return to a system of racially identifiable schools. In the case of Oklahoma City, this would mean overwhelmingly African American and white schools. Chief Justice Rehnquist, insisting that local control over education was desirable, said that federal judicial supervision should end once desegregation plans had resulted in eliminating the "vestiges of past discrimination." "In considering whether the vestiges of *de jure* segregation had been eliminated as far as practicable, the District Court should look not only at student assignments, but 'to every facet of school operations—faculty, staff, transportation, extra-curricular activities and facilities' " (498 U.S. at 250). In his final school desegregation case, Justice Marshall issued a vigorous dissent. He contended that the continued existence of racially identifiable schools established that the school district had not eliminated the vestiges of segregation and therefore the federal court should continue supervision.

While it was an important decision, *Dowell* did not provide federal courts or school districts with much guidance in determining whether racially identifiable schools are related to de jure segregation or in identifying the "vestiges of *de jure* segregation." One year later, in *Freeman v. Pitts* (1992), the Court attempted to address this issue further. The case involved the DeKalb County, Georgia, School System (DCSS), under federal court orders since 1969 to desegregate. In 1986 DCSS officials asked the federal district court to dismiss the litigation, asserting that the system had achieved unitary status with respect to four of the six *Green* factors: student assignments, transportation, physical facilities, and extracurricular activities.

By an 8-0 vote, the Supreme Court agreed with DCSS and authorized the district court to withdraw supervision over some aspects of school operations identified in *Green,* although the school system had not yet achieved unitary status in all areas. Justice Kennedy wrote, "upon a finding that a school system subject to a court-supervised desegregation plan is in compliance in some but not all areas, the court in appropriate cases may return control to the school system in those areas where compliance has been achieved, limiting further judicial supervision to operations that are not yet in full compliance with the court decree" (503 U.S. at 491). Moreover, Kennedy emphasized that where racial imbalance in student assignments is due to demographic factors, rather than to constitutional violations, federal courts have no authority or practical ability to remedy the imbalance. "Residential housing choices, and their attendant effects on the racial composition of schools, present an ever-changing pattern, one difficult to address through judicial remedies" (503 U.S. at 495). In a separate concurrence, Justice Scalia called for an *immediate* end to federal judicial supervision of schools that no longer practice intentional discrimination. On the other hand, Justices Souter, Blackmun, Stevens, and O'Connor cautioned federal courts to engage in an extensive analysis of all of the *Green* factors, including whether the school district's decisions contributed to racially identifiable schools, before they withdrew their supervision over desegregation plans.

FREEMAN V. PITTS

503 U.S. 467, 112 S.Ct. 1430, 118 L.Ed.2d 108 (1992)

■ After Pitts et al. charged the DeKalb County, Georgia, School System (DCSS) with segregation, in 1969 a federal district court approved a desegregation plan. The federal court was to maintain jurisdiction over the implementation of the plan. In 1986, Freeman and other DCSS officials petitioned the court for final dismissal of the litigation, maintaining that the DCSS had achieved unitary status. They based their claim on the school system's successful performance in four of six factors identified by the U.S. Supreme Court in *Green v. New Kent County School Board* (1968) as related to unitary status. The six factors identified in *Green* were: student assignments, transportation, physical facilities, extracurricular activities, faculty assignments, and resource allocation. The district court agreed that DCSS was unitary with respect to the first four factors and that no further action was required in that regard. In particular, the court said that the racial imbalance in student assignments was not a vestige of de jure segregation but was related to independent demographic changes. The court, however, refused to dismiss the case altogether, ordering the DCSS to address the remaining problems related to faculty assignments and resource allocation. A court of appeals reversed this decision, holding that full supervision must continue until the DCSS achieved unitary status in all six *Green* factors at the same time for several years. DCSS officials appealed to the U.S. Supreme Court.

This case is important primarily because it provides some guidance to the lower federal courts regarding the duration of their jurisdiction over school desegregation activities. As you read the case, consider these questions: 1) Is the problem of racial imbalance in student assignments attributable to the de jure/de facto distinction the Court has insisted on using? 2) Are the problems in achieving complete unitary status of the DCSS (and, presumably, other school systems) the inevitable consequence of the Court's decision in *Milliken v. Bradley* (1974)? 3) Will the decision here encourage federal judges to withdraw or retain their supervision of public school systems in the midst of desegregation orders?

VOTE:

8 justices upheld the district court's decision to withdraw its supervision over some areas of school operations although the school system had not achieved complete unitary status (Kennedy, Rehnquist, White, Scalia, Souter, Blackmun, Stevens, and O'Connor).

1 justice did not participate in the case (Thomas).

Justice Kennedy delivered the opinion of the Court.

* * *

In the extensive record that comprises this case, one fact predominates: remarkable changes in the racial composition of the county presented DCSS and the District Court with a student population in 1986 far different from the one they set out to integrate in 1969. Between 1950 and 1985, DeKalb County grew from 70,000 to 450,000 in total population, but most of the gross increase in student enrollment had occurred by 1969, the relevant starting date for our purposes. Although the public school population experienced only modest changes between 1969 and 1986 (remaining in the low 70,000's), a striking change occurred in the racial proportions of the student population. The school system that the District Court ordered desegregated in 1969 had 5.6% black students; by 1986 the percentage of black students was 47%.

To compound the difficulty of working with these radical demographic changes, the northern and southern parts of the county experienced much different growth patterns. The District Court found that "[a]s the result of these demographic shifts, the population of the northern half of DeKalb County is now predominantly white and the southern half of DeKalb County is predominantly black." * * *

* * *

Two principal questions are presented. The first is whether a district court may relinquish its supervision and control over those aspects of a school system in which there has been compliance with a desegregation decree if other aspects of the system remain in noncompliance. As we answer this question in the affirmative, the second question is whether the Court of Appeals erred in reversing the District Court's order providing for incremental withdrawal of supervision in all the circumstances of this case.

The duty and responsibility of a school district once segregated by law is to take all steps necessary to eliminate the vestiges of the unconstitutional *de jure* system. This is required in order to insure that the principal wrong of the *de jure* system, the injuries and stigma inflicted upon the race disfavored by the violation, is no longer present. This was the rationale and the objective of *Brown I* and *Brown II.*
* * *

The objective of *Brown I* was made more specific by our holding in *Green* that the duty of a former *de jure* district is to "take whatever steps might be necessary to convert to a unitary system in which racial discrimination would be eliminated root and branch." We also identified various parts of the school system which, in addition to student attendance patterns, must be free from racial discrimination before the mandate of *Brown* is met: faculty, staff, transportation, extracurricular activities and facilities. The *Green* factors are a measure of the racial identifiability of schools in a system that is not in compliance with *Brown,* and we instructed the District Courts to fashion remedies that address all these components of elementary and secondary school systems.

* * *

Today, we make explicit the rationale that was central in *[Pasadena City Board of Education v.] Spangler.* A federal court in a school desegregation case has the discretion to order an incremental or partial withdrawal of its supervision and control. This discretion derives both from the constitutional authority which justified its intervention in the first instance and its ultimate objectives in formulating the decree. The authority of the court is invoked at the outset to remedy particular constitutional violations. In construing the remedial authority of the district courts, we have been guided by the principles that "judicial powers may be exercised only on the basis of a constitutional violation," and that "the nature of the violation determines the scope of the remedy." A remedy is justifiable only insofar as it advances the ultimate objective of alleviating the initial constitutional violation.

* * * In *Dowell,* we emphasized that federal judicial supervision of local school systems was intended as a "temporary measure." Although this temporary measure has lasted decades, the ultimate objective has not changed—to return school districts to the control of local authorities. Just as a court has the obligation at the outset of a desegregation decree to structure a plan so that all available resources of the court are directed to comprehensive supervision of its decree, so too must a court provide an orderly means for withdrawing from control when it is shown that the school district has attained the requisite degree of compliance. A transition phase in which control is relinquished in a gradual way is an appropriate means to this end.

* * *

We hold that, in the course of supervising desegregation plans, federal courts have the authority to relinquish supervision and control of school districts in incremental stages, before full compliance has been achieved in every area of school operations. While retaining jurisdiction over the case, the court may determine that it will not order further remedies in areas where the school district is in compliance with the decree. That is to say, upon a finding that a school system subject to a court-supervised desegregation plan is in compliance in some but not all areas, the court in appropriate cases may return control to the school system in those areas where compliance has been achieved, limiting further judicial supervision to operations that are not yet in full compliance with the court decree. In particular, the district court may determine that it will not order further remedies in the area of student assignments where racial imbalance is not traceable, in a proximate way, to constitutional violations.

A court's discretion to order the incremental withdrawal of its supervision in a school desegregation case must be exercised in a manner consistent with the purposes and objectives of its equitable power. Among the factors which must inform the sound discretion of the court in ordering partial withdrawal are the following: whether there has been full and satisfactory compliance with the decree in those aspects of the system where supervision is to be withdrawn; whether retention of judicial control is necessary or practicable to achieve compliance with the decree in other facets of the school system; and whether the school district has demonstrated, to the public and to the parents and students of the once disfavored race, its good faith commitment to the whole of the court's decree and to those provisions of the law and the constitution that were the predicate for judicial intervention in the first instance.

In considering these factors a court should give particular attention to the school system's record of compliance. A school system is better positioned to demonstrate its good faith commitment to a constitutional course of action when its policies form a consistent pattern of lawful conduct directed to eliminating earlier violations. And with the passage of time the degree to which racial imbalances continue to represent vestiges of a constitutional violation may diminish, and the practicability and efficacy of various remedies can be evaluated with more precision.

* * *

We reach now the question whether the Court of Appeals erred in prohibiting the District Court from returning to DCSS partial control over some of its affairs. We decide that the Court of Appeals did err in holding that, as a matter of law, the District Court had no discretion to permit DCSS to regain control over student assignment, transportation, physical facilities, and extracurricular activities, while retaining court supervision over the areas of faculty and administrative assignments and the quality of education, where full compliance had not been demonstrated.

* * *

The Court of Appeals' rejection of the District Court's order rests on related premises: first, that given noncompliance in some discrete categories, there can be no partial withdrawal of judicial control; and second, until there is full compliance, heroic measures must be taken to ensure racial balance in student assignments systemwide. Under our analysis and our precedents, neither premise is correct.

* * *

That there was racial imbalance in student attendance zones was not tantamount to a showing that the school district was in noncompliance with the decree or with its duties under the law. Racial balance is not to be achieved for its own sake. It is to be pursued when racial imbalance has been caused by a constitutional violation. Once the racial imbalance due to the *de jure* violation has been remedied, the school district is under no duty to remedy imbalance that is caused by demographic factors. * * *

* * *

The findings of the District Court that the population changes which occurred in DeKalb County were not caused by the policies of the school district, but rather by independent factors, are consistent with the mobility that is a distinct characteristic of our society. * * * In such a society it is inevitable that the demographic makeup of school districts, based as they are on political subdivisions such as counties and municipalities, may undergo rapid change.

The effect of changing residential patterns on the racial composition of schools though not always fortunate is somewhat predictable. Studies show a high correlation between residential segregation and school segregation. The District Court in this case heard evidence tending to show that racially stable neighborhoods are not likely to emerge because whites prefer a racial mix of 80% white and 20% black, while blacks prefer a 50%-50% mix.

Where resegregation is a product not of state action but of private choices, it does not have constitutional implications. It is beyond the authority and beyond the practical ability of the federal courts to try to counteract these kinds of continuous and massive demographic shifts. To attempt such results would require ongoing and never-ending supervision by the courts of school districts simply because they were once *de jure* segregated. Residential housing choices, and their attendant effects on the racial composition of schools, present an ever-changing pattern, one difficult to address through judicial remedies.

* * *

To say, as did the Court of Appeals, that a school district must meet all six *Green factors* before the trial court can declare the system unitary and relinquish its control over school attendance zones, and to hold further that racial balancing by all necessary means is required in the interim, is simply to vindicate a legal phrase. The law is not so formalistic. A proper rule must be based on the necessity to find a feasible remedy that insures systemwide compliance with the court decree and that is directed to curing the effects of the specific violation.

We next consider whether retention of judicial control over student attendance is necessary or practicable to achieve compliance in other facets of the school system. Racial balancing in elementary and secondary school student assignments may be a legitimate remedial device to correct other fundamental inequities that were themselves caused by the constitutional violation. * * *

There was no showing that racial balancing was an appropriate mechanism to cure other deficiencies in this case. It is true that the school district was not in compliance with respect to faculty assignments, but the record does not show that student reassignments would be a feasible or practicable way to remedy this defect. To the contrary, the District Court suggests that DCSS could solve the faculty assignment problem by reassigning a few teachers per school. The District Court, not having our analysis before it, did not have the opportunity to make specific findings and conclusions on this aspect of the case, however. Further proceedings are appropriate for this purpose.

The requirement that the school district show its good faith commitment to the entirety of a desegregation plan so that parents, students and the public have assurance against further injuries or stigma also should be a subject for more specific findings. We stated in *Dowell* that the good faith compliance of the district with the court order over a reasonable period of time is a factor to be considered in deciding whether or not jurisdiction could be relinquished. * * *

* * *

The judgment is reversed and the case is remanded to the Court of Appeals. * * *

It is so ordered.

Justice Thomas took no part in the consideration or decision of this case.

Justice Scalia concurred. * *

At some time, we must acknowledge that it has become absurd to assume, without any further proof, that violations of the Constitution dating from the days when Lyndon Johnson was President, or earlier, continue to have an appreciable effect upon current operation of schools. We are close to that time. While we must continue to prohibit, without qualification, all racial discrimination in the operation of public schools, and to afford remedies that eliminate not only the discrimination but its identified consequences, we should consider laying aside the extraordinary, and increasingly counterfactual, presumption of *Green.* We must soon revert to the ordinary principles of our law, of our democratic heritage, and of our educational tradition: that plaintiffs alleging Equal Protection violations must prove intent and causation and not merely the existence of racial disparity; that public schooling, even in the South, should be controlled by locally elected authorities acting in conjunction with parents; and that it is "desirable" to permit pupils to attend "schools nearest their homes."

Justice Souter concurred.

* * *

We recognize that although demographic changes influencing the composition of a school's student population may well have no causal link to prior *de jure* segregation, judicial control of student assignments may still be necessary to remedy persisting vestiges of the unconstitutional dual system, such as remaining imbalance in faculty assignments. This is, however, only one of several possible causal relationships between or among unconstitutional acts of school segregation and various *Green*-type factors. I think it is worth mentioning at least two others: the dual school system itself as a cause of the demographic shifts with which the district court is faced when considering a partial relinquishment of supervision, and a *Green*-type factor other than student assignments as a possible cause of imbalanced student assignment patterns in the future.

The first would occur when demographic change toward segregated residential patterns is itself caused by past school segregation and the patterns of thinking that segregation creates. Such demographic change is not an independent, supervening cause of racial imbalance in the student body, and we have said before that when demographic change is not independent of efforts to segregate, the causal relationship may be considered in fashioning a school desegregation remedy. Racial imbalance in student assignments caused by demographic change is not insulated from federal judicial oversight where the demographic change is itself caused in this way, and before deciding to relinquish supervision and control over student assignments, a district court should make findings on the presence or absence of this relationship.

* * *

Justice Blackmun, with whom Justice Stevens and Justice O'Connor joined, concurred in the judgment.

It is almost 38 years since this Court decided *Brown v. Board of Education.* In those 38 years the students in DeKalb County, Ga., never have attended a desegregated school system even for one day. The majority of "black" students never have attended a school that was not disproportionately black. Ignoring this glaring dual character of the DeKalb County School System (DCSS), part "white" and part "black," the District Court relinquished control over student assignments, finding that the school district had achieved "unitary status" in that aspect of the system. No doubt frustrated by the continued existence of duality, the Court of Appeals ordered the school district to take extraordinary measures to correct all manifestations of this racial imbalance. Both decisions, in my view, were in error, and I therefore concur in the Court's decision to vacate the judgment and remand the case.

* * *

Whether a district court must maintain active supervision over student assignment, and order new remedial actions depends on two factors. As the Court discusses, the district court must order changes in student assignment if it "is necessary or practicable to achieve compliance in other facets of the school system." The district court also must order affirmative action in school attendance if the school district's conduct was a "contributing cause" of the racially identifiable schools. It is the application of this latter causation requirement that I now examine in more detail.

DCSS claims that it need not remedy the segregation in DeKalb County schools because it was caused by demographic changes for which DCSS has no responsibility. It is not enough, however, for DCSS to establish that demographics exacerbated the problem; it must prove that its own policies did not contribute. Such contribution can occur in at least two ways: DCSS may have contributed to the demographic changes themselves, or it may have contributed directly to the racial imbalance in the schools.

To determine DCSS' possible role in encouraging the residential segregation, the court must examine the situation with special care. "[A] connection between past segregative acts and present segregation may be present even when not apparent and . . . close examination is required before concluding that the connection does not exist." Close examination is necessary because what might seem to be purely private preferences in housing may in fact have been created, in part, by actions of the school district.

> People gravitate toward school facilities, just as schools are located in response to the needs of people. The location of schools may thus influence the patterns of residential development of a metropolitan area and have important impact on composition of inner-city neighborhoods.

This interactive effect between schools and housing choices may occur because many families are concerned about the racial composition of a prospective school and will make residential decisions accordingly. Thus, schools that are demonstrably African American or white provide a signal to these families, perpetuating and intensifying the residential movement.

* * *

In addition to exploring the school district's influence on residential segregation, the District Court here should examine whether school board actions might have contributed to school segregation. Actions taken by a school district can aggravate or eliminate school segregation independent of residential segregation. School board policies concerning placement of new schools and closure of old schools and programs such as magnet classrooms and majority-to-minority (M to M) transfer policies affect the racial composition of the schools. A school district's failure to adopt policies that effectively desegregate its schools continues the violation of the Fourteenth Amendment. The Court many times has noted that a school district is not responsible for all of society's ills, but it bears full responsibility for schools that have never been desegregated.

* * *

The District Court apparently has concluded that DCSS should be relieved of the responsibility to desegregate because such responsibility would be burdensome. To be sure, changes in demographic patterns aggravated the vestiges of segregation and made it more difficult for DCSS to desegregate. But an integrated school system is no less desirable because it is difficult to achieve, and it is no less a constitutional imperative because that imperative has gone unmet for 38 years.

* * *

Justice Thomas did not participate in *Freeman v. Pitts* because he was not yet confirmed at the time of oral argument, but he did join the Court in time to hear *United States v. Fordice* (1992). *Fordice,* not generally regarded as a case of major importance, was the first decision involving desegregation of higher education since *Sweatt v. Painter* and *McLaurin v. Oklahoma* had been decided in 1950. In *Fordice* the Court applied the general principles of *Green* to higher education. *Green* had held that, after maintaining a system of de jure segregation, a school board's adoption of a "freedom-of-choice" plan was an inadequate remedy for segregation. The Court extended this principle to higher education in *Fordice,* ruling that, although Mississippi had ended de jure segregation of its colleges and universities, its current admissions policies continued to perpetuate segregation in those institutions. Writing for the majority, Justice White ordered the state to take steps to remedy this problem. "[S]urely the State may not leave in place policies rooted in its prior officially segregated system that serve to maintain the racial identifiability of its universities if those policies can practicably be eliminated without eroding sound educational policies" (112 S.Ct. at 2743). Justice Thomas wrote a brief concurrence in which he emphasized his support for the maintenance of historically black colleges. In a solo dissent, Justice Scalia argued that *Green* "has no proper application in the context of higher education . . ." (112 S.Ct. at 2746).

By the time the Court heard its next school desegregation case, Justices Ginsburg and Breyer had succeeded Justices White and Blackmun, respectively. In *Missouri v. Jenkins II* (1995), they dissented from the majority's ruling that limited the authority of federal courts in remedying school desegregation. Here a federal district judge had ordered the state to fund 1) salary increases for the staff of the Kansas City, Missouri, School District and 2) remedial "quality education" programs because student achievement scores were lower than the national averages in various grade levels. As in *Missouri I* the judge's orders were designed to improve inner-city schools to attract white suburban students and to reverse "white flight" to the suburbs.

In a 5-4 decision, the Court held that the remedial authority of federal courts in school desegregation cases is limited to remedying the vestiges of past discrimination. Citing *Milliken v. Bradley* and *Freeman v. Pitts* as important precedents, Chief Justice Rehnquist wrote, ". . . [T]he proper response by the District Court should have been to eliminate to the extent practicable the vestiges of prior *de jure* segregation within the KCMSD: a system-wide reduction in student achievement and the existence of 25 racially identifiable schools with a population of over 90% black students" (115 S.Ct. at 2050). Rehnquist said that the district court's purpose was "to attract nonminority students from outside the KCMSD schools" and that this "*inter*district goal [was] beyond the scope of the *intra*district violation identified . . ." (115 S.Ct. at 2051).

This case attracted attention primarily because of Justice Thomas's concurrence, which implied that the district court's order smacked of paternalism and criticized the reasoning in the *Brown* decision.

> *It never ceases to amaze me that the courts are so willing to assume that anything that is predominantly black must be inferior. Instead of focusing on remedying the harm done to those black schoolchildren injured by segregation, the District Court sought to convert the Kansas City, Missouri, School District (KCMSD) into a "magnet district" that would reverse the "white flight" caused by desegregation. . . . [T]he court has read our cases to support the theory that black students suffer an unspecified psychological harm from segregation that retards their mental and educational development. This approach relies on questionable social science research rather than constitutional principle, but it also rests on an assumption of African American inferiority (115 S.Ct. at 2061-62).*

Discrimination in Jury Selection

In general, the Rehnquist Court extended the prohibition against racial discrimination in jury selection through its decisions in *Powers v. Ohio* (1991), *Edmondson v. Leesville Concrete Co.* (1991), and *Georgia v. McCollum* (1992). In *Powers* the Court held that *Batson*'s ban on the prosecution's use of peremptory challenges to exclude jurors on the basis of race applies even when the defendant and the potential juror are of different races. These principles were extended to federal civil trials with the Court's ruling in *Edmonson*. Finally, the *McCollum* decision held that the *Batson* prohibition on the use of peremptory challenges by prosecutors to exclude potential jurors on the basis of race extended to defense attorneys as well.

Voting Rights Cases

In *Shaw v. Reno* (1993), an important voting rights case, the Court held that white voters in North Carolina could use the Equal Protection Clause to challenge a redistricting plan that had resulted in the creation of two majority-black congressional districts in the state. The case arose when North Carolina gained an additional congressional seat after the 1990 census. The state legislature, with the approval of the United States Justice Department, developed a plan to create two majority-black districts, with a goal of maximizing the possibility of electing two African Americans to the U.S. House of Representatives. One of the districts was drawn in an irregular shape. After two African Americans were elected to the House in 1992, a group of white voters filed suit claiming that the plan was a "racial gerrymander" that prevented them from voting in a "color-blind" election. A three-judge federal district court rejected their claim, but the Supreme Court reversed by a 5-4 vote. Writing for the majority, Justice O'Connor held that the white voters could challenge the racially drawn districts as violative of their rights to equal protection and ordered the district court to apply strict scrutiny in examining their claims. That is, the plan could be permitted only if it served a "compelling interest" and was narrowly tailored to achieve that interest. Finally, in a rather strange passage, O'Connor contended, "A reapportionment plan that includes in one district individuals who belong to the same race, but who are otherwise widely separated by geographical and political boundaries, and who may have little in common with one another but the color of their skin, bears an uncomfortable resemblance to political apartheid" (113 S.Ct at 2827).

In dissent, Justice White, joined by Justices Blackmun and Stevens, maintained that the white voters had not been harmed by the plan, given that whites were a majority in 83 percent of the districts (ten of twelve), while constituting just 79 percent of the voting age population. Justice Souter criticized the majority for adopting the strict scrutiny test to examine the plan, stressing that the Court had always "analyzed equal protection claims involving race in electoral districting differently from equal protection claims involving other forms of governmental conduct . . ." (113 S.Ct. at 2845).

Court observers and voting rights experts maintained that the Court's ruling in *Shaw v. Reno* would have far-reaching implications. The 1992 congressional elections had resulted not only in the election of the two African American House members from North Carolina, but the total number of African Americans elected to the House rose dramatically from 26 to 38 (plus the nonvoting delegate from the District of Columbia). More importantly, a number of them were elected to seats created from redistricting after the 1990 census. There was much speculation about the survival of these voting districts, as *Shaw* spawned additional litigation challenging some of them on equal protection grounds.

The Court ruled on one such challenge in *Miller v. Johnson* (1995), a case arising from congressional redistricting efforts in Georgia in 1991 and 1992. Provisions of the Voting Rights Act of 1965 required Georgia (and other states) to have its redistricting plans approved by the Justice Department ("preclearance"). The Justice Department refused to approve plans containing two majority-black districts, holding that the legislature did not maximize the voting strength of African American voters. Finally, the state's revised plan creating three majority black districts—the Second, Fifth, and Eleventh—was approved. The Eleventh District, the one challenged in this case, was 60 percent African American. It was diagonally shaped, encompassing portions of urban Atlanta, Savannah, and Augusta, as well as predominantly African American rural areas. After Cynthia McKinney, an African American Democrat, was elected to this seat in 1992 and reelected in 1994, a group of white voters from the Eleventh District filed suit in federal district court, alleging that it was a racial gerrymander in violation of the Equal Protection Clause. Utilizing *Shaw* as the controlling precedent, the court agreed.

In a narrow ruling, the Supreme Court held the Georgia plan in violation of the Equal Protection Clause. Writing for a five-member majority, Justice Kennedy said that because race was the "predominant, overriding factor" in drawing the district lines, the redistricting plan could be upheld only if it was "narrowly tailored to achieve a compelling state interest" (115 S.Ct. at 2490). He conceded that "eradicating the effects of past racial discrimination" is significant, but he said that it was not the concern here. The State does not argue . . . that it created the Eleventh District to remedy past discrimination, and with good reason: there is little doubt that the State's true interest in designing the Eleventh District was creating a third majority-black district to satisfy the Justice Department's preclearance demands . . ." (115 S.Ct. at 2490). Moreover, Kennedy said that the Justice Department's maximization policy was based on a misinterpretation of the Voting Rights Act. "The congressional plan challenged here was not required . . . under a correct reading of the statute" (115 S.Ct. at 2491).

Dissenting from the ruling were Justices Stevens, Souter, Ginsburg, and Breyer. Writing for the four, Ginsburg rejected the majority's conclusion that race was the predominant factor in the redistricting plan.

> *[T]he Eleventh District's design reflects significant consideration of "traditional districting factors (such as keeping political subdivisions intact) and the usual political process of compromise and trades for a variety of nonracial reasons." . . . Evidence at trial . . . shows that considerations other than race went into determining the Eleventh District's boundaries. For a "political reason"—to accommodate the request of an incumbent State Senator regarding the placement of the precinct in which his son lived—the DeKalb County portion of the Eleventh District was drawn to include a particular (largely white) precinct. The corridor through Effingham County was substantially narrowed at the request of a (white) State Representative. In Chatham County, the District was trimmed to exclude a heavily black community in Garden City because a State Representative wanted to keep the city intact inside the neighboring First District. The Savannah extension was configured by "the narrowest means possible" to avoid splitting the city of Port Wentworth"* (115 S.Ct. at 2503-04).

In addition, emphasizing that ethnicity has long been a factor in districting decisions, Ginsburg pointed out that numbers of voting districts in U.S. cities are ethnically identifiable—Irish, Italian, Jewish, and so on. Finally, she warned the majority that its decision could inappropriately increase federal judicial intervention into state redistricting matters. "Only after litigation—under either the Voting Rights Act, the Court's new *Miller* standard, or both—will States now be assured that plans conscious of race are safe. Federal judges in large numbers may be drawn into the fray. This enlargement of the judicial role is unwarranted" (115 S.Ct. at 2507).

Miller will have a significant impact on redistricting plans for years to come, as more litigation challenging majority-minority congressional districts is expected. In fact, on the same day that *Miller* was handed down, the Court noted jurisdiction in similar cases from Texas and North Carolina.

Statutory Cases

In *Patterson v. McClean Credit Union* (1989), Brenda Patterson charged her employer with racial harassment in violation of the Civil Rights Act of 1866, which forbade discrimination in the making of contracts. Thirteen years earlier, the Court had held in *Runyon v. McCrary* (1976) that the 1866 act applied to discrimination by private individuals, not just to state discrimination. Although the Court did not overturn *Runyon* in the *Patterson* case, as it indicated it might do, the majority severely limited the application of the 1866 law. Over the strong objections of four dissenters, the Court held that the right to make contracts applied only at the hiring stage of employment and not to posthiring matters. In *Ward's Cove Packing Company v. Atonio* (1989), a sharply divided Court drastically altered the requirements for analyzing disparate impact employment discrimination claims under Title VII. The case had been brought by nonwhite workers in Alaskan salmon canneries who successfully demonstrated that they were concentrated in low-paying jobs while white workers were concentrated in higher-paying jobs. Previously, the burden had been on the employer to prove that it did not engage in discrimination, but here the Court's majority shifted the burden to employees, requiring, among other things, that they demonstrate which specific employment practice led to the statistical disparity.

The strong, negative reaction to *Patterson, Ward's Cove,* and other cases prompted Congress to pass the Civil Rights Act of 1991 to overrule these decisions. In 1994, however, the Court limited its utility in *Rivers v. Roadway Express.* By an 8-1 vote, the Court ruled that the 1991 act could not be applied retroactively to those racial discrimination cases which had been pending when the law was passed. In her first case in this area, Justice Ginsburg joined the majority's holding that Congress intended the act only to apply prospectively to new cases. Justice Blackmun issued the lone dissent in this case. He argued that a "natural reading" of the statute and the Court's precedents required that the act be applied retroactively.

Conclusion

At this point, with the exception of cases involving voting rights, the Rehnquist Court has not engaged in a conservative revolution in the area of equal protection and race. It is clear, nonetheless, that the Court is not apt to return to the liberal stance of the Warren Court. With the retirements of Justices Brennan, Marshall, and Blackmun, Justice Stevens is the only liberal remaining on the Court. Justice Souter seems to be moving in a liberal direction, and the most recent appointees—Ruth Bader Ginsburg and Stephen Breyer—although generally regarded as moderates, appear inclined to join with Souter in these cases. Despite the addition of these new justices to the Court's liberal minority, however, the Rehnquist Court is not likely to take expansive views of the Equal Protection Clause and civil rights statutes in deciding cases involving claims of racial discrimination.

REFERENCES

Anderson, Alan B., and George W. Pickering. *Confronting the Color Line: The Broken Promise of the Civil Rights Movement in Chicago.* Athens: University of Georgia Press, 1986.

Berry, Mary Frances. *Black Resistance, White Law: A History of Constitutional Racism in America.* New York: Appleton-Century-Crofts, 1971.

Carson, Clayborn, et al. *Eyes on the Prize: America's Civil Rights Years, A Reader and Guide.* New York: Penguin Books, 1987.

Ginger, Ann Fagan. *Law, the Supreme Court, and the People's Rights.* Woodbury, New York: Barron's Educational Series, 1974.

Irons, Peter, and Stephanie Guitton, eds. *May It Please the Court.* New York: The New Press, 1993.

Jordan, Winthrop D. *White over Black: American Attitudes toward the Negro, 1550-1812.* Chapel Hill, N.C.: University of North Carolina Press, 1968.

Lively, Donald E. *The Constitution and Race.* New York: Praeger, 1992.

Nieman, Donald G. *Promises to Keep: African-Americans and the Constitutional Order, 1776 to the Present.* New York: Oxford University Press, 1991.

Sickels, Robert J. *Race, Marriage, and the Law.* Albuquerque: University of New Mexico Press, 1972.

Wiecek, William M. *The Sources of Antislavery Constitutionalism in America, 1760-1848.* Ithaca, N.Y.: Cornell University Press, 1977.

Wilkinson, J. Harvie. *From Brown to Bakke: The Supreme Court and School Integration: 1954-1978.* New York: Oxford University Press, 1979.

CHAPTER 14

Equal Protection and Gender

CASE STUDY

Frontiero v. Richardson (1973)

Frontiero v. Richardson (1973) began in October, 1970, when Sharron Frontiero, a physical therapist at Maxwell Air Force Base Hospital in Montgomery, Alabama, attempted to take advantage of a housing benefit provided to military personnel. Federal military benefit statutes permitted married male members of the Air Force who lived off-base to receive a basic allowance for quarters (BAQ) without having to prove the actual dependency of their wives. The wives of male members also were entitled to certain medical benefits regardless of their actual dependence on their spouse for support. Sharron Frontiero, who lived off-base with her husband, Joseph Frontiero, a full-time college student, informed her commanding officer that she wanted to receive a BAQ. Her commanding officer instructed her to consult the base legal office. When she did this, Frontiero was told that she could not receive the BAQ because she did not meet the regulations' criteria. In order to receive a BAQ, female members of the armed services had to prove that their husbands were dependent on them for more than one-half of their support. Unfortunately for Lieutenant Frontiero, her husband's share of their monthly expenses totaled $354, but because he received $205 per month in G.I. benefits, he was not actually dependent on her for more than half his support.

Frontiero then consulted with both the base hospital commander and a member of the inspector general's staff, neither of whom could provide her assistance. The inspector general's office, however, advised her to file a formal complaint. She did so, but again was informed that nothing could be done.

Having exhausted all of these possibilities, the Frontieros contacted two well-known civil rights attorneys, Joseph J. Levin, Jr., and Morris S. Dees, Jr. They agreed that the Frontieros' sex discrimination complaint against the Air Force was legitimate. The Frontieros could not have contacted Levin and Dees at a more opportune time. The attorneys were in the process of establishing an organization specializing in class action litigation on behalf of the economically disadvantaged. This organization, the Southern Poverty Law Center, financed the *Frontiero* case.

On December 23, 1970, Levin and Dees filed a class action suit in federal district court on behalf of the Frontieros and other similarly situated military personnel. The complaint asserted that the statutes concerning housing and medical benefits constituted gender discrimination in violation of the Due Process Clause of the Fifth Amendment. Because the Fourteenth Amendment's Equal Protection Clause applies only to states, the Supreme Court has interpreted the Fifth Amendment's Due Process Clause to require the federal government to adhere to equal protection principles. The attorneys pointed out that in order to receive these benefits, female members had to show actual dependency of their spouses, while male members automatically received benefits for their spouses. The complaint, therefore, sought three things: 1) a judgment that the gender-based distinctions in the statutes were unconstitutional, 2) a permanent injunction against enforcement of the challenged provisions, and 3) back pay for those benefits which had been denied to Sharron Frontiero (Cortner 1975).

A three-judge district court was convened on January 7, 1971, and, over a year later, on April 5, 1972, the court announced its decision. By a 2-1 vote, the panel ruled in favor of the government and thereby denied that the challenged statutes were unconstitutional. Using the traditional equal protection test, Judges Rives and McFadden held that there was indeed a rational basis for the gender classification scheme at issue. They asserted that Congress was concerned about the administrative burden that would be created by requiring married male members to provide actual proof of their wives' dependency. Judge Johnson, the lone dissenter, argued that the majority failed to prove its own administrative convenience argument. He wrote, "If it is administratively convenient to provide a conclusive presumption for men, it is inconsistent to require a demonstration of dependency in fact for women" (344 F.Supp. at 210).

After losing in federal district court, Frontiero filed a notice of appeal to the U.S. Supreme Court in April 1972. The Court noted jurisdiction in October, and heard oral arguments in January 1973. By this time, the case had attracted the attention and support of the American Civil Liberties Union (ACLU). Thus, the ACLU's Women's Rights Project (WRP) filed an amicus curiae brief in support of Frontiero, urging the Court to reverse the lower court's decision (Cortner 1975). Moreover, Ruth Bader Ginsburg, the future Supreme Court justice and director of the WRP at the time, participated in oral arguments before the Court. She convinced Frontiero's attorneys to grant her ten of their allotted thirty minutes of oral argument in order to persuade the Court to adopt the suspect classification test to decide gender discrimination cases in the same manner as racial discrimination cases.

Attorneys Levin and Dees maintained that the sexual distinctions in the challenged statutes were invalid under the traditional rational basis test as well. They asserted that the government's desire for administrative convenience "cannot by any test justify the further visitation of inequalities upon women which present dependency definitions enact" (Cortner 1975, p. 203).

Government counsel relied primarily on the administrative convenience justification that had been accepted by the district court. In addition, counsel urged the Court not to place sexual classifications in the suspect category, because they were not comparable to classifications based on race or national origin. Finally, the government contended that the Court should not invalidate the challenged statutes but should wait for the political process to remedy the situation. Counsel noted that because Congress was working on legislation to change its policies on dependent benefits, and because the proposed Equal Rights Amendment (ERA) would bring about the necessary changes if ratified, it would be premature and improper for the Court to strike down the existing policies.

When the decision was announced several months later on May 14, 1973, each side could claim a partial victory (case excerpt on p. 678). The Court ruled 8-1 that the statutes in question were invalid, but a majority declined to place gender classifications in the suspect category. Justices Brennan, Douglas, Marshall, and White concluded that the dependency benefits statutes violated the Due Process Clause of the Fifth Amendment because the sexual classifications were inherently suspect. Justice Stewart concurred in the judgment, stating "the statutes before us work an invidious discrimination in violation of the Constitution" (*Frontiero v. Richardson*, 411 U.S. at 691). Justices Powell, Burger, and Blackmun agreed that the statutes were unconstitutional, but they were persuaded by the government's argument that gender classifications need not be placed in the suspect category. They concluded that the ERA, which was in the ratification stage, would indeed resolve the problem of gender classifications, and therefore judicial action on this matter was premature and unnecessary. Finally, Justice Rehnquist dissented for the reasons stated by Judge Rives in his opinion for the district court.

Several months after the ruling was announced, Sharron Frontiero, who had left the Air Force in 1972 when her enlistment was completed, received $2,095 in back pay and allowances. When asked for a reaction to the Court's decision, the Frontieros expressed a strong sense of accomplishment, of making an important contribution to the feminist movement. More importantly, for the larger society, *Frontiero* was an important victory in the legal fight against gender discrimination. Unfortunately though, *Frontiero* left unresolved the major question of whether to place gender classifications in the suspect category for purposes of equal protection analysis. And, contrary to the expectations of Justices Powell, Blackmun, and Burger, the ERA was eventually defeated when it fell three states short of the three-quarters needed for ratification. Thus, the issue was not resolved through the amendment process, leaving the Court to grapple with the question of what standard to use in examining gender-based discrimination.

Historical Origins and Contemporary Conflicts

The questions raised in *Frontiero* brought to the fore the issue of gender discrimination in American society, particularly as it relates to women. While there have been some Supreme Court decisions concerning discrimination against men, the bulk of gender discrimination litigation concerns discrimination against women. This is because the legal, political, and economic systems placed restrictions on women that were not extended to men. Although a small number of women could vote and own property during the colonial period, by the nineteenth century, gender discrimination was firmly entrenched in the law in many states. Hoff (1991) documented the various types of discrimination levied against women, particularly married women, in such areas as divorce, control over property, guardianship rights over their children, access to the courts, and control over their own wages. She noted that, in the first half of the nineteenth century, even when state laws were passed to protect the property rights of married women, "this legislation also tended to adhere to traditional ideas of patriarchal common law by denying women the right to sell, sue, or contract without their husbands' or other male relatives' approval" (p. 128).

In addition to state laws limiting women's equality and freedom, neither the original Constitution nor the Bill of Rights provided real protection for women's rights. Women are not mentioned in either of these documents, and it was not until the Nineteenth Amendment was ratified in 1920 that the Constitution made reference to women.

Although many women were never content with their subordinate status, the first *organized* women's rights movement did not occur until 1848, when feminists gathered at Seneca Falls, New York. At this convention, the participants (including a few men) adopted the Declaration of Sentiments, a document patterned after the Declaration of Independence. Following a preamble and a list of grievances related to the subordination of women in various aspects of life, the Declaration of Sentiments included a set of twelve resolutions to guide the participants in their reform efforts. Some of the resolutions were:

> *Resolved, that all laws which prevent woman from occupying such a station in society as her conscience shall dictate, or which place her in a position inferior to that of man, are contrary to the great precept of nature and therefore of no force or authority.*
>
> *Resolved, that woman is man's equal—was intended to be so by the Creator, and the highest good of the race demands that she should be recognized as such.*
>
> *Resolved, that it is the duty of the women of this country to secure to themselves their sacred right to elective franchise.*

> *Resolved, that the speedy success of our cause depends upon the zealous and untiring efforts of both men and women, for the overthrow of the monopoly of the pulpit, and for the security to woman an equal participation with men in the various trades, professions, and commerce.*

The last two of these resolutions involved matters that would ultimately be decided by the Supreme Court less than thirty years after the Seneca Falls meeting.

Early court cases concerned protective legislation directed at women in the labor force. These laws governed hours and wages of working women as well as restrictions on where they could work. They were based partly on a philosophy of "romantic paternalism," which emphasized that women are weak, delicate creatures who need the protection of strong men. The Court, endorsing these views, generally upheld such legislation.

Later cases decided in the 1970s and early 1980s included such matters as the exclusion of women from jury duty, laws giving preference in administrative matters to males over females, statutory rape laws that punish males but not females, and the exclusion of women from registration for the draft. More recent conflicts from the late 1980s and the 1990s have involved pregnancy disability benefits, sexual harassment, and fetal protection policies. Following a discussion of Supreme Court approaches to cases involving gender discrimination, the Court's decisions in these matters will be discussed in greater depth.

Supreme Court Approaches to Equal Protection and Gender

While the Court's approach to examining racial classifications under the Equal Protection Clause was fairly clear even in early cases, this was not so with respect to claims of gender discrimination. In *Korematsu v. United States,* decided in 1944, the Court held that racial classifications are automatically suspect, and that the Equal Protection Clause requires that they be subjected to rigid scrutiny. Consequently, when the first contemporary gender discrimination case reached the Supreme Court in 1971, many Court observers assumed that the same standard would apply. This was *not* the case, however. In *Reed v. Reed,* the Court indicated that the rational basis test was the appropriate standard for cases involving gender-based classifications. Nonetheless, women's rights groups and civil rights advocates continued to push the Court to place gender discrimination in the suspect category.

Two years after *Reed,* this issue was placed squarely before the Court in *Frontiero v. Richardson* (1973). Only four justices agreed that classifications on the basis of gender are inherently suspect and subject to strict scrutiny. Justices Brennan, Douglas, Marshall, and White noted that sex, like race and national origin, met the criteria for placement in the suspect category: 1) women were subject to a long history of discrimination; 2) sex is an immutable characteristic of birth; and 3) women lacked the ability to affect change through the elected branches of government. By contrast, Justices Powell, Blackmun, and Burger argued that the Equal Rights Amendment, which had been approved by Congress and had already been ratified by a number of states, would resolve the problem.

To the contrary, the ERA was not ratified, and the Court continued to face the question of the appropriate standard of review for gender-based classifications. While a majority never agreed to examine such classifications with strict scrutiny, in 1976 the Court announced that gender discrimination would be reviewed using an intermediate level of scrutiny. In *Craig v. Boren,* the majority set forth the important government objective test. Under this standard, "classifications by gender must serve important governmental objectives and must be substantially related to achievement of those objectives" (*Craig v. Boren,* 429 U.S. at 197, 1976).

This important government objective test is the current standard for reviewing gender-based discrimination under the Equal Protection Clause. Thus, although the Court refused to accord such classifications the highest level of scrutiny, it does not appear willing to return to the less stringent rational basis test.

Pre-Warren Court Period

The first gender discrimination cases heard by the Supreme Court were not decided under the Equal Protection Clause, but rather under the Privileges and Immunities Clause and the Due Process Clause of the Fourteenth Amendment. Conflicts in these cases derived from cultural attitudes about the proper role of women in American society. While discrimination against women in every facet of life was firmly entrenched, early feminists sought to bring about changes in the way that women were treated by that system, particularly in terms of political, social, and legal rights.

Pre-1937 Period

Two cases decided by the Supreme Court in the mid-nineteenth century, *Bradwell v. Illinois* (1873) and *Minor v. Happersett* (1875), were the first to challenge gender discrimination as a violation of the Fourteenth Amendment. Both cases involved the Privileges and Immunities Clause. In the first case, Myra Bradwell, a prominent women's rights activist, sought entrance into the legal profession in Illinois. After Bradwell's application to the Illinois bar was denied for the sole reason that she was a married woman, the case was appealed to the Supreme Court. Her attorney maintained that the "Fourteenth Amendment opens to every citizen of the United States, male or female, . . . the honorable professions as well as the servile employments of life" (Goldstein 1988 p. 68). The Supreme Court disagreed, however, ruling that the Privileges and Immunities Clause of the Fourteenth Amendment refers only to national citizenship, not state citizenship. Becoming a lawyer does not relate to national citizenship, unless the desire is to practice in the federal courts. Because Bradwell was seeking to practice in the state court of Illinois, the Privileges and Immunities Clause was not applicable to her.

Myra Bradwell v. Illinois

83 U.S. (16 Wall.) 130, 21 L. Ed. 442 (1873)

Myra Bradwell was a prominent women's rights activist in Illinois. After being trained for the Illinois bar exam by her attorney husband, she applied to the bar for a license to practice law in Illinois. Her application was denied because under state law women were not eligible to practice law. After a denial by the Supreme Court of Illinois, Bradwell appealed to the United States Supreme Court. Her attorney argued that this denial was a violation of the Fourteenth Amendment Privileges and Immunities Clause.

As you read the case, consider the following questions: 1) Would the decision have been different had the case been argued and decided using the Equal Protection Clause rather than the Privileges and Immunities Clause? 2) Given the view of women's roles at that time, as Bradley's concurrence indicates, was the decision here inevitable?

Vote:

8 justices agreed that there was no Fourteenth Amendment violation in the state action of denying Bradwell's application (Miller, Bradley, Field, Swayne, Davis, Strong, Hunt, Clifford).

1 justice dissented from the ruling (Chase).

Justice Miller delivered the opinion of the Court.

The supreme court [of Illinois] denied the application apparently upon the ground that it was a woman who made it.

* * *

In regard to that Amendment counsel for the plaintiff in this court truly says there are certain privileges and immunities which belong to a citizen

of the United States as such; otherwise it would be nonsense for the 14th Amendment to prohibit a state from abridging them, and he proceeds to argue that admission to the bar of a state, of a person who possesses the requisite learning and character, is one of those which a state may not deny.

In this latter proposition we are not able to concur with counsel. We agree with him that there are privileges and immunities belonging to citizens of the United States, in that relation and character, and that it is these and these alone which a state is forbidden to abridge. But the right to admission to practice in the courts of a state is not one of them. This right in no sense depends on citizenship of the United States. It has not, as far as we know, ever been made in any state or in any case to depend on citizenship at all. Certainly many prominent and distinguished lawyers have been admitted to practice, both in the state and Federal courts, who were not citizens of the United States or of any state. But, on whatever basis this right may be placed, so far as it can have any relation to citizenship at all, it would seem that, as to the courts of a state, and as to the Federal courts, it would relate to citizenship of the United States.

The judgment of the State Court is, therefore, affirmed.

Justice Bradley:

I concur in the judgment of the court in this case, by which the judgment of the supreme court of Illinois is affirmed, but not for the reasons specified in the opinion just read.

* * *

The claim that, under the 14th Amendment of the Constitution, which declares that no state shall make or enforce any law which shall abridge the privileges and immunities of citizens of the United States, and the statute law of Illinois, or the common law prevailing in that state, can no longer be set up as a barrier against the right of females to pursue any lawful employment for a livelihood (the practice of law included), assumes that it is one of the privileges and immunities of women as citizens to engage in any and every profession, occupation or employment in civil life.

It certainly cannot be affirmed, as a historical fact, that this has ever been established as one of the fundamental privileges and immunities of the sex. On the contrary, the civil law, as well as nature herself, has always recognized a wide difference in the respective spheres and destinies of man and woman. Man is, or should be, woman's protector and defender. The natural and proper timidity and delicacy which belongs to the female sex evidently unfits it for many of the occupations of civil life. The constitution of the family organization, which is founded in the divine ordinance, as well as in the nature of things, indicates the domestic sphere as that which properly belongs to the domain and functions of womanhood. The harmony, not to say identity, of interests and views which belong to the family institution, is repugnant to the idea of a woman adopting a distinct and independent career from that of her husband. So firmly fixed was this sentiment in the founders of the common law that it became a maxim of that system of jurisprudence that a woman had no legal existence separate from her husband, who was regarded as her head and representative in the social state; and, notwithstanding some recent modifications of this civil status, many of the special rules of law flowing from and dependent upon this cardinal principle still exist in full force in most states.

It is true that many women are unmarried and not affected by any of the duties, complications and incapacities arising out of the married state, but these are exceptions to the general rule. The paramount destiny and mission of woman are to fulfill the noble and benign offices of wife and mother. This is the law of the Creator. And the rules of civil society must be adapted to the general constitution of things, and cannot be based upon exceptional cases.

* * *

It is the prerogative of the legislator to prescribe regulations founded on nature, reason, and experience for the due admission of qualified persons to professions and callings demanding special skill and confidence. This fairly belongs to the police power of the state; and, in my opinion, in view of the peculiar characteristics, destiny, and mission of woman, it is within the province of the legislature to ordain what offices, positions, and callings shall be filled and discharged by men, and shall receive the benefit of those energies and responsibilities, and that decision and firmness which are presumed to predominate in the sterner sex.

For these reasons I think that the laws of Illinois now complained of are not obnoxious to the charge of abridging any of the privileges and immunities of citizens of the United States.

Justice Field and Justice Swayne:

We concur in the opinion of Mr. Justice Bradley.

Dissenting, Chief Justice Chase.

Perhaps as important as the outcome of the case is a passage from Justice Bradley's concurrence, which was cited in later cases to permit discrimination against women: "The civil law, as well as nature herself, has always recognized a wide difference in the respective spheres and destinies of man and woman. Man is, or should be, woman's protector and defender. The natural and proper timidity and delicacy which belong to the female sex evidently unfits it for many of the occupations of civil life. . . . The paramount destiny and mission of woman are to fulfill the noble and benign offices of wife and mother. This is the law of the Creator" (83 U.S. at 446). Chief Justice Chase dissented without comment from this ruling.

Two years after Myra Bradwell's case, the Court's attention was turned to the issue of suffrage. After the Civil War, women's rights activists began to focus their energies on securing for women the right to vote. They formed the National Woman Suffrage Association (NWSA) and the American Woman Suffrage Association (AWSA) to organize efforts in the various states and at the national level. The case *Minor v. Happersett* (1875) arose when Virginia Minor, president of her state chapter of the NWSA, was denied the opportunity to register to vote. She and about 150 members of this organization had attempted to register to vote in ten states where women were denied that right. After Reese Happersett, the St. Louis registrar, refused to allow her to register, Minor's husband filed a suit in civil court on her behalf. The case eventually reached the Supreme Court; once again it was argued and decided on the Privileges and Immunities Clause of the Fourteenth Amendment. Minor's counsel claimed that the right to vote was one of the privileges and immunities of national citizenship. In a unanimous ruling, the Court admitted that women are citizens of the United States, but it also maintained that in conferring citizenship, the Constitution did not necessarily confer the right of suffrage. The justices reasoned that the Fourteenth Amendment did not add to the privileges and immunities of citizens, but instead simply guaranteed those protections already held. Since many states restricted suffrage at the time of adoption of the Fourteenth Amendment, this right was not one of the privileges and immunities that already existed. With this momentous ruling, therefore, women were not *guaranteed* the right to vote in every state until ratification of the Nineteenth Amendment in 1920. Several states, however, extended suffrage to women prior to 1920.

After the *Bradwell* and *Happersett* rulings, the Court's next major decisions involving gender discrimination concerned the power of states to pass legislation to "protect" women. These cases came during an era (the late 1890s and early 1900s) when there were concerns about the working conditions in many factories and businesses. Progressive organizations such as the National Consumers' League (NCL) lobbied for legislative reforms regarding wages, hours of work, and hazardous conditions in the workplace. These reforms produced major conflicts between progressives and women's rights activists over the desirability of protective legislation. Progressives pushed for protective labor legislation for women as part of an overall strategy to obtain similar protection for *all* workers. Some women's rights activists, however, saw protective legislation for women as an obstacle to the goal of equality. Organizations such as the National Women's Party emphasized that, rather than helping women, protective legislation actually hindered women's employment opportunities because it characterized them as weak and vulnerable and therefore incapable of performing certain jobs.

To the delight of progressives and the dismay of some women's groups, the Supreme Court generally upheld this legislation, ruling that the Due Process Clause of the Fourteenth Amendment was not violated by these laws. First, the Court upheld a maximum hour law for women in *Muller v. Oregon* (1908). In *Muller*, an

Oregon statute prohibited women employed in factories, laundries, and other "mechanical" establishments from working more that ten hours a day. Muller, the owner of a small laundry, was convicted for violating the statute, and his subsequent appeal was accepted by the Supreme Court. Louis Brandeis, who would later become a Supreme Court justice, argued the case for Oregon. He relied primarily on studies showing that long work hours were deleterious to women's health and to their reproductive capabilities. The Court accepted Brandeis's argument, ruling unanimously that the maximum hour statute did not violate the Due Process Clause of the Fourteenth Amendment. Ironically, the Court had struck down maximum hour legislation for men three years earlier in *Lochner v. New York* (1905). Consequently, the justices reasoned in *Muller* that the differences in the sexes justified the difference in legislation. "Her physical structure and a proper discharge of her maternal functions—having in view not merely her own health, but the well-being of the race—justify legislation to protect her from the greed as well as the passion of man" (208 U.S. at 422).

Fifteen years later, however, the Court struck down a minimum wage law for women in *Adkins v. Children's Hospital* (1923). The case involved a District of Columbia statute that created and empowered a board to establish minimum wages for children and women workers. The wage for women was to be directed toward the necessary cost of living and to the maintenance of their physical and moral health. In a 5-3 decision, the Court declared the law in violation of the Fifth Amendment's Due Process Clause, as it constituted "undue" interference with the liberty of contract. The majority opinion relied to some extent on *Lochner*, which many observers thought had been overruled in an earlier case. Moreover, in a rather strange discussion, the Court claimed that the Nineteenth Amendment made special protection for women unnecessary. According to Justice Sutherland, maximum hour legislation was appropriate because it was related to women's physical weakness, whereas minimum wage legislation was premised on the notion that women cannot fend for themselves in the economy. He said that because women obtained the right to vote and to make contracts, protective legislation was not necessary regarding wages, and, indeed, the wage law actually limited women's freedom. Sutherland wrote, "[This] is simply and exclusively a price-fixing law, confined to adult women . . . who are legally as capable of contracting for themselves as men. It forbids two parties having lawful capacity . . . to freely contract with one another" (261 U.S. at 554).

Justices Taft and Holmes, in separate dissents, took the majority to task for striking down this legislation. Both maintained that the Court had previously upheld some laws that limited freedom of contract. Moreover, Holmes questioned the constitutional grounds for the freedom of contract doctrine, writing "pretty much all law consists in forbidding men to do some things that they want to do and contract is no more exempt from law than other acts" (261 U.S. at 568). Holmes also said that there was no meaningful difference between the power to fix wages (which the Court struck down) and the power to fix hours of work (which the Court sustained); both interfere with the freedom of contract. Finally, Taft and Holmes emphasized that the minimum wage law was a reasonable statute passed after study by intelligent minds, and the Court should have deferred to the legislature in this matter.

These two decisions, *Muller* and *Adkins,* although distinguished by the justices, seemed to be in conflict with one another. On the one hand, *Muller* protected women from being overworked and exploited by their employers, but on the other hand, *Adkins* allowed unscrupulous employers to exploit women workers by underpaying them.

In addition to decisions on maximum hour and minimum wage laws, the Court ruled on the validity of statutes regarding night work restrictions for women. In *Radice v. New York* (1924), the Court heard a challenge to a New York law that prohibited women from being employed between 10:00 P.M. and 6:00 A.M. in restaurants in large cities. While the statute did have some exceptions, Goldstein wrote, "It meant that women in major cities could not work as waitresses or cooks or hostesses in most restaurants after ten o'clock at night" (1988, p. 37). Because of these restrictions, the jobs that women did during the day or in smaller cities became "men's jobs" at night in large cities. Radice was convicted for violating the statute; and after the state court of appeals upheld his conviction, he appealed to the Supreme Court, arguing that the law violated both due process and equal protection. The Court unanimously upheld the law, accepting the legislature's argument that in large cities "night work is substantially and especially detrimental to the health of women" (264 U.S. at 294, 1924). Answering the contention that night work is harmful to all workers, not just to women, the Court reasoned that women's "delicate organism" makes them more vulnerable than men. Twelve years after *Radice* was decided, the Court again invalidated a minimum wage law for women. In *Morehead v. New York ex rel. Tipaldo* (1936), the Court ruled 5-4 that such legislation violates the Due Process Clause of the Fourteenth Amendment.

New Deal Era Until the Warren Court

Only one year after *Morehead,* however, the Court revisited this issue and came to a different conclusion. Some would argue that this change was due to the political environment. In addition to striking down minimum wage laws, the Court had been hostile to other social welfare legislation, including Franklin Roosevelt's New Deal programs. Following Roosevelt's victory in the 1936 presidential election, he introduced his controversial "court-packing plan." Under this plan, a new seat would be created on the Court for every justice over the age of 70. The effect would have been the addition of six new seats, which would have been filled by Roosevelt's appointees, who presumably would be more sympathetic to social welfare and economic regulation legislation. Thus with six new justices and three or four of the current justices voting together, Roosevelt's policies could be upheld. When the Court began to uphold New Deal legislation, however, the plan to increase the size of the Court became unnecessary. For example, Justice Roberts, who had provided the fifth vote to invalidate the minimum wage law challenged in *Morehead,* joined the majority in *West Coast Hotel v. Parrish* (1937) to uphold a statute similar to the one struck down in *Adkins*. Here, a Washington state law created a board to establish minimum wages for women and children workers. The case arose when Elsie Parrish sued her employer, West Coast Hotel, for back pay that would bring her wages up to the minimum that had been set by law. Those challenging the statute argued that mandating minimum wages deprived women of the freedom of contract. In a 5-4 decision, writing for the majority, Chief Justice Hughes said, "The Constitution does not speak of freedom of contract. It speaks of liberty and prohibits the devprivation of liberty without due process at law" (300 U.S. at 391). According to Hughes, this liberty is limited by legislation aimed at protecting the health, safety, morals, and welfare of the people. The minimum wage law at issue, Hughes maintained, was consistent with this interpretation of due process. To the dismay of those who opposed this type of legislation for women on the grounds that it actually hurt their opportunities for employment, Hughes's opinion contained language affirming the need to protect women. After quoting *Muller* and related precedents, Hughes concluded, "What can be closer to the public interest than the health of women and their protection from unscrupulous and overreaching employers? And if the protection of women is a legitimate end . . . , how can it be said that the requirements of the payments of a minimum wage . . . is not an admissible means to that end?" (300 U.S. at 398).

Not surprisingly, Justice Sutherland, author of the majority opinion in *Adkins,* scolded the majority for not abiding by that precedent because the statutes challenged in the two cases were basically the same. While conceding that there was no absolute freedom of contract, he said that such freedom could be limited only because of "exceptional circumstances." Lastly, Sutherland claimed that the statute was unnecessary because women had achieved legal and political equality with men, and, because it applied only to women, the statute discriminated arbitrarily against men. This decision explicitly overruled *Adkins* and implicitly nullified *Morehead* as well. Four years later, in *U.S. v. Darby* (1941), the Court would uphold minimum wage laws as applied to all workers, female or male, children or adults.

The next occasion for the Court to deal with the issue of sex discrimination came after World War II. This time the case involved the Equal Protection Clause rather than the Due Process Clause. Like other states concerned about the health and morals of women, Michigan passed a law that prevented women from serving as bartenders unless their husbands or fathers were the owners of the liquor establishments where they worked. In *Goesaert v. Cleary* (1948), decided by a 6-3 vote, the Court held that this legislation was consistent with the power of government to regulate liquor traffic. Justice Frankfurter's opinion for the majority was rather broad, as he emphasized that Michigan could, without violating the Constitution, prohibit *all* women from bartending. He maintained that despite changes in the social and legal status of women, states may make distinctions between the sexes. While claiming that the state could forbid all women from bartending, Frankfurter nonetheless argued that the state could not discriminate in favor of wives and daughters without a valid reason. The reason for this distinction, he found, was the protective oversight in bars that could be provided by a female bartender's husband or father.

Taking a somewhat different approach in examining the statute in question, the dissenters, led by Justice Rutledge, viewed the statute as arbitrarily discriminating against *female owners* of bars: "A male owner, although he himself is always absent from his bar, may employ his wife and daughter as barmaids. A female owner may neither work as a barmaid herself or employ her daughter in that position, even if a man is always present in the establishment to keep order" (335 U.S. at 468). Finding no justification for this discrimination, the dissenters would have ruled that the statute was indeed a violation of the Equal Protection Clause.

The Warren Court Era

In contrast to the plethora of decisions regarding racial discrimination, the Warren Court heard only one case concerning gender discrimination. And, to the disappointment of women's rights activists, even the "liberal" Warren Court permitted such discrimination to continue. In *Hoyt v. Florida* (1961), the Court ruled on the exclusion of women from juries. By a unanimous vote, the Court ruled that a statute automatically excluding women but not men from jury duty did not constitute a denial of equal protection. Justice Harlan, writing for a six-member majority, said the purpose of the statute was not to exclude women from jury duty but instead was an attempt to permit them to fulfill their home and family responsibilities. As in *Muller,* the Court's language was detrimental to the goals of those who pushed for women's equality in all spheres of public life—political, economic, and social. "Despite the enlightened emancipation of women from the restrictions and protections of bygone years, and their entry into many parts of community life formerly considered to be reserved to men, woman is still regarded as the center of home and family life" (368 U.S. at 61–62, 1961).

In a brief concurrence in the result, Justices Black, Douglas, and Warren concluded that there was no evidence that Florida was "not making a good faith effort to have women perform jury duty without discrimination on the ground of sex" (368 U.S. at 69). Perhaps more importantly, they did not join in the part of the majority opinion that perpetuated stereotypes about women and their roles in society.

Hoyt v. Florida

368 U.S. 57 (1961)

■ Under Florida law, women were automatically exempted from jury duty unless they requested to serve, while men were automatically included on jury lists unless they requested an exemption. A result of the law was a substantial overrepresentation of male jurors, and thus, a number of all-male juries. In this case, of ten thousand names on a list of eligible jurors, a mere ten were women. Following her conviction for second-degree murder by an all-male jury, Gwendolyn Hoyt claimed that she was denied equal protection of the laws because women jurors would have been more understanding given the circumstances of the murder. Hoyt had suspected her husband of adultery, and she killed him with a baseball bat during a subsequent fight. She had become enraged not simply over the adultery, but over the fact that he rejected her when she said she was willing to take him back. The Florida Supreme Court rejected her equal protection claims and affirmed her conviction.

This case is important because it is the only case in which the Warren Court considered whether the Equal Protection Clause prohibits discrimination on the basis of gender. Given the Court's "liberal" decisions in the area of racial discrimination, many people assumed that the justices would do the same with respect to gender discrimination. As you read the case, consider the following questions: 1) Is the fact that other states have laws similar to Florida's sufficient justification for upholding the challenged statute? 2) Would the three justices who concurred in the result have reached the opposite conclusion if the statute placed an outright ban on women jurors?

Vote:

9-0 to uphold the statute (Harlan, Warren, Black, Frankfurter, Brennan, Douglas, Clark, Whittaker, Stewart).

Justice Harlan delivered the opinion of the Court.

. . . Of course, [Mrs. Hoyt's] premises misconceive the scope of the right to an impartially selected jury assured by the Fourteenth Amendment. That right does not entitle one accused of crime to a jury tailored to the circumstances of the particular case, whether relating to the sex or other condition of the defendant, or to the nature of the charges to be tried. It requires only that the jury be indiscriminately drawn from among those eligible in the community for jury service, untrammelled by any arbitrary and systematic exclusions. The result of this appeal must therefore depend on whether such an exclusion of women from jury service has been shown.

We address ourselves first to appellant's challenge to the statute on its face.

Several observations should initially be made. We of course recognize that the Fourteenth Amendment reaches not only arbitrary class exclusions from jury service based on race or color, but also all other exclusions which "single out" any class of persons "for different treatment not based on some reasonable classification." We need not, however, accept appellant's invitation to canvass in this case the continuing validity of this Court's dictum in *Strauder v. West Virginia,* to the effect that a State may constitutionally "confine" jury duty to males. This constitutional proposition has gone unquestioned for more than eighty years in the decisions of the Court and had been reflected, until 1957, in congressional policy respecting jury service in the federal courts themselves. Even were it to be assumed that this question is still open to debate, the present case tenders narrower issues.

Manifestly, Florida's [statute] does not purport to exclude women from state jury service. Rather, the statute "gives to women the privilege to serve but does not impose service as a duty." It accords women an absolute exemption from jury service unless they expressly waive that privilege. This is not to say, however, that what in form may be only an exemption of a particular class of persons can in no circumstances be regarded as an exclusion of that class. Where, as here, an exemption of a class in the community is asserted to be in substance an exclusionary device, the relevant inquiry is whether the exemption itself is based on some reasonable classification and whether the manner in which it is exercisable rests on some rational foundation.

In the selection of jurors, Florida has differentiated between men and women in two respects. It has given women an absolute exemption from jury duty based solely on their sex, no similar exemption obtaining as to men. And it has provided for its effectuation in a manner less onerous than that governing exemptions exercisable by men: women are not to be put on the jury list unless they have voluntarily registered for such service; men, on the other hand, even if entitled to an exemption, are to be included on the list unless they have filed a written claim of exemption as provided by law.

In neither respect can we conclude that Florida's statute is not "based on some reasonable classification," and that it is thus infected with unconstitutionality. Despite the enlightened emancipation of women from the restrictions and protections of bygone years, and their entry into many parts of community life formerly considered to be reserved to men, woman is still regarded as the center of home and family life. We cannot say that it is constitutionally impermissible for a State, acting in pursuit of the general welfare, to conclude that a woman should be relieved from the civic duty of jury service unless she herself determines that such service is consistent with her own special responsibilities.

Florida is not alone in so concluding. Women are now eligible for jury service in all but three States of the Union. Of the forty-seven States where women are eligible, seventeen besides Florida, as well as the District of Columbia, have accorded women an absolute exemption based solely on their sex, exercisable in one form or another. In two of these States, as in Florida, the exemption is automatic, unless a woman volunteers for such service. It is true, of course, that Florida could have limited the exemption, as some other States have done, only to women who have family responsibilities. But we cannot regard it as irrational for a state legislature to consider preferable a broad exemption, whether born of the State's historic public policy or of a determination that it would not be administratively feasible to decide in each individual instance whether the family responsibilities of a prospective female juror were serious enough to warrant an exemption.

Likewise we cannot say that Florida could not reasonably conclude that full effectuation of this exemption made it desirable to relieve women of the necessity of affirmatively claiming it, while at the same time requiring of men an assertion of the exemptions available to them. Moreover, from the standpoint of its own administrative concerns the State might well consider that it was "impractical to compel large numbers of women, who have an absolute exemption, to come to the clerk's office for examination since they so generally assert their exemption."

Appellant argues that whatever may have been the design of this Florida enactment, the statute in practical operation results in an exclusion of women from jury service, because women, like men, can be expected to be available for jury service only under compulsion. . . .

This argument, however, is surely beside the point. Given the reasonableness of the classification involved, the relative paucity of women jurors does not carry the constitutional consequence appellant would have it bear. "Circumstances or chance may well dictate that no persons in a certain class will serve on particular jury or during some particular period."

We cannot hold this statute as written offensive to the Fourteenth Amendment.

Appellant's attack on the statute as applied in this case fares no better.

This case in no way resembles those involving race or color in which the circumstances shown were found by this Court to compel a conclusion of purposeful discriminatory exclusions from jury service. There is present here neither the unfortunate atmosphere of ethnic or racial prejudices which underlay the situations depicted in those cases, nor the long course of discriminatory administrative practice which the statistical showing in each of them evinced.

In the circumstances here depicted, it indeed "taxes our credulity" to attribute to these administrative officials a deliberate design to exclude the very class whose eligibility for jury service the state legislature, after many years of contrary policy, had declared only a few years before. It is sufficiently evident from the record that the presence on the jury list of no more than ten or twelve women in the earlier years, and the failure to add in 1957 more women to those already on the list, are attributable not to any discriminatory motive, but to a purpose to put on the list only those women who might be expected to be qualified for service if actually called. Nor is there the slightest suggestion that the list was the product of any plan to place on it only women of a particular economic or other community or organizational group.

Finding no substantial evidence whatever in this record that Florida has arbitrarily undertaken to exclude women from jury service, a showing which it was incumbent on appellant to make, we must sustain the judgment of the Supreme Court of Florida.

The Chief Justice, Justice Black, and Justice Douglas, concurring.

We cannot say from this record that Florida is not making a good faith effort to have women perform jury duty without discrimination on the ground of sex. Hence, we concur in the result, for the reasons set forth in Part II of the Court's opinion.

The Burger Court Era

Just as many of the Warren Court's decisions attacking racial discrimination came during the height of the Civil Rights Movement, so too the Burger Court's rulings redressing gender discrimination occurred during the contemporary feminist movement. By the end of the 1960s, women had entered the labor force in increasing numbers, where they encountered various forms of discrimination. Their increasing awareness of inequalities based on gender, along with their participation in civil rights, student, antiwar, and other protest movements of the 1950s and 1960s, resulted in a movement that sought to eradicate gender discrimination and to bring women into full equality in all aspects of American life. As part of their efforts, feminists adopted the legal strategy employed by African Americans in the Civil Rights Movement. Under the leadership of the NAACP Legal Defense and Education Fund, African Americans brought to the Court litigation challenging racial segregation in various areas of American life. The Women's Rights Project (WRP) of the American Civil Liberties Union (ACLU), directed by Ruth Bader Ginsburg, and other women's groups saw the success of the NAACP and created similar strategies for attacking gender discrimination. Some progress had already occurred in persuading Congress to begin to outlaw gender discrimination. Discrimination on the basis of gender was included in the Civil Rights Act of 1964 (although it was introduced in an effort to kill the entire bill), and Congress had passed the Equal Pay Act mandating equal wages for equal work a year earlier.

Reed v. Reed (1971) and Its Aftermath

In 1971, the Court heard the first contemporary case alleging that gender discrimination was a violation of the Equal Protection Clause. In *Reed v. Reed,* a divorced couple, Sally and Cecil Reed, competed for the right to administer their deceased son's estate. Under Idaho law, if men and women were equally qualified to administer estates, then courts were to appoint males over females. The Court struck down the statute in a unanimous ruling (7-0). Chief Justice Burger, writing for the Court, acknowledged that states may treat different classes of people differently, but he emphasized that the classification must be reasonable, not arbitrary. Moreover, the classification must have a relationship to the object of the legislation. He found unsatisfactory Idaho's rationale that the purpose of the statute was to reduce the workload of the probate courts by reducing the number of hearings held when people compete to administer an estate. He concluded, "To give a mandatory preference to members of either sex over members of the other merely to accomplish the elimination of hearings on the merits, is to make the very kind of arbitrary legislative choice forbidden by the Equal Protection Clause of the Fourteenth Amendment" (404 U.S. at 76, 1971).

For the ACLU which had sponsored the case, *Reed* was a bittersweet victory. In striking down the discriminatory statute, the Court for the first time declared a law to be unconstitutional because of gender discrimination. The justices failed to rule, however, that gender-based classifications are suspect and would be reviewed under strict scrutiny. By using the rational basis test instead, the Court made it difficult for individuals to prevail against the government in gender discrimination cases.

The next opportunity to convince the Court came two years later in the case of *Frontiero v. Richardson* (1973), which we examined in detail at the beginning of this chapter. Again, the Court refused to place gender-based classifications in the suspect category.

FRONTIERO V. RICHARDSON

411 U.S. 677, 93 S.Ct. 1764, 36 L. Ed. 2d 583 (1973)
[The facts of this case are omitted because they were presented in the case study at the beginning of the chapter.]

■ This case is important primarily because the Court addressed the question of whether gender discrimination should be treated as a suspect classification in the same way as discrimination based on race and national origin. As you read the case, consider the following questions: 1) Did Justice Brennan's plurality opinion present a convincing argument for characterizing gender discrimination as inherently suspect? 2) Was Justice Powell correct in assuming that ratification of the Equal Rights Amendment would make gender a suspect classification?

VOTE:

4 justices agreed to make gender a suspect class and found the laws unconstitutional (Brennan, Douglas, White, and Marshall).

4 justices found the laws unconstitutional but refused to make gender a suspect class (Stewart, Powell, Burger, and Blackmun).

1 justice found the laws constitutional (Rehnquist).

Justice Brennan announced the judgment of the Court and an opinion in which Justice Douglas, Justice White, and Justice Marshall join.

* * *

At the outset, appellants contend that classifications based upon sex, like classifications based upon race, alienage, and national origin, are inherently suspect and must therefore be subjected to close judicial scrutiny. We agree and, indeed, find at least implicit support for such an approach in our unanimous decision only last Term in *Reed v. Reed* (1971).

In *Reed,* the Court considered the constitutionality of an Idaho statute providing that, when two individuals are otherwise equally entitled to appointment as administrator of an estate, the male applicant must be preferred to the female. . . .

The Court noted that the Idaho statute "provides that different treatment be accorded to the applicants on the basis of their sex; it thus establishes a classification subject to scrutiny under the Equal Protection Clause." Under "traditional" equal protection analysis, a legislative classification must be sustained unless it is "patently arbitrary" and bears no rational relationship to a legitimate governmental interest.

In an effort to meet this standard, appellee contended that the statutory scheme was a reasonable measure designed to reduce the workload on probate courts by eliminating one class of contests. Moreover, appellee argued that the mandatory preference for male applicants was in itself reasonable since "men [are] as a rule more conversant with business affairs than . . . women." Indeed, appellee maintained that "it is a matter of common knowledge, that women still are not engaged in politics, the professions, business or industry to the extent that men are." And the Idaho Supreme Court, in upholding the constitutionality of this statute, suggested that the Idaho Legislature might reasonably have "concluded that in general men are better qualified to act as an administrators than are women."

Despite these contentions, however, the Court held the statutory preference for male applicants unconstitutional. In reaching this result, the Court implicitly rejected appellee's apparently rational explanation of the statutory scheme, and concluded that, by ignoring the individual qualifications of particular applicants, the challenged statute provided "dissimilar treatment for men and women who are . . . similarly situated." The Court therefore held that, even though the State's interest in achieving administrative efficiency "is not without some legitimacy, [t]o give a mandatory preference to members of either sex over members of the other, merely to accomplish the elimination of hearings on the merits, is to make the very kind of arbitrary legislative choice forbidden by the [Constitution]. . . ." This departure from "traditional" rational-basis analysis with respect to sex-based classifications is clearly justified.

There can be no doubt that our Nation has had a long and unfortunate history of sex discrimination. Traditionally, such discrimination was rationalized by an attitude of "romantic paternalism" which, in practical effect, put women, not on a pedestal, but in a cage. Indeed, this paternalistic attitude became so firmly rooted in our national consciousness that, 100 years ago, a distinguished Member of the Court was able to proclaim:

> Man is, or should be, woman's protector and defender. The natural and proper timidity and delicacy which belongs to the female sex evidently unfits it for many of the occupations of civil life. . . .
>
> . . . The paramount destiny and mission of woman are to fulfil the noble and benign offices of wife and mother. This is the law of the Creator. *Bradwell v. State,* (Bradley, J. concurring).

As a result of notions such as these, our statute books gradually became laden with gross, stereotyped distinctions between the sexes and, indeed, throughout much of the 19th century the position of women in our society was, in many respects, comparable to that of blacks under the pre-Civil War slave codes. Neither slaves nor women could hold office, serve on juries, or bring suit in their own names, and married women traditionally were denied the legal capacity to hold or convey property or to serve as legal guardians of their own children. And although blacks were guaranteed the right to vote in 1870, women were denied even that right—which is itself "preservative of their basic civil and political rights"—until adoption of the Nineteenth Amendment half a century later.

It is true, of course, that the position of women in America has improved markedly in recent decades. Nevertheless, it can hardly be doubted that, in part because of the high visibility of the sex characteristic, women still face pervasive, although at times more subtle, discrimination in our educational institutions, in the job market and perhaps most conspicuously, in the political arena.

Moreover, since sex, like race and national origin, is an immutable characteristic determined solely by the accident of birth, the imposition of special disabilities upon the members of a particular sex because of their sex would seem to violate "the basic concept of our system that legal burdens should bear some relationship to individual responsibility. . . ." And what differentiates sex from such nonsuspect statuses as intelligence or physical disability, and aligns it with the recognized suspect criteria, is that the sex characteristic frequently bears no relation to ability to perform or contribute to society. As a result, statutory distinctions between the sexes often have the effect of invidiously relegating the entire class of females to inferior legal status without regard to the actual capabilities of its individual members.

We might also note that, over the past decade, Congress has itself manifested an increasing sensitivity to sex-based classifications. In Title VII of the Civil Rights Act of 1964, for example, Congress expressly declared that no employer, labor union, or other organization subject to the provisions of the Act shall discriminate against any individual on the basis of "race, color, religion, *sex,* or national origin." Similarly, the Equal Pay Act of 1963 provides that no employer covered by the Act "shall discriminate . . . between employees on the basis of *sex*." And [Sect. 1] of the Equal Rights Amendment, passed by Congress on March 22, 1972, and submitted to the legislatures of the States for ratification declares that "[e]quality of rights under the law shall not be denied or abridged by the United States or by any state on account of sex." Thus, Congress itself has concluded that classifications based upon sex are inherently invidious, and this conclusion of a coequal branch of Government is not without significance to the question presently under consideration.

With these considerations in mind, we can only conclude that classifications based upon sex, like classifications based upon race, alienage, or national origin are inherently suspect, and must therefore be subjected to strict judicial scrutiny. Applying the analysis mandated by that stricter standard of review, it is clear that the statutory scheme now before us is constitutionally invalid.

The sole basis of the classification established in the challenged statutes is the sex of the individuals involved. Thus, a female member of the uniformed services seeking to obtain housing and medical benefits for her spouse must prove his dependency in fact, whereas no such burden is imposed upon male members. In addition, the statutes operate so as to deny benefits to a female member, such as appellant Sharron Frontiero, who provides less than one-half of her spouse's support, while at the same time granting such benefits to a male member who likewise provides less than one-half of his spouse's support. Thus, to this extent at least, it may fairly be said that these statutes command "dissimilar treatment for men and women who are . . . similarly situated."

Moreover, the Government concedes that the differential treatment accorded men and women under these statutes serves no purpose other than mere "administrative convenience." In essence, the Government maintains that, as an empirical matter, wives in our society frequently are dependent upon their husbands, while husbands rarely are dependent upon their wives. Thus, the Government argues that Congress might reasonably have concluded that it would be both cheaper and easier simply conclusively to presume that wives of male members are financially dependent upon their husbands, while burdening female members with the task of establishing dependency in fact.

The Government offers no concrete evidence, however, tending to support its view that such differential treatment in fact saves the Government any money. In order to satisfy the demands of strict judicial scrutiny, the Government must demonstrate, for example, that it is actually cheaper to grant increased benefits with respect to *all* male members, than it is to determine which male members are in fact entitled to such benefits and to grant increased benefits only to those members whose wives actually meet the dependency requirement. Here, however, there is substantial evidence that, if put to the test, many of the wives of male members would fail to qualify for benefits. And in light of the fact that the dependency determination with respect to the husbands of female members is presently made solely on the basis of affidavits, rather than through the more costly hearing process, the Government's explanation of the statutory scheme is, to say the least, questionable.

In any case, our prior decisions make clear that, although efficacious administration of governmental programs is not without some importance, "the Constitution recognizes higher values than speed and efficiency." And when we enter the realm of "strict judicial scrutiny," there can be no doubt that "administrative convenience" is not a shibboleth, the mere recitation of which dictates constitutionality. On the contrary, any statutory scheme which draws a sharp line between the sexes, *solely* for the purpose of achieving administrative convenience, necessarily commands "dissimilar treatment for men and women who are . . . similarly situated," and therefore involves the "very kind of arbitrary legislative choice forbidden by the [Constitution] . . . ." We therefore conclude that, by according differential treatment to male and female members of the uniformed services for the sole purpose of achieving administrative convenience, the challenged statutes violate the Due Process Clause of the Fifth Amendment insofar as they require a female member to prove the dependency of her husband.

Reversed.

Justice Stewart concurs in the judgment, agreeing that the statutes before us work an invidious discrimination in violation of the Constitution.

Justice Rehnquist dissents for the reasons stated by Judge Rives in his opinion for the District Court, Frontiero v. Laird, 341 F. Supp. 201 (1972).

Justice Powell with whom the Chief Justice and Justice Blackmun join, concurring in the judgment.

I agree that the challenged statutes constitute an unconstitutional discrimination against servicewomen in violation of the Due Process Clause of the Fifth Amendment, but I cannot join the opinion of Mr. Justice Brennan, which would hold that all classifications based upon sex, "like classifications based upon race, alienage, and national origin," are "inherently suspect and must therefore be subjected to close judicial scrutiny." It is unnecessary for the Court in this case to characterize sex as a suspect classification, with all of the far-reaching implications of such a holding. *Reed v. Reed* (1971), which abundantly supports our decision today, did not add sex to the narrowly limited group of classifications which are inherently suspect. In my view, we can and should decide this case on the authority of *Reed* and reserve for the future any expansion of its rationale.

There is another, and I find compelling, reason for deferring a general categorizing of sex classifications as invoking the strictest test of judicial scrutiny. The Equal Rights Amendment, which if adopted will resolve the substance of this precise question, has been approved by Congress and submitted for ratification by the States. If this Amendment is duly adopted, it will represent the will of the people accomplished in the manner prescribed by the Constitution. By acting prematurely and unnecessarily, as I view it, the Court has assumed a decisional responsibility at the very time when state legislatures, functioning within the traditional democratic process, are debating the proposed Amendment. It seems to me that this reaching out to pre-empt by judicial action a major political decision which is currently in process of resolution does not reflect appropriate respect for duly prescribed legislative processes.

There are times when this Court, under our system, cannot avoid a constitutional decision on issues which normally should be resolved by the elected representatives of the people. But democratic institutions are weakened, and confidence in the restraint of the Court is impaired, when we appear unnecessarily to decide sensitive issues of broad social and political importance at the very time they are under consideration within the prescribed constitutional processes.

Despite disagreement over the appropriate standard of review for gender-based classifications, the Court continued to hear cases in its next two terms alleging gender discrimination by both the federal government and state governments. Some of the cases involved discrimination against men rather than against women.

- In a 6-3 decision, the Court upheld a Florida law that granted widows but not widowers a $500 property-tax exemption. The Court reasoned that women who lost their spouses were more financially disabled than men who lost their spouses. *Kahn v. Shevin* 416 U.S. 351 (1974)

- By a 6-3 vote, the Court upheld California's program that allowed disability insurance benefits for private employees not covered by workmen's compensation laws, but that excluded pregnancy from coverage. According to the Court, the rational basis for the exclusion was that the cost of extending coverage to pregnancy might jeopardize the entire program. *Geduldig v. Aiello* 417 U.S. 484 (1974)
- In a 5-4 decision, the Court upheld a federal law that guaranteed to women in the Navy thirteen years of service before discharge, but that required the automatic discharge of men who failed twice to be promoted. The law was declared rational because it compensated for women's fewer opportunities for promotion, primarily denial of service in combat. *Schlesinger v. Ballard* 419 U.S. 498 (1975)
- In an 8-0 decision, the Court struck down a provision of federal law that allowed for payments of death benefits to the surviving spouse and minor children in the case of a husband's death, but permitted such benefits only to the children in the case of a wife's death. According to the Court, this gender-based distinction was indistinguishable from the classification declared to be invalid in *Frontiero*. *Weinberger v. Weisenfeld* 420 U.S. 636 (1975)
- In an 8-1 ruling, the Court struck down a Utah law requiring child-support payments for males until they reached the age of 21, but for females until they became 18. On the basis of *Reed,* this law was irrational. *Stanton v. Stanton* 421 U.S. 7 (1975)
- By an 8-1 vote, the Court invalidated a Louisiana law that excluded women from juries unless they requested in writing to serve. However, the decision was not based on gender discrimination but on Sixth Amendment grounds. The Court held that the right to an impartial jury was violated because the exclusion of women as a class meant that the jury was not drawn from a fair cross-section of the community. *Taylor v. Louisiana* 419 U.S. 522 (1975)

The Important Government Objective Test

Although its decisions after *Frontiero* made it appear that the Court would not be able to articulate a single standard for analyzing gender-based classifications, in 1976 a majority introduced a new test in the case of *Craig v. Boren*. This test, which requires that gender-based classifications be examined under "heightened" or "intermediate" scrutiny, was actually introduced to the Court by Ruth Bader Ginsburg in her brief in the case of *Weinberger v. Weisenfeld* (1975). She developed this approach after efforts to persuade the Court to use "strict scrutiny" proved unsuccessful in *Frontiero*. In *Craig,* then, Ginsburg advised the attorney representing the individuals challenging the statute to argue for the Court to use "heightened" or "intermediate" scrutiny and to play down the "strict scrutiny" approach. This strategy proved to be successful.

At issue in *Craig* was an Oklahoma law that permitted eighteen- to twenty-year-old females to purchase beer containing 3.2 percent alcohol ("near beer"), but that prohibited males in that age group from doing so. The state claimed that the law was passed because eighteen- to twenty-year-old males posed a greater threat to traffic safety than females of that age. The Supreme Court was unpersuaded, and it invalidated the statute by a 7-2 vote. Writing for the majority, Justice Brennan announced that the important government objective test would be used to review the statute. Under this standard, he said, "classifications by gender must serve important governmental objectives and must be substantially related to achievement of those objectives" (429 U.S. at 197). Thus, the Court held that while the promotion of traffic safety was an important objective, the means—the gender-based classification—were not substantially related to it. Brennan argued that the statistics regarding traffic safety that the state presented as supporting evidence were "insufficient and unpersuasive." Moreover, he concluded that traffic safety could be negatively affected because the statute prohibited only the sale, not the consumption, of 3.2 beer. Thus, a male's female companion could purchase the beer for him, and he could consume it and then proceed to operate a vehicle. In separate dissents, Chief Justice Burger and Justice Rehnquist claimed that the rational basis test was appropriate for the disposition of this case, and they would have applied it to uphold the statute. Justice Rehnquist went even further, arguing that because this case involved discrimination against males rather than against females, the Court's gender-discrimination precedents were not applicable.

Craig et al. v. Boren, Governor of Oklahoma, et al.

429 U.S. 190, 97 S.Ct. 451, 50 L. Ed. 2d 397 (1976)

■ Under Oklahoma law, eighteen- to twenty-year-old females were permitted to purchase beer containing 3.2 percent alcohol (near beer), but males in that age group were prohibited from doing so. Mark Walker and Curtis Craig, both under the age of twenty-one, and Carolyn Whitener, a beer vendor, challenged the law as a violation of equal protection. A three-judge district court upheld the law, citing *Reed,* and accepted the state's argument that the purpose of the gender-based distinction was to promote traffic safety. The state had presented statistical evidence to support its contention that eighteen- to twenty-year-old males posed a greater threat to traffic safety because of alcohol abuse than did females of that age.

This case is important because it was the first time since *Reed v. Reed* (1971) that a majority of the justices agreed upon a standard for determining the constitutional validity of gender-based classifications. As you read the case, consider the following questions: 1) Did the important government objective test really stem from *Reed v. Reed* as Justice Brennan seems to maintain? 2) Is it appropriate for the justices to use statistical evidence in making decisions? If so, how should such evidence be used? 3) Which standard of review is more likely to lead to greater subjectivity in the decision making of the justices—rational basis or important government objective?

Vote:

7 justices found the law unconstitutional (Blackmun, Brennan, Marshall, Powell, Stevens, Stewart, White).

2 justices found the law constitutional (Burger, Rehnquist).

Justice Brennan delivered the opinion of the Court.

* * *

Analysis may appropriately begin with the reminder that *Reed* emphasized that statutory classifications that distinguish between males and females are "subject to scrutiny under the Equal Protection Clause." To withstand constitutional challenge, previous cases establish that classifications by gender must serve important governmental objectives and must be substantially related to achievement of those objectives. Thus, in *Reed,* the objectives of "reducing the workload on probate courts," and "avoiding intrafamily controversy," were deemed of insufficient importance to sustain use of an overt gender criterion in the appointment of administrators of intestate decedents' estates. Decisions following *Reed* similarly have rejected administrative ease and convenience as sufficiently important objectives to justify gender-based classifications. . . .

Reed v. Reed has also provided the underpinning for decisions that have invalidated statutes employing gender as an inaccurate proxy for other, more germane bases of classification. Hence, "archaic and overboard" generalizations . . . could not justify use of a gender line in determining eligibility for certain governmental entitlements. Similarly, increasingly outdated misconceptions concerning the role of females in the home rather than in the "marketplace and world of ideas" were rejected as loose-fitting characterizations incapable of supporting state statutory schemes that were premised upon their accuracy. In light of the weak congruence between gender and the characteristic or trait that gender purported to represent, it was necessary that the legislatures choose either to realign their substantive laws in a gender-neutral fashion, or to adopt procedures for identifying those instances where the sex-centered generalization actually comported with fact.

In this case, too, ". . . we feel [*Reed*] is controlling. . . ." We turn then to the question whether, under *Reed,* the difference between males and females with respect to the purchase of 3.2% beer warrants the differential in age drawn by the Oklahoma statute. We conclude that it does not.

The District Court recognized that *Reed v. Reed* was controlling. In applying the teachings of that case, the court found the requisite important governmental objective in the traffic-safety goal proffered by the Oklahoma Attorney General. It then concluded that the statistics introduced by the appellees established that the gender-based distinction was substantially related to achievement of that goal.

We accept for purposes of discussion the District Court's identification of the objective underlying [the challenged sections of the statute] as the enhancement of traffic safety. Clearly, the protection of public health and safety represents an important function of state and local governments. However, appellees' statistics in our view cannot support the conclusion that the gender-based distinction closely serves to achieve that objective and therefore the distinction cannot under *Reed* withstand equal protection challenge.

The appellees introduced a variety of statistical surveys. First, an analysis of arrest statistics for 1973 demonstrated that 18-20-year-old male arrests for "driving under the influence" and "drunkenness" substantially exceeded female arrests for that same age period. Similarly, youths aged 17-21 were found to be overrepresented among those killed or injured in traffic accidents, with males again numerically exceeding females in this regard. Third, a random roadside survey in Oklahoma City revealed that young males were more inclined to drive and drink beer than were their female counterparts. Fourth, Federal Bureau of Investigation nationwide statistics exhibited a notable increase in arrests for "driving under the influence." Finally, statistical evidence gathered in other jurisdictions, particularly Minnesota and Michigan, was offered to corroborate Oklahoma's experience by indicating the pervasiveness of youthful participation in motor vehicle accidents following the imbibing of alcohol. . . .

Even were this statistical evidence accepted as accurate, it nevertheless offers only a weak answer to the equal protection question presented here. The most focused and relevant of the statistical surveys, arrests of 18-20-year-olds for alcohol-related driving offenses, exemplifies the ultimate unpersuasiveness of this evidentiary record. Viewed in terms of the correlation between sex and the actual activity that Oklahoma seeks to regulate—driving while under the influence of alcohol—the statistics broadly establish that .18% of females and 2% of males in that age group were arrested for that offense. While such a disparity is not trivial in a statistical sense, it hardly can form the basis for employment of a gender line as a classifying device. Certainly if maleness is to serve as a proxy for drinking and driving, a correlation of 2% must be considered an unduly tenuous "fit." Indeed, prior cases have consistently rejected the use of sex as a decisionmaking factor even though the statutes in question certainly rested on far more predictive empirical relationships than this.

Moreover, the statistics exhibit a variety of other shortcomings that seriously impugn their value to equal protection analysis. Setting aside the obvious methodological problems, the surveys do not adequately justify the salient features of Oklahoma's gender-based traffic-safety law. None purports to measure the use and dangerousness of 3.2% beer as opposed to alcohol generally, a detail that is of particular importance since, in light of its low alcohol level, Oklahoma apparently considers the 3.2% beverage to be "nonintoxicating." Moreover, many of the studies, while graphically documenting the unfortunate increase in driving under the influence of alcohol, make no effort to relate their findings to age-sex differentials as involved here. Indeed, the only survey that explicitly centered its attention upon young drivers and their use of beer—albeit apparently not of the diluted 3.2% variety—reached results that hardly can be viewed as impressive in justifying either a gender or age classification.

There is no reason to belabor this line of analysis. . . . Suffice it to say that the showing offered by the appellees does not satisfy us that sex represents a legitimate, accurate proxy for the regulation of drinking and driving. In fact, when it is further recognized that Oklahoma's statute prohibits only the selling of 3.2% beer to young males and not their drinking the beverage once acquired (even after purchase by their 18-20-year-old female companions), the relationship between gender and traffic safety becomes far too tenuous to satisfy *Reed's* requirement that the gender-based difference be substantially related to achievement of the statutory objective.

We hold, therefore, that under *Reed,* Oklahoma's 3.2% beer statute invidiously discriminates against males 18-20 years of age.

* * *

We conclude that the gender-based differential contained in [this statute] constitutes a denial of the equal protection of the laws to males aged 18-20 and reverse the judgment of the District Court.

It is so ordered.

Justice Powell concurred.

Justice Stevens concurred.

Justice Blackmun concurred in part.

Justice Stewart concurred in the judgment.

Chief Justice Burger dissented.

Justice Rehnquist dissenting.

The Court's disposition of this case is objectionable on two grounds. First is its conclusion that *men* challenging a gender-based statute which treats them less favorably than women may invoke a more stringent standard of judicial review than pertains to most other types of classifications. Second is the Court's enunciation of this standard, without citation to any source, as being that "classifications by gender must serve *important* governmental objectives and must be *substantially* related to achievement of those objectives." (emphasis added [by Rehnquist].) The only redeeming feature of the Court's opinion, to my mind, is that it apparently signals a retreat by those who joined the plurality opinion in *Frontiero v. Richardson* (1973) from their view that sex is a "suspect" classification for purposes of equal protection analysis. I think the Oklahoma statute challenged here need pass only the "rational basis" equal protection analysis and I believe that it is constitutional under that analysis.

In *Frontiero v. Richardson,* the opinion for the plurality sets forth the reasons of four Justices for concluding that sex should be regarded as a suspect classification for purposes of equal protection analysis. These reasons center on our Nation's "long and unfortunate history of sex discrimination," which has been reflected in a whole range of restrictions on the legal rights of women, not the least of which have concerned the ownership of property and participation in the electoral process. Noting that the pervasive and persistent nature of the discrimination experienced by women is in part the result of their ready identifiability, the plurality rested its invocation of strict scrutiny largely upon the fact that "statutory distinctions between the sexes often have the effect of invidiously relegating the entire class of females to inferior legal status without regard to the actual capabilities of its individual members."

Subsequent to *Frontiero,* the Court has declined to hold that sex is a suspect class, and no such holding is imported by the Court's resolution of this case. However, the Court's application here of an elevated or "intermediate" level scrutiny, like that invoked in cases dealing with discrimination against females, raises the question of why the statute here should be treated any differently from countless legislative classifications unrelated to sex which have been upheld under a minimum rationality standard.

Most obviously unavailable to support any kind of special scrutiny in this case, is a history or pattern of past discrimination, such as was relied on by the plurality in *Frontiero* to support its invocation of strict scrutiny. There is no suggestion in the Court's opinion that males in this age group are in any way peculiarly disadvantaged, subject to systematic discriminatory treatment, or otherwise in need of special solicitude from the courts.

* * *

The Court's conclusion that a law which treats males less favorably than females "must serve important governmental objectives and must be substantially related to achievement of those objectives" apparently comes out of thin air. The Equal Protection Clause contains no such language, and none of our previous cases adopt that standard. I would think we have had enough difficulty with the two standards of review which our cases have recognized—the norm of "rational basis," and the "compelling state interest" required where a "suspect classification" is involved—so as to counsel weightily against the insertion of still another "standard" between those two. How is this Court to divine what objectives are important? How is it to determine whether a particular law is "substantially" related to the achievement of such objective, rather than related in some other way to its achievement? Both of the phrases used are so diaphanous and elastic as to invite subjective judicial preferences or prejudices relating to particular types of legislation, masquerading as judgments whether such legislation is directed at "important" objectives or, whether the relationship to those objectives is "substantial" enough.

I would have thought that if this Court were to leave anything to decision by the popularly elected branches of the Government, where no constitutional claim other than that of equal protection is invoked, it would be the decision as to what governmental objectives to be achieved by law are "important," and which are not. As for the second part of the Court's new test, the Judicial Branch is probably in no worse position than the Legislative or Executive Branches to determine if there is *any* rational relationship between a classification and the purpose which it might be thought to serve. But the introduction of the adverb "substantially" requires courts to make subjective judgments as to operational effects, for which neither their expertise nor their access to data fits them. And even if we manage to avoid both confusion and the mirroring of our own preferences in the development of this new doctrine, the thousands of judges in other courts who must interpret the Equal Protection Clause may not be so fortunate.

* * *

The rationality of a statutory classification for equal protection purposes does not depend upon the statistical "fit" between the class and the trait sought to be singled out. It turns on whether there may be a sufficiently higher incidence of the trait within the

included class than in the excluded class to justify different treatment. . . . Notwithstanding the Court's critique of the statistical evidence, that evidence suggests clear differences between the drinking and driving habits of young men and women. Those differences are grounds enough for the State reasonably to conclude that young males pose by far the greater drunk-driving hazard, both in terms of sheer numbers and in terms of hazard on a per-driver basis. The gender-based difference in treatment in this case is therefore not irrational.

Although the Court created this new important government objective test in *Craig* in 1976, this standard was not used in a case decided shortly after *Craig*. In *Califano v. Goldfarb* (1976), the Court by a 5-4 vote struck down a provision of the Social Security Act that provided benefits for widows based on the earnings of their deceased husbands, but that provided no benefits to widowers unless they had received half of their financial support from deceased wives. A majority could not agree, however, on the reason for invalidating the statute. A plurality consisting of Justices Brennan, White, Marshall, and Powell stressed that the classification here was indistinguishable from those classifications struck down in *Weisenfeld* and *Frontiero*. Justice Stevens voted to strike the classification simply because it discriminated against the male survivors of female workers.

Shortly after *Goldfarb,* the Court *upheld* a gender-based classification in another section of the Social Security Act and used the *Craig* precedent in doing so. In a brief per curiam opinion, *Califano v. Webster* (1977), the Court sustained a provision permitting women to exclude more low-earning years from the calculation of their retirement benefits than men were allowed to do. Compensating women for past economic discrimination was accepted as an important government interest.

By 1979, the Court seemed to be more committed to applying consistently the important government objective test created in *Craig* to cases involving gender-based classifications. The Court used this standard to invalidate: 1) an Alabama law that made husbands but not wives liable for alimony payments following a divorce (*Orr v. Orr,* 1979), and 2) a New York law that permitted unwed mothers, but not unwed fathers, to withhold consent from the adoption of their children (*Caban v. Mohammed,* 1979). Similarly, in 1981, the Court struck down a Louisiana law that gave a husband the right to dispose of property jointly owned with his wife without first obtaining her consent (*Kirchberg v. Feenstra,* 1981).

While the Court was becoming more consistent in applying the new *Craig* rule, it did not always result in invalidation of the gender classification. For example, the Court sustained statutory rape laws that punished males for having sex with females under a specified age, but which excluded females from punishment for such actions. In *Michael M. v. Sonoma County* (1981), a seventeen-and-a-half-year old male was prosecuted under California law for having sex with a seventeen-and-a-half-year-old female. The Supreme Court, by a 5-4 vote, upheld the statute. Again, however, there was no majority opinion. A plurality consisting of Justices Rehnquist, Burger, Stewart, and Powell accepted the state's argument that the purpose of the law was to prevent illegitimate teenage pregnancies. In addition, the means of punishing males but not females was related to this objective because females are more negatively affected by teenage pregnancy than are males. In his opinion concurring in the judgment, Justice Blackmun first chastised the plurality for not seeing the similarity between the problems of teenage pregnancy and those related to abortion. He then cited the precedents of *Schlesinger v. Ballard* (1975), *Weinberger v. Weisenfeld* (1975), and *Kahn v. Shevin* (1974) to support his vote to uphold the statute. In dissent, Justices Brennan, White, and Marshall argued that the state did not prove that its goal of preventing teenage pregnancy could not be met by a gender-neutral law. Moreover, they even questioned the state's purpose in enacting the statute: "Indeed the historical development of [the statute] demonstrates that the law was initially enacted on the premise that young women, in contrast to young men, were to be deemed legally incapable of consenting to an act of sexual intercourse. Because their chastity was considered particularly precious, those young women were held to be uniquely in need of the State's protection" (450 U.S. at 494–95, 1981). Justice Stevens, also in dissent, held that the only justification for the statute would be if males were more guilty than females in participating in this conduct. Because this was not the case, in Stevens's view, the law should have been struck down.

In another important case from 1981, *Rostker v. Goldberg,* the Court used the important government objective test to sustain a gender distinction. At issue was the Military Selective Service Act (MSSA), which excluded females from registering for the draft. In a 6-3 decision, the Court voted to uphold the act. Justice Rehnquist, writing for the majority, maintained that the important government interest was raising and supporting armies and preparing for a draft of combat troops. The means—excluding women—were substantially related to the purpose because women were not eligible for combat. Rehnquist stated, "The fact that Congress and the Executive have decided that women should not serve in combat fully justifies Congress in not authorizing their registration since the purpose of registration is to develop a pool of potential combat troops" (453 U.S. at 79, 1981). In upholding this classification, the Court did not examine whether the exclusion of women from combat duty is itself a violation of equal protection.

On another point, it had been suggested by some military experts that if there were a draft, a number of women could be used to fill noncombat positions. In doing so, more men would be free for combat duty. The majority, however, did not accept this line of reasoning. Rehnquist pointed to the congressional hearings, which he said indicated that Congress had considered this option, but felt the extra burdens of including women in draft and registration plans were not worth the effort. The committee reports cited training problems as well as administrative problems concerning housing, financial hardship, and physical standards. In addition to these problems, Rehnquist said that Congress had determined that placing women in noncombat positions would impair military flexibility. "In peace and war, significant rotation of personnel is necessary. Large numbers of non-combat positions must be available to which combat troops can return for duty before being redeployed" (453 U.S. at 82). Another argument that seemed to persuade the majority was the determination by Congress that if women were needed for noncombat roles, that need could be met by volunteers.

In a dissent joined by Justice Brennan, Justice White rejected this line of argument, concluding that all noncombat positions need not be filled by combat ready personnel (men), but that women would be eligible for many of those positions. Furthermore, according to White, the legislative record indicated that during mobilization, the government could not rely solely on volunteers, but needed the draft to "secure the personnel needed for jobs that can be performed by persons ineligible for combat" (453 U.S. at 85). He said that military experts had concluded that this could be done without sacrificing military preparedness and effectiveness. Thus, by registering only men for these positions, the government was discriminating against women without "adequate justification."

Justice Marshall, joined by Justice Brennan, concluded that the MSSA satisfied the first part of the important government objective test, but failed the second part. They agreed that raising and supporting armies is an important government interest but claimed that the exclusion of women from registration is not substantially related to that goal. They said that because of combat restrictions already in place, registering women will not result in their being drafted for combat roles. In addition, Marshall noted that not all draftees must be available for combat duty; and he, like White, concluded from his reading of the legislative history that women would be eligible and qualified for some noncombat positions for which troops would be inducted.

Later that year, the first female justice began service on the Supreme Court. Despite her appointment by a conservative president, Ronald Reagan, some women's groups were optimistic that Sandra Day O'Connor's experiences would lead her to provide a strong voice against gender discrimination. While she has not proven to be an outspoken proponent of women's rights, her opinion in an important case from her first term indicated a willingness to examine gender-based classifications carefully. The case involved a male bringing charges of discrimination on account of gender. In *Mississippi University for Women v. Hogan* (1982), Joe Hogan was denied admission to the nursing program at MUW, an all-female, state-supported institution. In a 5-4 decision, the Court ruled that the admissions policy violated the Equal Protection Clause. Justice O'Connor, writing for the majority, ruled that the policy failed both parts of the important government objective test. First, she argued, despite the claims by the state that its single-sex admissions policy compensates for discrimination against women, the policy actually perpetuates the stereotype that nursing is a woman's job. Second, the means were not substantially related to the objective. The state had claimed that men were denied admission because the presence of men in classes negatively affects the performance of women students. O'Connor pointed out that this could not be the case because the University already allowed men to audit classes and to participate in continuing education courses.

In dissent, Chief Justice Burger emphasized that the decision was limited to a professional nursing school, so that other all-women programs might be upheld. Also in dissent, Justice Blackmun took the opposite view, fearing that the ruling could be extended beyond this case. "[This] ruling, it seems to me, places in constitutional jeopardy any state-supported educational institution that confines its student body in any area to members of one sex. . . ." (458 U.S. at 734, 1982). Blackmun also noted, as did Powell and Rehnquist in yet another dissent, that Hogan was not denied admission to nursing school altogether; other programs were open to him. It was just that it was inconvenient for him to go elsewhere. Finally, while arguing that the rational basis test was appropriate for deciding the case, Powell and Rehnquist nonetheless concluded that the admissions policy passed the important government objective test. Citing several studies illustrating the benefits of single-sex colleges and the number of students who prefer such institutions, they maintained that this policy did advance an important interest. Moreover, the means are related to the objective despite the fact that men are permitted to audit classes. Because the record showed that men audited on average 14 courses a year out of a possible 913, Rehnquist and Powell accepted the State's argument that the classroom environment for female students was not substantially affected.

Mississippi University for Women v. Hogan

458 U.S. 718, 102 S.Ct. 3331, 73 L. Ed. 2d 1090 (1982)

■ This case arose when Joe Hogan, a male registered nurse, attempted to pursue a Bachelor of Arts degree in Nursing at Mississippi University for Women (MUW), a state-supported school in Columbus, Mississippi. Hogan was denied admission to the program because of a state policy that maintained MUW as an all-women institution. He was informed that he could audit the courses in which he was interested, but he would not be allowed to enroll for credit. Hogan then filed suit in federal district court, claiming that MUW's

Nursing School's single-sex admissions policy was unconstitutional gender discrimination. The district court ruled in favor of the State, but the Court of Appeals reversed. The Supreme Court granted certiorari in the case.

As you read the case, consider these questions: (1) Does the majority's decision place in jeopardy all state-supported single-sex colleges and universities? (2) Would the majority's decision have been different had there been strong evidence that the presence of men in the nursing school classes affected the performance of women students? (3) Should the examination of discrimination against males require a less strict standard than that used in deciding cases where females have been discrimination victims?

VOTE:

5 justices agreed that MUW's single-sex admissions policy was a violation of the Equal Protection Clause (Brennan, Marshall, O'Connor, Stevens, and White).

4 justices voted to uphold the single-sex admissions policy (Blackmun, Burger, Powell, and Rehnquist).

Justice O'Connor delivered the opinion of the Court.

This case presents the narrow issue of whether a state statute that excludes males from enrolling in a state-supported professional nursing school violates the Equal Protection Clause of the Fourteenth Amendment.

* * *

We begin our analysis aided by several firmly established principles. Because the challenged policy expressly discriminates among applicants on the basis of gender, it is subject to scrutiny under the Equal Protection Clause of the Fourteenth Amendment. *Reed v. Reed* (1971). That this statutory policy discriminates against males rather than against females does not exempt it from scrutiny or reduce the standard of review. Our decisions also establish that the party seeking to uphold a statute that classifies individuals on the basis of their gender must carry the burden of showing an "exceedingly persuasive justification" for the classification. The burden is met only by showing at least that the classification serves "important governmental objectives and that the discriminatory means employed" are "substantially related to the achievement of those objectives."

Although the test for determining the validity of a gender-based classification is straightforward, it must be applied free of fixed notions concerning the roles and abilities of males and females. Care must be taken in ascertaining whether the statutory objective itself reflects archaic and stereotypic notions. Thus, if the statutory objective is to exclude or "protect" members of one gender because they are presumed to suffer from an inherent handicap or to be innately inferior, the objective itself is illegitimate.

If the State's objective is legitimate and important, we next determine whether the requisite direct, substantial relationship between objective and means is present. The purpose of requiring that close relationship is to assure that the validity of a classification is determined through reasoned analysis rather than through the mechanical application of traditional, often inaccurate, assumptions about the proper roles of men and women. The need for the requirement is amply revealed by reference to the broad range of statutes already invalidated by this Court, statutes that relied upon the simplistic, outdated assumption that gender could be used as a "proxy for other, more germane bases of classification," to establish a link between objective and classification.

Applying this framework, we now analyze the arguments advanced by the State to justify its refusal to allow males to enroll for credit in MUW's School of Nursing.

The State's primary justification for maintaining the single-sex admissions policy of MUW's School of Nursing is that it compensates for discrimination against women and, therefore, constitutes educational affirmative action. As applied to the School of Nursing, we find the State's argument unpersuasive.

* * *

. . . [A] State can evoke a compensatory purpose to justify an otherwise discriminatory classification only if members of the gender benefited by the classification actually suffer a disadvantage related to the classification. . . .

* * *

. . . Mississippi has made no showing that women lacked opportunities to obtain training in the field of nursing or to attain positions of leadership in that field when the MUW School of Nursing opened its door or that women currently are deprived of such opportunities. In fact, in 1970, the year before the School of Nursing's first class enrolled, women earned 94 percent of the nursing baccalaureate degrees conferred in Mississippi and 98.6 percent of the degrees earned nationwide. That year was not an aberration; one decade earlier, women had earned all the nursing degrees conferred in Mississippi and 98.9 percent of the degrees conferred nationwide. As one would expect, the labor force reflects the same predominance of women in nursing. When MUW's

School of Nursing began operation, nearly 98 percent of all employed registered nurses were female.

Rather than compensate for discriminatory barriers faced by women, MUW's policy of excluding males from admission to the School of Nursing tends to perpetuate the stereotyped view of nursing as an exclusively woman's job. By assuring that Mississippi allots more openings in its state-supported nursing schools to women than it does to men, MUW's admissions policy lends credibility to the old view that women, not men, should become nurses, and makes the assumption that nursing is a field for women a self-fulfilling prophecy. Thus, we conclude that, although the State recited a "benign, compensatory purpose," it failed to establish that the alleged objective is the actual purpose underlying the discriminatory classification.

The policy is invalid also because it fails the second part of the equal protection test, for the State has made no showing that the gender-based classification is substantially and directly related to its proposed compensatory objective. To the contrary, MUW's policy of permitting men to attend classes as auditors fatally undermines its claim that women, at least those in the School of Nursing, are adversely affected by the presence of men.

MUW permits men who audit to participate fully in classes. Additionally, both men and women take part in continuing education courses offered by the School of Nursing, in which regular nursing students also can enroll. The uncontroverted record reveals that admitting men to nursing classes does not affect teaching style, that the presence of men in the classroom would not affect the performance of the female nursing students, and that men in coeducational nursing schools do not dominate the classroom. In sum, the record in this case is flatly inconsistent with the claim that excluding men from the School of Nursing is necessary to reach any of MUW's educational goals.

Thus, considering both the asserted interest and the relationship between the interest and the methods used by the State, we conclude that the State has fallen short of establishing the "exceedingly persuasive justification" needed to sustain the gender-based classification. Accordingly, we hold that MUW's policy of denying males the right to enroll for credit in its School of Nursing violates the Equal Protection Clause of the Fourteenth Amendment.

* * *

. . . [W]e affirm the judgment of the Court of Appeals.

It is so ordered.

Chief Justice Burger, dissenting.

I agree generally with Justice Powell's dissenting opinion. I write separately, however, to emphasize that the Court's holding today is limited to the context of a professional nursing school. Since the Court's opinion relies heavily on its finding that women have traditionally dominated the nursing profession, it suggests that a State might well be justified in maintaining, for example, the option of an all-women's business school or liberal arts program.

Justice Blackmun, dissenting.

* * *

While the Court purports to write narrowly, declaring that it does not decide the same issue with respect to "separate but equal" undergraduate institutions for females and males or with respect to units of MUW other than its School of Nursing, there is inevitable spillover from the Court's ruling today. That ruling, it seems to me, places in constitutional jeopardy any state-supported educational institution that confines its student body in any area to members of one sex, even though the State elsewhere provides an equivalent program to the complaining applicant. The Court's reasoning does not stop with the School of Nursing of the Mississippi University for Women.

* * *

Justice Powell, with whom Justice Rehnquist joins, dissenting.

The Court's opinion bows deeply to conformity. Left without honor—indeed, held unconstitutional—is an element of diversity that has characterized much of American education and enriched much of American life. The Court in effect holds today that no State now may provide even a single institution of higher learning open only to women students. It gives no heed to the efforts of the State of Mississippi to provide abundant opportunities for young men and young women to attend coeducational institutions, and none to the preferences of the more than 40,000 young women who over the years have evidenced their approval of an all-women's college by choosing Mississippi University for Women over seven coeducational universities within the State. The Court decided today that the Equal Protection Clause makes it unlawful for the State to provide women with a traditionally popular and respected choice of educational environment. It does so in a case instituted by one man, who represents no class, and whose primary concern is personal convenience.

* * *

. . . His constitutional complaint is based upon a single asserted harm: that he must *travel* to attend the state-supported nursing schools that concededly are available to him. The Court characterizes this injury as one of "inconvenience." This description is fair and accurate, though somewhat embarrassed by the fact that there is, of course, no constitutional right to attend a state-supported university in one's home town. Thus the Court, to redresss respondent's injury of inconvenience, must rest its invalidation of MUW's single-sex program on a mode of "sexual stereotype" reasoning that has no application whatever to the respondent or to the "wrong" of which he complains. At best this is anomalous. And ultimately the anomaly reveals legal error—that of applying a heightened equal protection standard, developed in cases of genuine sexual stereotyping, to a narrowly utilized state classification that provides an *additional* choice for women. Moreover, I believe that Mississippi's educational system should be upheld in this case even if this inappropriate method of analysis is applied.

Coeducation, historically, is a novel educational theory. From grade school through high school, college, and graduate and professional training, much of the Nation's population during much of our history has been educated in sexually segregated classrooms. At the college level, for instance, until recently some of the most prestigious colleges and universities—including most of the Ivy League—had long histories of single-sex education. As Harvard, Yale, and Princeton remained all-male colleges well into the second half of this century, the "Seven Sister" institutions established a parallel standard of excellence for women's colleges. . . .

* * *

The arguable benefits of single-sex colleges also continue to be recognized by students of higher education. The Carnegie Commission on Higher Education has reported that it "favor[s] the continuation of colleges for women. They provide an element of diversity. . . and [an environment in which women] generally . . . speak up more in their classes, . . . hold more positions of leadership on campus, . . . and . . . have more role models and mentors among women teachers and administrators. . . ."

* * *

The issue in this case is whether a State transgresses the Constitution when—within the context of a public system that offers a diverse range of campuses, curricula, and educational alternatives—it seeks to accommodate the legitimate personal preferences of those desiring the advantages of an all-women's college. In my view, the Court errs seriously by assuming—without argument or discussion—that the equal protection standard generally applicable to sex discrimination is appropriate here. That standard was designed to free women from "archaic and overbroad generalizations. . . ." In no previous case have we applied it to invalidate state efforts to *expand* women's choices. Nor are there prior sex discrimination decisions by this Court in which a male plaintiff, as in this case, had the choice of an equal benefit.

The cases cited by the Court therefore do not control the issue now before us. In most of them women were given no opportunity for the same benefit as men. Cases involving male plaintiffs are equally inapplicable. . . .

By applying heightened equal protection analysis to this case, the Court frustrates the liberating spirit of the Equal Protection Clause. It prohibits the States from providing women with an opportunity to choose the type of university they prefer. And yet it is these women whom the Court regards as the *victims* of an illegal, stereotyped perception of the role of women in our society. The Court reasons this way in a case in which no woman has complained, and the only complainant is a man who advances no claims on behalf of anyone else. His claim, it should be recalled, is not that he is being denied a substantive educational opportunity, or even the right to attend an all-male or a coeducational college. It is *only* that the colleges open to him are located at inconvenient distances.

The Court views this case as presenting a serious equal protection claim of sex discrimination. I do not, and I would sustain Mississippi's right to continue MUW on a rational-basis analysis. But I need not apply this "lowest tier" of scrutiny. I can accept for present purposes the standard applied by the Court: that there is a gender-based distinction that must serve an important governmental objective by means that are substantially related to its achievement. The record in this case reflects that MUW has a historic position in the State's educational system dating back to 1884. More than 2,000 women presently evidence their preference for MUW by having enrolled there. The choice is one that discriminates invidiously against no one. And the State's purpose in preserving that choice is legitimate and substantial. Generations of our finest minds, both among educators and students, have believed that single-sex, college-level institutions afford distinctive benefits. There are many persons, of course, who have different views. But simply because there are these differences is no reason—certainly none of constitutional dimension—to conclude that no substantial state interest is served when such a choice is made available.

* * *

In sum, the practice of voluntarily chosen single-sex education is an honored tradition in our country, even if it now rarely exists in state colleges and universities. Mississippi's accommodation of such student choices is legitimate because it is completely consensual and is important because it permits students to decide for themselves the type of college education they think will benefit them most. Finally, Mississippi's policy is substantially related to its long-respected objective.

A distinctive feature of America's tradition has been respect for diversity. This has been characteristic of the peoples from numerous lands who have built our country. It is the essence of our democratic system. At stake in this case as I see it is the preservation of a small aspect of this diversity. But that aspect is by no means insignificant, given our heritage of available choice between single-sex and coeducational institutions of higher learning. The Court answers that there is discrimination—not just that which may be tolerable, as for example between those candidates for admission able to contribute most to an educational institution and those able to contribute less—but discrimination of constitutional dimension. But, having found "discrimination," the Court finds it difficult to identify the victims. It hardly can claim that women are discriminated against. A constitutional case is held to exist solely because one man found it inconvenient to travel to any of the other institutions made available to him by the State of Mississippi. In essence he insists that he has a right to attend a college in his home community. This simply is not a sex discrimination case. The Equal Protection Clause was never intended to be applied to this kind of case.

Gender and Disparate Impact

As was noted in Chapter 13: Equal Protection and Race, the Court has dealt with another type of discrimination case called disparate impact. Disparate impact cases involve policies that, though neutral on their face, have a disproportionately negative impact on certain groups such as racial minorities and women. Disparate impact cases can arise under either the Equal Protection Clause of the Fourteenth Amendment or the Civil Rights Act of 1964. In *Personnel Administrator v. Feeney* (1979), the Court had the opportunity to examine whether so-called "veterans' preference" policies, adopted by many states and the federal government, violate the Equal Protection Clause. Under Massachusetts laws, military veterans were provided a preference for state civil service jobs; as long as veterans passed the state's civil service exam, they received a higher eligibility rank than nonveteran applicants. The Supreme Court upheld this policy against a claim of gender discrimination by a 7-2 vote. Justice Stewart, writing for the majority, outlined the two-part inquiry developed in *Washington v. Davis* (1976) for deciding adverse impact cases: 1) Is the classification really neutral? 2) Does the adverse effect reflect purposeful, invidious discrimination? In applying these questions to this case, the Court held first that the veterans' preference laws were indeed neutral, that is, they were not gender-based. Then the Court ruled that Feeney had not proved that there was purposeful discrimination, in that no evidence existed that the laws were passed *because* they would have adverse effects upon women. "Nothing in the record demonstrates that this preference for veterans was originally devised or subsequently re-enacted because it would accomplish the collateral goal of keeping women in a stereotypic and predefined place in the Massachusetts Civil Service" (442 U.S. at 279). In a concurring opinion, Justices Stevens and White argued that a number of males were also disadvantaged by the veterans' preference. This was an additional reason to reject the claim that the purpose of the law was to benefit males over females. Justices Marshall and Brennan dissented from the ruling, claiming that the state's absolute veterans' preference system did show purposeful gender-based discrimination. They noted that, until 1971, certain traditionally female occupations were exempted from the preference policy, and this system "has created a gender-based civil service hierarchy, with women occupying low grade clerical and secretarial jobs and men holding more responsible and remunerative positions" (442 U.S. at 285).

Personnel Administrator of Massachusetts v. Feeney

442 U.S. 256, 99 S.Ct. 2282, 60 L. Ed. 2d 870 (1979)

■ A number of states and the federal government have enacted laws that give a preference to military veterans when filling civil service jobs. These laws have had the effect of excluding women from the most lucrative of these positions because they have not had the same opportunities to become veterans as men have had. Specifically, various federal policies placed restrictions on the enlistment of women in the armed forces, excluded them from registration for the draft, and confined those women who enlisted to noncombat and lower-level positions. This case arose when Helen Feeney, a twelve-year civil service employee in Massachusetts, challenged her state's law, which gave an *absolute* preference to veterans. Under Massachusetts law, veterans who passed the civil service examination automatically were ranked higher than any nonveteran applicant. When a vacancy occurred, the three top-ranking candidates were eligible. Feeney, who scored well on the exams (second or third in the state), competed for a number of jobs but always was ranked behind several veterans. After Feeney filed suit against the law, a federal district court declared it to be unconstitutional discrimination in violation of the Equal Protection Clause. The Supreme Court, however, remanded the case to the district court for reconsideration in light of the Court's decision in a similar case, *Washington v. Davis*. In *Davis*, the Court had held that, although racially neutral laws may have a racially discriminatory effect ("disparate impact"), they would not be decided under strict scrutiny unless the challengers could prove discriminatory intent. In many cases, of course, this would be difficult to prove. Nonetheless, the federal district court again declared the law to be unconstitutional. The case returned to the Supreme Court, where the district court's decision of unconstitutionality was reversed.

As you read the case, consider these questions: 1) In passing laws, are most legislatures going to be direct about their intentions to discriminate? 2) What is appropriate evidence of an intent to discriminate?

Vote:

7 justices agreed that there must be evidence of an intent to discriminate and voted to uphold the law (Stewart, Blackmun, Stevens, Burger, Rehnquist, Powell, and White).

2 justices agreed with the test used but saw an intent to discriminate and therefore voted to overturn the statute (Marshall and Brennan).

Justice Stewart delivered the opinion of the Court.

* * *

The veterans' hiring preference in Massachusetts, as in other jurisdictions, has traditionally been justified as a measure designed to reward veterans for the sacrifice of military service, to ease the transition from military to civilian life, to encourage patriotic service, and to attract loyal and well-disciplined people to civil service occupations.

* * *

The first Massachusetts veterans' preference statute defined the term "veterans" in gender-neutral language. Women who have served in official United States military units during wartime . . . have always been entitled to the benefit of this preference. In addition, Massachusetts, through a 1943 amendment to the definition of "wartime service," extended the preference to women who served in unofficial auxiliary women's units.

* * *

Notwithstanding the apparent attempts by Massachusetts to include as many military women as possible within the scope of the preference, the statute today benefits an overwhelmingly male class. This is attributable in some measure to the variety of federal statutes, regulations, and policies that have restricted the number of women who could enlist in the United States Armed Forces, and largely to the simple fact that women have never been subjected to a military draft.

* * *

The impact of the veterans' preference law upon the public employment opportunities of women has thus been severe. This impact lies at the heart of the appellee's federal constitutional claim.

The sole question for decision on this appeal is whether Massachusetts, in granting an absolute lifetime preference to veterans, has discriminated against women in violation of the Equal Protection Clause of the Fourteenth Amendment.

The equal protection guarantee of the Fourteenth Amendment does not take from the States all power of classification. Most laws classify, and many affect certain groups unevenly, even though the law itself treats them no differently from all other members of the class described by the law. When the basic classification is rationally based, uneven effects upon particular groups within a class are ordinarily of no constitutional concern. . . .

Certain classifications, however, in themselves supply a reason to infer antipathy. Race is the paradigm. A racial classification, regardless of purported motivation, is presumptively invalid and can be upheld only upon an extraordinary justification. This rule applies as well to a classification that is ostensibly neutral but is an obvious pretext for racial discrimination. But, as was made clear in *Washington v. Davis* and *Arlington Heights v. Metropolitan Housing Dev. Corp.,* even if a neutral law has a disproportionately adverse effect upon a racial minority, it is unconstitutional under the Equal Protection Clause only if that impact can be traced to a discriminatory purpose.

* * *

When a statute gender-neutral on its face is challenged on the ground that its effects upon women are disproportionably [sic] adverse, a twofold inquiry is thus appropriate. The first question is whether the statutory classification is indeed neutral in the sense that it is not gender based. If the classification itself, covert or overt, is not based upon gender, the second question is whether the adverse effect reflects invidious gender-based discrimination. In this second inquiry, impact provides an "important starting point," but purposeful discrimination is "the condition that offends the Constitution."

It is against this background of precedent that we consider the merits of the case before us.

The question whether [the statute] establishes a classification that is overtly or covertly based upon gender must first be considered. The appellee has conceded that [it] is neutral on its face. She has also acknowledged that state hiring preferences for veterans are not *per se* invalid, for she has limited her challenge to the absolute lifetime preference that Massachusetts provides to veterans. . . .

* * *

The distinction made by [the statute] is . . . quite simply between veterans and nonveterans, not between men and women.

The dispositive question, then, is whether the appellee has shown that a gender-based discriminatory purpose has, at least in some measure, shaped the Massachusetts veterans' preference legislation. As did the District Court, she points to two basic factors which in her view distinguish [it] from the neutral rules at issue in the *Washington v. Davis* and *Arlington Heights* cases. The first is the nature of the preference, which is said to be demonstrably gender-biased in the sense that it favors a status reserved under federal military policy primarily to men. The second concerns the impact of the absolute lifetime preference upon the employment opportunities of women, an impact claimed to be too inevitable to have been unintended. The appellee contends that these factors, coupled with the fact that the preference itself has little if any relevance to actual job performance, more than suffice to prove the discriminatory intent required to establish a constitutional violation.

The contention that this veterans' preference is "inherently nonneutral" or "gender-biased" presumes that the State, by favoring veterans, intentionally incorporated into its public employment policies the panoply of sex-based and assertedly discriminatory federal laws that have prevented all but a handful of women from becoming veterans. There are two serious difficulties with this argument. First, it is wholly at odds with the District Court's central finding that Massachusetts has not offered a preference to veterans for the purpose of discriminating against women. Second, it cannot be reconciled with the assumption made by both the appellee and the District Court that a more limited hiring preference for veterans could be sustained. Taken together, these difficulties are fatal.

* * *

The appellee's ultimate argument rests upon the presumption, common to the criminal and civil law, that a person intends the natural and foreseeable consequences of his voluntary actions. . . . The decision to grant a preference to veterans was of course "intentional." So, necessarily, did an adverse impact upon nonveterans follow from that decision. And it cannot seriously be argued that the Legislature of Massachusetts could have been unaware that most veterans are men. It would thus be disingenuous to say that the adverse consequences of this legislation for women were unintended, in the sense that they were not volitional or in the sense that they were not foreseeable.

"Discriminatory purpose," however, implies more than intent as volition or intent as awareness of consequences. It implies that the decisionmaker, in this case a state legislature, selected or reaffirmed a particular course of action at least in part "because of," not merely "in spite of," its adverse effects upon an identifiable group. Yet nothing in the record demonstrates that this preference for veterans was originally devised or subsequently re-enacted because it would accomplish the collateral goal of keeping women in a stereotypic and predefined place in the Massachusetts Civil Service.

* * *

The appellee . . . has simply failed to demonstrate that the law in any way reflects a purpose to discriminate on the basis of sex.

The judgment is reversed, and the case is remanded for further proceedings consistent with this opinion.

It is so ordered.

Justice Stevens, with whom Justice White joins, concurred.

Justice Marshall, with whom Justice Brennan joins, dissenting.

Although acknowledging that in some circumstances, discriminatory intent may be inferred from the inevitable or foreseeable impact of a statute, the Court concludes that no such intent has been established here. I cannot agree. In my judgment, Massachusetts' choice of an absolute veterans' preference system evinces purposeful gender-based discrimination. And because the statutory scheme bears no substantial relationship to a legitimate governmental objective, it cannot withstand scrutiny under the Equal Protection Clause.

The District Court found that the "prime objective" of the Massachusetts veterans' preference statute was to benefit individuals with prior military service. Under the Court's analysis, this factual determination "necessarily compels the conclusion that the state intended nothing more than to prefer 'veterans.' Given this finding, simple logic suggests that an intent to exclude women from significant public jobs was not at work in this law." I find the Court's logic neither simple nor compelling.

That a legislature seeks to advantage one group does not, as a matter of logic or of common sense, exclude the possibility that it also intends to disadvantage another. Individuals in general and lawmakers in particular frequently act for a variety of reasons. . . . Thus, the critical constitutional inquiry is not whether an illicit consideration was the primary or but-for cause of a decision, but rather whether it had an appreciable role in shaping a given legislative enactment. Where there is "proof that a discriminatory purpose has been *a* motivating factor in the decision, . . . judicial deference is no longer justified." [emphasis added by Justice Marshall]

Moreover, since reliable evidence of subjective intentions is seldom obtainable, resort to inference based on objective factors is generally unavoidable. To discern the purposes underlying facially neutral policies, this Court has therefore considered the degree, inevitability, and foreseeability of any disproportionate impact as well as the alternatives reasonably available.

In the instant case, the impact of the Massachusetts statute on women is undisputed. . . . Because less than 2% of the women in Massachusetts are veterans, the absolute-preference formula has rendered desirable state civil service employment an almost exclusively male prerogative.

As the District Court recognized, this consequence follows foreseeably, indeed inexorably, from the long history of policies severely limiting women's participation in the military. Although neutral in form, the statute is anything but neutral in application. It inescapably reserves a major sector of public employment to "an already established class which, as a matter of historical fact, is 98% male." Where the foreseeable impact of a facially neutral policy is so disproportionate, the burden should rest on the State to establish that sex-based considerations played no part in the choice of the particular legislative scheme.

Clearly, that burden was not sustained here. The legislative history of the statute reflects the Commonwealth's patent appreciation of the impact the preference system would have on women, and an equally evident desire to mitigate that impact only with respect to certain traditionally female occupations. Until 1971, the statute and implementing civil service regulations exempted from operation of the preference any job requisitions "especially calling for women." In practice, this exemption, coupled with the absolute preference for veterans, has created a gender-based civil service hierarchy, with women occupying low-grade clerical and secretarial jobs and men holding more responsible and remunerative positions.

* * *

To survive challenge under the Equal Protection Clause, statutes reflecting gender-based discrimination must be substantially related to the achievement of important governmental objectives. Appellants here advance three interests in support of the absolute-preference system: (1) assisting veterans in their readjustment to civilian life; (2) encouraging military enlistment; and (3) rewarding those who have served their country. Although each of those goals is unquestionably legitimate, the "mere recitation of a benign, compensatory purpose" cannot of itself insulate legislative classifications from constitutional scrutiny. And in this case, the Commonwealth has failed to establish a sufficient relationship between its objectives and the means chosen to effectuate them.

With respect to the first interest, facilitating veterans' transition to civilian status, the statute is plainly overinclusive. By conferring a permanent preference, the legislation allows veterans to invoke their advantage repeatedly, without regard to their date of discharge. . . .

Nor is the Commonwealth's second asserted interest, encouraging military service, a plausible justification for this legislative scheme. In its original and subsequent re-enactments, the statute extended benefits retroactively to veterans who had served during a prior specified period. If the Commonwealth's "actual purpose" is to induce enlistment, this legislative design is hardly well suited to that end. . . . Moreover, even if such influence could be presumed, the statute is still grossly overinclusive in that it bestows benefits on men drafted as well as those who volunteered.

Finally, the Commonwealth's third interest, rewarding veterans, does not "adequately justify the salient features" of this preference system. Where a particular statutory scheme visits substantial hardship on a class long subject to discrimination, the legislation cannot be sustained unless " 'carefully tuned to alternative considerations.' " Here, there are a wide variety of less discriminatory means by which Massachusetts could effect its compensatory purposes. For example, a point preference system, such as that maintained by many States and the Federal Government, or an absolute preference for a limited duration, would reward veterans without excluding all qualified women from upper level civil service positions. . . .

In its present unqualified form, the veterans' preference statute precludes all but a small fraction of Massachusetts women from obtaining any civil service position also of interest to men. Given the range of alternatives available, this degree of preference is not constitutionally permissible.

I would affirm the judgment of the court below.

Gender and Statutory Classifications

In addition to claims of gender discrimination as a violation of the Equal Protection Clause of the Fourteenth Amendment, a number of cases involve statutory claims, that is, the interpretation and application of federal laws that prohibit gender discrimination. To be specific, Title VII of the Civil Rights Act of 1964 prohibits gender discrimination in employment, while Title IX of the 1972 Education Amendments prohibits gender discrimination in educational programs receiving federal funds.

Phillips v. Martin Marietta Corp. (1971), decided in the same year as *Reed,* was the first case to involve the application of Title VII to gender discrimination. This case began when Ida Phillips applied for a position with the Martin Marietta Corporation. She was told that the company did not accept applications from women with preschool-age children; however, the company did hire men who were similarly situated. Phillips filed suit in federal district court, claiming that this action violated Title VII, which prevents employers from refusing to hire people on the basis of gender, unless it is a "bona-fide occupational qualification" (BFOQ) necessary to the normal operations of that business. The district court ruled in favor of the company, concluding that there was no pattern of bias against women because in the job category for which Phillips had applied, 75 to 80 percent of those hired were women. The court of appeals upheld this decision, but the Supreme Court remanded the case for further consideration. In a brief per curiam opinion, the justices ruled that under Title VII, individuals with similar qualifications must be provided employment opportunities irrespective of their gender. They continued by saying that Title VII does not permit different hiring policies for women and men with preschool-age children, but that the distinction in question might be allowed if there was evidence that "conflicting family obligations. . . [were] more relevant to the job performance for a woman than for a man" (400 U.S. at 544, 1971). The court of appeals was to examine the record to determine if the company's policy constituted a BFOQ.

Other early cases involving Title VII were decided as follows.

- By a 6-3 vote, the Court ruled that Title VII was not violated by an employer's denial of benefits for pregnancy disability leave. The Court reasoned that discrimination on the basis of pregnancy is not gender discrimination. *G.E. v. Gilbert* (1976) (overruled by Pregnancy Discrimination Act of 1978)
- In a unanimous decision, the Court held that Title VII prohibits employers from denying seniority to women who return to work after taking a pregnancy leave. *Nashville Gas Company v. Satty* (1977)

- In a split ruling, the Court ruled that the restriction of female prison guards to certain areas of a prison did not violate Title VII, but that height and weight requirements did. The former was a "bona fide occupational qualification" under the Civil Rights Act while the latter were not. *Dothard v. Rawlinson* (1977)
- In a 6-2 decision, the Court struck down as violative of Title VII a city policy that required female employees to make larger monthly pension fund contributions than their male counterparts. The policy was based on the fact that women on average live longer than men (so they would need pensions longer). This policy violated a provision of Title VII which prohibits gender discrimination "with respect to . . . compensation, terms, conditions, or privileges of employment." *LA Department of Water and Power v. Manhart* (1978)

Mississippi University for Women v. Hogan (1982) was not the only important case heard by the Burger Court regarding gender discrimination in the field of education. Unlike *Hogan,* however, *Grove City College v. Bell* (1984) involved Title IX of the Education Amendments of 1972 rather than the Equal Protection Clause. The case involved the appropriate interpretation of Title IX's proscription against gender discrimination in programs receiving federal financial assistance. Such programs are required to file forms with the federal government providing assurances that they are not engaging in such discrimination. The case began when Grove City College refused to file the appropriate forms with the Department of Education. Grove City did not receive federal funds directly, but some of its students received Basic Educational Opportunity Grants (BEOGs), which they used to pay tuition and other fees. The Department of Education threatened to cut off BEOGs available to Grove City students after the college refused to file the necessary forms. Grove City went to court to block this action, maintaining that it did not directly receive federal funds, so it should not have to comply with Title IX. The Supreme Court, by a unanimous vote, rejected Grove City's claim, contending that there was no meaningful distinction between direct and indirect aid. White's majority opinion relied on the language of the Education Amendments of 1972, congressional intent, and administrative practice in concluding that Grove City was indeed a recipient of federal aid and therefore was required to fill out the forms.

More importantly, however, the Court ruled on the scope of Title IX. The Department of Education had consistently interpreted it to apply institutionwide, and the Department argued this position through the district court and appeals court levels of the *Grove City* case. By the time the case reached the Supreme Court, however, President Reagan was in office and the executive branch's interpretation of Title IX changed. The Reagan administration asserted that it applied only to specific parts or programs within educational institutions. By a 6-3 vote, the Court agreed with the Reagan administration's interpretation, holding that Grove City needed to fill out forms only for the program that received federal monies, not for the entire college. Thus, the phrase "any education program or activity" was given a narrow interpretation. Justices Stevens, Brennan, and Marshall dissented from this part of the ruling. Stevens argued that the majority went beyond what was necessary to resolve the case because the question of institutionwide coverage was not raised by the parties. Brennan and Marshall contended that Title IX applied to the entire institution if it receives or benefits from federal funds. They reached this conclusion based upon their reading of the legislative history of Title IX and subsequent judicial interpretations as well as judicial and administrative interpretations of similar language in Title VI. Moreover, they argued that the BEOG monies received by Grove City were used to support most of its facilities and services.

The Court's ruling limiting the scope of Title IX sparked considerable controversy regarding its implications. Many civil rights groups alleged that under the ruling, educational institutions would be able to discriminate legally against females in some areas, most notably in athletics and vocational training programs. Subsequently, they launched a campaign to persuade Congress to pass legislation overturning the effects of *Grove City*. Unsuccessful at first, a broad-based coalition eventually persuaded Congress to pass the Civil Rights Restoration Act of 1988 over President Reagan's veto.

While *Grove City* was being decided, the last major gender discrimination case of the Burger era was making its way through the lower federal courts. *Meritor Savings Bank v. Vinson* (1986) was concerned with sexual harassment, an issue that was receiving considerable attention from feminists and other civil rights groups. The case began when Mechelle Vinson filed charges of sexual harassment against her supervisor and her employer (Meritor Savings Bank). In resolving this case, the Court was to decide three issues: 1) Is sexual harassment gender discrimination in violation of Title VII of the Civil Rights Act of 1964? 2) Is sexual harassment restricted to economic terms—so-called "quid pro quo," where employment and advancement in a job is the issue; or, does it encompass sexual misconduct that creates a "hostile" working environment? 3) To what extent are employers liable for sexual harassment by their supervisory personnel? A unanimous Court agreed that sexual harassment *is* gender discrimination in violation of Title VII and that sexual harassment includes more than "quid pro quo" behavior. Writing for the majority, Justice Rehnquist said that the language in Title VII indicates that Congress was concerned with more than economic discrimination, as it refers to "terms, conditions or privileges of employment." Furthermore, he noted that the guidelines developed by the Equal Employment Opportunities Commission (EEOC) included both "quid pro quo" and "hostile environment" sexual harassment. However, on the question of employer liability for sexual harassment practiced by their supervisors, the Court refused to issue a definitive rule, alleging that EEOC guidelines were unclear on this point. Rehnquist did say that the court of appeals was wrong in its conclusion that employers are always automatically liable for the sexual misconduct of their supervisory personnel, but he indicated that employer liability would depend upon the specific context in which the harassment occurs.

Justices Marshall, Brennan, Blackmun, and Stevens disagreed with this part of the Court's ruling, maintaining that the EEOC guidelines did address fairly clearly the question of employer liability. They concluded that the guidelines make employers responsible for the actions of their agents and supervisory employees. Moreover, the four argued that this rule should apply to both "quid pro quo" and "hostile environment" sexual harassment, not just to the former as the solicitor general had argued. While stating this general rule, they acknowledged that there may be some limits on liability, for example, when a supervisor and an employee work in different parts of the employer's business such that the supervisor has no authority over the employee.

Meritor Savings Bank was an important case in addressing the legal implications of sexual harassment in the workplace. The Court's decision that sexual harassment is gender discrimination and that it includes "hostile environment" claims cleared the way for employees, particularly women, to become more willing to challenge such conduct. Nonetheless, the Court's refusal to issue a standard on employer liability left a serious gap in the legal arena of sexual harassment.

Gender Discrimination and Freedom of Association

A final case from the Burger era deserves attention, although it was decided on freedom of association grounds rather than on gender discrimination grounds. *Roberts v. U.S. Jaycees* (1984) involved the question of whether the government could prevent private organizations from discriminating in membership on the basis of gender. Feminists and other civil rights activists had argued that many of these clubs were essential to women's advancement in the business world because they provided the context for making important business contacts. In *Roberts,* Minnesota's civil rights law, which prohibited gender discrimination in places of public accommodations, was challenged by the national Jaycees organization. The Jaycees limited regular membership to eighteen- to thirty-five-year-old men, but allowed women to participate in the organization as associate members. Associate membership status involved lower dues, and it prohibited women from voting, holding office, and participating in some activities. When the Minneapolis and St. Paul chapters admitted women as regular members, the national organization imposed sanctions against them and threatened to revoke their charters. The two chapters filed a complaint with the state human rights department, charging that the national bylaws, which excluded women, violated Minnesota law, and the state human rights commissioner ordered hearings. Subsequently, the national organization (U.S. Jaycees) filed suit claiming that the state law violated speech and association rights. The Jaycees lost the case in federal district court, and after the appeals court overturned that decision, Roberts (the state commissioner) appealed to the Supreme Court.

The Court upheld the Minnesota human rights law in a 7-0 decision, with Justices Blackmun and Burger not participating, and O'Connor concurring in the judgment only. In the majority opinion, Brennan addressed two questions—whether the law violated freedom of association and whether it abridged freedom of speech. On the freedom of association question, Brennan discussed the freedom of intimate association, stating that this liberty is generally accorded only to relationships that are distinguished by smallness, a high degree of selectivity, and the maintenance of seclusion from others. Further, other types of organizations such as large businesses do not have similar characteristics, and others are somewhere in the middle. With respect to the Jaycees, the local chapters were neither small nor selective organizations, given that women and other nonmembers of both genders are allowed to participate in some of the clubs' activities. Therefore, the Jaycees clubs did not have those distinctive features that would allow them the freedom to exclude women from membership. With respect to freedom of expression, Brennan maintained that this right is not absolute, but can be abridged if there is a compelling interest that is not related to suppressing ideas. In this case, Minnesota had a compelling interest in prohibiting discrimination against women in places of public accommodations and in providing them the benefits of participation in political, economic, and social activities. The Court also ruled that the Human Rights Law did not burden expression in that there was no evidence that the organization would have to alter its messages if women were admitted as full members. "The Act requires no change in the Jaycees' creed of promoting the interests of young men and it imposes no restrictions on the organization's ability to exclude individuals with ideologies or philosophies different from those of existing members" (468 U.S. at 627). Finally, Brennan said that stereotypes about differences in women's and men's attitudes regarding various issues were insufficient to conclude that any change in content of the organization's speech would be required by the Act.

In a very brief concurrence, O'Connor indicated that the Court should have placed this case in the commercial speech category. She said that since the Jaycees were a "commercial operation," they were not entitled to the same First Amendment rights accorded to expressive associations.

As the Burger era drew to an end, it seemed obvious that many of the most blatant forms of gender discrimination were not going to be permitted. The Court had struck down a number of policies that were based on stereotypes about the sexes, e.g.,

Reed, Frontiero, and *MUW v. Hogan.* On the other hand, the Court upheld some laws that were based upon traditional attitudes about women and men, e.g., *Michael M.* and *Rostker v. Goldberg.* Perhaps many of the cases, particularly the early ones decided by the Burger Court, were not very difficult, and by the end of this era, the cases involved more complex issues. This is what Mezey argued in her book *In Pursuit of Equality: Women, Public Policy, and the Federal Courts.* She wrote, "The decisions furthering sex equality, in which the Court struck down the sex-based laws, were mostly 'easy' cases because the laws under review were grounded in separate spheres thinking that defined women's and men's lives in old-fashioned, stereotypical roles" (1992, pp. 20–21). This is not to say, however, that these decisions were unimportant or insignificant, for they did indicate that the Court was not going to allow gender discrimination to go unchallenged. The Burger Court had gone beyond any of its predecessors in taking a critical look at laws and policies that made distinctions between women and men, and that were often instrumental in keeping women in a subordinate position in our society.

Finally, while the Burger Court refused to accord gender classifications the same strict scrutiny that had been applied to racial classifications, it appeared to settle on a heightened standard for examining such classifications. The Court had created the important government objective test, which required an intermediate level of scrutiny, and this was viewed by most women's rights activists as an improvement over the rational basis test.

The Rehnquist Court Era

With Warren Burger's retirement, William Rehnquist's elevation to chief justice, and Presidents Reagan and Bush's nominations to the Court, speculation arose that the Court would move to the right in matters involving gender discrimination, particularly discrimination against women. As in the previous chapters, the Rehnquist Court's decisions in the area of gender equality will be discussed from both quantitative and doctrinal perspectives. This will enable us to determine whether the Court has engaged in a constitutional counterrevolution in its decisions regarding gender discrimination. A conservative decision in a gender discrimination case is one in which the Court upholds the challenged classification, while a liberal outcome occurs when the Court supports the individual bringing a complaint of gender discrimination.

Surprisingly, the data suggest that the Rehnquist Court has been *more liberal* than either the Burger Court or the Warren Court. As seen in Table 14.1, the Rehnquist Court decided 80 percent of its gender discrimination cases in a liberal fashion, compared to 65 percent for the Burger Court and 0 percent for the Warren Court. These comparisons, however, may be misleading, given the number of cases decided by each Court. The Burger Court decided forty-three gender discrimination cases, while the Rehnquist and Warren Courts decided only ten and one cases, respectively. Nonetheless, of the ten cases heard by the Rehnquist Court, eight had liberal outcomes.

While these data do not indicate a conservative counterrevolution by the Rehnquist Court in the area of gender equality, our analysis needs to go further. The decision-making patterns of individual justices provide some useful information. Table 14.2 reveals that only Justice Powell cast a majority of votes against individuals in gender discrimination cases (67%). Powell, however, participated in only three cases on the Rehnquist Court. Chief Justice Rehnquist's votes were evenly split between conservative and liberal outcomes. The most liberal justices were Blackmun, Souter, Ginsburg, Stevens, Marshall, and Brennan with liberalism scores

TABLE 14.1: Liberal/Conservative Outcomes of Gender Discrimination Cases for the Warren, Burger, and Rehnquist Courts, 1953-94 Terms

	Outcomes		
Court Era	Liberal	Conservative	Totals
Warren Court 1953-68 Terms	0% (0)	100% (1)	1
Burger Court 1969-85 Terms	65% (28)	35% (15)	43
Rehnquist Court 1986-94 Terms	80% (8)	20% (2)	10
Totals	67% (36)	33% (18)	54

TABLE 14.2: Liberal/Conservative Voting Records of Justices of the Rehnquist Court in Gender Discrimination Cases, 1986-94 Terms

Justices	**Liberal Votes**	**Conservative Votes**
Blackmun	100% (8)	0% (0)
Souter	100% (4)	0% (0)
Ginsburg	100% (2)	0% (0)
Stevens	90% (9)	10% (1)
Marshall	86% (6)	14% (1)
Brennan	83% (5)	17% (1)
O'Connor	78% (7)	22% (2)
Kennedy	71% (5)	29% (2)
Thomas	67% (2)	33% (1)
White	62% (5)	38% (3)
Scalia	60% (6)	40% (4)
Rehnquist	50% (5)	50% (5)
Powell	33% (1)	67% (2)
Breyer	Did not Participate	

ranging from 100% (Blackmun, Souter, and Ginsburg) to 83% (Brennan). Justices Souter and Ginsburg, however, participated in only four and two cases, respectively.

The results of the bloc voting analysis in Table 14.3 are both complex and intriguing. Two overlapping liberal blocs can be identified. The most liberal bloc consists of Justices Brennan, Marshall, Blackmun, and Stevens, who have a perfect interagreement score of 100 percent. O'Connor barely misses joining this bloc, but her agreement scores are high enough with Blackmun and Stevens that these three justices form a separate liberal bloc. A third bloc also exists, consisting of Justices Scalia and Rehnquist who have an average interagreement rate of 90 percent; this can best be described as a moderate bloc with conservative tendencies, given the Court's overall liberal record in gender discrimination cases. The bloc voting analysis further supports the conclusion that the Rehnquist Court has not engaged in a conservative counterrevolution with respect to gender discrimination.

The doctrinal analysis supports this conclusion as well. As Table 14.4 indicates, the Court did not create any new precedents, conservative or liberal, in the area of

TABLE 14.3: Bloc Voting Analysis of the Rehnquist Court in Gender Discrimination Cases, 1986-94 Terms (Percent Agreement Rate)

	BR	MA	BL	ST	OC	KE	WH	RE	SC
Brennan	—	100	100	100	80	33	67	50	67
Marshall	100	—	100	100	83	50	71	57	71
Blackmun	100	100	—	100	88	71	67	50	63
Stevens	100	100	100	—	89	71	75	60	70
O'Connor	80	83	88	89	—	86	86	67	78
Kennedy	33	50	71	71	86	—	80	86	86
White	67	71	67	75	86	80	—	88	75
Rehnquist	50	57	50	60	67	86	88	—	90
Scalia	67	71	63	70	78	86	75	90	—

Court mean = 76
Sprague Criterion = 88
Liberal blocs: Brennan, Marshall, Blackmun, Stevens = 100
Blackmun, Stevens, O'Connor = 92
Moderate bloc: Rehnquist and Scalia = 90

gender discrimination. Of the ten cases heard, eight were decided on the basis of a liberal interpretation of existing precedent, and two were decided by the Court's conservative interpretation of existing precedent. Although all ten of the cases are included in the table, the following discussion will focus primarily on the major cases.

Our discussion will begin with an examination of two major cases from the Rehnquist Court's first term, 1986–87. In the first term, the justices were forced to interpret the relationship between federal and state laws regarding pregnancy disability benefits. This case involved a federal statute, the Pregnancy Discrimination Act of 1978 (PDA). *California Federal Savings and Loan v. Guerra* (1987) began in 1982, when Lillian Garland, a receptionist at California Federal Savings and Loan Bank, attempted to return to her job after her maternity leave. The bank refused to rehire her, arguing that its official policy permitted it to refuse to rehire any employee on a leave of absence. Under California law, employers were required to grant pregnancy leave for up to four months. The bank argued, however, that the state law was in conflict with the PDA, which forbids employers to discriminate against pregnant women. California Federal pointed to the section of the PDA that says, "women affected by pregnancy, childbirth, or related medical conditions, shall be treated the same for all employment-related purposes, including receipt of benefits under fringe benefit programs, as other persons not so affected but similar in their ability or inability to work. . ." (42 U.S.C.A. Sect. 2000e[k]). Because California Federal's policy applied equally to all of its employees and the PDA required that women "affected by pregnancy" be treated the same as other employees, California Federal argued that the state law that treated pregnant women differently than other employees must be held invalid.

After the district court agreed with California Federal that the PDA preempted California law and the appeals court reversed that decision, the case was appealed to the U.S. Supreme Court. In a 6-3 decision, the Court ruled that the California law regarding benefits provided to pregnant workers was not preempted by the PDA, but was consistent with its purposes. Justice Marshall, joined by Justices Blackmun, Brennan, O'Connor, and Stevens, wrote the majority opinion for the Court. Marshall

TABLE 14.4: A Framework for the Doctrinal Analysis of the Rehnquist Court's Gender Discrimination Cases, 1986-94 Terms

Major or Minor Importance	Majority or Plurality Opinion	Treatment of Precedent: Creation of New Liberal Precedent	Liberal Modification of Existing Precedent	Liberal Interpretation of Existing Precedent	Conservative Interpretation of Existing Precedent	Conservative Modification of Existing Precedent	Creation of New Conservative Precedent
Major	Majority			Cal. Fed. v. Guerra (1987) Rotary v. Rotary (1987) UAW v. Johnson Controls (1991)			
	Plurality			Price Waterhouse v. Hopkins (1989)			
Minor	Majority			NY Club Assn v. NY (1988) Franklin v. Gwin. Co. (1992) Harris v. Forklift (1993) JEB v.TB (1994)	Wimberly v. Labor Com. (1987) Florida v. Long (1988)		
	Plurality						

said that the legislative intent and history of the PDA demonstrated that it did not forbid the preferential treatment of pregnancy. He stated that the law was a reaction to the Court's decision in *G.E. v. Gilbert* (1976), which had held that discrimination on the basis of pregnancy was not gender discrimination. He emphasized that Congress was concerned with providing relief for working women who had been victimized by discrimination when they became pregnant, and that while the PDA did not *require* preferential treatment for pregnant workers, the law did not *prohibit* it either. In addition, he noted that at the time the PDA was being debated and approved, other state laws similar to California's existed, and Congress did not appear to find them in conflict with the PDA. Marshall then distinguished the California law from earlier protective legislation that was based on stereotypes about the roles and abilities of the sexes. The PDA, he argued, "does not reflect archaic or stereotypical notions about pregnancy and the abilities of pregnant workers" (479 U.S. 290 1987). It merely permits women, as well as men, to have a family life without fear of losing their jobs as a result. Finally, Marshall stressed that it was possible for California employers to comply with both state and federal law. The statute "does not compel California employers to treat pregnant workers *better* than other disabled employees. . . . Employers are free to give comparable benefits to other disabled employees, thereby treating 'women affected by pregnancy' no better than 'other persons not so affected but similar in their ability or inability to work' " (479 U.S. at 291).

While joining the majority opinion, Justice Stevens issued a brief concurrence, emphasizing that this case was similar to *United Steelworkers v. Weber* (1979), in which the Court interpreted Title VII to distinguish between "discrimination *against* members of the protected class and special preference *in favor of* members of that class" (479 U.S. at 294, emphasis added). Stevens argued that here, as in *Weber*, the preferential treatment is consistent with the goals and purposes of Title VII, and therefore, the California law is not preempted by the PDA. In a rather confusing concurrence in the judgment only, Scalia stated that the California statute could not be preempted because it did not require employers to do anything forbidden by Title VII.

The dissenters had a different interpretation of the legislative intent and history of the PDA. Justice White, joined by Justices Powell and Rehnquist, said that the PDA requires equal treatment for pregnant and nonpregnant workers, not preferential treatment. "Congress' silence in its consideration of the PDA with respect to preferential treatment of pregnant workers cannot fairly be interpreted to abrogate the plain statements in the legislative history, not to mention the language of the statute, that equality of treatment was to be the guiding principle of the PDA" (479 U.S. at 300).

In its second major case, decided in the same term, *Board of Directors of Rotary International v. Rotary Club* (1987), the Court revisited the issue of whether private organizations could legally discriminate in membership on the basis of gender. This case also involved a California statute, the Unruh Civil Rights Act. The law required nondiscrimination on the basis of sex, race, color, religion, ancestry, or national origin in business establishments in the state. Similar to the Jaycees organization, women were allowed to participate in a number of activities, but they were excluded from membership by the Rotary constitution. When a local chapter of Rotary International (the Duarte Club) admitted women to the organization, its charter was revoked and it was expelled from the parent organization. Subsequently, the Rotary Club of Duarte filed suit in the California Superior Court for the County of Los Angeles, charging that Rotary International's actions violated the Unruh Act. The trial court ruled in favor of Rotary International, declaring that it was not a business establishment, and therefore the Unruh Act was not applicable. The decision was reversed by the state court of appeals, and that judgment was appealed to the U.S. Supreme Court.

In a 7-0 decision with Justices O'Connor and Blackmun not participating, the Court upheld the nondiscrimination law. Justice Powell, writing for all except Scalia, relied upon the precedent established in *Roberts* three years earlier. In dismissing the claim that the law violated the group's freedom of intimate association, he said that "the relationship among Rotary Club members is not the kind of intimate or private relation that warrants constitutional protection" (481 U.S. at 546). As was the case in *Roberts,* the Court was influenced by the large size of the local chapters, the participation of nonmembers in club activities, and the wide publicity associated with the club's meetings and other activities. The freedom of expressive association claim by Rotary International was not persuasive either, as the Court ruled that admitting women will not significantly affect the "members' ability to carry out their various purposes" (481 U.S. at 548). Powell said that the state law did not require the club to change either its basic goals or its activities, particularly since the group does not take positions on "public questions" of the day. Furthermore, Powell emphasized the state's "compelling interest" of eliminating discrimination against women in public accommodations, and in ensuring that women have access to the business and professional contacts that are often made in these kinds of associations. Justice Scalia concurred in the judgment, without writing an opinion.

Thus, these two decisions did not signal a retreat from the Court's liberal decisions in previous gender discrimination cases, but neither did they break new ground. As Table 14.4 illustrates, in both *California Federal* and *Rotary International,* the liberal outcome was due simply to the Court's liberal interpretation of existing precedent. Nonetheless, *California Federal* and *Rotary Club* indicate that the Rehnquist Court did not embark on a conservative counterrevolution in the area of gender discrimination in its first term.

By the time the justices heard their next major gender discrimination case, Justice Powell had retired from the Court and had been replaced by Anthony Kennedy, a federal appeals judge from the Ninth Circuit. This change in membership was thought to be an important one, because Powell had been regarded as a moderate or "swing vote" on the Court. With the appointment of Kennedy by President Reagan, there was speculation that the conservative wing on the Court would have an additional ally. As Table 14.2 demonstrates, in the three gender discrimination cases in which Powell participated during the Rehnquist era, he took the conservative position in two of them. This is fairly consistent with his voting record in gender discrimination cases during the Burger era, as he had eighteen liberal (45%) and twenty-two conservative (55%) votes. Thus, these data suggest that Kennedy's appointment would not add a new justice to the conservative wing, but instead would allow the conservatives to maintain the votes that they already had if Kennedy was similarly disinclined to favor individuals in such cases.

Justice Kennedy's first gender discrimination case involved a very difficult problem for the Court to resolve. *Price Waterhouse v. Hopkins* (1989) arose when Ann Hopkins, a successful senior manager at the accounting firm of Price Waterhouse, was denied partnership status in the company. She claimed that gender discrimination played a significant role in this adverse decision. In considering her candidacy, the firm's policy board had invited partners to submit comments about Hopkins, and some of those comments were based on gender stereotypes. The evaluations said that she was too aggressive, macho, masculine, and the like. Also, one of the partners explained to her that her professional problems would be solved if she acted more femininely, for example, wore make-up and jewelry, and changed her hair style. Price Waterhouse alleged that the negative decision was based upon complaints about Hopkins' interpersonal skills, not on these gender-based kinds of comments. These facts presented the Court with an especially difficult question because the case differed from the normal "pretext" case in which employees claimed that adverse employment decisions were made *solely* because of illegal discrimination; in these types of cases, the rules regarding liability and the burden of proof had been fairly clear. The specific issue in *Price Waterhouse,* however, was the extent of employer liability and the burden of proof in "mixed motive" cases, where the evidence suggests that an employment action resulted from a mixture of legitimate and illegitimate (illegal discrimination) motives.

At the district court, Hopkins argued that once she demonstrated that gender played a part in the employment decision, the burden should be on Price Waterhouse to prove that the ultimate decision was not based upon gender discrimination, and the district court agreed with her on this question of liability. After the appeals court affirmed this ruling, Price Waterhouse appealed to the Supreme Court.

The Court accepted the case for review because the question of the burden of proof carried by the employer in these "mixed motives" cases had been the subject of conflict among the federal circuits. By a 6-3 vote, the Court ruled that the burden of proof is on the employer in "mixed motives" cases, but the correct standard is "preponderance of the evidence," not "clear and convincing evidence" as the lower courts had held. Justice Brennan wrote a plurality opinion that was joined by Justices Blackmun, Marshall, and Stevens, while Justices White and O'Connor wrote separate opinions, concurring in the judgment only. The plurality held, "When a plaintiff in a Title VII case proves that her gender played a motivating part in an employment decision, the defendant may avoid a finding of liability only by proving by a preponderance of the evidence that it would have made the same decision even if it had not taken the plaintiff's gender into account" (490 U.S. at 252). In examining the lower court records, the plurality was also persuaded that gender stereotyping, hence gender discrimination, was present in this case, and that it played a part in the decision not to propose Hopkins for partner. While O'Connor and White agreed that the burden of proof was on the employer and that "preponderance of the evidence" was the appropriate standard, they disagreed about the extent of the role played by illegitimate motives in the adverse employment action. They argued that the employee must demonstrate that the illegitimate motive was not simply present, but that it was "a *substantial* factor in the adverse employment action" (490 U.S. at 259).

In dissent, Justice Kennedy, writing for himself and Justices Rehnquist and Scalia, expressed concern that the Court's different rules for deciding "pretext" and "mixed-motives" cases would cause confusion in the lower courts. Moreover, they stressed that the burden should remain with the employee to prove that the employer made its adverse decision based upon illegal motives, not the reverse. Finally, the dissenters disagreed with the plurality's view that Hopkins had presented the appropriate evidence that gender discrimination was a real factor in Price Waterhouse's decision not to propose her for promotion to partner. They argued that there was uncertainty as to whether she would have been elected to partnership without the gender-based evaluations of her colleagues.

While the outcome of *Price Waterhouse* was liberal, the commentators' assumptions about Justice Kennedy seemed to be accurate, at least initially, given his conservative vote and, perhaps as important, his rather sharp dissent. Overall, however, the case suggested Kennedy's appointment was not going to affect the liberal direction of the Court in gender discrimination cases.

The Rehnquist Court heard its next major gender discrimination case, *International Union, UAW v. Johnson Controls, Inc.,* in the 1990–91 term. By this time, David Souter had joined the Court, replacing the liberal William Brennan. *Johnson Controls* was important because it marked the first time that the Court ruled on the legality of so-called fetal protection policies, which were sparking considerable controversy. Relying on medical evidence indicating that exposure to toxic substances is harmful to a developing fetus, Johnson Controls, a battery manufacturer, established a policy that excluded women of childbearing capability from jobs in the company where they would be exposed to lead. The Supreme Court invalidated this fetal protection policy by a 9-0 vote. Only five justices, however, joined the majority opinion: Blackmun, Marshall, O'Connor, Stevens, and Souter. Justices Kennedy, Rehnquist, and White concurred in the judgment and in the opinion in part. Justice Scalia concurred only in the judgment.

The majority, led by Blackmun, held that Johnson Controls' policy of excluding fertile women, but not fertile men, from certain jobs was obviously gender discrimination, particularly because medical evidence suggests that lead has harmful effects on the reproductive systems of males as well as females. The Court rejected the company's defense that the policy was a BFOQ, or "bona fide occupational qualification." Blackmun stressed that for gender distinctions to qualify as a BFOQ, they "must relate to ability to perform the duties of the job" (499 U.S. at 204), and the record indicates that "fertile women . . . participate in the manufacture of batteries as efficiently as anyone else" (499 U.S. at 206). In concluding, the majority responded to Johnson Controls' claim that the ruling would subject employers to increased tort liability. Rejecting this argument, Blackmun wrote that if employers are not negligent and take reasonable steps to inform their female employees about the risks of employment, then it would be difficult for a court to find the employer liable.

The Court ruled that *all* gender-specific fetal protection policies violate Title VII, and this was precisely the point rejected by Kennedy, Rehnquist, and White. They agreed that this particular policy was illegal, but they thought that fetal protection policies might be upheld in some situations. For example, they argued that women who are actually pregnant might be excluded from jobs where they would be exposed to highly toxic substances. Moreover, White wrote, "A fetal protection policy would be justified under terms of a statute, [if] employer[s] could show that exclusion of women from certain jobs was reasonably necessary to avoid substantial tort liability" (499 U.S. at 212). In addition, they asserted that increased tort liability was a legitimate concern for employers, and that the majority's language about negligence and warnings to employees was not sufficient to protect employers from liability.

Concurring in the judgment only, Justice Scalia asserted that considerations about the effects of lead on the male reproductive system and whether or not women would be unable to perform their job duties safely were irrelevant to the decision. He said that the Pregnancy Discrimination Act of 1978, which amended Title VII, required a decision that the fetal protection policy was illegal gender discrimination, and that under the terms of this act, pregnant women, as well as men, have the right to decide whether to take jobs that might place their children at risk. On the other hand, he agreed with White's concurrence that the majority had gone too far in its assertion that concerns about increased costs were not a sufficient BFOQ defense. "The Court goes far afield . . . in suggesting that increased cost alone—short of 'costs . . . so prohibitive as to threaten survival of the employer's business,' cannot support a BFOQ defense" (499 U.S. at 224).

INTERNATIONAL UNION, UAW v. JOHNSON CONTROLS, INC.

499 U.S. 187, 111 S.Ct. 1196, 113 L. Ed. 2d 158 (1991)

■ Johnson Controls, Inc., a manufacturer of batteries, adopted a broad fetal protection policy. Such policies have been created after medical evidence suggested that exposure to toxic substances is harmful to a developing fetus. The policy in question in this case generally excluded women of childbearing capability from company jobs where they would be exposed to lead. Women of childbearing capability were defined as "all women except those whose inability to bear children is medically documented" (499 U.S. at 192). Three employees of the company, two women and one man, filed a class-action suit in federal district court, alleging that the policy was sex discrimination in violation of Title VII of the Civil Rights Act. Mary Craig, one of the two women, became sterilized in order to keep her job, while the other woman, Elsie Nason, a 50-year-old divorcee, suffered a reduction in pay when she was transferred out of a job where she was exposed to lead. The male litigant, Donald Penney, applied for a leave of absence so that he could lower the level of lead in his body because he planned to become a father. His request was denied. Johnson Controls prevailed in district court on the basis of a "business necessity" defense, rather than the more stringent "bona fide occupational qualification" test. The federal court of appeals affirmed this ruling, deciding, however, that the company met the "bona fide occupational qualification" standard as well as the "business necessity" defense. The employees appealed to the Supreme Court.

In reading this case, ask yourselves these questions: (1) Should business necessity ever be a legitimate reason for discrimination on the basis of gender or other factors like race and religion? (2) Do you think that careful, non-negligent behavior by employers in this kind of situation will protect them against lawsuits?

VOTE:

9-0 to strike down the fetal protection policy. (Blackmun, Marshall, O'Connor, Stevens, Souter, White, Kennedy, Rehnquist, Scalia).

Justice Blackmun, joined by Justices Marshall, O'Connor, Stevens, and Souter, delivered the opinion of the Court.

In this case we are concerned with an employer's gender-based fetal-protection policy. May an employer exclude a fertile female employee from certain jobs because of its concern for the health of the fetus the woman might conceive?

Respondent Johnson Controls, Inc., manufactures batteries. In the manufacturing process, the element lead is a primary ingredient. Occupational exposure to lead entails health risks, including the risk of harm to any fetus carried by a female employee.

Before the Civil Rights Act of 1964 became law, Johnson Controls did not employ any woman in a battery-manufacturing job. In June 1977, however, it announced its first official policy concerning its employment of women in lead-exposure work:. . .

. . . [In this policy] Johnson Controls "stopped short of excluding women capable of bearing children from lead exposure" but emphasized that a woman who expected to have a child should not choose a job in which she would have such exposure. The company also required a woman who wished to be considered for employment to sign a statement that she had been advised of the risk of having a child while she was exposed to lead. . . .

Five years later, in 1982, Johnson Controls shifted from a policy of warning to a policy of exclusion. Between 1979 and 1983, eight employees became pregnant while maintaining blood lead levels in excess of 30 micrograms per deciliter. This appeared to be the critical level noted by the Occupational Health and Safety Administration (OSHA) for a worker who was planning to have a family. The company responded by announcing a broad exclusion of women from jobs that exposed them to lead:

> . . . [I]t is [Johnson Controls'] policy that women who are pregnant or who are capable of bearing children will not be placed into jobs involving lead exposure or which could expose them to lead through the exercise of job bidding, bumping, transfer or promotion rights.

The policy defined "women . . . capable of bearing children" as "[a]ll women except those whose inability to bear children is medically documented." It further stated that an unacceptable work station was one where, "over the past year," an employee had recorded a blood lead level of more than 30 micrograms per deciliter or the work site had yielded an air sample containing a lead level in excess of 30 micrograms per cubic meter.

In April 1984, petitioners filed in the United States District Court for the Eastern District of Wisconsin a class action challenging Johnson Controls' fetal-protection policy as sex discrimination that violated Title VII of the Civil Rights Act of 1964, as amended. . . .

* * *

The bias in Johnson Controls' policy is obvious. Fertile men, but not fertile women, are given a choice as to whether they wish to risk their reproductive health for a particular job. Section 703(a) of the Civil Rights Act of 1964 prohibits sex-based classifications in terms and conditions of employment, in hiring and discharging decisions, and in other employment decisions that adversely affect an employee's status. Respondent's fetal-protection policy explicitly discriminates against women on the basis of their sex. The policy excludes women with childbearing capacity from lead-exposed jobs and so creates a facial classification based on gender. Respondent assumes as much in its brief before this Court.

Nevertheless, the Court of Appeals assumed, as did the two appellate courts who already had confronted the issue, that sex-specific fetal-protection policies do not involve facial discrimination. These courts analyzed the policies as though they were facially neutral, and had only a discriminatory effect upon the employment opportunities of women. Consequently, the courts looked to see if each employer in question had established that its policy was justified as a business necessity. The business necessity standard is more lenient for the employer than the statutory BFOQ defense. The Court of Appeals here went one step further and invoked the burden-shifting framework set forth in *Wards Cove Packing Co. v. Atonio,* thus requiring petitioners to bear the burden of persuasion on all questions. The court assumed that because the asserted reason for the sex-based exclusion (protecting women's unconceived offspring) was ostensibly benign, the policy was not sex-based discrimination. That assumption, however, was incorrect.

First, Johnson Controls' policy classifies on the basis of gender and childbearing capacity, rather than fertility alone. Respondent does not seek to protect the unconceived children of all its employees. Despite evidence in the record about the debilitating effect of lead exposure on the male reproductive system, Johnson Controls is concerned only with the harms that may befall the unborn offspring of its female employees. . . . Johnson Controls' policy is facially discriminatory because it requires only a female employee to produce proof that she is not capable of reproducing.

Our conclusion is bolstered by the Pregnancy Discrimination Act of 1978 (PDA), in which Congress explicitly provided that, for purposes of Title VII, discrimination "on the basis of sex" includes discrimination "because of or on the basis of pregnancy, childbirth, or related medical conditions." "The Pregnancy Discrimination Act has now made clear that, for all Title VII purposes, discrimination based on a woman's pregnancy is, on its face, discrimination because of her sex."

* * *

Under section 703(e)(1) of Title VII, an employer may discriminate on the basis of "religion, sex, or national origin in those certain instances where religion, sex, or national origin is a bona fide occupational qualification reasonably necessary to the normal operation of that particular business or enterprise." We therefore turn to the question whether Johnson Controls' fetal-protection policy is one of those "certain instances" that come within the BFOQ exception.

* * *

The wording of the BFOQ defense contains several terms of restriction that indicate that the exception reaches only special situations. The statute thus limits the situations in which discrimination is permissible to "certain instances" where sex discrimination is "reasonably necessary" to the "normal operation" of the "particular" business. . . .

* * *

Johnson Controls argues that its fetal-protection policy falls within the so-called safety exception to the BFOQ. Our cases have stressed that discrimination on the basis of sex because of safety concerns is allowed only in narrow circumstances. . . .

* * *

Our case law . . . makes clear that the safety exception is limited to instances in which sex or pregnancy actually interferes with the employees's ability to perform the job. This approach is consistent with the language of the BFOQ provision itself, for it suggests that permissible distinctions based on sex must relate to ability to perform the duties of the job. . . .

* * *

We have no difficulty concluding that Johnson Controls cannot establish a BFOQ. Fertile women, as far as appears in the record, participate in the manufacture of batteries as efficiently as anyone else. Johnson Controls' professed moral and ethical concerns about the welfare of the next generation do not suffice to establish a BFOQ of female sterility. Decisions about the welfare of future children must be left to the parents who conceive, bear, support, and raise them rather than to the employers who hire those parents. Congress has mandated this choice through Title VII, as amended by the Pregnancy Discrimination Act. Johnson Controls has attempted to exclude women because of their reproductive capacity. Title VII and the PDA simply do not allow a woman's dismissal because of her failure to submit to sterilization.

* * *

A word about tort liability and the increased cost of fertile women in the workplace is perhaps necessary. One of the dissenting judges in this case expressed concern about an employer's tort liability and concluded that liability for a potential injury to a fetus is a social cost that Title VII does not require a company to ignore. It is correct to say that Title VII does not prevent the employer from having a conscience. The statute, however, does prevent sex-specific fetal-protection policies. These two aspects of Title VII do not conflict.

More than 40 States currently recognize a right to recover for a prenatal injury based either on negligence or on wrongful death. According to Johnson Controls, however, the company complies with the lead standard developed by OSHA and warns its female employees about the damaging effects of lead. . . . If, under general tort principles, Title VII bans sex-specific fetal-protection policies, the employer fully informs the woman of the risk, and the employer has not acted negligently, the basis for holding an employer liable seems remote at best.

* * *

Our holding today that Title VII, as so amended, forbids sex-specific fetal-protection policies is neither remarkable nor unprecedented. Concern for a woman's existing or potential offspring historically has been the excuse for denying women equal employment opportunities. Congress in the PDA prohibited discrimination on the basis of a woman's ability to become pregnant. We do no more than hold that the Pregnancy Discrimination Act means what it says.

It is no more appropriate for the courts than it is for individual employers to decide whether a woman's reproductive role is more important to herself and her family than her economic role. Congress has left this choice to the woman as hers to make.

The judgment of the Court of Appeals is reversed and the case is remanded for further proceedings consistent with this opinion.

It is so ordered.

Justice White, with whom Chief Justice Rehnquist and Justice Kennedy join, concurring in part and concurring in the judgment.

The Court properly holds that Johnson Controls' fetal protection policy overtly discriminates against women, and thus is prohibited by Title VII unless it falls within the bona fide occupational qualification (BFOQ) exception. The Court erroneously holds, however, that the BFOQ defense is so narrow that it could never justify a sex-specific fetal protection policy. I nevertheless concur in the judgment of reversal because on the record before us summary judgment in favor of Johnson Controls was improperly entered by the District Court and affirmed by the Court of Appeals.

In evaluating the scope of the BFOQ defense, the proper starting point is the language of the statute. Title VII forbids discrimination on the basis of sex, except "in those certain instances where . . . sex . . . is a bona fide occupational qualification reasonably necessary to the normal operation of that particular business or enterprise." For the fetal protection policy involved in this case to be a BFOQ, therefore, the policy must be "reasonably necessary" to the "normal operation" of making batteries, which is Johnson Controls' "particular business." Although that is a difficult standard to satisfy, nothing in the statute's language indicates that it could *never* support a sex-specific fetal protection policy.

On the contrary, a fetal protection policy would be justified under the terms of the statute if, for example, an employer could show that exclusion of women from certain jobs was reasonably necessary to avoid substantial tort liability. Common sense tells us that it is part of the normal operation of business concerns to avoid causing injury to third parties, as well as to employees, if for no other reason than to avoid tort liability and its substantial costs. This possibility of tort liability is not hypothetical; every State currently allows children born alive to recover in tort for prenatal injuries caused by third parties, and an increasing number of courts have recognized a right to recover even for prenatal injuries caused by torts committed prior to conception.

The Court dismisses the possibility of tort liability by no more than speculating that if "Title VII bans sex-specific fetal-protection policies, the employer fully informs the woman of the risk, and the employer has not acted negligently, the basis for holding an employer liable seems remote at best." Such speculation will be small comfort to employers. First, it is far from clear that compliance with Title VII will pre-empt state tort liability, and the Court offers no support for that proposition. Second, although warnings may preclude claims by injured *employees,* they will not preclude claims by injured children because the general rule is that parents cannot waive causes of action on behalf of their children, and the parents' negligence will not be imputed to the children. Finally, although state tort liability for prenatal injuries generally requires negligence, it will be difficult for employers to determine in advance what will constitute negligence. . . .

* * *

Prior decisions construing the BFOQ defense confirm that the defense is broad enough to include considerations of cost and safety of the sort that could form the basis for an employer's adoption of a fetal protection policy. . . .

* * *

In enacting the BFOQ standard, "Congress did not ignore the public interest in safety." The Court's narrow interpretation of the BFOQ defense in this case, however, means that an employer cannot exclude even *pregnant* women from an environment highly toxic to their fetuses. It is foolish to think that Congress intended such a result, and neither the language of the BFOQ exception nor our cases require it.

* * *

Justice Scalia, concurring in the judgment.

I generally agree with the Court's analysis, but have some reservations, several of which bear mention.

First, I think it irrelevant that there was "evidence in the record about the debilitating effect of lead exposure on the male reproductive system." Even without such evidence, treating women differently "on the basis of pregnancy" constitutes discrimination "on the basis of sex," because Congress has unequivocally said so.

Second, the Court points out that "Johnson Controls has shown no factual basis for believing that all or substantially all women would be unable to perform safely . . . the duties of the job involved." In my view, this is . . . entirely irrelevant. By reason of the Pregnancy Discrimination Act, it would not matter if all pregnant women placed their children at risk in taking these jobs, just as it does not matter if no men do so. . . .

* * *

Last, the Court goes far afield, it seems to me, in suggesting that increased cost alone—short of "costs . . . so prohibitive as to threaten survival of the employer's business," cannot support a BFOQ defense. I agree with Justice White's concurrence, that nothing in our prior cases suggests this, and in my view it is wrong. I think, for example, that a shipping company may refuse to hire pregnant women as crew members on long voyages because the on-board facilities for foreseeable emergencies, though quite feasible, would be inordinately expensive. In the present case, however, Johnson has not asserted a cost-based BFOQ.

I concur in the judgment of the Court.

Unlike Justices Kennedy and Souter, Clarence Thomas did not have the opportunity to participate in a *major* gender discrimination case during his first term. Because he had been an outspoken critic of the Court's liberal decisions in civil rights cases, most legal observers expected him to join the Court's conservative wing on gender discrimination issues. In addition, as a judge on the U.S. Court of Appeals for the District of Columbia Circuit, Thomas wrote a majority opinion which held that an FCC policy that gave preferences to women in the awarding of some broadcast licenses was unconstitutional (*Lamprecht v. FCC,* 1991). Therefore, his position in the relatively minor case of *Franklin v. Gwinnett County Public Schools* (1992) was not surprising. Thomas joined in a unanimous judgment that Title IX permits the award of monetary damages for sexual harassment of students in public schools.

The Rehnquist Court heard no gender discrimination cases in its 1992–93 term. At the end of that term, Justice White retired and was succeeded by federal appellate judge Ruth Bader Ginsburg, who earlier had been the chief litigator in gender discrimination cases for the Women's Rights Project of the ACLU. In Justice Ginsburg's first term, the Court decided two cases involving gender equality issues. In *Harris v. Forklift Systems* (1993), the Court unanimously ruled that litigants pursuing "hostile environment" sexual harassment claims under Title VII need not prove pyschological injury in order to win monetary damages. Justice O'Connor wrote, "So long as the environment would reasonably be perceived, and is perceived, as hostile or abusive, there is no need for it also to be psychologically injurious" (114 S.Ct. at 371). Justice Ginsburg joined a six-member majority which held that the Equal Protection Clause prohibits the systematic gender-based application of peremptory challenges to potential jurors (*J.E.B. v. Alabama ex rel. T.B.,* 1994). This was an extension of the *Batson v. Kentucky* (1986) line of cases prohibiting racial discrimination in jury selection.

Conclusion

At this point, the Rehnquist Court's position on gender discrimination issues is comparable to that of its immediate predecessor, the Burger Court. Both the quantitative and the doctrinal analyses indicate that the Court has not engaged in a conservative counterrevolution in this area in its first nine terms. The Court has favored individual claimants in the majority of gender discrimination cases that it has heard, and a strong liberal bloc has existed on the Court with respect to these cases. In addition, the Court has not overturned any of the liberal precedents of the Burger Court.

With the retirements of Justices Brennan, Marshall, and Blackmun, however, the liberal bloc on the Rehnquist Court has been diminished. At the same time, the concurrences and dissents in *California Federal, Price Waterhouse,* and *Johnson Controls* seem to indicate that some Rehnquist Court justices would prefer a more conservative interpretation of civil rights statutes and precedents. Therefore, future personnel changes on the Court could result in a serious reexamination and revision of some of the liberal precedents in the area of gender discrimination.

REFERENCES

Cortner, Richard C. *The Supreme Court and Civil Liberties Policy.* Palo Alto: Mayfield Publishing Company, 1975.

Goldstein, Leslie F. *The Constitutional Rights of Women: Cases in Law and Social Change.* 2d ed. Madison: The University of Wisconsin Press, 1988.

Hoff, Joan. *Law, Gender, and Injustice: A Legal History of U.S. Women.* New York: New York University Press, 1991.

Mezey, Susan Gluck. *In Pursuit of Equality: Women, Public Policy and the Federal Courts.* New York: St. Martin's Press, 1992.

O'Connor, Karen. "Gender." In *The Oxford Companion to the Supreme Court of the United States.* Edited by Kermit L. Hall, 328–35. New York: Oxford University Press, 1992.

CHAPTER

15 AFFIRMATIVE ACTION

CASE STUDY

REGENTS OF THE UNIVERSITY OF CALIFORNIA V. BAKKE (1978)

In many respects, Allan Bakke was the epitome of the American dream, illustrating the widely held belief that hard work and perseverance lead to success. He came from a middle-class family, in which his father was a mail carrier and his mother was a teacher. After graduating from high school, Bakke attended the University of Minnesota where he majored in mechanical engineering, graduating with a 3.5 grade point average. He was able to attend college with financial assistance from the Naval Reserve Officers Training Corps (ROTC), and upon graduation he joined the Marine Corps to fulfill his obligations. During his tenure in the marines, Bakke spent several months in Vietnam as commander of an antiaircraft missile unit. When he returned home from his military service, he became employed as an aerospace engineer at the Ames Research Center, a NASA laboratory near Palo Alto, California (Lindsey 1977; Wilkinson 1979).

Bakke's work at the NASA research center brought him into contact with a number of physicians who had combined their medical expertise with engineering. It was at this time that he decided that he really wanted to become a medical doctor. After making this decision, he spent his nonwork hours taking courses in biology and chemistry and working as a hospital emergency room volunteer in preparation for applying to medical school. Thus, Bakke was not the typical student seeking a medical degree when he applied for admission to medical school in 1973. At thirty-three years of age, with military service behind him and with a career in engineering, he was what we now refer to as a nontraditional student. At the time of application, Bakke was well aware that his age would be the primary barrier against his admission to medical school.

In attempting to fulfill his dream, Bakke applied to almost a dozen medical schools, but he was rejected by all of them. He was most angry, however, at being rejected by the University of California, Davis. After applying there, he was invited for an interview, which went very well, except that the faculty member who conducted the interview could sense Bakke's frustration when he asked him why he wanted to switch fields from engineering to medicine. Nonetheless, the faculty member was generally impressed with Bakke, and he recommended his admission to the school. Unfortunately for Bakke, his application was rejected. Admission was based on the applicant's grade point average, letters of recommendation, an essay, scores on the Medical School Admissions Test (MCAT), and the interview. A point scale was constructed using these items, where the highest possible score was 500 points. Bakke's rating was 468, but it was two points shy of the threshold score of 470 for automatic admission. Although some candidates with scores lower than 470 were admitted, Bakke was not one of them. After receiving a rejection letter, Bakke wrote to the chair of the admissions committee, Dr. George Lowrey, to ask for reconsideration of his application. After a month went by and he received no response, he wrote again. Lowrey did not respond, but he instructed one of his assistants to do so (Lindsey 1977).

At some point during the application process, Bakke discovered that the university had established a special admissions program that reserved 16 of the 100 total seats for minority applicants. He also learned that his undergraduate grades and scores on the medical school admissions tests were higher than those of the applicants admitted under this special program. Thus, in this second letter, Bakke was very critical of the special admissions program, and he indicated to the chair that he was considering pursuing legal action against the university.

The records indicate that Bakke received some information about the special program and his ranking from Lowrey's assistant, Peter Storandt, who served as an admissions counselor. Bakke's situation struck a nerve in Storandt, who was upset not only about the special admissions program but also about the practice of awarding admissions on the basis of friendship and political connections. In fact, he estimated that about a dozen slots were awarded on this basis to students who otherwise would not have qualified for admission. Moreover, he indicated that faculty members did not hold these students in high regard, and they did not view them as very skilled physicians upon graduation. At the same time, however, Storandt noted that many of the students admitted under the special program went on to do very well in their studies.

Nonetheless, Storandt's anger about the special admissions program weighed heavily on his mind, and he was determined to help Bakke gain admittance. He told him how close he had come to being accepted, and he encouraged him to reapply under the early admissions program. If that course of action failed, then Bakke was to file a lawsuit challenging the special admissions program. This is precisely what happened. Bakke's second application was also rejected, and he subsequently filed suit in a California court claiming that the special admissions program violated state and federal laws against discrimination. The attorney for the State Board of Regents argued, among other things, that Bakke would not have been admitted even without the special admissions program because other applicants with higher rankings than his were also rejected. Bakke's attorney, Reynold Colvin, said the only reason he was rejected was because of his race. In a twenty-three-page opinion, the trial judge agreed with both parties, ruling that the special admissions program was illegal, but denying Bakke admission because he did not prove that the program was the reason for his rejection. Both sides appealed the trial court's ruling, and the appeal bypassed the first appellate court and went directly to the California Supreme Court. In a 6-1 decision, the state supreme court held the program unconstitutional and ordered Bakke's admission to the medical school.

At this point, serious disagreement arose among supporters of the special admissions program over what course of action the Board of Regents should take. Some groups encouraged the Regents *not* to pursue the case further because its position was too weak, and a negative U.S. Supreme Court decision would endanger affirmative action programs across the country. Other groups argued that the Regents had a moral obligation to take the case to the Supreme Court; and furthermore, if they did not, it would become an excuse for universities to get rid of these programs altogether. The Regents decided to pursue the case, and after the Supreme Court agreed to grant certiorari, Bakke's admission was stayed pending review of the case.

By this time, the *Bakke* case had generated attention all over the country. Affirmative action had been labeled by its opponents as reverse discrimination against whites, and Allan Bakke became the symbol for those white males who alleged that they were now the targets of discrimination. The Court's decision was going to be significant and far reaching, because it would affect similar programs established at other universities and especially professional schools.

In addition to higher education, affirmative action programs were being considered and initiated by the federal government and by other public and private employers. Thus, the Court's decision could provide guidance to these employers regarding the general legality of such programs, as well as the form such programs might take if they were generally legal.

Given the significance of this case, it should not be surprising that the Court received a substantial number of amicus briefs attempting to persuade the justices in deciding the case. Most of the briefs were in support of the special admissions program, filed on behalf of such diverse organizations as the American Bar Association, the Association of American Medical Colleges, the NAACP Legal Defense and Education Fund, the

American Civil Liberties Union, the National Council of Churches, the National Education Association, Harvard University, Stanford University, and the United Auto Workers. Briefs supporting Alan Bakke were filed by several organizations, including such major groups as the Anti-Defamation League of B'nai B'rith, the American Jewish Committee, the American Federation of Teachers, the Chamber of Commerce, and the Fraternal Order of Police.

Oral argument was held on October 12, 1977. As he did at previous court levels, Reynold Colvin presented Bakke's case to the Supreme Court, while the Board of Regents secured the services of Archibald Cox, the former Watergate special prosecutor, to argue its case. In addition, the Court permitted the U.S. solicitor general, Wade McCree, to present arguments on behalf of the federal government.

Cox's presentation came first. He justified the special admissions program on several grounds, including the importance of racial diversity for both minority and nonminority students and faculty and the need for minority role models. When asked whether the program's designation of sixteen places for minority applicants was a quota, Cox replied that it was a "set-aside," not a quota. "[T]his was not pointing the finger at a group which had been marked as inferior in any sense, and it was not undifferentiated, it operated against a wide variety of people. So I think it was not stigmatizing in the sense that the old quota against Jews was stigmatizing, in any way" (Irons and Guitton 1993, pp. 307–8). This response did not satisfy the justices, and some justices continued to press the quota issue.

After Cox concluded his presentation, McCree came forward. He gave a brief history of racial discrimination and its continuing effects, and he stressed the importance of race-conscious affirmative action programs in rectifying this problem. Although he voiced his support of affirmative action in general, he indicated his opposition to strict quotas.

Unlike Cox and McCree, who gave considerable attention to societal concerns, Colvin focused primarily on individual rights. He argued that Bakke's qualifications for admission to medical school were greater than those of the students admitted under the special program. In fact, he spent so much time reciting the facts of the case that Justice Powell admonished him to move on to the constitutional issues. When he did so, Colvin contended that the Fourteenth Amendment simply did not allow for this racial classification. Justice Marshall, the Court's lone African American, asked him whether the university could reserve even one seat for minority applicants. His negative response led to a heated exchange between the two.

> *Marshall:* You are talking about your client's rights. Don't these underprivileged people have some rights?
>
> *Colvin:* They certainly have the right to compete. . . .
>
> *Marshall:* To eat cake. (Irons and Guitton 1993, p. 313)

This exchange marked the end of oral argument.

Over eight months later, on June 28, 1978, the Court finally issued its ruling on the validity of the Davis special admissions program (case excerpt on p. 718). It was a complex decision, with a serious split among the justices. One group of four, made up of Chief Justice Burger and Justices Stewart, Rehnquist, and Stevens, voted to strike down the program, while a second group of four, consisting of Justices Brennan, White, Marshall, and Blackmun, voted to uphold the special admissions program. Justice Powell provided the deciding vote. He agreed with the first plurality that the Davis program was invalid, but at the same time he joined the second plurality in concluding that race or ethnicity can be considered as a factor in admissions decisions.

A major shortcoming of the Court's decision, however, was that the justices could not agree on the appropriate standard for reviewing affirmative action or race-conscious programs. Justice Powell and the Brennan plurality both decided the case on equal protection (Fourteenth Amendment) grounds. Nonetheless, Powell utilized strict scrutiny, while Brennan argued that the important government objective test, an intermediate level of scrutiny, was the appropriate approach. The Stevens plurality, avoiding the equal protection question altogether, decided the case on statutory grounds, holding that Title VI of the Civil Rights Act prohibits racial discrimination in programs receiving federal financial assistance. As we will see in the remainder of this chapter, this problem is one that persisted far beyond the *Bakke* case.

In conclusion, while the Court's decision provided some insight into the validity of affirmative action, *Bakke* did not resolve this controversial issue. It was merely the beginning of a complex and sometimes confusing series of rulings on race-conscious (and later gender-conscious) affirmative action programs.

Historic Origins and Contemporary Conflicts

As *Bakke* illustrates, affirmative action has been one of the most controversial issues in this country since the Vietnam War. This concept, which has evoked a hostile response from its opponents, grew out of the Civil Rights Movement of the 1950s and 1960s. After passage of the Civil Rights Act of 1964, which prohibited racial discrimination in employment, public accommodations, and the like, civil rights advocates argued that additional, positive steps were necessary to address the inequalities that remained after legal discrimination was prohibited. President Johnson lent support to this idea when he issued Executive Order 11246 in 1965. This order, while not referring specifically to affirmative action, forbade those contracting with the federal government from discriminating on the basis of race, religion, or national origin. One year later, the Office of Federal Contract Compliance (OFCC) was created to monitor compliance with this executive order. In 1968, the OFCC issued regulations requiring federal contractors with fifty or more employees and contracts worth $50,000 or more to establish written affirmative action plans. The following year, such contractors were ordered to set goals and timetables for the recruitment and hiring of minority workers (Mezey 1992). Thus, affirmative action was not applied throughout the private sector but only to recipients of lucrative federal contracts.

After this initial development by the federal government, affirmative action was expanded to other areas. State and local governments, graduate and professional schools, and private employers instituted various forms of affirmative action. These included recruitment of minorities as well as goals for increasing minority representation in higher education and employment. Some of these programs were voluntarily established, others came in response to specific claims of discrimination, and some were mandated by the courts upon findings of discrimination. Affirmative action originally pertained to African Americans, but later was extended to include some other American minority groups and nonminority women.

Those advocating affirmative action offered several reasons why it was needed. The most basic reason pointed to affirmative action as a form of compensatory justice, that is, compensating African Americans for centuries of discrimination and unequal treatment. Some proponents viewed affirmative action as a necessary extension of civil rights activities. They said that while Title VII of the Civil Rights Act of 1964 prohibited future employment discrimination, this alone was insufficient to increase the representation of African Americans in various occupations. They pointed to such policies and practices as personal connections and seniority rules, which appeared to be race-neutral but often had discriminatory effects. In the absence of positive steps taken to alter these arrangements, the continuing effects of past discrimination would remain unabated. For example, studies have shown that most jobs, especially those that are higher paying, are found through personal contacts and informal networks. Because most African Americans lacked access to these information systems, high levels of black unemployment and underemployment would persist. Thus affirmative action advocates maintained that aggressive advertising, recruitment, and outreach efforts were necessary to remedy this problem. They pointed out that such actions also would benefit those whites who found themselves outside of job information loops.

While concluding that increased advertising, recruitment, and outreach efforts were important in remedying the effects of discrimination, affirmative action proponents did not view these as completely sufficient. They emphasized that in order to measure progress in this area, employers needed to develop specific goals and timetables for hiring and promoting African American employees. Such goals and timetables were not to be the same for every employer, but would be developed according to the specific employment situations of each.

Affirmative action came under increasing attack from many whites who believed that affirmative action amounted to "reverse discrimination" against them. They said that affirmative action programs were inconsistent with the American ideal of a "color-blind" society and that such programs conflicted with the idea that rewards and opportunities should be based on "merit." In response to these arguments, proponents of affirmative action contended that American society had never been "color-blind," and that rewards and opportunities were not always distributed on the basis of "merit," but on the basis of nepotism, patronage, and so on.

Opponents of this concept succeeded in bringing a number of legal challenges to affirmative action programs. Several of these cases made their way to the Supreme Court for decision, beginning in the late 1970s. The Court has been called upon to decide affirmative action disputes involving admission to educational institutions, government subcontracting, and employment practices related to hiring, promotions, and layoffs. These disputes have involved affirmative action programs of educational institutions, as well as those of public and private employers. The legal challenges to affirmative action have come under the Fourteenth Amendment Equal Protection Clause, the Fifth Amendment Due Process Clause, as well as various provisions of the Civil Rights Act of 1964. In the next sections, then, we will examine the Court's treatment of this controversial issue.

Supreme Court Decision Making in Affirmative Action Cases Decided under the Equal Protection Clause

The Court has had great difficulty agreeing upon an appropriate standard for examining affirmative action programs challenged under the Equal Protection Clause. In the 1978 *Bakke* decision, Justice Powell used strict scrutiny, the Brennan plurality advocated intermediate scrutiny, and the Stevens plurality completely avoided equal protection analysis. With strict scrutiny, an affirmative action plan would be upheld only if it were narrowly tailored to achieve a compelling interest. Under intermediate scrutiny, an affirmative action program would be valid if it were substantially related to achieving an important government interest.

Neither standard commanded a majority until 1989. In *Richmond v. J.A. Croson Co.,* which involved a local government's affirmative action plan, a narrow majority held that affirmative action plans were to be examined under strict scrutiny. One year later, however, in *Metro Broadcasting, Inc. v. FCC* (1990), a 5-4 majority used intermediate scrutiny in upholding an affirmative action program established by the Federal Communications Commission, an entity of the federal government. The result of these two decisions was that no *single* standard applied to affirmative action programs established by governmental bodies. Plans adopted by the federal government were to be analyzed under intermediate scrutiny, while strict scrutiny would be applied to those created by state and local governments. Five years after *Metro Broadcasting,* however, in *Adarand Constructors v. Pena* (1995), the Court changed course again. A narrow majority ruled that affirmative action plans established by the federal government must be examined under strict scrutiny as well.

Burger Court Era

As it became clear that challenges to affirmative action would reach the Supreme Court, advocates and opponents of affirmative action, along with legal commentators, speculated about the Court's response to these programs. Four of the Court's members—Warren Burger, Harry Blackmun, Lewis Powell, and William Rehnquist—had been appointed by President Nixon. Because none of these four had strong liberal records in the area of civil rights, it was questionable whether the Court would give approval to affirmative action programs. Furthermore, by the mid 1970s, it was obvious that the Burger Court was not as liberal in its racial discrimination decisions as was its predecessor. For example, while the Burger Court continued to order desegregation of schools that were segregated by law (de jure), it limited the power of the government, especially the federal courts, to remedy de facto school segregation. In addition, unlike its predecessor, the Burger Court was less likely to permit the government to use its powers to prohibit private discrimination (*Moose Lodge v. Irvis* 1972).

The Burger Court's record in this area is mixed, much like its record in racial discrimination cases in general. The Court approved of affirmative action in five of the seven cases it heard, but those cases were decided by narrow votes (5-4, 5-2, and 6-3). Thus, although the Burger Court upheld affirmative action in most of its cases, at no time did a decision amass more than six votes. In addition, even when a majority voted in favor of affirmative action, the justices were so badly divided on the reasoning that it was difficult to predict how future cases would be decided.

The Early Cases

The first time that affirmative action came to the Court, the justices were able to avoid the issue by invoking a technical rule of mootness. In *DeFunis v. Odegaard* (1974), Marco DeFunis, a white student, was denied admission to the University of Washington Law School. He alleged that minority applicants with lesser qualifications, primarily lower grades and lower scores on the Law School Admissions Test (LSAT), were admitted to the school, and this was a violation of the Equal Protection Clause. The university responded by arguing that factors other than grades and test scores were taken into consideration in admissions decisions, and that it could take steps to expand opportunities for minorities to enter the legal profession given their lack of access in the past. A state trial court ruled in favor of DeFunis and ordered his admission to the law school in 1971, but the state supreme court reversed that ruling. Subsequently, DeFunis appealed to the U.S. Supreme Court, which accepted the case for review. DeFunis, however, was allowed to remain in school, pending disposition of the appeal. By the time the Court considered the case in 1974, DeFunis was in his last year of law school and was presumed to be assured of graduating, so the Court dismissed the case on the grounds that the case was moot. Justices Brennan, Douglas, Marshall, and White dissented from the ruling of mootness, asserting that the case should have been given full consideration.

Although the Court was able to sidestep this issue in 1974, affirmative action returned to the Court four years later in *Regents of the University of California v. Bakke* (1978). (See the case study at the beginning of this chapter for a detailed discussion of the case.)

The Court made a confusing 5-4 decision, with Justice Powell's vote determining the outcome. Powell joined a plurality consisting of Chief Justice Burger, and Justices Rehnquist, Stevens, and Stewart in holding the special admissions program invalid, but he agreed with the other plurality of Justices Brennan, White, Marshall, and Blackmun that race or ethnicity could be a legitimate factor in the admissions process. While setting aside a specific number of seats for minority applicants was unconstitutional, race or ethnicity may be considered a "plus" in admissions considerations, but it may not be the only factor.

Regents of the University of California v. Bakke

438 U.S. 265, 98 S. Ct 2733, 57 .L Ed. 2d 750 (1978)
[The facts of this case are omitted because they were presented in the case study at the beginning of the chapter.]

■ This case is important because it represents the Court's first decision on the validity of affirmative action programs. As you read the case, consider the following questions: (1) Is Justice Powell correct in concluding that all racial classifications are related to personal or individual rights rather than membership in a particular group? (2) Would Justice Powell and the Stevens' plurality have decided the case differently had the medical school been found guilty of practicing discrimination? (3) Why is diversity a stronger justification in Powell's view than the other justifications presented by the medical school? (4) Which test is most appropriate for examining this case—strict scrutiny or intermediate scrutiny?

Vote:

4 justices held that the special admissions program was unlawful (Burger, Stewart, Rehnquist, and Stevens).

4 justices held that the special admissions program was valid (Brennan, White, Marshall, and Blackmun).

1 justice held that the special admissions program was invalid but that race could be considered as a factor in the admissions process (Powell).

Justice Powell announced the judgment of the Court.

* * *

Petitioner does not deny that decisions based on race or ethnic origin by faculties and administrations of state universities are reviewable under the Fourteenth Amendment. For his part, respondent does not argue that all racial or ethnic classifications are *per se* invalid. The parties do disagree as to the level of judicial scrutiny to be applied to the special admissions program. Petitioner argues that the court below erred in applying strict scrutiny, as this inexact term has been applied in our cases. That level of review, petitioner asserts, should be reserved for classifications that disadvantage "discrete and insular minorities." Respondent, on the other hand, contends that the California court correctly rejected the notion that the degree of judicial scrutiny accorded a particular racial or ethnic classification hinges upon membership in a discrete and insular minority and duly recognized that the "rights established [by the Fourteenth Amendment] are personal rights."

* * *

The guarantees of the Fourteenth Amendment extend to all persons. Its language is explicit: "No State shall . . . deny to any person within its jurisdiction the equal protection of the laws." It is settled beyond question that the "rights created by the first section of the Fourteenth Amendment are, by its terms, guaranteed to the individual. The rights established are personal rights." The guarantee of equal protection cannot mean one thing when applied to one individual and something else when applied to a person of another color. If both are not accorded the same protection, then it is not equal.

* * *

* * * Racial and ethnic distinctions of any sort are inherently suspect and thus call for the most exacting judicial examination.

* * *

Petitioner urges us to adopt for the first time a more restrictive view of the Equal Protection Clause and hold that discrimination against members of the white "majority" cannot be suspect if its purpose can be characterized as "benign." The clock of our liberties, however, cannot be turned back to 1868. It is far too late to argue that the guarantee of equal protection to *all* persons permits the recognition of special wards entitled to a degree of protection greater than that accorded others. "The Fourteenth Amendment is not directed solely against discrimination due to a 'two-class theory'—that is, based upon differences between 'white' and Negro."

* * *

We have held that in "order to justify the use of a suspect classification, a State must show that its purpose or interest is both constitutionally permissible and substantial, and that its use of the classification is 'necessary . . . to the accomplishment' of its purpose or the safeguarding of its interest." The special admissions program purports to serve the purposes of: (i) "reducing the historic deficit of traditionally disfavored minorities in medical schools and in the medical profession"; (ii) countering the effects of societal discrimination; (iii) increasing the number of physicians who will practice in communities currently underserved; and (iv) obtaining the educational benefits that flow from an ethnically diverse student body. It is necessary to decide which, if any, of these purposes is substantial enough to support the use of a suspect classification.

If petitioner's purpose is to assure within its student body some specified percentage of a particular group merely because of its race or ethnic origin, such a preferential purpose must be rejected not as insubstantial but as facially invalid. Preferring members of any one group for no reason other than race or ethnic origin is discrimination for its own sake. This the Constitution forbids.

The State certainly has a legitimate and substantial interest in ameliorating, or eliminating where feasible, the disabling effects of identified discrimination. The line of school desegregation cases, commencing with *Brown*, attests to the importance of this state goal and the commitment of the judiciary to affirm all lawful means toward its attainment. In the school cases, the States were required by court order to redress the wrongs worked by specific instances of racial discrimination. The goal was far more focused than the remedying of the effects of "societal discrimination," an amorphous concept of injury that may be ageless in its reach into the past.

We have never approved a classification that aids persons perceived as members of relatively victimized groups at the expense of other innocent individuals in the absence of judicial, legislative, or administrative findings of constitutional or statutory violations. After such findings have been made, the governmental interest in preferring members of the injured groups at the expense of others is substantial, since the legal rights of the victims must be vindicated. In such a case, the extent of the injury and the consequent remedy will have been judicially, legislatively, or administratively defined. * * *

Petitioner does not purport to have made, and is in no position to make, such findings. Its broad mission is education, not the formulation of any legislative policy or the adjudication of particular claims of illegality- . . . Before relying upon these sorts of findings in establishing a racial classification, a governmental body must have the authority and capability to establish, in the record, that the classification is responsive to identified discrimination. * * *

Hence, the purpose of helping certain groups whom the faculty of the Davis Medical School perceived as victims of "societal discrimination" does not justify a classification that imposes disadvantages upon persons like respondent, who bear no responsibility for whatever harm the beneficiaries of the special admissions program are thought to have suffered. To hold otherwise would be to convert a remedy heretofore reserved for violations of legal rights into a privilege that all institutions throughout the Nation could grant at their pleasure to whatever groups are perceived as victims of societal discrimination. That is a step we have never approved.

Petitioner identifies, as another purpose of its program, improving the delivery of health-care services to communities currently underserved. It may be assumed that in some situations a State's interest in facilitating the health care of its citizens is sufficiently compelling to support the use of a suspect classification. But there is virtually no evidence in the record indicating that petitioner's special admissions program is either needed or geared to promote that goal. * * *

Petitioner simply has not carried its burden of demonstrating that it must prefer members of particular ethnic groups over all other individuals in order to promote better health-care delivery to deprived citizens. Indeed, petitioner has not shown that its preferential classification is likely to have any significant effect on the problem.

The fourth goal asserted by petitioner is the attainment of a diverse student body. This clearly is a constitutionally permissible goal for an institution of higher education. Academic freedom, though not a specifically enumerated constitutional right, long has been viewed as a special concern of the First Amendment. The freedom of a university to make its own judgments as to education includes the selection of its student body. * * *

* * *

* * * The atmosphere of "speculation, experiment and creation"—so essential to the quality of higher education—is widely believed to be promoted by a diverse student body. As the Court noted in *Keyishian* [*v. Board of Regents* (1967)], it is not too much to say that the "nation's future depends upon leaders trained through wide exposure" to the ideas and mores of students as diverse as this Nation of many peoples.

Thus, in arguing that its universities must be accorded the right to select those students who will contribute the most to the "robust exchange of ideas," petitioner invokes a countervailing constitutional interest, that of the First Amendment. In this light, petitioner must be viewed as seeking to achieve a goal that is of paramount importance in the fulfillment of its mission.

It may be argued that there is greater force to these views at the undergraduate level than in a medical school where the training is centered primarily on professional competency. But even at the graduate level, our tradition and experience lend support to the view that the contribution of diversity is substantial. * * * Physicians serve a heterogeneous population. An otherwise qualified medical student with a particular background—whether it be ethnic, geographic, culturally advantaged or disadvantaged—may bring to a professional school of medicine experiences, outlooks, and ideas that enrich the training of its student body and better equip its graduates to render with understanding their vital service to humanity.

Ethnic diversity, however, is only one element in a range of factors a university properly may consider in attaining the goal of a heterogeneous student body. Although a university must have wide discretion in making the sensitive judgments as to who should be admitted, constitutional limitations protecting individual rights may not be disregarded. Respondent urges—and the courts below have held—that petitioner's dual admissions program is a racial classification that impermissibly infringes his rights under the Fourteenth Amendment. As the interest of diversity is compelling in the context of a university's admissions program, the question remains whether the program's racial classification is necessary to promote this interest.

It may be assumed that the reservation of a specified number of seats in each class for individuals from the preferred ethnic groups would contribute to the attainment of considerable ethnic diversity in the student body. But petitioner's argument that this is the only effective means of serving the interest of diversity is seriously flawed. In a most fundamental sense the argument misconceives the nature of the state interest that would justify consideration of race or ethnic background. It is not an interest in simple ethnic diversity, in which a specified percentage of the student body is in effect guaranteed to be members of selected ethnic groups, with the remaining percentage an undifferentiated aggregation of students. The diversity that furthers a compelling state interest encompasses a far broader array of qualifications and characteristics of which racial or ethnic origin is but a single though important element. Petitioner's special admissions program, focused *solely* on ethnic diversity, would hinder rather than further attainment of genuine diversity.

* * *

The experience of other university admissions programs, which take race into account in achieving the educational diversity valued by the First Amendment, demonstrates that the assignment of a fixed number of places to a minority group is not a necessary means toward that end. An illuminating example is found in the Harvard College program:

> In recent years Harvard College has expanded the concept of diversity to include students from disadvantaged economic, racial and ethnic groups. * * *
>
> In practice, this new definition of diversity has meant that race has been a factor in some admission decisions. When the Committee on Admissions reviews the large middle group of applicants who are "admissible" and deemed capable of doing good work in their courses, the race of an applicant may tip the balance in his favor just as geographic origin or a life spent on a farm may tip the balance in other candidates' cases. * * *

* * *

In such an admissions program, race or ethnic background may be deemed a "plus" in a particular applicant's file, yet it does not insulate the individual from comparison with all other candidates for the available seats. The file of a particular black applicant may be examined for his potential contribution to diversity without the factor of race being decisive when compared, for example, with that of an applicant identified as an Italian American if the latter is thought to exhibit qualities more likely to promote beneficial educational pluralism. Such qualities could include exceptional personal talents, unique work or service experience, leadership potential, maturity, demonstrated compassion, a history of overcoming disadvantage, ability to communicate with the poor, or other qualifications deemed important. In short, an admissions program operated in this way is flexible enough to consider all pertinent elements of diversity in light of the particular qualifications of each applicant, and to place them on the same footing for consideration, although not necessarily according them the same weight. Indeed, the weight attributed to a particular quality may vary from year to year depending upon the "mix" both of the student body and the applicants for the incoming class.

This kind of program treats each applicant as an individual in the admissions process. The applicant who loses out on the last available seat to another candidate receiving a "plus" on the basis of ethnic background will not have been foreclosed from all consideration for that seat simply because he was not the right color or had the wrong surname. It would mean only that his combined qualifications, which may have included similar nonobjective factors, did not outweigh those of the other applicant. His qualifications would have been weighed fairly and competitively, and he would have no basis to complain of unequal treatment under the Fourteenth Amendment.

* * *

In summary, it is evident that the Davis special admissions program involves the use of an explicit racial classification never before countenanced by this Court. It tells applicants who are not Negro, Asian, or Chicano that they are totally excluded from a specific percentage of the seats of an entering class. No matter how strong their qualifications, quantitative and extracurricular, including their own potential for contribution to educational diversity, they are never afforded the chance to compete with applicants from the preferred groups for the special admissions seats. At the same time, the preferred applicants have the opportunity to compete for every seat in the class.

The fatal flaw in petitioner's preferential program is its disregard of individual rights as guaranteed by the Fourteenth Amendment. Such rights are not absolute. But when a State's distribution of benefits or imposition of burdens hinges on ancestry or the color of a person's skin, that individual is entitled to a demonstration that the challenged classification is necessary to promote a substantial state interest. Petitioner has failed to carry this burden. For this reason, that portion of the California court's judgment holding petitioner's special admissions program invalid under the Fourteenth Amendment must be affirmed.

In enjoining petitioner from ever considering the race of any applicant, however, the courts below failed to recognize that the State has a substantial interest that legitimately may be served by a properly devised admissions program involving the competitive consideration of race and ethnic origin. For this reason, so much of the California court's judgment as enjoins petitioner from any consideration of the race of any applicant must be reversed.

With respect to respondent's entitlement to an injunction directing his admission to the Medical School, petitioner has conceded that it could not carry its burden of proving that, but for the existence of its unlawful special admissions program, respondent still would not have been admitted. Hence, respondent is entitled to the injunction, and that portion of the judgment must be affirmed.

* * *

Opinion of Justice Brennan, Justice White, Justice Marshall, and Justice Blackmun, concurring in the judgment in part and dissenting in part.

The Court today, in reversing in part the judgment of the Supreme Court of California, affirms the constitutional power of Federal and State Governments to act affirmatively to achieve equal opportunity for all. The difficulty of the issue presented—whether governments may use race-conscious programs to redress the continuing effects of past discrimination—and the mature consideration which each of our Brethren has brought to it have resulted in many opinions, no single one speaking for the Court. But this should not and must not mask the central meaning of today's opinions: Government may take race into account when it acts not to demean or insult any racial group, but to remedy disadvantages cast on minorities by past racial prejudice, at least when appropriate findings have been made by judicial, legislative, or administrative bodies with competence to act in this area.

* * *

* * * [T]he [Equal Protection] Clause [of the Fourteenth Amendment] was early turned against those whom it was intended to set free, condemning them to a "separate but equal" status before the law, a status always separate but seldom equal. Not until 1954—only 24 years ago—was this odious doctrine interred by our decision in *Brown v. Board of Education*, which proclaimed that separate schools and public facilities of all sorts were inherently unequal and forbidden under our Constitution. * * * [A] glance at our docket and at dockets of lower courts will show that even today officially sanctioned discrimination is not a thing of the past.

Against this background, claims that law must be "color-blind" or that the datum of race is no longer relevant to public policy must be seen as aspiration rather than as description of reality. This is not to denigrate aspiration; for reality rebukes us that race has too often been used by those who would stigmatize and oppress minorities. Yet we cannot—and, as we shall demonstrate, need not under our Constitution or Title VI, which merely extends the constraints of the Fourteenth Amendment to private parties who receive federal funds—let color blindness become myopia which masks the reality that many "created equal" have been treated within our lifetimes as inferior both by the law and by their fellow citizens.

* * *

In our view, Title VI prohibits only those uses of racial criteria that would violate the Fourteenth Amendment if employed by a State or its agencies; it does not bar the preferential treatment of racial minorities as a means of remedying past societal discrimination to the extent that such action is consistent with the Fourteenth Amendment. The legislative history of Title VI, administrative regulations interpreting the statute, subsequent congressional and executive action, and the prior decisions of this Court compel this conclusion. None of these sources lends support to the proposition that Congress intended to bar all race-conscious efforts to extend the benefits of federally financed programs to minorities who have been historically excluded from the full benefits of American life.

* * *

Respondent argues that racial classifications are always suspect and, consequently, that this Court should weigh the importance of the objectives served by Davis' special admissions program to see if they are compelling. In addition, he asserts that this Court must inquire whether, in its judgment, there are alternatives to racial classifications which would suit Davis' purposes. Petitioner, on the other hand, states that our proper role is simply to accept petitioner's determination that the racial classifications used by its programs are reasonably related to what it tells us are its benign purposes. We reject petitioner's view, but, because our prior cases are in many respects inapposite to that before us now, we find it necessary to define with precision the meaning of that inexact term, "strict scrutiny."

Unquestionably we have held that a government practice or statute which restricts "fundamental rights" or which contains "suspect classifications" is to be subjected to "strict scrutiny" and can be justified only if it furthers a compelling government purpose and, even then, only if no less restrictive alternative is available. But no fundamental right is involved here. Nor do whites as a class have any of the "traditional indicia of suspectness: the class is not saddled with such disabilities, or subjected to such a history of purposeful unequal treatment, or relegated to such a position of political powerlessness as to command extraordinary protection from the majoritarian political process."

* * *

On the other hand, the fact that this case does not fit neatly into our prior analytic framework for race cases does not mean that it should be analyzed by applying the very loose rational-basis standard of review that is the very least that is always applied in equal protection cases. " '[T]he mere recitation of a benign, compensatory purpose is not an automatic shield which protects against any inquiry into the actual purposes underlying a statutory scheme.' " Instead, a number of considerations—developed in gender-discrimination cases but which carry even more force when applied to racial classifications—lead us to conclude that racial classifications designed to further remedial purposes " 'must serve important governmental objectives and must be substantially related to achievement of those objectives.' "

* * *

Davis' articulated purpose of remedying the effects of past societal discrimination is, under our cases, sufficiently important to justify the use of race-conscious admissions programs where there is a sound basis for concluding that minority underrepresentation is substantial and chronic, and that the handicap of past discrimination is impeding access of minorities to the Medical School.

* * *

Certainly, on the basis of the undisputed factual submissions before this Court, Davis had a sound basis for believing that the problem of underrepresentation of minorities was substantial and chronic and that the problem was attributable to handicaps imposed on minority applicants by past and present racial discrimination. Until at least 1973, the practice of medicine in this country was, in fact, if not in law, largely the prerogative of whites. In 1950, for example, while Negroes constituted 10% of the total population, Negro physicians constituted only 2.2% of the total number of physicians. The overwhelming majority of these, moreover, were educated in two predominantly Negro medical schools, Howard and Meharry. By 1970, the gap between the proportion of Negroes in medicine and their proportion in the population had widened: The number of Negroes employed in medicine remained frozen at 2.2% while the Negro population had increased to 11.1%. The number of Negro admittees to predominantly white medical schools, moreover, had declined in absolute numbers during the years 1954 to 1964.

* * *

Davis clearly could conclude that the serious and persistent underrepresentation of minorities in medicine depicted by these statistics is the result of handicaps under which minority applicants labor as a consequence of a background of deliberate, purposeful discrimination against minorities in education and in society generally, as well as in the medical profession. * * *

* * * The generation of minority students applying to Davis Medical School since it opened in 1968—most of whom were born before or about the time *Brown I* was decided—clearly have been victims of this discrimination. Judicial decrees recognizing discrimination in public education in California testify to the fact of widespread discrimination suffered by California-born minority applicants; many minority group members living in California, moreover, were born and reared in school districts in Southern States segregated by law. * * *

* * *

The second prong of our test—whether the Davis program stigmatizes any discrete group or individual and whether race is reasonably used in the light of the program's objectives—is clearly satisfied by the Davis program.

It is not even claimed that Davis' program in any way operates to stigmatize or single out any discrete and insular, or even any identifiable, nonminority group. Nor will harm comparable to that imposed upon racial minorities by exclusion or separation on grounds of race be the likely result of the program. It does not, for example, establish an exclusive preserve for minority students apart from and exclusive of whites. Rather, its purpose is to overcome the effects of segregation by bringing the races together. True, whites are excluded from participation in the special admissions program, but this fact only operates to reduce the number of whites to be admitted in the regular admissions program in order to permit admission of a reasonable percentage—less than their proportion of the California population—of otherwise underrepresented qualified minority applicants.

Nor was Bakke in any sense stamped as inferior by the Medical School's rejection of him. Indeed, it is conceded by all that he satisfied those criteria regarded by the school as generally relevant to academic performance better than most of the minority members who were admitted. Moreover, there is absolutely no basis for concluding that Bakke's rejection as a result of Davis' use of racial preference will affect him throughout his life in the same way as the segregation of the Negro schoolchildren in *Brown I* would have affected them. Unlike discrimination against racial minorities, the use of racial preferences for remedial purposes does not inflict a pervasive injury upon individual whites in the sense that wherever they go or whatever they do there is a significant likelihood that they will be treated as second-class citizens because of their color. * * *

In addition, there is simply no evidence that the Davis program discriminates intentionally or unintentionally against any minority group which it purports to benefit. The program does not establish a quota in the invidious sense of a ceiling on the number of minority applicants to be admitted. Nor can the program reasonably be regarded as stigmatizing the program's beneficiaries or their race as inferior. The Davis program does not simply advance less qualified applicants; rather, it compensates applicants, who it is uncontested are fully qualified to study medicine, for educational disadvantages which it was reasonable to conclude were a product of state-fostered discrimination. Once admitted, these students must satisfy the same degree requirements as regularly admitted students; they are taught by the same faculty in the same classes; and their performance is evaluated by the same standards by which regularly admitted students are judged. * * *

We disagree with the lower courts' conclusion that the Davis program's use of race was unreasonable in light of its objectives. * * *

[T]he Davis admissions program does not simply equate minority status with disadvantage. Rather, Davis considers on an individual basis each applicant's personal history to determine whether he or she has likely been disadvantaged by racial discrimination. The record makes clear that only minority applicants likely to have been isolated from the mainstream of American life are considered in the special program; other minority applicants are eligible only through the regular admissions program.
* * *

Finally, Davis' special admissions program cannot be said to violate the Constitution simply because it has set aside a predetermined number of places for qualified minority applicants rather than using minority status as a positive factor to be considered in evaluating the applications of disadvantaged minority applicants. For purposes of constitutional adjudication, there is no difference between the two approaches. In any admissions program which accords special consideration to disadvantaged racial minorities, a determination of the degree of preference to be given is unavoidable, and any given preference that results in the exclusion of a white candidate is no more or less constitutionally acceptable than a program such as that at Davis. * * * There is no sensible, and certainly no constitutional, distinction between, for example, adding a set number of points to the admissions rating of disadvantaged minority applicants as an expression of the preference with the expectation that this will result in the admission of an approximately determined number of qualified minority applicants and setting a fixed number of places for such applicants as was done here.

* * *

Accordingly, we would reverse the judgment of the Supreme Court of California holding the Medical School's special admissions program unconstitutional and directing respondent's admission, as well as that portion of the judgment enjoining the Medical School from according any consideration to race in the admissions process.

The opinion of Justice White is omitted.

Justice Marshall.

I agree with the judgment of the Court only insofar as it permits a university to consider the race of an applicant in making admissions decisions. I do not agree that petitioner's admissions program violates the Constitution. For it must be remembered that, during most of the past 200 years, the Constitution as interpreted by this Court did not prohibit the most ingenious and pervasive forms of discrimination against the Negro. Now, when a State acts to remedy the effects of that legacy of discrimination, I cannot believe that this same Constitution stands as a barrier.

* * *

The position of the Negro today in America is the tragic but inevitable consequence of centuries of unequal treatment. Measured by any benchmark of comfort or achievement, meaningful equality remains a distant dream for the Negro.

A Negro child today has a life expectancy which is shorter by more than five years than that of a white child. The Negro child's mother is over three times more likely to die of complications in childbirth, and the infant mortality rate for Negroes is nearly twice that for whites. The median income of the Negro family is only 60% that of the median of a white family, and the percentage of Negroes who live in families with incomes below the poverty line is nearly four times greater than that of whites.

When the Negro child reaches working age, he finds that America offers him significantly less than it offers his white counterpart. For Negro adults, the unemployment rate is twice that of whites, and the unemployment rate for Negro teenagers is nearly three times that of white teenagers. A Negro male who completes four years of college can expect a median annual income of merely $110 more than a white male who has only a high school diploma. Although Negroes represent 11.5% of the population, they are only 1.2% of the lawyers and judges, 2% of the physicians, 2.3% of the dentists, 1.1% of the engineers and 2.6% of the college and university professors.

The relationship between those figures and the history of the unequal treatment afforded to the Negro cannot be denied. At every point from birth to death the impact of the past is reflected in the still disfavored position of the Negro.

In light of the sorry history of discrimination and its devastating impact on the lives of Negroes, bringing the Negro into the mainstream of American life should be a state interest of the highest order. To fail to do so is to ensure that America will forever remain a divided society.

* * *

While I applaud the judgment of the Court that a university may consider race in its admissions process, it is more than a little ironic that, after several hundred years of class-based discrimination against Negroes, the Court is unwilling to hold that a class-based remedy for that discrimination is permissible. In declining to so hold, today's judgment ignores the fact that for several hundred years Negroes have been discriminated against, not as individuals, but rather solely because of the color of their skins. It is unnecessary in 20th-century America to have individual Negroes demonstrate that they have been victims of racial discrimination; the racism of our society has been so pervasive that none, regardless of wealth or position, has managed to escape its impact. The experience of Negroes in America has been different in kind, not just in degree, from that of other ethnic groups. It is not merely the history of slavery alone but also that a whole people were marked as inferior by the law. And that mark has endured. The dream of America as the great melting pot has not been realized for the Negro; because of his skin color he never even made it into the pot.

* * *

It is because of a legacy of unequal treatment that we now must permit the institutions of this society to give consideration to race in making decisions about who will hold the positions of influence, affluence, and prestige in America. For far too long, the doors to those positions have been shut to Negroes. If we are ever to become a fully integrated society, one in which the color of a person's skin will not determine the opportunities available to him or her, we must be willing to take steps to open those doors. I do not believe that anyone can truly look into America's past and still find that a remedy for the effects of that past is impermissible.

* * *

The opinion of Justice Blackmun is omitted.

Justice Stevens, with whom The Chief Justice, Justice Stewart, and Justice Rehnquist join.

* * *

* * * Our settled practice . . . is to avoid the decision of a constitutional issue if a case can be fairly decided on a statutory ground. "If there is one doctrine more deeply rooted than any other in the process of constitutional adjudication, it is that we ought not to pass on questions of constitutionality... unless such adjudication is unavoidable." The more important the issue, the more force there is to this doctrine. In this case, we are presented with a constitutional question of undoubted and unusual importance. Since, however, a dispositive statutory claim was raised at the very inception of this case, and squarely decided in the portion of the trial court judgment affirmed by the California Supreme Court, it is our plain duty to confront it. Only if petitioner should prevail on the statutory issue would it be necessary to decide whether the University's admissions program violated the Equal Protection Clause of the Fourteenth Amendment.

Section 601 of the Civil Rights Act of 1964 provides:

> No person in the United States shall, on the ground of race, color, or national origin, be excluded from participation in, be denied the benefits of, or be subjected to discrimination under

any program or activity receiving Federal financial assistance.

The University, through its special admissions policy, excluded Bakke from participation in its program of medical education because of his race. The university also acknowledges that it was, and still is, receiving federal financial assistance. The plain language of the statute therefore requires affirmance of the judgment below. A different result cannot be justified unless that language misstates the actual intent of the Congress that enacted the statute or the statute is not enforceable in a private action. Neither conclusion is warranted.

Title VI is an integral part of the far-reaching Civil Rights Act of 1964. No doubt, when this legislation was being debated, Congress was not directly concerned with the legality of "reverse discrimination" or "affirmative action" programs. Its attention was focused on the problem at hand, the "glaring . . . discrimination against Negroes which exists throughout our Nation," and, with respect to Title VI, the federal funding of segregated facilities. The genesis of the legislation, however, did not limit the breadth of the solution adopted. Just as Congress responded to the problem of employment discrimination by enacting a provision that protects all races, so, too, its answer to the problem of federal funding of segregated facilities stands as a broad prohibition against the exclusion of *any* individual from a federally funded program "on the grounds of race." In the words of the House Report, Title VI stands for "the general principle that *no person* . . . be excluded from participation . . . on the ground of race, color, or national origin under any program or activity receiving Federal financial assistance." This same broad view of Title VI and section 601 was echoed throughout the congressional debate and was stressed by every one of the major spokesmen for the Act.

Petitioner contends, however, that exclusion of applicants on the basis of race does not violate Title VI if the exclusion carries with it no racial stigma. No such qualification or limitation of section 601's categorical prohibition of "exclusion" is justified by the statute or its history. The language of the entire section is perfectly clear; the words that follow "excluded from" do not modify or qualify the explicit outlawing of any exclusion on the stated grounds.

* * *

* * * In unmistakable terms the Act prohibits the exclusion of individuals from federally funded programs because of their race. As succinctly phrased during the Senate debate, under Title VI it is not "permissible to say 'yes' to one person; but to say 'no' to another person, only because of the color of his skin."

* * *

The University's special admissions program violated Title VI of the Civil Rights Act of 1964 by excluding Bakke from the Medical School because of his race. It is therefore our duty to affirm the judgment ordering Bakke admitted to the University.

Accordingly, I concur in the Court's judgment insofar as it affirms the judgment of the Supreme Court of California. To the extent that it purports to do anything else, I respectfully dissent.

Both sides could claim victory because while the Court did not allow the specific set-aside, it refused to rule that affirmative action was invalid in general. The Court's inability to make a definitive decision on this issue, however, assured that the subject of affirmative action would return for additional case decisions. Also, the *Bakke* case involved affirmative action in education, but affirmative action programs also involved employment, and these were beginning to be challenged in the lower courts as well. Only one year after *Bakke*, the Court had the opportunity to address this issue in *United Steelworkers v. Weber* (1979). *Weber* involved a voluntary affirmative action plan adopted by a private employer to address the discrimination that had been applied against African Americans in craft unions. Kaiser Aluminum and Chemical Company entered into an agreement with the steelworkers union to set up training programs in Kaiser plants across the country that would help to open more opportunities for black workers. This case involved the program set up at a Kaiser plant in Gramercy, Louisiana, an area where African Americans made up 39 percent of the workforce, but represented only 1.83 percent of the skilled craft workers. Under this program, half of the positions were reserved for African Americans and half for whites, and admission to the training program was based on seniority, within the two racial groups. Brian Weber, a white union member who had less seniority than any of the whites who were admitted, but more seniority than some African Americans who were admitted, filed suit in federal court alleging that this program violated Title VII of the Civil Rights Act, which prohibited discrimination in employment. The district court agreed with Weber that the training program was in violation of Title VII, its decision was affirmed by the appeals court, and the case was appealed to the Supreme Court.

In a 5-2 decision with Justices Powell and Stewart not participating, the Court overturned the appeals court ruling, holding that this voluntary, affirmative action training program did not violate Title VII. The Court held that although a literal reading of Title VII might appear to prohibit this program, it was consistent with the "spirit" of the Civil Rights Act. Writing for the majority, Justice Brennan said that Congress's primary concern in passing Title VII was with "the plight of the Negro in our economy," and that "it was clear to Congress that '[t]he crux of the problem [was] to open employment opportunities for Negroes in occupations which have been traditionally closed to them' " (443 U.S. at 202–3). The majority emphasized also that the program being challenged here was temporary, that it did not require white workers to be discharged, and that it did not bar them completely from admission to the program.

In a dissenting opinion, Justice Rehnquist and Chief Justice Burger argued that both the language and the legislative history of Title VII and the Court's precedents interpreting this legislation required that this affirmative action plan be struck down. Rehnquist wrote, "... *no* racial discrimination in employment is permissible under Title VII, not even preferential treatment of minorities to correct racial imbalance" [emphasis in original] (443 U.S. at 230).

Thus, in *Weber*, the Court approved affirmative action programs created by private employers, but what about such programs as established by public employers? The Court was able to address this issue one year after *Weber* in the case *Fullilove v. Klutznick* (1980). In *Fullilove*, the affirmative action program being challenged involved what became known as "set-asides." Here, Congress had established in the Public Works Employment Act of 1977 that when state and local governments contracted with the federal government, 10 percent of those contracts had to be set aside for minority business enterprises (MBEs). By a 6-3 vote, the Court upheld this set-aside provision, but a majority could not agree on the reasoning for the decision. One plurality, consisting of Chief Justice Burger and Justices Powell and White, relied on congressional power under the Spending and Commerce Clauses of Article I and the Enforcement Clause (section 5) of the Fourteenth Amendment. Section 5 reads "The Congress shall have power to enforce, by appropriate legislation, the provisions of this article." These three justices emphasized that the set-aside provision was based on legislative determinations that discrimination in the contracting industry had a negative effect on the opportunities of minority contractors. Moreover, they stressed that the set-aside did not amount to a rigid quota system, but was a flexible, temporary program designed to remedy the discrimination faced by minorities in contracting.

A second plurality consisting of Justices Marshall, Brennan, and Blackmun used the important government interest standard suggested by Brennan in the *Bakke* case. In their view, "the racial classifications employed in the set-aside provision [were] substantially related to the achievement of the important and congressionally articulated goal of remedying the present effects of past racial discrimination" (448 U.S. at 521). They emphasized that the provision required contracts to be awarded only to qualified MBEs, that neither minority nor nonminority firms were stigmatized by the program, and that a very small amount of funds were involved in the program.

Justices Rehnquist, Stevens, and Stewart dissented from the Court's judgment. Writing for himself and Rehnquist, Stewart said that the Court was endorsing racial classifications that violated the Constitution's requirement of strict race neutrality. He wrote that race-conscious remedies should be enacted only after courts have conducted proceedings to identify specific victims of discrimination and victimizers. Stevens objected to the set-aside provision for different reasons. He felt that there should have been hearings held on this provision and was disturbed that Congress was acting without specific findings of discriminatory practices. Also, he questioned the inclusion of minority groups other than African Americans in the provision, arguing that they did not have the discriminatory history faced by African Americans and therefore did not qualify for "special treatment."

Fullilove v. Klutznick

448 U.S. 448, 100 S. Ct. 2758, 65 L. Ed. 2d 902 (1980)

■ In the Public Works Employment Act (PWEA) of 1977, Congress provided that 10 percent of the funds granted to state and local governments for public works projects must be used to procure services or supplies from minority-owned businesses. A group of white contractors filed suit in federal district court, alleging that the MBE provision violated the equal protection component of the Due Process Clause of the Fifth Amendment. After the district court and the court of appeals upheld the MBE program, the contractors appealed to the Supreme Court.

This case is important because it is the first time that the Court examined an affirmative action program of the federal government. As you read the case, consider the following questions: (1) Is the racial classification contained here comparable to that involved in *Plessy v. Ferguson,* as Justice Stewart maintains? (2) Is it reasonable to conclude automatically that the nonminority contractors involved here are "innocent" parties, as some of the justices contend? (3) Why do you think Chief Justice Burger did not apply strict scrutiny in deciding this case?

Vote:

6 justices voted to uphold the MBE provision (Burger, White, Powell, Marshall, Brennan, and Blackmun).

3 justices voted to strike down the MBE provision (Stewart, Rehnquist, and Stevens).

Chief Justice Burger announced the judgment of the Court and delivered an opinion, in which Justice White and Justice Powell joined.

* * *

Our analysis proceeds in two steps. At the outset, we must inquire whether the *objectives* of this legislation are within the power of Congress. If so, we must go on to decide whether the limited use of racial and ethnic criteria, in the context presented, is a constitutionally permissible *means* for achieving the congressional objectives and does not violate the equal protection component of the Due Process Clause of the Fifth Amendment.

In enacting the MBE provision, it is clear that Congress employed an amalgam of its specifically delegated powers. The Public Works Employment Act of 1977, by its very nature, is primarily an exercise of the Spending Power. This Court has recognized that the power to "provide for the . . . general Welfare" is an independent grant of legislative authority, distinct from other broad congressional powers. Congress has frequently employed the Spending Power to further broad policy objectives by conditioning receipt of federal moneys upon compliance by the recipient with federal statutory and administrative directives. This Court has repeatedly upheld against constitutional challenge the use of this technique to induce governments and private parties to cooperate voluntarily with federal policy.

The MBE program is structured within this familiar legislative pattern. The program conditions receipt of public works grants upon agreement by the state or local governmental grantee that at least 10% of the federal funds will be devoted to contracts with minority businesses, to the extent this can be accomplished by overcoming barriers to access and by awarding contracts to bona fide MBE's. It is further conditioned to require that MBE bids on these contracts are competitively priced, or might have been competitively priced but for the present effects of prior discrimination. * * *

Here we need not explore the outermost limitations on the objectives attainable through such an application of the Spending Power. The reach of the Spending Power, within its sphere, is at least as broad as the regulatory powers of Congress. If, pursuant to its regulatory powers, Congress could have achieved the objectives of the MBE program, then it may do so under the Spending Power. * * *

We turn first to the Commerce Power. Had Congress chosen to do so, it could have drawn on the Commerce Clause to regulate the practices of prime contractors on federally funded public works projects. The legislative history of the MBE provision shows that there was a rational basis for Congress to conclude that the subcontracting practices of prime contractors could perpetuate the prevailing impaired access by minority businesses to public contracting opportunities, and that this inequity has an effect on interstate commerce. Thus Congress could take necessary and proper action to remedy the situation.

It is not necessary that these prime contractors be shown responsible for any violation of antidiscrimination laws. Our cases dealing with application of Title VII of the Civil Rights Act of 1964, as amended, express no doubt of the congressional authority to prohibit practices "challenged as perpetuating the effects of [not unlawful] discrimination occurring prior to the effective date of the Act." Insofar as the MBE program pertains to the actions of private prime contractors, the Congress could have achieved its objectives under the Commerce Clause. We conclude that in this respect the objectives of the MBE provision are within the scope of the Spending Power.

In certain contexts, there are limitations on the reach of the Commerce Power to regulate the actions of state and local governments. To avoid such complications, we look to section 5 of the Fourteenth Amendment for the power to regulate the procurement practices of state and local grantees of federal funds. A review of our cases persuades us that the objectives of the MBE program are within the power of Congress under section 5 "to enforce, by appropriate legislation," the equal protection guarantees of the Fourteenth Amendment.

* * *

With respect to the MBE provision, Congress had abundant evidence from which it could conclude that minority businesses have been denied effective participation in public contracting opportunities by procurement practices that perpetuated the effects of prior discrimination. Congress, of course, may legislate without compiling the kind of "record" appropriate with respect to judicial or administrative proceedings. Congress had before it, among other data, evidence of a long history of marked disparity in the percentage of public contracts awarded to minority business enterprises. This disparity was considered to result not from any lack of capable and qualified minority businesses, but from the existence and maintenance of barriers to competitive access which had their roots in racial and ethnic discrimination, and which continue today, even absent any intentional discrimination or other unlawful conduct. Although much of this history related to the experience of minority businesses in the area of federal procurement, there was direct evidence before the Congress that this pattern of disadvantage and discrimination existed with respect to state and local construction contracting as well. In relation to the MBE provision, Congress acted within its competence to determine that the problem was national in scope.

* * *

We now turn to the question whether, as a *means* to accomplish these plainly constitutional objectives, Congress may use racial and ethnic criteria, in this limited way, as a condition attached to a federal grant. * * *

* * *

Our review of the regulations and guidelines governing administration of the MBE provision reveals that Congress enacted the program as a strictly remedial measure; moreover, it is a remedy that functions prospectively, in the manner of an injunctive decree. Pursuant to the administrative program, grantees and their prime contractors are required to seek out all available, qualified, bona fide MBE's; they are required to provide technical assistance as needed, to lower or waive bonding requirements where feasible, to solicit the aid of the Office of Minority Business Enterprise, the SBA, or other sources for assisting MBE's to obtain required working capital, and to give guidance through the intricacies of the bidding process. The program assumes that grantees who undertake these efforts in good faith will obtain at least 10% participation by minority business enterprises. It is recognized that, to achieve this target, contracts will be awarded to available, qualified, bona fide MBE's even though they are not the lowest competitive bidders, so long as their higher bids, when challenged, are found to reflect merely attempts to cover costs inflated by the present effects of prior disadvantage and discrimination. There is available to the grantee a provision authorized by Congress for administrative waiver on a case-by-case basis should there be a demonstration that, despite affirmative efforts, this level of participation cannot be achieved without departing from the objectives of the program. There is also an administrative mechanism, including a complaint procedure, to ensure that only bona fide MBE's are encompassed by the remedial program, and to prevent unjust participation in the program by those minority firms whose access to public contracting opportunities is not impaired by the effects of prior discrimination.

As a threshold matter, we reject the contention that in the remedial context the Congress must act in a wholly "color-blind" fashion. In *Swann v. Charlotte-Mecklenburg Board of Education* (1971), we rejected this argument in considering a court-formulated school desegregation remedy on the basis that examination of the racial composition of student bodies was an unavoidable starting point and that racially based attendance assignments were permissible so long as no absolute racial balance of each school was required. * * *

In . . . school desegregation cases we dealt with the authority of a federal court to formulate a remedy for unconstitutional racial discrimination. However, the authority of a court to incorporate racial criteria into a remedial decree also extends to statutory violations. Where federal antidiscrimination laws have been violated, an equitable remedy may in the appropriate case include a racial or ethnic factor . . . .

* * *

Here we deal . . . not with the limited remedial powers of a federal court . . . but with the broad remedial powers of Congress. It is fundamental that in no organ of government, state or federal, does there repose a more comprehensive remedial power than in the Congress, expressly charged by the Constitution with competence and authority to enforce equal protection guarantees. Congress not only may induce voluntary action to assure compliance with existing federal statutory or constitutional antidiscrimination provisions, but also, where Congress has authority to declare certain conduct unlawful, it may, as here, authorize and induce state action to avoid such conduct.

A more specific challenge to the MBE program is the charge that it impermissibly deprives nonminority businesses of access to at least some portion of the government contracting opportunities generated by the Act. It must be conceded that by its objective of remedying the historical impairment of access, the MBE provision can have the effect of awarding some contracts to MBE's which otherwise might be awarded to other businesses, who may themselves be innocent of any prior discriminatory actions. Failure of nonminority firms to receive certain contracts is, of course, an incidental consequence of the program, not part of its objective; similarly, past impairment of minority-firm access to public contracting opportunities may have been an incidental consequence of "business as usual" by public contracting agencies and among prime contractors.

It is not a constitutional defect in this program that it may disappoint the expectations of nonminority firms. When effectuating a limited and properly tailored remedy to cure the effects of prior discrimination, such "a sharing of the burden" by innocent parties is not impermissible. The actual "burden" shouldered by nonminority firms is relatively light in this connection when we consider the scope of this public works program as compared with overall construction contracting opportunities. Moreover, although we may assume that the complaining parties are innocent of any discriminatory conduct, it was within congressional power to act on the assumption that in the past some nonminority businesses may have reaped competitive benefit over the years from the virtual exclusion of minority firms from these contracting opportunities.

* * *

The Congress has not sought to give select minority groups a preferred standing in the construction industry, but has embarked on a remedial program to place them on a more equitable footing with respect to public contracting opportunities. There has been no showing in this case that Congress has inadvertently effected an invidious discrimination by excluding from coverage an identifiable minority group that has been the victim of a degree of disadvantage and discrimination equal to or greater than that suffered by the groups encompassed by the MBE program. It is not inconceivable that on very special facts a case might be made to challenge the congressional decision to limit MBE eligibility to the particular minority groups identified in the Act. But on this record we find no basis to hold that Congress is without authority to undertake the kind of limited remedial effort represented by the MBE program. Congress, not the courts, has the heavy burden of dealing with a host of intractable economic and social problems.

* * *

* * * Even in the context of a facial challenge such as is presented in this case, the MBE provision cannot pass muster unless, with due account for its administrative program, it provides a reasonable assurance that application of racial or ethnic criteria will be limited to accomplishing the remedial objectives of Congress and that misapplications of the program will be promptly and adequately remedied administratively.

It is significant that the administrative scheme provides for waiver and exemption. * * *

The administrative program contains measures to effectuate the congressional objective of assuring legitimate participation by disadvantaged MBE's. Administrative definition has tightened some less definite aspects of the statutory identification of the minority groups encompassed by the program. There is administrative scrutiny to identify and eliminate from participation in the program MBE's who are not "bona fide" within the regulations and guidelines; for example, spurious minority-front entities can be exposed. A significant aspect of this surveillance is the complaint procedure available for reporting "unjust participation by an enterprise or individuals in the MBE program." And even as to specific contract awards, waiver is available to avoid dealing with an MBE who is attempting to exploit the remedial aspects of the program by charging an unreasonable price, i.e., a price not attributable to the present effects of past discrimination. We must assume that Congress intended close scrutiny of false claims and prompt action on them.

Grantees are given the opportunity to demonstrate that their best efforts will not succeed or have not succeeded in achieving the statutory 10% target for minority firm participation within the limitations of the program's remedial objectives. In these circumstances a waiver or partial waiver is available once compliance has been demonstrated. A waiver may be sought and granted at any time during the contracting process, or even prior to letting contracts if the facts warrant.

* * *

Congress, after due consideration, perceived a pressing need to move forward with new approaches in the continuing effort to achieve the goal of equality of economic opportunity. In this effort, Congress has necessary latitude to try new techniques such as the limited use of racial and ethnic criteria to accomplish remedial objectives; this is especially so in programs where voluntary cooperation with remedial measures is induced by placing conditions on federal expenditures. That the program may press the outer limits of congressional authority affords no basis for striking it down.

* * *

Any preference based on racial or ethnic criteria must necessarily receive a most searching examination to make sure that it does not conflict with constitutional guarantees. This case is one which requires, and which has received, that kind of examination. This opinion does not adopt, either expressly or implicitly, the formulas of analysis articulated in such cases as *University of California Regents v. Bakke* (1978). However, our analysis demonstrates that the MBE provision would survive judicial review under either "test" articulated in the several *Bakke* opinions. The MBE provision of the Public Works Employment Act of 1977 does not violate the Constitution.

* * *

Justice Powell concurred [omitted].

Justice Marshall, with whom Justice Brennan and Justice Blackmun join, concurred in the judgment.

My resolution of the constitutional issue in this case is governed by the separate opinion I coauthored in *University of California Regents v. Bakke* (1978). In my view, the 10% minority set-aside provision of the Public Works Employment Act of 1977 passes constitutional muster under the standard announced in that opinion.

In *Bakke*, I joined my Brothers Brennan, White, and Blackmun in articulating the view that "racial classifications are not *per se* invalid under [the Equal Protection Clause of] the Fourteenth Amendment." We acknowledged that "a government practice or statute which . . . contains 'suspect classifications' is to be subjected to 'strict scrutiny' and can be justified only if it furthers a compelling government purpose and, even then, only if no less restrictive alternative is available." Thus, we reiterated the traditional view that racial classifications are prohibited if they are irrelevant. In addition, we firmly adhered to "the cardinal principle that racial classifications that stigmatize—because they are drawn on the presumption that one race is inferior to another or because they put the weight of government behind racial hatred and separatism—are invalid without more."

We recognized, however, that these principles outlawing the irrelevant or pernicious use of race were inapposite to racial classifications that provide benefits to minorities for the purpose of remedying the present effects of past racial discrimination. Such classifications may disadvantage some whites, but whites as a class lack the " 'traditional indicia of suspectness: the class is not saddled with such disabilities, or subjected to such a history of purposeful unequal treatment, or relegated to such a position of political powerlessness as to command extraordinary protection from the majoritarian political process.' " Because the consideration of race is relevant to remedying the continuing effects of past racial discrimination, and because governmental programs employing racial classifications for remedial purposes can be crafted to avoid stigmatization, we concluded that such programs should not be subjected to conventional "strict scrutiny"—scrutiny that is strict in theory, but fatal in fact.

* * *

We concluded, therefore, that because a racial classification ostensibly designed for remedial purposes is susceptible to misuse, it may be justified only by showing "an important and articulated purpose for its use." "In addition, any statute must be stricken that stigmatizes any group or that singles out those least well represented in the political process to bear the brunt of a benign program." In our view, then, the proper inquiry is whether racial classifications designed to further remedial purposes serve important governmental objectives and are substantially related to achievement of those objectives.

Judged under this standard, the 10% minority set-aside provision at issue in this case is plainly constitutional. Indeed, the question is not even a close one.

As Mr. Chief Justice Burger demonstrates, it is indisputable that Congress' articulated purpose for enacting the set-aside provision was to remedy the present effects of past racial discrimination. * * * Congress had a sound basis for concluding that minority-owned construction enterprises, though capable, qualified, and ready and willing to work, have received a disproportionately small amount of public contracting business because of the continuing effects of past discrimination. * * * In these circumstances remedying these present effects of past racial discrimination is a sufficiently important governmental interest to justify the use of racial classification.

Because the means chosen by Congress to implement the set-aside provision are substantially related to the achievement of its remedial purpose, the provision also meets the second prong of our *Bakke* test. Congress reasonably determined that race-conscious means were necessary to break down the barriers confronting participation by minority enterprises in federally funded public works projects. * * *

* * *

* * * Today, by upholding this race-conscious remedy, the Court accords Congress the authority necessary to undertake the task of moving our society toward a state of meaningful equality of opportunity, not an abstract version of equality in which the effects of past discrimination would be forever frozen into our social fabric. I applaud this result. Accordingly, I concur in the judgment of the Court.

Justice Stewart, with whom Justice Rehnquist joins, dissents.

The equal protection standard of the Constitution has one clear and central meaning—it absolutely prohibits invidious discrimination by government. That standard must be met by every State under the Equal Protection Clause of the Fourteenth Amendment. And that standard must be met by the United States itself under the Due Process Clause of the Fifth Amendment. Under our Constitution, any official action that treats a person differently on account of his race or ethnic origin is inherently suspect and presumptively invalid.

The hostility of the Constitution to racial classifications by government has been manifested in many cases decided by this Court. And our cases have made clear that the Constitution is wholly neutral in forbidding such racial discrimination, whatever the race may be of those who are its victims. * * *

* * * Under our Constitution, the government may never act to the detriment of a person solely because of that person's race. * * * In short, racial discrimination is by definition invidious discrimination.

The rule cannot be any different when the persons injured by a racially biased law are not members of a racial minority. The guarantee of equal protection is "universal in [its] application, to all persons . . . without regard to any differences of race, or color, or of nationality." * * *

No one disputes the self-evident proposition that Congress has broad discretion under its spending power to disburse the revenues of the United States as it deems best and to set conditions on the receipt of the funds disbursed. No one disputes that Congress has the authority under the Commerce Clause to regulate contracting practices on federally funded public works projects, or that it enjoys broad powers under section 5 of the Fourteenth Amendment "to enforce by appropriate legislation" the provisions of that Amendment. But these self-evident truisms do not begin to answer the question before us in this case. For in the exercise of its powers, Congress must obey the Constitution just as the legislatures of all the States must obey the Constitution in the exercise of their powers. If a law is unconstitutional, it is no less unconstitutional just because it is a product of the Congress of the United States.

On its face, the minority business enterprise (MBE) provision at issue in this case denies the equal protection of the law. The Public Works Employment Act of 1977 directs that all project construction shall be performed by those private contractors who submit the lowest competitive bids and who meet established criteria of responsibility. One class of contracting firms—defined solely according to the racial and ethnic attributes of their owners—is, however, excepted from the full rigor of these requirements with respect to a percentage of each federal grant. The statute, on its face and in effect, thus bars a class to which the petitioners belong from having the opportunity to receive a government benefit, and bars the members of that class solely on the basis of their race or ethnic background. This is precisely the kind of law that the guarantee of equal protection forbids.

The Court's attempt to characterize the law as a proper remedial measure to counteract the effects of past or present racial discrimination is remarkably unconvincing. The Legislative Branch of government is not a court of equity. It has neither the dispassionate objectivity nor the flexibility that are needed to mold a race-conscious remedy around the single objective of eliminating the effects of past or present discrimination.

But even assuming that Congress has the power, under section 5 of the Fourteenth Amendment or some other constitutional provision, to remedy previous illegal racial discrimination, there is no evidence that Congress has in the past engaged in racial discrimination in its disbursement of federal contracting funds. * * *

* * * [The MBE provision's] legislative history suggests that it had at least two other objectives in addition to that of counteracting the effects of past or present racial discrimination in the public works construction industry. One such purpose appears to have been to assure to minority contractors a certain percentage of federally funded public works contracts. But, since the guarantee of equal protection immunizes from capricious governmental treatment "persons"—not "races"—it can never countenance laws that seek racial balance as a goal in and of itself. "Preferring members of any one group for no reason other than race or ethnic origin is discrimination for its own sake. This the Constitution forbids." Second, there are indications that the MBE provision may have been enacted to compensate for the effects of social, educational, and economic "disadvantage." No race, however, has a monopoly on social, educational, or economic disadvantage, and any law that indulges in such a presumption clearly violates the constitutional guarantee of equal protection. Since the MBE provision was in whole or in part designed to effectuate objectives other than the elimination of the effects of racial discrimination, it cannot stand as a remedy that comports with the strictures of equal protection, even if it otherwise could.

* * *

Justice Stevens dissented.

* * *

Our historic aversion to titles of nobility is only one aspect of our commitment to the proposition that the sovereign has a fundamental duty to govern impartially. When government accords different treatment to different persons, there must be a reason for the difference. Because racial characteristics so seldom provide a relevant basis for disparate treatment, and because classifications based on race are potentially so harmful to the entire body politic, it is especially important that the reasons for any such classification be clearly identified and unquestionably legitimate.

The statutory definition of the preferred class includes "citizens of the United States who are Negroes, Spanish-speaking, Orientals, Indians, Eskimos, and Aleuts." All aliens and all nonmembers of the racial class are excluded. No economic, social, geographical, or historical criteria are relevant for exclusion or inclusion. There is not one word in the remainder of the Act or in the legislative history that explains why any Congressman or Senator favored this particular definition over any other or that identifies the common characteristics that every member of the preferred class was believed to share. Nor does the Act or its history explain why 10% of the total appropriation was the proper amount to set aside for investors in each of the six racial subclasses.

* * *

In his eloquent separate opinion in *University of California Regents v. Bakke*, Mr. Justice Marshall recounted the tragic class-based discrimination against Negroes that is an indelible part of America's history. I assume that the wrong committed against the Negro class is both so serious and so pervasive that it would constitutionally justify an appropriate classwide recovery measured by a sum certain for every member of the injured class. Whether our resources are adequate to support a fair remedy of that character is a policy question I have neither the authority nor the wisdom to address. But that serious classwide wrong cannot in itself justify the particular classification Congress has made in this Act. Racial classifications are simply too pernicious to permit any but the most exact connection between justification and classification. Quite obviously, the history of discrimination against black citizens in America cannot justify a grant of privileges to Eskimos or Indians.

Even if we assume that each of the six racial subclasses has suffered its own special injury at some time in our history, surely it does not necessarily follow that each of those subclasses suffered harm of identical magnitude. Although "the Negro was dragged to this country in chains to be sold in slavery," the "Spanish-speaking" subclass came voluntarily, frequently without invitation, and the Indians, the Eskimos and the Aleuts had an opportunity to exploit America's resources before the ancestors of most American citizens arrived. There is no reason to assume, and nothing in the legislative history suggests, much less demonstrates, that each of the subclasses is equally entitled to reparations from the United States Government.

* * *

My principal objection to the reparation justification for this legislation, however, cuts more deeply than my concern about its inequitable character. We can never either erase or ignore the history that Mr.

Justice Marshall has recounted. But if that history can justify such a random distribution of benefits on racial lines as that embodied in this statutory scheme, it will serve not merely as a basis for remedial legislation, but rather as a permanent source of justification for grants of special privileges. For if there is no duty to attempt either to measure the recovery by the wrong or to distribute the recovery within the injured class in an evenhanded way, our history will adequately support a legislative preference for almost any ethnic, religious, or racial group with the political strength to negotiate "a piece of the action" for its members.

* * *

It is unfortunately but unquestionably true that irrational racial prejudice persists today and continues to obstruct minority participation in a variety of economic pursuits, presumably including the construction industry. But there are two reasons why this legislation will not eliminate, or even tend to eliminate, such prejudice. First, prejudice is less likely to be a significant factor in the public sector of the economy than in the private sector because both federal and state laws have prohibited discrimination in the award of public contracts for many years. Second, and of greater importance, an absolute preference that is unrelated to a minority firm's ability to perform a contract inevitably will engender resentment on the part of competitors excluded from the market for a purely racial reason and skepticism on the part of customers and suppliers aware of the statutory classification. It thus seems clear to me that this Act cannot be defended as an appropriate method of reducing racial prejudice.

* * *

Unlike Mr. Justice Stewart and Mr. Justice Rehnquist, however, I am not convinced that the [Due Process] Clause contains an absolute prohibition against any statutory classification based on race. I am nonetheless persuaded that it does impose a special obligation to scrutinize any governmental decisionmaking process that draws nationwide distinctions between citizens on the basis of their race and incidentally also discriminates against noncitizens in the preferred racial classes. * * *

* * *

* * * [R]ather than take the substantive position expressed in Mr. Justice Stewart's dissenting opinion, I would hold this statute unconstitutional on a narrower ground. It cannot fairly be characterized as a "narrowly tailored" racial classification because it simply raises too many serious questions that Congress failed to answer or even to address in a responsible way. The risk that habitual attitudes toward classes of persons, rather than analysis of the relevant characteristics of the class, will serve as a basis for a legislative classification is present when benefits are distributed as well as when burdens are imposed. In the past, traditional attitudes too often provided the only explanation for discrimination against women, aliens, illegitimates, and black citizens. Today there is a danger that awareness of past injustice will lead to automatic acceptance of new classifications that are not in fact justified by attributes characteristic of the class as a whole.* * *

I respectfully dissent.

The Later Cases

By 1980, the Court had heard three important cases regarding affirmative action and had given general approval to this policy. Nonetheless, the issue continued to be controversial, and when Ronald Reagan was elected president, much of the opposition to affirmative action came from the executive branch. The executive branch previously had favored such programs; for example, the solicitor general under the Carter administration filed amicus briefs in support of affirmative action in the *Bakke* and *Weber* cases. In addition, the assistant attorney general argued the *Fullilove* case, urging the Court to uphold the government's set-aside program. The Reagan Justice Department, however, was opposed to affirmative action, adopting the position that affirmative action was justified only to remedy specific, identifiable discrimination, and that this relief should be limited to the actual victims of intentional discrimination. Proponents of affirmative action contended that this would probably invalidate most affirmative action programs because intentional discrimination was exceedingly difficult to prove. They noted that it was unlikely for employers to admit to discrimination, even when they had intentionally discriminated.

The decisions in the first affirmative action cases to come before the Court during the Reagan administration led many to believe that the opponents of these programs were going to prevail. The first case was not decided until 1984, as the Court did not address affirmative action in 1981, 1982, or 1983. *Firefighters Local Union No. 1784 v. Stotts* (1984) involved an employment conflict between affirmative action and seniority rights. After a class-action suit by African American firefighters claiming discrimination by the city of Memphis in its hiring and promotion practices, the city entered into a consent decree to increase the proportion of African American employees in the fire department. Later, the city's fiscal crisis required that some employees would be laid off, and such layoffs were to be based on seniority or the "last hired, first fired" principle. This would have had a negative impact on the newly hired African American firefighters and would defeat the goals of the consent decree. Thus, a federal district judge modified the consent decree to preserve the jobs of African American employees although this contradicted the seniority plan. By a 6-3 vote, the Court held that the judge exceeded his powers under Title VII in modifying the consent decree to protect the African American workers from layoffs. Writing for the majority, Justice White held that under Title VII, bona fide seniority systems are valid even if they thwart the goals of affirmative action. Moreover, White accepted the argument made in an amicus brief by the Reagan Justice Department that affirmative action should be limited to individuals who can prove that "they have been actual victims of [a] discriminatory practice" (467 U.S. at 579). He added, "[e]ven when an individual shows that the discriminatory practice has had an impact on him, he is not automatically entitled to have a non-minority employee laid off to make room for him" (467 U.S. at 579). Although concurring in the judgment that the district court had exceeded its authority by modifying the consent decree, Justice Stevens took issue with the majority's treatment of Title VII. He concluded that the discussion was not necessary to resolve the case and was "wholly advisory."

In dissent, Justices Blackmun, Brennan, and Marshall argued that because the layoffs had ended and the preliminary injunction was no longer in effect, the issue was moot and therefore the appeals court decision should simply have been vacated. "Since the preliminary injunction was entered . . . the layoffs all have terminated and the city has taken back every one of the workers laid off pursuant to the modified plan. Accordingly, the preliminary injunction no longer restrains the city's conduct. . . ." (467 U.S. at 594)

Thus, the *Stotts* decision seemed to indicate that the Reagan administration's position on affirmative action had prevailed. The Court had held that interests in seniority outweighed goals of affirmative action, and perhaps more importantly, the majority opinion contained strong language seeming to limit affirmative action to those who could "prove" they were victimized by discrimination.

Two years later in *Wygant v. Jackson Board of Education* (1986), the Court again struck down an affirmative action policy that protected minority workers from layoffs. This time, however, there was no language by the majority indicating that affirmative action applied only to those who can prove actual discrimination. Here, a teachers' union had included in its collective bargaining agreement a layoff policy that required minority teachers to be retained over whites with more seniority. The Court, by a 5-4 vote, held that the race-conscious policy violated the Equal Protection Clause of the Fourteenth Amendment. Justice Powell, writing for a plurality including himself, and Chief Justice Burger, and Justices O'Connor and Rehnquist, rejected the Board's contention that the policy was justified because of societal discrimination and because it helped to provide minority students with role models in their classrooms. The plurality said that the policy could be upheld only if the Board presented convincing evidence of its own discrimination, and the policy was "narrowly tailored" to remedy that discrimination. Powell concluded that the Board had not presented such evidence and that there were alternative ways to meet its goals, for example, the adoption of hiring goals that were less disruptive to the white teachers involved. In a concurrence, Justice White reiterated his point from *Stotts*, that he would have limited the affirmative action remedy here to the "actual victims" of discrimination. On the other hand, in her concurrence, Justice O'Connor disagreed that affirmative action remedies had to be limited to specific instances of identified discrimination. She said that such a narrow reading "would severely undermine public employers' incentive to meet voluntarily their civil rights obligations" (476 U.S. at 290).

Justices Blackmun, Brennan, and Marshall dissented, arguing that the policy in question promoted "important governmental interests" and was substantially related to such interests. Marshall, writing for the threesome, said that the layoff policy was beneficial in preserving the faculty integration that had been achieved through the affirmative action hiring policy adopted in the previous decade. He stressed that the layoff policy did not absolutely benefit or burden one race, and that it did not completely ignore seniority. In another dissent, Justice Stevens also was persuaded that the policy was justified to preserve the faculty integration that had taken place in the Jackson public schools. Moreover, he saw a distinction between "*exclud[ing]* a member of a minority race because of his or her skin color and a decision to *include* more members of the minority in a school faculty for that reason" (476 U.S. at 316).

As might be expected, affirmative action proponents were disappointed with the Court's rulings in *Stotts* and *Wygant,* while its opponents were satisfied that the Court was on a path of increasing opposition to affirmative, race-conscious remedies for discrimination. Two decisions later in the term, however, indicated that the justices were not yet ready to curtail affirmative action.

Local 28 of the Sheet Metal Workers v. EEOC (1986) involved the scope of the federal courts' authority in remedying discrimination under Title VII. A federal district court had concluded that Local 28 violated Title VII by discriminating against nonwhite workers, primarily African Americans and Hispanics, in recruitment, selection, training, and admission to the union. After determining the area's relevant labor pool, the district court established a 29 percent nonwhite membership goal for the union. The union did not comply and subsequently was found guilty of contempt.

By a 5-4 vote, the Supreme Court upheld the affirmative action order by the district court as consistent with the purposes of Title VII, specifically to remedy the continuing effects of pervasive discrimination and to open occupations traditionally closed to African Americans. Joined by Justices Blackmun, Marshall, and Stevens, Justice Brennan wrote, "Where an employer or union has engaged in particularly long-standing or egregious discrimination, an injunction simply reiterating Title VII's prohibition against discrimination will often prove useless and will only result in endless enforcement litigation. In such cases, requiring recalcitrant employers or unions to hire and to admit qualified minorities in the workforce may be the only effective way to ensure the full enjoyment of the rights protected by Title VII . . ." (478 U.S. at 448, 449). According to Brennan, this was such a case where the union had a record of "pervasive and egregious discrimination," (478 U.S. at 476) as well as "foot-dragging resistance to court orders" (478 U.S. at 477) requiring it not to discriminate. Justice Powell joined the plurality in part, and wrote a separate concurrence emphasizing that the remedy here was "narrowly tailored" to the goal of eliminating the union's discriminatory practices. Perhaps most importantly, Powell agreed with the plurality that Title VII does not limit a court to applying affirmative action only to the identified victims of discrimination. This was a rebuff to the Reagan administration, which had argued through the solicitor general's brief that a district court could "award preferential relief only to the actual victims of unlawful discrimination" (478 U.S. at 444). Finally, the plurality was persuaded to approve the district court's action because the membership goal was flexible and not aimed at maintaining racial balance; the membership goal was temporary; and because no white union members were required to be laid off under the plan, it did not "unnecessarily trammel the interests of white employees" (478 U.S. at 479).

In dissent, Justice White said the remedy ordered here was excessive, but he seemed to back away from his earlier position which was consistent with the view of the Reagan administration. ". . . I agree that Section 706(g) [of Title VII] does not bar relief for nonvictims in all circumstances" (478 U.S. at 499). Justice O'Connor dissented because she believed the membership goal to be a strict racial quota which she said was prohibited by Title VII. Justice Rehnquist, joined by Chief Justice Burger, argued that despite an employer's pervasive discrimination, the legislative history of Title VII and the *Stotts* decision limit affirmative remedies to the actual victims of such discrimination.

The Court reiterated the principle that affirmative action is not limited to the actual victims of discrimination in *Local 93, Firefighters v. City of Cleveland* (1986), handed down on the same day. After admitting to a long history of racial discrimination, the city of Cleveland agreed to establish promotion goals to increase the numbers of minority firefighters in various ranks. The plan was to be in place for approximately four years, and in some situations it would have required some minority firefighters to be promoted over nonminority employees with more seniority. The firefighters union, Local 93, objected to this consent decree, alleging that it was impermissible under section 706(g) Title VII. This section reads, "No order of the court shall require the admission or reinstatement of an individual as a member of a union, or the hiring, reinstatement, or promotion of an individual as an employee . . . if such individual was refused admission, suspended, or expelled, or was refused employment or advancement or was suspended or discharged for any reason other than discrimination on account of race, color, religion, sex, or national origin...." Local 93 argued that this section required that the race-conscious relief under the consent decree apply only to those who were the actual victims of discrimination. The union's interpretation was supported by the solicitor general's amicus brief to the Court.

By a 6-3 vote, the Court rejected this interpretation of section 706(g), and it upheld the consent decree. The Court said that this provision of Title VII did not apply to consent decrees. The majority held that whether or not courts were prevented from imposing this type of race-conscious relief after litigation, it was "clear that voluntary action available to employers and unions seeking to eradicate race discrimination may include reasonable race-conscious relief that benefits individuals who were not actual victims of discrimination" (478 U.S. at 516). Justice O'Connor, who dissented in *Local 28,* joined the majority in this case. She wrote a separate concurrence, stressing the narrowness of the ruling, stating that the Court was only interpreting the applicability of section 706(g). She emphasized that the decision here left open the question of whether the relief provided for in the consent decree was prohibited by section 703 of Title VII or by the Fourteenth Amendment. She said that the nonminority employees involved here were free to challenge the consent decree on these grounds.

In a lone dissent, Justice White argued that Title VII forbids this type of practice—period. "An employer may not, without violating Title VII, simply decide for itself or in agreement with its employees to have a racially balanced workforce. . . . Even without displacing any present employees, Title VII would forbid quota hiring or promotion" (478 U.S. at 531–32). Therefore, he contended, this practice is not permitted under consent decrees as well.

Justice Rehnquist, writing for himself and Chief Justice Burger, argued that *Stotts* was the controlling precedent for this case. In their view, because *Stotts* held that race-conscious relief was limited to the actual victims of discrimination, and the consent decree did not meet this requirement, it was necessarily invalid.

As the Burger era drew to a close, only one thing seemed to be clear about the Court's position on affirmative action—the justices were deeply divided over this issue. Moreover, they could not agree on which standard to use if the case was challenged on equal protection grounds, and they were in disagreement over the interpretation of various sections of Title VII as they related to affirmative action plans.

Finally, while the Court had approved of affirmative action in five of the seven cases decided on the merits, the decisions were by such narrow votes that supporters of affirmative action believed such programs to be in jeopardy. At the same time, affirmative action opponents expressed some hope that these close votes foreshadowed the Court's increasing hostility to such programs. Thus, those on both sides of the issue looked with increasing interest to the Rehnquist Court.

The Rehnquist Court Era

As in previous chapters, the Rehnquist Court's decisions regarding affirmative action will be discussed from both quantitative and doctrinal perspectives. This will enable us to determine whether the Court has engaged in a conservative revolution in this area. A liberal decision is one in which the Court upholds affirmative action, while a conservative outcome occurs when the Court rules against affirmative action.

The quantitative analysis reveals that the Rehnquist Court was substantially more conservative than the Burger Court in affirmative action cases. As Table 15.1 shows, the Burger Court supported affirmative action in 71% of its cases, while the Rehnquist Court upheld affirmative action in only half of its cases.

Beyond the figures for the Rehnquist Court overall, the voting records of the individual justices indicate a deeply divided Court. As seen in Table 15.2, five justices have consistently supported affirmative action, and five justices have consistently disapproved of affirmative action. At one end of the spectrum, Justices Brennan, Marshall, and Blackmun, participating in five of the six cases, voted to uphold affirmative action in all of them. Justice Powell voted in favor of affirmative action in both cases in which he participated, while Justice Stevens supported affirmative

TABLE 15.1: Liberal/Conservative Outcomes of Affirmative Action Cases for the Burger and Rehnquist Courts, 1969-94 Terms

	Outcomes		
Court Era	Liberal	Conservative	Totals
Burger Court, 1969-1985 Terms	71% (5)	29% (2)	7
Rehnquist Court, 1986-1994 Terms	50% (3)	50% (3)	6
Totals	62% (8)	38% (5)	13

TABLE 15.2: Liberal/Conservative Voting Records of Justices of the Rehnquist Court in Affirmative Action Cases, 1986-94 Terms

Justices	Liberal Votes	Conservative Votes
Brennan	100% (5)	0% (0)
Marshall	100% (5)	0% (0)
Blackmun	100% (5)	0% (0)
Powell	100% (2)	0% (0)
Souter	100% (1)	0% (0)
Ginsburg	100% (1)	0% (0)
Breyer	100% (1)	0% (0)
Stevens	83% (5)	17% (1)
White	20% (1)	80% (4)
O'Connor	17% (1)	83% (5)
Thomas	0% (0)	100% (1)
Kennedy	0% (0)	100% (4)
Rehnquist	0% (0)	100% (6)
Scalia	0% (0)	100% (6)

action in five of the six cases. Three of the most recent appointees (Souter, Ginsburg, and Breyer) each participated in one case and voted to uphold affirmative action. At the other end of the spectrum, Chief Justice Rehnquist and Justice Scalia voted against affirmative action in all six cases, while Justice Kennedy did the same in the four cases in which he participated. Justices O'Connor and White consistently voted against affirmative action, in five of six cases and four of five cases, respectively. Finally, Justice Thomas voted against affirmative action in his only case.

The bloc analysis presented in Table 15.3 underscores the deep division that has existed on the Rehnquist Court in the area of affirmative action. The Court has been sharply divided into two blocs, one liberal and one conservative. The liberal bloc consists of four justices—Brennan, Marshall, Blackmun, and Stevens—who have a

TABLE 15.3: Bloc Voting Analysis of the Rehnquist Court in Affirmative Action Cases, 1986-94 Terms (Percent Agreement Rates)

	BR	MA	BL	ST	WH	RE	SC	KE	OC
Brennan	—	100	100	80	20	0	0	0	20
Marshall	100	—	100	80	20	0	0	0	20
Blackmun	100	100	—	80	20	0	0	0	20
Stevens	80	80	80	—	40	17	17	25	33
White	20	20	20	40	—	80	80	67	60
Rehnquist	0	0	0	17	80	—	100	100	83
Scalia	0	0	0	17	80	100	—	100	83
Kennedy	0	0	0	25	67	100	100	—	100
O'Connor	20	20	20	33	60	83	83	100	—

Court mean = 46
Sprague Criterion = 73
Liberal bloc: Brennan, Marshall, Blackmun, Stevens = 90
Conservative bloc: White, Rehnquist, Scalia, Kennedy, O'Connor = 85

high level of average interagreement at 90 percent. The conservative bloc's average interagreement score is somewhat lower at 85 percent, but the conservative bloc has constituted a majority of the Court: White, Rehnquist, Scalia, Kennedy, and O'Connor.

These data, then, indicate that the Rehnquist Court has had the potential voting alignment to undergo a conservative revolution in the area of affirmative action, and recent changes in the Court's membership have probably not changed this alignment. Three of the four most staunch supporters of affirmative action (Justices Brennan, Marshall, and Blackmun) are no longer on the Court. Justices Brennan and Blackmun were succeeded by justices who supported affirmative action in their initial case (Souter and Breyer), but Justice Marshall was succeeded by Thomas, whose earlier writings and whose vote in his first case indicate his opposition to affirmative action. Justice Ginsburg, who supported affirmative action in her first case, succeeded an opponent of affirmative action (White). Nonetheless, it appears that the conservatives have a majority willing to overturn affirmative action programs—Rehnquist, Scalia, Kennedy, O'Connor, and Thomas. Kennedy's succession of Powell is important in this respect because while Kennedy has consistently voted against affirmative action, Powell's record indicates general approval of this concept. When the Burger and Rehnquist Court cases are combined, Justice Powell voted in favor of affirmative action in six of the eight cases in which he participated. In the two cases in which he ruled against affirmative action, the plans being challenged were in conflict with seniority rights (*Stotts* and *Wygant v. Jackson*).

The results of the doctrinal analysis provide strong evidence that the Rehnquist Court has indeed engaged in a conservative revolution in its affirmative action jurisprudence. As Table 15.4 indicates, the Court has decided six substantive affirmative action cases, five of which have been classified as "major" or "important" cases. The Court decided the two 1987 cases *U.S. v. Paradise* and *Johnson v. Transportation Agency* by liberally interpreting existing precedent. In 1989, however, the Court shifted gears. It decided *Martin v. Wilks* on the basis of a conservative interpretation of existing precedent, and in *Richmond v. Croson*, the majority created a new conservative precedent when it adopted the strict scrutiny standard for examining affirmative action plans challenged as violating equal protection. Justice Kennedy's replacement of Powell probably did not make much of a difference here. While Kennedy joined the majority in adopting the strict scrutiny approach, Justice Powell had argued for this test in the *Bakke* case. The *Croson* ruling did not resolve this issue because a year later in *Metro Broadcasting v. FCC*, the majority used intermediate scrutiny in deciding the case—a liberal modification of existing precedent. The Court distinguished between plans of the federal government (intermediate scrutiny) and those of state and local governments (strict scrutiny). Five years later, however, the Court created a new conservative precedent, ruling that all governmental affirmative action plans would be examined using strict scrutiny (*Adarand Constructors v. Pena*). We now move to a discussion of these cases.

In a case decided during its first term, the Rehnquist Court dealt with a plan developed by a federal district court to remedy discrimination by a public employer, the Alabama Department of Public Safety. *U.S. v. Paradise* (1987) actually began in 1972, when a federal district court found that the department's hiring practices were discriminatory and in violation of the Equal Protection Clause. The court discovered that in its thirty-seven years of existence, the Department of Public Safety had never hired an African American trooper. In fact, the only jobs held by African Americans were as laborers. After finding a pattern of discrimination, the district court ordered the department to end its discriminatory practices in both hiring and promotion and

TABLE 15.4: A Framework for the Doctrinal Analysis of the Rehnquist Court's Affirmative Action Cases, 1986–94 Terms

Major or Minor Importance	**Majority or Plurality Opinion**	**Treatment of Precedent**					
		Creation of New Liberal Precedent	Liberal Modification of Existing Precedent	Liberal Interpretation of Existing Precedent	Conservative Interpretation of Existing Precedent	Conservative Modification of Existing Precedent	Creation of New Conservative Precedent
Major	Majority		Metro Broadcasting v. FCC (1990)	Johnson v. Transp Agency (1987)	Martin v. Wilks (1989)		Richmond v. Croson (1989) Adarand Constructors v. Pena (1995)
	Plurality						
Minor	Majority						
	Plurality			U.S. v. Paradise (1987)			

imposed a 50 percent hiring goal for African American troopers. Twelve years passed without the department reaching this goal; by 1984 no African Americans had been promoted to major, captain, lieutenant, or sergeant positions, and only four had been promoted to corporal. The district court then ordered a temporary plan in which the department was required to promote one African American for every one white promoted until African Americans made up 25 percent of officers in the corporal rank. A similar plan was enacted for promotions to the ranks above corporal. Over objections from the Reagan administration, the district court's actions were upheld by the court of appeals. The Reagan administration then petitioned the Supreme Court to review the case.

By a 5-4 vote, the Court ruled that the district court's plan was not in violation of the Equal Protection Clause. There was, however, no majority opinion as five justices did not agree on the appropriate standard of review. Normally an advocate of intermediate scrutiny, Justice Brennan wrote for a plurality which held that even under strict scrutiny, the plan was permissible. Writing for himself and Justices Blackmun, Marshall, and Powell, Brennan said that the district court had a compelling interest in remedying past and present discrimination by the state and that the remedy imposed was narrowly tailored for that purpose. The plurality emphasized the long history of pervasive discrimination by the department and found the 50 percent promotion goal appropriate given that history. Moreover, Brennan argued that the plan was temporary, flexible, and did not overly burden nonminority employees. "The features of the one-for-one requirement and its actual operation indicate that it is flexible in application at all ranks. The requirement may be waived if no qualified black candidates are available. * * * Further, it applies only when the Department needs to make promotions. Thus, if external forces, such as budget cuts, necessitate a promotion freeze, the Department will not be required to make gratuitous promotions to remain in compliance with the court's order" (480 U.S. at 177, 178). Although agreeing with the plurality that the district court had not exceeded its authority in issuing this plan, Justice Stevens argued that because of the department's pattern of egregious discrimination, the remedy did not need to be narrowly tailored to achieve a compelling governmental interest. He maintained that the department's discriminatory conduct permitted the district court to have broad authority to remedy the violations involved here.

Justice O'Connor issued a dissenting opinion, joined by Chief Justice Rehnquist and Justice Scalia. She agreed with the majority that the department was guilty of "pervasive, systematic, and obstinate discriminatory conduct" (480 U.S. at 196), but she argued that the district court had not narrowly tailored the plan to remedy that discrimination. She viewed the plan as a strict quota that was not necessary to remedy the discrimination and its effects. O'Connor said that the district court should have used alternative remedies, for example, appointing a trustee to develop promotion procedures, and issuing citations, fines, or other penalties for contempt of court decrees. In a separate dissent, Justice White simply concluded that the district court had exceeded its authority in imposing such a broad remedy in this case.

Several months after the *Paradise* ruling, the Court issued its first decision in an affirmative action case involving gender rather than race. *Johnson v. Transportation Agency* (1987) stemmed from a plan adopted by the Santa Clara County (California) Transportation Agency to redress gender and racial segregation in its job classifications. The plan provided that when positions in traditionally male-dominated occupations were to be filled, gender would be considered as one factor in examining qualified applicants. Diane Joyce and Paul Johnson applied for a promotion to road dispatcher, and they both were rated as well qualified. When gender was taken into account, the agency director chose Joyce for the position, and Johnson filed suit claiming gender discrimination in violation of Title VII.

The Court upheld the plan by a 6-3 vote. Justice Brennan wrote the majority opinion, using the *Weber* case as the controlling precedent. Brennan wrote, "Such a plan is fully consistent with Title VII, for it embodies the contribution that voluntary employer action can make in eliminating the vestiges of discrimination in the workplace" (480 U.S. at 642). In reaching this conclusion, the majority was influenced by several factors. First, the justices said that the plan did not require any rigid quotas, but merely established flexible promotion goals to achieve the purpose of correcting the imbalance in the agency's job classifications. Second, the plan permitted gender to be considered as *one* factor, but it was not the only consideration, and women had to compete with other qualified applicants for the promotions. Thus, males were not completely barred from advancement in the agency. Furthermore, Brennan wrote that Johnson was not absolutely entitled to the promotion here because the agency director was authorized to appoint any of seven qualified candidates who had been recommended for the position. "Thus, denial of the promotion unsettled no legitimate firmly rooted expectation on the part of the petitioner" (480 U.S. at 638). Lastly, the plan was temporary in nature, and it was not designed to "maintain a permanent racial and sexual balance" (480 U.S. at 640). While this case involved a public employer, it was decided on statutory grounds (Title VII) rather than constitutional grounds (equal protection).

In a spirited dissent, Justice Scalia, writing for himself, Chief Justice Rehnquist, and Justice White, chastised the majority for allowing this affirmative action remedy without evidence of specific discrimination by the employer. Scalia wrote that Title VII's purpose was to ensure a color-blind and gender-blind workplace, but the majority's decision in this case thwarted that goal. "The Court today completes the process of converting [Title VII] from a guarantee that race or sex will *not* be the basis for employment determinations, to a guarantee that it often *will* [emphasis in original]" (480 U.S. at 658). Moreover, Scalia argued that the Court's decision would result in employers hiring less-qualified employees because that would be less expensive than defending themselves against discrimination lawsuits. Finally, the dissenters emphasized that inasmuch as *Weber* encourages the decision reached here, it should be overruled so that the purposes of Title VII could be achieved.

Johnson v. Transportation Agency, Santa Clara County, California

480 U.S. 616, 107 S. Ct. 1442, 94 Ed. 2d 615 (1987)

■ A study by the Transportation Agency of Santa Clara County, California, found that while women made up 36 percent of the local labor market, they made up only 22 percent of the agency's labor force. More importantly, the women employed by the agency were concentrated in lower-paying, female-dominated jobs, particularly at the clerical levels. The agency developed a plan, therefore, to increase the number of women employed in higher-paying positions traditionally dominated by males, like skilled craft work. Annual hiring and promotion goals were established for this purpose, but no specific number of positions was set aside for women to fill.

The plan became the subject of controversy in 1979 when it was used in filling a vacancy for the job of road dispatcher, a skilled craft classification. When this vacancy occurred, the agency discovered that of 238 positions in this classification, no woman had ever held such a position. Two applicants, Diane Joyce and Paul Johnson, were both rated well qualified for the position, although Johnson's interview score was two points higher than Joyce's. Taking affirmative action into consideration, the agency promoted Joyce over Johnson, who then filed suit in federal district court, alleging that the agency's plan and actions violated Title VII. Although the district court decided in his favor, the court of appeals reversed that decision, and Johnson then appealed to the Supreme Court.

This case is significant because it is the first time the Court considered an affirmative action plan involving gender rather than race. As you read the case, consider these questions: (1) Would the case have arisen if Joyce and Johnson had earned identical scores on the interview? (2) Is Justice Scalia correct in his conclusion that gender segregation in various job classifications, such as road maintenance, is due primarily to women's lack of desire for this type of work? (3) Would the outcome have been different if the Transportation Agency had set aside a specific number of positions in male-dominated job classifications to be held by women?

VOTE:

6 justices agreed that the plan was consistent with Title VII (Brennan, Marshall, Blackmun, Powell, Stevens, and O'Connor).

3 justices viewed the plan as a violation of Title VII (White, Rehnquist, and Scalia).

Justice Brennan delivered the opinion of the Court.

* * * The question for decision is whether in making the promotion the agency impermissibly took into account the sex of the applicants in violation of Title VII of the Civil Rights Act of 1964. * * *

* * *

As a preliminary matter, we note that petitioner bears the burden of establishing the invalidity of the Agency's Plan. Only last Term, in *Wygant v. Jackson Board of Education* (1986), we held that "[t]he ultimate burden remains with the employees to demonstrate the unconstitutionality of an affirmative-action program," and we see no basis for a different rule regarding a plan's alleged violation of Title VII. This case also fits readily within the analytical framework set forth in *McDonnell Douglas Corp. v. Green* (1973). Once a plaintiff establishes a prima facie case that race or sex has been taken into account in an employer's employment decision, the burden shifts to the employer to articulate a nondiscriminatory rationale for its decision. The existence of an affirmative action plan provides such a rationale. If such a plan is articulated as the basis for the employer's decision, the burden shifts to the plaintiff to prove that the employer's justification is pretextual and the plan is invalid. As a practical matter, of course, an employer will generally seek to avoid a charge of pretext by presenting evidence in support of its plan. That does not mean, however, as petitioner suggests, that reliance on an affirmative action plan is to be treated as an affirmative defense requiring the employer to carry the burden of proving the validity of the plan. The burden of proving its invalidity remains on the plaintiff.

The assessment of the legality of the Agency Plan must be guided by our decision in *Weber*. In that case, the Court addressed the question whether the employer violated Title VII by adopting a voluntary affirmative action plan designed to "eliminate manifest racial imbalances in traditionally segregated job categories." * * *

We upheld the employer's decision to select less senior black applicants over the white respondent, for we found that taking race into account was consistent with Title VII's objective of "break[ing] down old patterns of racial segregation and hierarchy." * * *

We noted that the plan did not "unnecessarily trammel the interests of the white employees," since it did not require "the discharge of white workers and their replacement with new black hirees." Nor did the plan create "an absolute bar to the advancement of white employees," since half of those trained in the new program were to be white. Finally, we observed that the plan was a temporary measure, not designed to maintain racial balance, but to "eliminate a manifest racial imbalance." As Justice Blackmun's concurrence made clear, *Weber* held that an employer seeking to justify the adoption of a plan need not point to its own prior discriminatory practices, nor even to evidence of an "arguable violation" on its part. Rather, it need point only to a "conspicuous . . . imbalance in traditionally segregated job categories." Our decision was grounded in the recognition that voluntary employer action can play a crucial role in furthering Title VII's purpose of eliminating the effects of discrimination in the workplace, and that Title VII should not be read to thwart such efforts.

In reviewing the employment decision at issue in this case, we must first examine whether that decision was made pursuant to a plan prompted by concerns similar to those of the employer in *Weber*. Next, we must determine whether the effect of the Plan on males and nonminorities is comparable to the effect of the plan in that case.

The first issue is therefore whether consideration of the sex of applicants for Skilled Craft jobs was justified by the existence of a "manifest imbalance" that reflected underrepresentation of women in "traditionally segregated job categories." In determining whether an imbalance exists that would justify taking sex or race into account, a comparison of the percentage of minorities or women in the employer's work force with the percentage in the area labor market or general population is appropriate in analyzing jobs that require no special expertise. * * * Where a job requires special training, however, the comparison should be with those in the labor force who possess the relevant qualifications. * * * The requirement that the "manifest imbalance" relate to a "traditionally segregated job category" provides assurance both that sex or race will be taken into account in a manner consistent with Title VII's purpose of eliminating the effects of employment discrimination, and that the interests of those employees not benefiting from the plan will not be unduly infringed.

* * *

It is clear that the decision to hire Joyce was made pursuant to an Agency plan that directed that sex or race be taken into account for the purpose of remedying underrepresentation. The Agency Plan acknowledged the "limited opportunities that have existed in the past" for women to find employment in certain job classifications "where women have not been traditionally employed in significant numbers." As a result, observed the Plan, women were concentrated in traditionally female jobs in the Agency, and represented a lower percentage in other job classifications than would be expected if such traditional segregation had not occurred. * * * The Plan sought to remedy these imbalances through "hiring, training and promotion of . . . women throughout the Agency in all major job classifications where they are underrepresented."

As an initial matter, the Agency adopted as a benchmark for measuring progress in eliminating underrepresentation the long-term goal of a work force that mirrored in its major job classifications the percentage of women in the area labor market. Even as it did so, however, the Agency acknowledged that such a figure could not by itself necessarily justify taking into account the sex of applicants for positions in all job categories. * * * The Plan therefore directed that annual short-term goals be formulated that would provide a more realistic indication of the degree to which sex should be taken into account in filling particular positions. The Plan stressed that such goals "should not be construed as 'quotas' that must be met," but as reasonable aspirations in correcting the imbalance in the Agency's work force. These goals were to take into account factors such as "turnover, layoffs, lateral transfers, new job openings, retirements and availability of minorities, women and handicapped persons in the area work force who possess the desired qualifications or potential for placement." The Plan specifically directed that, in establishing such goals, the Agency work with the County Planning Department and other sources in attempting to compile data on the percentage of minorities and women in the local labor force that were actually working in the job classifications constituting the Agency work force. From the outset, therefore, the Plan sought annually to develop even more refined measures of the underrepresentation in each job category that required attention.

As the Agency Plan recognized, women were most egregiously underrepresented in the Skilled Craft job category, since *none* of the 238 positions was occupied by a woman. * * *

* * * The Agency's Plan emphasized that the long-term goals were not to be taken as guides for actual hiring decisions, but that supervisors were to consider a host of practical factors in seeking to meet affirmative action objectives, including the fact that in some job categories women were not qualified in numbers comparable to their representation in the labor force.

* * *

* * * Given the obvious imbalance in the Skilled Craft category, and given the Agency's commitment to eliminating such imbalances, it was plainly not unreasonable for the Agency to determine that it was appropriate to consider as one factor the sex of Ms. Joyce in making its decision. The promotion of Joyce thus satisfies the first requirement enunciated in *Weber*, since it was undertaken to further an affirmative action plan designed to eliminate Agency work force imbalances in traditionally segregated job categories.

We next consider whether the Agency Plan unnecessarily trammeled the rights of male employees or created an absolute bar to their advancement. In contrast to the plan in *Weber*, the Plan sets aside no positions for women. The Plan expressly states that "[t]he 'goals' established for each Division should not be construed as 'quotas' that must be met." Rather, the Plan merely authorizes that consideration be given to affirmative action concerns when evaluating qualified applicants. As the agency Director testified, the sex of Joyce was but one of numerous factors he took into account in arriving at his decision. * * * Similarly, the Agency Plan requires women to compete with all other qualified applicants. *No* persons are automatically excluded from consideration; *all* are able to have their qualifications weighed against those of other applicants.

In addition, petitioner had no absolute entitlement to the road dispatcher position. Seven of the applicants were classified as qualified and eligible, and the Agency Director was authorized to promote any of the seven. Thus, denial of the promotion unsettled no legitimate, firmly rooted expectation on the part of petitioner. Furthermore, while petitioner in this case was denied a promotion, he retained his employment with the Agency, at the same salary and with the same seniority, and remained eligible for other promotions.

Finally, the Agency's Plan was intended to *attain* a balanced work force, not to maintain one. The Plan contains 10 references to the Agency's desire to "attain" such a balance, but no reference whatsoever to a goal of maintaining it. * * *

The Agency acknowledged the difficulties that it would confront in remedying the imbalance in its work force, and it anticipated only gradual increases in the representation of minorities and women. It is thus unsurprising that the Plan contains no explicit end date, for the Agency's flexible, case-by-case approach was not expected to yield success in a brief period of time. Express assurance that a program is only temporary may be necessary if the program actually sets aside positions according to specific numbers. * * * In this case, however, substantial evidence shows that the Agency has sought to take a moderate, gradual approach to eliminating the imbalance in its work force, one which establishes realistic guidance for employment decisions, and which visits minimal intrusion on the legitimate expectations of other employees. Given this fact, as well as the Agency's express commitment to "attain" a balanced work force, there is ample assurance that the Agency does not seek to use its Plan to maintain a permanent racial and sexual balance.

* * *

We therefore hold that the Agency appropriately took into account as one factor the sex of Diane Joyce in determining that she should be promoted to the road dispatcher position. The decision to do so was made pursuant to an affirmative action plan that represents a moderate, flexible, case-by-case approach to effecting a gradual improvement in the representation of minorities and women in the Agency's work force. Such a plan is fully consistent with Title VII, for it embodies the contribution that voluntary employer action can make in eliminating the vestiges of discrimination in the workplace. Accordingly, the judgment of the Court of Appeals is affirmed.

Justice Stevens concurred [omitted].

Justice O'Connor concurred in the judgment [omitted].

Justice White dissented [omitted].

Justice Scalia, with whom the Chief Justice joins, and with whom Justice White joins in [p]art. . . , dissenting.

With a clarity which, had it not proven so unavailing, one might well recommend as a model of statutory draftsmanship, Title VII of the Civil Rights Act of 1964 declares:

> It shall be an unlawful employment practice for an employer—
>
> (1) to fail or refuse to hire or to discharge any individual, or otherwise to discriminate against any individual with respect to his compensation, terms, conditions, or privileges of employment, because of such individual's race, color, religion, sex, or national origin; or
>
> (2) to limit, segregate, or classify his employees or applicants for employment in any way which would deprive or tend to deprive any individual of employment opportunities or otherwise adversely affect his status as an employee, because of such individual's race, color, religion, sex, or national origin.

The Court today completes the process of converting this from a guarantee that race or sex will *not* be the basis for employment determinations, to a guarantee that it often *will*. Ever so subtly, without even alluding to the last obstacles preserved by earlier opinions that we now push out of our path, we effectively replace the goal of a discrimination-free society with the quite incompatible goal of proportionate representation by race and by sex in the workplace. * * *

* * *

The most significant proposition of law established by today's decision is that racial or sexual discrimination is permitted under Title VII when it is intended to overcome the effect, not of the employer's own discrimination, but of societal attitudes that have limited the entry of certain races, or of a particular sex, into certain jobs. * * *

* * *

In fact, however, today's decision goes well beyond merely allowing racial or sexual discrimination in order to eliminate the effects of prior societal *discrimination*. The majority opinion often uses the phrase "traditionally segregated job category" to describe the evil against which the plan is legitimately (according to the majority) directed. As originally used in *Steelworkers v. Weber*, that phrase described skilled jobs from which employers and unions had systematically and intentionally excluded black workers—traditionally segregated jobs, that is, in the sense of conscious, exclusionary discrimination. But that is assuredly not the sense in which the phrase is used here. It is absurd to think that the nationwide failure of road maintenance crews, for example, to achieve the agency's ambition of 36.4% female representation is attributable primarily, if even substantially, to systematic exclusion of women eager to shoulder pick and shovel. It is a "traditionally segregated job category" *not* in the *Weber* sense, but in the sense that, because of longstanding social attitudes, it has not been regarded *by women themselves* as desirable work. Or as the majority opinion puts the point, quoting approvingly the Court of Appeals: "'A plethora of proof is hardly necessary to show that women are generally underrepresented in such positions and that strong social pressures weigh against their participation.'" * * * There are, of course, those who believe that the social attitudes which cause women themselves to avoid certain jobs and to favor others are as nefarious as conscious, exclusionary discrimination. Whether or not that is so (and there is assuredly no consensus on the point equivalent to our national consensus against intentional discrimination), the two phenomena are certainly distinct. And it is the alteration of social attitudes, rather than the elimination of discrimination, which today's decision approves as justification for state-enforced discrimination. This is an enormous expansion, undertaken without the slightest justification or analysis.

* * *

Today's decision does more . . . than merely reaffirm *Weber*, and more than merely extend it to public actors. It is impossible not to be aware that the practical effect of our holding is to accomplish *de facto* what the law—in language even plainer than that ignored in *Weber*—forbids anyone from accomplishing *de jure*: in many contexts it effectively *requires* employers, public as well as private, to engage in intentional discrimination on the basis of race or sex. * * * A statute designed to establish a color-blind and gender-blind workplace has thus been converted into a powerful engine of racism and sexism, not merely *permitting* intentional race- and sex-based discrimination, but often making it, through operation of the legal system, practically compelled.

It is unlikely that today's result will be displeasing to politically elected officials, to whom it provides the means of quickly accommodating the demands of organized groups to achieve concrete, numerical improvements in the economic status of particular constituencies. Nor will it displease the world of corporate and governmental employers (many of whom have filed briefs as *amici* in the present case, all on the side of Santa Clara) for whom the cost of hiring less qualified workers is often substantially less—and infinitely more predictable—than the cost of litigating Title VII cases and of seeking to convince federal agencies by nonnumerical means that no discrimination exists. In fact, the only losers in the process are the Johnsons of the country, for whom Title VII has been not merely repealed but actually inverted. The irony is that these individuals—predominantly unknown, unaffluent, unorganized—suffer this injustice at the hands of a Court fond of thinking itself the champion of the politically impotent. I dissent.

The Rehnquist Court did not decide any affirmative action cases in the 1987–88 term, but the issue returned to its agenda in the 1988–89 term in the form of two cases. The first case, *Richmond v. J. A. Croson Co.* (1989), involved the use of set-asides in the awarding of contracts. The city of Richmond, Virginia established a set-aside program whereby prime contractors who received city construction contracts were to subcontract at least 30 percent of the dollar amount of the contract to minority business enterprises (MBEs). A contractor could receive a waiver if no qualified MBEs could be found. The plan was patterned after the federal government's program that the Court upheld in *Fullilove*.

By a 6-3 vote, the Supreme Court held that the Minority Utilization Plan was in violation of the Equal Protection Clause. For the first time, a majority of the justices adopted the strict scrutiny standard for examining affirmative action plans that are challenged on equal protection grounds. Justice O'Connor wrote an opinion that was joined by Chief Justice Rehnquist and Justice White, and in part by Justices Stevens and Kennedy. As noted earlier, Kennedy's replacement of Powell did not seem to have a major impact on the outcome of this case, especially with respect to the appropriate standard of review. Justice Powell had argued a decade earlier in *Bakke* that strict scrutiny should be applied in examining affirmative action plans. On the other hand, given his approval of a similar program that was challenged in *Fullilove*, Powell may have voted to uphold the Richmond plan. Nonetheless, the outcome would have been the same; the plan would have been struck down by a 5-4 vote rather than by a 6-3 vote.

O'Connor first addressed the applicability of the *Fullilove* precedent because Richmond had argued that its set-aside plan was patterned after that upheld in *Fullilove.* O'Connor concluded, however, that *Fullilove* did not apply here because the federal government had more latitude in remedying discrimination than did state and local governments. ". . . Congress, unlike any State or political subdivision, has a specific constitutional mandate to enforce the dictates of the Fourteenth Amendment" (488 U.S. at 490). Next, O'Connor argued that the appropriate standard for examining this plan was strict scrutiny. In a separate opinion, Justice Scalia agreed. Under this approach, racial classifications must be directed toward a compelling state interest and must be narrowly tailored to achieve that interest. O'Connor then applied this test, holding that the Richmond Plan violated both parts of this test. First, the city contended that the plan was aimed at remedying past discrimination that had resulted in the small number of local minority contractors. O'Connor rejected this point, arguing that Richmond had not demonstrated that the city itself was guilty of such discrimination, and "past discrimination in a particular industry cannot justify the use of an unyielding racial quota" (488 U.S. at 499). Moreover, the city's inclusion of minorities other than African Americans was viewed as evidence that there was no remedial purpose of the plan. "There is *absolutely no evidence* [emphasis in original] of past discrimination against Spanish-speaking, Oriental, Indian, Eskimo, or Aleut persons in any aspect of the Richmond construction industry" (490 U.S. at 506). Second, O'Connor wrote that the plan was not narrowly tailored to assist those who had suffered the effects of discrimination, given that minorities from all over the country were eligible for the program. In addition, she chided the city for not considering race-neutral alternatives to increase the participation of minority businesses in city contracting. She cited such possibilities as simplifying bidding procedures, relaxing bonding requirements, and providing training and financial aid for disadvantaged entrepreneurs of all races.

In an opinion concurring in the judgment only, Justice Scalia expressed his view that the Constitution is color-blind, and that race-conscious plans, even if benign or remedial, violate that principle. Thus, only a "social emergency" would justify an exception to it. While granting that discrimination has occurred and has been borne disproportionately by African Americans, Scalia made clear that he was adamantly opposed to race-conscious policies, opting instead for remedies that do not rely upon racial classifications. He argued that "any race-neutral remedial program aimed at the disadvantaged . . . will have a disproportionately beneficial impact on African Americans" (488 U.S. at 528). Thus, race-neutral programs should be preferred.

In a stinging dissent for himself and Justices Blackmun and Brennan, Justice Marshall criticized the majority for what he termed a "grapeshot attack" on affirmative action, and for discouraging government officials from acting to eradicate racial discrimination. He said that the Richmond Plan was analogous to that upheld in *Fullilove* and therefore should have been approved. More importantly, he chastised the majority for adopting the strict scrutiny approach, suggesting instead that the appropriate standard of review was whether the race-conscious remedy served important government objectives and was substantially related to those objectives. Marshall cited two legitimate objectives of the Richmond Plan: 1) to address the effects of past racial discrimination, and 2) to prevent the city from making financial decisions that reinforce and perpetuate the effects of that discrimination. Further, Marshall concluded that the testimony of Richmond's public officials regarding widespread racial discrimination in contracting in the Richmond area was sufficient proof that such discrimination existed. Marshall argued that the plan was substantially related to these objectives, much like the set-aside program in *Fullilove.* The Richmond Plan was limited in duration, it contained a waiver provision, and it did not unduly burden innocent third parties. In fact, Marshall claimed, although the plan affected 30 percent of public contracting funds, it involved only 3 percent of the total contracting monies in the Richmond area. Finally, in one of the opinion's most passionate passages, Marshall accused his colleagues of ignoring the continuing problem of racial discrimination. "In concluding that remedial classifications warrant no different standard of review under the Constitution than the most brute and repugnant forms of state-sponsored racism, a majority of this Court signals that it regards racial discrimination as largely a phenomenon of the past, and that government bodies need no longer preoccupy themselves with rectifying racial injustice. I, however, do not believe this Nation is anywhere close to eradicating racial discrimination or its vestiges (488 U.S. at 552).

City of Richmond v. J. A. Croson Co.

488 U.S. 469, 109 S. Ct. 706, 102 L. Ed. 2d 854 (1989)

■ The Richmond City Council adopted a set-aside program in 1983 after studies indicated that although the city's population was 50 percent African American, minority contractors received only .67% percent of the city's prime contracts. Also, there was evidence that the local contractors associations had practically no minority-owned businesses as members. The Minority Business Utilization Plan (Plan) required prime contractors who were awarded city contracts to subcontract at least 30 percent of the dollar amount of the contract to minority business enterprises (MBEs). The MBE could be owned by African American, Spanish-speaking, Oriental, Native American, or Eskimo citizens from anywhere in the United States. The plan was patterned after that of the federal government, which had been upheld by the Court in *Fullilove* and, like the program in *Fullilove,* a contractor could receive a waiver if no qualified MBEs could be found. The case arose when the J. A. Croson Company's application for such a waiver was denied. Croson filed suit in federal district court, challenging the set-aside plan as unconstitutional under the Equal Protection Clause. The district court upheld the plan, but the court of appeals reversed that decision. The city appealed to the Supreme Court.

This case is important primarily because it is the first time that a majority agreed to examine affirmative action policies under strict scrutiny. As you read the case, consider the following questions: (1) Is it reasonable and logical to conclude that Congress has greater powers to remedy the effects of societal discrimination than do state and local governments? (2) Would the Court have upheld this set-aside if the city had provided specific evidence of its own discrimination and if the plan had been limited to African Americans in the city? (3) What justifications do the justices present for using (or not using) strict scrutiny in deciding affirmative action cases?

Vote:

6 justices viewed the Plan as a violation of the Equal Protection Clause (O'Connor, Rehnquist, White, Stevens, Kennedy, and Scalia).

3 justices voted to uphold the Plan (Marshall, Brennan, and Blackmun).

* * *

Justice O'Connor announced the judgment of the Court and delivered the opinion of the Court.

* * *

The parties and their supporting *amici* fight an initial battle over the scope of the city's power to adopt legislation designed to address the effects of past discrimination. Relying on our decision in *Wygant*, appellee argues that the city must limit any race-based remedial efforts to eradicating the effects of its own prior discrimination. This is essentially the position taken by the Court of Appeals below. Appellant argues that our decision in *Fullilove* is controlling, and that as a result the city of Richmond enjoys sweeping legislative power to define and attack the effects of prior discrimination in its local construction industry. * * *

* * *

What appellant ignores is that Congress, unlike any State or political subdivision, has a specific constitutional mandate to enforce the dictates of the Fourteenth Amendment. * * *

That Congress may identify and redress the effects of society-wide discrimination does not mean that, *a fortiori*, the States and their political subdivisions are free to decide that such remedies are appropriate. Section 1 of the Fourteenth Amendment is an explicit *constraint* on state power, and the States must undertake any remedial efforts in accordance with that provision. * * *

* * *

The Equal Protection Clause of the Fourteenth Amendment provides that "[n]o State shall . . . deny to *any person* within its jurisdiction the equal protection of the laws." (Emphasis added. [by O'Connor]) As this Court has noted in the past, the "rights created by the first section of the Fourteenth Amendment are, by its terms, guaranteed to the individual. The rights established are personal rights." The Richmond Plan denies certain citizens the opportunity to compete for a fixed percentage of public contracts based solely upon their race. To whatever racial group these citizens belong, their "personal rights" to be treated with equal dignity and respect are implicated by a rigid rule erecting race as the sole criterion in an aspect of public decisionmaking.

Absent searching judicial inquiry into the justification for such race-based measures, there is simply no way of determining what classifications are "benign" or "remedial" and what classifications are in fact motivated by illegitimate notions of racial inferiority or simple racial politics. Indeed, the purpose of strict scrutiny is to "smoke out" illegitimate uses of race by assuring that the legislative body is pursuing a goal important enough to warrant use of a highly suspect tool. The test also ensures that the means chosen "fit" this compelling goal so closely that there is little or no possibility that the motive for the classification was illegitimate racial prejudice or stereotype.

Classifications based on race carry a danger of stigmatic harm. Unless they are strictly reserved for remedial settings, they may in fact promote notions of racial inferiority and lead to a politics of racial hostility. We thus reaffirm the view expressed by the plurality in *Wygant* that the standard of review under the Equal Protection Clause is not dependent on the race of those burdened or benefited by a particular classification.

* * *

Appellant argues that it is attempting to remedy various forms of past discrimination that are alleged to be responsible for the small number of minority businesses in the local contracting industry. Among these the city cites the exclusion of blacks from skilled construction trade unions and training programs. This past discrimination has prevented them "from following the traditional path from laborer to entrepreneur." The city also lists a host of nonracial factors which would seem to face a member of any racial group attempting to establish a new business enterprise, such as deficiencies in working capital, inability to meet bonding requirements, unfamiliarity with bidding procedures, and disability caused by an inadequate track record.

While there is no doubt that the sorry history of both private and public discrimination in this country has contributed to a lack of opportunities for black entrepreneurs, this observation, standing alone, cannot justify a rigid racial quota in the awarding of public contracts in Richmond, Virginia. Like the claim that discrimination in primary and secondary schooling justifies a rigid racial preference in medical school admissions, an amorphous claim that there has been past discrimination in a particular industry cannot justify the use of an unyielding racial quota.

It is sheer speculation how many minority firms there would be in Richmond absent past societal discrimination, just as it was sheer speculation how many minority medical students would have been admitted to the medical school at Davis absent past discrimination in educational opportunities. Defining these sorts of injuries as "identified discrimination" would give local governments license to create a patchwork of racial preferences based on statistical generalizations about any particular field of endeavor.

These defects are readily apparent in this case. The 30% quota cannot in any realistic sense be tied to any injury suffered by anyone. The District Court relied upon five predicate "facts" in reaching its conclusion that there was an adequate basis for the 30% quota: (1) the ordinance declares itself to be remedial; (2) several proponents of the measure stated their views that there had been past discrimination in the construction industry; (3) minority businesses received 0.67% of prime contracts from the city while minorities constituted 50% of the city's population; (4) there were very few minority contractors in local and state contractors' associations; and (5) in 1977, Congress made a determination that the effects of past discrimination had stifled minority participation in the construction industry nationally.

None of these "findings," singly or together, provide the city of Richmond with a "strong basis in evidence for its conclusion that remedial action was necessary." There is nothing approaching a prima facie case of a constitutional or statutory violation by *anyone* in the Richmond construction industry.

The District Court accorded great weight to the fact that the city council designated the Plan as "remedial." But the mere recitation of a "benign" or legitimate purpose for a racial classification is entitled to little or no weight. Racial classifications are suspect, and that means that simple legislative assurances of good intention cannot suffice.

The District Court also relied on the highly conclusionary statement of a proponent of the Plan that there was racial discrimination in the construction industry "in this area, and the State, and around the nation." It also noted that the city manager had related his view that racial discrimination still plagued the construction industry in his home city of Pittsburgh. These statements are of little probative value in establishing identified discrimination in the Richmond construction industry. The factfinding process of legislative bodies is generally entitled to a presumption of regularity and deferential review by the judiciary. But when a legislative body chooses to employ a suspect classification, it cannot rest upon a generalized assertion as to the classification's relevance to its goals. * * * The history of racial classifications in this country suggests that blind judicial deference to legislative or executive pronouncements of necessity has no place in equal protection analysis.

Reliance on the disparity between the number of prime contracts awarded to minority firms and the minority population of the city of Richmond is similarly misplaced. * * *

* * *

In this case, the city does not even know how many MBE's in the relevant market are qualified to undertake prime or subcontracting work in public construction projects. Nor does the city know what percentage of total city construction dollars minority firms now receive as subcontractors on prime contracts let by the city.

* * *

The city and the District Court also relied on evidence that MBE membership in local contractors' associations was extremely low. Again, standing alone this evidence is not probative of any discrimination in the local construction industry. There are numerous explanations for this dearth of minority participation, including past societal discrimination in education and economic opportunities as well as both black and white career and entrepreneurial choices. Blacks may be disproportionately attracted to industries other than construction. The mere fact that black membership in these trade organizations is low, standing alone, cannot establish a prima facie case of discrimination.

For low minority membership in these associations to be relevant, the city would have to link it to the number of local MBE's eligible for membership. If the statistical disparity between eligible MBE's and MBE membership were great enough, an inference of discriminatory exclusion could arise. In such a case, the city would have a compelling interest in preventing its tax dollars from assisting these organizations in maintaining a racially segregated construction market.

Finally, the city and the District Court relied on Congress' finding in connection with the set-aside approved in *Fullilove* that there had been nationwide discrimination in the construction industry. The probative value of these findings for demonstrating the existence of discrimination in Richmond is extremely limited. By its inclusion of a waiver procedure in the national program addressed in *Fullilove*, Congress explicitly recognized that the scope of the problem would vary from market area to market area.

Moreover, as noted above, Congress was exercising its powers under section 4 of the Fourteenth Amendment in making a finding that past discrimination would cause federal funds to be distributed in a manner which reinforced prior patterns of discrimination. While the States and their subdivisions may take remedial action when they possess evidence that their own spending practices are exacerbating a pattern of prior discrimination, they must identify that discrimination, public or private, with some specificity before they may use race-conscious relief. * * *

* * *

In sum, none of the evidence presented by the city points to any identified discrimination in the Richmond construction industry. We, therefore, hold that the city has failed to demonstrate a compelling interest in apportioning public contracting opportunities on the basis of race. To accept Richmond's claim that past societal discrimination alone can serve as the basis for rigid racial preferences would be to open the door to competing claims for "remedial relief" for every disadvantaged group. The dream of a Nation of equal citizens in a society where race is irrelevant to personal opportunity and achievement would be lost in a mosaic of shifting preferences based on inherently unmeasurable claims of past wrongs. * * * We think such a result would be contrary to both the letter and the spirit of a constitutional provision whose central command is equality.

The foregoing analysis applies only to the inclusion of blacks within the Richmond set-aside program. There is *absolutely no evidence* of past discrimination against Spanish-speaking, Oriental, Indian, Eskimo, or Aleut persons in any aspect of the Richmond construction industry. The District Court took judicial notice of the fact that the vast majority of "minority" persons in Richmond were black. It may well be that Richmond has never had an Aleut or Eskimo citizen. The random inclusion of racial groups that, as a practical matter, may never have suffered from discrimination in the construction industry in Richmond suggests that perhaps the city's purpose was not in fact to remedy past discrimination.

If a 30% set-aside was "narrowly tailored" to compensate black contractors for past discrimination, one may legitimately ask why they are forced to share this "remedial relief" with an Aleut citizen who moves to Richmond tomorrow? The gross overinclusiveness of Richmond's racial preference strongly impugns the city's claim of remedial motivation.

As noted by the court below, it is almost impossible to assess whether the Richmond Plan is narrowly tailored to remedy prior discrimination since it is not linked to identified discrimination in any way. We limit ourselves to two observations in this regard.

First, there does not appear to have been any consideration of the use of race-neutral means to increase minority business participation in city contracting. Many of the barriers to minority participation in the construction industry relied upon by the city to justify a racial classification appear to be race neutral. If MBE's disproportionately lack capital or cannot meet bonding requirements, a race-neutral program of city financing for small firms would, *a fortiori*, lead to greater minority participation. The principal opinion in *Fullilove* found that Congress had carefully examined and rejected race-neutral alternatives before enacting the MBE set-aside. There is no evidence in this record that the Richmond City Council has considered any alternatives to a race-based quota.

Second, the 30% quota cannot be said to be narrowly tailored to any goal, except perhaps outright racial balancing. It rests upon the "completely unrealistic" assumption that minorities will choose a particular trade in lockstep proportion to their representation in the local population.

Since the city must already consider bids and waivers on a case-by-case basis, it is difficult to see the need for a rigid numerical quota. As noted above, the congressional scheme upheld in *Fullilove* allowed for a waiver of the set-aside provision where an MBE's higher price was not attributable to the effects of past discrimination. Based upon proper findings, such programs are less problematic from an equal protection standpoint because they treat all candidates individually, rather than making the color of an applicant's skin the sole relevant consideration. Unlike the program upheld in *Fullilove*, the Richmond Plan's waiver system focuses solely on the availability of MBE's; there is no inquiry into whether or not the particular MBE seeking a racial preference has suffered from the effects of past discrimination by the city or prime contractors.

* * * Under Richmond's scheme, a successful black, Hispanic, or Oriental entrepreneur from anywhere in the country enjoys an absolute preference over other citizens based solely on their race. We think it obvious that such a program is not narrowly tailored to remedy the effects of prior discrimination.

Nothing we say today precludes a state or local entity from taking action to rectify the effects of identified discrimination within its jurisdiction. If the city of Richmond had evidence before it that nonminority contractors were systematically excluding minority businesses from subcontracting opportunities, it could take action to end the discriminatory exclusion. Where there is a significant statistical disparity between the number of qualified minority contractors willing and able to perform a particular service and the number of such contractors actually engaged by the locality or the locality's prime contractors, an inference of discriminatory exclusion could arise. Under such circumstances, the city could act to dismantle the closed business system by taking appropriate measures against those who discriminate on the basis of race or other illegitimate criteria. In the extreme case, some form of narrowly tailored racial preference might be necessary to break down patterns of deliberate exclusion.

* * *

Even in the absence of evidence of discrimination, the city has at its disposal a whole array of race-neutral devices to increase the accessibility of city contracting opportunities to small entrepreneurs of all races. Simplification of bidding procedures, relaxation of bonding requirements, and training and financial aid for disadvantaged entrepreneurs of all races would open the public contracting market to all those who have suffered the effects of past societal discrimination or neglect. Many of the formal barriers to new entrants may be the product of bureaucratic inertia more than actual necessity, and may have a disproportionate effect on the opportunities open to new minority firms. Their elimination or modification would have little detrimental effect on the city's interests and would serve to increase the opportunities available to minority business without classifying individuals on the basis of race. The city may also act to prohibit discrimination in the provision of credit or bonding by local suppliers and banks. Business as usual should not mean business pursuant to the unthinking exclusion of certain members of our society from its rewards.

* * *

* * * Because the city of Richmond has failed to identify the need for remedial action in the awarding of its public construction contracts, its treatment of

its citizens on a racial basis violates the dictates of the Equal Protection Clause. Accordingly, the judgment of the Court of Appeals for the Fourth Circuit is *affirmed.*

Justice Stevens concurred in part and concurred in the judgment [omitted].

Justice Kennedy concurred in part and concurred in the judgment [omitted].

Justice Scalia concurred in the judgment [omitted].

Justice Marshall, with whom Justice Brennan and Justice Blackmun joined, dissented.

It is a welcome symbol of racial progress when the former capital of the Confederacy acts forthrightly to confront the effects of racial discrimination in its midst. In my view, nothing in the Constitution can be construed to prevent Richmond, Virginia, from allocating a portion of its contracting dollars for businesses owned or controlled by members of minority groups. Indeed, Richmond's set-aside program is indistinguishable in all meaningful respects from—and in fact was patterned upon—the federal set-aside plan which this Court upheld in *Fullilove v. Klutznick* (1980).

A majority of this Court holds today, however, that the Equal Protection Clause of the Fourteenth Amendment blocks Richmond's initiative. The essence of the majority's position is that Richmond has failed to catalog adequate findings to prove that past discrimination has impeded minorities from joining or participating fully in Richmond's construction contracting industry. I find deep irony in second-guessing Richmond's judgment on this point. As much as any municipality in the United States, Richmond knows what racial discrimination is; a century of decisions by this and other federal courts has richly documented the city's disgraceful history of public and private racial discrimination. In any event, the Richmond City Council *has* supported its determination that minorities have been wrongly excluded from local construction contracting. Its proof includes statistics showing that minority-owned businesses have received virtually no city contracting dollars and rarely if ever belonged to area trade associations; testimony by municipal officials that discrimination has been widespread in the local construction industry; and the same exhaustive and widely publicized federal studies relied on in *Fullilove*, studies which showed that pervasive discrimination in the Nation's tight-knit construction industry had operated to exclude minorities from public contracting. These are precisely the types of statistical and testimonial evidence which, until today, this Court had credited in cases approving of race-conscious measures designed to remedy past discrimination.

More fundamentally, today's decision marks a deliberate and giant step backward in this Court's affirmative-action jurisprudence. Cynical of one municipality's attempt to redress the effects of past racial discrimination in a particular industry, the majority launches a grapeshot attack on race-conscious remedies in general. The majority's unnecessary pronouncements will inevitably discourage or prevent governmental entities, particularly States and localities, from acting to rectify the scourge of past discrimination. This is the harsh reality of the majority's decision, but it is not the Constitution's command.

* * *

"Agreement upon a means for applying the Equal Protection Clause to an affirmative-action program has eluded this Court every time the issue has come before us." My view has long been that race-conscious classifications designed to further remedial goals "must serve important governmental objectives and must be substantially related to achievement of those objectives" in order to withstand constitutional scrutiny. Analyzed in terms of this two-pronged standard, Richmond's set-aside, like the federal program on which it was modeled, is "plainly constitutional."

Turning first to the governmental interest inquiry, Richmond has two powerful interests in setting aside a portion of public contracting funds for minority-owned enterprises. The first is the city's interest in eradicating the effects of past racial discrimination. It is far too late in the day to doubt that remedying such discrimination is a compelling, let alone an important, interest. * * *

Richmond has a second compelling interest in setting aside, where possible, a portion of its contracting dollars. That interest is the prospective one of preventing the city's own spending decisions from reinforcing and perpetuating the exclusionary effects of past discrimination.

* * *

The remaining question with respect to the "governmental interest" prong of equal protection analysis is whether Richmond has proffered satisfactory proof of past racial discrimination to support its twin interests in remediation and in governmental nonperpetuation. * * *

* * *

The varied body of evidence on which Richmond relied provides a "strong," "firm," and "unquestionably legitimate" basis upon which the city council could determine that the effects of past racial discrimination warranted a remedial and prophylactic governmental response. As I have noted, Richmond acted against a backdrop of congressional and Executive Branch studies which demonstrated with such force the nationwide pervasiveness of prior discrimination that Congress presumed that " 'present economic inequities' " in construction contracting resulted from "'past discriminatory systems.'" The city's local evidence confirmed that Richmond's construction industry did not deviate from this pernicious national pattern. The fact that just 0.67% of public construction expenditures over the previous five years had gone to minority-owned prime contractors, despite the city's racially mixed population, strongly suggests that construction contracting in the area was rife with "present economic inequities." To the extent this enormous disparity did not itself demonstrate that discrimination had occurred, the descriptive testimony of Richmond's elected and appointed leaders drew the necessary link between the pitifully small presence of minorities in construction contracting and past exclusionary practices. That *no one* who testified challenged this depiction of widespread racial discrimination in area construction contracting lent significant weight to these accounts. The fact that area trade associations had virtually no minority members dramatized the extent of present inequities and suggested the lasting power of past discriminatory systems. In sum, to suggest that the facts on which Richmond has relied do not provide a sound basis for its finding of past discrimination simply blinks credibility.

* * *

When the legislatures and leaders of cities with histories of pervasive discrimination testify that past discrimination has infected one of their industries, armchair cynicism like that exercised by the majority has no place. * * * Disbelief is particularly inappropriate here in light of the fact that appellee Croson, which had the burden of proving unconstitutionality at trial, has *at no point* come forward with *any* direct evidence that the city council's motives were anything other than sincere.

* * *

In my judgment, Richmond's set-aside plan also comports with the second prong of the equal protection inquiry, for it is substantially related to the interests it seeks to serve in remedying past discrimination and in ensuring that municipal contract procurement does not perpetuate that discrimination. The most striking aspect of the city's ordinance is the similarity it bears to the "appropriately limited" federal set-aside provision upheld in *Fullilove*. Like the federal provision, Richmond's is limited to five years in duration and was not renewed when it came up for reconsideration in 1988. Like the federal provision, Richmond's contains a waiver provision freeing from its subcontracting requirements those nonminority firms that demonstrate that they cannot comply with its provisions. Like the federal provision, Richmond's has a minimal impact on innocent third parties. While the measure affects 30% of *public* contracting dollars, that translates to only 3% of overall Richmond area contracting.

Finally, like the federal provision, Richmond's does not interfere with any vested right of a contractor to a particular contract; instead it operates entirely prospectively. Richmond's initiative affects only future economic arrangements and imposes only a diffuse burden on nonminority competitors—here, businesses owned or controlled by nonminorities which seek subcontracting work on public construction projects. * * *

* * *

I would ordinarily end my analysis at this point and conclude that Richmond's ordinance satisfies both the governmental interest and substantial relationship prongs of our Equal Protection Clause analysis. However, I am compelled to add more, for the majority has gone beyond the facts of this case to announce a set of principles which unnecessarily restricts the power of governmental entities to take race-conscious measures to redress the effects of prior discrimination.

Today, for the first time, a majority of this Court has adopted strict scrutiny as its standard of Equal Protection Clause review of race-conscious remedial measures. This is an unwelcome development. A profound difference separates governmental actions that themselves are racist, and governmental actions that seek to remedy the effects of prior racism or to prevent neutral governmental activity from perpetuating the effects of such racism.

* * *

In concluding that remedial classifications warrant no different standard of review under the Constitution than the most brutal and repugnant forms of state-sponsored racism, a majority of this Court signals that it regards racial discrimination as largely a phenomenon of the past, and that government bodies need no longer preoccupy themselves with rectifying racial injustice. I, however, do not believe this Nation is anywhere close to eradicating racial discrimination or its vestiges. In constitutionalizing its wishful thinking, the majority today does a grave disservice not only to those victims of past and present racial discrimination in this Nation whom government has sought to assist, but also to this Court's long tradition of approaching issues of race with the utmost sensitivity.

* * *

The majority today sounds a full-scale retreat from the Court's longstanding solicitude to race-conscious remedial efforts "directed toward deliverance of the century-old promise of equality of economic opportunity." The new and restrictive tests it applies scuttle one city's effort to surmount its discriminatory past, and imperil those of dozens more localities. I, however, profoundly disagree with the cramped vision of the Equal Protection Clause which the majority offers today and with its application of that vision to Richmond, Virginia's, laudable set-aside plan. The battle against pernicious racial discrimination or its effects is nowhere near won. I must dissent.

Justice Blackmun, with whom Justice Brennan joined, dissented [omitted].

Legal commentators and scholars attested to the significance of the *Croson* decision. The Court's adoption of strict scrutiny and its invalidation of the Richmond set-aside plan, they declared, would make it exceedingly difficult for the voluntary affirmative action programs established by other local and state governments to withstand challenges. Moreover, *Croson* might discourage additional cities and states who were considering the creation of such programs from doing so. While it is difficult to determine precisely the validity of these predictions, lower federal courts have used *Croson* to strike down the set-aside plans of several local and state governments.

In the second case from the 1988 term, *Martin v. Wilks* (1989), the issue was not whether a specific affirmative action plan should be upheld, but rather who could challenge such plans and when those challenges could be brought. The case evolved from a suit brought by African American firefighters in Birmingham, Alabama, charging racial discrimination in hiring and promotion in violation of Title VII. The suit resulted in a consent decree between the city and the firefighters that established annual hiring and promotion goals. The decree was approved by a federal district court over the objections of the Birmingham Firefighters Association and a group of white firefighters. Later, another group of white fighters filed suit in federal district court, charging that the consent decree was invalid and that it discriminated against them in favor of less qualified African Americans. The district court dismissed their suit, but the appeals court reversed.

By a 5-4 vote, the Supreme Court affirmed the appeals court decision, ruling that the white firefighters were not bound by the consent decree because they were not involved in the original litigation which led to the decree. In a rather brief majority opinion, Chief Justice Rehnquist held that the African American plaintiffs in the original litigation should have identified all of the parties potentially affected by the lawsuit. "The parties to a lawsuit presumably know better than anyone else the nature and scope of relief sought in the action, and at whose expense such relief might be granted. It makes sense, therefore, to place on them a burden of bringing in additional parties where such a step is indicated, rather than placing on potential additional parties a duty to intervene when they acquire knowledge of the lawsuit" (490 U.S. at 765). The decision was based on the interpretation of the Federal Rules of Civil Procedure rather than on Title VII analysis.

Justices Stevens, Brennan, Marshall, and Blackmun dissented vigorously from the Court's ruling. Writing for the four, Justice Stevens argued that although their *interests* may have been affected by the consent decrees, the white firefighters were not deprived of any *legal rights.* "There is nothing unusual about the fact that litigation between adverse parties may, as a practical matter, seriously impair the interests of third parties who elect to the sit on the sidelines" (490 U.S. at 792). Furthermore, he said that the consent decrees were part of a valid effort to remedy discrimination by the city, and the district court approved them only after careful consideration. In Stevens's view, the white firefighters had failed to prove this conclusion incorrect. Stevens also addressed the white firefighters' claim that they were not responsible for the history of discrimination against African Americans in hiring and promotion in Birmingham. "[T]hey are nevertheless beneficiaries of the discriminatory practices that the litigation was designed to correct. * * * Just as white employees in the past were innocent beneficiaries of illegal discriminatory practices, so it is inevitable that some of the same white employees will be innocent victims who must share some of the burdens resulting from the redress of the past wrongs" (490 U.S. at 791, 792).

The Court's decisions against affirmative action in both cases led some observers to conclude that this controversial policy had suffered its final blows. This was not the case, however, as one year later in *Metro Broadcasting, Inc. v. FCC* (1990) the Court again upheld affirmative action. The Federal Communications Commission (FCC) enacted two affirmative action policies (minority preference) to be used in the process of awarding broadcast licenses for radio and television stations. The "minority enhancement" and "distress sale" policies were adopted to assist the FCC in achieving its responsibility of promoting broadcast diversity.

In a 5-4 decision, the Court upheld both minority ownership policies as consistent with the equal protection component of the Fifth Amendment Due Process Clause. Justice Brennan, joined by Justices Blackmun, Marshall, Stevens, and surprisingly, White, wrote the majority opinion. Unlike the previous *Croson* case, the majority here did not examine the policies under strict scrutiny. Drawing upon O'Connor's apparent distinction in the *Croson* case between federal powers and those of state and local governments, the majority held that when "benign race-conscious measures" have been ordered by Congress, the important government objective test is the appropriate standard of review. Justice Brennan accepted the government's claim that the minority ownership policies were enacted to increase broadcast diversity, that is, to contribute to a diversity of views and information for both minorities and nonminorities. Further, the majority held that the policies were substantially related to the achievement of broadcast diversity, in that the FCC determined and Congress agreed that "diversification of ownership will broaden the range of programming available to the broadcasting audience" (497 U.S. at 570). Brennan also rejected the claim that this conclusion was based on impermissible stereotyping. He said that in enacting the policies, the FCC and Congress did not assume that radio and television programs that appealed to minorities were necessarily "minority programming," nor that programs described as "minority" appeal only to minorities. In addition, the majority agreed that relevant evidence suggests "minority ownership does appear to have specific impact on the presentation of minority images in local news, inasmuch as minority-owned stations tend to devote more news time to topics of minority interest and to avoid racial and ethnic stereotypes in portraying minorities" (497 U.S. at 581).

The majority was also persuaded that these minority preference measures were undertaken by the FCC only after it found that race-neutral policies were ineffective, that they were limited in extent and duration, and they did not pose an undue burden on nonminorities. The Court said that because of the limited frequencies on the airwaves and the FCC's duty to grant licenses in the public interest, the First Amendment does not guarantee a broadcast license to anyone. Thus, there is no legitimate expectation that a license will be granted upon application.

In a dissent joined by Chief Justice Rehnquist and Justices Scalia and Kennedy, Justice O'Connor chastised the majority for refusing to apply the strict scrutiny standard to this case. She said that this standard of review applies to the federal government in the same way that it does to state and local governments. After subjecting the minority ownership policies to strict scrutiny, the dissenters concluded that there was no compelling interest because the policies were not designed to remedy identified discrimination, but rather to further an interest in broadcast diversity. "The interest in increasing the diversity of broadcast viewpoints is clearly not a compelling interest. It is simply too amorphous, too insubstantial, and too unrelated to any legitimate basis for employing racial classifications" (497 U.S. at 612). In addition, she said that the policies failed under intermediate scrutiny as well. She did not view broadcast diversity as an important interest. Moreover, O'Connor said that the policies were not narrowly tailored to remedy any identified discrimination, and further, they were not substantially related to the stated interest. She viewed the correlation between minority ownership and diversity in programming as quite tenuous, and said that it was based on a racial generalization or improper stereotype. O'Connor then asserted that the FCC had a race-neutral means at its disposal—it could require the owners of broadcast licenses to provide programming that would contribute to diversity. Finally, she contended that the policies did pose a significant burden to nonminorities, especially the distress sale program. "For the would-be purchaser or person who seeks to compete for the station, that opportunity depends entirely upon race or ethnicity" (497 U.S. at 630).

Metro Broadcasting, Inc. v. FCC

497 U.S. 547, 110 S. Ct. 2997, 111 L. Ed. 2d 445 (1990)

In attempting to increase minority ownership of broadcast licenses, the FCC established two policies. The first policy involved a minority enhancement plan whereby several criteria were set for awarding licenses, but minority-owned firms were to receive a "plus" in their applications. The second policy, called "distress sale," was used when the broadcast qualifications of the owner of a radio or television station were in question. Under regular procedures, that owner may not sell the license until the hearing process is completed. An exception, however, permits the license to be sold to a qualified minority-owned business for up to 75 percent of the fair market value.

The minority enhancement policy was upheld by a court of appeals over the objections of the Metro Broadcasting Company, which had applied for a new television license. An FCC order had awarded the license to a minority-owned firm. The distress sale policy was invalidated by a court of appeals after Shurberg Broadcasting opposed an FCC ruling that awarded an existing license to a minority applicant. The Supreme Court consolidated the two cases on appeal.

This case is important primarily because it rejected the strict scrutiny standard for federal affirmative action programs. Moreover, it indicated that, despite the decision in *Croson,* affirmative action had not received its death blow but had received a reprieve (at least temporarily). As you read the case, consider these questions: (1) Given his membership in the majority in *Croson,* which articulated strict scrutiny as the appropriate standard for review of affirmative action, why did Justice White join the Brennan majority here in applying the important government objective test? (2) Which side is correct about the relationship between minority ownership and broadcast diversity? That is, is there improper stereotyping involved here? (3) Is it logical to have one standard of review for federal programs and a different standard for state and local programs?

Vote:

5 justices voted to uphold the FCC policies (Brennan, White, Marshall, Blackmun, and Stevens).

4 justices would have invalidated the policies (O'Connor, Rehnquist, Scalia, and Kennedy).

Justice Brennan delivered the opinion of the Court.

* * *

It is of overriding significance in these cases that the FCC's minority ownership programs have been specifically approved—indeed, mandated—by Congress. In *Fullilove v. Klutznick* (1980), Chief Justice Burger, writing for himself and two other Justices, observed that although "[a] program that employs racial or ethnic criteria . . . calls for close examination," when a program employing a benign racial classification is adopted by an administrative agency at the explicit direction of Congress, we are "bound to approach our task with appropriate deference to the Congress, a co-equal branch charged by the Constitution with the power to 'provide for the . . . general Welfare of the United States' and 'to enforce, by appropriate legislation,' the equal protection guarantees of the Fourteenth Amendment."

* * *

A majority of the Court in *Fullilove* did not apply strict scrutiny to the race-based classification at issue. Three Members inquired "whether the *objectives* of th[e] legislation are within the power of Congress" and "whether the limited use of racial and ethnic criteria . . . is a constitutionally permissible *means* for achieving the congressional objectives." Three other Members would have upheld benign racial classifications that "serve important governmental objectives and are substantially related to achievement of those objectives." We apply that standard today. We hold that benign race-conscious measures mandated by Congress—even if those measures are not "remedial" in the sense of being designed to compensate victims of past governmental or societal discrimination—are constitutionally permissible to the extent that they serve important governmental objectives within the power of Congress and are substantially related to achievement of those objectives.

Our decision last Term in *Richmond v. J. A. Croson Co.* (1989), concerning a minority set-aside program adopted by a municipality, does not prescribe the level of scrutiny to be applied to a benign racial classification employed by Congress. * * * [M]uch of the language and reasoning in *Croson* reaffirmed the lesson of *Fullilove* that race-conscious classifications adopted by Congress to address racial and ethnic discrimination are subject to a different standard than such classifications prescribed by state and local governments. * * *

We hold that the FCC minority ownership policies pass muster under the test we announce today. First, we find that they serve the important governmental objective of broadcast diversity. Second, we conclude that they are substantially related to the achievement of that objective.

Congress found that "the effects of past inequities stemming from racial and ethnic discrimination have resulted in a severe underrepresentation of minorities in the media of mass communications." Congress and the Commission do not justify the minority ownership policies strictly as remedies for victims of this discrimination, however. Rather, Congress and the FCC have selected the minority ownership policies primarily to promote programming diversity, and they urge that such diversity is an important governmental objective that can serve as a constitutional basis for the preference policies. We agree.

We have long recognized that "[b]ecause of the scarcity of [electromagnetic] frequencies, the Government is permitted to put restraints on licensees in favor of others whose views should be expressed on this unique medium." * * *

Against this background, we conclude that the interest in enhancing broadcast diversity is, at the very least, an important governmental objective and is therefore a sufficient basis for the Commission's minority ownership policies. Just as a "diverse student body" contributing to a "'robust exchange of ideas'" is a "constitutionally permissible goal" on which a race-conscious university admissions program may be predicated, the diversity of views and information on the airwaves serves important First Amendment values. The benefits of such diversity are not limited to the members of minority groups who gain access to the broadcasting industry by virtue of the ownership policies; rather, the benefits redound in the opinion to all members of the viewing and listening audience. As Congress found, "the American public will benefit by having access to a wider diversity of information sources." * * *

We also find that the minority ownership policies are substantially related to the achievement of the Government's interest. One component of this inquiry concerns the relationship between expanded minority ownership and greater broadcast diversity. * * *

The FCC has determined that increased minority participation in broadcasting promotes programming diversity. As the Commission observed in its 1978 Statement of Policy on Minority Ownership of Broadcasting Facilities, "ownership of broadcasting facilities by minorities is [a] significant way of fostering the inclusion of minority views in the area of programming" and "[f]ull minority participation in the ownership and management of broadcast facilities results in a more diverse selection of programming." * * * The FCC's conclusion that there is an empirical nexus between minority ownership and broadcasting diversity is a product of its expertise, and we accord its judgment deference.

Furthermore, the FCC's reasoning with respect to the minority ownership policies is consistent with longstanding practice under the Communications Act. From its inception, public regulation of broadcasting has been premised on the assumption that diversification of ownership will broaden the range of programming available to the broadcast audience. Thus, "it is upon *ownership* that public policy places primary reliance with respect to diversification of content, and that historically has proved to be significantly influential with respect to editorial comment and the presentation of news." * * *

Congress also has made clear its view that the minority ownership policies advance the goal of diverse programming. In recent years, Congress has specifically required the Commission, through appropriations legislation, to maintain the minority ownership policies without alteration. We would be remiss, however, if we ignored the long history of congressional support for those policies prior to the passage of the appropriations acts because, for the past two decades, Congress has consistently recognized the barriers encountered by minorities in entering the broadcast industry and has expressed emphatic support for the Commission's attempts to promote programming diversity by increasing minority ownership. * * *

* * *

The judgment that there is a link between expanded minority ownership and broadcast diversity does not rest on impermissible stereotyping. Congressional policy does not assume that in every case minority ownership and management will lead to more minority-oriented programming or to the expression of a discrete "minority viewpoint" on the airwaves. Neither does it pretend that all programming that appeals to minority audiences can be labeled "minority programming" or that programming that might be described as "minority" does not appeal to nonminorities. Rather, both Congress and the FCC maintain simply that expanded minority ownership of broadcast outlets will, in the aggregate, result in greater broadcast diversity. A broadcasting industry with representative minority participation will produce more variation and diversity than will one whose ownership is drawn from a single racially and ethnically homogeneous group. * * *

Although all station owners are guided to some extent by market demand in their programming decisions, Congress and the Commission have determined that there may be important differences between the broadcasting practices of minority owners and those of their nonminority counterparts. This judgment—and the conclusion that there is a nexus between minority ownership and broadcasting diversity—is corroborated by a host of empirical evidence. Evidence suggests that an owner's minority status influences the selection of topics for news coverage and the presentation of editorial viewpoint, especially on matters of particular concern to minorities. "[M]inority ownership does appear to have specific impact on the presentation of minority images in local news," inasmuch as minority-owned stations tend to devote more news time to topics of minority interest and to avoid racial and ethnic stereotypes in portraying minorities. In addition, studies show that a minority owner is more likely to employ minorities in managerial and other important roles where they can have an impact on station policies. * * *

* * *

* * * [T]he Commission established minority ownership preferences only after long experience demonstrated that race-neutral means could not produce adequate broadcasting diversity. The FCC did not act precipitately in devising the programs we uphold today; to the contrary, the Commission undertook thorough evaluations of its policies *three* times—in 1960, 1971, and 1978—before adopting the minority ownership programs. In endorsing the minority ownership preferences, Congress agreed with the Commission's assessment that race-neutral alternatives had failed to achieve the necessary programming diversity.

Moreover, the considered nature of the Commission's judgment in selecting the particular minority ownership policies at issue today is illustrated by the fact that the Commission has rejected other types of minority preferences. For example, the Commission has studied but refused to implement the more expansive alternative of setting aside certain frequencies for minority broadcasters. * * *

* * *

Finally, we do not believe that the minority ownership policies at issue impose impermissible burdens on nonminorities. Although the nonminority challengers in these cases concede that they have not suffered the loss of an already-awarded broadcast license, they claim that they have been handicapped in their ability to obtain one in the first instance. But just as we have determined that "[a]s part of this Nation's dedication to eradicating racial discrimination, innocent persons may be called upon to bear some of the burden of the remedy," we similarly find that a congressionally mandated benign race-conscious program that is substantially related to the achievement of an important governmental interest is consistent with equal protection principles so long as it does not impose *undue* burdens on nonminorities. * * *

In the context of broadcasting licenses, the burden on nonminorities is slight. The FCC's responsibility is to grant licenses in the "public interest, convenience, or necessity," and the limited number of frequencies on the electromagnetic spectrum means that "[n]o one has a First Amendment right to a license." Applicants have no settled expectation that their applications will be granted without consideration of public interest factors such as minority ownership. Award of a preference in a comparative hearing or transfer of a station in a distress sale thus contravenes "no legitimate firmly rooted expectation[s]" of competing applicants.

* * * We disagree that the distress sale policy imposes an undue burden on nonminorities. By its

terms, the policy may be invoked at the Commission's discretion only with respect to a small fraction of broadcast licenses—those designated for revocation or renewal hearings to examine basic qualification issues—and only when the licensee chooses to sell out at a distress price rather than to go through with the hearing. The distress sale policy is not a quota or fixed quantity set-aside. Indeed, the nonminority firm exercises control over whether a distress sale will ever occur at all, because the policy operates only where the qualifications of an existing licensee to continue broadcasting have been designated for hearing and no other applications for the station in question have been filed with the Commission at the time of the designation. Thus a nonminority can prevent the distress sale procedures from ever being invoked by filing a competing application in a timely manner.

* * *

The Commission's minority ownership policies bear the imprimatur of longstanding congressional support and direction and are substantially related to the achievement of the important governmental objective of broadcast diversity. * * * [T]he cases are remanded for proceedings consistent with this opinion.

Justice Stevens concurred [omitted].

Justice O'Connor, with whom the Chief Justice, Justice Scalia, and Justice Kennedy join, dissented.

* * * To uphold the challenged programs, the Court departs from . . . our traditional requirement that racial classifications are permissible only if necessary and narrowly tailored to achieve a compelling interest. This departure marks a renewed toleration of racial classifications and a repudiation of our recent affirmation that the Constitution's equal protection guarantees extend equally to all citizens. The Court's application of a lessened equal protection standard to congressional actions finds no support in our cases or in the Constitution. I respectfully dissent.

As we recognized last Term, the Constitution requires that the Court apply a strict standard of scrutiny to evaluate racial classifications such as those contained in the challenged FCC distress sale and comparative licensing policies. * * *

* * *

The Constitution's guarantee of equal protection binds the Federal Government as it does the States, and no lower level of scrutiny applies to the Federal Government's use of race classifications. * * *

* * *

Our history reveals that the most blatant forms of discrimination have been visited upon some members of the racial and ethnic groups identified in the challenged programs. Many have lacked the opportunity to share in the Nation's wealth and to participate in its commercial enterprises. It is undisputed that minority participation in the broadcasting industry falls markedly below the demographic representation of those groups, and this shortfall may be traced in part to the discrimination and the patterns of exclusion that have widely affected our society. As a Nation we aspire to create a society untouched by that history of exclusion, and to ensure that equality defines all citizens' daily experience and opportunities as well as the protection afforded to them under law.

For these reasons, and despite the harms that may attend the Government's use of racial classifications, we have repeatedly recognized that the Government possesses a compelling interest in remedying the effects of identified race discrimination. We subject even racial classifications claimed to be remedial to strict scrutiny, however, to ensure that the Government in fact employs any race-conscious measures to further this remedial interest and employs them only when, and no more broadly than, the interest demands. The FCC or Congress may yet conclude after suitable examination that narrowly tailored race-conscious measures are required to remedy discrimination that may be identified in the allocation of broadcasting licenses. Such measures are clearly within the Government's power.

Yet it is equally clear that the policies challenged in these cases were not designed as remedial measures and are in no sense narrowly tailored to remedy identified discrimination. * * *

Under the appropriate standard, strict scrutiny, only a compelling interest may support the Government's use of racial classifications. Modern equal protection doctrine has recognized only one such interest: remedying the effects of racial discrimination. The interest in increasing the diversity of broadcast viewpoints is clearly not a compelling interest. It is simply too amorphous, too insubstantial, and too unrelated to any legitimate basis for employing racial classifications. * * *

An interest capable of justifying race-conscious measures must be sufficiently specific and verifiable, such that it supports only limited and carefully defined uses of racial classifications. * * *

* * *

Our traditional equal protection doctrine requires, in addition to a compelling state interest, that the Government's chosen means be necessary to accomplish and narrowly tailored to further the asserted interest. * * * The Court instead finds the racial classifications to be "substantially related" to achieving the Government's interest, a far less rigorous fit requirement. The FCC's policies fail even this requirement.

* * *

The FCC assumes a particularly strong correlation of race and behavior. The FCC justifies its conclusion that insufficiently diverse viewpoints are broadcast by reference to the percentage of minority owned stations. This assumption is correct only to the extent that minority owned stations provide the desired additional views, and that stations owned by individuals not favored by the preferences cannot, or at least do not, broadcast underrepresented programming. Additionally, the FCC's focus on ownership to improve programming assumes that preferences linked to race are so strong that they will dictate the owner's behavior in operating the station, overcoming the owner's personal inclinations and regard for the market. This strong link between race and behavior, especially when mediated by market forces, is the assumption that Justice Powell rejected in his discussion of health care service in *Bakke*. In that case, the state medical school argued that it could prefer members of minority groups because they were more likely to serve communities particularly needing medical care. Justice Powell rejected this rationale, concluding that the assumption was unsupported and that such individual choices could not be presumed from ethnicity or race.

The majority addresses this point by arguing that the equation of race with distinct views and behaviors is not "impermissible" in this particular case. * * * The Court embraces the FCC's reasoning that an applicant's race will likely indicate that the applicant possesses a distinct perspective, but notes that the correlation of race to behavior is "not a rigid assumption about how minority owners will behave in every case." The corollary to this notion is plain: individuals of unfavored racial and ethnic backgrounds are unlikely to possess the unique experiences and background that contribute to viewpoint diversity. Both the reasoning and its corollary reveal but disregard what is objectionable about a stereotype: the racial generalization inevitably does not apply to certain individuals, and those persons may legitimately claim that they have been judged according to their race rather than upon a relevant criterion. * * *

* * *

Moreover, the FCC's programs cannot survive even intermediate scrutiny because race-neutral and untried means of directly accomplishing the governmental interest are readily available. The FCC could directly advance its interest by requiring licensees to provide programming that the FCC believes would add to diversity. The interest the FCC asserts is in programming diversity, yet in adopting the challenged policies, the FCC expressly disclaimed having attempted *any* direct efforts to achieve its asserted goal. * * *

* * *

Finally, the Government cannot employ race classifications that unduly burden individuals who are not members of the favored racial and ethnic groups. The challenged policies fail this independent requirement, as well as the other constitutional requirements. The comparative licensing and distress sale programs provide the eventual licensee with an exceptionally valuable property and with a rare and unique opportunity to serve the local community. The distress sale imposes a particularly significant burden. The FCC has at base created a specialized market reserved exclusively for minority controlled applicants. There is no more rigid quota than a 100% set-aside. This fact is not altered by the observation that the FCC and seller have some discretion over whether stations may be sold through the distress program. For the would-be purchaser or person who seeks to compete for the station, that opportunity depends entirely upon race or ethnicity. The Court's argument that the distress sale allocates only a small percentage of all license sales also misses the mark. This argument readily supports complete preferences and avoids scrutiny of particular programs: it is no response to a person denied admission at one school, or discharged from one job, solely on the basis of race, that other schools or employers do not discriminate.

* * *

In sum, the Government has not met its burden even under the Court's test that approves of racial classifications that are substantially related to an important governmental objective. Of course, the programs even more clearly fail the strict scrutiny that should be applied. The Court has determined, in essence, that Congress and all federal agencies are exempted, to some ill-defined but significant degree, from the Constitution's equal protection requirements. This break with our precedents greatly undermines equal protection guarantees, and permits distinctions among citizens based on race and ethnicity which the Constitution clearly forbids. I respectfully dissent.

Justice Kennedy, with whom Justice Scalia joins, dissented [omitted].

Metro Broadcasting was important in that the Court, in addition to upholding affirmative action, backed away from the strict scrutiny approach (at least in part). By concluding that intermediate scrutiny applied to affirmative action programs of the federal government, the majority's ruling increased the likelihood that such programs would be upheld in the future. Legal analysts, however, noted that this decision probably would not have the same ramifications as the earlier *Croson* ruling, given *Metro Broadcasting*'s application only to the federal sector, rather than to all levels of government.

The Court did not hear another substantive affirmative action case until 1995 when it decided *Adarand Constructors v. Pena.* Two years earlier, the justices had ruled on a technical question regarding who has standing to challenge affirmative action programs (*Northeastern Florida Chapter of the Associated General Contractors of America v. City of Jacksonville, Florida* 1993). By the time the Court heard *Adarand,* Justices Ginsburg and Breyer had succeeded Justices White and Blackmun, respectively. There was much speculation about how they (and Justice Souter) would vote in their first affirmative action case. There seemed to be little doubt, however, that Thomas, unlike his predecessor, would vote to strike down affirmative action if given the opportunity. It appeared, therefore, that Thomas would join Rehnquist, Scalia, Kennedy, and O'Connor to form a majority that would invalidate all affirmative action programs.

Adarand involved a challenge to a federal affirmative action program regarding the awarding of federal contracts for highway construction. The program provides a monetary bonus to prime contractors if they subcontract at least 10 percent of the overall amount of the contract to "disadvantaged business enterprises" (DBEs). DBEs include small businesses owned and operated by African Americans, Hispanics, Asians, Native Americans, and other minority groups. Adarand Constructors filed suit in federal district court alleging that the program violated the Equal Protection Component of the Due Process Clause of the Fifth Amendment. The district court upheld the program, and the circuit court of appeals affirmed on the basis of *Metro Broadcasting.*

By a 5-4 vote, the Supreme Court overruled its previous *Metro Broadcasting* decision, holding that federal affirmative action programs, like those of state and local governments, must be examined under strict scrutiny. That is, they must be narrowly tailored to achieve a compelling interest. Writing for the majority, O'Connor said that relevant precedents show that "the Court understood the standards for federal and state racial classifications to be the same" (115 S.Ct. at 2107). Moreover, she emphasized that *all* racial classifications "must necessarily receive a most searching examination," and "the standard of review under the Equal Protection Clause is not dependent on the race of those burdened or benefited by a particular classification" (115 S.Ct. at 2108, 2110). She maintained, nonetheless, that government is not prevented from acting to eliminate racial discrimination and its lingering effects, and that it is possible for carefully drawn affirmative action programs to meet the strict scrutiny test. The majority did not invalidate this particular program, but remanded it to the lower courts for reexamination under the strict scrutiny standard.

In separate concurrences, Justices Scalia and Thomas concluded that affirmative action programs are never permissible. According to Scalia, "government can never have a 'compelling interest' in discriminating on the basis of race in order to 'make up' for past racial discrimination in the opposite direction" (115 S.Ct. at 2118). Thomas denounced government affirmative action as an unacceptable form of paternalism that conflicts with the consitutional principle of equality. Furthermore, he argued that "So-called benign discrimination teaches many that because of chronic and apparently immutable handicaps, minorities cannot compete with them without their patronizing indulgence" (115 S.Ct. at 2119). According to Thomas, affirmative action programs "stamp minorities with a badge of inferiority," and "government-sponsored racial discrimination based on benign prejudice is just as noxious as discrimination inspired by malicious prejudice" (115 S.Ct. at 2119).

The dissenters—Stevens, Souter, Ginsburg, and Breyer—argued that *Fullilove* was the appropriate precedent and that Congress, unlike state and local decisionmakers, is empowered by the Fourteenth Amendment to remedy discrimination and its lingering effects. In addition, Stevens criticized the majority for equating policies designed to oppress minorities with those crafted to eliminate the effects of oppression. "There is no moral or constitutional equivalence between a policy that is designed to perpetuate a caste system and one that seeks to eradicate racial subordination. Invidious discrimination is an engine of oppression, subjugating a disfavored group to enhance or maintain the power of the majority. Remedial race-based preferences reflect the opposite impulse: a desire to foster equality in society" (115 S.Ct. at 2120).

Adarand Constructors, Inc. v. Pena

U.S. 115 S.Ct. 2097, 132 L.Ed. 2d 158 (1995)

■ Most federal contracting programs contain a clause that provides prime contractors with monetary incentives to subcontract a certain portion of the overall contract to businesses owned by socially and economically disadvantaged individuals. This case, concerning contracting in the highway construction industry, involved the Department of Transportion, the Small Business Administration (SBA), and the Surface Transportation and Uniform Relocation Assistance Act (STURAA). Under STURAA, prime contractors would receive a monetary bonus if they subcontracted at least 10 percent of the total amount of the contract to businesses certified by the SBA as "disadvantaged business enterprises" (DBEs). Small businesses owned and operated by African Americans, Hispanic Americans, Asian Pacific Americans, Native Americans, and members of other minority groups are considered to be DBEs. Mountain Gravel and Construction Company was awarded a prime contract for a highway construction project in Colorado. This company accepted a bid for the guardrail portion of the contract from Gonzales Construction Company, a Hispanic-owned firm. Adarand Constructors, a white-owned company that submitted a lower bid, filed suit in federal district court challenging the program as a violation of the equal protection component of the Fifth Amendment's Due Process Clause. The district court rejected Adarand's claim, and the court of appeals affirmed, citing *Metro Broadcasting* as the controlling precedent.

This case is important because the Court adopted a single standard, strict scrutiny, for examining all governmental affirmative action programs. As you read the case, consider the following questions: (1) Which precedent(s) is most appropriate for deciding this case—*Fullilove, Croson,* or *Metro Broadcasting*? (2) Will most federal affirmative action programs be upheld or struck down as a result of this decision?

Vote:

5 justices voted to apply strict scrutiny to all governmental affirmative action programs (O'Connor, Rehnquist, Scalia, Kennedy, and Thomas).

4 justices rejected the application of strict scrutiny to federal affirmative action programs (Stevens, Souter, Ginsburg, and Breyer).

Justice O'Connor announced the judgment of the Court and delivered an opinion . . . which is for the Court except insofar as it might be inconsistent with the views expressed in Justice Scalia's concurrence.

* * *

Adarand's claim arises under the Fifth Amendment to the Constitution, which provides that "No person shall . . . be deprived of life, liberty, or property, without due process of law." Although this Court has always understood that Clause to provide some measure of protection against *arbitrary* treatment by the Federal Government, it is not as explicit a guarantee of equal treatment as the Fourteenth Amendment, which provides that "No *State* shall . . . deny to any person within its jurisdiction the equal protection of the laws" (emphasis added). Our cases have accorded varying degrees of significance to the difference in the language of those two Clauses. We think it necessary to revisit the issue here.

* * *

In *Bolling v. Sharpe*, the Court for the first time explicitly questioned the existence of any difference between the obligations of the Federal Government and the States to avoid racial classifications. * * *

Bolling's facts concerned school desegregation, but its reasoning was not so limited. The Court's observations that "[d]istinctions between citizens solely because of their ancestry are by their very nature odious," *Hirabayashi [v. U.S.* (1943)], and that "all legal restrictions which curtail the civil rights of a single racial group are immediately suspect," *Korematsu [v. U.S.* (1944)], carry no less force in the context of federal action than in the context of action by the States—indeed, they first appeared in cases concerning action by the Federal Government. * * *

Later cases in contexts other than school desegregation did not distinguish between the duties of the States and the Federal Government to avoid racial classifications. Consider, for example, the following passage from *McLaughlin v. Florida*, a 1964 case that struck down a race-based state law:

> [W]e deal here with a classification based upon the race of the participants, which must be viewed in light of the historical fact that the central purpose of the Fourteenth Amendment was to eliminate racial discrimination emanating from official sources in the States. This strong policy renders racial classifications "constitutionally suspect," *Bolling v. Sharpe,* and subject to the "most rigid scrutiny," *Korematsu v. United States,* and "in most circumstances irrelevant" to any constitutionally acceptable legislative purpose, *Hirabayashi v. United States.*

McLaughlin's reliance on cases involving federal action for the standards applicable to a case involving state legislation suggests that the Court understood the standards for federal and state racial classifications to be the same.

Cases decided after *McLaughlin* continued to treat the equal protection obligations imposed by the Fifth and the Fourteenth Amendments as indistinguishable. . . . *Loving v. Virginia*, [1967], which struck down a race-based state law, cited *Korematsu* for the proposition that "the Equal Protection Clause demands that racial classifications . . . be subjected to the 'most rigid scrutiny.' " The various opinions in *Frontiero v. Richardson*, (1973), which concerned sex discrimination by the Federal Government, took their equal protection standard of review from *Reed v. Reed*, (1971), a case that invalidated sex discrimination by a State, without mentioning any possibility of a difference between the standards applicable to state and federal action. Thus, in 1975, the Court stated explicitly that "[t]his Court's approach to Fifth Amendment equal protection claims has always been precisely the same as to equal protection claims under the Fourteenth Amendment." *Weinberger v. Wiesenfeld*. * * *

Most of the cases discussed above involved classifications burdening groups that have suffered discrimination in our society. In 1978, the Court confronted the question whether race-based governmental action designed to benefit such groups should also be subject to "the most rigid scrutiny." *Regents of Univ. of California v. Bakke* involved an equal protection challenge to a state-run medical school's practice of reserving a number of spaces in its entering class for minority students. The petitioners argued that "strict scrutiny" should apply only to "classifications that disadvantage 'discrete and insular minorities.' " *Bakke* did not produce an opinion for the Court, but Justice Powell's opinion announcing the Court's judgment rejected the argument. * * *

Two years after *Bakke*, the Court faced another challenge to remedial race-based action, this time involving action undertaken by the Federal Government. In *Fullilove v. Klutznick*, (1980), the Court upheld Congress' inclusion of a 10% set-aside for minority-owned businesses in the Public Works Employment Act of 1977. As in *Bakke*, there was no opinion for the Court. Chief Justice Burger, in an opinion joined by Justices White and Powell, observed that "[a]ny preference based on racial or ethnic criteria must necessarily receive a most searching examination to make sure that it does not conflict with constitutional guarantees." * * *

* * *

In *Wygant v. Jackson Board of Ed.*, (1986), the Court considered a Fourteenth Amendment challenge to another form of remedial racial classification. The issue in *Wygant* was whether a school board could adopt race-based preferences in determining which teachers to lay off. Justice Powell's plurality opinion observed that "the level of scrutiny does not change merely because the challenged classification operates against a group that historically has not been subject to governmental discrimination". . . . In other words, "racial classifications of any sort must be subjected to 'strict scrutiny.' " * * *

The Court's failure to produce a majority opinion in *Bakke*, *Fullilove*, and *Wygant* left unresolved the proper analysis for remedial race-based governmental action. * * *

The Court resolved the issue, at least in part, in 1989. *Richmond v. J. A. Croson Co.*, (1989), concerned a city's determination that 30% of its contracting work should go to minority-owned businesses. A majority of the Court in *Croson* held that "the standard of review under the Equal Protection Clause is not dependent on the race of those burdened or benefited by a particular classification," and that the single standard of review for racial classifications should be "strict scrutiny." * * *

With *Croson*, the Court finally agreed that the Fourteenth Amendment requires strict scrutiny of all race-based action by state and local governments. But *Croson* of course had no occasion to declare what standard of review the Fifth Amendment requires for such action taken by the Federal Government. * * *

Despite lingering uncertainty in the details, however, the Court's cases through *Croson* had established three general propositions with respect to governmental racial classifications. First, skepticism: " '[a]ny preference based on racial or ethnic criteria must necessarily receive a most searching examination.' " Second, consistency: "the standard of review under the Equal Protection Clause is not dependent on the race of those burdened or benefited by a particular classification." And third, congruence: "[e]qual protection analysis in the Fifth Amendment area is the same as that under the Fourteenth Amendment." Taken together, these three propositions lead to the conclusion that any person, of whatever race, has the right to demand that any governmental actor subject to the Constitution justify any racial classification subjecting that person to unequal treatment under the strictest judicial scrutiny. * * *

A year later, however, the Court took a surprising turn. *Metro Broadcasting, Inc. v. FCC*, (1990), involved a Fifth Amendment challenge to two race-based policies of the Federal Communications Commission. In *Metro Broadcasting*, the Court repudiated the long-held notion that "it would be unthinkable that the same Constitution would impose a lesser duty on the Federal Government" than it does on a State to afford equal protection of the laws, *Bolling*. It did so by holding that "benign" federal racial classifications need only satisfy intermediate scrutiny, even though *Croson* had recently concluded that such classifications enacted by a State must satisfy strict scrutiny. * * *

* * *

By adopting intermediate scrutiny as the standard of review for congressionally mandated "benign" racial classifications, *Metro Broadcasting* departed from prior cases in two significant respects. First, it turned its back on *Croson*'s explanation of why strict scrutiny of all governmental racial classifications is essential. . . .

* * *

Second, *Metro Broadcasting* squarely rejected one of the three propositions established by the Court's earlier equal protection cases, namely, congruence between the standards applicable to federal and state racial classifications, and in so doing also undermined the other two: skepticism of all racial classifications, and consistency of treatment irrespective of the race of the burdened or benefited group. Under *Metro Broadcasting*, certain racial classifications ("benign" ones enacted by the Federal Government) should be treated less skeptically than others; and the race of the benefited group is critical to the determination of which standard of review to apply. *Metro Broadcasting* was thus a significant departure from much of what had come before it.

The three propositions undermined by *Metro Broadcasting* all derive from the basic principle that the Fifth and Fourteenth Amendments to the Constitution protect *persons*, not *groups*. It follows from that principle that all governmental action based on race—a group classification long recognized as "in most circumstances irrelevant and therefore prohibited," *Hirabayashi*—should be subjected to detailed judicial inquiry to ensure that the *personal* right to equal protection of the laws has not been infringed. These ideas have long been central to this Court's understanding of equal protection, and holding "benign" state and federal racial classifications to different standards does not square with them. "[A] free people whose institutions are founded upon the doctrine of equality" should tolerate no retreat from the principle that government may treat people differently because of their race only for the most compelling reasons. Accordingly, we hold today that all racial classifications, imposed by whatever federal, state, or local governmental actor, must be analyzed by a reviewing court under strict scrutiny. In other words, such classifications are constitutional only if they are narrowly tailored measures that further compelling governmental interests. To the extent that *Metro Broadcasting* is inconsistent with that holding, it is overruled.

* * *

Finally, we wish to dispel the notion that strict scrutiny is "strict in theory, but fatal in fact." *Fullilove*. The unhappy persistence of both the practice and the lingering effects of racial discrimination against minority groups in this country is an unfortunate reality, and government is not disqualified from acting in response to it. * * * When race-based action is necessary to further a compelling interest, such action is within constitutional constraints if it satisfies the "narrow tailoring" test this Court has set out in previous cases.

Because our decision today alters the playing field in some important respects, we think it best to remand the case to the lower courts for further consideration in light of the principles we have announced. * * *

* * *

Accordingly, the judgment of the Court of Appeals is vacated, and the case is remanded for further proceedings consistent with this opinion.

It is so ordered.

Justice Scalia, concurring in part and concurring in the judgment.

I join the opinion of the Court, . . . except insofar as it may be inconsistent with the following: In my view, government can never have a "compelling interest" in discriminating on the basis of race in order to "make up" for past racial discrimination in the opposite direction. Individuals who have been wronged by unlawful racial discrimination should be made whole; but under our Constitution there can be no such thing as either a creditor or a debtor race. That concept is alien to the Constitution's focus upon the individual. To pursue the concept of racial entitlement—even for the most admirable and benign of purposes—is to reinforce and preserve for future mischief the way of thinking that produced race slavery, race privilege and race hatred. In the eyes of government, we are just one race here. It is American.

It is unlikely, if not impossible, that the challenged program would survive under this understanding of strict scrutiny, but I am content to leave that to be decided on remand.

Justice Thomas, concurring in part and concurring in the judgment.

I agree with the majority's conclusion that strict scrutiny applies to *all* government classifications based on race. I write separately, however, to express my disagreement with the premise underlying Justice Stevens' and Justice Ginsburg's dissents: that there is a racial paternalism exception to the principle of equal protection. I believe that there is a "moral [and] constitutional equivalence" between laws designed to subjugate a race and those that distribute benefits on the basis of race in order to foster some current notion of equality. Government cannot make us equal; it can only recognize, respect, and protect us as equal before the law.

That these programs may have been motivated, in part, by good intentions cannot provide refuge from the principle that under our Constitution, the government may not make distinctions on the basis of race. As far as the Constitution is concerned, it is irrelevant whether a government's racial classifications are drawn by those who wish to oppress a race or by those who have a sincere desire to help those thought to be disadvantaged. There can be no doubt that the paternalism that appears to lie at the heart of this program is at war with the principle of inherent equality that underlies and infuses our Constitution. See Declaration of Independence ("We hold these truths to be self-evident, that all men are created equal, that they are endowed by their Creator with certain unalienable Rights, that among these are Life, Liberty, and the pursuit of Happiness").

These programs not only raise grave constitutional questions, they also undermine the moral basis of the equal protection principle. Purchased at the price of immeasurable human suffering, the equal protection principle reflects our Nation's understanding that such classifications ultimately have a destructive impact on the individual and our society. Unquestionably, "[i]nvidious [racial] discrimination is an engine of oppression." It is also true that "[r]emedial" racial preferences may reflect "a desire to foster equality in society." But there can be no doubt that racial paternalism and its unintended consequences can be as poisonous and pernicious as any other form of discrimination. So-called "benign" discrimination teaches many that because of chronic and apparently immutable handicaps, minorities cannot compete with them without their patronizing indulgence. Inevitably, such programs engender attitudes of superiority or, alternatively, provoke resentment among those who believe that they have been wronged by the government's use of race. These programs stamp minorities with a badge of inferiority and may cause them to develop dependencies or to adopt an attitude that they are "entitled" to preferences. * * *

In my mind, government-sponsored racial discrimination based on benign prejudice is just as noxious as discrimination inspired by malicious prejudice. In each instance, it is racial discrimination, plain and simple.

* * *

Justice Stevens, with whom Justice Ginsburg joins, dissenting.

Instead of deciding this case in accordance with controlling precedent, the Court today delivers a disconcerting lecture about the evils of governmental racial classifications. For its text the Court has selected three propositions, represented by the bywords "skepticism," "consistency," and "congruence." * * *

* * *

The Court's concept of "consistency" assumes that there is no significant difference between a decision by the majority to impose a special burden on the members of a minority race and a decision by the majority to provide a benefit to certain members of that minority notwithstanding its incidental burden on some members of the majority. In my opinion that assumption is untenable. There is no moral or constitutional equivalence between a policy that is designed to perpetuate a caste system and one that seeks to eradicate racial subordination. Invidious discrimination is an engine of oppression, subjugating a disfavored group to enhance or maintain the power of the majority. Remedial race-based preferences reflect the opposite impulse: a desire to foster equality in society. No sensible conception of the Government's constitutional obligation to "govern impartially," *Hampton v. Mow Sun Wong*, (1976), should ignore this distinction.

* * *

The Court's explanation for treating dissimilar race-based decisions as though they were equally objectionable is a supposed inability to differentiate between "invidious" and "benign" discrimination. But the term "affirmative action" is common and well understood. Its presence in everyday parlance shows that people understand the difference between good intentions and bad. As with any legal concept, some cases may be difficult to classify, but our equal protection jurisprudence has identified a critical difference between state action that imposes burdens on a disfavored few and state action that benefits the few "in spite of" its adverse effects on the many.

* * *

The Court's concept of "congruence" assumes that there is no significant difference between a decision by the Congress of the United States to adopt an affirmative-action program and such a decision by a State or a municipality. In my opinion that assumption is untenable. It ignores important practical and legal differences between federal and state or local decisionmakers.

* * *

Ironically, after all of the time, effort, and paper this Court has expended in differentiating between federal and state affirmative action, the majority today virtually ignores the issue. It provides not a word of direct explanation for its sudden and enormous departure from the reasoning in past cases. Such silence, however, cannot erase the difference between Congress' institutional competence and constitutional authority to overcome historic racial subjugation and the States' lesser power to do so.

* * *

In my judgment, the Court's novel doctrine of "congruence" is seriously misguided. Congressional deliberations about a matter as important as affirmative action should be accorded far greater deference than those of a State or municipality.

The Court's concept of *stare decisis* treats some of the language we have used in explaining our decisions as though it were more important than our actual holdings. In my opinion that treatment is incorrect.

This is the third time in the Court's entire history that it has considered the constitutionality of a federal affirmative-action program. On each of the two prior occasions, the first in 1980, *Fullilove v. Klutznick*, and the second in 1990, *Metro Broadcasting, Inc. v. FCC*, the Court upheld the program. Today the Court explicitly overrules *Metro Broadcasting* (at least in part) and undermines *Fullilove* by recasting the standard on which it rested and by calling even its holding into question. * * *

* * *

The Court's holding in *Fullilove* surely governs the result in this case. * * * In no meaningful respect is the current scheme more objectionable than the 1977 Act. Thus, if the 1977 Act was constitutional, then so must be the SBA and STURAA. Indeed, even if my dissenting views in *Fullilove* had prevailed, this program would be valid.

* * *

My skeptical scrutiny of the Court's opinion leaves me in dissent. The majority's concept of "consistency" ignores a difference, fundamental to the idea of equal protection, between oppression and assistance. The majority's concept of "congruence" ignores a difference, fundamental to our constitutional system, between the Federal Government and the States. And the majority's concept of *stare decisis* ignores the force of binding precedent. I would affirm the judgment of the Court of Appeals.

Justice Souter, with whom Justice Ginsburg and Justice Breyer join, dissenting.

* * *

. . . I agree with Justice Stevens's conclusion that *stare decisis* compels the application of *Fullilove*. Although *Fullilove* did not reflect doctrinal consistency, its several opinions produced a result on shared grounds that petitioner does not attack: that discrimination in the construction industry had been subject to government acquiescence, with effects that remain and that may be addressed by some preferential treatment falling within the congressional power under Section 5 of the Fourteenth Amendment. Once *Fullilove* is applied, as Justice Stevens points out, it follows that the statutes in question here (which are substantially better tailored to the harm being remedied than the statute endorsed in *Fullilove*,) pass muster under Fifth Amendment due process and Fourteenth Amendment equal protection.

* * *

* * * The Court has long accepted the view that constitutional authority to remedy past discrimination is not limited to the power to forbid its continuation, but extends to eliminating those effects that would otherwise persist and skew the operation of public systems even in the absence of current intent to practice any discrimination. This is so whether the remedial authority is exercised by a court, the Congress, or some other legislature. Indeed, a majority of the Court today reiterates that there are circumstances in which Government may, consistently with the Constitution, adopt programs aimed at remedying the effects of past invidious discrimination.

When the extirpation of lingering discriminatory effects is thought to require a catch-up mechanism, like the racially preferential inducement under the statutes considered here, the result may be that some members of the historically favored race are hurt by that remedial mechanism, however innocent they may be of any personal responsibility for any discriminatory conduct. When this price is considered reasonable, it is in part because it is a price to be paid only temporarily; if the justification for the preference is eliminating the effects of a past practice, the assumption is that the effects will themselves recede into the past, becoming attenuated and finally disappearing. Thus, Justice Powell wrote in his concurring opinion in *Fullilove* that the "temporary nature of this remedy ensures that a race-conscious program will not last longer than the discriminatory effects it is designed to eliminate."

* * *

Justice Ginsburg, with whom Justice Breyer joins, dissenting.

For the reasons stated by Justice Souter, and in view of the attention the political branches are currently giving the matter of affirmative action, I see no compelling cause for the intervention the Court has made in this case. I further agree with Justice Stevens that, in this area, large deference is owed by the Judiciary to "Congress' institutional competence and constitutional authority to overcome historic racial subjugation." * * *

The statutes and regulations at issue, as the Court indicates, were adopted by the political branches in response to an "unfortunate reality": "[t]he unhappy persistence of both the practice and the lingering effects of racial discrimination against minority groups in this country." The United States suffers from those lingering effects because, for most of our Nation's history, the idea that "we are just one race" was not embraced. For generations, our lawmakers and judges were unprepared to say that there is in this land no superior race, no race inferior to any other. * * *

The divisions in this difficult case should not obscure the Court's recognition of the persistence of racial inequality and a majority's acknowledgement of Congress' authority to act affirmatively, not only to end discrimination, but also to counteract discrimination's lingering effects. Those effects, reflective of a system of racial caste only recently ended, are evident in our workplaces, markets, and neighborhoods. Job applicants with identical resumes, qualifications, and interview styles still experience different receptions, depending on their race. White and African American consumers still encounter different deals. People of color looking for housing still face discriminatory treatment by landlords, real estate agents, and mortgage lenders. Minority entrepreneurs sometimes fail to gain contracts though they are the low bidders, and they are sometimes refused work even after winning contracts. Bias both conscious and unconscious, reflecting traditional and unexamined habits of thought, keeps up barriers that must come down if equal opportunity and nondiscrimination are ever genuinely to become this country's law and practice.

Given this history and its practical consequences, Congress surely can conclude that a carefully designed affirmative action program may help to realize, finally, the "equal protection of the laws" the Fourteenth Amendment has promised since 1868.

* * *

The precise impact of *Adarand* on affirmative action plans of the federal government is unclear at this point. Some argue that such programs are unlikely to be sustainable under strict scrutiny, while others maintain that the demands of strict scrutiny can be met.

Conclusion

As our discussion illustrates, affirmative action is in a precarious position vis-a-vis the Supreme Court. A core group of justices either disapproves of affirmative action in general or takes very narrow views of the appropriateness of race-conscious remedies for overcoming discrimination and its lingering effects. Scalia and Thomas do not favor affirmative action in any circumstance. Rehnquist and Kennedy seem to believe that even when there is a pattern of discrimination, individuals must prove that they specifically were victims in order to benefit from an affirmative action program, which is difficult to do. Furthermore, even Justice O'Connor, who occasionally has approved of affirmative action, seems to prefer race-neutral alternatives for dealing with discrimination and its effects.

None of the three justices most supportive of affirmative action—Blackmun, Brennan, and Marshall—remains on the Court. Justice Stevens has been supportive of affirmative action, and Souter, Ginsburg, and Breyer demonstrated support for affirmative action in *Adarand.* Nevertheless, there are enough votes on the Rehnquist Court to restrict severely affirmative action programs, even if affirmative action is permitted in principle.

REFERENCES

Irons, Peter, and Stephanie Guitton, eds. *May It Please the Court.* New York: The New Press, 1993.

Lindsey, Robert. "White/Caucasian—and Rejected." *New York Times Magazine.* 3 April 1977, pp. 42-47, 95.

Mezey, Susan Gluck. *In Pursuit of Equality: Women, Public Policy and the Federal Courts.* New York: St. Martin's Press, 1992.

Wilkinson, J. Harvie. *From Brown to Bakke: The Supreme Court and School Integration 1954-1978.* Oxford: Oxford University Press, 1979.

CHAPTER 16

Equal Protection in Other Areas: Alienage, Poverty, Illegitimacy, Fundamental Rights

CASE STUDY

San Antonio v. Rodriguez (1973)

Demetrio Rodriguez wanted his children and others in their community to have a better education than he and those of his generation had obtained. Rodriguez, a forty-two-year-old veteran of the U.S. Navy and U.S. Air Force, lived in the Edgewood community, a Hispanic barrio on the west side of San Antonio, Texas. He was well aware of the inferior conditions in the schools in the Edgewood Independent School District. At the Edgewood Elementary School, which his three sons attended, for example, the building was dilapidated and crumbling, basic school supplies were lacking, and nearly 50 percent of the teachers were not certified by the state and were teaching with emergency permits. Rodriguez and other parents formed the Edgewood District Concerned Parents Association in an attempt to improve the quality of the schools in their community. After meeting with local school officials, they were informed by the district superintendent that there was no money for rebuilding schools, hiring more qualified teachers, or for any other improvements (Irons 1988).

On July 10, 1968, with the assistance of Arthur Gochman, a civil rights attorney, Rodriguez and six other parents decided to file suit in federal court challenging the state's school financing system as a violation of the Equal Protection Clause. They alleged that the inferior education provided to the students of Edgewood and other poor children in Texas was the result of the state's use of property taxes as the primary basis for funding its schools. The aim of the lawsuit was to obtain an order compelling the state to equalize the funding of all of the state's school districts. Given that these families had little money to pursue litigation, Gochman attempted to gain support for the suit from the Mexican American Legal Defense and Education Fund (MALDEF). The organization's limited resources precluded it from participating in the case, but Gochman agreed to pursue it nonetheless.

Gochman's brief before the federal court focused on two major claims. First, Gochman argued that education was a "fundamental right" guaranteed by the Fourteenth Amendment and that it must be provided equally to all students. Second, he claimed that under the Equal Protection Clause poor families were a "suspect class" deserving of special protection by the judiciary. Because more than 90 percent of the Edgewood students were Latino, Gochman made an additional claim—that Mexican Americans, like African Americans, were a distinct racial and ethnic group, and therefore the suspect classification should be applied to them.

Shortly after the suit was filed, attorneys for the state of Texas petitioned the federal court to dismiss the complaint, and over one year later, on October 15, 1969, the court finally made its decision. While the three-judge panel denied the motion to dismiss the case, it agreed to the state's proposal to allow the Texas legislature to act on school financing before intervening in the case. The legislature had authorized a committee study of education funding, but the legislature was not going to convene until January of 1971. The federal court agreed to postpone intervention even though the legislature had refused to act on similar reform proposals earlier in the year. Perhaps not surprisingly, the legislature took no action on school finance reform when it convened in 1971. This inaction by the state disturbed and angered the federal panel. In a hearing in December of 1971, Judge Spears admonished the state's attorneys, "I think it is a little disconcerting to a court, when it abstains and does it on specific grounds that it wishes for the legislature to do something about it, and with education as important as it is to the citizenry of our state and our nation, for the legislature to completely ignore it. It makes you feel that it just does no good for a court to do anything other than, if it feels these laws are suspect, declare them unconstitutional" (Irons 1988, p. 286).

The stage was then set for a full trial. To illustrate the wide disparities in educational funding in San Antonio, Gochman contrasted the Edgewood district, which was the poorest, with the Alamo Heights district, which was the wealthiest. Demographic factors indicated the differences in the economic status of the two communities. Fifty-four percent of the male workers in Alamo Heights were executives or professionals, compared to just 4 percent in Edgewood; similarly, about 75 percent of Alamo Heights residents had high school diplomas while less than 10 percent of Edgewood residents were high school graduates.

Gochman then illustrated the disparities in educational funding between the two districts. Like most other states, the Texas educational system was financed primarily by property taxes, with limited additional funding from state and federal programs. Districts with high local property values could often generate a large sum of money without high tax rates. Despite taxing itself at the highest rate in the city, the Edgewood district could raise only $26 per student, while Alamo Heights taxed itself at the lowest rate and provided $333 per pupil. After adding in state and federal funding for each, the disparities remained—$356 for each Edgewood student compared to $594 for each student in Alamo Heights. Gochman explained that in order for the Edgewood revenues from property taxes to equal those of Alamo Heights, Edgewood residents would have had to tax themselves at twenty times the rate of Alamo Heights. He pointed out that even if the Edgewood parents were interested in doing this, they were precluded by Texas law from doing so. A tax of almost $13 for each $100 of property value would have been necessary, but the state ceiling was $1.50. Thus, Gochman argued, "The Texas system makes it impossible for poor districts to provide quality education" (Irons 1988, p. 287).

On December 23, 1971, more than three years after the suit was initially filed, the federal court declared the Texas school finance system in violation of the Equal Protection Clause of the Fourteenth Amendment. The panel accepted Gochman's two major claims—discrimination on the basis of wealth or poverty is suspect, and education is a fundamental right. The judges ruled that Texas had not demonstrated a compelling reason for its system and, even more, that it had not even proven a rational basis for that system. The ruling was not completely satisfactory to Gochman and the Edgewood parents, however, because the court gave the state two more years to reform the system.

In preparing to appeal the case to the United States Supreme Court, the state's attorney general hired Charles Alan Wright, a University of Texas law professor with considerable expertise and experience in federal litigation. Gochman continued to represent Demetrio Rodriguez and the other Edgewood parents.

This case was of considerable significance across the nation, and it attracted amicus briefs from a variety of sources. Amicus briefs in support of the state were filed by the attorneys general of twenty-five states, and an additional brief was filed by lawyers representing the interests of those holding school bonds. Briefs filed on behalf of the Edgewood parents came from the ACLU, the NAACP Legal Defense and Educational Fund, the National Education Association, the California state controller, the Minnesota attorney general, and the San Antonio Independent School District itself.

Oral argument was held on October 12, 1972. Professor Wright began his arguments by acknowledging the imperfection of the Texas school finance system, but he contended that the system allowed for local control and the independence of school districts. This, in the state's view, constituted a rational basis for the funding system. Wright also conceded that the system had resulted in funding disparities, but he claimed that requiring state action to eliminate the disparities "would impose a constitutional straitjacket on the public schools of fifty states" (Irons and Guitton 1993, p. 323). Wright argued that the state was only required to give the Edgewood students a minimum level of education, not the same accorded to those in Alamo Heights. When asked by Justice Douglas about the racial aspect of the case, Wright conceded that it was there, but said it was purely coincidental. Finally, he urged the Court to use the rational basis test to decide the case, arguing that education was not a fundamental right under the Constitution. He asserted that the educational needs of poor people were no more fundamental than their needs for food or housing.

Gochman began by arguing that the record illustrated clearly the correlation between district wealth and district school funding. "[A]s to the poorest districts and the richest districts, the poorest people live in the poorest districts and the richest people live in the richest districts. And in Bexar County [where Edgewood was located], it perfectly correlates" (Irons and Guitton 1993, p. 326). In addition to focusing on discrimination based on wealth, he emphasized the racial aspect of the funding disparities, noting that minority districts received less money per student in Bexar county and statewide. As he did at the trial level, Gochman stressed that education was a fundamental right guaranteed by the Constitution. When asked by Chief Justice Burger whether other services such as police protection, fire protection, and public health facilities were also fundamental, Gochman responded, "I think what's important is the constitutional importance of education. That is, education affects matters guaranteed by the Bill of Rights. It's preservative of other rights, unlike some of these other services" (p. 328). Finally, Gochman sharply criticized Wright's claim that Texas was required to provide only a minimum level of education for the Edgewood students, alleging that this amounted to the creation of two classes—"minimum-opportunity citizens, and first-class citizens" (p. 329).

Several months later, on March 21, 1973, the Court issued its decision (case excerpt on p. 781). By a narrow 5-4 vote, the justices upheld the state's property tax scheme of school financing. Writing for a five-member majority, Justice Powell first refused to subject the property tax classification to strict scrutiny, ruling that it did not involve discrimination against a "suspect class," nor was education a fundamental right. He specifically rejected Gochman's argument that because education was so closely connected with the preservation of First Amendment freedoms it should be deemed fundamental. "How . . . is education to be distinguished from the significant personal interests in the basics of decent food and shelter?" (411 U.S. at 37). Applying the rational basis test, Powell argued that the Texas system of school finance was reasonably aimed at promoting local control of public education. In addition, he expressed concern that a ruling against the property tax scheme for public education could lead to similar conclusions with respect to other public services. Finally, Powell conceded that the Texas system (and presumably those of other states) was in need of reform to ensure higher quality and increased opportunity for all children, but he maintained that this task must be left to the discretion of state legislators.

In a bitter dissent, Justice Marshall attacked the majority for what he termed "a retreat from our historic commitment to equality of educational opportunity" (411 U.S. at 71). He accepted both of Gochman's major claims—that the children in poor districts were members of a "suspect class" deserving of special protection and that education was a fundamental right that could not be infringed absent a compelling state interest. Moreover, Marshall disagreed with the majority view that this matter was best left to state legislatures for resolution.

For Demetrio Rodriguez and other families, the Court's decision was a disappointing end to a difficult struggle. The 1973 ruling was not the end of this matter, however. Twelve years later, on behalf of Demetrio Rodriguez and other parents, the Mexican American Legal Defense and Education Fund (MALDEF) filed a suit alleging that the Texas school finance system violated the state constitution. The results were different this time. In 1989, the Texas Supreme Court found the property tax system in violation of the state constitution. Two years later, the state legislature finally acted to reform the system (Irons and Guitton, p. 330). Whether this reform has substantially eliminated the disparities remains in question.

School finance reform continues to be a hotly contested issue throughout the country. Although this issue has not returned to the U.S. Supreme Court, efforts have been undertaken at the state court levels to provide more equitable funding of public schools.

Historical Origins and Contemporary Conflicts

As we saw in Chapters 13 and 14, the Equal Protection Clause of the Fourteenth Amendment has been applied primarily to claims of racial and gender discrimination. Our case study above illustrates that the Equal Protection Clause has been used to challenge other types of discrimination. Claims of discrimination on the basis of indigency, alienage, illegitimacy, age, and mental retardation have all been addressed by the federal courts. In addition, the Equal Protection Clause has been used to invalidate government policies that infringe on what are termed "fundamental rights" or "fundamental interests." These rights or interests fall into four categories: 1) the right to marriage and procreation; 2) the right to vote; 3) the right to interstate travel; and 4) access to justice. These rights have been viewed by the Court as so vital to a free and democratic society that they must be guaranteed to everyone. Some have argued that other public needs such as the rights to education and housing should be deemed fundamental, but the Court has not agreed, ruling that fundamental rights are limited to matters explicitly or implicitly guaranteed by the Constitution. The Court has also heard several equal protection cases involving economic interests. Such cases, however, have not been included in standard treatments of equal protection, but rather within the context of economic regulation.[1]

Most of the Supreme Court cases regarding these "miscellaneous" claims of equal protection violations occurred during the Warren and Burger eras. A few cases regarding discrimination against aliens and infringements of fundamental rights were decided in the pre-Warren Court era. As more litigation was pursued, the Warren and Burger Courts undertook a more serious examination of claims that some government policies unconstitutionally discriminated against aliens, illegitimate children, and poor people and that others deprived people of their fundamental rights. At the same time, however, the Court has established no new fundamental rights since 1969. The Rehnquist Court has heard few cases involving discrimination against the poor, illegitimate children, or aliens. In the cases that it has decided, the Rehnquist Court has not broken any new ground with its decisions.

In the next few years, however, some of these issues may reach the Rehnquist Court for resolution. For example, gay and lesbian activists may challenge laws that discriminate on the basis of sexual orientation as violations of equal protection. In addition, the 1994 midterm congressional elections saw the passage in California of Proposition 187, which prohibits illegal aliens from receiving public education and health care services. Prop 187 is already being challenged in the lower courts, and unless this controversy is resolved there, it will likely end up at the U.S. Supreme Court.

---

[1]For example, *Allegheny Pittsburgh Coal Co. v. County Commission* 488 U.S. 336 (1989); *Nordlinger v. Hahn* 112 S.Ct. 2326 (1992); and *FCC v. Beach Communications* 113 S.Ct. 2096 (1993). In *Allegheny Pitsburgh Coal Co.,* using the rational basis test, the Court rejected an equal protection challenge to a county property tax assessment scheme that had resulted in wide disparities in assessments for comparable property. In *Nordlinger,* again applying minimal scrutiny, the Court upheld California's Proposition 13, an amendment to the state's constitution that severely limited property tax rates. The impact of Proposition 13 was that those who bought property after its passage were forced to pay significantly higher taxes than those who owned similar property before it passed. Finally, in *Beach Communications,* the Court upheld a federal cable television regulation that exempted some private cable systems from local franchising requirements over claims that the policy violated equal protection.

Decision Making on the Equal Protection Clause in Other Areas

As we noted in the introduction to this section of the book, the Court's original approach to evaluating claims under the Equal Protection Clause was two-tiered. That is, the Court used the rational basis/minimal scrutiny test for economic and social classifications and the strict scrutiny approach for racial classifications. However, the Court adopted a third approach, intermediate scrutiny, to examine gender classifications, which it had refused to place in the suspect category.

The Court has experienced great difficulty in deciding which approach to use in considering other types of equal protection claims. In fact, all three approaches or tests are used in deciding nonracial and nongender equal protection cases. The type of test used depends on the type of classification involved. Most clearly, cases involving claims of a deprivation of a fundamental right are decided using strict scrutiny. The Court has articulated four types of interests as fundamental and deserving of rigid scrutiny: 1) marriage and procreation (*Skinner v. Oklahoma,* 1942); 2) access to justice (*Griffin v. Illinois,* 1956); 3) voting rights (*Reynolds v. Sims,* 1964); and 4) interstate travel (*Shapiro v. Thompson,* 1969).

Perhaps most confusing is the Court's treatment of discrimination against aliens. In *Graham v. Richardson* (1971), the justices ruled that alienage, like race, was a suspect classification requiring the application of strict scrutiny. Here the majority struck down a state statute that denied welfare benefits to noncitizens. Two years later, however, the Court intimated that not all restrictions involving aliens need be examined under strict scrutiny (*Sugarman v. Dougall,* 1973), and by the late 1970s, the Court began to use minimal scrutiny in evaluating policies that prohibited the employment of aliens in some public sector jobs. A 1982 case indicated the Court's willingness to use the third standard, intermediate scrutiny, in examining some claims involving discrimination against aliens. In striking down a Texas law that permitted school districts to deny a free public education to the children of illegal aliens, the majority ruled that while strict scrutiny was not appropriate, the law could be justified only if "it further[ed] some substantial goal of the State" (*Plyler v. Doe,* 457 U.S. at 224).

With respect to policies discriminating against illegitimate children, it was unclear in the early cases whether minimal scrutiny or strict scrutiny was the approach used. In *Matthews v. Lucas* (1976) and *Trimble v. Gordon* (1977), however, the Court appeared to consider intermediate scrutiny as the appropriate standard. The majority said that although strict scrutiny is not required, minimal scrutiny is insufficient. This position was reaffirmed in *Clark v. Jeter* (1988). In *Lucas,* the Court upheld provisions of the Social Security Act that required illegitimate, but not legitimate, children to prove actual dependence on their deceased fathers before they could receive surviving children's benefits. In *Trimble,* the majority invalidated a state intestate succession statute that permitted legitimate children to inherit from both parents, but allowed illegitimate children to inherit only from their mothers. The Court's ruling in *Clark v. Jeter* struck down Pennsylvania's six-year statute of limitations for undertaking paternity actions on behalf of illegitimate children.

Equal protection claims alleging discrimination on the basis of indigency are subjected to minimal scrutiny unless they involve deprivation of a fundamental right. The Court has repeatedly refused to include wealth classifications in the suspect category (*Dandridge v. Williams,* 1970; *James v. Valtierra,* 1971; and *San Antonio v. Rodriguez,* 1973).

Finally, claims involving age discrimination and discrimination on the basis of mental retardation are examined using minimal scrutiny or the rational basis test. The Court refused to place age in the suspect category in *Massachusetts Board of Retirement v. Murgia* (1976). In upholding a state's mandatory retirement law, the Court held "even if the statute could be said to impose a penalty upon a class defined as the aged, it would not impose a distinction sufficiently akin to those classifications that we have found suspect to call for strict judicial scrutiny" (427 U.S. at 314). Similarly, the majority held in *Cleburne v. Cleburne Living Center* (1985) that the rational basis test was the appropriate standard for deciding cases involving discrimination against the mentally retarded.

Pre-Warren Court Period

As we noted in the introduction to this section, the Court's jurisprudence regarding the Fourteenth Amendment is of fairly recent vintage. Before the middle of the twentieth century, the Supreme Court did not hear many cases involving alleged violations of the Equal Protection Clause. The cases that were heard primarily involved matters of racial discrimination against African Americans, and not until later was gender discrimination addressed under equal protection. Two cases decided in 1886 and 1942, however, appeared to indicate the Court's willingness to include other types of discrimination in its equal protection analysis.

Yick Wo v. Hopkins (1886), as we explained in Chapter 13, concerned a San Francisco ordinance that discriminated against Chinese laundry owners in the city. The ordinance required the city's board of supervisors to approve laundry operating licenses, but it did not apply to laundries that were located in brick buildings. Given that the overwhelming majority of Chinese laundries were located in wooden buildings, the ordinance was clearly aimed at destroying Chinese-owned businesses. Yick Wo had been a resident of California for over twenty years, and he had operated a laundry for about that same time. He was not a U.S. citizen, however. After being arrested, convicted, and fined for operating his laundry without the required license, Yick Wo claimed that his rights to equal protection had been violated. In a unanimous opinion the Supreme Court agreed, ruling that the Equal Protection Clause applied to aliens as well as to citizens. Justice Matthews said that the Clause applied "to all persons within the territorial jurisdiction, without regard to any differences of race, of color, or of nationality; and the equal protection of the laws is a pledge of the protection of equal laws" (118 U.S. at 369).

Nearly sixty years later, the Court began to argue that the Equal Protection Clause also was meant to protect certain fundamental rights, and laws restricting such rights demanded strict scrutiny from the judiciary. In *Skinner v. Oklahoma* (1942) the Court was faced with a state law that authorized the compulsory sterilization of habitual criminals convicted of certain crimes. By a unanimous vote the Court found the statute in violation of equal protection. Justice Douglas wrote, "We are dealing here with legislation which involves one of the basic civil rights of man. Marriage and procreation are fundamental to the very existence and survival of the race. * * * [We emphasize] . . . that strict scrutiny of the classification which a State makes in a sterilization law is essential, lest unwittingly or otherwise invidious discriminations are made against groups or types of individuals in violation of the constitutional guaranty of just and equal laws" (316 U.S. at 541).

The Warren Court Era

We have indicated elsewhere that the Warren Court embarked on a civil rights revolution in the mid-1950s to late 1960s. With respect to the Equal Protection

Clause, we discussed the Court's landmark decisions in the area of racial discrimination (Chapter 13). In addition, the justices in the Warren era issued several important equal protection decisions that extended the clause beyond matters of racial discrimination. The Warren Court extended the fundamental rights standard to issues involving criminal justice, voting, and the right to travel freely among the states. In addition, discrimination against illegitimate children and the poor came under closer examination during this era.

Fundamental Rights

In 1964 the Warren Court issued a landmark decision that extended the fundamental rights standard to the electoral arena. *Reynolds v. Sims* involved the problem of malaportionment of state legislatures. In many states, although population shifts had occurred to make some areas more highly populated than others, state legislative districts had not been reapportioned to reflect those changes. Thus, more heavily populated urban districts were given the same number of seats in the legislature as were rural districts with substantially smaller populations. For example, in Alabama where *Reynolds* arose, senate districts ranged in population from 15,417 to 634,864, while the population of house districts varied from 6,731 to 104,767. Voters in the more highly populated urban districts charged that this apportionment scheme diluted and debased their votes and violated their right to equal protection.

By an 8-1 vote, the Supreme Court agreed, holding that both houses of state legislatures must be apportioned on the basis of population. This, the justices ruled, would further the "one person, one vote" principle and guarantee to all citizens an equal role in the election of state legislatures. Writing for the majority, Chief Justice Warren emphasized that voting rights are critical to a democratic society and must be protected. "Undoubtedly, the right of suffrage is a fundamental matter in a free and democratic society . . . . [A]ny infringement of the right of citizens to vote must be carefully and meticulously scrutinized" (377 U.S. at 561–62).

Justice Harlan, the lone dissenter in the case, criticized his colleagues for intervening in reapportionment questions, arguing that these matters were best left to the discretion of states. "[T]he Equal Protection Clause was never intended to inhibit the States in choosing any democratic method they pleased for the apportionment of their legislatures" (377 U.S. at 590–91).

Two years later, the Court reiterated its view that the right to vote is a fundamental interest protected by the Equal Protection Clause and subject to strict scrutiny. In *Harper v. Virginia Board of Elections* (1966), the justices declared poll taxes to be an unconstitutional infringement on the right of suffrage. Writing for a six-member majority, Justice Douglas declared, "wealth or fee paying has, in our view, no relation to voting qualifications; the right to vote is too precious, too fundamental to be so burdened or conditioned" (383 U.S. at 670).

In 1969, the Court added another right, that of interstate travel, to its fundamental interest doctrine when it invalidated durational residency requirements for eligibility for welfare benefits. *Shapiro v. Thompson* was brought by Vivian Thompson, a new resident of Connecticut who was denied welfare benefits because at the time of her application she had not lived in the state for one year.

In a 6-3 decision, the Court ruled that durational residency requirements for receiving welfare benefits unconstitutionally infringed on the freedom to travel among the states. "[T]he nature of our Federal Union and our constitutional concepts of personal liberty unite to require that all citizens be free to travel throughout the length and breadth of our land uninhibited by statutes, rules, or regulations which unreasonably burden or restrict this movement" (394 U.S. at 629). Because the right to travel was a fundamental right, the justices applied strict scrutiny in examining the residency requirement. Thus, it could be upheld only if the state could prove it was narrowly tailored to achieve a compelling interest. The state contended that the waiting period requirement preserved the fiscal integrity of its public assistance programs. First, if the waiting period deterred indigent newcomers from moving to the state, programs to assist long-term residents could be better maintained. Also, the objective was to discourage indigents who might enter the state for the sole purpose of obtaining larger benefits. The Court did not find these objectives sufficiently compelling.

In addition, government officials argued that the one-year waiting period requirement furthered several legitimate objectives: 1) assisted in planning of the welfare budget; 2) provided an objective test of residency; 3) minimized the possibility of fraud (receipt of payments from more than one state); and 4) encouraged new residents to enter into the labor force. The Court found none of these objectives to be strong enough to survive strict scrutiny. In fact, Brennan intimated that the statute failed even the weaker rational basis test. "[E]ven under traditional equal protection tests a classification of welfare applicants according to whether they have lived in the State for one year would seem irrational and unconstitutional" (394 U.S. at 638).

Chief Justice Warren and Justice Black dissented from the ruling, arguing that the statute did not substantially restrict the right to travel. Justice Harlan went further in his dissent, criticizing the majority for its expansion of the fundamental rights doctrine. "[W]hen a statute affects only matters not mentioned in the Federal Constitution and is not arbitrary or irrational, I . . . know of nothing which entitles this Court to pick out particular human activities, characterize them as 'fundamental,' and give them added protection under an unusually stringent equal protection test" (394 U.S. at 662).

Shapiro v. Thompson

394 U.S. 618, 89 S.Ct. 1322, 22 L. Ed. 2d 600 (1969)

■ After becoming pregnant with her second child, Vivian Thompson, a 19-year-old Massachusetts resident, moved to the state of Connecticut to live with her mother. When her mother no longer could support her financially, she applied for benefits under the AFDC (Aid to Families with Dependent Children) program, which is jointly funded by individual states and the federal government. Her application was rejected because she had not lived in Connecticut for at least one year, as required by state law. With the assistance of an OEO Neighborhood Legal Services Office, she filed a lawsuit challenging the constitutionality of Connecticut's residency requirement (Ginger 1973, pp. 587–88). After a three-judge federal district court ruled in Thompson's favor, the state sought review in the U.S. Supreme Court. Two similar cases from Pennsylvania and the District of Columbia were consolidated with this appeal.

This case is important primarily because it prohibited states from discriminating against new residents who apply for various forms of public assistance. As you read the case, consider these questions: 1) How would the residency requirements have fared under the rational basis test? 2) Would state residency requirements for AFDC benefits be upheld if they were required by federal law? 3) Are there any legitimate methods state officials could use to determine whether indigents have moved to their jurisdictions for the sole purpose of obtaining higher welfare benefits?

Vote:

6 justices found the residency requirements unconstitutional (Brennan, Douglas, Fortas, Stewart, White, and Marshall).

3 justices voted to uphold the residency requirements (Warren, Black, and Harlan).

Justice Brennan delivered the opinion of the Court.

* * *

Primarily, appellants justify the waiting-period requirement as a protective device to preserve the fiscal integrity of state public assistance programs. It is asserted that people who require welfare assistance during their first year of residence in a State are likely to become continuing burdens on state welfare programs. Therefore, the argument runs, if such people can be deterred from entering the jurisdiction by denying them welfare benefits during the first year, state programs to assist long-time residents will not be impaired by a substantial influx of indigent newcomers.

There is weighty evidence that exclusion from the jurisdiction of the poor who need or may need relief was the specific objective of these provisions. In the Congress, sponsors of federal legislation to eliminate all residence requirements have been consistently opposed by representatives of state and local welfare agencies who have stressed the fears of the States that elimination of the requirements would result in a heavy influx of individuals into States providing the most generous benefits. * * *

We do not doubt that the one-year waiting period device is well suited to discourage the influx of poor families in need of assistance. An indigent who desires to migrate, resettle, find a new job, and start a new life will doubtless hesitate if he knows that he must risk making the move without the possibility of falling back on state welfare assistance during his first year of residence, when his need may be most acute. But the purpose of inhibiting migration by needy persons into the State is constitutionally impermissible.

This Court long ago recognized that the nature of our Federal Union and our constitutional concepts of personal liberty unite to require that all citizens be free to travel throughout the length and breadth of our land uninhibited by statutes, rules, or regulations which unreasonably burden or restrict this movement. * * *

* * *

Thus, the purpose of deterring the in-migration of indigents cannot serve as justification for the classification created by the one-year waiting period, since that purpose is constitutionally impermissible. If a law has "no other purpose . . . than to chill the assertion of constitutional rights by penalizing those who choose to exercise them, then it [is] patently unconstitutional."

Alternatively, appellants argue that even if it is impermissible for a State to attempt to deter the entry of all indigents, the challenged classification may be justified as a permissible state attempt to discourage those indigents who would enter the State solely to obtain larger benefits. We observe first that none of the statutes before us is tailored to serve that objective. Rather, the class of barred newcomers is all-inclusive, lumping the great majority who come to the State for other purposes with those who come for the sole purpose of collecting higher benefits. In actual operation, therefore, the three statutes enact what in effect are non-rebuttable presumptions that every applicant for assistance in his first year of residence came to the jurisdiction solely to obtain higher benefits. Nothing whatever in any of these records supplies any basis in fact for such a presumption.

More fundamentally, a State may no more try to fence out those indigents who seek higher welfare benefits than it may try to fence out indigents generally. Implicit in any such distinction is the notion that indigents who enter a State with the hope of securing higher welfare benefits are somehow less deserving than indigents who do not take this consideration into account. But we do not perceive why a mother who is seeking to make a new life for herself and her children should be regarded as less deserving because she considers, among other factors, the level of a State's public assistance. Surely such a mother is no less deserving than a mother who moves into a particular State in order to take advantage of its better educational facilities.

Appellants argue further that the challenged classification may be sustained as an attempt to distinguish between new and old residents on the basis of the contribution they have made to the community through the payment of taxes. We have difficulty seeing how long-term residents who qualify for welfare are making a greater present contribution to the State in taxes than indigent residents who have recently arrived. If the argument is based on contributions made in the past by the long-term residents, there is some question, as a factual matter, whether this argument is applicable in Pennsylvania where the record suggests that some 40% of those denied public assistance because of the waiting period had lengthy prior residence in the State. But we need not rest on the particular facts of these cases. Appellants' reasoning would logically permit the State to bar new residents from schools, parks, and libraries or deprive them of police and fire protection. Indeed it would permit the State to apportion all benefits and services according to the past tax contributions of its citizens. The Equal Protection Clause prohibits such an apportionment of state services.

We recognize that a State has a valid interest in preserving the fiscal integrity of its programs. It may legitimately attempt to limit its expenditures, whether for public assistance, public education, or any other program. But a State may not accomplish such a purpose by invidious distinctions between classes of its citizens. It could not, for example, reduce expenditures for education by barring indigent children from its schools. Similarly, in the cases before us, appellants must do more than show that denying welfare benefits to new residents saves money. The saving of welfare costs cannot justify an otherwise invidious classification.

In sum, neither deterrence of indigents from migrating to the State nor limitation of welfare benefits to those regarded as contributing to the State is a constitutionally permissible state objective.

Appellants next advance as justification certain administrative and related governmental objectives allegedly served by the waiting-period requirement. They argue that the requirement (1) facilitates the planning of the welfare budget; (2) provides an objective test of residency; (3) minimizes the opportunity for recipients fraudulently to receive payments from more than one jurisdiction; and (4) encourages early entry of new residents into the labor force.

* * *

The argument that the waiting-period requirement facilitates budget predictability is wholly unfounded. The records in all three cases are utterly devoid of evidence that either State or the District of Columbia in fact uses the one-year requirement as a means to predict the number of people who will require assistance in the budget year. * * *

The argument that the waiting period serves as an administratively efficient rule of thumb for determining residency similarly will not withstand scrutiny. The residence requirement and the one-year waiting-period requirements are distinct and independent prerequisites for assistance under these three statutes, and the facts relevant to the determination of each are directly examined by the welfare authorities. Before granting an application, the welfare authorities investigate the applicant's employment, housing, and family situation and in the course of the inquiry necessarily learn the facts upon which to determine whether the applicant is a resident.

Similarly, there is no need for a State to use the one-year waiting period as a safeguard against fraudulent receipt of benefits; for less drastic means are available, and are employed, to minimize that hazard.

* * *

Pennsylvania suggests that the one-year waiting period is justified as a means of encouraging new residents to join the labor force promptly. But this logic would also require a similar waiting period for long-term residents of the State. A State purpose to encourage employment provides no rational basis for imposing a one-year waiting-period restriction on new residents only.

We conclude therefore that appellants in these cases do not use and have no need to use the one-year requirement for the governmental purposes suggested. Thus, even under traditional equal protection tests a classification of welfare applicants according to whether they have lived in the State for one year would seem irrational and unconstitutional. But, of course, the traditional criteria do not apply in these cases. Since the classification here touches on the fundamental right of interstate movement, its constitutionality must be judged by the stricter standard of whether it promotes a *compelling* state interest. Under this standard, the waiting-period requirement clearly violates the Equal Protection Clause.

* * *

Affirmed.

Justice Stewart concurred [omitted].

Chief Justice Warren, with whom Justice Black joins, dissenting.

In my opinion the issue before us can be simply stated: May Congress, acting under one of its enumerated powers, impose minimal nationwide residence requirements or authorize the States to do so? Since I believe that Congress does have this power and has constitutionally exercised it in these cases, I must dissent.

* * *

* * * I am convinced that Congress does have power to enact residence requirements of reasonable duration or to authorize the States to do so and that it has exercised this power.

The Court's decision reveals only the top of the iceberg. Lurking beneath are the multitude of situations in which States have imposed residence requirements including eligibility to vote, to engage in certain professions or occupations or to attend a state-supported university. Although the Court takes pains to avoid acknowledging the ramifications of its decision, its implications cannot be ignored. I dissent.

Justice Harlan, dissenting.

* * *

In upholding the equal protection argument, the Court has applied an equal protection doctrine of relatively recent vintage: the rule that statutory classifications which either are based upon certain "suspect" criteria or affect "fundamental rights" will be held to deny equal protection unless justified by a "compelling" governmental interest.

* * *

I think that this branch of the "compelling interest" doctrine is sound when applied to racial classifications, for historically the Equal Protection Clause was largely a product of the desire to eradicate legal distinctions founded upon race. However, I believe that the more recent extensions have been unwise.

* * *

The second branch of the "compelling interest" principle is even more troublesome. For it has been held that a statutory classification is subject to the "compelling interest" test if the result of the classification may be to affect a "fundamental right." * * *

I think this branch of the "compelling interest" doctrine particularly unfortunate and unnecessary. It is unfortunate because it creates an exception which threatens to swallow the standard equal protection rule. Virtually every state statute affects important rights. This Court has repeatedly held, for example, that the traditional equal protection standard is applicable to statutory classifications affecting such fundamental matters as the right to pursue a particular occupation, the right to receive greater or smaller wages or to work more or less hours, and the right to inherit property. Rights such as these are in principle indistinguishable from those involved here, and to extend the "compelling interest" rule to all cases in which such rights are affected would go far toward making this Court a "super-legislature." * * * But when a statute affects only matters not mentioned in the Federal Constitution and is not arbitrary or irrational, I must reiterate that I know of nothing which entitles this Court to pick out particular human activities, characterize them as "fundamental," and give them added protection under an unusually stringent equal protection test. * * *

* * *

I do not consider that the factors which have been urged to outweigh these considerations are sufficient to render unconstitutional these state and federal enactments. It is said, first, that this Court . . . has acknowledged that the right to travel interstate is a "fundamental" freedom. Second it is contended that the governmental objectives mentioned above either are ephemeral or could be accomplished by means which do not impinge as heavily on the right to travel, and hence that the requirements are unconstitutional because they "sweep unnecessarily broadly and thereby invade the area of protected freedoms."

* * *

Taking all of these competing considerations into account, I believe that the balance definitely favors constitutionality. In reaching that conclusion, I do not minimize the importance of the right to travel interstate. However, the impact of residence conditions upon that right is indirect and apparently quite insubstantial. On the other hand, the governmental purposes served by the requirements are legitimate and real, and the residence requirements are clearly suited to their accomplishment. To abolish residence requirements might well discourage highly worthwhile experimentation in the welfare field. * * * Moreover, although the appellees assert that the same objectives could have been achieved by less restrictive means, this is an area in which the judiciary should be especially slow to fetter the judgment of Congress and of some 46 state legislatures in the choice of methods. Residence requirements have advantages, such as administrative simplicity and relative certainty, which are not shared by the alternative solutions proposed by the appellees. In these circumstances, I cannot find that the burden imposed by residence requirements upon ability to travel outweighs the governmental interests in their continued employment. Nor do I believe that the period of residence required in these cases—one year—is so excessively long as to justify a finding of unconstitutionality on that score.

* * *

The Court's fundamental rights doctrine also includes the concept of access to justice. Beginning with *Griffin v. Illinois* (1956), the Court applied the Equal Protection Clause to guarantee that poor criminal defendants have access to the courts. In *Griffin,* two indigent defendants convicted of armed robbery were denied a free transcript of their trial, which they needed for preparing an appeal. By a 5-4 vote, the Supreme Court agreed that the refusal to supply them with the transcript denied them due process and equal protection. Justice Black wrote a four-person plurality opinion, while Justice Frankfurter, in a separate opinion, concurred only in the judgment. Black argued, "Both equal protection and due process emphasize the central aim of our entire judicial system—all people charged with crime must, so far as the law is concerned, 'stand on an equality before the bar of justice in every American court.' . . .[I]n criminal trials a State can no more discriminate on account of poverty than on account of religion, race, or color" (351 U.S. at 17).

The dissenters—Justices Burton, Minton, Reed, and Harlan—saw no violations of due process or equal protection, because the state followed its established procedure for appeals and its procedure was open to all relevant defendants. "The Constitution requires the equal protection of the law, but it does not require the States to provide equal financial means for all defendants to avail themselves of such laws" (351 U.S. at 29).

Language in the plurality and majority opinions in *Griffin, Harper,* and *Shapiro* led some commentators to conclude that the Warren Court might declare classifications based on wealth/indigency as suspect and deserving of strict scrutiny. This did not occur, however. Laws discriminating against poor people were subjected to minimal scrutiny unless they deprived such persons of a fundamental right.

Illegitimacy

The Warren Court also applied the Equal Protection Clause to classifications that discriminated against illegitimate children. In *Levy v. Louisiana* (1968) the Court invalidated a state law that permitted only legitimate children to recover damages for the wrongful death of their mother. It was unclear, however, what standard would be used in examining classifications regarding illegitimacy, because Justice Douglas's majority opinion contained language referring both to the rational basis test and the compelling interest doctrine.

The Burger Court Era

While the Warren Court heard several equal protection cases that did not involve claims of racial and gender discrimination, a litigation explosion occurred during the Burger era. The Burger Court heard a substantial number of cases involving miscellaneous equal protection claims, particularly those regarding classifications based on alienage and illegitimacy. It was not clear, however, what the personnel changes on the Court would mean for the Court's equal protection analysis in these matters. The justices remaining from the Warren era—Brennan, Douglas, White, and Marshall—appeared willing to extend the Equal Protection Clause to protect against various forms of discrimination, while Justice Stewart's position seemed less certain. It was also unclear how Chief Justice Burger and Justices Blackmun, Powell, and Rehnquist would interpret the Clause to deal with other forms of discrimination.

Indigency or Poverty

The Burger Court, like its predecessor, refused to accord suspect status and strict scrutiny to classifications based on wealth or poverty. First, in *Dandridge v. Williams* (1970) a six-person majority upheld as rational a Maryland law that limited AFDC benefits to $250 per month, irrespective of family size or needs. In ruling against the claim that the law discriminated against large families, the Court refused to apply strict scrutiny, holding that the law rationally furthered the state's interest in "encouraging employment and in avoiding discrimination between welfare families and the families of the working poor" (397 U.S. at 486). One year later, the Court rejected an equal protection challenge to a California constitutional provision that required low-rent housing projects to be first approved in a local referendum. Writing for a slim majority in *James v. Valtierra* (1971), Justice Black held that although the referendum procedure posed a disadvantage for poor people, that did not constitute a violation of equal protection. In a dissent joined by Justices Brennan and Blackmun, Justice Marshall advocated strict scrutiny for wealth-based classifications, arguing that "singling out the poor to bear a burden not placed on any other class of citizens tramples the values the Fourteenth Amendment was designed to protect" (402 U.S. at 145).

The Court once again met the issue of wealth as a suspect classification in the 1973 landmark case *San Antonio Independent School District v. Rodriguez,* which was the topic of our case study beginning this chapter. Justice Powell's majority opinion refused to place wealth classifications in the suspect category, maintaining that there was no evidence that the Texas system "discriminate[d] against any definable category of 'poor' people or that it result[ed] in the absolute deprivation of education. . ." (411 U.S. at 25).

San Antonio Independent School District v. Rodriguez

411 U.S. 1, 93 S.Ct. 1278, 36 L. Ed. 2d 16 (1973)

[The facts of this case are omitted because they were presented in the case study at the beginning of the chapter.]

■ This case is important because the Court again refused to place discrimination based on poverty in the suspect classification. Moreover, the majority ruled that education was not a fundamental right and, as such, government policies restricting it were not subject to strict scrutiny. As you read the case, consider these questions: 1) Is Justice Marshall correct in concluding that the Court's narrow approach to equal protection analysis—that is, its reliance on either the rational basis or the compelling interest test—makes it more difficult to decide cases such as this one? 2) Do you think that the majority was concerned that a ruling against the Texas system would have implications for school financing in other states?

Vote:

5 justices voted to uphold the Texas school finance system (Powell, Stewart, Burger, Blackmun, and Rehnquist).

4 justices voted to strike down the Texas system (Douglas, Brennan, White, and Marshall).

Justice Powell delivered the opinion of the Court.

* * *

Texas virtually concedes that its historically rooted dual system of financing education could not withstand the strict judicial scrutiny that this Court has found appropriate in reviewing legislative judgments that interfere with fundamental constitutional rights or that involve suspect classifications. If, as previous decisions have indicated, strict scrutiny means that the State's system is not entitled to the usual presumption of validity, that the State rather than the complainants must carry a "heavy burden of justification," that the State must demonstrate that its educational system has been structured with "precision" and is "tailored" narrowly to serve legitimate objectives and that it has selected the "least drastic means" for effectuating its objectives, the Texas financing system and its counterpart in virtually every other State will not pass muster. The State candidly admits that "[n]o one familiar with the Texas system would contend that it has yet achieved perfection." Apart from its concession that educational finance in Texas has "defects" and "imperfections," the State defends the system's rationality with vigor and disputes the District Court's finding that it lacks a "reasonable basis."

This, then, establishes the framework for our analysis. We must decide, first, whether the Texas system of financing public education operates to the disadvantage of some suspect class or impinges upon a fundamental right explicitly or implicitly protected by the Constitution, thereby requiring strict judicial scrutiny. If so, the judgment of the District Court should be affirmed. If not, the Texas scheme must still be examined to determine whether it rationally furthers some legitimate, articulated state purpose and therefore does not constitute an invidious discrimination in violation of the Equal Protection Clause of the Fourteenth Amendment.

The District Court's opinion does not reflect the novelty and complexity of the constitutional questions posed by appellees' challenge to Texas' system of school financing. In concluding that strict judicial scrutiny was required, that court relied on decisions dealing with the rights of indigents to equal treatment in the criminal trial and appellate processes, and on cases disapproving wealth restrictions on the right to vote. Those cases, the District Court concluded, established wealth as a suspect classification. Finding that the local property tax system discriminated on the basis of wealth, it regarded those precedents as controlling. It then reasoned, based on decisions of this Court affirming the undeniable importance of education, that there is a fundamental right to education and that, absent some compelling state justification, the Texas system could not stand.

We are unable to agree that this case, which in significant aspects is *sui generis,* may be so neatly fitted into the conventional mosaic of constitutional analysis under the Equal Protection Clause. Indeed, for the several reasons that follow, we find neither the suspect-classification nor the fundamental-interest analysis persuasive.

The wealth discrimination discovered by the District Court in this case, and by several other courts that have recently struck down school-financing laws in other States, is quite unlike any of the forms of wealth discrimination heretofore reviewed by this Court. Rather than focusing on the unique features of the alleged discrimination, the courts in these cases have virtually assumed their findings of a suspect classification through a simplistic process of analysis: since, under the traditional systems of financing public schools, some poorer people receive less expensive educations than other more affluent people, these systems discriminate on the basis of wealth. This approach largely ignores the hard threshold questions, including whether it makes a difference for purposes of consideration under the Constitution that the class of disadvantaged "poor" cannot be identified or defined in customary equal protection terms, and whether the relative—rather than absolute—nature of the asserted deprivation is of significant consequence. Before a State's laws and the justifications for the classifications they create are subjected to strict judicial scrutiny, we think these threshold considerations must be analyzed more closely than they were in the court below.

* * *

* * * First, in support of their charge that the system discriminates against the "poor," appellees have made no effort to demonstrate that it operates to the peculiar disadvantage of any class fairly definable as indigent, or as composed of persons whose incomes are beneath any designated poverty level. Indeed, there is reason to believe that the poorest families are not necessarily clustered in the poorest property districts. A recent and exhaustive study of school districts in Connecticut concluded that . . . the poor were clustered around commercial and industrial areas—those same areas that provide the most attractive sources of property tax income for school districts. Whether a similar pattern would be discovered in Texas is not known, but there is no basis on the record in this case for assuming that the poorest people—defined by reference to any level of absolute impecunity—are concentrated in the poorest districts.

Second, neither appellees nor the District Court addressed the fact that, unlike each of the foregoing cases, lack of personal resources has not occasioned an absolute deprivation of the desired benefit. The argument here is not that the children in districts having relatively low assessable property values are receiving no public education; rather, it is that they are receiving a poorer quality education than that available to children in districts having more assessable wealth. Apart from the unsettled and disputed question whether the quality of education may be determined by the amount of money expended for it, a sufficient answer to appellees' argument is that, at least where wealth is involved, the Equal Protection Clause does not require absolute equality or precisely equal advantages. * * *

For these two reasons—the absence of any evidence that the financing system discriminates against any definable category of "poor" people or that it results in the absolute deprivation of education—the disadvantaged class is not susceptible of identification in traditional terms.

* * *

However described, it is clear that appellees' suit asks this Court to extend its most exacting scrutiny to review a system that allegedly discriminates against a large, diverse, and amorphous class, unified only by the common factor of residence in districts that happen to have less taxable wealth than other districts. The system of alleged discrimination and the class it defines have none of the traditional indicia of suspectness: the class is not saddled with such disabilities, or subjected to such a history of purposeful unequal treatment, or relegated to such a position of political powerlessness as to command extraordinary protection from the majoritarian political process.

We thus conclude that the Texas system does not operate to the peculiar disadvantage of any suspect class. But in recognition of the fact that this Court has never heretofore held that wealth discrimination alone provides an adequate basis for invoking strict scrutiny, appellees have not relied solely on this contention. They also assert that the State's system impermissibly interferes with the exercise of a "fundamental" right and that accordingly the prior decisions of this Court require the application of the strict standard of judicial review. It is this question—whether education is a fundamental right, in the sense that it is among the rights and liberties protected by the Constitution—which has so consumed the attention of courts and commentators in recent years.

In *Brown v. Board of Education* (1954), a unanimous Court recognized that "education is perhaps the most important function of state and local governments." * * *

Nothing this Court holds today in any way detracts from our historic dedication to public education. We are in complete agreement with the conclusion of the three-judge panel below that "the grave significance of education both to the individual and to our society" cannot be doubted. But the importance of a service performed by the State does not determine whether it must be regarded as fundamental for purposes of examination under the Equal Protection Clause. * * *

* * * It is not the province of this Court to create substantive constitutional rights in the name of guaranteeing equal protection of the laws. Thus, the key to discovering whether education is "fundamental" is not to be found in comparisons of the relative societal significance of education as opposed to subsistence or housing. Nor is it to be found by weighing whether education is as important as the right to travel. Rather, the answer lies in assessing whether there is a right to education explicitly or implicitly guaranteed by the Constitution.

Education, of course, is not among the rights afforded explicit protection under our Federal Constitution. Nor do we find any basis for saying it is implicitly so protected. As we have said, the undisputed importance of education will not alone cause this Court to depart from the usual standard for reviewing a State's social and economic legislation. It is appellees' contention, however, that education is distinguishable from other services and benefits provided by the State because it bears a peculiarly close relationship to other rights and liberties accorded protection under the Constitution. Specifically, they insist that education is itself a fundamental personal right because it is essential to the effective exercise of First Amendment freedoms and to intelligent utilization of the right to vote. In asserting a nexus between speech and education, appellees urge that the right to speak is meaningless unless the speaker is capable of articulating his thoughts intelligently and persuasively. The "marketplace of ideas" is an empty forum for those lacking basic communicative tools. Likewise, they argue that the corollary right to receive information becomes little more than a hollow privilege when the recipient has not been taught to read, assimilate, and use available knowledge.

* * *

We need not dispute any of these propositions. The Court has long afforded zealous protection against unjustifiable governmental interference with the individual's rights to speak and to vote. Yet we have never presumed to possess either the ability or the authority to guarantee to the citizenry the most *effective* speech or the most *informed* electoral choice. That these may be desirable goals of a system of freedom of expression and of a representative form of government is not to be doubted. These are indeed goals to be pursued by a people whose thoughts and beliefs are freed from governmental interference. But they are not values to be implemented by judicial intrusion into otherwise legitimate state activities.

* * *

. . . [T]he logical limitations on appellees' nexus theory are difficult to perceive. How, for instance, is education to be distinguished from the significant personal interests in the basics of decent food and shelter? Empirical examination might well buttress an assumption that the ill-fed, ill-clothed, and ill-housed are among the most ineffective participants in the political process, and that they derive the least enjoyment from the benefits of the First Amendment. * * *

* * *

We need not rest our decision, however, solely on the inappropriateness of the strict scrutiny test. A century of Supreme Court adjudication under the Equal Protection Clause affirmatively supports the application of the traditional standard of review, which requires only that the State's system be shown to bear some rational relationship to legitimate state purposes. This case represents far more than a challenge to the manner in which Texas provides for the education of its children. We have here nothing less than a direct attack on the way in which Texas has chosen to raise and disburse state and local tax revenues. We are asked to condemn the State's judgment in conferring on political subdivisions the power to tax local property to supply revenues for local interests. In so doing, appellees would have the Court intrude in an area in which it has traditionally deferred to state legislatures. This Court has often admonished against such interferences with the State's fiscal policies under the Equal Protection Clause. * * *

* * *

The foregoing considerations buttress our conclusion that Texas' system of public school finance is an inappropriate candidate for strict judicial scrutiny. These same considerations are relevant to the determination whether that system, with its conceded imperfections, nevertheless bears some rational relationship to a legitimate state purpose. * * *

* * *

* * * While assuring a basic education for every child in the State, it [the Texas system of school finance] permits and encourages a large measure of participation in and control of each district's schools at the local level. In an era that has witnessed a consistent trend toward centralization of the functions of government, local sharing of responsibility for public education has survived. * * *

The persistence of attachment to government at the lowest level where education is concerned reflects the depth of commitment of its supporters. In part, local control means . . . the freedom to devote more money to the education of one's children. Equally important, however, is the opportunity it offers for participation in the decisionmaking process that determines how those local tax dollars will be spent. Each locality is free to tailor local programs to local needs. Pluralism also affords some opportunity for experimentation, innovation, and a healthy competition for educational excellence. * * *

* * *

Appellees . . . urge that the Texas system is unconstitutionally arbitrary because it allows the availability of local taxable resources to turn on "happenstance." They see no justification for a system that allows, as they contend, the quality of education to fluctuate on the basis of the fortuitous positioning of the boundary lines of political subdivisions and the location of valuable commercial and industrial property. But any scheme of local taxation—indeed the very existence of identifiable local governmental units—requires the establishment of jurisdictional boundaries that are inevitably arbitrary. It is equally inevitable that some localities are going to be blessed with more taxable assets than others. Nor is local wealth a static quantity. Changes in the level of taxable wealth within any district may result from any number of events, some of which local residents can and do influence. For instance, commercial and industrial enterprises may be encouraged to locate within a district by various actions—public and private.

Moreover, if local taxation for local expenditures were an unconstitutional method of providing for education then it might be an equally impermissible means of providing other necessary services customarily financed largely from local property taxes, including local police and fire protection, public health and hospitals, and public utility facilities of various kinds. We perceive no justification for such a severe denigration of local property taxation and control as would follow from appellees' contentions. It has simply never been within the constitutional prerogative of this Court to nullify statewide measures for financing public services merely because the burdens or benefits thereof fall unevenly depending upon the relative wealth of the political subdivisions in which citizens live.

In sum, to the extent that the Texas system of school financing results in unequal expenditures between children who happen to reside in different districts, we cannot say that such disparities are the product of a system that is so irrational as to be invidiously discriminatory. Texas has acknowledged its shortcomings and has persistently endeavored—not without some success—to ameliorate the differences in levels of expenditures without sacrificing the benefits of local participation. The Texas plan is not the result of hurried, ill-conceived legislation. It certainly is not the product of purposeful discrimination against any group or class. * * *

* * *

* * * We hardly need add that this Court's action today is not to be viewed as placing its judicial imprimatur on the status quo. The need is apparent for reform in tax systems which may well have relied too long and too heavily on the local property tax. And certainly innovative thinking as to public education, its methods, and its funding is necessary to assure both a higher level of quality and greater uniformity of opportunity. These matters merit the continued attention of the scholars who already have contributed much by their challenges. But the ultimate solutions must come from the lawmakers and from the democratic pressures of those who elect them.

Reversed.

Justice Stewart concurred [omitted].

Justice Brennan dissented [omitted].

Justice White, with whom Justice Douglas and Justice Brennan join, dissenting.

* * *

I cannot disagree with the proposition that local control and local decisionmaking play an important part in our democratic system of government. Much may be left to local option, and this case would be quite different if it were true that the Texas system, while insuring minimum educational expenditures in every district through state funding, extended a meaningful option to all local districts to increase their per-pupil expenditures and so to improve their children's education to the extent that increased funding would achieve that goal. The system would then arguably provide a rational and sensible method of achieving the stated aim of preserving an area for local initiative and decision.

The difficulty with the Texas system, however, is that it provides a meaningful option to Alamo Heights and like school districts but almost none to Edgewood and those other districts with a low per-pupil real estate tax base. In these latter districts, no matter how desirous parents are of supporting their schools with greater revenues, it is impossible to do so through the use of the real estate property tax. In these districts, the Texas system utterly fails to extend a realistic choice to parents because the property tax, which is the only revenue-raising mechanism extended to school districts, is practically and legally unavailable. * * *

* * *

The Equal Protection Clause permits discriminations between classes but requires that the classification bear some rational relationship to a permissible object sought to be attained by the statute. It is not enough that the Texas system before us seeks to achieve the valid, rational purpose of maximizing local initiative; the means chosen by the State must also be rationally related to the end sought to be achieved. * * *

* * * If the State aims at maximizing local initiative and local choice, by permitting school districts to resort to the real property tax if they choose to do so, it utterly fails in achieving its purpose in districts with property tax bases so low that there is little if any opportunity for interested parents, rich or poor, to augment school district revenues. Requiring the State to establish only that unequal treatment is in

furtherance of a permissible goal, without also requiring the State to show that the means chosen to effectuate that goal are rationally related to its achievement, makes equal protection analysis no more than an empty gesture. In my view, the parents and children in Edgewood, and in like districts, suffer from an invidious discrimination violative of the Equal Protection Clause.

* * *

Justice Marshall, with whom Justice Douglas concurs, dissenting.

The Court today decides, in effect, that a State may constitutionally vary the quality of education which it offers its children in accordance with the amount of taxable wealth located in the school districts within which they reside. The majority's decision represents an abrupt departure from the mainstream of recent state and federal court decisions concerning the unconstitutionality of state educational financing schemes dependent upon taxable local wealth. More unfortunately, though, the majority's holding can only be seen as a retreat from our historic commitment to equality of educational opportunity and as unsupportable acquiescence in a system which deprives children in their earliest years of the chance to reach their full potential as citizens. The Court does this despite the absence of any substantial justification for a scheme which arbitrarily channels educational resources in accordance with the fortuity of the amount of taxable wealth within each district.

In my judgment, the right of every American to an equal start in life, so far as the provision of a state service as important as education is concerned, is far too vital to permit state discrimination on grounds as tenuous as those presented by this record. Nor can I accept the notion that it is sufficient to remit these appellees to the vagaries of the political process which, contrary to the majority's suggestion, has proved singularly unsuited to the task of providing a remedy for this discrimination. I, for one, am unsatisfied with the hope of an ultimate "political" solution sometime in the indefinite future while, in the meantime, countless children unjustifiably receive inferior educations that "may affect their hearts and minds in a way unlikely ever to be undone." I must therefore respectfully dissent.

* * *

In my view, . . . it is inequality—not some notion of gross inadequacy—of educational opportunity that raises a question of denial of equal protection of the laws. I find any other approach to the issue unintelligible and without directing principle. Here, appellees have made a substantial showing of wide variations in educational funding and the resulting educational opportunity afforded to the schoolchildren of Texas. This discrimination is, in large measure, attributable to significant disparities in the taxable wealth of local Texas school districts. This is a sufficient showing to raise a substantial question of discriminatory state action in violation of the Equal Protection Clause.

* * *

* * * I must voice my disagreement with the Court's rigidified approach to equal protection analysis. The Court apparently seeks to establish today that equal protection cases fall into one of two neat categories which dictate the appropriate standard of review—strict scrutiny or mere rationality. But this Court's decisions in the field of equal protection defy such easy categorization. A principled reading of what this Court has done reveals that it has applied a spectrum of standards in reviewing discrimination allegedly violative of the Equal Protection Clause. This spectrum clearly comprehends variations in the degree of care with which the Court will scrutinize particular classifications, depending, I believe, on the constitutional and societal importance of the interest adversely affected and the recognized invidiousness of the basis upon which the particular classification is drawn. I find in fact that many of the Court's recent decisions embody the very sort of reasoned approach to equal protection analysis for which I previously argued—that is, an approach in which "concentration [is] placed upon the character of the classification in question, the relative importance to individuals in the class discriminated against of the governmental benefits that they do not receive, and the asserted state interests in support of the classification."

I therefore cannot accept the majority's labored efforts to demonstrate that fundamental interests, which call for strict scrutiny of the challenged classification, encompass only established rights which we are somehow bound to recognize from the text of the Constitution itself. To be sure, some interests which the Court has deemed to be fundamental for purposes of equal protection analysis are themselves constitutionally protected rights. * * * But it will not do to suggest that the "answer" to whether an interest is fundamental for purposes of equal protection analysis is *always* determined by whether that interest "is a right . . . explicitly or implicitly guaranteed by the Constitution." * * *

* * *

The majority is, of course, correct when it suggests that the process of determining which interests are fundamental is a difficult one. But I do not think the problem is insurmountable. And I certainly do not accept the view that the process need necessarily degenerate into an unprincipled, subjective "picking-and-choosing" between various interests or that it must involve this Court in creating "substantive constitutional rights in the name of guaranteeing equal protection of the laws." Although not all fundamental interests are constitutionally guaranteed, the determination of which interests are fundamental should be firmly rooted in the text of the Constitution. The task in every case should be to determine the extent to which constitutionally guaranteed rights are dependent on interests not mentioned in the Constitution. As the nexus between the specific constitutional guarantee and the nonconstitutional interest draws closer, the nonconstitutional interest becomes more fundamental and the degree of judicial scrutiny applied when the interest is infringed on a discriminatory basis must be adjusted accordingly. * * *

* * *

* * * It is true that this Court has never deemed the provision of free public education to be required by the Constitution. Indeed, it has on occasion suggested that state-supported education is a privilege bestowed by a State on its citizens. Nevertheless, the fundamental importance of education is amply indicated by the prior decisions of this Court, by the unique status accorded public education by our society, and by the close relationship between education and some of our most basic constitutional values.

* * *

The nature of our inquiry into the justification for state discrimination is essentially the same in all equal protection cases: We must consider the substantiality of the state interests sought to be served, and we must scrutinize the reasonableness of the means by which the State has sought to advance its interests. Differences in the application of this test are, in my view, a function of the constitutional importance of the interests at stake and the invidiousness of the particular classification. * * * Here, both the nature of the interest and the classification dictate close judicial scrutiny of the purposes which Texas seeks to serve with its present educational financing scheme and of the means it has selected to serve that purpose.

The only justification offered by appellants to sustain the discrimination in educational opportunity caused by the Texas financing scheme is local educational control. * * *

* * *

In Texas, statewide laws regulate in fact the most minute details of local public education. * * *

Moreover, even if we accept Texas' general dedication to local control in educational matters, it is difficult to find any evidence of such dedication with respect to fiscal matters. * * * If Texas had a system truly dedicated to local fiscal control, one would expect the quality of the educational opportunity provided in each district to vary with the decision of the voters in that district as to the level of sacrifice they wish to make for public education. In fact, the Texas scheme produces precisely the opposite result. Local school districts cannot choose to have the best education in the State by imposing the highest tax rate. Instead, the quality of the educational opportunity offered by any particular district is largely determined by the amount of taxable property located in the district—a factor over which local voters can exercise no control.

* * *

In my judgment, any substantial degree of scrutiny of the operation of the Texas financing scheme reveals that the State has selected means wholly inappropriate to secure its purported interest in assuring its school districts local fiscal control. At the same time, appellees have pointed out a variety of alternative financing schemes which may serve the State's purported interest in local control as well as, if not better than, the present scheme without the current impairment of the educational opportunity of vast numbers of Texas schoolchildren. I see no need, however, to explore the practical or constitutional merits of those suggested alternatives at this time for, whatever their positive or negative features, experience with the present financing scheme impugns any suggestion that it constitutes a serious effort to provide local fiscal control. If for the sake of local education control, this Court is to sustain interdistrict discrimination in the educational opportunity afforded Texas school children, it should require that the State present something more than the mere sham now before us.

* * *

The Court seeks solace for its action today in the possibility of legislative reform. The Court's suggestions of legislative redress and experimentation will doubtless be of great comfort to the schoolchildren of Texas' disadvantaged districts, but considering the vested interests of wealthy school districts in the preservation of the status quo, they are worth little more. * * *

Fundamental Rights

In general, the Burger Court continued to scrutinize closely classifications that impinged on fundamental rights already established by previous Court decisions. It refused, however, to make any additions to the fundamental rights category.

In *Dunn v. Blumstein* (1972) the Court struck down a Tennessee law that established residency requirements as a condition for voting. The residency requirements violated two fundamental rights—the right to vote and the right to interstate travel. The majority could find no compelling interests to justify the residency requirements.

In the *Rodriguez* case, in addition to the suspect classification arguments, the plaintiffs contended that education is a fundamental right deserving of special recognition and protection. The majority disagreed, however, holding that the right to education is neither explicitly nor implicitly guaranteed by the Constitution. Justice Marshall disagreed, arguing that "the fundamental importance of education is amply indicated by the . . . unique status accorded public education by our society, and by the close relationship between education and some of our most basic constitutional values" (411 U.S. at 111).

Memorial Hospital v. Maricopa County (1974) was another case involving the right to travel. By an 8-1 vote, the Court struck down an Arizona law that established a one-year residency requirement for indigents to receive nonemergency medical services provided at the county's expense.

Illegitimacy

The Burger Court's equal protection decisions concerning discrimination against illegitimate children were among the most confusing, primarily because it was unclear whether such classifications would be examined under the rational basis standard or some higher level of scrutiny. In addition, similar classifications seemed to be upheld in some instances but invalidated in others.

In *Labine v. Vincent* (1971), a five-member majority used the rational basis test to uphold a state law restricting the inheritance rights of illegitimate children. The majority accepted as reasonable the state's interest in promoting the legally recognized family. One year later, however, the Court invalidated a state workers' compensation law that prohibited dependent illegitimate children from recovering damages for the wrongful death of their parents (*Weber v. Aetna Casualty & Surety Company,* 1972).

Four years later in a case involving the federal government, the Court again upheld a legal restriction placed on illegitimacy (*Matthews v. Lucas,* 1976). At the same time, however, the majority ruled that while such classifications were not subject to strict scrutiny, the rational basis test was inadequate. One year later the Court appeared to reaffirm this principle in *Trimble v. Gordon* (1977). "Despite the conclusion that classifications based on illegitimacy fall in a 'realm of less than strictest scrutiny,' *Lucas* . . . establishes that the scrutiny 'is not a toothless one'" (430 U.S. at 767). In *Trimble,* the justices struck down a provision of an Illinois statute regarding intestate succession, which permitted legitimate children to inherit from both parents, but allowed illegitimate children to inherit only from their mothers. The majority rejected the state's claimed interest in "the promotion of [legitimate] family relationships," emphasizing that states may not "attempt to influence the actions of men and women by imposing sanctions on the children born of their illegitimate relationships" (430 U.S. at 769).

Trimble v. Gordon

430 U.S. 762, 97 S.Ct. 1459, 52 L. Ed. 2d 31 (1977)

■ Deta Trimble, the illegitimate daughter of Sherman Gordon, claimed heirship after Gordon died without a will (intestate). A probate court rejected her claim on the basis of Section 12 of the Illinois Probate Act. According to this provision, legitimate children could inherit by intestate succession from both parents, but illegitimate children could inherit by intestate succession only from their mothers. Her appeal of the probate court ruling was dismissed by the Illinois Supreme Court. Subsequently, Trimble petitioned the U.S. Supreme Court for review.

This case is important because it limited the authority of the states to discriminate against illegitimate children and because it appeared to affirm the intermediate level of scrutiny as the appropriate test for illegitimacy classification. As you read the case, consider these questions: 1) Does Justice Powell state clearly that intermediate scrutiny is the standard being applied? 2) What are the implications of laws that distinguish between "legitimate" and "illegitimate" children?

Vote:

5 justices declared the challenged provision unconstitutional (Powell, Brennan, White, Marshall, and Stevens).

4 justices voted to uphold the challenged provision (Burger, Stewart, Blackmun, and Rehnquist).

Justice Powell delivered the opinion of the Court.

* * *

* * * In weighing the constitutional sufficiency of these justifications, we are guided by our previous decisions involving equal protection challenges to laws discriminating on the basis of illegitimacy. "[T]his Court requires, at a minimum, that a statutory classification bear some rational relationship to a legitimate state purpose." In this context, the standard just stated is a minimum; the Court sometimes requires more. "Though the latitude given state economic and social regulation is necessarily broad, when state statutory classifications approach sensitive and fundamental personal rights, this Court exercises a stricter scrutiny. . . ."

Appellants urge us to hold that classifications based on illegitimacy are "suspect," so that any justifications must survive "strict scrutiny." We considered and rejected a similar argument last Term in *Mathews v. Lucas* (1976). As we recognized in *Lucas,* illegitimacy is analogous in many respects to the personal characteristics that have been held to be suspect when used as the basis of statutory differentiations. We nevertheless concluded that the analogy was not sufficient to require "our most exacting scrutiny." Despite the conclusion that classifications based on illegitimacy fall in a "realm of less than strictest scrutiny," *Lucas* also establishes that the scrutiny "is not a toothless one," a proposition clearly demonstrated by our previous decisions in this area.

* * *

The Illinois Supreme Court relied in part on the State's purported interest in "the promotion of [legitimate] family relationships." * * *

In a case like this, the Equal Protection Clause requires more than the mere incantation of a proper state purpose. No one disputes the appropriateness of Illinois' concern with the family unit, perhaps the most fundamental social institution of our society. The flaw in the analysis lies elsewhere. As we said in *Lucas,* the constitutionality of this law "depends upon the character of the discrimination and its relation to legitimate legislative aims." * * * [W]e have expressly considered and rejected the argument that a State may attempt to influence the actions of men and women by imposing sanctions on the children born of their illegitimate relationships.

* * *

The Illinois Supreme Court also noted that the decedents whose estates were involved in the consolidated appeals could have left substantial parts of their estates to their illegitimate children by writing a will. * * *

* * *

By focusing on the steps that an intestate might have taken to assure some inheritance for his illegitimate children, the analysis loses sight of the essential question: the constitutionality of discrimination against illegitimates in a state intestate succession law. If the decedent had written a will devising property to his illegitimate child, the case no longer would involve intestate succession law at all. * * *

Finally, appellees urge us to affirm the decision below on the theory that the Illinois Probate Act, including § 12, mirrors the presumed intentions of the citizens of the State regarding the disposition of their property at death. Individualizing this theory, appellees argue that we must assume that Sherman Gordon knew the disposition of his estate under the Illinois Probate Act and that his failure to make a will shows his approval of that disposition. We need not resolve the question whether presumed intent alone can ever justify discrimination against illegitimates, for we do not think that § 12 was enacted for this purpose. * * *

* * *

* * * [W]e find in § 12 a primary purpose to provide a system of intestate succession more just to illegitimate children than the prior law, a purpose tempered by a secondary interest in protecting against spurious claims of paternity. In the absence of a more convincing demonstration, we will not hypothesize an additional state purpose that has been ignored by the Illinois Supreme Court.

For the reasons stated above, we conclude that § 12 of the Illinois Probate Act cannot be squared with the command of the Equal Protection Clause of the Fourteenth Amendment. Accordingly, we reverse the judgment of the Illinois Supreme Court and remand the case for further proceedings not inconsistent with this opinion.

So ordered.

The Chief Justice, Justice Stewart, Justice Blackmun, and Justice Rehnquist dissent. Like the Supreme Court of Illinois, they find this case constitutionally indistinguishable from *Labine v. Vincent* (1971). They would, therefore, affirm the judgment.

Justice Rehnquist, dissenting.

* * *

The essential problem of the Equal Protection Clause is . . . the one of determining where the courts are to look for guidance in defining "equality" as that word is used in the Fourteenth Amendment. Since the Amendment grew out of the Civil War and the freeing of the slaves, the core prohibition was early held to be aimed at the protection of blacks. If race was an invalid sorting tool where blacks were concerned, it followed logically that it should not be valid where other races were concerned either. A logical, though not inexorable, next step, was the extension of the projection to prohibit classifications resting on national origin.

The presumptive invalidity of all of these classifications has made decisions involving them, for the most part, relatively easy. But when the Court has been required to adjudicate equal protection claims not based on race or national origin, it has faced a much more difficult task. * * *

Illegitimacy, which is involved in this case, has never been held by the Court to be a "suspect classification." Nonetheless, in several opinions of the Court, statements are found which suggest that although illegitimates are not members of a "suspect class," laws which treat them differently from those born in wedlock will receive a more far-reaching scrutiny under the Equal Protection Clause than will other laws regulating economic and social conditions. The Court's opinion today contains language to that effect. In one sense this language is a source of consolation, since it suggests that parts of the Court's analysis used in this case will not be carried over to traditional "rational basis" or "minimum scrutiny" cases. At the same time, though, it is a source of confusion, since the unanswered question remains as to the precise sort of scrutiny to which classifications based on illegitimacy will be subject.

* * *

The "difficulty" of the "judicial task" is, I suggest, a self-imposed one, stemming not from the Equal Protection Clause but from the Court's insistence on reading so much into it. * * *

* * *

But a graver defect than this in the Court's analysis is that it . . . requires a conscious second-guessing of legislative judgment in an area where this Court has no special expertise whatever. Even assuming that a court has properly accomplished the difficult task of identifying the "purpose" which a statute seeks to serve, it then sits in judgment to consider the so-called "fit" between that "purpose" and the statutory means adopted to achieve it. In most cases, and all but invariably if the Court insists on singling out a unitary "purpose," the "fit" will involve a greater or lesser degree of imperfection. Then the Court asks itself: How much "imperfection" between means and ends is permissible? In making this judgment it must throw into the judicial hopper the whole range of factors which were first thrown into the legislative hopper. What alternatives were reasonably available? What reasons are there for the legislature to accomplish this "purpose" in the way it did? What obstacles stood in the way of other solutions?

The fundamental flaw, to me, in this approach is that there is absolutely nothing to be implied from the fact that we hold judicial commissions that would enable us to answer any one of these questions better than the legislators to whose initial decision they were committed. Without any antecedent constitutional mandate, we have created on the premises of the Equal Protection Clause a school for legislators, whereby opinions of this Court are written to instruct them in a better understanding of how to accomplish their ordinary legislative tasks.

* * *

Here the Illinois Legislature was dealing with a problem of intestate succession of illegitimates from their fathers, which as the Court concedes frequently presents difficult problems of proof. The provisions of Illinois Probate Act § 12, as most recently amended, alleviate some of the difficulties which previously stood in the way of such succession. The fact that the Act in question does not alleviate all of the difficulties, or that it might have gone further than it did, is to me wholly irrelevant under the Equal

Protection Clause. The circumstances which justify the distinction between illegitimates and legitimates contained in § 12 are apparent with no great exercise of imagination; they are stated in the opinion of the Court, though they are there rejected as constitutionally insufficient. Since Illinois' distinction is not mindless and patently irrational, I would affirm the judgment of the Supreme Court of Illinois.

Only one year later, however, the Court again upheld the importance of the state's emphasis on promoting traditional family relationships. In *Lalli v. Lalli* (1978), a narrow majority sustained a state law that prevented illegitimate children from inheriting from their intestate fathers unless the father had previously acknowledged his paternity in a court proceeding.

Alienage

The Burger Court's decisions regarding discrimination against aliens also have been quite confusing. Despite declaring alienage a suspect classification in 1971, the Court's decisions since then have not all followed strict scrutiny. Depending upon the types of issues involved, the justices have used strict scrutiny, the intermediate level of review, and the rational basis test.

In *Graham v. Richardson* (1971) the Court was faced with an Arizona statute that limited welfare benefits to U.S. citizens and to aliens who had resided in the United States for at least fifteen years. In striking down the statute by a unanimous vote, the Court declared that "classifications based on alienage, like those based on nationality or race, are inherently suspect and subject to close judicial scrutiny. Aliens as a class are a prime example of a 'discrete and insular' minority . . . for whom such heightened judicial solicitude is appropriate" (403 U.S. at 372). The state's asserted interest in preserving welfare benefits for its own residents was not deemed sufficiently compelling to justify the classification.

Two years later, applying strict scrutiny, the high court invalidated a Connecticut law that prohibited resident aliens from practicing law (*In Re Griffiths,* 1973). That same year, in *Sugarman v. Dougall* the Court again used strict scrutiny and voided a New York statute that barred aliens from competing for certain policy-making positions in the state civil service. At the same time, in dicta the Court suggested that not all restrictions on aliens were suspect and, more specifically, that aliens might legitimately be excluded from other types of public employment. Writing for the majority, Justice Blackmun intimated that states could require that only citizens be allowed to hold "state elective or important nonelective executive, legislative, and judicial positions" (413 U.S. at 647) or positions that involve the development, implementation, or review of public policy.

Five years later, apparently relying on the dicta from *Sugarman,* the Court applied minimal scrutiny in upholding a New York law that prohibited aliens from becoming state troopers. In *Foley v. Connelie* (1978) Chief Justice Burger said that application of strict scrutiny to all alienage classifications "would obliterate all the distinctions between citizens and aliens, and thus depreciate the historic value of citizenship" (435 U.S. at 295). According to Burger, the decision to "confine the employment of police officers to citizens" was justified because they are important nonelective officers who participate in executing policy, and "the State may reasonably presume [them] to be more familiar with and sympathetic to American traditions" (435 U.S. at 299–300).

Similarly, in *Ambach v. Norwick* (1979), the Court used the rational basis test to sustain a New York law that prevented aliens from being certified as public school teachers, unless they had earlier established their intentions to apply for citizenship. In the majority's view, because an important task of public school teachers was to teach students about their government and society, this occupation was "bound up with the operation of the State as a governmental entity" (441 U.S. at 73–74). Thus, they concluded, these jobs could be legitimately restricted to citizens. Using similar reasoning, the Court upheld a California law that prevented aliens from becoming deputy probation officers (*Cabell v. Chavez-Salido,* 1982). On the other hand, employing strict scrutiny, the justices struck down a Texas law that barred aliens from the position of notary public on the grounds that this did not involve a "political function" as was present in the previous cases (*Bernal v. Fainter,* 1984).

In an important 1982 case involving public education, the high court did not use either the rational basis test or the compelling interest standard in examining the alienage classification. *Plyler v. Doe* concerned a Texas law that withheld from school districts funds for educating the children of illegal aliens and that authorized school districts to deny a free public education to these children. By a 5-4 vote, the Court invalidated the law. Writing for the majority, Justice Brennan rejected the state's argument that *illegal* aliens were not protected by the Equal Protection Clause. He also maintained that strict scrutiny was not the appropriate standard of review. Brennan wrote, "Undocumented aliens cannot be treated as a suspect class because their presence in this country in violation of federal law is not a 'constitutional irrelevancy'" (457 U.S. at 223). Furthermore, education was not considered to be a fundamental right. At the same time, however, minimal scrutiny was insufficient because the classification was directed against undocumented children who were not responsible for their illegal status and who would be harmed substantially by the statute. "By denying these children a basic education, we deny them the ability to live within the structure of our civic institutions, and foreclose any realistic possibility that they will contribute in even the smallest way to the progress of our Nation" (457 U.S. at 223). Therefore, the Texas law could be upheld only if it furthered a substantial state interest. The state asserted three main interests in support of the statute—protecting against an influx of illegal immigrants, improving the overall quality of education, and ensuring that those educated by the state put their education to productive use within the state. Finding none of these to be substantial, the majority declared the law in violation of the Equal Protection Clause.

In a sharp dissent for himself and Justices White, Rehnquist, and O'Connor, Chief Justice Burger contended that the rational basis test was the appropriate standard of review, and he criticized the majority for intruding on the functions of the political branches of government. He said that in making decisions about the allocation of "finite resources," "a state has a legitimate reason to differentiate between persons who are lawfully within the state and those who are unlawfully there" (457 U.S. at 243–44). In a rather caustic passage Burger argued, "[T]he Constitution does not constitute us as 'Platonic Guardians' nor does it vest in this Court the authority to strike down laws because they do not meet our standards of desirable social policy, 'wisdom,' or 'common sense' " (457 U.S. 242). In his view, while it may be wrong for society to deny undocumented children the benefit of an education, the Court should defer to the political branches to remedy the problem.

PLYLER V. DOE

457 U.S. 202, 102 S.Ct. 2382, 72 L. Ed 2d 786 (1982)

■ In 1975, the Texas legislature amended its Education Code to authorize public school districts to deny enrollment to the children of illegal (undocumented) aliens. The law also withheld from school districts funds for educating these children. The state's rationale was that the presence of these children in public schools drained resources and decreased the schools' ability to provide a quality education for other children. Two years later, a class action suit was filed in federal court challenging the law as a violation of the Equal Protection Clause. The district court held that the law in fact did deprive these children of equal protection of the laws. After the court of appeals affirmed this decision, the state sought review in the U.S. Supreme Court.

This case is important because the Court affirmed that the equal protection guarantee extends to all persons within a state's jurisdiction, regardless of citizenship status. As you read the case, consider these questions: 1) For purposes of equal protection analysis, is it appropriate to use different tests for illegal versus legal aliens? 2) Would the dissenters have voted differently had there been evidence that the children of legal aliens were harmed by this law? 3) Which side is correct about the proper role of the Court in deciding issues not resolved by the political branches of government?

VOTE:

5 justices voted to strike down the Texas law (Brennan, Marshall, Blackmun, Powell, and Stevens).

4 justices voted to uphold the Texas law (Burger, White, Rehnquist, and O'Connor).

Justice Brennan delivered the opinion of the Court.

* * *

The Equal Protection Clause directs that "all persons similarly circumstanced shall be treated alike." But so too, "[t]he Constitution does not require things which are different in fact or opinion to be treated in law as though they were the same." The initial discretion to determine what is "different" and what is "the same" resides in the legislatures of the States. A legislature must have substantial latitude to establish classifications that roughly approximate the nature of the problem perceived, that accommodate competing concerns both public and private, and that account for limitations on the practical ability of the State to remedy every ill. In applying the Equal Protection Clause to most forms of state action, we thus seek only the assurance that the classification at issue bears some fair relationship to a legitimate public purpose.

But we would not be faithful to our obligations under the Fourteenth Amendment if we applied so deferential a standard to every classification. The Equal Protection Clause was intended as a restriction on state legislative action inconsistent with elemental constitutional premises. Thus we have treated as presumptively invidious those classifications that disadvantage a "suspect class," or that impinge upon the exercise of a "fundamental right." With respect to such classifications, it is appropriate to enforce the mandate of equal protection by requiring the State to demonstrate that its classification has been precisely tailored to serve a compelling governmental interest. In addition, we have recognized that certain forms of legislative classification, while not facially invidious, nonetheless give rise to recurring constitutional difficulties; in these limited circumstances we have sought the assurance that the classification reflects a reasoned judgment consistent with the ideal of equal protection by inquiring whether it may fairly be viewed as furthering a substantial interest of the State. * * *

Sheer incapability or lax enforcement of the laws barring entry into this country, coupled with the failure to establish an effective bar to the employment of undocumented aliens, has resulted in the creation of a substantial "shadow population" of illegal migrants—numbering in the millions—within our borders. This situation raises the specter of a permanent caste of undocumented resident aliens, encouraged by some to remain here as a source of cheap labor, but nevertheless denied the benefits that our society makes available to citizens and lawful residents. The existence of such an underclass presents most difficult problems for a Nation that prides itself on adherence to principles of equality under law.

The children who are plaintiffs in these cases are special members of this underclass. Persuasive arguments support the view that a State may withhold its beneficence from those whose very presence within the United States is the product of their own unlawful conduct. These arguments do not apply with the same force to classifications imposing disabilities on the minor *children* of such illegal entrants. At the least, those who elect to enter our territory by stealth and in violation of our law should be prepared to bear the consequences, including, but not limited to, deportation. But the children of those illegal entrants are not comparably situated. Their "parents have the ability to conform their conduct to societal norms," and presumably the ability to remove themselves from the State's jurisdiction; but the children who are plaintiffs in these cases "can affect neither their parents' conduct nor their own status." Even if the State found it expedient to control the conduct of adults by acting against their children, legislation directing the onus of a parent's misconduct against his children does not comport with fundamental conceptions of justice. * * *

Of course, undocumented status is not irrelevant to any proper legislative goal. Nor is undocumented status an absolutely immutable characteristic since it is the product of conscious, indeed unlawful, action. But § 21.031 is directed against children, and imposes its discriminatory burden on the basis of a legal characteristic over which children can have little control. It is thus difficult to conceive of a rational justification for penalizing these children for their presence within the United States. Yet that appears to be precisely the effect of § 21.031.

Public education is not a "right" granted to individuals by the Constitution. But neither is it merely some governmental "benefit" indistinguishable from other forms of social welfare legislation. Both the importance of education in maintaining our basic institutions, and the lasting impact of its deprivation on the life of the child, mark the distinction. The "American people have always regarded education and [the] acquisition of knowledge as matters of supreme importance." * * *

In addition to the pivotal role of education in sustaining our political and cultural heritage, denial of education to some isolated group of children poses an affront to one of the goals of the Equal Protection Clause: the abolition of governmental barriers presenting unreasonable obstacles to advancement on the basis of individual merit. Paradoxically, by depriving the children of any disfavored group of an education, we foreclose the means by which that group might raise the level of esteem in which it is held by the majority. But more directly, "education prepares individuals to be self-reliant and self-sufficient participants in society." * * *

These well-settled principles allow us to determine the proper level of deference to be afforded § 21.031. Undocumented aliens cannot be treated as a suspect class because their presence in this country in violation of federal law is not a "constitutional irrelevancy." Nor is education a fundamental right; a State need not justify by compelling necessity every variation in the manner in which education is provided to its population. But more is involved in these cases than the abstract question whether § 21.031 discriminates against a suspect class, or whether education is a fundamental right. Section 21.031 imposes a lifetime hardship on a discrete class of children not accountable for their disabling status. The stigma of illiteracy will mark them for the rest of their lives. By denying these children a basic education, we deny them the ability to live within the structure of our civic institutions, and foreclose any realistic possibility that they will contribute in even the smallest way to the progress of our Nation. In determining the rationality of § 21.031, we may appropriately take into account its costs to the Nation and to the innocent children who are its victims. In light of these countervailing costs, the discrimination contained in § 21.031 can hardly be considered rational unless it furthers some substantial goal of the State.

It is the State's principal argument, and apparently the view of the dissenting Justices, that the undocumented status of these children *vel non* [or not] establishes a sufficient rational basis for denying them benefits that a State might choose to afford other residents. * * * Indeed, in the State's view, Congress' apparent disapproval of the presence of these children within the United States, and the evasion of the federal regulatory program that is the mark of undocumented status, provides authority for its decision to impose upon them special disabilities. Faced with an equal protection challenge respecting the treatment of aliens, we agree that the courts must be attentive to congressional policy; the exercise of congressional power might well affect the State's prerogatives to afford differential treatment to a particular class of aliens. But we are unable to find in the congressional immigration scheme any statement of policy that might weigh significantly in arriving at an equal protection balance concerning the State's authority to deprive these children of an education.

* * *

To be sure, like all persons who have entered the United States unlawfully, these children are subject to deportation. But there is no assurance that a child subject to deportation will ever be deported. An illegal entrant might be granted federal permission to continue to reside in this country, or even to become a citizen. In light of the discretionary federal power to grant relief from deportation, a State cannot realistically determine that any particular undocumented child will in fact be deported until after deportation proceedings have been completed. It would of course be most difficult for the State to justify a denial of education to a child enjoying an inchoate federal permission to remain.

* * *

* * * Apart from the asserted state prerogative to act against undocumented children solely on the basis of their undocumented status—an asserted prerogative that carries only minimal force in the circumstances of these cases—we discern three colorable state interests that might support § 21.031.

First, appellants appear to suggest that the State may seek to protect itself from an influx of illegal immigrants. While a State might have an interest in mitigating the potentially harsh economic effects of sudden shifts in population, § 21.031 hardly offers an effective method of dealing with an urgent demographic or economic problem. There is no evidence in the record suggesting that illegal entrants impose any significant burden on the State's economy. To the contrary, the available evidence suggests that illegal aliens underuse public services, while contributing their labor to the local economy and tax money to the state fisc. The dominant incentive for illegal entry into the State of Texas is the availability of employment; few if any illegal immigrants come to this country, or presumably to the State of Texas, in order to avail themselves of a free education. Thus, even making the doubtful assumption that the net impact of illegal aliens on the economy of the State is negative, we think it clear that "[c]harging tuition to undocumented children constitutes a ludicrously ineffectual attempt to stem the tide of illegal immigration," at least when compared with the alternative of prohibiting the employment of illegal aliens.

Second, while it is apparent that a State may "not . . . reduce expenditures for education by barring [some arbitrarily chosen class of] children from its schools," appellants suggest that undocumented children are appropriately singled out for exclusion because of the special burdens they impose on the State's ability to provide high-quality public education. But the record in no way supports the claim that exclusion of undocumented children is likely to improve the overall quality of education in the State. * * * And, after reviewing the State's school financing mechanism, the District Court concluded that barring undocumented children from local schools would not necessarily improve the quality of education provided in those schools. Of course, even if improvement in the quality of education were a likely result of barring some *number* of children from the schools of the State, the State must support its selection of *this* group as the appropriate target for exclusion. In terms of education cost and need, however, undocumented children are "basically indistinguishable" from legally resident alien children.

Finally, appellants suggest that undocumented children are appropriately singled out because their unlawful presence within the United States renders them less likely than other children to remain within the boundaries of the State, and to put their education to productive social or political use within the State. Even assuming that such an interest is legitimate, it is an interest that is most difficult to quantify. The State has no assurance that any child, citizen or not, will employ the education provided by the State within the confines of the State's borders. In any event, the record is clear that many of the undocumented children disabled by this classification will remain in this country indefinitely, and that some will become lawful residents or citizens of the United States. It is difficult to understand precisely what the State hopes to achieve by promoting the creation and perpetuation of a subclass of illiterates within our boundaries, surely adding to the problems and costs of unemployment, welfare, and crime. It is thus clear that whatever savings might be achieved by denying these children an education, they are wholly insubstantial in light of the costs involved to these children, the State, and the Nation.

If the State is to deny a discrete group of innocent children the free public education that it offers to other children residing within its borders, that denial must be justified by a showing that it furthers some substantial state interest. No such showing was made here. Accordingly, the judgment of the Court of Appeals in each of these cases is

Affirmed.

[The concurring opinions of Justices Marshall, Blackmun, and Powell each have been omitted.]

Chief Justice Burger, with whom Justice White, Justice Rehnquist, and Justice O'Connor join, dissenting.

Were it our business to set the Nation's social policy, I would agree without hesitation that it is senseless for an enlightened society to deprive any children—including illegal aliens—of an elementary education. I fully agree that it would be folly—and wrong—to tolerate creation of a segment of society made up of illiterate persons, many having a limited or no command of our language. However, the Constitution does not constitute us as "Platonic Guardians" nor does it vest in this Court the authority to strike down laws because they do not meet our standards of desirable social policy, "wisdom," or "common sense." We trespass on the assigned function of the political branches under our structure of limited and separated powers when we assume a policymaking role as the Court does today.

The Court makes no attempt to disguise that it is acting to make up for Congress' lack of "effective leadership" in dealing with the serious national problems caused by the influx of uncountable millions of illegal aliens across our borders. The failure of enforcement of the immigration laws over more than a decade and the inherent difficulty and expense of sealing our vast borders have combined to create a grave socioeconomic dilemma. It is a dilemma that has not yet even been fully assessed, let alone addressed. However, it is not the function of the Judiciary to provide "effective leadership" simply because the political branches of government fail to do so.

The Court's holding today manifests the justly criticized judicial tendency to attempt speedy and wholesale formulation of "remedies" for the failures—or simply the laggard pace—of the political processes of our system of government. The Court employs, and in my view abuses, the Fourteenth Amendment in an effort to become an omnipotent and omniscient problem solver. That the motives for doing so are noble and compassionate does not alter the fact that the Court distorts our constitutional function to make amends for the defaults of others.

In a sense, the Court's opinion rests on such a unique confluence of theories and rationales that it will likely stand for little beyond the results in these particular cases. Yet the extent to which the Court departs from principled constitutional adjudication is nonetheless disturbing.

I have no quarrel with the conclusion that the Equal Protection Clause of the Fourteenth Amendment *applies* to aliens who, after their illegal entry into this country, are indeed physically "within the jurisdiction" of a state. However, as the Court concedes, this "only begins the inquiry." The Equal Protection Clause does not mandate identical treatment of different categories of persons.

The dispositive issue in these cases, simply put, is whether, for purposes of allocating its finite resources, a state has a legitimate reason to differentiate between persons who are lawfully within the state and those who are unlawfully there. The distinction the State of Texas has drawn—based not only upon its own legitimate interests but on classifications established by the Federal Government in its immigration laws and policies—is not unconstitutional.

* * *

Denying a free education to illegal alien children is not a choice I would make were I a legislator. Apart from compassionate considerations, the long-range costs of excluding any children from the public schools may well outweigh the costs of educating them. But that is not the issue; the fact that there are sound *policy* arguments against the Texas Legislature's choice does not render that choice an unconstitutional one.

The Constitution does not provide a cure for every social ill, nor does it vest judges with a mandate to try to remedy every social problem. Moreover, when this Court rushes in to remedy what it perceives to be the failings of the political processes, it deprives those processes of an opportunity to function. When the political institutions are not forced to exercise constitutionally allocated powers and responsibilities, those powers, like muscles not used, tend to atrophy. Today's cases, I regret to say, present yet another example of unwarranted judicial action which in the long run tends to contribute to the weakening of our political processes.

* * *

Age

In the 1970s, individuals began challenging mandatory retirement laws as age discrimination in violation of the Equal Protection Clause. In contrast to its analysis of classifications regarding illegitimacy and alienage, the Burger Court's position regarding the test for age classifications was very clear. In *Massachusetts Board of Retirement v. Murgia* (1976) the Court held that the rational basis test was the appropriate standard of review. Using that standard, in a per curiam opinion the justices upheld a Massachusetts law that required state police officers to retire at the age of fifty. The high court refused to place age classifications in the suspect category, maintaining that "old age does not define a 'discrete and insular' group . . . in need of 'extraordinary protection from the majoritarian political process' " (427 U.S. at 313). The opinion continued, "Even if the [Massachusetts] statute could be said to impose a penalty upon the class defined as the aged, it would not impose a distinction sufficiently akin to those classifications that we have found suspect to call for strict judicial scrutiny" (427 U.S. at 314).

In his lone dissent, Justice Marshall reiterated his dissatisfaction with the Court's two-tiered approach to equal protection analysis. In addition, he claimed that the mandatory retirement statute deprived individuals of their right "to engage in . . . the common occupations of life," which "has been repeatedly recognized by this Court as falling within the concept of liberty guaranteed by the Fourteenth Amendment" (427 U.S. at 322).

Three years later, applying minimal scrutiny, the Court sustained a federal law requiring members of the Foreign Service to retire at age sixty (*Vance v. Bradley*, 1979). Despite these adverse decisions, age discrimination is prohibited by federal statutory law, most notably by the Age Discrimination in Employment Act (ADEA).

Mental Retardation

In the mid-1980s, the Burger Court was forced to decide whether mental retardation is a classification that requires more than minimal scrutiny. In *Cleburne v. Cleburne Living Center* (1985), the Court heard a challenge to a city ordinance requiring a special use permit for the operation of a group home for the mentally retarded. The city of Cleburne, Texas, declared that in accordance with its zoning regulations, such permits were required for the construction of "[h]ospitals for the insane or feeble-minded, or alcoholic [sic] or drug addicts, or penal or correctional institutions" (473 U.S. at 436). The Cleburne Living Center was classified as a "hospital for the feeble-minded," and its application for the special use permit was denied by the city council after a public hearing. A federal district court upheld the council's decision, but the court of appeals reversed, holding that mental retardation is a "quasi-suspect" classification, requiring the intermediate scrutiny standard. Using this test, the appellate court invalidated the ordinance.

By a 6-3 vote, the Supreme Court reversed the appellate holding that intermediate scrutiny was the appropriate level of review. Writing for the majority, Justice White said, "The lesson of [*Massachusetts v.*] *Murgia* is that where individuals in the group affected by a law have distinguishing characteristics relevant to interests the state has the authority to implement, the courts have been very reluctant . . . to closely scrutinize legislative choices as to whether, how and to what extent those interests should be pursued. In such cases, the Equal Protection Clause requires only a rational means to serve a legitimate end" (473 U.S. at 441–42). Nonetheless, the Court ruled that the ordinance as applied here was invalid. The justices first noted that the zoning ordinance did not require special permits for other types of multiple dwellings, for example, boarding houses, fraternity or sorority houses, and nursing homes for the aged. While recognizing that mentally retarded individuals "may be different from those who would occupy other facilities that would be permitted in . . . [the same] zone without a special permit," Justice White argued, "the record does not reveal any rational basis for believing that the . . . home would pose any special threat to the city's legitimate interests" (473 U.S. at 448). Justices Marshall, Brennan, and Blackmun concurred in the judgment that the ordinance as applied here was invalid, but they agreed with the appellate court's conclusion that cases involving discrimination against the mentally retarded demand a higher level of scrutiny.

The Rehnquist Court Era

Unlike its predecessor, the Rehnquist Court decided only four equal protection cases involving classifications based on indigency, illegitimacy, age, and mental retardation. Therefore, no data analysis was conducted because there were not enough cases to make meaningful comparisons between the Rehnquist, Burger, and Warren Courts. We will focus our attention instead on the doctrinal analysis of the relevant cases. As Table 16.1 illustrates, the four cases were considered to be minor, and they all were decided on the basis of existing precedent.

Clark v. Jeter (1988) concerned Pennsylvania's six-year statute of limitations for undertaking paternity actions. Tiffany Clark, the illegitimate daughter of Cherlyn Clark, was born in 1973. Ten years later, Tiffany's mother filed a child support complaint in common pleas court naming Gene Jeter as the child's father. Following court ordered blood tests showing a high probability that Jeter was Tiffany's father, he asked that the complaint be dismissed because it was filed after the statute of limitations had run out. Cherlyn Clark contended that the six-year statute of limitations violated the Equal Protection Clause. The court's decision against Clark

TABLE 16.1: A Framework for the Doctrinal Analysis of the Rehnquist Court's Equal Protection Cases in Other Areas, 1986-94 Terms

		Treatment of Precedent					
Major or Minor Importance	**Majority or Plurality Opinion**	Creation of New Liberal Precedent	Liberal Modification of Existing Precedent	Liberal Interpretation of Existing Precedent	Conservative Interpretation of Existing Precedent	Conservative Modification of Existing Precedent	Creation of New Conservative Precedent
Major	Majority						
	Plurality						
Minor	Majority			Clark v. Jeter (1988)	Kadrmas v. Dickinson Public Schools (1988) Gregory v. Ashcroft (1991) Heller v. Doe (1993)		
	Plurality						

was affirmed by the Superior Court of Pennsylvania, and her petition for appeal was denied by the Pennsylvania Supreme Court.

By a unanimous vote, the U.S. Supreme Court invalidated the Pennsylvania statute. Writing for the Court, Justice O'Connor reiterated that intermediate scrutiny was the appropriate standard of review for classifications based on illegitimacy. To survive intermediate scrutiny, a statute must be substantially related to an important government objective. The Pennsylvania six-year statute of limitations failed this test, however, because it was "not substantially related to Pennsylvania's interest in avoiding the litigation of stale or fraudulent claims. In a number of circumstances, Pennsylvania permit[ted] the issue of paternity to be litigated more than six years after the birth of an illegitimate child" (486 U.S. at 464).

That same year, the Court decided a case regarding the equality claims of poor people. In *Kadrmas v. Dickinson Public Schools* (1988), by a 5-4 vote the majority upheld as reasonable a North Dakota statute permitting school districts to charge a user fee for school bus transportation. No violation of the Equal Protection Clause was found despite the fact that poor children whose families could not afford the fee were precluded from using the bus.

Three years later, in *Gregory v. Ashcroft* (1991), the Rehnquist Court was faced with a mandatory retirement law. A group of state judges alleged that a mandatory retirement provision in the Missouri Constitution violated both the ADEA and the Equal Protection Clause. By a 7-2 vote, the high court rejected these claims. In her majority opinion, Justice O'Connor first addressed the ADEA claim, ruling that state judges were excluded from the act's coverage. With respect to the equal protection claim, she emphasized that the provision would be subject only to minimal scrutiny. "This Court has said repeatedly that age is not a suspect classification under the Equal Protection Clause. Nor do petitioners claim that they have a fundamental interest in serving as judges. The State need therefore assert only a rational basis for its age classification" (501 U.S. at 470). The rationale set forth by the state was an interest in maintaining a judiciary that was competent to carry out its functions. Because voluntary retirement, impeachment, and the election process were inadequate for meeting this goal, the state turned to mandatory retirement. The majority accepted these explanations as sufficient to sustain the provision. "The people of Missouri rationally could conclude that the threat of deterioration at age 70 is sufficiently great, and the alternatives for removal sufficiently inadequate, that they will require all judges to step aside at age 70. This classification does not violate the Equal Protection Clause" (501 U.S. at 473).

GREGORY V. ASHCROFT

501 U.S. 452, 111 S.Ct. 2395, 115 L. Ed. 2d 410 (1991)

■ The Missouri Constitution contains a provision that requires all state judges except municipal judges to retire at the age of seventy. Ellis Gregory, an associate circuit judge, along with three other state judges, filed suit against the governor, claiming that this mandatory retirement provision violated both the federal Age Discrimination in Employment Act (ADEA) and the Equal Protection Clause. A federal district court dismissed the suit, ruling that the judges were excluded from ADEA coverage. Also, using the rational basis test, the district court found no equal protection violation. After the court of appeals affirmed the suit's dismissal, Gregory petitioned the U.S. Supreme Court for review.

This case is important because the Court reaffirmed that age classifications are not subject to strict scrutiny. As you read the case, consider these questions: 1) Is there any rationale for using intermediate scrutiny rather than the rational basis test for examining age classifications? 2) Would the Court have decided differently had the mandatory retirement age been set at sixty-five rather than at seventy?

VOTE:

7 justices found no violation of the ADEA or the Equal Protection Clause (O'Connor, Rehnquist, Scalia, Kennedy, Souter, White, and Stevens).

2 justices voted to strike the mandatory retirement provision as violative of the ADEA (Blackmun and Marshall).

Justice O'Connor delivered the opinion of the Court.

[O'Connor first addressed the ADEA claim, ruling that state judges were excluded from its coverage. "In light of the ADEA's clear exclusion of most important public officials, it is at least ambiguous whether Congress intended that appointed judges nonetheless be included. In the face of such ambiguity, we will not attribute to Congress an intent to intrude on state governmental functions. . . ."]

* * *

Petitioners argue that, even if they are not covered by the ADEA, the Missouri Constitution's mandatory retirement provision for judges violates the Equal Protection Clause of the Fourteenth Amendment to the United States Constitution. Petitioners contend that there is no rational basis for the decision of the people of Missouri to preclude those age 70 and over from serving as their judges. They claim that the mandatory retirement provision makes two irrational distinctions: between judges who have reached age 70 and younger judges, and between judges 70 and over and other state employees of the same age who are not subject to mandatory retirement.

Petitioners are correct to assert their challenge at the level of rational basis. This Court has said repeatedly that age is not a suspect classification under the Equal Protection Clause. Nor do petitioners claim that they have a fundamental interest in serving as judges. The State need therefore assert only a rational basis for its age classification. In cases where a classification burdens neither a suspect group nor a fundamental interest, "courts are quite reluctant to overturn governmental action on the ground that it denies equal protection of the laws." In this case, we are dealing not merely with government action, but with a state constitutional provision approved by the people of Missouri as a whole. This constitutional provision reflects both the considered judgment of the state legislature that proposed it and that of the citizens of Missouri who voted for it. "[W]e will not overturn such a [law] unless the varying treatment of different groups or persons is so unrelated to the achievement of any combination of legitimate purposes that we can only conclude that the [people's] actions were irrational."

* * *

The people of Missouri have a legitimate, indeed compelling, interest in maintaining a judiciary fully capable of performing the demanding tasks that judges must perform. It is an unfortunate fact of life that physical and mental capacity sometimes diminish with age. The people may therefore wish to replace some older judges. Voluntary retirement will not always be sufficient. Nor may impeachment—with its public humiliation and elaborate procedural machinery—serve acceptably the goal of a fully functioning judiciary.

The election process may also be inadequate. Whereas the electorate would be expected to discover if their governor or state legislator were not performing adequately and vote the official out of office, the same may not be true of judges. Most voters never observe state judges in action, nor read judicial opinions. State judges also serve longer terms of office than other public officials, making them—deliberately—less dependent on the will of the people. * * * Most of these judges do not run in ordinary elections. The people of Missouri rationally could conclude that retention elections—in which state judges run unopposed at relatively long intervals—do not serve as an adequate check on judges whose performance is deficient. Mandatory retirement is a reasonable response to this dilemma.

This is also a rational explanation for the fact that state judges are subject to a mandatory retirement provision, while other state officials—whose performance is subject to greater public scrutiny, and who are subject to more standard elections—are not. Judges' general lack of accountability explains also the distinction between judges and other state employees, in whom a deterioration in performance is more readily discernible and who are more easily removed.

The Missouri mandatory retirement provision, like all legal classifications, is founded on a generalization. It is far from true that all judges suffer significant deterioration in performance at age 70. It is probably not true that most do. It may not be true at all. But a State " 'does not violate the Equal Protection Clause merely because the classifications made by its laws are imperfect.' " "In an equal protection case of this type . . . those challenging the . . . judgment [of the people] must convince the court that the . . . facts on which the classification is apparently based could not reasonably be conceived to be true by the . . . decisionmaker." The people of Missouri rationally could conclude that the threat of deterioration at age 70 is sufficiently great, and the alternatives for removal sufficiently inadequate, that they will require all judges to step aside at age 70. This classification does not violate the Equal Protection Clause.

* * *

Affirmed.

[*The opinion of Justice White, joined by Justice Stevens, concurring in part, dissenting in part, and concurring in the judgment, is omitted.*]

Justice Blackmun, with whom Justice Marshall joins, dissenting.

* * *

The Missouri constitutional provision mandating the retirement of a judge who reaches the age of 70 violates the ADEA and is, therefore, invalid. Congress enacted the ADEA with the express purpose "to promote employment of older persons based on their ability rather than age; to prohibit arbitrary age discrimination in employment; to help employers and workers find ways of meeting problems arising from the impact of age on employment." Congress provided for only limited exclusions from the coverage of the ADEA, and exhorted courts applying this law to construe such exclusions narrowly. The statute's structure and legislative history reveal that Congress did not intend an appointed state judge to be beyond the scope of the ADEA's protective reach. Further, the EEOC, which is charged with the enforcement of the ADEA, has determined that an appointed state judge is covered by the ADEA. This Court's precedent dictates that we defer to the EEOC's permissible interpretation of the ADEA.

I dissent.

Heller v. Doe (1993) required the high court to examine the constitutionality of different standards for committing mentally retarded and mentally ill individuals. Under Kentucky law, "clear and convincing evidence" was required to commit the mentally retarded, while a more stringent test, proof "beyond a reasonable doubt," was necessary to commit mentally ill individuals. The case was brought on behalf of a group of mentally retarded individuals who had been committed involuntarily.

The Supreme Court, by a 5-4 vote, upheld the law. Writing for a five-person majority, Justice Kennedy first declared the rational basis test to be the appropriate standard of review. He concluded that the law satisfied this standard and therefore did not violate the Equal Protection Clause. According to Kennedy, the distinction in tests for commitment was reasonable because of differences in both diagnosis of and treatment for the mentally ill and the mentally retarded. He said that mental retardation was generally easier to diagnose than mental illness, and more importantly, "[t]he prevailing methods of treatment for the mentally retarded, as a general rule, are much less invasive than are those given the mentally ill" (113 S.Ct. at 2645). A separate provision of the law regarding participation by family members and legal guardians in commitment proceedings was also challenged. Such persons were permitted to participate in proceedings involving the mentally retarded but not the mentally ill. By a 6-3 vote, the Court found a rational basis for this distinction also. Kennedy wrote, "[M]ental retardation has its onset during a person's developmental period. * * * Based on these facts, Kentucky may have concluded that close relatives and guardians, both of whom likely have intimate knowledge of a mentally retarded person's abilities and experiences, have valuable insights which should be considered during the involuntary commitment process. Mental illness, by contrast, may arise or manifest itself with suddenness only after minority, when the afflicted person's immediate family members have no knowledge of the medical condition and have long ceased to provide care and support" (113 S.Ct. at 2647).

Conclusion

The paucity of Rehnquist Court decisions in equal protection cases concerning classifications based on indigency, alienage, illegitimacy, age, and mental retardation makes it difficult to predict future trends in decisions affecting these and related issues. Based on the few cases it has decided and on its general equal protection jurisprudence, we may speculate that the Rehnquist Court will continue to take a cautious approach to those cases that do not involve claims of racial or gender discrimination.

REFERENCES

Ginger, Ann Fagan. *The Law, the Supreme Court, and the People's Rights*. Woodbury, N.Y.: Barron's Educational Series, 1973.

Irons, Peter. *The Courage of Their Convictions*. New York: The Free Press, 1988.

Irons, Peter, and Stephanie Guitton. *May It Please The Court*. New York: The New Press, 1993.

CHAPTER

17 PRIVACY AND ABORTION

CASE STUDY

BOWERS V. HARDWICK (1986)

In the early hours of August 3, 1982, Atlanta police officer K. R. Torick went to the home of Michael Hardwick to serve him with an arrest warrant. The warrant, which apparently had expired, concerned Hardwick's failure to appear in court to answer charges of drinking in public. The officer had ticketed him a few weeks earlier for having an open beer bottle in public. This occurred outside a gay bar where Hardwick worked as a bartender. Officer Torick said that he was let in the house by Hardwick's roommate, who, Torick claimed, told him that he was not sure if Hardwick was at home but that it was all right for the officer to go in and look for him. Torick said that as he walked down the hallway, he saw a bedroom door partially open. In it, he observed Hardwick and another man having oral sex. Torick arrested the two men for violating a Georgia statute that criminalized acts of sodomy, even those between consenting adults. Michael Hardwick has a different story of the events leading up to his arrest, including the claim that Torick initially approached him at the bar because he knew he was gay and simply wanted to hassle him. [See Peter Irons (1988), *The Courage of Their Convictions,* for Hardwick's complete account of the case.] Whatever the circumstances of his arrest, Hardwick became embroiled in a controversy that gained national prominence.

After his arrest, the Georgia chapter of the American Civil Liberties Union (ACLU) approached Hardwick about using his case to challenge the state sodomy law. Two ACLU attorneys, John Sweet and Louis Levenson, told him about all of the risks involved: the possibility of a twenty-year prison term, the publicity that certainly would follow, and the possibility of violence against him. Having worked in gay bars, Hardwick was well aware of the harassment and intimidation of Atlanta's gay community. He thought about the proposal for a few days and agreed to have Sweet and Levenson go ahead with the legal challenge.

His attorneys assumed that he would be convicted for violating the sodomy law and that they then could begin the appeals process. After the initial hearing, however, District Attorney Lewis Slaton refused to send the case to the grand jury for indictment. Irons (1988) speculates that Slaton did not prosecute Hardwick because "he did not want to arouse the Atlanta gay community and its enemies" and because he "knew that Officer Torick's expired warrant, his earlier arrest of Michael, and disputes over how he gained entrance to Michael's house might embarrass the police and prosecutors" (p. 383). This explanation seems plausible, given that the original warrant never was served and that Hardwick had paid the fine for drinking in public three weeks before he was arrested for violating the sodomy law.

After Slaton declined to prosecute Hardwick, the ACLU filed a suit in federal district court, charging that the Georgia sodomy statute violated the constitutional right of privacy. At this level, Hardwick was represented by a different ACLU attorney, Kathleen Wilde. Named in the complaint were Michael Bowers, the state attorney general; Lewis Slaton, the district attorney; and George Napier, Atlanta police commissioner. On April 18, 1983, Judge Robert Hall ruled against Hardwick, citing a 1975 precedent from a federal appeals court. In *Doe v. Commonwealth's Attorney*, a federal panel had upheld a Virginia sodomy statute nearly identical to Georgia's. Wilde appealed Hall's decision to a federal appellate court, and, more than two years later, Hardwick obtained a favorable ruling. A three-judge panel struck down the Georgia law as a violation of the right of privacy, arguing that the Constitution protected "consensual sexual behavior among adults" (Irons 1988, p. 386). Georgia appealed this ruling to the Supreme Court.

The high court granted certiorari, and oral arguments were scheduled for March 31, 1986. Amicus briefs in support of Hardwick's position were filed by two states, New York and California, as well as by several organizations, including the American Psychological Association (joined by the American Public Health Association), the American Jewish Congress, the National Organization for Women, and the Presbyterian Church (U.S.A.). The Catholic League for Religious and Civil Rights and the Rutherford Institute filed amicus briefs urging the Court to uphold the sodomy law. Two general amicus briefs were filed by the Lesbian Rights Project and the National Gay Rights Advocates.

At oral argument, the state was represented by Michael Hobbs, its deputy attorney general, while Laurence Tribe, a Harvard law professor and constitutional law expert, argued on behalf of Hardwick. Hobbs presented his arguments first. He began by framing the issue as "whether or not there is a fundamental right under the Constitution of the United States to engage in consensual private homosexual sodomy" (Irons and Guitton 1993, p. 363). Although the statute was written in universal terms, upon questioning by the justices about whether married couples could be prosecuted for violations, he said that those prosecutions would be unconstitutional. Hobbs reasoned that the right of marital privacy recognized in *Griswold* would extend to sodomy between married heterosexuals. In his view, *Griswold* and other privacy precedents were not relevant here because they were concerned only with relationships involving marriage, the family, procreation, abortion, childrearing, and child education. He emphasized that the prohibition against homosexual sodomy involved an issue of morality and argued that the Court should defer to the wishes of the people, represented by their legislators, in such matters. Moreover, Hobbs argued that if the Court invalidated laws against consensual, private homosexual sodomy, the Court would ". . . soon be confronted with questions concerning the legitimacy of statutes which prohibit polygamy; homosexual, same-sex marriage; consensual incest; prostitution; fornication; adultery; and possibly even personal possession in private of illegal drugs" (p. 365).

In his arguments, Tribe tried to reframe the issues. He said that the case was not about laws against polygamy, bigamy, or incest but simply was "about the limits of governmental power" (Irons and Guitton 1993, p. 365). Tribe suggested that the Court had to determine whether the state can dictate how adults should behave in their bedrooms in their intimate, personal associations with each other. In response to questioning from Justice Powell about whether the state might prohibit sodomy in the back of an automobile, in a public toilet, or in a hotel room overnight, Tribe conceded that those places are not "entitled to the same degree of protection" but said he could not draw a precise line for acceptable and unacceptable regulations. Nonetheless Tribe maintained, ". . . there is a fundamental right to restrict government's intimate regulation of the privacies of association like in the home" (p. 368).

Three months later, on June 30, 1986, the Court issued its ruling in *Bowers v. Hardwick* (case excerpt on p. 829). By a 5-4 vote, the justices upheld the Georgia sodomy law against this challenge. The majority opinion, written by Justice White, contained reasoning that appeared to echo the arguments made by Hobbs. First, in declining to rule on the Georgia law as applied to heterosexual sodomy, White wrote, "The issue presented is whether the Federal Constitution confers a fundamental right upon homosexuals to engage in sodomy . . ." (478 U.S. at 190). Second, he stated that *Griswold, Roe,* and other privacy precedents were not applicable to this case because "[n]o connection between family, marriage, or procreation on the one hand and homosexual activity on the other has been demonstrated . . . by respondent" (478 U.S. at 191). Next, he pointed to the number of state laws that criminalized sodomy to support his conclusion that consensual homosexual sodomy was not a fundamental right. Finally, in rejecting Tribe's "privacy of the home" argument, White accepted Hobbs's "Pandora's box" claim.

The dissenters—Justices Blackmun, Brennan, Marshall, and Stevens—criticized the majority for misconstruing the issue. Blackmun wrote, "This case is . . . [not] about 'a fundamental right to engage in homosexual sodomy' . . . . Rather, this case is about 'the most comprehensive of rights and the right most valued by civilized men,' namely 'the right to be let alone' " (478 U.S. at 199).

Just how close the decision was in this case is revealed by the concurring opinion of Justice Powell. Powell indicated that, had Hardwick been convicted and imprisoned for his conduct, his decision might have been different. Because the statute provided for a prison sentence of up to twenty years, an Eighth Amendment cruel and unusual punishment issue would have been raised. Hardwick was not tried and convicted, however, and he did not raise this issue, so Powell saw no reason to address it. Powell initially voted in conference to support Hardwick's challenge based on the Eighth Amendment issue, but later switched sides and provided the decisive vote for White's majority opinion. After he retired from the Court, Powell admitted that he had made a mistake in supporting the majority in Hardwick's case (Jeffries 1994, p. 530). By that time, it was, of course, too late to shift his decisive vote to support the privacy right and thus the precedent supporting Georgia's statute remained intact.

Although Michael Hardwick lost his case, he expressed no regrets about becoming involved in this controversial issue. This is particularly remarkable in light of the emotional and physical harassment he experienced between his initial arrest in 1982 and the Supreme Court's decision in 1986. Moreover, after the decision he reluctantly agreed to go public and began appearing on talk shows, in newspaper interviews, and at public rallies. While Hardwick initially was fearful of possible negative repercussions, public understanding and support increased his confidence in speaking out. Although the 1986 decision has not been reexamined by the high court in any subsequent cases, Hardwick continued to maintain his right to privacy. "There's no way the Supreme Court can say that I can't have sex with a consenting adult in the privacy of my own bedroom" (Irons 1988, p. 403).

Historical Origins and Contemporary Conflicts

Although the concept of a right to privacy may appear to be straightforward, it actually has complex implications. Many people agree that government should not interfere with certain aspects of their lives, but, as *Bowers v. Hardwick* (1986) illustrates, there is widespread disagreement over the extent of this freedom. More importantly, there are continuing debates about whether this right is constitutionally protected, because the right of privacy is not enumerated in the Bill of Rights or other constitutional provisions. As we noted in the case study in Chapter 1, Robert Bork, a former Supreme Court nominee, was a leading opponent of the constitutional right of privacy. In fact, Bork's position on this controversial issue was a major factor in the defeat of his nomination to the Court.

The constitutional provision most related to the right of privacy is the Fourth Amendment protection against unreasonable searches and seizures. It reads, "The right of the people to be secure in their persons, houses, papers, and effects, against unreasonable searches and seizures, shall not be violated." This provision is concerned primarily with the area of criminal law. A general right of privacy, however, was stressed by Justice Louis Brandeis in his dissent in an important government surveillance case from 1928. In *Olmstead v. U.S,* the Court upheld a defendant's conviction where the government had obtained incriminating evidence through wiretapping. In support of overturning the conviction, Brandeis wrote, "[T]he makers of our Constitution . . . conferred as against the government the right to be let alone—the most comprehensive of rights and the right most valued by civilized men. To protect that right, every unjustifiable intrusion by the government upon the *privacy* [emphasis added] of the individual, whatever the means employed, must be deemed a violation of the Fourth Amendment" (277 U.S. at 478).

Although privacy concerns were implicated in cases decided on other grounds, no independent right of privacy was established until *Griswold v. Connecticut* (1965). In *Griswold,* the Court struck down a state law that made the sale and possession of contraceptive devices a crime. The Court held that this law violated the right of privacy, which could be inferred from the various provisions of the Bill of Rights and the spirit of those amendments. The decision in *Griswold* applied to married people only, but seven years later the Court extended this protection to single individuals in *Eisenstadt v. Baird* (1972).

The greatest controversy over the Court's treatment of privacy arose in its landmark decision in *Roe v. Wade* (1973), when the Burger Court ruled that the right of privacy encompassed a woman's decision to have an abortion. Most of the Court's privacy decisions continue to involve reproductive freedom, specifically abortion, but the justices have heard a few cases concerning other issues. For example, the Court issued rulings regarding state restrictions on the private sexual practices of consenting adults (*Bowers v. Hardwick,* 1986) and the right of patients to refuse medical treatment when they have no hope of recovery (*Cruzan v. Missouri Department of Public Health,* 1990).

Decision Making in Privacy Cases

As noted above, most of the Court's privacy decisions have involved government restrictions on abortion. The first test or doctrine used to examine regulations on abortion was the compelling state interest test. As you will recall from previous chapters, this test has been used in several areas, including, for example, free exercise and equal protection. The compelling interest test places a significant burden on the government to prove that its interest(s) outweigh an individual's constitutional rights. In *Roe v. Wade* (1973), Justice Blackmun extended this test to abortion regulations, ruling that such regulations would be upheld only if there were a "compelling state interest." This "compelling state interest" was tied to the trimesters of pregnancy, the health of the woman, and the viability of the fetus. Viability is the point when the fetus is able to live outside of the mother. Thus, in the first trimester, because the abortion procedure is as safe, if not safer, for women than childbirth and because the fetus is not viable, there is no compelling state interest in regulating abortion. Therefore, there is no basis for impeding the woman's right to privacy by permitting government regulations. In the second trimester, abortions are more dangerous to the woman, so the state has a compelling interest in protecting maternal health. Thus, regulations narrowly tailored to achieve this purpose may be upheld. In the third trimester, viability comes into play and dangers to the woman increase, so the state has a compelling interest in protecting both maternal health and fetal life. Consequently, during the third trimester, the state may regulate and even prohibit abortions, except when an abortion is necessary to save a woman's life.

The trimester framework was abandoned and the compelling state interest test for abortion regulations was modified significantly in 1992. This modification was first posited by Justice O'Connor in 1983, but it did not gain acceptance until *Planned Parenthood v. Casey* (1992). According to *Casey,* an abortion regulation will be examined first to determine if it poses an "undue burden" on a pregnant woman's right to abortion. A regulation presents an undue burden "if its purpose or effect is to place a substantial obstacle in the path of a woman seeking an abortion before the fetus attains viability" (505 U.S. at 878). If the regulation poses an undue burden, the state must prove a compelling interest for it to be upheld. If the regulation is not "unduly burdensome," however, it will be upheld if it has a rational basis.

With respect to the few nonabortion-related privacy cases, the Court utilizes the rational basis test unless the government policy conflicts with a fundamental right. Under the rational basis test, the justices determine whether the policy is arbitrary or capricious and the burden is on the individual to prove that it is irrational. Because it involves deference to the government's policy decision, the rational basis approach frequently results in the regulation being upheld. In addition to *Bowers v. Hardwick* (1986), for example, the Court used the rational basis test to uphold regulations on the hairstyle of police officers in *Kelley v. Johnson* (1976).

Pre-Warren Court Period

Five years before the *Olmstead* case discussed above, the Supreme Court made a decision that later would be used as precedent in the *Griswold* case to establish an independent right of privacy. Although the case did not specifically refer to privacy, the Court discussed the importance of preventing the government from acting in ways that obstruct people's rights to conduct their lives as they see fit. *Meyer v. Nebraska* (1923) involved a state law that prohibited the teaching of modern languages other than English to children prior to ninth grade. By a 7-2 vote, the Court struck down this statute holding that it violated the liberty guaranteed by the Fourteenth Amendment. Justice McReynolds, writing for the majority, said that this liberty "denotes not merely freedom from bodily restraint but also the right of the individual to contract, to engage in any of the common occupations of life, to acquire useful knowledge, to marry, establish a home and bring up children, to worship God according to the dictates of his own conscience, and generally to enjoy those privileges long recognized at common law as essential to the orderly pursuit of happiness by free men" (262 U.S. at 399). Some forty-two years later, this decision was cited by the majority in *Griswold* as an important precedent for the right of privacy.

Meyer v. Nebraska

262 U.S. 390, 43 S.Ct. 625, 67 L.Ed.1042 (1923)

In 1919, Nebraska passed a law that prohibited the teaching of modern languages other than English to children who had not yet passed the eighth grade. Exempted from the statute were classical languages such as Latin, Greek, and Hebrew. Meyer was convicted under this statute of using the German language to teach a ten-year-old boy the subject of reading. The Nebraska Supreme Court affirmed the conviction, and Meyer appealed to the U.S. Supreme Court.

This case is important because forty years later it was used as a precedent to establish an independent constitutional right of privacy. As you read the case, consider these questions: 1) Would the outcome have been different if this case had been decided during World War I or II? 2) Could the case have been argued and decided on First Amendment freedom of speech grounds, rather than on the basis of the Fourteenth Amendment? 3) If so, what might the result have been?

Vote:

7 justices voted to strike the law (McReynolds, Taft, McKenna, Van Devanter, Brandeis, Butler, Sanford).

2 justices found the law constitutional (Holmes and Sutherland).

Justice McReynolds delivered the opinion of the Court.

* * *

The problem for our determination is whether the statute as construed and applied unreasonably in-

fringes the liberty guaranteed to the plaintiff in error by the Fourteenth Amendment:

> No state . . . shall deprive any person of life, liberty or property without due process of law.

While this court has not attempted to define with exactness the liberty thus guaranteed, the term has received much consideration and some of the included things have been definitely stated. Without doubt, it denotes not merely freedom from bodily restraint but also the right of the individual to contract, to engage in any of the common occupations of life, to acquire useful knowledge, to marry, establish a home and bring up children, to worship God according to the dictates of his own conscience, and generally to enjoy those privileges long recognized at common law as essential to the orderly pursuit of happiness by free men. The established doctrine is that this liberty may not be interfered with, under the guise of protecting the public interest, by legislative action which is arbitrary or without reasonable relation to some purpose within the competency of the state to effect. Determination by the Legislature of what constitutes proper exercise of police power is not final or conclusive but is subject to supervision by the courts.

The American people have always regarded education and acquisition of knowledge as matters of supreme importance which should be diligently promoted. The Ordinance of 1787 declares: "Religion, morality and knowledge being necessary to good government and the happiness of mankind, schools and the means of education shall forever be encouraged."

Corresponding to the right of control, it is the natural duty of the parent to give his children education suitable to their station in life; and nearly all the states, including Nebraska, enforce this obligation by compulsory laws.

Practically, education of the young is only possible in schools conducted by especially qualified persons who devote themselves thereto. The calling always has been regarded as useful and honorable, essential, indeed, to the public welfare. Mere knowledge of the German language cannot reasonably be regarded as harmful. Heretofore it has been commonly looked upon as helpful and desirable. Plaintiff in error taught this language in school as part of his occupation. His right thus to teach and the right of parents to engage him so to instruct their children, we think, are within the liberty of the amendment.

* * *

It is said the purpose of the legislation was to promote civic development by inhibiting training and education of the immature in foreign tongues and ideals before they could learn English and acquire American ideals, and "that the English language should be and become the mother tongue of all children reared in this state." It is also affirmed that the foreign born population is very large, that certain communities commonly use foreign words, follow foreign leaders, move in a foreign atmosphere, and that the children are thereby hindered from becoming citizens of the most useful type and the public safety is imperiled.

That the state may do much, go very far, indeed, in order to improve the quality of its citizens, physically, mentally and morally, is clear; but the individual has certain fundamental rights which must be respected. The protection of the Constitution extends to all, to those who speak other languages as well as to those born with English on the tongue. Perhaps it would be highly advantageous if all had ready understanding of our ordinary speech, but this cannot be coerced by methods which conflict with the Constitution—a desirable end cannot be promoted by prohibited means.

* * *

The desire of the Legislature to foster a homogeneous people with American ideals prepared readily to understand current discussions of civic matters is easy to appreciate. Unfortunate experiences during the late war and aversion toward every character of truculent adversaries were certainly enough to quicken that aspiration. But the means adopted, we think, exceed the limitations upon the power of the state and conflict with rights assured to plaintiff in error. The interference is plain enough and no adequate reason therefor in time of peace and domestic tranquility has been shown.

The power of the state to compel attendance at some school and to make reasonable regulations for all schools, including a requirement that they shall give instructions in English, is not questioned. Nor has challenge been made of the state's power to prescribe a curriculum for institutions which it supports. Those matters are not within the present controversy. Our concern is with the prohibition approved by the Supreme Court. Adams v. Tanner [1917], pointed out that mere abuse incident to an occupation ordinarily useful is not enough to justify its abolition, although regulation may be entirely proper. No emergency has arisen which renders knowledge by a child of some language other than English so clearly harmful as to justify its inhibition with the consequent infringement of rights long freely enjoyed. We are constrained to conclude that the statute as applied is arbitrary and without reasonable relation to any end within the competency of the state.

As the statute undertakes to interfere only with teaching which involves a modern language, leaving complete freedom as to other matters, there seems no adequate foundation for the suggestion that the purpose was to protect the child's health by limiting his mental activities. It is well known that proficiency in a foreign language seldom comes to one not instructed at an early age, and experience shows that this is not injurious to the health, morals or understanding of the ordinary child.

The Judgment of the court below must be reversed and the cause remanded for further proceedings not inconsistent with this opinion.

Reversed.

Justice Holmes and Justice Sutherland dissented.

Two years after *Meyer*, in *Pierce v. Society of Sisters* (1925) the Court struck down an Oregon law that prohibited parents from sending their children to private schools. "The fundamental theory of liberty . . . excludes any general power of the State to standardize its children by forcing them to accept instruction from public teachers only" (268 U.S. at 535). *Pierce* was also cited in *Griswold* as an important precedent.

The *Griswold* case was preceded by two other cases involving matters of procreation, although they were not decided on privacy grounds. First, in *Buck v. Bell* (1927) the Court ruled that laws providing for compulsory sterilization of mentally retarded persons did not violate the Fourteenth Amendment. Justice Holmes wrote, "It is better for all the world, if instead of waiting to execute degenerate offspring for crime, or to let them starve for their imbecility, society can prevent those who are manifestly unfit from continuing their kind" (274 U.S. at 207). Referring specifically to Carrie Buck, her mother, and her daughter, Holmes declared, "[t]hree generations of imbeciles are enough" (274 U.S. at 207). Fifteen years later, however, in *Skinner v. Oklahoma* (1942) the Court struck down a law authorizing the sterilization of the "feeble-minded" and habitual criminals. In doing so, the justices held that the right to procreation was a fundamental right protected by the Equal Protection Clause. This case was also cited in *Griswold* as a significant precedent for the right of privacy.

The Warren Court Era

It probably is not surprising that the Warren Court, which was responsible for expanding civil liberties and civil rights in a variety of issues, would interpret the Constitution to provide a general right of privacy. The Court actually had the opportunity to rule on the Connecticut law struck down in *Griswold* (1965) in a 1961 case, but the justices voted 5-4 at that time to dismiss the case on technical grounds (*Poe v. Ullman*). The law being challenged in *Griswold* criminalized the sale, possession, or use of contraceptive devices, and it prohibited anyone from counseling others in the use of such devices. Those who violated the law would be subject to fines and/or imprisonment.

By a 7-2 vote, the Court reversed the lower courts and held the Connecticut law unconstitutional. In an opinion joined by four of his colleagues, Justice Douglas said that the law forbidding the use of contraceptives was an inappropriate government invasion of the right of marital privacy. Although a general right of privacy was not expressly stated in the Constitution or the Bill of Rights, Douglas asserted that various provisions of the Bill of Rights created this right. "[S]pecific guarantees in the Bill of Rights have penumbras, formed by emanations from those guarantees that help give them life and substance. Various guarantees create zones of privacy" (381 U.S. at 484). He referred to the First Amendment right of association, the Third Amendment protection against quartering soldiers, the Fourth Amendment protection against unreasonable search and seizure, and the Fifth Amendment protection against self-incrimination. Douglas also emphasized the Ninth Amendment, which reads, "The enumeration in the Constitution, of certain rights, shall not be construed to deny or disparage others retained by the people." Having established this right of privacy, Douglas argued that the Connecticut law was an obvious violation of that right. "Would we allow the police to search the sacred precincts of marital bedrooms for telltale signs of the use of contraceptives? The very idea is repulsive to the notions of privacy surrounding the marriage relationship" (381 U.S. at 485–86).

In a concurring opinion for himself, Chief Justice Warren, and Justice Brennan, Justice Goldberg accepted Douglas's penumbra approach to the right of privacy, but he placed more emphasis on the Ninth Amendment as the source of this privacy right. Goldberg said that the language and history of the Ninth Amendment demonstrated that it was intended to protect basic and fundamental rights, even if they were not mentioned specifically in the first eight amendments to the Constitution. In separate opinions concurring in the judgment only, Justices Harlan and White argued that there is indeed a right of privacy, but they found its source in the liberty guaranteed by the Fourteenth Amendment.

Justices Black and Stewart dissented from the Court's ruling, arguing that although the Connecticut statute was offensive, it did not violate any fundamental right contained in the U.S. Constitution. Black wrote, "[I] get nowhere in this case by talk about a constitutional 'right of privacy' as an emanation from one or more constitutional provisions. I like my privacy as well as the next one, but I am nevertheless compelled to admit that government has a right to invade it unless prohibited by some specific constitutional provision" (381 U.S. at 509–10).

GRISWOLD V. CONNECTICUT

381 U.S. 479, 85 S.Ct. 1678, 14 L.Ed.2d 510 (1965)

■ In 1961, Estelle Griswold, executive director of Planned Parenthood in Connecticut, and James Buxton, medical director of the clinic, were arrested and convicted for violating a Connecticut contraceptive law. The 1879 statute made it a crime to sell, possess, or use contraceptive devices, and it also prohibited anyone from counseling others in the use of contraceptives. Griswold and Buxton had given information to a married couple about the appropriate birth control device to be used by the wife. They were fined $100 apiece, and the Connecticut appellate courts upheld their convictions. They appealed to the U.S. Supreme Court.

This case is important because it was the first to discover an independent right of privacy protected by the Constitution. As you read the case, consider the following questions: 1) Which argument regarding the source of this privacy right is more persuasive: Douglas's penumbra argument, the Ninth Amendment argument, or the liberty guarantee of the Fourteenth Amendment? 2) What is the appropriate way to discern whether a right is "basic" or "fundamental" if the Constitution does not explicitly mention it? 3) Is there any danger in deferring to the wishes of legislatures in such situations?

VOTE:

7 justices held that the law violated the right of privacy (Douglas, Clark, Goldberg, Warren, Brennan, Harlan, and White).

2 justices voted to uphold the law and found no constitutional right of privacy (Black and Stewart).

Justice Douglas delivered the opinion of the Court.

* * *

. . . [W]e are met with a wide range of questions that implicate the Due Process Clause of the Fourteenth Amendment. Overtones of some arguments suggest that *Lochner v. New York* should be our guide. But we decline that invitation. . . . We do not sit as a super-legislature to determine the wisdom, need, and propriety of laws that touch economic problems, business affairs, or social conditions. This law, however, operates directly on an intimate relation of husband and wife and their physician's role in one aspect of that relation.

The association of people is not mentioned in the Constitution nor in the Bill of Rights. The right to educate a child in a school of the parents' choice—whether public or parochial—is also not mentioned. Nor is the right to study any particular subject or any foreign language. Yet the First Amendment has been construed to include certain of those rights.

By *Pierce v. Society of Sisters* [1925], the right to educate one's children as one chooses is made applicable to the States by the force of the First and Fourteenth Amendments. By *Meyer v. Nebraska* [1923], the same dignity is given the right to study the German language in a private school. In other words, the State may not, consistently with the spirit of the First Amendment, contract the spectrum of available knowledge. The right of freedom of speech and press includes not only the right to utter or to print, but the right to distribute, the right to receive, the right to read, and freedom of inquiry, freedom of thought, and freedom to teach—indeed the freedom of the entire university community. Without those peripheral rights the specific rights would be less secure. And so we reaffirm the principle of the *Pierce* and the *Meyer* cases.

In *NAACP v. Alabama* [1958], we protected the "freedom to associate and privacy in one's associations," noting that freedom of association was a peripheral First Amendment right. Disclosure of membership lists of a constitutionally valid association, we held, was invalid "as entailing the likelihood of a substantial restraint upon the exercise by petitioner's members of their right to freedom of association." In other words, the First Amendment has a penumbra where privacy is protected from governmental intrusion. In like context, we have protected forms of "association" that are not political in the customary sense but pertain to the social, legal, and economic benefit of the members. * * *

* * *

The foregoing cases suggest that specific guarantees in the Bill of Rights have penumbras, formed by emanations from those guarantees that help give them life and substance. Various guarantees create zones of privacy. The right of association contained in the penumbra of the First Amendment is one, as we have seen. The Third Amendment in its prohibition against the quartering of soldiers "in any house" in time of peace without the consent of the owner is another facet of that privacy. The Fourth Amendment explicitly affirms the "right of the people to be secure in their persons, houses, papers, and effects, against unreasonable searches and seizures." The Fifth Amendment in its Self-Incrimination Clause enables the citizen to create a zone of privacy which government may not force him to surrender to his detriment. The Ninth Amendment provides: "The enumeration in the Constitution, of certain rights, shall not be construed to deny or disparage others retained by the people."

The Fourth and Fifth Amendments were described in *Boyd v. United States* [1886] as protection against all governmental invasions "of the sanctity of a man's home and the privacies of life." We recently referred in *Mapp v. Ohio* [1961] to the Fourth Amendment as creating a "right to privacy, no less important than any other right carefully and particularly reserved to the people."

We have had many controversies over these penumbral rights of "privacy and repose." * * * These cases bear witness that the right of privacy which presses for recognition here is a legitimate one.

The present case, then, concerns a relationship lying within the zone of privacy created by several fundamental constitutional guarantees. And it concerns a law which, in forbidding the *use* of contraceptives rather than regulating their manufacture or sale, seeks to achieve its goals by means having a maximum destructive impact upon that relationship. Such a law cannot stand in light of the familiar principle, so often applied by this Court, that a "governmental purpose to control or prevent activities constitutionally subject to state regulation may not be achieved by means which sweep unnecessarily broadly and thereby invade the area of protected freedoms." Would we allow the police to search the sacred precincts of marital bedrooms for telltale signs of the use of contraceptives? The very idea is repulsive to the notions of privacy surrounding the marriage relationship.

We deal with a right of privacy older than the Bill of Rights—older than our political parties, older than our school system. Marriage is a coming together for better or for worse, hopefully enduring, and intimate to the degree of being sacred. It is an association that promotes a way of life, not causes; a harmony in living, not political faiths; a bilateral loyalty, not commercial or social projects. Yet it is an association for as noble a purpose as any involved in our prior decisions.

Reversed.

Justice Goldberg, whom the Chief Justice and Justice Brennan join, concurred.

I agree with the Court that Connecticut's birth-control law unconstitutionally intrudes upon the right of marital privacy, and I join in its opinion and judgment. Although I have not accepted the view that "due process" as used in the Fourteenth Amendment incorporates all of the first eight Amendments, I do agree that the concept of liberty protects those personal rights that are fundamental, and is not confined to the specific terms of the Bill of Rights. My conclusion that the concept of liberty is not so restricted and that it embraces the right of marital privacy though that right is not mentioned explicitly in the Constitution is supported both by numerous decisions of this Court, referred to in the Court's opinion, and by the language and history of the Ninth Amendment. In reaching the conclusion that the right of marital privacy is protected as being within the protected penumbra of specific guarantees of the Bill of Rights, the Court refers to the Ninth Amendment. I add these words to emphasize the relevance of that Amendment to the Court's holding.

* * *

The Ninth Amendment reads, "The enumeration in the Constitution, of certain rights, shall not be construed to deny or disparage others retained by the people." * * * It was proffered to quiet expressed fears that a bill of specifically enumerated rights could not be sufficiently broad to cover all essential rights and that the specific mention of certain rights would be interpreted as a denial that others were protected.

* * *

While this Court has had little occasion to interpret the Ninth Amendment, "[i]t cannot be presumed that any clause in the constitution is intended to be without effect." * * * The Ninth Amendment to the Constitution may be regarded by some as a recent discovery and may be forgotten by others, but since 1791 it has been a basic part of the Constitution which we are sworn to uphold. To hold that a right so basic and fundamental and so deep-rooted in our society as the right of privacy in marriage may be infringed because that right is not guaranteed in so many words by the first eight amendments to the Constitution is to ignore the Ninth Amendment and to give it no effect whatsoever. Moreover, a judicial construction that this fundamental right is not protected by the Constitution because it is not mentioned in explicit terms by one of the first eight amendments or elsewhere in the Constitution would violate the Ninth Amendment, which specifically states that "[t]he enumeration in the Constitution, of certain rights, shall not be *construed* to deny or disparage others retained by the people." (Emphasis added.)

* * *

Justice Harlan concurred in the judgment.

* * *

In my view, the proper constitutional inquiry in this case is whether this Connecticut statute infringes the Due Process Clause of the Fourteenth Amendment because the enactment violates basic values "implicit in the concept of ordered liberty." For reasons stated at length in my dissenting opinion in *Poe v. Ullman* [1961], I believe that it does. While the relevant inquiry may be aided by resort to one or more of the provisions of the Bill of Rights, it is not dependent on them or any of their radiations. The Due Process Clause of the Fourteenth Amendment stands, in my opinion, on its own bottom.

* * *

Justice White concurred in the judgment.

In my view this Connecticut law as applied to married couples deprives them of "liberty" without due process of law, as that concept is used in the Fourteenth Amendment. I therefore concur in the judgment of the Court reversing these convictions under Connecticut's aiding and abetting statute.

* * *

As I read the opinions of the Connecticut courts and the argument of Connecticut in this Court, the State claims but one justification for its anti-use statute. * * * [T]he statute is said to serve the State's Policy against all forms of promiscuous or illicit sexual relationships, be they premarital or extramarital, concededly a permissible and legitimate legislative goal.

. . . I wholly fail to see how the ban on the use of contraceptives by married couples in any way reinforces the State's ban on illicit sexual relationships. Connecticut does not bar the importation or possession of contraceptive devices; they are not considered contraband material under state law, and their availability in that State is not seriously disputed. The only way Connecticut seeks to limit or control the availability of such devices is through its general aiding and abetting statute whose operation in this context has been quite obviously ineffective and whose most serious use has been against birth-control clinics rendering advice to married, rather than unmarried, persons. * * *

In these circumstances one is rather hard pressed to explain how the ban on use by married persons in any way prevents use of such devices by persons engaging in illicit sexual relations and thereby contributes to the State's policy against such relationships. Neither the state courts nor the State before the bar of this Court has tendered such an explanation. * * * I find nothing in this record justifying the sweeping scope of this statute, with its telling effect on the freedoms of married persons, and therefore conclude that it deprives such persons of liberty without due process of law.

Justice Black, with whom Justice Stewart joined, dissented.

* * *

The Court talks about a constitutional "right of privacy" as though there is some constitutional provision or provisions forbidding any law ever to be passed which might abridge the "privacy" of individuals. But there is not. There are, of course, guarantees in certain specific constitutional provisions which are designed in part to protect privacy at certain times and places with respect to certain activities. Such, for example, is the Fourth Amendment's guarantee against "unreasonable searches and seizures." But I think it belittles that Amendment to talk about it as though it protects nothing but "privacy." * * * The average man would very likely not have his feelings soothed any more by having his property seized openly than by having it seized privately and by stealth. He simply wants his property left alone. And a person can be just as much, if not more, irritated, annoyed and injured by an unceremonious public arrest by a policeman as he is by a seizure in the privacy of his office or home.

One of the most effective ways of diluting or expanding a constitutionally guaranteed right is to substitute for the crucial word or words of a constitutional guarantee another word or words, more or less flexible and more or less restricted in meaning. This fact is well illustrated by the use of the term "right of privacy" as a comprehensive substitute for the Fourth Amendment's guarantee against "unreasonable searches and seizures." "Privacy" is a broad, abstract and ambiguous concept which can easily be shrunken in meaning but which can also, on the other hand, easily be interpreted as a constitutional ban against many things other than searches and seizures. I have expressed the view many times that First Amendment freedoms, for example, have suffered from a failure of the courts to stick to the simple language of the First Amendment in construing it, instead of invoking multitudes of words substituted for those the Framers used. For these reasons I get nowhere in this case by talk about a constitutional "right of privacy" as an emanation from one or more constitutional provisions. I like my privacy as well as the next one, but I am nevertheless compelled to admit that government has a right to invade it unless prohibited by some specific constitutional provision. For these reasons I cannot agree with the Court's judgment and the reasons it gives for holding this Connecticut law unconstitutional.

* * *

[The dissenting opinion of Justice Stewart, in which Justice Black joined, is omitted.]

The Burger Court Era

Reproductive Rights Cases

The decision in *Griswold,* which established that the right of privacy includes the right to use contraceptives, applied only to married couples. Seven years later, the Burger Court extended this right to single individuals in *Eisenstadt v. Baird* (1972). At issue was a Massachusetts law that prohibited the distribution of birth control devices to single persons. William Baird, a state Planned Parenthood official, was convicted for violating the statute. In a 6-1 decision, the Court invalidated the Massachusetts law. (Justices Powell and Rehnquist were not yet confirmed at the time of oral arguments.) In the majority opinion, Justice Brennan wrote, "If the right to privacy means anything, it is the right of the *individual,* married or single, to be free from unwarranted governmental intrusion into matters so fundamentally affecting a person as the decision whether to beget a child" (405 U.S. at 453). Five years later, the Court held that the right to privacy with respect to contraceptives extends to minors. In *Carey v. Population Services, International* (1977), the Court struck down a New York statute that prohibited the distribution of contraceptive devices to persons under the age of sixteen.

Griswold and *Eisenstadt* paved the way for the Court's decisions in *Roe v. Wade* (1973) and its lesser known companion case, *Doe v. Bolton* (1973), which extended the right of privacy in reproductive matters to the abortion decision. (See Chapter 2 for an extensive case study of *Roe v. Wade.*) *Roe* is without a doubt the most well known and most controversial of the Court's privacy cases. This case occurred during the women's rights movement, when feminists were challenging restrictive laws and practices in a number of areas, including abortion policies. Many feminists sought to reform restrictive abortion laws because they viewed women's rights to control their own bodies as crucial to women's independence and autonomy. They were successful in getting abortion legalized by the legislatures in a few states—Hawaii, Alaska, New York, and Washington—and they were assisted by lower court rulings which, on the basis of *Griswold,* held abortion laws unconstitutional in California, Texas, Wisconsin, Georgia, the District of Columbia, Illinois, Florida, New Jersey, and Connecticut (Goldstein 1988). Thus, there was much activity on the issue of abortion before the Supreme Court decided *Roe* and *Doe* in 1973.

In *Roe v. Wade,* the Court was faced with a Texas statute that prohibited abortions except when necessary to save the life of the woman. Jane Roe, an unmarried pregnant woman, challenged this law on the ground that it violated her right of privacy. The Court, by a 7-2 vote, ruled the Texas law an unconstitutional invasion of the right of privacy. Justice Harry Blackmun wrote the majority opinion. He first acknowledged the difficulty of resolving this important issue and then discussed the history of abortion in ancient times and its treatment under common law and English statutory law and in American law. Blackmun emphasized that abortion, especially in the early stages of pregnancy, was not always restricted or prohibited. "[A]t common law, at the time of adoption of our Constitution, and throughout the major portion of the 19th century, abortion was viewed with less disfavor than under most American statutes currently in effect. Phrasing it another way, a woman enjoyed a substantially broader right to terminate a pregnancy than she does in most States today" (410 U.S. at 140). Blackmun then explained that when criminal abortion laws were passed in the mid-to-late nineteenth century, medical concerns primarily prompted their enactment. That is, the abortion procedure itself was a very hazardous one for women. Because of modern medical techniques, Blackmun argued, the hazards once prevalent were no longer present. In fact, according to medical experts, abortions performed in the first trimester are as safe, if not safer, than normal childbirth.

Blackmun then considered the constitutional issue of whether the right of privacy extends to a woman's decision to have an abortion. He acknowledged that this privacy right is not specifically mentioned in the Constitution, but he stressed the importance of precedents that have recognized this right of personal privacy. He concluded, "This right of privacy, whether it be founded in the Fourteenth Amendment's concept of personal liberty and restrictions upon state action, as we feel it is, or as the District Court determined, in the Ninth Amendment's reservation of rights to the people, is broad enough to encompass a woman's decision whether or not to terminate a pregnancy" (410 U.S. at 153). Because it is a fundamental right, the compelling state interest test applies. At the same time, the right to choose to have an abortion is not absolute but instead is qualified by state interests in the health of the woman and in protecting the potential life of the fetus. Those state interests, Blackmun explained, become compelling at different points in the pregnancy, and therefore some state regulation is legitimate. Before explaining when and why these state interests become compelling enough for government regulation, Blackmun responded to Texas's argument that, under the Fourteenth Amendment, the fetus is a person and that life begins at conception. He asserted that the Constitution does not define "person," but that in most instances, the word applies postnatally. On the question of when life begins, Blackmun responded, "We need not resolve th[is] difficult question. * * * When those trained in the respective disciplines of medicine, philosophy, and theology are unable to arrive at any consensus, the judiciary, at this point in the development of man's knowledge, is not in a position to speculate as to the answer" (410 U.S. at 159).

Using the trimester approach to pregnancy (dividing the pregnancy into three thirteen-week periods), Blackmun explained when the state interests become compelling and the degree of government regulation that is appropriate at each stage. During the first trimester, because the abortion procedure is a safe one, the state has no compelling interest. Therefore, the abortion decision is left to the woman and her physician. In the second trimester, the state's interest in the health of the mother becomes compelling such that regulations reasonably related to preserving maternal health are permissible. These may include such things as qualifications and licensing of persons performing abortion and the types of facilities where second-trimester abortions may be performed, for example, outpatient clinics or hospitals. The state interest in the life of the fetus becomes compelling in the third trimester, normally the point of viability (when the fetus can survive outside of the womb), and at this stage, the state may regulate and even prohibit abortions to achieve its interest. Applying this framework to the Texas statute under attack, Blackmun held the law unconstitutional because it did not distinguish between abortions in earlier and later stages of pregnancy, and it permitted them only to save the life of the woman.

In his dissenting opinion, Justice Rehnquist maintained that "the claim of a person to be free from unwanted state regulation of consensual transactions may be a form of 'liberty' protected by the Fourteenth Amendment" (410 U.S. at 878). However, this liberty is not absolute, but is merely guaranteed against deprivation without due process. Thus, he claimed, the compelling state interest test is not appropriate, but "[t]he test traditionally applied in the area of social and economic legislation is whether or not a law such as that challenged has a rational relation to a valid state objective" (410 U.S. at 173). He would have left abortion matters up to state legislators to decide.

Roe v. Wade

410 U.S. 113, 93 S.Ct. 705, 35 L.Ed.2d 147 (1973)

■ Jane Roe (a pseudonym), an unmarried pregnant woman in the state of Texas, sought an abortion from her doctor. He informed her that, under Texas law, abortions were illegal except to save the life of the mother. Roe was not in that situation, and she could not afford to travel to a state where abortion was legal. Her physician referred her to an attorney who could assist her with adoption procedures, and the attorney referred her to two other lawyers, Sarah Weddington and Linda Coffee, who were looking for an appropriate case to challenge the Texas law. They accepted Roe's case and attacked the law as a violation of the right of privacy. A three-judge panel ruled that the law did violate the right of privacy protected by the Ninth Amendment but refused to issue an injunction prohibiting enforcement of the law.

This case is important because it extended the right of privacy to include a woman's decision to have an abortion. As you read the case, consider these questions: 1) Is the trimester framework a reasonable method for accommodating both a woman's right to privacy and the state's interests in protecting maternal health and fetal life? 2) Which is the appropriate standard for examining this abortion statute: the rational basis test suggested by Justice Rehnquist or the compelling state interest test utilized by the majority?

Vote:

7 justices found the Texas law unconstitutional (Blackmun, Brennan, Marshall, Douglas, Stewart, Burger, and Powell).

2 justices voted to uphold the Texas statute (White and Rehnquist).

Justice Blackmun delivered the opinion of the Court.

* * *

We forthwith acknowledge our awareness of the sensitive and emotional nature of the abortion controversy, of the vigorous opposing views, even among physicians, and of the deep and seemingly absolute convictions that the subject inspires. One's philosophy, one's experiences, one's exposure to the raw edges of human existence, one's religious training, one's attitudes toward life and family and their values, and the moral standards one establishes and seeks to observe, are all likely to influence and to color one's thinking and conclusions about abortion.

In addition, population growth, pollution, poverty, and racial overtones tend to complicate and not to simplify the problem.

Our task, of course, is to resolve the issue by constitutional measurement, free of emotion and of predilection. We seek earnestly to do this, and, because we do, we have inquired into, and in this opinion place some emphasis upon, medical and medical-legal history and what that history reveals about man's attitudes toward the abortion procedure over the centuries. * * *

* * *

The principal thrust of appellant's attack on the Texas statutes is that they improperly invade a right, said to be possessed by the pregnant woman, to choose to terminate her pregnancy. Appellant would discover this right in the concept of personal "liberty" embodied in the Fourteenth Amendment's Due Process Clause; or in personal, marital, familial, and sexual privacy said to be protected by the Bill of Rights or its penumbras, or among those rights reserved to the people by the Ninth Amendment. Before addressing this claim, we feel it desirable briefly, to survey, in several aspects, the history of abortion, for such insight as that history may afford us, and then to examine the state purposes and interests behind the criminal abortion laws.

It perhaps is not generally appreciated that the restrictive criminal abortion laws in effect in a majority of States today are of relatively recent vintage. Those laws, generally proscribing abortion or its attempt at any time during pregnancy except when necessary to preserve the pregnant woman's life, are not of ancient or even of common-law origin. Instead, they derive from statutory changes effected, for the most part, in the latter half of the 19th century.

[Justice Blackmun discussed the history of abortion in five sections: ancient attitudes, the Hippocratic Oath, the Common Law, the English Statutory Law, and the American Law.]

* * *

It is . . . apparent that at common law, at the time of the adoption of our Constitution, and throughout the major portion of the 19th century, abortion was viewed with less disfavor than under most American statutes currently in effect. Phrasing it another way, a woman enjoyed a substantially broader right to terminate a pregnancy than she does in most States today. At least with respect to the early stage of pregnancy, and very possibly without such a limitation, the opportunity to make this choice was present in this country well into the 19th century. Even later, the law continued for some time to treat less punitively an abortion procured in early pregnancy.

[Blackmun then summarized the position of the American Medical Association, the American Public Health Association, and the American Bar Association.]

* * *

Three reasons have been advanced to explain historically the enactment of criminal abortion laws in the 19th century and to justify their continued existence.

It has been argued occasionally that these laws were the product of a Victorian social concern to discourage illicit sexual conduct. Texas, however, does not advance this justification in the present case, and it appears that no court or commentator has taken the argument seriously. * * *

A second reason is concerned with abortion as a medical procedure. When most criminal abortion laws were first enacted, the procedure was a hazardous one for the woman. This was particularly true prior to the development of antisepsis. Antiseptic techniques . . . were not generally accepted and employed until about the turn of the century. Abortion mortality was high. Even after 1900, and perhaps until as late as the development of antibiotics in the 1940's, standard modern techniques such as dilation and curettage were not nearly so safe as they are today. Thus, it has been argued that a State's real concern in enacting a criminal abortion law was to protect the pregnant woman, that is, to restrain her from submitting to a procedure that placed her life in serious jeopardy.

Modern medical techniques have altered this situation. Appellants and various *amici* refer to medical data indicating that abortion in early pregnancy, that is, prior to the end of the first trimester, although not without its risk, is now relatively safe. Mortality rates for women undergoing early abortions, where the procedure is legal, appear to be as low as or lower than the rates for normal childbirth. Consequently, any interest of the State in protecting the woman from an inherently hazardous procedure, except when it would be equally dangerous for her to forgo it, has largely disappeared. Of course, important state interests in the areas of health and medical standards do remain. The State has a legitimate interest in seeing to it that abortion, like any other medical procedure, is performed under circumstances that insure maximum safety for the patient. * * * Moreover, the risk to the woman increases as her pregnancy continues. Thus, the State retains a definite interest in protecting the woman's own health and safety when an abortion is proposed at a late stage of pregnancy.

The third reason is the State's interest—some phrase it in terms of duty—in protecting prenatal life. Some of the argument for this justification rests on the theory that a new human life is present from the moment of conception. The State's interest and general obligation to protect life then extends, it is argued, to prenatal life. Only when the life of the pregnant mother herself is at stake, balanced against the life she carries within her, should the interest of the embryo or fetus not prevail. Logically, of course, a legitimate state interest in this area need not stand or fall on acceptance of the belief that life begins at conception or at some other point prior to live birth. In assessing the State's interest, recognition may be given to the less rigid claim that as long as at least *potential* life is involved, the State may assert interests beyond the protection of the pregnant woman alone.

Parties challenging state abortion laws have sharply disputed in some courts the contention that a purpose of these laws, when enacted, was to protect prenatal life. Pointing to the absence of legislative history to support the contention, they claim that most state laws were designed solely to protect the woman. Because medical advances have lessened this concern, at least with respect to abortion in early pregnancy, they argue that with respect to such abortions the laws can no longer be justified by any state interest. There is some scholarly support for this view of original purpose. The few state courts called upon to interpret their laws in the late 19th and early 20th centuries did focus on the State's interest in protecting the woman's health rather than in preserving the embryo and fetus. Proponents of this view point out that in many States, including Texas, by statute or judicial interpretation, the pregnant woman herself could not be prosecuted for self-abortion or for cooperating in an abortion performed upon her by another. They claim that adoption of the "quickening" distinction through received common law and state statutes tacitly recognizes the greater health hazards inherent in late abortion and impliedly repudiates the theory that life begins at conception.

It is with these interests, and the weight to be attached to them, that this case is concerned.

The Constitution does not explicitly mention any right of privacy. In a line of decisions, however, . . . the Court has recognized that a right of personal privacy, or a guarantee of certain areas or zones of privacy, does exist under the Constitution. In varying contexts, the Court or individual Justices have, indeed, found at least the roots of that right in the First Amendment, in the Fourth and Fifth Amendments, in the penumbras of the Bill of Rights, in the Ninth Amendment, or in the concept of liberty guaranteed by the first section of the Fourteenth Amendment. These decisions make it clear that only personal rights that can be deemed "fundamental" or "implicit in the concept of ordered liberty" are included in this guarantee of personal privacy. They also make it clear that the right has some extension to activities relating to marriage, procreation, contraception, family relationships, and child rearing and education.

This right of privacy, whether it be founded in the Fourteenth Amendment's concept of personal liberty and restrictions upon state action, as we feel it is, or, as the District Court determined, in the Ninth Amendment's reservation of rights to the people, is broad enough to encompass a woman's decision whether or not to terminate her pregnancy. The detriment that the State would impose upon the pregnant woman by denying this choice altogether is apparent. Specific and direct harm medically diagnosable even in early pregnancy may be involved. Maternity, or additional offspring, may force upon the woman a distressful life and future. Psychological harm may be imminent. Mental and physical health may be taxed by child care. There is also the distress, for all concerned, associated with the unwanted child, and there is the problem of bringing a child into a family already unable, psychologically and otherwise, to care for it. In other cases, as in this one, the additional difficulties and continuing stigma of unwed motherhood may be involved. All these are factors the woman and her responsible physician necessarily will consider in consultation.

On the basis of elements such as these, appellant and some *amici* argue that the woman's right is absolute and that she is entitled to terminate her pregnancy at whatever time, in whatever way, and for whatever reason she alone chooses. With this we do not agree. Appellant's arguments that Texas either has no valid interest at all in regulating the abortion decision, or no interest strong enough to support any limitation upon the woman's sole determination, are unpersuasive. The Court's decisions recognizing a right of privacy also acknowledge that some state regulation in areas protected by that right is appropriate. As noted above, a State may properly assert important interests in safeguarding health, in maintaining medical standards, and in protecting potential life. At some point in pregnancy, these respective interests become sufficiently compelling to sustain regulation of the factors that govern the abortion decision. The privacy right involved, therefore, cannot be said to be absolute. * * *

We therefore, conclude that the right of personal privacy includes the abortion decision, but that this right is not unqualified and must be considered against important state interests in regulation.

* * *

Where certain "fundamental rights" are involved, the Court has held that regulation limiting these rights may be justified only by a "compelling state interest," and that legislative enactments must be narrowly drawn to express only the legitimate state interests at stake. * * *

* * *

The District Court held that the appellee failed to meet his burden of demonstrating that the Texas statute's infringement upon Roe's rights was necessary to support a compelling state interest, and that, although the appellee presented "several compelling justifications for state presence in the area of abortions," the statutes outstripped these justifications and swept "far beyond any areas of compelling state interest." Appellant and appellee both contest that holding. Appellant, as has been indicated, claims an absolute right that bars any state imposition of criminal penalties in the area. Appellee argues that the State's determination to recognize and protect prenatal life from and after conception constitutes a compelling state interest. As noted above, we do not agree fully with either formulation.

The appellee and certain *amici* argue that the fetus is a "person" within the language and meaning of the Fourteenth Amendment. * * *

The Constitution does not define "person" in so many words. Section 1 of the Fourteenth Amendment contains three references to "person." The first, in defining "citizens," speaks of "persons born or naturalized in the United States." The word also appears both in the Due Process Clause and in the Equal Protection Clause. "Person" is used in other places in the Constitution. . . . But in nearly all these instances, the use of the word is such that it has application only postnatally. None indicates, with any assurance, that it has any possible pre-natal application.

All this, together with our observation that throughout the major portion of the 19th century prevailing legal abortion practices were far freer than they are today, persuades us that the word "person," as used in the Fourteenth Amendment, does not include the unborn. * * *

This conclusion, however, does not of itself fully answer the contentions raised by Texas, and we pass to other considerations.

The pregnant woman cannot be isolated in her privacy. She carries an embryo and, later, a fetus, if one accepts the medical definitions of the developing young in the human uterus. * * * The situation therefore is inherently different from marital intimacy, or bedroom possession of obscene material, or marriage, or procreation, or education. . . . As we have intimated above, it is reasonable and appropriate for a State to decide that at some point in time another interest, that of health of the mother or that of potential human life, becomes significantly involved. The woman's privacy is no longer sole and any right of privacy she possesses must be measured accordingly.

Texas urges that, apart from the Fourteenth Amendment, life begins at conception and is present throughout pregnancy, and that, therefore, the State has a compelling interest in protecting that life from and after conception. We need not resolve the difficult question of when life begins. When those trained in the respective disciplines of medicine, philosophy, and theology are unable to arrive at any consensus, the judiciary, at this point in the development of man's knowledge, is not in a position to speculate as to the answer.

* * *

In view of all this, we do not agree that, by adopting one theory of life, Texas may override the rights of the pregnant woman that are at stake. We repeat, however, that the State does have an important and legitimate interest in preserving and protecting the health of the pregnant woman, whether she be a resident of the State or a nonresident who seeks medical consultation and treatment there, and that it has still *another* important and legitimate interest in protecting the potentiality of human life. These interests are separate and distinct. Each grows in substantiality as the woman approaches term and, at a point during pregnancy, each becomes "compelling."

With respect to the State's important and legitimate interest in the health of the mother, the "compelling" point, in the light of present medical knowledge, is at approximately the end of the first trimester. This is so because of the now-established medical fact . . . that until the end of the first trimester mortality in abortion may be less than mortality in normal childbirth. It follows that, from and after this point, a State may regulate the abortion procedure to the extent that the regulation reasonably relates to the preservation and protection of maternal health. Examples of permissible state regulation in this area are requirements as to the qualifications of the person who is to perform the abortion; as to the licensure of that person; as to the facility in which the procedure is to be performed, that is, whether it must be a hospital or may be a clinic or some other place of less-than-hospital status; as to the licensing of the facility; and the like.

This means, on the other hand, that, for the period of pregnancy prior to this "compelling" point, the attending physician, in consultation with his patient, is free to determine, without regulation by the State, that, in his medical judgment, the patient's pregnancy should be terminated. If that decision is reached, the judgment may be effectuated by an abortion free of interference by the State.

With respect to the State's important and legitimate interest in potential life, the "compelling" point is at viability. This is so because the fetus then presumably has the capability of meaningful life outside the mother's womb. State regulation protective of fetal life after viability thus has both logical and biological justifications. If the State is interested in protecting fetal life after viability, it may go so far as to proscribe abortion during that period, except when it is necessary to preserve the life or health of the mother.

Measured against these standards, Art. 1196 of the Texas Penal Code, in restricting legal abortions to those procured or attempted by medical advice for the purpose of saving the life of the mother," sweeps too broadly. The statute makes no distinction between abortions performed early in pregnancy and those performed later, and it limits to a single reason, "saving" the mother's life, the legal justification for the procedure. The statute, therefore, cannot survive the constitutional attack made upon it here.

* * *

To summarize and to repeat:

1. A state criminal abortion statute of the current Texas type, that excepts from criminality only a *lifesaving* procedure on behalf of the mother, without regard to pregnancy stage and without recognition of the other interests involved, is violative of the Due Process Clause of the Fourteenth Amendment.

(a) For the stage prior to approximately the end of the first trimester, the abortion decision and its effectuation must be left to the medical judgment of the pregnant woman's attending physician.

(b) For the stage subsequent to approximately the end of the first trimester, the State, in promoting its interest in the health of the mother, may, if it chooses, regulate the abortion procedure in ways that are reasonably related to maternal health.

(c) For the stage subsequent to viability, the State in promoting its interest in the potentiality of human life may, if it chooses, regulate, and even proscribe, abortion except where it is necessary, in appropriate medical judgment, for the preservation of the life or health of the mother.

* * *

This holding, we feel, is consistent with the relative weights of the respective interests involved, with the lessons and examples of medical and legal history, with the lenity of the common law, and with the demands of the profound problems of the present day. The decision leaves the State free to place increasing restrictions on abortion as the period of pregnancy lengthens, so long as those restrictions are tailored to the recognized state interests. The decision vindicates the right of the physician to administer medical treatment according to his professional judgment up to the points where important state interests provide compelling justifications for intervention. Up to those points, the abortion decision in all its aspects is inherently, and primarily, a medical decision, and basic responsibility for it must rest with the physician. If an individual practitioner abuses the privilege of exercising proper medical judgment, the usual remedies, judicial and intraprofessional, are available.

* * *

It is so ordered.

[The concurring opinions of Chief Justice Burger and Justice Douglas, which appear in Doe v. Bolton, Roe's companion, each are omitted.]

[Justice White's dissent is omitted.]

[The concurring opinion of Mr. Justice Stewart is omitted.]

Justice Rehnquist dissented.

* * *

* * * I have difficulty in concluding, as the Court does, that the right of "privacy" is involved in this case. Texas, by the statute here challenged, bars the performance of a medical abortion by a licensed physician on a plaintiff such as Roe. A transaction resulting in an operation such as this is not "private" in the ordinary usage of that word. Nor is the "privacy" that the Court finds here even a distant relative of the freedom from searches and seizures protected by the Fourth Amendment to the Constitution, which the Court has referred to as embodying a right to privacy.

If the Court means by the term "privacy" no more than that the claim of a person to be free from unwanted state regulation of consensual transactions may be a form of "liberty" protected by the Fourteenth Amendment, there is no doubt that similar claims have been upheld in our earlier decisions on the basis of that liberty. I agree with the statement of Mr. Justice Stewart in his concurring opinion that the "liberty," against deprivation of which without due process the Fourteenth Amendment protects, embraces more than the rights found in the Bill of Rights. But that liberty is not guaranteed absolutely against deprivation, only against deprivation without due process of law. The test traditionally applied in the area of social and economic legislation is whether or not a law such as that challenged has a rational relation to a valid state objective. The Due Process Clause of the Fourteenth Amendment undoubtedly does place a limit, albeit a broad one, on legislative power to enact laws such as this. If the Texas statute were to prohibit an abortion even where the mother's life is in jeopardy, I have little doubt that such a statute would lack a rational relation to a valid state objective. . . . But the Court's sweeping invalidation of any restrictions on abortion during the first trimester is impossible to justify under that standard, and the conscious weighing of competing factors that the Court's opinion apparently substitutes for the established test is far more appropriate to a legislative judgment than to a judicial one.

* * *

While the Court's opinion quotes from the dissent of Mr. Justice Holmes in *Lochner v. New York* (1905), the result it reaches is more closely attuned to the majority opinion of Mr. Justice Peckham in that case. As in *Lochner* and similar cases applying substantive due process standards to economic and social welfare legislation, the adoption of the compelling state interest standard will inevitably require this Court to examine the legislative policies and pass on the wisdom of these policies in the very process of deciding whether a particular state interest put forward may or may not be "compelling." The decision here to break pregnancy into three distinct terms and to outline the permissible restrictions the State may impose in each one, for example, partakes more of judicial legislation than it does of a determination of the intent of the drafters of the Fourteenth Amendment.

The fact that a majority of the States reflecting, after all, the majority sentiment in those States, have had restrictions on abortions for at least a century is a strong indication, it seems to me, that the asserted right to an abortion is not "so rooted in the traditions and conscience of our people as to be ranked as fundamental." Even today, when society's views on abortion are changing, the very existence of the debate is evidence that the "right" to an abortion is not so universally accepted as the appellant would have us believe.

* * *

For all of the foregoing reasons, I respectfully dissent.

The Georgia statute challenged in *Doe v. Bolton* (1973) was not as restrictive as the Texas law from *Roe,* but nonetheless it placed major obstacles in the paths of women seeking to obtain abortions. The law permitted "necessary" abortions under three types of circumstances: 1) if the pregnancy was dangerous to the woman's life or if it would cause serious or permanent injury, 2) if it appeared that the fetus would be born with a serious and permanent mental or physical defect, and 3) if the pregnancy resulted from rape (Mezey 1992). The law contained several other provisions as well. First, two physicians in addition to the woman's doctor had to certify that the abortion was necessary. Second, abortions could be performed only in licensed and accredited hospitals, and the procedure required advance approval from the hospital's abortion committee. Finally, the statute applied only to residents of the state of Georgia.

By a 7-2 vote, using the framework set forth in *Roe,* the Court invalidated the two independent physicians requirement, the accredited hospital provision, the hospital abortion committee requirement, and the residency requirement. (The three situations permitting "necessary" abortions had already been struck at the district court.) Justice Blackmun, again writing for the majority, ruled that the requirement of approval by the hospital committee and the independent physicians provision infringed on a woman's right to privacy and on her physician's right to practice without legitimate reasons. The accredited hospital requirement provision was struck "because it fail[ed] to exclude the first trimester of pregnancy" (410 U.S. at 195). The residency requirement violated the right to travel that had been established four years earlier in *Shapiro v. Thompson* (1969).

Justice White's dissent, joined by Justice Rehnquist, covered both the *Roe* and *Doe* cases. He accused the majority of blatant judicial activism, stressing that in abortion matters the Court should defer to the decisions of state legislatures. Moreover, he criticized the majority for placing more value on the "convenience" of the woman seeking an abortion than on the life of the fetus. In his view, it was constitutionally appropriate for states to deny abortions unless the health or life of the woman was in some danger.

While the Court's decision in *Roe* (and by extension, *Doe*) was critical to abortion reform in this country, it by no means ended the debate over this emotionally charged issue. To the contrary, *Roe* intensified the debate. Abortion opponents bitterly attacked both the decision and the justices in the majority. More importantly, they stepped up their efforts to get new restrictive statutes passed by state legislatures. According to Mezey (1992), "[F]ollowing *Roe,* almost two hundred abortion bills were introduced in state legislatures. Within two years, 32 states enacted a total of 62 abortion-related laws" (p. 220). Mezey placed the statutes in seven categories: "performance regulations (where abortions could be performed and by whom), consent requirements, recordkeeping and reporting requirements, advertising prohibitions, funding restrictions (state and federal), conscience laws (allowing hospitals or physicians to refuse to perform abortions), and fetal protection" (p. 220).

The first of these new statutes to reach the Court was a comprehensive piece of legislation from the state of Missouri. In *Planned Parenthood v. Danforth* (1976), the statute under challenge contained provisions pertaining to first-trimester abortions as well as those performed later in the pregnancy. Planned Parenthood of Central Missouri and two physicians involved in performing abortions challenged eight specific provisions of the statute:

1. the broad definition of viability as "that stage of fetal development when the life of the unborn child may be continued indefinitely outside the womb by natural or artificial life-supportive systems;"
2. a provision requiring a woman's written consent for an abortion during the first trimester of pregnancy;

3 & 4. provisions requiring spousal consent for married women and parental consent for unmarried women under eighteen for a first-trimester abortion, unless the abortion is necessary to preserve the woman's life;

5. a requirement that persons who perform abortions or assist in them exercise the same standard of care that would be applicable to a live birth, including taking steps to preserve the life of the aborted fetus;

6 & 7. a requirement that reports of all abortions performed be recorded for statistical and public health purposes and that those records be kept for a period of seven years; and

8. a provision prohibiting abortion by method of saline amniocentesis after the first trimester.

At the district court level, all of the provisions were upheld except the one relating to the standard of care for preserving the life of an aborted fetus. The Supreme Court's decision was more complex, as it invalidated some provisions and upheld others in various alignments of the justices. By a unanimous vote, the Court upheld the provisions related to the viability definition, the written consent of the woman, and the recordkeeping and reporting requirements. By a 6-3 vote, the Court struck down the spousal consent requirement, the saline amniocentesis prohibition, and the standard of care provision. The parental consent provision was held invalid by a 5-4 vote. Justice Blackmun wrote the majority opinion, and he was joined by Justices Brennan, Marshall, Stewart, and Powell. Justice Stevens, concurring in part and dissenting in part, agreed with the majority on all of the provisions except the one that required parental consent for minors. Chief Justice Burger and Justice Rehnquist joined a separate opinion by Justice White concurring in the judgment in part and dissenting in part. The latter three would have upheld all of the challenged provisions as reasonably related to the preservation of maternal health and potential life.

According to Justice Blackmun, Missouri's definition of viability was consistent with *Roe,* and the requirement of written consent of the woman seeking an abortion was a legitimate method of ensuring that the decision was made with complete knowledge about the procedure and its consequences. The recordkeeping and reporting requirements were upheld because they were related to preserving maternal health, the information was to be kept confidential, and they had no significant impact on the woman's abortion decision. Blackmun struck both the spousal and parental consent provisions, arguing that states cannot permit third parties (husbands or parents) to have veto power over decisions properly made between the patient and her physician. Acknowledging that it would be desirable for the abortion decision to be made by both spouses, Blackmun said that when there is a disagreement between the two, the woman's decision must prevail. "Inasmuch as it is the woman who physically bears the child and who is the more directly and immediately affected by the pregnancy, as between the two, the balance weighs in her favor" (428 U.S. at 71).

On the question of prohibiting the use of saline amniocentesis after the first twelve weeks of pregnancy, the majority held that it was actually *adversely* related to the preservation of maternal health. Noting that this method was a commonly used medical procedure for post first-trimester abortions, that it was viewed by physicians as safer than continuing the pregnancy until normal childbirth, and that there were no safer alternatives available in the state, Blackmun said this provision "fail[ed] as a reasonable regulation for the protection of maternal health" (428 U.S. at 79). Finally, the majority struck the standard of care requirement because it did not distinguish between abortions performed before and after viability. Three years later in *Colautti v. Franklin* (1979), the Court invalidated a similar Pennsylvania statute that required physicians to preserve the lives of viable or "possibly viable" fetuses.

After *Danforth,* another type of abortion regulation that made its way to the Court involved policies restricting public funds from being used for abortion expenses. The policies involved medical care for indigent people under Medicaid, a joint federal-state program governed by Title XIX of the Social Security Act. Under Title XIX, "A State plan for medical assistance must . . . include reasonable standards . . . of determining eligibility for and the extent of medical assistance under the plan which . . . are consistent with the objectives of this [Title]" (42 U.S.C. Sect. 1396 [a][17]). States, therefore, had some discretion in determining which medical procedures would be funded. Using this discretion, some states prohibited the use of Medicaid funds for "nontherapeutic" or elective abortions, that is, abortions that were not medically necessary. The precise meaning of these terms varied from state to state.

In two companion cases decided in 1977, *Beal v. Doe* and *Maher v. Roe,* the Court sanctioned these abortion restrictions by 6-3 votes. In *Beal,* which was decided on statutory grounds, the majority upheld the right of states under Title XIX to fund only "medically necessary" abortions. Justice Powell wrote, "[N]othing in the statute suggests that participating States are required to fund every medical procedure that falls within the delineated categories of medical care" (432 U.S. at 444). Moreover, even if abortions were safer and cheaper than childbirth, the state's refusal to fund nontherapeutic abortions was justified by its "strong and legitimate interest in encouraging normal childbirth" (446). *Maher v. Roe,* which also involved a state policy limiting Medicaid funds to "medically necessary" abortions, was challenged and decided on constitutional grounds. The issue was whether the regulation, by funding the expenses connected with childbirth but not those connected with abortion, violated a fundamental right protected by the Equal Protection Clause. If a fundamental right were involved, the Court would have examined the regulation using strict scrutiny, where the state would have to prove a compelling interest to justify the policy. The majority, however, ruled that there was no fundamental right involved and that the state policy was reasonably related to its "strong and legitimate" interest in childbirth. In attempting to distinguish between the Connecticut law and abortion restrictions previously invalidated, Justice Powell wrote, "The Connecticut regulation places no obstacles—absolute or otherwise—in the pregnant woman's path to an abortion. An indigent woman who desires an abortion suffers no disadvantage as a consequence of Connecticut's decision to fund childbirth; she continues as before to be dependent on private sources for the service she desires. * * * The indigency that may make it difficult—and in some cases, perhaps, impossible--for some women to have abortions is neither created nor in any way affected by the Connecticut regulation" (432 U.S. at 474).

A third case, *Poelker v. Doe,* decided along with *Beal* and *Maher,* involved not Medicaid funds but a city policy (St. Louis, Missouri) which prohibited public hospitals from performing elective abortions while allowing them to be used for services connected with childbirth. The same 6-3 majority upheld this regulation as consistent with *Roe.* In a short per curiam opinion, the justices held, "the Constitution does not forbid a State or city, pursuant to democratic processes, from expressing a preference for normal childbirth . . ." (432 U.S. at 521).

The dissenters in the three cases—Justices Brennan, Marshall, and Blackmun—criticized the majority for "a distressing insensitivity to the plight of impoverished pregnant women" (*Maher,* 432 U.S. at 483) and for making it more difficult for some women to exercise their rights under *Roe.* In his dissent for the three in *Beal,* Brennan argued that the majority's decision would "forc[e] penniless pregnant women to have children they would not have borne if the State had not weighted the scales to make their choice to have abortions substantially more onerous" (432 U.S. at 454).

Beal, Maher, and *Poelker* involved state and city restrictions on public funds for abortions, but in the mid 1970s Congress entered this area and passed similar federal legislation. Congressional efforts were led by Henry Hyde, a Republican member of the House of Representatives, who was successful in attaching antiabortion amendments to annual appropriations bills. These amendments restricted federal funds from being used to pay for abortions for Medicaid recipients. Although some who supported this legislation claimed that it was simply aimed at preventing public monies from being used in abortions, it was clear that these amendments were part of an overall strategy to restrict access to abortion. Hyde himself stated, "I certainly would like to prevent, if I could legally, anybody having an abortion, a rich woman, a middle-class woman, or a poor woman. Unfortunately, the only vehicle available is the HEW [M]edicaid bill" (Mezey 1992, p. 247). Early versions of the Hyde Amendment contained exemptions for pregnancies that resulted from rape or incest "promptly reported," as well as those that would result in "severe and long-lasting physical health damage" to the woman (p. 248). This latter provision involving "health damage" seemed to include "medically necessary" abortions, not simply those that were necessary to save the life of the woman. When the Hyde Amendment reached the Supreme Court in 1980, however, the version being challenged did not contain the "health damage" provision. The amendment allowed Medicaid coverage of abortions only for life-threatening pregnancies; therefore, "medically necessary" abortions were no longer funded. It continued, however, to include a provision for victims of rape and incest.

A lower federal court judge invalidated the Hyde Amendment, but the Supreme Court upheld it in *Harris v. McRae* (1980) by a 5-4 vote. Justice Stewart, writing for the majority, relied extensively on the *Maher* precedent in holding that the amendment did not violate a woman's constitutional right to an abortion. "[A]lthough government may not place obstacles in the path of a woman's exercise of her freedom of choice, it need not remove those not of its own creation. Indigency falls into the latter category. The financial constraints that restrict an indigent woman's ability to enjoy the full range of constitutionally protected freedom of choice are the product not of governmental restrictions on access to abortions, but rather of her own indigency" (448 U.S. at 316). In short, Stewart declared, a woman may have the constitutional right to have an abortion, but that does not require the government to provide her with the funds to do so.

As in the three earlier cases, Justices Brennan, Marshall, and Blackmun dissented from the Court's ruling. This time, Justice Stevens dissented as well. Once again they accused the majority of allowing the government to discriminate against poor women in the exercise of their constitutional rights. In their view, the funding restriction in the Hyde Amendment was no different from other restrictions that had been placed on abortion. Justice Brennan wrote, "The fundamental flaw in the Court's . . . analysis . . . is its failure to acknowledge that the discriminatory distribution of the benefits of governmental largesse can discourage the exercise of fundamental liberties just as effectively as can outright denial of those rights through criminal and regulatory sanctions" (448 U.S. at 334). In *Williams v. Zbaraz* (1980), a companion case to *Harris,* the Court upheld a state statute (Illinois) which was similar to the Hyde Amendment.

After the Court struck the parental consent provision in *Danforth,* states continued to pass laws requiring some level of parental involvement in a minor's abortion decision. One type of law involved a "judicial bypass" procedure, whereby a minor could get permission from a judge to have an abortion. The other required parental notification rather than consent. Opponents of parental notification laws argued that they would have the same effect as parental consent laws—minors would have difficulty in gaining access to abortions. These two types of abortion regulations were examined by the Court in *Bellotti v. Baird II* (1979) and *H.L. v. Matheson* (1981). In *Bellotti II,* the Court rejected a Massachusetts parental consent law that included a judicial bypass procedure because the procedure was inadequate to protect the minors' privacy right. Justice Powell's plurality opinion set forth three criteria for a legitimate judicial bypass procedure: 1) the minor must be permitted to show either that she is mature enough to decide to have an abortion or that an abortion is in her best interests, 2) the procedure must guarantee the minor's anonymity, and 3) an expedited appeals process must be provided. In *Matheson,* a six-member majority upheld a Utah parental notification law, holding that it did not give parents veto power over their daughters' abortion decision. Moreover, it was a legitimate method for the state to "promote the family unit" and to allow parents to provide physicians with important information about their daughters' medical histories.

The cases concerning parental consent/notification and funding restrictions involved fairly narrow types of restrictions on abortion. The most comprehensive and restrictive abortion regulations since *Danforth* involved a city ordinance examined by the Court in *Akron v. Akron Center for Reproductive Health* (1983), *Akron I.* This was also the first abortion case in which Justice Sandra Day O'Connor participated. At the time of her appointment and confirmation, she was criticized by anti-choice activists who claimed that she was supportive of abortion. Her position in *Akron I* indicated that they were wrong. O'Connor led the three dissenters who voted to uphold the regulations being challenged. Her opinion will be discussed shortly.

The following five provisions of the Akron abortion ordinance were challenged at the Supreme Court:

1. a hospital requirement for all post first-trimester abortions;
2. parental consent for unmarried minors under the age of fifteen;
3. an "informed consent" provision requiring physicians to make specific statements to abortion patients, including, among other things, telling them that a

fetus is a human life from the moment of conception (clearly an attempt to undercut *Roe*'s admonition against defining when life begins), the abortion technique to be used, the particular risks of the woman's pregnancy, and agencies available to assist the woman if she chooses to continue the pregnancy;

4. a twenty-four-hour waiting period between the time the consent form is signed and the abortion is performed; and
5. a requirement that fetal remains be "disposed of in a humane and sanitary manner."

By a 6-3 vote, the Supreme Court struck down all five provisions as inconsistent with the requirements of *Roe v. Wade*. Justice Powell wrote the majority opinion, joined by Chief Justice Burger and Justices Brennan, Marshall, Blackmun, and Stevens. In dissent were Justices O'Connor, White, and Rehnquist.

In striking down the hospitalization requirement, Powell indicated that medical experts did not recommend hospital abortions for the first sixteen weeks of pregnancy, which would include several weeks of the second trimester. Moreover, this hospitalization requirement presented a significant obstacle to women seeking abortions because the costs increased dramatically (more than doubled), and Akron hospitals performed very few second-trimester abortions.

The parental consent provision was invalidated on the basis of *Bellotti II,* and the informed consent requirement was deemed to be an attempt "not to inform the woman's consent but rather to persuade her to withhold it altogether" (462 U.S. at 444). In addition, some of the information required to be given, for example, development of the fetus, date of possible viability, and abortion alternatives including adoption and childbirth, infringed on physicians' discretion in advising their patients. Information about risks associated with the woman's own pregnancy, the abortion technique to be used, and medical instructions related to her recovery were permitted. However, the city could not mandate that only physicians give this information, for they could "delegate the counseling task to another qualified individual" (462 U.S. at 448). Similarly, the majority viewed the twenty-four-hour waiting period as an unnecessary obstacle in the paths of women seeking to obtain abortions. Powell said that the waiting period was "arbitrary and inflexible," and there was no evidence that an abortion would be safer because of it. Finally, the majority saw the provision regarding disposal of fetal remains in a "humane and sanitary manner" as suggestive of a requirement of "decent burial" even at early stages of fetal development. Thus, it was held unconstitutional as well.

In the most important part of her dissent, O'Connor went beyond the Akron regulations to attack the trimester approach from *Roe,* urging the Court to reexamine this precedent. Arguing that advances in technology made second-trimester abortions safer and at the same time moved viability to an earlier point in pregnancy, O'Connor found the trimester approach "unworkable" and "clearly on a collision course with itself" (462 U.S. at 458). Furthermore, she contended that the state had a compelling interest in maternal health and the potential life of the fetus throughout the pregnancy, not just in the second and third trimesters. "[*P*]*otential* life is no less potential in the first weeks of pregnancy than it is at viability or afterward" (462 U.S. at 461). Subsequently, O'Connor explained her approach for examining the constitutionality of abortion regulations. She said the Court should begin its analysis by determining whether the regulation posed an undue burden on the pregnant woman's right to an abortion. If so, the state would have to prove a compelling interest for the regulation to be upheld. If the regulation was not "unduly burdensome," the regulation should be upheld if it had a rational basis. After examining the Akron regulations under this standard, she found none of them to be unduly burdensome, and she viewed them as reasonably related to preserving maternal health and protecting potential life.

Two cases were decided along with *Akron*. In *Planned Parenthood v. Ashcroft* (1983), a case from Missouri, the Court invalidated a similar hospital requirement for second-trimester abortions, but upheld such a requirement in *Simopoulous v. Virginia* (1983) because the statute defined hospital to include "outpatient surgical hospitals." Also in *Ashcroft,* the Court upheld a requirement that a second physician be present at all abortions performed after viability.

As these cases illustrate, except for funding restrictions and parental consent and notification requirements, the Burger Court was skeptical of abortion regulations. This did not, however, prevent states from passing more laws designed to restrict access to abortion. In the final case from the Burger era, *Thornburgh v. American College of Obstetricians and Gynecologists* (1986), the Court upheld *Roe* and *Akron* and invalidated more regulations, but by only a 5-4 margin. Chief Justice Burger, who was in the majority in *Akron,* switched sides and joined the dissenters in *Thornburgh*.

The Pennsylvania statute challenged in *Thornburgh* was quite similar to the Akron ordinance. It contained an informed consent provision requiring specific information to be given to the woman both orally and in print, and the information had to be provided at least twenty-four hours before consent could be given. Physicians were required to file detailed reports, including "identification of the performing and referring physicians and of the facility or agency; information as to the woman's political subdivision and State of residence, age, race, marital status, and number of prior pregnancies; the date of her last menstrual period and the probable gestational age; the basis for any determination of nonviability; and the method of payment for the abortion" (476 U.S. at 765). The final sections of the act being challenged concerned the degree of care to be exercised by physicians in postviability abortions and the presence of a second physician during abortions performed when "viability is possible." The degree of care exercised was to be the same as if the fetus were "intended to be born and not aborted," and physicians were to use the abortion method that maximized protection of the fetus unless it was significantly more risky to the life or health of the woman. Violators would be subject to imprisonment and a fine of up to $15,000. The second physician was to take steps necessary to preserve the fetus's life and health if the abortion resulted in a live birth.

Justices Blackmun, Brennan, Marshall, Powell, and Stevens voted to strike all of these provisions, while Justices White, Rehnquist, O'Connor, and Chief Justice Burger dissented from this ruling. Justice Blackmun wrote the majority opinion. He said that the informed consent requirement was really intended to obstruct the woman's choice, and it impermissibly infringed on the doctor-patient relationship. "Under the guise of informed consent, the Act requires the dissemination of information that is not relevant to such consent, and, thus, it advances no legitimate state interest" (476 U.S. at 763). Because the required reports were so detailed and were available to the public, women who chose to exercise their right to abortion ran the risk of "public exposure and harassment." This would be a serious invasion of privacy. Blackmun ruled that the degree of care standard presented a trade-off between maternal health and fetal survival, when maternal health must take precedence. Lastly, he invalidated the second physician requirement because it provided no exception "for the situation where the health of the mother was endangered by delay in the arrival of the second physician" (476 U.S. at 770).

In several dissents, Chief Justice Burger and Justices White, O'Connor, and Rehnquist contended that the Pennsylvania statute was constitutionally permissible, and they called for the Court to reexamine *Roe v. Wade*. Justices White and

Rehnquist went further, calling for the Court to reverse *Roe* altogether and leave abortion policy up to the states. "[T]he time has come to recognize that *Roe v. Wade* . . . 'departs from a proper understanding' of the Constitution and to overrule it. * * * Abortion is a hotly contested moral and political issue. Such issues, in our society, are to be resolved by the will of the people, either as expressed through legislation or through the general principles they have already incorporated into the Constitution they have adopted" (476 U.S. at 788, 796). Justice O'Connor did not call for *Roe* to be reversed; instead, she continued to press her "undue burden" test as the appropriate standard for examining abortion regulations.

Nonreproductive Rights Cases

As we noted earlier, the overwhelming majority of the Supreme Court's privacy cases have involved reproductive matters, particularly abortion. Two nonreproductive rights cases decided by the Burger Court merit discussion. In the first case, *Kelley v. Johnson,* decided in 1976, the Court upheld a police department regulation concerning hair length and hairstyle against a claim by police officers that it violated their privacy rights. By a 6-2 vote, with Justice Stevens not participating and Justice Rehnquist writing for the majority, the high court ruled that the regulation did not violate any "liberty" interest guaranteed by the Fourteenth Amendment. Distinguishing the *Roe, Eisenstadt,* and *Griswold* precedents from the issue presented in this case, Rehnquist wrote, "Each of those cases involved a substantial claim of infringement on the individual's freedom of choice with respect to certain basic matters of procreation, marriage, and family life" (425 U.S. at 244). Also of importance to the majority was the fact that the claim was brought by a public employee rather than by a member of the general public. The majority viewed the hair-length regulation as reasonably related to the organizational structure chosen by police departments to carry out their law enforcement functions. "This choice may be based on a desire to make police officers readily recognizable to the members of the public, or a desire for the esprit de corps which such similarity is felt to inculcate within the police force itself. Either one is a sufficiently rational justification . . ." (425 U.S. at 248).

Dissenting for himself and Justice Brennan, Justice Marshall contended that the regulation was a violation of the police officers' constitutional rights. Citing *Roe* and *Griswold* among others, Marshall declared, "To say that the liberty guarantee of the Fourteenth Amendment does not encompass matters of personal appearance would be fundamentally inconsistent with the values of privacy, self-identity, autonomy, and personal integrity that I have always assumed the Constitution was designed to protect" (425 U.S. at 251).

Kelley v. Johnson

425 U.S. 238, 96 S.Ct. 1440, 47 L.Ed.2d 708 (1976)

■ The Suffolk County Police Commissioner adopted regulations concerning the hair grooming of its police officers. The regulations pertained to the length and style of hair, sideburns, and mustaches, and prohibited the wearing of beards, goatees, and wigs except for medical and cosmetic reasons. The president of the patrolmen's association of Suffolk County filed suit in federal district court, alleging that the regulations violated the officers' Fourteenth Amendment rights. The district court dismissed the complaint, but the court of appeals reversed and remanded the case to the district court for reconsideration. After reconsideration, the district court ruled in favor of the police officers, and the court of appeals affirmed that decision. Kelley, the police commissioner, appealed to the Supreme Court.

This case is important because it is one of the few privacy cases decided by the Court that does not involve matters of reproductive freedom, Fourth Amendment search and seizure, or other Bill of Rights guarantees. As you read the case, consider these questions: 1) Why did the Court agree to hear this case? That is, how important is the issue presented here? 2) Is the rational basis test appropriate for examining the regulation being challenged? 3) Is it reasonable to conclude, as Justices Brennan and Marshall did, that the authors of the Bill of Rights considered some rights to be so clear that they did not need to be stated explicitly in that document?

VOTE:

6 justices voted to uphold the regulation (Rehnquist, Burger, Stewart, White, Blackmun, and Powell).

2 justices found the regulation a violation of the Fourteenth Amendment (Marshall and Brennan).

1 justice did not participate (Stevens).

Justice Rehnquist delivered the opinion of the Court.

* * *

Section 1 of the Fourteenth Amendment to the United States Constitution provides in pertinent part: "No State shall . . . deprive any person of life, liberty, or property, without due process of law."

This section affords not only a procedural guarantee against the deprivation of "liberty," but likewise protects substantive aspects of liberty against unconstitutional restrictions by the State.

The "liberty" interest claimed by respondent here, of course, is distinguishable from the interests protected by the Court in *Roe v. Wade* (1973), *Eisenstadt v. Baird* (1972), *Stanley v. Illinois* (1972), *Griswold v. Connecticut* [1965], and *Meyer v. Nebraska* (1923). Each of those cases involved a substantial claim of infringement on the individual's freedom of choice with respect to certain basic matters of procreation, marriage, and family life. But whether the citizenry at large has some sort of "liberty" interest within the Fourteenth Amendment in matters of personal appearance is a question on which this Court's cases offer little, if any, guidance. We can, nevertheless, assume an affirmative answer for purposes of deciding this case, because we find that assumption insufficient to carry the day for respondent's claim.

Respondent has sought the protection of the Fourteenth Amendment, not as a member of the citizenry at large, but on the contrary as an employee of the police department of Suffolk County, a subdivision of the State of New York. While the Court of Appeals made passing reference to this distinction, it was thereafter apparently ignored. We think, however, it is highly significant. * * * [W]e have sustained comprehensive and substantial restrictions upon activities of both federal and state employees lying at the core of the First Amendment. If such state regulations may survive challenges based on the explicit language of the First Amendment, there is surely even more room for restrictive regulations of state employees where the claim implicates only the more general contours of the substantive liberty interest protected by the Fourteenth Amendment.

The hair-length regulation here touches respondent as an employee of the county and, more particularly, as a policeman. Respondent's employer has, in accordance with its well-established duty to keep the peace, placed myriad demands upon the members of the police force, duties which have no counterpart with respect to the public at large. Respondent must wear a standard uniform, specific in each detail. When in uniform he must salute the flag. He may not take an active role in local political affairs by way of being a party delegate or contributing or soliciting political contributions. He may not smoke in public. All of these and other regulations of the Suffolk County Police Department infringe on respondent's freedom of choice in personal matters, and it was apparently the view of the Court of Appeals that the burden is on the State to prove a "genuine public need" for each and every one of these regulations.

This view was based upon the Court of Appeals' reasoning that the "unique Judicial deference" accorded by the judiciary to regulation of members of the military was inapplicable because there was no historical or functional justification for the characterization of the police as "para-military." But the conclusion that such cases are inapposite, however correct, in no way detracts from the deference due Suffolk County's choice of an organizational structure for its police force. Here the county has chosen a mode of organization which it undoubtedly deems the most efficient in enabling its police to carry out the duties assigned to them under state and local law. Such a choice necessarily gives weight to the overall need for discipline, esprit de corps, and uniformity.

The county's choice of an organizational structure, therefore, does not depend for its constitutional validity on any doctrine of historical prescription. Nor, indeed, has respondent made any such claim. His argument does not challenge the constitutionality of the organizational structure, but merely asserts that the present, hair-length regulation infringes his asserted liberty interest under the Fourteenth Amendment. We believe, however, that the hair-length regulation cannot be viewed in isolation, but must be rather considered in the context of the county's chosen mode of organization for its police force.

The promotion of safety of persons and property is unquestionably at the core of the State's police power, and virtually all state and local governments employ a uniformed police force to aid in the accomplishment of that purpose. Choice of organization, dress, and equipment for law enforcement personnel is a decision entitled to the same sort of presumption of legislative validity as are state choices designed to promote other aims within the cognizance of the State's police power. * * * Thus the question is not . . . whether the State can "establish" a "genuine public need" for the specific regulation. It is whether respondent can demonstrate that there is no rational connection between the regulation, based as it is on the county's method of organizing its police force, and the promotion of safety of persons and property.

We think the answer here is so clear that the District Court was quite right in the first instance to have dismissed respondent's complaint. * * * The constitutional issue to be decided . . . is whether petitioner's determination that such regulations should be enacted is so irrational that it may be branded "arbitrary," and therefore a deprivation of respondent's "liberty" interest in freedom to choose his own hairstyle. The overwhelming majority of state and local police of the present day are uniformed. This fact itself testifies to the recognition by those who direct those operations, and by the people of the States and localities who directly or indirectly choose such persons, that similarity in appearance of police officers is desirable. This choice may be based on a desire to make police officers readily recognizable to the members of the public, or a desire for the esprit de corps which such similarity is felt to inculcate within the police force itself. Either one is a sufficiently rational justification for regulations so as to defeat respondent's claim based on the liberty guarantee of the Fourteenth Amendment.

* * *

The judgment of the Court of Appeals is *Reversed.*

Justice Stevens took no part in the consideration or decision of this case.

[The concurring opinion of Justice Powell is omitted.]

Justice Marshall, with whom Justice Brennan joined, dissented.

* * *

As the Court recognizes, the Fourteenth Amendment's guarantee of liberty "protects substantive aspects of liberty against unconstitutional restrictions by the State." And we have observed that "[l]iberty under law extends to the full range of conduct which the individual is free to pursue." It seems to me manifest that that "full range of conduct" must encompass one's interest in dressing according to his own taste. * * * To say that the liberty guarantee of the Fourteenth Amendment does not encompass matters of personal appearance would be fundamentally inconsistent with the values of privacy, self-identity, autonomy, and personal integrity that I have always assumed the Constitution was designed to protect.

* * *

To my mind, the right in one's personal appearance is inextricably bound up with the historically recognized right of "every individual to the possession and control of his own person," and perhaps even more fundamentally, with "the right to be let alone—the most comprehensive of rights and the right most valued by civilized men." In an increasingly crowded society in which it is already extremely difficult to maintain one's identity and personal integrity, it would be distressing, to say the least, if the government could regulate our personal appearance unconfined by any constitutional strictures whatsoever.

Acting on its assumption that the Fourteenth Amendment does encompass a right in one's personal appearance, the Court justifies the challenged hair-length regulation on the grounds that such regulations may "be based on a desire to make police officers readily recognizable to the members of the public, or a desire for the esprit de corps which such similarity is felt to inculcate within the police force itself." While fully accepting the aims of "identifiability" and maintenance of esprit de corps, I find no rational relationship between the challenged regulation and these goals.

As for the first justification offered by the Court, I simply do not see how requiring policemen to maintain hair of under a certain length could rationally be argued to contribute to making them identifiable to the public as policemen. Surely, the fact that a uniformed police officer is wearing his hair below his collar will make him no less identifiable as a policeman. * * *

As for the Court's second justification, the fact that it is the president of the Patrolmen's Benevolent Association, in his official capacity, who has challenged the regulation here would seem to indicate that the regulation would if anything, decrease rather than increase the police force's esprit de corps. And even if one accepted the argument that substantial similarity in appearance would increase a force's esprit de corps, I simply do not understand how implementation of this regulation could be expected to create any increment in similarity of appearance among members of a uniformed police force. While the regulation prohibits hair below the ears or the collar and limits the length of sideburns, it allows the maintenance of any type of hairstyle, other than a ponytail.

* * *

The Court cautions us not to view the hair-length regulation in isolation, but rather to examine it "in the context of the county's chosen mode of organization for its police force." While the Court's caution is well taken, one should also keep in mind, as I fear the Court does not, that what is ultimately under scrutiny is neither the overall structure of the police force nor the uniform and equipment requirements to which its members are subject, but rather the regulation which dictates acceptable hair lengths. The fact that the uniform requirement, for instance, may be rationally related to the goals of increasing police officer "identifiability" and the maintenance of esprit de corps does absolutely nothing to establish the legitimacy of the hair-length regulation. I see no connection between the regulation and the offered rationales and would accordingly affirm the judgment of the Court of Appeals.

In the other case, *Bowers v. Hardwick* (1986), the Court heard a challenge to a Georgia law prohibiting sodomy between consenting adults. (See the case study at the beginning of this chapter.) This case, handed down at the end of the 1985–86 term, was the final privacy case in which Chief Justice Burger participated. He joined four of his colleagues—Justices White, Powell, Rehnquist, and O'Connor—to hold that the Georgia statute did not violate the right of privacy.

Bowers v. Hardwick

478 U.S. 186, 106 S.Ct. 2841, 92 L.Ed.2d 140 (1986)
[The facts of this case are omitted because they were presented in the case study at the beginning of this chapter.]

■ This case is important because it upheld the authority of the government to regulate matters concerning the sexual activities of consenting adults. As you read the case, consider the following questions: 1) Should the Court have examined the sodomy law in terms of its application to heterosexuals as well as to homosexuals? 2) If so, could the Court have justified two different decisions? 3) Does Justice White present an adequate explanation for the majority's conclusion that this statute passes the rational basis test?

Vote:

5 justices found the Georgia statute constitutional (White, Burger, Powell, Rehnquist, and O'Connor).

4 justices voted to strike the law as a violation of the right of privacy (Blackmun, Brennan, Marshall, and Stevens).

Justice White delivered the opinion of the Court.

* * *

* * * The issue presented is whether the Federal Constitution confers a fundamental right upon homosexuals to engage in sodomy and hence invalidates the laws of the many States that still make such conduct illegal and have done so for a very long time. The case also calls for some judgment about the limits of the Court's role in carrying out its constitutional mandate.

We first register our disagreement with the Court of Appeals and with respondent that the Court's prior cases have construed the Constitution to confer a right of privacy that extends to homosexual sodomy and for all intents and purposes have decided this case. The reach of this line of cases was sketched in *Carey v. Population Services International* (1977). *Pierce v. Society of Sisters* (1925) and *Meyer v. Nebraska* (1923) were described as dealing with child rearing and education; *Prince v. Massachusetts* (1944) with family relationships; *Skinner v. Oklahoma ex rel. Williamson* (1942) with procreation; *Loving v. Virginia* (1967) with marriage; *Griswold v. Connecticut* [1965] and *Eisenstadt v. Baird* [1972] with contraception; and *Roe v. Wade* (1973) with abortion. The latter three cases were interpreted as construing the Due Process Clause of the Fourteenth Amendment to confer a fundamental individual right to decide whether or not to beget or bear a child.

Accepting the decisions in these cases and the above description of them, we think it evident that none of the rights announced in those cases bears any resemblance to the claimed constitutional right of homosexuals to engage in acts of sodomy that is asserted in this case. No connection between family, marriage, or procreation on the one hand and homosexual activity on the other has been demonstrated, either by the Court of Appeals or by respondent. Moreover, any claim that these cases nevertheless stand for the proposition that any kind of private sexual conduct between consenting adults is constitutionally insulated from state proscription is unsupportable. Indeed, the Court's opinion in *Carey* twice asserted that the privacy right . . . did not reach so far.

Precedent aside, however, respondent would have us announce, as the Court of Appeals did, a fundamental right to engage in homosexual sodomy. This we are quite unwilling to do. It is true that despite the language of the Due Process Clauses of the Fifth and Fourteenth Amendments, which appears to focus only on the processes by which life, liberty, or property is taken, the cases are legion in which those Clauses have been interpreted to have substantive content, subsuming rights that to a great extent are immune from federal or state regulation or proscription. Among such cases are those recognizing rights that have little or no textual support in the constitutional language. * * *

Striving to assure itself and the public that announcing rights not readily identifiable in the Constitution's text involves much more than the imposition of the Justices' own choice of values on the States and the Federal Government, the Court has sought to identify the nature of the rights qualifying for heightened judicial protection. In *Palko v. Connecticut* (1937) it was said that this category includes those fundamental liberties that are "implicit in the concept of ordered liberty," such that "neither liberty nor justice would exist if [they] were sacrificed." A different description of fundamental liberties appeared in *Moore v. East Cleveland* (1977), where they are characterized as those liberties that are "deeply rooted in this Nation's history and tradition."

It is obvious to us that neither of these formulations would extend a fundamental right to homosexuals to engage in acts of consensual sodomy. Proscriptions against that conduct have ancient roots. * * * Sodomy was a criminal offense at common law and was forbidden by the laws of the original 13 States when they ratified the Bill of Rights. In 1868, when the Fourteenth Amendment was ratified, all but 5 of the 37 States in the Union had criminal sodomy laws. In fact, until 1961, all 50 States outlawed sodomy, and today, 24 States and the District of Columbia continue to provide criminal penalties for sodomy performed in private and between consenting adults. * * * Against this background, to claim that a right to engage in such conduct is "deeply rooted in this Nation's history and tradition" or "implicit in the concept of ordered liberty" is, at best, facetious.

Nor are we inclined to take a more expansive view of our authority to discover new fundamental rights imbedded in the Due Process Clause. The Court is most vulnerable and comes nearest to illegitimacy when it deals with judge-made constitutional law having little or no cognizable roots in the language or design of the Constitution. * * *

Respondent, however, asserts that the result should be different where the homosexual conduct occurs in the privacy of the home. He relies on *Stanley v. Georgia* (1969), where the Court held that the First Amendment prevents conviction for possessing and reading obscene material in the privacy of one's home. . . .

Stanley did protect conduct that would not have been protected outside the home, and it partially prevented the enforcement of state obscenity laws; but the decision was firmly grounded in the First Amendment. The right pressed upon us here has no similar support in the text of the Constitution, and it does not qualify for recognition under the prevailing principles for construing the Fourteenth Amendment. Its limits are also difficult to discern. Plainly enough, otherwise illegal conduct is not always immunized whenever it occurs in the home. Victimless crimes, such as the possession and use of illegal drugs, do not escape the law where they are committed at home. *Stanley* itself recognized that its holding offered no protection for the possession in the home of drugs, firearms, or stolen goods. And if respondent's submission is limited to the voluntary sexual conduct between consenting adults, it would be difficult, except by fiat, to limit the claimed right to homosexual conduct while leaving exposed to prosecution adultery, incest, and other sexual crimes even though they are committed in the home. We are unwilling to start down that road.

Even if the conduct at issue here is not a fundamental right, respondent asserts that there must be a rational basis for the law and that there is none in this case other than the presumed belief of a majority of the electorate in Georgia that homosexual sodomy is immoral and unacceptable. This is said to be an inadequate rationale to support the law. The law, however, is constantly based on notions of morality, and if all laws representing essentially moral choices are to be invalidated under the Due Process Clause, the courts will be very busy indeed. Even respondent makes no such claim, but insists that majority sentiments about the morality of homosexuality should be declared inadequate. We do not agree, and are unpersuaded that the sodomy laws of some 25 States should be invalidated on this basis.

Accordingly, the judgment of the Court of Appeals is *Reversed.*

[The concurring opinion of Chief Justice Burger is omitted.]

Justice Powell concurred.

I join the opinion of the Court. I agree with the Court that there is no fundamental right—i.e., no substantive right under the Due Process Clause—such as that claimed by respondent Hardwick, and found to exist by the Court of Appeals. This is not to suggest, however, that respondent may not be protected by the Eighth Amendment of the Constitution. The Georgia statute at issue in this case authorizes a court to imprison a person for up to 20 years for a single private, consensual act of sodomy. In my view, a prison sentence for such conduct—certainly a sentence of long duration—would create a serious Eighth Amendment issue. Under the Georgia statute a single act of sodomy, even in the private setting of a home, is a felony comparable in terms of the possible sentence imposed to serious felonies such as aggravated battery, first-degree arson, and robbery.

In this case, however, respondent has not been tried, much less convicted and sentenced. Moreover, respondent has not raised the Eighth Amendment issue below. For these reasons this constitutional argument is not before us.

Justice Blackmun, with whom Justice Brennan, Justice Marshall, and Justice Stevens joined, dissented.

This case is no more about "a fundamental right to engage in homosexual sodomy," as the Court purports to declare, than *Stanley v. Georgia* (1969) was about a fundamental right to watch obscene movies, or *Katz v. United States* (1967) was about a fundamental right to place interstate bets from a telephone booth. Rather, this case is about "the most comprehensive of rights and the right most valued by civilized men," namely, "the right to be let alone."

The statute at issue denies individuals the right to decide for themselves whether to engage in particular forms of private, consensual sexual activity. The Court concludes that [the statute] is valid essentially because "the laws of . . . many States . . . still make such conduct illegal and have done so for a very long time." But the fact that the moral judgments expressed by statutes like [this one] may be " 'natural and familiar . . . ought not to conclude our judgment upon the question whether statutes embodying them conflict with the Constitution of the United States.' " * * * I believe we must analyze respondent Hardwick's claim in the light of the values that underlie the constitutional right to privacy. If that right means anything, it means that, before Georgia can prosecute its citizens for making choices about the most intimate aspects of their lives, it must do more than assert that the choice they have made is an " 'abominable crime not fit to be named among Christians.' "

* * *

. . . [T]he Court's almost obsessive focus on homosexual activity is particularly hard to justify in light of the broad language Georgia has used. Unlike the Court, the Georgia Legislature has not proceeded on the assumption that homosexuals are so different from other citizens that their lives may be controlled in a way that would not be tolerated if it limited the choices of those other citizens. Rather, Georgia has provided that "[a] person commits the offense of sodomy when he performs or submits to any sexual act involving the sex organs of one person and the mouth or anus of another." The sex or status of the persons who engage in the act is irrelevant as a matter of state law. In fact, to the extent I can discern a legislative purpose for Georgia's 1968 enactment of [the statute], that purpose seems to have been to broaden the coverage of the law to reach heterosexual as well as homosexual activity. * * *

* * *

Only the most willful blindness could obscure the fact that sexual intimacy is "a sensitive, key relationship of human existence, central to family life, community welfare, and the development of human personality." The fact that individuals define themselves in a significant way through their intimate sexual relationships with others suggests, in a Nation as diverse as ours, that there may be many "right" ways of conducting those relationships, and that much of the richness of a relationship will come from the freedom an individual has to *choose* the form and nature of these intensely personal bonds.

In a variety of circumstances we have recognized that a necessary corollary of giving individuals freedom to choose how to conduct their lives is acceptance of the fact that different individuals will make different choices. * * * The Court claims that its decision today merely refuses to recognize a fundamental right to engage in homosexual sodomy; what the Court really has refused to recognize is the fundamental interest all individuals have in controlling the nature of their intimate associations with others.

* * *

The core of petitioner's defense of [the statute] . . . is that respondent and others who engage in the conduct prohibited . . . interfere with Georgia's exercise of the " 'right of the Nation and of the States to maintain a decent society.' " Essentially, petitioner argues, and the Court agrees, that the fact that the acts described . . . "for hundreds of years, if not thousands, have been uniformly condemned as immoral" is a sufficient reason to permit a State to ban them today.

I cannot agree that either the length of time a majority has held its convictions or the passions with which it defends them can withdraw legislation from this Court's scrutiny. * * *

The assertion that "traditional Judeo-Christian values proscribe" the conduct involved cannot provide an adequate justification . . . . That certain, but by no means all, religious groups condemn the behavior at issue gives the State no license to impose their judgments on the entire citizenry. The legitimacy of secular legislation depends instead on whether the State can advance some justification for its law beyond its conformity to religious doctrine. * * *

* * * Statutes banning public sexual activity are entirely consistent with protecting the individual's liberty interest in decisions concerning sexual relations: the same recognition that those decisions are intensely private which justifies protecting them from governmental interference can justify protecting individuals from unwilling exposure to the sexual activities of others. But the mere fact that intimate behavior may be punished when it takes place in public cannot dictate how States can regulate intimate behavior that occurs in intimate places.

This case involves no real interference with the rights of others, for the mere knowledge that other individuals do not adhere to one's value system cannot be a legally cognizable interest, let alone an interest that can justify invading the houses, hearts, and minds of citizens who choose to live their lives differently.

* * *

[The dissenting opinion of Justice Stevens, in which Justices Brennan and Marshall joined, is omitted.]

THE REHNQUIST COURT ERA

As the Burger Era ended, speculation continued about the future of *Roe v. Wade* and abortion rights for women. The decision in *Thornburgh* upheld that landmark precedent and invalidated significant regulations on the abortion decision, but the vote was so close that many assumed that with the Reagan and Bush appointees the Court would begin to uphold state restrictions on abortion. More specifically, pro-choice advocates were worried that *Roe v. Wade* was in great danger of being overruled altogether. Both Presidents Reagan and Bush had announced on more than one occasion their disapproval of *Roe v. Wade* and their desire to have that decision overturned. Moreover, many Court observers alleged that the abortion issue became a major litmus test for potential Supreme Court nominees. The Reagan and Bush appointments to the Court gave abortion rights advocates reason to be alarmed. Chief Justice Burger, who joined the *Roe* majority and voted to strike some abortion regulations in later cases, was succeeded by Justice Rehnquist, a dissenter in *Roe*. In post-*Roe* cases, Justice Rehnquist voted to uphold all of the challenged restrictions on abortions. The record also indicates that Antonin Scalia, Rehnquist's successor, was an opponent of abortion rights in general, and of *Roe v. Wade* in particular. The later appointments of Justices Kennedy, Souter, and Thomas increased the concerns of pro-choice advocates as to the future for abortion rights in this country. In addition, the Justice Departments in the Reagan and Bush administrations were increasingly aggressive in filing amicus briefs in Supreme Court cases encouraging the justices to uphold various regulations on abortion and ultimately to overrule *Roe*. Just how has the Rehnquist Court treated this sensitive and difficult issue? Has the Court dealt with privacy rights in other contexts, and, if so, how has it responded? As we have done throughout this book, we will examine these questions from both quantitative and doctrinal perspectives.

The results of the quantitative analysis are reported in Tables 17.1 through 17.3. The data here pertain to the Court's decisions in abortion cases. A conservative decision is one in which the Court upheld government regulations on abortion, while a liberal decision favors those persons and groups claiming that the regulation violates the right of privacy. As Table 17.1 indicates, the Rehnquist Court was more conservative (60%) than the Burger Court, whose decisions were evenly split between conservative and liberal outcomes. A word of caution is in order, however,

TABLE 17.1: Liberal/Conservative Outcomes of Abortion Cases for the Burger and Rehnquist Courts, 1969-94 Terms

	Outcomes		
Court Era	Liberal	Conservative	Totals
Burger Court, 1969-85 Terms	50% (9)	50% (9)	18
Rehnquist Court, 1986-94 Terms	40% (2)	60% (3)	5*
Totals	48% (11)	52% (12)	23

*Two cases from the United States Supreme Court Judicial Database set were excluded from this analysis: *National Organization for Women v. Scheidler* (1994) and *Madsen v. Women's Health Center* (1994). These cases did not involve abortion regulations per se. *Scheidler* was concerned with whether a federal antiracketeering law could be applied to the unlawful demonstrations of antiabortion protestors. *Madsen* is generally treated as a freedom of expression case involving the extent to which federal judges can limit the activities of antiabortion protestors around abortion clinics.

given the number of cases heard by each Court. The Burger Court heard 18 cases in this area, while the Rehnquist Court heard only five cases. Nevertheless, the Rehnquist Court issued a conservative decision in three of its five abortion cases. Moreover, the Court's record may be even more conservative than the data actually indicate because in two of the cases, several different provisions of statutes were involved. While the Court struck down parts of the statutes, the overall result was to uphold the regulation. This will be seen more clearly in the discussions of the cases themselves.

With respect to the individual justices on the Rehnquist Court, Table 17.2 illustrates the serious polarization that exists on the issue of abortion. At one end of the spectrum, Chief Justice Rehnquist and Justices Scalia, and White voted for conservative outcomes in all five cases, while at the other end, Justices Blackmun, Marshall, and Brennan cast liberal votes in all of the cases in which they

TABLE 17.2: Liberal/Conservative Voting Records of Justices of the Rehnquist Court in Abortion Cases, 1986-94 Terms

Justices	Liberal Votes	Conservative Votes
Blackmun	100% (5)	0% (0)
Marshall	100% (4)	0% (0)
Brennan	100% (3)	0% (0)
Stevens	80% (4)	20% (1)
O'Connor	60% (3)	40% (2)
Souter	50% (1)	50% (1)
Kennedy	20% (1)	80% (4)
Thomas	0% (0)	100% (1)
Rehnquist	0% (0)	100% (5)
White	0% (0)	100% (5)
Scalia	0% (0)	100% (5)
Powell	Did not participate	
Ginsburg	Did not participate	
Breyer	Did not participate	

participated—five, four, and three, respectively. Justice Kennedy joined his conservative colleagues in four of the five cases, while Justice Stevens took a liberal position in four of the five cases. Justices Souter and Thomas participated in the fewest cases, two and one, respectively, with Souter casting one vote each way, and Thomas casting his in a conservative manner. While Justice O'Connor's scores indicate that she voted for a conservative outcome in only two of the five cases, this is somewhat misleading. In two of the three cases where she is reported to have taken the liberal position, this is only partially correct. While she voted to invalidate part of a challenged statute, the overall result in these cases was to preserve most of the other regulations being challenged. This also was true for Kennedy and Souter in one of the cases. We will illustrate this more clearly when the cases themselves are discussed.

The final aspect of the quantitative analysis is reported in Table 17.3. There we find that three voting blocs existed on the Rehnquist Court in its 1986–93 terms: 1) a four-person liberal bloc consisting of Justices Brennan, Marshall, Blackmun, and Stevens, 2) a four-member conservative bloc made up of Chief Justice Rehnquist and Justices White, Scalia, and Kennedy, and 3) one two-person bloc, consisting of Justices Stevens and O'Connor. The significance of this latter bloc, however, is uncertain, given the concerns raised above regarding O'Connor's votes.

The doctrinal analysis in Table 17.4 supports the conclusion that the Rehnquist Court has made significant conservative modifications in constitutional law with respect to abortion rights. In three of the five cases, the Court's decision was based on either a conservative interpretation of existing precedent (*Akron II* and *Rust*) or a conservative modification of existing precedent (*Webster*). In addition, while *Hodgson* appears to involve a liberal interpretation of existing precedent because the Court struck down one section of a parental notification statute, one can argue that the outcome was actually conservative. This is so because in approving the second section of the statute, the Court effectively upheld the challenged regulation. Finally, *Casey* represents a liberal interpretation of existing precedent in that the Court explicitly affirmed *Roe* but, again, most of the challenged provisions were upheld. We move now to a more detailed discussion of these cases.

TABLE 17.3: Bloc Voting Analysis of the Rehnquist Court in Abortion Cases, 1986-94 Terms (Percent Agreement Rates)

	BR	MA	BL	ST	OC	KE	WH	RE	SC
Brennan	—	100	100	67	33	0	0	0	0
Marshall	100	—	100	75	50	0	0	0	0
Blackmun	100	100	—	80	60	20	0	0	0
Stevens	67	75	80	—	80	40	20	20	20
O'Connor	33	50	60	80	—	60	40	40	40
Kennedy	0	0	20	40	60	—	80	80	80
White	0	0	0	20	40	80	—	100	100
Rehnquist	0	0	0	20	40	80	100	—	100
Scalia	0	0	0	20	40	80	100	100	—

Court Mean = 44
Sprague Criterion = 72
Liberal bloc: Brennan, Marshall, Blackmun, Stevens = 87
Conservative bloc: Kennedy, White, Rehnquist, Scalia = 90
Additional bloc: Stevens, O'Connor = 80

TABLE 17.4: A Framework for the Doctrinal Analysis of the Rehnquist Court's Abortion Cases, 1986-94 Terms

		Treatment of Precedent					
Major or Minor Importance	**Majority or Plurality Opinion**	Creation of New Liberal Precedent	Liberal Modification of Existing Precedent	Liberal Interpretation of Existing Precedent	Conservative Interpretation of Existing Precedent	Conservative Modification of Existing Precedent	Creation of New Conservative Precedent
Major	Majority				Akron II (1990) Rust v. Sullivan (1991)		
	Plurality			Hodgson v. Minn (1990) Planned Parenthood v. Casey (1992)		Webster v. Reprod Health Services (1989)	
Minor	Majority						
	Plurality						

Reproductive Rights Cases

The Rehnquist Court did not hear its first privacy case until its third term, 1988–89, and, as expected, the case involved abortion regulations. Perhaps not surprisingly, the case arose in Missouri, a state that has been at the center of the abortion controversy in previous Supreme Court decisions. *Webster v. Reproductive Health Services* (1989) was closely watched by legal observers and activists on both sides because a host of anti-choice groups, state legislators, members of Congress, and the Bush administration filed amicus briefs urging the Court to uphold the regulations and, more importantly, to overturn *Roe*. In fact, the Bush administration was granted ten minutes of oral argument to present its views. Because the new solicitor general was not yet confirmed at the time of oral argument, Charles Fried, President Reagan's solicitor general, argued on behalf of the Bush administration. In his presentation Fried declared, "What is necessary is for the Court to return to legislatures an opportunity in some substantial way to express their preference, which the Court says they may express, for normal childbirth over abortion, and *Roe* stands as a significant barrier to that" (Craig and O'Brien 1993, p. 229). Given the close vote in *Thornburgh* (5-4) and the appointments of Justices Scalia and Kennedy, it seemed a distinct possibility that Fried and others would be successful in their efforts. This was not the case, however, because although the Court refused to invalidate any of the regulations being challenge, a majority did not agree to overturn *Roe*.

In *Webster*, four sections of a Missouri statute were challenged: 1) the preamble, which declared that "life begins at conception," 2) a prohibition on the use of public facilities or employees to perform abortions, 3) a prohibition on public funding of abortion counseling, and 4) a requirement that physicians conduct viability tests prior to performing abortions.

By a 5-4 vote, the Court upheld the fetal viability testing provision and the section prohibiting public facilities and employees from being used in abortions, and chose not to rule on the preamble or the prohibition on public funding of abortion counseling. There was no majority opinion, however. Chief Justice Rehnquist announced the decision in a plurality opinion joined by Justices White and Kennedy, while Justices O'Connor and Scalia agreed with the result reached but issued separate opinions concurring in part. Justice Blackmun issued a dissenting opinion for himself and Justices Brennan and Marshall, while Justice Stevens wrote an additional dissent. With respect to the preamble's declaration regarding the beginning of life, Rehnquist argued that it did not regulate abortion but merely expressed the state's value judgment favoring childbirth over abortion. Thus, he said, there was no need to decide on its constitutionality. "It will be enough for federal courts to address the meaning of the preamble should it be applied to restrict the activities of appellees in some concrete way" (492 U.S. at 506). Similarly, the plurality dismissed the part of the complaint regarding the prohibition on public funds for abortion counseling after the state's interpretation of that section persuaded the appellees that they were not "adversely affected" by it. Rehnquist used the precedents from *Maher*, *Poelker*, and *McRae* in accepting the prohibition of public facilities and employees from being used in performing abortions. "As in those cases, the State's decision here to use public facilities and staff to encourage childbirth over abortion 'places no government obstacle in the path of a woman who chooses to terminate her pregnancy.' * * * *Maher*, *Poelker*, and *McRae* all support the view that the State need not commit any resources to facilitating abortions . . ." (492 U.S. at 509, 511).

The controversy over fetal viability testing stemmed from different interpretations of what that section of the law required. The challengers argued, and the court of appeals agreed, that these tests for gestational age, fetal weight, and lung maturity were mandated for *all* women seeking abortions at the twenty-week stage of gestation or beyond. On the other hand, the state contended that the law was not so rigid but provided the physician with discretion in making decisions about viability and in prescribing these tests. Accepting the state's interpretation, Rehnquist wrote, "We think the viability testing provision makes sense only if the second sentence is read to require only those tests that are useful to making subsidiary findings as to viability. If we construe this provision to require a physician to perform those tests needed to make the three specified findings *in all circumstances,* . . . the second sentence . . . would conflict with the first sentence's *requirement* that a physician apply his reasonable professional skill and judgment" (492 U.S. at 514–515). In addition, in examining the validity of this viability-testing provision, the plurality ignited a firestorm by implicating *Roe*. The provision was aimed at promoting fetal life, which *Roe* permits only in the third trimester. Because the twenty-week stage falls in the second trimester of pregnancy, Rehnquist claimed that the *Roe* trimester approach had to be abandoned. Despite this significant change, Rehnquist insisted that *Roe* had not been overruled and that there was no need to do so.

This treatment of *Roe* is where Justice O'Connor parted company with the plurality. She concluded that the viability-testing provision was constitutional because it did not "impose an undue burden on a woman's abortion decision" (492 U.S. at 530), but she denied that *Roe* had to be implicated in order to reach this conclusion. "I do not understand these viability testing requirements to conflict with any of the Court's past decisions concerning state regulation of abortion. Therefore, there is no necessity to accept the State's invitation to reexamine . . . *Roe v. Wade* (1973). * * * When the constitutional invalidity of a State's abortion statute actually turns on the constitutional validity of *Roe v. Wade,* there will be time enough to reexamine *Roe*. And to do so carefully" (492 U.S. at 525–26). On the other hand, Justice Scalia attacked the plurality for not explicitly overruling *Roe*. "It thus appears that the mansion of constitutionalized abortion-law, constructed overnight in *Roe v. Wade,* must be disassembled door-jamb by door-jamb, and never entirely brought down, no matter how wrong it may be" (492 U.S. at 537).

Writing for himself and Justices Brennan and Marshall, Justice Blackmun declared that all four of the challenged provisions were unconstitutional, but he directed most of his dissent to the fetal viability-testing section. In his view, the provision was clearly invalid because it required these tests for every twenty-week fetus. Medical evidence suggested that these tests were dangerous for both the woman and the fetus, and therefore they were not related to promoting maternal and fetal health. Furthermore, he criticized the plurality for attacking the trimester framework and undercutting *Roe,* insisting that it was the most workable approach to deciding cases involving abortion regulations. In a particularly striking passage, Blackmun expressed his pessimism about the impact of the decision both on women and on the legitimacy of the Court. "I fear for the future. I fear for the liberty and equality of the millions of women who have lived and come of age in the 16 years since *Roe* was decided. I fear for the integrity of, and public esteem for, this Court" (492 U.S. at 538).

Webster v. Reproductive Health Services

492 U.S. 490, 109 S.Ct. 3040, 106 L.Ed.2d 410 (1989)

■ In 1986, the Missouri legislature passed a law placing a number of restrictions on abortion. Upon a challenge by a group of physicians, nurses, and abortion clinics, a federal district court invalidated several provisions of the act. A court of appeals affirmed the district court's decision almost in its entirety. The state appealed to the U.S. Supreme Court, and the Court agreed to address four sections of the act: First, the preamble stated that "life begins at conception" and "unborn children have protectable interests in life, health, and well-being." Second, the statute prohibited the use of public facilities or employees to perform or assist in abortions except those necessary to save the life of the mother. This would prevent even those women who could pay for their own abortions from being able to obtain one if their private doctors worked in public hospitals. Third, a section of the law prohibited public funds from being used to "encourage or counsel a woman to have an abortion not necessary to save her life." Fourth, a section on tests for determining fetal viability read as follows: "Before a physician performs an abortion on a woman he has reason to believe is carrying an unborn child of twenty or more weeks gestational age, the physician shall first determine if the unborn child is viable. . . . * * * In making this determination of viability, the physician shall perform or cause to be performed such medical examinations and tests as are necessary to make a finding of the gestational age, weight, and lung maturity of the unborn child . . ." (492 U.S. at 513).

This case is important because it is the first decision to undercut severely the provisions of *Roe v. Wade* (1973). As you read this case, consider these questions: 1) Is the Rehnquist plurality disingenuous in stating that *Roe* was not being overruled, given its attack upon the trimester framework? 2) Were Justice Blackmun's concerns about the implications of *Webster* for the future of abortion rights well founded, or was he overreacting to the decision?

VOTE:

5 justices voted to uphold the law (Rehnquist, White, O'Connor, Scalia, and Kennedy).

4 justices found the law unconstitutional (Blackmun, Brennan, Marshall, and Stevens).

Chief Justice Rehnquist announced the judgment of the Court and delivered the opinion of the Court.

* * *

The state contends that the preamble itself is precatory and imposes no substantive restrictions on abortions, and that appellees therefore do not have standing to challenge it. Appellees, on the other hand, insist that the preamble is an operative part of the Act intended to guide the interpretation of other provisions of the Act. * * *

* * *

We think the extent to which the preamble's language might be used to interpret other state statutes or regulations is something that only the courts of Missouri can definitively decide. * * * It will be time enough for federal courts to address the meaning of the preamble should it be applied to restrict the activities of appellees in some concrete way. Until then, this Court "is not empowered to decide . . . abstract propositions, or to declare, for the government of future cases, principles or rules of law which cannot affect the result as to the thing in issue in the case before it." We therefore need not pass on the constitutionality of the Act's preamble.

Section 188.210 provides that "[i]t shall be unlawful for any public employee within the scope of his employment to perform or assist an abortion, not necessary to save the life of the mother," while section 188.215 makes it "unlawful for any public facility to be used for the purpose of performing or assisting an abortion not necessary to save the life of the mother." The Court of Appeals held that these provisions contravened this Court's abortion decisions. We take the contrary view.

* * * In *Maher v. Roe* [1977], the Court upheld a Connecticut welfare regulation under which Medicaid recipients received payments for medical services related to childbirth, but not for nontherapeutic abortions. The Court rejected the claim that this unequal subsidization of childbirth and abortion was impermissible under *Roe v. Wade*. * * * Relying on *Maher*, the Court in *Poelker v. Doe* (1977) held that the city of St. Louis committed "no constitutional violation . . . in electing, as a policy choice, to provide publicly financed hospital services for childbirth without providing corresponding services for nontherapeutic abortions."

More recently, in *Harris v. McRae* (1980), the Court upheld "the most restrictive version of the Hyde Amendment," which withheld from States federal funds under the Medicaid program to reimburse the costs of abortions, " 'except where the life of the mother would be endangered if the fetus were carried to term.' " As in *Maher* and *Poelker*, the Court required only a showing that Congress' authorization of "reimbursement for medically necessary services generally, but not for certain medically necessary abortions" was rationally related to the legitimate governmental goal of encouraging childbirth.

* * *

* * * As in those cases, the State's decision here to use public facilities and staff to encourage childbirth over abortion "places no governmental obstacle in the path of a woman who chooses to terminate her pregnancy." Just as Congress' refusal to fund abortions in *McRae* left "an indigent woman with at least the same range of choice in deciding whether to obtain a medically necessary abortion as she would have had if Congress had chosen to subsidize no health care costs at all," Missouri's refusal to allow public employees to perform abortions in public hospitals leaves a pregnant woman with the same choices as if the State had chosen not to operate any public hospitals at all. The challenged provisions only restrict a woman's ability to obtain an abortion to the

extent that she chooses to use a physician affiliated with a public hospital. This circumstance is more easily remedied, and thus considerably less burdensome, than indigency, which "may make it difficult—and in some cases, perhaps, impossible—for some women to have abortions" without public funding. Having held that the State's refusal to fund abortions does not violate *Roe v. Wade,* it strains logic to reach a contrary result for the use of public facilities and employees. * * *

* * *

Maher, Poelker, and *McRae* all support the view that the State need not commit any resources to facilitating abortions, even if it can turn a profit by doing so. In *Poelker,* the suit was filed by an indigent who could not afford to pay for an abortion, but the ban on the performance of nontherapeutic abortions in city-owned hospitals applied whether or not the pregnant woman could pay. * * * Thus we uphold the Act's restrictions on the use of public employees and facilities for the performance or assistance of nontherapeutic abortions.

The Missouri Act contains three provisions relating to "encouraging or counseling a woman to have an abortion not necessary to save her life." Section 188.205 states that no public funds can be used for this purpose; section 188.210 states that public employees cannot, within the scope of their employment, engage in such speech; and section 188.215 forbids such speech in public facilities. The Court of Appeals did not consider section 188.205 separately from sections 188.210 and 188.215. It held that all three of these provisions were unconstitutionally vague, and that "the ban on using public funds, employees, and facilities to encourage or counsel a woman to have an abortion is an unacceptable infringement of the woman's Fourteenth Amendment right to choose an abortion after receiving the medical information necessary to exercise the right knowingly and intelligently."

Missouri has chosen only to appeal the Court of Appeals' invalidation of the public funding provision, section 188.205. * * * We accept, for purposes of decision, the State's claim that section 188.205 "is not directed at the conduct of any physician or health care provider, private or public," but "is directed solely at those persons responsible for expending public funds."

Appellees contend that they are not "adversely" affected under the State's interpretation of section 188.205, and therefore that there is no longer a case or controversy before us on this question. * * * We accordingly direct the Court of Appeals to vacate the judgment of the District Court with instructions to dismiss the relevant part of the complaint. * * *

Section 188.029 of the Missouri Act provides:

> "Before a physician performs an abortion on a woman he has reason to believe is carrying an unborn child of twenty or more weeks gestational age, the physician shall first determine if the unborn child is viable by using and exercising that degree of care, skill, and proficiency commonly exercised by the ordinarily skillful, careful, and prudent physician engaged in similar practice under the same or similar conditions. In making this determination of viability, the physician shall perform or cause to be performed such medical examinations and tests as are necessary to make a finding of the gestational age, weight, and lung maturity of the unborn child and shall enter such findings and determination of viability in the medical record of the mother."

* * *

The Court of Appeals read section 188.029 as requiring that after 20 weeks "doctors *must* perform tests to find gestational age, fetal weight and lung maturity." The court indicated that the tests needed to determine fetal weight at 20 weeks are "unreliable and inaccurate" and would add $125 to $250 to the cost of an abortion. It also stated that "amniocentesis, the only method available to determine lung maturity, is contrary to accepted medical practice until 28-30 weeks of gestation, expensive, and imposes significant health risks for both the pregnant woman and the fetus."

* * *

We think the viability-testing provision makes sense only if the second sentence is read to require only those tests that are useful to making subsidiary findings as to viability. If we construe this provision to require a physician to perform those tests needed to make the three specified findings *in all circumstances,* including when the physician's reasonable professional judgment indicates that the tests would be irrelevant to determining viability or even dangerous to the mother and the fetus, the second sentence of section 188.029 would conflict with the first sentence's *requirement* that a physician apply his reasonable professional skill and judgment. It would also be incongruous to read this provision, especially the word "necessary," to require the performance of tests irrelevant to the expressed statutory purpose of determining viability. * * *

The viability-testing provision of the Missouri Act is concerned with promoting the State's interest in potential human life rather than in maternal health. Section 188.029 creates what is essentially a presumption of viability at 20 weeks, which the physician must rebut with tests indicating that the fetus is not viable prior to performing an abortion. It also directs the physician's determination as to viability by specifying consideration, if feasible, of gestational age, fetal weight, and lung capacity. * * *

In *Roe v. Wade,* the Court recognized that the State has "important and legitimate" interests in protecting maternal health and in the potentiality of human life. During the second trimester, the State "may, if it chooses, regulate the abortion procedure in ways that are reasonably related to maternal health." * * * After viability, when the State's interest in potential human life was held to become compelling, the State "may, if it chooses, regulate, and even proscribe, abortion except where it is necessary, in appropriate medical judgment, for the preservation of the life or health of the mother."

* * *

We think that the doubt cast upon the Missouri statute . . . is not so much a flaw in the statute as it is a reflection of the fact that the rigid trimester analysis of the course of a pregnancy enunciated in *Roe* has resulted in . . . making constitutional law in this area a virtual Procrustean bed. * * *

Stare decisis is a cornerstone of our legal system, but it has less power in constitutional cases, where, save for constitutional amendments, this Court is the only body able to make needed changes. We have not refrained from reconsideration of a prior construction of the Constitution that has proved "unsound in principle and unworkable in practice." We think the *Roe* trimester framework falls into that category.

In the first place, the rigid *Roe* framework is hardly consistent with the notion of a Constitution cast in general terms, as ours is, and usually speaking in general principles, as ours does. The key elements of the *Roe* framework—trimesters and viability—are not found in the text of the Constitution or in any place else one would expect to find a constitutional principle. Since the bounds of the inquiry are essentially indeterminate, the result has been a web of legal rules that have become increasingly intricate, resembling a code of regulations rather than a body of constitutional doctrine. * * *

In the second place, we do not see why the State's interest in protecting potential human life should come into existence only at the point of viability, and that there should therefore be a rigid line allowing state regulation after viability but prohibiting it before viability. * * * "[T]he State's interest, if compelling after viability, is equally compelling before viability."

The tests that section 188.029 requires the physician to perform are designed to determine viability. The State here has chosen viability as the point at which its interest in potential human life must be safeguarded. It is true that the tests in question increase the expense of abortion, and regulate the discretion of the physician in determining the viability of the fetus. Since the tests will undoubtedly show in many cases that the fetus is not viable, the tests will have been performed for what were in fact second-trimester abortions. But we are satisfied that the requirement of these tests permissibly furthers the State's interest in protecting potential human life, and we therefore believe section 188.029 to be constitutional.

* * *

Both appellants and the United States as *Amicus Curiae* have urged that we overrule our decision in *Roe v. Wade.* The facts of the present case, however, differ from those at issue in *Roe.* Here, Missouri has determined that viability is the point at which its interest in potential human life must be safeguarded. In *Roe,* on the other hand, the Texas statute criminalized the performance of *all* abortions, except when the mother's life was at stake. This case therefore affords us no occasion to revisit the holding of *Roe,* which was that the Texas statute unconstitutionally infringed the right to an abortion derived from the Due Process Clause, and we leave it undisturbed. To the extent indicated in our opinion, we would modify and narrow *Roe* and succeeding cases.

Because none of the challenged provisions of the Missouri Act properly before us conflict with the Constitution, the judgment of the Court of Appeals is *Reversed.*

Justice O'Connor concurred in part and concurred in the judgment.

* * *

Unlike the plurality, I do not understand these viability testing requirements to conflict with any of the Court's past decisions concerning state regulation of abortion. Therefore, there is no necessity to accept the State's invitation to reexamine the constitutional validity of *Roe v. Wade* (1973). Where there is no need to decide a constitutional question, it is a venerable principle of this Court's adjudicatory processes not to do so for "[t]he Court will not 'anticipate a question of constitutional law in advance of the necessity of deciding it.' " Neither will it generally "formulate a rule of constitutional law broader than is required by the precise facts to which it is to be applied." Quite simply, "[i]t is not the habit of the court to decide questions of a constitutional nature unless absolutely necessary to a decision of the case." The Court today has accepted the State's every interpretation of its abortion statute and has upheld, under our existing precedents, every provision of that statute which is properly before us. Precisely for this reason reconsideration of *Roe* falls not into any "good-cause exception" to this "fundamental rule of judicial restraint. . . ." When the constitutional invalidity of a State's abortion statute actually turns on the constitutional validity of *Roe v. Wade,* there will be time enough to reexamine *Roe.* And to do so carefully.

* * *

Justice Scalia concurred in part and concurred in the judgment.

* * * As to Part II-D [of the plurality's opinion], I share Justice Blackmun's view that it effectively would overrule *Roe v. Wade* (1973). I think that should be done, but would do it more explicitly. * * *

* * *

* * * The result of our vote today is that we will not reconsider that prior opinion, even if most of the Justices think it is wrong, unless we have before us a statute that in fact contradicts it—and even then (under our newly discovered "no-broader-than-necessary" requirement) only minor problematical aspects of *Roe* will be reconsidered, unless one expects State legislatures to adopt provisions whose compliance with *Roe* cannot even be argued with a straight face. It thus appears that the mansion of constitutionalized abortion-law, constructed overnight in *Roe v. Wade,* must be disassembled door-jamb by door-jamb, and never entirely brought down, no matter how wrong it may be.

* * *

Justice Blackmun, with whom Justice Brennan and Justice Marshall joined, concurred in part and dissented in part.

Today, *Roe v. Wade* (1973), and the fundamental constitutional right of women to decide whether to terminate a pregnancy, survive but are not secure. Although the Court extricates itself from this case without making a single, even incremental, change in the law of abortion, the plurality and Justice Scalia would overrule *Roe* (the first silently, the other explicitly) and would return to the States virtually unfettered authority to control the quintessentially intimate, personal, and life-directing decision whether to carry a fetus to term. Although today, no less than yesterday, the Constitution and the decisions of this Court prohibit a State from enacting laws that inhibit women from the meaningful exercise of that right, a plurality of this Court implicitly invites every state legislature to enact more and more restrictive abortion regulations in order to provoke more and more test cases, in the hope that sometime down the line the Court will return the law of procreative freedom to the severe limitations that generally prevailed in this country before January 22, 1973. Never in my memory has a plurality announced a judgment of this Court that so foments disregard for the law and for our standing decisions.

* * *

I fear for the future. I fear for the liberty and equality of the millions of women who have lived and come of age in the 16 years since *Roe* was decided. I fear for the integrity of, and public esteem for, this Court.

I dissent.

* * * Although I disagree with the plurality's consideration of sections 1.205, 188.210, and 188.215, and am especially disturbed by its misapplication of our past decisions in upholding Missouri's ban on the performance of abortions at "public facilities," the plurality's discussion of these provisions is merely prologue to its consideration of the statute's viability-testing requirement, section 188.029—the only section of the Missouri statute that the plurality construes as implicating *Roe* itself. There, tucked away at the end of its opinion, the plurality suggests a radical reversal of the law of abortion; and there, primarily, I direct my attention.

In the plurality's view, the viability-testing provision imposes a burden on second-trimester abortions as a way of furthering the State's interest in protecting the potential life of the fetus. Since under the *Roe* framework, the State may not fully regulate abortion in the interest of potential life (as opposed to maternal health) until the third trimester, the plurality finds it necessary, in order to save the Missouri testing provision, to throw out *Roe*'s trimester framework. In flat contradiction to *Roe,* the plurality concludes that the State's interest in potential life is compelling before viability, and upholds the testing provision because it "permissibly furthers" that state interest.

* * *

Had the plurality read the statute as written, it would have had no cause to reconsider the *Roe* framework. As properly construed, the viability-testing provision does not pass constitutional muster under even a rational-basis standard, the least restrictive level of review applied by this Court. By mandating tests to determine fetal weight and lung maturity for every fetus thought to be more than 20 weeks gestational age, the statute requires physicians to undertake procedures, such as amniocentesis, that, in the situation presented, have no medical justification, impose significant additional health risks on both the pregnant woman and the fetus, and bear no rational relation to the State's interest in protecting fetal life. As written, section 188.029 is an arbitrary imposition of discomfort, risk, and expense, furthering no discernible interest except to make the procurement of an abortion as arduous and difficult as possible. Thus, were it not for the plurality's tortured effort to avoid the plain import of section 188.029, it could have struck down the testing provision as patently irrational irrespective of the *Roe* framework.

* * *

[T]he plurality asserts that the trimester framework cannot stand because the State's interest in potential life is compelling throughout pregnancy, not merely after viability. The opinion contains not one word of rationale for its view of the State's interest. This "it-is-so-because-we-say-so" jurisprudence constitutes nothing other than an attempted exercise of brute force; reason, much less persuasion, has no place.

* * *

For my own part, I remain convinced, as six other Members of this Court 16 years ago were convinced, that the *Roe* framework, and the viability standard in particular, fairly, sensibly, and effectively functions to safeguard the constitutional liberties of pregnant women while recognizing and accommodating the State's interest in potential human life. The viability line reflects the biological facts and truths of fetal development; it marks that threshold moment prior to which a fetus cannot survive separate from the woman and cannot reasonably and objectively be regarded as a subject of rights or interests distinct from, or paramount to, those of the pregnant woman. At the same time, the viability standard takes account of the undeniable fact that as the fetus evolves into its postnatal form, and as it loses its dependence on the uterine environment, the State's interest in the fetus' potential human life, and in fostering a regard for human life in general, becomes compelling. As a practical matter, because viability follows "quickening"—the point at which a woman feels movement in her womb—and because viability occurs no earlier than 23 weeks gestational age, it establishes an easily applicable standard for regulating abortion while providing a pregnant woman ample time to exercise her fundamental right with her responsible physician to terminate her pregnancy. * * *

Having contrived an opportunity to reconsider the *Roe* framework, and then having discarded that framework, the plurality finds the testing provision unobjectionable because it "permissibly furthers the State's interest in protecting potential human life." This newly minted standard is circular and totally meaningless. Whether a challenged abortion regulation "permissibly furthers" a legitimate state interest is the *question* that courts must answer in abortion cases, not the standard for courts to apply. In keeping with the rest of its opinion, the plurality makes no attempt to explain or to justify its new standard, either in the abstract or as applied in this case. Nor could it. * * * One thing is clear, however: were the plurality's "permissibly furthers" standard adopted by the Court, for all practical purposes, *Roe* would be overruled.

* * *

Thus, "not with a bang, but a whimper," the plurality discards a landmark case of the last generation, and casts into darkness the hopes and visions of every woman in this country who had come to believe that the Constitution guaranteed her the right to exercise some control over her unique ability to bear children. The plurality does so either oblivious or insensitive to the fact that millions of women, and their families, have ordered their lives around the right to reproductive choice, and that this right has become vital to the full participation of women in the economic and political walks of American life. The plurality would clear the way once again for government to force upon women the physical labor and specific and direct medical and psychological harms that may accompany carrying a fetus to term. The plurality would clear the way again for the State to conscript a woman's body and to force upon her a "distressful life and future."

The result, as we know from experience, would be that every year hundreds of thousands of women, in desperation, would defy the law, and place their health and safety in the unclean and unsympathetic hands of back-alley abortionists, or they would attempt to perform abortions upon themselves, with disastrous results. Every year, many women, especially poor and minority women, would die or suffer debilitating physical trauma, all in the name of enforced morality or religious dictates or lack of compassion, as it may be.

* * *

For today, at least, the law of abortion stands undisturbed. For today, the women of this Nation still retain the liberty to control their destinies. But the signs are evident and very ominous, and a chill wind blows.

* * *

[The opinion of Justice Stevens, concurring in part and dissenting in part, is omitted.]

The *Webster* decision effectively invited states to pass additional regulations on abortion, and they could be fairly confident that those regulations would be upheld. There were only a few states that did so, however, because groups opposed to abortion lacked sufficient political influence in most states (Smith 1993).

In two decisions handed down on the same day in the term following *Webster*, the Court returned to the subject of parental notification of minors seeking to obtain abortions. The first of these, *Hodgson v. Minnesota* (1990), concerned two sections of a Minnesota law requiring such notification. The first section, Subdivision 2, required physicians to notify both parents of a minor before performing an abortion on her, and it ordered physicians to wait forty-eight hours after notification before performing the abortion. The section applied even to minors whose parents were separated or divorced, as well as in cases of desertion by one parent. Exemptions were made for medical emergencies, for situations where both parents had consented in writing, and for cases when the minor was a victim of parental abuse or neglect. Subdivision 6 established a judicial bypass procedure to take effect if the first section were declared unconstitutional. Under this provision, "If the pregnant minor can convince 'any judge of a court of competent jurisdiction' that she is 'mature and capable of giving informed consent to the proposed abortion,' or that an abortion without notice to both parents would be in her best interest, the court can authorize the physician to proceed without notice" (497 U.S. at 427). A federal district court struck down both sections of the law, and the court of appeals invalidated the first section but upheld the section establishing the judicial bypass procedure.

The Supreme Court affirmed the judgment of the court of appeals. Five justices—Stevens, Brennan, Marshall, Blackmun, and O'Connor—declared Subdivision 2 unconstitutional, while O'Connor joined Chief Justice Rehnquist and Justices Kennedy, Scalia, and White to uphold Subdivision 6. Because Subdivision 6 was put in place in case Subdivision 2 was declared unconstitutional, the effect of the ruling then was to allow a two-parent notification requirement as long as a judicial bypass procedure was included. Writing for the majority on Subdivision 2, Justice Stevens, who previously had voted to sustain parental consent and parental notification laws, distinguished those cases on the grounds that they required consent or notification of only one parent. Moreover, he emphasized lower court findings that the law could subject minors to "major trauma" as well as to family violence. Finally, he saw no legitimate state interest being achieved by the two-parent notification requirement. "The usual justification for a parental consent or notification provision is that it supports the authority of a parent who is presumed to act in the minor's best interest. * * * To the extent that such an interest is legitimate, it would fully be served by a requirement that the minor notify one parent who can then seek the counsel of his or her mate or any other party . . ." (497 U.S. at 450).

With regard to both Subdivisions 2 and 6, Justice Kennedy wrote for a plurality that included Chief Justice Rehnquist and Justices White and Scalia. These four saw the two-parent requirement as consistent with the standards set forth in *Bellotti II*. Furthermore, they would uphold it with or without the judicial bypass procedure. Justice O'Connor, however, voted to uphold the law only because it included the bypass provision. From her perspective, "Subdivision 6 passes constitutional muster because the interference with the internal operation of the family required by subdivision 2 simply does not exist where the minor can avoid notifying one or both parents by use of the bypass procedure" (497 U.S. at 461).

In *Hodgson*'s companion case, *Ohio v. Akron Center for Reproductive Health* (1990), *Akron II*, the Court also ruled on a one-parent notification requirement that included a judicial bypass procedure. Under this Ohio law, physicians were to notify one parent and then to wait twenty-four hours before performing an abortion on a minor. The law permitted another relative to be notified upon testimony from that individual that the minor could be subject to physical or emotional abuse by the parent. The statute was invalidated at the district and appellate levels.

A six-member majority consisting of Chief Justice Rehnquist and Justices Kennedy, White, O'Connor, Scalia, and Stevens reversed the lower courts' rulings, holding that the Ohio statute was consistent with *Bellotti II* and similar precedents. The major contention over the law concerned the judicial bypass procedure, which the challengers argued did not satisfy the requirements of *Bellotti II.* Justice Kennedy, writing for the majority, disagreed. To begin with, Kennedy contended that the Court had never *required* parental notification laws to contain judicial bypass procedures, and he said there was no reason to address that issue in this case. Nonetheless, he wrote, "whether or not the Fourteenth Amendment requires notice statutes to contain bypass procedures, [Ohio's] bypass procedure meets the requirements identified for parental consent statutes in *Danforth, Bellotti, Ashcroft,* and *Akron*" (497 U.S. at 510). Finally, using language associated most with Justice O'Connor, Kennedy said that the Ohio law did not "impose an undue burden" on minors seeking to obtain abortions.

The dissenters, Justices Blackmun, Brennan, and Marshall, saw the statute as simply a way for the state to obstruct pregnant minors' abortion decisions, and they claimed that the state did not demonstrate any important interest being furthered by the law. "The language of the Ohio statute," Justice Blackmun contended, "purports to follow the standards for a bypass procedure that are set forth in *Bellotti II,* but at each stage along the way, the statute deliberately places 'substantial state-created obstacles in the pregnant [minor's] path to an abortion,' in the legislative hope that she will stumble, perhaps fall, and at least ensuring that she 'conquer a multi-faceted obstacle course' before she is able to exercise her constitutional right to an abortion" (497 U.S. at 527).

Except for the *Harris v. McRae* (1980) decision regarding public funding of abortion, abortion cases decided by the Supreme Court generally involved state regulations. In *Rust v. Sullivan* (1991), however, the Court was faced with a federal restriction on abortion. This was David Souter's first abortion case, and there was much interest regarding his position on this issue given the record of his predecessor, William Brennan, as a strong supporter of abortion rights. The case arose over regulations developed and implemented by the Reagan administration with respect to family-planning clinics receiving federal funds. Under a section of a 1970 statute, family-planning clinics were allotted federal financial support, provided that the funds not be used in programs where abortion was a method of family planning. The early interpretation of this provision was that clinics receiving federal monies could not provide abortions, but could provide abortion counseling. In 1988, the Reagan administration issued stricter regulations, prohibiting clinics receiving federal monies from counseling pregnant women about abortions or from even broaching the subject of abortion. This "gag rule," as it was called, was challenged by Planned Parenthood on the grounds that it was not authorized by the statute and that it violated First Amendment freedom of speech and abortion rights guaranteed by *Roe v. Wade.* The court of appeals upheld the "gag rule" against this challenge.

By a 5-4 vote, with Justice O'Connor surprisingly joining the dissenters, the Court affirmed the appellate court's ruling. Chief Justice Rehnquist delivered the majority opinion, joined by Justices White, Scalia, Kennedy, and Souter. Souter's presence on the Court clearly made a difference in this case. He provided the fifth vote to uphold the "gag rule," while his predecessor would have voted to strike it down. In his majority opinion, Rehnquist first accepted the Reagan administration's interpretation of the statute, arguing that the language in the statute was ambiguous. "Title X does not define the term 'method of family planning,' nor does it enumerate what types of medical and counseling services are entitled to Title X funding" (500 U.S. at 184). Therefore, the "gag rule" was a permissible interpretation of the statute. Second, he rejected the claim that the rule violated freedom of speech, ruling that the government may attach conditions to programs it funds. Furthermore, Rehnquist claimed, the rule did not force staff members in the affected family-planning clinics to give up their freedom of speech, because they "remain free . . . to pursue abortion-related activities when they are not acting under the auspices of the Title X project" (500 U.S. at 198). Third, the majority concluded that the rule did not unconstitutionally interfere with a woman's right to choose to have an abortion. Although acknowledging that obtaining information from family-planning clinics would make a woman's decision easier, Rehnquist held, "the Constitution does not require that the Government distort the scope of its mandated program in order to provide that information" (500 U.S. at 203).

After criticizing the majority for its construction of the statute and for unnecessarily addressing the constitutional claims, Justice Blackmun asserted that the "gag rule" did indeed violate freedom of speech and interfere with the abortion decision. He viewed the rule as an unconstitutional content-based and viewpoint-based restriction upon protected speech because it clearly required the affected family-planning clinics to provide counseling and referral about childbirth related services, while prohibiting them from discussing the topic of abortion. This also impermissibly "manipulat[ed] the content of the doctor/patient dialogue . . ." (500 U.S. at 212). Finally, Blackmun argued that the "gag rule" imposed a significant obstacle to poor women seeking abortions who receive their only information about abortion from family-planning clinics funded by the federal government. Justice Marshall joined Blackmun's dissent fully, but Justices Stevens and O'Connor would not have addressed the constitutional arguments at all, asserting that the "gag rule" was not a reasonable interpretation of the statute. The "gag rule" subsequently was repealed by an executive order issued by President Clinton two days after his inauguration.

After the 1990–91 term, abortion rights advocates lost another supporter when Thurgood Marshall retired from the Court and was replaced by Clarence Thomas. Because of some earlier speeches, Thomas was considered to be an opponent of abortion rights in general and of *Roe v. Wade* in particular, despite claiming during his confirmation hearings that he had never even discussed the case or the issue of abortion. Thus with Justices Brennan and Marshall no longer on the Court, the odds were increasing that *Roe* would be overturned. The opportunity for the Court to reexamine *Roe* came in the 1991–92 term.

In *Planned Parenthood v. Casey* (1992), the justices heard a challenge to a Pennsylvania law containing provisions almost identical to the ones previously struck down in *Akron I* and *Thornburgh*: informed consent, a twenty-four-hour waiting period, parental consent for minors, spousal notification, and public reporting and disclosure requirements. In a complicated and fragmented decision in which there was no majority opinion, the Pennsylvania statute withstood a challenge by Planned Parenthood. Chief Justice Rehnquist, along with Justices White, Scalia, and Thomas, voted to uphold all of the provisions, and they called for *Roe* to be overturned. Justice Blackmun, not surprisingly, voted to invalidate all of the provisions, while Justice Stevens would have struck all but the informed consent and reporting requirements. The outcome was determined by a trio of justices—O'Connor, Kennedy, and Souter—who refused to overturn *Roe* and voted to uphold all of the provisions except for the spousal notification requirement. Kennedy's membership in this trio is especially surprising given that he was a member of the

Webster plurality that severely criticized and undercut *Roe*. O'Connor, Kennedy, and Souter announced the judgment of the Court in a joint opinion, and it is this opinion that determined the outcome of the case.

In refusing to overrule *Roe,* the trio emphasized the need to follow the principle of stare decisis and their concern to avoid damaging the integrity and legitimacy of the Court. "A decision to overrule *Roe*'s essential holding under the existing circumstances would address error, if error there was, at the cost of both profound and unnecessary damage to the Court's legitimacy, and to the Nation's commitment to the rule of law" (505 U.S. at 869). While the three justices claimed to reaffirm the "central holding" of *Roe v. Wade,* the opinion departed significantly from the standards set in that decision. Specifically, they rejected *Roe*'s trimester framework, although continuing to use the point of viability as the line for the most restrictive regulations. Instead of the trimester approach, they opted for the "undue burden" analysis that had been encouraged by O'Connor since the *Akron* case. Under this approach, an abortion regulation will be examined first to determine if it poses an "undue burden" on a pregnant woman's right to abortion. A regulation presents an undue burden "if its purpose or effect is to place a substantial obstacle in the path of a woman seeking an abortion before the fetus attains viability" (505 U.S. at 878). If the regulation poses an undue burden, the state must prove a compelling interest for it to be upheld. If the regulation is not "unduly burdensome," however, the rational basis test applies.

Having set forth the undue burden analysis, the trio examined the provisions of the Pennsylvania statute. Only the spousal notification requirement was deemed to unduly burden a woman's choice to have an abortion. The trio was persuaded that numbers of women face physical and psychological abuse from their husbands, and requiring these same women to notify their spouses about an abortion would further endanger them.

Justice Blackmun praised the trio of O'Connor, Kennedy, and Souter for what he termed their "act of personal courage and constitutional principle" in refusing to overturn *Roe* and in helping to reaffirm that "the Constitution protects a woman's right to terminate her pregnancy in its early stages" (505 U.S. at 923). At the same time, he expressed his concern about the future of abortion rights, particularly criticizing Chief Justice Rehnquist and Justice Scalia, who emphasize that the right to choose to have an abortion is not a fundamental liberty. In his concluding passage, Blackmun lamented, "In one sense, the Court's approach is worlds apart from that of the Chief Justice and Justice Scalia. And yet, in another sense, the distance between the two approaches is short—the distance is but a single vote. I am 83 years old. I cannot remain on this Court forever, and when I do step down, the confirmation process for my successor well may focus on the issue before us today. That, I regret, may be exactly where the choice between the two worlds will be made" (505 U.S. at 943).

Planned Parenthood of Southeastern Pennsylvania v. Casey

505 U.S. 833, 120 L.Ed.2d 674 (1992)

■ A state chapter of Planned Parenthood filed suit challenging a Pennsylvania abortion law that contained provisions almost identical to the ones invalidated in *Akron v. Akron Center for Reproductive Health* (1983) and *Thornburgh v. American College of Obstetricians and Gynecologists* (1986). Physicians were required to inform women about fetal development, women had to give their consent, and they had to wait twenty-four hours after giving such consent before the abortion could be performed. The law mandated parental consent for minors and spousal notification for married women. It also contained detailed reporting and public disclosure requirements for doctors who perform abortions. A court of appeals upheld all but the spousal notification provision. Planned Parenthood appealed to the U.S. Supreme Court.

This case is important in two respects: 1) Although it had been widely expected, *Roe* was not explicitly overruled, and 2) the "undue burden" standard advocated by Justice O'Connor emerged as the controlling doctrine. As you read the case, consider the following questions: 1) Given the abandonment of the trimester framework, is the "central holding" of *Roe* really affirmed, as the plurality maintained? 2) Does the "undue burden" test leave the protection of abortion rights, for all practical purposes, up to the will of state and local legislators? 3) Given the modification of *Roe* by O'Connor, Kennedy, and Souter and their refusal to invalidate the Pennsylvania statute, why does Justice Blackmun praise their joint opinion?

VOTE:

4 justices agreed to uphold all of the challenged restrictions (Rehnquist, White, Scalia, and Thomas).

3 justices voted to uphold all of the challenged provisions except the ones relating to spousal notification and reporting of spousal notification (O'Connor, Kennedy, and Souter).

1 justice voted to uphold the informed consent and reporting provisions but to strike the requirements relating to spousal notification, reporting of spousal notification, abortion counseling, and the twenty-four-hour waiting period (Stevens).

1 justice voted to strike all of the challenged provisions (Blackmun).

Justice O'Connor, Justice Kennedy, and Justice Souter announced the judgment of the Court and delivered the opinion of the Court.

Liberty finds no refuge in a jurisprudence of doubt. Yet 19 years after our holding that the Constitution protects a woman's right to terminate her pregnancy in its early stages, *Roe v. Wade* (1973), that definition of liberty is still questioned. Joining the respondents as *amicus curiae,* the United States, as it has done in five other cases in the last decade, again asks us to overrule *Roe.*

* * *

After considering the fundamental constitutional questions resolved by *Roe* [*v. Wade* (1973)], principles of institutional integrity, and the rule of *stare decisis,* we are led to conclude this: the essential holding of *Roe v. Wade* should be retained and once again reaffirmed.

It must be stated at the outset and with clarity that *Roe*'s essential holding, the holding we reaffirm, has three parts. First is a recognition of the right of the woman to choose to have an abortion before viability and to obtain it without undue interference from the State. Before viability, the State's interests are not strong enough to support a prohibition of abortion or the imposition of a substantial obstacle to the woman's effective right to elect the procedure. Second is a confirmation of the State's power to restrict abortions after fetal viability, if the law contains exceptions for pregnancies which endanger a woman's life or health. And third is the principle that the State has legitimate interests from the outset of the pregnancy in protecting the health of the woman and the life of the fetus that may become a child. These principles do not contradict one another; and we adhere to each.

* * *

Our law affords constitutional protection to personal decisions relating to marriage, procreation, contraception, family relationships, child rearing, and education. Our cases recognize "the right of the individual, married or single, to be free from unwarranted governmental intrusion into matters so fundamentally affecting a person as the decision whether to bear or beget a child." Our precedents "have respected the private realm of family life which the state cannot enter." These matters, involving the most intimate and personal choices a person may make in a lifetime, choices central to personal dignity and autonomy, are central to the liberty protected by the Fourteenth Amendment. At the heart of liberty is the right to define one's own concept of existence, of meaning, of the universe, and of the mystery of human life. * * *

* * *

While we appreciate the weight of the arguments made on behalf of the State in the case before us, arguments which in their ultimate formulation conclude that *Roe* should be overruled, the reservations any of us may have in reaffirming the central holding of *Roe* are outweighed by the explication of individual liberty we have given combined with the force of *stare decisis.* * * *

* * *

The Court's duty in the present case is clear. In 1973, it confronted the already-divisive issue of governmental power to limit personal choice to undergo abortion, for which it provided a new resolution based on the due process guaranteed by the Fourteenth Amendment. Whether or not a new social consensus is developing on that issue, its divisiveness is no less today than in 1973, and pressure to overrule the decision, like pressure to retain it, has grown only more intense. A decision to overrule *Roe*'s essential holding under the existing circumstances would address error, if error there was, at the cost of both profound and unnecessary damage to the Court's legitimacy, and to the Nation's commitment to the rule of law. It is therefore imperative to adhere to the essence of *Roe*'s original decision, and we do so today.

From what we have said so far it follows that it is a constitutional liberty of the woman to have some freedom to terminate her pregnancy. We conclude that the basic decision in *Roe* was based on a constitutional analysis which we cannot now repudiate. The woman's liberty is not so unlimited, however, that from the outset the State cannot show its concern for the life of the unborn, and at a later point in fetal development the State's interest in life has sufficient force so that the right of the woman to terminate the pregnancy can be restricted.

That brings us, of course, to the point where much criticism has been directed at *Roe,* a criticism that always inheres when the Court draws a specific rule from what in the Constitution is but a general standard. * * * And it falls to us to give some real substance to the woman's liberty to determine whether to carry her pregnancy to full term.

We conclude the line should be drawn at viability, so that before that time the woman has a right to choose to terminate her pregnancy. We adhere to this principle for two reasons. First, as we have said, is the doctrine of *stare decisis.* Any judicial act of line-drawing may seem somewhat arbitrary, but *Roe* was a reasoned statement, elaborated with great care. We have twice reaffirmed it in the face of great opposition. Although we must overrule those parts of *Thornburgh* [1986] and *Akron I* [1983] which, in our view, are inconsistent with *Roe*'s statement that the State has a legitimate interest in promoting the life or potential life of the unborn, the central premise of those cases represents an unbroken commitment by this Court to the essential holding of *Roe.* It is that premise which we reaffirm today.

The second reason is that the concept of viability, as we noted in *Roe,* is the time at which there is a realistic possibility of maintaining and nourishing a life outside the womb, so that the independent existence of the second life can in reason and all fairness be the object of state protection that now overrides the rights of the woman. Consistent with other constitutional norms, legislatures may draw lines which appear arbitrary without the necessity of offering a justification. But courts may not. We must justify the lines we draw. And there is no line other than viability which is more workable. * * *

The woman's right to terminate her pregnancy before viability is the most central principle of *Roe v. Wade.* It is a rule of law and a component of liberty we cannot renounce. * * *

* * *

Though the woman has a right to choose to terminate or continue her pregnancy before viability, it does not at all follow that the State is prohibited from taking steps to ensure that this choice is thoughtful and informed. Even in the earliest stages of pregnancy, the State may enact rules and regulations designed to encourage her to know that there are philosophic and social arguments of great weight that can be brought to bear in favor of continuing the pregnancy to full term and that there are procedures and institutions to allow adoption of unwanted children as well as a certain degree of state assistance if the mother chooses to raise the child herself. "The Constitution does not forbid a State or city, pursuant to democratic processes, from expressing a preference for normal childbirth." It follows that States are free to enact laws to provide a reasonable framework for a woman to make a decision that has such profound and lasting meaning. This, too, we find consistent with *Roe*'s central premises, and indeed the inevitable consequence of our holding that the State has an interest in protecting the life of the unborn.

We reject the trimester framework, which we do not consider to be part of the essential holding of *Roe.* * * * The trimester framework suffers from these basic flaws: in its formulation it misconceives the nature of the pregnant woman's interest; and in practice it undervalues the State's interest in potential life, as recognized in *Roe.*

* * *

* * * Because we set forth a standard of general application to which we intend to adhere, it is important to clarify what is meant by an undue burden.

A finding of an undue burden is a shorthand for the conclusion that a state regulation has the purpose or effect of placing a substantial obstacle in the path of a woman seeking an abortion of a nonviable fetus. * * * [W]e answer the question, left open in previous opinions discussing the undue burden formulation, whether a law designed to further the State's interest in fetal life which imposes an undue burden on the woman's decision before fetal viability could be constitutional. The answer is no.

Some guiding principles should emerge. What is at stake is the woman's right to make the ultimate decision, not a right to be insulated from all others in doing so. Regulations which do no more than create a structural mechanism by which the State, or the parent or guardian of a minor, may express profound respect for the life of the unborn are permitted, if they are not a substantial obstacle to the woman's exercise of the right to choose. Unless it has that effect on her right of choice, a state measure designed to persuade her to choose childbirth over abortion will be upheld if reasonably related to that goal. Regulations designed to foster the health of a woman seeking an abortion are valid if they do not constitute an undue burden.

* * * We give this summary:

(a) To protect the central right recognized by *Roe v. Wade* while at the same time accommodating the State's profound interest in potential life, we will employ the undue burden analysis as explained in this opinion. An undue burden exists, and therefore a provision of law is invalid, if its purpose or effect is to place a substantial obstacle in the path of a woman seeking an abortion before the fetus attains viability.

(b) We reject the rigid trimester framework of *Roe v. Wade.* To promote the State's profound interest in potential life, throughout pregnancy the State may take measures to ensure that the woman's choice is informed, and measures designed to advance this interest will not be invalidated as long as their purpose is to persuade the woman to choose childbirth over abortion. These measures must not be an undue burden on the right.

(c) As with any medical procedure, the State may enact regulations to further the health or safety of a woman seeking an abortion. Unnecessary health regulations that have the purpose or effect of presenting a substantial obstacle to a woman seeking an abortion impose an undue burden on the right.

(d) Our adoption of the undue burden analysis does not disturb the central holding of *Roe v. Wade,* and we reaffirm that holding. Regardless of whether exceptions are made for particular circumstances, a State may not prohibit any woman from making the ultimate decision to terminate her pregnancy before viability.

(e) We also reaffirm *Roe*'s holding that "subsequent to viability, the State in promoting its interest in the potentiality of human life may, if it chooses, regulate, and even proscribe, abortion except where it is necessary, in appropriate medical judgment, for the preservation of the life or health of the mother."

These principles control our assessment of the Pennsylvania statute, and we now turn to the issue of the validity of its challenged provisions.

* * *

We . . . consider the informed consent requirement. Except in a medical emergency, the statute requires that at least 24 hours before performing an abortion a physician inform the woman of the nature of the procedure, the health risks of the abortion and of childbirth, and the "probable gestational age of the unborn child." * * *

Our prior decisions establish that as with any medical procedure, the State may require a woman to give her written informed consent to an abortion. In this respect, the statute is unexceptional. Petitioners challenge the statute's definition of informed consent because it includes the provision of specific information by the doctor and the mandatory 24-hour waiting period. The conclusions reached by a majority of the justices in the separate opinions filed today and the undue burden standard adopted in this opinion require us to overrule in part some of the Court's past decisions, decisions driven by the trimester framework's prohibition of all previability regulations designed to further the State's interest in fetal life.

* * *

To the extent *Akron I* and *Thornburgh* find a constitutional violation when the government requires, as it does here, the giving of truthful, nonmisleading information about the nature of the procedure, the attendant health risks and those of childbirth, and the "probable gestational age" of the fetus, those cases go too far, are inconsistent with *Roe*'s acknowledgment of an important interest in potential life, and are overruled. * * *

* * *

Section 3209 of Pennsylvania's abortion law provides, except in cases of medical emergency, that no physician shall perform an abortion on a married woman without receiving a signed statement from the woman that she has notified her spouse that she is about to undergo an abortion. The woman has the option of providing an alternative signed statement certifying that her husband is not the man who impregnated her; that her husband could not be located; that the pregnancy is the result of spousal sexual assault which she has reported; or that the woman believes that notifying her husband will cause him or someone else to inflict bodily injury upon her. A physician who performs an abortion on a married woman without receiving the appropriate signed statement will have his or her license revoked, and is liable to the husband for damages.

* * *

* * * [T]here are millions of women in this country who are the victims of regular physical and psychological abuse at the hands of their husbands. Should these women become pregnant, they may

have very good reasons for not wishing to inform their husbands of their decision to obtain an abortion. Many may have justifiable fears of physical abuse, but may be no less fearful of the consequences of reporting prior abuse to the Commonwealth of Pennsylvania. Many may have a reasonable fear that notifying their husbands will provoke further instances of child abuse; these women are not exempt from Section 3209's notification requirement. Many may fear devastating forms of psychological abuse from their husbands, including verbal harassment, threats of future violence, the destruction of possessions, physical confinement to the home, the withdrawal of financial support, or the disclosure of the abortion to family and friends. These methods of psychological abuse may act as even more of a deterrent to notification than the possibility of physical violence, but women who are the victims of the abuse are not exempt from Section 3209's notification requirement. And many women who are pregnant as a result of sexual assaults by their husbands will be unable to avail themselves of the exception for spousal sexual assault, because the exception requires that the woman have notified law enforcement authorities within 90 days of the assault, and her husband will be notified of her report once an investigation begins. * * *

* * *

* * * The unfortunate yet persisting conditions we document above will mean that in a large fraction of the cases in which Section 3209 is relevant, it will operate as a substantial obstacle to a woman's choice to undergo an abortion. It is an undue burden, and therefore invalid.

* * *

We next consider the parental consent provision. Except in a medical emergency, an unemancipated young woman under 18 may not obtain an abortion unless she and one of her parents (or guardian) provides informed consent as defined above. If neither a parent nor a guardian provides consent, a court may authorize the performance of an abortion upon a determination that the young woman is mature and capable of giving informed consent and has in fact given her informed consent, or that an abortion would be in her best interests.

We have been over most of this ground before. Our cases establish, and we reaffirm today, that a State may require a minor seeking an abortion to obtain the consent of a parent or guardian, provided that there is an adequate judicial bypass procedure. Under these precedents, in our view, the one-parent consent requirement and judicial bypass procedure are constitutional.

* * *

In *Danforth* [1976], we held that recordkeeping and reporting provisions "that are reasonably directed to the preservation of maternal health and that properly respect a patient's confidentiality and privacy are permissible." We think that under this standard, all the provisions at issue here except that relating to spousal notice are constitutional. * * *

Subsection (12) of the reporting provision requires the reporting of, among other things, a married woman's "reason for failure to provide notice" to her husband. This provision in effect requires women, as a condition of obtaining an abortion, to provide the Commonwealth with the precise information we have already recognized that many women have pressing reasons not to reveal. Like the spousal notice requirement itself, this provision places an undue burden on a woman's choice, and must be invalidated for that reason.

* * *

[The opinion of Justice Stevens, concurring in part and dissenting in part, is omitted.]

Justice Blackmun concurred in part, concurred in the judgment in part, and dissented in part.

* * *

Make no mistake, the joint opinion of Justices O'Connor, Kennedy, and Souter is an act of personal courage and constitutional principle. In contrast to previous decisions in which Justices O'Connor and Kennedy postponed reconsideration of *Roe v. Wade,* the authors of the joint opinion today join Justice Stevens and me in concluding that "the essential holding of *Roe* should be retained and once again reaffirmed." In brief, five Members of this Court today recognize that "the Constitution protects a woman's right to terminate her pregnancy in its early stages."

* * *

Today, no less than yesterday, the Constitution and decisions of this Court require that a State's abortion restrictions be subjected to the strictest of judicial scrutiny. Our precedents and the joint opinion's principles require us to subject all non-de minimis abortion regulations to strict scrutiny. Under this standard, the Pennsylvania statute's provisions requiring content-based counseling, a 24-hour delay, informed parental consent, and reporting of abortion-related information must be invalidated.

* * *

* * * If there is much reason to applaud the advances made by the joint opinion today, there is far more to fear from the Chief Justice's opinion.

The Chief Justice's criticism of *Roe* follows from his stunted conception of individual liberty. While recognizing that the Due Process Clause protects more than simple physical liberty, he then goes on to construe this Court's personal-liberty cases as establishing only a laundry list of particular rights, rather than a principled account of how these particular rights are grounded in a more general right of privacy. * * *

* * *

The Chief Justice's narrow conception of individual liberty and *stare decisis* leads him to propose the same standard of review proposed by the plurality in *Webster.* "States may regulate abortion procedures in ways rationally related to a legitimate state interest." * * *

* * *

But, we are reassured, there is always the protection of the democratic process. While there is much to be praised about our democracy, our country since its founding has recognized that there are certain fundamental liberties that are not to be left to the whims of an election. A woman's right to reproductive choice is one of those fundamental liberties. Accordingly, that liberty need not seek refuge at the ballot box.

In one sense, the Court's approach is worlds apart from that of the Chief Justice and Justice Scalia. And yet, in another sense, the distance between the two approaches is short—the distance is but a single vote.

I am 83 years old. I cannot remain on this Court forever, and when I do step down, the confirmation process for my successor well may focus on the issue before us today. That, I regret, may be exactly where the choice between the two worlds will be made.

Chief Justice Rehnquist, with whom Justice White, Justice Scalia, and Justice Thomas joined, concurred in the judgment in part and dissented in part.

The joint opinion . . . retains the outer shell of *Roe v. Wade* but beats a wholesale retreat from the substance of that case. We believe that *Roe* was wrongly decided, and that it can and should be overruled consistently with our traditional approach to *stare decisis* in constitutional cases. We would adopt the approach of the plurality in *Webster V. Reproductive Health Services* [1989] and uphold the challenged provisions of the Pennsylvania statute in their entirety.

* * *

We think . . . that the Court was mistaken in *Roe* when it classified a woman's decision to terminate her pregnancy as a "fundamental right" that could be abridged only in a manner which withstood "strict scrutiny." * * *

We believe that the sort of constitutionally imposed abortion code of the type illustrated by our decisions following *Roe* is inconsistent "with the notion of a Constitution cast in general terms, as ours is, and usually speaking in general principles, as ours does." * * *

The joint opinion of Justices O'Connor, Kennedy, and Souter cannot bring itself to say that *Roe* was correct as an original matter, but the authors are of the view that "the immediate question is not the soundness of *Roe*'s resolution of the issue, but the precedential force that must be accorded to its holding." Instead of claiming that *Roe* was correct as a matter of original constitutional interpretation, the opinion therefore contains an elaborate discussion of *stare decisis.* This discussion of the principle of *stare decisis* appears to be almost entirely dicta, because the joint opinion does not apply that principle in dealing with *Roe. Roe* decided that a woman had a fundamental right to an abortion. The joint opinion rejects that view. *Roe* decided that abortion regulations were to be subjected to "strict scrutiny" and could be justified only in the light of "compelling state interests." The joint opinion rejects that view. *Roe* analyzed abortion regulation under a rigid trimester framework, a framework which has guided this Court's decisionmaking for 19 years. The joint opinion rejects that framework.

* * * While purporting to adhere to precedent, the joint opinion instead revises it. *Roe* continues to exist, but only in the way a storefront on a western movie set exists: a mere facade to give the illusion of reality. Decisions following *Roe,* such as *Akron v. Akron Center for Reproductive Health, Inc.* [1983] and *Thornburgh v. American College of Obstetricians and Gynecologists* [1986] are frankly overruled in part under the "undue burden" standard expounded in the joint opinion.

In our view, authentic principles of *stare decisis* do not require that any portion of the reasoning in *Roe* be kept intact. * * *

* * *

The sum of the joint opinion's labors in the name of *stare decisis* and "legitimacy" is this: *Roe v. Wade* stands as a sort of judicial Potemkin Village, which may be pointed out to passers by as a monument to the importance of adhering to precedent. But behind the facade, an entirely new method of analysis, without any roots in constitutional law, is imported to decide the constitutionality of state laws regulating abortion. Neither *stare decisis* nor "legitimacy" are truly served by such an effort.

* * *

For the reasons stated, we therefore would hold that each of the challenged provisions of the Pennsylvania statute is consistent with the Constitution. * * *

Justice Scalia, with whom the Chief Justice, Justice White, and Justice Thomas joined, concurred in the judgment in part and dissented in part.

My views on this matter are unchanged from those I set forth in my separate opinions in *Webster v. Reproductive Health Services* (1989) and *Ohio v. Akron Center for Reproductive Health* (1990). The States may, if they wish, permit abortion-on-demand, but the Constitution does not require them to do so. * * *

* * * The issue is whether [a woman's claim to a constitutional right to have an abortion] is liberty protected by the Constitution of the United States. I am sure it is not. I reach that conclusion not because of anything so exalted as my views concerning the "concept of existence, of meaning, of the universe, and of the mystery of human life." Rather, I reach it . . . because of two simple facts: (1) the Constitution says absolutely nothing about it, and (2) the longstanding traditions of American society have permitted it to be legally proscribed. * * *

* * *

Casey and *Webster* are evidence of the Rehnquist Court's willingness to permit greater restrictions on abortion, without allowing states to ban them altogether. While this is an important development in abortion policy, such laws will not prevent abortions. Smith (1993) argues, for example, "Because pro-choice political interests and pro-choice public opinion are so strong in many states, these states will not restrict abortions" (p. 122). Thus, the primary impact of these decisions, particularly *Casey,* will be upon young women and poor women who live in states where there are significant restrictions on abortion and who cannot afford to travel to states with less restrictive laws. One could argue that for these women, *Casey*'s reaffirmation of *Roe* is meaningless.

While *Casey* is the most recent case involving substantive abortion regulations, in its 1992 and 1993 terms, the Court decided three cases involving antiabortion protestors and their efforts to limit the operations of abortion clinics. In *Bray v. Alexandria Women's Health Clinic* (1993) a majority held that the federal courts could not use the Civil Rights Act of 1871 to prohibit blockades of abortion clinics by antiabortion demonstrators. One year later, however, a unanimous court ruled that a federal antiracketeering law (RICO) could be applied to antiabortion protesters who engage in conspiracies to harm abortion clinics (*National Organization for Women v. Scheidler,* 1994). Finally, the Court approved a federal judge's creation of a buffer zone around an abortion clinic to permit patients to have access to the clinic's services without undue interference by antiabortion protestors (*Madsen v. Women's Health Center,* 1994).

Nonreproductive Rights Cases

The Rehnquist Court's only nonabortion-related privacy decision concerned the right of dying medical patients to refuse medical treatment. By the time the Court heard *Cruzan v. Missouri Department of Health* (1990), the situation of Nancy Cruzan was fairly well known, as it had gained national media attention. Cruzan had suffered severe brain injuries in an automobile accident, injuries that left her in a "permanent vegetative state." Her parents' request to have her taken off life-support systems was refused by hospital personnel and ultimately by the Missouri Supreme Court. By a 5-4 vote, the Court affirmed this decision. The majority, led by Chief Justice Rehnquist, ruled that the state's requirements of a living will or "clear and convincing" evidence before terminal decisions can be made on behalf of incompetent patients did not violate any constitutional rights of those patients. Rehnquist held that these requirements were reasonable efforts by the state to protect incompetent patients against erroneous decisions by others. "Not all incompetent patients will have loved ones available to serve as surrogate decisionmakers. And even where family members are present, '[t]here will, of course, be some unfortunate situations in which family members will not act to protect a patient.' A State is entitled to guard against potential abuses in such situations" (497 U.S. at 281). Thus the right of incompetent patients to have medical treatment withdrawn can be limited by states to those instances where there is "clear and convincing" evidence of the patient's will. At the same time, however, the majority opinion seemed to affirm the constitutional right of *competent* patients to reject life-preserving medical treatment. It is important to note that the decision here was not based on the right of privacy, but on a right to individual liberty guaranteed by the Due Process Clause of the Fourteenth Amendment.

In dissent, Justice Brennan, joined by Justices Marshall and Blackmun, contended that the standard prescribed by the Missouri Supreme Court was too stringent. Brennan argued that requiring specific statements by the patient when the person is competent and requiring that evidence to be "clear and convincing" interferes with the patient's wishes. He insisted that testimony from close friends and relatives "may often be the best evidence available of what the patient's choice would be" (497 U.S. at 325). Therefore, the statements made by Nancy Cruzan in conversations with her family and friends were, in the dissenters' view, sufficient evidence of her wishes. In a separate dissent, Justice Stevens stressed that his concern was not the "clear and convincing evidence" standard per se. For Stevens, the proper consideration was "not how to prove the controlling facts but rather what proven facts should be controlling" (497 U.S. at 350). From his perspective, the critical concern was the best interest of the patient. Applying this to Nancy Cruzan's situation, Stevens said the evidence showed that keeping her alive in a "persistent vegetative state" was not in her own best interest.

Cruzan by Cruzan v. Director, Missouri Dept. of Public Health

497 U.S. 261, 110 S.Ct. 2841, 111 L.Ed.2d 224 (1990)

■ In 1983, Nancy Cruzan had become permanently incapacitated due to severe brain injuries incurred in an automobile accident. When informed by doctors that their daughter would be in a "persistent vegetative condition," Cruzan's parents requested that she be taken off the hydration and nutrition systems keeping her alive. Removal of these would result in her death. They insisted that they were simply following their daughter's wishes, because, before the accident, she had indicated informally to friends and relatives her desire not to be kept alive unless she could lead a reasonably normal life. The hospital personnel, however, refused the parents' request, so the Cruzans petitioned a trial court to authorize disconnection of the life-support systems. The trial court agreed with the Cruzans, but the state supreme court reversed this decision upon the state's appeal. The Missouri Supreme Court said that the informal oral statements by Nancy Cruzan, now incompetent, were insufficient to establish her preferences. The court ruled that there must exist either a formal living will or "clear and convincing" evidence of a patient's wishes before a guardian is allowed to withdraw life-sustaining medical treatment. The Cruzans appealed to the U.S. Supreme Court.

This case is important because it is the first time that the Court ruled on the constitutional rights of dying patients to refuse medical treatment. As you read the case, consider these questions: 1) Is the balancing test used by the majority appropriate for deciding this dispute, or should an increased burden be placed on the state to justify its policy? 2) What kind of evidence might be accepted as "clear and convincing"? 3) Which of the dissents is more persuasive in arguing that the Cruzans' request should have been granted?

Vote:

5 justices voted to affirm the decision of the Missouri Supreme Court (Rehnquist, White, O'Connor, Scalia, and Kennedy).

4 justices voted to overturn the decision of the Missouri Supreme Court (Brennan, Marshall, Blackmun, and Stevens).

Chief Justice Rehnquist delivered the opinion of the Court.

* * *

The Fourteenth Amendment provides that no State shall "deprive any person of life, liberty, or property, without due process of law." The principle that a competent person has a constitutionally protected liberty interest in refusing unwanted medical treatment may be inferred from our prior decisions. * * *

* * *

But determining that a person has a "liberty interest" under the Due Process Clause does not end the inquiry; "whether respondent's constitutional rights have been violated must be determined by balancing his liberty interests against the relevant state interests."

Petitioners insist that under the general holdings of our cases, the forced administration of life-sustaining medical treatment, and even of artificially-delivered food and water essential to life, would implicate a competent person's liberty interest. Although we think the logic of the cases ... would embrace such a liberty interest, the dramatic consequences involved in refusal of such treatment would inform the inquiry as to whether the deprivation of that interest is constitutionally permissible. But for purposes of this case, we assume that the United States Constitution would grant a competent person a constitutionally protected right to refuse lifesaving hydration and nutrition.

Petitioners go on to assert that an incompetent person should possess the same right in this respect as is possessed by a competent person. * * *

The difficulty with petitioners' claim is that in a sense it begs the question: an incompetent person is not able to make an informed and voluntary choice to exercise a hypothetical right to refuse treatment or any other right. Such a "right" must be exercised for her, if at all, by some sort of surrogate. Here, Missouri has in effect recognized that under certain circumstances a surrogate may act for the patient in electing to have hydration and nutrition withdrawn in such a way as to cause death, but it has established a procedural safeguard to assure that the action of the surrogate conforms as best it may to the wishes expressed by the patient while competent. Missouri requires that evidence of the incompetent's wishes as to the withdrawal of treatment be proved by clear and convincing evidence. The question, then, is whether the United States Constitution forbids the establishment of this procedural requirement by the State. We hold that it does not.

Whether or not Missouri's clear and convincing evidence requirement comports with the United States Constitution depends in part on what interests the State may properly seek to protect in this situation. Missouri relies on its interest in the protection and preservation of human life, and there can be no gainsaying this interest. As a general matter, the States—indeed, all civilized nations—demonstrate their commitment to life by treating homicide as serious crime. Moreover, the majority of States in this country have laws imposing criminal penalties on one who assists another to commit suicide. We do not think a State is required to remain neutral in the face of an informed and voluntary decision by a physically-able adult to starve to death.

But in the context presented here, a State has more particular interests at stake. The choice between life and death is a deeply personal decision of obvious and overwhelming finality. We believe Missouri may legitimately seek to safeguard the personal element of this choice through the imposition of heightened evidentiary requirements. It cannot be disputed that the Due Process Clause protects an interest in life as well as an interest in refusing life-sustaining medical treatment. Not all incompetent patients will have loved ones available to serve as surrogate decisionmakers. And even where family members are present, "[t]here will, of course, be some unfortunate situations in which family members will not act to protect a patient." A State is entitled to guard against potential abuses in such situations. Similarly, a State is entitled to consider that a judicial proceeding to make a determination regarding an incompetent's wishes may very well not be an adversarial one, with the added guarantee of accurate factfinding that the adversary process brings with it. Finally, we think a State may properly decline to make judgments about the "quality" of life that a particular individual may enjoy, and simply assert an unqualified interest in the preservation of human life to be weighed against the constitutionally protected interests of the individual.

In our view, Missouri has permissibly sought to advance these interests through the adoption of a "clear and convincing" standard of proof to govern such proceedings. * * * "This Court has mandated an intermediate standard of proof—'clear and convincing evidence'—when the individual interests at stake in a state proceeding are both 'particularly important' and 'more substantial than mere loss of money.' " * * *

We think it self-evident that the interests at stake in the instant proceedings are more substantial, both on an individual and societal level, than those involved in a run-of-the-mine civil dispute. But not only does the standard of proof reflect the importance of a particular adjudication, it also serves as "a societal judgment about how the risk of error should be distributed between the litigants." The more stringent the burden of proof a party must bear, the more that party bears the risk of an erroneous decision. We believe that Missouri may permissibly place an increased risk of an erroneous decision on those seeking to terminate an incompetent individual's life-sustaining treatment. An erroneous decision not to terminate results in a maintenance of the status quo; the possibility of subsequent developments such as advancements in medical science, the discovery of new evidence regarding the patient's intent, changes in the law, or simply the unexpected death of the patient despite the administration of life-sustaining treatment, at least create the potential that a wrong decision will eventually be corrected or its impact mitigated. An erroneous decision to withdraw life-sustaining treatment, however, is not susceptible of correction. * * *

* * *

In sum, we conclude that a State may apply a clear and convincing evidence standard in proceedings where a guardian seeks to discontinue nutrition and hydration of a person diagnosed to be in a persistent vegetative state. * * *

The Supreme Court of Missouri held that in this case the testimony adduced at trial did not amount to clear and convincing proof of the patient's desire to have hydration and nutrition withdrawn. In so doing, it reversed a decision of the Missouri trial court which had found that the evidence "suggest[ed]" Nancy Cruzan would not have desired to continue such measures, but which had not adopted the standard of "clear and convincing evidence" enunciated by the Supreme Court. The testimony adduced at trial consisted primarily of Nancy Cruzan's statements made to a housemate about a year before her accident that she would not want to live should she face life as a "vegetable," and other observations to the same effect. The observations did not deal in terms with withdrawal of medical treatment or of hydration and nutrition. We cannot say that the Supreme Court of Missouri committed constitutional error in reaching the conclusion that it did.

Petitioners alternatively contend that Missouri must accept the "substituted judgment" of close family members even in the absence of substantial proof that their views reflect the views of the patient. * * *

No doubt is engendered by anything in this record but that Nancy Cruzan's mother and father are loving and caring parents. If the State were required by the United States Constitution to repose a right of "substituted judgment" with anyone, the Cruzans would surely qualify. But we do not think the Due Process Clause requires the State to repose judgment on these matters with anyone but the patient herself. Close family members may have a strong feeling—a feeling not at all ignoble or unworthy, but not entirely disinterested, either—that they do not wish to witness the continuation of the life of a loved one which they regard as hopeless, meaningless, and even degrading. But there is no automatic assurance that the view of close family members will necessarily be the same as the patient's would have been had she been confronted with the prospect of her situation while competent. All of the reasons previously discussed for allowing Missouri to require clear and convincing evidence of the patient's wishes lead us to conclude that the State may choose to defer only to those wishes, rather than confide the decision to close family members.

The judgment of the Supreme Court of Missouri is *Affirmed.*

[The concurring opinions of Justices O'Connor and Scalia are each omitted.]

Justice Brennan, with whom Justice Marshall and Justice Blackmun joined, dissented.

* * *

Although the right to be free of unwanted medical intervention, like other constitutionally protected interests, may not be absolute, no State interest could outweigh the rights of an individual in Nancy Cruzan's position. Whatever a State's possible interests in mandating life-support treatment under other circumstances, there is no good to be obtained here by Missouri's insistence that Nancy Cruzan remain on life-support systems if it is indeed her wish not to do so. Missouri does not claim, nor could it, that society as a whole will be benefited by Nancy's receiving medical treatment. No third party's situation will be improved and no harm to others will be averted.

The only state interest asserted here is a general interest in the preservation of life. But the State has no legitimate general interest in someone's life, completely abstracted from the interest of the person living that life, that could outweigh the person's choice to avoid medical treatment. * * * Thus, the State's general interest in life must accede to Nancy Cruzan's particularized and intense interest in self-determination in her choice of medical treatment. There is simply nothing legitimately within the State's purview to be gained by superseding her decision.

* * *

This is not to say that the State has no legitimate interests to assert here. . . . Missouri has a *parens patriae* interest in providing Nancy Cruzan, now incompetent, with as accurate as possible a determination of how she would exercise her rights under these circumstances. Second, if and when it is determined that Nancy Cruzan would want to continue treatment, the State may legitimately assert an interest in providing that treatment. But *until* Nancy's wishes have been determined, the only state interest that may be asserted is an interest in safeguarding the accuracy of that determination.

Accuracy, therefore, must be our touchstone. Missouri may constitutionally impose only those procedural requirements that serve to enhance the accuracy of a determination of Nancy Cruzan's wishes or are at least consistent with an accurate determination. The Missouri "safeguard" that the Court upholds today does not meet that standard. The determination needed in this context is whether the incompetent person would choose to live in a persistent vegetative state on life-support or to avoid this medical treatment. * * * Only evidence of specific statements of treatment choice made by the patient when competent is admissible to support a finding that the patient, now in a persistent vegetative state, would wish to avoid further medical treatment. Moreover, this evidence must be clear and convincing. * * *

* * *

The testimony of close friends and family members . . . may often be the best evidence available of what the patient's choice would be. It is they with whom the patient most likely will have discussed such questions and they who know the patient best. * * *

The Missouri court's disdain for Nancy's statements in serious conversations not long before her accident, for the opinions of Nancy's family and friends as to her values, beliefs and certain choice, and even for the opinion of an outside objective factfinder appointed by the State evinces a disdain for Nancy Cruzan's own right to choose. The rules by which an incompetent person's wishes are determined must represent every effort to determine those wishes. * * *

* * *

There are various approaches to determining an incompetent patient's treatment choice in use by the several States today and there may be advantages and disadvantages to each and other approaches not yet envisioned. The choice, in largest part, is and should be left to the States, so long as each State is seeking, in a reliable manner, to discover what the patient would want. But with such momentous interests in the balance, States must avoid procedures that will prejudice the decision. * * *

* * *

. . . Missouri and this Court have displaced Nancy's own assessment of the processes associated with dying. They have discarded evidence of her will, ignored her values, and deprived her of the right to a decision as closely approximating her own choice as humanly possible. They have done so disingenuously in her name, and openly in Missouri's own. That Missouri and this Court may truly be motivated only by concern for incompetent patients makes no matter. As one of our most prominent jurists warned us decades ago: "Experience should teach us to be most on our guard to protect liberty when the government's purposes are beneficent. . . . The greatest dangers to liberty lurk in insidious encroachment by men of zeal, well meaning but without understanding."

I respectfully dissent.

Justice Stevens dissented.

* * *

The Court . . . permits the State's abstract, undifferentiated interest in the preservation of life to overwhelm the best interests of Nancy Beth Cruzan, interests which would, according to an undisputed finding, be served by allowing her guardians to exercise her constitutional right to discontinue medical treatment. Ironically, the Court reaches this conclusion despite endorsing three significant propositions which should save it from any such dilemma. First, a competent individual's decision to refuse life-sustaining medical procedures is an aspect of liberty protected by the Due Process Clause of the Fourteenth Amendment. Second, upon a proper evidentiary showing, a qualified guardian may make that decision on behalf of an incompetent ward. Third, in answering the important question presented by this tragic case, it is wise "not to attempt by any general statement, to cover every possible phase of the subject." Together, these considerations suggest that Nancy Cruzan's liberty to be free from medical treatment must be understood in light of the facts and circumstances particular to her.

I would so hold: in my view, the Constitution requires the State to care for Nancy Cruzan's life in a way that gives appropriate respect to her own best interests.

* * *

* * * [I]f Nancy Cruzan has no interest in continued treatment, and if she has a liberty interest in being free from unwanted treatment, and if the cessation of treatment would have no adverse impact on third parties, and if no reason exists to doubt the good faith of Nancy's parents, then what possible basis could the State have for insisting upon continued medical treatment? * * *

* * *

* * * [T]he dying patient's best interests are put to one side and the entire inquiry is focused on her prior expressions of intent. An innocent person's constitutional right to be free from unwanted medical treatment is thereby categorically limited to those patients who had the foresight to make an unambiguous statement of their wishes while competent. The Court's decision affords no protection to children, to young people who are victims of unexpected accidents or illnesses, or to the countless thousands of elderly persons who either fail to decide, or fail to explain, how they want to be treated if they should experience a similar fate. Because Nancy Beth Cruzan did not have the foresight to preserve her constitutional right in a living will, or some comparable "clear and convincing" alternative, her right is gone forever and her fate is in the hands of the state legislature instead of in those of her family, her independent neutral guardian *ad litem,* and an impartial judge—all of whom agree on the course of action that is in her best interests. The Court's willingness to find a waiver of this constitutional right reveals a distressing misunderstanding of the importance of individual liberty.

* * *

To be constitutionally permissible, Missouri's intrusion upon these fundamental liberties must, at a minimum, bear a reasonable relationship to a legitimate state end. Missouri asserts that its policy is related to a state interest in the protection of life. In my view, however, it is an effort to define life, rather than to protect it, that is the heart of Missouri's policy. Missouri insists, without regard to Nancy Cruzan's own interests, upon equating her life with the biological persistence of her bodily functions. Nancy Cruzan, it must be remembered, is not now simply incompetent. She is in a persistent vegetative state, and has been so for seven years. The trial court found, and no party contested, that Nancy has no possibility of recovery and no consciousness.

* * *

In short, there is no reasonable ground for believing that Nancy Beth Cruzan has any *personal* interest in the perpetuation of what the State has decided is her life. * * *

* * *

My disagreement with the Court is thus unrelated to its endorsement of the clear and convincing standard of proof for cases of this kind. Indeed, I agree that the controlling facts must be established with unmistakable clarity. The critical question, however, is not how to prove the controlling facts but rather what proven facts should be controlling. In my view, the constitutional answer is clear: the best interests of the individual, especially when buttressed by the interests of all related third parties, must prevail over any general state policy that simply ignores those interests. * * * The failure of Missouri's policy to heed the interests of a dying individual with respect to matters so private is ample evidence of the policy's illegitimacy.

* * *

While the Cruzans lost this case, their initial request was honored several months after the Court's decision. After the state withdrew from the case, the Cruzans presented new evidence to a county court about their daughter's wishes. The court granted their request to have the feeding tube disconnected, and Nancy Cruzan died twelve days later.

Despite the Court's decision in *Cruzan,* the issue of the "right to die" may return to the Court for consideration. As we noted in *Cruzan,* the Court ruled that the right of privacy does not include the "right to die." It did rule, however, that competent adults, because of individual liberty interests, do have the right to make medical decisions about themselves, including decisions that would result in their own death. Thus, future Supreme Court cases in this area are likely to be argued on individual liberty grounds rather than on the right of privacy. A potential case could arise as a result of a state ballot proposal involving the "right to die." In November of 1994, Oregon became the first state to approve "physician-assisted suicide." According to Measure 16, physicians will be allowed to prescribe a lethal dose of drugs to terminally ill patients (under strict conditions). A federal district judge issued an injunction against this law, and the case is under consideration by a federal appeals court.

Other potential cases are making their way through the courts. The states of New York and Washington are involved in litigation in the federal courts concerning their laws that ban assisted suicide. At the district court level, the New York law was upheld, but the Washington statute was invalidated. Both of these cases are being reviewed by their respective federal courts of appeals. The most publicized "right to die" dispute involves Dr. Jack Kevorkian, a Michigan physician who has admitted to assisting a number of terminally ill patients in committing suicide. He was arrested for violating the state law that makes assisted suicide a felony. Although juries have acquitted Dr. Kevorkian in two different cases, the county prosecutor has made plans to pursue additional prosecutions because Dr. Kevorkian has continued to assist other terminally ill people in ending their own lives. The law under which Dr. Kevorkian was prosecuted was held unconstitutional by lower state courts, including the Michigan Court of Appeals, but the Michigan Supreme Court reversed these rulings. After the Michigan high court reinstated the ban and ordered the prosecution of Dr. Kevorkian, his attorneys appealed to the U.S. Supreme Court. Again, the arguments were based on an individual's liberty interests, rather than on the right of privacy. Although the Court refused to accept this case for review, the fact that three other "right to die" cases (Oregon, New York, and Washington) are pending in the federal appeals courts makes it likely that the Court will eventually have to rule on this controversial issue.

Conclusion

It is clear that during the Rehnquist era, the Court's treatment of abortion policy has undergone some important changes. The Reagan and Bush appointees from the late 1980s to the early 1990s—Justices Scalia, Kennedy, Souter, and Thomas—joined with Chief Justice Rehnquist and Justices White and O'Connor to uphold more restrictive abortion regulations. In addition, despite the plurality assertion in *Casey* that *Roe v. Wade* remains in principle, *Casey* represents a significant departure from *Roe*. Moreover, if *Casey* is really the controlling precedent, advocates of abortion rights will have great difficulty in getting restrictive statutes invalidated. Under the *Casey* definition of an "undue burden," it is likely that most abortion regulations would pass the Court's scrutiny.

These changes in abortion policy do seem to be related to the personnel changes that have occurred on the Court. Two of the strongest supporters of abortion rights, Justices Brennan and Marshall, were succeeded by Justices Souter and Thomas, respectively. Despite agreeing to preserve *Roe,* Souter upheld the regulations being challenged in *Rust* and *Casey*. In *Casey,* Thomas's lone privacy decision, he joined a plurality calling for *Roe* to be explicitly overruled. Justice Kennedy succeeded Justice Powell, who had authored the majority opinion in *Akron I,* where the Court struck down regulations that were very similar to the ones Kennedy agreed to uphold in *Casey*.

The most recent personnel changes are due to the retirements of Justices White and Blackmun. Justice White, a dissenter in *Roe* and a sustainer of strict abortion regulations, was succeeded by Ruth Bader Ginsburg, who strongly supports abortion rights, despite expressing some concerns about the reasoning in *Roe*. She has argued that the *Roe* decision would have been stronger if it were based on the Equal Protection Clause rather than the right of privacy. Justice Blackmun, *Roe*'s author and the Court's most passionate defender of a woman's right to choose, was succeeded by Stephen Breyer, a federal appeals court judge. Breyer also appears to be a supporter of abortion rights.

In sum, the only personnel change in recent years that has resulted in a liberal justice replacing a conservative one in this area was Justice Ginsburg's succession of Justice White. Most importantly, it appears that, for the foreseeable future, a majority exists who will permit greater restrictions on abortions. At the same time, however, the appointments of Ginsburg and Breyer will most certainly strengthen the Court's general commitment to recognizing the abortion decision as a fundamental right and to preventing some forms of government interference with that decision.

REFERENCES

Craig, Barbara Hinkson, and David M. O'Brien. *Abortion and American Politics.* Chatham, N.J.: Chatham House Publishers, 1993.

Goldstein, Leslie. *The Constitutional Rights of Women: Cases in Law and Social Change.* 2d ed. Madison: The University of Wisconsin Press, 1988.

Irons, Peter. *The Courage of Their Convictions.* New York: The Free Press, 1988.

Irons, Peter, and Stephanie Guitton. *May It Please the Court.* New York: The New Press, 1993.

Mezey, Susan Gluck. *In Pursuit of Equality: Women, Public Policy, and the Federal Courts.* New York: St. Martin's Press, 1992.

Smith, Christopher E. *Courts and Public Policy.* Chicago: Nelson-Hall, 1993.

American Civil Rights/Liberties and the Changing Supreme Court:

Conclusions

American Civil Rights/Liberties and the Changing Supreme Court: Conclusions

A central inquiry of this book has been whether the civil rights and liberties policies of the United States Supreme Court have changed in dramatic ways since 1986 when William Rehnquist became chief justice. Republican presidents Ronald Reagan and George Bush had the opportunity to remake the Court in the eighties and nineties. Reagan was able to appoint Sandra Day O'Connor in 1981 as the Court's first woman justice; in 1986 he had the opportunity to elevate Rehnquist to the position of chief justice to replace Warren Burger and then to appoint Antonin Scalia to Rehnquist's associate justice seat; and in 1987 Reagan appointed Anthony Kennedy to the high court. Many Court observers thought that the four Reagan appointees would join with Byron White to form a five-person conservative majority that would move American civil rights and liberties in a much more conservative direction despite the presence of four liberals on the Court—Brennan, Marshall, Blackmun, and Stevens.

President Bush had the opportunity to expand this conservative grouping even further. The Court's two leading liberals—Brennan and Marshall—retired in 1990 and 1991, respectively. Bush appointed David Souter to replace Brennan in 1990, and the next year Bush named Clarence Thomas to replace Marshall. This seemed to provide an overwhelming conservative coalition of seven justices that would create a conservative counterrevolution in American civil rights and liberties policies.

Democrat William Clinton's election to the presidency in 1992 and his two Supreme Court appointments seemed to be a situation of "too little, too late" for liberals. Clinton's appointment in 1993 of Ruth Bader Ginsburg to replace Harry Blackmun was not viewed as affecting the balance on the Court, and the replacement of Byron White by Stephen Breyer in 1994 was not seen by most Court observers as a change which would have major effects on Court policies.

What do the results of our quantitative and doctrinal analyses in this book suggest regarding this question of the effect of changing membership on the civil rights and liberties policies of the Supreme Court since 1986? Based upon our examination of the Court's decisions though the 1994–95 term, we conclude that the Rehnquist Court has not engaged in a constitutional counterrevolution against the civil rights and liberties policies of the Warren and Burger Courts. The Rehnquist Court can more accurately be characterized as a moderately conservative Court which has moved in more conservative directions in some areas but which has not repudiated most of the major precedents and doctrines of past Courts.

In First Amendment cases, the Rehnquist Court has been more liberal than conservative in its freedom of expression cases and has adhered to the major principles of the Warren and Burger Courts. More volatility can be seen in regard to the religious guarantees, especially with the Free Exercise Clause where the liberal *Sherbert* test has been substantially undercut by the introduction of the far more conservative *Smith* test. The Rehnquist Court continues to struggle with the Establishment Clause; the *Lemon* test has been neglected but not yet rejected, and the Court seems evenly balanced between justices advocating neutrality and accommodationist approaches to the Establishment Clause.

A somewhat similar pattern can be seen in regard to the guarantees of the criminally accused. The Fourth Amendment jurisprudence of the Rehnquist Court has been characterized by major conservative changes, specifically the relaxed standards for certain categories of warrantless searches. With respect to the Fifth, Sixth, and Eighth Amendments, the Rehnquist Court has generally continued the pattern established by the Burger Court in further reducing the scope of various protections. However, the Rehnquist Court has not engaged in a wholesale counterrevolution because the Warren Court's important precedents remain intact, albeit in less expansive form, and, despite the creation of various weakening exceptions, important doctrines such as the exclusionary rule and *Miranda* warnings survive.

In the area of equal protection, the Rehnquist Court has again established a somewhat mixed record. The Court has been surprisingly liberal in regard to gender discrimination cases. With respect to racial discrimination cases, however, the Court has been more conservative. In its school desegregation decisions, the Rehnquist Court has taken a narrow view of the role of the federal courts, ruling that federal judges are limited to remedying segregation that results from de jure segregation. Moreover, judges may withdraw supervision from school desegregation cases even if racially identifiable schools continue to exist in systems previously under court orders to desegregate. In the area of voting rights, the Court has made it difficult for majority-minority districts to be upheld, ruling that if race is the predominant factor in drawing the district lines, the redistricting plan must be subject to strict scrutiny. With respect to affirmative action, the Rehnquist Court has engaged in a conservative counterrevolution, ruling that all governmental affirmative action programs—local, state, and federal—must be examined under strict scrutiny.

Finally, in the area of privacy the Rehnquist Court has significantly modified but not overturned the controversial abortion decision of *Roe v. Wade* (1973). The Court's new undue burden standard provides states with greater authority to regulate abortions than existed under the original trimester formula of *Roe,* but a woman's fundamental right of choice remains.

All of these conclusions must necessarily be tentative. This book covers the Court's decisions through the 1994–95 term, but new decisions in subsequent terms could profoundly affect these conclusions. More definitive assessments on the Rehnquist Court will not be possible until Chief Justice Rehnquist resigns and a new chief justice is appointed.

Regardless of who sits on the Supreme Court, however, American civil rights and liberties will remain an important and fascinating subject. The justices are continually confronted with novel, difficult, and important issues regarding the meaning of the American Constitution. As students of the Court, we are continually impressed with the abilities and efforts of the members of the Supreme Court. We certainly do not always agree with the outcomes or the reasoning of the Court's decisions. However, we readily acknowledge that the justices approach their responsibilities with seriousness of purpose and a desire to protect what they see as important constitutional values.

APPENDIX

Doctrinal Framework

Introduction

The doctrinal framework presented in Chapter 1 and utilized throughout the book is a technique we have developed to assist in assessing the direction and magnitude of policy changes by the Rehnquist Court in the area of civil rights and liberties. A central theme of this book is whether the changing membership of the Court since 1986 has led to significantly more conservative policies. This is an issue which has dominated much of the recent scholarship on the Court (e.g., Kairys 1993; Domino 1994; and Friedelbaum 1994), but none of the existing studies has set forth explicit criteria by which to assess the extent to which the Rehnquist Court has altered previous civil rights and liberties policies.

We specify three variables in our framework which are directly relevant to assessing policy changes. One factor involves the Court's treatment of existing precedent. In assessing this factor, we analyze not only whether the Court's judgment was liberal or conservative but also whether the Court's opinion was based upon existing precedent, modified existing precedent, or created a new precedent by overruling an existing precedent. A second variable involves the importance of the case, and we classify all cases as being either major or minor in importance. Finally, the third criterion we examine is whether a case involves a majority or plurality opinion.

After classifying each case decided by the Rehnquist Court according to these three variables, we then group the cases into common areas (e.g., the Establishment Clause, gender discrimination, etc.) and place each case into its appropriate cell in the table. The patterns in the table allow us to offer judgments about the extent of change associated with the Rehnquist Court. *In order to conclude that significant policy change has occurred, a table must contain one or more cases in which a Court majority has modified existing precedent or created a new precedent in a decision of major importance.*

Court's Treatment of Existing Precedent

We need to explain precisely how we have measured each of the three variables used in the doctrinal framework. The most complex variable is the Court's treatment of existing precedent, which involves two considerations: whether the Court's decision was liberal or conservative and whether the Court followed, modified, or overturned existing precedent. We have followed closely the techniques developed by Harold Spaeth (1995) in the *United States Supreme Court Judicial Database,* a project supported by the National Science Foundation.

The criteria we have utilized for classifying case outcomes as liberal or conservative follow closely those used by Spaeth. Spaeth (1995, p. 103) states that decisions which favor the individual claiming a civil rights or civil liberties violation by the government are considered to be liberal; those decisions favoring the government are classified as conservative. This definitional approach to the concepts of liberalism and conservatism is widely utilized in studies on Supreme Court decision making (e.g., Segal and Spaeth 1989 and Smith and Hensley 1993).

Although this approach to defining liberalism and conservatism is valid for most decisions, various complexities do arise. The most important exception involves affirmative action cases where a liberal decision is one that favors the government's program and a conservative decision is one that favors the individual challenging the affirmative action policy. Establishment Clause cases can also present difficulties when the government is trying to assure the separation of church and state, for example by refusing to provide a state-paid sign language interpreter in a parochial school (*Zobrest v. Catalina Hills School District,* 1993). If the government is trying to promote the separation of church and state, then a Supreme Court decision favoring the government is considered liberal. Because of the unique circumstances which can arise in each area of civil rights and liberties policies, we are careful to define the concepts of liberalism and conservatism in each chapter.

We also follow Spaeth's guidelines in regard to measuring the Court's treatment of precedent. The justice who writes the majority opinion in a case will typically state that the Court is basing its decision upon existing precedent and these decisions are classified as involving the interpretation of existing precedent. Occasionally, however, the justice writing the majority opinion will state explicitly that the Court is modifying or overruling existing precedent. Thus, if the justice authoring a majority opinion states that an existing precedent has been overruled, then the case is classified as one in which the Court has created a new precedent. Also, a justice writing the majority opinion in a case may occasionally state that a precedent is being formally altered but not overruled; in this situation, the case is classified as the modification of existing precedent. Finally, on rare occasion, a dissenting opinion will argue persuasively that the majority opinion either modified or overruled an existing precedent even though this was not acknowledged in the majority opinion. These criteria mean that relatively few cases will be classified as modifying existing precedent or creating new precedent because the Court is very reluctant to admit to this type of activity, which goes against the principle of *stare decisis,* adhering to precedent. Thus, the presence of cases in the categories of the modification of existing precedent and the creation of new precedent may signal important policy changes by the Court.

Importance of the Case

The second major variable involves the importance of the cases, and we classify the cases as being of either major or minor importance. Although all Supreme Court decisions can be viewed as important, substantial variation does exist in the legal and social significance of the cases decided by the Court. Political scientists have given considerable attention to the issue of measuring the importance of Supreme Court cases (e.g., Cook 1993), but no clear consensus exists regarding this measurement issue. Numerous criteria can be utilized to assess the importance of Supreme Court cases, depending upon the purposes and requirements of the researcher. Our research requires that we use sources which have several characteristics: (1) the source should be familiar and legitimate to researchers in the field, (2) the source should be current, allowing us to classify recently decided cases, (3) the source should be reliable, allowing researchers to produce the same list of important cases, and (4) the source should be consistent over time. Based upon these criteria, we have chosen to utilize two sources which identify the Court's most important cases each term: (1) *New York Times* and (2) *United States Supreme Court Reports: Lawyers' Edition* published by Lawyers Cooperative Publishing.

Each of these sources needs to be discussed briefly. Each Sunday after the Supreme Court completes its term, the *New York Times* publishes an extensive analysis of the recently completed term. This analysis includes a listing and description of the most significant cases decided in the previous year. In utilizing *United States Supreme Court Reports: Lawyers' Edition,* we draw upon two different listings. Hardbound volume of *Lawyers' Edition* contain annual summaries of each term of the Court, and a section of this summary is entitled "Landmark Decisions" where the most important decisions are listed and described. The hardbound volumes are typically published two years after the Court has completed a term, however, and thus for more recent decisions we identify the major cases as those which are highlighted (by being enclosed in a box) in the paperback, advanced copies of *Lawyer's Edition.*

In order to be classified as a major case, *both* sources must identify the case as being important. The two sources are in agreement on a majority of the cases each term, but substantial disagreement can also exist. By requiring a case to make both lists, we can have considerable confidence that the case is indeed of major importance. On rare occasion, however, we have asserted our own judgment that a case should be considered major even though both sources did not list it. For example, we did list *Oregon v. Smith* (1990) as a major free exercise of religion case even though this was not included in the group of the 1989-90 term cases by the *New York Times.* The Court, the popular media, and the scholarly community have clearly acknowledged this as a landmark case because it changed the level of Court protection of free exercise claims from strict scrutiny to minimal scrutiny, and hence we have included it in our list of major cases.

A final caution needs to be added regarding our classification of cases as being of major or minor importance. This caution relates to our lack of historic perspective on contemporary cases. Although certain cases may seem to be of great significance when the Court decides them, their importance may be overrated; as time passes, these cases may come to be viewed by legal experts as relatively minor cases. Similarly, cases which initially may be considered of minor importance may be viewed as major cases from a longer historical perspective.

Majority or Plurality Opinion

The third and final variable of our doctrinal framework involves the majority or plurality status of the controlling opinion of a case. In most cases, no ambiguity exists in the determination of whether the Court has issued a majority opinion. If five or more justices join all parts of the controlling opinion, then the case is classified as involving a majority opinion. Conversely, if four or fewer justices join the controlling opinion, then the decision is classified as being a plurality opinion. Ambiguity can arise, however, when less than a majority of the justices joint the controlling opinion and one or more justices concur in part in the controlling opinion. In such situations, the opinions must be read with great care to determine if five or more justices agreed with the central legal reasoning supporting the decision, which means that the decision can be classified as a majority opinion. A good example of a difficult decision to classify on the basis of a majority or plurality opinion is *Richmond v. Croson* (1989), the case in which the Court applied the strict scrutiny approach to state affirmative action programs. O'Connor wrote the controlling opinion, but she was not joined by four other justices in all parts of her opinion. In the critical doctrinal part of the case (Section III.A.), she was joined only by Rehnquist, Kennedy, and White. Scalia did not join any of O'Connor's opinion; instead, he wrote a separate concurring opinion in which he stated explicitly that he agreed with O'Connor that the strict scrutiny approach should be used in state affirmative action cases. Thus, *Richmond v. Croson* is classified as involving a majority opinion.

References

Cook, Beverly Blair. 1993. "Measuring the Significance of United States Supreme Court Decisions." *Journal of Politics* 55: 1127-1140.

Domino, John C. 1994. *Civil Rights and Liberties: Toward the 21st Century.* New York: Harper Collins.

Friedelbaum, Stanley H. 1994. *The Rehnquist Court: In Pursuit of Judicial Conservativism.* Westport, Connecticut: Greenwood Press.

Kairys, David. 1993. *With Liberty and Justice for Some.* New York: The New Press.

Spaeth, Harold J. 1995. *United States Supreme Court Judicial Database, 1953-1993 Terms.* Ann Arbor, Michigan: Inter-University Consortium for Political and Social Research.

APPENDIX B
Quantitative Techniques of Analysis

Introduction

We utilize quantitative techniques extensively throughout the book as one approach to describing and analyzing Supreme Court civil rights and liberties policies. Quantitative analysis is rarely used in textbooks such as this, however. We therefore think it is important to provide a justification for our utilization of quantitative data as well as a somewhat detailed description of the quantitative techniques we are employing.

Advantages of Quantitative Analysis

Numerous advantages are associated with the use of quantitative techniques to analyze Supreme Court decision making. Quantitative analysis enables us to be comprehensive, precise, efficient, and reliable.

Quantitative techniques are *comprehensive*. Because the Supreme Court has issued thousands of civil rights and liberties decisions in its history, it is a practical impossibility to describe and analyze all of these cases through traditional, narrative methods. Quantitative analysis does allow for comprehensive analysis, however. By classifying case outcomes and justices' votes into liberal and conservative categories, statistical summaries can be easily produced. Thus, for example, in one table we can compare the liberal/conservative voting patterns of the Warren, Burger, and Rehnquist Courts for *all* the civil rights and liberties cases decided during these Court eras.

A second advantage in the use of quantitative data is the *precision* attained. In the non-quantitative analysis of Supreme Court decision making patterns, the best a researcher can do is to make a broad, general statement regarding decisional trends. Thus, a researcher may state that the Court has become "somewhat" or "substantially" more conservative, but no precise information can be supplied. What does the word "somewhat" mean? How much more conservative has the Court become? Quantitative techniques allow for precision. Our voting data will allow us, for example, to compare exactly how liberal the Warren Court was in regard to obscenity cases and to compare directly the percentage of liberal outcomes of the Burger and Rehnquist Courts in the area of obscenity.

Quantitative techniques are also *efficient*. Although short, summary conclusions can be stated in non-quantitative research, the justification of these conclusions is typically a long, complicated process because numerous decisions have to be described and analyzed. In quantitative research, however, important conclusions can be reached and explained based upon the information in a single table.

Finally, quantitative techniques are also highly *reliable*. Explicit criteria are set forth for coding cases, the results of the coding process can be examined by other researchers for accuracy, the analysis of the data follows widely accepted procedures, and the results are reported in a clear, quantitative format. In contrast, non-quantitative research tends to have low reliability. Conclusions are offered based upon research techniques which lack explicit criteria regarding what cases are to be analyzed and how they will be analyzed; therefore, the research cannot be reliably reproduced, and the conclusions offered are more subject to challenge.

Limitations of Quantitative Methods of Analysis

Despite the major advantages of quantitative techniques of analysis, they also have important limitations: (1) treating all cases as being of equal importance when in reality they vary substantially in importance, (2) oversimplifying the decisions of the Court and the justices, and (3) disregarding the legal reasoning of the justices.

One significant limitation of quantitative analysis is the lack of consideration of the *relative importance* of Supreme Court cases. Some cases have far greater significance—legal, political, social, or economic—than others. Quantitative techniques weigh all cases equally, however, while a non-quantitative approach can give substantial emphasis to cases assessed to be of great importance while minimizing or disregarding cases thought to be of minor significance.

A second limitation of quantitative techniques is the *over-simplification* which can occur. In classifying cases in quantitative analysis, the Court's judgment and the votes of the justices are typically dichotomized as being for one side and against the other side. Although this type of classification system is generally satisfactory, complexities do arise. For example, a justice might concur in part and dissent in part regarding the majority opinion of the Court. Whichever way the justice is classified as voting, some inaccuracy is going to exist; the complexity of the justice's position cannot be fully represented by the coding system.

The most important weakness of quantitative techniques is the failure to take into account the *written opinions* of the justices. The justices of the Supreme Court not only have to vote for one side or the other in a case but also have to offer explanations through written opinions for their votes. The opinions are more important than the votes because the votes affect only the direct parties in the case whereas the opinions can set forth guidelines and policies for the entire country. In the case of *Miranda v. Arizona* (1966), for example, the 5-4 vote that Ernesto Miranda's rights were violated directly affected only Miranda and his state prosecutors. The majority opinion in the case, however, directly affected the activities of police and prosecutors throughout the country by specifying precise statements that had to be made to arrested suspects before interrogation could begin.

Do these limitations mean that we should not undertake quantitative methods of analyzing Supreme Court civil rights and liberties cases? The answer is no. The many advantages of quantitative analysis provide more than adequate justification for its use. The limitations we have acknowledged do require us, however, to exercise caution in offering conclusions based upon purely quantitative data. Even more importantly, however, these limitations require that we also utilize nonquantitative techniques which can address the weakness and limitations of quantitative techniques of analysis. Thus, throughout the book we combine not only quantitative techniques of analysis but also a unique doctrinal framework discussed in Appendix A as well as in-depth analysis of the justices' opinions in the major cases decided by the Court.

Having justified our utilization of quantitative techniques to study the Supreme Court's civil rights and civil liberties decisions, we now need to discuss these techniques. More specifically, we will discuss the primary source of our data—the United States Supreme Court Judicial Database—and also the research questions and quantitative techniques we will employ to analyze the data.

The Spaeth Data: The United States Supreme Court Judicial Database

The primary source of our data is the *United States Supreme Court Judicial Database*. This data set has been compiled by Harold J. Spaeth (1995) under grants from the National Science Foundation. The data are available through the Inter-University Consortium for Political and Social Research at Ann Arbor, Michigan. We want to point out that this discussion of the Spaeth data is probably more detailed than most students want or need to know. We present it for interested faculty members and students who wish to attain an understanding of the source of the numbers we discuss.

The "Spaeth data" cover the decisions of the United States Supreme Court for all terms of the Warren Court (1953-1968), the Burger Court (1969-1985), and the Rehnquist Court (1986-1993). The data set is updated each year as the Court completes its most recent term, but a time lag of one to two years can exist because of the time it takes to code all the cases and then for the ICPSR to make the data available for public use. Because we need to include the most recent data in our book, we code each term of the Court as soon as it is completed, utilizing the key variables identified by Spaeth in his codebook.

Spaeth gathers an extraordinary amount of information about each case. He measures 39 variables which are classified under six distinctive categories: identification variables, background variables, chronological variables, substantive variables, outcome variables, and voting and opinion variables. We only use a few of these variables, and thus we will discuss only those variables which we employ in our analyses.

Unit of Analysis and Form of Decision

Two critically important and closely related variables are the unit of analysis (ANALU) and the form of decision (DEC_TYPE). Supreme Court cases can be very complex and confusing, and therefore it is important to know exactly what you are analyzing when you use this data set. The unit of analysis variable enables the researcher to choose between using either the case citation or the docket number of a case as the basic unit of analysis. In most decisions there will only be one case citation and one docket number, and thus it will make no difference which unit of analysis is employed. Not all cases are so simple, however. For example, several times each term the Court will consolidate two or more cases, each of which has a separate docket number, and issue a single decision, with a single case citation, which covers all of the consolidated cases. Many other complications can arise regarding cases, docket numbers, case citations, and decisions. No single approach can resolve all of the possible problems.

Our approach is to use case citation as our basic unit of analysis because this seems to minimize any difficulties and to serve our purposes most fully. The problem with using docket numbers as the basic unit of analysis is that it tends to inflate the importance of some cases. For example, four cases with separate docket numbers might be consolidated together by the Court because they raise the same issue, and this means that they are identified by one case citation, typically the first case alphabetically. If case citation is the unit of analysis, then the Court outcome and the individual justices' votes are counted only once; if a docket number is the unit of analysis, then the Court outcome and the individual justices' votes would be counted four times, once for each docket number.

The variable of the form of the decision is also important and can affect dramatically the number of cases being examined. Decisions can take seven different forms: (1) cases with oral arguments and a signed majority opinion, (2) *per curiam* cases with an unsigned opinion and without oral argument, (3) memorandum cases, (4) decrees, (5) cases decided by an equally divided vote, (6) *per curiam* cases with an unsigned opinion and with oral argument, and (7) judgments of the Court, which involve cases with oral arguments and a signed opinion joined by less than a majority of the Court. Researchers are free to analyze any single form or any combination of forms. We have chosen to analyze all cases which involve oral arguments, whether the Court issues a signed or unsigned opinion. These cases seem to be the ones to which the Court assigns particular importance because they allocate time for oral arguments by the attorneys, and they are also important cases because the Court has provided written explanations for their decisions.

Civil Rights and Liberties Cases

Our book focuses on the Supreme Court's civil rights and liberties cases, and therefore we are only concerned with these types of decisions contained in the Spaeth data. Two variables—ISSUE AREAS and ISSUE—are relevant here.

Spaeth identifies thirteen issue areas in a variable labeled as "VALUE." These are criminal procedures, civil rights, First Amendment, due process, privacy, attorneys, unions, economic activity, judicial power, federalism, interstate relations, federal taxation, and miscellaneous. The first five of these are associated with civil rights and liberties and are therefore the categories on which we focus our attention.

Each issue area or value is divided by Spaeth into numerous specific issues, which are our major concern in this book because they involve the major, specific civil rights and liberties policies decided by the Court. Within the ISSUE variable, Spaeth identifies 58 specific issues under the heading of criminal procedure, 41 specific issues within the category of civil rights, 20 First Amendment issues, 7 issues under due process, and 3 issues under the heading of privacy. The ISSUE variable enables us to engage in a wide variety of analyses regarding Supreme Court decision making in civil rights and liberties. For example, under the heading of civil rights issues we can analyze the Court's decisions in such areas as race discrimination, gender discrimination, and affirmative action.

We are constrained somewhat by the limitations of the ISSUE variable, however. These restrictions are relatively few, but some of the more important ones need to be mentioned. Perhaps most significantly, the First Amendment category does not differentiate between freedom of speech and freedom of the press cases. Some civil rights and liberties textbooks have separate chapters on these two subjects. We have chosen to analyze freedom of speech and press together under the broad category of freedom of expression, and part of the reason for this choice relates to the nature of the Spaeth data. More importantly, however, freedom of speech and of the press need to be treated together because the Supreme Court itself recognizes that these are closely related, overlapping areas rather than distinct and separate forms of expression. An additional limitation created by the ISSUE variable is the absence of the issues of warrantless searches or the exclusionary rule under the criminal procedure issue area. Thus, we have not been able to undertake separate, quantitative analyses on these subjects.

Direction of Decisions and Justices' Votes (Liberalism-Conservatism)

The final variables in the Spaeth data that are of importance for our purposes involve the *direction* of the Court's decisions and the *direction* of the votes of the individual justices. The basic concern in regard to direction is whether the Court upheld or rejected the civil rights or liberties claim. These directional variables are of critical importance because they identify whether the Court and the individual justices are voting liberally or conservatively. As noted in Appendix A, Spaeth (1995, p. 103) states that a liberal decision is one which favors the individual claiming a civil rights or liberties violation by the government; conversely, those decisions favoring the government are considered to be conservative. The terms liberal and conservative can be ambiguous concepts, however, and may vary in their meaning depending upon the civil right or liberty under discussion; thus, we specify the exact meaning of these terms when we use them in the respective chapters of this book.

Research Questions and Data Analysis

In analyzing the voting data on the Supreme Court's civil rights and liberties policies, we are guided by a common set of questions in each chapter, and we utilize a common data analysis format in each chapter for answering these questions.

The first question we raise in the quantitative analysis section of the various chapters is whether the Rehnquist Court has been more conservative than the preceding Warren and Burger Courts. In analyzing this issue, we create a simple table in which we compare the percentage of liberal and conservative outcomes for the three Court eras.

Having examined the overall patterns of Supreme Court decision making across time, we then turn to a more detailed analysis of the Rehnquist Court period by looking at the liberal/conservative voting records of the individual justices who have served during the Rehnquist Court era. The table containing this information allows us to assess the extent to which changes in membership may affect the direction of the Court's decision making through a comparison of the voting record of new appointees with the voting record of the justices being replaced. This table containing the liberal/conservative voting records of the individual justices can also provide us with insights into whether a majority of closely aligned justices exists which can dominate Court decision making in that particular area of civil rights and liberties.

The question of judicial voting alignments—voting blocs—is an interesting and important issue. If a majority of the justices form a highly cohesive voting bloc in a particular area, then this majority coalition has the potential to bring about significant policy change on the Court. We therefore need to examine closely the issue of bloc voting. Determining the liberal and conservative voting patterns of the individual justices is not an adequate method of determining bloc voting patterns because such data do not tell us the extent to which justices voted together in the same cases. In other words, two justices could both have 80 percent conservative voting records in a particular area of civil rights and liberties, but they might have voted together in the same cases only 60 percent of the time.

Specific procedures do exist for undertaking bloc voting analysis which enable us to assess the extent to which groups of justices form cohesive voting blocs. Before we discuss these procedures, however, we need to emphasize that bloc voting on the Supreme Court does not mean that the justices consciously align with one another, swap votes, or engage in any type of unethical behavior. Bloc voting recognizes that the justices arrive at their decisions through their independent judgments, although these may be influenced by the bargaining and persuasion that occurs as the justices exchange ideas in conference and in written communications. The justices eventually cast their votes, however, and bloc voting analysis determines if particular groups of justices tend to vote together to an unusually high degree.

Bloc voting analysis is widely used in studying the Supreme Court (e.g. Smith, Baugh, Hensley, and Johnson 1994; Bowen and Scheb 1993; and Dudley 1993), and Murphy and Tanenhaus (1973) have laid out specific criteria for undertaking bloc analysis. The initial step in bloc voting analysis is to select a relatively stable Court period and an issue area of interest. Because we are examining the Rehnquist Court era, we have a period characterized by some turnover in personnel; five new justices—Kennedy, Souter, Thomas, Ginsburg, and Breyer—have been appointed to the Court since Rehnquist became chief justice in 1986. Some justices—especially Powell, Ginsburg, and Breyer—have participated in relatively few decisions during this era, and thus they must be excluded from our bloc voting analysis. In regard to issue areas, the Court has handed down a sufficient number of decisions for us to do bloc voting analysis in every chapter of the book except Chapter 16, which deals with a small number of equal protection cases not involving race or gender.

Having selected a particular Court period and an issue area, the next step is to determine an index of agreement score for each pair of justices in all relevant cases. This score is determined by taking the number of cases in which the justices voted together—both liberal or both conservative—and dividing by the total number of cases in which they participated. Thus, if two justices voted similarly in 15 of 20 cases, they would have an interagreement score of 75 percent.

Once the index of agreement scores for all pairs of justices are determined, the next step is to create a bloc voting matrix containing the names of all justices and their interagreement scores. The initial task in constructing this matrix is to create a master list of the interagreement scores of all pairs of justices, ranked from the highest score to the lowest. As a general guideline, a pair of justices should only be included in the list if they have participated in at least one-half of the total cases. Having completed the list, the pair of justices with the highest level of agreement is placed in the first two spots in the upper left-hand corner of the matrix. In the Establishment Clause bloc voting matrix in Table 5.4, for example, Justices Brennan and Marshall were in 100 percent agreement, and therefore they were placed in the first two places in the matrix. The next task is to search the list of the pairs of justices for the highest score which includes one of the justices already in the matrix. In the Establishment Clause bloc voting matrix in Table 5.4, this justice was Stevens, who had an 89 percent agreement score with Marshall. (Blackmun also had an 89 percent agreement score with Marshall and could have been placed third rather than fourth.) This same process occurs until all the justices have been placed in the matrix and all of the respective scores have been entered.

The final stage is to determine if one or more voting blocs exist and which justices belong to which bloc.

This involves several steps. The first step is to determine the overall average agreement score for all the justices, i.e., the Court mean. This is done by adding together all the scores for every pair of justices and then dividing this summation by the number of pairs of justices. Thus, in Table 5.4 all of the numbers (percentages) in the matrix are added together and divided by 36, the number of scores. This resulted in a Court mean of 62.86; this can be interpreted to show that the average interagreement score of the justices was 63 percent.

This number by itself is not very helpful, however, because a voting bloc implies that two or more justices have an extraordinarily high level of agreement. We therefore need a way to determine if a significantly high level of agreement exists. The Sprague Criterion can be used for this purpose.

The Sprague Criterion can be calculated easily. First, the Court mean is subtracted from 100. Second, the resulting number is divided by two. Third, the number that results from the division in step two is added to the Court mean. The resulting number is the Sprague Criterion. We can again turn to Table 5.4 for an illustrative example. The Court mean of 62.86 is subtracted from 100.00, resulting in 37.14. This number is then divided by two, which produces a result of 18.57. This number (18.57) is then added to the Court mean (62.86), producing a Sprague Criterion of 81.43.

Two or more justices with an interagreement average greater than the Sprague Criterion are considered to be a voting bloc. The size of the Sprague Criterion will vary, but it will always be substantially larger than the Court mean, giving us confidence that the blocs we identify will involve justices who share common views about the civil rights/liberties policy being examined. Table 5.4 shows an unusually complex group of voting blocs. The largest voting bloc during the Rehnquist Court era consisted of Brennan, Marshall, Blackmun, and Stevens, who had an average agreement score of 92 percent. O'Connor and Blackmun also formed a two-person bloc with an 85 percent agreement rate. O'Connor could not be added to the larger, four-person bloc, however, because the majority of her interagreement scores with the members of the bloc were below the Sprague Criterion. Finally, two small conservative blocs existed, each involving only two justices, Rehnquist and Scalia with a 92 percent interagreement and Rehnquist and White at 83 percent.

References for Appendix B

Bowen, Terry and John M. Scheb II. 1993. "Freshman Opinion Writing on the United States Supreme Court, 1921-1991." *Judicature* 76: 239-243.

Dudley, Robert L. 1992. "The Freshman Effect and Voting Alignments: A Reexamination of Judicial Folklore." *American Politics Quarterly* 21: 360-367.

Murphy, Walter and Joseph Tanenhaus. 1973. *The Study of Public Law.* New York: Random House.

Segal, Jeffrey A. and Harold J. Spaeth. 1989. "Decisional Trends on the Warren and Burger Courts: Results from the Supreme Court Database Project." *Judicature* 73: 103-107.

Smith, Christopher E. and Thomas R. Hensley. 1993. "Assessing the Conservatism of the Rehnquist Court." *Judicature* 77: 83-89.

Smith, Christopher E., Joyce A. Baugh, Thomas R. Hensley, and Scott P. Johnson. 1994. "The First-Term Performance of Justice Ruth Bader Ginsburg." *Judicature* 78: 74-80.

Spaeth, Harold J. 1995. *United States Supreme Court Judicial Database, 1953-1993 Terms.* Ann Arbor, Michigan: Inter-university Consortium for Political and Social Research.

APPENDIX

The Justices of the United States Supreme Court

Justice (Party)	President (Party)	Justice Replaced	Years of Service	State of Justice	Law School
*Jay, John (Fed.)	Washington (Fed.)		1789-1795	N.Y.	
Rutledge, John (Fed.)	Washington (Fed.)		1789-1791	S.C.	
Cushing, William (Fed.)	Washington (Fed.)		1789-1810	Mass.	
Wilson, James (Fed.)	Washington (Fed.)		1789-1798	Penn.	
Blair, John (Fed.)	Washington (Fed.)		1789-1795	Va.	
Iredell, James (Fed.)	Washington (Fed.)		1790-1799	N.C.	
Johnson, Thomas (Fed.)	Washington (Fed.)	Rutledge	1791-1793	Md.	
Paterson, William (Fed.)	Washington (Fed.)	Johnson	1793-1806	N.J.	
*Rutledge, John (Fed.)	Washington (Fed.)	Jay	1795	S.C.	
Chase, Samuel (Fed.)	Washington (Fed.)	Blair	1796-1811	Md.	
*Ellsworth, Oliver (Fed.)	Adams (Fed.)	Rutledge	1796-1800	Conn.	
Washington, Bushrod (Fed.)	Adams (Fed.)	Wilson	1798-1829	Pa.	
Moore, Alfred (Fed.)	Adams (Fed.)	Iredell	1799-1804	N.C.	

*Chief Justice

Justice (Party)	President (Party)	Justice Replaced	Years of Service	State of Justice	Law School
*Marshall, John (Fed.)	Adams (Fed.)	Ellsworth	1801-1835	Va.	
Johnson, William (Dem.-Rep.)	Jefferson (Dem.-Rep.)	Moore	1804-1834	S.C.	
Livingston, Henry Brockholst (Dem.-Rep.)	Jefferson (Dem.-Rep.)	Paterson	1806-1823	N.Y.	
Todd, Thomas (Dem.-Rep.)	Jefferson (Dem.-Rep.)	(new seat)	1807-1826	Ky.	
Duvall, Gabriel (Dem.-Rep.)	Madison (Dem.-Rep.)	Chase	1811-1835	Md.	
Story, Joseph (Dem.-Rep.)	Madison (Dem.-Rep.)	Cushing	1811-1845	Mass.	
Thompson, Smith (Dem.-Rep.)	Monroe (Dem.-Rep.)	Livingston	1823-1843	N.Y.	
Trimble, Robert (Dem.-Rep.)	Quincy Adams (Dem.-Rep.)	Todd	1826-1828	Ky.	
McLean, John (Dem., later Rep.)	Jackson (Dem.)	Trimble	1829-1861	Ohio	
Baldwin, Henry (Dem.)	Jackson (Dem.)	Washington	1830-1844	Penn.	
Wayne, James M. (Dem.)	Jackson (Dem.)	Johnson	1835-1867	Ga.	
*Taney, Roger B. (Dem.)	Jackson (Dem.)	Marshall	1836-1864	Md.	
Barbour, Philip P. (Dem.)	Jackson (Dem.)	Duval	1836-1841	Va.	
Catron, John (Dem.)	Van Buren (Dem.)	(new seat)	1837-1865	Tenn.	
McKinley, John (Dem.)	Van Buren (Dem.)	(new seat)	1837-1852	Ky.	
Daniel, Peter V. (Dem.)	Van Buren (Dem.)	Barbour	1841-1860	Va.	
Nelson, Samuel (Dem.)	Tyler (Dem.)	Thompson	1845-1872	N.Y.	
Woodbury, Levi (Dem.)	Polk (Dem.)	Story	1845-1851	N.H.	

Justice (Party)	President (Party)	Justice Replaced	Years of Service	State of Justice	Law School
Grier, Robert C. (Dem.)	Polk (Dem.)	Baldwin	1846-1870	Penn.	
Curtis, Benjamin R. (Whig)	Fillmore (Whig)	Woodbury	1851-1857	Mass.	
Campbell, John A. (Dem.)	Pierce (Dem.)	McKinley	1853-1861	Ala.	
Clifford, Nathan (Dem.)	Buchanan (Dem.)	Curtis	1858-1881	Maine	
Swayne, Noah H. (Rep.)	Lincoln (Rep.)	McLean	1862-1881	Ohio	
Miller, Samuel F. (Rep.)	Lincoln (Rep.)	Daniel	1862-1890	Iowa	
Davis, David (Rep., later Dem.)	Lincoln (Rep.)	Campbell	1862-1877	Ill.	
Field, Stephen J. (Dem.)	Lincoln (Rep.)	(new seat)	1863-1897	Calif.	
*Chase, Salmon P. (Rep.)	Lincoln (Rep.)	Taney	1864-1873	Ohio	
Strong, William (Rep.)	Grant (Rep.)	Grier	1870-1880	Penn.	
Bradley, Joseph (Rep.)	Grant (Rep.)	Wayne	1870-1892	N.J.	
Hunt, Ward (Rep.)	Grant (Rep.)	Nelson	1872-1882	N.Y.	
*Waite, Morrison (Rep.)	Grant (Rep.)	Chase	1874-1888	Ohio	
Harlan, John Marshall (Rep.)	Hayes (Rep.)	Davis	1877-1911	Ky.	
Woods, William B. (Rep.)	Hayes (Rep.)	Strong	1880-1887	Ga.	
Matthews, Stanley (Rep.)	Garfield (Rep.)	Swayne	1881-1889	Ohio	
Gray, Horace (Rep.)	Arthur (Rep.)	Clifford	1881-1902	Mass.	
Blatchford, Samuel (Rep.)	Arthur (Rep.)	Hunt	1882-1893	N.Y.	
Lamar, Lucius Q.C. (Dem.)	Cleveland (Dem.)	Woods	1888-1893	Miss.	

Justice (Party)	President (Party)	Justice Replaced	Years of Service	State of Justice	Law School
*Fuller, Melville (Dem.)	Cleveland (Dem.)	Waite	1888-1910	Ill.	
Brewer, David J. (Rep.)	Harrison (Rep.)	Matthews	1889-1910	Kan.	
Brown, Henry B. (Rep.)	Harrison (Rep.)	Miller	1890-1906	Mich.	
Shiras, George (Rep.)	Harrison (Rep.)	Bradley	1892-1903	Penn.	
Jackson, Howell E. (Dem.)	Harrison (Rep.)	Lamar	1893-1895	Tenn.	
White, Edward D. (Dem.)	Cleveland (Dem.)	Blatchford	1894-1910	La.	
Peckham, Rufus W. (Dem.)	Cleveland (Dem.)	Jackson	1895-1909	N.Y.	
McKenna, Joseph (Rep.)	McKinley (Rep.)	Field	1898-1925	Calif.	
Holmes, Oliver Wendell Jr. (Rep.)	T. Roosevelt (Rep.)	Gray	1902-1932	Mass.	Harvard
Day, William R. (Rep.)	T. Roosevelt (Rep.)	Shiras	1903-1922	Ohio	
Moody, William H. (Rep.)	T. Roosevelt (Rep.)	Brown	1906-1910	Mass.	
Lurton, Horace H. (Dem.)	Taft (Rep.)	Peckham	1910-1916	Tenn.	Cumberland
Hughes, Charles Evans (Rep.)	Taft (Rep.)	Brewer	1910-1916	N.Y.	Columbia
*White, Edward D. (Dem.)	Taft (Rep.)	Fuller	1910-1921	La.	
*Van Devanter, Willis (Rep.)	Taft (Rep.)	White	1910-1937	Wyo.	Cincinnati
Lamar, Joseph R. (Dem.)	Taft (Rep.)	Moody	1910-1916	Ga.	
Pitney, Mahlon (Rep.)	Taft (Rep.)	Harlan	1912-1922	N.J.	
McReynolds, James C. (Dem.)	Wilson (Dem.)	Lurton	1914-1940	Tenn.	Virginia

Justice (Party)	President (Party)	Justice Replaced	Years of Service	State of Justice	Law School
Brandeis, Louis D. (Rep.)	Wilson (Dem.)	Lamar	1916-1939	Mass.	Harvard
Clarke, John H. (Dem.)	Wilson (Dem.)	Hughes	1916-1922	Ohio	
*Taft, William Howard (Rep.)	Harding (Rep.)	White	1921-1930	Ohio	Cincinnati
Sutherland, George (Rep.)	Harding (Rep.)	Clarke	1922-1938	Utah	
Butler, Pierce (Dem.)	Harding (Rep.)	Day	1922-1939	Minn.	
Stanford, Edward T. (Rep.)	Harding (Rep.)	Pitney	1923-1930	Tenn.	Harvard
Stone, Harlan F. (Rep.)	Coolidge (Rep.)	McKenna	1925-1941	N.Y.	Columbia
*Hughes, Charles Evans (Rep.)	Hoover (Rep.)	Taft	1930-1941	N.Y.	Columbia
Roberts, Owen J. (Rep.)	Hoover, (Rep.)	Stanford	1930-1945	Penn.	Pennsylvania
Cardozo, Benjamin (Dem.)	Hoover (Rep.)	Holmes	1932-1938	N.Y.	
Black, Hugo L. (Dem.)	F. Roosevelt (Dem.)	VanDevanter	1937-1971	Ala.	Alabama
Reed, Stanley F. (Dem.)	F. Roosevelt (Dem.)	Sutherland	1938-1957	Ky.	
Frankfurter, Felix (Ind.)	F. Roosevelt (Dem.)	Cardozo	1939-1962	Mass.	Harvard
Douglas, William O. (Dem.)	F. Roosevelt (Dem.)	Brandeis	1939-1975	N.Y.	Columbia
Murphy, Frank (Dem.)	F. Roosevelt (Dem.)	Butler	1940-1949	Mich.	Michigan
Byrnes, James F. (Dem.)	F. Roosevelt (Dem.)	McReynolds	1941-1942	S.C.	

Justice (Party)	President (Party)	Justice Replaced	Years of Service	State of Justice	Law School
*Stone, Harlan F. (Rep.)	F. Roosevelt (Dem.)	Hughes	1941-1946	N.Y.	Columbia
Jackson, Robert H. (Dem.)	F. Roosevelt (Dem.)	Stone	1941-1954	N.Y.	
Rutledge, Wiley B. (Dem.)	F. Roosevelt (Dem.)	Byrnes	1943-1949	Iowa	Colorado
Burton, Harold H. (Rep.)	Truman (Dem.)	Roberts	1945-1958	Ohio	Harvard
*Vinson, Fred M. (Dem.)	Truman (Dem.)	Stone	1946-1953	Ky.	Centre College, Ky.
Clark, Tom C. (Dem.)	Truman (Dem.)	Murphy	1949-1967	Tex.	Texas
Minton, Sherman (Dem.)	Truman (Dem.)	Rutledge	1949-1956	Ind.	Indiana
*Warren, Earl (Rep.)	Eisenhower (Rep.)	Vinson	1953-1969	Calif.	California
Harlan, John Marshall (Rep.)	Eisenhower (Rep.)	Jackson	1955-1971	N.Y.	New York Law School
Brennan, William J. (Dem.)	Eisenhower (Rep.)	Minton	1956-1990	N.J.	Harvard
Whittaker, Charles E. (Rep.)	Eisenhower (Rep.)	Reed	1957-1962	Mo.	U. of Kansas City
Steward, Potter (Rep.)	Eisenhower (Rep.)	Burton	1958-1981	Ohio	Yale
White, Byron R. (Dem.)	Kennedy (Dem.)	Whittaker	1962-1993	Colo.	Yale
Goldberg, Arthur J. (Dem.)	Kennedy (Dem.)	Frankfurter	1962-1965	Ill.	Northwestern
Fortas, Abe (Dem.)	Johnson, (Dem.)	Goldberg	1965-1969	Tenn.	Yale
Marshall, Thurgood (Dem.)	Johnson, (Dem.)	Clark	1967-1991	N.Y.	Howard
*Warren E. Burger (Rep.)	Nixon (Rep.)	Warren	1969-1986	Minn.	St. Paul College of Law

Justice (Party)	President (Party)	Justice Replaced	Years of Service	State of Justice	Law School
Blackmun, Harry A. (Rep.)	Nixon (Rep.)	Fortas	1970-1994	Minn.	Harvard
Powell, Lewis Jr. (Dem.)	Nixon (Rep.)	Black	1972-1987	Va.	Washington & Lee
Rehnquist, William H. (Rep.)	Nixon (Rep.)	Harlan	1972-1986	Ariz.	Stanford
Stevens, John Paul (Rep.)	Ford (Rep.)	Douglas	1975-	Ill.	Northwestern
O'Connor, Sandra Day (Rep.)	Reagan (Rep.)	Stewart	1981-	Ariz.	Stanford
*Rehnquist, William H. (Rep.)	Reagan (Rep.)	Burger	1986-	Ariz.	Stanford
Scalia, Antonin (Rep.)	Reagan (Rep.)	Rehnquist	1986-	D.C.	Harvard
Kennedy, Anthony M. (Rep.)	Reagan (Rep.)	Powell	1988-	Calif.	Harvard
Souter, David H. (Rep.)	Bush (Rep.)	Brennan	1990-	N.H.	Harvard
Thomas, Clarence (Rep.)	Bush (Rep.)	Marshall	1991-	Geor.	Yale
Ginsburg, Ruth Bader (Dem.)	Clinton (Dem.)	White	1993-	D.C.	Columbia
Breyer, Stephen G. (Dem.)	Clinton (Dem.)	Blackmun	1994-	Mass.	Harvard

APPENDIX D

Twentieth Century Natural Court Periods

1900-1901

Chief: Fuller (D)
Associates:
Harlan I (R)
Gray (R)
Brewer (R)
Brown (R)
Shiras (R)
E. White (D)
Peckham (D)
McKenna (R)

1902

Chief: Fuller (D)
Associates:
Harlan I (R)
Brewer (R)
Brown (R)
Shiras (R)
E. White (D)
Peckham (D)
McKenna (R)
Holmes (R)

1903-1905

Chief: Fuller (D)
Associates:
Harland (Ky.) (R)
Brewer (R)
Brown (R)
E. White (D)
Peckham (D)
McKenna (R)
Holmes (R)
Day (R)

1906-1908

Chief: Fuller (D)
Associates:
Harland (Ky.) (R)
Brewer (R)
E. White (D)
Peckham (D)
McKenna (R)
Holmes (R)
Day (R)
Moody (R)

1909

Chief: Fuller (D)
Associates:
Harland (Ky.) (R)
Brewer (R)
E. White (D)
McKenna (R)
Holmes (R)
Day (R)
Moody (R)
Lurton (D)

1910-1911

Chief: E. White (D)
Associates:
Harland (Ky.) (R)
McKenna (R)
Holmes (R)
Day (R)
Lurton (D)
Hughes (R)
VanDevanter (R)
J. Lamar (D)

1912-1913

Chief: E. White (D)
Associates:
McKenna (R)
Holmes (R)
Day (R)
Lurton (D)
Hughes (R)
VanDevanter (R)
J. Lamar (D)
Pitney (R)

1914-1915

Chief: E. White (D)
Associates:
McKenna (R)
Holmes (R)
Day (R)
Hughes (R)
VanDevanter (R)
J. Lamar (D)
Pitney (R)
McReynolds (D)

1916-1920

Chief: E. White (D)
Associates:
McKenna (R)
Holmes (R)
Day (R)
VanDevanter (R)
Pitney (R)
McReynolds (D)
Brandeis (R)
Clarke (D)

1921	1922	1923-1924
Chief: Taft (R)	*Chief: Taft (R)*	*Chief: Taft (R)*
Associates:	*Associates:*	*Associates:*
McKenna (R)	McKenna (R)	McKenna (R)
Holmes (R)	Holmes (R)	Holmes (R)
Day (R)	VanDevanter (R)	VanDevanter (R)
VanDevanter (R)	Pitney (R)	McReynolds (D)
Pitney (R)	McReynolds (D)	Brandeis (R)
McReynolds (D)	Brandeis (R)	Sutherland (R)
Brandeis (R)	Sutherland (R)	Butler (D)
Clarke (D)	Butler (D)	Sanford (R)

1925-1929	1930-1931	1932-1936
Chief: Taft (R)	*Chief: Hughes (R)*	*Chief: Hughes (R)*
Associates:	*Associates:*	*Associates:*
Holmes (R)	Holmes (R)	VanDevanter (R)
VanDevanter (R)	VanDevanter (R)	McReynolds (D)
McReynolds (D)	McReynolds (D)	Brandeis (R)
Brandeis (R)	Brandeis (R)	Sutherland (R)
Sutherland (R)	Sutherland (R)	Butler (D)
Butler (D)	Butler (D)	Stone (R)
Sanford (R)	Stone (R)	Roberts (R)
Stone (R)	Roberts (R)	Cardozo (D)

1937	1938	1939
Chief: Hughes (R)	*Chief: Hughes (R)*	*Chief: Hughes (R)*
Associates:	*Associates:*	*Associates:*
McReynolds (D)	McReynolds (D)	McReynolds (D)
Brandeis (R)	Brandeis (R)	Butler (D)
Sutherland (R)	Butler (D)	Stone (R)
Butler (D)	Stone (R)	Roberts (R)
Stone (R)	Roberts (R)	Black (D)
Roberts (R)	Cardozo (D)	Reed (D)
Cardozo (D)	Black (D)	Frankfurter (I)
Black (D)	Reed (D)	Douglas (D)

1940	1941-1942	1943-1944
Chief: Hughes (R)	*Chief: Stone (R)*	*Chief: Stone (R)*
Associates:	*Associates:*	*Associates:*
McReynolds (D)	Roberts (R)	Roberts (R)
Stone (R)	Black (D)	Black (D)
Roberts (R)	Reed (D)	Reed (D)
Black (D)	Frankfurter (I)	Frankfurter (I)
Reed (D)	Douglas (D)	Douglas (D)
Frankfurter (I)	Murphy (D)	Murphy (D)
Douglas (D)	Byrnes (D)	R. Jackson (D)
Murphy (D)	R. Jackson (D)	W. Rutledge (D)

1945

Chief: Stone (R)
Associates:
Black (D)
Reed (D)
Frankfurter (I)
Douglas (D)
Murphy (D)
R. Jackson (D)
W. Rutledge (D)
Burton (R)

1946-1948

Chief: Vinson (D)
Associates:
Black (D)
Reed (D)
Frankfurter (I)
Douglas (D)
Murphy (D)
R. Jackson (D)
W. Rutledge (D)
Burton (R)

1949-1952

Chief: Vinson (D)
Associates:
Black (D)
Reed (D)
Frankfurter (I)
Douglas (D)
R. Jackson (D)
Burton (R)
Clark (D)
Minton (D)

1953-1954

Chief: Warren (R)
Associates:
Black (D)
Reed (D)
Frankfurter (I)
Douglas (D)
R. Jackson (D)
Burton (R)
Clark (D)
Minton (D)

1955

Chief: Warren (R)
Associates:
Black (D)
Reed (D)
Frankfurter (I)
Douglas (D)
Burton (R)
Clark (D)
Minton (D)
Harlan (R)

1956

Chief: Warren (R)
Associates:
Black (D)
Reed (D)
Frankfurter (I)
Douglas (D)
Burton (R)
Clark (D)
Harlan (R)
Brennan (D)

1957

Chief: Warren (R)
Associates:
Black (D)
Frankfurter (I)
Douglas (D)
Burton (R)
Clark (D)
Harlan (R)
Brennan (D)
Whittaker (R)

1958-1961

Chief: Warren (R)
Associates:
Black (D)
Frankfurter (I)
Douglas (D)
Clark (D)
Harlan (R)
Brennan (D)
Whittaker (R)
Stewart (R)

1962-1965

Chief: Warren (R)
Associates:
Black (D)
Douglas (D)
Clark (D)
Harlan (R)
Brennan (D)
Stewart (R)
B. White (D)
Goldberg (D)

1965-1967

Chief: Warren (R)
Associates:
Black (D)
Douglas (D)
Clark (D)
Harlan (R)
Brennan (D)
Stewart (R)
B. White (D)
Fortas (D)

1967-1969

Chief: Warren (R)
Associates:
Black (D)
Douglas (D)
Harlan (R)
Brennan (D)
Stewart (R)
B. White (D)
Fortas (D)
T. Marshall (D)

1969

Chief: Burger (D)
Associates:
Black (D)
Douglas (D)
Harlan (R)
Brennan (D)
Stewart (R)
B. White (D)
Fortas (D)
T. Marshall (D)

1969-1970

Chief: Burger (R)
Associates:
Black (D)
Douglas (D)
Harlan (R)
Brennan (D)
Stewart (R)
B. White (D)
T. Marshall (D)

1970

Chief: Burger (R)
Associates:
Black (D)
Douglas (D)
Harlan (R)
Brennan (D)
Stewart (R)
B. White (D)
T. Marshall (D)
Blackmun (R)

1971

Chief: Burger (R)
Associates:
Douglas (D)
Brennan (D)
Stewart (R)
B. White (D)
T. Marshall (D)
Blackmun (R)

1972-1975

Chief: Burger (R)
Associates:
Douglas (D)
Brennan (D)
Stewart (R)
B. White (D)
T. Marshall (D)
Blackmun (R)
Powell (D)
Rehnquist (R)

1975-1981

Chief: Burger (R)
Associates:
Brennan (D)
Stewart (R)
B. White (D)
T. Marshall (D)
Blackmun (R)
Powell (D)
Rehnquist (R)
Stevens (R)

1981-1986

Chief: Burger (R)
Associates:
Brennan (D)
B. White (D)
T. Marshall (D)
Blackmun (R)
Powell (D)
Rehnquist (R)
Stevens (R)
O'Connor (R)

1986-1987

Chief: Rehnquist (R)
Associates:
Brennan (D)
B. White (D)
T. Marshall (D)
Blackmun (R)
Powell (D)
Stevens (R)
O'Connor (R)
Scalia (R)

1988-1990

Chief: Rehnquist (R)
Associates:
Brennan (D)
B. White (D)
T. Marshall (D)
Blackmun (R)
Stevens (R)
O'Connor (R)
Scalia (R)
Kennedy (R)

1990-1991

Chief: Rehnquist (R)
Associates:
B. White (D)
T. Marshall (D)
Blackmun (R)
Stevens (R)
O'Connor (R)
Scalia (R)
Kennedy (R)
Souter (R)

1991-1993

Chief: Rehnquist (R)
Associates:
B. White (D)
Blackmun (R)
Stevens (R)
O'Connor (R)
Scalia (R)
Kennedy (R)
Souter (R)
Thomas (R)

1993-1994

Chief: Rehnquist (R)
Associates:
Blackmun (R)
Stevens (R)
O'Connor (R)
Scalia (R)
Kennedy (R)
Souter (R)
Thomas (R)
Ginsburg (D)

1994-

Chief: Rehnquist (R)
Associates:
Stevens (R)
O'Connor (R)
Scalia (R)
Kennedy (R)
Souter (R)
Thomas (R)
Ginsburg (D)
Breyer (D)

APPENDIX

E The Constitution of the United States

We the People of the United States, in Order to form a more perfect Union, establish Justice, insure domestic Tranquility, provide for the common defence, promote the general Welfare, and secure the Blessings of Liberty to ourselves and our Posterity, do ordain and establish this Constitution for the United States of America.

Article I

Section 1. All legislative Powers herein granted shall be vested in a Congress of the United States, which shall consist of a Senate and House of Representatives.

Section 2. [1] The House of Representatives shall be composed of Members chosen every second Year by the People of the several States, and the Electors in each State shall have the Qualifications requisite for Electors of the most numerous Branch of the State Legislature.

[2] No Person shall be a Representative who shall not have attained to the Age of twenty five Years, and been seven Years a Citizen of the United States, and who shall not, when elected, be an Inhabitant of that State in which he shall be chosen.

[3] Representatives and direct Taxes shall be apportioned among the several States which may be included within this Union, according to their respective Numbers, which shall be determined by adding to the whole Number of free Persons, including those bound to Service for a Term of Years, and excluding Indians not taxed, three fifths of all other Persons. The actual Enumeration shall be made within three Years after the first Meeting of the Congress of the United States, and within every subsequent Term of ten Years, in such Manner as they shall by Law direct. The Number of Representatives shall not exceed one for every thirty Thousand, but each State shall have at Least one Representative; and until such enumerations shall be made, the State of New Hampshire shall be entitled to chuse three, Massachusetts eight, Rhode Island and Providence Plantations one, Connecticut five, New-York six, New Jersey four, Pennsylvania eight, Delaware one, Maryland six, Virginia ten, North Carolina five, South Carolina five, and Georgia three.

[4] When vacancies happen in the Representation from any State, the Executive Authority thereof shall issue Writs of Election to fill such Vacancies.

[5] The House of Representatives shall chuse their Speaker and other Officers; and shall have the sole Power of Impeachment.

Section 3. [1] The Senate of the United States shall be composed of two Senators from each State, chosen by the Legislature thereof, for six Years; and each Senator shall have one Vote.

[2] Immediately after they shall be assembled in Consequence of the first Election, they shall be divided as equally as may be into three Classes. The Seats of the Senators of the first Class shall be vacated at the Expiration of the Second Year, of the second Class at the Expiration of the fourth Year, and of the third Class at the Expiration of the sixth Year, so that one third may be chosen every second Year; and if Vacancies happen by Resignation, or otherwise, during the Recess of the Legislature of any State, the Executive thereof may make temporary Appointments until the next Meeting of the Legislature, which shall then fill such Vacancies.

[3] No Person shall be a Senator who shall not have attained to the Age of thirty Years, and been nine Years a Citizen of the United States, and who shall not, when elected, be an Inhabitant of that State for which he shall be chosen.

[4] The Vice President of the United States shall be President of the Senate, but shall have no Vote, unless they be equally divided.

[5] The Senate shall chuse their other Officers, and also a President pro tempore, in the Absence of the Vice President, or when he shall exercise the Office of President of the United States.

[6] The Senate shall have the sole Power to try all Impeachments. When sitting for that Purpose, they shall be on Oath or Affirmation. When the President of the United States is tried, the Chief Justice shall preside: And

no Person shall be convicted without the Concurrence of two thirds of the Members present. Judgment in Cases of Impeachment shall not extend further than to removal from Office, and disqualification to hold and enjoy any Office of honor, Trust, or Profit under the United States: but the Party convicted shall nevertheless be liable and subject to Indictment, Trial, Judgment, and Punishment, according to Law.

Section 4. [1] The Times, Places and Manner of holding Elections for Senators and Representatives, shall be prescribed in each State by the Legislature thereof; but the Congress may at any time by Law make or alter such Regulations, except as to the Places of chusing Senators.

[2] The Congress shall assemble at least once in every Year, and such Meeting shall be on the first Monday in December, unless they shall by Law appoint a different Day.

Section 5. [1] Each House shall be the Judge of the Elections, Returns, and Qualifications of its own Members, and a Majority of each shall constitute a Quorum to do business; but a smaller Number may adjourn from day to day, and may be authorized to compel the Attendance of absent Members, in such Manner, and under such Penalties as each House may provide.

[2] Each House may determine the Rules of its Proceedings, punish its Members for disorderly Behaviour, and, with the Concurrence of two thirds, expel a Member.

[3] Each House shall keep a Journal of its Proceedings, and from time to time publish the same, excepting such Parts as may in their Judgment require Secrecy; and the yeas and Nays of the Members of either House on any question shall, at the Desire of one fifth of those Present, be entered on the Journal.

[4] Neither House, during the Session of Congress, shall, without the Consent of the other, adjourn for more than three days, nor to any other Place than that in which the two Houses shall be sitting.

Section 6. [1] The Senators and Representatives shall receive a Compensation for their Services, to be ascertained by Law, and paid out of the Treasury of the United States. They shall in all Cases, except Treason, Felony and Breach of the Peace, be privileged from Arrest during their Attendance at the Session of their respective Houses, and in going to and returning from the same; and for any Speech or Debate in either House, they shall not be questioned in any other Place.

[2] No Senator or Representative shall, during the Time for which he was elected, be appointed to any civil Office under the Authority of the United States, which shall have been created, or the Emoluments whereof shall have been increased during such time; and no Person holding any Office under the United States, shall be a Member of either House during his Continuance in Office.

Section 7. [1] All Bills for raising Revenue shall originate in the House of Representatives; but the Senate may propose or concur with Amendments as on other Bills.

[2] Every Bill which shall have passed the House of Representatives and the Senate, shall, before it becomes a Law, be presented to the President of the United States; If he approve he shall sign it, but if not he shall return it, with his Objections to the House in which it shall have originated, who shall enter the Objections at large on their Journal, and proceed to reconsider it. If after such Reconsideration two thirds of that House shall agree to pass the Bill, it shall be sent, together with the Objections, to the other House, by which it shall likewise be reconsidered, and if approved by two thirds of that House, it shall become a Law. But in all such Cases the Votes of both Houses shall be determined by yeas and Nays, and the Names of the Persons voting for and against the Bill shall be entered on the Journal of each House respectively. If any Bill shall not be returned by the President within ten Days (Sundays excepted) after it shall have been presented to him, the Same shall be a Law, in like Manner as if he had signed it, unless the Congress by their Adjournment prevent its Return, in which Case it shall not be a Law.

[3] Every Order, Resolution, or Vote to which the Concurrence of the Senate and House of Representatives may be necessary (except on a question of Adjournment) shall be presented to the President of the United States; and before the Same shall take Effect, shall be approved by him, or being disapproved by him, shall be repassed by two thirds of the Senate and House of Representatives, according to the Rules and Limitations prescribed in the Case of a Bill.

Section 8. [1] The Congress shall have Power To lay and collect Taxes, Duties, Imposts and Excises, to pay the Debts and provide for the common Defence and general Welfare of the United States; but all Duties, Imposts and Excises shall be uniform throughout the United States;

[2] To borrow Money on the Credit of the United States;

[3] To regulate Commerce with foreign Nations, and among the several States, and with the Indian Tribes;

[4] To establish an uniform Rule of Naturalization, and uniform Laws on the subject of Bankruptcies throughout the United States;

[5] To coin Money, regulate the Value thereof, and of foreign Coin, and fix the Standard of Weights and Measures;

[6] To provide for the Punishment of counterfeiting the Securities and current Coin of the United States;

[7] To establish Post Offices and post Roads;

[8] To promote the Progress of Science and useful Arts, by securing for limited Times to Authors and Inventors the exclusive Right to their respective Writings and Discoveries;

[9] To constitute Tribunals inferior to the supreme Court;

[10] To define and punish Piracies and Felonies committed on the high Seas, and Offences against the Law of Nations;

[11] To declare War, grant Letters of Marque and Reprisal, and make rules concerning Captures on Land and Water;

[12] To raise and support Armies, but no Appropriation of Money to that Use shall be for a longer Term than two Years;

[13] To provide and maintain a Navy;

[14] To make Rules for the Government and Regulation of the land and naval Forces;

[15] To provide for calling forth the Militia to execute the Laws of the Union, suppress Insurrections and repel Invasions;

[16] To provide for organizing, arming, and disciplining, the Militia, and for governing such Part of them as may be employed in the Service of the United States, reserving to the States respectively, the Appointment of the Officers, and the Authority of training the Militia according to the discipline prescribed by Congress;

[17] To exercise exclusive Legislation in all Cases whatsoever, over such District (not exceeding ten Miles square) as may, by Cession of particular States, and the Acceptance of Congress, become the Seat of the Government of the United States, and to exercise like Authority over all Places purchased by the Consent of the Legislature of the State in which the Same shall be for the Erection of Forts, Magazines, Arsenals, dock-Yards, and other needful Buildings;—And

[18] To make all Laws which shall be necessary and proper for carrying into Execution the foregoing Powers, and all other Powers vested by this Constitution in the Government of the United States, or in any Department or Officer thereof.

Section 9. [1] The Migration or Importation of such Persons as any of the States now existing shall think proper to admit, shall not be prohibited by the Congress prior to the Year one thousand eight hundred and eight, but a Tax or duty may be imposed on such Importation, not exceeding ten dollars for each Person.

[2] The privilege of the Writ of Habeas Corpus shall not be suspended, unless when in Cases of Rebellion or Invasion the public Safety may require it.

[3] No Bill of Attainder or ex post facto Law shall be passed.

[4] No Capitation, or other direct, Tax shall be laid, unless in Proportion to the Census or Enumeration herein before directed to be taken.

[5] No Tax or Duty shall be laid on Articles exported from any State.

[6] No Preference shall be given by any Regulation of Commerce or Revenue to the Ports of one State over those of another: nor shall Vessels bound to, or from, one State be obliged to enter, clear, or pay Duties in another.

[7] No money shall be drawn from the Treasury, but in Consequence of Appropriations made by Law; and a regular Statement and Account of the Receipts and Expenditures of all public Money shall be published from time to time.

[8] No Title of Nobility shall be granted by the United States: And no Person holding any Office of Profit or Trust under them, shall, without the Consent of the Congress, accept of any present, Emolument, Office, or Title, of any kind whatever, from any King, Prince, or foreign State.

Section 10. [1] No State shall enter into any Treaty, Alliance, or Confederation; grant Letters of Marque and Reprisal; coin Money; emit Bills of Credit; make any Thing but gold and silver Coin a Tender in Payment of Debts; pass any Bill of Attainder, ex post facto Law, or Law impairing the Obligation of Contracts, or grant any Title of Nobility.

[2] No State shall, without the Consent of the Congress, lay any Imposts or Duties on Imports or Exports, except what may be absolutely necessary for executing it's inspection Laws: and the net Produce of all Duties and Imposts, laid by any State on Imports or Exports, shall be for the Use of the Treasury of the United States; and all such Laws shall be subject to the Revision and Controul of the Congress.

[3] No State shall, without the Consent of Congress, lay any Duty of Tonnage, keep Troops, or Ships of War in time of Peace, enter into any Agreement or Compact with another State, or with a foreign Power, or engage in War, unless actually invaded, or in such imminent Danger as will not admit of delay.

Article II

Section 1. [1] The executive Power shall be vested in a President of the United States of America. He shall hold his Office during the Term of four Years, and, together with the Vice President, chosen for the same term, be elected, as follows

[2] Each State shall appoint, in such Manner as the Legislature thereof may direct, a Number of Electors, equal to the whole Number of Senators and Representatives to which the State may be entitled in the Congress; but no Senator or Representative, or Person holding an Office of Trust or Profit under the United States, shall be appointed an Elector.

[3] The Electors shall meet in their respective States, and vote by Ballot for two Persons, of whom one at least shall not be an Inhabitant of the same State with themselves. And they shall make a List of all the Persons voted for, and of the Number of Votes for each; which List they shall sign and certify, and transmit sealed to the Seat of the Government of the United States, directed to the President of the Senate. The President of the Senate shall, in the Presence of the Senate and House of Representatives, open all the Certificates, and the Votes shall then be counted. The Person having the greatest Number of Votes shall be the President, if such Number be a Majority of the whole Number of Electors appointed; and if there be more than one who have such Majority, and have an equal Number of Votes, then the House of Representatives shall immediately chuse by Ballot one of them for President; and if no Person have a Majority, then from the five highest on the List the said House shall in like Manner chuse the President. But in chusing the President, the Votes shall be taken by States the Representation from each State having one Vote; A quorum for this Purpose shall consist of a Member or Members from two thirds of the States, and a Majority of all the States shall be necessary to a Choice. In every Case, after the Choice of the President, the Person having the greatest Number of Votes of the Electors shall be the Vice President. But if there should remain two or more who have equal Votes, the Senate shall chuse from them by Ballot the Vice President.

[4] The Congress may determine the Time of chusing the Electors, and the Day on which they shall give their Votes; which Day shall be the same throughout the United States.

[5] No person except a natural born Citizen, or a Citizen of the United States, at the time of the Adoption of this Constitution, shall be eligible to the Office of President; neither shall any Person be eligible to that Office who shall not have attained to the Age of thirty-five Years, and been fourteen Years a Resident within the United States.

[6] In case of the Removal of the President from Office, or of his Death, Resignation, or Inability to discharge the Powers and Duties of the said Office, the Same shall devolve on the Vice President, and the Congress may by Law provide for the Case of Removal, Death, Resignation or Inability, both of the President and Vice President, declaring what Officer shall then act as President, and such Officer shall act accordingly, until the Disability be removed, or a President shall be elected.

[7] The President shall, at stated Times, receive for his Services, a Compensation, which shall neither be encreased nor diminished during the Period for which he shall have been elected, and he shall not receive within that Period any other Emolument from the United States, or any of them.

[8] Before he enter on the Execution of his Office, he shall take the following Oath or Affirmation:—"I do solemnly swear (or affirm) that I will faithfully execute the Office of President of the United States, and will to the best of my Ability, preserve, protect and defend the Constitution of the United States."

Section 2. [1] The President shall be Commander in Chief of the Army and Navy of the United States, and of the Militia of the several States, when called into the actual Service of the United States; he may require the Opinion, in writing, of the principal Officer in each of the executive Departments, upon any Subject relating to the Duties of their respective Offices, and he shall have Power to grant Reprieves and Pardons for Offences against the United States, except in Cases of Impeachment.

[2] He shall have Power, by and with the Advice and Consent of the Senate, to make Treaties, provided two thirds of the Senators present concur; and he shall nominate, and by and with the Advice and Consent of the Senate, shall appoint Ambassadors, other public Ministers and Consuls, Judges of the supreme Court, and all other Officers of the United States, whose Appointments are not herein otherwise provided for, and which shall be established by Law; but the Congress may by Law vest the Appointment of such inferior Officers, as they think proper, in the President alone, in the Courts of Law, or in the Heads of Departments.

[3] The President shall have Power to fill up all Vacancies that may happen during the Recess of the Senate, by granting Commissions which shall expire at the End of their next Session.

Section 3. He shall from time to time give to the Congress Information of the State of the Union, and recommend to their Consideration such Measures as he shall judge necessary and expedient; he may, on extraordinary Occasions, convene both Houses, or either of them, and in Case of Disagreement between them, with Respect to the Time of Adjournment, he may adjourn them to such Time as he shall think proper; he shall receive Ambassadors and other public Ministers; he shall take Care that the Laws be faithfully executed, and shall Commission all the Officers of the United States.

Section 4. The President, Vice President and all civil Officers of the United States, shall be removed from Office on Impeachment for, and Conviction of, Treason, Bribery, or other High Crimes and Misdemeanors.

Article III

Section 1. The judicial Power of the United States, shall be vested in one supreme Court, and in such inferior Courts as the Congress may from time to time ordain and establish. The Judges, both of the supreme and inferior Courts, shall hold their Offices during good Behaviour, and shall, at stated Times, receive for their Services a Compensation, which shall not be diminished during their Continuance in Office.

Section 2. [1] The judicial Power shall extend to all Cases, in Law and Equity, arising under this Constitution, the Laws of the United States, and Treaties made, or which shall be made, under their Authority;—to all Cases affecting Ambassadors, other public Ministers and Consuls;—to all Cases of admiralty and maritime Jurisdiction;—to Controversies to which the United States shall be a Party;—to Controversies between two or more States; between a State and Citizens of another State;—between Citizens of different States;—between Citizens of the same State claiming Lands under Grants of different States, and between a State, or the Citizens thereof, and foreign States, Citizens or Subjects.

[2] In all Cases affecting Ambassadors, other public Ministers and Consuls, and those in which a State shall be a Party, the supreme Court shall have original Jurisdiction. In all the other Cases before mentioned, the supreme Court shall have appellate Jurisdiction, both as to Law and Fact, with such Exceptions, and under such Regulations as the Congress shall make.

[3] The Trial of all Crimes, except in Cases of Impeachment, shall be by Jury; and such Trial shall be held in the State where the said Crimes shall have been committed; but when not committed within any State, the Trial shall be at such Place or Places as the Congress may by Law have directed.

Section 3. [1] Treason against the United States, shall consist only in levying War against them, or in adhering to their Enemies, giving them Aid and Comfort. No Person shall be convicted of Treason unless on the Testimony of two Witnesses to the same overt Act, or on Confession in open Court.

[2] The Congress shall have Power to declare the Punishment of Treason, but no Attainder of Treason shall work Corruption of Blood, or Forfeiture except during the Life of the Person attainted.

Article IV

Section 1. Full Faith and Credit shall be given in each State to the public Acts, Records, and judicial Proceedings of every other State. And the Congress may by general Laws prescribe the Manner in which such Acts, Records and Proceedings shall be proved, and the Effect thereof.

Section 2. [1] The Citizens of each State shall be entitled to all Privileges and Immunities of Citizens in the several States.

[2] A Person charged in any State with Treason, Felony, or other Crime, who shall flee from Justice, and be found in another State, shall on Demand of the executive Authority of the State from which he fled, be delivered up, to be removed to the State having Jurisdiction of the Crime.

[3] No Person held to Service or Labour in one State, under the Laws thereof, escaping into another, shall, in Consequence of any Law or Regulation therein, be discharged from such Service or Labour, but shall be delivered up on Claim of the Party to whom such Service or Labour may be due.

Section 3. [1] New States may be admitted by the Congress into this Union; but no new State shall be formed or erected within the Jurisdiction of any other State; nor any State be formed by the Junction of two or more States, or Parts of States, without the Consent of the Legislatures of the States concerned as well as of the Congress.

[2] The Congress shall have Power to dispose of and make all needful Rules and Regulations respecting the Territory or other Property belonging to the United States; and nothing in this Constitution shall be so construed as to Prejudice any Claims of the United States, or of any particular State.

Section 4. The United States shall guarantee to every State in this Union a Republican Form of Government, and shall protect each of them against Invasion; and on Application of the Legislature, or of the Executive (when the Legislature cannot be convened) against domestic Violence.

Article V

The Congress, whenever two thirds of both Houses shall deem it necessary, shall propose Amendments to this Constitution, or, on the Application of the Legislatures of two thirds of the several States, shall call a Convention for proposing Amendments, which, in either Case, shall be valid to all Intents and Purposes, as Part of this Constitution, when ratified by the Legislatures of three fourths of the several States, or by Conventions in three fourths thereof, as the one or the other Mode of Ratification may be proposed by the Congress; Provided that no Amendment which may be made prior to the Year One thousand eight hundred and eight shall in any Manner affect the first and fourth Clauses in the Ninth Section of the first Article; and that no State, without its Consent, shall be deprived of its equal Suffrage in the Senate.

Article VI

[1] All Debts contracted and Engagements entered into, before the Adoption of this Constitution, shall be as

valid against the United States under this Constitution, as under the Confederation.

[2] This Constitution, and the Laws of the United States which shall be made in Pursuance thereof; and all Treaties made, or which shall be made, under the Authority of the United States, shall be the supreme Law of the Land; and the Judges in every State shall be bound thereby, any Thing in the Constitution or Laws of any State to the Contrary notwithstanding.

[3] The Senators and Representatives before mentioned, and the Members of the several State Legislatures, and all executive and judicial Officers, both of the United States and of the several States, shall be bound by Oath or Affirmation, to support this Constitution; but no religious Test shall ever be required as a Qualification to any Office or public Trust under the United States.

Article VII

The Ratification of the Conventions of nine States, shall be sufficient for the Establishment of this Constitution between the States so ratifying the Same.

Amendments

(The first 10 Amendments were ratified December 15, 1791, and form what is known as the "Bill of Rights")

Amendment 1

Congress shall make no law respecting an establishment of religion, or prohibiting the free exercise thereof; or abridging the freedom of speech, or of the press; or the right of the people peaceably to assemble, and to petition the Government for a redress of grievances.

Amendment 2

A well regulated Militia, being necessary to the security of a free State, the right of the people to keep and bear Arms, shall not be infringed.

Amendment 3

No Soldier shall, in time of peace be quartered in any house, without the consent of the Owner, nor in time of war, but in a manner to be prescribed by law.

Amendment 4

The right of the people to be secure in their persons, houses, papers, and effects, against unreasonable searches and seizures, shall not be violated, and no Warrants shall issue, but upon probable cause, supported by Oath or affirmation, and particularly describing the place to be searched, and the persons or things to be seized.

Amendment 5

No person shall be held to answer for a capital, or otherwise infamous crime, unless on a presentment or indictment of a Grand Jury, except in cases arising in the land or naval forces, or in the Militia, when in actual service in time of War or public danger; nor shall any person be subject for the same offence to be twice put in jeopardy of life or limb; nor shall be compelled in any criminal case to be a witness against himself, nor be deprived of life, liberty, or property, without due process of law; nor shall private property be taken for public use, without just compensation.

Amendment 6

In all criminal prosecutions, the accused shall enjoy the right to a speedy and public trial, by an impartial jury of the State and district wherein the crime shall have been committed, which district shall have been previously ascertained by law, and to be informed of the nature and cause of the accusation; to be confronted with the witnesses against him; to have compulsory process for obtaining witnesses in his favor, and to have the Assistance of Counsel for his defence.

Amendment 7

In Suits at common law, where the value in controversy shall exceed twenty dollars, the right of trial by jury shall be preserved, and no fact tried by jury, shall be otherwise re-examined in any Court of the United States, than according to the rules of the common law.

Amendment 8

Excessive bail shall not be required, nor excessive fines imposed, nor cruel and unusual punishments inflicted.

Amendment 9

The enumeration in the Constitution, of certain rights, shall not be construed to deny or disparage others retained by the people.

Amendment 10

The powers not delegated to the United States by the Constitution, nor prohibited by it to the States, are reserved to the States respectively, or to the people.

Amendment 11
(Ratified February 7, 1795)

The Judicial power of the United States shall not be construed to extend to any suit in law or equity, commenced or prosecuted against one of the United States by Citizens of another State, or by Citizens or Subjects of any Foreign State.

Amendment 12
(Ratified July 27, 1804)

The Electors shall meet in their respective states and vote by ballot for President and Vice-President, one of whom, at least, shall not be an inhabitant of the same state with themselves; they shall name in their ballots the person voted for as President, and in distinct ballots the person voted for as Vice-President, and they shall make distinct lists of all persons voted for as President, and of all persons voted for as Vice-President, and of the number of votes for each, which lists they shall sign and certify, and transmit sealed to the seat of the government of the United States, directed to the President of the Senate;—The President of the Senate shall, in the presence of the Senate and House of Representatives, open all the certificates and the votes shall then be counted;—The person having the greatest number of votes for President, shall be the President, if such number be a majority of the whole number of Electors appointed; and if no person have such majority, then from the persons having the highest numbers not exceeding three on the list of those voted for as President, the House of Representatives shall choose immediately, by ballot, the President. But in choosing the President, the votes shall be taken by states, the representation from each state having one vote; a quorum for this purpose shall consist of a member or members from two-thirds of the states, and a majority of all the states shall be necessary to a choice. [And if the House of Representatives shall not choose a President whenever the right of choice shall devolve upon them, before the fourth day of March next following, then the Vice-President shall act as President, as in the case of the death or other constitutional disability of the President.—]* The person having the greatest number of votes as Vice-President, shall be the Vice-President, if such number be a majority of the whole number of Electors appointed, and if no person have a majority, then from the two highest numbers on the list, the Senate shall choose the Vice-President; a quorum for the purpose shall consist of two-thirds of the whole number of Senators, and a majority of the whole number shall be necessary to a choice. But no person constitutionally ineligible to the office of President shall be eligible to that of Vice-President of the United States.

Amendment 13
(Ratified December 6, 1865)

Section 1. Neither slavery nor involuntary servitude, except as a punishment for crime whereof the party shall have been duly convicted, shall exist within the United States, or any place subject to their jurisdiction.

Section 2. Congress shall have power to enforce this article by appropriate legislation.

Amendment 14
(Ratified July 9, 1868)

Section 1. All persons born or naturalized in the United States, and subject to the jurisdiction thereof, are citizens of the United States and of the State wherein they reside. No State shall make or enforce any law which shall abridge the privileges or immunities of citizens of the United States; nor shall any State deprive any person of life, liberty, or property, without due process of law; nor deny to any person within its jurisdiction the equal protection of the laws.

Section 2. Representatives shall be apportioned among the several States according to their respective numbers, counting the whole number of persons in each State, excluding Indians not taxed. But when the right to vote at any election for the choice of electors for President and Vice President of the United States, Representatives in Congress, the Executive and Judicial officers of a State, or the members of the Legislature thereof, is denied to any of the male inhabitants of such State, being twenty-one years of age, and citizens of the United States, or in any way abridged, except for participation in rebellion, or other crime, the basis of representation therein shall be reduced in the proportion which the number of such male citizens shall bear to the whole number of male citizens twenty-one years of age in such State.

Section 3. No person shall be a Senator or Representative in Congress, or elector of President and Vice President, or hold any office, civil or military, under the United States, or under any State, who, having previously taken an oath, as a member of Congress, or as an officer of the United States, or as a member of any State legislature, or as an executive or judicial officer of any State, to support the Constitution of the United States, shall have engaged in insurrection or rebellion against the same, or given aid or comfort to the enemies thereof. But Congress may by a vote of two-thirds of each House, remove such disability.

Section 4. The validity of the public debt of the United States, authorized by law, including debts incurred for payment of pensions and bounties for services in suppressing insurrection or rebellion, shall not be questioned. But neither the United States nor any State shall assume or pay any debt or obligation incurred in aid of insurrection or rebellion against the United States, or

*Superseded by section 3 of the Twentieth Amendment.

any claim for the loss or emancipation of any slave; but all such debts, obligations and claims shall be held illegal and void.

Section 5. The Congress shall have power to enforce, by appropriate legislation, the provisions of this article.

Amendment 15
(Ratified February 3, 1870)

Section 1. The right of citizens of the United States to vote shall not be denied or abridged by the United States or by any State on account of race, color, or previous condition of servitude.

Section 2. The Congress shall have power to enforce this article by appropriate legislation.

Amendment 16
(Ratified February 3, 1913)

The Congress shall have power to lay and collect taxes on incomes, from whatever source derived, without apportionment among the several States, and without regard to any census or enumeration.

Amendment 17
(Ratified April 8, 1913)

[1] The Senate of the United States shall be composed of two Senators from each State, elected by the people thereof, for six years; and each Senator shall have one vote. The electors in each State shall have the qualifications requisite for electors of the most numerous branch of the State legislatures.

[2] When vacancies happen in the representation of any State in the Senate, the executive authority of such State shall issue writs of election to fill such vacancies: *Provided,* That the legislature of any State may empower the executive thereof to make temporary appointments until the people fill the vacancies by election as the legislature may direct.

[3] This amendment shall not be so construed as to affect the election or term of any Senator chosen before it becomes valid as part of the Constitution.

Amendment 18
(Ratified January 16, 1919. Repealed December 5, 1933 by Amendment 21)

Section 1. After one year from the ratification of this article the manufacture, sale, or transportation of intoxicating liquors within, the importation thereof into, or the exportation thereof from the United States and all territory subject to the jurisdiction thereof for beverage purposes is hereby prohibited.

Section 2. The Congress and the several States shall have concurrent power to enforce this article by appropriate legislation.

Section 3. This article shall be inoperative unless it shall have been ratified as an amendment to the Constitution by the legislatures of the several States as provided in the Constitution, within seven years from the date of the submission hereof to the States by the Congress.

Amendment 19
(Ratified August 18, 1920)

[1] The right of citizens of the United States to vote shall not be denied or abridged by the United States or by any State on account of sex.

[2] Congress shall have power to enforce this article by appropriate legislation.

Amendment 20
(Ratified January 23, 1933)

Section 1. The terms of the President and Vice President shall end at noon on the 20th day of January, and the terms of Senators and Representatives at noon on the 3d day of January, of the years in which such terms would have ended if this article had not been ratified; and the terms of their successors shall then begin.

Section 2. The Congress shall assemble at least once in every year, and such meeting shall begin at noon on the 3d day of January, unless they shall by law appoint a different day.

Section 3. If, at the time fixed for the beginning of the term of the President, the President elect shall have died, the Vice President elect shall become President. If the President shall not have been chosen before the time fixed for the beginning of his term, or if the President elect shall have failed to qualify, then the Vice President elect shall act as President until a President shall have qualified; and the Congress may by law provide for the case wherein neither a President elect nor a Vice President elect shall have qualified, declaring who shall then act as President, or the manner in which one who is to act shall be selected, and such person shall act accordingly until a President or Vice President shall have qualified.

Section 4. The Congress may by law provide for the case of the death of any of the persons from whom the House of Representatives may choose a President whenever the right of choice shall have devolved upon them, and for the case of the death of any of the persons from whom the Senate may choose a Vice President whenever the right of choice shall have devolved upon them.

Section 5. Sections 1 and 2 shall take effect on the 15th day of October following the ratification of this article.

Section 6. This article shall be inoperative unless it shall have been ratified as an amendment to the Constitution by the legislatures of three-fourths of the several States within seven years from the date of its submission.

Amendment 21
(Ratified December 5, 1933)

Section 1. The eighteenth article of amendment to the Constitution of the United States is hereby repealed.

Section 2. The transportation or importation into any State, Territory, or possession of the United States for delivery or use therein of intoxicating liquors, in violation of the laws thereof, is hereby prohibited.

Section 3. This article shall be inoperative unless it shall have been ratified as an amendment to the Constitution by conventions in the several States, as provided in the Constitution, within seven years from the date of the submission hereof to the States by the Congress.

Amendment 22
(Ratified February 27, 1951)

Section 1. No person shall be elected to the office of the President more than twice, and no person who has held the office of President, or acted as President, for more than two years of a term to which some other person was elected President shall be elected to the office of President more than once. But this Article shall not apply to any person holding the office of President when this Article was proposed by the Congress, and shall not prevent any person who may be holding the office of President, or acting as President, during the term within which this Article becomes operative from holding the office of President or acting as President during the remainder of such term.

Section 2. This article shall be inoperative unless it shall have been ratified as an amendment to the Constitution by the legislatures of three-fourths of the several States within seven years from the date of its submission to the States by the Congress.

Amendment 23
(Ratified March 29, 1961)

Section 1. The District constituting the seat of Government of the United States shall appoint in such manner as the Congress may direct:

A number of electors of President and Vice President equal to the whole number of Senators and Representatives in Congress to which the District would be entitled if it were a State, but in no event more than the least populous state; they shall be in addition to those appointed by the States, but they shall be considered, for the purposes of the election of President and Vice President, to be electors appointed by a state; and they shall meet in the District and perform such duties as provided by the twelfth article of amendment.

Section 2. The Congress shall have power to enforce this article by appropriate legislation.

Amendment 24
(Ratified January 23, 1964)

Section 1. The right of citizens of the United States to vote in any primary or other election for President or Vice President, for electors for President or Vice President, or for Senator or Representative in Congress, shall not be denied or abridged by the United States or any State by reason of failure to pay any poll tax or other tax.

Section 2. The Congress shall have power to enforce this article by appropriate legislation.

Amendment 25
(Ratified February 10, 1967)

Section 1. In case of the removal of the President from office or of his death or resignation, the Vice President shall become President.

Section 2. Whenever there is a vacancy in the office of the Vice President, the President shall nominate a Vice President who shall take office upon confirmation by a majority vote of both Houses of Congress.

Section 3. Whenever the President transmits to the President pro tempore of the Senate and the Speaker of the House of Representatives his written declaration that he is unable to discharge the powers and duties of his office, and until he transmits to them a written declaration to the contrary, such powers and duties shall be discharged by the Vice President as Acting President.

Section 4. Whenever the Vice President and a majority of either the principal officers of the executive departments or of such other body as Congress may by law provide, transmit to the President pro tempore of the Senate and the Speaker of the House of Representatives their written declaration that the President is unable to discharge the powers and duties of his office, the Vice President shall immediately assume the powers and duties of the office as Acting President.

Thereafter, when the President transmits to the President pro tempore of the Senate and the Speaker of the House of Representatives his written declaration that no inability exists, he shall resume the powers and duties of his office unless the Vice President and a majority of either the principal officers of the executive department or of such other body as Congress may by law provide, transmit within four days to the President pro tempore of the Senate and the Speaker of the House of Representatives their written declaration and the President is unable to discharge the powers and duties of his office. Thereupon Congress shall decide the issue, assembling within forty-eight hours for that purpose if not in session. If the Congress, within twenty-one days after receipt of the latter written declaration, or, if Congress is not in session, within twenty-one days after Congress is required to assemble, determines by two-thirds vote of both Houses that the President is unable to discharge the powers and duties of his office, the Vice President shall continue to discharge the same as Acting President; otherwise, the President shall resume the powers and duties of his office.

Amendment 26
(Ratified July 1, 1971)

Section 1. The right of citizens of the United States, who are eighteen years of age or older, to vote shall not be denied or abridged by the United States or by any State on account of age.

Section 2. The Congress shall have power to enforce this article by appropriate legislation.

Amendment 27
(Ratified May 7, 1992)

No law varying the compensation for the services of the Senators and Representatives shall take effect, until an election of Representatives shall have intervened.

The Supreme Court and American Politics

Introduction and Overview

GLOSSARY

A

Absolutism An approach to interpreting the First Amendment which emphasizes the language stating that Congress shall pass *no* laws interfering with First Amendment rights, thus meaning that any form of governmental interference with these guarantees is unconstitutional.

Actual malice A standard used in libel cases which requires that material must be published with knowledge that it was false or with a reckless disregard of the truth.

Advisory opinion An opinion or interpretation of the law which lacks binding effect. The Supreme Court does not give advisory opinions but only decides actual cases or controversies.

Affirm For an appellate court to reach a decision in agreement with the result produced in a case decided by a lower court.

Affirmative action A concept embodied in programs which seek to address the effects of discriminatory practices against minority groups and women. These programs can take a wide variety of forms but can only be justified if the government is pursuing a compelling interest through narrowly tailored means.

Amicus curiae A Latin term meaning "friend of the court," a person or group not a litigant in the case but who provides information to a court in the form of a brief.

Appeal The process of taking a case to a higher court for review. A party losing in a trial court generally has the right to appeal a case once to an appellate court. The further appeal of a case usually depends upon the discretion of the next court.

Appellant The party that appeals a decision of a lower court to a higher court. Because most of the Supreme Court's cases arrive via a petition for a writ of certiorari rather than an appeal, the first-listed party who brought the case to the Supreme Court is usually called the petitioner. The appellant's name appears first in the title of the case.

Appellate jurisdiction The authority of a higher court to review the decisions of a lower court.

Appellee The party that responds to the appeal to a higher court made by the party that lost at the lower court level. If the party is responding to a petition to a higher court, as in most U.S. Supreme Court cases, then the party is called the respondent and, like the appellant in a usual appeal, is listed second in the case title.

Arguendo For the sake of argument; assuming something is so, without accepting its truth, in order to extend further a line of argument.

Arraignment An early step in the criminal justice process where formal charges are read to the defendant and the defendant enters a plea of "guilty" or "not guilty."

B

Balancing test A general approach to interpreting many areas of constitutional law in which the civil rights and liberties of the individual are weighed against the interests asserted by the government. The government typically wins in cases in which this test is used. This is closely associated with the minimal scrutiny approach and the rational basis test.

Bench trial A trial conducted by a judge alone without a jury. A bench trial occurs when a defendant waives the constitutional right to a trial by jury for serious charges or when the defendant is charged with petty offenses and therefore has no right to a jury trial.

Bill of attainder A statutory law which imposes a penalty upon an individual without a hearing or trial. This is prohibited by Article III, Section 9 of the Constitution.

Brandeis brief A written document presented by an attorney to a court which emphasizes social science rather than or in addition to citation to legal authority.

Brief A formal document submitted to a court by counsel presenting the facts and the legal argument for one of the parties to the case.

C

Capital offense A crime which is punishable by the death penalty.

Capital punishment Imposition of the death penalty upon a criminal defendant found guilty of a crime for which death can be imposed.

Case A legal dispute brought before a court for resolution involving parties with a live controversy.

Case law The law as interpreted through prior cases rather than from other sources such as statutes or historical materials.

Censorship An action by the government which prevents expression from occurring. This is also called prior restraint. The government can engage in censorship only under the most extreme circumstances.

Certification, Writ of A rarely used method of seeking Supreme Court review of a case in which a lower court asks the Court to clarify some point of law.

Certiorari, Writ of An order from the Supreme Court to a lower court to send forward the records of a case for review. This is the procedure by which the Court determines which cases it will hear to review actions by lower courts. A writ is issued if at least four justices so decide, and no reasons have to be given regarding this decision. When the Court issues a writ, it is said to "grant cert."

Circuit courts Thirteen courts in the federal judicial system which constitute an intermediate system between the federal district courts of original jurisdiction and the Supreme Court. Most states also have an intermediate system of appellate courts, but these are not always called "circuit courts" as in the federal judicial system.

Civil law The body of law which deals with the legal relationships, rights, and duties of private persons. Civil law is distinguished from criminal law, which deals with crimes against the government.

Civil rights The guarantees associated with the Equal Protection Clause of the Fourteenth Amendment, especially as applied to government discrimination based upon race, alienage, and gender. Civil rights can also be protected through statutory enactments.

Class action A lawsuit filed by a single person or group on behalf of all other parties similarly situated.

Clemency An action by an executive official which modifies the severity of a court-imposed punishment.

Comity The deference shown by federal courts to state courts in interpreting state law.

Commercial speech Another name for advertising, a form of expression that is protected under the First Amendment through intermediate scrutiny.

Common law The body of rules and principles based upon long-standing practices and customs which have been recognized and enforced by the courts. This system had its origins in the English courts and was brought to America by the colonists. Common law can be distinguished from statutory law, which is created by legislatures.

Compelling state interest A test which requires the government to show an extremely important objective achieved through narrowly tailored means in order to interfere with a constitutional right or liberty. This test is used in a variety of areas, especially in freedom of expression and equal protection cases. It is also called the strict scrutiny test.

Concurring opinion An opinion issued by a justice who agrees with the judgment of the Court but disagrees with parts or all of the reasoning supporting the judgment.

Consent decree A court order in which the parties to the decree agree to act in accordance with the terms set by the order; generally used to settle lawsuits before they go to trial.

Conspiracy An agreement or association created for criminal purposes.

Constitutional courts Federal courts which derive their power from Article III of the Constitution as opposed to being created by legislative enactment under Article I.

Contempt An act that in some way shows disrespect for a court or obstructs the activities of the court. Contempt can occur in both civil and criminal law and is usually a punishable offense.

Criminal law The body of law which is concerned with enforcing laws defined as crimes by the state and with punishing those persons who are found guilty of violating these laws. Criminal law is contrasted with civil law which deals with the legal relationships between private persons.

D

Declaratory judgment A court decision which states an interpretation of the law but does not order a special action.

De facto segregation "In fact;" a status or situation that has been created by private actions and decisions rather than by governmental laws and actions. De facto civil rights situations are generally considered to be beyond the jurisdiction of the courts because no state action was involved.

Defamation The harming of a person's reputation. This is one of the elements that must be proven in a libel action.

Defendant The individual in a court case, either civil or criminal, against whom the suit is being instituted.

De jure segregation "In law;" a status or situation that has been created by legislative or executive actions. De jure civil rights situations are subject to court challenges because state action is involved.

Dicta See obiter dicta.

Dissenting opinion An opinion by a justice that disagrees with the judgment of the Court and expresses the reasons for the disagreement.

Docket A listing of all the cases filed in a court.

Double jeopardy The trying of a person twice for the same offense. This is prohibited by the Fifth Amendment.

Due process Fairness; a complex concept contained in both the Fifth and Fourteenth Amendments that requires that government treat citizens fairly. Most due process issues involve the procedures that government must follow, especially in criminal cases, but the courts have occasionally addressed substantive due process issues as well.

E

Eminent domain The principle that the government may take private property for public use if just compensation is paid. This principle is stated in the Fifth Amendment.

En banc The hearing of a case by all of the members of a circuit court rather than the normal process of a three-judge panel reviewing a case.

Error, Writ of An order sent from an appellate court to a lower court that asks for the record in a case which can be reviewed for error.

Exclusionary rule A rule that any evidence obtained in violation of a constitutional guarantee for the criminally accused must be excluded from the trial.

Executive privilege The exemption of the executive from disclosure requirements that exist for ordinary citizens based upon the executive's need for confidentiality in undertaking the duties of office.

Ex parte A judicial action in which only one party is involved.

Ex post facto law A law that makes something a crime which was not illegal at the time when the action occurred. This is prohibited by Article I, Section 9 of the Constitution.

F

Federalism A system of government in which there are at least two levels of units, each with defined areas of responsibility and authority. In the United States federal system of government, the national government and the state governments have both independent and shared areas of power.

Federal preemption The exclusive power of the federal government to override state authority in certain areas, for example, interstate commerce.

Felony A serious criminal offense usually involving a penalty of at least one year in state or federal prison.

G

Gerrymander Redrawing the boundaries of a legislative district in order to maximize certain advantages.

Grand jury A jury composed of 12 to 23 people that meets in private to determine if there is sufficient evidence to issue an indictment, a formal charge which begins a criminal case.

H

Habeas corpus, Writ of An order to an incarcerating official to bring a person held in custody before the court to determine if the person is being held lawfully.

Harmless error A decision by an appellate court that a mistake made by a lower court did not sufficiently affect the rights of a party alleging the error to justify a reversal of the judgment.

I

Immunity A grant to a person of exemption from prosecution on the condition that testimonial evidence is provided.

In camera A court hearing that occurs in private—typically in a judge's chambers—without any spectators.

Incorporation The process by which the Supreme Court has made most of the Bill of Rights guarantees applicable to the states through the Due Process Clause of the Fourteenth Amendment.

Indictment A formal charge issued by a grand jury in a criminal case listing specific offenses by a defendant.

In forma pauperis A Latin term meaning in the manner of a pauper. This is a mechanism by which a poor person can file papers before a court without any costs being involved. Prisoners frequently use this method to appeal cases to the Supreme Court.

Information A formal set of charges filed by a prosecutor in a criminal case indicating the specific offenses by a defendant. This is used in some states instead of a grand jury indictment.

In haec verba A Latin term meaning "in these words."

Injunction A court order which requires someone to do something or to restrain from certain actions.

In re A Latin term meaning "in the affair of." This refers to a judicial proceeding in which there are no adversary parties, but judicial action is required.

Intermediate scrutiny A judicial test used in both freedom of expression and equal protection cases which provides heightened but not the highest level of protection. When this test is used, the government must establish that it has an important government objective that is being pursued through means that are substantially related to this objective. This is also called the important government objective test.

Interpretivism A theory of interpreting the Constitution which seeks to control the influence of justices' personal attitudes and values by requiring that decisions be based upon the language of the Constitution, the intent of the framers, and the original understanding of the provisions of the Constitution.

J

Judgment The official decision of a court in regard to the disposition of the case.

Judicial review The power of the courts to rule unconstitutional any legislation or other governmental action on the grounds that it violates a constitutional provision.

Jurisdiction The authority of a court to hear and decide a case based upon a set of specific conditions, including a live controversy occurring in a defined geographical area between specific parties directly affected by the controversy to which the court can provide an appropriate solution. Courts frequently refuse to hear cases on jurisdictional grounds.

Jurisprudence The accumulated body of law on a given topic, e.g., the Court's Fourth Amendment jurisprudence.

L

Legislative courts Federal courts that derive their authority from Article I of the Constitution dealing with the legislative branch rather than from Article III dealing with the judiciary.

Libel Harming the reputation of another person through written material which is false and which was written with a knowledge of its falseness or with a reckless disregard of the truth.

Litigant A person who is a party to a lawsuit.

M

Majority opinion An opinion in a case that has the support of a majority of the members of the Court and thus becomes controlling precedent for future cases.

Mandamus, Writ of A Latin term for "we command." An order from an appellate court to a lower court or to a governmental official requiring the performance of a particular act.

Minimal scrutiny test Also called the rational basis test, this test is used in numerous areas of constitutional law and usually results in the government prevailing against individuals' claimed violations of constitutional rights and liberties. The government is required under this test only to show that it is pursuing a legitimate objective through means that are rationally related to the objective.

Misdemeanor A criminal act which is considered to be less serious, usually punishable by less than a one-year period of incarceration.

Moot A situation in which a legal question has already been resolved, the situation has changed so that the legal issue no longer exists, or a hypothetical issue is under consideration.

Motion A request to a judicial official for some type of action.

N

Natural rights Rights based not upon statutory law but based instead upon a higher law transcending human sources, whether it be nature, a deity, or some other source.

O

Obiter dictum A statement in a judicial opinion which is not essential to the resolution of the case before the court. Typically called simply dicta, these statements are not binding in subsequent cases, but they may be utilized and may eventually become part of a controlling precedent.

Obscenity Sexual expression that is beyond the protection of the First Amendment. The Court has struggled to achieve a precise definition of obscenity, and the three-part *Miller* test embodies the Court's current criteria.

Opinion of the court The opinion which announces the decision of a court, whether it is a majority or plurality opinion.

Original intent The purpose or intended meaning of a constitutional provision by those who wrote it.

Original jurisdiction The authority of a court to hear a case in the first instance. The Supreme Court has both original and appellate jurisdiction, the authority to hear a case on appeal from a lower court.

Overbreadth A freedom of expression doctrine that stipulates that any government regulation of expression must not extend beyond the legitimate authority to control expression.

P

Per curiam opinion Latin term for "by the court." A judicial opinion by a court which is not signed by an individual judge but which expresses the judgment of the court as a whole.

Peremptory challenge During the process of jury selection, the discretionary removal of a prospective juror which does not require any reason for the removal. In contrast, removal for cause requires a showing as to why a juror would not be impartial.

Petitioner A party that initiates a legal action based on a petition, such as a petition for a writ of certiorari in the Supreme Court. The petitioner is listed first in the name of the case.

Petit jury A jury that hears a trial. A petit jury is contrasted with a grand jury which determines if there is sufficient evidence to bring charges against a defendant.

Plea bargain An agreement reached between a defendant and a prosecutor in which the defendant pleads guilty in exchange for a reduced charge or a lesser sentence. The Court has ruled that plea bargains are consistent with the requirements of the Sixth Amendment.

Plenary review The process by which the Supreme Court agrees to hear a case and then requires attorneys for both sides to prepare written briefs and to present oral arguments to the justices.

Plurality opinion An opinion announcing the judgment and reasoning of the Court but which lacks a majority consensus in regard to the reasoning. A plurality opinion is not considered to be binding precedent.

Political questions A method by which the Court declines to hear certain cases on the basis that they involve essentially political rather than legal questions and thus should be left to the other branches of government, the "political" branches.

Pornography A rather general and imprecise term referring to sexual expression ranging from nudity, which is often constitutionally protected, to the obscene, which is beyond constitutional protection.

Precedent A previous court decision which is applicable to a new case before a court. The doctrine of stare decisis maintains that judicial officials should be guided in their decision making by adherence to precedent.

Probable cause A term contained in the Fourth Amendment of the Constitution which sets the standard for judicial officials to determine if a warrant should be issued in a criminal case. Probable cause exists if a reasonable person would believe based upon the totality of the circumstances that a crime has occurred and that evidence could be discovered.

Probation A status in which a person convicted of a crime is freed from incarceration before finishing a complete sentence, although the person remains under supervision.

Procedural due process The constitutional requirement embedded in the Due Process Clauses of the Fifth and Fourteenth Amendments that government must follow fair procedures in dealing with citizens. The procedural guarantees of the Constitution are generally considered to be embodied in the rights of the criminally accused in the Fourth, Fifth, Sixth, and Eighth Amendments.

R

Rational basis test A test used to interpret the constitutionality of government legislation and actions in cases involving freedom of expression, the free exercise of religion, and equal protection. This test places a strong burden of proof on the individual claiming a government violation of a constitutional right or liberty because the government only needs to establish that it is pursuing a legitimate objective through means that are rationally related to the objective. This is also called the minimal scrutiny test.

Reapportionment An alteration in the boundaries of electoral districts based upon changes in the population. The principle of one person, one vote is supposed to guide the reapportionment process.

Remand To send a case back to a lower court which previously heard the case with instructions to rehear the case based upon the guidelines provided by the higher court.

Respondent The party in a legal action initiated by a petition which is forced to respond to the arguments by the party filing the petition. In U.S. Supreme Court cases initiated by a petition for a writ of certiorari, the respondent is listed second in the case title.

Restrictive covenant A provision in a deed which bars the sale or rental of property to certain classes of people, typically racial minorities. Enforcement of restrictive covenants by the government is prohibited.

Reverse An action by an appellate court that disagrees with and overturns the decision of a lower court.

Ripeness The status of a case in which it is ready for hearing and adjudication. If one or more procedural matters—for example, failure to exhaust lower court remedies—is not satisfied, then a case may be considered not to be "ripe."

S

Search warrant A term specified in the Fourth Amendment which is an authorization by a judicial official who believes probable cause exists to allow a law enforcement officer to search and seize evidence relating to a crime. The search warrant must be specific in regard to the place to be searched and the items to be seized.

Self-incrimination Giving testimony that could implicate oneself in a crime. The Fifth Amendment guarantees protection against self-incrimination.

Separation of powers The formal division of authority specified in the Constitution among the three branches of government, with the legislative branch authorized to make laws, the executive branch authorized to implement the laws, and the judicial branch empowered to interpret the laws. In reality, the separation of powers among the three branches of government is very complex and overlapping.

Seriatim Latin term meaning individually or one-by-one. This was a practice in the early history of the Supreme Court where each justice would write his opinion of a case. Chief Justice John Marshall changed this procedure to one in which the Court as an entity would issue an opinion.

Slander Causing harm to the reputation of another through the spoken word that contains false statements.

Sovereignty The exercise by a governmental unit of ultimate political authority. The Constitution gives the federal government sovereignty over the state governments, but reserves certain areas for control by the states.

Speech plus conduct Freedom of expression that involves activities by groups of people, such as demonstrations, protests, rallies, etc. The government can issue reasonable time, place, and manner restrictions in regard to speech plus conduct.

Standing to sue Sometimes simply called standing, this is the condition in which a party meets the required conditions to initiate a lawsuit. This typically includes having a personal interest in the controversy and its outcome.

Stare decisis A Latin term meaning "let the decision stand." Closely tied to the concept of precedent, this idea means that courts should base their actions closely on prior decisions in closely related cases. The principle of stare decisis is supposed to give legitimacy and stability to the law by controlling judicial discretion.

State action Those activities which are done by the state or which are closely associated with state authority. Constitutional rights and liberties claims can generally only be brought against state action not private action.

Statute A written law enacted by a legislative body.

Strict scrutiny The highest level of protection that the Court applies in civil rights and liberties cases, this test requires the government to show that it is pursuing a compelling government interest through narrowly tailored means. This is also known as the suspect classification test in equal protection cases.

Subpoena A judicial order to appear before a grand jury, a court, or a legislative hearing.

Substantive due process An ambiguous concept based upon the due process clauses found in the Fifth and Fourteenth Amendments that involves the substantive fairness of government laws as opposed to the procedural fairness of government actions. The Supreme Court has created controversy throughout its history by using the idea of substantive due process to invalidate government economic regulation in the early part of the twentieth century and to invalidate laws interfering with a right of privacy in the latter part of the twentieth century.

Summary decision An action by the Supreme Court issuing a decision in a case without receiving written briefs or hearing oral arguments.

Suspect classification test A doctrine associated with equal protection cases which requires any government law or action involving race or alienage to be justified by a compelling governmental interest achieved through narrowly tailored means. This is also called the strict scrutiny test.

Symbolic speech A form of freedom of expression which involves the use of symbols, such as a flag, to communicate ideas. Symbolic expression is generally given an intermediate level of protection.

T

Tort A civil wrong or injury inflicted by one person on the person or property of another.

V

Vacate To set aside or annul the decision of a lower court.

Vagueness A doctrine that requires any government law to be sufficiently precise and clear so that a reasonable person can understand what is prohibited and what is permitted.

Venue The place where a trial is held.

Voire dire A Latin term meaning "to speak the truth;" this is the process by which a jury is selected.

W

War Power The grant of authority in the Constitution to the national government to declare and wage war.

Writ An order issued by a court commanding some type of action.

Subject Index